CLASSICS OF INDUSTRIAL AND ORGANIZATIONAL PSYCHOLOGY

Edited by
DON MANKIN
RUSSELL E. AMES, JR.
MILTON A. GRODSKY
University of Maryland
University College

MOORE PUBLISHING COMPANY, INC.

OAK PARK, ILLINOIS

Library of Congress Cataloging in Publication Data

Main entry under title:

Classics of industrial and organizational psychology.

Includes bibliographic references.
1. Psychology, Industrial—Addresses, essays, lectures. I. Mankin, Donald A. II. Ames, Russell E. III. Grodsky, Milton A.
HF5548.8.C56   658.3'001'9   80-15699
ISBN 0-935610-11-1

Classics of Industrial and Organizational Psychology, First Edition

Moore Publishing Company, Inc.
701 South Gunderson Avenue, Oak Park, Illinois 60304

Topical Contents

IV. TRAINING

V. MOTIVATION, SATISFACTION, AND JOB DESIGN

VI. ENGINEERING PSYCHOLOGY

VII. LEADERSHIP

Chronological Contents

Preface

As with most contemporary disciplines and fields, particularly those in the social and behavioral sciences, defining the nature, purposes, and domain of industrial and organizational (I/O) psychology is a difficult and precarious task. Nonetheless, a general definition is possible and can function as a useful point of departure for the selections included in this volume. The definition offered by Blum and Naylor (1968) should serve this function well:

> Industrial psychology is simply the application or extension of psychological facts and principles to the problems concerning human beings operating within the context of business and industry. (p. 4)

There are at least two respects, however, in which this definition is seriously dated. First, the expression "industrial psychology" has since been replaced in general use by "industrial and organizational psychology," which better represents the recent elaboration and integration of the issues and content within the field and is, therefore, much more descriptive of present perspectives and practice. We will have more to say about this difference shortly. Second, the expression "business and industry" might create the mistaken impression that I/O psychology is limited to the concerns of the private sector. In addition, while it is clearly not intended by the authors, the mental images associated with this expression might not appropriately reflect the kind of knowledge and information-based service organizations—health, research, financial, educational, government agencies, etc.—that increasingly characterize advanced industrialized societies (e.g., see Bell, 1973). With these interpretations of the expressions "industrial psychology" and "business and industry," the definition presented above should be timeless enough to span the field of I/O psychology from its earliest years to its most contemporary concerns.

Now that we have defined the focus of the book, the next issue to deal with is our definition of "classic" works in this field and our criteria for selecting the articles included in this volume. Again, we will begin with a definition and identify our interpretations of this definition. The *American Heritage Dictionary of the English Language* (Morris, 1975) defines a classic as "serving as an outstanding representative of its kind; model . . . Having lasting significance or recognized worth . . . Of or in accordance with established principles and methods" (p. 249). For the older works in this volume, which make up a substantial majority of the articles included, this meant that each selection is either a classic work in and of itself, particularly representative of the highest quality work addressing an issue of especially enduring importance, or representative of an individual author's work that is, in total, of great significance and lasting value.

Two other criteria that strongly influenced our choices were readability and usefulness. For example, in some cases we passed over an early work that had identified a previously overlooked issue and precipitated a great deal of subsequent research in favor of a later work that would give students a retrospective overview and, perhaps, a resolution of the issue. In our opinion, the later work is of more use to students although the earlier one may be of greater historical interest. By the same token, we have not included excerpts from books that are acknowledged classics except where these excerpts can stand on their own as useful selections.

Several selections of relatively modern origin have been included, although they may be too recent for an adequate judgment of their enduring value. At the risk of being pretentious, the editors feel that an attempt should be made to identify some of the "classics of the future" to keep this volume from being prematurely dated and, perhaps, to spark some lively debate.

Finally, these are by no means *the* classics. For reasons of space, balance, and continuity many important works and authors have not been included. In our introductions to each selection, several of these other works may be cited in our attempt to provide as full a picture as possible of the development of a particular issue, idea, or controversy. Even with that, however, it was inevitable that we would overlook some.

The selections in this volume are organized into nine sections. Within each section the selections are arranged chronologically, except where considerations of cohesiveness and continuity dictated otherwise. The first section is basically historical in nature—the selections are from several of the "earliest voices" in the field and present some of the first attempts to deal explicitly, formally, and systematically with the person as a component in the industrial system. The remaining eight sections reflect the three independent movements that have been primarily responsible for shaping I/O psychology over the years—i.e., the personnel psychology, human relations, and the applied experimental/industrial engineering movements (see Landy and Trumbo, 1976, p. 106). The emphasis of the personnel psychology movement—represented by the sections on Criterion Development and Performance Appraisal (II), Personnel Selection (III), and Training (IV)—was on individual differences, testing, training, personnel decisions, and criteria-related issues. This was the earliest (and for many years dominant) emphasis of I/O psychology. Indeed, until relatively recently this *was* I/O psychology. The Hawthorne studies (see the selection by Roethlisberger in Section I) precipitated the human relations movement which eventually became instrumental in the development of the field of organizational psychology. In 1970, this new field formally merged with the earlier personnel psychology when Division 14 of the American Psychological Association changed its name from "Division of Industrial Psychology" to "Division of Industrial and Organizational Psychology." The sections on Motivation, Satisfaction and Job Design (V), Leadership (VII), Organizational Communications and Decision Making (VIII), and Organizational Assessment and Change (IX) reflect these more recent concerns.

The applied experimental/industrial engineering movement played a somewhat different role than the other two movements in the development of I/O psychology. While some of its earliest roots are similar, particularly the work of F. W. Taylor (see his selection in Section I), this movement received its principal impetus during World War II (as psychologists became increasingly concerned with the performance of human operators in complex military systems) and has since evolved into the separate but closely related field of engineering psychology. In addition to being classics in their own right, the selections in Section VI were chosen to reflect several of the important issues that overlap both fields.

The assistance of several people made this book possible. First, we wish to thank the authors and publishers of each selection for permission to reprint their work. We also wish to thank Jay Shafritz for his guidance throughout the project and Irwin Goldstein, Nancy Hedberg, Edward Locke, and Marshall Sashkin for their invaluable suggestions and critiques. Jan Jones, Nello Caporossi, and Frank Gangi did much of the uninteresting and bothersome detail work that made it easier for us to focus on the selection process itself. Finally, we would like to thank Pepa Boliek, Molly Oppenheim, and Ruth Reeves for their patient secretarial assistance.

DONALD A. MANKIN
RUSSELL E. AMES, JR.
MILTON A. GRODSKY

REFERENCES

Bell, D. 1973. *The coming of the post-industrial society: A venture in social forecasting.* New York: Basic Books.

Blum, M. L., and Naylor, J. C. 1968. *Industrial psychology: Its theoretical and social foundations* (rev. ed.). New York: Harper & Row.

Landy, F. J., & Trumbo, D. A. 1976. *Psychology of work behavior.* Homewood, IL: Dorsey.

Morris, W. (ed.) 1975. *The American heritage dictionary of the English language.* New York: American Heritage Publishing Co.

I

The Origins of Industrial and Organizational Psychology

Introduction. An examination of the origins of industrial and organizational (I/O) psychology reveals two names, Walter Dill Scott and Hugo
Münsterberg, that stand out as the most frequently mentioned and widely
acknowledged candidates for having "fathered" this field. Rather than engage in an interesting but, in this context, irrelevant discussion as to which
of the two most deserves the honor, it should be sufficient to recognize the
prominent role each of them played in the creation of I/O psychology. Both
men were instrumental in shaping an applied psychology out of what had
been an exclusively theoretical science barely out of its infancy, and both
are represented here.

If one had to pick a date to mark the founding of I/O psychology, a good
choice would be December 20, 1901. On that date Scott, a psychology
professor at Northwestern University, addressed a group of advertising professionals and outlined the potential contributions of psychology to the
field of advertising. Over the next several years, Scott published several
articles and books that elaborated a psychological theory of advertising and
provided guidelines for its application, especially his book *The Theory of
Advertising* (Scott, 1903), which is generally acknowledged as the first
book to address the application of psychological principles to industry. He
later expanded the domain of his interests to include a wider range of
business concerns (Scott, 1911). The selection presented here, "How
Suggestion Works on the Prospect's Brain," is a later and more succinct
summary of his views on the psychology of advertising.

Scott's writings on advertising influenced the work of the other "founding father" of industrial psychology, Hugo Münsterberg. Münsterberg was
born in Germany and educated at Wilhelm Wundt's laboratory in Leipzig.
After emigrating to the United States in 1892 to direct the psychological
laboratory at Harvard, he began to explore seriously the application of
psychological principles to such practical problems as education, law,
psychotherapy, and, of course, to the issues with which his name is most
frequently associated, business and industrial efficiency. The article in-

cluded here, "The Market and Psychology," originally appeared in *McClures Magazine* in 1909 and is one of his earliest publications on this topic and the related topics of personnel selection, equipment design, product packaging and design, and advertising. These topics were covered in considerably more detail in a later book, *Psychology and Industrial Efficiency* (1913), which served as an early model for the rapidly developing field of industrial psychology.

Münsterberg was also influenced by the work of another individual, Frederick W. Taylor, who was an industrial engineer. Had he been a psychologist, one might be tempted to call Taylor the father of industrial psychology for, as Wren (1979) notes, "scientific management"—the system and philosophy developed by Taylor—"gave industrial psychology its ethic, its scope and its direction for research" (p. 211). Beginning in the latter part of the 19th century, Taylor systematically investigated the influence of financial incentives, tool design, and work layout on job performance. Based on these investigations, Taylor devised his system of scientific management, which included among its primary goals the determination of "the one best way" (the one that was most efficient and least fatiguing) to do a job and the standardization of work operations to make every worker easily replaceable. To fulfill these goals, scientific management focused on the effects of financial incentives and the physical aspects of the job on worker performance. Taylor's best known work is his book, *The Principles of Scientific Management* (first published in 1911 and reprinted in 1947). A summary article with the same title, published in 1916, is included here.

The limitations of Taylor's system were dramatically demonstrated in the series of studies conducted at the Hawthorne Works of the Western Electric Co. by Harvard sociologist Elton Mayo and several of his associates beginning in 1924 and continuing into the 1930s. The purpose of the Hawthorne studies was to assess the effects of such working conditions as workroom illumination, length of working day, and rest periods on worker productivity. The researchers were surprised to find that productivity increased *regardless of the experimental manipulation*. Although the explanation for these findings is still very much a subject of debate, at the time, for many years following, and to a certain extent today, the Hawthorne results have been interpreted in terms of such previously unrecognized social-psychological phenomena as need for affiliation, group pressure, and personal attitudes. Regardless of how these results are ultimately interpreted, these studies were largely responsible for transforming the prevailing paradigm of industrial psychology from its emphasis on financial incentives, the physical conditions of work, and the individual worker as the relevant unit of analysis to a more complex perspective that recognized the motivational and affective importance of the informal network of social relationships that typically develop in formal organizations. Indeed, the earliest roots of the "organizational" aspect of I/O psychology can be found in these studies. A concise description of the Hawthorne studies is presented in the chapter reprinted here from F. J. Roethlisberger's book *Management and Morale* (1941). A more complete discussion can be found in Roethlisberger and Dickson (1939).

REFERENCES

Münsterberg, H. 1913. *Psychology and industrial efficiency.* Boston: Houghton-Mifflin.

Roethlisberger, F. J. 1941. *Management and morale.* Cambridge, MA: Harvard University Press.

Roethlisberger, F. J., and Dickson, W. J. 1939. *Management and the worker.* Cambridge, MA: Harvard University Press.

Scott, W. D. 1903. *The theory of advertising.* Boston: Small, Maynard and Company.

Scott, W. D. 1911. *Increasing human efficiency in business.* New York: Macmillan.

Taylor, F. W. 1947. *Principles of scientific management.* New York: Harper & Row.

Wren, D. A. 1979. *The evolution of management thought* (2nd ed.). New York: Wiley.

1. How Suggestion Works on the Prospect's Brain*

WALTER DILL SCOTT

All down the ages of the world, from Aristotle down to modern times, when people wanted to know how to influence men in business or any other place, the syllogism was what they had to make use of.

A syllogism is the giving of one statement, which men are accustomed to accept, and then another, and then the logical conclusion. The illustration which has come down from the days of Aristotle is this one: "All men are mortal. Socrates is a man. Therefore, Socrates is going to die." The syllogism is not a method of advancing knowledge; it is a method of putting knowledge in such a way that it compels assent on the part of every rational being who considers it. Now, the difficulty of the syllogism is that it puts people in a hostile attitude. Aristotle defined man as a reasoning animal, and there was the fallacy. Man is not fundamentally and essentially a reasoning animal. When people have already made up their minds upon a subject, then the syllogism appeals to them; but it is not the way to get action.

*Source: From *Advertising & Selling* (May 1914), pp. 11 and 59. An abstract of an address before the Detroit Board of Commerce.

Because of the particular mental attitude a man had to take to accept the definition, there have been revolts all along the line. People have swung to the opposite extreme and have thought of many abnormal methods of convincing men. People in all ages have believed in some influences such as stars or demons, or something that could get people to act in unison.

MESSMERISM AND SUGGESTION

Let me show just how a single man started something here, and the effect of it. Dr. Messmer, of Vienna, was raised in the atmosphere of Aristotelian logic on one side, and the belief in some method of producing great influences on people, on the other, namely, that of the stars. He believed that the use of a magnet would concentrate the effect of the stars. He experimented with this and discovered that he could actually cure a large number of patients, and he performed a large number of very important cures. Later on he came to believe that the effect was not caused by the magnet, but the man himself, and that he was a magnetic man. A Scotch doctor, by the name of Braid, saw this demonstration of Messmer producing such a wonderful effect on the people, and he came to the conclusion that it was not animal magnetism, or the influence of the stars, but it was the influence of the idea in the mind of the subject. This was the method of suggestion. Then the theory developed that all the control that one man has over another is developed through suggestion.

THE POWER OF IDEAS

What do I mean by suggestion? By suggestion I mean an activity which is produced by the dynamic impulse and nature of the idea. Ideas are dynamic things: they are the things that get the action. Our idea of an act will result in that act, unless it is hindered by some impeding, inhibiting or contradicting act. Every idea results in an act, but not all ideas lead to acts in the same degree. If a thing seems clear, it results, and if it doesn't seem clear, it does not result in the same extent. If you think of the letter O and then the letter Z, when you think of the letter O there is tension in your lips, and when you think of the letter Z there is tension at the base of your tongue. You cannot think of anything in any way without some incipient beginning of that action. For instance, if you try to imagine right now the holding of a ripe peach in your mouth, and then crushing the skin and pulp in your mouth, the thought in that case is a reality and you are eating the peach. That idea induces the activity of the salivary gland, and that is a fact, and you cannot think that without starting that action.

It is not necessary to give a person an idea and then convince him of the truth of it. The giving him the idea is all that is necessary and the idea will be held as true unless a contradictory idea arises with it. Every man in Germany and most of Europe believes that monarchy is the divine method of controlling men; in America the people believe that democracy is the divine method for governing men. Millions of people hold those faiths and would be willing to sacrifice their lives to defend them. They have never reasoned them out; they have merely taken them on faith.

GROUP OR SOCIAL SUGGESTION

Historically we seem to have developed in groups. It was quite important in ancient times that, if one man went to attack an enemy, the others would immediately join in the fight; and if one man would start to run, the other would do so, too. If one man held an idea, it was important that the others hold the same idea, or else the group would be annihilated. Those were forces during the development of all mankind, and thus mankind has come out of the workshop of nature an imitator, and credulous beyond belief. We do the things we see other people do, and we believe what they say.

Now, here is the suggestion in advertising; as I read the advertisement I feel that a whole lot of people are also reading it. Now, that is important. I must feel that the other people are being convinced. It is social suggestion that convinces me; it is not that the advertiser put it out; it is because I feel that other people believe it.

William Jennings Bryan is a great orator. Now, as I heard Bryan I was convinced of the truth of his statements, but, if I felt that other people were not, it would not have much effect on me. But if I heard him speak and he convinced me and I believed other people were convinced, the effect would be tremendous. Now, the function of advertising is that very same thing. As you see the advertising it is the big suggestion, not coming from the paper, but coming from all the public that you believe are having that thought at that time.

WHY ARGUMENT HAS DANGER

My third point is this: In suggestion there is an absence of deliberation or criticism that is sometimes regarded as the most important point of all. Certain ideas are readily criticised and certain others are not. Any idea that corresponds to your ambition, your purposes of life, your emotions, your instincts, those ideas are not criticized. Again, ideas which in the first perspective are criticized, later on are not. I believe that Ivory Soap is 99 percent pure; the first time that I read that advertisement I did not. I have come to believe that White

Rock is America's best table water. I have come to believe a lot of things which I first resented, but the advertiser has cleverly overcome my tendency to criticize by the skillful force of repetition. As Mr. Dooley says, "I'll belave annything if ye tell it to me often enough." These three things are the characteristic of suggestion: First, no act is an act of suggestion unless it illustrates in a high degree the dynamic impulsive nature of it; second, no act is properly called suggestion unless it comes from the actions or words of another person; third, nothing is called suggestion if it is critical in any way whatever. Argument puts people in a critical attitude, and therefore is dangerous.

Now, what can you do to carry out these principles in your task right now? In the first place we must get ideas which are dynamic and impulsive, which carry to action and carry to belief. In your particular activity, what is the idea which is dynamic? Is it the service the store renders? Is it the price? Is it the quality of the goods? The function of the advertiser is to get the idea into the mind of the public.

Now, my second point, on the nature of personality; what kind of a personality is it that can give suggestion? It is the personality that seems to know, that is the standard in its particular line. If your store and your advertising correspond, then your advertising will be strong. If your advertising is strong and the personality is weak, you are in a hopeless condition. You must make the advertising correspond to the personality. Until that is done, the advertising cannot be strong.

2. The Market and Psychology*

HUGO MÜNSTERBERG

A long time before New York and Chicago were discovered, there lived an alchemist who sold an unfailing prescription for making gold from eggs. He sold it at a high price, on a contract that he was to refund the whole sum in case the prescription was carried through and did not yield the promised result. It is said that he never broke the contract and yet became a very rich man. His prescription was that the gold-seeker should hold a pan over the fire with the yolks of a dozen eggs in it and stir them for half an hour without ever thinking of the word hippopotamus. Many thousands tried, and yet no one succeeded. The fatal word, which perhaps they never had thought of before, now always unfortunately rushed into their minds, and the more they tried to suppress it, the more it was present. That good man was a fair psychologist. He knew something of the laws of the mind, and although he may have been unable to transform eggs into gold, he understood instead how to transform psychology into gold. Psychology has made rapid progress since those times in which the alchemist cornered the market, but our modern commerce and industry so far have profited little from the advance. Goods are manufactured and distributed, bought and sold; at every stage the human mind is at work, since human minds are the laborers, are the salesmen, are the buyers; and yet no one consults the exact knowledge of the science that deals with the laws and characteristics of the human mind.

How curiously this situation contrasts with our practical application of physical science! We can hardly imagine a state in which we should allow the scholarly physicist to have steam engines and telegraphs in his laboratory rooms and yet make no effort to put these inventions to practical use in the world of industry and commerce. But just that is the situation in the world of mental facts. The laboratories for the study of inner life flourish, experiments are made, inventions are tested, new vistas are opened; but practical life goes on without making use of all these psychological discoveries. It is, indeed, as if the steam engine were confined to the laboratory table, while in the practical world work were still done clumsily by the arms of slaves.

The only fields in which the psychical experiment has been somewhat translated into practical use are those of education and medicine. The educational expert has slowly begun to understand that the attention and the interest of the school child, his imitations and his play, his memory and his fatigue, deserve careful psychological study. The painstaking studies of the laboratory have shown how the old teacher, in spite of his common sense, too often worked with destructive methods. Whole school plans had to be revised, the mental hygiene of the school-room had to be changed, educational prejudices had to be swept away.

In a similar way psychological knowledge gradually leaked into the

*Source: From American Problems by Hugo Münsterberg, Chapter 7, pp. 151-73. New York: Moffat, Yard and Co., 1910.

medical world also. The power of suggestion, with all its shadings, from slight psychotherapeutic influence to the deepest hypnotic control, is slowly becoming a tool of the physician. The time has come when it is no longer excusable that our medical students should enter professional life without a knowledge of scientific psychology. They do not deserve sympathy if they stand aghast when quacks and mystics are successful where their own attempts at curing have failed. It can be foreseen that reform in this field is near, and it may be admitted that even those healing knights errant have helped to direct the public interest to the overwhelming importance of psychology in medicine. For education and medicine alike the hope seems justified that the laboratory work of the psychologist for the practical needs of men will not be in vain.

We are much farther from this end in the field of law. Certainly the psychologist knows better than any one that he has neither a prescription to remove crime from the world nor an instrument to see to the bottom of the mind of the defendant or to make the witness speak nothing but the truth. Nevertheless, he knows that an abundance of facts has been secured by experimental methods which might be helpful in the prevention of crime, in the sifting of evidence, and in the securing of truthful confession. Every word of the witness depends on his memory, on his power of perception, on his suggestibility, on his emotion; and yet no psychological expert is invited to make use of the psychological achievements in this sphere. But even here there are signs of progress, for interest in the problems involved seems wide awake.

It is strikingly different with the whole field of economic activity. The thousandfold importance of psychological studies to the life of the workshop and the mill, of the store and the household, has not yet attracted public attention. On the whole, commerce and industry seem to take good care of themselves, and seem little in the mood to philosophize or to beg advice of a psychological expert. Here and there they have taken a bit of laboratory knowledge and profited from it, without realizing that such a haphazard plunge into psychology can hardly be sufficient. For instance, no railway or steamship company would employ a man who is to look out for signals until he has been examined for color-blindness. The variations of the color sense in men are typical discoveries of psychological experimentation. But even here the expert knows that the practical tests of today represent, on the whole, an earlier stage of knowledge, and do not progress parallel to laboratory study of the varieties of color-blindness. Further, the transportation companies ought not to limit their signal tests to trials of the color sense. It is perhaps no less important that the man on the engine should be tested as to the rapidity of his reactions, or the accuracy of his perceptions, or the quickness of his decisions. For the examination of each of such mental capacities the psychological laboratory can furnish exact methods. Moreover, the transportation companies should have no less interest in studying with psychological experiments the question of what kind of signals may be most appropriate. For instance, psychologists have raised the important query whether it is advisable to have different railroad signals in the daytime from those at night. The safety of the service demands that the correct handling be done automatically, and this will be secured the more easily, the more uniform the outer conditions. Experiment alone can determine the influence of such variations.

Even this small psychological group, the use of signals for transportation companies, is not confined to visible impressions. An abundance of effort is nowadays concentrated on the fog-horn signals of ships, but no one gives any attention to the psychological conditions for discriminating the direction from which a sound comes. In our psychological laboratories widely different experiments have been made concerning the perception of sounds with reference to direction and distance. We know, for instance, that certain illusions constantly enter into this field, and that the conditions of the ear, and even of the ear-shell, may produce important modifications. Yet no one thinks of studying with all the available psychological means the hearing capacities of the ship officer. A difference in the two ears of the captain may be no less disastrous than the inability to discriminate red and green.

Another field in which a slight tendency to consult the modern psychologist has set in is that of advertising. Many hundreds of millions are probably wasted every year on advertisements that are unsuccessful because they do not appeal to the mind of the reader. They may be unfit to draw his attention, or may be unable to impress the essentials on his memory, or, above all, may not succeed in giving the desired suggestion. The reader glances at them without being impressed by the desirable qualities of the offered wares.

The evident need of psychological guidance has affected a certain contact between empirical psychology and business in this field. The professional advertisement writer today looks into the psychology of suggestion and attention, of association of ideas and apperception, and profits from the interesting books that cover the theory of advertising. Yet every row of posters on the billboards affords plenty of material for studying sins against the spirit of psychology. Perhaps there sits in life-size the guest at the restaurant table and evidently rejects the wrong bottle, which the waiter is bringing. The advertiser intends to suggest that every passer-by should be filled with disgust for the wrong brand, while the only desirable one is printed in heavy letters above. What really must happen is that the advertised name will associate itself with the imitated inner movement of rejection, and the rival company alone can profit from the unpsychological poster.

But, anyhow, the application of general psychology to the problem of advertising can be only the beginning. What is needed is the introduction of systematic experiment which will cover the whole ground of display, not only in pictures and text, but in the shop windows and the stores. The experiment may refer to the material itself. Before an advertisement is printed, the arrangement of words, the kind of type, the whole setting of the content, may be tested experimentally. The electric chronoscope of the psychological laboratory can easily show how many thousandths of a second the average reader needs for reading one or another type, and other experiments may demonstrate how much is apperceived during a short exposure, and how much kept in memory, and what kind of involuntary emotional response and muscle reaction is started by every kind of arrangement. The trade journals not seldom show specimens of skillful and of clumsy schemes of advertising, and yet all this remains dogmatic until experiment has brought out the subtle points.

But much more important than experimenting with the concrete material is the experimental study of the principles involved. This is, after all, the strength of the experimental method in all fields, that the complex facts of life are transformed into neat, simple schemes in which everything is left out but the decisive factor. If the jeweler wants to display his rings and watches in the window in such a way that the effect of the largest possible number will be produced, it is not necessary that we experiment for him with costly timepieces and jewelry. For instance, we may place twenty little squares of paper on one sheet of black cardboard, and on another from sixteen to twenty-four. After short exposures we ask our subjects to decide on which sheet there are more squares. If the squares on both sheets are arranged in the same way the observer will see at a glance that eighteen are less than twenty, or twenty-two more than twenty. But by trying very different combinations and studying the effect of different groupings, we shall soon discover that with certain arrangements the twenty look like only seventeen, or, with better arrangements, like twenty-two or twenty-three. In the same way we may study the effect if we mix squares and circles, or have squares of various sizes, or some of uniform, some of different color. In short, in the most simple form of experiment we can find out the principles that control the impression of the passer-by as to the greater or smaller number he believes himself to see.

The effort to attract the customer begins, of course, not with the storekeeper and the salesman, but with the manufacturer. He, too, must know psychology in order to make his article as persuasive as possible. Since I began to give my attention to the application of psychology to commerce and labor, I have collected a large number of wrappings and packings in which the various industrial establishments sell their goods, and have received plenty of confidential information as to the success or failure of the various labels and pictures. Not a few of them can be tested quite exactly, inasmuch as the article itself remains the same, while the make-up for the retail sale changes. The same quality and kind of toilet soap or chocolate or breakfast food or writing paper that in the one packing remained a dead weight on the store shelves, in another packing found a rapid sale.

Much depends upon the habits and traditions and upon the development of taste among the special group of customers. But I am inclined to think that if the material is analyzed carefully the psychological laboratory can predict beforehand failure or success with a certain safety. As a matter of course, such factors cannot be reduced to a few simple equations. There is no special color combination that is suitable for chocolates and soap and chewing-gum alike, and the same color combination is not even equally fitting for both summer and winter. And still less can the same head of a girl be successfully used to advertise side-combs and patent medicines and ketchup. But this associative factor is equally open to scientific experiment.

Yet, after all, the make-up of the article and its paper cover are less important than the quality and construction of the goods themselves. The manufacturer too easily forgets that his product is to be used for the purposes of human minds, and that a real perfection of his output can never be reached unless the subtlest adjustment to the mental functions is secured. This is true for the most trivial as well as the most refined and complex thing that is to satisfy human interests. To be sure, small effect would be gained if the seller were simply to look over a text-book of psychology. He might easily be misled. The psychologist can show that a square filled with horizontal lines looks tall and one filled with vertical lines looks broad, but woe to the tailoring establishment that should dress its customers in accordance with that psychological prescription. If the tailor were to dress the stout woman who wants to appear tall in costumes with horizontal stripes and the thin one who wants to look plump in a dress with vertical stripes, the effect would be the opposite of that which was desired. It is not that psychology is wrong, but the application of the principle is out of order. We never look at a woman as we look at a square, comparing the height with the breadth. The vertical stripes in the gown force our eyeballs to move upward and downward and reënforce by that our perception of height, while the horizontal stripes simply suggest to us the idea of breadth. Or, to point to a similar misapplication: There was a painter who had learned from the psychologists that we see singly only those things upon which we focus, while everything in the background is seen by the two eyes in a double image. He thought for this reason that he would reach a more natural effect if he drew double lines for the background things in his pictures. The effect was absurd, as his double picture was now seen with each of the two eyes, while in reality we get a double image by developing one in each eye.

Half-baked psychology certainly cannot help us, but the fact that misunderstandings may come up in every corner of psychology is no argument against its proper use. We should not like to eat the meal which a cook might prepare from bits of chemical knowledge gathered from a hand-book of physiology. The well-trained expert must always remain the middleman between science and the needs of practical life. But if special laboratories for applied psychology could examine the market demands with careful study of all the principles involved, the gain for practical life would be certain.

To analyze the case a little more fully, I may point to a product of our factories that is indispensable to our modern life—the typewriting machine. It may serve as an illustration just as well as a hundred other industrial articles, and it has the advantage that the varieties of the machines are popularly well known. Everybody knows that there are machines with or without visible writing, machines with ideal keyboards and machines with universal keyboards, machines with the double keyboard and machines with the single keyboard on which the capital letters demand the pressure of a shift-key to change the position of the carriage. Psychologists nowadays, especially in Germany, have started to examine carefully the claims of the various systems, and the results differ greatly from what the man on the street presupposes. Thus we stand before a curious conflict. The manufacturer must shape his article in such a way that it attracts the customer, but while this holds without restriction for questions of external shape and outfit and packing and name, it may interfere with the greatest usefulness of the article and therefore with the real advantage of the buyer. Yet ultimately the advantage of the men who use the article must be the strongest advertisement, and it may thus be quite possible that it lies more in the interest of the manufacturer to bring to the market a product that pleases less at the first approach and by a surface appearance, but more in the long run.

The visible writing of the typewriter is a case in point. He who is not accustomed to typewriting and wants to begin it will naturally prefer the writing with visible letters. He thinks of his ordinary handwriting; he knows how essential it is for him to follow the point of his pen with his eyes. He forgets that in the visible writing the very letter that he is writing is, of course, invisible at that moment, and the touch of the key perfectly produces the complete letter. The real effect is, therefore, that he sees the letters that he is no longer writing. The case is thus fundamentally different from that of handwriting. On the other hand, the amount of attention that is given to looking at the visible words is withdrawn from the only field that is essential—the keyboard or the copy. The visible machine may appear more attractive to one who does not know, but may be less effective through starting bad and distracting habits. Yet again this may have psychological exceptions. In the case of those individuals who are absolutely visualizers, the visible writing may be a help when they are writing, not from a copy, but on dictation or from their own thoughts. In that case the seeing of the preceding letters would help in the organization of the motor impulses needed for pressing the keys for the next syllable. It would, therefore, demand a careful experimental analysis to determine those persons who would profit and those who would suffer by the visibility of the writing. The instinctive feeling can never decide it.

But this difference of individual disposition plays no less a part with reference to the other qualities of the various types of machines. The double keyboard demands a distribution of attention over a very large field. The psychological laboratory can easily demonstrate that individuals exist whose attention is concentrated and cannot stretch out much beyond the focus, and others whose attention is wide and moves easily. On the other hand, the shift-key is not merely one of the many keys, but demands an entirely different kind of effort, which interrupts the smooth running flow of finger movements. The psychophysical experiment demonstrates how much more slowly and with how much more effort the shift-key movement must be performed. Again, the analysis of the laboratory shows that there are individuals who can easily interrupt their regular movement habits by will impulses of an entirely different kind, but others who lose much of their psychological energy by so sudden a change. For these the breaking in of the shift-key process means an upsetting of the mental adjustment and therefore a great loss in their effectiveness. Accordingly, the machine that is excellent for the one is undesirable for the other, and the market would fare better if all this were not left to chance.

Even as to the keyboard, it seems that psychological principles are involved which demand reference to individual tendencies. For some it is best if the letters that frequently occur together in the language are in near neighborhood on the keyboard; for other minds such an arrangement is the least desirable. These writers mix up the motor impulses that belong to similar and correlated ideas, and they fare better if the intimately associated letters demand a movement in an entirely different direction, with the greatest possible psychological contrast.

There is hardly any instrument on the market for which a similar analysis of the interplay of mental energies could

not be carried out. But let us rather turn to another aspect, the work in the factory itself. I feel sure that the time will come when the expert psychologist will become the most helpful agent in this sphere of industrial life. The farmers have tilled the ground for thousands of years without scientific chemistry, but we know how indispensable the aid of the chemist appears to the agriculturist today. A new period of farming has begun through the help of the scientific expert. A similar service to labor and industry might be rendered by experimental psychology. It would even be quite conceivable that governments should organize this help in a similar way to that by which they have secured agricultural laboratories for the farms of the country. The Department of Agriculture at Washington has experimental stations all over the land, and not a little of the great harvest is due to their effectiveness. The Department of Commerce and Labor at a future time may establish experimental stations which will bring corresponding help to the mills and factories and even to the artisans everywhere. There is no establishment that produces without making use of human minds and brains. The mill-owner must learn how to use the mental energies of his laborers in the same way that the farmer knows how to use the properties of the soil. And such help is not only to the economic interest of the producer; it would be perhaps still more to the interest of the workingman and his market price.

The first thought might turn to the safety of the laborer, which is indeed dependent upon various psychological conditions. For instance, the mill-owner is not expected to know what mental factors determine the correct perception of distance, and yet it is evident that a laborer is in constant danger if he cannot estimate correctly his distance from a moving machine. He may be able to see correctly with one eye every part of the machine, but if the other eye is somewhat defective, though he himself may not notice it, his plastic interpretation of his impressions will be insufficient. He will constantly be in danger of putting his hands into the buzzing wheels. Only careful consideration of such psychological elements as build up the idea of distance, and exact tests of the workingman's senses, could eliminate such ever-present dangers.

The captain of industry may feel more interested in bringing out the fullest efficiency of his laborer; but, again, as yet nothing indicates that he is willing to put scientific exactitude into the service of this dominant psychological question. An experimental test alone can decide under what conditions the greatest continuity of effective work can be secured and under what mental conditions the individual can do his best. Methods for studying the curve of fatigue in the individual laborer, or the conditions for his most accurate muscle work, and a hundred similar devices, are today already at the disposal of the mental workshop; but probably for a long time to come the foreman will be thought to know better than the expert.

Moreover, it is evident that as soon as this contact between the mill and the experimental psychological laboratory has been perfected, new questions will arise corresponding to the special needs of industrial activity. The technical conditions of every industry in the country can easily be imitated in the laboratory with the simplest means. So far we have not the least really scientific investigation of the psychological effect of specializing, of the division of labor, of the influence of changes in the machines, of the complexity of machines, of the effect of temperature, food, light, color, noise, odor, of discipline, reward, imitation, piece work, of repetition, of distribution of attention, of emotion, and hundreds of other mental factors that enter into the workingman's life. It is simply untrue to say that those things regulate themselves. On the contrary, traditions and superficial tendencies, short-sighted economy and indifference, a thousand times establish methods that are to nobody's interest. The employer and the employee alike have to suffer from them.

We may get an idea of the help that could be brought if, for instance, we think of the methods of learning the handling of machines. There are many industrial activities that demand most complicated technique, and yet the learning is left to most haphazard methods. So far, we know practically nothing as to the most profitable methods of learning these industrial activities. But we have only to compare this situation with the excellent work that modern experimental psychology has performed in the fields of handwriting, typewriting, telegraphy, piano-playing, and drawing. In every one of these fields most careful experiments have been carried on for months under the most subtle conditions. With complex instruments the growth and development of the process were analyzed, and the influences that retarded progress and hampered the most efficient learning were disentangled.

Again we may learn from the case of typewriting work. Anyone who writes with the forefingers may finally reach a certain rapidity in handling the machine. Yet no one masters it who has not learned it in a systematic way which must ultimately be controlled by the studies of experimental psychologists. Such experimental analyses of the processes in learning to run the typewriter have been carried through with the greatest carefulness, and have demonstrated that the student passes through a number of different stages. He is not only doing the thing more and more quickly: the essential factor lies in the development of habits—habits of manipulation, habits of feeling attitude, habits of attention, habits of association, habits of decisions in overcoming difficulties; and every insight into this formation of mental connections offers guidance for a proficient training. The experiments indicate the psychological conditions for a spurt in effort, for fluctuations in efficiency, for the lasting gain in speed and accuracy, for their relations to the activity of the heart and to motor activities. In short, we now know scientifically the psychological processes by which the greatest possible economy in typewriting can be secured. There is no industrial machine in our factories and mills for which a similar study has been performed; and yet every effort in this direction would increase the effectiveness of the laborer and the profit of the employer.

Our psychological educators nowadays have studied with all the methods of the laboratory the effects of pauses during the school day. We know how certain pauses work as real recreation in which exhausted energies are restituted, but that other kinds of pauses work as disturbing interruptions by which the acquired adjustment to the work is lost. It would need most accurate investigations with the subtlest means of the psychological workshop to determine for each special industry what rhythm of work and what recesses, what rapidity and what method of recreation, would secure the fullest effect. The mere subjective feeling of the workingman himself or the common-sense judgment of the onlooker may be entirely misleading.

Does not everyone know how this inner sensation of strength has deceived the workingman in the case of alcohol? His bottle supplies him with an illusory feeling of energy; the careful experiment demonstrates that his effectiveness suffers under the immediate influence of whiskey. The scientific inquiry in every such case must replace the superficial impression. Moreover, a systematic study would not only inquire how the laborer is to learn the most efficient use of the existing machines, but the machines themselves would then be adjusted to the results of the psychological experiment. The experiment would have to determine which muscles could produce the effect that is demanded

with the greatest accuracy and speed and perseverance, and the handles and levers and keys would have to be distributed accordingly. Even the builder of the motor-car relies on most superficial, common-sense judgment when he arranges the levers as they seem most practical for quick handling. The psychological laboratory, which would study in thousandths of a second the movements of the chauffeur with the various cars, might find that here also illusions too easily enter. Industry ought to have outgrown the stage of unscientific decisions, and it is inexcusable if physics and chemistry are considered the only sciences that come into question, and experimental psychology is ignored, when every single business, every wheel to be turned and every lever to be moved, are dependent upon the psychical facts of attention and memory, of will and feeling, of perception and judgment.

It would probably be more difficult to help the actual sale of the commercial products by exact scientific methods, except as far as advertisements and display are concerned. And yet it is evident that every man behind the counter and every sales-girl who wants to influence the customer works with psychological agencies. The study of the psychology of attention and suggestion, of association of ideas and of emotion, may systematically assist the commercial transaction. The process certainly has two sides, but if we think of the interest of the salesman only, we might say that he has to hypnotize his victim. He has to play skilfully on the attention of his shopping customer, he must slowly inhibit in her mind the desire for anything that the store cannot offer, he must cleverly fix the emotions on a particular choice, and finally he must implant the conviction that life is not worth living without this particular shirt-waist. How much the stores would profit if every employee should learn the careful avoidance of opposing suggestions! Whether shop-girls in a department store are advised to ask after every sale: "Do you want to take it with you?" or are instructed to ask first: "Do you want to have it sent to your home?" makes no difference to the feeling of the customers. They are unconscious sufferers from the suggestion, but for the store it may mean a difference of thousands for the delivery service. The newspaper boy at the subway entrance who simply asks: "Paper, sir?" cannot hope for the success of his rival who with forceful suggestion asks: "Which paper?"

The experimental study of the commercial question may finally bring new clearness into the relations of trade and law. To give one illustration from many, I may mention the case of commercial imitation. Everyone who studies the court cases in restraint of trade becomes impressed with the looseness and vagueness of the legal ideas involved. There seems nowhere a definite standard. In buying his favorite article the purchaser is sometimes expected to exert the sharpest attention in order not to be deceived by an imitation. In other cases, the court seems to consider the purchaser as the most careless, stupid person, who can be tricked by any superficial similarity. The evidence of the trade witnesses is an entirely unreliable, arbitrary factor. The so-called ordinary purchaser changes his mental qualities with every judge, and it seems impossible to foresee whether a certain label will be construed as an unallowed imitation of the other or as a similar but independent trademark.

In the interest of psychology applied to commerce and labor, I have collected in my laboratory a large number of specimens which show all possible degrees of imitation. In every case it is evident that the similarity of form or color or name or packing is used in a conscious way in order to profit from the reputation of another article which has won its popularity by quality or by advertisement. I have a bottle of Moxie among a dozen imitations of similar names in bottles of a similar shape and with the beverage similar in color to the successfully advertised Moxie. Tomato ketchups and sardine boxes, cigarette cases and talcum powders, spearmint gums and plug tobaccos, glove labels and vaudeville posters, patent medicines and gelatines, appear in interesting twin and triplet forms. The cigarette boxes of Egyptian Deities are accompanied by the Egyptian Prettiest and the Egyptian Daintiest; Rupena stands at the side of Peruna; and the Pain Expeller is packed and bottled like the Pain Killer.

Not a few of the specimens of my imitation museum have kept the lawyers busy. Yet all this is evidently at first a case for the psychologist. The whole problem belongs to the psychology of recognition. There would be no difficulty in producing in the laboratory conditions under which the mental principles involved could be repeated and brought under exact observation. Many obstacles would have to be overcome, but certainly the experiment could determine the degree of difficulty or ease with which the recognition of a certain impression can be secured. As soon as such a scale of the degrees of attention were gained, we could have an objective standard and could determine whether or not too much attention was needed to distinguish an imitation from the original. Then we might find by objective methods whether the village drug-store or our lack of attention was to blame when we were anxious for a glass of Moxie and the clerk gave us instead the brown bitter fluid from a bottle of Noxie, Hoxie, Non-Tox, Modox, Nox-All, Noxemall, Noxie-Cola, Moxine, or Sod-Ox, all of which stand temptingly in my little museum for applied psychology.

3. The Principles of Scientific Management*

FREDERICK WINSLOW TAYLOR

By far the most important fact which faces the industries of our country, the industries, in fact, of the civilized world, is that not only the average worker, but nineteen out of twenty workmen throughout the civilized world firmly believe that it is for their best interests to go slow instead of to go fast. They firmly believe that it is for their interest to give as little work in return for the money that they get as is practical. The reasons for this belief are two-fold, and I do not believe that the workingmen are to blame for holding these fallacious views.

If you will take any set of workmen in your own town and suggest to those men that it would be a good thing for them in their trade if they were to double their output in the coming year, each man turn out twice as much work and become twice as efficient, they would say, "I do not know anything about other people's trades; what you are saying about increasing efficiency being a good thing may be good for other trades, but I know that the only result if you come to our trade would be that half of us would be out of a job before the year was out." That to the average workingman is an axiom; it is not a matter subject to debate at all. And even among the average business men of this country that opinion is almost universal. They firmly believe that that would be the result of a great increase in efficiency, and yet directly the opposite is true.

THE EFFECT OF LABOR-SAVING DEVICES

Whenever any labor-saving device of any kind has been introduced into any trade—go back into the history of any trade and see it—even though that labor-saving device may turn out ten, twenty, thirty times that output that was originally turned out by men in that trade, the result has universally been to make work for more men in that trade, not work for less men.

Let me give you one illustration. Let us take one of the staple businesses, the cotton industry. About 1840 the power loom succeeded the old hand loom in the cotton industry. It was invented many years before, somewhere about 1780 or 1790, but it came in very slowly. About 1840 the weavers of Manchester, England, saw that the power loom was coming, and they knew it would turn out three times the yardage of cloth in a day that the hand loom turned out. Ant what did they do, these five thousand weavers of Manchester, England, who saw starvation staring them in the face? They broke into the establishments into which those machines were being introduced, they smashed them, they did everything possible to stop the introduction of the power loom. And the same result followed that follows every attempt to interfere with the introduction of any labor-saving device, if it is really a labor-saving device. Instead of stopping

*Source: Bulletin of the Taylor Society (December 1916). An abstract of an address given by the late Dr. Taylor before the Cleveland Advertising Club, March 3, 1915, two weeks prior to his death. It was repeated the following day at Youngstown, Ohio, and this presentation was Dr. Taylor's last public appearance.

the introduction of the power loom, their opposition apparently accelerated it, just as opposition to scientific management all over the country, bitter labor opposition today, is accelerating the introduction of it instead of retarding it. History repeats itself in that respect. The power loom came right straight along.

And let us see the result in Manchester. Just what follows in every industry when any labor-saving device is introduced. Less than a century has gone by since 1840. The population of England in that time has not more than doubled. Each man in the cotton industry in Manchester, England, now turns out, at a restricted estimate ten yards of cloth for every yard of cloth that was turned out in 1840. In 1840 there were 5,000 weavers in Manchester. Now there are 265,000. Has that thrown men out of work? Has the introduction of labor-saving machinery, which has multiplied the output per man by tenfold, thrown men out of work?

What is the real meaning of this? All that you have to do is to bring wealth into this world and the world uses it. That is the real meaning. The meaning is that where in 1840 cotton goods were a luxury to be worn only by rich people when they were hardly ever seen on the street, now every man, woman and child all over the world wears cotton goods as a daily necessity.

Nineteen-twentieths of the real wealth of this world is used by the poor people, and not the rich, so that the workingman who sets out as a steady principle ' to restrict output is merely robbing his own kind. That group of manufacturers which adopts as a permanent principle restriction of output, in order to hold up prices, is robbing the world. The one great thing that marks the improvement of this world is measured by the enormous increase in output of the individuals in this world. There is fully twenty times the output per man now that there was three hundred years ago. That marks the increase in the real wealth of the world; that marks the increase of the happiness of the world, that gives us the opportunity for shorter hours, for better education, for amusement, for art, for music, for everything that is worthwhile in this world—goes right straight back to this increase in the output of the individual. The workingmen of today live better than the king did three hundred years ago. From what does the progress the world has made come? Simply from the increase in the output of the individual all over the world.

THE DEVELOPMENT OF SOLDIERING

The second reason why the workmen of this country and of Europe deliberately restrict output is a very simple one. They, for this reason, are even less to blame than they are for the other. If, for example, you are manufacturing a pen, let us assume for simplicity that a pen can be made by a single man. Let us say that the workman is turning out ten pens per day, and that he is receiving $2.50 a day for his wages. He has a progressive foreman who is up to date, and that foreman goes to the workman and suggests, "Here, John, you are getting $2.50 a day, and you are turning out ten pens. I would suggest that I pay you 25 cents for making that pen." The man takes the job, and through the help of his formean, through his own ingenuity, through his increased work, through his interest in his business, through the help of his friends, at the end of the year he finds himself turning out twenty pens instead of ten. He is happy, he is making $5, instead of $2.50 a day. His foreman is happy because, with the same room, with the same men he had before, he has doubled the output of his department, and the manufacturer himself is sometimes happy, but not often. Then someone on the board of directors asks to see the payroll, and he finds that we are paying $5 a day where other similar mechanics are only getting $2.50, and in no uncertain terms he announces that we must stop ruining the labor market. We cannot pay $5 a day when the standard rate of wages is $2.50; how can we hope to compete with surrounding towns? What is the result? Mr. Foreman is sent for, and he is told that he has got to stop ruining the labor market of Cleveland. And the foreman goes back to his workman in sadness, in depression, and tells his workman, "I am sorry, John, but I have got to cut the price down for that pen; I cannot let you earn $5 a day; the board of directors has got on to it, and it is ruining the labor market; you ought to be willing to have the price reduced. You cannot earn more than $3 or $2.75 a day, and I will have to cut your wages so that you will only get $3 a day." John, of necessity accepts the cut, but he sees to it that he never makes enough pens to get another cut.

CHARACTERISTICS OF THE UNION WORKMAN

There seem to be two divergent opinions about the workmen of this country. One is that a lot of the trade unions' workmen, particularly in this country, have become brutal, have become dominatinf, careless of any interests but their own, and are a pretty poor lot. And the other opinion which those same trade unionists hold of themselves is that they are pretty close to little gods. Whichever view you may hold of the workingmen of this country, and my personal view of them is that they are a pretty fine lot of fellows, they are just about the same as you and I. But whether you hold the bad opinion or the good opinion, it makes no difference. Whatever the workingmen of this country are or whatever they are not, they are not fools. And all that is necessary is for a workingman to have but one object lesson, like that I have told you, and he soldiers for the rest of his life.

There are a few exceptional employ-

ers who treat their workmen differently, but I am talking about the rule of the country. Soldiering is the absolute rule with all workmen who know their business. I am not saying it is for their interest to soldier. You cannot blame them for it. You cannot expect them to be large enough minded men to look at the proper view of the matter. Nor is the man who cuts the wages necessarily to blame. It is simply a misfortune in industry.

THE DEVELOPMENT OF SCIENTIFIC MANAGEMENT

There has been, until comparatively recently, no scheme promulgated by which the evils of rate cutting could be properly avoided, so soldiering has been the rule.

Now the first step that was taken toward the development of those methods, of those principles, which rightly or wrongly have came to be known under the name of scientific management—the first step that was taken in an earnest endeavor to remedy the evils of soldiering; an earnest endeavor to make it unnecessary for workmen to be hypocritical in this way, to deceive themselves, to deceive their employers, to live day in and day out a life of deceit, forced upon them by conditions—the very first step that was taken toward the development was to overcome that evil. I want to emphasize that, because I wish to emphasize the one great fact relating to scientific management, the greatest factor: namely, that scientific management is no new set of theories that has been tried on by any one at every step. Scientific management at every step has been an evolution, not a theory. In all cases the practice has preceded the theory, not succeeded it. In every case one measure after another has been tried out, until the proper remedy has been found. That series of proper eliminations, that evolution, is what is called scientific management. Every element of it has had to fight its way against the elements that preceded it, and prove itself better or it would not be there tomorrow.

All the men that I know of who are in any way connected with scientific management are ready to abandon any scheme, any theory in favor of anything else that could be found that is better. There is nothing in scientific management that is fixed. There is no one man, or group of men, who have invented scientific management.

What I want to emphasize is that all of the elements of scientific management are an evolution, not an invention. Scientific management is in use in an immense range and variety of industries. Almost every type of industry in this country has scientific management working successfully. I think I can safely say that on the average in those establishments in which scientific management has been introduced, the average workman is turning out double the output he was before. I think that is a conservative statement.

THE WORKMAN THE CHIEF BENEFICIARIES

Three or four years ago I could have said there were about fifty thousand men working under scientific management, but now I know there are many more. Company after company is coming under it, many of which I know nothing about. Almost universally they are working successfully. This increasing of the output per individual in the trade, results, of course, in cheapening the product; it results, therefore, in larger profit usually to the owners of the business; it results also, in many cases, in a lowering of the selling price, although that has not come to the extent it will later. In the end the public gets the good. Without any question, the large good which so far has come from scientific management has come to the worker. To the workman has come, practically right off as soon as scientific management is introduced, an increase

in wages amounting from 33 to 100 per cent, and yet that is not the greatest good that comes to the workmen from scientific management. The great good comes from the fact that, under scientific management, they look upon their employers as the best friends they have in the world; the suspicious watchfulness which characterizes the old type of management, the semi-antagonism, or the complete antagonism between workmen and employers is entirely superseded, and in its place comes genuine friendship between both sides. That is the greatest good that has come under scientific management. As a proof of this in the many businesses in which scientific management has been introduced, I know of not one single strike of workmen working under it after it had been introduced, and only two or three while it was in process of introduction. In this connection I must speak of the fakers, those who have said they can introduce scientific management into a business in six months or a year. That is pure nonsense. There have been many strikes stirred up by that type of man. Not one strike has ever come, and I do not believe ever will come, under scientific management.

WHAT SCIENTIFIC MANAGEMENT IS

What is scientific management? It is no efficiency device, nor is it any group of efficiency devices. Scientific management is no new scheme for paying men, it is no bonus system, no piecework system, no premium system of payment; it is no new method of figuring costs. It is no one of the various elements by which it is commonly known, by which people refer to it. It is not time study nor man study. It is not the printing of a ton or two of blanks and unloading them on a company and saying, "There is your system, go ahead and use it." Scientific management does not exist and cannot exist until there has been a complete mental revolution on the part of the workmen working under it, as to their duties toward themselves and toward their employers, and a complete mental revolution in the outlook for the employers, toward their duties, toward themselves, and toward their workmen. And until this great mental change takes place, scientific management does not exist. Do you think you can make a great mental revolution in a large group of workmen in a year, or do you think you can make it in a large group of foremen and superintendents in a year? If you do, you are very much mistaken. All of us hold mighty close to our ideas and principles in life, and we change very slowly toward the new, and very properly too.

Let me give you an idea of what I mean by this change in mental outlook. If you are manufacturing a hammer or a mallet, into the cost of that mallet goes a certain amount of raw materials, a certain amount of wood and metal. If you will take the cost of the raw materials and then add to it that cost which is frequently called by various names— overhead expenses, general expense, indirect expense; that is, the proper share of taxes, insurance, light, heat, salaries of officers and advertising—and you have a sum of money. Subtract that sum from the selling price, and what is left over is called the surplus. It is over this surplus that all of the labor disputes in the past have occurred. The workman naturally wants all he can get. His wages come out of that surplus. The manufacturer wants all he can get in the shape of profits, and it is from the division of this surplus that all the labor disputes have come in the past—the equitable division.

The new outlook that comes under scientific management is this: The workmen, after many object lessons, come to see and the management come to see that this surplus can be made so great, providing both sides will stop their pulling apart, will stop their fighting and will push as hard as they can to get as cheap an output as possible, that

there is no occasion to quarrel. Each side can get more than ever before. The acknowledgment of this fact represents a complete mental revolution.

INTELLIGENT OLD-STYLE MANAGEMENT

There is one more illustration of the new and great change which comes under scientific management. I can make it clearer, perhaps, by contrasting it with what I look upon as the best of the older types of management. If you have a company employing five hundred or a thousand men, you will have in that company perhaps fifteen different trades. The workmen in those trades have learned absolutely all that they know, not from books, not by being taught, but they have learned it traditionally. It has been handed down to them, not even by word of mouth in many cases, but by seeing what other men do. One man stands alongside of another man and imitates him. That is the way the trades are handed down, and my impression is that trades are now picked up just as they were in the Middle Ages.

The manufacturer, the manager, or the foreman who knows his business realizes that his chief function as a manager—I am talking now of the old-fashioned manager—ought to be to get the true initiative of his workman. He wants the initiative of the workman, their hard work, their good will, their ingenuity, their determination to do all they can for the benefit of his firm. If he knows anything about human nature, if he has thought over the problems, he must realize that in order to get the initiative of his workman, in order to modify their soldiering, he must do something more for his men than other employers are doing for their men under similar circumstances. The wise manager, under the old type of management, deliberately sets out to do something better for his workmen than his competitors are doing, better than he himself has ever done before. It takes a good while for the workmen to stop looking for that "nigger in the woodpile," but if the manager keeps at them long enough he will get the confidence of the men, and when he does workmen of all kinds will respond by giving a great increase in output. When he sets out to do better for his men than other people do for theirs, the workmen respond liberally when that time comes. I refer to this case as being the highest type of management, the case in which the managers deliberately set out to do something better for their workmen than other people are doing, and to give them a special incentive of some kind, to which the workmen respond by giving a share at least of their initiative.

WHAT SCIENTIFIC MANAGEMENT WILL DO

I am going to try to prove to you that the old style of management has not a ghost of a chance in competition with the principles of scientific management. Why? In the first place, under scientific management, the initiative of the workmen, their hard work, their goodwill, their best endeavors are obtained with absolute regularity. There are cases all the time where men will soldier, but they become the exception, as a rule, and they give their true initiative under scientific management. That is the least of the two sources of gain. The greatest source of gain under scientific management comes from the new and almost unheard-of duties and burdens which are voluntarily assumed, not by the workmen, but by the men on the management side. These are the things which make scientific management a success. These new duties, these new burdens undertaken by the management have rightly or wrongly been divided into four groups, and have been called the principles of scientific management.

The first of the great principles of scientific management, the first of the new burdens which are voluntarily under-

taken by those on the management side is the deliberate gathering together of the great mass of traditional knowledge which, in the past, has been in the heads of the workmen, recording it, tabulating it, reducing it in most cases to rules, laws, and in many cases to mathematical formulae, which, with these new laws, are applied to the co-operation of the management to the work of the workmen. This results in an immense increase in the output, we may say, of the two. The gathering in of this great mass of traditional knowledge, which is done by the means of motion study, time study, can be truly called the science.

Let me make a prediction. I have before me the first book, so far as I know, that has been published on motion study and on time study. That is, the motion study and time study of the cement and concrete trades. It contains everything relating to concrete work. It is of about seven hundred pages and embodies the motions of men, the time and the best way of doing that sort of work. It is the first case in which a trade has been reduced to the same condition that engineering data of all kinds have been reduced, and it is this sort of data that is bound to sweep the world.

I have before me something which has been gathering for about fourteen years, the time or motion study of the machine shop. It will take probably four or five years more before the first book will be ready to publish on that subject. There is a collection of sixty or seventy thousand elements affecting machine-shop work. After a few years, say three, four or five years more, some one will be ready to publish the first book giving the laws of the movements of men in the machine shop—all the laws, not only a few of them. Let me predict, just as sure as the sun shines, that is going to come in every trade. Why? Because it pays, for no other reason. That results in doubling the output in any shop. Any device which results in an increased output is bound to come in spite of all oposition, whether we want it or not. It comes automatically.

THE SELECTION OF THE WORKMAN

The next of the four principles of scientific management is the scientific selection of the workman, and then his progressive development. It becomes the duty under scientific management of not one, but of a group of men on the management side, to deliberately study the workmen who are under them; study them in the most careful, thorough and painstaking way; and not just leave it to the poor, overworked foreman to go out and say, "Come on, what do you want? If you are cheap enough I will give you a trial."

That is the old way. The new way is to take a great deal of trouble in selecting the workmen. The selection proceeds year after year. And it becomes the duty of those engaged in scientific management to know something about the workmen under them. It becomes their duty to set out deliberately to train the workmen in their employ to be able to do a better and still better class of work than ever before, and to then pay them higher wages than ever before. This deliberate selection of the workmen is the second of the great duties that devolve on the management under scientific management.

BRINGING TOGETHER THE SCIENCE AND THE MAN

The third principle is the bringing together of this science of which I have spoken and the trained workmen. I say bringing because they don't come together unless some one brings them. Select and train your workmen all you may, but unless there is some one who will make the men and the science come together, they will stay apart. The "make" involves a great many elements. They are not all disagreeable elements. The most important and largest way of "making" is to do something nice for the man whom you wish to make come together with the science. Offer him a plum, something that is worthwhile. There are many plums offered to those who come under scientific management—better treatment, more kindly treatment, more consideration for their wishes, and an opportunity for them to express their wants freely. That is one side of the "make." An equally important side is, whenever a man will not do what he ought, to either make him do it or stop it. If he will not do it, let him get out. I am not talking of any mollycoddle. Let me disabuse your minds of any opinion that scientific management is a mollycoddle scheme.

I have a great many union friends. I find they look with especial bitterness on this word "make." They have been used to doing the "making" in the past. That is the attitude of the trade unions, and it softens matters greatly when you can tell them the facts, namely, that in our making the science and the men come together, nine-tenths of our trouble comes with the men on the management side in making them do their new duties. I am speaking of those who have been trying to change from the old system to the new. Nine-tenths of our troubles come in trying to make the men on the management side do what they ought to do, to make them do the new duties, and take on these new burdens, and give up their old duties. That softens this word "make."

THE PRINCIPLE OF THE DIVISION OF WORK

The fourth principle is the plainest of all. It involves a complete re-division of the work of the establishment. Under the old scheme of management, almost all of the work was done by the workmen. Under the new, the work of the establishment is divided into two large parts. All of that work which formerly was done by the workmen alone is divided into two large sections, and one of those sections is handed over to the management. They do a whole division of the work formerly done by the workmen. It is this real cooperation, this genuine division of the work between the two sides, more than any other element which accounts for the fact that there never will be strikes under scientific management. When the workman realizes that there is hardly a thing he does that does not have to be preceded by some act of preparation on the part of management, and when that workman realizes when the management falls down and does not do its part, that he is not only entitled to a kick, but that he can register that kick in the most forcible possible way, he cannot quarrel with the men over him. It is team work. There are more complaints made every day on the part of the workmen that the men on the management side fail to do their duties than are made by the management that the men fail. Every one of the complaints of the men have to be heeded, just as much as the complaints from the management that the workmen do not do their share. That is characteristic of scientific management. It represents a democracy, co-operation, a genuine division of work which never existed before in this world.

THE PROOF OF THE THEORY

I am through now with the theory. I will try to convince you of the value of these four principles by giving you some practical illustrations. I hope that you will look for these four elements in the illustrations. I shall begin by trying to show the power of these four elements when applied to the greatest kind of work I know of that is done by man. The reason I have heretofore chosen pig-iron for an illustration is that it is the lowest form of work that is known.

A pig of iron weighs about ninety-two pounds on an average. A man stoops down and, with no other implement than his hands, picks up a pig of iron, walks a few yards with it, and drops it on a pile. A large part of the community

has the impression that scientific management is chiefly handling pig-iron. The reason I first chose pig-iron for an illustration is that, if you can prove to any one the strength, the effect, of those four principles when applied to such rudimentary work as handling pig-iron, the presumption is that it can be applied to something better. The only way to prove it is to start at the bottom and show those four principles all along the line. I am sorry I cannot, because of lack of time, give you the illustration of handling pig-iron. Many of you doubt whether there is much of any science in it. I am going to try to prove later with a high class mechanic that the workman who is fit to work at any type of work is almost universally incapable of understanding the principles without the help of some one else. I will use shoveling because it is a shorter illustration, and I will try to show what I mean by the science of shoveling, and the power which comes to the man who knows the science of shoveling. It is a high art compared with pig-iron handling.

THE SCIENCE OF SHOVELING

When I went to the Bethlehem Steel Works, the first thing I saw was a gang of men unloading rice coal. They were a splendid set of fellows, and they shoveled fast. There was no loafing at all. They shoveled as hard as you could ask any man to work. I looked with the greatest of interest for a long time, and finally they moved off rapidly down into the yard to another part of the yard and went right at handling iron ore. One of the main facts connected with that shoveling was that the work those men were doing was that, in handling the rice coal, they had on their shovels a load of 3¾ pounds, and when the same men went to handling ore with the same shovel, they had over 38 pounds on their shovels. Is it asking too much of anyone to inquire whether 3¾ pounds is the right load for a shovel, or whether 38 pounds is the right load for a shovel?

Surely if one is right the other must be wrong. I think that is a self-evident fact, and yet I am willing to bet that that is what workmen are doing right now in Cleveland.

That is the old way. Suppose we notice that fact. Most of us do not notice it because it is left to the foreman. At the Midvale works, we had to find out these facts. What is the old way of finding them out? The old way was to sit down and write one's friends and ask them the question. They got answers from contractors about what they thought it ought to be, and then they averaged them up, or took the most reliable man, and said, "That is all right; now we have a shovel load of so much." The more common way is to say, "I want a good shovel foreman." They will send for the foreman of the shovelers and put the job up to him to find what is the proper load to put on a shovel. He will tell you right off the bat. I want to show you the difference under scientific management.

Under scientific management you ask no one. Every little trifle,—there is nothing too small,—becomes the subject of experiment. The experiments develop into a law; they save money; they increase the output of the individual and make the thing worthwhile. How is this done? What we did in shoveling experiments was to deliberately select two first class shovelers, the best we knew how to get. We brought them into the office and said, "Jim and Mike, you two fellows are both good shovelers. I have a proposition to make to you. I am going to pay you double wages if you fellows will go out and do what I want you to do. There will be a young chap go along with you with a pencil and a piece of paper, and he will tell you to do a lot of fool things, and you will do them, and he will write down a lot of fool things, and you will think it is a joke, but it is nothing of the kind. Let me tell you one thing: if you fellows think that you can fool that chap you are very much mistaken, you cannot

fool him at all. Don't get it through your heads you can fool him. If you take this double wages, you will be straight and do what you are told." They both promised and did exactly what they were told. What we told them was this: "We want you to start in and do whatever shoveling you are told to do, and work at just the pace, all day long, that when it comes night you are going to be good and tired, but not tired out. I do not want you exhausted or anything like that, but properly tired. You know what a good day's work is. In other words, I do not want any loafing business or any overwork business. If you find yourself overworked and getting too tired, slow down." Those men did that and did it in the most splendid kind of way day in and day out. We proved their cooperation because they were in different parts of the yard, and they both got near enough the same results. Our results were duplicated.

I have found that there are a lot of schemes among my working friends, but no more among them than among us. They are good, straight fellows if you only treat them right, and put the matter up squarely to them. We started in at a pile of material, with a very large shovel. We kept innumerable accurate records of all kinds, some of them useless. Thirty or forty different items were carefully observed about the work of those two men. We counted the number of shovelfuls thrown in a day. We found with a weight of between thirty-eight and thirty-nine pounds on the shovel, the man made a pile of material of a certain height. We then cut off the shovel, and he shoveled again and with a thirty-four pound load his pile went up and he shoveled more in a day. We again cut off the shovel to thirty pounds, and the pile went up again. With twenty-six pounds on the shovel, the pile again went up, and at twenty-one and one-half pounds the men could do their best. At twenty pounds the pile went down, at eighteen it went down, and at fourteen it went down, so that they were at the peak of twenty-one and one-half pounds. There is a scientific fact. A first class shoveler ought to take twenty-one and one-half pounds on his shovel in order to work to the best possible advantage. You are not giving that man a chance unless you give him a shovel which will hold twenty-one pounds.

The men in the yard were run by the old fashioned foreman. He simply walked about with them. We at once took their shovels away from them. We built a large labor tool room which held ten to fifteen different kinds of shoveling implements so that for each kind of material that was handled in that yard, all the way from rice coal, ashes, coke, all the way up to ore, we would have a shovel that would just hold twenty-one pounds, or average twenty-one. One time it would hold eighteen, the next twenty-four, but it will average twenty-one.

When you have six hundred men laboring in the yard, as we had there, it becomes a matter of quite considerable difficulty to get, each day, for each one of those six hundred men, engaged in a line one and one-half to two miles long and a half mile wide, just the right shovel for shoveling material. That requires organization to lay out and plan for those men in advance. We had to lay out the work each day. We had to have large maps on which the movements of the men were plotted out a day in advance. When each workman came in the morning, he took out two pieces of paper. One of the blanks gave them a statement of the implements which they had to use, and the part of the yard in which they had to work. That required organization planning in advance.

One of the first principles we adopted was that no man in that labor gang could work on the new way unless he earned sixty per cent higher wages than under the old plan. It is only just to the workman that he shall know right off whether he is doing his work right or not. He must not be told a week or month after, that he fell down. He must know it the next morning. So the next slip that came out of the pigeon hole was either a white or yellow slip. We used the two colors because some of the men could not read. The yellow slip meant that he had not earned his sixty per cent higher wages. He knew that he could not stay in that gang and keep on getting yellow slips.

TEACHING THE MEN

I want to show you again the totally different outlook there is under scientific management by illustrating what happened when that man got his yellow slips. Under the old scheme, the foreman could say to him, "You are no good, get out of this; no time for you, you cannot earn sixty per cent higher wages; get out of this! Go!" It was not done politely, but the foreman had no time to palaver. Under the new scheme what happened? A teacher of shoveling went down to see that man. A teacher of shoveling is a man who is handy with a shovel, who has made his mark in life with a shovel, and yet who is a kindly fellow and knows how to show the other fellow what he ought to do. When that teacher went there he said, "See here, Jim, you have a lot of those yellow slips, what is the matter with you? What is up? Have you been drunk? Are you tired? Are you sick? Anything wrong with you? Because if you are tired or sick we will give you a show somewhere else." "Well, no, I am all right." "Then if you are not sick, or there is nothing wrong with you, you have forgotten how to shovel. I showed you how to shovel. You have forgotten something, now go ahead and shovel and I will show you what is the matter with you." Shoveling is a pretty big science, it is not a little thing.

If you are going to use the shovel right you should always shovel off an iron bottom; if not an iron bottom, a wooden bottom; and if not a wooden bottom a hard dirt bottom. Time and again the conditions are such that you have to go right into the pile. When that is the case, with nine out of ten materials it takes more trouble and more time and more effort to get the shovel into the pile than to do all the rest of the shoveling. That is where the effort comes. Those of you again who have taught the art of shoveling will have taught your workmen to do this. There is only one way to do it right. Put your forearm down onto the upper part of your leg, and when you push into the pile, throw your weight against it. That relieves your arm of work. You then have an automatic push, we will say, about eighty pounds, the weight of your body thrown on to it. Time and again we would find men whom we had taught to shovel right were going at it in the old way, and of course they could not do a day's work. The teacher would simply stand over that fellow and say, "There is what is the matter with you, Jim, you have forgotten to shovel into the pile."

You are not interested in shoveling, you are not interested in whether one way or the other is right, but I do hope to interest you in the difference of the mental attitude of the men who are teaching under the new system. Under the new system, if a man falls down, the presumption is that it is our fault at first, that we probably have not taught the man right, have not given him a fair show, have not spent time enough in showing him how to do his work.

Let me tell you another thing that is characteristic of scientific management. In my day, we were smart enough to know when the boss was coming, and when he cam up we were apparently really working. Under scientific management, there is none of that pretense. I cannot say that in the old days we were delighted to see the boss coming around. We always expected some kind of roast if he came too close. Under the

new, the teacher is welcomed; he is not an enemy, but a friend. He comes there to try to help the man get bigger wages, to show him how to do something. It is the great mental change, the change in the outlook that comes, rather than the details of it.

DOES SCIENTIFIC MANAGEMENT PAY?

It took the time of a number of men for about three years to study the art of shoveling in that yard at the Bethlehem Steel Works alone. They were carefully trained college men, and they were busy all the time. That costs money, the tool room costs money, the clerks we had to keep there all night figuring up how much the men did the day before cost money, the office in which the men laid out and planned the work cost money. The very fair and proper question, the only question to ask is "Does it pay?" because if scientific management does not pay, there is nothing in it; if it does not pay in dollars and cents, it is the rankest kind of nonsense. There is nothing philanthropic about it. It has got to pay, because business which cannot be done on a profitable basis ought not to be done on a philanthropic basis, for it will not last. At the end of three and one-half years we had a very good chance to know whether or not it paid.

Fortunately in the Bethlehem Steel Works they had records of how much it cost to handle the materials under the old system, where the single foreman led a group of men around the works. It costs them between seven and eight cents a ton to handle materials, on an average throughout the year. After paying for all this extra work I have told you about, it cost between three and four cents a ton to handle materials, and there was a profit of between seventy-five and eighty thousand dollars a year in that yard by handling those materials in the new way. What the men got out of it was this: Under the old system there were between four and six hundred men handling the material in that yard, and when we got through there were about one hundred and forty. Each one was earning a great deal more money. We made careful investigation and found they were almost all saving money, living better, happier; they are the most contented set of laborers to be seen anywhere. It is only by this kind of justification, justification of a profit for both sides, an advantage to both sides, that scientific management can exist.

I would like to give you one more illustration. I want to try to prove to you that even the highest class mechanic cannot possibly understand the philosophy of his work, cannot possibly understand the laws under which he has to operate. There is a man who has had a high school education, an ingenious fellow who courts variety in life, to whom it is pleasant to change from one kind of work to another. He is not a cheap man, he is rather a high grade man among the machinists of this country. The case of which I am going to tell you is one in which my friend Barth went to introduce scientific management in the works of an owner, who, at between 65 and 70 years of age, had built up his business from nothing to almost five thousand men. They had a squabble, and after they got through, Mr. Barth made the proposition, "I will take any machine that you use in your shop, and I will show you that I can double the output of that machine." A very fair machine was selected. It was a lathe on which the workman had been working about twelve years. The product of that shop is a patented machine with a good many parts, 350 men working making those parts year in and year out. Each man had ten or a dozen parts a year.

The first thing that was done was in the presence of the foreman, the superintendent and the owner of the establishment. Mr. Barth laid down the way in which all of the parts were to be machined on that machine by the workman. Then Mr. Barth, with one of his small slide rules, proceeded to analyze the machine. With the aid of this analysis, which embodies the laws of cuttimg metals, Mr. Barth was able to take his turn at the machine; his gain was from two and one-half times to three times the amount of work turned out by the other man. This is what can be done by science as against the old rule of thumb knowledge. That is not exaggeration; the gain is as great as that in many cases.

Let me tell you something. The machines of this country, almost universally in the machine shops of our country, are speeded two or three hundred percent wrong. I made that assertion before the tool builders in Atlantic City. I said, "Gentlemen, in your own shops, many of your machines are two and three hundred percent wrong in speeds. Why? Because you have guessed at it." I am trying to show you what are the losses under the old opinions, the difference between knowledge on the one hand and guesswork on the other.

In 1882, at the end of a long fight with the machinists of the Midvale Steel Works, I went there as a laborer, and finally became a machinist after serving my apprenticeship outside. I finally got into the shop, and worked up to the place of a clerk who had something wrong with him. I then did a little bit more work than the others were doing, not too much. They came to me and said, "See here, Fred, you are not going to be a piecework hog." I said, "You fellows mean that you think I am not going to try to get any more work off these machines? I certainly am. Now I am on the other side, and I am going to be straight with you, and I will tell you so in advance." They said, "All right then, we will give you fair notice you will be outside the fence inside of six weeks." Let me tell you gentlemen, if any of you have been through a fight like that, trying to get workmen to do what they do not want to do, you will know the meanness of it, and you will never want to go into another one. I never would have gone into it if I had known what was ahead of me. After the meanest kind of a bitter fight, at the end of three years, we fairly won out and got a big increase in output. I had no illusion at the end of that time as to my great ability or anything else. I knew that those workmen knew about ten times as much as I did about doing the work. I set out deliberately to get on our side some of that knowledge that those workmen had.

Mr. William Sellers was the president, and he was a man away beyond his generation in progress. I went to him and said, "I want to spend quite a good deal of money trying to educate ourselves on the management side of our works. I do not know much of anything, and I am just about in the same condition as all the rest of the foremen around here." Very reluctantly, I may say, he allowed us to start to spend money. That started the study of the art of cutting metals. At the end of six months, from the standpoint of how to cut the metal off faster, the study did not amount to anything, but we unearthed a gold mine of information. Mr. Sellers laughed at me, but when I was able to show him the possibilities that lay ahead of us, the number of things we could find out, he said, "Go ahead." So until 1889, that experiment went straight ahead day in and day out. That was done because it paid in dollars and cents.

After I left the Midvale Steel Works, we had no means of figuring those experiments except the information which we had already gotten. Ten different machines were built to develop the art of cutting metals, so that almost continuously from 1882 for twenty-six years, all sorts of experiments went on to determine the twelve great elements that go to make up the art of cutting metals. I am trying to show you just what is going to take place in every industry throughout this world. You must know those facts if you are going to

manufacture cheaply, and the only way to know them is to pay for them.

THE DISCOVERY OF HIGH SPEED STEEL

Twelve elements do not sound very many, but they are difficult elements. One of the twelve elements was the discovery of high speed steel, that is, it resulted from a careful series of experiments to determine the proper chemical composition, plus the proper heat treatment of tool steel in order to get the highest cutting speed out of it. It was a series of most carefully tried scientific experiments lasting through three years, which led gradually up to the discovery of high speed steel. Most people think it was an accident. Not at all. It was at the expense of about $50,000 in work, in wages, and in the manufacture of steels. That is one of the twelve elements. There are eleven others. Among the others is this one, simplest of all. We found very early that if we threw a heavy stream of cold water on the tip of the tool, the cooling effect was such that we could run forty percent faster. Mr. Sellers was skeptical, and it was pretty hard to make him believe the truth. He tore down the old shop and built an entirely new shop in order to get that forty percent increase. He had his overhead supply of water brought down to each machine so that it could be adjusted quickly, and by means of that it gave us that forty percent increase. Gentlemen, think of it, only one machine shop in twenty years followed that. It was explained to the manufacturers, and the average man said, "Oh, hell, what's the use." There is the answer.

I also want to try to show you why the high class mechanic cannot possibly compete with this science. The working out of those twelve elements resulted in the development of twelve large mathematical formulas, and in order to figure out the two great things that every mechanic has to know when he sets a tool in a lathe and goes to cutting metals,—what speed and what feed shall be used,—requires the solution of a mathematical problem containing twelve unknown quantities. If any one tries to solve those twelve unknown quantities with a pencil and paper, it takes about six hours. For eighteen years we had mathematicians all the time employed trying to solve that problem, and it paid because we got nearer and nearer to the solution. At the end of eighteen years, instead of taking six hours to solve the problem, it can be solved in twenty seconds by all of the workmen. That brings this problem right down to the level of every day practical common sense.

THE EFFECT ON THE WORKMAN

Almost every one says, "Why, yes, that may be a good thing for the manufacturer, but how about the workmen? You are taking all the initiative away from that workman, you are making a machine out of him; what are you doing for him? He becomes merely a part of the machine." That is the almost universal impression. Again let me try to sweep aside the fallacy of that view by an illustration. The modern surgeon without a doubt is the finest mechanic in the world. He combines the greatest manual dexterity with the greatest knowledge of implements and the greatest knowledge of the materials on which he is working. He is a true scientist, and he is a very highly skilled mechanic.

How does the surgeon teach his trade to the young men who come to the medical school? Does he say to them, "Now, young men, we belong to an older generation than you do, but the new generation is going to far outstrip anything that has been done in our generation; therefore, what we want of you is your initiative. We must have your brains, your thought, with your initiative. Of course, you know we old fellows have certain prejudices. For example, if we were going to amputate a leg, when we come down to the bone we are accustomed to take a saw, and we use it in that way and saw the bone off. But, gentlemen, do not let that fact one minute interfere with you originality, with your initiative, if you prefer an axe or a hatchet." Does the surgeon say this? He does not. He says, "You young men are going to outstrip us, but we will show you how. You shall not use a single implement in a single way until you know just which one to use, and we will tell you which one to use, and until you know how to use it, we will tell you how to use that implement, and after you have learned to use that implement our way, if you then see any defects in the implements, any defects in the method, then invent; but, invent so that you can invent upwards. Do not go inventing things which we discarded years ago."

That is just what we say to our young men in the shops. Scientific Management makes no pretense that there is any finality in it. We merely say that the collective work of thirty or forty men in this trade through eight or ten years has gathered together a large amount of data. Every man in the establishment must start that way, must start our way, then if he can show us any better way, I do not care what it is, we will make an experiment to see if it is better. It will be named after him, and he will get a prize for having improved on one of our standards. There is the way we make progress under scientific management. There is your justification for all this. It does not dwarf initiative, it makes true initiative. Most of our progress comes through our workmen, but it comes in a legitimate way.

4. The Hawthorne Experiments*

F. J. ROETHLISBERGER

At a recent meeting the researches in personnel at the Hawthorne plant of the Western Electric Company were mentioned by both a management man and a union man. There seemed to be no difference of opinion between the two regarding the importance or relevance of these research findings for effective management-employee relations. This seemed to me interesting because it suggested that the labor situation can be discussed at a level where both sides can roughly agree. The question of what this level is can be answered only after closer examination of these studies.

In the February, 1941, issue of the *Reader's Digest* there appeared a summary statement of these researches by Stuart Chase, under the title, "What Makes the Worker Like to Work?" At the conclusion of his article, Stuart Chase said, "There is an idea here so big that it leaves one gasping." Just what Mr. Chase meant by this statement is not explained, but to find out one can go back to the actual studies and see what was learned from them. In my opinion, the results were very simple and obvious—as Sherlock Holmes used to say to Dr. Watson, "Elementary, my dear Watson." Now this is what may have left Stuart Chase "gasping"—the systematic exploitation of the simple and the obvious which these studies represent.

There seems to be an assumption today that we need a complex set of ideas to handle the complex problems of this complex world in which we live. We assume that a big problem needs a big idea; a complex problem needs a complex idea for its solution. As a result, our thinking tends to become more and more tortuous and muddled. Nowhere is this more true than in matters of human behavior. It seems to me that the road back to sanity—and here is where my title comes in—lies

(1) In having a few simple and clear ideas about the world in which we live.

(2) In complicating our ideas, not in a vacuum, but only in reference to things we can observe, see, feel, hear, and touch. Let us not generalize from verbal definitions; let us know in fact what we are talking about.

(3) In having a very simple method by means of which we can explore our complex world. We need a tool which will allow us to get the data from which our generalizations are to be drawn. We need a simple skill to keep us in touch with what is sometimes referred to as "reality."

(4) In being "tough-minded," i.e., in not letting ourselves be too disappointed because the complex world never quite fulfills our most cherished expectations of it. Let us remember that the concrete phenomena will always elude any set of abstractions that we can make of them.

(5) In knowing very clearly the class of phenomena to which our ideas and methods relate. Now, this is merely a way of saying, "Do not use a saw as a hammer." A saw is a useful tool precisely because it is limited and designed for a certain purpose. Do not criticize the usefulness of a saw because it does not make a good hammer.

*Source: Reprinted by permission of the publishers from *Management and Morale* by F. J. Roethlisberger, Cambridge, Mass.: Harvard University Press, Copyright © 1941 by the President and Fellows of Harvard College; © 1969 by Fritz Jules Roethlisberger. Selection has been retitled and originally appeared as Chapter II, "The Road Back to Sanity," pp. 7-26.

Although this last statement is obvious with regard to such things as "saws" and "hammers," it is less well understood in the area of human relations. Too often we try to solve human problems with nonhuman tools and, what is still more extraordinary, in terms of nonhuman data. We take data from which all human meaning has been deleted and then are surprised to find that we reach conclusions which have no human significance.

It is my simple thesis that a human problem requires a human solution. First, we have to learn to recognize a human problem when we see one; and, second, upon recognizing it, we have to learn to deal with it as such and not as if it were something else. Too often at the verbal level we talk glibly about the importance of the human factor; and too seldom at the concrete level of behavior do we recognize a human problem for what it is and deal with it as such. *A human problem to be brought to a human solution requires human data and human tools.* It is my purpose to use the Western Electric researches as an illustration of what I mean by this statement, because, if they deserve the publicity and acclaim which they have received, it is because, in my opinion, they have so conclusively demonstrated this point. In this sense they are the road back to sanity in management-employee relations.

EXPERIMENTS IN ILLUMINATION

The Western Electric researches started about sixteen years ago, in the Hawthorne plant, with a series of experiments on illumination. The purpose was to find out the relation of the quality and quantity of illumination to the efficiency of industrial workers. These studies lasted several years, and I shall not describe them in detail. It will suffice to point out that the results were quite different from what had been expected.

In one experiment the workers were divided into two groups. One group, called the "test group," was to work under different illumination intensities. The other group, called the "control group," was to work under an intensity of illumination as nearly constant as possible. During the first experiment, the test group was submitted to three different intensities of illumination of increasing magnitude, 24, 46, and 70 foot candles. What were the results of this early experiment? Production increased in both rooms—in both the test group and the control group—and the rise in output was roughly of the same magnitude in both cases.

In another experiment, the light under which the test group worked was decreased from 10 to 3 foot candles, while the control group worked, as before, under a constant level of illumination intensity. In this case the output rate in the test group went up instead of down. It also went up in the control group.

In still another experiment, the workers were allowed to believe that the illumination was being increased, although, in fact, no change in intensity was made. The workers commented favorably on the improved lighting condition, but there was no appreciable change in output. At another time, the workers were allowed to believe that the intensity of illumination was being decreased, although again, in fact, no actual change was made. The workers complained somewhat about the poorer lighting, but again there was no appreciable effect on output.

And finally, in another experiment, the intensity of illumination was decreased to .06 of a foot candle, which is the intensity of illumination approximately equivalent to that of ordinary moonlight. Not until this point was reached was there any appreciable decline in the output rate.

What did the experimenters learn? Obviously, as Stuart Chase said, there was something "screwy," but the experimenters were not quite sure who or what was screwy—they themselves, the subjects, or the results. One thing was clear: the results were negative. Nothing of a positive nature had been learned about the relation of illumination to industrial efficiency. If the results were to be taken at their face value, it would appear that there was no relation between illumination and industrial efficiency. However, the investigators were not yet quite willing to draw this conclusion. They realized the difficulty of testing for the effect of a single variable in a situation where there were many uncontrolled variables. It was thought therefore that another experiment should be devised in which other variables affecting the output of workers could be better controlled.

A few of the tough-minded experimenters already were beginning to suspect their basic ideas and assumptions with regard to human motivation. It occurred to them that the trouble was not so much with the results or with the subjects as it was with their notion regarding the way their subjects were supposed to behave—the notion of a simple cause-and-effect, direct relationship between certain physical changes in the workers' environment and the responses of the workers to these changes. Such a notion completely ignored the human meaning of these changes to the people who were subjected to them.

In the illumination experiments, therefore, we have a classic example of trying to deal with a human situation in nonhuman terms. The experimenters had obtained no human data; they had been handling electric-light bulbs and plotting average output curves. Hence their results had no human significance. That is why they seemed screwy. Let me suggest here, however, that the results were not screwy, but the experimenters were—a "screwy" person being by definition one who is not acting in accordance with the customary human values of the situation in which he finds himself.

THE RELAY ASSEMBLY TEST ROOM

Another experiment was framed, in which it was planned to submit a segregated group of workers to different kinds of working conditions. The idea was very simple: A group of five girls were placed in a separate room where their conditions of work could be carefully controlled, where their output could be measured, and where they could be closely observed. It was decided to introduce at specified intervals different changes in working conditions and to see what effect these innovations had on output. Also, records were kept, such as the temperature and humidity of the room, the number of hours each girl slept at night, the kind and amount of food she ate for breakfast, lunch, and dinner. Output was carefully measured, the time it took each girl to assemble a telephone relay of approximately forty parts (roughly a minute) being automatically recorded each time; quality records were kept; each girl had a physical examination at regular intervals. Under these conditions of close observation the girls were studied for a period of five years. Literally tons of material were collected. Probably nowhere in the world has so much material been collected about a small group of workers for such a long period of time.

But what about the results? They can be stated very briefly. When all is said and done, they amount roughly to this: A skillful statistician spent several years trying to relate variations in output with variations in the physical circumstances of these five operators. For example, he correlated the hours that each girl spent in bed the night before with variations in output the following day. Inasmuch as some people said that the effect of being out late one night was not felt the following day but the day after that, he correlated variations in output with the amount of rest the operators had had two nights before. I mention this just to point out the fact that he missed no obvious tricks and that he did a careful job and a thorough one, and it took him many years to do it. The attempt to relate changes in physical circumstances to variations in output resulted in not a single correlation of enough statistical significance to be recognized by any competent statistician as having any meaning.

Now, of course, it would be misleading to say that this negative result was the only conclusion reached. There were positive conclusions, and it did not take the experimenters more than two years to find out that they had missed the boat. After two years of work, certain things happened which made them sit up and take notice. Different experimental conditions of work, in the nature of changes in the number and duration of rest pauses and differences in the length of the working day and week, had been introduced in this Relay Assembly Test Room. For example, the investigators first introduced two five-minute rests, one in the morning and one in the afternoon. Then they increased the length of these rests, and after that they introduced the rests at different times of the day. During one experimental period they served the operators a specially prepared lunch during the rest. In the later periods, they decreased the length of the working day by one-half hour and then by one hour. They gave the operators Saturday morning off for a while. Altogether, thirteen such periods of different working conditions were introduced in the first two years.

During the first year and a half of the experiment, everybody was happy, both the investigators and the operators. The investigators were happy because as conditions of work improved the output rate rose steadily. Here, it appeared, was strong evidence in favor of their preconceived hypothesis that fatigue was the major factor limiting output. The operators were happy because their conditions of work were being improved, they were earning more money, and they were objects of considerable attention from top management. But then one investigator—one of those tough-minded fellows—suggested that they restore the original conditions of work, that is, go back to a full forty-eight-hour week without rests, lunches and what not. This was Period XII. Then the happy state of affairs, when everything was going along as it theoretically should, went sour. Output, instead of taking the expected nose dive, maintained its high level.

Again the investigators were forcibly reminded that human situations are likely to be complex. In any human situation, whenever a simple change is introduced—a rest pause, for example—other changes, unwanted and unanticipated, may also be brought about. What I am saying here is very simple. If one experiments on a stone, the stone does not know it is being experimented upon—all of which makes it simple for people experimenting on stones. But if a human being is being experimented upon, he is likely to know it. Therefore, his attitudes toward the experiment and toward the experimenters become very important factors in determining his responses to the situation.

Now that is what happened in the Relay Assembly Test Room. To the investigators, it was essential that the workers give their full and wholehearted coöperation to the experiment. They did not want the operators to work harder or easier depending upon their attitude toward the conditions that were imposed. They wanted them to work as they felt, so that they could be sure that the different physical conditions of work were solely responsible for the variations in output. For each of the experimental changes, they wanted subjects whose responses would be uninfluenced by so-called "psychological factors."

In order to bring this about, the investigators did everything in their power to secure the complete coöperation of their subjects, with the result that almost all the practices common to the shop were altered. The operators were consulted about the changes to be made, and, indeed, several plans were abandoned because they met with the disapproval of the girls. They were questioned sympathetically about their reactions to the conditions imposed, and many of these conferences took place in the office of the superintendent. The girls were allowed to talk at work; their "bogey" was eliminated. Their physical health and well-being became matters of great concern. Their opinions, hopes, and fears were eagerly sought. What happened was that in the very process of setting the conditions for the test—a so-called "controlled" experiment—the experimenters had completely altered the social situation of the room. Inadvertently a change had been introduced which was far more important than the planned experimental innovations: the customary supervision in the room had been revolutionized. This accounted for the better attitudes of the girls and their improved rate of work.

THE DEVELOPMENT OF A NEW AND MORE FRUITFUL POINT OF VIEW

After Period XII in the Relay Assembly Test Room, the investigators decided to change their ideas radically. What all their experiments had dramatically and conclusively demonstrated was the importance of employee attitudes and sentiments. It was clear that the responses of workers to what was happening about them were dependent upon the significance these events had for them. In most work situations the meaning of a change is likely to be as important, if not more so, than the change itself. This was the great éclaircissement, the new illumination, that came from the research. It was an illumination quite different from what they had expected from the illumination studies. Curiously enough, this discovery is nothing very new or startling. It is something which anyone who has had some concrete experience in handling other people intuitively recognizes and practices. Whether or not a person is going to give his services whole-heartedly to a group depends, in good part, on the way he feels about his job, his fellow workers, and supervisors—the meaning for him of what is happening about him.

However, when the experimenters began to tackle the problem of employee attitudes and the factors determining such attitudes—when they began to tackle the problem of "meaning"—they entered a sort of twilight zone where things are never quite what they seem. Moreover, overnight, as it were, they were robbed of all the tools they had so carefully forged; for all their previous tools were nonhuman tools concerned with the measurement of output, temperature, humidity, etc., and these were no longer useful for the human data that they now wanted to obtain. What the experimenters now wanted to know was how a person felt, what his intimate thinking, reflections, and preoccupations were, and what he liked and disliked about his work environment. In short, what did the whole blooming business—his job, his supervision, his working conditions—mean to him? Now this was human stuff, and there were no tools, or at least the experimenters knew of none, for obtaining and evaluating this kind of material.

Fortunately, there were a few courageous souls among the experimenters. These men were not metaphysicians, psychologists, academicians, professors, intellectuals, or what have you. They were men of common sense and of practical affairs. They were not driven by any great heroic desire to change the world. They were true experimenters, that is, men compelled to follow the implications of their own monkey business. All the evidence of their studies was pointing in one direction. Would they take the jump? They did.

EXPERIMENTS IN INTERVIEWING WORKERS

A few tough-minded experimenters decided to go into the shops and—completely disarmed and denuded of their elaborate logical equipment and in all humility—to see if they could learn how to get the workers to talk about things that were important to them and could learn to understand what the workers were trying to tell them. This was a revolutionary idea in the year 1928, when this interviewing program started—the idea of getting a worker to talk to you and to listen sympathetically, but intelligently, to what he had to say. In that year a new era of personnel relations began. It was the first real attempt to get human data and to forge human tools to get them. In that year a novel idea was born; dimly the experimenters perceived a new method of human control. In that year the Rubicon was crossed from which there could be no return to the "good old days." Not that the experimenters ever wanted to return, because they now entered a world so exciting, so intriguing, and so full of promise that it made the "good old days" seem like the prattle and play of children.

When these experimenters decided to enter the world of "meaning," with very few tools, but with a strong sense of curiosity and a willingness to learn, they had many interesting adventures. It would be too long a story to tell all of them, or even a small part of them. They made plenty of mistakes, but they were not afraid to learn.

At first, they found it difficult to learn to give full and complete attention to what a person had to say without interrupting him before he was through. They found it difficult to learn not to give advice, not to make or imply moral judgments about the speaker, not to argue, not to be too clever, not to domi-

nate the conversation, not to ask leading questions. They found it difficult to get the person to talk about matters which were important to him and not to the interviewer. But, most important of all, they found it difficult to learn that perhaps the thing most significant to a person was not something in his immediate work situation.

Gradually, however, they learned these things. They discovered that sooner or later a person tends to talk about what is uppermost in his mind to a sympathetic and skillful listener, and they became more proficient in interpreting what a person is saying or trying to say. Of course they protected the confidences given to them and made absolutely sure that nothing an employee said could ever be used against him. Slowly they began to forge a simple human tool—imperfect, to be sure—to get the kind of data they wanted. They called this method "interviewing." I would hesitate to say the number of manhours of labor which went into the forging of this tool. There followed from studies made through its use a gradually changing conception of the worker and his behavior.

A NEW WAY OF VIEWING EMPLOYEE SATISFACTION AND DISSATISFACTION

When the experimenters started to study employee likes and dislikes, they assumed, at first, that they would find a simple and logical relation between a person's likes or dislikes and certain items and events in his immediate work situation. They expected to find a simple connection, for example, between a person's complaint and the object about which he was complaining. Hence, the solution would be easy: correct the object of the complaint, if possible, and presto! the complaint would disappear. Unfortunately, however, the world of human behavior is not so simple as this conception of it; and it took the investigators several arduous and painful years to find this out. I will mention only a few interesting experiences they had.

Several times they changed the objects of the complaint only to find that the attitudes of the complainants remained unchanged. In these cases, correcting the object of the complaint did not remedy the complaint or the attitude of the person expressing it. A certain complaint might disappear, to be sure, only to have another one arise. Here the investigators were running into so-called "chronic kickers," people whose dissatisfactions were more deeply rooted in factors relating to their personal histories. For such people the simple remedy of changing the object of the complaint was not enough.

Several times they did absolutely nothing about the object of the complaint, but after the interview, curiously enough, the complaint disappeared. A typical example of this was that of a woman who complained at great length and with considerable feeling about the poor food being served in the company restaurant. When, a few days later, she chanced to meet the interviewer, she commented with great enthusiasm upon the improved food and thanked the interviewer for communicating her grievance to management and for securing such prompt action. Here no change had been made in the thing criticized; yet the employee felt that something had been done.

Many times they found that people did not really want anything done about the things of which they were complaining. What they did want was an opportunity to talk about their troubles to a sympathetic listener. It was astonishing to find the number of instances in which workers complained about things which had happened many, many years ago, but which they described as vividly as if they had happened just a day before.

Here again, something was "screwy," but this time the experimenters realized that it was their assumptions which were screwy. They were assuming that the meanings which people assign to their experience are essentially logical. They were carrying in their heads the notion of the "economic man," a man primarily motivated by economic interest, whose logical capacities were being used in the service of this self-interest.

Gradually and painfully in the light of the evidence, which was overwhelming, the experimenters had been forced to abandon this conception of the worker and his behavior. Only with a new working hypothesis could they make sense of the data they had collected. The conception of the worker which they developed is actually nothing very new or startling; it is one which any effective administrator intuitively recognizes and practices in handling human beings.

First, they found that the behavior of workers could not be understood apart from their feelings or sentiments. I shall use the word "sentiment" hereafter to refer not only to such things as feelings and emotions, but also to a much wider range of phenomena which may not be expressed in violent feelings or emotions—phenomena that are referred to by such words as "loyalty," "integrity," "solidarity."

Secondly, they found that sentiments are easily disguised, and hence are difficult to recognize and to study. Manifestations of sentiment take a number of different forms. Feelings of personal integrity, for example, can be expressed by a handshake; they can also be expressed, when violated, by a sitdown strike. Moreover, people like to rationalize their sentiments and to objectify them. We are not so likely to say "I feel bad," as to say "The world is bad." In other words, we like to endow the world with those attributes and qualities which will justify and account for the feelings and sentiments we have toward it; we tend to project our sentiments on the outside world.

Thirdly, they found that manifestations of sentiment could not be understood as things in and by themselves, but only in terms of the total situation of the person. To comprehend why a person felt the way he did, a wider range of phenomena had to be explored. The following three diagrams illustrate roughly the development of this point of view.

It will be remembered that at first the investigators assumed a simple and direct relation between certain physical changes in the worker's environment and his responses to them. This simple state of mind is illustrated in diagram I. But all the evidence of the early experiments showed that the responses of employees to changes in their immediate working environment can be understood only in terms of their attitudes—the "meaning" these changes have for them. This point of view is represented in diagram II. However, the "meaning" which these changes have for the worker is not strictly and primarily logical, for they are fraught with human feelings and values. The "meaning," therefore, which any individual worker assigns to a particular change depends upon (1) his social "conditioning," or what sentiments (values, hopes, fears, expectations, etc.) he is bringing to the work situation because of his previous family and group associations, and hence the relation of the change to these sentiments; and (2) the kind of human satisfactions he is deriving from his social participation with other workers and supervisors in the immediate work group of which he is a member, and hence the effect of the change on his customary interpersonal relations. This way of regarding the responses of workers (both verbal and overt) is represented in diagram III. It says briefly: Sentiments do not appear in a vacuum; they do not come out of the blue; they appear in a social context. They have to be considered in terms of that context, and apart from it they are likely to be misunderstood.

One further point should be made about that aspect of the worker's environment designated "Social Situation at

I. Change————Response

II. Change————Response
                    ＼
         Attitudes (Sentiments)

III. Change   Response
           ＼   ／
         Attitudes (Sentiments)
           ／   ＼
Personal   Social Situation
History   at Work

Work" in diagram III. What is meant is that the worker is not an isolated, atomic individual; he is a member of a group, or of groups. Within each of these groups the individuals have feelings and sentiments toward each other, which bind them together in collaborative effort. Moreover, these collective sentiments can, and do, become attached to every item and object in the industrial environment—even to output. Material goods, output, wages, hours of work, and so on, cannot be treated as things in themselves. Instead, they must be interpreted as carriers of social value.

OUTPUT AS A FORM OF SOCIAL BEHAVIOR

That output is a form of social behavior was well illustrated in a study made by the Hawthorne experimenters, called the Bank Wiring Observation Room. This room contained fourteen workmen representing three occupational groups—wiremen, soldermen, and inspectors. These men were on group piecework, where the more they turned out the more they earned. In such a situation one might have expected that they would have been interested in maintaining total output and that the faster workers would have put pressure on the slower workers to improve their efficiency. But this was not the case. Operating within this group were four basic sentiments, which can be expressed briefly as follows: (1) You should not turn out too much work; if you do, you are a "rate buster." (2) You should not turn out too little work; if you do, you are a "chiseler." (3) You should not say anything to a supervisor which would react to the detriment of one of your associates; if you do, you are a "squealer." (4) You should not be too officious; that is, if you are an inspector you should not act like one.

To be an accepted member of the group a man had to act in accordance with these social standards. One man in this group exceeded the group standard of what constituted a fair day's work. Social pressure was put on him to conform, but without avail, since he enjoyed doing things the others disliked. The best-liked person in the group was the one who kept his output exactly where the group agreed it should be.

Inasmuch as the operators were agreed as to what constituted a day's work, one might have expected rate of output to be about the same for each member of the group. This was by no means the case; there were marked differences. At first the experimenters thought that the differences in individual performance were related to differences in ability, so they compared each worker's relative rank in output with his relative rank in intelligence and dexterity as measured by certain tests. The results were interesting: the lowest producer in the room ranked first in intelligence and third in dexterity; the highest producer in the room was seventh in dexterity and lowest in intelligence. Here surely was a situation in which the native capacities of the men were not finding expression. From the viewpoint of logical, economic behavior, this room did not make sense. Only in terms of powerful sentiments could these individual differences in output level be explained. Each worker's level of output reflected his position in the informal organization of the group.

WHAT MAKES THE WORKER NOT WANT TO COOPERATE?

As a result of the Bank Wiring Observation Room, the Hawthorne researchers became more and more interested in the informal employee groups which tend to form within the formal organization of the company, and which are not likely to be represented in the organization chart. They became interested in the beliefs and creeds which have the effect of making each individual feel an integral part of the group and which make the group appear as a single unit, in the social codes and norms of behavior by means of which employees automatically work together in a group without any conscious choice as to whether they will or will not coöperate. They studied the important social functions these groups perform for their members, the histories of these informal work groups, how they spontaneously appear, how they tend to perpetuate themselves, multiply, and disappear, how they are in constant jeopardy from technical change, and hence how they tend to resist innovation. In particular, they became interested in those groups whose norms and codes of behavior are at variance with the technical and economic objectives of the company as a whole. They examined the social conditions under which it is more likely for the employee group to separate itself out in opposition to the remainder of the groups which make up the total organization. In such phenomena they felt that they had at last arrived at the heart of the problem of effective collaboration. They obtained a new enlightenment of the present industrial scene; from this point of view, many perplexing problems became more intelligible.

Some people claim, for example, that the size of the pay envelope is the major demand which the employee is making of his job. All the worker wants is to be told what to do and to get paid for doing it. If we look at him and his job in terms of sentiments, this is far from being as generally true as we would like to believe. Most of us want the satisfaction that comes from being accepted and recognized as people of worth by our friends and work associates. Money is only a small part of this social recognition. The way we are greeted by our boss, being asked to help a newcomer, being asked to keep an eye on a difficult operation, being given a job requiring special skill—all of these are acts of social recognition. They tell us how we stand in our work group. We all want tangible evidence of our social importance. We want to have a skill that is socially recognized as useful. We want the feeling of security that comes not so much from the amount of money we have in the bank as from being an accepted member of a group. A man whose job is without social function is like a man without a country; the activity to which he has to give the major portion of his life is robbed of all human meaning and significance.

If this is true—and all the evidence of the Western Electric researches points in this direction—have we not a clue as to the possible basis for labor unrest and disputes? Granted that these disputes are often stated in terms of wages, hours of work, and physical conditions of work, is it not possible that these demands are disguising, or in part are the symptomatic expression of, much more deeply rooted human situations which we have not as yet learned to recognize, to understand, or to control? It has been said there is an irresistible urge on the part of workers to tell the boss off, to tell the boss to go to hell. For some workers this generalization may hold, and I have no reason to believe it does not. But, in those situations where it does, it is telling us something very important about these particular workers and their work situations. Workers who want to tell their boss to go to hell sound to me like people whose feelings of personal integrity have been seriously injured. What in their work situations has shattered

their feelings of personal integrity? Until we understand better the answer to this question, we cannot handle effectively people who manifest such sentiments. Without such understanding we are dealing only with words and not with human situations—as I fear our over-logicized machinery for handling employee grievances sometimes does.

The matters of importance to workers which the Hawthorne researches disclosed are not settled primarily by negotiating contracts. If industry today is filled with people living in a social void and without social function, a labor contract can do little to make coöperation possible. If, on the other hand, the workers are an integral part of the social situations in which they work, a legal contract is not of the first importance. Too many of us are more interested in getting our words legally straight than in getting our situations humanly straight.

In summary, therefore, the Western Electric researches seem to me like a beginning on the road back to sanity in employee relations because (1) they offer a fruitful working hypothesis, a few simple and relatively clear ideas for the study and understanding of human situations in business; (2) they offer a simple method by means of which we can explore and deal with the complex human problems in a business organization—this method is a human method: it deals with things which are important to people; and (3) they throw a new light on the precondition for effective collaboration. Too often we think of collaboration as something which can be logically or legally contrived. The Western Electric studies indicate that it is far more a matter of sentiment than a matter of logic. Workers are not isolated, unrelated individuals; they are social animals and should be treated as such.

This statement—the worker is a social animal and should be treated as such—is simple, but the systematic and consistent practice of this point of view is not. If it were systematically practiced, it would revolutionize present-day personnel work. Our technological development in the past hundred years has been tremendous. Our methods of handling people are still archaic. If this civilization is to survive, we must obtain a new understanding of human motivation and behavior in business organizations—an understanding which can be simply but effectively practiced. The Western Electric researches contribute a first step in this direction.

II

Criterion Development and Performance Appraisal

Introduction. The development of job performance criteria and the methods for measuring and evaluating individuals' job behavior with respect to these criteria is a significant issue for many I/O psychologists, because job performance and behavior are generally the dependent or outcome variables we try to predict by personnel selection, develop by training programs, influence by designing jobs and reward systems, inspire by leadership, and improve by changing organizations. In effect, job performance is the *sine qua non* of I/O psychology, and criterion development and performance appraisal are processes on which many other activities of I/O psychologists ultimately depend. Therefore, it is only fitting that we begin our review of the substantive areas of I/O psychology with this fundamentally important topic.

One of the oldest and most widely used techniques for measuring job behavior is the critical incident technique. This technique was first described by James C. Flanagan in an article published in 1949 and was later elaborated on in some detail by Flanagan in the 1954 article, "The Critical Incident Technique," which is included here as our opening selection. The first step in this procedure is to ask supervisors, subordinates and coworkers to identify for particular jobs specific behaviors that were critical in satisfactory or unsatisfactory job performance. These "critical incidents" are then used to identify basic dimensions or areas of performance. The results may be as complex as a rating scale or as simple as a checklist of important job behaviors that a supervisor can use to evaluate an employee's performance by observing and recording those behaviors, both "good" and "bad," that the employee exhibits. An overall rating based on the number and relative desirability of the employee's observed behavior can be used as a measure of his or her job performance.

The next paper in this section, "Dimensional Problems of Criteria" by Edwin E. Ghiselli, addresses a controversy that for some time dominated issues concerning criterion measurement. Most of the early work relating to this issue reflected the assumption that for any given work situation there was an "ultimate criterion" that was the single best measure of job performance. The problem with this view is that job performance is multidimensional; that is, there is more than one kind of behavior involved in successful job performance. For example, assembly line workers must keep up with the pace of the line. They should also work carefully enough to keep product defects to a minimum, be on time, get along with their co-workers, miss few work days, and remain in the job for an extended period of time. As a result, attention subsequently shifted away from attempts to identify a single measure of job success to the development of "composite criteria" that combined several components of success into an overall measure.

Ghiselli was one of the first to criticize the composite approach and argue for the adoption of multiple criteria that deal separately with the individual dimensions of job performance. In his article, he identifies three ways in which the multidimensionality of criteria need to be considered. First, at any given time, a worker's performance can be measured along several different dimensions. In addition, the relations among different criteria and between tests and criteria may change over time. And, finally, different individuals may perform successfully in different ways by using different abilities and behaviors.

One of the most promising developments in recent years has been the assessment center approach to the evaluation of managerial performance and potential. The next article, "The Assessment Center Method," is written by Douglas Bray, a pioneer in the development and use of this technique. The technique played a central role in Bray's Management Progress Study at AT&T, which is still the most extensive, long-term, and well documented research on assessment centers (Bray, 1964; Grant and Bray, 1966).

While there are many variations of the assessment center technique, there are several features they usually have in common. First, the job related behavior of participants is assessed away from their jobs in a highly structured situation where these behaviors can be more easily observed. Second, the assessment activities generally include the direct observation of participants' performance on situational tests and simulations. And third, the technique has been used almost exclusively for assessing behaviors in managerial jobs, although there appears to be no a priori reason why it could not be adopted for other kinds of jobs as well.

Three other features of the assessment center approach should be pointed out: first, this approach reflects the emphasis of Flanagan's critical incident technique on the direct observation of behavior; second, it is in accordance with Ghiselli's advocacy of the multidimensionality of job performance; and third, it has been used as a predictor of future job performance in personnel selection and, as such, is consistent with current interest in the use of work samples for this purpose (see the Wernimont and Campbell article in the section to follow).

One of the most elusive and enduring problems in criterion development and performance appraisal has been the description and classification of tasks in terms that are general enough to allow their applicability to a wide variety of jobs, yet specific enough to be meaningful. Without a taxonomy of basic dimensions, it is frequently necessary to develop new criterion and performance appraisal systems from scratch for each job. The last article in this section, "Toward a Taxonomy of Human Performance" by Edwin Fleishman, describes one of the most extensive and successful attempts to develop just such a taxonomy. One of the features of Fleishman's work that appears particularly useful is his effort to describe the taxonomy of tasks in terms of the abilities needed to perform them. (For other work on this issue see Fine, 1974 and McCormick, Jeanneret and Mecham, 1972.)

REFERENCES

Bray, D. W. 1964. The management progress study. *American Psychologist,* **19,** 419-420.

Fine, S. A. 1974. Functional job analysis: An approach to a technology for manpower planning. *Personnel Journal,* **53,** 813-818.

Grant, D. L., and Bray, D. W. 1966. The assessment center in the measurement of potential for business management. *Psychological Monographs,* **80** (Whole No. 625).

McCormick, E. J., Jeanneret, P. R., and Mecham, R. C. 1972. A study of job characteristics and job dimensions as based on the Position Analysis Questionnaire (PAQ). *Journal of Applied Psychology,* **56,** 347-368.

5. The Critical Incident Technique*

JOHN C. FLANAGAN

During the past ten years the writer and various collaborators have been engaged in developing and utilizing a method that has been named the "critical incident technique." It is the purpose of this article to describe the development of this methodology, its fundamental principles, and its present status. In addition, the findings of a considerable number of studies making use of the critical incident technique will be briefly reviewed and certain possible further uses of the technique will be indicated.

The critical incident technique consists of a set of procedures for collecting direct observations of human behavior

*Source: From *Psychological Bulletin,* vol. 51 (July 1954), pp. 327-58. Copyright © 1954 by the American Psychological Association. Reprinted by permission.

in such a way as to facilitate their potential usefulness in solving practical problems and developing broad psychological principles. The critical incident technique outlines procedures for collecting observed incidents having special significance and meeting systematically defined criteria.

By an incident is meant any observable human activity that is sufficiently complete in itself to permit inferences and predictions to be made about the person performing the act. To be critical, an incident must occur in a situation where the purpose or intent of the act seems fairly clear to the observer and where its consequences are sufficiently definite to leave little doubt concerning its effects.

Certainly in its broad outlines and basic approach the critical incident technique has very little which is new about it. People have been making observations on other people for centuries. The work of many of the great writers of the past indicates that they were keen observers of their fellow men. Some of these writers must have relied on detailed notes made from their observations. Others may have had unusual abilities to reconstruct memory images in vivid detail. Some may have even made a series of relatively systematic observations on many instances of a particular type of behavior. Perhaps what is most conspicuously needed to supplement these activities is a set of procedures for analyzing and synthesizing such observations into a number of relationships that can be tested by making additional observations under more carefully controlled conditions.

BACKGROUND AND EARLY DEVELOPMENTS

The roots of the present procedures can be traced back directly to the studies of Sir Francis Galton nearly 70 years ago, and to later developments such as time sampling studies of recreational activities, controlled observation tests, and anecdotal records. The critical incident technique as such, however, can best be regarded as an outgrowth of studies in the Aviation Psychology Program of the United States Army Air Forces in World War II. The Aviation Psychology Program was established in the summer of 1941 to develop procedures for the selection and classification of aircrews.

One of the first studies (40) carried out in this program was the analysis of the specific reasons for failure in learning to fly that were reported for 1,000 pilot candidates eliminated from flight training schools in the summer and early fall of 1941. The basic source used in this analysis was the proceedings of the elimination boards. In these proceedings the pilot instructors and check pilots reported their reasons for eliminating the particular pilot. It was found that many of the reasons given were clichés and stereotypes such as "lack of inherent flying ability" and "inadequate sense of sustentation," or generalizations such as "unsuitable temperament," "poor judgment," or "insufficient progress." However, along with these a number of specific observations of particular behaviors were reported. This study provided the basis for the research program on selecting pilots. Although it was found very useful, it also indicated very clearly the need for better procedures for obtaining a representative sample of factual incidents regarding pilot performance.

A second study (13), which emphasized the importance of factual reports on performance made by competent observers, was carried out in the winter of 1943-1944 in the 8th, 9th, 12th, and 15th Air Forces. This study collected the reasons for the failures of bombing missions as reported in the Group Mission Reports. Although in the preparation of these reports much greater emphasis was given to determining the precise facts in the case, it was apparent that in many instances the official reports did not provide a complete

record of all the important events. Even
with these limitations, the information
given was found to be of considerable
value, and the systematic tabulations
that were prepared provided the basis
for a series of recommendations that resulted in important changes in Air Force
selection and training procedures.

In the summer of 1944 a series of
studies (74) was planned on the problem of combat leadership in the United
States Army Air Forces. These represent
the first large-scale, systematic effort to
gather specific incidents of effective or
ineffective behavior with respect to a
designated activity. The instructions
asked the combat veterans to report incidents observed by them that involved
behavior which was especially helpful
or inadequate in accomplishing the assigned mission. The statement finished
with the request, "Describe the officer's
action. What did he do?" Several
thousand incidents were collected in
this way and analyzed to provide a relatively objective and factual definition of
effective combat leadership. The resulting set of descriptive categories was
called the "critical requirements" of
combat leadership.

Another study (74) conducted in the
Aviation Psychology Program involved
a survey of disorientation while flying.[1]
Disorientation in this study was defined
to include any experience denoting uncertainty as to one's spatial position in
relation to the vertical. In this study
pilots returning from combat were asked
"to think of some occasion during combat flying in which you personally experienced feelings of acute disorientation or strong vertigo." They were then
asked to describe what they "saw,
heard, or felt that brought on the ex-

perience." This study led to a number of
recommendations regarding changes in
cockpit and instrument panel design
and in training in order to overcome
and prevent vertigo while flying.

In a project carried out in the Aviation Psychology Program in 1946, Fitts
and Jones (12) collected descriptions of
specific experiences from pilots in taking off, flying on instruments, landing,
using controls, and using instruments.
These interviews with pilots were electrically recorded. They provided many
factual incidents that were used as a
basis for planning research on the design of instruments and controls and the
arrangement of these within the cockpit.

In addition to the collection of
specific incidents and the formulation of
critical requirements, as outlined above,
the summary volume (13) for the Aviation Psychology Program Research Reports contained a discussion of the
theoretical basis of procedures for obtaining the critical requirements of a
particular activity. Perhaps the best
method of describing the status of these
procedures at the close of the war is to
quote from the discussion in this summary volume, which was written in the
late spring of 1946. In the section on
techniques for defining job requirements, the present author wrote as follows:

The principal objective of job analysis
procedures should be the determination of
critical requirements. These requirements
include those which have been demonstrated to have made the difference between success and failure in carrying out
an important part of the job assigned in a
significant number of instances. Too often,
statements regarding job requirements are
merely lists of all the desirable traits of
human beings. These are practically no
help in selecting, classifying, or training
individuals for specific jobs. To obtain
valid information regarding the truly critical requirements for success in a specific
assignment, procedures were developed in
the Aviation Psychology Program for making systematic analyses of causes of good
and poor performance.

---

1. This study was planned by Paul M.
Fitts, Jr., who also contributed to the previously mentioned USAAF studies and planned
and carried out the interview study with
pilots described below on the design of instruments, controls, and arrangements.

Essentially, the procedure was to obtain first-hand reports, or reports from objective records, of satisfactory and unsatisfactory execution of the task assigned. The cooperating individual described a situation in which success or failure was determined by specific reported causes.

This procedure was found very effective in obtaining information from individuals concerning their own errors, from subordinates concerning errors of their superiors, from supervisors with respect to their subordinates, and also from participants with respect to co-participants (13, pp. 273-274).

DEVELOPMENTAL STUDIES AT THE AMERICAN INSTITUTE FOR RESEARCH

At the close of World War II some of the psychologists who had participated in the USAAF Aviation Psychology Program established the American Institute for Research, a nonprofit scientific and educational organization. The aim of this organization is the systematic study of human behavior through a coordinated program of scientific research that follows the same general principles developed in the Aviation Psychology Program. It was in connection with the first two studies undertaken by the Institute in the spring of 1947 that the critical incident technique was more formally developed and given its present name.

These studies were natural extensions of the previous research in the Aviation Psychology Program. The study reported by Preston (52) dealt with the determination of the critical requirements for the work of an officer in the United States Air Force. In this study, many of the procedural problems were first subjected to systematic tryout and evaluation. Six hundred and forty officers were interviewed, and a total of 3,029 critical incidents were obtained. This led to the development of a set of 58 critical requirements classified into six major areas. The second study, reported by Gordon (27, 28), was carried out to de-

termine the critical requirements of a commercial airline pilot. In this study, several different sources were used to establish the critical requirements of the airline pilot. These included training records, flight check records including the specific comments of check pilots, critical pilot behaviors reported in accident records, and critical incidents reported anonymously in interviews by the pilots themselves. From this study, 733 critical pilot behaviors were classified into 24 critical requirements of the airline pilot's job. These were used to develop selection tests to measure the aptitudes and other personality characteristics found critical for success in the job. They also provided the basic data for the formulation of an objective flight check to determine the eligibility of applicants for the airline transport rating.

The third application of the critical incident technique by the staff of the American Institute for Research was in obtaining the critical requirements for research personnel on a project sponsored by the Psychological Sciences Division of the Office of Naval Research. In this study (20), about 500 scientists in 20 research laboratories were interviewed. These scientists reported more than 2,500 critical incidents. The critical behaviors were used to formulate inductively a set of 36 categories, which constitutes the critical requirements for the effective performance of the duties of research personnel in the physical sciences. This initial study provided the basis for the development of selection tests, proficiency measures, and procedures for evaluating both job performance and the research report.

Another project undertaken by the American Institute for Research in the spring of 1948 provided valuable experience with the critical incident technique. This study, reported by Nagay (48), was done for the Civil Aeronautics Administration under the sponsorship of the Committee on Aviation Psychology of the National Research Council. It was concerned with the air route traffic controller's job. One of the innovations in this study was the use of personnel of the Civil Aeronautics Administration who had no previous psychological training in collecting critical incidents by means of personal interviews. In previous studies all such interviewing had been conducted by psychologists with extensive training in such procedures. In this study, aeronautical specialists from each of the seven regions conducted the interviews in their regions after a brief training period. An interesting finding from this study was the clear reflection of seasonal variations in flying conditions in the types of incidents reported. The study also demonstrated the selective recall of dramatic or other special types of incidents. This bias was especially noticeable in the incidents reported several months after their occurrence. The incidents obtained in this study were used to develop procedures for evaluating the proficiency of air route traffic controllers and also for developing a battery of selection tests for this type of personnel.

In the spring of 1949 the American Institute for Research undertook a study to determine the critical job requirements for the hourly wage employees in the Delco-Remy Division of the General Motors Corporation. This study, reported by Miller and Flanagan (46), was the first application of these techniques in an industrial situation. Foremen who were members of a committee appointed to develop employee evaluation procedures collected 2,500 critical incidents in interviews with the other foremen in the plants. On the basis of these data a form was prepared for collecting incidents on a day-to-day basis as a continuous record of job performance.

Using this form, the Performance Record for Hourly Wage Employees (21), three groups of foremen kept records on the performance of their employees for a two-week period. A group of 24 foremen recorded incidents daily; another group of 24 foremen reported incidents at the end of each week; and a third group containing the same number of foremen reported incidents only at the end of the two-week period. The three groups of foremen represented comparable conditions of work and supervision. The foremen reporting daily reported 315 critical incidents; the foremen reporting weekly, 155 incidents; and the foremen reporting only once at the end of two weeks reported 63 incidents. Thus, foremen who reported only at the end of the week had forgotten approximately one half of the incidents they would have reported under a daily reporting plan. The foremen who reported only at the end of the two-week period appeared to have forgotten 80 percent of the incidents observed. Although it is possible that the findings may be partially attributed to the fact that the foremen making daily records actually observed more critical incidents because of the daily reminder at the time of recording, it is clear that much better results can be expected when daily recording is used.

Another analysis based on data collected at the Delco-Remy Division compared the number of critical incidents of various types obtained from interviews with those recorded daily by the foremen on the performance records. Although there were some differences in the relative frequencies for specific categories, the general patterns appeared to be quite similar. These results suggest that critical incidents obtained from interviews can be relied on to provide a relatively accurate account of job performance if suitable precautions are taken to prevent systematic bias.

In addition to the development of the performance record described above, the critical incidents collected in this study were used as the basis for constructing selection tests covering both aptitude (18) and attitude (2) factors.

STUDIES CARRIED OUT AT THE UNIVERSITY OF PITTSBURGH

A substantial number of studies have been carried out in the department of psychology at the University of Pittsburgh by students working for advanced degrees under the author's direction. Most of these studies had as their objective the determination of the critical requirements for a specific occupational group or activity. Many of them also included contributions to technique. In 1949 Wagner (66) completed a dissertation on the critical requirements for dentists. In this study, critical incidents were obtained from three sources: patients, dentists, and dental school instructors. The incidents were classified into four main aspects of the dentist's job: (a) demonstrating technical proficiency; (b) handling patient relationships; (c) accepting professional responsibility; and (d) accepting personal responsibility. As might be expected, the patients did not report as large a proportion of incidents for demonstrating technical proficiency or accepting professional responsibility as did the other two groups, and the instructors reported only a relatively small proportion of their incidents in the area of handling patient relationships.

On the basis of the findings from this study, a battery of selection tests was developed for use by the University of Pittsburgh School of Dentistry. A number of proficiency tests for measuring ability with respect to certain of the critical requirements were also developed using these results as a basis.

Another dissertation completed in 1949 was Finkle's (11) study of the critical requirements of industrial foremen. This study was conducted in the East Pittsburgh plant of the Westinghouse Electric Corporation. Critical incidents were obtained from foremen, general foremen, and staff personnel. A number of points pertaining to technique were studied.

One finding was in reference to the effect on the types of incidents obtained of the degree of importance or exceptionalness set up as a criterion for reporting or ignoring incidents. The incidents obtained from the use of questions that asked for incidents only slightly removed from the norm were compared with incidents obtained from questions intended to elicit more definitely effective or ineffective behaviors. Some examples of these questions are:

1. Think of a time when a foreman has done something that you felt should be encouraged because it seemed to be in your opinion an example of good foremanship. (Effective—slight deviation from norm.)

2. Think of a time when a foreman did something that you thought was not up to par. (Ineffective—slight deviation from norm.)

3. Think of a time when a foreman has, in your opinion, shown definitely good foremanship—the type of action that points out the superior foreman. (Effective—substantial deviation from the norm.)

4. Think of a time when a foreman has, in your opinion, shown poor foremanship—the sort of action which if repeated would indicate that the man was not an effective foreman. (Ineffective—substantial deviation from norm.)

The frequencies of incidents obtained in each of the 40 categories into which the effective behaviors were classified were compared for the questions requesting slight and substantial deviations from the norm, and the significance of the differences was tested by means of the chi-square test. Two of the differences were significant at the 1 percent level and one at the 5 percent level. Comparisons of the frequencies in each of the 40 categories for ineffective incidents failed to reveal any chi squares significant at either the 5 percent or the 1 percent level.

The questions involving only a slight deviation from the norm resulted in more effective incidents concerned with gaining the respect and loyalty of the workers and also in more incidents that involved making, encouraging, and accepting suggestions. They produced significantly fewer incidents regarding fitting men to jobs. The small number of significant differences—only three in 80 comparisons—suggests that the types of incidents obtained are not very greatly changed by variations in wording of the questions comparable to those shown above. It seems likely that this is at least partially due to the fact that the persons interviewed report only incidents that represent a fairly substantial deviation from the norm regardless of the precise wording of the question asked.

Another comparison made in this study related to the influence of asking for an effective or an ineffective incident first. About 10 percent more incidents were obtained from booklets requesting effective incidents first than from booklets requesting ineffective incidents first. This difference was sufficiently small so that it could reasonably be attributed to chance sampling fluctuations.

The incidents collected in this study were used, along with other data, in the preparation of a Performance Record for Foremen and Supervisors (23).

A study was conducted by Nevins (50) on the critical requirements of bookkeepers in sales companies. She collected incidents relating to applicants for bookkeeping positions as well as for employees working in this capacity.

For the collection of the information about the practicing bookkeepers, a modification in the critical incident technique was made. This was done because, in the bookkeeping profession, success and failure are usually defined in terms of persistent behavioral patterns. Occasional mistakes in adding and balancing accounts are expected, but repeated errors are considered serious. Instead of the single incident, there-

fore, many of the items included represented either a pattern of behaviors or a series of similar behaviors.

Weislogel (72) determined the critical requirements for life insurance agency heads. A principal feature of his study related to the comparison of two types of agency heads—managers and general agents. It was believed that the critical behaviors for one type of agency head might provide a different pattern than that obtained for the other. This hypothesis was not confirmed by the analysis of the obtained incidents. The patterns of critical requirements were found to be quite similar for the two types of administrators.

Smit (58) carried out a study to determine the critical requirements for instructors of general psychology courses. Perhaps the finding of most general importance in this study was the existence of substantial differences between the patterns of critical incidents reported by students and faculty. The faculty reported a significantly larger percentage of effective behaviors in the following areas: giving demonstrations or experiments, using discussion group techniques, encouraging and ascertaining students' ideas and opinions.

The students, on the other hand, contributed a larger percentage of behaviors in the following areas: reviewing examinations, distributing grades, and explaining grades; using lecture aids such as drawings, charts, movies, models, and apparatus; using project techniques; giving test questions on assigned material; helping students after class and during class recess; the manner of the instructor.

The faculty reported a larger percentage of ineffective behaviors concerning maintaining order. The ineffective behaviors that were reported in a larger percentage by students involved these areas: presenting requirements of the course, using effective methods of expression, dealing with students' questions, pointing out fallacies, reviewing and summarizing basic facts and principles, using project techniques, using verbal diagnostic teaching techniques, achievement testing students on assigned material, objective type achievement testing, using humor.

This is a good illustration of the problem of the competence of various types of available observers to evaluate the contribution to the general aim of the activity of a specific action. Examination of the reports from students indicated a somewhat limited sphere of competence. Apparently one of the principal reasons for this was the lack of perspective on the part of the students and their inability to keep the general aim of the instructor clearly in mind because of its divergence from their own immediate aims. In many cases, this latter aim seemed to be directed toward achieving a satisfactory grade in the course.

Eilbert (7) developed a functional description of emotional immaturity. The contributors of critical incidents included psychiatrists, psychologists, psychiatric social workers, occupational therapists, nurses, and corpsmen from a military hospital, plus 13 psychologists in nonmilitary organizations. The subjects of the incidents were primarily patients under psychiatric care.

The contributors were given a form that oriented them to the concept "emotional immaturity" by suggesting that it was revealed generally by childlike modes of behavior. The questions used to elicit incidents were: Have you recently thought of someone as being emotionally immature (regardless of diagnosis)? What specifically happened that gave you this impression? What would have been a more mature reaction to the same situation?

Because of the indefinite nature of the concept, it was felt that a check should be made on the contributor's understanding of his task. Twenty of the participating persons were asked to summarize briefly their interpretation of what they had been asked to do. This

appeared to be very useful in developing the phrasing of the questions so that they were uniformly interpreted by the various observers.

The author of the study classified all the immaturities on the basis of a classification system developed from preliminary categorizations prepared by six of the contributors. This classification was submitted to 14 psychiatrists for review. They were asked to indicate which of the categories they were willing to accept as a type of immaturity as the term had been defined in an official document. More than half the categories were accepted by at least 13 of the 14 judges, and none was rejected by more than 50 percent of the judges. It was felt then that the system was acceptable.

This study illustrates the application of the critical incident technique to the study of personality. It is believed that this study provides an excellent example of the possibilities for developing more specific behavioral descriptions.

Folley (24) reported on the critical requirements of sales clerks in department stores. The behaviors were abstracted from narrative records of individual shopping incidents written by shoppers who were relatively inexperienced in evaluating sales personnel. For various reasons, including the competence of the observers, their training, and their limited point of view, the resulting description must be regarded as only partial.

In the past few years, many other individuals and groups have made use of the techniques described above, or modifications of them, in a wide variety of studies. Some of these studies on which reports are being published will be reviewed briefly in the section on applications.

THE PROCEDURE IN ITS PRESENT FORM

From the foregoing discussion, it is

clear that the critical incident technique is essentially a procedure for gathering certain important facts concerning behavior in defined situations. It should be emphasized that the critical incident technique does not consist of a single rigid set of rules governing such data collection. Rather it should be thought of as a flexible set of principles which must be modified and adapted to meet the specific situation at hand.

The essence of the technique is that only simple types of judgments are required of the observer, reports from only qualified observers are included, and all observations are evaluated by the observer in terms of an agreed upon statement of the purpose of the activity. Of course, simplicity of judgments is a relative matter. The extent to which a reported observation can be accepted as a fact depends primarily on the objectivity of this observation. By objectivity is meant the tendency for a number of independent observers to make the same report. Judgments that two things have the same effect or that one has more or less effect than the other with respect to some defined purpose or goal represent the simplest types of judgments that can be made. The accuracy and therefore the objectivity of the judgments depend on the precision with which the characteristic has been defined and the competence of the observer in interpreting this definition with relation to the incident observed. In this latter process, certain more difficult types of judgments are required regarding the relevance of various conditions and actions on the observed success in attaining the defined purpose for this activity.

It is believed that a fair degree of success has been achieved in developing procedures that will be of assistance in gathering facts in a rather objective fashion with only a minimum of inferences and interpretations of a more subjective nature. With respect to two other steps that are essential if these incidents are to be of value a comparable degree of ob-

jectivity has not yet been obtained. In both instances, the subjective factors seem clearly due to current deficiencies in psychological knowledge.

The first of these two other steps consists of the classification of the critical incidents. In the absence of an adequate theory of human behavior, this step is usually an inductive one and is relatively subjective. Once a classification system has been developed for any given type of critical incidents, a fairly satisfactory degree of objectivity can be achieved in placing the incidents in the defined categories.

The second step refers to inferences regarding practical procedures for improving performance based on the observed incidents. Again, in our present stage of psychological knowledge, we are rarely able to deduce or predict with a high degree of confidence the effects of specific selection, training, or operating procedures on future behaviors of the type observed. The incidents must be studied in the light of relevant established principles of human behavior and of the known facts regarding background factors and conditions operating in the specific situation. From this total picture hypotheses are formulated. In only a few types of activities are there both sufficient established principles and sufficient information regarding the effective factors in the situation to provide a high degree of confidence in the resulting hypotheses regarding specific procedures for improving the effectiveness of the results.

In the sections which follow, the five main steps included in the present form of the procedures will be described briefly. In order to provide the worker with maximum flexibility at the present stage, in addition to examples of present best practice, the underlying principles for the step will be discussed and also the chief limitations with, wherever possible, suggestions for studies that may result in future improvements in the methods.

1. GENERAL AIMS

A basic condition necessary for any work on the formulation of a functional description of an activity is a fundamental orientation in terms of the general aims of the activity. No planning and no evaluation of specific behaviors are possible without a general statement of objectives. The trend in the scientific field toward operational statements has led a number of writers to try to describe activities or functions in terms of the acts or operations performed, the materials acted on, the situations involved, the results or products, and the relative importance of various acts and results. These analyses have been helpful in emphasizing the need for more specific and detailed descriptions of the requirements of activities. Typically, however, such discussions have failed to emphasize the dominant role of the general aim in formulating a description of successful behavior or adjustment in a particular situation.

In its simplest form, the functional description of an activity specifies precisely what it is necessary to do and not to do if participation in the activity is to be judged successful or effective. It is clearly impossible to report that a person has been either effective or ineffective in a particular activity by performing a specific act unless we know what he is expected to accomplish. For example, a supervisor's action in releasing a key worker for a half a day to participate in a recreational activity might be evaluated as very effective if the general aim of the foreman was to get along well with the employees under him. On the other hand, this same action might be evaluated as ineffective if the primary general aim is the immediate production of materials or services.

In the case of the usual vocational activities the supervisors can be expected to supply this orientation. In certain other types of activities, such as civic, social, and recreational activities, there frequently is no supervisor. The objectives of participation in the activity must then be determined from the participants themselves. In some instances, these may not be verbalized to a sufficient extent to make it possible to obtain them directly.

Unfortunately, in most situations there is no one general aim which is the correct one. Similarly, there is rarely one person or group of persons who constitute an absolute, authoritative source on the general aim of the activity. In a typical manufacturing organization the foreman, the plant manager, the president, and the stockholders might define the general aim of the workers in a particular section somewhat differently. It is not possible to say that one of these groups knows the correct general aim and the others are wrong. This does not mean that one general aim is as good as another and that it is unimportant how we define the purpose of the activity. It does mean that we cannot hope to get a completely objective and acceptable general aim for a specific activity. The principal criterion in formulating procedures for establishing the general aim of the activity should be the proposed use of the functional description of the activity which is being formulated. Unless the general aim used is acceptable to the potential users of the detailed statement of requirements, the whole effort in formulating this statement will have been wasted.

The most useful statements of aims seem to center around some simple phrase or catchword which is slogan-like in character. Such words provide a maximum of communication with only a minimum of possible misinterpretation. Such words as "appreciation," "efficiency," "development," "production," and "service" are likely to be prominent in statements of general aims. For example, the general aim of a teacher in elementary school art classes might be the development of an appreciation of various visual art forms on the part of the students. The general aim of the good citizen might be taken as effective participation in the development and application of the rules and procedures by which individuals and groups are assisted in achieving their various goals.

With the aid of a form of the type shown in Figure 1, the ideas of a number of well-qualified authorities can be collected. It is expected that in response to the question on the primary purpose of the activity many persons will give a fairly lengthy and detailed statement. The request to summarize is expected to get them to condense this into a brief usable statement. These should be pooled and a trial form of the statement of general aim developed. This statement should be referred either to these authorities or to others to obtain a final statement of the general aim that is acceptable to them. Necessary revisions should be made as indicated by these discussions. Usually considerable effort is required to avoid defeating the purpose of the general aim by cluttering up the statement with specific details and qualifying conditions.

Fig. 1

OUTLINE FOR INTERVIEW TO ESTABLISH THE GENERAL AIM FOR AN ACTIVITY

1. *Introductory statement:* We are making a study of (specify activity). We believe you are especially well qualified to tell us about (specify activity).
2. *Request for general aim:* What would you say is the primary purpose of (specify activity)?
3. *Request for summary:* In a few words, how would you summarize the general aim of (specify activity)?

In summary, the general aim of an activity should be a brief statement obtained from the authorities in the field which expresses in simple terms those

objectives to which most people would agree. Unless a brief, simple statement has been obtained, it will be difficult to get agreement among the authorities. Also it will be much harder to convey a uniform idea to the participants. This latter group will get an over-all impression and this should be as close to the desired general aim as possible.

2. PLANS AND SPECIFICATIONS

To focus attention on those aspects of behavior which are believed to be crucial in formulating a functional description of the activity, precise instructions must be given to the observers. It is necessary that these instructions be as specific as possible with respect to the standards to be used in evaluation and classification. The group to be studied also needs to be specified.

One practical device for obtaining specific data is to obtain records of "critical incidents" observed by the reporting personnel. Such incidents are defined as extreme behavior, either outstandingly effective or ineffective with respect to attaining the general aims of the activity. The procedure has considerable efficiency because of the use of only the extremes of behavior. It is well known that extreme incidents can be more accurately identified than behavior which is more nearly average in character.

One of the primary aims of scientific techniques is to insure objectivity for the observations being made and reported. Such agreement by independent observers can only be attained if they are all following the same set of rules. It is essential that these rules be clear and specific. In most situations the following specifications will need to be established and made explicit prior to collecting the data:

a. *The situations observed.* The first necessary specification is a delimitation of the situations to be observed. This specification must include information about the place, the persons, the conditions, and the activities. Such specifications are rather easily defined in many instances. For example, such brief specifications as observations of "the behavior in classrooms of regularly employed teachers in a specified high school while instructing students during class periods," constitute a fairly adequate definition of a situation of this type.

In complex situations it is probably essential not only that the specifications with respect to the situation be relatively complete and specific, but also that practical examples be provided to assist the observer in deciding in an objective fashion whether or not a specific behavior should be observed and recorded.

b. *Relevance to the general aim.* After the decision has been made that a particular situation is an appropriate one for making observations, the next step is to decide whether or not a specific behavior which is observed is relevant to the general aim of the activity as defined in the section above. For example, if the general aim of the activity was defined as sustained high quality and quantity of production, it might be difficult to decide whether or not to include an action such as encouraging an unusually effective subordinate to get training that would assist him in developing his ability in an avocational or recreational activity not related to his work. In this case, it might be specified that any action which either directly or indirectly could be expected over a long period of time to have a significant effect on the general aim should be included. If it could not be predicted with some confidence whether this effect would be good or bad, it should probably not be considered.

The extent of detail required to obtain objectivity with respect to this type of decision depends to a considerable degree on the background and experiences of the observers with respect to this activity. For example, supervisors with substantial experience in a particular company can be expected to agree on whether or not a particular behavior is relevant to the attainment of the general aim. On the other hand, if outside observers were to be used, it would probably be necessary to specify in considerable detail the activities that can be expected to have an effect on the general aim.

c. *Extent of effect on the general aim.* The remaining decision that the observer must make is how important an effect the observed incident has on the general aim. It is necessary to specify two points on the scale of importance: (a) a level of positive contributions to the general aim in specific terms, preferably including a concrete example, and (b) the corresponding level of negative effect on the general aim expressed in similar terms.

A definition which has been found useful is that an incident is critical if it makes a "significant" contribution, either positively or negatively, to the general aim of the activity. The definition of "significant" will depend on the nature of the activity. If the general aim of the activity is in terms of production, a significant contribution might be one which caused, or might have caused, an appreciable change in the daily production of the department either in the form of an increase or a decrease.

In certain specific situations, it might be desirable and possible to set up a quantitative criterion such as saving or wasting 15 minutes of an average worker's production. In some situations, a definition of significance might be set up in terms of dollars saved or lost both directly and indirectly.

Actions which influence the attitudes of others are more difficult to evaluate objectively. Perhaps the best we might be able to do is to state it in terms of a probability estimate. For example, one such criterion might be that the minimum critical level would be an action that would have an influence such that at least one person in ten might change his vote on an issue of importance to the company.

d. *Persons to make the observations.* One additional set of specifications refers to the selection and training of the observers who are to make and report the judgments outlined in the steps above.

Wherever possible, the observers should be selected on the basis of their familiarity with the activity. Special consideration should be given to observers who have made numerous observations on persons engaged in the activity. Thus, for most jobs, by far the best observers are supervisors whose responsibility it is to see that the particular job being studied is done. However, in some cases very useful observations can be contributed by consumers of the products and services of the activity. For example, for a study of effective sales activities, the customers may have valuable data to contribute. For a study of effective parental activity, the children may be able to make valuable contributions.

In addition to careful selection of the persons to make observations, attention should be given to their training. Minimal training should include a review of the nature of the general aim of the activity and a study of the specifications and definitions for the judgments they will be required to make. Where the situation is complex or the observers are not thoroughly familiar with the activity, supervised practice in applying these definitions should be provided. This can be done by preparing descriptions of observations and asking the observers to make judgments about these materials. Their judgments can be immediately confirmed or corrected during such supervised practice periods.

In Figure 2 is shown a form for use in developing specifications regarding observations. The use of this form in making plans for the collection of critical incidents or other types of observational data should aid in objectifying these specifications.

Fig. 2

SPECIFICATIONS REGARDING OBSERVATIONS

1. Persons to make the observations.
   a. Knowledge concerning the activity.
   b. Relation to those observed.
   c. Training requirements.
2. Groups to be observed.
   a. General description.
   b. Location.
   c. Persons.
   d. Times.
   e. Conditions.
3. Behaviors to be observed.
   a. General type of activity.
   b. Specific behaviors.
   c. Criteria of relevance to general aim.
   d. Criteria of importance to general aim (critical points)

3. COLLECTING THE DATA

If proper plans and specifications are developed, the data collection phase is greatly simplified. A necessary condition for this phase is that the behaviors or results observed be evaluated, clas-sified, and recorded while the facts are still fresh in the mind of the observer. It would be desirable for these operations to be performed at the time of observation so that all requisite facts could be determined and checked. Memory is improved if it is known in advance that the behavior to be observed is to be remembered. It is greatly improved if the specific aspects of what is to be observed are defined and if the operations to be performed with respect to evaluation and classification are clearly specified.

The critical incident technique is frequently used to collect data on observations previously made which are reported from memory. This is usually satisfactory when the incidents reported are fairly recent and the observers were motivated to make detailed observations and evaluations at the time the incident occurred.

The importance of obtaining recent incidents to insure that the incidents are representative of actual happenings was demonstrated in the study on air route traffic controllers by Nagay (48) reported above. However, as also discussed in that study, in some situations adequate coverage cannot be obtained if only very recent incidents are included.

Evidence regarding the accuracy of reporting is usually contained in the incidents themselves. If full and precise details are given, it can usually be assumed that this information is accurate. Vague reports suggest that the incident is not well remembered and that some of the data may be incorrect. In several situations there has been an opportunity to compare the types of incidents reported under two conditions (a) from memory and without a list of the types of incidents anticipated, and (b) those reported when daily observations were being made in a routine work situation, and the evaluations and classifications were made and recorded on a prepared check list within 24 hours of the time of observation. The results of one such comparison were discussed briefly above in connection with the American Institute for Research study of factory employees.

During the observational period a negligible number of incidents were reported by the foremen as not fitting into the general headings included on the list. Although the proportions of incidents for the various items on the list are not identical, they are reasonably close for most of the items. Items on such matters as meeting production requirements and accepting changes in jobs are higher in terms of the recorded than the recalled incidents. The fact that items such as wasting time and assisting on problems are lower for the recalled incidents suggests that part of this discrepancy lies in the interpretations of the category definitions. The classifying of recorded incidents was done by the foremen, while the classification of the recalled incidents was done by the research workers. In fairness, it should also be noted that the definitions used by the research workers were rewritten before they were incorporated in the foremen's manuals.

On the whole, it seems reasonable to assume that, if suitable precautions are taken, recalled incidents can be relied on to provide adequate data for a fairly satisfactory first approximation to a statement of the requirements of the activity. Direct observations are to be preferred, but the efficiency, immediacy, and minimum demands on cooperating personnel which are achieved by using recalled incident data frequently make their use the more practical procedure.

Another practical problem in collecting the data for describing an activity refers to the problem of how it should be obtained from the observers. This applies especially to the problem of collecting recalled data in the form of critical incidents. Four procedures have been used and will be discussed briefly below:

a. *Interviews*. The use of trained personnel to explain to observers precisely what data are desired and to record the incidents, making sure that all necessary details are supplied, is probably the most satisfactory data collection procedure. This type of interview is somewhat different from other sorts of interviews and a brief summary of the principal factors involved will be given.

(i) *Sponsorship of the study*. If a stranger to the observers is collecting the data, it is ordinarily desirable to indicate on what authority the interview is being held. This part should be as brief as possible to avoid any use of time for a prolonged discussion of a topic irrelevant to the purpose of the interview. In many instances all that needs to be said is that someone known and respected by the observer has suggested the interview.

(ii) *Purpose of the study*. This should also be brief and ordinarily would merely involve a statement that a study was being made to describe the requirements of the activity. This would usually be cast in some such informal form as, "We wish to find out what makes a good citizen," or, "We are trying to learn in detail just what successful work as a nurse includes." In cases where there is some hesitation about cooperating or a little more explanation seems desirable, a statement can be added concerning the value and probable uses of the results. This frequently takes the form of improving selection and training procedures. In some instances, it would involve improving the results of the activity. For example, the interviewer might say, "In order to get better sales clerks we need to know just what they do that makes them especially effective or ineffective," or, "If parents are to be more effective, we need to be able to tell them the things they do that are effective and ineffective."

(iii) *The group being interviewed*. If there is any likelihood of a person feeling, "But, why ask me?" it is desirable to forestall this by pointing out that he is a member of a group which is in an unusually good position to observe and report on this activity. The special qualifications of members of this group as observers can be mentioned briefly, as, "Supervisors such as yourself are constantly observing and evaluating the work of switchboard girls," or, "Students are in an unusually good position to observe the effectiveness of their teachers in a number of ways."

(iv) *The anonymity of the data.* Especially for the collection of information about ineffective behavior, one of the principal problems is to convince the observer that his report cannot harm the person reported on in any way. Usually he also needs to be convinced that the person reported on will never know that he has reported the incident. Assurances are not nearly so effective in this situation as actual descriptions of techniques to be used in handling the data, which enable the observer to judge for himself how well the anonymity of the data will be guarded. Under no circumstances should the confidences of the reportees be violated in any way. The use of sealed envelopes, avoidance of identifying information, the mailing of data immediately to a distant point for analysis, and similar techniques are helpful in establishing the good faith of the interviewer in taking all possible precautions to safeguard the incidents reported.

(v) *The question.* The most crucial aspect of the data collection procedure is the questions asked the observers. Many studies have shown that a slight change in wording may produce a substantial change in the incidents reported. For example, in one study the last part of one of the specific questions asked was, "Tell just how this employee behaved which caused a noticeable decrease in production." This question resulted in almost all incidents reported having to do with personality and attitude behaviors. This part of the question was changed to, "Tell just what this employee did which caused a noticeable decrease in production." This second question produced a much broader range of incidents. To the question writer "how he behaved" and "what he did" seemed like about the same thing. To the foremen who were reporting incidents "how he behaved" sounded as if personality and attitudes were being studied. The subtle biases involved in the wording of questions are not always so easily found. Questions should always be tried out with a small group of typical observers before being put into general use in a study.

The question should usually refer briefly to the general aim of the activity.

This aim might be discussed more fully in a preliminary sentence. It should usually state that an incident, actual behavior, or what the person did is desired. It should briefly specify the type of behavior which is relevant and the level of importance which it must reach to be reported. It should also tie down the selection of the incidents to be reported by the observer in some way, such as asking for the most recent observation, in order to prevent the giving of only the more dramatic or vivid incidents, or some other selected group, such as those which fit the observer's stereotypes.

An effective procedure for insuring that the interpretation of the persons being interviewed is close to that intended is to request a sample of persons typical of those to be interviewed to state in their own words what they understand they have been asked to do. These persons should be selected so as to represent all types who will be interviewed. From a study of their interpretations, necessary revisions can be made to insure that all interviewees will be in agreement as to the nature of the incidents they are to provide.

(vi) *The conversation.* The interviewer should avoid asking leading questions after the main question has been stated. His remarks should be neutral and permissive and should show that he accepts the observer as the expert. By indicating that he understands what is being said and permitting the observer to do most of the talking, the interviewer can usually get unbiased incidents. If the question does not seem to be understood, it can be repeated with some reference to clarifying just what is meant by it. If the observer has given what seems like only part of the story, he should be encouraged by restating the essence of his remarks. This usually tends to encourage him to continue and may result in his bringing out many relevant details that the interviewer did not know the situation well enough to ask for. In some cases, it is desirable to have the interviews recorded electrically and transcribed. This increases the work load substantially, and trained interviewers can usually get satisfactory reports at the time or by editing their notes shortly after the interview.

Usually the interviewer should apply certain criteria to the incidents while they are being collected. Some of the more important criteria are: (a) is the actual behavior reported; (b) was it observed by the reporter; (c) were all relevant factors in the situation given; (d) has the observer made a definite judgment regarding the criticalness of the behavior; (e) has the observer made it clear just why he believes the behavior was critical.

In Figure 3 is shown a sample of the type of form used by interviewers to collect critical incidents. Of course the form must be adapted to the needs of the specific situation.

b. *Group interviews.* Because of the cost in time and personnel of the individual interview, a group interview technique has been developed. This retains the advantages of the individual interview in regard to the personal contact, explanation, and availability of the interviewer to answer questions. To some extent it also provides for a check on the data supplied by the interviewees. Its other advantages are that the language of the actual observer is precisely reproduced and the time for editing the interviews is virtually eliminated.

The method consists of having the interviewer give his introductory remarks to a group very much as he would do in an individual interview. There is an opportunity for questions and clarification. Then each person is asked to write incidents in answer to specific questions contained on a specially prepared form. The size of the group which can be handled effectively will vary with the situation. If the group is fairly small, it is usually possible for the interviewer to read the responses of each member of the group to the first question and make sure that he understands what is wanted. There seems to be a certain amount of social facilitation, and the results in most situations have been excellent. In the report of the first use of this procedure by Wagner (65), the amount of interviewer time required per usable incident was 4.3 minutes for the group interview procedure as compared with 15.7 minutes for individual interviews. The quality of these incidents, obtained from officers in the United States Air Force, appeared to be about the same for the two situations.

Fig. 3

SAMPLE OF A FORM FOR USE BY AN INTERVIEWER IN COLLECTING EFFECTIVE CRITICAL INCIDENTS

"Think of the last time you saw one of your subordinates do something that was very helpful to your group in meeting their production schedule." (Pause till he indicates he has such an incident in mind.) "Did his action result in increase in production of as much as one per cent for that day?—or some similar period?"

(If the answer is "no," say) "I wonder if you could think of the last time that someone did something that did have this much of an effect in increasing production." (When he indicates he has such a situation in mind, say) "What were the general circumstances leading up to this incident?" _____

_____

_____

"Tell me exactly what this person did that was so helpful at that time."

_____

_____

"Why was this so helpful in getting your group's job done?" _____

_____

_____

"When did this incident happen?"

_____

"What was this person's job?"

_____

"How long has he been on this job?"

_____

"How old is he?" _____

c. *Questionnaires.* If the group becomes large, the group interview procedure is more in the nature of a questionnaire procedure. There are, of course, all types of combinations of procedures that can be used. The one that is most different from those discussed is the mailed questionnaire. In situations where the observers are motivated to read the instructions carefully and answer conscientiously, this technique seems to give results which are not essentially different from those obtained by the interview method. Except for the addition of introductory remarks, the forms used in collecting critical incidents by means of mailed questionnaires are about the same as those used in group interviews.

d. *Record forms.* One other procedure for collecting data is by means of written records. There are two varieties of recording: one is to record details of incidents as they happen. This situation is very similar to that described in connection with obtaining incidents by interviews above, except that the observation and giving of incidents are delayed following the introductory remarks and the presentation of the questions until an incident is observed to happen.

A variation of this procedure is to record such incidents on forms which describe most of the possible types of incidents by placing a check or tally in the appropriate place.

As additional information becomes available on the nature of the components which make up activities, observers may thus collect data more efficiently by using forms for recording and classifying observations. In the meantime, because of the inadequacy of the information currently available regarding these components, it seems desirable to ask observers to report their observations in greater detail and have the classification done by specially trained personnel.

e. *Size of sample.* A general problem which overlaps the phases of collecting the incidents and analyzing the data relates to the number of incidents required. There does not appear to be a simple answer to this question. If the activity or job being defined is relatively simple, it may be satisfactory to collect only 50 or 100 incidents. On the other hand, some types of complex activity appear to require several thousand incidents for an adequate statement of requirements.

The most useful procedure for determining whether or not additional incidents are needed is to keep a running count on the number of new critical behaviors added to the classification system with each additional 100 incidents. For most purposes, it can be considered that adequate coverage has been achieved when the addition of 100 critical incidents to the sample adds

only two or three critical behaviors. For jobs of a supervisory nature, it appears that between 2,000 and 4,000 critical incidents are required to establish a comprehensive statement of requirements that includes nearly all of the different types of critical behaviors. For semiskilled and skilled jobs between 1,000 and 2,000 incidents seem to be adequate to cover the critical behaviors.

Coverage of all or nearly all of the various critical behaviors is not the only criterion as to whether or not a sufficient number of critical incidents has been collected. If a relatively precise definition of each critical behavior category is required, it may be necessary to get at least three or four examples of each critical behavior. Similarly, if the critical incidents are to be used as a basis for developing selection tests, training materials, and proficiency measures, more incidents may be required to provide a sufficient supply of usable ideas for the development of these materials.

In summary, although there is no simple formula for determining the number of critical incidents that will be required, this is a very important consideration in the plan of the study; checks should be made both on the first hundred or so incidents and again after approximately half of the number of incidents believed to be required have been obtained in order to make it possible to revise the preliminary estimates, if necessary, with a minimum loss in effort and time.

4. ANALYZING THE DATA

The collection of a large sample of incidents that fulfill the various conditions outlined above provides a functional description of the activity in terms of specific behaviors. If the sample is representative, the judges well qualified, the types of judgments appropriate and well defined, and the procedures for observing and reporting such that incidents are reported accurately, the stated requirements can be expected to be comprehensive, detailed, and valid in this form. There is only one reason for going further and that is practical utility. The purpose of the data analysis stage is to summarize and describe the data in an efficient manner so that it can be effectively used for many practical purposes.

In the discussion which follows, it should be kept in mind that the process of description has been completed. The specific procedures to be discussed are not concerned with improving on the comprehensiveness, specificity of detail, or validity of the statement of the requirements of the activity. Rather, they are concerned with making it easier to report these requirements, to draw inferences from them, and to compare the activity with other activities.

The aim is to increase the usefulness of the data while sacrificing as little as possible of their comprehensiveness, specificity, and validity. It appears that there are three primary problems involved: (a) the selection of the general frame of reference that will be most useful for describing the incidents; (b) the inductive development of a set of major area and subarea headings; and (c) the selection of one or more levels along the specificity-generality continuum to use in reporting the requirements. Each of these problems will be discussed below:

a. *Frame of reference.* There are countless ways in which a given set of incidents can be classified. In selecting the general nature of the classification, the principal consideration should usually be that of the uses to be made of the data. The preferred categories will be those believed to be most valuable in using the statement of requirements. Other considerations are ease and accuracy of classifying the data, relation to previously developed definitions or classification systems, and considerations of interpretation and reporting, which will be discussed in a later section.

For job activities, the choice of a frame of reference is usually dominated by considerations of whether the principal use of the requirements will be in relation to selection, training, measurement of proficiency, or the development of procedures for evaluating on-the-job effectiveness. For selection purposes, the most appropriate classification system is a psychological one. The main headings have to do with types of psychological traits that are utilized in the selection process. For training uses, the best classification system follows a set of headings that is easily related to training courses or broad training aims. For proficiency measurement, the headings tend to be similar to those for training except that there is less attention to possible course organization and aims and greater attention to the components of the job as it is actually performed. For the development of procedures for evaluating on-the-job effectiveness to establish a criterion of success, the classification system is necessarily directed at presenting the on-the-job behaviors under headings that represent either well-marked phases of the job or provide a simple framework for classifying on-the-job activities that is either familiar to or easily learned by supervisors.

Similarly, in nonvocational activities the frame of reference depends on the uses planned for the findings. For example, if a study is being made to define immaturity reactions in military personnel, the frame of reference would depend somewhat on whether the functional description is to be used primarily to identify personnel showing this type of maladjustment or whether the principal use will be to try to prepare specifications for types of situations in which immaturity reactions would not lead to serious difficulties.

b. *Category formulation.* The induction of categories from the basic data in the form of incidents is a task requiring insight, experience, and judgment. Unfortunately, this procedure is, in the present stage of psychological knowledge, more subjective than objective. No simple rules are available, and the quality and usability of the final product are largely dependent on the skill and sophistication of the formulator. One rule is to submit the tentative categories to others for review. Although there is no guarantee that results agreed on by several workers will be more useful than those obtained from a single worker, the confirmation of judgments by a number of persons is usually reassuring. The usual procedure is to sort a relatively small sample of incidents into piles that are related to the frame of reference selected. After these tentative categories have been established, brief definitions of them are made, and additional incidents are classified into them. During this process, needs for redefinition and for the development of new categories are noted.

The tentative categories are modified as indicated and the process continued until all the incidents have been classified.

The larger categories are subdivided into smaller groups and the incidents that describe very nearly the same type of behavior are placed together. The definitions for all the categories and major headings should then be re-examined in terms of the actual incidents classified under each.

c. *General behaviors.* The last step is to determine the most appropriate level of specificity-generality to use in reporting the data. This is the problem of weighing the advantages of the specificity achieved in specific incidents against the simplicity of a relatively small number of headings. The level chosen might be only a dozen very general behaviors or it might be several hundred rather specific behaviors. Practical considerations in the immediate situation usually determine the optimal level of generality to be used.

Several considerations should be kept in mind in establishing headings for major areas and in stating critical requirements at the selected level of generality. These are listed below:

(i) The headings and requirements should indicate a clear-cut and logical organization. They should have a discernible and easily remembered structure.

(ii) The titles should convey meanings in themselves without the necessity of detailed definition, explanation, or differentiation. This does not mean that they should not be defined and explained. It does mean that these titles, without the detailed explanation, should still be meaningful to the reader.

(iii) The list of statements should be homogeneous; *i.e.*, the headings for either areas or requirements should be parallel in content and structure. Headings for major areas should be neutral, not defining either unsatisfactory or outstanding behaviors. Critical requirements should ordinarily be stated in positive terms.

(iv) The headings of a given type should all be of the same general magnitude or level of importance. Known biases in the data causing one area or one requirement to have a disproportionate number of incidents should not be reflected in the headings.

(v) The headings used for classifica-

tion and reporting of the data should be such that findings in terms of them will be easily applied and maximally useful.

(vi) The list of headings should be comprehensive and cover all incidents having significant frequencies.

5. INTERPRETING AND REPORTING

It is never possible in practice to obtain an ideal solution for each of the practical problems involved in obtaining a functional description of an activity. Therefore, the statement of requirements as obtained needs interpretation if it is to be used properly. In many cases, the real errors are made not in the collection and analysis of the data but in the failure to interpret them properly. Each of the four preceding steps, (a) the determination of the general aim, (b) the specification of observers, groups to be observed, and observations to be made, (c) the data collection, and (d) the data analysis, must be studied to see what biases have been introduced by the procedures adopted. If there is a division of opinion as to the general aim and one of the competing aims is selected, this should be made very clear in the report. If the groups on whom the observations are made are not representative of the relevant groups involved, they must be described as precisely as possible. The aim of the study is usually not a functional description of the activity as carried on by this sample but rather a statement relating to all groups of this type. In order to avoid faulty inferences and generalizations, the limitations imposed by the group must be brought into clear focus. Similarly, the nature of judgments made in collecting and analyzing the data must be carefully reviewed.

While the limitations need to be clearly reported, the value of the results should also be emphasized. Too often the research worker shirks his responsibility for rendering a judgment concerning the degree of credibility which should be attached to his findings. It is a difficult task, but if the results are to be used, someone will have to make such a judgment, and the original investigator is best prepared to make the necessary evaluations either for the general case or for certain typical specific examples.

USES OF THE CRITICAL INCIDENT TECHNIQUE

The variety of situations in which the collection of critical incidents will prove of value has only been partially explored. In the approximately eight years since the writer and his colleagues began a systematic formulation of principles and procedures to be followed in collecting this type of data, a fairly large number of applications has been made. The applications will be discussed under the following nine headings: (a) measures of typical performance (criteria); (b) measures of proficiency (standard samples); (c) training; (d) selection and classification; (e) job design and purification; (f) operating procedures; (g) equipment design; (h) motivation and leadership (attitudes); (i) counseling and psychotherapy.

Space is not available here to describe these various applications in detail. However, a brief description of the types of application that have been made, along with brief illustrative examples and references, will be presented. Some of the studies involve several of the types of applications to be discussed. The presentation is not intended to be complete, but rather to give the reader interested in further study some orientation and guidance.

MEASURES OF TYPICAL PERFORMANCE (CRITERIA)

The simplest and most natural application of a systematically collected set of critical incidents is in terms of the preparation of a statement of critical requirements and a check list or some similar type of procedure for evaluating the typical performance of persons engaged in this activity. If an observational check list that includes all of the impor-

tant behaviors for the activity is available, the performance of the individual can be objectively evaluated and recorded by merely making a single tally mark for each observation. Such records provide the essential basis for criterion data which are sufficiently detailed and specific for special purposes but at the same time can be combined into a single over-all evaluation when this is desirable. Such a procedure was first suggested and tried out in connection with developmental studies of the American Institute for Research. These included: Preston's study of officers for the United States Air Force (52); Nagay's study on air route traffic controllers for the Civil Aeronautics Administration (49); and M. H. Weislogel's study on research personnel for the Office of Naval Research (69). Another American Institute for Research study was reported by R. B. Miller and the present author (21). This was a performance record form for hourly wage employees developed in cooperation with personnel of the Delco-Remy Division of the General Motors Corporation, the Employment Practices Division of that corporation, and the Industrial Relations Center of the University of Chicago. The same authors have developed similar performance records for salaried employees, and foremen and supervisors (22, 23). The principles and procedures underlying this type of evaluation of performance have been published elsewhere (14, 15, 17).

A number of important contributions to the development of functional descriptions and standards of performance have been made by other groups using the critical incident technique. One of the most notable of these is the development by Hobbs et al. (3, 31), of *Ethical Standards of Psychologists*. More than 1,000 critical incidents involving ethical problems of psychologists were contributed by the members of the American Psychological Association. It is believed that this represents the first attempt to use empirical methods to establish ethical standards. Because of the importance of this study, and the generality of some of the problems involved, certain of the conclusions reported by the Committee on Ethical Standards for Psychology in their introductory statement will be quoted here.

First, it is clear that psychologists believe that ethics are important; over two thousand psychologists were sufficiently concerned with the ethical obligations of their profession to contribute substantially to the formulation of these ethical standards. Second, psychologists believe that the ethics of a profession cannot be prescribed by a committee; ethical standards must emerge from the day-by-day value commitments made by psychologists in the practice of their profession. Third, psychologists share a conviction that the problems of men, even those involving values, can be studied objectively; this document summarizes the results of an effort to apply some of the techniques of social science to the study of ethical behavior of psychologists. Fourth, psychologists are aware that a good code of ethics must be more than a description of the current status of ethics in the profession; a code must embody the ethical aspirations of psychologists and encourage changes in behavior, bringing performance ever closer to aspiration. Fifth, psychologists appreciate that process is often more important than product in influencing human behavior; the four years of widely-shared work in developing this code are counted on to be more influential in changing ethical practices of psychologists than will be the publication of this product of their work. Finally, psychologists recognize that the process of studying ethical standards must be a continuing one; occasional publications such as this statement mark no point of conclusion in the ongoing process of defining ethical standards—they are a means of sharing the more essential discipline of examining professional experience, forming hypotheses about professional conduct, and testing these hypotheses by reference to the welfare of the people affected by them (3, p. v).

In addition to the study by Smit mentioned in a previous section (58), several other studies on the use of the critical incident procedures as a basis for evaluating teaching effectiveness have been reported. One of these was a study conducted under the joint sponsorship of the Educational Research Corporation and the Harvard University Graduate School of Education with funds provided by the New England School Development Council and the George F. Milton Fund. This was an exploratory study of teacher competence reported by Domas (6). Approximately 1,000 critical incidents were collected from teachers, principals, and other supervisors. Although this was an exploratory study, it was felt that it made an important contribution to the general problem of relating salary to teacher competence.

The second of these studies was conducted as part of the teacher characteristics study sponsored by the American Council on Education and subsidized by the Grant Foundation. This study is reported by Jensen (32). Teachers, administrators, and teachers in training in the Los Angeles area contributed more than 1,500 critical incidents of teacher behavior. The incidents were classified under personal, professional, and social qualities. The category formulation indicated that there were about 20 distinct critical requirements. These were recommended as a basis for teacher evaluation and as an aid to the in-service growth of teachers.

Another study was that of Smith and Staudohar (59), which determined the critical requirements for basic training of tactical instructors in the United States Air Force. From 130 training supervisors, 555 tactical instructors, and 3,082 basic trainees, a total of 6,615 usable incidents were obtained. The authors comment that:

The training supervisors report a predominance of ineffective incidents in the major areas of: Sets a good example and maintains effective personal relations. The tactical instructors report more ineffective incidents in the area of Makes his expectations clear. Basic trainees show a predominance of ineffective incidents in three areas: Sets a good example, Considers trainee's needs, and Maintains effective personal relations (59, p. 5).

Another study on the evaluation of instructor effectiveness was carried out by Konigsburg (33). This study involved the development of an instructor check list for college instructors based on the critical incident technique and a comparison of techniques for recording observations. Its principal findings were the very low correlation coefficients between the total scores from the Purdue Rating Scale for Instruction and the instructor check list. When these two instruments were each given to half the class on the same day, the average correlation coefficient was found to be .29. The other principal finding is that the planned performances of a total of 46 predetermined behaviors were better reflected by the results obtained on the instructor check list than by the results on the Purdue Rating Scale.

A somewhat related study has been reported by Barnhart (4). This study collected a large number of critical incidents for the purpose of establishing the critical requirements for school board membership. The author applied his findings to the problem of evaluating the effectiveness of school board members.

Another type of application of the critical incident technique to the development of bases for evaluating behavior is the previously mentioned study of Eilbert (7). His list of 51 types of immature reaction based on a collection of several hundred critical incidents describing manifestations of emotional immaturity is believed to provide a useful guide to further investigation and appraisal of persons with behavior problems. It is believed that the results of this study provide substantial encouragement to the application of the critical incident technique to similar problems in the field of clinical diagnosis and evaluation.

MEASURES OF PROFICIENCY (STANDARD SAMPLES)

A closely related use of critical incidents is to provide a basis for evaluating the performance of persons by use of standard samples of behavior involving important aspects of the activity. Such evaluations are called proficiency measures and are differentiated from the evaluation of typical performance on the job primarily on the basis that a test situation rather than a real job situation is used. Measures of this sort are especially useful at the end of training courses as checks on the maintenance of proficiency, and when the tasks assigned to participants vary a great deal in difficulty or are not directly observed by the supervisors.

One of the first applications of critical incidents to the development of proficiency measures was Gordon's study on the development of a standard flight check for the airline transport rating (28, 29). This study was done by the American Institute for Research under the sponsorship of the National Research Council Committee on Aviation Psychology with funds provided by the Civil Aeronautics Administration. In this study data from analyses of airline accidents were combined with critical incidents reported by airline pilots to provide the basis for developing an objective measure of pilot proficiency. The flight check consisted of the presentation of situations providing uniformly standardized opportunities to perform the critical aspects of the airline pilot's job as indicated from the study of the accidents and critical incidents reported. The new check was found to yield 88 percent agreement on the decision to pass or fail a particular pilot when examined on flights on successive days by different check pilots. The previous flight check when used on the same flights gave only 63 percent agreement, which was little better than chance under the conditions of the study.

Similar studies on the development of flight checks at the American Institute for Research have been carried out by Marley (36, 37), G. S. Miller (39), and Ericksen (9). These studies, sponsored by the United States Air Force and the Civil Aeronautics Administration, were concerned respectively with objective flight checks for B-29 bombing crew members, B-36 bombing crew members, and private pilots flying light civilian aircraft. Ericksen also developed a light plane proficiency check to predict military flying success (10) on a similar project sponsored by the U.S. Air Force Human Resources Research Center.

A similar set of proficiency measures was developed by Krumm for Air Force pilot instructors (34, 35), also under the sponsorship of the Human Resources Research Center. These measures were based on more than 4,000 critical incidents collected from student pilots, flight instructors, and supervisors. The critical incidents were classified under three main headings: (a) proficiency as a pilot; (b) proficiency as a teacher; and (c) proficiency in maintaining effective personnel relations. The proficiency measures developed in connection with this study included paper-and-pencil tests presenting critical situations and requiring the instructor to select one of several proposed solutions.

Another development of this type carried on at the American Institute for Research was the construction of tests for evaluating research proficiency in physics and chemistry for the Office of Naval Research by M. H. Weislogel (71). This study was based on the critical incidents for research personnel (20) discussed in a previous section. The items for these proficiency measures were based on detailed rationales. The items described a practical research situation in considerable detail and outlined five specific choices concerning such matters as the best thing to do next, suggestions for improving the procedure as reported, etc. The critical behaviors tested in the items were taken directly from the critical incidents. The method of developing tests through the use of comprehensive rationales has been discussed generally in another paper (16).

Three studies have been reported by the American Institute for Research in which critical incidents were used as a basis for developing situational performance tests for measuring certain aspects of the proficiency of military personnel. These included the study of Sivy and Lange on the development of an objective form of the Leaders Reaction Test for the Personnel Research Branch, Department of the Army (57). This test included 20 situational problems based on the critical requirements of the noncommissioned combat infantry leader as determined on the basis of critical incidents collected in military maneuvers and during combat operations at the front in Korea. A second proficiency measure of a somewhat similar sort was developed for other types of personnel by R. L. Weislogel (73). The third study of this type was carried out by Suttell (61) for the Human Resources Research Center. This study was based on critical incidents collected in previous studies of the American Institute for Research and reported the development and preliminary evaluation of the Officer Situations Test. This test was designed to measure nonintellectual aspects of officer performance through the use of 16 situational problems requiring about six hours of testing time.

Because of the great difficulty in obtaining valid and reliable measures of typical performance, accurate measures of proficiency are essential for many types of activities. It is apparent that a comprehensive set of critical incidents can be of great value in constructing such measures.

TRAINING

Many of the applications of the critical incident technique to training problems have been carried out for the military in special situations so that the reports are classified security information. In addition to work by Preston, Glaser, and R. L. Weislogel, R. B. Miller and Folley have utilized critical incidents in establishing training requirements for specific types of maintenance mechanics (47) in a study for the Human Resources Research Center.

Similarly, Ronan has used critical incidents as a basis for developing a program of training for emergency procedures in multi-engine aircraft (54) in a study for the United States Air Force Human Factors Operations Research Laboratory. On the basis of several thousand incidents reported by aircrew personnel regarding emergencies, three evaluation devices were prepared. These involved a conventional type multiple-choice test; a special multiple-choice test designed to measure the individual's information concerning the important cues in the emergency situation, the appropriate actions to be taken, and the basic troubles or causes of the emergency; and a "flight check" to be used in evaluating the performance of aircrew members in electronic flight simulators.

The obvious relevance of the behaviors involved in critical incidents and the specific details included make such incidents an ideal basis for developing training programs and training materials.

A recent study by Collins (5) uses critical incidents as a basis for evaluating the effectiveness of a training program. The types of incidents reported by mothers after a two-week training course were significantly different from those reported at the beginning of the program in a number of aspects relevant to the objectives of the program. The critical incidents appeared to provide a much more sensitive basis for revealing changes than other procedures used.

SELECTION AND CLASSIFICATION

Until recently, the customary approach of the research psychologist to the development of tests for selection and classification purposes has been as follows: A very brief period was given to study of the job. Following this, a wide variety of selection procedures was administered to a group of applicants or employees, and follow-up data were gathered. Since the research psychologist had little confidence in the accuracy of his analysis of the psychological elements required by the job, there was a tendency to try everything that was available and seemed even remotely related to the tasks involved. This has been called the "shotgun approach." It was hoped that with a wide scatter at least a few of the tests would pay off. The critical incident technique has lent substantial support to the more thorough study of the job prior to initiating testing procedures. There is increasing feeling at the present time that a much larger percentage of the investigator's time should be spent on determining the critical requirements of the job, so that the psychologist will have sufficient confidence in his tentative conclusions as to the nature of the important selection procedures to permit their use on a tentative basis prior to the collection of empirical follow-up data. This is especially important in those situations where the follow-up requires a very long period of time or where the number of cases that can be followed up is so small that definitive findings cannot be anticipated.

One of the most important requirements for developing a system of job analysis that will facilitate a relatively accurate identification of the important job elements for a specific task is to establish a clear and specific set of definitions for these job elements in behavioral terms. The American Institute for Research has carried out a series of projects on this problem. The first of these was a study undertaken by Wagner under the sponsorship of the United States Air Force School of Aviation Medicine to define the requirements of aircrew jobs in terms of specific job elements (67, 68). Several thousand critical incidents were gathered from aircrew members, and these were classified into 24 job elements. These job elements were inductively formulated from the critical incidents and were grouped under the four area headings: (a) learning and thinking; (b) observation and visualization; (c) sensory-motor coordination; and (d) motives, temperament, and leadership.

The development of more than 100 proficiency tests to measure each of the various critical behaviors included in the 24 tentatively proposed job elements was reported by Hahn (30) for the School of Aviation Medicine. These tests were administered to a group of approximately 500 high school senior boys, and the intercorrelations were used to reformulate the tentative job elements. In a study just completed by Taylor (62) for the Human Resources Research Center, the results of applying an analytical procedure developed by Horst to study the interrelationships involved are reported. This analysis led to the formulation of a new set of 20 job elements for each of which a selection test has been developed. These tests have been administered to several hundred aviation cadets and follow-up data on their success in aircrew training should be available soon.

A similar project based on critical incidents collected from various civilian jobs has been reported by the present author (2, 18, 19). The Flanagan Aptitude Classification Test Series, published in 1953, provides aptitude measures for 14 critical job elements. The Applicant Inventory, also published in 1953, measures attitudes predictive of job adjustment for hourly wage employees.

An effort to adapt the critical incident technique to the problem of developing civil service examinations is reported by Wager and Sharon (64). In an exploratory study they collected about 100 incidents regarding on-the-job behaviors of maintenance technicians. These incidents were used as a basis for determin-

ing job requirements in terms of behavior, and test items were developed for use in selecting applicants who could be expected to meet these requirements.

Another study that used critical incidents as a basis for developing tests to predict performance was carried out by O'Donnell (51). His test, designed to predict success in dentistry, was based on critical incidents collected by Wagner. The test includes items designed to predict, in part, the following three general areas: (a) demonstrating technical proficiency; (b) handling patient relationships; and (c) accepting professional responsibility. A follow-up study indicated moderate validity for these materials.

One of the few studies known to the author in which the critical incident technique was used in a project carried on outside the United States is Emons' doctor's dissertation (8). This study, carried out at the University of Liége, investigated the aptitudes of effective sales personnel in a large department store. A group of 40 supervisors provided 228 critical incidents. Nine categories were formulated from this group of incidents and recommendations made for an aptitude test to improve current selection procedures.

JOB DESIGN AND PURIFICATION

Inadequate attention has been given to the scientific design of jobs to promote over-all efficiency. Where a team has several different types of tasks to perform, it is frequently possible to design each of the team member's jobs so that only a few of the several tasks are involved. If the jobs have been studied by use of the critical incident technique, it may be possible to select and train each team member for only two or three of the critical job elements. This tends to maximize the effectiveness of performance with respect to each of the various types of tasks. Although such procedures have nearly always been informally used in planning the work of teams, the critical incident technique facilitates the collection of the data essential to this type of job purification.

Some preliminary work on this problem has been carried out at the American Institute for Research. Recommendations resulting from these studies for reducing the number of job elements required in certain common maintenance jobs are expected to lead to a saving of millions of dollars in training costs as well as to improving the effectiveness of job performance.

OPERATING PROCEDURES

Another application of critical incidents which has not been adequately exploited is the study of operating procedures. Detailed factual data on successes and failures that can be systematically analyzed are of great importance in improving the effectiveness and efficiency of operations. Such information can be efficiently collected by means of the critical incident technique.

Examples of such studies are provided by a series of three projects carried out by the American Institute for Research under the sponsorship of the United States Air Force School of Aviation Medicine. The first of these involves the collection of critical incidents relating to near accidents in flying reported by Vasilas, Fitzpatrick, DuBois, and Youtz (63). More than 1,700 critical incidents were collected from pilots and other aircrew members by procedures developed for this study. These incidents pointed to possible improvements in training job design and equipment design as well as in operating procedures.

The second of these studies was specifically concerned with the effect of the age of pilots and other crew members on aircrew operations. This study was reported by Shriver (56), and included tentative suggestions regarding various modifications in operating procedures.

The third study in this series, reported by Goodenough and Suttell (26), involved the collection of critical incidents regarding the impairment of

human efficiency in emergency operations. These incidents provide a detailed statement of both the types of stresses that impair performance and the types of performance that are impaired under specific conditions. More than 2,000 critical incidents were collected in which impairment in performance on operational assignments was observed. These incidents were collected in Alaska and the Far East as well as in operational commands in the United States. This report contains suggestions for improving operations in emergency situations.

EQUIPMENT DESIGN

An application closely related to that just discussed involves the collection of critical incidents to improve the design of equipment. Reports of specific incidents from the field have always been a basis for equipment modifications. The critical incident technique facilitates the collection and processing of this type of information. Too often in the past action was taken on the basis of informal reports from operating personnel. The collection of large numbers of critical incidents representative of operating experience provides a sound basis for modifying existing equipment and designing new models.

In the study by Fitts and Jones (12), mentioned above, which was carried out at the Aero-Medical Laboratory, 270 critical incidents relating to errors in reading and interpreting aircraft instruments were collected and analyzed. These led to a number of specific suggestions regarding modifications in instrument displays.

Other recent studies conducted at the American Institute for Research have used data from the critical incident technique along with other sources to develop procedures for designing jobs. The reports on these projects are classified for military security reasons.

Other projects at the American Institute for Research have used the critical incident technique as a supplemental procedure for task analysis of equipment in the design stage of development (9, 10, 34, 35, 39). These procedures have been found very effective when used by psychologists working closely with engineers on the preparation of design specifications for new equipment.

MOTIVATION AND LEADERSHIP

The study of attitudes has been somewhat limited and difficult to interpret because of the almost exclusive reliance on verbal statements of opinions and preferences. The critical incident technique has been applied in a few instances to gather factual data regarding specific actions involving decisions and choices. These studies suggest that critical incidents of this type may be a very valuable supplementary tool for the study of attitudes.

A recent study carried out by Preston of the American Institute for Research for the Air Force's Human Resources Research Center (53) used critical incidents as a basis for studying decisions of airmen to re-enlist in the Air Force. It is believed that these specific incidents provide valuable information not contained in studies utilizing only data on opinions.

A series of reports by Ruch (55) contains critical incidents on combat leadership collected from senior officers in the Far East Air Forces. These incidents provide a factual basis for the study of motivation and leadership of Air Force personnel engaged in combat operations.

COUNSELING AND PSYCHOTHERAPY

Another field in which current techniques emphasize over-all impressions, opinions, and reports of single cases is counseling and psychotherapy. There appears to be a trend, however, in this field toward emphasizing the collection of factual incidents. This suggests that the critical incident technique may be useful in this area also.

Exploratory work has recently been done at the University of Pittsburgh with the critical incident technique to establish areas of change accompanying psychotherapy. A series of three master's theses were carried out by Speth, Goldfarb, and Mellett (25, 38, 60). They collected 243 critical incidents from 11 psychotherapists. These incidents were collected about patients who had shown improvement and were replies to the question, "What did the patient do that was indicative of improvement?" Although these studies were primarily exploratory in nature, the tentative finding that different therapists stress different criteria of improvement and nonimprovement suggests that the critical incident approach may be of use not only in developing objective measures of improvement but also in experimental studies of the types of improvement resulting from the therapists' use of specific procedures.

A somewhat related type of study initiated by Diederich and reported by Allen (1) describes the use of the technique to obtain critical incidents from students reporting things that caused them to like a fellow high school student either more or less than before. This study is being continued to provide the basis for tests of specific value areas. An incidental finding of the study was that when an example of the kind of incident desired was shown on the form, 53 percent of the positive and 23 percent of the negative behaviors reported were in the same category as the example given.

SUMMARY AND CONCLUSIONS

This review has described the development of a method of studying activity requirements called the critical incident technique. The technique grew out of studies carried out in the Aviation Psychology Program of the Army Air Forces in World War II. The success of the method in analyzing such activities as combat leadership and disorientation in pilots resulted in its extension and further development after the war. This developmental work has been carried out primarily at the American Institute for Research and the University of Pittsburgh. The reports of this work are reviewed briefly.

The five steps included in the critical incident procedure as most commonly used at the present time are discussed. These are as follows:

a. Determination of the general aim of the activity. This general aim should be a brief statement obtained from the authorities in the field which expresses in simple terms those objectives to which most people would agree.

b. Development of plans and specifications for collecting factual incidents regarding the activity. The instructions to the persons who are to report their observations need to be as specific as possible with respect to the standards to be used in evaluating and classifying the behavior observed.

c. Collection of the data. The incident may be reported in an interview or written up by the observer himself. In either case it is essential that the reporting be objective and include all relevant details.

d. Analysis of the data. The purpose of this analysis is to summarize and describe the data in an efficient manner so that it can be effectively used for various practical purposes. It is not usually possible to obtain as much objectivity in this step as in the preceding one.

e. Interpretation and reporting of the statement of the requirements of the activity. The possible biases and implications of decisions and procedures made in each of the four previous steps should be clearly reported. The research worker is responsible for pointing out not only the limitations but also the degree of credibility and the value of the final results obtained.

It should be noted that the critical incident technique is very flexible and the principles underlying it have many types of applications. Its two basic principles may be summarized as follows: (a) reporting of facts regarding behavior is preferable to the collection of interpretations, ratings, and opinions based on general impressions; (b) reporting should be limited to those behaviors which, according to competent

observers, make a significant contribution to the activity.

It should be emphasized that critical incidents represent only raw data and do not automatically provide solutions to problems. However, a procedure which assists in collecting representative samples of data that are directly relevant to important problems such as establishing standards, determining requirements, or evaluating results should have wide applicability.

The applications of the critical incident technique which have been made to date are discussed under the following nine headings: (a) measures of typical performance (criteria); (b) measures of proficiency (standard samples); (c) training; (d) selection and classification; (e) job design and purification; (f) operating procedures; (g) equipment design; (h) motivation and leadership (attitudes); (i) counseling and psychotherapy.

In summary, the critical incident technique, rather than collecting opinions, hunches, and estimates, obtains a record of specific behaviors from those in the best position to make the necessary observations and evaluations. The collection and tabulation of these observations make it possible to formulate the critical requirements of an activity. A list of critical behaviors provides a sound basis for making inferences as to requirements in terms of aptitudes, training, and other characteristics. It is believed that progress has been made in the development of procedures for determining activity requirements with objectivity and precision in terms of well-defined and general psychological categories. Much remains to be done. It is hoped that the critical incident technique and related developments will provide a stable foundation for procedures in many areas of psychology.

NOTES

1. Allen, C. D. Critical requirements in in-

terpersonal behavior. Unpublished senior thesis, Princeton Univer., 1950.

2. American Institute for Research. *The applicant inventory.* Pittsburgh: American Institute for Research, 1954.

3. American Psychological Association, Committee on Ethical Standards for Psychology. *Ethical standards of psychologists.* Washington, D.C.: Amer. Psychol. Assn., 1953.

4. Barnhart, R. E. The critical requirements for school board membership based upon an analysis of critical incidents. Unpublished doctor's dissertation, Indiana Univer., 1952.

5. Collins, Marjorie G. Selected methods applied to the evaluation of a parent training course in child management. Unpublished doctor's dissertation, Univer. of Pittsburgh, 1954.

6. Domas, S. J. *Report of an exploratory study of teacher competence.* Cambridge: New England School Development Council, 1950.

7. Eilbert, L. R. A study of emotional immaturity utilizing the critical incident technique. *Univer. Pittsburgh Bull.,* 1953, **49,** 199-204.

8. Emons, V. L'analyse de la fonction de vendeuse de grand magasin par la méthode des exigencies critiques. Unpublished doctor's dissertation, Univ. of Liége, Belgium, 1952.

9. Ericksen, S. C. Development of an objective proficiency check for private pilot certification. Washington: Civil Aeronautics Administration, 1951. *(Div. of Res., Rep.* No. 95.)

10. Ericksen, S. C. Development of a light plane proficiency check to predict military flying success. *USAF, Hum. Resour. Res. Cent., Tech. Rep.,* 1952, No. 52-6.

11. Finkle, R. B. A study of the critical requirements of foremanship. *Univer. Pittsburgh Bull.,* 1950, **46,** 291-297. (Abstract)

12. Fitts, P. M., & Jones, R. E. Psychological aspects of instrument display. 1. Analysis of 270 "pilot error" experiences in reading and interpreting aircraft instruments. Dayton, O.: U.S. Air Force, Air Materiel Command, Wright-Patterson Air Force Base, 1947. *(Mem. Rep.* TSEAA-694-12A.)

13. Flanagan, J. C. The aviation psychology program in the Army Air Forces.

Washington: U.S. Government Printing Office, 1947. *(AAF Aviat. Psychol. Program Res. Rep.* No. 1.)

14. Flanagan, J. C. A new approach to evaluating personnel. *Personnel,* 1949, **26,** 35-42.

15. Flanagan, J. C. Critical requirements: a new approach to employee evaluation. *Personnel Psychol.,* 1949, **2,** 419-425.

16. Flanagan, J. C. Use of comprehensive rationales. *Educ. Psychol. Measmt.,* 1951, **11,** 151-155.

17. Flanagan, J. C. Principles and procedures in evaluating performance. *Personnel,* 1952, **28,** 373-386.

18. Flanagan, J. C. *Flanagan aptitude classification tests.* Chicago: Science Research Associates, 1953.

19. Flanagan, J. C. Improving personnel selection. *Publ. Personnel Rev.,* 1953, **14,** 107-112.

20. Flanagan, J. C., et al. *Critical requirements for research personnel.* Pittsburgh: American Institute for Research, 1949.

21. Flanagan, J. C., et al. *The performance record for hourly employees.* Chicago: Science Research Associates, 1953.

22. Flanagan, J. C., et al. *The performance record for non-supervisory salaried employees.* Chicago: Science Research Associates, 1953.

23. Flanagan, J. C., et al. *The performance record for foremen and supervisors.* Chicago: Science Research Associates, 1953.

24. Folley, J. D., Jr. Development of a list of critical requirements for retail sales personnel from the standpoint of customer satisfaction. Unpublished master's thesis, Univer. of Pittsburgh, 1953.

25. Goldfarb, A. Use of the critical incident technique to establish areas of change accompanying psychotherapy: II. Relationship to diagnostic group. Unpublished master's thesis, Univer. of Pittsburgh, 1952.

26. Goodenough, D. R., & Suttell, Barbara J. *The nature and extent of impairment of human efficiency in emergency operations: the field study.* Pittsburgh: American Institute for Research, 1952.

27. Gordon, T. The airline pilot: a survey of the critical requirements of his job and of pilot evaluation and selection pro-

cedures. Washington: Civil Aeronautics Administration, 1947. *(Div. of Res., Rep. No. 73.)*

28. Gordon, T. The development of a standard flight-check for the airline transport rating based on the critical requirements of the airline pilot's job. Washington: Civil Aeronautics Administration, 1949. *(Div. of Res., Rep. No. 85.)*

29. Gordon, T. The development of a method of evaluating flying skill. *Personnel Psychol.,* 1950, **3,** 71-84.

30. Hahn, C. P. Measurement of individual differences with respect to critical job requirements. *USAF Sch. Aviat. Med.,* 1954, Proj. No. 21-29-014, No. 2.

31. Hobbs, N. The development of a code of ethical standards for psychology. *Amer. Psychologist,* 1948, **3,** 80-84.

32. Jensen, A. C. Determining critical requirements for teachers. *J. Exp. Educ.,* 1951, **20,** 79-86.

33. Konigsburg, D. The development and preliminary evaluation of an instructor check list based on the critical incident technique. Unpublished doctor's dissertation, Univer. of Pittsburgh, 1954.

34. Krumm, R. L. Critical requirements of pilot instructors. *USAF, Hum. Resour. Res. Cent., Tech. Rep.,* 1952, No. 52-1.

35. Krumm, R. L. *Development of a measure of pilot instructor proficiency based on the critical requirements of the instructor's job.* Pittsburgh: American Institute for Research, 1953.

36. Marley, F. W. Individual differences in critical aircrew elements: I. The determination of critical proficiency requirements for B-29 combat crews. *USAF Sch. Aviat. Med.,* 1952, Proj. No. 21-29-014, No. 1.

37. Marley, F. W. The development of performance flight checks for B-29 combat crews. *USAF, Hum. Resour. Res. Lab.,* 1952, Rep. No. 19.

38. Mellett, T. P. Use of the critical incident technique to establish areas of change accompanying psychotherapy: III. Differences among therapists. Unpublished master's thesis, Univer. of Pittsburgh, 1952.

39. Miller, G. S. *Development of B-36 bombardment objective flight checks and proficiency measures for use with re-*

connaissance crews. Pittsburgh: American Institute for Research, 1953.

40. Miller, N. E. Psychological research on pilot training. Washington: U.S. Government Printing Office, 1947. *(AAF Aviat. Psychol. Program Res. Rep. No. 8.)*

41. Miller, R. B. Anticipating tomorrow's maintenance job. *USAF, Hum. Resour. Res. Cent., Res. Rev.,* 1953, No. 53-1.

42. Miller, R. B. A method for determining human engineering design requirements for training equipment. Dayton, O.: U.S. Air Force, Air Development Center, Wright-Patterson Air Force Base, 1953. *(Tech. Rep. 53-135.)*

43. Miller, R. B. Handbook on training and training equipment design. Dayton, O.: U.S. Air Force, Air Development Center, Wright-Patterson Air Force Base, 1953. *(Tech. Rep. 53-136.)*

44. Miller, R. B. A method for man-machine task analysis. Dayton, O.: U.S. Air Force, Air Development Center, Wright-Patterson Air Force Base, 1953. *(Tech. Rep. 53-137.)*

45. Miller, R. B. Human engineering design schedule for training equipment. Dayton, O.: U.S. Air Force, Air Development Center, Wright-Patterson Air Force Base, 1953. *(Tech. Rep. 53-138.)*

46. Miller, R. B., & Flanagan, J. C. The performance record: an objective merit-rating procedure for industry. *Amer. Psychologist,* 1950, **5,** 331-332. (Abstract)

47. Miller, R. B., & Folley, J. D., Jr. *The validity of maintenance job analysis from the prototype of an electronic equipment.* Pittsburgh: American Institute for Research, 1952.

48. Nagay, J. A. The development of a procedure for evaluating the proficiency of air route traffic controllers. Washington: Civil Aeronautics Administration, 1949. *(Div. of Res., Rep. No. 83.)*

49. Nagay, J. A. The airline tryout of the standard flight-check for the airline transport rating. Washington: Civil Aeronautics Administration, 1949. *(Div. of Res., Rep. No. 88.)*

50. Nevins, Charlotte I. An analysis of reasons for the success or failure of bookkeepers in sales companies. Un-

published master's thesis, Univer. of Pittsburgh, 1949.

51. O'Donnell, R. J. The development and evaluation of a test for predicting dental student performance. *Univer. Pittsburgh Bull.*, 1953, **49**, 240-245. (Abstract)

52. Preston, H. O. *The development of a procedure for evaluating officers in the United States Air Force.* Pittsburgh: American Institute for Research, 1948.

53. Preston, H. O. *Events affecting reenlistment decisions.* Pittsburgh: American Institute for Research, 1953.

54. Ronan, W. W. *Training for emergency procedures in multi-engine aircraft.* Pittsburgh: American Institute for Research, 1953.

55. Ruch, F. L. Incidents of leadership in combat. *USAF, Hum. Resour. Res. Inst., Res. Memo*, 1953, No. 3.

56. Shriver, Beatrice M. Age and behavior: a study of the effects of aging on aircrew performance. *USAF Sch. Aviat. Med.*, 1953, Proj. No. 21-0202-0005, No. 3.

57. Sivy, J., & Lange, C. J. Development of an objective form of the Leaders Reaction Test. *AGO, Personnel Res. Branch, PRS Rep.*, 1952, No. 930.

58. Smit, JoAnne. A study of the critical requirements for instructors of general psychology courses. *Univer. Pittsburgh Bull.*, 1952, **48**, 279-284. (Abstract)

59. Smith, R. G., Jr., & Staudohar, F. T. Technical requirements of basic training tactical instructors. *USAF, Hum. Resour. Res. Cent., Tech. Rep.*, 1954, No. 54-7.

60. Speth, E. W. The use of the critical incident technique to establish areas of change accompanying psychotherapy: I. Function of age and education. Unpublished master's thesis, Univer. of Pittsburgh, 1952.

61. Suttell, Barbara J. *Development of a situation test to measure non-intellectual officer qualities.* Pittsburgh: American Institute for Research, 1953.

62. Taylor, M. V., Jr. *The development of aircrew job element aptitude tests.* Pittsburgh: American Institute for Research, 1953.

63. Vasilas, J. N., Fitzpatrick, R., DuBois, P. H., & Youtz, R. P. Human factors in near accidents. *USAF Sch. Aviat. Med.*, 1953, Proj. No. 21-1207-0001, No. 1.

64. Wager, C. E., & Sharon, M. I. Defining job requirements in terms of behavior. *Personnel Admin.*, 1951, **14**, 18-25.

65. Wagner, R. F. A group situation compared with individual interviews for securing personnel information. *Personnel Psychol.*, 1948, **1**, 93-107.

66. Wagner, R. F. A study of the critical requirements for dentists. *Univer. Pittsburgh Bull.*, 1950, **46**, 331-339. (Abstract)

67. Wagner, R. F. Development of standardized procedures for defining the requirements of aircrew jobs in terms of testable traits. *USAF Sch. Aviat. Med.*, 1951, Proj. No. 21-29-010, No. 1.

68. Wagner, R. F. Using critical incidents to determine selection test weights. *Personnel Psychol.*, 1951, **4**, 373-381.

69. Weislogel, Mary H. *Development of a test for selecting research personnel.* Pittsburgh: American Institute for Research, 1950.

70. Weislogel, Mary H. *Procedures for evaluating research personnel with a performance record of critical incidents.* Pittsburgh: American Institute for Research, 1950.

71. Weislogel, Mary H. *The development of tests for evaluating research proficiency in physics and chemistry.* Pittsburgh: American Institute for Research, 1951.

72. Weislogel, R. L. Critical requirements for life insurance agency heads. *Univer. Pittsburgh Bull.*, 1952, **48**, 300-305. (Abstract)

73. Weislogel, R. L., & Schwarz, P. A. Some practical and theoretical problems in situation testing. Unpublished manuscript. Pittsburgh: American Institute for Research, 1953.

74. Wickert, F. Psychological research on problems of redistribution. Washington: U.S. Government Printing Office, 1947. (*AAF Aviat. Psychol. Program Res. Rep.* No. 14.)

6. Dimensional Problems of Criteria*

EDWIN E. GHISELLI

The discussions by Otis (8), Toops (12), Bellows (1), and Thorndike (11) constitute the fundamental conceptual formulations of the criterion problem, yet all have been published within the last decade and a half. While others have considered matters connected with the development of criteria for use in validating selective devices, by and large their concern has been with technical details or some restricted phase. Thus the broader aspects of the criterion problem have not received attention they deserve.

In a way it is unfortunate that the term criteria has been used to denote measurements of job success. This term refers to standards for the evaluation of something else, and the implication is that the something else is of greater importance than the standards themselves. In the present context selective devices are the something else. It is certainly true that far more attention has been devoted to the development of predictive devices than to the understanding and evaluation of criteria.

Since criteria are means for quantitatively describing workers' performance, an examination of the dimensional problems of criteria would seem both legitimate and necessary. While such an examination may raise new and as yet unanswerable questions, at least those who are concerned with the selection of workers will be in a better position to see the kinds of problems that confront them. This paper will deal with certain matters connected with the dimension-ality of criteria—static dimensionality, dynamic dimensionality, and individual dimensionality.

STATIC DIMENSIONALITY

As it is ordinarily stated, the selection problem involves the prediction of a single variable—the criterion. The presumption is that the job proficiency of workers can be described completely by a single dimension. But for almost any job there are a number of dimensions on which workers' performance can be measured. Thus typists can be evaluated not only in terms of speed of typing, but also in terms of errors, neatness of product, absences, etc. When confronted with this situation the common procedure is to select one of the criterion variables and say that it is the best, the most pertinent, or the most representative.

When there are several criterion variates for a given job, sometimes the decision is to combine all measures into a single composite. This presents a series of technical problems and also a series of theoretical ones. Mere assignment of equal weight to all components is seldom satisfactory, because other grounds, perhaps purely intuitive ones, suggest that they are not equally important. Almost all of those who have attempted rational solutions to the differential weighting of a set of independent variables fall back upon some notion of a general factor. The objectives may be stated differently. For example,

*Source: From Journal of Applied Psychology, vol. 40 (February 1956), pp. 1-4. Copyright © 1956 by the American Psychological Association. Reprinted by permission.

Edgerton and Kolbe (4) and Horst (6) say that the purpose is to maximize differences between individuals in terms of composite criterion scores and to minimize differences in scores on the different criterion variables within the individual. However, the end result is the same, and the various criterion variates are thereby weighted in terms of their principal component.

This would be a satisfactory solution if it could be demonstrated that all of the different measures of performance for any given job are determined largely by the same general factors. However, such evidence as there is suggests that if there are general factors at work, at best they are of minor importance (e.g., 2, 9). In other words, it would appear that workers' performance on any given job is best described in terms of several dimensions, and one dimension is not sufficient.

If the proposition is accepted that criteria are multidimensional with the dimensions being independent, or at least relatively so, then the situation is not an easy one. There is no way to combine the independent scores of an individual into a single value that will describe him uniquely. Rather it will be necessary to locate his position in the multidimensional criterion space. This can be accomplished in either of two ways: each criterion dimension can be predicted separately and the individual's position in the space estimated, or the space can be divided into parts and that portion of the space in which the individual is most likely to fall could be estimated by the discriminate function.

These solutions require judgments as to which portions of the space contain most desirable individuals. When a single criterion variable is being predicted, the problem is simple. All that needs be said in making a decision with respect to candidates for a job is that the higher the score the better. But with the multidimensional situation it is necessary to define which parts of the space contain satisfactory persons who should be hired, and which parts contain those individuals who should be rejected. It might be argued that those people who are high on every criterion variate are successful and hence should be selected. The criterion space then would be divided into two parts, one at the upper right-hand corner containing only individuals who are high on all variables and therefore to be classed as satisfactory, and all of the remaining area of the space containing all of the rest of the individuals who would then be classified as unsatisfactory. Persons who fall into this second part would necessarily be classified as unsatisfactory even if they were high on all but one of the dimensions.

Procedures such as these clearly presume that all criterion dimensions are equally important and that a low score on any one is tantamount to complete failure. This situation may hold in certain circumstances but probably not too many. In most cases the notion of equality among criterion dimensions cannot be supported, and compensation for low scores on one dimension must be allowed for by high scores on another.

Kurtz has provided a rational solution of a very different kind (7). He has proposed that when criteria are multidimensional they need not be combined, nor need the individuals' unique positions in the multidimensional space be described. Rather predictors can be weighted so that the highest possible average of the validity coefficients with all of the criterion variates is obtained. This solution simply ignores the problem of differential importance of criteria. Yet a kind of compromise is effected which in many situations may be as good as or even better than arbitrarily combining all criterion variates into an equally weighted composite and predicting it.

Undoubtedly there are still other kinds of solutions to the multivariate criterion problem, but few have given it systematic consideration. It is obvious that new ideas are necessary and that ingenuity should be the order of the day.

DYNAMIC CRITERIA

The foregoing criteria have been called static since in dealing with them the matter of change is not considered. For any given type of criterion, data are collected for a period of time and then merely summed. Yet it is apparent that the performance of workers does change as they learn and develop on the job. The length of time during which such change occurs generally seems to be underestimated. The tendency is to think that most improvement occurs within the first few weeks or months after the individual is placed on the job. However, increases in job proficiency have been noted over quite long periods of time. Farmer and Chambers report significant improvements in the performance of bus drivers even after five years on the job (5). Haire and the present writer found that the performance of investment salesmen improved at a constant rate during the first six years of employment with no suggestion of a leveling off.

The obvious thing to do is to examine the intercorrelations among criterion measurements taken at different periods of time in order to ascertain the kind of pattern that holds. For example, analysis of the intercorrelations among monthly production records for a period of several years would give some indication of the extent to which dimensionality changes with time.

Pertinent facts are few, but generalizing from the results of laboratory experiments on learning one would expect to find the intercorrelations among measures of proficiency taken at different periods fairly uniform in magnitude, with the relationships among extreme periods perhaps being somewhat lower than the relationships among near periods. Haire and the present writer found just this state of affairs holding for the intercorrelations among the monthly

sales of investment salesmen for a two-year period, and for the intercorrelations among the weekly production records of taxicab drivers for an 18-week period. This uniformity in magnitude of intercorrelations is most easily accounted for on the basis of a single set of general factors equally important throughout time.

If this be the true state of affairs, it would mean that the selection problem is quite simple. When those individuals who are superior in the early phases are differentiated accurately, those who will be superior later on are thereby located, since they are the same individuals. However, even if the intercorrelations among criteria taken at different times are exactly the same in magnitude, since they will not be perfect they could be accounted for just as well by a variety of different factors changing in importance as time passes.

For the taxicab drivers described earlier, the scores earned by the men on a series of tests administered at the time of hiring were available. The scores on the various tests were correlated with production on each of the first 18 weeks of employment. If the uniform correlations among production records for the various weeks were the result of general factors of uniform importance, then the validities of the tests should be the same throughout the entire period. While for some of the tests the magnitude of the validity coefficients did remain practically unchanged throughout the period, other tests showed a gradual reduction in validity, still others a gradual increase, and one even showed regular and significant cyclical changes in validity from about zero to .40.

If this be the state of affairs with criteria, then the prediction problem is a difficult one indeed. The general predictions of job success that one desires to make, predictions of performance whether success occurs early or late in employment, would necessarily be relatively poor. To be of substantial magnitude, predictions would have to be of performance fairly closely pin-pointed in time.

CRITERION DIMENSIONALITY OF THE INDIVIDUAL

Some 15 years ago Otis made a most challenging statement about the criterion problem (8). In effect, he said that several workers on the same job might be considered equally good and yet the nature of their contributions to their organization might be quite different. In other words, the idea is that workers on the same job might be evaluated in terms of different criterion dimensions. Thus one college professor is considered good because he is an excellent teacher, and another because his research is very significant. This is not saying that an individual is to be considered good if he is high on any one criterion variable. Rather the notion is that while certain criterion variables are appropriate in describing the performance of some workers, they just are not pertinent in describing the performance of other workers on exactly the same job.

It would appear, therefore, that the criterion dimensionality of the individual should be investigated in the same way that Stephenson (10), Cattell (3), and others, investigate the personality dimensionality of the individual. It is quite possible that workers assigned to the same job perform quite differently in a qualitative as well as in a quantitative sense. For example, one clerk in a department store may perceive his job as seller of the merchandise assigned to him. Another sales clerk may view his job as builder of general good will. The number of dollars the store receives as a result of the efforts of the two workers might be exactly the same, in the one case because the clerk himself sells a lot of merchandise, and in the other case because the clerk gets the customers to buy throughout the entire store. Under these circumstances, the factors leading to successful performance of the one kind would be quite different from those

leading to successful performance of the other kind. It follows, then, that different types of tests necessarily would have to be used in order to predict the two different kinds of performances.

It might be argued that what is being considered here is not one job but two. However, in an administrative sense there is just one job, and it is only in a psychological sense that the jobs are qualitatively different. Studies of criterion dimensionality of the individual are one way of determining whether different positions in the same job in fact are psychologically the same or different.

SOME CONCLUSIONS CONCERNING THE DIMENSIONALITY OF CRITERIA

The matters discussed here are merely translations and formalizations of the kinds of problems that are commonly raised in connection with criteria. They are embarrassing and confusing questions, but nonetheless legitimate, and the psychologist should be prepared to provide answers to them. The questions are termed embarrassing because satisfactory answers have not been provided, and confusing because their full implications and the possible scope of answers are not well understood.

The evaluation of selective devices merely by simple correlations with single criterion variables is insufficient. It is apparent that the description of workers' job performance is a complex matter. Satisfactory statements concerning validity, therefore, cannot be made until rational solutions are developed for the various dimensional problems of criteria.

NOTES

1. Bellows, R. M. Procedures for evaluating vocational criteria. *J. Appl. Psychol.*, 1941, **25,** 499-513.
2. Carter, L. F. Psychological research on

navigator training. Washington: Government Printing Off., 1947. *(AAF Aviat. Psychol. Prog. Res. Rep. No. 10.)*

3. Cattell, R. B. *Factor analysis.* Harper, 1952.
4. Edgerton, H. A., & Kolbe, L. E. The method of minimum variation for the coordination of criteria. *Psychometrika,* 1936, **1,** 185-187.
5. Farmer, E., & Chambers, E. G. A study of accident proneness among motor coach drivers. *Rep. Indus. Hlth. Res. Bd., Lond.,* 1939, No. 84.
6. Horst, A. P. Obtaining a composite measure from different measures of the same attributes. *Psychometrika,* 1936, 1, 53-60.
7. Kurtz, A. B. The simultaneous prediction of any number of criteria by the use of a unique set of weights. *Psychometrika,* 1937, **2,** 95-101.
8. Otis, J. L. The criterion. In W. H. Stead, et al., *Occupational counseling techniques.* New York: American Book, 1940.
9. Rush, C. H. A factorial study of sales criteria. *Personnel Psychol.,* 1953, **6,** 9-24.
10. Stephenson, W. *The study of behavior; Q-technique and its methodology.* Chicago: Univer. of Chicago Press, 1953.
11. Thorndike, R. L. *Personnel selection.* New York: Wiley, 1949.
12. Toops, H. A. The criterion. *Educ. Psychol. Measmt.,* 1944, **4,** 271-297.

7. The Assessment Center Method*

DOUGLAS W. BRAY

The recent spread of the assessment center method throughout business and governmental organizations has been phenomenal. In 1960 only one American business organization was using assessment centers, and even in the mid-1960s only a handful of companies were running them. By the early 1970s, however, the method was being applied in several hundred organizations and many more were waiting in the wings to join the rush to add the technique to their personnel selection and development repertoire.

NATURE OF ASSESSMENT CENTERS

The term "assessment center" is somewhat of a misnomer since it implies that there must be a building or some other semipermanent physical location for the activity. Although this is often the case, there is nothing mandatory about it. What is really involved in assessment is the application of various methods of observing and evaluating behavior in a variety of situations. Such methods can be applied in nearly any location, including a business office set aside for a day for the purpose. The methodology is what is important, not the physical setting.

The purpose of an assessment center is to provide an objective off-the-job evaluation of developed abilities, potential, strengths and weaknesses, and motivation. (The degree to which evaluation of motivation is an aspect of assessment varies considerably from organization to organization.) The assessment center leads to these evaluations through the observation of behavior in a variety of standardized performance situations, the rating of that behavior on a number of predetermined dimensions,

Source: "The Assessment Center Method, by Douglas W. Bray, pp. 16-1–16-15, from *Training and Development Handbook,* 2nd Ed. Edited by Robert L. Craig. Copyright © 1976 by McGraw-Hill Book Company. Reprinted by permission. Tables renumbered.

the drawing of conclusions concerning potential for certain levels and types of work, and the diagnosis of developmental needs.

EMERGENCE OF THE MANAGEMENT ASSESSMENT CENTER

The assessment center first came to public attention in the United States at the conclusion of World War II, when it was revealed that the method had been used during the war to select intelligence operatives for the Office of Strategic Services. This use was publicized in an article in *Fortune* magazine[1] and in a book entitled *Assessment of Men.*[2] These reports generated considerable interest because of the imaginative and exciting nature of many of the simulations used and also because the elaborateness of the method contrasted sharply with the simplicity of paper-and-pencil methods of selection so widely used in nearly all other contexts, military and otherwise.

The OSS reports led to a few other attempts to apply the method, notably to the selection of clinical psychologists at a time when great numbers of them were being trained for the Veterans Administration and to the selection of psychiatrists at the Menninger Clinic. The results of these applications, as well as several outside the United States, were summarized in the mid-1950s.[3] Most psychologists viewed the results reported as disappointing, and the assessment center appeared not to be destined to play much of a role in either personnel selection or personnel development. Certainly very few suggested that it was a promising method for business use.

In 1956 the American Telephone and Telegraph Company undertook a longitudinal study of the development of young managers.[4]

In order to form a base for the years of follow-up to come, it was necessary to determine the abilities, aptitudes, values, and motivations of the study sample at the time when they first became managers. A 3½-day assessment center process was designed, and the 422 subjects of the study were assessed in the years 1956 to 1960. The assessment center had been introduced into American business.

This first AT&T assessment center was staffed by professional psychologists and thus was similar to the OSS center and other professional centers which had preceded the Bell System application. An important breakthrough occurred in 1958, when Michigan Bell management suggested that the assessment center might be modified to make it usable by laypersons. The specific purpose in mind was to aid in making the promotion decision involving craftsmen nominated for first-line management. The proposed assessment center started operations in the fall of 1958 with a staff consisting entirely of laypersons. Thus the assessment center method was freed of its reliance on professional assessors and freed of the barrier to widespread use which this requirement imposed. The way was open for the assessment center movement.

There was little immediate reaction: other organizations were slow to follow the Bell System's lead. During the 1960s, however, several companies became interested and started making serious use of the assessment center method, although on a smaller scale than AT&T. The first of these was Standard Oil of Ohio,[5] followed by General Electric and IBM. Momentum gradually increased up to the rapid proliferation of the late '60s and early '70s. Such expansion was supported by basic scientific studies[6] and by popular articles in publications read by many business executives.[7]

THE TYPICAL ASSESSMENT CENTER

Since the assessment center is an extremely flexible method, a description of the typical center may be misleading. Centers may run from less than a day to three or more days, they may or may not involve paper-and-pencil testing or measures of personality, and, in special instances, they may not even include that staple of the assessment center method—a group exercise. There is, nevertheless, a model which is representative of most centers.

The usual center occupies two days of the subject's time. Subjects are assessed in groups of six or twelve because most group exercises are constructed to accommodate six participants. While at the center the subjects undergo an extensive interview, an in-basket, and two group exercises. These are the basics, frequently embellished with additional individual performance situations and by paper-and-pencil tests and questionnaires.

THE BUSINESS GAME

Most assessment centers include a business game which, surprisingly enough, requires extremely little knowledge of business. The participants, usually six in number, try to make a profit by buying materials, putting them together in prescribed combinations, and selling them back to the staff members administering the exercise. The first assessment center business game used Tinker Toys. Others have involved the buying of digits and the resale of two- or three-digit number combinations, shares of stock in stock trading and conglomerate games, or simple electronic parts. The purpose of such games is not to determine business knowledge or experience, and a definite effort is made in designing games to keep them simple enough so that no assessee will have any particular advantage over the others because of past business experience. The game conditions are intended to be a stimulus for interpersonal behavior so that the assessors can observe evidences of leadership, decisiveness, resistance to stress, planning and organizing ability, and other characteristics relevant to performance as a manager. All the games

have definite time limits and, in addition, include stressful or uncertain periods so as to heighten interest and involvement. The games are, in fact, involving, and many assessees report that they enjoy going through them.

THE LEADERLESS GROUP DISCUSSION

An extremely common component of the assessment center is a leaderless group discussion. The original and most common format called for the six participants to act as the members of a board or committee, each of whom had an assigned point of view concerning the matter up for decision. The assessee was to promote this point of view as successfully as possible in the discussion period. In one example the six participants adopt the roles of members of the city council of a small city. They are to meet to decide what to do with additional federal funds which have suddenly come their way. Each participant is told that he or she has looked into the needs of a different city department and is attending the meeting hoping to obtain as much of the money as possible for that particular interest. Each participant is provided with briefing materials which give needed information about the city, its budget, etc., and a special briefing sheet outlining his or her particular project. Once again, as in the business game, an effort is made to provide materials which will fall within the experience of all the participants so that no special advantage will accrue to any of them. Behavior in the presentations and discussion is observed for such dimensions as oral communication skill, leadership, planning and organizing ability, resistance to stress, interpersonal sensitivity, and judgment. Other group discussion exercises have the participants play the roles of members of school boards, scholarship committees, supervisors meeting on a possible promotion, compensation committees, etc.

Not all leaderless group discussions are of the assigned-role variety. In some the participants are told that they are members of a task force or a special committee of some sort considering one problem or a series of problems. In this type of discussion the participants come to their own conclusions about the issues involved and the extent to which they wish to make a forceful presentation of a particular point of view. The participants are therefore not required to be as definitely competitive as they are when individual roles are assigned. Both types of group discussions are useful, depending on the particular dimensions which one desires to observe.

THE IN-BASKET

The in-basket presents management problems to the individual assessee in the form of written materials which might come across a manager's desk. These include letters, memorandums, notes from the boss, records of telephone calls, appraisal forms, routine reports, etc. The assessee is usually told that he or she has come into a new job which has been vacant for several weeks. Things have piled up, and the assessee has come in for the first time on a Sunday afternoon to spend a few hours getting on top of things. Some of the materials, which are in no particular order, are quite important and call for early action. Others are routine and may well be ignored. Assessees are instructed to deal with the materials as they think they would in the real situation except to make more of a record than they otherwise might of the actions they intend to take.

Although the in-basket can be treated simply as a written exercise, it is usually followed by an intensive interview. In this interview the assessor digs into the assessee's reasoning and perceptions about the various items in the basket and into the causes of his or her decisiveness or indecisiveness. The interviewer may also ask questions about the assessee's perception of the whole situation: How good a boss was the previous incumbent? What problems does the

organization have? What does the assessee plan to do to correct them? The in-basket interview is often conducted as a third-party inquiry. In other applications the staff members may play the role of the assessee's new boss and thus introduce a power relationship and perhaps somewhat more stress. The interview and the review of the written material itself form the basis for evaluating such dimensions as planning and organizing skills, decision-making ability, judgment, attention to detail, and perception.

THE INTERVIEW

An extensive interview is inevitably a part of the assessment process. Such interviews are usually quite lengthy, running from one to two hours, and often rove freely over many areas of the assessee's past and current life. Childhood and school experiences are, of course, prominent among the areas covered. Aspirations and expectations about the future are usually a matter of particular interest. In some centers interviews follow a prescribed format which specifies the questions to be asked. At the other extreme are interview methods which allow the interviewer complete freedom in formulating questions and interacting with the interviewee. In such cases the interviewer is expected to have a good grasp of the dimensions about which the interview is to provide information. A personal history blank is often administered early in the assessment process or even before the assessee reports to the center. The interviewer reviews this blank prior to the interview to help formulate the general approach and specific questions. Although some of the dimensions for which the interview provides good data are observable elsewhere in the assessment process, such as personal impact and oral communication skills, the interview makes a unique contribution in respect to some dimensions not easily observed elsewhere.[8] These include advancement motivation, the importance of job security, goal flexibility, and range of interests.

PAPER-AND-PENCIL TESTS

Although many assessment centers rely entirely on simulations and interviews, a considerable number include at least some paper-and-pencil testing as part of the battery of techniques. The Bell System assessment centers for the selection of first-line supervisors, for example, have long included a test of general mental ability and a current-events test. Centers elsewhere have used similar tests, and some have also used personality and motivational inventories. The cognitive instruments are used to obtain objective measures of learning capacity, range of interests, etc. The personality blanks are used for the purpose of evaluating motivational characteristics, an area which is tapped at most assessment centers only by the interview.

OTHER METHODS

The above types of techniques— business games, group discussions, in-baskets, interviews, and paper-and-pencil tests—are those most commonly seen in the typical assessment center. Other types of simulations have, however, appeared and will no doubt be added to in the future. One of these is the analysis/presentation exercise, in which the assessee must do an extensive analysis of a problem (often as an evening assignment) and then make a formal presentation of recommendations. Another simulation—individual fact-finding and decisionmaking— requires the assessee to dig out the facts in an ambiguous decision-making situation by face-to-face questioning and then defend the decision under vigorous cross-examination by an assessor.

A few centers have added projective personality tests, such as the Thematic Apperception Test. Such a step obviously requires the services of a professional staff member for the administration and particularly the interpretation of the responses to these instruments.

The reason for adding such tests is, of course, to find out more about the motivation of the assessees. The techniques have been shown to be helpful in throwing light on dimensions such as achievement motivation, desire to hold a leadership role, and independence.[9]

ASSESSMENT-STAFF ACTIVITIES

The purpose of the assessment exercises is to elicit behavior so that the candidate can later be judged on a variety of characteristics. It is obvious, then, that a trained staff must be on hand to observe the behavior. Although, as has been noted, early assessment centers relied almost completely on professional observers, most business assessment centers are staffed entirely by laypersons. These individuals are usually managers in the assessee's own company two levels above the level of those being assessed. (This requirement may have to be relaxed at higher levels of the organization.) These managers are trained for three to ten days to administer the assessment techniques and, more importantly, to carefully observe and record behavior so that their observations can later be made available to all members of the assessment staff. Behavior in a particular exercise may be observed by only one or two assessors, who must then prepare a report on their observations for later use by the entire staff. The nature of this report varies according to the software used and the training of the assessor. In some instances, the assessor report form provides the framework for the report, and the assessor completes the final report by answering fully all the questions on the form. More experienced assessors may simply record behavior in any manner they wish and write a report which they structure and organize completely on their own.

After the assessees have returned to their jobs and all the assessment reports are written, a most important phase of the assessment process takes place. This is the assessment staff meeting in which the performance of each candidate in all the exercises is reviewed and rated. The consideration of each candidate never occupies less than an hour and frequently takes closer to two hours. One candidate at a time is considered. The entire assessment staff listens to the reports of the candidate's behavior in all the exercises, interviews, etc., and then rates the candidate on the dimensions around which the assessment center is organized. These dimensions, such as face-to-face leadership skill, proficiency in planning and organizing, and decision-making ability, usually number from 15 to 25. Differences in ratings are discussed and adjudicated with the goal of achieving as much consensus as possible.

Following the rating of the dimensions, the assessment staff turns its attention to final recommendations. These may have to do with selection, placement, advancement, or development. In the case of advancement, the assessors usually place the candidate into one of several categories depending on whether they consider him or her to be completely acceptable for promotion, questionable, or unacceptable. Once again, there is considerable discussion of differences of opinion among the assessors in an effort to make sure that the reasons for the final recommendation are completely clear.

USES OF ASSESSMENT

The first operational use of assessment centers in the Bell System was as an aid in determining the promotability of nonmanagement employees who had been recommended by their organizations as candidates for first-line management. Although this is still a very common application of the assessment center method, much experience has accumulated about its use for other purposes. Uses have differed in respect to the level of the employee evaluated, the type of job for which the person is being evaluated, and the general purposes of the assessment.

EMPLOYMENT

A few organizations have used the assessment center to aid in employment decisions. These applications have concerned themselves with recent college graduates being considered for general management employment and persons applying for sales jobs. Several Bell System telephone companies as well as Sears, Roebuck[10] have used assessment centers in the college employment process. These centers have been similar to the typical one described above or have been some condensation thereof. Of practical importance is the fact that candidates for employment not only are willing to undergo assessment but also are often greatly impressed that a company devotes so much care and attention to its employment process. Logistics are sometimes a problem; it may be difficult to assemble groups of candidates to undergo assessment at the same time. Some type of prescreening before assessment may also be necessary to reduce large pools of applicants to smaller numbers for more serious consideration. Applicants for sales positions, including experienced salespeople, have also shown a clear willingness to be assessed even when the process may require a day of their own time.

EARLY IDENTIFICATION

Although it is the newest application of the method, early-identification assessment is logically considered next since it concerns the employee who has been hired only recently. The purpose of early identification, as used so far, has been to uncover potential for management-level work among new nonmanagement employees. Assessment is condensed into one day, and staff procedures are much shortened so that a high volume of assessees can be processed. The purpose of the assessment is not to render a final judgment of the candidates' promotability to management levels, but rather to identify those who have promise for the future. The intent is to give those with high potential special development opportunities and accelerated treatment so that they can reach target positions significantly earlier than might otherwise be the case. Early-identification processes have been worked out not only for management and sales jobs but also for the job of engineering assistant. In this application the assessment techniques are all individual in nature. There are no group exercises.

PLACEMENT

Placement has been used only sparingly as a purpose of assessment. This is most likely because assessment has usually been done on a general management model rather than for specific jobs. Assessment does, however, influence placement decisions in some cases. In the Standard Oil of Ohio application an important aspect of assessment is to decide the next assignment an assessee should have, given the overall pattern of strengths and weaknesses revealed by assessment. The point here is that assessment often leads to an assignment for developmental purposes rather than because the person is a "better fit" in the job to which he or she is to be moved. Assessment has also played a role in interdepartmental transfers, where it has proved to be a powerful way of breaking down traditional barriers. This application is especially helpful in instances where some departments are rich in talent and others are hard up for managers. The New York Telephone Company used assessment in such a circumstance with the highly successful transfer of managers across departmental lines.

ADVANCEMENT

By far the most frequent use of assessment is as part of the promotion process. The most usual pattern is for those who have been appraised by management as good candidates for advancement to go to the assessment center for a final check. This type of assessment is done at many different levels of man-

agement. It is probably most common at the lower levels, but many organizations restrict their assessment to middle managers. A few use it even at close to the vice-presidential level. Although attendance at the assessment center by nomination is by far the most frequent pattern, some organizations have assessed all incumbents at given levels of management to aid not only in selecting the most capable but also in evaluating the amount of potential available and in highlighting the developmental needs of the organization.

DEVELOPMENT

Recommendations for development are nearly always one of the outputs of the assessment center process. Not only may new assignments and different career paths be indicated for a particular individual, but formal training may also be suggested. Assessment which is done purely for the purpose of development is, however, rare. The original General Electric program had a strong emphasis on development and currently involves the preparation of a developmental plan during the manager's week at the center.[11] Several other organizations have also combined assessment and development experiences. In one department of IBM, for example, those attending the sessions spend the first two days being assessed and the next three days in management development activities. It has proved difficult for organizations to stick to a strict developmental model in their assessment activities. Once extensive evaluative information on individuals is available, the pressure to use that information as a guide to advancement and placement is extremely strong.

AFFIRMATIVE ACTION

A new purpose for assessment centers have been found in affirmative-action programs, which seek to speed the advancement of minority-group members and women. Early-identification programs are particularly relevant in this regard. Many organizations are hiring increased numbers of minority-group members into entry-level jobs. Normal processes of identification, development, and advancement are often lengthy, and it is particularly necessary to identify minority-group members with higher potential so that they can be moved along more quickly. The use of assessment centers (whether in early-identification programs or otherwise) can also serve to reduce the anxiety of some operating people that affirmative action may result in the advancement of individuals who are not fully capable of effective performance. Operating people tend to believe that nothing but the traditional approach of long service in a variety of jobs can produce a capable worker. Certification through an assessment center can provide evidence that the person really is capable of doing the level of work in question.

An interesting aspect of the consent agreement between AT&T and the EEOC and other government agencies was the provision of special regional assessment centers for women already in telephone company management. The problem consisted in the assertion by the government agencies that many women college graduates hired directly into management in the telephone business had not been put on the same "fast-track" program that many males had entered during the years in question. Since, however, many of the women managers had not been hired against the same standards as the men assigned to the special program, it was necessary to find a means of identifying those women of comparable potential. It was agreed that three regional assessment centers would be established to process all the 2,000 women who were covered by the agreement and who elected to attend.

ESSENTIALS OF ASSESSMENT

An obvious first step in starting an assessment center is to decide the level and type of job to which assessment is to be applied. Is the center to be used for employment or advancement, or will it be primarily developmental in nature? Is it to be concerned with lower-, middle-, or even upper-level management? Is the center to assess general management ability or certain specialist skills, such as sales? Answers to these questions will depend on a variety of factors including dissatisfaction with current methods, the importance of the job in question, resistances to certain applications, and the availability of appropriate staff.

SELECTING DIMENSIONS

Once the type and level of job are decided upon, the next most important step is identifying, defining, and getting organizational acceptance of the characteristics that the assessment center is to measure. These characteristics are called *dimensions, variables,* or *qualities.* It is these dimensions which will form the focus of assessment, will be reported on to management in terms of strengths and weaknesses, and will be discussed with assessees in feedback sessions. Obviously, the dimensions must make sense to the management of the organization, or management people—whether assessors, assessees, or supervisors—will not take them seriously.

Methods of identifying the dimensions to be used may include formal job analysis and descriptions, but they are most often based on special interviews with line and staff managers in the organization who supervise the level of work in question or who have special staff knowledge thereof. The process is often iterative in nature: that is, those building the assessment center construct a list of dimensions from the first round of interviewing and then play these back to management for revision. Second and third drafts may then be made until there is general satisfaction with the list.

With so many organizations now involved in assessment, the number of dimensions used somewhere or other is quite large. The following are some samples:

Oral communication skill
Leadership skills
Personal impact
Sensitivity
Flexibility
Independence
Work standards
Career ambition
Work involvement
Resistance to stress
Energy
Decisiveness
Planning and organizing ability
Tenacity

CHOOSING EXERCISES

A next step is the selection of assessment center exercises (including interviews and tests, if appropriate) designed to elicit behavior relevant to the dimensions around which the center is organized. Examples of the most common techniques have been given above, but it may be appropriate to design new ones for specific situations. For instance, one retail store chain has a special exercise known as the "irate customer phone call," and another organization has a special individual case for those to be employed as salespeople of printed advertisements. In planning the assessment center, there should be a good amount of redundancy between exercises so that a particular dimension can be seen in more than one setting. The more of this the better, since it adds to the reliability of judgments of the various dimensions.

STAFFING

Although a few assessment centers depend heavily on professionals, nearly all are staffed by managers from the organization itself. These managers are usually two levels above the assessees in the organization: that is, they supervise the level of management for which the assessee is a candidate. This is not universal, however. In some instances the assessors are only one level above the assessees.

An important decision relative to staffing is the number of times an assessor is likely to serve. In the original Bell System applications, it was anticipated that assessors would serve for several months or more. Few organizations have followed this lead, however, and many use assessors for only one or two assessee groups. Both extremes have their advantages. When assessors are to serve a long time, it is feasible to train them very thoroughly since the cost of training will be written off over many weeks of assessment. It is also likely that the more experienced the assessors, the better the quality of assessment. On the other hand, it may be very difficult to persuade management to release personnel for long periods, although they might be quite willing to have them serve a time or two. Considerable turnover of assessors also accomplishes the permeation of the organization with knowledge and sophistication about assessment since many managers will have been trained and will have served on the staff. They thus will be in a better position to appreciate assessment reports and to be guided by them.

FEEDBACK

Once the assessment of a candidate has been completed, the ratings made, and the reports prepared, the findings must then be played back to the organization. This is clearly what the assessment center is all about, and although it comes at the conclusion of a description of the essentials of assessment, it is clear that what is going to happen at this point should be decided long before the assessment center is started. One aspect of feedback concerns the form of the report to management and the question of who in management should receive the report. The most usual form is a short summary of the assessee's performance at the assessment center, paying particular attention to strengths and weaknesses demonstrated. This report is often sent to a manager in the assessee's organization several levels above the assessee. In other instances, it is sent directly to the assessee's boss. It would seem to make most sense to send the report to that level of the organization which actually controls the promotion or transfer of people at the assessee's level. For development purposes, however, it is usually expected that the information will eventually reach the candidate's supervisor.

Nearly all assessment center applications provide for the feedback of the assessment results to the assessees themselves. This is often done by a member of the assessment staff, but is sometimes carried out by a specialist who has learned assessment center methods and who handles all feedbacks within the organization. This would seem to be especially appropriate if that person is also in charge of management development, career counseling, or some similar function. The report to the assessee is usually private, although some organizations permit—at the assessee's request—that his or her boss be present; some organizations even require this. A variation tried by a few organizations is to have the assessment center administrator and the boss agree on a feedback which encompasses both assessment results and job performance, and this feedback is given jointly.

OUTSIDE ASSISTANCE

The assessment center is a sophisticated intervention into an organization's personnel management system, both in the operation of the center and in its various impingements on the organization. It is therefore essential that advice and assistance be obtained from those experienced in the method during the process of introducing a center into a new setting.

A number of organizations have come into being in order to fill this need. Their services fall into one or more of three categories: (1) consultation and assistance in training assessors and assessment center administrators, (2) the provision of assessment center techniques on either a ready-made or a

tailor-made basis, and (3) assessment of candidates on a per-head basis. Development Dimensions, Inc., provides services of all three types, has an extensive catalog of assessment exercises, and conducts regular conferences and workshops on the assessment center method. Cabot Jafee and Associates and an interlocking organization, Assessment Designs (both of Orlando, Florida), provide consultation services and materials. Personnel Decisions (Minneapolis) both assists organizations in installing centers and conducts "public" centers.

Other sources of assistance include Hilton Wasserman and Associates (New York), Assessment Associates (Baltimore), Consulting Associates (Southfield, Michigan), Humber, Mundie & McClary (Milwaukee), John Paisios & Associates (Chicago), and Canadian Management Assessment Centres Ltd. (Toronto). Some other consulting firms, originally established to provide different kinds of services, have now included assessment centers in their areas of work. The American Management Association has marketed a package including films and software to enable organizations to introduce centers for selecting first-level managers. Educational Testing Service has developed tailor-made in-baskets for a number of years.

The growing international scope of assessment center activities is creating a demand for consulting assistance overseas. For example, Development Dimensions has affiliates as far afield as Tokyo, Rio de Janeiro, and Johannesburg, and many of their exercises have been translated into French, Japanese, Portuguese, and Afrikaans.

VALIDITY STUDIES

The validation of the assessment center process poses special problems. Since most assessment centers have been used as the basis for decisions relative to advancement or development, criteria such as promotion soon after assessment are seriously contaminated. Comparing assessment results with ordinary management appraisals is not a good basis for validity studies; if one had confidence in management appraisals, one would not be conducting assessment centers in the first place.

In spite of these and other difficulties, however, there have been many convincing studies of the predictive power of assessment ratings. Assessment centers were introduced into business as part of the Bell System's Management Progress Study.[12] Individual assessment results in that study were fed back neither to management nor to the assessees themselves, and the data thus provide an excellent basis for the determination of long-term predictive validity. The study assessment staffs made a final rating of whether each subject would reach middle management within 10 years from the time of initial employment as a management trainee or, in the case of up-from-the ranks managers, from the time of assessment. Eight years after the assessment of the candidates, the management level of each was determined. The results are shown in Table 1. Of the college graduate management trainees rated likely to reach middle management within 10 years, some 64 percent had, in fact, reached middle management. Of those not so predicted, only 32 percent had reached the target level. In the case of the non-

college persons, the corresponding percentages were 39 and 9. These results show very definite predictive power for the assessment center in a situation in which assessment results were known to no one except the researchers.

In another Bell System study, of the personnel assessment program used to help select first-line managers, an attempt was made to overcome the contamination problem by using two or more promotions, rather than just the initial promotion, as the criterion.[13] A sample of almost 6,000 assessees was followed, with the results shown in Table 2. At the extremes of the table, those who were rated more than acceptable at initial assessment had received two or more promotions in slightly over 40 percent of the cases, while those who were rated not acceptable had been promoted twice or more only about 4 percent of the time. A study of this sort does not completely overcome the contamination problem. However, it is argued that although assessment recommendations may play a considerable role in the decision to promote from nonmanagement into management, further advancement is unlikely to be very much affected because of the strong influence of perceived performance as a first-level manager and because of changes in supervisors from year to year.

Another Bell System study, this time of a sales assessment center,[14] used a carefully controlled research design.

Table 1

MANAGEMENT PROGRESS STUDY PREDICTIONS AND PROGRESS IN MANAGEMENT

Staff Predictions	Management Level Eight Years Later			
	Third Level or Higher	Second Level	First Level	Total
College recruits:				
Will reach third level	64%	36%	—	100%
Will not reach third level	32	68	—	100
Non-college managers:				
Will reach third level	39	61	—	100
Will not reach third level	9	41	50%	100

Table 2

PERCENT OF NONMANAGEMENT ASSESSEES PROMOTED TO
SECOND-LEVEL OR HIGHER MANAGEMENT

Assessment Rating	Number of Assessees	Number Receiving Two or More Promotions	Percent Receiving Two or More Promotions
More than acceptable	410	166	40.5
Acceptable	1,466	321	21.9
Questionable	1,910	220	11.5
Not acceptable	2,157	91	4.2
Total	5,943	798	13.4

There was no feedback of assessment center results, and the criterion was observation of on-the-job performance by a team of trained managers. Seventy-eight men who had been hired by ordinary employment methods as communications consultants were sent to a sales assessment center, where they received a final rating as to their acceptability for sales employment. Six months or more after they had completed sales training and were out on the job, they were carefully observed by a team of specially trained sales managers who rated them dichotomously on whether they did or did not meet standards of sales performance. The raters had no knowledge of the assessment predictions. Table 3 shows the relationship between assessment judgments and the ratings of job performance. It will be seen that there is a strong relationship, with all those few men who had been rated more than acceptable meeting performance standards, as compared with only 10 percent of the unacceptable group.

An IBM study[15] used the technique of following the later careers of assessment candidates who were promoted to first-line management. The promotion to first-line manager had been made partially as the result of an assessment center report. Table 4 shows the combined results for three departments— sales, service, and administration. The IBM center placed the candidate in one of six categories reflecting the assessors' opinion of the degree of management potential possessed. The top category, as the table shows, was that of executive management, and the lowest category was a recommendation that the person remain in nonmanagement. Once again a wide difference is observed between those in the higher and

Table 3

PERCENT OF SALES ASSESSEES MEETING FIELD REVIEW
PERFORMANCE STANDARDS

Assessment Rating	Number of Assessees	Number Meeting Review Standards	Percent Meeting Review Standards
More than acceptable	9	9	100
Acceptable	32	19	60
Questionable	16	7	44
Not acceptable	21	2	10
Total	78	37	47

Table 4

PERCENT OF ASSESSEES RECEIVING FURTHER ADVANCEMENT
AFTER BECOMING FIRST-LINE MANAGERS*

Assessed Potential	Number of Managers	Number Promoted a Second Time	Percent Promoted a Second Time
Executive management	41	14	34
Higher management	85	27	32
Second-line management	110	30	27
First-line management	88	11	12
Remain nonmanagement	71	5	7
Total	395	87	22

*Adapted from data shown in the IBM study.

those in the lower assessment categories.

A unique criterion used by IBM for those of the above managers in the sales department was demotion after advancement to first-line management.[15] Table 5 shows the results, and it will be noted that demotion among those in the highest assessment ratings was strikingly less frequent than among those rated less optimistically.

A special type of validity study is that comparing the later performance of minority- and non-minority-group assessees. A recent doctoral dissertation used data from a Michigan Bell Telephone Company assessment program.[16] The study compared careful job performance and potential for promotion ratings with assessment ratings for black and white female assessees. Table 6 shows the resulting correlations. Very

Table 5

SALES MANAGERS DEMOTED AFTER ADVANCEMENT TO
FIRST-LINE MANAGEMENT

Assessed Potential	Number of Managers	Number Demoted	Percent Demoted
Higher management	46	2	4
Second-line management	50	7	14
First-line or nonmanagement	71	14	20
Total	167	23	14

Table 6

CORRELATIONS BETWEEN OVERALL ASSESSMENT RATING AND LATER
PERFORMANCE AND POTENTIAL RATINGS

	Whites (assessment rating with $N = 91$)	Blacks (assessment rating with $N = 35$)
Job performance	41*	35†
Potential for further advancement	59*	54*

†Statistically significant at the 0.05 level.
*Statistically significant at the 0.01 level.

little difference, and certainly no statistically significant difference, between the two groups appeared. The dissertation also presents data showing that the supervisor's knowledge that his or her subordinate has been assessed does not affect ratings of performance or potential.

IMPLICATIONS FOR TRAINING AND DEVELOPMENT

The spread of the assessment center method has great implications for those concerned with training and development. One effect of assessment is the identification of those toward whom training should be directed and some good leads as to what their training needs are. Where successful performance at an assessment center is, for example, a precondition for training or for advancement to a job which will require training, trainers can expect to have more capable groups of trainees than they otherwise would. Training time can be reduced, or higher goals for training can be established. On the other hand, assessment often identifies a group of candidates who do not perform well enough at the assessment center to merit recommendation for immediate promotion, but who do not fail badly. This is a group that might profit from training enough so that they could qualify for advancement later. Since assessment centers rate a number of dimensions important to performance in management, the trainer can focus training more on the actual needs of the individual or groups of individuals. There is no point in providing leadership training for a person who has already achieved the highest possible rating on that dimension.

Not only can individual needs be targeted, but also the training organization can determine the needs of whole levels of individuals. In assessing a group of middle managers for one of its subsidiary companies, some 45 percent were judged not promotable by an AT&T assessment staff. A review of

these cases showed five general categories of deficiency. Table 7 shows the percent of the group manifesting each weakness; many of these managers who were assessed poorly clearly had more than one deficiency.

Table 7
DEFICIENCIES MANIFESTED BY MIDDLE MANAGERS ASSESSED AS HAVING LOW POTENTIAL FOR FURTHER ADVANCEMENT (N = 22)

Area of Deficiency	Percent
Leadership skills	82
Administrative skills	73
Achievement motivation	45
Interpersonal conflicts	45
Intellectual ability	32

The table suggests the uncomfortable observation that far from all these managers are good bets for development. How much can one hope to accomplish with a trainee who has distinctly less intellectual ability than those at his or her level and who also has little achievement motivation?

The possible motivational effects of assessment feedback have been noted earlier. If the assessee has received an objective statement of his or her strengths and weaknesses shortly before entering a training experience, it is reasonable to expect more motivation for profiting from the training experience.

A final and completely different opportunity which assessment gives training organizations is the use of assessment as a criterion. Reviewers of management training and development programs over the years have bewailed the lack of objective evidence that the programs accomplish anything. Trainers have often responded that they are, in fact, accomplishing something but that it is extremely difficult to trace the effects of the training into ultimate criteria such as turnover or productivity. Since many of the goals of management training parallel the dimensions utilized for evaluation in assessment centers, it seems logical that assessment may provide a criterion for the effectiveness of training. Managers could be assessed before and after training, or, in a more experimental design, they could be assigned randomly to training or no-training conditions, or to different types of training, and assessed some time after taining. It may be that the assessment center approach can finally throw some light on the overall effectiveness of management training and assist in pinpointing its strengths and weaknesses.

NOTES

1. "A Good Man Is Hard to Find." *Fortune,* March 1946.
2. Office of Strategic Services Assessment Staff: *Assessment of Men,* Rinehart & Company, Inc., New York, 1948.
3. Taft, R.: "Multiple Methods of Personality Assessment." *Psychological Bulletin,* vol. 56, pp. 333-352, 1959.
4. Bray, D. W., D. L. Grant, and R. J. Campbell: "Studying Careers and Assessing Ability," in A. J. Marrow (ed.), *The Failure of Success,* AMACOM, New York, pp. 154-169, 1972.

   Bray, D. W., D. L. Grant, and R. J. Campbell: *Formative Years in Business: A.T. & T's Long-Term Study of Managerial Lives,* Interscience Publishers, a division of John Wiley & Sons, Inc., New York, 1974.
5. Finkle, R. D., and W. S. Jones: *Assessing Corporate Talent: A Key to Managerial Manpower Planning,* Interscience Publishers, a division of John Wiley & Sons, Inc., New York, 1970.
6. Bray, D. W., and D. L. Grant: "The Assessment Center in the Measurement of Potential for Business Management." *Psychological Monographs,* vol. 80, pp. 1-27, 1966.
7. Byham, W. C.: "Assessment Centers for Spotting Future Managers." *Harvard Business Review,* pp. 150-160, 1970.
8. Grant, D. L., and D. W. Bray: "Contributions of the Interview to Assessment of Management Potential." *Journal of Applied Psychology,* vol. 53, pp. 24-34, 1969.
9. Grant, D. L., W. Katkovsky, and D. W. Bray: "Contributions of Projective Techniques to Assessment of Management Potential." *Journal of Applied Psychology,* vol. 51, pp. 226-232, 1967.
10. Bentz, V. J.: "Validity Studies at Sears," paper presented before the American Psychological Association, annual convention, 1971.
11. General Electric Company, Corporate Education Services: *Talent Development Program,* January 1972. (Internal publication.)
12. Bray, D. W.: "The Management Progress Study." *American Psychologist,* vol. 19, pp. 419-420, 1964.
13. Moses, J. L.: "Assessment Center Performance and Management Progress." *Studies in Personnel Psychology,* vol. 4, pp. 7-12, 1972.
14. Bray, D. W., and R. J. Campbell: "Selection of Salesmen by Means of an Assessment Center." *Journal of Applied Psychology,* vol. 52, pp. 36-41, 1968.
15. Kraut, A. I., and G. J. Scott: "Validity of an Operational Management Assessment Program." *Journal of Applied Psychology,* vol. 56, pp. 124-129, 1972.
16. Huck, J. R.: "Determinants of Assessment Center Ratings for White and Black Females and the Relationship of these Dimensions to Subsequent Performance Effectiveness," unpublished doctoral dissertation, Wayne State University, Detroit, 1973.

8. Toward a Taxonomy of Human Performance*

EDWIN A. FLEISHMAN

Much research in the behavioral sciences is concerned with the study of factors affecting human task performance. Thus, we may study the effects on task performance of different training methods, different environments and conditions of work, attitudinal and group factors, and individual differences in abilities. It is surprising, therefore, that more attempts have not been made to conceptualize a set of variables common to these areas, namely, those associated with the kinds of *tasks* that people perform.

For some years, a number of us have been concerned with the need to develop a set of concepts that might help us make more dependable generalizations of research results to new tasks. The essential problem is the need to generalize the effect of some training, environmental, or procedural condition, from knowledge of its effect on one task, to its probable effect on some other task. What has been lacking is a system for classifying such tasks that would lead to improved generalizations and predictions about how such factors affect human performance (cf. Fleishman, 1967b; Gagné, 1964). In particular, what is needed is a learning and performance theory that ascribes a central role to task dimensions.

Not too long ago a favorite distinction in psychology textbooks was between "mental" and "motor" tasks or between "cognitive" and "noncognitive" tasks. Such broad distinctions are clearly too all-inclusive for generalizing results obtained on the effect of some learning or other condition to some new task. Job analysts, on the other hand, have developed highly detailed task analysis systems, but these are often too specific to particular jobs to help us arrive at general task dimensions applicable across many different tasks and jobs. Other psychologists (such as Alluisi, 1967; Gagné, 1964; Miller, 1966) have proposed categories of tasks in terms of broad human functions required to perform them. For example, such categories as *identification, discrimination, sequence learning, motor skill, scanning,* and *problem solving* are terms that have been used in the literature. However, everything we know from actual correlations among human performances indicates a considerable diversity of functions *within* each of these broad areas. The recent work by McCormick and his associates (e.g., McCormick, Jeanneret, & Mecham, 1972) explicitly recognizes this.

The need for a better conceptualization of task dimensions relates to some other pressing problems of our field. The recent challenges to our selection methodology intensify the need to search for better methods of job analysis conceptually linked to more analytical criterion measures of job performance. A taxonomic system of task dimensions should assist in this.

It has been my feeling over the years that some kind of taxonomy of human

*Source: From *American Psychologist*, vol. 30 (December 1975), pp. 1127-49. Copyright © 1975 by the American Psychological Association. Reprinted by permission. Footnotes renumbered.

performance is required which provides an integrative framework and common language applicable to a variety of basic and applied areas. Such a taxonomy should have certain characteristics. It should identify important correlates of learning, criterion performance levels, and individual differences *and* should be applicable to laboratory tasks and to tasks encountered in on-the-job situations.

Although the need has been recognized (e.g., Fitts, 1962; Melton & Briggs, 1960; Miller, 1962), it is only recently that concerted attempts have been made to explore more intensively some of the issues and alternatives in taxonomic development in psychology and to proceed on an *empirical* basis in the evaluation of these alternatives. I would like to review a program of research that has made at least some beginnings in this area.

Specifically, this article discusses briefly some general problems in the development of taxonomic systems applicable to descriptions of human performance and tasks. Some alternative approaches and provisional classification schemes developed are described. Then, some attempts to *evaluate* the utility and validity of these systems are reviewed.

SOME TAXONOMIC ISSUES

Early in our research program we reviewed the literature bearing on taxonomic approaches and concepts in the behavioral sciences as well as related developments in other sciences (Chambers, 1973; Farina, 1973; Theologus, 1973; Wheaton, 1973). We cannot provide the details of this review here, but we can indicate some issues that stood out.

PURPOSE OF CLASSIFICATION

We need to be clear on why we are interested in task classification. The question is important because individuals who attempt such classification usually do not view the development of such a system as an end, in and of itself. Rather, they view the system of classification as a tool to increase their ability to interpret or predict some facet of human performance (Cotterman, Note 1). This goal is to be achieved by seeking relationships between that which is classified (e.g., tasks, processes mediating performance) and selected variables of interest to a particular investigator (e.g., distribution of practice, training regimens, environmental stressors).

We can elect to develop a system of classification having utility for a limited area (e.g., the classification of tasks with respect to which certain training methods are found most effective in promoting high levels of task performance), or we may look for a system from which a *variety* of applications may stem. For example, we might first classify tasks and *only then* relate stressors, learning principles, training regimens, etc., to each class of tasks in this system. In this case, classification is designed from inception to be general and to serve a variety of users by aiding in the interpretation, prediction, or control of a broad range of human performance phenomena.

With respect to systems having rather specific applied objectives, classifications dealing with training are most numerous. A number of investigators (Annett & Duncan, 1967; Gagné, 1962; Miller, 1966; Cotterman, Note 1; Eckstrand, Note 2; Folley, Note 3; Stolurow, Note 4) have called for systems intended to permit the classification of tasks into sets of categories that are relatively homogeneous with respect to principles of learning, training techniques, etc. Bloom (1956) has attempted to develop a similar taxonomic system for the educational community. However, few empirical evaluations of such systems have been attempted.

Where broad task classification systems are developed as autonomous structures, which are only some time later to be applied to other variables, the classification exercise is an integral step in the development of theory. The resultant system provides a consistent conceptual framework, the elements of which eventually are to be used in the interpretation or prediction of human performance. One is not precluded from seeking specific applications for such classifications. The point is that a specific application does not dictate the composition and structure of the system.

Learning theorists have engaged in these pursuits (see Melton, 1964), but as yet there is no comprehensive system that effectively compares, contrasts, and interrelates the various human learning "categories."[1] Consequently, we have been unable to formulate a general theory of learning which allows dependable generalizations of learning principles to particular classes of tasks. Gagné (1964) has been the most systematic in the specification of general "learning categories" and their potential implications for ordering principles of learning.

The ability theorists also have attempted to isolate basic dimensions of behavior on which a general theory of human performance might be based. Guilford (1967) and I (Fleishman, 1964) have been perhaps the most explicit in attempting to integrate the ability dimensions identified within the general framework of experimental psychology. Thus, my associates and I have conducted research relating ability dimensions identified in research on individual differences to stages of learning (Fleishman & Hempel, 1954, 1955), stimulus–response relations (Fleishman, 1957), skill retention (Fleishman & Parker, 1962), part–whole task relations (Fleishman, 1965), effects of drugs (Elkin, Freedle, Van Cott, & Fleishman, Note 5), etc. This variety of studies was possible because we first attempted to develop a standard and consistent clas-

sificatory structure of human abilities and then attempted to test the feasibility of this framework across different areas of human performance. This approach is examined later in this article.

CONCEPTUAL BASES OF CLASSIFICATION

After the consideration of the purposes of task classification, one needs to examine the descriptive bases of taxonomy. A concern here is with the definition and meaning of the concept *task*.

● *Definition of the task.* Task definitions vary greatly with respect to their breadth of coverage. At one end of this dimension are definitions that view the task as the totality of the situation imposed on the subject. For example, this definition would consider ambient stimuli an integral part of the task. The other end of this dimension is represented by definitions that treat a task as a specific *performance*. In this case, for example, one task could be to "depress the button whenever the light comes on." Suffice it to say that very different concepts may underlie definitions falling at either end of this dimension.

This diversity of opinion is also reflected in the extent to which tasks are defined as being external to or an intrinsic part of the subject. Some definitions take into account the propensity of subjects to redefine an imposed task in terms of their own needs, values, experiences, etc. In the grossest sense, these definitions treat a task as whatever it is the subject *perceives* the task to be. Other investigators (e.g., Hackman, 1970) define the task in terms of stimulus materials and instruction to the subject. The instructions indicate the activities to be performed with respect to the stimuli and the goals to be achieved. Merely giving a person a broken radio would not be assigning him a task.

Most investigators treat tasks as consisting of interrelated processes and activities. For example, Miller (1966) stated that "A task is any set of activities, occurring at about the same

---

1. For a recent attempt in the area of instrumental conditionings, see Wood (1974).

time, sharing some common purpose that is recognized by the task performer" (p. 11).

Our conclusion was that we should not debate about *the* definition of a "task" as if only one were possible. Rather, we must adopt or develop a definition that will permit the derivation of terms that reliably describe tasks and distinguish among them. These derived terms can provide the conceptual basis for classification, as we shall see later.

There appear to be four major conceptual bases underlying current task description and classification.

• *Behavior description approach.* In this conceptual approach to task classification, categories of tasks are formulated based on observations and descriptions of what operators actually do while performing a task. Most often, overt behaviors such as dial setting, meter reading, and soldering are employed. In spite of the large number of terms available for this approach to task description, relatively few descriptive systems have been developed that are based exclusively on operator behaviors or activities. McCormick (Note 6) has employed this descriptive approach in his studies of worker-oriented job variables (e.g., handling objects, personal contact with customers), and Fine (Note 7) has used this approach as a basis for describing worker functions in terms of handling (things), analyzing (data), and negotiating (with people).

• *Behavior requirements approach.* A second approach to "task" description emphasizes the cataloging of behaviors that are assumed to be *required* in order to achieve criterion levels of performance. The human operator is assumed to possess a large repertoire of processes that will serve to *intervene* between stimulus events and responses. There has been a great deal of interest in codifying the required intervening processes (functions, behaviors, etc.), cataloging tasks in terms of the types of processes required for successful performance, and then relating to particular

training methodologies the types of tasks that emerge (see Annett & Duncan, 1967; Gagné & Bolles, 1963; Miller, 1966; and Eckstrand, Note 2). Typical of the functions used to differentiate among tasks are scanning function, short-term memory, long-term memory, decision making, and problem solving.

• *Ability requirements approach.* The third conceptual basis for the description and classification of tasks, which we call the ability requirements approach (e.g., see Fleishman, 1972), is in many respects similar to the behavioral requirements concept. Tasks are to be described, contrasted, and compared in terms of the abilities that a given task requires of the operator. These abilities are relatively enduring attributes of the individual performing the task. The assumption is made that specific tasks will require certain abilities if performance is to be maximized. Tasks requiring similar abilities would be placed within the same category or would be said to be similar.

The abilities approach differs from the behavior requirements approach primarily in terms of concept derivation and level of description. The ability concepts are empirically derived through factor-analytic studies and are treated as more basic units than the behavior functions.

• *Task characteristics approach.* A fourth approach differs from the preceding approaches in terms of the type of task description that is attempted. This approach (see Farina & Wheaton, 1973; Hackman, 1970) is predicated on a definition that treats the task as a set of conditions that elicit performance. These conditions are imposed on the individual and have an objective existence quite apart from the activities they may trigger, the processes they may call into play, or the abilities they may require. Having adopted this point of view, appropriate descriptive terms are those that focus on the task per se. The assumption is made that tasks can be described and differentiated in terms of intrinsic, objective properties they may possess. These properties or characteristics may pertain to the goal toward which the operator works, relevant task stimuli, instructions, procedures, or even to characteristics of the response(s) or the task content. The obvious problem is the selection of those task components that are to be described, as well as the particular terms or parameters by means of which description is to be accomplished.

We have seen that tasks can be defined in several ways, particularly in regard to the scope of definition; the extent to which tasks may be treated as objective entities, clearly apart from the operators who perform them; and the extent to which tasks are viewed as processes or structures.

SOME METHODOLOGICAL ISSUES

Within the scope of this article I cannot dwell on the more general problems of "how" to proceed with classification. I shall discuss instead a number of criteria for evaluating such systems.

The requirement for operational definition of terms becomes increasingly critical if the system is to be used by a broad range of specialists. The descriptive terms may be completely unfamiliar to many of these individuals, or even too familiar as in the case of the popular terms *decision making* and *problem solving*. Although homage is paid to the need for operational definitions, few investigators have actually generated such definitions. Also, as a minimum requirement, the descriptors employed in the differentiation and classification of tasks must permit *nominal scaling*. That is, a judge must at least be able to ascertain whether each descriptor applies or does not apply to the particular task being examined.

Also, descriptors must be defined and treated within a system of measurement so that they can be reliably evaluated. Another criterion requires that classes

within the system be mutually exclusive and exhaustive.

A major criterion is that classes are desired that have specific behavioral implications, as with the interest of Annett & Duncan (1967) in classifying "tasks" so that each category or class of tasks has specific training requirements associated with it. Ultimately, of course, any behavioral classification scheme must make the "match" between specific categories and behavioral effects. The degree to which the "match" can be made will determine the predictive power of the system. At one level, a statement might concern *whether or not* a particular environmental variable would affect performance. At another and more sophisticated level it might be possible to predict the *direction* and *magnitude* of the effect.

A final set of criteria includes efficiency and utility. The taxonomy should promote communication among its users, be they researchers in different areas or specialists who must use research findings in applied settings.

In our own program we found it useful to lay out these general issues, which we have elaborated elsewhere. In no sense can we say that our subsequent efforts met the rigorous standards called for. However, they at least provide indications of where we fell short and allow for successive iterations toward meeting these criteria.

In the remainder of this article, I illustrate some developments with two provisional systems, one based on the *ability requirements approach* and another on the *task characteristics approach*. I conclude with some attempts to link these two approaches.

THE ABILITIES APPROACH

Much of what is known today about the categorization of human skills, at least that which is based on empirical research, comes from correlational and factor analysis studies. Such correlational studies are typically carried out in the psychometric tradition, and until recently, little attempt has been made to integrate the ability concepts developed there into the more general body of psychological theory. Here the fact of individual differences is exploited to gain insights about common processes required to perform different groups of tasks. Abilities are defined by empirically determined relations among observed separate performances.

It has been my feeling, over many years, that research using combinations of experimental and correlational methods, properly conducted, can lead to the development of a taxonomy of human performance which is applicable to a variety of basic and applied problems and that ability concepts may provide an integrative framework.

Elsewhere (e.g., Fleishman, 1962) I have elaborated on the concepts of *ability* and *skill*. Briefly, ability refers to a more general capacity of the individual, related to performance in a variety of human tasks. For example, the fact that spatial visualization has been found related to performance on such diverse tasks as aerial navigation, blueprint reading, and dentistry makes this ability somehow more basic.

My interest in this area began when I was responsible for developing psychomotor tests to select pilots for the Air Force. Figure 1a shows a test found valid for pilot selection. The test requires simultaneous manipulations of stick and rudder pedals and has a great deal of face validity. However, Figure 1b shows another test found equally valid. This test, the familiar pursuit roter, has little face validity. The subject is required to keep a stylus tip in contact with a moving target. My feeling was that we needed basic research on the dimensions of perceptual-motor ability to identify what factors in these tests were common to the criterion performance in more complex tasks such as piloting.

An extensive series of interlocking experimental–factor-analytic studies, which we have conducted over many years, has attempted to isolate and identify the ability factors common to a wide range of perceptual–motor performances. Essentially, this is laboratory research in which tasks are specifically designed or selected to test certain hypotheses about the organization of abilities in a certain range of tasks. The experimental battery of tasks is administered to several hundred subjects, and

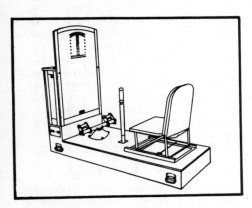

a. COMPLEX COORDINATION   b. ROTARY PURSUIT

Figure 1. Examples of tests found valid for pilot selection

the correlation patterns are examined through factor analysis methods. Subsequent studies tend to introduce task variations aimed at sharpening or limiting our ability factor definitions.

Through our investigation of a wide range of several hundred different tasks, we have been able to account for performance in terms of a relatively small number of abilities. The following display gives the labels of 11 perceptual–motor factors that consistently appear to account for the common variance in such tasks. In subsequent studies, definitions of these abilities and their distinctions from one another have become more clearly delineated. I will not define all of these here, but extensive definitions of each ability exist with illustrations of the tasks that best measure them (Fleishman, 1964).

PERCEPTUAL–MOTOR ABILITIES

Control precision
Multilimb coordination
Response orientation
Reaction time
Speed of arm movement
Rate control (timing)
Manual dexterity
Finger dexterity
Arm–hand steadiness
Wrist–finger speed
Aiming

Similar studies have been carried out in the physical proficiency area, and nine factors have been identified that account for performance in several hundred physical performance tasks:

PHYSICAL PROFICIENCY ABILITIES

Extent flexibility
Dynamic flexibility
Static strength
Dynamic strength
Explosive strength
Trunk strength
Gross body coordination
Equilibrium
Stamina

Perhaps it might be useful to provide some examples of how one examines the generality of an ability category and how one defines its limits. The specifi-

cation of an ability category is an arduous task. The definition of the rate control factor may provide an illustration.

In early studies it was found that this factor was common to compensatory tracking, for example, keep a horizontal line in the center of the dial, by compensatory movements of a control, as well as to following pursuit tasks, for example, keep a gun sight in line with a moving target (see Figure 2a). To test the generality of this factor, further tasks were developed to emphasize responses to stimuli moving at different rates, where the tasks were not conventional tracking tasks. For example, Figure 2b shows a task in which the subject had to time his movements in relation to different stimulus rates, but he did not have to follow a target or to compensate for the target's movement. The factor was found to extend to such tasks.

Later studies attempted to discover if emphasis on this ability is in judging the rate of the stimulus as distinguished from ability to respond at the appropriate rate. Thus, Figure 2c shows a task developed where the only response was the timing of button pressing in response to judgments about the location of stimuli moving at different rates. Performance on this task did not correlate with other rate control tasks. Finally, several motion picture tasks, such as the one in Figure 2d, were adapted in which the subject was required to extrapolate the course of an airplane moving across a screen. The only response required was on an IBM answer sheet. (At what point did the planes meet? Points 1, 2, 3, 4, or 5?) These moving picture tests involving only judgments about stimulus rate did not correlate with the group of tasks previously found to measure "rate control." Thus, our definition of this rate control ability was expanded to include measures beyond tracking and pursuit tasks, but was restricted to tasks requiring the timing of an actual adjustive movement to the changing stimulus.

A similar history can be sketched for

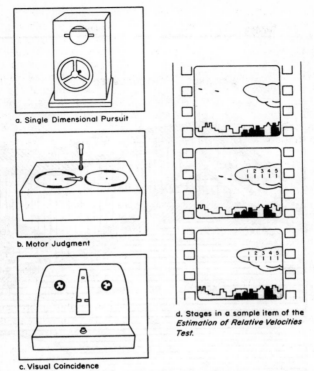

a. Single Dimensional Pursuit

b. Motor Judgment

c. Visual Coincidence

d. Stages in a sample item of the *Estimation of Relative Velocities Test.*

Figure 2. Examples of tasks used to evaluate the generality and limitations of rate control ability. (From "On the Relation Between Abilities, Learning, and Human Performance" by Edwin A. Fleishman, *American Psychologist*, 1972, 27, 1017–1032. Copyright 1972 by the American Psychological Association. Reprinted by permission.)

each ability variable identified, and a great number of principles relating task characteristics and abilities measured can now be described. For example, we know that multilimb coordination is common to tasks involving simultaneous control actions of two hands, two feet, or hands and feet, but some feedback indicator of coordination is required. Furthermore, this factor does not extend to tasks involving the body in motion, such as in athletic tasks. And we know that fast reaction times are general to auditory and visual stimuli,

but as soon as more than one stimulus or response is involved in such tasks, the ability required shifts to response orientation. And it is useful to know that there are four primary strength factors, not confined to muscle groups but dependent on specific task requirements (see Fleishman, 1964).

ABILITIES PREDICTIVE OF LEARNING

Our subsequent work (e.g., Fleishman, 1957, 1960; Fleishman & Ellison, 1969; Fleishman & Hempel, 1955) attempted to use the ability concepts developed to

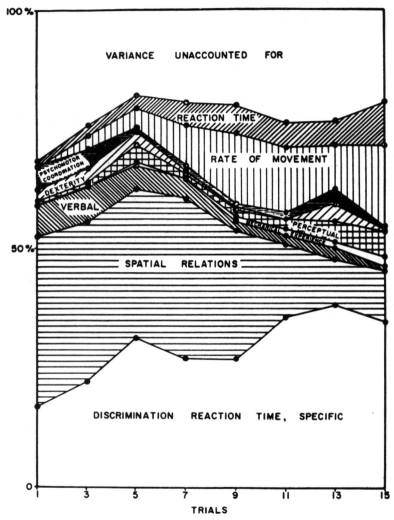

Figure 3. Percentage of variance represented by loadings on each factor at different stages of practice on the discrimination reaction time task. Note: Percentage of variance is represented by the size of the shaded areas for each factor. (From "The Relation Between Abilities and Improvement with Practice in a Visual Discrimination Reaction Task" by Edwin A. Fleishman and Walter E. Hempel, Jr., *Journal of Experimental Psychology*, 1955, *49*, 301–312. Copyright 1955 by the American Psychological Association. Reprinted by permission.)

predict various learning measures and other aspects of task performance, with encouraging results. The basic method is to give subjects a battery of reference ability tests and then have them train on a criterion task. Loadings of performance achieved at various states of learning, on the factors defined by the ability factors, are then examined. In general, these studies, with a great variety of practice tasks, show that (a) the particular combinations of abilities contributing to performance on a task change as practice on this task continues; (b) these changes are progressive and systematic and eventually become stabilized; (c) in perceptual–motor tasks, for example, the contribution of nonmotor abilities (e.g., verbal, spatial) may play a role early in learning, but their contribution decreases systematically with practice, relative to motor abilities; and finally (d) there is also an increase in a factor specific to the task itself not common to the more general abilities. Figure 3 illustrates one set of findings for a task involving the manipulation of different switches in response to different patterns of stimulus lights.

Figure 4 depicts these same results in terms of learning curves. Where the total group of subjects is stratified into those high and low on one ability (e.g., spatial), their learning curves for this task converge as practice continues. When the same subjects are stratified according to high and low scores on another ability (e.g., reaction time), their learning curves diverge. Our work relating abilities to more general performance phenomena led us to feel that this kind of taxonomic system might be worth future development. For one review of this work, see Fleishman (1967a).

USE OF TASK STANDARDIZED BY ABILITY MEASURED

As one illustration, we have carried out a number of studies in which "standardized tasks" representing such ability dimensions have been used in laboratory studies of factors affecting human performance. For example, we have observed the effects of a variety of drugs and dosages on measures of a variety of reference ability tasks. These measures sample the perceptual, motor, sensory, and cognitive areas.

Figure 5 gives a few illustrations of these events for a given dosage of the drug scopolamine (Fleishman, 1967b; Elkin et al., Note 5). As can be seen, we are getting differential effects; that is, some abilities within each area were more affected than others. The absolute performance decrement, time to reach maximum effect, and time to recover depended on the ability measured. For example, the physical abilities of dynamic flexibility and explosive strength showed only slight effects, whereas the motor abilities of multilimb coordination and finger dexterity showed marked effects. Such findings indicate why the category "motor skill" is too broad. Similar findings have been reported for other drugs (Baker, Geist, & Fleishman, Note 8). The goal here is to develop what might be called "behavioral toxicity profiles" for different classes of drugs.

We have also conducted similar studies on the effects of different *noise* stressors (Theologus, Wheaton, & Fleishman, 1974). The rationale of this program is that different components of human task performance will be affected differently as a function of the type and level of stressor, and that measurement of changes in these components will provide quantitative evaluations of the disruptive effects of the stressor and of man's vulnerability to it.

We used a device, shown in Theologus et al. (1974), designed to measure 10 of the different psychomotor abilities identified. We found that intermittent, moderate-intensity noise (85 db.) is more likely to affect performance on tasks emphasizing some of these abilities than others. Figure 6 shows the significant effect of the *random* intermittent noise on the mean reaction time

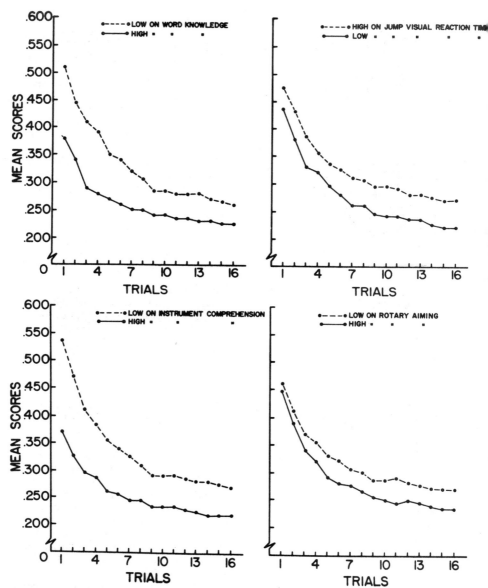

Figure 4. Comparison of learning curves on the discrimination reaction time task for groups scoring high and low on different ability test measures. (From "The Relation Between Abilities and Improvement with Practice in a Visual Discrimination Reaction Task" by Edwin A. Fleishman and Walter E. Hempel, Jr., *Journal of Experimental Psychology*, 1955, *49*, 301–312. Copyright 1955 by the American Psychological Association. Reprinted by permission.)

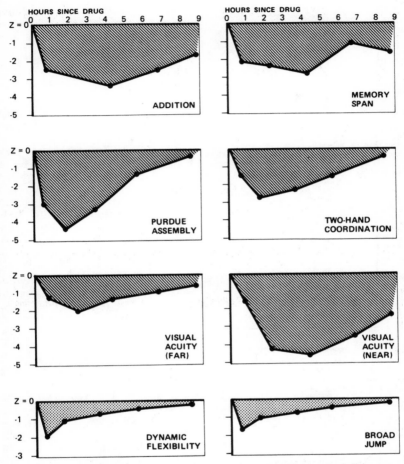

Figure 5. Effects of a given dosage of scopolamine in degrading performance on several different tasks involving different abilities. (Adapted from "Performance Assessment Based on an Empirically Derived Task Taxonomy" by Edwin A Fleishman, *Human Factors*, 1967, *9*, 349–366. Copyright 1967 by the Human Factors Society. **Reprinted by permission.**)

and the absence of any effect on this measure for the patterned noise of the same intensity. However, Figure 7 shows that on the rate control task (tracking), no effect of either type of noise is demonstrated. Figure 8 illustrates that for a time-sharing task there is no noise effect at first, but the effects appear to be cumulative during continued exposure. The results are illustrative of differential effects according to task category.

Our feeling was that improved generalizations of research data might

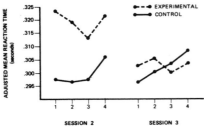

Figure 6. Adjusted mean reaction time at each block of trials on the reaction time task (Session 2 = random 85-db. noise; Session 3 = patterned 85-db. noise). (From "Effects of Intermittent, Moderate Intensity Noise Stress on Human Performance" by George C. Theologus, George R. Wheaton, and Edwin A. Fleishman, *Journal of Applied Psychology*, 1974, *59*, 539–547. Copyright 1974 by the American Psychological Association. Reprinted by permission.)

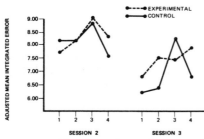

Figure 7. Adjusted mean integrated error at each block of trials on the rate control task (Session 2 = random 85-db. noise; Session 3 = patterned 85-db. noise). (From "Effects of Intermittent, Moderate Intensity Noise Stress on Human Performance" by George C. Theologus, George R. Wheaton, and Edwin A. Fleishman, *Journal of Applied Psychology*, 1974, *59*, 539–547. Copyright 1974 by the American Psychological Association. Reprinted by permission.)

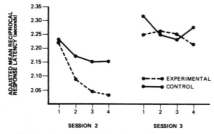

Figure 8. Adjusted transformed mean response latency at each block of trials on the time-sharing task (Session 2 = random 85-db. noise; Session 3 = patterned 85-db. noise). (From "Effects of Intermittent, Moderate Intensity Noise Stress on Human Performance" by George C. Theologus, George R. Wheaton, and Edwin A. Fleishman, *Journal of Applied Psychology*, 1974; *59*, 539–547. Copyright 1974 by the American Psychological Association. Reprinted by permission.)

be possible if careful specifications of our task categories were utilized, with ability concepts holding the key.

METHODS OF ESTIMATING ABILITY REQUIREMENTS

Another phase of our program has involved extensive reviews of the factor-analytic ability literature. One of the striking findings in this review was the difficulty in moving from the factor analysts' definition to a more operational definition which could be used reliably by observers in estimating the ability requirements of a new task. A large effort in our program involved the successive refinement of such definitions to improve the utility of these concepts in describing tasks. A host of different reliability studies have been conducted in which task descriptions have been examined by individuals who rated them in terms of cognitive, perceptual, and motor abilities (Theologus & Fleishman, 1973). These descriptions have ranged from descriptions of laboratory apparatus to descriptions of jobs. The attempt has been to use the same ability concepts to *bridge the gap in describing laboratory and real-world tasks* within the same conceptual framework.

Scaling techniques have been developed which include precise definitions of the abilities, distinctions from other abilities, and behaviorally anchored scales (Theologus & Fleishman, 1973; Theologus, Romashko, & Fleishman, 1973). Figure 9 gives an example of one such scale. The scale values of the task examples have been empirically determined.

We have examined questions of number of raters needed, training required, etc., with regard to reliability achieved using these techniques, when applied to different kinds of tasks. All of the answers are not in, but successful refinements have been made, and the scales have been found useful for a number of purposes, including the estimation of ability requirements in com-

1. VERBAL COMPREHENSION

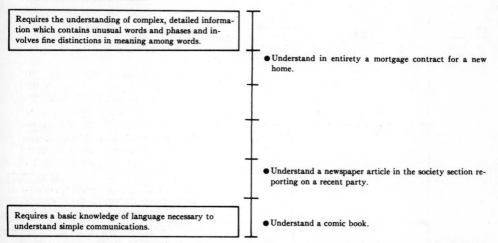

Figure 9. Example of an ability requirement scale; task statements have empirically determined scale values. (From *Development of a Taxonomy of Human Performance: A Feasibility Study of Ability Dimensions for Classifying Human Tasks* [AIR Tech. Rep. 726-5] by George C. Theologus, Tania Romashko, and Edwin A. Fleishman.)

plex jobs (e.g., see Romashko, Brumback, & Fleishman, Note 9, Note 10).

Another method for estimating ability requirements of tasks is in a preliminary state of development. This approach requires the observer to make binary decisions and to follow through a series of minor decisions until the ability definition is reached. Figure 10 gives an example of one such system for one ability area.

EVALUATING THE UTILITY OF ABILITY REQUIREMENTS IN CLASSIFYING TASKS

One way to evaluate a taxonomic system is in terms of its capacity to organize a portion of the data found in the human performance literature. In one study (Levine, Romashko, & Fleishman, 1973) our objective was to examine the feasibility of structuring an area of literature according to the "abilities" required for task performance. The area of human performance selected for examination was that of sustained attention in monitoring tasks, in the so-called vigilance literature. Vigilance is generally

considered to involve a change in the detection of infrequent signals over prolonged periods of time. Our idea was to examine the tasks used in these previous studies, to rate them in terms of the abilities taxonomy, using our scales, and to classify the studies in terms of the *abilities* required by the tasks used. The next step was to examine the data within and between these categories of tasks to see if improved generalizations could be made about factors affecting vigilance performance.

The vigilance area was selected for study for several reasons. First, while a variety of different tasks have been used in previous vigilance research, the range of tasks is not as great as in many other areas. Consequently, the number of different abilities involved is not likely to be large, and this in turn would reduce the complexity of the evaluation. Second, a reasonably large number of studies have been reported on the effects of several selected independent variables on vigilance performance, and it is important that enough studies be

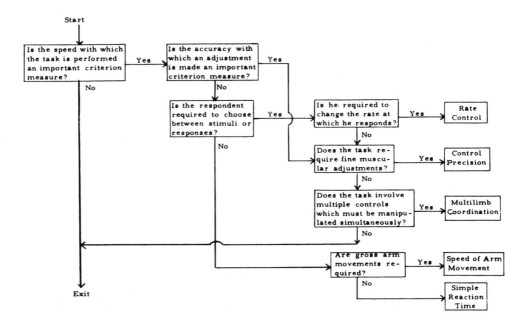

Figure 10. Portion of a tentative binary flow diagram used to make decisions about the relevance of selected abilities for performing particular tasks. (From *Development of a Taxonomy of Human Performance: A Review of the Third Year's Progress* [AIR Tech. Rep. 726-TPR3] by Edwin A. Fleishman and Robert W. Stephenson.)

available to provide a sufficient number of data points within task categories. Third, a common dependent measure is employed in nearly all vigilance studies, that is, detection accuracy.

The study was designed to examine (a) the extent to which performance in vigilance tasks could be differentiated on the basis of abilities and (b) whether improved generalizations about the effects of independent variables in vigilance performance were possible as a result of such task classifications.

Four abilities were found to be required for the different task performances in this area, with two, perceptual speed and flexibility of closure, predominating.

Figure 11 provides some illustrative results when the data for such tasks were partitioned according to levels of an independent variable (whether the

signals were auditory, visual, or both). We have plotted percent of target detections at 30-minute intervals throughout the first 180 minutes of the vigilance task. It can be seen that regardless of whether the ability category was perceptual speed or flexibility of closure, overall performance was superior under auditory conditions than under visual conditions. Furthermore, the visual plus auditory condition was markedly superior in number of targets detected to either auditory or visual presentation.

The important results show that the functions obtained vary with the type of task as defined by our ability ratings. For the auditory condition, perceptual speed tasks show a severe performance decrement with time in the task. On the other hand, there was a very small performance decrement for flexibility of closure tasks within the first 90 minutes,

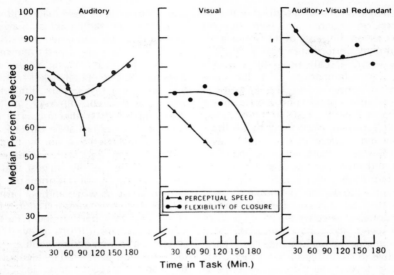

Figure 11. Median percentage of correct detections as a function of time in the task and ability category for different sensory modes. (From "Evaluation of an Abilities Classification System for Integrating and Generalizing Human Performance Research Findings: An Application to Vigilance Tasks" by Jerrold M. Levine, Tania Romashko, and Edwin A. Fleishman, *Journal of Applied Psychology*, 1973, *58*, 149–157. Copyright 1973 by the American Psychological Association. **Reprinted by permission.**)

and an increment in performance accuracy beyond that time. For the visual condition, the function describing performance with time in the task for perceptual speed studies was similar to that obtained for the auditory condition. However, for tasks requiring flexibility of closure, the function in the visual condition is almost the reverse of that for the auditory condition.

Similar analyses were made for other variables, such as signal rate. Although the data provided are preliminary, and in several instances functions are based upon only a few data points, it was nevertheless possible to infer that the effects of the independent variables on performance in a vigilance task are in part a function of the class of task imposed upon the subjects. It has been demonstrated that when studies are categorized by abilities required by the task, relationships between performance and time in the task differ markedly as a function of the selected independent variables. It should be emphasized that despite the differences among specific tasks in terms of equipment, displays, response requirements, etc., the classification system enabled an integration of results and the development of functional relationships that were otherwise obscured.

A more recent study by our staff, along these same general lines, was conducted on the effects of alcohol on human performance (Levine, Kramer, & Levine, 1975). As before, the effort was designed to categorize the existing literature on alcohol effects into task groups in order to determine whether alcohol effects differ as a function of different types of tasks. Tasks described in the literature on alcohol effects were grouped together on the basis of the abilities required to perform the task using the ability rating scale procedures developed. A preliminary set of abilities was chosen representing the cognitive, sensory-perceptual, and psychomotor domains. After the tasks in these studies were grouped according to abilities measured, performance on these tasks as a function of amount of alcohol dosage and time since dosage was examined for each class of tasks.

Figure 12 depicts performance as a function of dosage, for the ability categories of selective attention, perceptual speed, and control precision. What is plotted is the performance decrement, relative to control groups, for increasing dosage levels. The plots are in terms of grams of alcohol per kilogram of body weight. The number of data points are small, dependent on studies found in the literature, and therefore conclusions

and interpretations were made with caution. However, each point is an average of several studies, and there is a striking similarity in the rate of performance deterioration with increasing alcohol dosages for the perceptual speed and control precision tasks. This situation is somewhat different, however, for tasks involving selective attention. The data suggest that performance on tasks involving this cognitive ability is more seriously impaired with increases in dosage. Other results suggest that the greatest impact of alcohol on performance occurs when an hour or more elapses between administration of alcohol and task performance. Further, when these conditions prevail, the selective attention and perceptual speed tasks are most hampered by alcohol and the control precision tasks least hampered.

Taken together these results indicate that the rate and degree of deterioration are a function of both dosage levels and

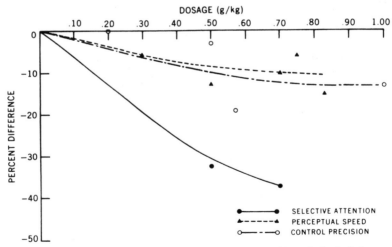

Figure 12. Median percent decrement as a function of alcohol dosage and predominant ability. (From "Effects of Alcohol on Human Performance: An Integration of Research Findings Based on an Abilities Classification" by Jerrold M. Levine, Gloria G. Kramer, and Ellen N. Levine, *Journal of Applied Psychology*, 1975, *60*, 285–293. Copyright 1975 by the American Psychological Association. Reprinted by permission.)

task categories. Knowledge of the task categories improves the prediction that can be made about human performance. Again, despite differences among the specific tasks in the literature in terms of displays, response requirements, performance index, technique of alcohol administration in different studies, etc., the categorization of tasks used in these studies, according to ability requirements, appears to allow an integration of results and the development of functional relationships that otherwise might be obscured.

Several other kinds of evaluation of the abilities taxonomy have been made. One has involved validating the ability ratings made by observers against actual factor loadings obtained on the same tasks (Theologus & Fleishman, 1973). Such evaluations have led to further refinements of the scales.

TASK CHARACTERISTICS APPROACH

In a second general approach to taxonomic development, our project staff (Farina & Wheaton, 1973) has worked with what has been termed the *task characteristics approach*. As mentioned earlier, this approach attempts to provide for the description of tasks in terms of a variety of task-intrinsic properties including goals, stimuli, procedures, etc. Knowledge of how performance varies, as a result of manipulating the characteristics of tasks, might provide a basis for estimating performance on other tasks whose characteristics could be described.

The development of task characteristics received initial guidance from a definition of the term *task*. A task was conceived of as having several components: an explicit goal, procedures, input stimuli, responses, and stimulus–response relationships. In order to differentiate among tasks, the components of a task were treated as categories within which to devise task characteristics or descriptors.

Figure 13 clarifies the relationship among the terms *task, task components,*

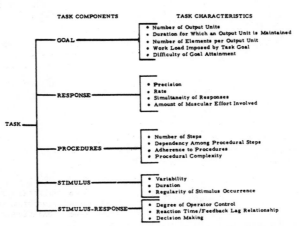

Figure 13.   Conceptual scheme of task characteristics: Relationship among the terms *task, components,* and *characteristic.*   (From *Development of a Taxonomy of Human Performance: The Task Characteristics Approach to Performance Prediction* [AIR Tech. Rep. 726-7] by Alfred J. Farina, Jr., and George R. Wheaton.)

and *characteristics*. Each characteristic was cast into a rating scale format that presented a definition of the characteristic and provided a seven-point scale with defined anchor points and midpoints along with examples for each point (Smith & Kendall, 1963). A sample rating scale is shown in Figure 14.

Many different reliability studies have been conducted. Relations between values obtained from three-judge groups and larger groups were high, and a human factors background by raters was found helpful. Of primary interest here are studies in which ratings of task characteristics have predicted actual task performance. In an illustrative study (Farina & Wheaton, 1973), judges rated 37 tasks on 19 scales. The criterion performance score reported for each task was converted to obtain the average number of units produced per unit time.

The six most reliable scales were chosen for analysis. For each of these scales, the ratings provided by three judges were averaged to obtain a single value on each scale for each of the tasks. The specific task descriptive scales employed in the study were (a) stimulus duration, (b) number of output units, (c) duration for which an output unit is maintained, (d) simultaneity of responses, (e) number of procedural steps, and (f) variability of stimulus location.

The results showed that four predictors accounted for approximately 70 percent of the variance in the criterion measure (after correction for small sample bias). It was possible to specify those task characteristics that contributed most to performance. Several replications of such studies have been completed, the most recent of which have employed more complex training devices used by the Navy (Mirabella & Wheaton, Note 11) where it was possible to predict *learning time* through a knowledge of the ratings of the tasks on critical task dimensions.

Overall these efforts have tentatively demonstrated that it is possible to de-scribe tasks in terms of a task-characteristics language and that these task characteristics may represent important correlates of performance.

LINKING ABILITIES AND TASK REQUIREMENTS

We now present a final set of results, relevant to task taxonomy and human performance.

We have encouraging results from studies which indicate that it is possible to build up a body of principles about interactions of task characteristics with ability requirements through experimental-correlational studies in the laboratory. The approach is to develop tasks that can be varied along specified task dimensions, to administer these tasks to groups of subjects who also receive a series of "reference" ability tasks known to sample certain more general abilities (e.g., spatial orientation, control precision). Correlations between these reference tasks and scores on variations of the criterion task specify the ability requirements (and changes in these requirements) as a function of task variations.

In earlier studies (see Fleishman, 1957, 1972), subjects were required to press a button within a circular arrangement of buttons on the control panel in response to particular lights that appeared in a circular arrangement of lights on a display panel. The correct button depended on the position of the light. Subjects performed under seven different conditions of display-control compatibility, where the display panel was rotated from 0°, 45°, 90°, 135°, and 270°. These same subjects also performed on a series of spatial, perceptual, and psychomotor reference tasks.

We were able to show systematic changes in the ability factors sampled by the criterion task as a function of degree of rotation of the display panel, from the fully compatible (0°) condition. Progressive rotation of the light panel was found to shift the ability require-

Rate the present task on this dimension.

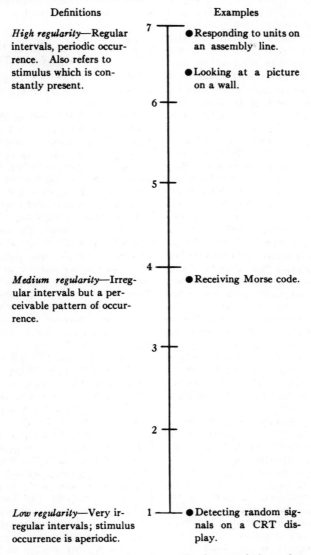

Definitions	**Examples**
High regularity—Regular intervals, periodic occurrence. Also refers to stimulus which is constantly present.	● Responding to units on an assembly line. ● Looking at a picture on a wall.
Medium regularity—Irregular intervals but a perceivable pattern of occurrence.	● Receiving Morse code.
Low regularity—Very irregular intervals; stimulus occurrence is aperiodic.	● Detecting random signals on a CRT display.

Figure 14. Example of a task characteristic scale. (From *Development of a Taxonomy of Human Performance: The Task Characteristics Approach to Performance Prediction* [AIR Tech. Rep. 726-7] by Alfred J. Farina, Jr., and George R. Wheaton.)

ments from perceptual speed to two other factors: response orientation and spatial orientation. Perceptual speed was measured in the upright and slight displacement conditions. The other abilities were measured at larger display rotations. Here, individual differences along known ability dimensions are used to explore the relations between tasks and the characteristics of people who can perform the tasks most effectively. Of course, these are problems faced every day by personnel, training, engineering, and systems psychologists.

A study just completed (Wheaton, Shaffer, Mirabella, & Fleishman, Note 12) has taken us a step closer in applying this paradigm to an operational task. The task used was that of the Navy sonar operator. The task consisted of auditory signal identification in which subjects were to determine the identity of a variety of complex sounds representing various types of ships. Each time a signal was presented, subjects had to determine whether it belonged to a cargo ship, warship, submarine, or light craft. Used in this form, the criterion task had the added virtue of high face validity, inasmuch as it closely resembled the task of a passive sonar operator.

Two task characteristics were selected for manipulation: signal duration and signal-to-noise ratio. Nine different task conditions were generated according to a factorial arrangement of these two variables. Stimuli were presented for either 9, 6, or 3 seconds, and under one of three signal-to-noise ratios. Background noise was set at −5 dB, 0 dB, or +5 dB referenced to the intensity of the signal to be identified. Each of the nine different task conditions generated in this manner was represented by a tape containing 100 signals, 25 for each ship category.

The experimental procedure which was followed was to administer a battery of 24 specifically selected tests to all subjects prior to their involvement in the auditory signal identification crite-

rion task. The battery contained tests representing a variety of well-established factors in the perceptual, cognitive, and memory domains of performance.

Upon completion of the battery and following extensive training in identifying the ship sounds, subjects performed under the nine different criterion task conditions. Figure 15 shows that variations in the two task characteristics really made a difference in actual performance. But what of the relation of the ability factors to these changes in task characteristics?

Of the five separate ability factors that were identified in the test battery, the auditory perceptual ability was found to be most related to criterion task performance. Figure 16 shows that within each signal duration, the loadings on this factor increased as background noise grew louder. The same was generally true within each level of background noise where loadings on the auditory perceptual factor increased in magnitude as signal durations grew shorter. In other words, the contribution of this ability to individual differences in performance increased as the criterion task became more difficult. There appeared to be two critical levels for each task dimension. Thus, signals can be decreased from 9 to 6 seconds without much change in the auditory perceptual requirement, but a further decrease to 3 seconds increases this ability requirement substantially. It is also shown that at this short signal level, an increase in background noise to equal intensity produces a further requirement for this ability, beyond which an additional increase in sound level produces little effect on the ability requirement. Knowledge of these task conditions allows us to be much more precise in specifying the ability requirements for effective criterion performance. Loadings on this ability also were shown to vary according to the type of signals (cargo ships, light craft, warships, and submarine) to be identified. These findings can be ex-

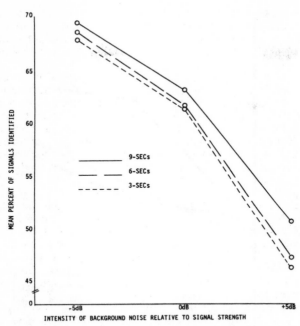

Figure 15. Identification accuracy as a function of the task conditions, background noise, and signal duration. (From *Methods for Predicting Job-Ability Requirements: 1. Ability Requirements as a Function of Changes in the Characteristics of an Auditory Signal Identification Task* [AIR Tech. Rep. 73-5] by George R. Wheaton, Ellen J. Shaffer, Angelo Mirabella, and Edwin A. Fleishman.)

plained on the basis of the task characteristics of these particular auditory stimuli.

The final study to be described involved the extension of this paradigm to cognitive or "higher order" reasoning tasks (Rose, Fingerman, Wheaton, Eisner, & Kramer, Note 13). In the present instance, we examined representative tasks faced by electronic troubleshooters and maintenance personnel.

The criterion task was an analog of a fault-finding or troubleshooting situation. Working with wiring diagrams, the subjects' task was to determine which one of a number of possible breakpoints was actually faulty. Each wiring diagram

contained a number of logic gates, switches, and probe points *(see Figure 17)*. In Figure 17, the small boxes (1, 2, 3, 4, and 5) represent switches, the lettered points (A through L) represent light-bulb sockets, and the starred points (1 through 9) indicate the possible locations of faults (or breaks) in the wires. The logic gates operate simply: Current will flow through the OR gate if *either* Switch 1 or Switch 2 is on. For current to flow through the AND gate (on figure), current must enter the gate along both input wires.

The subjects tested the points by placing a light bulb at various points in the circuit and pressing a switch or combi-

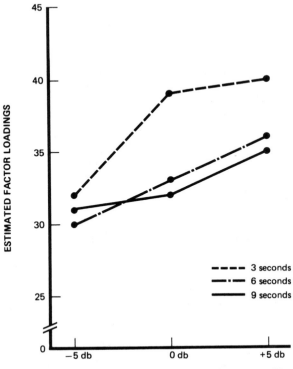

Figure 16. Estimated loadings of the auditory perceptual factor as a function of background noise level for each signal duration. (Adapted from *Methods for Predicting Job-Ability Requirements: 1. Ability Requirements as a Function of Changes in the Characteristics of an Auditory Signal Identification Task* [AIR Tech. Rep. 73-5] by George R. Wheaton, Ellen J. Shaffer, Angelo Mirabella, and Edwin A. Fleishman.)

nation of switches. For example, (on figure) to see if Point 9 is faulty you would place a bulb at B and press Switch 9. Other points are more difficult to test. For example, it takes two probes to see if Point 1 is faulty: first, you should put the bulb at C and press Switches 1 and 9. If the bulb does not light, either 1 or 9 is faulty. Second, you should put the bulb at B and press Switch 9. If the bulb lights, 9 is not faulty and 1 must be the breakpoint.

This basic task was varied along two dimensions: formal difficulty and perceptual complexity. Variations in formal difficulty involved increasing the number of possible breakpoints and the number of logic gates. Figure 18 is a third-level problem with 6 gates and 24 possible breakpoints.

Variations in the second task dimension involved changing the perceptual organization of the circuits. The first level is a straightforward, left to right circuit with no crossed wires. The second level rearranges the locations of the switches on the same circuit, creating several crossed wires. The third level (see Figure 19) changes the locations of both the switches and the logic gates. Although this looks confusing, the actual circuit in Figure 19 is exactly the same as the one in the last two figures.

Subjects were first given training in the mechanics of using the diagrams to test for breakpoints. Several criterion measures of performance were collected, including how fast the problems were solved, how many trials were required, and how efficiently subjects solved them. The efficiency measure was defined as the proportion of breakpoints that were eliminated by each test the subject used relative to the maximum breakpoints he could have eliminated on that test.

The task was analyzed according to the abilities hypothesized to contribute to task performance. A comprehensive battery of 21 ability tests was selected and administered to all subjects who then performed on the 18 troubleshooting problems in a replicated 3 × 3 design. The order of presentation was counterbalanced.

Without going into the details of the results and many different analyses, we can illustrate the important findings with a few figures. First, we will examine different criterion measures of performance. Figure 20 shows that changes in levels of the task dimensions of both formal difficulty and perceptual complexity made a difference in criterion performance. Here we have plotted mean time to solution across all problems. Figure 21 shows that for another criterion measure, namely, number of trials to solution, formal difficulty made a difference, but perceptual complexity made less of a difference.

Figure 22 shows that for a third criterion measure, efficiency of performance, both task dimensions made a difference, with the greatest effects occurring at the highest level of complexity

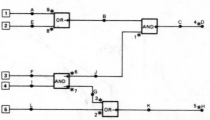

Figure 17. Circuit diagram problem representing first levels of formal difficulty and perceptual complexity. (From *Methods for Predicting Job-Ability Requirements: II. Ability Requirements as a Function of Changes in the Characteristics of an Electronic Fault-Finding Task* [AIR Tech. Rep. 74-6] by Andrew M. Rose, Paul W. Fingerman, George R. Wheaton, Ellen J. Eisner, and Gloria G. Kramer.)

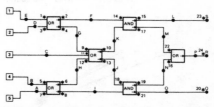

Figure 18. Circuit diagram problem representing the third level of formal difficulty and first level of perceptual complexity. (From *Methods for Predicting Job-Ability Requirements: II. Ability Requirements as a Function of Changes in the Characteristics of an Electronic Fault-Finding Task* [AIR Tech. Rep. 74-6] by Andrew M. Rose, Paul W. Fingerman, George R. Wheaton, Ellen J. Eisner, and Gloria G. Kramer.)

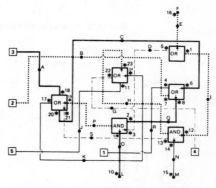

Figure 19. Circuit diagram problem representing the third levels of both formal difficulty and perceptual complexity. (From *Methods for Predicting Job-Ability Requirements: II. Ability Requirements as a Function of Changes in the Characteristics of an Electronic Fault-Finding Task* [AIR Tech. Rep. 74-6] by Andrew M. Rose, Paul W. Fingerman, George R. Wheaton, Ellen J. Eisner, and Gloria G. Kramer.)

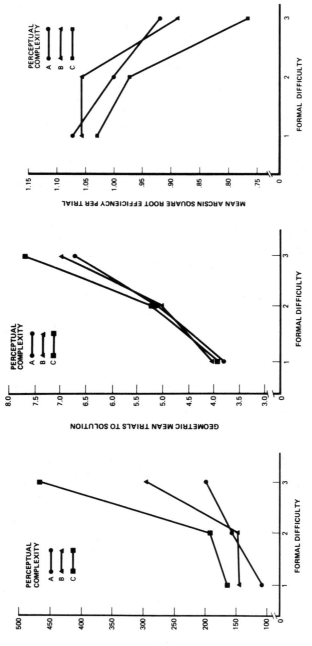

Figure 20. Geometric mean time to solution as a function of changes in formal difficulty and perceptual complexity. (From *Methods for Predicting Job-Ability Requirements: II. Ability Requirements as a Function of Changes in the Characteristics of an Electronic Fault-Finding Task* [AIR Tech. Rep. 74-6] by Andrew M. Rose, Paul W. Fingerman, George R. Wheaton, Ellen J. Eisner, and Gloria G. Kramer.)

Figure 21. Geometric mean trials to solution as a function of changes in formal difficulty and perceptual complexity. (From *Methods for Predicting Job-Ability Requirements: II. Ability Requirements as a Function of Changes in the Characteristics of an Electronic Fault-Finding Task* [AIR Tech. Rep. 74-6] by Andrew M. Rose, Paul W. Fingerman, George R. Wheaton, Ellen J. Eisner, and Gloria G. Kramer.)

Figure 22. Mean arcsin square root efficiency per trial as a function of changes in formal difficulty and perceptual complexity. (From *Methods for Predicting Job-Ability Requirements: II. Ability Requirements as a Function of Changes in the Characteristics of an Electronic Fault-Finding Task* [AIR Tech. Rep. 74-6] by Andrew M. Rose, Paul W. Fingerman, George R. Wheaton, Ellen J. Eisner, and Gloria G. Kramer.)

on both dimensions. These results, of course, underscore the need to look at different criterion measures.

But what about the linkage of ability requirements to these criterion performances, as a function of differences in these task characteristics? Several clear factors emerged in the factor analysis of the ability tests, but I will confine our results to those abilities found most related to task performance. Figure 23 shows clear relations between the task characteristics and particular ability requirements, where mean trials to solution is used as the criterion measure. The ability flexibility of closure was related to performance and increased in importance as difficulty increased on both dimensions. Associative memory was critical only at the first level of perceptual complexity.

Figure 24 illustrates the findings using the efficiency criterion measure of performance. First of all, it is evident that this criterion was the most predictable. Again, we see that flexibility of closure is the most important ability in this task, and its importance increases with increased difficulty on both task dimensions. A reasoning ability remains stable across conditions, and associative memory and induction drop out, but at different levels of perceptual complexity.

There were some differences depending on the criterion measure, and some measures were clearly more predictable than others. But there are common results across criterion measures. The contribution of one ability, flexibility of closure, increased across all criterion measures with changes in both task dimensions. The requirement for a second ability, syllogistic reasoning, remained constant for most measures across all conditions. For most criterion measures, memory ability showed low or decreasing predictions as conditions were made more difficult.

We can say that results with this cognitive task confirm the findings with psychomotor and with perceptual tasks and extend the principles to more realistic job-related tasks. If one were to predict from these abilities which individuals would do well on these tasks, the choices would depend on the task characteristics and the criterion measure selected.

There are two general types of training or selection decisions implied by the data. One type, typified by the pattern of loadings of the flexibility of closure factor, occurs when a change in task characteristic results in a change in importance of particular abilities but does not require different abilities. Here a change in cutoff value on the relevant test is the appropriate decision. The second type of decision occurs when changes in task demands change the combinations of abilities involved (as with our efficiency measure). In such situations, the implication is that different individuals would be selected if the nature of the task changed, or the training would need modification, or the task would need to be redesigned to be in accordance with the trainee population.

These studies have demonstrated empirically that the patterns of abilities related to criterion performance may undergo changes as specific characteristics of a task are systematically manipulated. We are currently determining whether such relationships can be inferred and what information is needed by task analysts who must estimate the ability requirements for a given task configuration.

In the general case, such judgments occur when a job is analyzed to determine what abilities may serve as a basis for selection of personnel or, given that personnel will not be preselected, to serve as a basis for formulating training programs. In the special case, these same kinds of selection and training decisions will be required when a new task is encountered which bears some specifiable resemblance to an old task for which selection and training programs have been developed. In either

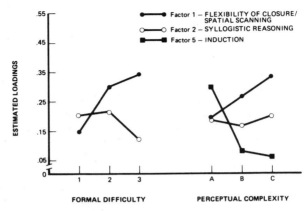

Figure 23. Estimated loadings of the criterion measure, geometric mean trials to solution for different ability factors under the different task conditions. (From *Methods for Predicting Job-Ability Requirements: II. Ability Requirements as a Function of Changes in the Characteristics of an Electronic Fault-Finding Task* [AIR Tech. Rep. 74-6] by Andrew M. Rose, Paul W. Fingerman, George R. Wheaton, Ellen J. Eisner, and Gloria G. Kramer.)

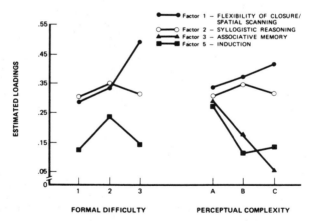

Figure 24. Estimated loadings of the criterion measure, arcsin square root efficiency per trial, for different ability factors under the different task conditions. (From *Methods for Predicting Job-Ability Requirements: II. Ability Requirements as a Function of Changes in the Characteristics of an Electronic Fault-Finding Task* [AIR Tech. Rep. 74-6] by Andrew M. Rose, Paul W. Fingerman, George R. Wheaton, Ellen J. Eisner, and Gloria G. Kramer.)

case, task analysts need a method for predicting job-ability requirements which shortcuts the process of studying each situation empirically, with little generalization across cases. This need was, of course, anticipated by Lawshe (1952) and Guion (1965), in their work on synthetic validity, and by Primoff (1957) at the Civil Service Commission. To be of real utility, such a method must also permit assessment of the impact that systematic changes in the nature of a task have on job-ability requirements.

SUMMARY STATEMENT

I have tried to lay out some general issues in taxonomic development and to give some examples of measurement approaches and methods of evaluation of taxonomic systems. Some studies were shown in which predictions and generalizations about human performance may be enhanced through applications of such task classification systems. I think we have gained some additional understanding of criterion performance as a result of this work. From our work thus far, a few additional observations are possible. The search for a single general taxonomy is not likely to be successful for all purposes. We may, indeed, need several task classification systems for several purposes, with the linkage between them understood and specified. A taxonomic system linking ability requirements and task characteristics appears to hold promise for providing an organizing framework. The process will be an iterative one. Taxonomies are not out there to be discovered; some invention is required. However, this invention must be grounded in empirical data, research, and evaluation. The research paradigm described, which includes combinations of experimental and correlational methods, seems a useful way to go about it.

NOTES

1. Cotterman, T. E. *Task classification: An approach to partially ordering information on human learning* (WADC TN 58-374). Wright-Patterson Air Force Base, Ohio: Wright-Patterson Air Development Center, 1959.

2. Eckstrand, G. A. *Current status of the technology of training* (AMRL-TR-64-86). Wright-Patterson Air Force Base, Ohio: Aerospace Medical Division, September 1964.

3. Folley, J. D., Jr. *Development of an improved method of task analysis and beginnings of a theory of training* (NAVTRADEVCEN 1218-1). Port Washington, N.Y.: U.S. Naval Training Devices Center, June 1964.

4. Stolurow, L. *A taxonomy of learning task characteristics* (AMRL-TD 12-64-2). Wright-Patterson Air Force Base, Ohio: Aerospace Medical Research Laboratories, January 1964.

5. Elkin, E. H., Freedle, R. O., Van Cott, H. P., & Fleishman, E. A. *Effects of drugs on human performance: The effects of scopolamine on representative human performance tests* (AIR Tech. Rep. E-25). Washington, D.C.: American Institutes for Research, August 1965.

6. McCormick, E. J. *The development, analysis, and experimental application of worker-oriented job variables* (Final report; ONR Nonr-1100 [19]). Lafayette, Ind.: Purdue University, 1964.

7. Fine, S. A. *A functional approach to a broad scale map of work behaviors* (HSR-RM-63/2). McLean, Va.: Human Sciences Research, September 1963.

8. Baker, W. J., Geist, A. M., & Fleishman, E. A. *Effects of cylert (magnesium-pemoline) on physiological, physical proficiency, and psychomotor performance measures* (AIR Tech. Rep. F-31). Washington, D.C.: American Institutes for Research, August 1967.

9. Romashko, T., Brumback, G. B., & Fleishman, E. A. *The development of a procedure to validate physical tests: Physical requirements of the fireman's job* (AIR Tech. Rep. 375-1). Washington, D.C.: American Institutes for Research, June 1974.

10. Romashko, T., Brumback, G. B., & Fleishman, E. A. *The development of a procedure to validate physical tests: Physical requirements of the sanitation man's job* (AIR Tech. Rep. 375-2). Washington, D.C.: American Institutes for Research, October 1973.

11. Mirabella, A., & Wheaton, G. R. *Effects of task index variations on transfer of training criteria* (NAVTRAEQUIPCEN 72-C-0126-1; American Institutes for Research Contract N61339-72-C-0126). Orlando, Fla.: U.S. Navy Training Equipment Center, September 1973.

12. Wheaton, G. R., Shaffer, E. J., Mirabella, A., & Fleishman, E. A. *Methods for predicting job-ability requirements: 1. Ability requirements as a function of changes in the characteristics of an auditory signal identification task* (AIR Tech. Rep. 73-5). Washington, D.C.: American Institutes for Research, September 1973.

13. Rose, A.M., Fingerman, P. W., Wheaton, G. R., Eisner, E., & Kramer, G. *Methods for predicting job-ability requirements: II. Ability requirements as a function of changes in the characteristics of an electronic fault-finding task* (AIR Tech. Rep. 74-6). Washington, D.C.: American Institutes for Research, August 1974.

REFERENCES

Alluisi, E. A. Methodology in the use of synthetic tasks to assess complex performance. *Human Factors,* 1967, **9,** 375-384.

Annett, J., & Duncan, K. D. Task analysis and training design. *Occupational Psychology,* 1967, **41,** 211-221.

Bloom, B. S. (Ed.). *Taxonomy of educational objectives. Handbook I: Cognitive domain.* New York: McKay, 1956.

Chambers, A. N. Development of a taxonomy of human performance: A heuristic model for the development of classification systems. JSAS *Catalog of Selected Documents in Psychology,* 1973, **3,** 24-25. (Ms. No. 320) (Also available as AIR Tech. Rep. 726-4. Washington, D.C.: American Institutes for Research, October 1969.)

Farina, A. J., Jr. Development of a taxonomy of human performance: A review of descriptive schemes for human task behavior. JSAS *Catalog of Selected Documents in Psychology,* 1973, **3,** 23. (Ms. No. 318) (Also available as AIR Tech. Rep. 726-2. Washington, D.C.: American Institutes for Research, January 1969.)

Farina, A. J., Jr., & Wheaton, G. R. Development of a taxonomy of human performance: The task characteristics approach to performance prediction. JSAS *Catalog of Selected Documents in Psychology,* 1973, **3,** 26-27. (Ms. No. 323) (Also available as AIR Tech. Rep. 726-7. Washington, D.C.: American Institutes for Research, February 1971.)

Fitts, P. M. Factors in complex skill training. In R. Glaser (Ed.), *Training research and education.* Pittsburgh, Pa.: University of Pittsburgh Press, 1962.

Fleishman, E. A. Factor structure in relation to task difficulty in psychomotor performance. *Educational and Psychological Measurement,* 1957, **17,** 522-532.

Fleishman, E. A. Abilities at different stages of practice in rotary pursuit performance. *Journal of Experimental Psychology,* 1960, **60,** 162-171.

Fleishman, E. A. The description and prediction of perceptual-motor skill learning. In R. Glaser (Ed.), *Training research and education.* Pittsburgh, Pa.: University of Pittsburgh Press, 1962.

Fleishman, E. A. *The structure and measurement of physical fitness.* Englewood Cliffs, N.J.: Prentice-Hall, 1964.

Fleishman, E. A. The prediction of total task performance from prior practice on task components. *Human Factors,* 1965, **7,** 18-27.

Fleishman, E. A. Individual differences and motor learning. In R. M. Gagné (Ed.), *Learning and individual differences.* Columbus, Ohio: Charles E. Merrill, 1967. (a)

Fleishman, E. A. Performance assessment based on an empirically derived task taxonomy. *Human Factors,* 1967, **9,** 349-366. (b)

Fleishman, E. A. On the relation between abilities, learning, and human performance. *American Psychologist,* 1972, **27,** 1017-1032.

Fleishman, E. A., & Ellison, G. D. Prediction of transfer and other learning phenomena from ability and personality measures. *Journal of Educational Psychology,* 1969, **60,** 300-314.

Fleishman, E. A., & Hempel, W. E., Jr. Changes in factor structure of a complex psychomotor test as a function of practice. *Psychometrika,* 1954, **18,** 239-252.

Fleishman, E. A., & Hempel, W. E., Jr. The relation between abilities and improvement with practice in a visual discrimination reaction task. *Journal of Experimental Psychology,* 1955, **49,** 301-312.

Fleishman, E. A., Kinkade, R. G., & Chambers, A. N. Development of a taxonomy of human performance: A review of the first year's progress. JSAS *Catalog of Selected Documents in Psychology,* 1972, **2,** 39. (Ms. No. 111) (Also available as AIR Tech. Rep. 726-TPR1. Washington, D.C.: American Institutes for Research, November 1968.)

Fleishman, E. A., & Parker, J. F. Factors in the retention and relearning of perceptual-motor skill. *Journal of Experimental Psychology,* 1962, **64,** 215-226.

Fleishman, E. A., & Stephenson, R. W. Development of a taxonomy of human performance: A review of the third year's progress. JSAS *Catalog of Selected Documents in Psychology,* 1972, **2,** 40-41. (Ms. No. 113) (Also available as AIR Tech. Rep. 726-TPR3. Washington, D.C.: American Institutes for Research, September 1970.)

Fleishman, E. A., Teichner, W. H., & Stephenson, R. W. Development of a taxonomy of human performance: A review of the second year's progress. JSAS *Catalog of Selected Documents in Psychology,* 1972, **2,** 39-40. (Ms. No. 112) (Also available as AIR Tech. Rep. 726-TPR2. Washington, D.C.: American Institutes for Research, January 1970.)

Gagné, R. M. Human functions in systems. In R. M. Gagné (Ed.), *Psychological principles in system development.* New York: Holt, Rinehart & Winston, 1962.

Gagné, R. M. *Conditions of learning.* New York: Holt, Rinehart & Winston, 1964.

Gagné, R. M., & Bolles, R. C. A review of factors in learning efficiency. In E. Galanter (Ed.), *Automatic teaching: The state of the art.* New York: Wiley, 1963.

Guilford, J. P. *Nature of human intelligence.* New York: McGraw-Hill, 1967.

Guion, R. M. Synthetic validity in a small company: A demonstration. *Personnel Psychology,* 1965, **18,** 49-63.

Hackman, J. R. Tasks and task performance in research on stress. In J. E. McGrath (Ed.), *Social and psychological factors in stress.* New York: Holt, Rinehart & Winston, 1970.

Lawshe, C. H. What can industrial psychology do for small business (a symposium)? 2. Employee selection. *Personnel Psychology,* 1952, **5,** 31-34.

Levine, J. M., Kramer, G. G., & Levine, E. N. Effects of alcohol on human performance: An integration of research findings based on an abilities classification. *Journal of Applied Psychology,* 1975, **60,** 285-293.

Levine, J. M., Romashko, T., & Fleishman, E. A. Evaluation of an abilities classification system for integrating and generalizing human performance research findings: An application to vigilance tasks. *Journal of Applied Psychology,* 1973, **58,** 149-157.

McCormick, E. J., Jeanneret, P. R., & Mecham, R. C. A study of job characteristics and job dimensions as based on the position analysis questionnaire (PAQ). *Journal of Applied Psychology,* 1972, **56,** 347-368.

Melton, A. W. The taxonomy of human learning: Overview. In A. Melton (Ed.), *Categories of human learning.* New York: Academic Press, 1964.

Melton, A. W., & Briggs, G. Engineering psychology. In P. R. Farnsworth & Q. McNemar (ed.), *Annual review of psychology* (Vol. 11). Palo Alto, Calif.: Annual Reviews, 1960.

Miller, R. B. Analysis and specification of behavior in training. In R. Glaser (Ed.), *Training research and education.* Pittsburgh, Pa.: University of Pittsburgh Press, 1962.

Miller, R. B. *Task taxonomy: Science or technology?* Poughkeepsie, N.Y.: IBM, 1966.

Primoff, E. S. The J-coefficient approach to jobs and tests. *Personnel Administration,* 1957, **20,** 34-40.

Smith, P. C., & Kendall, L. M. Retranslation of expectations: An approach to the construction of unambiguous anchors for rating scales. *Journal of Applied Psychology,* 1963, **47,** 149-155.

Theologus, G. C. Development of a taxonomy of human performance: A review of biological taxonomy and classification. JSAS *Catalog of Selected Documents in Psychology,* 1973, **3,** 23-24. (Ms. No. 319) (Also available as AIR Tech. Rep. 726-3. Washington, D.C.: American Institutes for Research, December 1969.)

Theologus, G. C., & Fleishman, E. A. Development of a taxonomy of human performance: Validation study of ability scales for classifying human tasks. JSAS *Catalog of Selected Documents in Psychology,* 1973, **3,** 29. (Ms. No. 326) (Also available as AIR Tech. Rep. 726-10. Washington, D.C.: American Institutes for Research, April 1971.)

Theologus, G. C., Romashko, T., & Fleishman, E. A. Development of a taxonomy of human performance: A feasibility study of ability dimensions for classifying human tasks. JSAS *Catalog of Selected Documents in Psychology,* 1973, **3,** 25-26. (Ms. No. 321) (Also available as AIR Tech. Rep. 726-5. Washington, D.C.: American Institutes for Research, January 1970.)

Theologus, G. C., Wheaton, G. R., & Fleishman, E. A. Effects of intermittent, moderate intensity noise stress on human performance. *Journal of Applied Psychology,* 1974, **59,** 539-547.

Wheaton, G. R. Development of a taxonomy of human performance: A review of classificatory systems relating to tasks and performance. JSAS *Catalog of Selected Documents in Psychology,* 1973, **3,** 22-23. (Ms. No. 317) (Also available as AIR Tech. Rep. 726-1. Washington, D.C.: American Institutes for Research, December 1968.)

Wood, P. J. A taxonomy of instrumental conditioning. *American Psychologist,* 1974, **29,** 584-597.

III

Personnel Selection

Introduction. Personnel selection—the task of choosing individuals from a larger group of applicants for a job, promotion, training program, or for that matter, any situation where the number of applicants exceeds the available opportunities—has been one of the principal concerns of I/O psychology from its earliest days. Since these decisions are frequently based on psychological tests—to assess individual characteristics from which future job behaviors can be predicted—the roots of personnel selection go back still further, to Terman, Binet, Cattell, Galton, and even as far back as Plato (see Hull, 1928).

Hugo Münsterberg's work on the selection of streetcar motormen for the Boston Elevated Railway Company was one of the first systematic attempts to use psychological tests for personnel selection (Münsterberg, 1913). The next significant development in the history of personnel selection was the adoption of Otis' paper-and-pencil tests by the Army for the selection and classification of recruits during World War I (Hull, 1928). The success of this effort led to widespread interest after the war in the development and use of tests and procedures for employee selection by industry. The growing optimism about the efficacy of scientific personnel selection was reinforced further by its continued success in both the military and industry.

However, several discordant notes were also sounded during this period. In 1928, Clark Hull expressed pessimism concerning the utility of tests as a predictor of occupational performance, noting that $r = .50$ seemed to be the upper limit for predictive validities in personnel selection. Furthermore, as Ghiselli (1966) points out, testing was considerably less successful in industry than it was in the military during the war. Ghiselli's (1955) comprehensive review of selection studies was consistent with Hull's earlier finding, and his two updates of this review—the first in 1966 and the most recent in 1973—tended to confirm this disappointing conclusion. In the studies reviewed in the latter paper, "The Validity of Aptitude Tests in Personnel Selection," which is the first paper reprinted in this section, the highest average validity coefficient for proficiency in a wide variety of jobs ranged from $r = .24$ to .46 with an overall average of $r = .35$.

These disturbing results led many personnel psychologists to question and reexamine the very assumptions and model upon which the processes of job performance prediction and personnel selection was based. This led Marvin D. Dunnette to conclude that the classic validation and prediction model was far too simplistic. Specifically, Dunnette stated that the classical model

> sought simply to link predictors, on the one hand, with criteria, on the other, through a simple index of relationship, the correlation coefficient. Such a simple linkage of predictors and criteria is grossly oversimplified in comparison with the complexities actually involved in predicting human behavior . . . It seems wise, therefore, to consider a prediction model which more fully presents the complexities which are only implied by the classic model. (1963, p. 318)

The article from which this quote is taken, "A Modified Model for Test Validation and Selection Research," is the next paper included here. In this selection, Dunnette offers an alternative to the classic prediction model, an alternative that illustrates the complex interactions that are possible among predictors, individuals, job behaviors, situations and organizational consequences. As such, his model suggests ways to improve personnel decisions and research by a variety of means which are more subtle, involved, and potentially more powerful than the straightforward but elusive search for better predictors that marked the earlier period in the history of personnel selection.

At approximately the same time that Dunnette was developing his comprehensive, general, and abstract heuristic model, other researchers were also exploring alternatives to the classical prediction model. An approach that has attracted a considerable degree of interest over the years involves the identification of logically different subgroups in an applicant population and the development of separate—and, therefore, more accurate— prediction equations for each. For example, a particular combination of measures may be a more accurate predictor of job performance for women than the same combination would be for men. (In effect, this strategy is a concrete, specific and immediately pragmatic example of the overall model proposed by Dunnette.) The variables used to identify and differentiate among subgroups are generally referred to as moderators—age, sex, and, more recently, race (to be discussed shortly) are some of the most widely used.

One of the early precursors of this approach was a paper written by Edwin Ghiselli, the same researcher who was also primarily responsible for the search for alternatives to the classical model. In this paper, "The Differentiation of Individuals in Terms of Their Predictability," which is our next selection, he proposes and demonstrates that it is possible to differentiate between individuals whose future job performance can be predicted by a specified set of procedures and individuals for whom these procedures are not effective. While he does not attempt to identify the kinds of variables that could be employed to divide applicant populations into subgroups for which different prediction procedures might be used, the seeds of the moderator variable concept are contained in this important, seminal paper.

The use of, and interest in, moderator variables are perhaps best illustrated by their application to the problems of unfair discrimination in personnel selection. In the early to mid-1960s, a newly developing sense of social conscience—spawned by the civil rights movement, ghetto riots and widespread public demonstrations by disenfranchised minorities and their sympathizers—led many personnel psychologists to examine the ways in which their models, assumptions, and practices may have contributed to the social and economic inequities that were the root cause of much of the turmoil of the time. The growing spectre of government regulation and legal sanctions—Title VII of the 1964 Civil Rights Act in particular—inspired those not moved by social conscience.

In essence, the problem was—and to a considerable extent still is today—that some minorities and women were underrepresented in the most desirable occupational categories and overrepresented in the lowest level jobs and among the ranks of the unemployed. At first, the search for causes and solutions focused on the pervading stereotypes of the abilities of minorities and women and the institutionalization of these beliefs in job recruiting, performance evaluation, and job promotion practices of many organizations. In later years, as the incidence of many of these abuses decreased, albeit *not* disappeared, attention shifted to issues of a far more complex and ambiguous nature.

Specifically, since some minorities consistently score lower on paper-and-pencil tests than the white middle-class majority, particularly on those tests that measure cognitive abilities, they have less chance of being selected for jobs that use these tests as predictors of future job performance. In light of these results, some I/O psychologists began to explore the possibility of "differential validity"—that is, the situation in which predictors and selection procedures found to be valid for some groups (e.g., middle-class white males) are not necessarily valid indicators of future job performance for other groups (e.g., blacks and women).

Robert M. Guion was one of the first personnel psychologists to consider seriously this possibility and also one of the first to suggest the use of race and ethnicity as a moderator variable for improving upon both the effectiveness and fairness of selection procedures. His article, "Employment Tests and Discriminatory Hiring," a classic for other reasons as well, is included here. It was one of the first attempts to define *unfair discrimination* and to distinguish it from the kind of discrimination that is necessarily and appropriately inherent to the selection process itself.

Employment practice is by nature discriminatory, and it must be so. An employer cannot be expected to take on all applicants regardless of their qualifications; he is expected to be able to distinguish between those who are qualified and those who are not . . .

In talking about discrimination, then, a clear distinction must be made between discrimination which is necessary and right and discrimination which is unfair. *Unfair discrimination exists when persons with equal probabilities of success on the job have unequal probabilities of being hired for the job.* (1966, pp. 25-26)

Perhaps most important is that this article was one of the first published by a prominent I/O psychologist to deal in depth with the problems of personnel selection and racial discrimination. As such, it inspired many others to address these problems and led to more than a decade of lively, frequently frustrating, and occasionally productive research and debate. In fact, much of this research and debate later led Guion to temper his earlier optimism regarding the pervasiveness of differential validity and, consequently, the utility of the moderator variable concept in addressing the problems of unfair discrimination (Guion, 1972). More recent research (e.g., Katzell and Dyer, 1977) and judicial decisions (e.g., the Supreme Court cases, *Bakke* v. *Regents of the University of California* and *United Steelworkers of America* v. *Weber*) attest to the enduring significance of these issues and, therefore, the classic status of Guion's paper.

The next paper, "Signs, Samples, and Criteria," illustrates another approach to the problems of unfair discrimination, in particular, and the accuracy of job performance predictions, in general. In this paper, Wernimont and Campbell suggest that the prediction of future job behavior might be greatly aided by using the notion of "behavioral consistency," which, in their words, means "little more than that familiar bit of conventional wisdom, 'the best indicator of future performance is past performance'" (1968, p. 372). In place of paper-and-pencil tests, they propose the development and use of "samples" of present job behavior to predict future behavior. In essence, these work samples approximate the tasks a potential employee might have to perform on the job and would use or simulate the actual tools, materials, and processes found on the job. They could run the gamut of complexity from simple mechanical and clerical operations to the assessment center techniques described by Bray in Section II of this book. As the preceding discussion suggests, the work sample approach differs from the one illustrated by Dunnette, Ghiselli, and Guion in that it is essentially consistent with the classical prediction model since it emphasizes the development of more effective predictors rather than the elaboration of a more complex prediction model.

With respect to the problems of unfair discrimination, work samples as nonverbal, relatively culture-free measures might be less subject, it is argued, to the inherent cultural biases of most paper-and-pencil tests. In addition, since work samples are close simulations of actual job situations, they should be more effective and fairer predictors of future work performance than paper-and-pencil tests measuring abstractly defined traits, abilities, and skills that may have only an indirect relationship to the requirements of the job. The promise of the "behavioral consistency" approach vis-a-vis unfair discrimination has yet to be fully realized, and there is reason to doubt that it ever will (e.g., see Blood, 1974). Nonetheless, it does represent an important advance in the development of a more effective and fair technology of personnel selection.

The last selection, reprinted as an appendix to this book, is the entire latest version of the *Standards for Educational and Psychological Tests and Manuals* published by the American Psychological Association in 1974. This document supercedes the previous version published in 1966 and is an essential reference for any professional interested in the development and use of employment tests. It is interesting to note that the initial version, published in 1954, was entitled *Technical Recommendations for Psychological Tests and Diagnostic Techniques* and to reflect on how and why we have moved from "recommendations" to "standards" in two decades. Any careful reading of the recent history of personnel selection and the articles in this section should reveal the unmistakable link between this field—the oldest and most traditional within I/O psychology—and the major currents of recent social change. This link should provide some reassurance to those concerned with the adaptability and relevance of our discipline to a dynamic and frequently turbulent world.

REFERENCES

American Psychological Association, American Educational Research Association, and National Council on Measurement Used in Education (Joint Committee). 1954. Technical recommendations for psychological tests and diagnostic techniques. *Psychological Bulletin,* **51**, 201-238.

Blood, M. R. 1974. Job samples: A better approach to selection testing? *American Psychologist,* **29**, 218-219.

Dunnette, M. D. 1963. A modified model for test validation and selection research. *Journal of Applied Psychology,* **47**, 251-254.

Ghiselli, E. E. 1955. *The measurement of occupational aptitude.* Berkeley: University of California Press.

Ghiselli, E. E. 1966. *The validity of occupational aptitude tests.* New York: Wiley.

Guion, R. M. 1966. Employment tests and discriminatory hiring. *Industrial Relations,* **5**, 20-37.

Guion, R. M. 1972. Implications for governmental regulatory agencies. In L. A. Crooks (ed.), *An investigation of sources of bias in the prediction of job performance.* Princeton: Educational Testing Service.

Hull, C. L. 1928. *Aptitude testing.* Yonkers, N.Y.: World Book.

Katzell, R. A., and Dyer, F. J. 1977. Differential validity revived. *Journal of Applied Psychology,* **62**, 137-145.

Münsterberg, H. 1913. *Psychology and industrial efficiency.* Boston: Houghton-Mifflin.

Wernimont, P. S., and Campbell, J. 1968. Signs, samples, and criteria. *Journal of Applied Psychology,* **5**, 372-376.

9. The Validity of Aptitude Tests in Personnel Selection*

EDWIN E. GHISELLI

Traditionally Munsterberg's experiment with motormen is taken to be the beginning of research in the use of tests for personnel selection. Nevertheless, anecdotal evidence strongly suggests that even before 1910 other psychologists conducted similar studies with tests, studies which were small in scope and which went unpublished and unpublicized. Furthermore, under the impetus of the scientific management movement some of the so-called efficiency experts at about that time were using a few simple tests for evaluating applicants for jobs, and even reported fragmentary evidence of validity in the attempt to justify and to publicize their activities. During World War I the large scale testing both of soldiers and industrial workers provided stimulation, methodology, and respectability to the examination of the utility of tests in the assessment of occupational aptitude. This all led to a great post-war surge of systematic research in personnel testing. So beginning about 1920 substantial amounts of data pertaining to the validity of various sorts of tests for the evaluation of workers in many different jobs began to become available.

For something over half a century, then, there has been an accumulation of experience with the use of tests as devices for assessing men and women for positions in business and industrial establishments, and an enormous amount of information has been collected. The purpose here is to summarize this information in as simple and compact form as is possible. Such a summary will at least permit an examination of general trends in the validity of tests for personnel selection.

METHOD

The description of the utility of a particular test for the selection of personnel for a given job is commonly given as the Pearsonian coefficient of correlation between test and criterion scores, the familiar validity coefficient. The findings of the different researches which have to do with the occupational validity of tests, then, have the unique quality of being expressed in the form of the same numerical index. As a consequence, they can be quite conveniently summarized by means of averages, the averages of the validity coefficients that have been reported for each type of test for each type of job. On an earlier occasion the author (1966) has summarized the literature pertaining to the occupational validity of tests in this way. The present report brings up to date the most recent of these summaries.

The classification of tests which was used is as follows:

TESTS OF INTELLECTUAL ABILITIES

Intelligence: This category includes all tests which are termed intelligence or mental alertness tests, as for example, the Otis and Wessman tests.

Immediate Memory: These tests present material, e.g., five-to ten-place

*Source: From *Personnel Psychology*, vol. 26 (1973), pp. 461-77. Copyright © 1973 by Personnel Psychology, Inc. Reprinted by permission.

numbers, which the individual studies and after a very short period of time tries to recall.

Substitution: With these tests the individual learns and applies a code.

Arithmetic: These devices involve the computation of arithmetic problems of various kinds, which are presented in simple form or as practical problems such as making change.

TESTS OF SPATIAL AND MECHANICAL ABILITIES

Spatial Relations: Spatial judgments about the size and form of figures are required by these tests. The Minnesota Paper Form Board is a good illustration.

Location: With these tests the individual must identify the location of a series of points, and make judgements about the distances between them. Examples are furnished by the copying and location subtests of the Mac Quarrie Mechanical Ability Tests.

Mechanical Principles: Tests of this sort, such as the Bennett Mechanical Comprehension Test, present in pictorial form problems which require knowledge of various mechanical principles to solve.

TESTS OF PERCEPTUAL ACCURACY

Number Comparison: The stimulus material in these tests consist of a series of pairs of numbers, both members of each pair consisting of the same number of digits. The digits in some of the pairs are exactly the same, and in others one digit is different. As in the number comparison part of the Minnesota Clerical Test the individual is required to indicate which pairs are the same and which are different.

Name Comparison: These tests are similar to the number comparison tests except that they consist of pairs of names instead of pairs of numbers. The Minnesota Clerical Test includes items of this sort.

Cancellation: A continuous series of numbers of letters in random order is presented by these tests, and the individual crosses out all numbers or letters of a specified sort.

Pursuit: This type of test presents a tangle of lines, and by eye alone the individual is required to follow each line from its beginning to its end. The pursuit subtest of the MacQuarrie Mechanical Ability Test is an example.

Perceptual Accuracy: The speed and accuracy with which similarities and differences between simple figures can be perceived is measured by these tests.

TESTS OF MOTOR ABILITIES

Tracing: With measuring devices of this sort the individual is required to follow a path with a pencil, both speed and accuracy being important in the performance. The tracing subtest of the MacQuarrie Mechanical Ability Test is an illustration.

Tapping: These tests present a series of circles or squares into each of which the individual places two, or perhaps three, dots with a pencil. The tapping part of the MacQuarrie Mechanical Ability Test is representative.

Dotting: These tests are similar to the tapping tests except that by using smaller circles or squares precision of movement is stressed. For instance, in the dotting subtest the MacQuarrie Mechanical Ability Test the individual places a single pencil dot in each of a series of quite small circles.

Finger Dexterity: This category includes all pegboard tests, together with tests which involve mating simple assemblies such as placing washers on rivets which are then inserted into holes. The O'Connor Finger Dexterity Test and the Purdue Pegboard Test are examples.

Hand Dexterity: While to some extent these tests do involve finger dexterity, their purpose is to measure grosser manual motions involving the wrist. In The Minnesota Turning Test, for example, blocks are picked up, turned over, and replaced in their original positions.

Arm Dexterity: As in the Minnesota Placing Test, these tests involve the very gross movements of picking up blocks and placing them in another position.

PERSONALITY TRAITS

Personality: Included here are all of the sundry inventories that ask questions which presumably are indicative of one or another of the many personality characteristics. A number of different trait names are used to distinguish the various aspects of personality. In some cases different names are used to denote the same, or very nearly the same, quality, and in others the same name is used to denote quite different qualities. As a consequence it is impossible to classify the measured traits into specific categories. Furthermore, in some instances inventories are developed for a given job and are not identified by a specific trait name. Therefore, only those results were included in the present summary where the trait seemed pertinent to the job in question, or where the inventory was developed specifically for the job through item analysis, and cross-validation data were reported. An example of this category of tests is the Guilford-Zimmerman Temperament Survey.

Interest: Inventories of this sort ask questions about interests in, and preferences for, such matters as avocations, occupations, and school subjects. Interest inventories were included in this summary on the same basis as were personality inventories.

The following classification of occupations was used:

Managerial occupations
  Executives and administrators (e.g., plant managers, department heads)
  Foremen (e.g., first-line industrial supervisors)
Clerical occupations
  General clerks (e.g., coding clerks)
  Recording clerks (e.g., typist, stenographers)
  Computing clerks (e.g., bookkeepers, calculating machine operators)
Sales occupations
  Salesclerks (e.g., retail sales persons)
  Salesmen (e.g., insurance salesmen, industrial salesmen)

Protective occupations (e.g., policemen, firemen)
Service occupations (e.g., waiters, hospital attendants)
Vehicle operators (.e.g., taxicab drivers, bus drivers)
Trades and crafts
  Mechanical repairmen (e.g., automobile mechanics, typewriter repairmen)
  Electrical workers (e.g., electricians, radio repairmen)
  Structural workers (e.g., carpenters)
  Processing workers (e.g., petroleum refinery workers, electric substation operators)
  Complex machine operators (e.g., printers, weaving machine operators)
  Machine workers (e.g., machinists, turret lathe operators)
Industrial occupations
  Machine tenders (e.g., punch press operators, bottle-capping machine operators)
  Bench workers (e.g., assemblers)
  Inspectors (e.g., pottery inspectors, gaugers)
  Packers and wrappers (e.g., package wrappers)
  Gross manual workers (e.g., unskilled laborers)

The literature summarized here includes reports which pertain to the occupational validity tests that were published during the period from 1920 through 1971. To these published findings was added a great amount of unpublished material which was obtained from private sources in a number of business, industrial, and governmental organizations. In all instances validity was expressed as the coefficient of correlation between test and criterion scores. The criterion, of course, was different for different jobs. In all but a very few instances the criterion was intended to be a measure of overall success, and was generally in the form of ratings, although occasionally they consisted of objective measures or combinations of different kinds of measures. The validity coefficients were differentiated in terms of whether they referred to the prediction of success in training, or to the level of proficiency attained on the actual job itself. Only those cases were included in the prediction of training where the training was preparation given the individual before he was actually placed on the job, and was not refresher training.

For each of the 20 types of tests, 21 types of jobs, and two types of criteria, the means of the validity coefficients were calculated. Because of the nature of the Pearsonian coefficient, the means were obtained through Fisher's z transformation, the coefficients entering into a mean being weighted in terms of the number of persons on which each of those coefficients were determined.

The circumstances in which studies of validity of occupational aptitude tests are conducted are of such a nature that in almost all instances, if not all, their findings were attenuated. As a consequence the validity coefficients that are reported for the tests almost invariably are underestimates of their true predictive power.

To begin with the criteria ordinarily used are global, covering all aspects of job performance and consequently a broad spectrum of traits. A single test, measuring as it does a restricted range of traits, cannot possibly be highly related to such a variable. Secondly, there is almost certain to be a restricted range both in test and criterion scores. If scores on the test being examined are not themselves used to select and reject candidates for the job, it is quite possible that they will have some relationship to whatever assessments are used for this purpose. Furthermore, poor workers on a job tend to be eliminated and superior ones to be promoted out of it. Since criterion scores must be obtained on workers who stay on the job for extended periods, those available for a validation study will have a smaller range of criterion scores than will those who are working on it at any given time. Restriction in the range of scores of variables being related, of course, results in a reduction in the magnitude of the coefficient of correlation between

them. Measures of human performance invariably have some degree of unreliability. The reliability coefficients of indices of job performance rarely reach as high as .90, while not infrequently they are less than .50. Values of the order of .60 to .80 can be taken to be characteristic of the reliability with which job performance is measured. It is, therefore, apparent that the magnitude of the reliability of the criteria which are used substantially limits the validity of tests which are used to predict them.

In view of the foregoing it is apparent that the average validity coefficients presented here must be considered to be understatements of the predictive power of occupational aptitude tests. Furthermore, the very process utilized here of classifying both tests and jobs into broad categories further diminishes the magnitude of those average coefficients. The sheer size of Buros' *Mental Measurements Yearbook* and the *Dictionary of Occupational Titles* is ample testimony to the fact that the types of tests and jobs can be numbered into the hundreds if not thousands. Yet in the summary here, a mere 20 classes of tests and 21 classes of jobs were used. Had more refined rubrics been employed the average validity coefficients would, of course, have been smaller in some instances, but in others they would have been much larger. Furthermore, the heterogeneity resulting from bundling together studies conducted at different times in different organizations, and utilizing widely different samples of individuals varying markedly in education, age, and social and ethnic backgrounds, while giving the findings a good deal of generality also certainly attenuates them.

It is to be recalled that in the studies summarized here validity is described solely by means of the Pearsonian coefficient of correlations. Thus a linear model, with at least the implication of homoscedasticity, is forced upon all relationships between test and criterion scores. Certainly in some instances nonlinear heteroscedastic models would give a much more favorable picture of the validity of occupational aptitude tests.

As will be seen in the following discussion and in the tables, while there is a wealth of information it is not equally distributed among the various types of tests, jobs, and criteria. For some jobs there are no data at all in important areas of aptitude, and for others it is quite limited. Nevertheless, it is possible to ascertain at least general trends for most jobs, and for many of them the data are quite complete.

RESULTS

MANAGERIAL OCCUPATIONS

The average validity coefficients for the managerial occupations are given in Table 1. It should be noted that the studies of the prediction of trainability which were included here were only those wherein the attempt was made to provide total training for the job and not just training in some specific area such as leadership.

In Table 1 it will be observed that in general the prediction of training criteria is better for foremen than it is for executives and administrators, whereas the reverse is true for job proficiency criteria. For both types of criteria, tests of intellectual abilities, spatial and mechanical abilities, and perceptual accuracy tend to be the best, and are of moderate validity for both types of managerial occupations. Tests of motor abilities have lesser, though apparently some, validity for proficiency criteria. Measures of personality and interest also are of moderate value in predicting the level of proficiency executives and administrators attain on their jobs, but they are much less useful for foremen.

Table 1

VALIDITY COEFFICIENTS FOR MANAGERIAL OCCUPATIONS

	Executives and Administrators		Foremen		All Managers	
	Train.	Prof.	Train.	Prof.	Train.	Prof.
Intellectual Abilities	.27b	.30e	.33b	.26e	.30c	.27f
Intelligence	.28b	.30e	.31b	.28e	.29b	.29f
Arithmetic	.25b	.29c	.36b	.20d	.33b	.23d
Spatial and Mechanical						
Abilities	.25b	.23e	.36a	.22e	.28b	.22e
Spatial Relations	.25b	.22e	.36a	.21d	.28b	.21d
Mechanical Principles		.42a		.23e		.23e
Perceptual Accuracy	.18b	.24c	.26b	.27b	.23b	.25e
Number Comparison		.14a		.37b		.31b
Name Comparison	.18b	.23b	.26a	.14b	.21b	.21c
Cancellation		.32b				.22b
Pursuit			.25a		.25a	
Motor Abilities	.02b	.13d	.38a	.15b	.02b	.14d
Tapping	.09b	.17b	.04a	.20a	.07b	.18c
Finger Dexterity	−.02b	.13b		.23a	−.02b	.14c
Hand Dexterity	−.02b	.10b		.02a	−.02b	.09c
Personality Traits	.53a	.29e		.16e	.53a	.22f
Personality		.28e		.15e		.21f
Interest	.53a	.30d		.17c	.53a	.28d

a. Less than 100 cases.
b. 100 to 499 cases.
c. 500 to 999 cases.
d. 1,000 to 4,999 cases.
e. 5,000 to 9,999 cases.
f. 10,000 or more cases.

Table 2
VALIDITY COEFFICIENTS FOR CLERICAL OCCUPATIONS

	General Clerks		Recording Clerks		Computing Clerks		All Clerks	
	Train.	Prof.	Train.	Prof.	Train.	Prof.	Train.	Prof.
Intellectual Abilities	.47[f]	.28[f]	.46[f]	.26[f]	.52[e]	.25[e]	.47[f]	.28[f]
Intelligence	.46[f]	.32[f]	.43[f]	.26[e]	.54[d]	.23[d]	.46[f]	.30[f]
Immediate Memory	.21[b]	.29[d]	.32[d]	.36[b]	.46[a]	.26[c]	.32[d]	.31[d]
Substitution		.24[d]	.24[c]	.23[c]	.34[b]	.24[c]	.25[d]	.24[e]
Arithmetic	.49[f]	.25[f]	.50[f]	.27[d]	.51[d]	.29[d]	.50[f]	.26[f]
Spatial and Mechanical Abilities	.35[f]	.12[e]	.30[f]	.17[d]	.52[d]	.26[d]	.34[f]	.17[f]
Spatial Relations	.39[e]	.11[d]	.32[e]	.15[d]	.55[c]	.25[d]	.35[f]	.16[e]
Location		.05[b]	.24[c]	.12[c]	.49[a]	.30[b]	.27[c]	.16[d]
Mechanical Principles	.32[e]	.20[c]	.29[f]	.23[d]	.50[c]	.26[c]	.32[f]	.23[d]
Perceptual Accuracy	.36[b]	.27[e]	.41[f]	.27[d]	.31[b]	.31[d]	.40[e]	.29[f]
Number Comparison	.42[b]	.28[e]	.28[b]	.29[d]	.35[b]	.32[d]	.34[c]	.30[e]
Name Comparison	.34[b]	.25[d]	.35[b]	.35[d]	.19[b]	.33[d]	.33[c]	.30[e]
Cancellation		.22[c]	.58[b]	.19[d]	.19[b]	.24[c]	.49[b]	.22[d]
Pursuit		-.17[a]	.21[b]	.12[b]	.11[a]	.35[b]	.15[b]	.12[b]
Perceptual Speed	.07[b]	.40[e]	.42[e]	.18[d]		.46[b]	.42[e]	.45[c]
Motor Abilities		.16[e]	.14[d]	.11[b]	.14[b]	.14[d]	.14[d]	.16[f]
Tracing	.00[b]	-.09[a]	.17[b]	.25[c]	.08[a]	.42[b]	.16[b]	.16[b]
Tapping	.32[b]	.20[d]	.23[b]	.17[c]	.16[b]	.15[c]	.21[c]	.20[d]
Dotting	.01[b]	.14[c]	.15[b]	.18[c]	.16[a]	.03[c]	.18[b]	.12[d]
Finger Dexterity	.06[b]	.16[d]	.09[c]	.17[c]		.18[b]	.08[d]	.17[d]
Hand Dexterity		.14[d]	.30[a]	-.09[a]		.12[c]	.14[b]	.14[d]
Arm Dexterity	.17[d]	.13[b]	.09[a]	.15[c]		.34[a]	.09[a]	.14[b]
Personality Traits		.17[d]				.19[b]	.17[d]	.22[d]
Personality	.17[d]	.30[c]		.18[c]		.17[b]		.24[d]
Interest		.30[c]		-.01[b]		.23[b]	.17[d]	.12[b]

a. Less than 100 cases.
b. 100 to 499 cases.
c. 500 to 999 cases.
d. 1,000 to 4,999 cases.
e. 5,000 to 9,999 cases.
f. 10,000 or more cases.

CLERICAL OCCUPATIONS

As may be seen in Table 2, while there are some differences in terms of the validity of the various sorts of tests for the three types of jobs which constitute the clerical occupations, there is, nevertheless, a considerable degree of consistency among them. Success in training for the clerical occupations is exceptionally well predicted by tests of intellectual abilities, and nearly as well by those indicative of perceptual accuracy. Oddly enough, tests of spatial and mechanical abilities also give rather good prediction of training success. More limited validity for training criteria is exhibited by measures of motor abilities. The personality and interest inventories which have been tried for this purpose have not proven to be of any great value.

Forecasts of success attained on the actual job is equally well given by tests of intellectual ability and perceptual accuracy, both of which have moderately high validity coefficients. Tests which measure spatial and mechanical abilities, and motor abilities, and inventories which are designed to measure various personality traits have much more restricted utility.

SALES OCCUPATIONS

No investigations of the validity of tests for training in the sales occupations were found that met the standards adopted in this study. The average validity coefficients for job proficiency criteria are listed in Table 3. An examination of the data present in this table will show that there is a sharp distinction between the lower sales occupations, the sales clerks, and the higher ones, the salesmen, in the utility of the

Table 3
VALIDITY COEFFICIENTS FOR SALES OCCUPATIONS

	Sales Clerks Prof.	Salesmen Prof.	All Sales Occups. Prof.
Intellectual Abilities	−.03[d]	.33[d]	.19[e]
Intelligence	−.06[d]	.34[d]	.19[e]
Immediate Memory	−.06[b]		−.06[b]
Substitution	−.16[a]		−.16[a]
Arithmetic	.10[b]	.29[d]	.25[d]
Spatial and Mechanical Abilities			
Spatial Relations	.14[b]	.20[b]	.18[c]
Mechanical Principles	.14[b]	.20[b]	.18[c]
		.16[a]	.16[a]
Perceptual Accuracy	−.02[d]	.23[b]	.04[d]
Number Comparison	−.14[b]	.27[b]	.05[b]
Name Comparison	.00[b]	.19[b]	.05[c]
Cancellation	.02[c]		.02[c]
Motor Abilities	.09[c]	.16[b]	.12[d]
Tapping	.21[b]	.17[b]	.19[b]
Finger Dexterity	−.05[b]	.18[b]	.06[b]
Hand Dexterity	.11[b]	.13[b]	.12[b]
Personality Traits	.35[d]	.30[c]	.32[e]
Personality	.36[d]	.29[d]	.31[d]
Interest	.34[c]	.31[d]	.32[d]

a. Less than 100 cases.
b. 100 to 499 cases.
c. 500 to 999 cases.
d. 1,000 to 4,999 cases.
e. 5,000 to 9,999 cases.
f. 10,000 or more cases.

various kinds of tests. For all practical purposes tests of intellectual abilities, perceptual accuracy, and motor abilities are of no value for the selection of sales clerks, whereas tests of intellectual abilities are rather good for the assessment of applicants for the job of salesman, and tests of perceptual accuracy and of motor abilities are of modest, but some, value. Measures of spatial and mechanical abilities have moderate validity for the job of salesman, and are of somewhat lesser value for the job of sales clerk. For both types of sales occupations measures of personality are rather good, perhaps being better for sales clerks than for salesmen.

PROTECTIVE OCCUPATIONS

The available information pertaining to the validity of various tests for the protective occupations is summarized in Table 4. It will be observed that good to very good predictions of trainability are provided by tests of intellectual abilities,

spatial and mechanical abilities, and perceptual accuracy. Measures of personality apparently are of no use at all for this purpose. None of the various individual types of tests have more than modest predictive power for proficiency criteria in the protective occupations. Yet all apparently do have some, though perhaps small, value.

SERVICE OCCUPATIONS

The average validity coefficients for the sundry jobs that are grouped together in the service occupations are shown in Table 5. The best predictions in these occupations, whether for trainability or job proficiency, are given by tests of intellectual abilities. In the case of trainability the validity is substantial, and it is considerably less for job proficiency. Tests of spatial and mechanical abilities, perceptual accuracy, and motor abilities in that order have reasonably good to moderate utility as measures of aptitude for training in the service occupations.

Table 4
VALIDITY COEFFICIENTS FOR PROTECTIVE OCCUPATIONS

	Train.	Prof.
Intellectual Abilities	.42[d]	.22[d]
Intelligence	.65[b]	.23[d]
Immediate Memory	.28[a]	.26[b]
Arithmetic	.30[c]	.18[c]
Spatial and Mechanical	.35[c]	.18[d]
Spatial Relations	.31[b]	.17[d]
Mechanical Principles	.38[b]	.23[b]
Perceptual Accuracy	.30[b]	.21[c]
Number Comparison		.16[b]
Name Comparison		.23[c]
Perceptual Speed	.30[b]	
Motor Abilities		.14[d]
Tapping		.16[b]
Finger Dexterity		.15[c]
Hand Dexterity		.08[b]
Personality Traits	−.11[b]	.21[c]
Personality	−.11[b]	.24[c]
Interest		−.01[b]

a. Less than 100 cases.
b. 100 to 499 cases.
c. 500 to 999 cases.
d. 1,000 to 4,999 cases.
e. 5,000 to 9,999 cases.
f. 10,000 or more cases.

Table 5
VALIDITY COEFFICIENTS FOR SERVICE OCCUPATIONS

	Train.	Prof.
Intellectual Abilities	.42[d]	.27[d]
Intelligence	.42[d]	.26[d]
Arithmetic	.42[d]	.28[d]
Spatial and Mechanical Abilities	.31[d]	.13[d]
Spatial Relations	.31[d]	.13[d]
Perceptual Accuracy	.25[c]	.10[d]
Number Comparison		.14[b]
Name Comparison	.25[c]	.15[c]
Cancellation		−.27[b]
Motor Abilities	.21[d]	.15[d]
Tapping	.18[c]	.22[c]
Finger Dexterity	.21[c]	.13[c]
Hand Dexterity	.23[c]	.13[c]
Arm Dexterity		−.01[b]
Personality Traits		.16[b]
Personality		.16[b]

a. Less than 100 cases.
b. 100 to 499 cases.
c. 500 to 999 cases.
d. 1,000 to 4,999 cases.
e. 5,000 to 9,999 cases.
f. 10,000 or more cases.

These same three tests together with measures of personality traits all have low validity for job proficiency.

VEHICLE OPERATORS

The findings for the relatively homogenous occupation of vehicle operator are given in Table 6. Tests of spatial relations and mechanical ability, and of motor abilities have average validity coefficients of moderate magnitude for training criteria. Tests of intellectual abilities have much lower validity, and tests of perceptual accuracy have little or no validity. In the prediction of job proficiency tests of motor abilities and of personality traits are the best, though having only modest validity. Measures of intellectual ability and of perceptual accuracy while not completely without value, have relatively low validity.

Table 6
VALIDITY COEFFICIENTS FOR VEHICLE OPERATORS

	Train.	Prof.
Intellectual Abilities	.18[d]	.16[d]
Intelligence	.21[d]	.15[d]
Immediate Memory	.10[b]	
Arithmetic	.17[d]	.25[c]
Spatial and Mechanical Abilities	.31[d]	.20[d]
Spatial Relations	.23[d]	.16[c]
Location		.18[b]
Mechanical Principles	.38[d]	.22[d]
Perceptual Accuracy	.09[c]	.17[b]
Number Comparison		.37[a]
Name Comparison	.11[a]	.15[b]
Perceptual Speed	.08[c]	
Motor Abilities	.31[b]	.25[d]
Tapping	.27[a]	.28[c]
Dotting		.28[b]
Finger Dexterity	.44[a]	.22[b]
Hand Dexterity	.21[a]	.16[b]
Personality Traits		.26[b]
Interest		.26[b]

a. Less than 100 cases.
b. 100 to 499 cases.
c. 500 to 999 cases.
d. 1,000 to 9,999 cases.
e. 5,000 to 9,999 cases.
f. 10,000 or more cases.

TRADES AND CRAFTS

While the jobs included in the category of the trades and crafts are rather different from each other in their specific nature they all do involve the exercise of a high degree of skill, and require an extensive preparation through training. The average validity coefficients for these various jobs are to be found in Table 7.

As would be expected from the characteristics of the jobs which constitute the trades and crafts, tests of intellectual abilities and of spatial and mechanical abilities have fairly substantial validity for the prediction of trainability. Tests of perceptual accuracy are almost as good, and those measuring motor abilities and personality traits have only limited validity. When it comes to measuring aptitude for performing the actual job itself, tests of intellectual abilities, spatial and mechanical abilities, perceptual accuracy, and personality traits are all found to be equally effective, having moderate validity. The validity of tests of motor abilities is more restricted.

INDUSTRIAL OCCUPATIONS

The many semiskilled and unskilled jobs which are to be found in industrial organizations are grouped together here to form the industrial occupations. The effectiveness of the various sorts of tests for these occupations are to be found in Table 8.

Measures of intellectual abilities, and of spatial and mechanical abilities are quite good measures of aptitude for training in the industrial occupations, being nearly as good for this purpose as they are in the case of the trades and crafts. The utility of tests of motor abilities is somewhat lesser, but still satisfactory. While the validity of tests of perceptual accuracy is still lower, they, too, are not without some value. Tests of intellectual abilities, spatial and mechanical abilities, perceptual accuracy, and motor abilities all have just about the same level of validity for pro-

Table 7
VALIDITY COEFFICIENTS FOR TRADES AND CRAFTS

	Mechanical Repairmen		Electrical Workers		Structural Workers		Processing Workers		Complex Machine Operators		Machine Workers		All Trades and Crafts	
	Train.	Prof.	Train.	Prof.	Train.	Prof.	Train.	Prof.	Train.	Prof.	Train.	Prof.	Train.	Prof.
Intellectual Abilities	.41[f]	.23[e]	.49[f]	.29[e]	.31[f]	.25[f]	.46[e]	.24[d]	.26[e]	.26[e]	.35[e]	.19[d]	.41[f]	.25[f]
Intelligence	.40[f]	.23[d]	.47[f]	.31[d]	.33[e]	.25[d]	.36[d]	.24[d]	.34[d]	.25[d]	.34[d]	.18[d]	.41[f]	.25[f]
Immediate Memory	.30[d]		.31[c]	.21[a]	.13[c]	.13[b]	.31[b]	.15[b]		.30[b]	.12[b]	-.02[b]	.28[e]	.17[c]
Substitution	.34[a]		.34[a]	-.17[a]	.31[c]	.31[a]		.34[a]		.26[b]	.27[b]	.21[b]	.31[e]	.21[b]
Arithmetic	.42[f]	.24[d]	.53[f]	.28[d]	.30[e]	.25[d]	.50[e]	.22[c]	.28[b]	.27[d]	.39[d]	.22[c]	.43[f]	.25[f]
Spatial and Mechanical Abilities	.40[f]	.20[d]	.47[f]	.21[d]	.33[e]	.22[d]	.33[d]	.24[d]	.35[d]	.25[e]	.40[e]	.27[d]	.41[f]	.23[f]
Spatial Relations	.42[f]	.18[d]	.46[e]	.19[d]	.33[e]	.23[d]	.35[d]	.25[d]	.35[d]	.25[d]	.44[d]	.28[d]	.41[f]	.23[f]
Location	.24[b]	.28[a]	.24[a]	.23[b]	.23[b]	.23[b]	.24[b]	.21[b]	.28[a]	.25[d]	.24[b]	.04[b]	.25[d]	.20[d]
Mechanical Principles	.40[f]	.28[a]	.49[f]	.25[d]	.34[d]	.10[b]	.13[c]	.28[b]		.40[a]	.38[d]	.44[b]	.41[f]	.26[d]
Perceptual Accuracy	.40[f]	.25[d]	.27[f]	.24[d]	.28[d]	.25[d]	.29[c]	.25[c]	.26[c]	.26[d]	.27[d]	.13[c]	.35[f]	.24[e]
Number Comparison	.22[a]	.20[d]	.25[c]	.17[a]	-.04[b]	.08[b]	.24[b]	.21[a]	.42[a]	.14[b]	.10[b]	.12[a]	.20[d]	.14[c]
Name Comparison	.34[b]	.23[a]	.25[b]	.21[c]	.31[d]	.25[b]	.14[b]	.31[b]	.30[b]	.26[b]	.21[b]	.23[b]	.28[d]	.25[e]
Cancellation		.20[d]		.21[a]		.21[a]			.20[b]	.23[a]	.28[b]		.24[d]	.16[b]
Pursuit	.17[c]	.36[b]	.16[c]	.29[b]	.18[a]	.24[a]	-.13[a]	.17[d]	.41[a]	.33[b]	.20[b]	.01[b]	.16[d]	.25[c]
Perceptual Speed	.40[f]	.03[a]	.43[c]	.36[a]	.29[b]	.35[b]	.34[c]	.19[b]	.28[a]	.28[a]	.35[c]	-.12[a]	.40[f]	.25[c]
Motor Abilities	.15[d]	.16[d]	.15[d]	.16[d]	.26[d]	.21[e]	.17[c]	.27[d]	.26[d]	.19[d]	.17[d]	.12[d]	.20[f]	.19[f]
Tracing	.21[b]	.27[a]	.24[b]	.15[a]	.24[a]	.30[c]	.17[b]	.24[b]	.22[a]	.19[d]	.21[b]	.06[b]	.22[d]	.20[c]
Tapping	.05[c]	.16[d]	.20[c]	.17[c]	.14[d]	.18[d]	-.01[b]	.31[b]	.24[b]	.20[d]	.10[b]	.14[c]	.17[d]	.19[c]
Dotting	.20[b]	.11[a]	-.14[a]	.01[a]	.13[b]	.20[b]	.02[b]		.26[a]	.11[b]	.08[b]	.06[b]	.13[c]	.11[c]
Finger Dexterity	.21[c]	.18[d]	.15[d]	.17[d]	.26[d]	.20[d]	.22[c]	.28[d]	.27[c]	.18[d]	.22[d]	.10[d]	.21[c]	.19[f]
Hand Dexterity	.11[b]	.13[d]	.03[b]	.12[c]	.33[c]	.22[c]		.25[c]	.27[c]	.18[d]	.20[b]	.21[b]	.23[d]	.18[e]
Arm Dexterity	.08[a]	.07[a]	-.10[a]			.24[a]		.22[a]	.34[a]	.33[a]	-.03[b]	.11[b]	.06[b]	.15[c]
Personality Traits	.16[e]		.16[e]			.28[b]		.27[c]	.31[a]	.24[b]		-.13[b]	.16[f]	.24[c]
Personality								.30[b]		.24[b]				.29[b]
Interest	.16[e]		.16[e]	.16[e]		.28[b]		.22[b]	.31[a]	.22[b]		-.13[b]	.16[f]	.17[b]

a. Less than 100 cases.
b. 100 to 499 cases.
c. 500 to 999 cases.
d. 1,000 to 4,999 cases.
e. 5,000 to 9,999 cases.
f. 10,000 or more cases.

Table 8
VALIDITY COEFFICIENTS FOR INDUSTRIAL OCCUPATIONS

	Machine Tenders		Bench Workers		Inspectors		Packers and Wrappers		Gross Manual Workers		All Industrial Workers	
	Train.	Prof.	Train.	Prof.	Train.	Prof.	Train.	Prof.	Train.	Prof.	Train.	Prof.
Intellectual Abilities	-.31a	.21f	.27d	.18f	.24c	.21d	.49f	.18d	.25b	.22e	.38e	.20f
Intelligence	-.31a	.21e	.20d	.18f	.22c	.23d	.50d	.17d	.23b	.21d	.38e	.20f
Immediate Memory		.17d		.06d		.14b		.24b				.15d
Substitution		.19c		.12d		-.01b		.16b				.14d
Arithmetic		.21e	.37c	.20e	.26b	.24d	.43c	.16f	.37a	.24d	.38e	.21f
Spatial and Mechanical Abilities		.20f	.35d	.22f	.25d	.22d	.46e	.15d	.30b	.19d	.40e	.20f
Spatial Relations		.22f	.32d	.21f	.28d	.24d	.43d	.15d	.30b	.19d	.40e	.21f
Location		.11d		.19e	.19c	.18c		.16c			.19c	.15e
Mechanical Principles			.63b	.41b		.42b	.50d	.14b			.50d	.24d
Perceptual Accuracy		.20f	.22c	.21f	.18d	.19d		.19d	.24a	.21d	.20d	.20f
Number Comparison		.20d	.38a	.15d		.04b		.13d			.38a	.13d
Name Comparison		.21c	.05b	.21e	.13b	.24c		.22d	.24a	.21d	.11b	.21f
Cancellation		.25b		.36c	.09b	-.11a		.24b				.31d
Pursuit		.15d	.29b	.15d	.22c	.09b		.16b			.15b	.15d
Perceptual Speed	.21a	.24b	.26b	.27d	.07d	.58a					.24d	.29d
Motor Abilities		.20f	.36d	.25f	.09a	.14e		.17e	.24b	.27e	.28d	.22f
Tracing		.16d	.16d	.18b	.11b	.20b		.12b			.14b	.16e
Tapping		.22e	.13b	.22e	.08a	.14c		.22d	.16b	.23d	.13c	.22f
Dotting		.15d	.22b	.16d	.02b	.06b		.13b			.18b	.15d
Finger Dexterity	.21a	.18f	.41d	.26f	.03b	.16d		.10d	.29b	.26d	.34d	.22f
Hand Dexterity		.27d	.41c	.27e		.25c		.20d	.25b	.30d	.33c	.26f
Arm Dexterity		.15c	.54b	.24c		.00d		.24d		.43b	.69b	.18d
Personality Traits		.26a		.26a								.26a
Personality				.50a								.50a
Interest		.26a		.02a								.14a

a. Less than 100 cases.
b. 100 to 499 cases.
c. 500 to 999 cases.
d. 1,000 to 4,999 cases.
e. 5,000 to 9,999 cases.
f. 10,000 or more cases.

ficiency criteria. Though this falls short of what is ordinarily desired, nonetheless it is apparent that these tests do give predictions of job proficiency which clearly are better than chance.

THE PREDICTIVE POWER OF OCCUPATIONAL APTITUDE TESTS

Considering the considerable differences in the times when the investigations summarized here were performed, together with the large differences in the nature of the organizations in which they were conducted, and the marked variations among the samples in such factors as age, sex, education, and background, the average validity coefficients presented here can be said to have a good deal of generality. Furthermore, since most of them are based upon a number of separate and distinct determinations they have a substantial measure of dependability and meaningfulness.

The general run of the validity coefficients is quite respectable for training criteria, and it is somewhat less so for proficiency criteria. The grand average of the validity coefficients for all tests for all jobs taken together is .39 for training criteria and .22 for proficiency criteria. However, for every job there is at least one type of test which has at least moderate validity. If for each job the highest average validity coefficient is observed, it will be found that for the 21 jobs these values range from .28 to .65 for training criteria, and from .24 to .46 for proficiency criteria. The averages of these maximal validity coefficients are .45 for training criteria and .35 for proficiency criteria. In view of the attenuating effects upon validity coefficients which were discussed earlier the foregoing values clearly are conservative as descriptions of the predictive power of occupational aptitude tests. It will be recalled that single tests are being considered here, and that judiciously selected combinations of tests would have been higher validity.

NOTE

Ghiselli, E. E. *The validity of occupational aptitude tests.* Wiley, 1966.

10. A Modified Model for Test Validation and Selection Research*

MARVIN D. DUNNETTE

Nearly 35 years ago, Clark Hull (1928) discussed the level of forecasting efficiency shown by the so-called modern tests of the time. He noted that the upper limit for tests was represented by validity coefficients of about .50 corresponding to a forecasting efficiency of only 13 percent. He regarded the region of forecasting efficiency lying above this point as being inaccessible to the test batteries of the day, and he viewed with pessimism the use of test batteries for predicting occupational criteria. Hull, of course, failed to emphasize that the ac-

*Source: From *Journal of Applied Psychology*, vol. 47 (October 1963), pp. 317-23. Copyright © 1963 by the American Psychological Association. Reprinted by permission. Footnotes renumbered.

curacy of practical decisions might better be assessed against zones of behavior (e.g., passing versus failing in a training program) rather than against the metrical continuum assumed in the calculation of his index of forecasting efficiency. Further, he gave no attention to the varying effects of different selection ratios on the accuracies obtainable with even rather low correlation coefficients. Even so, we should be somewhat dismayed by the fact that today our tests have still not penetrated the region of inaccessibility defined so long ago by Hull. Ghiselli's (1955) comprehensive review of both published and unpublished studies showed average validities ranging in the .30s and low .40s; an average validity of .50 or above was a distinct rarity. These low validities have apparently led many psychologists to become disenchanted with test and selection research. Some have disappeared into other endeavors such as the study of group influences, interaction patterns, and the like. Others have sought refuge in the hypothesis testing models of statistical inference and have implied validity for tests showing *statistically* (but often not *practically*) significant differences between contrasting groups (see Dunnette & Kirchner, 1962). Nunnally (1960) comments:

> We should not feel proud when we see the psychologist smile and say "the correlation is significant beyond the .01 level." Perhaps that is the most he can say, but he has no reason to smile [p. 649].

Even less defensible, perhaps, has been the tendency for many to persist in doing selection *without* conducting selection research or test validation. The ordinary defenses for such practice run the gamut—from claiming near miracles of clinical insight in personnel assessment to the recounting of anecdotes about instances of selective accuracy (counting the "hits" and forgetting the "misses") and finally to the old cliché that "management is well-satisfied with the methods being employed." We cannot and should not try to avoid the

fact that the statistics of selection (i.e., validity coefficients) are far from gratifying and offer little support to anyone claiming to do *much* better than chance in the selection process.

It seems wise, therefore, to discuss the possibility of improving our batting average in test validation and selection research. Selection programs will go on—with or without psychologists—but I believe we now have the capability for penetrating the region of inaccessibility outlined by Hull.

First, let us examine the classic validation or prediction model. This model has sought simply to link predictors, on the one hand, with criteria, on the other, through a simple index of relationship, the correlation coefficient. Such a simple linkage of predictors and criteria is grossly oversimplified in comparison with the complexities actually involved in predicting human behavior. Most competent investigators readily recognize this fact and design their validation studies to take account of the possible complexities—job differences, criterion differences, etc.—present in the prediction situation. Even so, the appealing simplicity, false though it is, of the classic model has led many researchers to be satisfied with a correspondingly simplified design for conducting selection research. Thus, the usual validation effort has ignored the events—on the job behavior, situational differences, dynamic factors influencing definitions of success, etc.—intervening between predictor and criterion behavior. I believe that the lure of this seemingly simple model is, to a great extent, responsible for the low order of validities reported in the Ghiselli (1955) review. It is noteworthy that the studies reviewed by Ghiselli show no typical level of prediction for any given test or type of job. In fact, there seems to be little consistency among various studies using similar tests amd purporting to predict similar criteria. The review also suggests that the magnitude of validity coefficients is inversely proportional to the sample size employed in the studies. This can perhaps be explained, in part, by sampling error, but it may also be due to the relatively greater homogeneity possible within smaller groups of subjects. It appears, in other words, that the varying levels of prediction shown by the various studies are related somehow to the appropriateness (or lack thereof) of the classic prediction model for the particular set of conditions in the study being reported. It seems wise, therefore, to consider a prediction model which more fully presents the complexities which are only implied by the classic model.

Guetzkow and Forehand (1961) have suggested a modification of the classic validation model which provides a richer schematization for prediction research and which offers important implications for the direction of future research. Their model along with certain additional modifications is shown in Figure 1. Note that the modified predic-

tion model takes account of the complex interactions which may occur between predictors and various predictor combinations, different groups (or types) of individuals, different behaviors on the job, and the consequences of these behaviors relative to the goals of the organization. The model permits the possibility of predictors being differentially useful for predicting the behaviors of different subsets of individuals. Further, it shows that similar job behaviors may be predictable by quite different patterns of interaction between groupings of predictors and individuals or even that the same level of performance on predictors can lead to substantially different patterns of job behavior for different individuals. Finally, the model recognizes the annoying reality that the same or similar job behaviors can, after passing through the situational filter, lead to quite different organizational consequences.

This modified and more complex

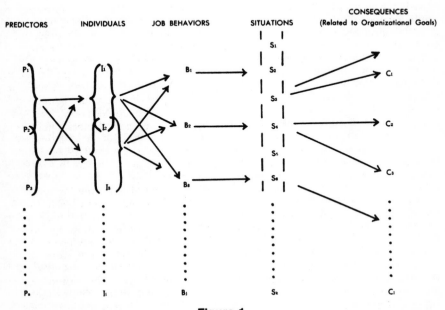

Figure 1
A MODIFIED MODEL FOR TEST VALIDATION AND SELECTION RESEARCH

prediction model leads to a number of important considerations involving the emphases to be followed by future validation research:

First, we must be willing to back off a step or two from global measures of occupational effectiveness—ratings, volume of output, and other so-called criteria of organizational worth, and do a more careful job of studying actual job behavior—with particular focus on behavioral or stylistic variations among different individuals with the same jobs. Most previous validation research has been overly concerned with predicting organizational consequences without first determining the nature of possible linkages between such consequences and differences in actual job behavior. It is true that industrial psychologists should continue to be concerned about predicting organizational consequences. Certainly, the modified model implies no lessening of such an interest. What is hoped, however, is that the more careful analysis of the behavioral correlates of differences in organizational consequences will lead to broader understanding of them and, eventually, to their more accurate prediction.

Secondly, as implied by the point just made, the modified model demands that we give up our worship of the criterion (Dunnette, 1963). I believe that our concept of the criterion has suggested the existence of some single, all encompassing measure of occupational success against which predictors must be compared. Our modified model demands that we work with multiple measures of individual behavior and organizational consequences. I suggest therefore that we cease talking about the criterion problem and that we discard the notion of a so-called ultimate criterion. Such action should result in a research emphasis which will be less restrictive and less simple-minded and more aware of the necessity of analyzing and predicting the many facets of occupational success.

Thirdly, the modified model implies

nothing concerning the form of the relationships to be expected. One of the unfortunate consequences of utilizing the classic validation model was its overemphasis on the correlation coefficient as almost the sole statistic of validation research. The notion of a simple linkage between predictor and criterion led easily to the equally simple assumption of the applicability of the linear, homoscedastic model for expressing the magnitude of relationships. Kahneman and Ghiselli (1962), in investigating relationships between 60 aptitude variables and various criteria, showed that 40 percent of the scatter diagrams departed significantly from the linear, homoscedastic model, and 90 percent of these departures held up on cross-validation. This is an important finding for it points up the necessity in future validation research of adopting a methodology taking account of the very great likelihood of nonlinear, heteroscedastic models. Our more complex prediction model, focusing as it does on the complex linkages between predictors and consequences, implies also the necessity of adopting more complex and sophisticated tools of analysis in studying these linkages.

Fourth, and most obviously, our modified model demands that we develop a sort of typology for classifying people, tests, job situations, and behaviors according to their relative predictability. Future validation research must define the unique conditions under which certain predictors may be used for certain jobs and for certain purposes. Research studies should, therefore, be devoted to the definition of homogeneous subsets within which appropriate prediction equations may be developed and cross-validated. This idea is not particularly startling nor even new. But it has not been applied widely in the conduct of selection research. The modified model rather explicitly directs us to carry out such subgrouping studies in order to learn more about the complex linkages between predictors and consequences. Fortunately several studies already are available which confirm the advantages of studying differential patterns of validity for various subgroups. A brief review of some of these research approaches should illustrate the utility of applying our more complicated model to validation research.

With respect to job groupings, Dunnette and Kirchner (Dunnette, 1958; Dunnette & Kirchner, 1958, 1960) have studied the different patterns of validities obtained when careful techniques of job analysis are used to discover groupings of jobs which are relatively homogeneous in terms of actual responsibilities. Substantially different validities were obtained for engineers grouped according to functional similarities (research, development, production, and sales), salesmen (industrial and retail), and clerical employees (stenographers and clerk typists). These studies highlight the necessity of studying job differences and the differential predictability of effectiveness in various job groupings. More generally, an emphasis on the varying predictability of different job activities is inherent in the methods of synthetic validity (Balma, Ghiselli, McCormick, Primoff, & Griffin, 1959) and in the use of the J coefficient developed by Primoff (1955).

Everyone recognizes the possibility of situational effects on the validity of psychological predictions, but there is a paucity of research designed to estimate systematically the magnitude of such effects. Perhaps the best example of such research is provided by Vroom (1960). He showed that various aptitude tests (verbal and nonverbal reasoning, arithmetic reasoning) predicted ratings of job success most effectively for persons who were highly motivated. Job effectiveness in nonmotivating situations showed either no relationship or negative relationships with tested abilities. In a second study with Mann (Vroom & Mann, 1960), it was shown that the size of work groups strongly influenced employee attitudes toward their supervisors. Employees in small groups

preferred democratic or equalitarian supervisors; employees in large work groups preferred authoritarian supervisors. In a significant series of studies, Porter (1962) is also investigating situational factors such as hierarchical level, firm size, and job function as they affect managerial perceptions of their jobs. More emphasis needs to be given to these and other situational factors in validation studies, particularly as they serve to operate as moderating variables (Saunders, 1956) in behavioral predictions.

Many studies have shown different validities for different subgroups of individuals. For example, Seashore (1961) summarized a vast number of scholastic success studies which show almost uniformly that the grades of women (in both high school and college) are significantly more predictable than those of men. It is also well established that differing patterns of validity are typically obtained for subgroups differing in amounts of education and/or years of job experience. It may seem obvious that such factors as sex, education, and experience provide useful moderating variables in validation research. However, researchers also have identified variables which are much less *obvious* but which *do* make substantial differences in the patterns and magnitudes of validities obtained. For example, Grooms and Endler (1960) showed that the grades of anxious college students were much more predictable ($r = .63$) with aptitude and achievement measures than were the grades of nonanxious students ($r = .19$); and Frederiksen, Melville, and Gilbert (Frederiksen & Gilbert, 1960; Frederiksen & Melville, 1954) have shown that interest in engineering (as measured by the Strong test) has a higher validity for predicting grades for noncompulsive engineers than for compulsive ones. Berdie (1961) showed that the grades of engineering students with relatively consistent scores on an algebra test were more predictable from the total test score than were the grades of students with less consistent scores.[1] Ghiselli (1956, 1962) has developed a method for dividing persons, on the basis of a screening test, into more and less predictable subgroups. The advantage of his method is that no a priori basis is necessary for the identification of subgroups; the method depends simply on the development of one or more predictor tests to facilitate the subgrouping process.

The identification of more and less predictable subgroups of persons, whether based on logical factors (such as sex, education, or experience) or on methods such as those employed by Berdie and Ghiselli, places a special burden on the investigator to demonstrate the stability of his results. Although the studies cited above were cross-validated (i.e., checked on holdout groups), the validity generalization and/or extension of such results has not often been measured. This needs to be done. The results so far reported with these methods are promising indeed, but they will take on greatly added significance when it is demonstrated that they hold up over time.

Less research has been directed at identifying subsets of predictors showing differential patterns of validity. However, Ghiselli (1960, 1962) has also contributed methodology in this area and has succeeded in significantly enhancing prediction by identifying, again through the development and use of screening tests, the particular predictor which will do the most valid job for each individual.

General approaches to the development of "types" have been made by a number of investigators. Gaier and Lee (1953) and Cronbach and Gleser (1953) summarize a variety of methods of assessing profile similarity and conclude that available indexes are simply variants of the general Pythagorean formula for the linear distance between two points in n-dimensional space. Lykken (1956) has questioned the psychological meaning of such "geometric similarity" and he proposes a method of actuarial pattern analysis which requires no assumptions concerning the form of the distribution and which defines similarity in psychological rather than geometric terms. His method consists simply of investigating criterial outcomes for subjects classified together into cells on the basis of similar test scores. In a recent study, he and Rose (Lykken & Rose, in press) demonstrate that the method is more accurate in discriminating between neurotics and psychotics on the basis of MMPI scores than either clinicians' judgments or a statistical technique based on equations derived from a discriminant function analysis. Lykken's method of actuarial pattern analysis is the same as Toops' (1959) method of developing subgroups or "ulstriths" based on biographical and test similarities and then writing different prediction equations for each of the subgroups so identified. It is interesting to note that computers have now given us the capability for carrying out many of Toops' suggestions—which at one time were regarded as wild-eyed, idealistic, and unrealistic. McQuitty (1957, 1960, 1961) also has developed methods for discovering the diagnostic and predictive significance of various response patterns. His techniques, in addition to the methods proposed by Lykken and Toops, constitute the most extensive attack made to date on the problem of developing differentially predictable subsets or types.

These studies and methods mark the bare beginnings of efforts to take account of complexities which have been ignored by the oversimplified prediction model of the past. It appears that subgrouping of tests, people, jobs, situations, and consequences is necessary to

---

1. The algebra test of 100 items was divided into 10 subtests of equal difficulty. The measure of consistency for each student was simply the sum of squares of the deviations of his 10 scores from his mean score on all 10 subtests.

a thorough understanding of what is going on in a prediction situation. The widespread acceptance of the modified model which we have been discussing should lead to a new and refreshing series of questions about problems of selection and placement. Instead of asking whether or not a particular selection technique (test, interview, or what have you) is any good, we will ask under *what circumstances* different techniques may be useful. What sorts of persons should be screened with each of the methods available, and how may the various subgroups of persons be identified and assigned to optimal screening devices? Finally, what job behaviors may be expected of various people and how may these behaviors be expected to aid or to detract from accomplishing different organizational objectives which may, in turn, vary according to different value systems and preferred outcomes?

What are the implications of these trends for the selection function in industry? Primarily, I believe they suggest the possibility of a new kind of selection process in the firm of the future. The selection expert of tomorrow will no longer be attempting to utilize the same procedure for all his selection problems. Instead, he will be armed with an array of prediction equations. He will have developed, through research, a wealth of evidence showing the patterns of validities for different linkages in the modified prediction model—for different predictors, candidates, jobs, and criteria. He will be a flexible operator, attentive always to the accumulating information on any given candidate, and ready to apply, at each stage, the tests and procedures shown to be optimal.

NOTES

Balma, M. J., Ghiselli, E. E., McCormick, E. J., Primoff, E. S., & Griffin, C. H. The development of processes for indirect or synthetic validity: A symposium. *Personnel Psychol.*, 1959, **12**, 395-400.

Berdie, R. F. Intra-individual variability and predictability. *Educ. Psychol. Measmt.*, 1961, **21**, 663-676.

Cronbach, L. J., & Gleser, Goldine. Assessing similarity between profiles. *Psychol. Bull.*, 1953, **50**, 456-473.

Dunnette, M. D. Validity of interviewer's ratings and psychological tests for predicting the job effectiveness of engineers. St. Paul: Minnesota Mining and Manufacturing Company, 1958. (Mimeo)

Dunnette, M. D. A note on the criterion. *J. Appl. Psychol.*, 1963, **47**, 251-254.

Dunnette, M. D., & Kirchner, W. K. Validation of psychological tests in industry. *Personnel Admin.*, 1958, **21**, 20-27.

Dunnette, M. D., & Kirchner, W. K. Psychological test differences between industrial salesmen and retail salesmen. *J. Appl. Psychol.*, 1960, **44**, 121-125.

Dunnette, M. D., & Kirchner, W. K. Validities, vectors, and verities. *J. Appl. Psychol.*, 1962, **46**, 296-299.

Frederiksen, N., & Gilbert, A. C. Replication of a study of differential predictability. *Educ. Psychol. Measmt.*, 1960, **20**, 759-767.

Frederiksen, N., & Melville, S. D. Differential predictability in the use of test scores. *Educ. Psychol. Measmt.*, 1954, **14**, 647-656.

Gaier, E. L., & Lee, Marilyn. Pattern analysis: The configural approach to predictive measurement. *Psychol. Bull.*, 1953, **50**, 140-148.

Ghiselli, E. E. The measurement of occupational aptitude. Berkeley: Univer. California Press, 1955.

Ghiselli, E. E. Differentiation of individuals in terms of their predictability. *J. Appl. Psychol.*, 1956, **40**, 374-377.

Ghiselli, E. E. Differentiation of tests in terms of the accuracy with which they predict for a given individual. *Educ. Psychol. Measmt.*, 1960, **20**, 675-684.

Ghiselli, E. E. The prediction of predictability and the predictability of prediction. Paper read at American Psychological Association, St. Louis, September 1962.

Grooms, R. R., & Endler, N. S. The effect of anxiety on academic achievement. *J. Educ. Psychol.*, 1960, **51**, 299-304.

Guetzkow, H., & Forehand, G. A. A research strategy for partial knowledge useful in the selection of executives. In R. Taguiri (Ed.), *Research needs in executive selection*. Boston: Harvard Graduate School of Business Administration, 1961.

Hull, C. L. Aptitude testing. Yonkers, N.Y.: World Book, 1928.

Kahneman, D., & Ghiselli, E. E. Validity and nonlinear heteroscedastic models. *Personnel Psychol.*, 1962, **15**, 1-11.

Lykken, D. T. A method of actuarial pattern analysis. *Psychol. Bull.*, 1956, **53**, 102-107.

Lykken, D. T., & Rose, R. J. Psychological prediction from actuarial tables. *J. Clin. Psychol.*, in press.

McQuitty, L. L. Isolating predictor patterns associated with major criterion patterns. *Educ. Psychol. Measmt.*, 1957, **17**, 3-42.

McQuitty, L. L. Hierarchical linkage analysis for the isolation of types. *Educ. Psychol. Measmt.*, 1960, **20**, 55-67.

McQuitty, L. L. A method for selecting patterns to differentiate categories of people. *Educ. Psychol. Measmt.*, 1961, **21**, 85-94.

Nunnally, J. The place of statistics in psychology. *Educ. Psychol. Measmt.*, 1960, **20**, 641-650.

Porter, L. W. Some recent explorations in the study of management attitudes. Paper read at American Psychological Association, St. Louis, September 1962.

Primoff, E. S. *Test selection by job analysis.* Washington, D. C.: United States Civil Service Commission, Test Development Section, 1955.

Saunders, D. R. Moderator variables in prediction. *Educ. Psychol. Measmt.*, 1956, **16**, 209-222.

Seashore, H. G. Women are more predictable than men. Presidential address, Division 17, American Psychological Association, New York, September 1961.

Toops, H. A. A research utopia in industrial psychology. *Personnel Psychol.*, 1959, **12**, 189-227.

Vroom, V. H. *Some personality determinants of the effects of participation.* Englewood Cliffs, N.J.: Prentice-Hall, 1960.

Vroom, V. H., & Mann, F. C. Leader authoritarianism and employee attitudes. *Personnel Psychol.*, 1960, **13**, 125-139.

11. Differentiation of Individuals in Terms of Their Predictability*

EDWIN E. GHISELLI

When scores on a test are unrelated to criterion scores or are related to them only to a very low degree, the presumption is that the test is of little value. Hence in a prediction or selection situation tests with low validity are quickly discarded and the entire effort is directed to the development of tests which will yield scores that are substantially related to the criterion.

Even though the validity coefficient of a test is negligible, there is the possibility that at least with certain individuals reasonably accurate predictions of criterion performance nevertheless may be made from scores on the test. As one regards the scatter diagram of the scores on two variables that exhibit a low relationship, it is apparent that some individuals fall on or very close to the line of relations while others depart markedly from it. Thus for some individuals there is quite close correspondence between standard scores on the test and standard scores on the criterion. The reminder of the individuals display to varying degrees differences between standard test and standard criterion scores.

Suppose, as the author has suggested

*Source: From *Journal of Applied Psychology*, vol. 40, no. 6 (1956), pp. 374-77. Copyright © 1956 by the American Psychological Association. Reprinted by permission.

elsewhere (5), that it were possible by some other means, perhaps another test, to differentiate those individuals whose test and criterion scores show small discrepancies from those individuals whose test and criterion scores are markedly different. Then it would be possible to screen out a group for which at least reasonably accurate predictions can be made. Thus even though the validity of the test for the entire group is low, for some individuals who can be differentiated beforehand, the test would have some practical utility.

In a somewhat different form this notion is implicit in dealing with individual cases in clinical and guidance work. Consider the case of a counselor attempting to decide whether a young person should seek education above the secondary school level. If it appears that motivation or interests seem inappropriate, he might not recommend college even though the intelligence test score is high. In effect, what is being said is that when the individual possesses certain other characteristics, there will be little correspondence between test performance and college achievement.

Therefore there is nothing new in the notion that it is possible to differentiate between those individuals for whom a test is a good predictor and those for whom it is a poor one. However, it remains to be seen whether it is possible to make such a differentiation in a systematic and objective fashion. It is the purpose of the present investigation to examine this possibility.

METHODS AND PROCEDURES

Scores from one test and two inventories were obtained on candidates for the job of taxicab driver at the time of hiring. The test consisted of tapping and dotting items, and the inventories consisted of 24 pairs of forced-choice items which sought to get at appropriateness of occupational level and interest in jobs involving personal relationships. The details of these devices have been described elsewhere (1). Previous investigations have indicated that these devices have some, though modest, validity for various aspects of the job of taxicab drivers (2, 3, 4).

In the present investigation the criterion of job proficiency consisted of production during the first 12 weeks of employment. Raw production figures were corrected for temporal variation and differences in division in which the driver operated. Records were obtained on 193 men who were randomly divided into two groups, 100 comprising an experimental group, and 93 a cross-validation group.

RESULTS

The validity coefficients of the three predictors together with their intercorrelations for the experimental group are given in Table 1. The validity of the tapping and dotting test at best can be characterized as limited. Neither of the two inventories has any appreciable value as a selective device. It is apparent that any combination of scores on the test and either of the inventories, as through multiple correlation, would have no greater validity than that of the test alone.

For each individual in the experimental group the difference between his standard score on the tapping and dot-

Table 1

VALIDITY COEFFICIENTS OF AND INTERCORRELATIONS AMONG PREDICTOR VARIABLES FOR THE EXPERIMENTAL GROUP

Variables	Tapping and Dotting	Occupational Level Inventory	Personal Relationships Inventory
Criterion	.259	.055	.125
Difference Score		.318	.126
Tapping and Dotting		.029	.283

ting test and his standard criterion score was computed. Differences in sign were ignored; hence an individual with a low difference score was one whose standard test and criterion scores were very similar, and an individual with a large difference score was one whose standard test and criterion scores were very different. The coefficients of correlation between these difference scores and scores on the two inventories are given in Table 1. The coefficient of correlation was found to be of moderate size for the occupational level scale and low for the personal relationships scale. Therefore there was a tendency for those individuals who made a low score on the occupational level inventory to display a correspondence between standard test and criterion scores, and for those individuals who made a high score to show a discrepancy between test and criterion scores. There was little such tendency in the case of the personal relationship inventory.

From the foregoing it would appear that if only those individuals who made low scores on the occupational level inventory were used, the coefficient of correlation between scores on the tapping and dotting test and the criterion would be greater than the value of .259 obtained for the entire group. However, no such tendency should result from a similar selection on the basis of the personal relationship inventory.

To examine this notion, the validity coefficients for the tapping and dotting test were calculated for the cross-validation group using three degrees of selectivity on the basis of the two inventories. The validity of the test scores was calculated for the one-third and two-thirds earning the lowest scores on the two inventories. The first of these groups should be composed of the one-third of the individuals whose performance is quite predictable with the least predictable two-thirds discarded. The second group should be composed of the individuals whose performance is fairly well predictable with the least predictable one-third discarded.

For the one-third of the individuals in the cross validation whose scores on the occupational level inventory indicated their job performance should be quite predictable from the tapping and dotting test the validity coefficient was found to be .664, whereas the validity coefficient for the most predictable two-thirds of the individuals was .323, and that for all cases only .220. On the other hand, for the one-third of the individuals whose scores on the personal relationships inventory indicated their job performance should be most predictable, the validity of the test was .000, for the most predictable two-thirds it was only .130, and for all cases it was .100.

In a practical selection situation, such as the present one with taxicab drivers, a first elimination of applicants can be made by dropping out those individuals for whom prediction of job success by means of the selection test is likely to be poor. Then a second elimination can be made on the basis of the selection test, picking those individuals whose scores are high. Thus in the present case those candidates scoring high on the occupational level inventory could be first eliminated. This process would leave those whose performance is substantially related to scores on the tapping and dotting test. Then those scoring low in this test could be eliminated resulting in the retention of a group whose average criterion performance is high. If the personal relationship inventory were used, no such benefits should accrue.

The question then is raised as to what proportion of candidates should be dropped out by the first screening and what proportion by the second screening. For example, if it is desired to obtain from a group of individuals 20 percent whose criterion performance will be significantly better than average, should 40 percent be dropped in the first screening and 40 percent in the second screening or should 20 percent be dropped in the first screening and 60 percent in the second screening? No definitive answer to this question can be offered at the present time. Undoubtedly the optimal percentages to be eliminated in the two screenings will be a function of the magnitude of the correlations between the tests, the criterion, and the difference scores.

On purely rational grounds it would appear that the optimal percentages eliminated in the two screenings would be nearly the same. If a very high proportion is eliminated in the first screening, while to be sure the prediction of success of the remainder will be good, there will be so few individuals left to eliminate in the second screening that there will be very little improvement in criterion scores. On the other hand, if very few are eliminated in the initial screening, then the validity of the selection test for the second screening will be so low that even with a high proportion eliminated the gain will be small.

To illustrate the problem an example using the cross-validation group is presented in Figure 1. The objective of the selection process is taken as the selection of the best 20 percent of candidates. Then various distributions of elimination between the two screenings can be made of the remaining 80 percent. At one extreme none can be elim-

inated in the first screening and the entire 80 percent can be eliminated on the basis of the second screening. At the other extreme 80 percent could be eliminated on the basis of the first screening and none in the second screening. The mean of the standard criterion scores of the "best" 20 percent of individuals selected by various distributions of percentages of elimination at the two stages were calculated. The mean criterion scores of the individuals remaining after elimination are shown in Figure 1.

Reference to Figure 1 will show that using the occupational level inventory as the basis for the first elimination, when the very large proportion of individuals is eliminated either in the first screening or in the second screening, the final results are poorest. A more equitable division of elimination between first screening and second screening is superior. Best results were obtained when a somewhat larger proportion was eliminated in the first than in the second screening. The personal relationship inventory, which has little or no value in selecting predictable individuals, does nothing to improve the selection of high performers on the criterion.

DISCUSSION

The results of this study point to the possibility of distinguishing applicants whose job performance can be predicted by ordinary selective procedures from those whose performance is poorly predicted. Selective procedures, therefore, can be improved not only by the addition of highly valid predictors to present procedures, but also by the addition of devices to screen out individuals whose levels of aptitude and job proficiency show little correspondence.

The investigation reported here is not sufficiently extensive to furnish many clues concerning the kinds of variables that will be useful in this type of screening. It seems likely that such variables

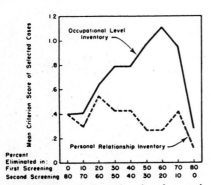

FIG. 1. Mean criterion scores of workers surviving the selection process under various conditions of selection.

will have a considerable degree of specificity for each particular selection situation. However, the results obtained with the occupational level inventory do suggest one interesting possibility. Each item in the inventory called for a choice to be made between two jobs in terms of their interest to the testee. The two jobs were similar in nature but one was at a lower and the other at a higher level, e.g., bookkeeping and accounting. Since the job of taxicab driver is only at the semi-skilled level, presumably it would not provide sufficient challenge for a person with higher occupational ambitions. Therefore low scores on the inventory were taken as the most appropriate.

As was seen, scores on the occupational inventory were unrelated to proficiency, yet they did distinguish those individuals whose aptitude and achievement levels were similar from those whose levels were different. If the inventory does measure occupational goals, then it would appear that inclu-

sion both of individuals whose goals are appropriate and individuals whose goals are inappropriate in a validation study masks the predictive power of the aptitude measure being evaluated.

NOTES

1. Brown, C. W., & Ghiselli, E. E. Age of semi-skilled workers in relation to abilities and interests. *Personnel Psychol.*, 1949, **2**, 497-511.
2. Brown, C. W., & Ghiselli, E. E. Prediction of labor turnover by aptitude tests. *J. Appl. Psychol.*, 1953, **37**, 9-12.
3. Brown, C. W., & Ghiselli, E. E. The prediction of proficiency of taxicab drivers. *J. Appl. Psychol.*, 1953, **37**, 437-439.
4. Ghiselli, E. E., & Brown, C. W. The prediction of accidents in taxicab drivers. *J. Appl. Psychol.*, 1949, **33**, 540-546.
5. Ghiselli, E. E. Worker selection: concepts and problems. *Personnel Psychol.*, 1956, **9**, 1-16.

12. Employment Tests and Discriminatory Hiring*

ROBERT M. GUION

The celebrated *Myart v. Motorola* case focused attention dramatically on the possibility that employment tests might be used, deliberately or inadvertently, as instruments of racial discrimination.[1] Paradoxically, the evidence of the case suggests that the test score apparently played only an obscure role in influencing the employment decision.

Nevertheless, many testers jumped to an immediate and often irrational de-

fense of testing, and many critics of testing began to regard the employment test as the clever subterfuge of confirmed racists. Both reactions are unfortunate, and it is to be hoped that they will be superseded by a more realistic and moderate view. A less emotional appraisal of the current state of the art should bring forth certain admissions from both camps. Testers must admit that most companies using psychological tests in their employment proce-

*Source: From *Industrial Relations* (February 1966), Vol. 5, pp. 20-37. Copyright © 1966 *Industrial Relations*. Reprinted by permission.

dures do not use them competently; more often than not tests are used with no knowledge at all of their validities for a particular situation. Conversely, critics must admit that other employment procedures are also typically misused and accepted on faith.

These remarks are devoted to test technology to the virtual exclusion of other employment procedures—with, I think, sufficient reason. Any procedure which can be used to discover, disprove, or verify claims of unfair discrimination through testing can also be applied to such other employment tools as interviewers' judgments, reference statements, or work histories. And let me clearly assert at the outset that despite many pitfalls, both obvious and hidden, competent psychological testing is better than any other hiring practice currently available. Such employment tools are designed to reduce the frequency of wrong decisions—hiring applicants who cannot do the job or rejecting those who could have done it well. Where tests have been used competently, they have been far more successful in reducing the number of mistakes than have, for example, such venerated practices as employment interviews.

The task of the tester is not to argue, but to develop procedures for reducing the mistakes still further. Now that our attention has been directed to the problem, it seems likely that many employment decision errors attributable to tests have resulted in unfair discrimination. There is no virtue in arguing whether this is so; investigation, not argument, is necessary for the task of minimizing such errors. The word is minimizing, not *eliminating;* it is unreasonable and unrealistic to expect perfection.

It should also be clearly understood at the outset that the target of this article is *inadvertent* discrimination. As Ash has pointed out, any competent psychologist who wishes to do so can easily develop a selection process that will discriminate in illegal ways.[2] The dedicated discriminator, like an assassin, will find a way, and it may be through testing. However, we can leave it to judical process to deal with blatant, deliberate discrimination. Our first concern must be with the fact that it is so easy to stumble into illegal discrimination inadvertently. It is when there is uncertainty—when one honestly does not know whether a test is an instrument of illegal discrimination—that tester and adjudicator alike need guides to follow.

SOME PRINCIPLES OF EMPLOYMENT TESTING

Illegal discrimination is largely an ethical matter, but it should be recognized that the fulfillment of ethical responsibility begins with technical competence; it is not enough to "mean well."

Competence begins when one clarifies the variables in a given employment situation. Some variables—traits, ratings, test scores—are used in making employment decisions; these are called predictors. Others—performance, job satisfaction, survival on the job—may be used in evaluating the outcome of such decisions; these are called criteria.

Before any predictor variable is used as a basis for making decisions about actual people who apply for jobs, it should be evaluated against appropriate criteria by some sort of systematic research; the evaluation is known as validation.

Validation cannot be carried out unless both kinds of variables are specified. For example, the predictor to be validated may be a test or an interviewer's rating system. The appropriate outcome (criterion) may be long-range competence, or it may be supervisory ratings after three weeks on the job. Whatever the variables, the validation study ends with a translation of the predictor (e.g., test scores) into expectancies, *i.e.*, statements of the probabilities of given criterion levels.[3]

A hypothetical example is given in Table 1. Let it be assumed here that the criterion—some measure of job success—yields an expectancy that about one-fourth of the people hired will be clearly superior, about half will do satisfactory work without being outstanding, and another fourth will be unsatisfactory. Then, if we know nothing about a person except that he has been hired according to "existing procedures," we can say that he has a 25 percent chance to be superior, a 50 percent chance to be satisfactory, and a 25 percent chance to be unsatisfactory.

Now if the test in Table 1 is added to the "existing employment procedure" and we know an individual's test score, the expectancies are different; they depend on the range within which his score lies. If he scores in the highest quarter of the test distribution, we say that he has a 50 percent rather than a 25 percent chance of being superior; if he scores in the lowest quarter he has only a 4 percent chance of being superior.

Expectancies, of course, do not apply literally to individuals; they apply to groups. Even so, two things seem immediately obvious about the use of a test with such a level of validity; (1) systematic use of the test in employment decision-making will result in an increase in the level of performance within the work force, and (2) the number of selection errors—the hiring of people who cannot work satisfactorily or the rejecting of those who can—will be reduced.

Validation should not be just a matter of setting up expectancies from whatever data are conveniently at hand. Validation research requires systematic data collection and analysis according to several principles, some of which seem especially relevant to concern over potentially unfair discrimination.

1. *Tests must be validated as predictors.* This is the heart of competence in employment testing. Prediction is not to be confused with description. One applicant may be tall, thin, and dark-haired; another, short, fat, and blonde. Since these are easy descriptions, it may be assumed that they are valid as *descriptions*—but this does not make then valid as *predictors*. The descriptions are useful for predictive purposes only if height, obesity, and hair color show some relationship, singly or in combination, to identified outcomes and goals.

2. *Validities must be recognized as situation-bound.* One cannot assure, without further research, that the results of a validity study done in one setting would be found in another apparently similar setting. Competence calls for situational validities, and there are no substitutes. The requirement of situational validation is simply a recognition

Table 1

HYPOTHETICAL EXPECTANCIES OF JOB SUCCESS LEVELS FOR FOUR RANGES OF A TEST SCORE DISTRIBUTION

Score range	Chances in 100 of attaining designated level of success		
	Unsatisfactory	Satisfactory	Superior
Highest quarter	8	42	50
Second quarter	14	56	30
Third quarter	24	60	16
Lowest quarter	54	42	4
Total distribution	25	50	25

that the obtained evidence of validity is dependent on a wide variety of factors, many of which are probably unknown. Different validities can be expected in different populations, however; it follows that any new source of applicants demands that new validation data be obtained. Suppose, for example, that a company has been drawing applicants principally from an urban environment and begins to recruit among farm people. There is no assurance that the tests with high predictive validity in the urban group would have the same predictive validity, or any validity, for rural applicants.

3. *Validities of a predictor should be investigated.* A test may be highly valid for predicting quantity of output and have no validity for all for predicting quality. Worse, a test may do beautifully in predicting production level, with high scores indicating high levels of production, and also do beautifully in predicting turnover, with high scores also identifying those who will probably not stay on the job very long. Competent validation does not stop with a single correlation between test scores and a single criterion; it studies the relationship of test scores to all important outcomes.

4. *Even a valid test should not be the sole basis for decision.* No test, whatever the criterion, is perfectly valid. The lack of even theoretically perfect validity, along with the actual unreliability of both predictor and criteria, cast considerable doubt on the utility and wisdom of a single, rigidly established cutting score. Too often a cutting score is treated as if it were a magical number. Those achieving the score or exceeding it are the "good guys" and all others, even those barely below the score, are the "bad guys." The competent test specialist recognizes the standard error of measurement and worries about it. Because he worries, he looks for additional information about people, especially those who score somewhere near the critical score.

All of these general considerations of technical competence in testing relate to the specific question of unfair discrimination. It may be an interesting intellectual exercise to demonstrate that an applicant's general mental ability can be described—without contamination by cultural background—by a certain "culture-free" test, but such an exercise is not by itself of much practical value. The important question is whether the scores on the test have any utility for predicting subsequent outcomes. The answer to the question must be derived from data collected within the situation itself, because there are no scientifically generalized answers available. If special recruiting efforts bring in applicants from different populations, or if new problems call for predicting different kinds of outcomes, then validation requires research with each of the various populations and each of the various criteria. Finally, at the moment of decision on an individual applicant, the competent specialist looks to the applicant's background and any other relevant information for guidance in interpreting the score: the score of a Negro high school dropout from a slum area may have somewhat different meaning from the same score obtained by the white, "respectably" educated son of the town's leading citizen—even if, for statistical purposes, both have been treated as coming from the same population.

UNFAIR DISCRIMINATION: NATURE OF THE PROBLEM

The employment plight of the Negro—"last hired, first fired"—is well-documented. During the last half century there have been advances in Negro employment opportunities without corresponding increases in relative incomes; in fact, the gap between Negro and white income seems to have widened during the fifties.[4]

This is not, by itself, direct evidence of discrimination. The fact is that Negro applicants are often less qualified than their white counterparts. The 1963 Report on Civil Rights listed such reasons for Negro unemployment as "inadequate education, inferior job training, discrimination by private employers, and discrimination in the state and local administration of federal programs."[5] A survey conducted under the auspices of Industrial Relations Counselors identified four areas in which Negro applicants generally seemed to be deficient: scores on achievement and aptitude tests, attentiveness to grooming and general attitudes during selection interviews, educational background, and work experience.[6] It has been observed that few Negroes are employed at higher organizational levels. Once again, this is partly due to the scarcity of Negro personnel qualified for managerial and executive work. However, the shortage can be attributed to the fact that capable Negroes have rarely seen much point in preparing themselves for executive positions; as Whitlow has put it, "The teaching professions grew in interest to the Negro because of the fact that there were no alternatives. We either went into teaching or nothing."[7] Now that many companies are actively, and many quite sincerely, seeking Negro managerial personnel, they must reckon with the consequences of the dry years which preceded the present situation in which it is a distinct advantage to be an intelligent Negro interested in professional management.[8]

That there is a vicious cycle is evident, and some employers are supporting or sponsoring programs to compensate for deficiencies in early experience. This is commendable, but neither law nor sound business practice demands it. However, both law and good sense demand that employers cease practices of unfair discrimination, including those that are inadvertent, which lead to unemployment. Perhaps the best way to break the cycle is to be sure that qualified Negroes get jobs they are qualified for.

Employment practice is by nature discriminatory, and it must be so. An employer cannot be expected to take on all applicants regardless of their qualifications; he is expected to be able to distinguish between those who are qualified and those who are not. The test of Table 1 is discriminatory; it discriminates between those with high and those with low probability of success. For a different illustration, women characteristically score lower than men on tests of mechanical aptitudes. Where such tests are used in making employment decisions, the effect is that women are less likely to be hired than men. The effect of the mechanical aptitude test is therefore discriminatory, but it can hardly be said to be discriminating against women unfairly unless low scoring women can actually perform the job as well as higher scoring men.[9]

In talking about discrimination, then, a clear distinction must be made between discrimination which is necessary and right and discrimination which is unfair. *Unfair discrimination exists when persons with equal probabilities of success on the job have unequal probabilities of being hired for the job.*

CIVIL RIGHTS ACT OF 1964: TITLE VII

It is against the law to discriminate on the basis of race, color, religion, national origin, or sex.[10] Despite some of the static from the Motorola incident, tests cannot be considered unlawful unless "intended *or used* to discriminate because of race, color, religion, sex, or national origin."[11] The phrase "or used" is especially interesting. When the courts interpret this phrase, a test will probably be considered unlawfully discriminating in any situation in which the *effect* is unlawful discrimination. The basic question is what constitutes an unlawful discriminatory effect. I propose that a reasonable interpretation of the law will hold a test to be illegally discriminatory only when a specified group exhibits inferior performance on the test, but *not* on the job for which the test is a predictor. Conversely, a test is not unlawfully discriminatory when a group characteristic that depresses test scores also tends to depress job performance.

Much is heard about the effect of cultural deprivation on test performance, but less is heard about the effect of cultural deprivation on job performance. As Ash has pointed out, "neither the Illinois Fair Employment Practices Act nor any other similar act protects 'culturally deprived persons' as such from discrimination employment."[12] He went on to say that it is likely that complaining applicants, their attorneys, and the courts will become sophisticated enough to distinguish between standards of *test* performance and standards of *job* performance.

The principal implication of Title VII, then, seems clear enough: test specialists had better be able to make the same distinction! People using employment tests had better gather data to demonstrate that their tests are valid as predictors of relevant aspects of job behavior for all classes of applicants. And if these tests are found to be invalid, they ought not to be used.

SMOKE SCREENS

The basic issue of validity has been obscured by a vast smoke screen of irrelevancies. The solution to the problem of eliminating unfair discrimination through testing is obscured by these smoke screens, some of which are identified and commented on below.

1. *Debate over the reality of racial differences.* Even if it could be unambiguously demonstrated that one racial group is inherently inferior to another, the problem of unfair discrimination would persist. The overlap in any set of distributions showing ethnic differences is such that many people in the "inferior" group score higher than the average member of the "superior" group.

2. *Debate over whether race or cultural deprivation is the villain.* Many whites are culturally deprived; many nonwhites are not. It is not sensible to jump to the conclusion that cultural deprivation is the source of unfair discrimination. Such a jump is scientifically unjustified. Since racial identification is one variable and deprivation is a different one, both deserve study. The linking of the two is also legally of questionable use: the mere demonstration that a test does not discriminate unfairly against the culturally deprived may not be deemed competent evidence in court that it does not discriminate against racial groups.

3. *Debate over moral values.* The word "unfair" admittedly implies a moral judgment. However, if one can accept the definition of "unfair discrimination" offered here and can agree that the aim is to discover whether a test is or is not acting as an instrument of unfair discrimination within that definition, then the whole thing becomes more a technical than a moral matter, regardless of whether one's motive is to stay clear of the law, to redress earlier wrongs done by one segment of society to another, or to achieve a more complete utilization of society's manpower resources.

4. *Questions about why nonwhites are underemployed or unemployed more often than whites.* Answers are needed; the questions are important. Too often, however, the answers offered are unsubstantiated opinions serving as excuses for denying the problem of unfair discrimination.

5. *Concern over the social consequences of integration in employment.* Even where the concern is genuine, it does not solve the problems. Moreover, the predicted dire consequences seem never to materialize in organizations actually providing equal opportunities.

RESEARCH ON DISCRIMINATION

Thorough, competent validation is not especially easy. Research which combines the ordinary task of validation with the less charted task of research on discrimination accents ordinary problems and finds some new ones.

Perhaps the most serious problem is the almost universal willingness to use unvalidated tests. An utterly disgusting phrase is all too common: "We feel that our tests are very good." Such feelings may be comforting, but they serve neither as evidence nor as a substitute for knowing what one is doing. Even many companies that routinely validate their tests shy away from any kind of research dealing with racial discrimination; it is a potato that is much too hot. Whether because of fear or inertia, testers seem to be hoping that they will never be called for evidence that their tests are nondiscriminatory, rather than doing something to seek evidence one way or the other.

The criterion problem is stickier in research on discrimination than in ordinary validation. Most personnel research relies on ratings; the ratings of a potentially prejudiced supervisor can hardly be used in research on discrimination. Fortunately, some special criterion variables have been provided by folklore and some of them are not too difficult to measure. In the selection of salesmen or other public-contact personnel, for example, customer reaction may well be one criterion. Here ratings of customers seem justified, although observations of customer behavior would be better. Or it may be said that minority group applicants are more likely to quit their jobs; turnover is an appropriate criterion measure, as are other personal variables: absenteeism, lateness, health and accident data, and so on. In general, however, one should develop objective measures of the same criterion variables that would be used in any other validation research. Other considerations aside, the current emphasis on equal opportunity in employment will have immeasurable value because it will cause organizations to consider carefully the outcomes they seek through all of their employment practices.

Another problem is that there are differences in test performances of different ethnic groups. Although this fact should not be used as a smoke screen to obscure the matter of predictive validation, it does pose special problems—principally because of the lack of scientific understanding of the basis of such differences. Group differences are often attributed to cultural deprivation. This is probably due to contemporary concern with Negro applicants who, a century after the Emancipation Proclamation, still carry with them the vestigial remains of slavery. Test differences are also found, however, for Jewish, Oriental, and certain national groups. Some of these groups may be culturally favored in some respects; others may have their own rich, though different, sorts of cultures. Can these differences be attributed to "cultural deprivation"?

Too much has been said about cultural *deprivation,* not enough about cultural *difference.* Certainly the ghetto and its attendent lack of communication with the outside—even when schools are integrated—fossilizes cultural differences. Some of the population differences may be due to suspiciousness; what has passed for cultural deprivation may be better described as cultural alienation. While the choice of term—deprivation, difference, or alienation—becomes relatively unimportant for the search for evidence of predictive validity, the question of cause poses genuine, long-range research problems.

For one thing, the nature of the differences in test performance needs to be better established. One should be rather cautious, for example, about such statements as "on the average, Negroes score lower than whites." The fact that this has generally been true may be more a reflection of test specialists' lack of imagination than of any underlying reality. It has been noted for several years that research on individual differences has been done with a rather archaic notion of the nature of intelligence. Dreger and Miller cite a study showing (among four ethnic groups each divided into low- and middle-class subgroups) differential patterns of scores on factorial test batteries.[13] The direction of differences between groups may prove to be much less important in future research than the kinds or patterns of differences that exist.

A further research problem is that of recruiting. In many organizations, there will be no opportunity to do any research at all unless there is a special effort to recruit from minority groups. For example, it has been shown that there is often a discrepancy between the attitudes of top management toward hiring Jewish college graduates and the actual practice of campus recruiters.[14] Clearly, managements must take unusual steps if they are to convince their recruiters that they are sincere in an equal opportunity program.

If a manager is embarking on a new push to hire Negroes, he must advertise in Negro periodicals, he must make direct contact with local Negro organizations, and he should have personal contact with leaders of the Negro community. These are extraordinary recruiting procedures: the result is an extraordinary applicant population. If there are

differences in validity, should these differences be attributed to racial differences or to differences in the recruiting procedures?

Despite the many problems and questions, the research must be done if an organization is to know whether it is guilty of unfair discrimination in its employment tests. There are several research models which can be used.

THE USE OF MODERATOR VARIABLES

A moderator variable may markedly influence validity. Most moderator variables have been used to describe or define differences between two or more groups which may have different patterns of validity. In a pioneer study, for example, Frederiksen and Melville[15] classified college students as either compulsive or noncompulsive and found interest test scores significantly more valid for the noncompulsive group. Compulsiveness in this example is a moderator variable; it "moderates" the effect of interest on academic performance.

Elsewhere, I have advocated investigating race as a moderator variable and suggested that different expectancy tables be developed for Negro and white applicants.[16] Table 2 offers, in schematic form, the kinds of results that might be found if expectancies were distinctly different for the two groups. It is

Table 2

RELATIONSHIP OF TWO HYPOTHETICAL DISTRIBUTIONS TO SPECIFIED EXPECTANCIES OF JOB SUCCESS WHERE STANDARDS MAY BE DEFINED ONLY BY EXPECTANCIES

| | Minimum test score for each expectancy | |
Expectancy	White distribution	Negro distribution
80	100	78
70	85	60
60	70	45
50	55	32
40	40	22
30	25	15
20	10	10

designed to illustrate several possible research results and inferences: (1) that scores of the Negro sample may actually be systematically lower than those of the white sample, (2) that the kinds of relationships may be different for the two groups (linear for whites and non-linear for Negroes), (3) that interpretations of very low scores may be the same for the two groups, while the interpretation of scores at another range may need to be different, and (4) that hiring standards can be expressed in terms of probabilities of success rather than in terms of test scores. Where distinctly different validities are found, hiring standards expressed as minimum test scores constitute unfair discrimination.

Table 3 offers a slightly different set of plausible results; it is like Table 2 only in that it assumes that scores in the Negro sample may actually be systematically lower than scores in the white sample. However, the kinds of relationships are the same and the interpretations of individual scores are the same. Where the validities are this similar, there is no evidence of unfair discrimination, even if hiring standards are expressed in terms of test scores.

These two different kinds of results have important implications for employment practice. If one wishes to hire only those applicants whose expectancy of success is of the order of 50 percent, the situation in Table 2 calls for different cutting scores for the two groups (55 for whites and 32 for Negroes), whereas the situation depicted in Table 3 calls for the same cutting score (60) in each group.

Other moderator variables could be substituted for race—with, of course, the proviso that they can be shown to be relevant to the legal issues as well as to scientific investigation. Measures of cultural deprivation should certainly be investigated; Lockwood has proposed the use of personal history or motivational variables as potential moderators.[17] Ignoring the pressure of the legal issues for the moment, it seems likely that some of these might ultimately serve better than race as moderators.

There are several objections to, or potential restrictions on, the moderator variable approach. If race is to be the moderator, one stumbles immediately over the scientific difficulty of establishing clear yardsticks by which people can be classified into convenient racial categories. Returning to the legal pressures, however, and to the social problems which precipitated them, such yardsticks do not seem to be a really serious problem for the test specialist.

Table 3

TEST SCORE INTERPRETATIONS FOR TWO HYPOTHETICAL DISTRIBUTIONS

Test score	Percentile rank		Expectancy	
	White	Negro	White	Negro
100	99	—	95	—
90	80	99	83	85
80	65	90	76	75
70	55	72	65	63
60	50	60	50	50
50	45	52	41	42
40	35	48	37	36
30	20	40	27	28
20	1	28	19	20

He can classify as Negro anyone whom an employment interviewer so identifies; and he can do the same in classifying others as whites. Discrimination is not such a big problem to those Negroes who can be identified as such only by their own statements, genetic histories, or anthropological measurements!

A more general limitation to the moderator variable approach has been identified by Campbell. He distinguishes between indirect validity, where the trait measured is related to job success but not essential to it, and intrinsic validity, where any factor changing test performance (such as training) also changes job performance. He points out that the value of moderator variables is probably limited to situations of indirect validity.[18] Parenthetically, it might be noted that most employment tests fit this category—a fact of which employment testers are not very proud.

A practical objection is that the moderator variable approach intensifies two ordinary and difficult validation problems. The first of these is the frequent inability to identify the criterion variables; the second is the more prosaic problem of finding enough cases. It is not easy to find situations in which both Negroes and whites are being hired to do the same type of work at a rapid enough rate to gather the kind of data that one would desire. In one organization which attempted research on discrimination in employment testing, the design called for at least 60 Negro applicants. In a full year they were unable to find that many, despite systematic recruiting efforts—and their research, not involving validation, utilized all applicants whether hired or not.

A social or ethical objection sometimes offered is that the moderator variable approach establishes different standards for applicants of different ethnic groups. This objection does not deserve to be taken seriously, since it betrays a confused refusal or inability to make the necessary distinction between standards of test performance and standards of job performance.

USE OF CULTURE-FREE TESTS

Some investigators, assuming that unfair discrimination has cultural deprivation as its roots, are looking for ways to utilize the so-called culture-free tests. The use of such a test by itself does not seem to be very promising; however, culture-free tests might be used as something other than straightforward predictors. For example, such tests might be used where scores are marginal on ordinarily valid tests. The procedure would be to identify, probably in standard error terms, the range of scores around a cutting score in which additional information should be sought. That information would include the score on a culture-free test. The original test and the culture-free test, expressed in standard score units, would be compared. The degree of discrepancy between the two could be a measure of cultural deprivation; such a measure could be a moderator or it could by itself, prove to be a valid predictor. Since these tests are typically measures of intelligence, their use seems especially worth considering where the criterion is trainability.

Krug has suggested two other classes of predictors, not intended to measure mental ability, which he considers to be relatively culture-free.[19] One of these is biographical information—a category more commonly thought to be especially biased. His argument is that the biographical inventory usually seeks indication of achievement or achievement motivation, of leadership experience, of breadth of interest, or of self-sufficiency. Items that reflect these variables, he says, have cultural equivalents. That is, whether one went to a Negro school, a white school, or an integrated school, questions about class offices held or subject matter clubs joined are essentially unbiased. The biographical inventory items that Krug is looking for, then, are those in which there is a "relative standard imbedded in the item"—*i.e.*, the response is relative to the culture from which the applicant has come. Although the idea seems worthy of investigation, I would personally have serious reservations about the validity of the assumption of the unbiased relative standard.

Krug's second suggestion is the use of situation tests, which, he asserts, have high promise of validity, partly because of their realism and partly because of their novelty.[20] This is a depressing point of view; it suggests that any effort in employment testing is probably self-defeating. The argument is that ordinary paper-and-pencil tests are easier for the white applicant than for the culturally deprived Negro because the white applicant has encountered them quite frequently in the past; they are in no sense an unusual experience for him, whereas the situational test is novel to both. Unanswered is the question of what happens to situational tests, however, when they become commonplace enough so that they are no longer novel.

COMPENSATORY MODELS

Traditional prediction through multiple regression has been essential compensatory; a deficiency in one characteristic can be overcome in the equation by an overbundance of some other characteristics. The compensatory model has worked in a wide variety of situations; it might well be the most useful solution to the problem of unfair racial discrimination in testing. Essentially, what is needed is an indentification of the variables through which an individual can overcome an initial handicap that he may have, from whatever cause.

Traditional multiple regression can also be combined with the moderator variable idea for a different sort of compensation. That is, a variable might be identified that is relevant to one group and not to another; it might, where it is relevant, compensate for

"underqualification." For example, commitment to the civil rights movement might, for a Negro youth, be the sort of motivational variable that could be called "the Avis syndrome"—being number two, he tries harder! Perhaps the discrepancy between an applicant's level of aspiration and the father's occupational level could be measured and used in multiple prediction equations for one or both groups.

COACHING

Although the idea of coaching people on tests is usually repugnant to test specialists, there have been some indications that it might be useful. Hay once developed a "warm-up" test that served somewhat as a coaching device.[21] In an unpublished study, this writer once improved the validity of a psychomotor test by providing enough preliminary practice trials so that learning tended to level off by the time a trial was officially "scored." Perhaps more to the point, it has been shown in Israel (where there are wide individual differences in exposure to test and test-like situations) that straightforward coaching increases the validity of intelligence tests.[22]

DEVELOPMENTAL MODELS

Personnel research is typically concerned with static measurement. In effect, the researcher takes two snapshots, one of the individual as an applicant and another when this performance is evaluated. Perhaps it would be better to take movies: look at patterns of change, identify processes of change, and measure the magnitudes of changes that have occurred. With such an approach, perhaps an applicant's future growth could be predicted from the kinds of choices he had made earlier in certain sorts of inevitable situations, or from persistent reactions to identifiable challenge situations. This concept is vague, but it seems worth some thought.

A slightly different developmental approach integrates selection with training. Here the argument is that full utilization of Negro manpower resources cannot be achieved without establishing extraordinary training programs to compensate for the effects of a history of discrimination. The selection problem is to identify those who will profit most from such training. There are two prediction problems: (1) to identify variables in the training situation (grades, rate of learning, etc.) that are valid predictors of later performance, and (2) to find employment tests that are valid predictors of these variables in training.

THE OUTLOOK IN RESEARCH

There is no evidence now available to indicate which models will be most useful for finding and eliminating unfair discrimination in testing; nor will such evidence become available until more equal-opportunity employers conduct the necessary research and publish the results. It is easy to be pessimistic and wonder whether the research will get done. If it is done, however, one can say quite optimistically that one by-product will be a general improvement in the state of test technology. At the very least, such research should result in a technically defensible individualization of employment testing in contrast to the more conventional group orientation. Furthermore, it is reasonable to hope that such research will move toward the identification of predictors with intrinsic validities.

POSTSCRIPT

The point of view of this article may be identified by its omissions as well as by the topics discussed. For example, the concept of clinical prediction, as distinguished from statistical prediction, was given no place in the discussion of competence.

There are two reasons. First, clinical prediction is most necessary in hiring for positions where statistical validation is impossible because of the small numbers of people hired, e.g., executives. While discrimination is indeed a problem at these levels, the more pressing problem is probably at levels requiring less in the way of personal and background qualifications. The income gap between white and Negro, for example, is unlikely to be closed by intensive efforts to recruit executives from the centers of cultural deprivation; it is more likely to be closed first in the blue-collar and office occupations where "underemployment" is a numerically greater problem and where the necessary skills can soon be learned. At these levels, statistical prediction is possible, preferable, and essential.

In the second place, statistical prediction provides actual data—data which can be unambiguously presented to fair employment commissions or to courts as the legal issues relating to testing are examined. In contrast, clinical prediction depends on "expert judgment"—a less demonstrable quality.

Another important omission from this article is the lack of serious mention of discrimination against women, Jews, the Irish, American Indians, Spanish-Americans, Unitarians, and Seventh Day Adventists. Such discrimination can exist and is illegal whether deliberate or not. The models suggested for identifying it in testing apply to these groups as well as to Negroes. Moreover, such discrimination may well pose serious social problems; probably all—and more—that has been said about the plight of the Negro can be said about the plight of the American Indian.

The focus on employment opportunities of the Negro may be attributed, first of all, to the trend of the times. There is a special urgency about Negro employment. Contemporary civil rights movements are essentially Negro civil rights movements. The moral issues of discrimination against Negroes are known and vehemently debated, although both the moral decisions and the technical ones may be as applicable to other objects of unfair discrimination as to Negroes.

More than this, however, the focus on Negro employment may partly be due to a fear time is running out, if indeed it has not already done so.[23] The civil rights movement is more aptly described as a civil rights revolution; all segments of the American community may be thankful that it has been, in the main, a nonviolent revolution.

Industry, the source of jobs, tends to be concentrated in northern communities—communities that have observed but have not participated in the upheavals of sit-ins, freedom rides, and voter registrations. Despite the drama of sit-ins, however, the basic issue has never really been equality in eating or riding as much as equality of economic opportunity. That means jobs—jobs in the industrial North as well as in the South. Civil rights leadership in the South has been nonviolent. Will it also be nonviolent in the North?

I doubt it. Nonviolence has not been a tradition in many industrial communities, and one can already observe parallels between today's civil rights movement and the labor strife of the thirties.[24] If major, catastrophic upheaval is to be avoided, there must be a concerted, intelligent effort to eliminate pretense and defense of the status quo—to seek out and to develop job competence and employment stability among Negro citizens. This means that industrial leaders—as individuals or as corporations—must take the initiative in (1) removing any removable causes of the lack of qualified Negroes in responsible positions and (2) removing the obstacles society has placed between the qualified Negro and the job he can do. Specifically, industrial leaders must take the initiative in the elimination of hope-destroying ghettoes, in the development of better schools for all children, and in the creation of technical and apprenticeship training centers where none now exist. Not the least of the needs is for industrial leaders to take the lead in authorizing or sponsoring research on possible discriminatory employment practices and seeing that it gets done.

It seems unfortunate that much industrial leadership must wait for demonstrations, laws, or riots to stimulate it to do what it ought to have done long ago; it seems unfortunate that efforts to eliminate the evils of unfair discrimination may take on the coloration of self-protection rather than concern for the welfare of others in a common society. Regardless of the motives, however, appropriate actions must be taken. But first they must be identified, and this calls for programs—crash programs—of research.

It is also to be hoped that the effect of the Negro civil rights movement will be more general, and that the broader question of unfair discrimination against those groups specifically included in the Civil Rights Act of 1964—women and other racial or ethnic groups—and against groups not specifically named in the act (e.g., recent high school graduates, older workers, epileptics) can be approached more effectively.

NOTES

1. "Hiring tests wait for the score: Myart vs. Motorola," *Business Week*, February 13, 1965, pp. 45-46. Less easily obtainable, but much more detailed and complete is the account by Robert L. French, "The Motorola Case," *Industrial Psychologist* 2 (August, 1965): 20-50.

2. Philip Ash, "The Implications of the Civil Rights Act of 1964 for Psychological Assessment in Industry," presented in the symposium, *Legal Issues Which Confront the Psychologist and the Community*, at the convention of the American Psychological Association in Chicago, September 5, 1965.

3. Validation is commonly carried out in terms of statistical summary statements, such as correlations or significance levels. This is only half of the task; validation is incomplete if it does not also provide a means for predicting whatever criterion is used. Where validity is determined by correlations, pre-

diction can be based on regression equations; expectancy tables are, however, superior in several respects to prediction from such equations. This is, of course, a dogmatic assertion of the rightness of my own preferences. For the sake of both brevity and clarity, I have been equally dogmatic throughout the discussion of competence without bothering to justify my assertions. For a more complete presentation of my views, see my text, *Personnel Testing* (New York: McGraw-Hill, 1965). The arguments concerning expectancies may be found on pp. 148-157.

4. Daniel E. Diamond, "Occupational Shifts in Negro Employment," *Business Topics* 12 (Summer, 1965): 32-44.

5. *Civil Rights '63*, U.S. Commission on Civil Rights (Washington, D.C.: 1963), p. 90.

6. Paul H. Norgren, Albert N. Webster, Roger D. Borgeson, and Maud B. Patten, *Employing the Negro in American Industry: A Study of Management Practices*, Industrial Relations Monograph No. 17 (New York: Industrial Relations Counselors, 1959).

7. Edward W. Whitlow, "The Placement of Negro College Graduates in Business Organizations," in *Selecting and Training Negroes for Managerial Positions* (Princeton, N.J.: Educational Testing Service, 1964), pp. 41-50.

8. Robert Mallory, "On-the-Job Experiences of Negro Managers," *Ibid.*, pp. 131-134.

9. Sometimes a generalization stemming from research on tests becomes the basis for employment decisions, even if the research had nothing to do with an employment problem. In the present example, such a generalization might be the basis for a general policy that a woman cannot be hired, no matter how high her score, because women are in general inferior (in this regard!) to men. An analogous illustration might be a verbal test on which the mean score of nonwhites is lower than the mean of whites, with the resulting policy being the automatic rejection of all nonwhite applicants. In either case, the prejudicial discrimination is manifestly unfair, but the fault is not with the test or with the use of tests in general. This kind of policy is simply not followed where there is competent use of tests.

10. People who have not bothered to look at the provisions of the law have been making some rather unfunny jokes about female attendants in men's rooms or male "bunnies" in nightclubs or Nordic blondes

playing the parts of African tribal rulers—as if all of these absurdities were made necessary by adherence to the law. Special requirements of sex, religion, or national origin are clearly permitted in circumstances where they are explicitly relevant and necessary for a particular lawful enterprise.

11. Tower amendment to the 1964 Civil Rights Act, as quoted by Ash, *op. cit.,* italics mine.

12. Ash, *loc. cit.*

13. Ralph Mason Dreger and Kent S. Miller, *Recent Research in Psychological Comparisons of Negroes and Whites in the United States*, presented at the convention of the Southeastern Psychological Association in Atlanta, April 2, 1965.

14. Lewis B. Ward, "The Ethnics of Executive Selection," *Harvard Business Review* 43 (March-April, 1965): 6-8.

15. Norman Frederiksen and S. Donald Melville, "Differential Predictability in the Use of Test Scores," *Educational and Psychological Measurement* 14 (Winter, 1954): 647-656.

16. Guion, *op. cit.,* pp. 491-193. This is not an unusual suggestion; however, it is usually offered in terms of different regressions rather than different expectancies.

17. Howard C. Lockwood, "Testing Minority Applicants for Employment," *Personnel Journal* 44 (July-August, 1965): 356-360.

18. Joe. T. Campbell, "The Problem of Cultural Bias in Selection: I. Background and Literature," *Selecting and Training Negroes . . . , pp.* 57-64.

19. *Robert E. Krug, "The Problem of Cultural Bias in Selection: III. Possible Solutions to the Problem of Cultural Bias in Tests," Ibid.,* pp. 77-85.

20. A situation test is one in which a person is placed in some kind of problem situation and his performance in that situation is observed and scored. A characteristic feature of the test is that the subject either does not know he is being observed or is unaware of the nature of the observations. For example, the subject might be placed in a situation in which he is supposed to exercise leadership in getting a task completed; at the same time, one might create in the situation essential obstacles to the completion of the task. The subject would probably be aware that he is being observed, but would not be aware that the obstacles were deliberately introduced for the sake of observing his reactions to them.

21. Edward N. Hay, "A Warm-up Test," *Personnel Psychology* 3 (Summer, 1950): 221-223.

22. Gina R. Ortar, "Improving Test Validity by Coaching," *Educational Research* 2 (June, 1960): 137-142.

23. Consider the pessimism of Stewart Alsop who, following his trip to the scene of the Watts riot, said that America's racial problem may not have a solution; he compared it to a painful, incurable disease. "Watts: The Fire Next Time," *Saturday Evening Post* (November 6, 1965): 20.

24. Robert B. McKersie, "The Civil Rights Movement and Employment," *Industrial Relations* 3 (May, 1964): 1-21.

13. Signs, Samples, and Criteria*

PAUL F. WERNIMONT
JOHN P. CAMPBELL

Many writers (e.g., Dunnette, 1963; Ghiselli & Haire, 1960; Guion, 1965; Wallace, 1965) have expressed concern about the difficulties encountered in trying to predict job performance, and in establishing the validity of tests for this purpose. In general, their misgivings center around the low validities obtained and misapplications of the so-called "classic validity model." To help ameliorate these difficulties it is proposed here that the concept of validity be altered as it is now applied to predictive and concurrent situations and introduce the notion of "behavioral consistency." By consistency of behavior is meant little more than that familiar bit of conventional wisdom, "The best indicator of future performance is past performance." Surprisingly few data seem to exist to either support or refute this generalization. It deserves considerably more attention.

SOME HISTORY

It is perhaps not too difficult to trace the steps by which applied psychologists arrived at their present situation. During both World War I and World War II general intelligence and aptitude tests were effectively applied to military personnel problems. Largely as the result of these successes, the techniques developed in the armed services were transported to the industrial situation and applied to the personnel problems of the business organization. From a concentration on global measures of mental ability, validation efforts branched out to include measures of specific aptitudes, interests, and personality dimensions. The process is perhaps most clearly illustrated by the efforts of the United States Employment Service to validate the General Aptitude Test Battery across a wide range of jobs and occupations. In general, testing seemed to be a quick, economical, and easy way of obtaining useful information which removed the necessity for putting an individual on the job and observing his performance over a trial period.

It was in the context of the above efforts that an unfortunate marriage oc-

*Source: From *Journal of Applied Psychology*, vol. 52 no. 5, pp. 372-76. Copyright © 1968 by the American Psychological Association. Reprinted by permission.

curred, namely, the union of the classic validity model with the use of tests as signs, or indicators, of predispositions to behave in certain ways (Cronbach, 1960, p. 457), rather than as samples of the characteristic behavior of individuals. An all too frequent procedure was to feed as many signs as possible into the classic validity framework in hopes that the model itself would somehow uncover something useful. The argument here is that it will be much more fruitful to focus on meaningful samples of behavior, rather than signs of predispositions, as predictors of later performance.

THE CONSISTENCY MODEL

To further illustrate the point, consider a hypothetical prediction situation in which the following five measures are available:

1. Scores on a mental ability test;
2. School grade-point average (GPA);
3. Job-performance criterion at Time 1;
4. Job-performance criterion at Time 2;
5. Job-performance criterion at Time 3.

Obviously, a number of prediction opportunities are possible. Test scores could be correlated with GPA; school achievement could be correlated with first-year job success; or the test scores and GPA could be combined in some fashion and the composite used to predict first-, second-, or third-year job performance. All of these correlations would be labeled validity coefficients and all would conform to the classic validity model. It is less clear what label should be attached to the correlation between two different measures of job performance. Few would call it validity; many would probably refer to it as reliability. There seems to be a tendency among applied psychologists to withhold the term validity from correlations between measures of essentially the same behavior, even if they were obtained at two different points in time. That is, the subtleties of the concept of

reliability and the ingredients of the classic validity model seem to have ingrained the notion that validity is a correlation between a predictor and a criterion and the two should somehow be dissimilar.

However, each of the 10 correlations that one could compute from the above situation represents the degree of common variation between the two variables, given the appropriateness of the linear correlation model. After all, that is what correlation is all about. In this sense there is no logical reason for saying that some of the coefficients represent validity and others reliability, although there certainly may be in other contexts. An implicit or explicit insistence on the predictor being "different" seems self-defeating. Rather one should really be trying to obtain measures that are as similar to the criterion or criteria as possible. This notion appears to be at least implicit in much of the work on prediction with biographical data where many of the items represent an attempt to assess previous achievement on similar types of activities. Behavior sampling is also the basis on which simulation exercises are built for use in managerial assessment programs.

At this point it should be emphasized that for the consistency notion to be consistent, the measures to be predicted must also be measures of behavior. For example, it would be something less than consistent to use a behavior sample to predict such criteria as salary progression, organizational level achieved, or subunit production. The individual does not always have substantial control over such variables, and, even with the more obvious biasing influences accounted for, they place a ceiling on the maximum predictive efficiency to be expected. Furthermore, they are several steps removed from actual job behavior. In this respect, the authors are very much in accord with Dunnette (1966) who argues strongly for the measurement of observable job behavior in terms of its effect on meaningful dimensions of performance effectiveness. A recently developed method for accomplishing this aim is the behavior retranslation technique of Smith and Kendall (1964). The applied psychologist should reaffirm his mandate and return to the measurement of behavior. Only then will one learn by what means, and to what extent, an individual has influenced his rate of promotion, salary increases, or work group's production.

In general terms, what might the selection or prediction procedure look like if one tried to apply a consistency model? First, a comprehensive study of the job would be made. The results of this effort would be in the form of dimensions of job performance well defined by a broad range of specific behavior incidents which in turn have been scaled with respect to their "criticalness" for effective or ineffective performance.

Next, a thorough search of each applicant's previous work experience and educational history would be carried out to determine if any of the relevant behaviors or outcomes have been required of him or have been exhibited in the past. Items and rating methods would be developed to facilitate judging the frequency of such behaviors, the intensity with which they were manifested, the similarity of their context to the job situation, and the likelihood that they will show up again. These judgments can than be related to similar judgments concerning significant and consistent aspects of an individual's job behavior.

Such a procedure places considerable emphasis on background data and is similar in form to the "selection by objectives" concept of Odiorne and Miller (1966). However, the aim is to be considerably more systematic and to focus on job behavior and not summary "objectives."

After the analysis of background data it might be found that the required job behaviors have not been a part of the applicant's past repertoire and it would be necessary to look for the likelihood of that job behavior in a variety of work-sample tests or simulation exercises. A number of such behavior measures are already being used in various management assessment programs.

Finally, individual performance measures of psychological variables would be given wider use where appropriate. For example, the Wechsler Adult Intelligence Scale (Wechsler, 1955) might be used to assess certain cognitive functions. Notice that such a measure is a step closer to actual performance sampling than are the usual kinds of group intelligence tests.

How does the above procedure compare to conventional practice? The authors hope they are not beating at a straw man if the usual selection procedure is described as follows. First, a thorough job analysis is made to discover the types of skills and abilities necessary for effective performance. This is similar to the consistency approach except that the objective seems to be to jump very quickly to a generalized statement of skills and abilities rather than remaining on the behavioral level. The conventional approach next entails a search for possible predictors to try out against possible criteria. Based on knowledge of the personnel selection and individual differences literature, personal experience, and "best guesses," some decisions are made concerning what predictors to include in the initial battery. It is the authors' contention that the classic validity model has forced an undue amount of attention on test and inventory measures at this stage. Witness the large amount of space devoted to a discussion of "test validation" in most books dealing with the selection problem. Again, signs seem to take precedence over samples. Lastly, one or more criterion measures are chosen. Too often the choice seems to be made with little reference to the previous job analysis and is based on a consideration of "objectivity" and relevance to the "ultimate" criterion. Unfortunately, even a slight misuse of these considerations can lead to criteria which are poorly understood. In contrast, working within the framework of a consistency model requires consideration of dimensions of actual job behavior.

It might be added that the above characterization of the conventional approach is meant to be somewhat idealized. Certain departures from the ideal might reinforce the use of signs to an even greater extent. For example, there is always the clear and present danger that the skill requirements will be stated in terms of "traits" (e.g., loyalty, resourcefulness, initiative) and thus lead even more directly to criteria and predictors which are oriented toward underlying predispositions.

RELATIONSHIP TO OTHER ISSUES

The consistency notion has direct relevance for a number of research issues that appear frequently in the selection and prediction literature. One important implication is that selection research should focus on individuals to a much greater extent than it has. That is, there should be more emphasis on intraindividual consistency of behavior. In their insightful discussion of the criterion problem, Ghiselli and Haire (1960) point out that intraindividual criterion performance sometimes varies appreciably over time, that is, is "dynamic." They give two examples of this phenomenon. However, after an exhaustive review of the literature, Ronan and Prien (1966) concluded that a general answer to the question, "Is job performance reliable?" is not really possible with present data. They go on to say that previous research has not adequately considered the relevant dimensions that contribute to job performance and very few studies have ac-

tually used the same criterion measure to assess performance at two or more points in time. In the absence of much knowledge concerning the stability of relevant job behaviors it seems a bit dangerous to apply the classic validation model and attempt to generalize from a one-time criterion measure to an appreciable time span of job behavior. Utilizing the consistency notion confronts the problem directly and forces a consideration of what job behaviors are recurring contributors to effective performance (and therefore predictable) and which are not.

In addition, the adoption of signs as predictors in the context of the classic model has undoubtedly been a major factor contributing to the lack of longitudinal research. It makes it far too easy to rely on concurrent studies, and an enormous amount of effort has been expended in that direction. Emphasis on behavior samples and behavior consistency requires that a good deal more attention be devoted to the former, along with very explicit consideration of the crucial parameters of a longitudinal study.

The moderator or subgrouping concept also seems an integral part of the consistency approach. The basic research aim is to find subgroups of people in a particular job family for whom behavior on a particular performance dimension is consistent. Subgrouping may be by individual or situational characteristics but the necessity is clear and inescapable. Only within such subgroups is longitudinal prediction possible.

Lastly, the process the authors are advocating demands a great deal in terms of being able to specify the contextual or situational factors that influence performance. It is extremely important to have some knowledge of the stimulus conditions under which the job behavior is emitted such that a more precise comparison to the predictor behavior sample can be made. Because of present difficulties in specifying the stimulus conditions in an organization (e.g., Sells, 1964), this may be the weakest link in the entire procedure. However, it is also a severe problem for any other prediction scheme, but is usually not made explicit.

It is important to note that the authors' notion of a consistency model does not rest on a simple deterministic philosophy and is not meant to preclude taking account of so-called "emergent" behaviors. Relative to "creativity," for example, the question becomes whether or not the individual has ever exhibited in similar contexts the particular kind of creative behavior under consideration. If a similar context never existed, the research must investigate creative performance and outputs obtained in a test situation which simulates the contextual limitations and requirements in the job situation.

An additional advantage of the consistency approach is that a number of old or persistent problems fortunately appear to dissipate, or at least become significantly diminished. Consider the following:

1. Faking and response sets—Since the emphasis would be on behavior samples and not on self-reports of attitudes, beliefs, and interests, these kinds of response bias would seem to be less of a problem.

2. Discrimination in testing—According to Doppelt and Bennett (1967) two general charges are often leveled at tests as being discriminatory devices:

(a) Lack of relevance—It is charged that test items are often not related to the work required on the job for which the applicant is being considered, and that even where relationships can be shown between test scores and job success there is no need to eliminate low-scoring disadvantaged people since they can be taught the necessary skills and knowledge in a training period after hiring.

(b) Unfairness of content—It is further maintained that most existing tests, especially verbal measures, emphasize middle-class concepts and information

and are, therefore, unfair to those who have not been exposed to middle-class cultural and educational influences. Consequently, the low test scores which are earned are not indicative of the "true" abilities of the disadvantaged, Predictions of job success made from such scores are therefore held to be inaccurate.

The examination of past behaviors similar in nature to desired future behavior, along with their contextual ramifications, plus the added techniques of work samples and simulation devices encompassing desired future behavior, should markedly reduce both the real and imagined severity of problems of unfairness in prediction.

3. Invasion of privacy—The very nature of the consistency approach would seem to almost entirely eliminate this problem. The link between the preemployment or prepromotion behavior and job behavior is direct and obvious for all to see.

CONCLUDING COMMENTS

The preceding discussion is meant to be critical of the concepts of predictive and concurrent validity. Nothing that has been said here should be construed as an attack on construct validity, although Campbell (1960) has pointed out that reliability and validity are also frequently confused within this concept. Neither do the authors mean to give the impression that a full-scale application of the consistency model would be without difficulty. Using available criteria and signs of assumed underlying determinants within the framework of the classic model is certainly easier; however, for long-term gains and the eventual understanding of job performance, focusing on the measurement of *behavior* would almost certainly pay a higher return on investment.

Some time ago, Goodenough (1949) dichotomized this distinction by referring to signs versus samples as indicators of future behavior. Between Hull's (1928) early statement of test validities and Ghiselli's (1966) more recent review, almost all research and development efforts have been directed at signs. Relatively small benefits seem to have resulted. In contrast, some recent research efforts directed at samples seem to hold out more promise. The AT&T studies, which used ratings of behavior in simulated exercises (Bray & Grant, 1966), and the In-basket studies reported by Lopez (1965) are successful examples of employing behavior samples with management and administrative personnel. Frederiksen (1966) has reported considerable data contributing to the construct validity of the In-basket. In addition, Ghiselli (1966) has demonstrated that an interview rating based on discussion of specific aspects of an individual's previous work and educational history had reasonably high validity, even under very unfavorable circumstances. In a nonbusiness setting, Gordon (1967) found that a work sample yielded relatively high validities for predicting final selection into the Peace Corps and seemed to be largely independent of the tests that were also included as predictors.

Hopefully, these first few attempts are the beginning of a whole new technology of behavior sampling and measurement, in both real and simulated situations. If this technology can be realized and the consistencies of various relevant behavior dimensions mapped out, the selection literature can cease being apologetic and the prediction of performance will have begun to be understood.

NOTES

Bray, D. W., & Grant, D. L. The assessment center in the measurement of potential for business management. *Psychological Monographs*, 1966, **80**(17, Whole No. 625).

Campbell, D. T. Recommendations for APA test standards regarding construct, trait, and discriminant validity. *American Psychologist*, 1960, **15**, 546-553.

Cronbach, L. J. *Essentials of psychological testing.* (2nd ed.) New York: Harper & Row, 1960.

Doppelt, J. P., & Bennett, G. K. Testing job applicants from disadvantaged groups. *Test Service Bulletin* (No. 57). New York: Psychological Corporation, 1967. Pp. 1-5.

Dunnette, M. D. A modified model for test validation and research. *Journal of Applied Psychology*, 1963, **47**, 317-323.

Dunnette, M. D. *Personnel selection and placement.* Belmont, Calif.: Wadsworth, 1966.

Frederiksen, N. Validation of a simulation technique. *Organizational Behavior and Human Performance*, 1966, **1**, 87-109.

Ghiselli, E. E. *The validity of occupational aptitude tests.* New York: Wiley, 1966.

Ghiselli, E. E., & Haire, M. The validation of selection tests in the light of the dynamic character of criteria. *Personnel Psychology*, 1960, **13**, 225-231.

Goodenough, F. *Mental testing: Its history, principles, and applications.* New York: Holt, Rinehart & Winston, 1949.

Gordon, L. V. Clinical, psychometric, and work sample approaches in the prediction of success in Peace Corps training. *Journal of Applied Psychology*, 1967, **51**, 111-119.

Guion, R. M. Synthetic validity in a small company: A demonstration. *Personnel Psychology*, 1965, **18**, 49-65.

Hull, C. L. *Aptitude testing.* New York: Harcourt, Brace & World, 1928.

Lopez, F. M., Jr. *Evaluating executive decision making: The In-basket technique.* New York: American Management Association, 1965.

Odiorne, G. S., & Miller, E. L. Selection by objectives: A new approach to managerial selection. *Management of Personnel Quarterly*, 1966, **5**(3), 2-10.

Ronan, W. W., & Prien, E. P. *Toward a criterion theory: A review and analysis of research and opinion.* Greensboro, N.C.: Richardson Foundation, 1966.

Sells, S. B. Toward a taxonomy of organizations. In W. W. Cooper, H. J. Leavitt, & W. W. Shelly, II (Eds.), *New perspectives in organization research.* New York: Wiley, 1964.

Smith, P. C., & Kendall, L. M. Retranslation of expectations: An approach to the construction of unambiguous anchors for rating scales. *Journal of Applied Psychology,* 1963, **47,** 149-155.

Wallace, S. R. Criteria for what? *American Psychologist,* 1965, **20,** 411-417.

Wechsler, D. *Manual for the Wechsler Adult Intelligence Scale.* New York: Psychological Corporation, 1955.

IV

Training

Introduction. Because it is frequently impossible to select individuals who perfectly "fit" the requirements of particular jobs, programs for developing and adding to an employee's existing skills and attitudes are often necessary. This is true for new employees and those already on the job, who may require additional training as their jobs change in response to technological innovation and organizational restructuring. In addition, promotions and transfers to different jobs may place new skill demands on employees and further increase the need for training programs.

The diversity of the literature on personnel training make the identification and selection of "classics" in this area an especially difficult task. For one thing, the bulk of the literature deals with very specific training techniques or the training needs of particular population and occupational subgroups (e.g., minorities, military, and women). Furthermore, much of this material is essentially non-theoretical and non-empirical and amounts to little more than descriptions of existing programs. In one of the first and most influential textbooks on the subject, McGehee and Thayer (1961) called for systematic research to make training an effective managerial tool. However, as indicated by Campbell's comprehensive review ten years later, their admonition seemed to have gone largely unheeded.

> By and large, the training and development literature . . . is faddish to an extreme. The fads center around the introduction of new techniques and follow a characteristic pattern. A new technique appears on the horizon and develops a large stable of advocates who first describe its "successful" use in a number of situations. A second wave of advocates busy themselves trying out numerous modifications of the basic technique. A few empirical studies may be carried out to demonstrate that the method "works." Then the inevitable backlash sets in and a few vocal opponents begin to criticize the usefulness of the technique, most often in the absence of data. Such criticism typically has very little effect. What does have an effect is the appearance of another new technique and a repetition of the same cycle. (1971, pp. 565-566)

More recent reviews by Hinrichs (1976) and Goldstein (1980) indicate that the bulk of the literature still has an essentially faddish flavor. Because of this situation, we have selected articles that deal primarily with issues applicable to personnel training in general and not just to specific techniques. While one of the articles does address a particular technique, it was selected because it illustrates the importance of the careful and objective evaluation of a highly touted and popular training technique.

Our first selection, the article by Robert M. Gagné entitled, "Military Training and Principles of Learning," represents one of the first serious attempts to relate training to learning theory. It also illustrates the important role the military played at that time in supporting much of the research in this area. In essence, Gagné concludes that the "principles of learning," as identified, articulated, and examined in laboratory research, are of less importance in training than a thorough analysis of the task components to be learned, the particular training content appropriate for each component, and the sequencing of the components to facilitate the transfer of training to the actual work situation. He also stresses the evaluation of training by some performance based instrument and the use of simulators ("concept trainers" or "teaching machines") as training devices. Thus, he presents within the confines of this one article the basic elements of training programs for the acquisition of basic skills.

The next article, "A Systematic Approach to Training" by Irwin Goldstein, is similar to the preceding article in that it describes an approach to training rather than a specific training program, technique, or subject population. The systems approach is now widely accepted among personnel psychologists, and this selection is one of the most succinct and accessible among many describing the approach. While there are many different systems approaches to training, they share several features: the assessment of training needs and objectives; the development of particular training experiences to fulfill these objectives; the evaluation of the effectiveness of the training program; and a consideration of the complex interactions of the program with the organizational context including personnel selection, managerial style, and work procedures. It is important to note that the approaches described by Gagné and Goldstein are complementary not discrepant. Taken together, they comprise a good normative model for training research and development.

The final article in this section is "Effectiveness of T-Group Experience in Managerial Training and Development" by John P. Campbell and M. D. Dunnette. During the 1960s, the T-groups and sensitivity training programs of which they were part were among the most popular, highly-touted, and widely used techniques for managerial development, focusing particularly on the skills necessary for effective interpersonal interaction. The interest in and applications of this technique are perfect illustrations of the faddish nature of personnel training described by Campbell earlier in this introduction. The careful analysis and evaluation of the technique conducted by

Campbell and Dunnette is a perfect illustration of the kind of assessment and scrutiny needed to move from training fads to training technology.

In spite of the limitations and diversity of the training literature today, the recent growth in articles that are more theoretical, empirical, and thoughtful has led one reviewer to express a measure of optimism concerning the future of training (Goldstein, 1980). If so, subsequent versions of this book will no doubt see an expanded list of classics on this subject.

REFERENCES

Campbell, J. P. 1971. Personnel training and development. *Annual Review of Psychology,* **22,** 565-602.
Goldstein, I. L. 1980. Training in work organizations. *Annual Review of Psychology,* **31,** in press.
Hinrichs, J. R. 1976. Personnel training. In M. D. Dunnette (ed.), *Handbook of Industrial and Organizational Psychology.* Chicago: Rand-McNally.
McGehee, W., and Thayer, P. W. 1961. *Training in business and industry.* New York: Wiley.

14. Military Training and Principles of Learning*

ROBERT M. GAGNÉ

The subject chosen for this address is one which I think I can view with a certain perspective. Stated very briefly, this circumstance arises from the fact of my changes in occupation, from that of an investigator of learning principles in academic laboratories, to a research administrator of programs of military training research in government laboratories, and back again to an academic laboratory. In making the remarks to follow, I claim nothing more than this perspective, which perhaps carries with it a certain detachment, or freedom from involvement with particular learning theory, as well as with particular training problems.

What I should like to talk about are some general impressions concerning the applicability of learning principles to military training. In the time available to me, I cannot really do more than this. It would be satisfying to think that I could review and marshal the evidence from military studies of training in a truly systematic manner. I am not sure that this can be done even with unlimited time. But at any rate, my aim is much more limited than this. Perhaps it can be stated in the following way. Suppose that I were a learning psychologist, fresh out of an academic laboratory, who was to take a new job in charge of a program of research on

*Source: From *American Psychologist*, vol. 17 (December 1962), pp. 83-91. Copyright © 1962 by the American Psychological Association. Reprinted by permission. Footnotes deleted.

some type of military training. What principles of learning would I look for to bring to bear on training problems? What kinds of generalizations from laboratory studies of learning would I search for and attempt to make use of in training situations? The answers I shall suggest for these questions require first a consideration of what kinds of principles have been tried, and how they have fared.

SOME REPRESENTATIVE MILITARY TASKS

First, we need to have in mind certain representative military tasks for which training either is or has been given, in order that we can consider in detail the kinds of learning principles that are applicable. Here are three which will serve well as examples: (1) flexible gunnery; (2) putting a radar set into operation; (3) finding malfunctions in an electronic system.

FLEXIBLE GUNNERY

The gunner of a now obsolete type of bomber aircraft was typically located in the waist or the tail of the plane, and aimed and fired a gun at fighter aircraft attacking on what was called a "pursuit course." To do this he looked at the attacking fighter through a reticle containing a central dot, which he lined up with the target by rotating his gunsight horizontally and vertically. At the same time, he had to "frame" the aircraft within a set of dots arranged in a circle whose circumference could be varied by rotating the round hand-grip by means of which he grasped the gunsight. This is the kind of task the psychologist calls "tracking," on which a great many laboratory studies have been carried out. It was, of course, tracking simultaneously in the three dimensions of azimuth, elevation, and range. To perform this task, the individual had to learn a motor skill.

PUTTING A RADAR SET IN OPERATION

This kind of task is typically what is called a "fixed procedure." That is, the individual is required to push buttons, turn switches, and so on, in a particular sequence. Here, for example, is a set of steps in a procedure used by radar operators to check the transmitter power and frequency of an airborne radar (Briggs & Morrison, 1956):

1. Turn the radar set to "Stand-by" operation
2. Connect power cord of the TS-147
3. Turn power switch on
4. Turn the test switch to transmit position
5. Turn DBM dial fully counterclockwise
6. Connect an RF cable to the RF jack on the TS-147

There are 14 more steps in this procedure. Notice that each of the steps by itself is easy enough; the individual is quite capable of turning a switch or connecting a cable. What he must learn to do, however, is to perform each step in the proper sequence. The sequence is important, and doing step 5 before step 4 may be not only an error, it may be dangerous. What must be learned, then, is a sequence of acts in the proper order.

FINDING MALFUNCTIONS IN COMPLEX EQUIPMENT

This is in many respects a most complex kind of behavior. There are of course some very simple kinds of equipment in which this activity can be reduced to a procedure; and when this is true, the task is one that can be learned from that point of view. But the major job, for complex equipment, is one of troubleshooting, a problem-solving activity that has considerable formal resemblance to medical as well as other kinds of diagnosis. Suppose this is a radar set, again, and that the initial difficulty (symptom) is that no "range sweep" appears on the oscilloscope tube face. Beginning at this point, the troubleshooter must track down a malfunctioning component. He does this first by making a decision as to how he will check the operation of subordinate parts of the system, next by carrying out the check and noting the information it yields, next by making another decision about a next check, and so on through a whole series of stages until he finds the malfunctioning unit. In each of these stages, he presumably must be formulating hypotheses which affect his actions at the next stage, in the typical and classically described manner of problem solving. What does the individual have to learn in order to solve such problems? This is indeed a difficult question to answer, but the best guess seems to be that he must acquire concepts, principles, rules, or something of that nature which he can arouse within himself at the proper moment and which guide his behavior in diagnosing malfunctions.

Here are, then, three types of activities that are not untypical of military jobs, and which are aimed at in military training: a motor skill like flexible gunnery; a procedure like putting a radar set into operation; and troubleshooting, the diagnosing of malfunctions in complex electronic equipment. Each one of these tasks has been examined more or less intensively by military psychologists and learning specialists. Among other things, each of these tasks can be shown to be not entirely unique, but to represent a rather broad class of tasks, in its formal characteristics, which cuts across particular content or occupational areas. For example, flexible gunnery is a tracking skill, which formally resembles many others, like maneuvering an airplane, sewing a seam on a sewing machine, hovering a helicopter, and many others. As for procedures, these are common indeed, and may be found in jobs such as that of a clerk in filling in or filing forms, a cook preparing food, or a pilot preflighting an airplane. Diagnosing difficulties is certainly a widely occurring kind of activity, which may be engaged in by the leader of a group who detects the symptom of low morale, as well as by a variety of mechanics who "fix" equipment of all sorts. Accordingly, one should probably not consider these particular examples as peculiar ones; instead, they appear to be representative of a wide variety of human activities.

LEARNING

How are these three kinds of tasks learned? What is it that the learning psychologist can say about them which will enable anyone (the teacher, the curriculum builder, the training manager) to undertake to arrange the external conditions in such a way that the desired performances will be acquired with the minimal expenditure of time, money, and wasted effort?

Suppose that you were, in fact, a psychologist who had studied learning, both animal and human, from the standpoint of experiment and theory, and that you were faced with this problem. How can scientific knowledge of learning be used to improve the process of training? Notice how I have stated this question. I am not asking, how can a scientific approach be applied to the study of training? Nor am I asking, how can experimental methodology be applied to the study of training? There are certainly answers to these questions, which have been provided by several people, notably Crawford (1962). The question is, rather, how can what you know about learning *as an event,* or as a *process,* be put to use in designing training so that it will be maximally effective?

The psychologist who is confronted with this question is likely to appeal, first, to a basic point of view towards learning which is so highly ingrained it may be called an *assumption.* Beyond this, and secondly, he looks for certain *principles* which have been well established by experiment. These are principles which relate certain variables in the learning situation, like time intervals between trials, sequence of trials, kind of feedback after each trial, and so on, to such dependent variables as rate of learning or goodness of performance.

Let us try to see what can be done both with the basic assumption and with some of the more important of the principles.

THE ASSUMPTION

The assumption that many learning psychologists would bring to the problem of designing training is something like this: "The best way to learn a performance is to practice that performance." I should like to show, later on, that this assumption is by no means a good one. But before I do that, I want to consider the question, where does this assumption come from, anyhow? First, it seems to have a cultural basis, by derivation from the writings of John Dewey, preserved in the educational catch-phrase "learning by doing." Second, it appears to come by unwarranted generalization from laboratory prototypes of learning such as the conditioned response. In conditioning, classical or otherwise, one observes learning only *after* the animal has made the first *response*. Thus, performance comes first, and learning is often considered to result from practice of this performance. Third, the assumption comes from theory which deals with conditioning, and which conceives of what is learned as either a response or an association terminating in a response, in either case established by *practicing the response* (with reinforcement). Without going into the matter further at the moment, the basic reason that generalization of this notion to the learning of the human tasks I have mentioned seems questionable is simply that the responses required (turning switches, inserting plugs, moving handles) do not have to be learned at all—they are already there in the human's repertoire.

PRINCIPLES

Beyond this assumption that learning comes about when performances are practiced, what *principles* can the learning psychologist depend on? What kinds

of conditions have been found to affect the rate of learning? What findings can he bring to bear on the problem of designing training to be maximally effective?

Let me mention some of the best-known of these principles, not necessarily all of them, using various sources. In part, I shall depend on an excellent article by Underwood (1959). First of all, there is *reinforcement*, the principle that learning will be more rapid the greater the amount of reinforcement given during practice. Other principles include *distribution of practice, meaningfulness*, increasing the *distinctiveness* of the elements of a task, and *response availability*.

These principles would appear to provide the learning psychologist with a fairly adequate bag of tricks with which he can approach the job of designing effective training. There is much evidence in the experimental literature that one can in fact alter the rate of learning by manipulating these variables in the learning situation, whether one is working with single conditioned responses or with verbal material having a somewhat more complex organization. Each of these variables, so far as is known, can be manipulated to make a dependable difference on learning, in the direction of increased as well as decreased effectiveness.

USING THESE ASSUMPTIONS AND PRINCIPLES IN TRAINING DESIGN

How does one fare if he seriously attempts to use this basic assumption and these principles to design effective training situations? *Not particularly well.* The assumption that the most effective learning is provided by practice on the final task leads one astray on many occasions. As for the principles, sometimes they can clearly not be applied, that is, there is no way to manipulate the training situation in the manner suggested by the principle. In other instances, the evidence simply fails to support the principle. When this happens, there may be good theoretical reasons for the event, but this still does not restore one's faith in the usefulness of the principle.

It will be possible here only to give a few examples of military training situations in which these assumptions and principles failed to work, but I have chosen them to be as representative as possible. Let me emphasize again that I do not maintain that these examples demonstrate that the principles are invalid. I simply want to show that they are strikingly inadequate to handle the job of designing effective training situations.

MOTOR SKILL

First let's consider what is perhaps the most difficult case, the learning of a motor skill like gunnery. What happens if we try to employ the assumption that the best way to learn gunnery is to practice gunnery? Using the kind of task required of a flexible gunner, a number of studies were made of the conditions of learning for this performance. One of the earliest ones, during World War II, reported by Melton (1947), showed that different amounts of practice in firing at sleeve targets during one through ten gun-camera missions made no significant difference in the measured proficiency of gunners. A number of other studies of gunnery also indicate the very small and often insignificant effects of practice continued beyond the first three trials or so (Rittenhouse & Goldstein, 1954). Furthermore, several such studies confirm the finding that the major improvement in this performance comes as a result of informing the learners of the correct picture to be achieved in ranging (i.e., so that the dots just touch the wing tips of the target aircraft) (Goldstein & Ellis, 1956). In other words, to summarize the finding very briefly, the evidence is that simple practice on the gunnery task is not a particularly effective training method; instructions about the correct sighting picture for ranging is much more effective in bringing about improved performance. Perhaps there are good theoretical reasons for this. But the fact remains that practicing the performance is *not* the best way to learn.

What about the principles of learning? Well, let's consider the one which a learning psychologist might be inclined to think of first—reinforcement, or the introduction of knowledge of results during practice. Translated into a form applicable to motor skills learning, the principle is that the more adequate are the knowledge of results, the more rapid the learning. This variable, too, has been tried out in a number of studies. Typically what was done was to augment the knowledge of results that come to the gunner through his observing his own tracking performance on a screen, by providing an extra cue, such as a buzzer, which sounded whenever the gunner was exactly on target in all three dimensions. The effect of this extra cue, it was found, was to improve the performance during learning. But did this mean that the learning itself was more effective, or simply that the buzzer "propped up" the performance? One seeks the answer to this question by comparing the performance of buzzer-trained and non-buzzer-trained groups on a standard criterion task without the buzzer. When this was done, the findings in several studies were negative (cf. Goldstein & Ellis, 1956), and one (Goldstein & Rittenhouse, 1954) actually showed that learners who had the advantage of augmented knowledge of results (reinforcement) exhibited a lower performance on a second gunnery task.

Other learning principles were unconfirmed in training situations. For example, a carefully executed study could find no evidence for changes in learning as a result of alterations in conditions of practice and rest periods (Rittenhouse & Goldstein, 1954). Still other variables simply cannot be used in the training situation. For example, the meaningfulness of the task is set by the task itself, and cannot be altered by changing the conditions of training. Similarly, the internal similarity of the elements of the task are fixed by the task; one cannot, for example, change the degree of resemblance of the aircraft or of the tracks they follow by simply redesigning the training, without setting about to change the nature of the task itself. (I omit here a discussion of the transfer effects of training with an easy discrimination to performance on a hard discrimination, and vice versa. This is a different principle than the one under discussion, and the evidence about it is not clear-cut.) What about response availability or familiarity? From the evidence on practice previously cited, as well as studies on part-training (cf. Goldstein & Ellis, 1956) it seems fairly clear that the responses in this task (turning knobs, moving the gunsight up and down with a handle) were highly familiar in the first place. No one, so far as I know, ever seriously proposed that they were not.

Perhaps these examples are sufficient to at least raise doubts about the usefulness of the learning psychologist's assumptions and principles, when he attempts to apply them to the practical job of designing training for motor skills. On the whole, it may fairly be said, I think, that the assumption was often wrong and the principles were seldom useful in bringing about training improvement. I caution you again that I am not saying the learning psychologist was unsuccessful in improving training. In many instances, he was very successful. What I am trying to answer is the question, when he was successful, what knowledge or set of principles was he using?

PROCEDURES

There are not many analytical studies of the learning of procedures. Perhaps the reason for this is that learning procedures is relatively such an easy matter, and the methods used to train them seem so obvious, that little work was

done on them. Consequently, I shall have to base my arguments primarily on these obvious features, rather than on a great deal of experimental evidence.

Suppose one is faced with the task of training someone to "turn on" a radar set by turning and pushing a series of fifteen switches in a particular sequence. (This is taken to be a simplified version of a representative procedural task.) How does one go about it? If one proposes to conduct training simply by "practicing the task" it becomes obvious almost immediately that this is an inefficient method to use. What is usually done is this: the learner is provided with a *list*, which states, in effect, "First, turn on power switch; second, depress voltage switch; third, set voltage knob to reading 10; etc." (e.g., Briggs & Morrison, 1956). Now the individual may be required to commit the list to memory first, and then proceed to the task; or, he may be allowed to use the list while he practices going through the sequence. The important thing is, however, that it is the *learning of the list* that contributes most to the performance of the task, not the practice of the switch-pressing responses, another example contrary to the principle that the best way to learn is to practice the required performance. I do not say that the performance should never be practiced, simply that something other than direct practice of the final task is more effective for learning procedures, just as is true for motor skills in the example previously described.

Learning principles applied to the training of procedures do not fare very well, either, although again I must note the absence of experimental evidence. One cannot alter meaningfulness, and in most cases the responses required are highly familiar. When they are not, as may be the case when a single step requires the use of an unfamiliar tool, this principle may actually have some limited usefulness. Sometimes the principle of increasing the distinctiveness of the elements of the task can be used, and one would indeed expect it to work. For example, one could put distinctive cues or labels on each of the switches in the 15-switch procedure, and this might be expected to speed up the rate of learning. However, it may be noted that this becomes a matter of changing the task (*i.e.*, the equipment), rather than of changing the conditions of learning. From evidence on the learning of nonsense-syllable lists, one would not expect a variable like distribution of practice to make much difference as a training variable, as Underwood (1959) has noted. Again a review of learning assumptions and principles has indicated limited usefulness.

DIAGNOSING MALFUNCTIONS

When we turn to a consideration of troubleshooting complex equipment, even the most theoretically-dedicated learning psychologist is forced to recognize, almost from the start, that the idea of learning to troubleshoot by simply practicing troubleshooting verges on the ridiculous. The most obvious reason is that one cannot identify a single *task* to be practiced. The troubleshooter is faced with a great variety of initial problem situations, each of which may have a great variety of causes. He cannot possibly practice solving all of them. In fact, it is clear that he must learn not a single task, but a *class of tasks*, or perhaps even several classes of tasks. Yet people do learn to do them, quite successfully, without ever doing anything that can legitimately be called "practicing the final performance."

What they do learn, among other things, is an elaborate set of rules pertaining to the flow of signals through a complex circuit. To a large extent, they learn these rules by looking at and responding to a circuit diagram which is a representation of the equipment rather than the equipment itself. And they use the rules in thinking about the signal flow, that is to say, in making successive decisions leading to a solution of the problem (finding the malfunction).

Since, as I have said, it is impossible to define a single task to be practiced in learning troubleshooting, it is just about equally difficult to apply the principles of reinforcement, meaningfulness, internal differentiation, and so on, to the design of training. If one accepts the task of "learning the rules" as what must be done, it is of course possible to ask the question as to whether such learning variables would apply to that task. This is a job that may some day be done by those interested in research on "learning programming." But it has not been done as yet. The evidence to date (such as it is) has not indicated strong effects, or even significant ones, for the variable of reinforcement in connection with learning programs (Goldbeck & Briggs, 1960). Other variables have not yet been investigated in relation to the learning of rules and principles.

WHAT IS APPLICABLE TO THE DESIGN OF TRAINING?

Does this mean that the psychologist has virtually nothing to offer to the problem of designing effective training? Have the results of psychologists' efforts to improve training been entirely negative? Quite to the contrary, it seems to me that efforts can be identified which were quite effective in producing significant improvements in training, and which led to some demonstrably useful designs for training. But the principles which were found to be effective for such purposes were not those that have been mentioned.

Here are the psychological principles that seem to me to be useful in training:

1. Any human task may be analyzed into a set of component tasks which are quite distinct from each other in terms of the experimental operations needed to produce them.

2. These task components are mediators of the final task performance; that is, their presence insures positive transfer to a final performance, and their absence reduces such transfer to near zero.

3. The basic principles of training design consist of: (a) identifying the component tasks of a final performance; (b) insuring that each of these component tasks is fully achieved; and (c) arranging the total learning situation in a sequence which will insure optimal mediational effects from one component to another.

These statements certainly imply a set of principles which would have very different names from those we are now most familiar with. They are concerned with such things as *task analysis, intratask transfer, component task achievement,* and *sequencing* as important variables in learning, and consequently in training. These principles are not set in opposition to the traditional principles of learning, such as reinforcement, differentiation of task elements, familiarity, and so on, and do not deny their relevance, only their *relative importance.* They are, however, in complete opposition to the previously mentioned assumption "the best way to learn a task is to practice the task."

It should also be pointed out here that I am unable to refer to any well-organized body of experimental evidence for these newly proposed principles. They come instead by inference and generalization from a wide variety of instances of learning and military training. I do not claim more for them than this. But they have to be stated before any systematic experimental work can be done on them.

Let me try now to illustrate a definite meaning for these principles with some examples. Consider first the procedural task described previously.

1. Turn radar set to "standby" operation
2. Connect power cord of the TS-147
3. Turn power switch on
4. Turn test switch to transmit position, etc.

The first step to be undertaken here is to analyze this task; and (with certain minor assumptions on our part), this is seen to be, first, the learning of an order series of responses to things; and second and subordinate to this, the locating

of these things. These two *component tasks* have a hierarchical relationship to each other, and immediately suggest the proper *sequencing* for the arrangement of the learning (or training) situation. That is to say, what must first be undertaken is that the learner learn what and where the "things" are (the "standby operation" switch, the "TS-147," the power switch, the test switch, and so forth). This is a matter of identification learning, which has considerable resemblance to the paired-associate learning of the psychological laboratory. Having achieved this subordinate task, it is then possible for the learner to undertake the second, or "serial order of things" task. According to the principle proposed here, maximal positive transfer to this task would be predicted following completely adequate performance on the subordinate task of identifying the "things."

Laboratory experiments which have undertaken to test such a hypothesis seem to be scarce. It is possible, however, to make reference to two studies (Primoff, 1938; Young, 1959) which have some suggestive findings. Generally speaking, when one learns a set of paired associates first, and then undertakes the learning of these units serially, there is high positive transfer; but when one learns units serially first, the amount of transfer to paired associate learning is very low indeed. These results strongly suggest that there is a *more efficient* and a *less efficient* sequence which can be arranged for the learning of a procedural task, and that this sequence involves learning one subtask before the total task is undertaken. A procedure is a task that can be analyzed into at least two component tasks, one of identification, and the other of serial ordering. The first is subordinate to the second in the sense that it mediates positive transfer to the second, provided it is first completely mastered.

Can this kind of analysis be applied to a more complex task like troubleshooting? Indeed it can, and those psychologists who thought about the problem of training troubleshooting came close to the kind of analysis I have suggested. Generally speaking, they recognized that troubleshooting some particular equipment as a final performance was supported by two broad classes of subordinate tasks. First, there was knowledge of the rules of signal flow in the system, and second, the proper use of test instruments in making checks. The rules of signal flow themselves constitute an elaborate hierarchy of subordinate tasks, if one wants to look at it that way. For example, if the signal with which the mechanic is concerned is the output of an amplifier, then it may be necessary that he know some of the rules about data flow through an amplifier. Thus the task may be progressively analyzed into subordinate components which support each other in the sense that they are predicted to mediate positive transfer.

The task of using test instruments in making checks provides an even clearer example, perhaps. Obviously, one subordinate task is "choosing the proper check to make" (presumably a matter of knowing some "rules"); another is "selecting the proper test instrument" (an identification task); still another is "setting up the test instrument" (a procedural task, which in its turn has components like those previously described); and another is "interpreting the instrument reading" (another task involving a "rule"). Even identifying these component tasks brings to troubleshooting a vast clarification of the requirements for training. If one is able to take another step of arranging the proper sequencing of these tasks in a training program, the difference which results is remarkable. This is the interpretation I should be inclined to make of the studies which have demonstrated significant improvements in troubleshooting training, such as those of Briggs and Besnard (1956); of Highland, Newman and Waller (1956); and

of French, Crowder, and Tucker (1956). In providing training which was demonstrably successful, these investigators were giving instruction on a carefully analyzed set of subordinate tasks, arranged in a sequence which, so far as they could tell, would best insure positive transfer to the variety of problem situations encountered in troubleshooting. It was *the identification of these tasks and this sequence* which I believe was the key to training improvement.

A good deal of other work also proceeded along these lines, although not always with a terminal phase of measured training effectiveness. For example, a whole series of studies by Miller and Folley, and their associates, were concerned with what was called *task analysis*. They had such titles as these: Line maintenance of the A-3A fire control system: III. Training characteristics (Folley & Miller, 1955); Job anticipation procedures applied to the K-1 system (Miller, Folley, & Smith, 1953); A comparison of job requirements for the line maintenance of two sets of electronic equipment (Miller, Folley, & Smith, 1954). What was all this talk about task analysis? Did it have anything to do with training? My answer is that it had to do with training more than with anything else. These were thoroughgoing and highly successful attempts to identify the variety of tasks contained in a job, and the variety of subtasks which contributed to each task. There was in fact explicit recognition of the idea that successful final performance must be a matter of attaining competence on these subtasks. So here again was the notion that effective training somehow depended on the identification of these subordinate tasks, as well as on their arrangement into a suitable sequence to insure positive transfer to the final performance.

A third source of these ideas in military training research should be mentioned. This was the development of training devices applicable to such jobs as electronic maintenance. It came to be recognized that these devices were in some respects very different from the traditional trainers such as those for developing skill in aircraft maneuvers. They were called "concept trainers," and this, as Briggs' (1959) discussion of them implies, was another name for "teaching machines." As such, they were developed independently of Skinner's ideas, and they were in fact based upon an entirely different set of principles, as is clear from the accounts provided by Briggs (1956), Crowder (1957), and French (1956). Each of these training devices (or teaching machines), aside from its hardware engineering, was developed on the basis of a painstaking task analysis, which identified the subordinate tasks involved in a total task like troubleshooting a particular electronic system. The subordinate tasks thus identified were then incorporated into a sequence designed to insure maximal positive transfer to the final task. There were certainly some programming principles, but they bore little resemblance to those which are most frequently mentioned in recent literature; in my opinion, they were much more important than these.

Still a fourth area of effort in training research was related to these ideas. This was the development of techniques to provide behavioral guides, or "jobs aids" in support of performance in various technical jobs (Hoehn, Newman, Saltz, & Wulff, 1957). In order to do this, it was found necessary to distinguish between those kinds of capabilities which could best be established by thorough training, and those kinds which could be established by minimal training plus the provision of a check list or handbook. Obviously, here again there had to be a detailed task analysis. Subordinate tasks had to be identified which would mediate transfer either to the kind of performance required without a handbook, or the kind required with a handbook. Besides the initial task analysis, it is again evident that this line of work was making use of ideas about

component task achievement and intratask transfer.

SUMMARY

Now that I have conveyed the message, my summary can be quite brief. If I were faced with the problem of improving training, I should not look for much help from the well-known learning principles like reinforcement, distribution of practice, response familiarity, and so on. I should look instead at the technique of task analysis, and at the principles of component task achievement, intratask transfer, and the sequencing of subtask learning to find those ideas of greatest usefulness in the design of effective training. Someday, I hope, even the laboratory learning psychologist will know more about these principles.

NOTES

Briggs, L. J. A troubleshooting trainer for the E-4 Fire Control System. USAF Personnel Train. Res. Cent. Tech. Note, 1956, No. 56-94.

Briggs, L. J. Teaching machines for training of military personnel in maintenance of electronic equipment. In E. Galanter (Ed.), Automatic teaching: The state of the art. New York: Wiley, 1959. Ch. 12.

Briggs, L. J., & Besnard, G. G. Experimental procedures for increasing reinforced practice in training Air Force mechanics for an electronic system. In G. Finch & F. Cameron (Eds.), Research symposium on Air Force human engineering, personnel, and training research. Washington, D.C.: National Academy of Sciences-National Research Council, 1956. Pp. 48-58.

Briggs, L. J., & Morrison, E. J. An assessment of the performance capabilities of fire control system mechanics. USAF Personnel Train. Res. Cent. Tech. Memo., 1956, No. ML-56-19.

Crawford, M. P. Concepts of training. In R. M. Gagné (Ed.), Psychological principles in system development. New York: Holt, Rinehart, & Winston, 1962. Ch. 9.

Crowder, N. A. A part-task trainer for troubleshooting. *USAF Personnel Train. Res. Cent. Tech. Note,* 1957, No. 57-71.

Folley, J. D., Jr., & Miller, R. B. Line maintenance of the A-3A Fire Control System: III. Training characteristics. *USAF Personnel Train. Res. Cent. Tech. Memo.,* 1955, No. 55-5.

French, R. S. The K-System MAC-1 troubleshooting trainer: I. Development, design, and use. *USAF Personnel Train. Res. Cent. Tech. Note,* 1956, No. 56-119.

French, R. S., Crowder, N. A., & Tucker, J. A., Jr. The K-System MAC-1 troubleshooting trainer: II. Effectiveness in an experimental training course. *USAF Personnel Train. Res. Cent. Tech. Note,* 1956, No. 56-120.

Goldbeck, R. A., & Briggs, L. J. An analysis of response mode and feedback factors in automated instruction. Santa Barbara, Calif.: American Institute for Research, 1960. (AIR Tech. Rep. No. 2)

Goldstein, M., & Ellis, D. S. Pedestal sight gunnery skills: A review of research. *USAF Personnel Train. Res. Cent. Tech. Note,* 1956, No. 56-31.

Goldstein, M., & Rittenhouse, C. H. Knowledge of results in the acquisition and transfer of a gunnery skill. *J. Exp. Psychol.,* 1954, **48,** 187-196.

Highland, R. W., Newman, S. E., & Waller, H. S. A descriptive study of electronic troubleshooting. In G. Finch & F. Cameron (Eds.), *Research symposium on Air Force*

human engineering, personnel, and training research. Washington, D.C.: National Academy of Sciences-National Research Council, 1956. Pp. 48-58.

Hoehn, A. J., Newman, S. E., Saltz, E., & Wulff, J. J. A program for providing maintenance capability. *USAF Personnel Train. Res. Cent. Tech. Memo.,* 1957, No. ML-57-10.

Melton, A. W. (Ed.) Apparatus tests. *USAAF Aviat. Psychol. Program. Res. Rep.,* 1947, No. 4, pp. 917-921.

Miller, R. B., Folley, J. D., Jr., & Smith, P. R. Job anticipation procedures applied to the K-1 system. *USAF Hum. Resources Res. Cent. Tech. Rep.,* 1953, No. 53-20.

Miller, R. B., Folley, J. D., Jr., & Smith, P. R. A comparison of job requirements for line maintenance of two sets of electronics equipment. *USAF Personnel Train. Res. Cent. Tech. Rep.,* 1954, No. 54-83.

Primoff, E. Backward and forward association as an organizing act in serial and in paired associate learning. *J. Psychol.,* 1938, **5,** 375-395.

Rittenhouse, C. H., & Goldstein, M. The role of practice schedule in pedestal sight gunnery performance. *USAF Personnel Train. Res. Cent. Tech. Rep.,* 1954, No. 54-97.

Underwood, B. J. Verbal learning in the educative processes. *Harvard Educ. Rev.,* 1959, **29,** 107-117.

Young, R. K. A comparison of two methods of learning serial associations. *Amer. J. Psychol.,* 1959, **72,** 554-559.

15. A Systematic Approach to Training*

IRWIN L. GOLDSTEIN

INSTRUCTIONAL TECHNOLOGY

While the term *technology* commonly refers to the development of hardware, *instructional technology* refers to the systematic development of programs in training and education. The systems approach to instruction emphasizes the specification of instructional objectives, precisely controlled learning experiences to achieve these objectives, criteria for performance, and evaluative information. Other characteristics of instructional technology would include the following:

1. The systems approach uses feedback

*Source: From *Training: Program Development and Evaluation* by I. L. Goldstein, Chapter 2, pp. 17-25. Copyright © 1974 by Wadsworth, Inc. Reprinted by permission of the publisher, Brooks/Cole Publishing Company, Monterey, California. Extraneous cross references omitted.

to continually modify instructional processes. From this perspective, training programs are never finished products; they are
continually adaptive to information that
indicates whether the program is meeting
its stated objectives.

2. The instructional-systems approach
recognizes the complex interaction among
the components of the system. For example, one particular medium, like television,
might be effective in achieving one set of
objectives, while another medium might
be preferable for a second set of objectives. Similar interactions could involve
learning variables and specific individual
characteristics of the learner. The systems
view stresses a concern with the total system rather than with the objectives of any
single component.

3. Systematic analysis provides a frame
of reference for planning and for remaining
on target. In this framework, a research
approach is necessary to determine which
programs are meeting their objectives.

4. The instructional-systems view is just
one of a whole set of interacting systems.
Training programs interact with and are directly affected by a larger system involving
corporate policies (for example, selection
and management philosophy). Similarly,
educational programs like the *Sesame
Street* TV program are affected by the social values of society.

The various components of the
instructional-systems approach are not
new. Evaluation was a byword years before systems approaches were in vogue.
Thus, the systems approach cannot be
considered a magic wand for all the
problems that were unsolved before its
inception. If the training designer were
convinced that his program worked, a
systems approach would be unlikely to
convince him that his program required
examination. However, the systems approach does provide a model that emphasizes important components and
their interactions, and there is good evidence that this model is an important
impetus for the establishment of objectives and evaluation procedures. As
such, it is a useful tool that enables designers of instructional programs (as
well as authors of books like this one) to
examine the total training process.

Figure 2-1 presents one model of an
instructional system. Most of the components of this model (for example, derive objectives and develop criteria) are
considered important to any instructional system, although the degree of
emphasis changes for different programs. The chapters that follow discuss
material related to each of these model
components. This chapter provides an
overview of the complete system and
the relationships among the components.

ASSESSMENT PHASE

ASSESSMENT OF INSTRUCTIONAL NEED

This phase of the instructional process
provides the information necessary to
design the entire program. An examination of the model indicates that the
training and evaluation phases are dependent upon the input from the development phase. Unfortunately, many
programs are doomed to failure because
trainers are more interested in conducting the training program than in assessing the needs of their organizations.
Educators have been seduced by pro-
gramed instruction and industrial trainers by sensitivity training before they
have determined the needs of their organization and the way the techniques
will meet those needs. The need-
assessment phase consists of organization analysis, task analysis, and person
analysis.

● *Organizational analysis.* Organizational analysis begins with an examination of the short- and long-term goals of
the organization, as well as of the trends
that are likely to affect these goals. Often, this analysis requires that upper-
level management examine their own
expectations concerning their training
programs. Training designed to produce
proficient sales personnel must be structured differently from programs to train
sales personnel who are capable of
moving up the corporate ladder to managerial positions. As school systems examine their goals, they recognize that

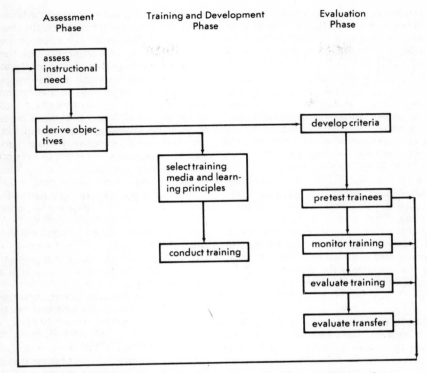

Figure 2-1. An instructional system. There are many other instructional-system models for military, business, and educational systems. Some of the components of this model were suggested by these other systems.

their programs are designed for academically oriented students, and it becomes clearer why vocationally oriented students feel like second-class citizens. When organizational analysis is ignored, planning difficulties abound. Many corporations have spent considerable sums of money retraining personnel because the original training programs and decisions on performance capabilities were based on a system that soon became obsolete. Another aspect of the organizational analysis focuses on training programs and supporting systems—for example, selection, human-factors engineering, and work procedures. Particular operating problems might best be resolved by changes in selection standards or redesign of the work environment.

● Task analysis. The second part of the need-assessment program is a careful analysis of the job to be performed by the trainees upon completion of the training program. The task analysis is usually divided into two separate procedures. The first step is a job description in behavioral terms. It is not a description of the worker. The narrative specifies the individual's duties and the special conditions under which the job is performed. The second procedure, most commonly referred to as task specification, further denotes all the tasks required on the job so that eventually the particular skills, knowledge, and attitudes required to perform the job will become clear. Thus, a brief description of the job of a gas-station attendant might state that the employee supplies cars and trucks with oil, water, air, and gas, changes oil, and lubricates autos and trucks. The task specification provides a list of tasks that includes: collects money, makes change, and provides directions to customers. These statements supply information about the behaviors required regardless of the individual performing the task.

• *Person analysis.* The organizational analysis and task analysis provide a picture of the task and the organizational setting. One critical consideration is missing—that is, the behaviors required of the individual who will be in the training program. Job requirements must be translated into the human attributes necessary to perform the task. This is a difficult but necessary job that must be based on inferences drawn from the analysis of the organizational and task components. The determination of the learning environment and instructional media is directly dependent on the particular types of behavior necessary to perform the task.

Another facet of person analysis is the examination of the performance standards and the capabilities of the target population. It is important to determine which necessary behavioral characteristics have already been learned by the prospective trainees. Too many training programs are exercises in boredom, because they focus on skills already acquired. The determination of the target population is also necessary. Some training programs are designed for individuals who are already in the system, while others are for trainees who are not yet part of the organization. In any case, it is senseless to design the training environment without acknowledging the characteristics of the groups to be trained.

BEHAVIORAL OBJECTIVES

From information obtained in the as-sessment of instructional needs, a blueprint emerges that describes the behavioral objectives to be achieved by the trainee upon completion of the training program. These behavioral objectives provide the input for the design of the training program as well as for the measures of success (criteria) that will be used to judge the program's adequacy. The following is an example of one behavioral objective for our gas-station attendant.

By reading the gasoline pump, the employee can determine the cost of the product and provide correct change to the customer without resorting to paper and pencil for computations. Performance will be judged adequate if the employee:

1. always provides correct change for single items (for example, gas) up to the total cost of $10;
2. always provides correct change when the customer pays cash ranging up to $100;
3. successfully completes 20 trials by providing the correct change.

Similar statements could be designed for instructional systems in a variety of settings. For example, the following behavioral objective is appropriate to the solution of a particular servicing aspect of a Xerox machine (Cicero, 1973).

Given a tool kit and a service manual, the technical representative will be able to adjust the registration (black line along paper edges) on a Xerox 2400 duplicator within 20 minutes according to the specifications stated in the manual [p. 15].

Well-written behavioral objectives specify what the trainee will be able to accomplish when he successfully completes the instructional program. They also indicate the conditions under which the performance must be maintained and the standards by which the trainee will be evaluated (Mager, 1962). Thus, objectives communicate the goals of the program to both the learner and the training designer. From these goals, the designers can determine the appropriate learning environment and the criteria for examining the achievement of the objectives. . . .

TRAINING-DEVELOPMENT PHASE

THE TRAINING ENVIRONMENT

Once the objectives have been specified, the next step is designing the environment to achieve the objectives. This is a delicate process that requires a blend of learning principles and media selection, based on the tasks that the trainee is eventually expected to perform. Gilbert (1960) described the temptations that often lead to a poor environment.

If you don't have a gadget called a teaching machine, don't get one. Don't buy one; don't borrow one; don't steal one. If you have such a gadget, get rid of it. Don't give it away, for someone else might use it. This is a most practical rule, based on empirical facts from considerable observation. If you begin with a device of any kind, you will try to develop the teaching program to fit that device [p. 478].

Gilbert's remarks are equally appropriate for any device or method, from airline simulators to educational television.

From the assessment of instructional need, the skills and knowledge necessary to perform the job become apparent. Now the performance required must be matched with the characteristics of the various media.

The best available basis for the needed matching of media with objectives . . . is a rationale by which the kind of learning involved in each educational objective is stated in terms of the learning conditions required (Briggs, Campeau, Gagné, May, 1967, p. 3).

This is the same process that gardeners use when they choose a certain tool for a certain job. In the same manner, trainers choose airline simulators that create the characteristics of flight in order to teach pilots; however, the simulator is not usually considered appropriate to teach an adult a foreign language. The analysis of job tasks and performance requirements, and the matching of these behaviors to those produced by the training environment, is, at this point, as much an art as a technology. Although the preceding examples of pilot training and language learning are misleading because they represent obvious differences between tasks, there could be significant improvements in the design of training environments if more emphasis were placed on this matching of training environments to required behaviors.

LEARNING PRINCIPLES

In training environments, the instructional process involves the acquisition of skills, concepts, and attitudes that are transferred to a second setting (for example, on the job or in another classroom). The acquisition phase emphasizes learning a new task. Performance on the job and in the next environment focuses on transfer of learning to a second setting. Both theoretical and empirical sources of information are available to aid in the design of environments to improve worker performance. Unfortunately, a definitive list of principles from the learning environment that could be adapted to the training setting has not completely emerged. The learning literature is weak in describing the variables that affect man, especially those pertaining to various forms of skilled behavior. Basic research has centered on the more simple behaviors for which there are available laboratory tasks. However, learning theorists have progressed to a stage of development at which it is clear that the choice of the proper learning variable or level of that variable cannot be based on random option. Learning variables interact with the training environment. Thus, it is not appropriate to ignore the information from the learning literature or to accept a particular variable (for example, feedback or knowledge of results) as useful for all tasks. An illustration of these interactions is provided in a review by Gagné (1962), which suggests that feedback—one of the most sacred variables—is not effective in improving performance on some types of motor-skill training. This does not mean that feedback is not a potent variable for some tasks. It does, however, imply that there are complex interactions that will require consistent research before definitive answers can be found. . . .

EVALUATION PHASE

Since the development of a training program involves an assessment of needs and a careful design of the training environment, the trainee is expected to perform his job at acceptable criterion levels. Unfortunately, this statement of faith displays a sense of self-confidence that is far from justified. Careful examinations of the instructional process disclose numerous pitfalls resulting from mistakes or deficiencies in our present state of knowledge. The assessment of the instructional need might have omitted important job components, or the job itself might have changed since the program was designed. In other instances, there are uncertainties about the most appropriate training technique to establish the required behaviors.

Unfortunately, few programs are evaluated. Indeed, the word *evaluation* raises all sorts of emotional defense reactions. In many cases, the difficulties seem related to a failure to understand that instructional programs are research efforts that must be massaged and treated until the required results are produced. An experience of mine may illuminate this problem.

A community agency was offering a program for previously unemployed individuals to help them obtain jobs. A colleague and I were invited to visit and offer suggestions about improvements to the program. Our questions about the success of the program were answered by reference to the excellent curricula and the high attendance rate of the participants. A frank discussion ensued related to the objectives of the program,

with particular emphasis on the criteria being utilized to measure the adequacy of the program—that is, how successful the participants were in obtaining and holding jobs. This discussion led to the revelation that the success level simply was not known, because such data had never been collected. Of course, it was possible that the program was working successfully, but the information to make such a judgment was unavailable. Thus, there was no way to judge the effectiveness of the program or to provide information that could lead to improvements.

The evaluation process centers around two procedures—establishing measures of success (criteria) and using experimental and nonexperimental designs to determine what changes have occurred during the training and transfer process. The criteria are based on the behavioral objectives, which were determined by the assessment of instructional need. As standards of performance, these criteria should describe: the behavior required to demonstrate the trainee's skill, the conditions under which the trainee is to perform, and the lowest limit of acceptable performance (Mager, 1962).

Criteria must be established for both the evaluation of trainees at the conclusion of the training program and the evaluation of on-the-job performance (referred to as transfer evaluation in the model). In educational settings, the criteria must pertain to performance in later courses as well as to performance in the original environment where the instructional program was instituted. One classification (Kirkpatrick, 1959, 1960) for this purpose suggests that several different measures are necessary, including reaction of participants, learning of participants in training, behavior changes on the job, and final results of the total program. Other serious issues pertain to the integration of the large number of criteria often needed to evaluate a program and to the difficulties (for example, biased estimates of performance) associated with the collection of criterion information. . . .

In addition to criterion development, the evaluation phase must also focus on the necessary design to assess the training program. Some designs use proficiency measures before and after training (pre- and post-tests) as well as continual monitoring to be certain that the program is being implemented as originally designed. Other designs include control groups to determine if any of the training effects could be caused by factors that are unrelated to the training program. For instance, some startled trainers have discovered that their control group performed as well as trainees enrolled in an elaborately designed training program. This often occurred because the control groups could not be permitted to do the job without training. Thus, they either had on-the-job training or were instructed through a program that existed before the implementation of the new instructional system. . . . the rigor of the design affects the quality and quantity of information available for evaluation. There are situations in which it is not possible to use the most rigorous design because of cost or because of the particular setting. In these cases, it is important to use the best design available and to recognize those factors that affect the validity of the information.

A training program should be a closed-loop system in which the evaluation process provides for continual modification of the program. An open-loop system, in contrast, either does not have any feedback or is not responsive to such information. In order to develop training programs that achieve their purpose, it is necessary to obtain the evaluative information and to use this information for program modifications.

The information may become available at many different stages in the evaluation process. For example, an effective monitoring program might show that the training program has not been implemented as originally planned. In other instances, different conclusions might be supported by comparing data obtained from the training evaluation or transfer evaluation. If the participant performs well in training but poorly in the transfer setting, the adequacy of the entire program must be assessed. As indicated by the feedback loops in the model (refer again to Figure 2-1), the information derived from the evaluation process is utilized to reassess the instructional need, thus creating input for the next stage of development.

Even in those instances in which the training program achieves its stated objectives, there are continual developments that can affect the program, including the addition of new media techniques and changes in the characteristics of trainees. These changes often cause previous objectives to become obsolete. The development of training programs must be viewed as a continually evolving process.

One purpose of this overview of the instructional process is to provide the reader with a model that can be used to organize the material in the following chapters. We shall begin the more comprehensive discussion of the components of instructional programs in the next chapter by examining the first step—assessment of instructional need.

NOTES

Briggs, L. J., Campeau, P. L., Gagné, R. M., & May, M. A. *Instructional media: A procedure for the design of multi-media instruction, a critical review of research, and suggestions for future research.* Palo Alto, Calif.: American Institutes for Research, 1967.

Cicero, J. P. Behavioral objectives for technical training systems. *Training and Development Journal*, 1973, **28**, 14-17.

Gagné, R. M. Military training and principles of learning. *American Psychologist,* 1962, **17,** 83-91.

Gilbert, T. F. On the relevance of laboratory investigation of learning to self-instructional programming. In A. A. Lumsdaine & R. Glaser (Eds.), *Teaching machines and programmed instruction.*

Washington, D.C.: National Education Association, 1960.

Kirkpatrick, D. L. Techniques for evaluating training programs. *Journal of the American Society of Training Directors,* 1959, **13,** 3-9, 21-26; 1960, **14,** 13-18, 28-32.

Mager, R. F. *Preparing instructional objectives.* Belmont, Calif.: Fearon, 1962.

16. Effectiveness of T-Group Experiences in Managerial Training and Development*

JOHN P. CAMPBELL

MARVIN D. DUNNETTE

At the fifth meeting the group's feelings about its own progress became the initial focus of discussion. The "talkers" participated as usual, conversation shifting rapidly from one point to another. Dissatisfaction was mounting, expressed through loud, snide remarks by some and through apathy by others.

George Franklin appeared particularly disturbed. Finally pounding the table, he exclaimed, "I don't know what is going on here! I should be paid for listening to this drivel? I'm getting just a bit sick of wasting my time here. If the profs don't put out—I quit!" George was pleased; he was angry, and he had said so. As he sat back in his chair, he felt he had the group behind him. He felt he had the guts to say what most of the others were thinking! Some members of the group applauded loudly, but others showed obvious disapproval. They wondered why George was excited over so insignificant an issue, why he hadn't done something constructive rather than just sounding off as usual. Why, they wondered, did he say their comments were "drivel"?

George Franklin became the focus of discussion. "What do you mean, George, by saying this nonsense?" "What do you

expect, a neat set of rules to meet all your problems?" George was getting uncomfortable. These were questions difficult for him to answer. Gradually he began to realize that a large part of the group disagreed with him; then he began to wonder why. He was learning something about people he hadn't known before. ". . . How does it feel, George, to have people disagree with you when you thought you had them behind you? . . ."

Bob White was first annoyed with George and now with the discussion. He was getting tense, a bit shaky perhaps. Bob didn't like anybody to get a raw deal, and he felt that George was getting it. At first Bob tried to minimize George's outburst, and then he suggested that the group get on to the real issues; but the group continued to focus on George. Finally Bob said, "Why don't you leave George alone and stop picking on him. We're not getting anywhere this way."

With the help of the leaders, the group focused on Bob. "What do you mean, 'picking' on him?" "Why, Bob, have you tried to change the discussion?" "Why are you so protective of George?" Bob began to realize that the group wanted to focus on George; he also saw that George didn't

---

*Source: From *Psychological Bulletin,* vol. 70 (August 1968), pp. 73-104. Copyright © 1968 by the American Psychological Association. Reprinted by permission. Footnotes renumbered.

think he was being picked on, but felt he was learning something about himself and how others reacted to him. "Why do I always get upset," Bob began to wonder, "when people start to look at each other? Why do I feel sort of sick when people get angry at each other?" . . . Now Bob was learning something about how people saw him, while gaining some insight into his own behavior [Tannenbaum, Wechsler, & Massarik, 1961, p. 123].

This short episode taken from a management-development session illustrates many of the features of an educational technique referred to as the T-group method of sensitivity training. When integrated with other techniques such as lectures and group problem-solving exercises, the complete program is usually relabeled "laboratory education."

There is little doubt that T groups have become a popular management-development device (House, 1967). The National Training Laboratories (NTL) and the Western Training Laboratories conduct programs for several hundred managers and executives each year (National Training Laboratories, 1967), a number of consulting firms have made this type of training a standard part of their repertoire, and many colleges and universities incorporate T groups as part of the curriculum in business education, public administration, education, or psychology. In addition, a number of university institutes such as Boston University's Human Relations Center and UCLA's Institute of Industrial Relations conduct T groups for business personnel. There are also instances, and here a trend is impossible to document, of line managers being trained to conduct T groups as an ongoing part of their organization's management-development program. It seems accurate to say that a T group is within easy reach of almost any manager.

This paper is devoted to an analysis and appraisal of the application of this technique to problems of managerial development. The focus is on the published literature surrounding the topic and not upon the authors' personal experiences. The authors are academic psychologists interested in organizational behavior and not T-group or laboratory-education practitioners.

In brief, this paper attempts to: (a) identify and summarize the crucial elements of the T-group method, (b) call attention to some of the difficulties in researching both the dynamics and the effects of the method, and (c) summarize in some detail the research evidence bearing on the utility of T groups for training and development purposes.

It is acknowledged at the outset that no single explicitly defined set of experiences can be labeled the laboratory method. There are many variations, or "training designs," depending upon the characteristics of certain parameters. However, at the heart of most efforts is a common core of experience known as the T group, usually regarded as the crucial part of the program (Bradford, Gibb, & Benne, 1964, p. 2; Schein & Bennis, 1965, p. 15). It is this common core which receives most of the attention from practitioners, researchers, and critics and which is the focus of this review.[1]

FORM AND NATURE OF THE T-GROUP METHOD

Two elements used to distinguish the T group from other training methods are the learning goals involved and the processes used to accomplish these goals. Advocates of T grouping tend to focus on goals at two different levels (Buchanan, 1965; Schein & Bennis, 1965). Flowing from certain scientific and democratic values are several metagoals, or goals which exist on a very general level. Schein and Bennis mentioned five, which they asserted to be the ultimate aims of all T-group training:

---

1. See also the "debate" between Argyris and Odiorne reported in the *Training Directors Journal*, 1963, **17**(10), 4-37.

a) a spirit of inquiry or a willingness to hypothesize and experiment with one's role in the world;

b) an "expanded interpersonal consciousness" or an increased awareness of more things about more people;

c) an increased authenticity in interpersonal relations or simply feeling freer to be oneself and not feeling compelled to play a role;

d) an ability to act in a collaborative and interdependent manner with peers, superiors, and subordinates rather than in authoritative or hierarchical terms; and

e) an ability to resolve conflict situations through problem solving rather than through horse trading, coercion, or power manipulation.

According to Schein and Bennis (1965), these metagoals are seldom articulated, but are implicit in the functioning of most T groups. A number of more proximate objectives usually are made explicit and are regarded by most authors as the direct outcomes of a properly functioning T group. It is true that not *all* practitioners would agree that *all* T groups try to accomplish *all* of these aims, but they are sufficiently common to most discussions of the T-group method that the authors feel relatively few qualms in listing them as the direct or proximate outcomes desired. The list is drawn from a variety of sources (Argyris, 1964; Bradford et al., 1964; Buchanan, 1965; Miles, 1960; Schein & Bennis, 1965; Tannenbaum et al., 1961):

1. *Increased self-insight or self-awareness concerning one's own behavior and its meaning in a social context.* This refers to the common aim of learning how others see and interpret one's behavior and gaining insight into why one acts in certain ways in different situations.

2. *Increased sensitivity to the behavior of others.* This goal is closely linked with the above. It refers first, to the development of an increased awareness of the full range of communicative stimuli emitted by other persons (voice inflections, facial expressions, bodily positions, and other contextual factors, in addition to the actual choice of words) and second, to the development of the ability to infer accurately the emotional or noncognitive bases for interpersonal communications. This goal is very similar to the concept of empathy as it is used by clinical and counseling psychologists, that is, the ability to infer correctly what another person is feeling.

3. *Increased awareness and understanding of the types of processes that facilitate or inhibit group functioning and the interactions between different groups—* specifically, why do some members participate actively while others retire to the background? Why do subgroups form and wage war against each other? How and why are pecking orders established? Why do different groups, who may actually share the same goals, sometimes create seeming insoluble conflict situations?

4. *Heightened diagnostic skill in social, interpersonal, and intergroup situations.* Achievement of the first three objectives should provide an individual with a set of explanatory concepts to be used in diagnosing conflict situations, reasons for poor communication, and the like.

5. *Increased action skill.* Although very similar to No. 4, it was mentioned separately by Miles (1960) and refers to a person's ability to intervene successfully in inter- or intragroup situations so as to increase member satisfactions, effectiveness, or output. The goal of increased action skill is toward intervention at the interpersonal rather than simply the technological level.

6. *Learning how to learn.* This does not refer to an individual's cognitive approach to the world, but rather to his ability to analyze continually his own interpersonal behavior for the purpose of helping himself and others achieve more effective and satisfying interpersonal relationships.

Differential emphasis among the above objectives constitutes one of the most important dimensions for distinguishing among variations in T groups. Some groups tend to emphasize the individual's goals of fostering self-awareness and sensitivity. Others orient toward the more organizational objectives of understanding interaction phenomena and intergroup processes (Buchanan, 1965) with the ultimate aim of improving organizational effectiveness. The evolution of different forms of T groups designed to achieve these two major emphases is discussed at length by Benne (1964) and Schein and Bennis (1965).

What processes and structural elements does the T group use to achieve these goals? The technology of any given group depends, in part, on the goals held to be paramount, but the thrust of the literature emphasizes a common core of experiences around which specialized variations may be developed.

Thus, the T-group learning experience has as its focal point the small, unstructured, face-to-face group, usually consisting of 10-15 people. Typically, no activities or topics for discussion are planned. A trainer is usually present, but he does not accept, in fact he overtly rejects, any leadership role. The participants are to discuss themselves and the way they portray themselves in the group. In the language of T grouping, the focus is on the "here and now," that is, on behavior emitted in the group rather than behavior involving past experiences or future problems. The here and now includes the feelings and emotions experienced by the group members. In fact, the cognitive aspects of problems are ancillary to this affect-laden orientation. Focusing on the here and now is facilitated by the trainer's abdication of the leadership role and his lack of responsiveness to the status symbols brought to the group by the participants (e.g., company position, education, family background, etc.). Frequently, the trainer merely specifies the length of time the group will be meeting and that the major concern is with seeking to understand one's own and others' behaviors. He then falls silent or otherwise refuses further guidance.

The vacuum is often filled by feelings of frustration, expressions of hostility, and eventual attempts by some members to impose an organized, and usually hierarchical (leaders, committees, etc.), structure on the group. These initial attempts to assume a leadership role

are usually represented by other members, and, either spontaneously or because of the trainer's intervention, they begin to consider why the self-appointed leader has tried to force his will on the group. If events follow their proper course, the behavior of the other group members also becomes a basis for discussion such that every participant has an opportunity to learn how his own within-group behavior is perceived. This process is illustrated by the episode quoted at the beginning of the present paper. More complete narrative accounts of what goes on in a T group are given by Klaw (1961), Weschler and Reisel (1959), and Kuriloff and Atkins (1966).

Given the unstructured group as the vehicle and the behavior emitted in the group as the principal topic of conversation, the success of the venture depends on the crucial process of feedback. Thus, the participants must be able to inform each other how their behavior is being seen and interpreted and to describe the kinds of feelings generated. This is the primary process by which the delegates "learn." They must receive articulate and meaningful feedback about their own behavior, including their own feedback attempts (feedback on feedback) and their efforts to interpret group processes. (E.g., did the other group members think Individual X was correct when he observed that Y and Z were forming a clique because they both felt rejected?)

For the feedback process to contribute to the goals of the training, at least two additional elements are believed necessary. First, a certain amount of anxiety or tension must be generated, particularly in the early part of the group's life. Anxiety supposedly results when an individual discovers how deficient his previous role-bound methods of interacting are for successful functioning in this new type of group situation.

A possible explanation for this type of anxiety generation flows from some of the stimulus-response formulations of Dollard and Miller (1950). Almost every individual has an established self-image protected by a number of defense mechanisms. Such mechanisms have become resistant to change because of their repeated association with the reinforcing properties of anxiety reduction; that is, they protect the self-image from threat. Thus, in the T group when an individual's usual mode of interacting is thwarted and his defense mechanisms are made a direct topic of conversation, considerable anxiety results. Such anxiety then constitutes a force for new learning because, if the group experience is a successful one, new methods of anxiety reduction will be learned. If the T group is successful, these methods will be more in line with the goals of the training and will have more utility for the individual in coping with his environment than his old methods which may indeed have been dysfunctional. Thus, anxiety serves the purpose of shaking up or jarring loose the participant from his preconceived notions and habitual forms of interacting so that feedback may have its maximum effect. Without such "unfreezing," feedback may be ineffectual (Schein, 1964).

The second element necessary for assuring effective feedback is what Schein and Bennis (1965) referred to as a climate of "psychological safety" and Bradford et al. (1964) called "permissiveness." That is, no matter what an individual does in a group or what he reveals about himself, the group must act in a supportive and nonevaluative way. Each individual must feel that it is safe to expose his feelings, drop his defenses, and try out new ways of interacting. Such an atmosphere has its obvious counterpart in any constructive clinical or therapeutic relationship.

The role of the trainer also constitutes a dominant technological element bearing on the group's effectiveness for giving feedback and promoting psychological support. The trainer serves as a model for the participants to imitate; that is, he absorbs feelings of hostility and frustration without becoming defensive, provides feedback for others, expresses his own feelings openly and honestly, and is strongly supportive of the expression of feelings in others. In short, he exhibits for consideration the very processes deemed necessary for maximum learning to occur.

However, in the so-called "instrumented" T group (Berzon & Solomon, 1966; Blake & Mouton, 1962) there may be no trainer. The function of a behavior model is accomplished by a series of questionnaires requiring the participants to rate themselves and each other on how supportive they are, how freely they express feelings, and how skillfully they give feedback.

Another structural ingredient of the T-group method bearing on the accomplishment of its goals is the organizational affiliation of the participants. So-called "stranger" groups (such as the groups conducted by the NTL) are composed of individuals from a number of different organizations and seem to emphasize self-insight and sensitivity as the primary goals. In contrast, "family" groups are composed of individuals drawn from a vertical slice of a particular unit of an organization, and, for them, goals relevant to group processes and intergroup interaction in the organization are more salient (Tannenbaum et al., 1961). Other types of group composition are possible. Members may be drawn from a horizontal slice of the organization or they may constitute an intact work group (Schein & Bennis, 1965). Organizational development rather than just individual development is paramount for these latter types of groups.

SOME ASSUMPTIONS

The training technology just described seems to make a number of assumptions, both explicitly and implicitly. The authors offer the following list for consideration:

1. A substantial number of group members, when confronted with others' behaviors and feelings in an atmosphere of psychological safety, can produce articulate and constructive feedback.

2. A significant number of the group members can agree on the major aspects of a particular individual's behavior exhibited in the group situation. Certainly a complete consensus is not to be expected, but neither must the feedback go off in all directions. A certain degree of communality is necessary if the feedback is to be helpful for the individual.

3. Feedback is relatively complete and deals with significant aspects of the individual's behavior.

4. The behavior emitted in the group is sufficiently representative of behavior outside the group so that learning occurring within the group will carry over or transfer.

5. Psychological safety can be achieved relatively quickly (in the matter of a few hours) among either complete strangers or among associates who have had varying types and degrees of interpersonal interaction.

6. Almost everyone initially lacks interpersonal competence; that is, individuals tend to have distorted self-images, faulty perceptions, and poor communication skills.

7. Anxiety facilitates new learning.

8. Finally, transfer of training occurs between the cultural island and the "back home" situation.

Little can be said about the validity of such assumptions since they involve extremely complex processes with as yet only a very thin research context. However, a few points seem relevant. The first four assumptions must be substantially met if the T group is to achieve the goals regarding self-insight, sensitivity, and understanding of group process; each of these assumptions places severe demands on individual abilities in observing and communicating. Maslow (1965) suggested that because of the skills demanded of individuals in this type of learning situation perhaps only a very small percentage of the population can hope to benefit. Further, a consideration of these four assumptions points up a potentially troublesome paradox underlying the T-group method—their close resemblance to the major T-group objectives themselves. That is, it appears that some of the interpersonal skills most important for accomplishing the T group's objectives are also the very skills constituting the major learning goals of the method.

Thus, some critical issues that must be resolved concern how rapidly such observational and communicative skills can be developed, whether or not a few relatively skilled participants can "carry" the rest of the group for the time necessary for others to develop minimal capability, and, finally, the degree to which all members profit from the group experience even if they initially differ greatly in these interpersonal abilities.

Assumption 5 is also related to the above. People must certainly differ greatly in their ability to accept the guarantee of psychological safety. To the extent that the feeling of safety cannot be achieved—and quickly—the prime basic ingredient for this form of learning is absent. Its importance cannot be overemphasized, nor can the difficulty of its being accomplished.

It would be informative to have normative data about Assumption 6; however, this encompasses certain definitional and measurement problems that will be touched on later. It should be noted that if Assumption 6 is strongly supported the demands of Assumptions 1 through 4 for "quick learning" become even more severe.

Assumption 7 also raises a number of difficult questions. The bulk of the evidence bearing on the relationship of anxiety and learning has been obtained from animal studies or from experiments using human subjects and relatively simple psychomotor tasks (Deese, 1958; Kimble, 1961). No firm generalizations have emerged from these investigations except that the relationship is a complex one and dependent on various parameters such as relative level of anxiety, motivational state prior to learning, complexity of the task, and a number of others. On the other hand, for complex human learning of the academic variety, Skinner (1953) argued that a complete absence of anxiety is desirable. In sum, the previous literature on the topic is equivocal.

Although no data directly relevant to the role of anxiety in inducing interpersonal learning are available, it might be informative to review Solomon's (1964) insightful analysis of the probable effects of punishment on learning. Based on his and others' research, Solomon theorized that learning as a consequence of punishment occurs in a two-stage process: First, a conditioned emotional reaction must be established to temporarily suppress the unwanted behavior. Second, and most important, responses incompatible with the punished response must then be reinforced and established; only in this way can one guard against the rapid extinction of the conditioned emotional reaction and the corresponding reappearance of the unwanted behavior. In the context of the T group, this means that "punishment" in the form of anxiety arousal must be accompanied by the reinforcement and shaping of responses incompatible with those responsible for originally inducing the anxiety. In a sense this is what the T group tries to do; however, it seems reasonable to ask whether or not the usual T group is sufficiently structured to assure the sophisticated control of stimuli and reinforcement configurations necessary in the two-stage process suggested by Solomon. Given the variability in contingencies that this lack of structure probably produces, some possible alternative outcomes might be either simply that no permanent learning occurs or that some of the negative side effects are incurred. The reality of their occurrence in other learning situations is well documented by Yates (1962).

The authors are not arguing that such negative outcomes are almost certain to occur. No empirical data exist on which to base such an argument. However, research results in other learning contexts suggest it is a potential danger for the T-group situation that should not be ignored.

PROBLEMS FACING T-GROUP RESEARCH

Before reviewing research results, the authors shall comment on some of the problems faced by investigators who wish to conduct research on the T group and its effects. Many of these difficulties are certainly not peculiar to the T group, but it is believed that T-group research faces certain unique problems which severely constrain any effort to explicate the effects of the method.

One of the major difficulties mentioned by Schein and Bennis (1965) is the lack of an explicit theory of learning for use in specifying the relation between learning experiences and learning outcomes. Nine individuals presented their formulations of the T-group change process in Bradford et al. (1964), and all were very different. Schein and Bennis attributed this diversity of theory to the wide range of learning outcomes seen as possible. Outcomes may include increased awareness, increased knowledge, changes in values, changes in attitudes, changes in motivation, or changes in actual behavior. Organizing all these into a single coherent system specifying relationships between training elements and learning outcomes is difficult indeed—probably more difficult for laboratory education than for other training methods. Presently, it is unclear what kinds of outcomes to expect from any specific T-group effort.

A second problem, not unique to T groups, is the ever-present question of transfer of learning from the training group to the individual's life outside the group. More specifically, does what is learned in a T-group transfer to the organizational setting? According to its practitioners, a crucial aspect of the T group is the creation of anxiety and the open expression of feelings in an atmosphere of psychological safety. Schein and Bennis (1965) speculated that the conditions which facilitate the necessary climate of safety are:

a) a T group which meets for a relatively long time in an isolated environment;

b) a heterogeneous group which will probably not meet again and which thus does not constitute such a threatening audience;

c) continual reinforcement by the staff that the laboratory culture is supportive, nonevaluative, nonthreatening, and, therefore, "different" than the world back home; and

d) an attitude on the part of the participants that the T group is something of a temporary "game" to be played with relative abandon because it is not "for keeps."

As Schein and Bennis recognized, all these conditions heighten the differences between the work group and the T group and would seem to work against transfer to the work situation. Groups conducted closer to the work situation, involving people from the same organization or subunit, and incorporating particular organizational problems for discussion may enhance the probability of transfer, but they may also lessen the probability of achieving many of the goals of a T group. Many of the supporting elements seen as facilitating open expression of feeling, accurate feedback, and psychological safety have been removed.

Assuming that transfer does occur, the problem of observing and measuring it remains. The measurement problem involves two major steps: (a) assessing what changes have occurred over the course of the training, and (b) determining how such changes are manifested in the organizational setting. For example, do people really become more sensitive to the feelings of others during the course of the T group, and are they then also more sensitive to the feelings of others on the job? Both these questions must be examined empirically.

The measurement problems involved in assessing the cognitive, attitudinal, and behavioral effects sought by the T-group experience are considerable. All the difficulties cannot be elaborated here nor can all potential areas of interpersonal change be discussed separately, but the magnitude of the problem can be illustrated by giving brief attention to the many difficulties involved in measuring interpersonal awareness. This factor has been chosen because nearly all T groups strive, either explicitly or implicitly, toward increasing members' empathy, interpersonal sensitivity, or interpersonal accuracy as a first and crucial step on the road toward developing improved interpersonal competence. T-group advocates forcefully and rightly call attention to the important role played by interpersonal perception in getting to know and learning to work constructively with other people. They make it the key to developing mature and understanding interaction in nearly all human relationships. As a consequence, the central focus of T-group training is to increase the level of accuracy with which persons discern the attributes, attitudes, opinions, feelings, and reactions of others in their social and work environments.

Any assessment or measurement of what goes on in T-group training must first cope with the problems involved in measuring this elusive phenomenon called interpersonal sensitivity. The problems are many, and they have already been well documented by Cronbach (1955), Gage and Cronbach (1955), Cline (1964), and H. C. Smith (1966). The major difficulty grows out of the plethora of strategies available to anyone who seeks to discern accurately the attributes, feelings, and reactions of others.

First, he may truly know each and every person in his environment *perfectly* and be able to make ideographic behavioral predictions for each one. This is probably the metagoal of most T-group training, but few would claim that it is realistically possible. A somewhat easier way of increasing the interpersonal accuracy of T-group participants might be by training them in the "art" of forming accurate stereotypes about people in general or about persons belonging to various subgroups in society. That is, one strategy for accomplishing a modicum of interpersonal accuracy is simply to know the base rates of particular behavior patterns, reactions, and feelings typically shown by different subgroups. The authors believe that most T-group advocates might be distressed if they were charged with seeking to develop accurate stereotypes instead of helping participants to "know" each and every person in their environment. Nonetheless, prediction of base rates has repeatedly been shown to be one of the most likely avenues for successfully predicting the responses of other persons.

Another strategy yielding accurate predictions for some persons is the "assumed similarity strategy" or, for want of a better name, *projective sensitivity*. Here, an effective and accurate interpersonal perceiver might be "sensitive" in the sense that he can accurately identify that subset of persons whose reactions, feelings, and attitudes are similar to his own. Then, simply by projecting his own feelings and behavior tendencies onto them, he can accomplish the desirable goal of "knowing others" in his environment. In this case, the successful T group will be one that manages to make persons more similar to one another in their behavioral tendencies, attitudes, opinions, feelings, and reactions or that teaches people to recognize individuals who are like themselves. However, this latter strategy is rather narrow and would appear to have limited utility for the development of interpersonal perceptual accuracy. T-group advocates might also be distressed if they were charged with training for conformity, but here again, assumed similarity (or projective sensitivity) has been repeatedly shown to be an important component of accurate inter-

personal perception (Cronbach, 1955; H. C. Smith, 1966).

Many other strategies for accomplishing accurate interpersonal prediction could be mentioned. Some may be artifactual (such as "accuracy" related to pervasive response sets—e.g., social desirability), and others may be illusory (such as the unwillingness of a perceiver to "go out on a limb" or to deviate from the average in predicting for others).

The major purpose here is simply to emphasize that interpersonal sensitivity is not only an elusive, but also a highly complex phenomenon. Persons involved in a T-group training program may indeed become more "sensitive," but the nature and underlying strategies of the sensitivities developed may differ widely from person to person and from program to program. Unless the various components and strategies involved in interpersonal sensitivity are taken into account during the design of measuring instruments and during the design and implementation of research investigations, little new knowledge concerning T-group training effects or the likelihood of transferring skills back to the work setting will accrue. So far (as will be seen in subsequent sections), most investigators have not attempted to cope with the serious measurement and design problems inherent in this area.

A REVIEW OF THE EMPIRICAL LITERATURE

Three reviews (Buchanan, 1965; House, 1967; Stock, 1964) of the T-group literature have previously appeared. Each has incorporated a somewhat different emphasis, either in type and breadth of studies reviewed or in conclusions drawn from the results. Stock (1964) devoted attention to investigations of how individuals behave in a T group, the relationship between personality and perceptions of other group members, the perceptions of the group by its members, the relationship of group composition to the course of group development, and the relationship of group composition to subgroup structure, group anxiety level, and member satisfaction. She also gave some attention to the role of the trainer and the impact of a T group on individual learning, but no studies were reviewed relative to the development of people in their organizational roles or to the complex question of transfer of learning. In sum, Stock's principal emphasis was on the behavior of individuals in the group setting rather than on the influence of T-group training on members' behavior in their organizations. In contrast, House (1967) and Buchanan (1965) discussed a sampling of studies aimed at evaluating the T group as a development technique; however, their treatment and conclusions differed somewhat from those in the present paper. The range of their citations was a bit narrower, and they tended to be more positive in their conclusions.

The present review is focused primarily on studies of the usefulness of the T-group technique for influencing the behavior of people in organizations. That is, of principal interest here is the relationship of T-group training to appropriate criterion measures. In addition, studies bearing on the viability of the assumptions underlying the method and investigations showing how successful the technique has been in capitalizing on the essential features of its technology have also been included. For example, investigations of the utility of interpersonal feedback in a group or studies of the effects of different trainer styles are relevant. The authors have also tried to limit citations to studies employing subjects who have some sort of management or supervisory responsibility. However, in the interest of including all potentially relevant research, the authors have also reviewed studies using students in business administration or related fields that imply an interest in management or administrative careers.

The discussion is organized according to the type and quality of criteria used. Martin's (1957) distinction between internal and external measures of training effects has been adopted. *Internal criteria* are measures linked directly to the content and processes of the training program, but which have no direct linkage to actual job behavior or to the goals of the organization. Examples of internal criteria include measures of attitude change, performance in simulated problem-solving situations, and opinions of trainees concerning what they thought they had learned. Obviously, changes in internal criteria need imply no necessary change in job behavior; for example, a change in attitudes toward employees may or may not be accompanied by different behavioral patterns back on the job.

External criteria are those linked directly with job behavior. Superior, subordinate, or peer ratings, unit production, or unit turnover are examples of external criteria that have been used. Neither of these two classes of criteria is regarded as more important than the other. It will subsequently be argued that a thorough knowledge of both is essential for a full understanding of training effects. The relationship between internal and external criteria is the essence of the problem of transfer to the organizational setting.

EXTERNAL CRITERIA

Studies by Boyd and Elliss (1962), Bunker (1965), and Miles (1965) are the three research efforts most frequently cited in support of the ability of the T-group experience to change job behavior. Valiquet (1964) carried out a similar study. All four investigations used a "perceived change" measure as the basic external criterion. This measure is an open-ended question asking a superior, subordinate, or peer of the subject to report any changes in the subject's behavior in the job situation during some specified period of time. The specific question used in the Bunker (1965), Miles (1965), and Valiquet (1964) studies is as follows:

> Over a period of time people may change in the ways they work with other people. Do you believe that the person you are describing has changed his/her behavior in working with people over the last year as compared with the previous year in any specific ways? If YES, please describe:

Estimates of change were usually obtained from several (three to seven) observers for each subject. In the Boyd and Elliss (1962) study, the observers were interviewed by the researchers, while in the other three studies, data were obtained by including the above question in a mailed questionnaire. Observers were not asked to judge the positive or negative aspects of the behavior changes, but merely to describe those which had occurred. In all four studies the perceived-change data were obtained several months after completion of training.

All studies used at least one control group, and in the Bunker, Miles, and Valiquet studies they were chosen in a similar, but unusual, fashion. Controls were matched with experimental subjects by asking each person in the experimental group to nominate a "control" individual who was in a similar organizational position and who had never participated in a T group. It is not clear from the report how the control subjects were chosen in the Boyd and Elliss study.

Subjects in the Miles (1965) and Bunker (1965) studies were participants in NTL programs. Miles used 34 high school principals as an experimental group and two groups of principals as controls. One "matched" group of 29 was chosen via the nomination procedure, and a second group of 148 was randomly selected from a national listing. Responses to the perceived-change measure were solicited from six to eight associates of each experimental and control subject and from the subjects themselves approximately 8 months

after the training. Returns were obtained from an average of five observers per subject.

Two other external criterion measures also were used: the Leadership Behavior Description Questionnaire (LBDQ—Stogdill & Coons, 1957), which was completed by observers, and the Group Participation Scale, a peer-nomination form originally developed by Pepinsky, Siegel, and Van Alta (1952) as a counseling criterion measure. Data from both these instruments were collected before and after the training for one-half of the experimental group and the matched-pair control group. To check any Treatment × Measurement interaction effects, data for the second half of the experimental group were collected posttraining only. There were no interactions.

A large number of other measures were also included in the study. Ratings of various training behaviors (internal criteria) were obtained from trainers, peers, and the participants themselves. These ratings were analyzed via the multitrait, multimethod (Campbell & Fiske, 1959) technique and subsequently collapsed into an overall "trainee effectiveness" score. More importantly, five measures of the individual's organizational situation were obtained: (a) security, as measured by length of tenure in present job; (b) power, as measured by the number of teachers in the participant's school; (c) autonomy, as measured by length of time between required reports to the immediate superior; (d) perceived power, as measured by a Likert-type scale; and (e) perceived adequacy of organizational functioning, as measured by a Likert-type scale. In addition, a number of personality measures were administered, including items intended to assess ego strength, flexibility, and self-insight. The participants were also asked to rate their "desire for change" before starting the training.

No significant results were found with the LBDQ or the Group Participation

Scale; and the personality measures were not predictive of anything. However, results obtained with the perceived-change measure were statistically significant. The observers reported perceived behavioral changes for 30 percent of the experimentals, 10 percent of the matched controls, and 12 percent of the randomly selected controls. The corresponding percentages for self-reported changes are 82 percent, 33 percent, and 21 percent for the three groups. The participants tended to report considerably more changes than the observers. An informal content analysis was carried out, and Miles (1965) concluded that the nature of the changes reported included increased sensitivity to others, heightened equalitarian attitudes, greater communication and leadership skills, and patterns of increased consideration and relaxed attitudes in their jobs. No details are given as to how the content analysis was performed.

With certain exceptions, most of the other relationships were not significant. One of the exceptions was a correlation of .55 between the perceived-change measure and trainer ratings of amount of change during the T group. Also, two of the situational variables, security and power, correlated .30 and .32 with the perceived-change measure; that is, more changes in job behavior tended to be observed for the high school principals with longer tenure and more subordinates.

Bunker's (1965) experimental group included 229 people from six different laboratories conducted at the NTL during 1960 and 1961. The participants were presumably rather heterogeneous, but a substantial proportion had leadership or managerial responsibilities. The matching-by-nomination procedure yielded 112 control subjects. Perceptions of behavior change were obtained from each experimental and control subject and from five to seven associates of each subject approximately a year after the training period. The 229 experimentals and 112 controls represented return rates of approximately 75 percent and 67 percent. Eighty-four percent of the observers returned questionnaires.

Bunker presented a list of 15 inductively derived categories that were used for content analyzing the perceived-change data. The 15 categories were grouped within three major classes labeled: (a) overt operational changes, that is, communication, relational facility, risk taking, increased interdependence, functional flexibility, self-control; (b) inferred changes in insight and attitudes, that is, awareness of human behavior, sensitivity to group behavior, sensitivity to others' feelings, acceptance of other people, tolerance of new information, self-confidence, comfort, insight into self and role; and (c) global judgments, really a catchall for changes with no specific referent. No details were given concerning how this classification scheme was developed. However, an agreement rate of 90 percent was reported when trained independent judges used the categories to classify the responses. Eleven of the 15 subcategories yielded statistically significant differences between experimental and control groups with the trained group showing greater change in each category. The greatest differences (ranging up to 20 percent-25 percent) were in areas related to increased openness, receptivity, tolerance of differences, increased operational skill in interpersonal relationships, and improved understanding of self and others. Again, about one-third (ranging up to 40 percent) of the members of the experimental group were reported to have changed in comparison with 15 percent-20 percent in the control group. Categories showing no differences between the groups reflected such things as effective initiation of action, assertiveness, and self-confidence. However, Bunker (1965) emphasized that changes among the trainees differed greatly from person to person and that actually there was "no standard learning outcome and no stereotyped ideal toward which conformity is induced [p. 42]."

Both the Boyd and Elliss (1962) study and Valiquet's (1964) investigation used managerial personnel from a single organization. Boyd and Elliss employed an experimental group of 42 managers selected from three different T groups conducted during 1961 at a large Canadian public utility. Their two control groups consisted of 12 control individuals who received no training and 10 managers who received a conventional human-relations training program employing lectures and conference techniques. Perceived changes were collected by interviewing each manager's superior, two of his peers, and two of his subordinates. The percentages of observers reporting changes for the laboratory-trained group, the conventionally trained group, and the no-training group were 65 percent, 51 percent, and 34 percent, respectively. The percentage of subjects showing changes "substantially" agreed upon by two or more observers was 64 percent for the experimental group and 23 percent for the two control groups taken together. All the above differences are statistically significant. For all subjects a total of 351 statements of perceived change was reported, but only 137 changes were agreed upon by two or more observers. Of twenty-two reported changes judged to be unfavorable (e.g., an increase in irritability or loss of tolerance) by the researchers, 20 were attributed to members of the laboratory-trained group. The observers were also asked to Q sort a deck of 80 statements describing different kinds of job-behavior changes. No significant differences were found with this instrument. In their conclusions, Boyd and Elliss emphasized the great heterogeneity among the trainees in their behavorial outcomes. They also argued that no particular pattern could be regarded as a typical training outcome.

Valiquet (1964) randomly selected 60 participants from an ongoing laboratory-type training program conducted in certain divisions of a large multiproduct corporation. The program was a continuing one and included T-group meetings at various management levels and follow-up meetings designed to promote the effective use of interpersonal skills for solving current organizational problems and planning future activities. Difficulties encountered in choosing an appropriate control group coupled with a low rate of response to the questionnaire resulted in a serious loss of subjects. Final results were available for 34 trained subjects and only 15 matched control-group subjects. On the average about five observers were nominated by each experimental and control subject. The change categories developed by Bunker were used to content analyze the descriptions obtained from each observer. Statistically significant differences were obtained between experimentals and controls on total number of changes observed, total changes agreed upon by two or more observers, and total number of changes reported by the subjects themselves. Results by category were much the same as in the Bunker study except that differences were greater in this study for the categories of "risk taking" and "functional flexibility," defined as the ability to accept change and to be an effective group member. Valiquet believes these differences occurred because the program involved inplant training conducted with co-workers, and the trainers were from within the firm, thereby facilitating the transfer of actual behavior to the work situation.

The above investigations, primarily the first three, seem to form the backbone of the evidence used to support the utility of the T-group method for the development of individuals in organizations. Certain summary statements can be made. In all the studies, between two and three times as many "changes" were reported for the experimental groups as for the control groups. In absolute terms about 30–40 percent of the trained individuals were reported as exhibiting some sort of perceptible change. The percentage was somewhat higher in the Boyd and Elliss (1962) study where the observer opinions were gathered by means of an interview rather than by questionnaire. Within the limits of the method, the types of perceived changes which seemed to discriminate best between experimentals and controls have to do with increased sensitivity, more open communication, and increased flexibility in role behavior.

The studies suffer from a number of obvious methodological limitations: The observers responding to the criterion measures apparently knew whether or not the individual they were describing had been through T-group training. Several of the authors suggested that the effects of such contamination were probably not serious, arguing that the variance in the types of changes was always greater for the experimental groups than for the control groups and that the proportion of changes verified by more than one observer was always higher for the trained group. Such arguments may or may not soothe the stomachaches of those who worry about this type of bias. There is a second potential source of error in that the multiple describers for each subject were nominated by the subject and probably had varying degrees of interaction with each other. It is not known to what extent the observers might have discussed the fact that they had been asked to describe a particular individual and thus contaminated each other's observations. Also, no before measures were used, and the estimation of change depended solely on recollection by the observers. The pervasive influence of perceiver bias on what is remembered and reported is a well-documented phenomenon in psychological research. Further, it is difficult even to speculate how the above potential biases might interact with the practice of having individuals in the experimental groups suggest subjects for the control group who in turn nominate their own observers. A suggestion of such a troublesome interaction is reported in the Valiquet (1964) study. The group of subjects for whom the least changes were reported had originally nominated a significantly higher percentage of peers as describers, rather than superiors or subordinates.

Moreover, it is important to remember that the kinds of changes reported in these four studies have no direct or established connection with job effectiveness. Even if an individual does actually exhibit more "sensitivity" or "functional flexibility" on the job, one still knows nothing about how these constructs may be related to performance effectiveness. The relationship between such measures and job effectiveness constitutes an additional research question. . . .

Underwood (1965) did ask observers to rate behavior changes according to their effects on job performance, but his study used fewer subjects and describers than those discussed above. Fifteen volunteers from a group of 30 supervisors who had participated in 30 hours of inplant T-group training were assigned to the experimental group. The control group consisted of 15 supervisors who had not been in the course, but who were matched on department, organization level, and age with those in the experimental group. Each subject was asked to recruit one observer who was then given a sealed envelope containing instructions for observing and reporting on any behavioral changes in the subject's "characteristic behavior pattern." Thirty-six reports of behavior change were gathered over a 15-week period. Some observers made no reports; several made more than one.

Nine individuals in the experimental group were reported to have changed in some fashion versus seven in the control group; however, there were nearly 2½ times as many changes reported for the experimental group as for the control group. The changes were classified into three categories relating to interpersonal behavior, personal behavior, and nonpersonal behavior. The bulk (32 of 36) were classified in the first two categories. Although the frequencies are small, it is interesting to note that in the control group the ratio of changes judged to increase effectiveness to those judged to decrease effectiveness was 4:1, while in the experimental group the ratio was only 2:1. In other words, the suggestion is that while the T group produced more observable changes in its members' job behavior it also produced a higher percentage of unfavorable changes with respect to their rated effects on job effectiveness. This is the only study of its kind, and it is unfortunate that the Ns are so small and the sources of observer bias so prevalent.

Finally, a study by Morton and Bass (1964) also dealt with perceived changes in job behavior. Conducted in an aerospace corporation, the study focused on a T-group-type program (referred to as an organizational training laboratory) for managers from different levels within the same department. Feedback was speeded by requiring written descriptions from the trainees as to what they were thinking and feeling. Three months after the training, the 107 managers who attended the laboratory were asked to report any critical job incidents which had occurred since the training and which they considered a consequence of the laboratory. Replies listing 359 incidents were received from 97 of the original trainees, and almost all of the incidents were judged by the researchers to have a favorable influence on job behavior. Almost two thirds of the incidents dealt with personal improvement and improved working relationships. Unfortunately, the criterion measure relied on self-report by the trainees, and there were no attempts at experimental control.

$N = 1$ STUDIES

Another type of external criterion study might be labeled the $N = 1$ (Dukes, 1965) investigation. Its distinguishing feature is that the criteria used to evaluate the effectiveness of the training consist of summary data reflecting the overall performance of the organization or organizational subunit. For example, changes in the firm's profit picture or changes in a subunit's turnover rate over the course of the training period might be used as criterion measures. Such a procedure is probably most appropriate for T-group and laboratory programs aimed at increasing organizational effectiveness by means of inplant training sessions and the incorporation of actual organizational problems as topics of discussion during the latter stages of the program. If only one organization is studied, N does indeed equal 1, and, in a statistical sense, there are zero degrees of freedom. Of course, basing observations on just one case precludes any estimation of sampling error. This is not to say that studies based on one observation have no use. Dukes (1965) has recently summarized several instances of interesting and fruitful $N = 1$ studies in the history of psychology. For example, a sample of one is appropriate if the measure used to assess the dependent variable is highly reliable, and the variable itself shows little variation in the population. Perhaps a more frequent situation amenable to an $N = 1$ strategy is when the research aim is to establish that a particular event is indeed possible. Thus, a particular study is used to reject a generalization. Another use of one observation studies is for the generation of hypotheses to guide future research. Unfortunately, none of the studies cited below serves any of the functions discussed in the Dukes' paper.

The most frequently cited study relevant to T-group training was reported by Blake, Mouton, Barnes, and Greiner (1964). The training experience was the Management Grid program which progresses in several stages. Initially, a series of T-group-like sessions is conducted for the purpose of exploring interpersonal relationships among peers and giving managers feedback about their particular management styles. A certain amount of structure and theory is also introduced in an attempt to move individual managers toward what Blake and Mouton (1964) called the 9,9 style of management, a style roughly akin to a maximum concern for both interpersonal relations and production problems. Over the course of a year or more, other training phases consisting of group examination of authority relationships between management levels, practice in the resolution of intergroup conflict, and collaborative problem solving are implemented. The program is intended to involve all managerial personnel from a particular firm.

Blake et al. (1964) presented the first phases of the grid program to all 800 managers in a 4,000-employee division of a large petroleum corporation. A large number of evaluation criteria were used with some being applied both before and after training and others only after the program had been completed. The measures obtained after completion of the program were such things as perceived changes in work-group performance (e.g., "boss' work effort," "quality of group decisions," and "profit and loss consciousness"), perceived changes in working relationships, and a number of items concerning attitudes toward specific management values and techniques. The above data were gathered from approximately 600 managers, and each respondent also was asked to estimate the change in his perceptions from 1962 to 1963, the year that included the grid program. The before-and-after measures included indexes of net profit, controllable operating costs, unit production per employee, frequency of management meetings, management-promotion criteria, frequency of transfers, and relative success in solving a number of persistent organizational problems (e.g., high maintenance costs, high utility costs, plant safety, and management communication). The data concerning the effectiveness of problem solutions were quite subjective and largely anecdotal in nature.

In general, the results were interpreted positively. For example, over the course of the training program the firm experienced a considerable increase in profits and a decrease in costs. The investigators attributed 56 percent of the profit increase to noncontrollable factors, 31 percent to a reduction in manpower, and 13 percent (amounting to several million dollars) to improved operating procedures and higher productivity per man-hour. The substantial increase in productivity per employee was said to have been achieved without increased investment in plant and equipment. Other criterion changes cited were an increased frequency of meetings, increased transfers within the plant and to other parts of the organization, a higher frequency of promotion for young line managers as opposed to staff men with more tenure, and a greater degree of success in solving the organizational problems discussed above. Besides these summary criteria, the individual measures of values and attitudes suggested a shift toward the attitudinal goals of the grid program, and the perceptual measures indicated a change toward the 9,9 style of managing. Recall, however, that these individual measures were obtained posttraining only, and the respondent was asked to estimate the amount of change that had taken place over a year's time.

Studies by Blansfield (1962) and Buchanan (1964) are also of the $N = 1$ type. Both involved lengthy laboratory-type programs, but both are described rather sketchily. Blansfield deals almost entirely with anecdotal evidence about those organizational developments reflecting favorably on the training program. No objective data besides the percentage of favorable trainee opinions are reported. Buchanan's (1964) study (reported in Buchanan, 1965) points to a shift from centralized to decentralized decision making, increased cooperation among work units, and a substantial increase in profits as evidence for the utility of the development program.

The utility of these results is difficult to judge. Neither the Blansfield nor the Buchanan study is reported in sufficient detail to allow careful consideration. However, more important difficulties in interpreting $N = 1$ studies are illustrated in the Blake et al. (1964) report. For example, the index showing a rise in productivity per employee appeared to be the result of an almost constant level of output with an accompanying substantial decrease in the size of the work force during the 12-month period. The crucial question of whether or not total productivity would have fallen along with the size of the work force if the training program had not been functioning is an unanswerable one. In addition, a development program that relies heavily on group participation and team spirit must live constantly in the shadow of the Hawthorne effect. The specific theoretical content or technology of the program may make little difference.

QUESTIONNAIRE MEASURES OF INDIVIDUAL PERCEPTIONS

Most of the criterion measures used in these investigations are individual perceptions obtained by means of standardized questionnaires. In some cases it is stretching a point to classify them as external criteria. For example, a measure of job satisfaction may have little or no relationship to measures of job behavior, but it is still a job-centered rather than a training-centered measure. A number of other ambiguities will be evident.

Beer and Kleisath (1967) studied the effects of the laboratory phase of the Management Grid program on the 230 managerial and professional personnel in one corporate division. Several questionnaire measures of perceptions of organizational functioning were obtained

before and approximately a year after the one-week grid program.

One of these was composed of established subscales developed in previous research at Ohio State University and the University of Michigan. A total of 14 scales was included: representation of department to people outside, persuasiveness, initiating structure, consideration for subordinates, tolerance of freedom, assumption of leadership role, production emphasis, integration of group members, participation of subordinates in decision making, emphasis on group rather than individual discussion, degree of employee influence on work, responsibility delegated to subordinates, authority delegated to subordinates, and the degree to which the supervisor perceives he delegates authority and responsibility. Since people from several levels had been through the grid program, all the subjects responded in terms of how they perceived their superiors' behavior.

Other questionnaire measures were used to assess changes in perceptions of group processes (integration, peer supportiveness of achievement, peer supportiveness of affiliation, and group norms), perceptions of intergroup processes (intergroup dependence, intergroup cooperation, and definition among departments), perceptions of communication patterns (informal, upward, downward, intergroup), job satisfaction (11 dimensions), and commitment to the organization. Voluntary turnover was also included as a criterion measure.

The questionnaires provided a total of 41 scales with which to assess perceptual changes, and the authors pointed out that 37 of these changed in the predicted direction. However, only 14 of the 37 were statistically significant, and a number of significant differences were quite small. The change in turnover is difficult to interpret in that the index decreased over the experimental period, but only back to the level it had been two years, before. Turnover had increased prior to the implementation of the grid program.

In sum, the results of the study tend to be in the predicted directions, but not overwhelmingly so. Unfortunately, there are competing explanations. No control groups were used, and the grid cannot be isolated as the course of the changes. Even if it were, the same criticism applies here as with the Blake et al. (1964) study regarding Hawthorne-type effects. Perhaps any kind of group human-relations program would produce similar outcomes.

Beer and Kleisath (1967) also reported that some of the results were in line with the objectives of later phases of the grid program which had not yet been implemented. This was interpreted as evidence for the pervasive effects of the initial phase of the grid. It could just as well be used as evidence for a pervasive Hawthorne effect.

Zand, Steele, and Zalkind (1967) studied 90 middle and top managers in a company employing 2,000 people. Two criterion measures were used. One consisted of a 42-item questionnaire designed to assess a manager's perceptions of his own behavior, his relations with his superior, the situation in his work group, the organizational climate, and the behavior norms in the company. No details were given as to how the instrument was constructed. The second criterion was an eight-item questionnaire originally developed by Haire, Ghiselli, and Porter (1966) to measure an individual's attitudes toward Theory X versus Theory Y (McGregor, 1960), a dichotomy roughly akin to authoritarian and directive management versus democratic and participative management.

The first questionnaire was administered before, immediately after, and one year after a one-week laboratory consisting of T groups, lectures, and group exercises, while the Theory X-Theory Y measure was given before and one year after. Perceptions of trust of others,

openness in communication, seeking help, and superior receptivity to others' ideas declined significantly immediately posttraining and then returned to pretraining levels on the one year follow-up. No changes were found on the Theory X-Theory Y measure. These results were interpreted as supportive of the laboratory program. The less favorable perceptions immediately after training were seen as reflecting the adoption of "more realistic" standards, and the return to former levels after one year represented perceptions of real behavior change, given the lower standards. Obviously, there are strong competing explanations which cannot be ruled out because of the lack of control.

The lack of change toward Theory Y was explained on the basis of the already strong orientation toward Theory Y for the managers in the sample. Almost all the initial item means were between 3.0 and 4.0 on a 5-point scale.

One other finding deserves comment because of its unique interpretation. Individuals who were rated as most "involved" in the laboratory also tended to be rated as the most involved in follow-up activities back in the organization. Again this was seen as evidence for the ability of the laboratory to change behavior. However, it could also be interpreted as simply consistency of behavior. The training program may not have changed anything.

Some of the difficulties involved in using perceptual data as criteria are illustrated in a study reported by Taylor (1967). The primary criterion measures were 20 semantic differential scales used to describe the trainee, 25 pairs of statements defining scales for describing the trainee's work group, and the eight-item Likert scale for measuring the trainee's orientation toward Theory Y or Theory X (Haire et al., 1966).

All the measures were completed before and six months after a one-week T-group laboratory conducted for 32 managers in a single organization. Some of the measures were also administered one month after the T group. An average of four associates of each subject also responded to the criterion measures with the aim of describing the participants' observed behavior. While the results tended to show a number of significant changes in the participants' own responses, corresponding changes were not observed by the trainees' associates. This general result was also true regarding the Theory Y-Theory X measure.

Friedlander (1968) used perceptual measures to evaluate the impact of still another kind of training group. Four work groups (total $N = 31$) from a large governmental research facility met in off-site locations for four-five days and tried to accomplish three objectives: (a) identify problems facing the work-group system, (b) develop solutions, and (c) plan implementation of the solutions. During the course of the sessions, interpersonal and intergroup processes affecting the work system were explored with the help of a trainer.

The questionnaire used to assess change was composed of six scales developed factor analytically (group problem-solving effectiveness, approach vs. withdrawal from leader, degree of mutual influence, personal involvement, intragroup trust vs. competitiveness, general evaluation of meetings). The item pool for the factor analysis originally was obtained from interview data, discussions with other groups, and a search of the literature. The questionnaire was administered to the four training groups and eight "comparison" groups before and six months after the group training sessions.

An analysis of covariance procedure was used to control for pretraining differences between trained and non-trained groups. While it was reasonable to predict posttraining differences between the individuals in experimental and comparison groups on all the dimensions, the results were mixed. The subjects felt they had achieved greater participation, mutual influence, and problem-solving effectiveness. Somewhat paradoxically, however, there were no changes on the competitiveness or general evaluation dimensions. Friedlander (1968) interpreted the results as "complex," but generally in support of the utility of the training effort.

Buchanan and Brunstetter (1959) used trainees' perceptions of how their work units changed as a measure of the effects of an intraorganizational laboratory program directed at organization development. All the managers in one large department ($N = 224$) were used as an experimental group, and all the managers in a second department ($N = 133$) constituted a control group. Three to seven months after the completion of the training, the participants were asked via a questionnaire to rate changes in the effectiveness of various functions occurring in their own subunits during the previous year. No before measure was used. On those functions judged by the researchers to be under the control of the manager, the experimental group reported a greater number of effective changes. Unfortunately, it is difficult to draw conclusions from the results of such a study. There is no way to estimate how comparable the two departments were before the training began. Also, the trainees were actually being asked to judge what kind of an effect they themselves had had on the department, since it was only through them that the training could have an impact.

While the questionnaire studies cited above have yielded a relatively vast amount of data, the results are quite mixed and are open to numerous alternative explanations. Statistically significant differences are not abundant, and even these tend to be quite small. Over it all hangs the constant threat of response biases that have no parallel in actual behavior change.

INTERNAL CRITERIA

A variety of internal criteria has been

incorporated in studies varying widely in sophistication. Because of the larger number of studies in this category, they will be dealt with more briefly; however, this does not imply a lower opinion of such research. As noted above, an understanding of both types of criteria is essential.

PERCEPTIONS OF SELF

Several investigations have focused on the change in an individual's self-perception occurring during training. Such a criterion flows directly from one of the major aims of T-group training—increasing the clarity and accuracy of individuals' perceptions of their own behavior. Studies by Bass (1962a), Bennis, Burke, Cutter, Harrington, and Hoffman (1957), Burke and Bennis (1961), Clark and Culbert (1965), Gassner, Gold, and Snadowsky (1964), Grater (1959), and Stock (1964) are relevant. A number of these were designed to assess discrepancies between descriptions of "actual self," "ideal self," and "others" (either a specific or some generalized other) and to measure any changes in these discrepancies produced by the T-group experience.

Two such studies are the ones by Burke and Bennis (1961) and Gassner et al. (1964). Burke and Bennis asked 84 participants from six different NTL groups to use 19 bipolar, adjectival rating scales to describe three concepts: (a) "The way I actually am in this T-group," (b) "The way I would like to be in this T-group," and (c) "Each of the other people in this group." The series of ratings of others was used to develop a pooled (or average) description of each subject on each of the 19 scales. The rating scales were administered during the middle of the first week and readministered at the next-to-last session of the third week. Changes were in the direction of greater agreement between actual and ideal self-descriptions and toward subjects' seeing themselves more nearly as others described them. The changes were statistically signifi-

cant on all rating scales for all groups combined, but not for each of the six groups. No control group was used.

The results by Gassner et al. (1964) illustrate the dangers of making inferences from studies without control groups. They conducted three experiments using undergraduate students at CCNY as subjects, and each of the experiments employed a control group which received no training. Sample sizes were 45-50 for the experimental groups and 25-30 for the controls. The principal measure was the Bills Index of Adjustment and Values (a checklist of 40 descriptive adjectives). It was completed by each subject for each of three sets: (a) "This is most characteristic of me," (b) "I would like this to be most characteristic of me," and (c) "Most CCNY students my age would like this to be characteristic of them." As in the previous study, members of the experimental groups reduced their discrepencies between actual and ideal self-descriptions. They also tended to see themselves as being more similar to the average student. However, the control groups showed similar changes, and there were no differences between the two groups on the postmeasures.

Although tangential to the present review because the training group was not really a T group, a study by Grater (1959) also used the Bills Index of Adjustment and Values to obtain descriptions of "real self," "ideal self," and "average group member" before and after a 22-session leadership-training course. The trainer attempted to keep interpersonal evaluation to a minimum, and discussion of emotional reactions was avoided. The group discussion focused mostly on leadership problems the participants had faced in the past and, to a lesser degree, on behavior shown in the group situation. However, a climate of psychological safety was consciously emphasized. Even though this training experience lacked many of the elements of a T group, results similar to those of Burke and Bennis (1961) were obtained. That is, self-perceived discrepencies between real self and ideal self were significantly reduced over the course of training (due primarily to changes in descriptions of the real self), and differences between descriptions of the ideal self and the average group member were reduced, but not significantly so.

However, even with a bona fide T group, significant changes in the self-image are not always found. The Bennis et al. (1957) study was carried out on 12 business-administration students participating in a semester-long T group, and changes in perceptions of actual self and ideal self were assessed by means of a 34-item inventory of possible role behaviors. The items were culled from a wide variety of sources and represented such role behaviors as, "tries hard to understand the contributions of others . . . ," "uses group setting to express nongroup oriented feelings . . . ," etc. The subjects rated each of the possible role behaviors on a seven-point scale according to how descriptive they felt it was of their real or ideal self. Over the course of the T group, there was no significant change in the discrepancy between actual and ideal self-descriptions. However, the authors pointed out that the study was intended to be exploratory, and only 12 subjects were used.

A study by Stock (1964) serves to muddy the waters a bit more. On the basis of her own data, she suggested that individuals who change the most in terms of their self-percept actually become more variable and seem less sure of what kinds of people they really are. Again, however, no control group was employed.

Bass (1962a) asked 30 trainees participating in a ten-day T-group laboratory to describe their mood at five different times during the training period. They did this by indicating on a four-point scale how well each of 27 adjectives (previously selected to reflect nine different moods such as pleasantness,

anxiety, etc.) fit their feelings. Four of nine mood factors showed statistically significant trends. Skepticism decreased throughout the period, concentration increased initially and then declined, depression increased initially and then declined, and activation decreased, went up, and then came down again. Contrary to Bass' expectations, very little anxiety was expressed at any time, and it showed no significant trend either up or down over the period of the training.

In summary it seems relatively well established that the way in which an individual sees himself may indeed change during the course of a T group. However, there is no firm evidence indicating that such changes are produced by T-group training as compared with other types of training, merely by the passage of time, or even by the simple expedient of retaking a self-descriptive inventory after a period of thinking about one's previous responses to the same inventory.

INTERPERSONAL SENSITIVITY

Relative to a somewhat different type of criterion measure, a major aim of the T-group method is to increase skill and accuracy in interpersonal perception, in addition to increasing the clarity of self-perceptions. In spite of the complex measurement problems involved, several studies have attempted to assess how a T group affects the accuracy of interpersonal perception.

In the Bennis et al. (1957) study cited above, a measure of "social sensitivity" was derived by first computing the discrepancy between an individual's prediction of another subject's response and the subject's actual response. For each individual the discrepancies were then summed over all the items and all the other group members. While there was a slight tendency for the accurate predictors to be predicted more accurately themselves, no changes occurred in this measure over the course of the T group.

Gage and Exline (1953) also attempted to assess how well T-group participants could predict the questionnaire responses of the other group members. Two NTL groups of 15 and 18 persons, respectively, responded to a 50-item questionnaire before and after a 3-week laboratory. The items were opinion statements concerning group processes, leadership styles, the scientific study of human relations, and so on. To control for the effects of taking the same items twice, two 50-item forms judged to be "equivalent" by the researchers were administered before and after. The subjects were asked to give their own opinions and also to predict how they thought the group as a whole would respond. An accuracy score for each person was obtained by correlating his predictions on each of the 50 items with the group's composite response on each of the items. Thus, each correlation, or accuracy index, was based on an N of 50. In addition to the accuracy measure, a "similarity" index was obtained by correlating the actual responses of each subject with the group response. The actual responses of the subjects were also correlated with their predictions of the group response to yield a measure of "assumed similarity." None of these three indexes changed significantly over the course of the training.

Lohman, Zenger, and Weschler (1959) gave the Gordon Personal Profile to 65 students at UCLA before and after their participation in semester-long courses using T groups. The students filled out the inventory themselves and for how they thought the trainer did. There was a slight increase in the degree of agreement between students' predictions and the trainer's responses, but, as has been seen, this could be due to any number of different prediction strategies. Fortunately, Lohman et al. placed little emphasis on the finding. No change occurred in the students' self-descriptions. No control group was used, and no attempt was made to account for the effects of taking the same

items twice. In sum, the studies incorporating a measure of how well an individual can predict the attitudes and values of others before and after T-group training have yielded largely negative results.

In his report of a laboratory program conducted by Argyris, Harrison (1962) found that T-group participants (19 middle and top managers) used a larger number of interpersonal terms in describing others than did 12 control-group managers selected from the same organizational levels. However, the trained managers did this only when they were describing individuals who had been in the T group.

In a later study employing a larger sample ($N = 115$) but no control group, Harrison (1966) used a modified version of Kelly's Role Construct Repertory Test to secure self-descriptions and descriptions of ten associates before, three weeks after, and three months after participation in NTL training. The modified form of the Kelly test asks the describer to respond to triads of individuals by selecting a word or phrase that discriminates one member of the triad from the other two and then to give its opposite. The concepts used by the subjects were coded into two categories: (a) concrete-instrumental, and (b) inferential-expressive. The former included such bipolar terms as man-woman, has power-has little power, and knows his job-incompetent. Some examples from the latter category are: afraid of people-confident, tries to get personal-formal and correct, and warm-cold. Interrater agreement for coding terms was 94 percent, and 83 percent of the bipolar terms used by the subjects were classified into one of the two categories, 29 percent as concrete-instrumental and 54 percent as inferential-expressive. In sharp contrast to the usual finding of an effect shortly after training with a subsequent drop off over time, Harrison found significant increases in the frequency of subjects' use of interpersonal concepts to describe associates three months after training, but no short-term (three-week) differences.

Oshry and Harrison (1966) asked 46 middle managers to evaluate some possible causes of unresolved interpersonal work problems, and the resources available for dealing with them, before and after they participated in a two-week NTL program. The problems were actual situations faced by the subjects in their back home work situation. The subjects were given a standard set of 45 items which listed a number of antecedent causes and possible ways of dealing with such problems. According to Oshry and Harrison, the managers, after training, viewed their work as more "human" and less impersonal, and they saw more distinct connections between getting work done and the satisfaction of interpersonal needs than before training. Moreover, after training the managers tended more often to see themselves as the most significant cause or contributor to their own work problems, but they failed to see how these new views of problem causes could be translated into managerial action.

In a similar study, Bass (1962b) showed the film *Twelve Angry Men* to 34 executives before and after two weeks of T-group training. The subjects were asked to finish a series of incomplete sentences describing the behavior of the characters portrayed in the film. Bass concluded that the training resulted in participants becoming more sensitive to the interpersonal relationships exhibited in the film. Although no control group was used, two other groups of trainees were shown the film only after training in order to assess possible effects of seeing the film twice. All groups responded similarly on the posttraining questionnaire, suggesting that the increased sensitivity to interpersonal relations was due to the training and not merely to seeing the film twice.

Stock (1964) discussed an unpublished study by Miles, Cohen, and Whitam in which participants were asked at various stages during T-group training to rank ten statements describing the trainer's behavior and to complete a questionnaire about group interactions. Responses were compared to the trainer's diagnosis of the group's difficulties. Some change seemed to occur on a variable labeled "sensitivity to feelings," but other results were negligible or uninterpretable because no control group was available for comparison. Few details were given.

Finally, in another study without a control group, Clark and Culbert (1965) analyzed the content of nine college students' verbalizations when interviewed before and after participating in a T group as part of a course requirement. Clark and Culbert concluded that four of the nine subjects were better perceivers of group processes at the end of the training than they had been at the beginning.

In contrast to the negative findings regarding perceptual accuracy scores, the six studies cited above establish fairly well that people who have been through a T group describe other people and situations in more interpersonal terms. However, there is still the more important question of whether this finding actually represents increased sensitization to interpersonal events or merely the acquisition of a new vocabulary.

ATTITUDE CHANGE

Turning to another type of internal criterion, the authors were surprised to find relatively few studies relating T-group experiences to attitude changes. This is in contrast to recent reviews of other areas of management-development research (J. P. Campbell, 1966; Miner, 1965) which have shown a rather heavy reliance on attitude measures as criteria. P. B. Smith (1964), Schutz and Allen (1966), and Baumgartel and Goldstein (1967) used the Fundamental Interpersonal Relations Orientation-Behavior questionnaire (FIRO-B; Schutz, 1958) as the primary dependent variable to assess the impact of T-group training. FIRO-B includes a series of attitude items designed to measure six relatively homogeneous dimensions related to three major types of an individual's behavior in groups: control (*i.e.*, attempting to influence the proceedings), inclusion (*i.e.*, initiating contacts with others in a group), and affection (*i.e.*, moving toward others in a close and personal way). The questionnaire contains a pair of scales for each behavior category: one to assess the respondent's own tendency or desire to show the behavior, and the other to assess how much he wants others in the group to show it.

Using only the four scales measuring attitudes toward affection and control, P. B. Smith (1964) obtained responses from 108 English managers and students before and after they had been trained in T groups (11 groups in all) and compared them with responses obtained from a control group of 44 students (six groups in all) who merely took part in a series of discussions. The overall disparity between one's own behavioral tendencies and that desired in others decreased for the T-group trainees, but showed no change for those in the control group. The largest changes occurred for those who initially showed strong control and weak affection tendencies and who desired low control and high affection from others in the groups. These changes are consonant with the aims of the T-group method.

Schutz and Allen (1966) used FIRO-B to study possible attitude changes among 71 persons of widely varied backgrounds who participated in a Western Training Laboratories sensitivity program. Thirty students in an education class at the University of California (Berkeley) were used as a control group. FIRO-B was administered before training, immediately after the two-week session, and again by mail six months after the session had been completed.

Correlations between pre- and posttest scores for the various FIRO-B scales were much lower for the experimental group than for the control group, indicating that the training induced greater changes in the attitudes measured by FIRO-B. The lowest correlations on all six scales (*i.e.*, most change) were obtained between the pretest and six-month posttest scores obtained by the trainee group. This outcome reinforces Harrison's results showing that T-group effects may be manifested only after some time. Unfortunately, the investigators did not report the specific nature or direction of the changes occurring on the various scales of the FIRO-B.

Baumgartel and Goldstein (1967) also used FIRO-B as a criterion measure, in addition to the Allport-Vernon-Lindzey Study of Values (Allport, Vernon, & Lindzey, 1960). Subjects were 100 students (59 male, 41 female) in five sections of a semester-long human-relations course (including T-group experiences) conducted at the University of Kansas. The two criterion instruments were administered pre and post, and the results were analyzed for males versus females and for high-valued versus low-valued participants identified by peer nominations. The data for the latter dichotomy were gathered at the conclusion of the course. No control group was used. The researchers predicted changes in the direction of more expressed control, lower religious values, and higher political values—especially for the participants who were seen as high valued by their peers. Only the prediction for the religious scale was supported; however, there were a number of significant results not predicted by the investigators. Overall, there was a significant increase in wanted control and a significant decrease in wanted affection. Most of the changes could be attributed to the high-valued females and low-valued males. The statistical significance of these interactions was not subjected to a direct test; however, the implication is clear that taking account of individual differences is a necessity when evaluating the effects of such training experiences.

The Baumgartel and Goldstein (1967) study illustrates another serious difficulty in evaluating T-group research. In a large number of the studies cited in this review the training program presented the T group in conjunction with other learning experiences such as reading assignments, lectures, simulated problem exercises, and the like. Thus, it is difficult to attribute any positive or negative results unequivocally to the influence of the T group, although this is often the implication given by investigators. The difficulty is compounded by descriptions of training programs which are usually so incomplete as to preclude any careful assessment of the role played by these other methods.

An attitude measure derived from the goals of the Management Grid program was used by Blake and Mouton (1966) to assess changes in union and management attitudes toward supervisory practices. Only the first phase (the part most analogous to a T group) of the grid program was evaluated, and the researcher's attention was concentrated on changes in attitudes toward five "distinct" managerial styles: maximum concern for both production and people (9,9), minimum concern for both production and people (1,1), maximum concern for production and minimum concern for people (9,1), maximum concern for people and minimum concern for production (1,9), and a moderate but balanced concern for both production and people (5,5). The criterion measure consisted of 40 attitude items in a force-choice format. Each item presented a pair of statements describing how subordinates could be used in a production setting to solve a problem in supervision. Each statement of the pair represented one of the five management styles, and each style was paired with every other style a total of

four times. The respondent was instructed not to indicate which of the two alternatives he preferred but rather to distribute a total of three points between the two alternatives according to his preference. The inventory was given before and after identical grid programs conducted for 33 management personnel and 23 union representatives, all of whom had management or staff responsibilities within the local. The analysis consisted of examining mean scores on all the alternatives pertaining to a particular management style. Significant differences in the predicted directions were obtained between the two groups on the pretest. Managers scored higher than union members on the styles with a high production orientation and lower on those with a low production orientation. No initial differences were found on the 5,5 style. Relative to the before and after comparisons, the managers tended to exhibit more shifts than the union personnel although both groups tended to move in the same direction. The management group increased on 9,9 (the largest difference), decreased on 5,5, and decreased on 1,9. The differences for the other two styles were not significant. Union members increased on 9,1 and decreased on 1,9.

While these results are encouraging, several problems remain. There were no comparison groups, and the strong possibility that any one of a number of other human-relations training methods would produce similar results cannot be entirely discounted. Also, the items appeared to be geared to the stated goals and content of the training program. Thus, the "correct" answer was apparent to the respondent, and a positive response bias may have been elicited which would account for the results.

Kernan (1964) used the Leadership Opinion Questionnaire (LOQ— Fleishman, Harris, & Burtt, 1955) to study possible attitude changes resulting from T-group training. The LOQ yields scores labeled "Consideration" and "Initiating Structure," corresponding roughly to a concern for employee human relations and a concern for getting the work out. It was administered before and after a three-day laboratory-training program conducted within a single organization. Experimental and control groups consisted of 40 and 20 engineering supervisors, respectively. No significant before-after differences were obtained for either group on either of the scales of the LOQ.

In contrast, significant before and after differences were found on the LOQ in the previously cited study by Beer and Kleisath (1967). Recall, however, that no control group was used.

Finally, Kassarjian (1965) attempted to assess changes in inner- versus other-directedness in four student and six adult extension T groups (N = 125) and observed no significant differences. His criterion measure was a 36-item force-choice inventory, which had yielded predicted relationships with other variables in previous research. The items, generated from Riesman's formulations (Riesman, Glazer, & Denny, 1950), yielded a test-retest reliability of .85 and on pervious occasions had discriminated significantly (and in the expected direction) between foreign-born and native-born United States citizens, urban and rural groups, occupational categories, and age groups. In addition, the inventory yielded significant and expected correlations with the Allport-Vernon-Lindzey Study of Values. Control groups (N = 55) similar in composition to the experimental groups were also used, and no significant differences were observed.

Again, the scarcity of research relating laboratory education to attitude change is disappointing and rather hard to understand.

PERSONALITY CHANGE

An internal criterion, which so far has yielded completely negative results, is the standardized personality measure. Massarik and Carlson (cited in Dunnette, 1962) administered the CPI (Gough, 1957) before and after a relatively long sensitivity-training course conducted with a group of students (N = 70) at UCLA. No significant changes were observed. Kernan (1964) also administered the F scale (Adorno, Frenkel-Brunswik, Levinson, & Sanford, 1950) before and after the three-day T-group laboratory. Again, no significant differences were obtained between scores before and after training for the 40 engineering supervisors. However, as the authors of both these studies are quick to point out, changes in such basic personality variables may be just too much to expect from such a relatively short experience, even if the T group is a "good" one.

SIMULATIONS

The last class of criteria to be considered is the situational test or artificial task which is intended to simulate job activities or job behavior. Performance in a business game or on a case problem is an example of this kind of dependent variable.

Bass (1967) used the Carnegie Institute of Technology Management Game (Cohen, Dill, Kuehn, & Winters, 1964) to study the effects of T-group training on the simulated managerial behavior of a number of University of Pittsburgh graduate students in business administration. The Carnegie Tech game is extremely complex and is designed to simulate the activities of several firms in a multiproduct industry. A number of students compose each firm, and they must interact effectively if the company is to prosper. Nine T groups (without trainers) met for 15 weeks. At the end of the 15 weeks three of the groups were divided into thirds and reformed into three new groups, three of the groups were split in half and reassembled, and three of the nine groups remained intact. The nine teams then competed with one another in the game. The splintered groups broke even or made a profit, but the intact groups lost an average of 5.37 million dollars over the

15-week trial period even though the intact groups gave the most positive descriptions of their openness, communication, and cooperation. On the basis of his own subjective observation, Bass attributed the lower performance of the intact groups to their neglect of the management-control function. In his opinion, the members of the intact groups never bothered to ask each other if they were carrying out their respective assignments. These results are somewhat difficult to assimilate into an evaluation of the T-group experience per se since both the splinter and intact groups had identical training. However, the study does demonstrate the danger of assuming relatively straightforward transfer from the T group to another setting.

Argyris (1965) used a case discussion as a situational task and then attempted to measure, via observational techniques, the changes in interpersonal competence over the course of a laboratory program conducted for executives in a university setting. On the basis of previous work, an extremely complex method for content analyzing sound tape recordings of group sessions was developed such that scores on various dimensions of interpersonal competence could be assigned to each individual. The dimensions were originally derived by rationally grouping discrete individual verbalizations and were given such labels as "owning up vs. not owning up," "experimenting vs. rejecting experimentation," "helping others to be open vs. not helping others be open," etc. Certain logically defined group norms such as trust versus conformity are also scored. The dimensions are all bipolar, and rationally assigned integers carrying pluses and minuses are used to represent magnitude. Behaviors are also categorized according to their expression of cognitive ideas versus feelings, and the feelings component is given much greater weight. Case discussions were scored before and after the T-group experience, which was part

of a six-week "living-in" executive development program. There were 57 managers in the experimental group and 56 in the control group. In general, the results were mixed and fell short of what the author considered to be success. As reflected in the content analysis, the norms which evolved in the experimental groups seemed to reflect greater overall competence than the controls. However, differences on the individual dimensions were much more difficult to interpret and seemed to offer no clear pattern. One frustrating aspect of the article is that the nature of the difference between the experimental and control groups is never actually described. Such an oversight was obviously unintentional, and the joint probability of such an error by both author and editor must be fantastically small; however, the effect is to leave the definition of experimental and control to the interpretive powers of the reader.

There are, of course, many other studies purporting to evaluate the effectiveness of laboratory training by using trainee opinion gathered at the conclusion of the training program. Almost without exception such studies are favorable. However, in the absence of at least a control group or before and after measures, such studies are not reviewed here.

INDIVIDUAL DIFFERENCES

So far research focused on the "average" effects of T-group or laboratory training has been considered. That is, the crucial question has been whether or not the training makes a difference for the group as a whole. Such a generalized interpretation may cover up important interactions between individual differences and training methods. Given a particular kind of outcome, certain kinds of people may benefit from T-group training while others may actually be harmed. The same reasoning may be applied to the interaction of differences in situational and organizational variables with the training experience. However, very few studies have investigated interactive effects.

The previously mentioned study by Bennis et al. (1957) used standardized personality measures to make differential predictions about the possible influences of T-group training. The personality measures included Cattell's 16 PF, the EPPS, and Harrington's Self-Sort Test. Schutz' FIRO-B was also administered. Relationships between these variables and the perceptual data were negligible.

Essentially negative results were also found by Steele (in press) who used the Sensation-Intuition (S-N) scale from the Myers-Briggs Type Indicator (Myers, 1962) to predict changes for 72 participants in an NTL program, 39 middle managers in a two-week Managerial Grid laboratory, and 45 students in a course employing a T group. The S-N scale is conceptualized as measuring a preference for basic modes of perceiving or becoming aware of the world, with the sensation end of the scale corresponding to preferences for facts, realism, practicality, and thoroughness, while intuition represents preferences for multiple causation, abstractness, experimentation with stimuli, and a chance to generate individualistic ideas and association about stimuli.

The criteria were trainer ratings and a questionnaire consisting of seven open-ended items designed to measure interpersonal values by posing a hypothetical conflict situation and asking for a course of action. In general, the S-N scale was related to the value orientation of the participants and to their general style of group behavior, as rated by the trainer. However, it was not related to changes on any of these variables.

Still in the personality realm, Mathis (1958) developed an index of T-group trainability using a sentence-completion format. From the theories of group development formulated by Bion (1959) and Lewin (1947), he reasoned that the existence of intrapersonal conflicts and tendencies toward the open communication of both aggression and affection would signify greater receptivity to the training, and the sentence-completion scale was scored to reflect these factors. The scale was then administered to 50 people at the beginning of a T group, and the ten highest and ten lowest scorers were interviewed at the conclusion of the sessions. The individuals scoring high on the trainability index were rated higher on sensitivity, sophistication, and productivity. Again, it must be remembered that these ratings were based on what the subject said in an interview immediately following the T-group program. There was no control group and no interviews before training.

Finally, Harrison and Lubin (1965) divided 69 people in a 1962 Western Training Laboratories program into two categories based on their orientations toward people versus tasks expressed via a questionnaire. Judgments of learning during training were made by the trainers. The investigators concluded that while the person-oriented members were more expressive, warm, and comfortable the task- or work-oriented members learned the most over the course of the laboratory program. However, the authors did not report if the work-oriented participants were still judged to be less effective than the person-oriented individuals, in spite of what they had learned, or were equal or superior to the person-oriented group after training. They were only "observed" to exhibit more "change." The data are quite subjective.

T-GROUP TECHNOLOGY

Research concerning the relative contributions of specific technological features of the T group is also sparse. For example, there are no systematic studies examining the influence of differences in trainer personality and/or style on the outcomes achieved by participants. Case reports and anecdotal evidence are all that exist.

Stock (1964) reported a number of studies focusing on differences in group composition as an independent variable; however, the dependent variable usually consisted of observations of the type of behavior going on in the group. No studies were found designed to relate differences in group composition to differences on either external or internal criterion measures. The authors do not mean to imply that descriptions of the behavior emitted in the group are not of considerable interest; they are simply not the focus of this review.

Feedback is one of the few T-group elements that has been examined empirically, but the evidence from two unpublished studies reported in Stock (1964) is equivocal. Both evaluated effectiveness of T-group feedback indirectly by observing the effects of providing additional feedback at the completion of the T-group experience. Large effects from additional feedback would imply that T-group feedback was not sufficient. Lippitt selected 14 pairs of individuals from two different T groups. The members of each pair were described in similar fashion by the other members of their group. One person of each pair was told in a counseling interview what the other group members thought of him and how they would like him to change. Trained observers rated the behavior of all the T-group members before and after the additional feedback was given. Thirteen of the 14 counseled subjects changed in the desired direction, but only eight of the noncounseled individuals changed in the desired direction. This would appear to be negative evidence for the sufficiency of T-group feedback.

In contrast, Roberts, Schopler, Smith, and Gibb studied 26 small problem-solving groups composed of college students. Twelve of the groups had T-group experience and 14 had not. Half of the trained and untrained groups received only "feelings" oriented feedback, and the other half received only "task" oriented feedback. In general,

the feelings-oriented feedback increased the efficiency and decreased the defensiveness of problem-solving behavior more in the untrained groups than in the trained groups. This was interpreted as positive evidence for the utility of T-group-type feedback.

A more recent study (French, Sherwood, & Bradford, 1966) also tends to argue for the insufficiency of T-group feedback. Twenty middle managers from a large organization participating in a two-week laboratory program were asked, at the outset, to rate themselves on 19 bipolar scales (e.g., reserved vs. talkative). Each subject then chose the four scales on which he wanted to change most. All 19 scales were readministered five times over the two-week training period and again ten months after the completion of training. The experimental manipulation consisted of four different levels of additional feedback ranging from Level A—being rated on one of the four salient scales by all other group members, being told the results of the rating, and discussing it with two other group members—through Levels B and C—which omitted discussion of the rating and feedback of the rating, respectively—to Level D—where the subject was asked to focus on one of the four scales, but other group members did not rate him nor was there any discussion of the scale. In a fifth condition (Level E) none of the four originally chosen scales was selected for attention and no feedback was given. Thus, for Level E, changes were measured on the 15 scales not originally chosen as important by an individual. Although it is not very clearly specified, the sample size for each treatment condition was apparently 20; that is, all the subjects received every treatment condition, but for a different scale. Feedback Levels A, B, and C produced greater changes in the self-ratings than Levels D and E for the selected scale, and this difference was statistically significant. This outcome (like Lippitt's results) may be interpreted as demonstrating the insufficiency of purely T-group feedback. But the results also seem rather obvious because they are based on self-ratings of "change" instead of behavior observations of others as in the Lippitt study.

Finally, some of the problems involved in the transfer of T-group skills back to the work role are illustrated in a quasi case study by Wagner (1965). A nine-member T group composed of managers from different organizations played the UCLA Executive Decision Game No. 2 immediately following a four-day sensitivity-training laboratory. At the end of each business "quarter" the participants were asked to rate the adequacy of the group's decision processes and the extent to which various individuals helped or hindered decision making. During the first quarter of the game, considerable regression from T-group norms took place. After this was pointed out to the group members, they apparently overcompensated during the second quarter by becoming overly conscious of interpersonal factors. Only after a second critique session in which regression and overcompensation were both discussed did the group seem to make efficient use of its T-group skills. Wagner freely pointed out the many qualifications that must be appended to conclusions drawn from such a study.

SUMMARY AND CONCLUSIONS

Argyris (1964) has commented that probably more research has been conducted on the effects of the T-group method than on any other specific management-development technique. A comparison of the present paper with a recent review of evaluation research on all types of management-development methods (J. P. Campbell, 1966) supports the validity of Argyris' statement. Thirty-seven of the 44 studies cited in the present review were focused on evaluating the outcomes of T groups. Of these 37, the majority (23) used internal

criteria. Based on the results of these studies, the following comments seem warranted:

1. The evidence, though limited, is reasonably convincing that T-group training does induce behavioral changes in the "back home" setting. This statement is based primarily on results from the first five studies reviewed. However, the subjective probability estimate of the truth of this generalization is not 1.00 because of the confounding elements already discussed, namely, the manner of choosing control groups, and the fact that most observers probably knew who had or had not received the T-group experience.

The $N = 1$ studies can contribute very little to any general conclusions. Their lack of control, zero degrees of freedom, and susceptibility to contaminating influences such as the Hawthorne effect cast considerable doubt on the utility of their results.

Given the fact of actual behavioral changes attributable to the T-group method, there remains the vexing problem of specifying the nature of these changes. Here the data are even less conclusive. Several researchers (e.g., Boyd & Elliss, 1962; Bunker, 1965) strongly resisted discussing the nature of any "typical" training effect; they implied that each trainee's pattern of change on various behavioral dimensions is unique. If this is true, the present lack of knowledge about how individual difference variables interact with training-program variables makes it nearly impossible for anyone to spell out ahead of time the outcomes to be expected from any given development program. That is, if training outcomes are truly unique and unpredictable, no basis exists for judging the potential worth of T-group training from an institutional or organizational point of view. Instead, its success or failure must be judged by each individual trainee in terms of his own personal goals.

However, in spite of this strong focus on uniqueness, it is true that group differences have been obtained which seem to be compatible with some of the major objectives of laboratory training.

Still another problem in evaluating the back home changes is that the perceived-change measures have not usually related observed changes to actual job effectiveness. Observers have been asked to report changes in behavior, not changes in performance. The only study to attack this problem directly was Underwood's (1965). His results lead to the suggestion that while laboratory training seems to produce more actual changes than the simple passage of time the relative proportion of changes detrimental to performance is also higher for the laboratory method.

2. Results with internal criteria are more numerous but even less conclusive. For example, evidence concerning changes in self-perceptions remains unequivocal. It still cannot be said with any certainty whether T groups lead to greater or lesser changes in self-perceptions than other types of group experience, the simple passage of time, or the mere act of filling out a self-description questionnaire.

The special problems of measuring changes in sensitivity and accuracy of interpersonal perception have already been touched upon. People who have been in a T group do apparently use more interpersonally oriented words to describe certain situations, but this says nothing about their general level of "sensitivity" or the relative accuracy of their interpersonal perceptions.

Again, the authors lament the small number of studies using well-researched attitude measures and/or situational measures as criteria. If such criteria were more widely used, one might have a clearer idea of exactly what kinds of attitudes and skills are fostered by laboratory education. As it is, no conclusions can be drawn. The P. B. Smith (1964) and Schutz and Allen (1966) studies using FIRO-B are suggestive of positive effects, but the studies by Kernan (1964) and Beer and Kleisath (1967)

using the LOQ yielded mixed results. Bass' (1967) use of a simulated exercise has rather negative implications.

NEEDED RESEARCH APPROACHES

Since the research results for both external and internal criteria tend to be equivocal, one might properly speculate on how research *should* proceed if one is to gain a better understanding of what the effects of T-group training are. Only with such an understanding can one judge the relative worth of T-group training as a personnel-development technique. Hopefully, future research will take into account at least seven major considerations:

1. Researchers must devote more effort to specifying the behavioral outcomes they expect to observe as a result of T-group training. The specifications should include the kinds of situations in which the behavior will or will not be exhibited. The loophole of being able to explain either behavior change or lack of change as supportive of the training method must be avoided.

2. More measures of individual differences must be incorporated in future T-group studies. Quite simply, the question is, for what kinds of people are particular training effects observed? Initially, most current researchers seem to act as if laboratory training should have similar effects for everyone. However, this seems hardly likely, and considerably more effort must be expended toward mapping the relevant interactions with individual differences. Only then can investigators avoid the embarrassment of having to conclude that the effects of the learning experience were unpredictably "unique."

3. More attention must be given to interactions between organizational characteristics, leadership climates, organizational goals, and training outcomes and effects. Obviously, the things learned in a development program are not transferred to a vacuum.

4. The effects of T-group training should be compared more fully with the behavioral effects stemming from other training methods. Perhaps the same behavioral objectives can be realized at less cost to

the individual and to the organization by using different methods. Research results specifying the conditions when T-group training should be used and when other methods should be used are needed.

5. A corollary to the above is the need to explore the *interaction* of T-group training and other learning experiences. This has immediate relevance because of the frequent practice of combining the T group with other methods in a laboratory program. The only investigation dealing with such an interaction is Bunker's recent re-analysis of his original data obtained from the 1960 and 1961 Bethel laboratories (Bunker & Knowles, 1967). Between these two sets of summer programs, the total length of the laboratory was reduced from three to two weeks. However, the total time devoted to T-group sessions remained almost constant, while the cutback was at the expense of theory sessions, lectures, and problem exercises. Taking advantage of this built-in difference, Bunker and Knowles compared the perceived-change scores (described earlier) for 52 people in the three-week laboratories and 101 people in the two-week laboratories. On both the total change score and the verified change score the three-week group was significantly superior to the two-week group. The two-week group fell about midway between the three-week group and the control group on the total change index. Bunker and Knowles argued that these results illustrate the necessity of providing additional transfer-facilitating experiences so as to take full advantage of the T group's power. Adopting a different view, one might also argue that it is these other learning experiences which are producing the changes, not the T group. Also, as Bunker and Knowles pointed out, there may have been systematic pretraining differences between the groups since there was no random assignment of subjects. Only further research can decide among these alternatives.

6. It is imperative that the relative contributions of various technological elements in the T-group method be more fully understood. It is surprising indeed that essentially no research has been done on the differential effects of changes in the trainer role, in spite of frequent allusions in the literature to the crucial role played in a T group by the trainer's behavior. Questions concerning the optimal procedures for giving feedback, for enhancing feelings of psychological safety, and for stimulating individuals to try new behaviors should also be investigated. In addition, Schein and Bennis (1965, p. 312) pointed to the necessity of studying the effects of variation in such parameters as the total amount of time the participants spend in the T group, how the total time is distributed, the degree of the laboratory's isolation, and the nature of the participant population. The array of variants in these technological features seems endless, but this should serve to stimulate rather than to inhibit research. At present, the development of new and different training designs seems to be based on a total lack of research evidence.

7. Finally, more effort should be directed toward forging the link between training-induced behavior changes and changes in job-performance effectiveness. Perceived-change measures as they have been used stop far short of this goal. In trying to define the link between job behavior and job effectiveness, researchers will need to make much more use of a wider variety of internal criterion measures flowing directly from the behavioral objectives of the T-group method.

Once again, one should emphasize that neither internal nor external measures are the more "important." Considerable research is needed on both; most important, the relationships between changes in internal criteria and changes in external criteria must be investigated thoroughly. For example, if a T group produces a change in interpersonal sensitivity, will the change be accompanied by improved performance in certain job dimensions or will it not? Is a particular attitude change induced by the laboratory method related to an increase or decrease in job effectiveness or is it entirely independent of performance? These, and others like them, are the crucial "payoff" questions in this whole area of research. So far, the literature offers only one example of an effort to link these two classes of criteria. In a study already cited, Miles (1965) reported that judgments by trainers of the degree of learning shown by participants correlated .55 with the degree of change observed back in their job situations. However, the trainees' own judgments made at the conclusion of the training period were not related to the amount of change their observers reported. Such a finding suggests that self-insight was not achieved and was not, therefore, the mediator of the observed behavior changes.

To sum up, the assumption that T-group training has positive utility for organizations must necessarily rest on shaky ground. It has been neither confirmed nor disconfirmed. The authors wish to emphasize again that utility for the organization is not necessarily the same as utility for the individual.

It should also be strongly emphasized that many if not all the points leading to the above statement can be applied equally to other methods of management development. The entire field suffers from a lack of research attention. However, the objectives of the T-group method are considerably more far reaching than other techniques, and the types of behavior changes desired are, by their very nature, more difficult to observe and measure. These two features serve to place greater research demands on the T-group method than on other techniques, dealing with more restricted, and perhaps less important, behavior domains. For the time being, the T group must remain a very interesting and challenging research area, which is where the energies of its proponents should be applied.

AN ADDENDUM

In the opinion of the present authors, one cannot come away from an examination of the T-group literature without a strong impression of its humanistic and sometimes existential flavor, even when the intended focus is the development of individuals in their organizational roles. This impression is fostered by a sometimes heavy reliance on anecdotal evidence (e.g., Argyris, 1962, 1964; Blake & Mouton, 1963; Foundation for Research on Human Behavior, 1960), by the emphasis often placed on purely personal development (Bugental & Tannenbaum, 1963), and by explicit attempts to conceptualize T-group learning in an existential framework (Hampden-Turner, 1966). To practitioners with this sort of bias, the present treatment of the research literature probably seems unduly mechanistic and sterile.

There are at least two possible replies to the perceived sterility of controlled systematic research. On the one hand, it is an unfortunate fact of scientific life that the reduction of ambiguity in behavioral data to tolerable levels demands systematic observations, measurement, and control. Often the unwanted result seems to be a dehumanization of the behavior being studied. That is, achieving unambiguous results may generate dependent variables that are somewhat removed from the original objectives of the development program and seem, thereby, to lack relevant content. This is not an unfamiliar problem in psychological research. As always, the constructive solution is to increase the effort and ingenuity devoted to developing criteria that are *both* meaningful and amenable to controlled observation and measurement. Such a solution must be found if T-group research is ever to contribute to an understanding of human behavior or eventually establish scientifically the utility of laboratory education as a training and development device. In this respect, people doing research on T-group effects deserve considerable encouragement and, because of the many difficulties involved, a great deal of sympathy.

On the other hand, negative feelings about the sterility of research results may reflect a rejection of both the scientific and organizational points of view. That is, it may be argued that the crucial factor in T-group training is how each *individual* feels at the end of the training program, and that investigating hypotheses concerning human behavior or assessing performance change is of little consequence. This view is quite legitimate so long as the T group assumes a status similar to that enjoyed by other purely individual events such as aesthetic appreciation or recreational enjoyment—events from which each individual takes what he chooses. These are events to be experienced for their own sake, and the individual decides whether they are "life enhancing" or not.

The danger in all of this is that the scientific and existential orientations may not be kept distinct. Argyris (1967) and Bass (1967) argued strongly that the distinction has become blurred at a number of key points, to the detriment of laboratory education. The present authors' view is that a normative or scientific orientation definitely cannot be used to argue against an individual's positive feelings about his own experiences in a T group, and it is hoped that any such connotation has been avoided. However, it is equally inappropriate to claim that a program has utility for accomplishing organizational goals and then to justify such a statement on existential grounds.[2]

---

2. For further discussion of these points the reader should consult the responses to the Argyris and Bass articles published in the *Journal of Applied Behavioral Science*, 1967, 2(3).

NOTES

Adorno, T. W., Frenkel-Brunswik, E., Levinson, D. J., & Sanford, R. M. *The authoritarian personality.* New York: Harper, 1950.

Allport, G. W., Vernon, P. E., & Lindzey, G. *Manual Study of Values.* (3rd ed.) Boston: Houghton-Mifflin, 1960.

Argyris, C. *Interpersonal competence and organizational behavior.* Homewood, Ill.: Irwin, 1962.

Argyris, C. T-groups for organizational effectiveness. *Harvard Business Review,* 1964, 42(2), 60-74.

Argyris, C. Explorations in interpersonal competence—II. *Journal of Applied Behavioral Science,* 1965, 1, 255-269.

Argyris, C. On the future of laboratory education. *Journal of Applied Behavioral Science,* 1967, 3, 153-182.

Bass, B. M. Mood changes during a management training laboratory. *Journal of Applied Psychology,* 1962, 46, 361-364. (a)

Bass, B. M. Reactions to *Twelve Angry Men* as a measure of sensitivity training. *Journal of Applied Psychology,* 1962, 46, 120-124. (b)

Bass, B. M. The anarchist movement and the T-group. *Journal of Applied Behavioral Science,* 1967, 3, 211-226.

Baumgartel, H., & Goldstein, J. W. Need and value shifts in college training groups. *Journal of Applied Behavioral Science,* 1967, 3, 87-101.

Beer, M., & Kleisath, S. W. The effects of the Managerial Grid lab on organizational and leadership dimensions. In S. S. Zalkind (Chm.), Research on the impact of using different laboratory methods for interpersonal and organizational change. Symposium presented at the meeting of the American Psychological Association, Washington, D.C., September 1967.

Benne, K. D. History of the T-group in the laboratory setting. In L. D. Bradford, J. R. Gibb, & K. D. Benne (Eds.), *T-group theory and laboratory method.* New York: Wiley, 1964.

Bennis, W., Burke, R., Cutter, H., Harrington, H., & Hoffman, J. A note on some problems of measurement and prediction in a training group. *Group Psychotherapy,* 1957, 10, 328-341.

Berzon, B., & Solomon, L. N. Research frontier: The self-directed therapeutic group—three studies. *Journal of Counseling Psychology,* 1966, 13, 491-497.

Bion, W. R. *Experiences in groups.* New York: Basic Books, 1959.

Blake, R. R., & Mouton, J. S. The instrumented training laboratory. In I. R. Wechsler & E. H. Schein (Eds.), *Issues in human relations training.* Washington, D.C.: National Training Laboratories-National Education Association, 1962.

Blake, R. R., & Mouton, J. S. Improving organizational problem solving through increasing the flow and utilization of new ideas. *Training Directors Journal,* 1963, **17**(9), 48-57.

Blake, R. R., & Mouton, J. S. *The Management Grid.* Houston: Gulf, 1964.

Blake, R. R., & Mouton, J. S. Some effects of Managerial Grid seminar training on union and management attitudes toward supervision. *Journal of Applied Behavioral Science,* 1966, **2,** 387-400.

Blake, R. R., Mouton, J. S., Barnes, L. B., & Greiner, L. E. Breakthrough in organization development. *Harvard Business Review,* 1964, **42**(6), 133-155.

Blansfield, M. G. Depth analysis of organizational life. *California Management Review,* 1962, **5,** 29-42.

Boyd, J. B., & Elliss, J. D. *Findings of research into senior management seminars.* Toronto: Hydro-Electric Power Commission of Ontario, 1962.

Bradford, L. P., Gibb, J. R., & Benne, K. D. *T-group theory and laboratory method.* New York: Wiley, 1964.

Buchanan, P. C. *Organizational development following major retrenchment.* New York: Yeshiva, 1964. (Mimeo)

Buchanan, P. C. Evaluating the effectiveness of laboratory training in industry. In, *Explorations in human relations training and research.* No. 1. Washington, D.C.: National Training Laboratories-National Education Association, 1965.

Buchanan, P. C., & Brunstetter, P. H. A research approach to management development: II. *Journal of the American Society of Training Directors,* 1959, **13,** 18-27.

Bugental, J. R. T., & Tannenbaum, R. *Sensitivity training and being motivation.* Los Angeles: University of California, Institute of Industrial Relations, 1963.

Bunker, D. R. Individual applications of laboratory training. *Journal of Applied Behavioral Science,* 1965, **1,** 131-148.

Bunker, D. R., & Knowles, E. S. Comparison of behavioral changes resulting from human relations training laboratories of different lengths. *Journal of Applied Behavioral Science,* 1967, **2,** 505-524.

Burke, H. L., & Bennis, W. G. Changes in perception of self and others during human relations training. *Human Relations,* 1961, **14,** 165-182.

Campbell, D. T., & Fiske, D. W. Convergent and discriminant validation by the multitrait, multi-method matrix. *Psychological Bulletin,* 1959, **56,** 81-105.

Campbell, J. P. *Management training: The development of managerial effectiveness.*

Greensboro, N.C.: The Richardson Foundation, 1966.

Clark, J. V., & Culbert, S. A. Mutually therapeutic perception and self awareness in a T-group. *Journal of Applied Behavioral Science,* 1965, **1,** 180-194.

Cline, V. B. Interpersonal perception. In B. A. Maher (Ed.), *Progress in experimental personality research.* New York: Academic Press, 1964.

Cohen, K. J., Dill, W. R., Kuehn, A. A., & Winters, P. R. *The Carnegie Tech Management Game: An experiment in business education.* Homewood, Ill.: Irwin, 1964.

Cronbach, L. J. Processes affecting scores on "understanding of others" and "assumed similarity." *Psychological Bulletin,* 1955, **52,** 177-193.

Deese, J. *The psychology of learning.* New York: McGraw-Hill, 1958.

Dollard, J., & Miller, N. E. *Personality and psychotherapy: An analysis in terms of learning, thinking, and culture.* New York: McGraw-Hill, 1950.

Dukes, W. F. $N = 1$. *Psychological Bulletin,* 1965, **64,** 74-79.

Dunnette, M. D. Personnel management. *Annual Review of Psychology,* 1962, **13,** 285-314.

Fleishman, E. A., Harris, F. F., & Burtt, H. E. *Leadership and supervision in industry.* Columbus: Ohio State University, Personnel Research Board, 1955.

Foundation for Research on Human Behavior. *An action research program for organization improvement.* Ann Arbor, Mich.: Author, 1960.

French, J. R. P., Jr., Sherwood, J. J., & Bradford, D. L. Changes in self-identity in a management training conference. *Journal of Applied Behavioral Science,* 1966, **2,** 210-218.

Friedlander, F. The impact of organizational training laboratories upon the effectiveness and interaction of ongoing work groups. *Personnel Psychology,* 1968, in press.

Gage, N. L., & Cronbach, L. J. Conceptual and methodological problems in interpersonal perception. *Psychological Review,* 1955, **62,** 411-422.

Gage, N. L., & Exline, R. V. Social perception and effectiveness in discussion groups. *Human Relations,* 1953, **6,** 381-396.

Gassner, S., Gold, J., & Snadowsky, A. M. Changes in the phenomenal field as a result of human relations training. *Journal of Psychology,* 1964, **58,** 33-41.

Gough, H. *California Psychological Inven-*

tory manual. Palo Alto, Calif.: Consulting Psychologists Press, 1957.

Grater, M. Changes in self and other attitudes in a leadership training group. *Personnel and Guidance Journal*, 1959, **37**, 493-496.

Haire, M., Ghiselli, E. E., & Porter, L. W. *Managerial thinking*. New York: Wiley, 1966.

Hampden-Turner, C. H. An existential "learning theory" and the integration of T-group research. *Journal of Applied Behavioral Science*, 1966, **2**, 367-386.

Harrison, R. Import of the laboratory on perceptions of others by the experimental group. In C. Argyris, *Interpersonal competence and organizational behavior*. Homewood, Ill.: Irwin, 1962.

Harrison, R. Cognitive change and participation in a sensitivity training laboratory. *Journal of Consulting Psychology*, 1966, **30**, 517-520.

Harrison, R., & Lubin, B. Personal style, group composition, and learning. *Journal of Applied Behavioral Science*, 1965, **1**, 286-301.

House, R. J. T-group education and leadership effectiveness: A review of the empirical literature and a critical evaluation. *Personnel Psychology*, 1967, **20**, 1-32.

Kassarjian, H. H. Social character and sensitivity training, *Journal of Applied Behavioral Science*, 1965, **1**, 433-440.

Kernan, J. P. Laboratory human relations training: Its effect on the "personality" of supervisory engineers. *Dissertation Abstracts*, 1964, **25**(1), 665-666.

Kimble, G. A. *Hilgard and Marquis' "Conditioning and learning."* (2nd ed.) New York: Appleton-Century-Crofts, 1961.

Klaw, S. Two weeks in a T-group. *Fortune*, 1961, **64**(8), 114-117.

Kuriloff, A. H., & Atkins, S. T-group for a work team. *Journal of Applied Behavioral Science*, 1966, **2**, 63-94.

Lewin, K. Group decision and social change. In T. Newcomb & E. Hartley (Eds.), *Readings in social psychology*. New York: Holt, Rinehart & Winston, 1947.

Lohman, K., Zenger, J. H., & Weschler, I. R. Some perceptual changes during sensitivity training. *Journal of Educational Research*, 1959, **53**, 28-31.

Martin, H. O. The assessment of training. *Personnel Management*, 1957, **39**, 88-93.

Maslow, A. H. *Eupsychian management: A journal*. Homewood, Ill.: Irwin, 1965.

Mathis, A. G. "Trainability" as a function of individual valency pattern. In D. Stock &

H. A. Thelen (Eds.), *Emotional dynamics and group culture*. Washington, D.C.: National Training Laboratories-National Education Association, 1958.

McGregor, D. *The human side of enterprise*. New York: McGraw-Hill, 1960.

Miles, M. B. Human relations training: Processes and outcomes. *Journal of Counseling Psychology*, 1960, **7**, 301-306.

Miles, M. B. Changes during and following laboratory training: A clinical-experimental study. *Journal of Applied Behavioral Science*, 1965, **1**, 215-242.

Miner, J. B. *Studies in management education*. New York: Springer, 1965.

Morton, R. B., & Bass, B. M. The organizational training laboratory. *Journal of the American Society of Training Directors*, 1964, **18**(10), 2-15.

Myers, I. B. *Manual for the Myers-Briggs Type Indicator*. Princeton, N.J.: Educational Testing Service, 1962.

National Training Laboratories. *21st annaul summer laboratories*. Washington, D.C.: Author, 1967.

Oshry, B. I., & Harrison, R. Transfer from here-and-now—to there-and-then: Changes in organizational problem diagnosis stemming from T-group training. *Journal of Applied Behavioral Science*, 1966, **2**, 185-198.

Pepinsky, H. B., Siegel, L., & Van Alta, E. L. The criterion in counseling: A group participation scale. *Journal of Abnormal and Social Psychology*, 1952, **47**, 415-419.

Riesman, D., Glazer, N., & Denny, R. *The lonely crowd*. New Haven: Yale University Press, 1950.

Schein, E. H. Management development as a process of influence. In H. J. Leavitt & L. R. Pondy (Eds.), *Readings in management psychology*. Chicago: University of Chicago Press, 1964.

Schein, E. H., & Bennis, W. G. *Personal and organizational changes through group methods: The laboratory approach*. New York: Wiley, 1965.

Schutz, W. C. *FIRO: A three-dimensional theory of interpersonal behavior*. New York: Holt, Rinehart & Winston, 1958.

Schutz, W. C., & Allen, V. L. The effects of a T-group laboratory on interpersonal behavior. *Journal of Applied Behavioral Science*, 1966, **2**, 265-286.

Skinner, B. F. *Science and human behavior*. New York: Macmillan, 1953.

Smith, H. C. *Sensitivity to people*. New York: McGraw-Hill, 1966.

Smith, P. B. Attitude changes associated with training in human relations. *British Journal of Social and Clinical Psychology*, 1964, **3**, 104-113.

Solomon, R. L. Punishment. *American Psychologist*, 1964, **19**, 239-253.

Steele, F. I. Personality and the "laboratory style." *Journal of Applied Behavioral Science*, in press.

Stock, D. A survey of research on T-groups. In L. P. Bradford, J. R. Gibb, & K. D. Benne (Eds.), *T-group theory and laboratory method*. New York: Wiley, 1964.

Stogdill, R. M., & Coons, A. E. *Leader behavior: Its description and measurement*. (Business Res. Monogr. No. 88) Columbus: Ohio State University, Bureau of Business Research, 1957.

Tannenbaum, R., Weschler, I. R., & Massarik, F. *Leadership and organization: A behavioral science approach*. New York: McGraw-Hill, 1961.

Taylor, F. C. Effects of laboratory training upon persons and their work groups. In S. S. Zalkind (Chm.), Research on the impact of using different laboratory methods for interpersonal and organizational change. Symposium presented at the meeting of the American Psychological Association, Washington, D.C., September 1967.

Underwood, W. J. Evaluation of laboratory method training. *Training Directors Journal*, 1965, **19**(5), 34-40.

Valiquet, I. M. Contribution to the evaluation of a management development program. Unpublished master's thesis, Massachusetts Institute of Technology, 1964.

Wagner, A. B. The use of process analysis in business decision games. *Journal of Applied Behavioral Science*, 1965, **1**, 387-408.

Weschler, I. R., & Reisel, J. *Inside a sensitivity training group*. Los Angeles: University of California, Institute of Human Relations, 1959.

Yates, A. J. *Frustration and conflict*. New York: Wiley, 1962.

Zand, D. E., Steele, F. I., & Zalkind, S. S. The impact of an organizational development program on perceptions of interpersonal, group, and organizational functioning. In S. S. Zalkind (Chm.), Research on the impact of using different laboratory methods for interpersonal and organizational change. Symposium presented at the meeting of the American Psychological Association, Washington, D.C., September 1967.

V
Motivation, Satisfaction and Job Design

Introduction. With this section we begin to explore the organizational aspect of I/O psychology, an aspect with which we will become increasingly involved as we progress through the remaining sections of this book. The topics of work motivation and job satisfaction have probably been the most thoroughly researched topics in I/O psychology in the last two decades. While interest in job design is of more recent origin, it shows signs of matching the vitality, interest, and controversy generated by the other two. All three topics are closely related, and their theoretical, empirical, and pragmatic issues overlap and inform each other. They are not one and the same, however, and the distinctions among them, particularly between satisfaction and motivation, as we shall shortly see, are important but frequently overlooked or misunderstood.

Two of the most important roots of the study of work motivation, job satisfaction and job design were Taylor's scientific management and the Hawthorne studies (see Section I). As noted in the Introduction to Section I, Taylor's work reflected, reinforced, and became a principal source of the then prevailing view that financial incentives and the physical conditions of work were the major factors in employee satisfaction and behavior. The Hawthorne studies led to a modification of this view that emphasized the social and interpersonal aspects of the job.

Despite the significant differences between these views, there was one characteristic they had in common, the implicit underlying assumption that a satisfied worker was a more highly motivated worker than one who was not. This widely-held and ostensibly logical belief was severely shaken by Brayfield and Crockett's 1955 research review "Employee Attitudes and Employee Performance," the first selection reprinted here. Their conclusion, which has since been confirmed by more recent studies (e.g., Herzberg, Mausner, Peterson, and Capwell, 1957; Vroom, 1964), was that a strong, pervasive, and direct influence of job satisfaction on performance had not been demonstrated despite many years of research. Within the field of I/O psychology, Brayfield and Crockett helped to draw attention to the distinction between the two concepts and forced many researchers to define more carefully the terms and to develop theories and conduct research that more accurately reflected the distinction between them. Unfortunately, many people outside of I/O psychology, including some managers and executives, are still not aware of this distinction and continue to believe that "a happy worker is a better worker."

The publication of the Brayfield and Crockett paper came at the beginning of a period that saw the emergence of a third view on the nature, sources, and processes of work motivation and job satisfaction. Locke (1976) calls it the *"Work Itself* (or *Growth) School,"* a view which "emphasizes the attainment of satisfaction through growth in skill, efficacy, and responsibility made possible by mentally challenging work" (Locke, 1976, p. 1300). The publication of the monograph by Herzberg, Mausner and Snyderman in 1959 and the interest, controversy, and sheer volume of research it spawned transformed this view from the germ of a belief held by a few into a major school of thought that dominated the study of motivation and satisfaction for years to come. In the article included here, a more up-to-date summary of Herzberg's work, he recounts his famous "two factor" theory in which he differentiates between hygiene factors (or extrinsic factors as they were called in his earlier work)—e.g., pay, job security, working conditions, and relations with co-workers and supervisors—and motivators (intrinsic factors)—i.e., conditions of the work itself including responsibility, advancement, recognition and achievement. According to Herzberg, the hygiene factors can only prevent or minimize job dissatisfaction but cannot lead to enduring *satisfaction,* a state that can only be produced by the motivators. In other words, he views satisfaction and dissatisfaction as independent dimensions with different causes rather than as opposite ends of the same continuum. On the basis of his theory, Herzberg argues that the only way to create job satisfaction is to design jobs to reflect the motivators, *i.e.,* to make them more challenging, to give more responsibility to the workers, etc. He uses the expression "job enrichment" to differentiate his proposal from the "job enlargement" efforts of others which he characterized as little more than adding routine, fragmented tasks to other routine, fragmented tasks to create a "larger" job just as routine and not significantly less fragmented.

The two selections that follow Herzberg's represent the next important step in the research on the nature and processes of job satisfaction and motivation, the development of "expectancy" theory, a theory that has since continued to gain in popularity and importance. In the first article, "The Effect of Performance on Job Satisfaction," Lawler and Porter examine the satisfaction–performance relationship once again. They note that in spite of the apparent agreement between the Brayfield and Crockett review and the more recent paper by Vroom (1964), the latter did identify a small but consistent relationship between the two. Most of the prevailing theories of the time, including Herzberg's, could not account for this relationship or for that matter did not even deal specifically and explicitly with the role of satisfaction in employee motivation. But Lawler and Porter did find a promising explanation in the newly-emerging "path goal" theories (e.g., Georgopoulos, Mahoney, and Jones, 1957; Vroom, 1964), which they themselves were in the process of modifying into "expectancy theory" (Porter and Lawler, 1968). They conclude that rather than satisfaction leading to performance, the influence is in the other direction—from performance to satisfaction. In their words, "good performance may lead to rewards, which in turn lead to satisfaction; this formulation then would say that satisfaction, rather than causing performance, as was previously assumed, is caused by it" (p. 272). For example, if pay were contingent on good performance, then employees would be motivated to perform well on the job and would experience satisfaction from the financial rewards for good performance. On the other hand, good performance in challenging jobs would be satisfying in itself because of the feelings of accomplishment and competence for doing difficult work well.

The next selection, an excerpt from the book by Campbell, Dunnette, Lawler, and Weick (1970), is one of the most cogent descriptions of expectancy theory presently available. To put this selection in the proper context, in an excerpt from their book that is not included here, the authors distinguish between process theories of motivation and content theories.

> The former [process theories] try to explain and describe the process of how behavior is energized, how it is directed, how it is sustained, and how it is stopped . . . Such theories attempt to specify how the variables interact and influence one another to produce certain kinds of behavior . . . By contrast content theories are more concerned with the specific identity of what it is within an individual or his environment that energizes and sustains behavior. That is, what specific things motivate people . . . The content theories are not centrally concerned with specifying the precise form of the interactions between variables. (Campbell, et al., 1970, p. 341)

Expectancy theory, then, is clearly a process theory, while Herzberg's two-factor theory is a content theory. Although there are several versions of expectancy theory (see Campbell and Pritchard, 1976 for a review), there is a certain commonality to all of them—they all postulate that the effort an individual exerts is a function of his or her expectation that the effort will lead to an outcome and the attractiveness ("valence") of the outcome.

At approximately the same time that expectancy theory was being fully developed and elaborated, an issue of a somewhat more pragmatic sort was generating considerable controversy. Partly as a result of Herzberg's work, job enrichment began to be promoted with an almost missionary zeal as a panacea for a variety of work-related problems, particularly those related to employee motivation and satisfaction (e.g., see Ford, 1969;

Myers, 1964). A note of caution was sounded, however, by a series of studies (Blood and Hulin, 1967; Hulin and Blood, 1968) that seemed to demonstrate that not all workers respond favorably to jobs that are challenging, allow more discretion, and require more worker responsibility. Indeed, it became increasingly apparent that very little was actually known about what kinds of work outcomes are associated with particular job characteristics and the effect of individual differences and organizational context on these relationships. Much of this uncertainty was finally resolved by the 1971 publication of the extensive study by Hackman and Lawler entitled, "Employee Reactions to Job Characteristics," which is the next article reprinted in this collection. In their study, Hackman and Lawler identified four core job dimensions—variety, autonomy, task identity and feedback—that are related to increased job satisfaction, motivation, work quality, and decreased absenteeism. They found that for workers who desire "higher order need satisfaction" (e.g., the motivator factors proposed by Herzberg) the core job dimensions would produce these favorable outcomes. Subsequent research has added considerably to our understanding of the facilitative conditions and expected results of job enrichment, to a degree that a technology of job design now appears possible and widely applicable (Hackman and Oldham, 1975 and 1976; Hackman, Oldham, Janson and Purdy, 1975; Oldham, Hackman and Pearce, 1976).

One of the major contributions to the technology of job design has been the research conducted at the Tavistock Institute of Human Relations in London since the early 1950s. The importance of the "sociotechnical systems" school of thought, as this research tradition is frequently called, was the attention it focused on the implications of job redesign and technological change for human relations on the job. The 1951 article by Trist and Bamforth, "Some Social and Psychological Consequences of the Longwall Method of Coal-Getting," in many respects marks the "birth" of the sociotechnical systems school and is still one of the best examples of this research available. It appears here out of chronological order because it anticipated and reflects the contemporary view of job redesign as one element in a broader systemic strategy for organizational change, a strategy that considers the interactions between job changes and their social and organizational context. As such, it complements the Hackman and Lawler articles. Indeed, these two articles taken together probably characterize present perspectives on job design more effectively than any other two "classics."

The last selection, "Job Satisfaction Reconsidered" by Walter R. Nord, is clearly the most unusual in this section, possibly in the entire collection, and is also the one that is most likely to raise questions concerning its inclusion. While it is true that the article is too recent for an adequate assessment of its enduring value to be made at this time, the authors of this book feel that the issues it raises, if not this particular article itself, will significantly influence I/O psychology for the next several years. What Nord does in this article is reexamine several of the basic assumptions that underlie most of the research on job satisfaction. Specifically, he argues that the study of job satisfaction has taken for granted the desirability of economic competition, growth, utilitarianism, individualism, and the existing distribution of power in the organization. An alternative perspective would, in his words, "be more macro in scope, take the express interests of lower level participants as a point of departure, and focus on ways to alter the existing distribution of power in organizations. In a word, it will be more radical" (1977, p. 1034). In effect, he is proposing that we examine the implications of alternative political and economic idealogies for research and practice in I/O psychology. His discussion of systems for workers' participation and control seems particularly relevant and contemporary in light of the growing interest in these systems in this country and their widespread acceptance in Western Europe and Scandinavia. Therefore, the reader is urged to consider this article carefully, as well as the rebuttal by Locke (1978) and Nord's subsequent response (Nord, 1978), to get an idea as to the kinds of value-dependent and socially-relevant issues that I/O psychologists may increasingly have to deal with in the turbulent years ahead.

REFERENCES

Blood, M. R., and Hulin, C. L. 1967. Alienation, environmental characteristics, and worker responses. *Journal of Applied Psychology*, **51**, 284-290.

Campbell, J. P., and Pritchard, R. D. 1976. Motivation theory in industrial and organizational psychology. In M. D. Dunnette (ed.), *Handbook of industrial and organizational psychology*. Chicago: Rand-McNally.

Campbell, J. P., Dunnette, M. D., Lawler, E. E., III, and Weick, K. E., Jr. 1970. *Managerial behavior, performance, and effectiveness*. New York: McGraw-Hill.

Ford, R. N. 1969. *Motivation through the work itself*. New York: American Management Associations.

Georgopoulos, B. S., Mahoney, G. M., and Jones, N. W. 1957. A path–goal approach to productivity. *Journal of Applied Psychology*, **41**, 345-353.

Hackman, J. R., and Oldham, G. R. 1975. Development of the job diagnostic survey. *Journal of Applied Psychology*, **60**, 159-170.

Hackman, J. R., and Oldham, G. R. 1976. Motivation through the design of work: Test of a theory. *Organizational Behavior and Human Performance*, **16**, 250-279.

Hackman, J. R., Oldham, G. R., Janson, R., and Purdy, K. 1975. A new strategy for job enrichment. *California Management Review*, **17**(4), 57-71.

Herzberg, F., Mausner, B., Peterson, R. O., and Capwell, D. F. 1957. *Job attitudes: A review of research and opinion*. Pittsburgh: Psychological Service of Pittsburgh.

Herzberg, F., Mausner, B., and Snyderman, B. 1959. *The motivation to work*. (2nd ed.) New York: Wiley.

Hulin, C. L., and Blood, M. R. 1968. Job enlargement, individual differences, and worker responses. *Psychological Bulletin*, **69**, 41-45.

Locke, E. A. 1976. The nature and causes of job satisfaction. In M. D. Dunnette (ed.), *Handbook of industrial and organizational psychology.* Chicago: Rand-McNally.

Locke, E. A. 1978. "Job satisfaction reconsidered"—reconsidered. *American Psychologist,* **33**, 854-855.

Myers, M. S. 1964. Who are your motivated workers. *Harvard Business Review,* **42(1)**, 73-88.

Nord, W. R. 1977. Job satisfaction reconsidered. *American Psychologist,* **32**, 1026-1035.

Nord, W. R. 1978. On Locke's "revision" of "job satisfaction reconsidered." *American Psychologist,* **33**, 855-857.

Oldham, G. R., Hackman, J. R., and Pearce, J. L. 1976. Conditions under which employees respond positively to enriched work. *Journal of Applied Psychology,* **61**, 395-403.

Porter, L. W., and Lawler, E. E., III. 1968. *Managerial attitudes and performance.* Homewood, Ill. Dorsey Press.

Vroom, V. H. 1964. *Work and motivation.* New York: Wiley.

17. Employee Attitudes and Employee Performance*

ARTHUR H. BRAYFIELD

WALTER H. CROCKETT

The systematic investigation of employee attitudes is a relatively recent development in American business and industry. Although Houser and his associates (26) pioneered in this field in the early 1920's there was little active interest until early in World War II when employee attitude surveys began to flourish (49, p. 7). Currently there is an abundant and growing literature on the use of this personnel tool (56).

Only infrequently, however, are discussions of the correlates of employee attitudes found and these are almost never substantiated by empirical evidence. Where we have located relevant discussions in the personnel and psychological literature a common assumption predominates—employee attitudes bear a significant relationship to employee performance. These are sample quotations:

> ... morale is not an abstraction. Rather it is concrete in the sense that it directly affects the quality and quantity of an individual's output.

> Numerous investigations have established the certainty that productive efficiency fluctuates with variations in interest and morale.

> ... employee morale ... reduces turnover. It makes labor trouble and strikes less likely. It cuts down absenteeism and tardiness; lifts production.

It is of some practical and theoretical interest to establish the relationships

*Source: From *Psychological Bulletin*, vol. 52, no. 5, 1955, pp. 396-424. Copyright © 1955 by the American Psychological Association. Reprinted by permission. Footnotes renumbered.

which exist between employee attitudes and employee performance. The purpose of this review is to examine and summarize the empirical literature which bears upon these relationships and to engage in some discussion of the methodological and theoretical considerations involved in such investigations.

Examination of the literature reveals that it is (a) recent, and (b) frequently peripheral in the sense that relevant data were collected and analyzed incidental to some other objective.

We have established certain conditions for the inclusion of materials in this review. First, the indices of employee attitudes must permit classification of respondents along some attitude continuum. Second, the indices of employee attitudes must have been obtained directly from the employees themselves. Although we are willing to include ratings of job performance by supervisors and others, if no other criteria of performance are available, we are not willing to accept estimates of *attitudes* by someone other than the individuals themselves. Performances, we would contend, are less easily disguised by the individual and less readily distorted by the observer than are attitudes. Third, the investigations must have been conducted in industrial or occupational settings. Within the limitations of interlibrary loan service our coverage is complete through July, 1954. We have made no effort to unearth unpublished studies although we report several including three studies by one of us.

The following scheme was adopted as a convenient and meaningful way of categorizing the literature.

1. Daniel Katz and Robert Kahn (33, p. 657) have suggested that "in social structures it is important to distinguish between: (1) the motivation to stay within the system, to remain a part of the group and (2) the motivation to act in a differential manner within that system." We have thus distinguished between those studies which involve performance on the job and those which involve withdrawal from the job (absences, accidents, turnover).

2. Within the above breakdown we have made a further differentiation based upon research design. One major design relates the attitudes of individuals to their performances as individuals. A second design relates the attitudes of the members of groups to their performances as groups.

3. A still further classificiation differentiates between studies in which a single index of attitudes either as a single item or as a summation of items was used and those few in which multiple indices were used.

We have not attempted to define such terms as job satisfaction or morale. Instead, we have found it necessary to assume that the measuring operations define the variables involved. Definitions are conspicuous by their absence in most current work in this area.

Where reliability data are reported for the attitude and performance measures, we have included them in our summaries. We also have attempted to specify whether or not the attitude data were collected under conditions which preserved the anonymity of the subjects. Throughout the first section of the paper we have tried to hold comments on methodology to a minimum, postponing detailed methodological considerations until the substantive material has been covered.

Before summarizing and discussing the literature it may be appropriate to describe the investigation which, as far as we can determine, initiated research in this area of industrial psychology. The classic study relating attitudes and performance in an industrial setting was conducted by Kornhauser and Sharp (39) in 1930 in Neenah, Wisconsin, in the mill operated by the Kimberly-Clark Corporation. Between 200 and 300 young girls engaged in routine repetitive jobs at machines were studied. Both questionnaires and interviews were used. The questionnaires were patterned after those developed by Houser and covered a range of specific attitudes— toward supervisors, repetitiveness and speed of work, personnel policies, wages, and the like. Scores were computed for groups of items and item responses were analyzed. Intercorrelations among different item groups ran about .4 to .5. Reliabilities were thought to be somewhat higher.

The finding on relationship of attitudes to performance is summed up in the statement that "Efficiency ratings of employees showed no relationship to their attitudes." No description is given of the rating system. Further, the authors say,

> In one group of 20 girls for whom we had comparable output records, three of the four with the most unfavorable attitudes were first, second, and fourth in production and the two most favorable were near the bottom in production.

With respect to the criterion of withdrawal from the job, Kornhauser and Sharp reported that "Unfavorableness of job attitudes is slightly correlated with lost time because of sickness."

Relations between attitudes and intelligence, age, schooling, marital status, home life, emotional adjustment, and supervision also were studied. This early report should be read by anyone seriously interested in this area of investigation.

PERFORMANCE ON THE JOB

INDIVIDUAL ANALYSIS

Three unpublished studies have used the Brayfield-Rothe Job Satisfaction Blank as an index of job satisfaction. In 1943 Brayfield (4) started work on the development of a scale intended to give what might be called a global measure of job satisfaction. It was predicated on attitude theory and applied the Thurstone scaling technique. After some preliminary work Likert's scoring technique was applied to 18 Thurstone-scaled items to produce an index which had a range of scores from 18 through 90 with a neutral or indifferent point at 54. The resulting scale gave a corrected split-half reliability coefficient of .87 when used with 231 women office employees. It differentiated between adults enrolled in a night class in personnel psychology who were employed in personnel jobs and similar students who were employed in non-personnel jobs. For the same group, a correlation of .91 was obtained between the Brayfield-Rothe and the Hoppock Job Satisfaction Blank.

In 1944, in connection with a larger study Brayfield collected data on 231 women office employees working for the same firm but employed in 22 different offices throughout the country. The scale was administered to small groups of individuals as part of a test battery. All materials were signed. At the same time supervisor's ratings on a graphic rating scale were obtained for all employees in the sample. A total score was computed from three items covering quantity, quality, and over-all worth to the company. About two-thirds of the employees were rated by two supervisors and the ratings were averaged. Reliabilities of ratings are unknown although in one office it was possible to compare two supervisors who had rated the same 23 women. The intercorrelation was in the low seventies.

When job satisfaction scores for these women clerical workers were compared with their performance ratings a correlation of .138, significant at the 5 percent level, was found. To control for the influence of job level, the 231 women were classified into six groups as follows: Stenographers (50); General Clerical (40); Typists (38); High Level Machine Clerical (36); Low Level Machine Clerical (34); Entry (33). The correlations for the first five groups ranged from − .06 to + .13. None were significant. The correlation for the group of 33 inexperienced and untrained girls (Entry) was .387, significant at the 5 percent level. An additional group of 35 women telephone order clerks provided a correlation of .26 which was not significant.

In 1950, Brayfield and Mangelsdorf obtained data on 55 second-, third-, and fourth-year plumber apprentices employed in a number of firms in Oakland, California. All were enrolled four hours per week in a public vocational school. The subjects completed the Brayfield-Rothe job satisfaction scale during classes as part of a testing program in which all the materials were identified by name of respondent. The corrected split-half reliability coefficient was .83. Performance ratings were obtained for each plumber from his foreman or employer. The rating form consisted of 25 scaled items in check list form developed by Goertzel (19, p. 117) who attempted to provide a generalized scale that could be used for assessment of workers on any type of job. For various groups of workers Goertzel found a correlation of approximately .80 between ratings on two forms of 25 items each. The correlation between job satisfaction scores and ratings was .203 which is not significant.

In 1953, Brayfield and Marsh studied the measured characteristics of 50 farmers enrolled four hours per week in a veterans' on-job training program. The median age of the subjects was in the early thirties. They had lived on farms most of their lives; all were managing their own farms. Among other materials they completed the Brayfield-Rothe job satisfication scale. All materials were signed. The corrected split-half reliability coefficient was .60; if the three subjects with the most inconsistent responses had been eliminated, the reliability coefficient would have become .77.

The subjects' performance as farmers was rated by their instructors who ranked them in order of effectiveness. Sixteen farmers were ranked by one instructor, 14 by a second, and the remaining 20 by another. Ranks were transmuted into "scores" (18) and cast into a single distribution. Re-rankings after several months, when similarly

treated, correlated .86 with the original rankings. Instructors were not aware that they would be asked to re-rank their students.

For the 50 farmers the correlation between job satisfaction scores and performance ratings was .115 which is not significant. If the three "erratic" subjects had been eliminated, the correlation would have become .133.

The same job satisfaction scale was used in 1953 in an unpublished study by Roger Bellows and associates of 109 Air Force control tower operators.[1] The correlation with individual proficiency ratings was .005.

Gadel and Kriedt (17) report a study employing a design similar to that used in the investigations just described. One hundred and ninety-three male IBM operators working in the machine rooms of numerous divisions of the Prudential Insurance Company home office completed and signed a 10-item job satisfaction questionnaire "designed to cover a variety of attitudes related to work duties." The performance criterion consisted of rank-order ratings on overall job performance made by the immediate supervisor. Ratings were converted to standard scores and correlations were computed for each of the groups. The resulting correlations were averaged using the Fisher z transformation. The relationship between job satisfaction and performance was found to be .08.

The Life Insurance Agency Management Association has engaged in job satisfaction studies since the early 1940s. A report of their work which falls into the research classification under consideration was published by Habbe (23) in 1947. Job satisfaction questionnaires were mailed out to 9,353 insurance agents. Seventy-five percent were returned of which more than 90 percent

---

1. R. M. Bellows. Personal communication. June 30, 1954.

were usable. Signatures were not requested although quite a few agents did identify themselves. The blank contained questions asking about single phases of the job to be answered by one of five alternatives indicating satisfaction or dissatisfaction. A single question asked "How do you feel about your job as a life underwriter?" The performance rating was in the form of a self-report since each agent was asked to check whether his previous year's production was "under $200,000" of insurance or "$200,000 or over." Agents producing under $200,000 scored 4.15 on what evidently was the single general satisfaction item as compared to 4.11 for the high producers. The "Extremely Satisfied" score is 5.00. The relationship is insignificant or slightly in favor of the lower producers. It should be noted that this performance criterion is a self-report and that the break at the $200,000 point might not be the best point for analyzing the relationship.

Baxter and his associates (1) have recently reported a training evaluation study concerned with new debit insurance agents (service and sell weekly and monthly premium, ordinary, and group insurance for families within a specific geographical territory). Included in the data collected were responses to a comprehensive job satisfaction attitude questionnaire with items varying in number from 32 to 43 depending upon when it was administered. Respondents apparently were identified. Supervisor ratings on a 5-point, 9-item graphic rating scale were collected. Sales volume figures were obtained for each agent for his first year on the job. Although the correlations between the job satisfaction index and the performance criteria were not reported, the investigators have made them available.[2] For 223 agents the correlation between satisfaction and supervisor's rat-

ing is .23, significant at the 1 percent level. The correlation between satisfaction and sales volume is .26 also significant at the 1 percent level. This is the only study in this classification which uses an objective performance criterion. The incentive situation is also more clear-cut here except perhaps for the farmers. Although this correlation is significant, it is quite low.

One of the most carefully done studies which we have inspected is Mossin's (48) investigation of the selling performance and what he termed contentment of 94 teenage female retail sales clerks in a large New York department store. His performance criteria of 12 items were based on the ratings of four experienced and specially trained shoppers. Ratings on five items formed a composite labeled "Selling Attitudes." Ratings on three other items were combined as an index of "Selling Skills." The intercorrelation was .76. In addition, the entire 12 items formed a composite which correlated beyond .9 with each of the other criteria. Several detailed analyses of the reliability of the criteria were made including intercorrelations among the four shoppers. A minimum estimate of the reliability of the criteria would be that they exceeded .7 and might actually have been somewhat higher.

Mossin used two job satisfaction measures. One was an over-all composite rating secured by combining the scores on six attitude items inquiring about "affective dispositions" toward departmental assignment, merchandise assignment, relations with customers, relations with fellow salesgirls, relations with supervisors, and working conditions, along with one item regarding intention to remain in retail selling plus one item requiring a self-appraisal of sales ability. The second index was a single multiple-response item asking "How you REALLY feel toward your job." Responses on these two indices of job satisfaction were obtained during an individual data collection session with

---

2. B. Baxter. Personal communication. February 17, 1954.

the investigator. Therefore, the respondents were identified. The correlation between the two satisfaction criteria was
.53.

The composite job satisfaction score
correlated − .07 with the Attitudes criterion and − .03 with the Skill criterion.
The single item job satisfaction index
correlated .15 and .06, respectively.
None of these is significant. No results
were reported for the 12-item composite
performance criterion although it may
be inferred that they would be of approximately the same magnitude since it
was highly correlated with the other two
criteria. This is a carefully executed investigation and should be consulted by
anyone working in this general area.

The final major investigation in this
series, by Bernberg (2), is the only one
to use differentiated attitude measures.
He included a measure of group morale
as identified by 34 "indirect method"
items, a 12-item scale presumed to
measure an employee's acceptance of
the formal organization (e.g., "I think
this company treats its employees worse
than any other company does"), a
0-100 thermometer scale with seven
verbal referent points based on the single statement, "On the whole, I believe
that the supervisor in my group is a man
who knows his job and is a leader," and
a similar thermometer scale for the self-
rating statement, "On the whole, I believe that my group has a high degree of
morale. By that, I mean the men work
willingly and cheerfully as a well organized team." The intercorrelations
among the four indices as computed for
890 hourly paid workers in a large aircraft manufacturing plant ranged from
.47 to .77 with the median at .5. Split-
half reliabilities for the two multi-item
scales were approximately .8.

Questionnaires embodying these
measures were sent home with more
than 1,000 employees of an aircraft
plant. No returns were accepted after 48
hours by which time 88 percent were
back. Presumably the respondents were
identified. The performance criterion

was the average weighted score of a
graphic rating scale with the five dimensions of adaptability, dependability, job
knowledge, quality, quantity. The split-
half reliability was .8.

The correlations between the four attitude measures and the performance
criterion ranged from .02 to .05.

Four miscellaneous studies warrant
brief mention only. An English doctoral
dissertation (40) is reported to include
the finding that it was clearly determined that "there is almost no relationship between proficiency and satisfaction among (British) post office counter
clerks."[3] Kerr (38) reports a master's
study finding of a correlation of − .76
between a 10-item job satisfaction
measure and employer reports on the
frequency of what he termed grievance,
advice, and catharsis conferences with
employees in two very small Indiana
plants. The study is relevant mainly as
suggesting a possible performance criterion for investigation. Chase (7) has a
very inadequately described study
which purports to find a small positive
relationship between superintendent's
ratings and teacher's satisfaction.
Brody's (5) master's thesis at New York
University describes an investigation in
which the relationship between Hoppock Job Satisfaction Blank scores and
production under a piece work incentive plan correlated .68 for 40 employees. This is an extraordinary finding.
However, examination of the raw data
in the Appendix casts serious doubt on
the meaningfulness of the correlation.
Two groups working under different incentive conditions are lumped together.
For the 22 cases which might actually
be legitimate subjects, the Hoppock
scores do not conform to any known
appropriate scoring system for that particular Blank. The production data are
bimodal.

3. Reported by Heron, A. Industrial
psychology. *Ann. Rev. Psychol.,*1954, 5,
203-228.

At this point we can summarize the findings for this research design. The prototype study used a single overall index of employee attitudes variously titled job satisfaction or morale. Respondents were identified. A distribution of individual scores was related to some index of individual performance on the job. Customarily, a single occupational group was studied. When 14 homogeneous occupational groups and one large sample of assorted hourly factory workers were studied, statistically significant low positive relationships between job satisfaction and job performance were found in two of the 15 comparisons. These results, pointing to an absence of relationships, are in line with the findings of the pioneering Kornhauser and Sharp investigation.

GROUP ANALYSIS

The essentials of this design are as follows. Employee attitudes are determined individually but the average for the group or the percentage responding in a certain manner is related to some estimate of performance or productivity for the group as a whole. This arrangement requires at least two groups. Characteristically, comparisons are by departments within a firm rather than by occupation.

The antecedents of this approach are to be found in a study by Rensis Likert which was reported in a privately circulated document in 1941. We have not examined the report. According to a reference to it in one of Katz's (30) papers, the morale of insurance agents in 10 agencies rated superior in operational efficiency by the home offices of nine companies was compared to that of agents in 20 agencies rated below average. We infer that some form of attitude questionnaire was used since Likert conducted the study although interviews may have been involved. Katz says that "Morale was found to be significantly related to the criterion." This study is mainly of historical interest.

Three studies employing this design or a modification of it utilized a single index of employee attitudes. Katz and Hyman (32) report a study which they supervised during World War II under the general direction of Likert. Their concern was with employee morale in shipyards and its relation to productivity, among other considerations. Two summary measures of morale were used, both of which were obtained from personal interview protocols. One was a yes–no answer to the question: "Have you ever felt like quitting the yards?" The rank order of the percentage who had felt like quitting was compared with an index of productivity (time to turn out a ship) for the five shipyards being studied. The two rank orders agreed fairly well. The second measure of employee attitudes was furnished by the responses to seven items regarding specific aspects of the working situation and environment. The relationship to productivity was somewhat less marked than the first comparison although the authors comment that "In general the yards with high productivity were the yards with high worker morale." It should be remarked that, although productivity differences were very great among the yards, the morale differences were really quite small; the morale scores for the five yards were 9.3, 9.4, 10.0, 10.0, 10.9.

Giese and Ruter (20) employed this design in a study of employees of a small national mail order company. It is one of the few studies which had as its primary purpose the determination of the relationship in which we are interested. In fact, the aim of the study was to devise a method for predicting the morale of departments from objective data. The only description of the attitude measure is "A morale questionnaire was scored so that a quantitative score was available." There is no statement regarding the anonymity of the subjects. Three objective measures of efficiency were available. For each of 25 departments there were available three average measures of efficiency and one average morale score. When correlations based on group averages were computed they were found to range between .15 and .27. None of these is significant (our determination).

The Triple Audit studies (62) of the Industrial Relations Center at the University of Minnesota fall into this research design category. Here the firm was the basic unit of comparison. Since the number of firms studied was small, only seven, the authors advise that it is impossible to draw any conclusions about the relationships obtained.

The next series of studies reviewed here used the same design but differ from the three just mentioned in that they make some differentiation among employee attitudes. That is, they make some attempt to specify component parts.

The early work of Likert and Katz has been continued by them at the University of Michigan since the war. The prototype study was undertaken in 1947 in the Prudential Insurance Company and findings were reported in some detail in 1950 (34). Although the objectives were broad, an important portion of the study was devoted to exploring the relationships between employee attitudes and productivity.

One-and-one-half-hour free-answer interviews covering 53 questions were held with 419 nonsupervisory clerical workers in 24 different sections. Responses were coded. The sections were arranged in parallel pairs in order to hold constant as many factors as possible. One set of 12 sections was designated as high productivity on the basis of production records while the parallel set was composed of low productivity sections. The authors note that productivity differences between the pairs were not great, rarely more than 10 percent. Each of the high–low productivity pairs consisted of two sections handling the same type of work with the same type of

people at the same job levels and were very similar on a number of factors.

A unique feature was the construction of four indices of attitudinal variables. The differentiations were made on a theoretical basis with some empirical confirmation for the relationship among the items used in each index. Four variables were specified: (a) pride in work group; (b) intrinsic job satisfaction; (c) company involvement; and (d) financial and job status satisfaction. Pride in work group was the most independent of the four; the remaining three intercorrelated around .4.

When these morale indices were related to productivity, only pride in work group showed a distinct relationship. Productivity groups were also differentiated by three specific attitude items not included in the morale indices.

A second study of similar design investigated these relationships among section hand employees of the Chesapeake & Ohio Railroad (35). Somewhat different morale items with more emphasis upon individual items were used in intensive interviews. Productivity criteria consisted of overall quality and quantity ratings by supervisors. There was some slight support for the previous finding of a relationship between pride in work group and productivity. The authors emphasize the lack of relationships found between employee attitudes and productivity.

Both Michigan studies, but particularly the insurance company one, may be studied with profit. The investigators are self-critical and also provide hypotheses for further investigation. The investigations are excellent examples of both the virtues and the shortcomings of survey techniques. Both illustrate attempts to measure a large number of variables with less precision perhaps than is ultimately desirable. These well-publicized studies are important in our present context because they have called into question a common assumption about an important relationship, have perhaps stimulated research elsewhere, and have produced a great amount of theorizing about motivation in industry.

Three recent investigations are patterned somewhat after the Michigan inquiries. Two studies by Comrey and associates (9, 10) are considerably less well reported. The findings, among Forest Service and Employment Service personnel, lend some slight support to the Michigan report of a relationship between attitudes toward the group and performance. Weschler (60) found a slightly negative relationship between a single-item index of job satisfaction and production among employees in two comparable groups of a Naval research laboratory. He obtained a similar result for a single item index of work group morale.

A recent study by Lawshe and Nagle (41) warrants extended comment. Two hundred and eight nonsupervisory office employees in 14 work groups at a plant of the International Harvester Company completed a 22-item questionnaire which was described by the authors as an attitude toward supervisor measure. The corrected split-half reliability was .92. There is no report regarding the anonymity of the respondents. The scores were related to group productivity.

A paired comparison rating of productivity by six plant executives was used. Each executive compared from 8 to 14 work groups under instructions to indicate ". . . The department in each pair which is, in your opinion, doing its job better." Ratings were converted to standard scores and averaged. The reliability of the means of all six raters was estimated to be .88. The authors are careful to point out that "one does not know for sure what the raters really had in mind when they rated." They suggest that

> How little trouble the work group caused, whether or not it had the answers when called upon, whether or not it could cope

with rush situations, and similar considerations are believed to have been the prime factors in the executives' ratings.

The average rating of each work group was correlated with average attitude toward the supervisor score in the work group. The resulting Pearson coefficient was .86, significant at the 1 percent level for $N = 14$. This is, of course, a remarkable result. A whole superstructure of industrial psychology could well be erected on this finding; stranger things have happened. However, the authors sound a note of caution:

> On the basis of this study it can be concluded only that the behavior of the supervisor, as perceived by the employees, is highly related to the productivity of the group as perceived by higher management.

It occurs to us that it may be a misnomer to call the questionnaire an attitude questionnaire. It might well be considered to be a supervisor behavior- or performance-rating device. For example, the questions included such things as, does he: give you straight answers, avoid you when he knows you want to see him about a problem, criticze you for happenings over which you have no control, delay in taking care of your complaints, keep you informed, give you recognition, show interest in your ideas, follow through on his promises, explain to you the "why" of an error to prevent recurrence, give you sufficient explanation of why a work change is necessary. There is supporting evidence for a finding that supervisory performance is related to productivity (34). It might be suggested further that the obtained correlation really expresses the relationship between supervisor performance ratings by employees and supervisor performance ratings by the executives since the performance of a work group may be judged in part at least on the basis of the observation of the supervisor and certainly on his reports. We suggest that the finding is relevant to current work on supervisor performance and productivity but we are skeptical of its direct relationship to the area of research being examined in this review despite the title.

The results from the study design which we have described in this section are substantially in agreement with the previous findings of minimal or no relationship between employee attitudes and performance. They do supply the hint that morale, as a group phenomenon, may bear a positive relationship to performance on the job.

WITHDRAWAL FROM THE JOB

As indicated earlier we have differentiated between performance on the job and withdrawal from the job. In this section we briefly summarize the trend of the evidence when employee attitudes are related to some form of withdrawal from the job. Withdrawal is indicated by absence and tardiness, by accidents (under one assumption), and by turnover or employment stability.

ABSENCES

● *Individual analysis*. The individual analysis design has been used in four studies. In another of the Triple Audit studies, Yoder and associates (62) employed a 66-item employee attitude questionnaire which yielded a total score as an index of general attitude. Respondents apparently were unidentified. Absence and tardiness data were *furnished by the respondents* on the questionnaire face sheet. Five groups of employees were studied including office workers, department store personnel, and manufacturing employees. No statistically significant relationships were found between the attitude index and absences. One significant relationship was found for tardiness. Four others were insignificant.

In a study of worker attitudes toward merit rating, Van Zelst and Kerr (55) include data relevant to our topic. Three hundred and forty employees selected by their employers in 14 firms out of the 50 invited to participate furnished a *self-report* of their absences and tar-

dinesses. Two Hoppock-type job satisfaction items were combined to give a single index. Respondents apparently were anonymous. Job satisfaction correlated .31 with a favorable absentee record and .26 with a favorable tardiness record. These are significant at the 1 percent level.

Bernberg (2) used four different measures of absence and tardiness which had split-half reliabilities in the seventies. These data were taken from the company records. The intercorrelations with the four measures of employee attitudes of the 890 aircraft plant workers ranged from − .05 to + .07.

● *Group analysis*. The group analysis design also has been used in four studies. Giese and Ruter (20) found an insignificant relation between tardiness and a single morale score when the group averages of employees in 25 departments of a mail order house were correlated. However, the correlation of − .47 between the morale index and absences is significant at the 5 percent level (our determination).

Kerr and associates (38) obtained mean scores on his 10-item Tear Ballot job satisfaction blank for the employees in 30 departments of a Chicago plant presumably under conditions of anonymity. They used six measures of absenteeism. This is a major contribution of the study since there are numerous problems in indexing absenteeism. The importance of such an analytical approach is evident when it is observed that job satisfaction correlated .51 with total absenteeism rate but correlated − .44 with unexcused absenteeism. One other relationship was statistically significant.

In their wartime morale studies, Katz and Hyman (31) used six specific attitude items. These morale indices were positively related to absenteeism. The magnitude of the relationship is typified by responses to this item: 33 percent of the workers disliking their jobs were categorized as absentees as compared with 36 percent who like their jobs.

Perhaps the most extensive investigation has been made by Metzner and Mann (46) of the Michigan Survey Research Center. The data were collected in the Detroit Edison Company according to a design similar to the Prudential and Chesapeake & Ohio studies. Anonymous questionnaires provided the attitudinal data. White-collar and blue-collar men and white-collar women were the subjects. The most striking finding was that there was no relationship between absences and attitudes toward any aspect of the work situation for white-collar women. Among white-collar men, 10 out of 15 attitudinal measures showed significant relationships at the 10 percent level. Eight of these were significant at the 5 percent or 1 percent levels. However, when job level or grade was controlled to some extent by grouping into high- and low-skill levels, there was practically no relationship between attitudes and absences for the high-skill level jobs. For the seven items it was possible to study. A fairly consistent relationship remained for the low-skill level jobs. Among the 18 items used with the 251 blue-collar men, nine were significant at the 10 percent level or better, six being at the 5 percent level or better. Incidentally, these are all percentage differences among various absence categories and the adjacent category differences are not particularly impressive although the differences between the extreme categories are appreciable.

ACCIDENTS

Hill and Trist (25), English investigators, have recently suggested that

> Accidents (may) be considered as a means of withdrawal from the work situation through which the individual may take up the role of absentee in a way acceptable both to himself and to his employing organization.

Accidents are considered to involve the "quality of the relationship obtaining between employees and their place of work." In an empirical test of this hypothesis they found accident rates to be positively associated with other forms of absences and to be most strongly associated with the least sanctioned forms of absence. Their study does not, of course, bear directly on our immediate concern. We include it to indicate a possible linkage with absence data.

● *Group analysis.* We have found two studies on the relationship between employee attitudes and accidents. Stagner and associates (53) used a group analysis design to study the job satisfaction of railroad employees. A total of 715 employees in 10 divisional groups, 2 accounting offices, and 12 shops were included. Fifteen specific items of an apparently anonymously administered questionnaire were given arbitrary weights based on the percentage of employees checking and were summed to give a single job satisfaction index. Mean satisfaction scores by groups were correlated with group accident rates. The obtained correlations are negative and small. Surprisingly, the authors conclude that

> We thus feel considerable confidence in the conclusion that working in a group with a high accident rate will tend to make the individual worker anxious, and reduce his satisfaction with his job.

However, the correlations are not statistically significant (our determination) and the causal sequence indicated in the quote is speculation.

The Triple Audit (62) studies also considered accidents. Although the authors have entered a general disclaimer as to the significance of their group design findings, the accident finding is intriguing. Employees in the three firms with fewer than average accidents had a mean attitude score of 133 while the employees in the three firms with more than average accidents had a mean score of 143. From these limited data it appears that there is a tendency for the firms with higher accident rates to have more favorable attitude scores. The data are interesting but should not be given disproportionate emphasis.

EMPLOYMENT STABILITY

● *Individual analysis.* Employment stability remains to be studied. In a study comparing indirect and direct methods of appraising employee attitudes, Weitz and Nuckols (59) provide relevant although peripheral data. This is an individual analysis design. Two attitude questionnaires, one composed of 18 indirect items and one consisting of 10 direct questions, were mailed to more than 1,200 insurance agents representing one company in the southern states. Forty-seven percent submitted answers. The respondents were identified. Total scores for each of the questionnaires were then related to survival during a one-year period. The direct method correlated .20, significant at the 1 percent level; the indirect method correlated insignificantly with survival. There was some sample bias resulting from the fact that a disproportionately small number of men, who subsequently terminated, responded.

Kerr (37) correlated total Tear Ballot job satisfaction scores obtained individually but without identification from 98 miscellaneous wage earners with an index of *self-reported* past job tenure (number of years on labor market divided by number of employers). The result for an unweighted total satisfaction score was .25, significant at the 5 percent level. Thus there seems to be a slight positive relationship between attitude toward present employment and past employment stability among the members of a heterogeneous group making self-reports on their employment records.

Van Zelst and Kerr (55) correlated total score on two Hoppock-type items with *employee reports* of previous job tenure. The obtained correlation was .09.

Friesen (16) recently has attempted to measure employee attitudes using an incomplete sentences technique. He developed four scales comprising a total of 81 items. These he labeled Working Situation, Work, Self, Leisure. He studied women office workers from one company with N's ranging from 38 to 70. The blanks were signed. Split-half reliability coefficients for the four scales ranged from .68 to .82. Intercorrelations among the scales ranged from .26 to .72 with Working Situation and Work being the two most highly correlated. Friesen attempted to validate the scales by obtaining modified "Guess Who" ratings from seven to nine fellow employees for each member of his sample. These ratings had uncorrected reliability coefficients ranging from .57 to .78. Their obtained correlations with the attitude scales were moderately high being .59, .67, .45, and .52, respectively. When the four attitude scales were related to a criterion of employment stability (two or more years with each employer versus less than two years with each employer) the biserial correlations were .43, .53, .37, and .22, respectively. All were significant at the 4 percent level or better. This is a *retrospective* measure of employment stability.

Two attitude items, chance to make decisions on the job, and a feeling they were making or had made an important contribution to the success of the company, were significantly related to turnover in a study by Wickert (61). This study has the limitation that the employees who had left the company were interviewed after their departure.

● *Group analysis.* The group analysis design has been used in three studies previously described. In the Giese and Ruter (20) investigation, morale scores correlated − .42 with a percent turnover criterion for 25 departments. This is significant at the 5 percent level (our determination). Kerr (38) found the relationship between total Tear Ballot score and turnover in 30 departments to be − .13 which is not significant. The Triple Audit studies (62) found average monthly turnover to be unrelated to attitudes in seven companies.

With respect to withdrawal from the job, then, there is some evidence, mainly from the group design studies, of a significant but complex relationship between employee attitudes and absences. The investigations reviewed here also lend some support to the assumption that employee attitudes and employment stability are positively related. The data on accidents and attitudes are extremely limited, but they do not support any significant relationships.

In summary, it appears that there is little evidence in the available literature that employee attitudes of the type usually measured in morale surveys bear any simple—or, for that matter, appreciable—relationship to performance on the job. The data are suggestive mainly of a relationship between attitudes and two forms of withdrawal from the job. This tentative conclusion, contrary as it is to rather widely held beliefs, warrants an attempt to identify and evaluate some of the factors which may account for these results.

We have chosen to comment on some methodological considerations, followed by a discussion of theoretical issues, and concluding with some possible implications for future research.

METHODOLOGICAL CONSIDERATIONS

The methodological questions which might be raised about any field study are legion (15, 27, 28, 36, 44). We shall comment briefly on some methodological limitations of the studies we have reviewed and on some fairly general problems of analysis and design of field study which are relevant to our topic.

LIMITATIONS OF THE CURRENT LITERATURE

It is difficult to know whether inadequacies in research reports reflect faults in research design, or whether space limitations in journals force authors to omit a considerable part of the methodological detail of their studies. This problem is apparent in the following discussion of three methodological areas: sampling, measurements, and the general procedure of the study.

● *Sampling.* In most industrial studies there is sampling of both respondents and items. With regard to the sampling of respondents, reports frequently fail to state how respondents were selected, the possible selective biases, or the population which the sample is supposed to represent. It is possible that conflicting results from two studies may reflect differences in the characteristics of the populations sampled. This would be of considerable interest theoretically and practically, but it is unlikely to be detected unless the respective populations are described in some detail.

With regard to sampling of items, it is not uncommon for questionnaires administered to industrial workers to contain 150 or more items, and for research reports to mention results from only a few of these items. One is left in doubt as to whether the items reported upon were selected on the basis of some theoretical analysis, in which case the other items presumably were not theoretically relevant to the issue in question, or whether the items were selected on the basis of statistical significance and the theoretical orientation developed in retrospect. The latter procedure obviously capitalizes on chance and the results should be subjected to further research before being accepted with any great confidence. Unless researchers inform the reader when they have operated on an *ad hoc* basis the tentative nature of the results will not be apparent.

● *Criterion measures.* Research reports sometimes fail to describe the specific measurements that were used! In addition, there is extreme diversity in the kinds of employee attitudes that are measured, and in the questionnaires and interview schedules that are used to identify or measure them. This means that disparity in results between two or more studies may sometimes reflect differences in operational definitions, rather than differences between the populations being studied. We shall deal in greater detail with the measurement of attitudes in a subsequent section. Here we shall concentrate for the moment on criteria of job performance and of withdrawal from the job.

It is not our purpose to present a definitive report on problems involved in the selection and measurement of criteria. This area is well covered in current books in the field (19, ch. 3; 54, ch. 5). However, it is obviously impossible to assess the relation between employee attitudes and job performance without some measure of the latter. Therefore, it is appropriate to dwell briefly on the criterion problem.

Let us consider, first, criteria of job performance. On production-line jobs as well as in sales and many other white-collar jobs, the criterion which seems, at first glance, best to reflect adequacy of job performance is productivity. Yet the measurement of productivity is much less simple than it may seem initially.

To be valid, a comparison of output between two individuals must equate the conditions under which the individuals operate. One salesman's territory may be potentially more fruitful than another's and his higher sales may cause, rather than result from, his greater satisfaction with his job. Two machines may vary in their potential output, in their state of repair, and in many other ways. Frequently there are, in addition, external restraints on productivity. Output in a factory may be determined by the speed of the assembly line or the speed of the machine, by the amount of material provided to an individual by some feeder line, or by the quality of the material being processed. Variation in situational factors such as these will affect total productivity no matter what the level of individual job performance.

Furthermore, on many jobs, white-collar as well as production-line, it is impossible to get a measure of productivity because a certain amount of work is required during the day and no more is produced, because adequate records are not kept, because the product depends on group rather than individual performance, or for a variety of other reasons.

Where output data are questionable or unobtainable as a performance criterion, it is sometimes suggested that other objective criteria such as quality of production as measured by number of errors, amount of scrap, and the like, be used. However, many of the above considerations such as machine variation, availability of records, and comparability of materials processed also apply to quality data.

Relevance, reliability, freedom from contamination, and practicality are criterion requisites which are not easily satisfied even when objective performance indices are available.

In the absence of direct counting measures of job performance, researchers are likely to obtain subjective evaluations, usually by superiors in the organization, of the performance levels of individuals or groups. Such ratings frequently were used in the investigations we have reviewed. The limitations and the precautions necessary in the use of ratings are well known and adequately documented (19, ch. 4; 22, ch. 11). Problems such as the selection of factors to be rated, the errors of human judgment-making, contamination, and reliability plague the investigator who is forced to rely upon ratings.

Criterion selection is a problem also in studies attempting to predict absenteeism and turnover. Sex differences, differences of position in the organization, and similar factors influence absences in such a way that differences in absence rate between two groups may reflect many things other than differences in employee attitudes. The same thing may be said of turnover. General employment and wage levels, selective service policies, and similar factors will all affect the rate of turnover and may mask the effect of employee attitudes on turnover.

The selection of criteria, then, involves a choice among a number of possible measurements all of which may be affected by situational factors over which the investigator has little if any control.

● *Procedural problems.* A frequent drawback of reports of the type summarized in this paper is a failure to report reliability data for the measurements, both of attitudes and of criteria of performance.

For the most part, the validity of the measures employed is unreported. With respect to the criterion measures this takes the form of failure to discuss the relevance of the particular criteria used. Usually employee attitude indices are assumed to have some form of face validity; empirical validation is seldom attempted. The reader is expected to assume that the questionnaires measured what they were intended to measure. In view of the history of measurement in psychology, however, experienced readers may hesitate to make this assumption.

We are indebted to S. Rains Wallace for the suggestion that a spurious factor may be present in studies which employ interviews or the extensive interpretation of questionnaires for determining morale in groups and relating it to the rated efficiency of the group.[4] It is not always clear whether the interviewers or interpreters had foreknowledge of the rated efficiency and thus might have contaminated their attitude measures.

Another procedural defect of some industrial studies is the use of self-reports or similar criterion data rather

than independently obtained measures. Thus, in studies of absence and of turnover, respondents may be asked to tell how many times they have been absent in the last six months or how many jobs they have held in the last five years. Absence material, at least, could be collected in a more straightforward and probably more valid manner by looking at the individual's attendance record unless an attempt is being made to preserve anonymity.

Sometimes, furthermore, the data collection is unsupervised, or is conducted incidentally to some other operation within the company. While there is no intrinsic objection to such projects, experience indicates that they frequently suffer from errors and extraneous factors and the reader should be warned of their tentative nature.

Finally, an important procedural issue concerns the practical problem of whether or not to identify the individual respondents. If we are to relate employee attitudes to measures or estimates of individual performance, it is necessary to be able to identify individual workmen. Frequently this means that the subject is required to sign the questionnaire or is interviewed individually. Although this is a crucial problem it has not been widely investigated or, sometimes, even considered. Thus it merits extended discussion.

We have located seven studies in industrial settings which bear upon the question of the influence of anonymity upon morale or job satisfaction (3, 14, 17, 24, 29, 45, 58). Two studies from the Survey Research Center, University of Michigan, compare responses made by employees to morale items when the items are contained in an anonymous questionnaire and when they are part of an interview. In Kahn's (29) study, comparisons were available for 65 items which were worded identically and were presented in the same context and sequence. In general, his findings support the conclusion that identification, at least via interview, produces dif-

---

4. S. R. Wallace. Personal communication. October, 1954.

ferential responses. For example, the questionnaire items elicited more expressions of criticism and dissatisfaction and more extreme responses. A somewhat similar study by Metzner and Mann (45), although much more limited, gave comparable results. Both studies contain possible defects in the matching of respondents as well as insufficient attention to interviewer differences.

A related study by Wedell and Smith (58) compared interviewer ratings of responses and coded ratings of the interview protocols with questionnaire responses of approximately 200 employees of a chemical company on three attitude questions. Interviewer ratings of responses differed significantly from questionnaire responses on the two questions dealing with attitude toward company and toward job. Coded ratings of the interview protocols differed significantly from questionnaire responses on the item dealing with attitude toward the company. In each instance of significant findings the interviews produced the most favorable attitude ratings as compared to the employees' actual questionnaire responses. The most interesting finding was the differences among interviewers. By and large, the more experienced and better trained interviewers showed the greatest discrepancies! The interview versus questionnaire methodological studies do not, of course, provide a crucial test of the anonymity factor since many other variables may be operating to confound the results (27).

In an abstract, Evans (14) reports a study of salaried employees which he says "provided for testing the hypothesis that employee anonymity should be preserved in management-conducted surveys." One major finding of his early analysis indicated that "employees are not particularly concerned about anonymity." He concludes that "the unwarranted popular assumption that employees must be anonymous is open to serious question." The brevity of the report makes it difficult to evaluate the significance of this conclusion.

In an early investigation of the problem in an industrial setting, Brayfield (3) compared the distribution of scores on a job satisfaction questionnaire obtained from female stenographers employed in private industry with those for a similar group employed in state civil service. The members of the industrial group identified themselves under good rapport conditions and the civil service group was anonymous. It was apparent by inspection that the two groups gave similar responses. The results are inconclusive particularly since the groups were not working under strictly comparable conditions.

Gadel and Kriedt (17) report briefly upon a test of the effect of anonymity upon employee attitude questionnaires. They found that the distributions of answers obtained under the differing conditions of anonymity and identification were almost identical for several groups of employees. The small differences present were inconsistent from group to group and from item to item.

In a carefully controlled study, Hamel and Reif (24) administered a 65-item employee attitude questionnaire to two random samples of all employees in a large department store. The members of one sample remained anonymous; those in the second sample identified themselves by name and department number. The mean scores for the two groups were not significantly different. When the group responses to each individual item were compared only two item responses in 65 were significantly different. For the number of comparisons involved the authors state that "this finding is slightly smaller than expected."

The results from studies outside the industrial situation using such diverse materials as attitude scales, opinion polls and ballots, and personality tests are equivocal. Hyman (27, p. 185), in a considered treatment of the issue, says the foregoing discussion should serve to make clear the complexity in estimating the nature and direction of effects due to identification or anonymity of the respondent.

Our own review of the dozen or so relevant nonindustrial investigations along with the industrial studies already cited leads us to agree with Kahn's (29, p. 8) conclusion that

the studies on the effect of anonymity of response conducted during the past two decades compel us to conclude that there is no predictable effect of anonymity *per se.*

We would sound the caution that, in any study of the problem, it is necessary to differentiate literal anonymity from psychological anonymity, as Hyman (27) has suggested, since even the questionnaire studies usually require identification at least to the extent of naming one's department, and sometimes even more extensive data are called for. These requirements and situational factors may influence responses to what the investigator considers to be anonymously answered materials.

We do hazard the opinion, however, that in a situation where rapport has been carefully nurtured in all steps of the investigation, the identification of *questionnaire* materials will not necessarily result in serious distortion of responses. Yet the dilemma remains. The investigator who asks for identification on the questionnaire, and perhaps especially the investigator who relies upon the interview, risks distortion in responses, while the one who does not ask for identification is unable to make certain crucial analyses. The ethical and practical consequences of coding and disguised identification of respondents are such as to render that particular solution debatable.

GENERAL PROBLEMS OF ANALYSIS AND DESIGN

We shall be concerned here with a discussion of scaling and statistical techniques commonly in use in psychology, with the general problem of operational definitions as applied to the specific area of industrial research, and with the validity of certain group measures.

● *Statistical and scaling techniques.* In the typical industrial study the psychologist asks a group of workers to fill out a questionnaire which is designed to measure "morale," he ranks the same employees on some aspects of their job performance, and he then runs a *t* test or a product-moment correlation between morale, on the one hand, and performance, on the other. We believe that too little recognition has been given to the assumptions about the nature of the data which are built into these measurements and into the statistical tests.

Thus, for example, the typical morale scale makes the assumption that a unidimensional continuum is being measured and that the items of the scale are equally important in contributing to the individual's position on the continuum. Except for item analysis in the initial construction of the scales, it is doubtful whether the validity of these assumptions is ever tested and item analysis does not guarantee unidimensionality, nor is it often used for differential weighting of items. The use of mean scores and of product-moment correlation adds such further assumptions as that the intervals between points on the scale are of equal magnitude, that the parent population is normally distributed on the variables concerned, that homoscedasticity exists in the case of the Pearsonian coefficient, and so on. To the extent that these assumptions are violated, the results become ambiguous. It is doubtful if the validity of the assumptions is routinely tested.

However, since these comments hold true generally for much research in all fields of psychology, it would be unreasonable to expect a different type of analysis among observers studying morale.

● *Measurement of morale.* McNemar (44) has commented at length upon the tendency for attitude researchers to "measure" a concept by applying a particular label (say conservatism-radicalism) to a set of questions without concern for other operational definitions of the same concept. "Morale" has probably been as greatly subject to this procedure as any other concept in psychology today. The lack of consistent definition of the term "morale" has led us to title this article "Employee *attitudes* and employee performance" in the hope that the term "attitude" provides the general and ambiguous connotation that is required to describe measurement in this field.

One likely cause of this proliferation of operational definitions is that morale is a global concept. Researchers tend to consider any area of satisfaction as important for the employee's overall morale, for his satisfaction with his job and his company. This has led to attempts, logically and through factor analysis, to specify particular aspects of morale. Frequently subareas of morale are identified, such as satisfaction with the work group, satisfaction with pay, with supervision, with promotion, with type of work, with physical aspects of the job, or with any other component of the working environment. Questions are then developed to provide an indication of the degree of employee satisfaction in each of these areas.

This move toward increased specification of the components of the concept, and toward the development of unidimensional scales probably should be applauded. However, a problem arises of how to use the subscales. Frequently the items within a subscale are summed to provide a score on the scale, and then the individuals' positions on the subscales are summed to provide an "index" of overall morale. In such an event, the subscales constitute simply a means of weighting items, and subscales are assumed to be equally important in producing whatever overall morale is supposed to be. The possibility remains that a more fruitful method of analysis would be to consider the

subscales independently or as configurations rather than to combine them additively.

The reason usually given for using multi-item scales in measuring morale is the same as that given for using many items in tests of ability: the greater reliability of longer scales. It is assumed that increasing the number of attitude items increases the likelihood that respondents will be ordered in the same way on a second administration of the questionnaire. Yet the analogy to ability tests is not necessarily a good one. While there may be an infinite population of arithmetic problems, for example, from which test items may be chosen, the inclusion of additional items in attitude scales is likely to introduce new attitude dimensions. Unless these dimensions are highly correlated, the scores on the questionnaire may be ambiguous. For example, a person could achieve a moderate morale score by indicating moderate satisfaction with his pay and with the type of work he is doing, or by indicating great satisfaction with the type of work he is doing and great dissatisfaction with his pay. It is not unlikely that these different patterns of response would be differently related to job performance, to absence, and to turnover.

Concern with unidimensionality, rather than with reliability as traditionally conceived, would lead to the use of such scaling techniques as Guttman's, Loevinger's, or Coombs's, or to the use of single items. It is interesting that many of the studies we have reported above have made at least partial use of the single-item approach (32, 35, 46, 48, 60, 61).

● *Use of group measurements.* Frequently, members of a work group or a department fill out morale questionnaires individually, but have group, rather than individual, performance or productivity records. In such situations it is customary to test the significance of the difference between the morale scores of the two groups to determine whether the higher producing group also has higher morale. We shall comment upon only one aspect of this procedure by pointing out that a relationship which exists at the individual level between satisfaction and productivity may be obscured when the individuals are lumped together. There may be a positive relationship between satisfaction and performance within each group even though the two groups as a whole do not differ significantly with regard to mean satisfaction. Such a relationship obviously is not revealed in this type of analysis and lack of individual performance records makes the appropriate analysis impossible.

The degree to which these and other methodological issues may have beclouded the relationships between employee attitudes, performance, absenteeism, and employment stability is an open question. Certainly, as must be obvious to the careful reader, the studies we have reviewed are subject to some or, occasionally, most of the shortcomings described above. However, the scarcity of relationships, either positive or negative, demonstrated to date even among the best designed of the available studies leads us to question whether or not methodological changes alone would lead to a substantial increase in the magnitude of the obtained relationships. We are led, then, from consideration of the current status of research on this topic to a discussion of the relationships on the conceptual level. Much of what we will say has previously been elaborated by Katz and Kahn (33) and by Morse (47).

THEORETICAL CONSIDERATIONS

MORALE AS AN EXPLANATORY
CONCEPT IN INDUSTRIAL PSYCHOLOGY

One principal generalization suffices to set up an expectation that morale should be related to absenteeism and turnover, namely, that organisms tend to avoid those situations which are punishing and to seek out situations that are rewarding. To the extent that worker dissatisfaction indicates that the individual is in a punishing situation, we should expect dissatisfied workers to be absent more often and to quit the job at a higher rate than individuals who are satisfied with their work. Since the general proposition about the effects of reward has received a great amount of verification in psychology, it is not strange that it has been carried to the analysis of absenteeism and turnover.

A plausible connection between satisfaction and performance on the job is less obvious. Let us consider specifically the possible relationship between satisfaction and productivity. Under conditions of marked dissatisfaction it is likely that low productivity may serve as a form of aggression which reflects worker hostility toward management. But the hypothesis that production should increase monotonically with increases in satisfaction apparently rests on the assumption that the worker will demonstrate his gratitude by increased output, or that the increased satisfaction frees certain creative energies in the worker, or that the satisfied employee accepts management's goals, which include high production.

In any event, it is commonly hypothesized that, whatever the causes, increased satisfaction makes workers more motivated to produce. Given this condition, it should follow that increased productivity can be attained by increasing worker satisfaction. We are going to advance the proposition that the motivational structure of industrial workers is not so simple as is implied in this formula. We feel that research workers have erred by overlooking individual differences in motivations and perceptions because of their concern with discovering important and applicable generalizations. Most of what follows is an effort to point out areas in which differences between workmen may make a difference in their adjustment to the situation.

At the outset let us make it clear that

we expect the relation between satisfaction and job performance to be one of concomitant variation, rather than cause and effect. It makes sense to us to assume that individuals are motivated to achieve certain environmental goals and that the achievement of these goals results in satisfaction. Productivity is seldom a goal in itself but is more commonly a means to goal attainment. Therefore, as G. M. Mahoney has suggested,[5] we might expect high satisfaction and high productivity to occur together when productivity is perceived as a path to certain important goals and when these goals are achieved. Under other conditions, satisfaction and productivity might be unrelated or even negatively related.

In the light of this consideration, we shall center our discussion on an analysis of industrial motivation as it relates specifically to employee satisfaction and to productivity.

For the sake of convenience we may distinguish between threats and rewards as incentives to productivity. Goode and Fowler (21) have described a factory in which morale and productivity were negatively related but productivity was kept high by the continuance of threats to workers. Here the essential workers—people with considerable skill—were marginal to the labor force because of their sex or because of physical handicaps. Since the plant was not unionized, it was possible for management to demand high productivity from these workers on threat of discharge. This meant that the workers, although most dissatisfied with their jobs, produced at a very high rate because of the difficulty they would face in finding another position should they be discharged.

There is little doubt that threat was widely used as a motivating device in our own society in the past and is presently used in more authoritarian

societies. However, it is doubtful if any great amount of at least explicit threat is currently used by industries in this country in efforts to increase productivity or reduce absenteeism. First of all, considerable change has occurred in management philosophy over the past 50 years, and such tactics are repugnant to many industrial concerns. Secondly, the growth of unions has virtually outlawed such tendencies except in small, semi-marginal industries which are not unionized.

Threats of discharge, then, probably do not operate as incentives unless the worker falls considerably below the mean in quantity and/or quality of output. For a number of reasons management has settled upon rewards for motivating workers to produce, including such tangible incentives as increased pay and promotion, as well as verbal and other symbolic recognition. Let us examine whether this system of rewards actually provides motivation for increased productivity by the worker.

It is a commonplace observation that motivation is not a simple concept. It is a problem which may be attacked at a number of different levels and from many theoretical points of view. Whatever their theoretical predilection, however, psychologists generally are agreed that human motivation is seldom directed only toward goals of physical well-being. Once a certain minimum level of living has been achieved, human behavior is directed largely toward some social goal or goals. Thus, in our own society, goals such as achievement, acceptance by others, dominance over others, and so on, probably are of as great concern to the average workman as the goals of finding sufficient food and shelter to keep body and psyche together.

We assume that social motives are of considerable importance in industry. We assume, further, that the goals as individual pursues will vary, depending upon the social systems within which he is behaving from time to time. Most

---

5. G. M. Mahoney. Personal communication. March, 1953.

industrial workers probably operate in a number of social systems. Katz and Kahn (33) suggest four such systems: first, the system of relations outside the plant; and, within the plant, the systems of relationship with fellow workers on the job, with members of the union, and with others in the company structure. We may ask whether job performance, and particularly productivity, is a path to goal achievement within these various sets of social relations.

● *Outside the plant.* It is often argued that any worker who is motivated to increase his status in the outside community should be motivated toward higher productivity within the plant. Productivity frequently leads directly to more money on the job, or involves movement to jobs with higher prestige or with authority over others. If productivity does result in such in-plant mobility, increased output may enable the individual to achieve a higher level of living, to increase his general status in the community, and to attempt such social mobility as he may desire. In this way productivity may serve as a path to the achievement of goals outside the plant.

The operation of this chain of relationships, however, depends not only upon the rewards given the high producer, but also upon the original motivation of the workman to increase his status position in the outside community. The amount of status motivation among production-line employees is open to question. Certainly the findings of Warner (57), Davis and Gardner (12), and others (6, 11, 13), indicate that there are systematic differences in the goals which are pursued in the different segments of our society. It is not impossible that a very large proportion of America's work force is only minimally motivated toward individual social achievement. The assumption that such a motivation does exist may reflect in considerable part a projection of certain middle-class aspirations onto working-class employees.

Furthermore, it is not unlikely that the reference group against which an individual workman evaluates his success may be only a segment of the community, rather than the community as a whole. An individual whose accomplishments are modest at best when compared with the range of possible accomplishments in the community may have a feeling of great accomplishment when he compares his achievements with those of others in his environment. If this is true, and if he desires to continue to operate within this segment of society, any further increase in rewards within the plant might lead to his exclusion from personally important groups outside the plant rather than to increased prestige in such groups.

Finally, there are many goals outside the industrial plant which may be socially rewarding to the individual and which require only minimal financial and occupational rewards inside the plant. Active participation in veterans' organizations, in churches, in recreational programs and similar activities may be and frequently are carried out by individuals at all positions in the industrial hierarchy. As a matter of fact, to the extent that the individual receives extensive social rewards from such activities he may have only slight interest in his work on the job, and he may continue to remain in industry only to maintain some minimum economic position while carrying out his outside functions. For such an individual, high productivity may lead to *no* important goals.

● *Relations with other workers in the plant.* The studies by Elton Mayo and his associates (43, 50, 51) introduced the work group into the analysis of industry, and a wealth of subsequent investigations have confirmed the importance of on-the-job groups. Throughout these studies has run the observation that members of the work group develop group standards of productivity and attempt to force these standards upon those workmen who deviate.

Thus, in the Bank Wiring Room (51) it was the socially maladjusted individual, the deviant from the work group, who maintained a level of production above that of the group even though his native ability was considerably below that of many of the others.

Mathewson's (42) classic study of restriction of output among unorganized workers was an early demonstration of the operation of group norms.

Schachter and associates (52) have conducted an experiment which indicates that in cohesive groups an individual's productivity may be either raised or lowered, depending upon the kind of communications directed toward him by congenial co-workers. In an actual factory setting, Coch and French (8) presented existent groups with evidence that a change in job methods and in productivity was necessary if the factory was to remain in a favorable position relative to other, competing factories. These groups, through group discussion, arrived at a decision as to the proper job set up, and modified the group judgment of "fair" output markedly upward.

There is evidence, then, that the level of performance on the job frequently depends upon a group norm, and that performance level may be changed by changing the group norm in a direction desired by management. This change in the norm probably results from a conviction among the workers that higher production is in their own interest as well as management's, *i.e.*, that their interests and management's interests coincide. This raises the perplexing question of whether, with regard to productivity, the interests of management and labor do, in fact, coincide.

Management, presumably, is interested in higher production as a way of reducing the ratio of cost to output, and thereby bettering management's financial and competitive position. In an expanding market, the argument goes, this makes possible the expansion of the company, increased wages, a larger labor force, and general prosperity not only for the corporation but for the employees as well.

The case may not be so attractive to the workers, especially when the market is not expanding and demand for the product is constant, nearly constant, or declining. In this event, higher productivity per worker means that fewer people are required for the same level of output, or that fewer hours are worked by the same number of workers. In either case, many workers may lose, rather than gain, by the increase in productivity. It may be argued that in normal times such individuals usually find fairly rapid employment in some other segment of the economy. However true this may be, from the viewpoint of the individual workman this involves a considerable disruption in working habits and in his social life in general, and is to be avoided wherever possible. Viewed in this light the interests of management and labor are inimical.

As psychologists we steer clear of such arguments. But we should be sensitive to the fact that the question is a debatable one, that a final decision will probably rest upon values rather than data, that each side is capable of convincing arguments, and that the perception of a certain inevitable conflict of interests between the two groups is honestly and intelligently held by many people. We should also recognize that any reduction in work force after a joint labor-management effort to increase productivity will likely be interpreted as resulting from the increased productivity, and may lead to a future avoidance not only of high productivity levels but also of labor-management cooperation.

At any rate, we often find that individual workers interpret higher productivity as counter to the interests of the employees. To the extent that this perception constitutes a group norm, such motives as are rewarded through the individual's social relationships with other workmen may be blocked by increased productivity. In such cases, productivity may serve as a path to certain goals, but as a block to social acceptance.

• *The union structure.* One system of relationships of considerable importance in many industrial concerns is the union. In many companies much of what was said in the preceding section may be extended to refer also to the relations of the worker in the system of social relations within the union.

In some plants high productivity is not a deterrent to active union participation. Nevertheless, it probably is true that productivity is seldom a prerequisite for advancement within the union hierarchy. If the individual is oriented toward the union structure, it is unlikely that high productivity will serve as a path to such goals, whatever its effect on other goals he may pursue.

• *The company structure.* We have indicated above that many of the worker's social motives outside the plant, as well as his desires for inplant associations with fellow workmen and within the union, may be only slightly affected by increases in productivity and sometimes may be blocked by increased productivity. The apparent range of goals that a worker may have is so wide that productivity may be a path to only a few of them.

However, workers are often motivated toward goals within the plant such as turning out a quality product, higher wages, and promotion. Let us examine the relationship between satisfaction and productivity for workers who are motivated toward these inplant goals.

At the start it is evident that productivity and quality are sometimes mutually exclusive. If the individual must concentrate on maintaining high quality work, speed of production probably plays a secondary role. Conversely, if he must emphasize speed, quality often must be reduced to some degree. The speed-quality dilemma is sometimes resolved by making the individual work units so routine and concerned with such minute changes in the material that increased speed will not affect the quality of the product. However, if a worker is more highly motivated when he is performing some meaningful job, the above procedure may be resolving one dilemma by raising another. At any rate, the artisan, motivated toward the goal of quality, may be highly satisfied with his job while turning out a very limited number of finished pieces per unit of time. If he is forced to increase productivity and lower in some measure the quality, we might expect his satisfaction to decrease. For such a person satisfaction and productivity would be negatively related.

Consider now the individual who is motivated toward higher wages and promotion. While these rewards may not be exclusively dependent upon job performance, at the same time productivity and other aspects of performance often are weighted heavily at promotion time in most companies. In other words, productivity and other aspects of job performance constitute a path to the goal of promotion and wage increases.

Now it is likely that people with aspirations to change position in the company structure will often be quite dissatisfied with their present position in the company. Aspiration to move within a system implies not only a desire for some different position in the future, but some degree of dissatisfaction with the position one is presently occupying. The amount of dissatisfaction probably depends upon the length of time the individual has occupied this position. Thus, although productivity may be a path to the goal, failure to achieve the goal to date may result in dissatisfaction and the high producer may be less satisfied than the low producer.

Evidence sustaining this point of view is to be found in Katz and associates' (34) report of a large insurnace company in which the best, most productive workers were also considerably more critical of company policy than were less productive workers. S. Lieberman reports a similar finding in a large appliance factory.[6] A year after all workers in the factory had filled out a questionnaire, Lieberman compared the earlier responses of those who had been promoted to foreman with a matched group of workers who were not promoted. Those promoted had been significantly less satisfied with company practices at the earlier time than had the control group.

Once again the question arises as to what is meant by satisfaction. It may be that extremely high satisfaction is indicative of a certain amount of complacency, a satisfaction with the job as it is, which may be only slightly related to job performance, if it is related at all. On the other hand, individuals who are highly motivated may perceive productivity as a path to their goals, but may also be more realistically critical of whatever deficiencies exist within the organization. They may feel, in addition, that their output is not being rewarded as rapidly as it deserves.

IMPLICATIONS FOR FUTURE RESEARCH

We have arrived at two conclusions: first, that satisfaction with one's position in a network of relationships need not imply strong motivation to outstanding performance within that system, and, second, that productivity may be only peripherally related to many of the goals toward which the industrial worker is striving. We do not mean to imply that researchers should have known all along that their results would be positive only infrequently and in particular circumstances. We have been operating on the basis of hindsight and have attempted to spell out some of the factors which may have accounted for the failure of industrial investigators to find positive relationships in their data.

---

6. S. Lieberman. Personal communication. July 15, 1954.

However, certain implications seem logical from the foregoing sections of this report. Foremost among these implications is the conclusion that it is time to question the strategic and ethical merits of selling to industrial concerns an assumed relationship between employee attitudes and employee performance. In the absence of more convincing evidence than is now at hand with regard to the beneficial effects on job performance of high morale, we are led to the conclusion that we might better forego publicizing these alleged effects.

The emphasis on predicting job performance, and particularly productivity, rests upon the acceptance of certain values. That is, the many studies that have used productivity as the criterion to be predicted have been performed because productivity has direct economic value to industry, and, presumably, to society at large. But the fact that it has economic value does not mean that job performance is the only, or even the most important, aspect of organizational behavior. From the viewpoint of studying, analyzing, and understanding the industrial setting and individual reactions thereto, productivity and other aspects of job performance may be only one of several important factors. It would seem worthwhile to study the causes, correlates, and consequence of satisfaction, per se. It seems possible, for example, that conditions conducive to job satisfaction will have an effect on the quality of the workman drawn into the industry, the quality of job performance, and the harmony of labor-management relations. Such potential correlates, among others, merit exploration.

Another potentially fruitful approach involves studying the differential effect of particular kinds of management practices upon the attitudes and performances of workers with different motives, aspirations, and expectations. The appropriate questions may concern how, for particular workers, productivity comes to be perceived as instrumental to the achievement of some goals but not others, while for other workers a different perception develops.

The experimental approach has largely been neglected in this area of industrial research, yet the control of variables that it provides seems essential to the development and refinement of our knowledge in the area. Certainly, where experimentation has been used, as by Schachter and associates (52) and by Coch and French (8), the results have been both enlightening for the understanding of present problems and encouraging for its future application. As our concepts become increasingly precise, we may expect an increased use of experimentation both within the industrial setting and in the laboratory.

Perhaps the most significant conclusion to be drawn from this survey of the literature is that the industrial situation is a complex one. We have suggested that an analysis of the situation involves analysis not only of the individual's relation to the social system of the factory, the work group, and the union, but the community at large as well. It is important to know what motives exist among industrial workers, how they are reflected in the behavior of the workers, and how the motives develop and are modified within the framework of patterned social relationships in the plant and in the larger community.

We seem to have arrived at the position where the social scientist in the industrial setting must concern himself with a full-scale analysis of that situation. Pursuit of this goal should provide us with considerable intrinsic job satisfaction.

NOTES

1. Baxter, B., Taaffe, A. A., & Hughes, J. F. A training evaluation study. *Personnel Psychol.*, 1953, **6**, 403-417.
2. Bernberg, R. E. Socio-psychological fac-

tors in industrial morale: I. The prediction of specific indicators. *J. Soc. Psychol.*, 1952, **36**, 73-82.
3. Brayfield, A. H. *The interrelation of measures of ability, aptitude, interests, and job satisfaction among clerical employees.* Unpublished doctor's dissertation, Univer. of Minnesota, 1946.
4. Brayfield, A. H., & Rothe, H. F. An index of job satisfaction. *J. Appl. Psychol.*, 1951, **35**, 307-311.
5. Brody, Mildred. *The relationship between efficiency and job satisfaction.* Unpublished master's thesis, New York Univer., 1945.
6. Centers, R. *The psychology of social classes.* Princeton: Princeton Univer. Press, 1949.
7. Chase, F. S. Factors for satisfaction in teaching. *Phi Delta Kappan*, 1951, **33**, 127-132.
8. Coch, L., & French, J. R., Jr. Overcoming resistance to change. *Hum. Relat.*, 1948, **1**, 512-532.
9. Comrey, A. L., Pfiffner, J. M., & Beem, Helen P. Factors influencing organizational effectiveness. I. The U.S. Forest Survey. *Personnel Psychol.*, 1952, **5**, 307-328.
10. Comrey, A. L., Pfiffner, J. M., & Beem, Helen P. Factors influencing organizational effectiveness. II. The Department of Employment Survey. *Personnel Psychol.*, 1953, **6**, 65-79.
11. Davis, A. *Social class influences upon learning.* Cambridge: Harvard Univer. Press, 1948.
12. Davis, A., Gardner, B. B., & Gardner, Mary R. *Deep south: A social and anthropological study of caste and class.* Chicago: Univer. of Chicago Press, 1941.
13. Ericson, Martha C. Social status and child rearing practices. In T. M. Newcomb & E. L. Hartley (Eds.), *Readings in social psychology.* New York: Holt, 1947. Pp. 494-501.
14. Evans, C. E. Item structure variation as a methodological problem in an employee survey. *Amer. Psychologist*, 1949, **4**, 280. (Abstract)
15. Festinger, L., & Katz, D. (Eds.) *Research methods in the behavioral sciences.* New York: Dryden Press, 1953.
16. Friesen, E. P. The incomplete sentences technique as a measure of employee attitudes. *Personnel Psychol.*, 1952, **5**, 329-345.

17. Gadel, Marguerite S., & Kriedt, P. H. Relationships of aptitude, interest, performance, and job satisfaction of IBM operators. *Personnel Psychol.*, 1952, **5**, 207-212.

18. Garrett, H. E. *Statistics in psychology and education.* New York: Longmans, Green, 1947.

19. Ghiselli, E. E., & Brown, C. W. *Personnel and industrial psychology.* New York: McGraw-Hill, 1948.

20. Giese, W. J., & Ruter, H. W. An objective analysis of morale. *J. Appl. Psychol.*, 1949, **33**, 421-427.

21. Goode, W. J., & Fowler, I. Incentive factors in a low morale plant. *Amer. Sociol. Rev.*, 1949, **14**, 618-624.

22. Guilford, J. P. *Psychometric methods.* New York: McGraw-Hill, 1954.

23. Habbe, S. Job attitudes of life insurance agents. *J. Appl. Psychol.*, 1947, **31**, 111-128.

24. Hamel, L., & Reif, H. G. Should attitude questionnaires be signed? *Personnel Psychol.*, 1952, **5**, 87-91.

25. Hill, J. M. M., & Trist, E. L. A consideration of industrial accidents as a means of withdrawal from the work situation. *Hum. Relat.*, 1953, **6**, 357-380.

26. Houser, J. D. *What the employer thinks.* Cambridge: Harvard Univer. Press, 1927.

27. Hyman, H. H. *Interviewing in social research.* Chicago: Univer. of Chicago Press, 1954.

28. Jahoda, Marie, Deutsch, M., & Cook, S. W. (Eds.) *Research methods in social relations.* New York: Dryden Press, 1951.

29. Kahn, R. L. *A comparison of two methods of collecting data for social research: The fixed-alternative questionnaire and the open-ended interview.* Unpublished doctor's dissertation, Univer. of Michigan, 1952.

30. Katz, D. Morale and motivation in industry. In W. Dennis (Ed.), *Current trends in industrial psychology.* Pittsburgh: Univer. of Pittsburgh Press, 1949. Pp. 145-171.

31. Katz, D., & Hyman, H. Industrial morale and public opinion methods. *Int. J. Opin. Attit. Res.*, 1947, **1**, 13-30.

32. Katz, D., & Hyman, H. Morale in war industry. In T. M. Newcomb & E. L. Hartley (Eds.), *Readings in social psychology.* New York: Holt, 1947. Pp. 437-447.

33. Katz, D., & Kahn, R. L. Some recent findings in human relations research in industry. In G. E. Swanson, T. M. Newcomb & E. L. Hartley (Eds.), *Readings in social psychology.* New York: Holt, 1952, Pp. 650-665.

34. Katz, D., Maccoby, N., & Morse, Nancy. *Productivity, supervision and morale in an office situation.* Univer. of Michigan: Survey Research Center, 1950.

35. Katz, D., Maccoby, N., Gurin, G., & Floor, L. G. *Productivity, supervision and morale among railroad workers.* Univer. of Michigan: Survey Research Center, 1951.

36. Kendall, Patricia L., & Lazarsfeld, P. F. Problems in survey analysis. In R. K. Merton & P. F. Lazarsfeld (Eds.), *Continuities in social research.* Glencoe, Ill.: Free Press, 1950.

37. Kerr, W. A. On the validity and reliability of the job satisfaction Tear Ballot. *J. Appl. Psychol.*, 1948, **32**, 275-281.

38. Kerr, W. A. Summary of validity studies of the Tear Ballot. *Personnel Psychol.*, 1952, **5**, 105-113.

39. Kornhauser, A., & Sharp, A. Employee attitudes: suggestions from a study in a factory. *Personnel J.*, 1932, **10**, 393-401.

40. Kristy, N. F. *Criteria of occupational success among post office counter clerks.* Unpublished doctor's thesis, Univer. of London, 1952.

41. Lawshe, C. H., & Nagle, B. F. Productivity and attitude toward supervisor. *J. Appl. Psychol.*, 1953, **37**, 159-162.

42. Mathewson, S. B. *Restriction of output among unorganized workers.* New York: Viking Press, 1931.

43. Mayo, E. *The social problems of an industrial civilization.* Cambridge: Graduate School of Business Administration, Harvard Univer., 1945.

44. McNemar, Q. Opinion-attitude methodology. *Psychol. Bull.*, 1946, **43**, 289-374.

45. Metzner, Helen, & Mann, F. A limited comparison of two methods of data collection: the fixed alternative questionnaire and the open-ended interview. *Amer. Sociol. Rev.*, 1952, **17**, 486-491.

46. Metzner, Helen, & Mann, F. Employee attitudes and absences. *Personnel Psychol.*, 1953, **6**, 467-485.

47. Morse, Nancy C. *Satisfactions in the*

white-collar job. Univer. of Michigan Survey Research Center, 1953.

48. Mossin, A. C. *Selling performance and contentment in relation to school background.* New York: Bureau of Publications, Teachers Coll., Columbia Univer., 1949.

49. Raube, S. A. *Experience with employee attitude surveys* (Studies in Personnel Policy, No. 115). New York: National Industrial Conference Board, 1951.

50. Roethlisberger, F. J. *Management and morale.* Cambridge: Harvard Univer. Press, 1943.

51. Roethlisberger, F. J., & Dickson, W. J. *Management and the worker.* Cambridge: Harvard Univer. Press, 1939.

52. Schachter, S., Ellertson, N., McBride, D., & Gregory, D. An experimental study of cohesiveness and productivity. *Hum. Relat.*, 1951, **4**, 229-238.

53. Stagner, R., Flebbe, D. R., & Wood, E. F. Working on the railroad: a study of job satisfaction. *Personnel Psychol.*, 1952, **5**, 293-306.

54. Thorndike, R. L. *Personnel selection.* New York: Wiley, 1949.

55. Van Zelst, R. H., & Kerr, W. A. Workers' attitudes toward merit rating. *Personnel Psychol.*, 1953, **6**, 159-172.

56. Viteles, M. S. *Motivation and morale in industry.* New York: Norton, 1953.

57. Warner, W. L., & Lunt, P. S. *The social life of a modern community.* New Haven: Yale Univer. Press, 1941.

58. Wedell, C., & Smith, K. U. Consistency of interview methods in appraisal of attitudes. *J. Appl. Psychol.*, 1951, **35**, 392-396.

59. Weitz, J., & Nuckols, R. C. The validity of direct and indirect questions in measuring job satisfaction. *Personnel Psychol.*, 1953, **5**, 487-494.

60. Weschler, I. R., Kahane, M., & Tannenbaum, R. Job satisfaction, productivity and morale: a case study. *Occupational Psychol.*, 1952, **26**, 1-14.

61. Wickert, F. R. Turnover, and employees' feelings of ego-involvement in the day-to-day operations of a company. *Personnel Psychol.*, 1951, **4**, 185-197.

62. Yoder, D., Heneman, H., Jr., & Cheit, E. F. *Triple audit of industrial relations.* Minneapolis: Univer. of Minnesota Press, 1951.

18. One More Time: How Do You Motivate Employees?*

FREDERICK HERZBERG

How many articles, books, speeches, and workshops have pleaded plaintively, "How do I get an employee to do what I want him to do?"

The psychology of motivation is tremendously complex, and what has been unraveled with any degree of assurance is small indeed. But the dismal ratio of knowledge to speculation has not dampened the enthusiasm for new forms of snake oil that are constantly coming on the market, many of them with academic testimonials. Doubtless this article will have no depressing impact on the market for snake oil, but since the ideas expressed in it have been tested in many corporations and other organizations, it will help—I hope—to redress the imbalance in the aforementioned ratio.

"MOTIVATING" WITH KITA

In lectures to industry on the problem, I have found that the audiences are anxious for quick and practical answers, so I will begin with a straightforward, practical formula for moving people.

What is the simplest, surest, and most direct way of getting someone to do something? Ask him? But if he responds that he does not want to do it, then that calls for a psychological consultation to determine the reason for his obstinancy. Tell him? His response shows that he does not understand you, and now an expert in communication methods has to be brought in to show you how to get through to him. Give him a monetary incentive? I do not need to remind the reader of the complexity and difficulty involved in setting up and administering an incentive system. Show him? This means a costly training program. We need a simple way.

Every audience contains the "direct action" manager who shouts, "Kick him!" And this type of manager is right. The surest and least circumlocuted way of getting someone to do something is to kick him in the pants—give him what might be called the KITA.

There are various forms of KITA, and here are some of them.

NEGATIVE PHYSICAL KITA

This is a literal application of the term and was frequently used in the past. It has, however, three major drawbacks: (1) it is inelegant; (2) it contradicts the precious image of benevolence that most organizations cherish; and (3) since it is a physical attack, it directly stimulates the autonomic nervous system, and this often results in negative feedback—the employee may just kick you in return. These factors give rise to certain taboos against negative physical KITA.

The psychologist has come to the rescue of those who are no longer permitted to use negative physical KITA. He has uncovered infinite sources of psychological vulnerabilities and the appropriate methods to play tunes on them. "He took my rug away"; "I wonder what he meant by that"; "The boss is always going around me"—these symptomatic expressions of ego sores that have been rubbed raw are the result of application of:

NEGATIVE PSYCHOLOGICAL KITA

This has several advantages over negative physical KITA. First, the cruelty is not visible; the bleeding is internal and comes much later. Second, since it affects the higher cortical centers of the brain with its inhibitory powers, it reduces the possibility of physical backlash. Third, since the number of psychological pains that a person can feel is almost infinite, the direction and site possibilities of the KITA are increased many times. Fourth, the person administering the kick can manage to be above it all and let the system accomplish the dirty work. Fifth, those who practice it receive some ego satisfaction (one-upmanship), whereas they would find drawing blood abhorrent. Finally, if the employee does complain, he can always be accused of being paranoid, since there is no tangible evidence of an actual attack.

Now, what does negative KITA accomplish? If I kick you in the rear (physically or psychologically), who is motivated? *I* am motivated; *you* move! Negative KITA does not lead to motivation, but to movement. So:

POSITIVE KITA

Let us consider motivation. If I say to you, "Do this for me or the company, and in return I will give you a reward, an incentive, more status, a promotion, all the quid pro quos that exist in the industrial organization," am I motivating you? The overwhelming opinion I receive from management people is, "Yes, this is motivation."

I have a year-old Schnauzer. When it was a small puppy and I wanted it to move, I kicked it in the rear and it moved. Now that I have finished its obedience training, I hold up a dog biscuit when I want the Schnauzer to move. In this instance, who is motivated—I or the dog? The dog wants the biscuit, but it is I who want it to move. Again, I am the one who is motivated, and the dog is the one who moves. In this instance all I did was apply KITA frontally; I exerted a pull instead of a push. When industry wishes to use such positive KITAs, it has available an incredible number and variety of dog biscuits (jelly beans for humans) to wave in front of the employee to get him to jump.

Why is it that managerial audiences are quick to see that negative KITA is *not* motivation, while they are almost unanimous in their judgment that positive KITA *is* motivation? It is because negative KITA is rape, and positive KITA is seduction. But it is infinitely worse to be seduced than to be raped; the latter is an unfortunate occurrence, while the former signifies that you were a party to your own downfall. This is why positive KITA is so popular; it is a tradition; it is in the American way. The organization does not have to kick you; you kick yourself.

MYTHS ABOUT MOTIVATION

Why is KITA not motivation? If I kick my dog (from the front or the back), he will move. And when I want him to move again, what must I do? I must kick him again. Similarly, I can charge a man's battery, and then recharge it, and recharge it again. But it is only when he has his own generator that we can talk about motivation. He then needs no outside stimulation. He *wants* to do it.

With this in mind, we can review some positive KITA personnel practices that were developed as attempts to instill "motivation."

1. REDUCING TIME SPENT AT WORK

This represents a marvelous way of motivating people to work—getting them off the job! We have reduced (formally and informally) the time spent on the job over the last 50 or 60 years until we are finally on the way to the "6½-day weekend." An interesting variant of this approach is the development of off-hour recreation programs. The philosophy here seems to be that those who play together, work together. The fact is that motivated people seek more hours of work, not fewer.

2. SPIRALING WAGES

Have these motivated people? Yes, to seek the next wage increase. Some medievalists still can be heard to say that a good depression will get employees moving. They feel that if rising wages don't or won't do the job, perhaps reducing them will.

3. FRINGE BENEFITS

Industry has outdone the most welfare-minded of welfare states in dispensing cradle-to-the-grave succor. One company I know of had an informal "fringe benefit of the month club" going for a while. The cost of fringe benefits in this country has reached approximately 25 percent of the wage dollar, and we still cry for motivation.

People spend less time working for more money and more security than ever before, and the trend cannot be reversed. These benefits are no longer rewards; they are rights. A 6-day week is inhuman, a 10-hour day is exploitation, extended medical coverage is a basic decency; and stock options are the salvation of American initiative. Unless the ante is continuously raised, the psychological reaction of employees is that the company is turning back the clock.

When industry began to realize that both the economic nerve and the lazy nerve of their employees had insatiable appetites, it started to listen to the behavioral scientists who, more out of a humanist tradition than from scientific study, criticized management for not knowing how to deal with people. The next KITA easily followed.

4. HUMAN RELATIONS TRAINING

Over 30 years of teaching and, in many instances, of practicing psychological approaches to handling people have resulted in costly human relations programs and, in the end, the same question: How do you motivate workers? Here, too, escalations have taken place. Thirty years ago it was necessary to request, "Please don't spit on the floor." Today the same admonition requires three "please"'s before the employee feels that his superior has demonstrated the psychologically proper attitudes toward him.

The failure of human relations training to produce motivation led to the conclusion that the supervisor or manager himself was not psychologically true to himself in his practice of interpersonal decency. So an advanced form of human relations KITA, sensitivity training, was unfolded.

5. SENSITIVITY TRAINING

Do you really, really understand yourself? Do you really, really, really trust the other man? Do you really, really, really, really cooperate? The failure of sensitivity training is now being explained, by those who have become opportunistic exploiters of the technique, as a failure to really (five times) conduct proper sensitivity training courses.

With the realization that there are only temporary gains from comfort and economic and interpersonal KITA, personnel managers concluded that the fault lay not in what they were doing, but in the employee's failure to appreciate what they were doing. This opened up the field of communications, a whole new area of "scientifically" sanctioned KITA.

6. COMMUNICATIONS

The professor of communications was invited to join the faculty of management training programs and help in making employees understand what management was doing for them. House organs, briefing sessions, supervisory instruction on the importance of communication, and all sorts of propaganda have proliferated until today there is even an International Council of Industrial Editors. But no motivation resulted, and the obvious thought occurred that perhaps management was not hearing what the employees were saying. That led to the next KITA.

7. TWO-WAY COMMUNICATION

Management ordered morale surveys, suggestion plans, and group participation programs. Then both employees and management were communicating and listening to each other more than ever, but without much improvement in motivation.

The behavioral scientists began to take another look at their conceptions and their data, and they took human relations one step further. A glimmer of truth was beginning to show through in the writings of the so-called higher-order-need psychologists. People, so they said, want to actualize themselves. Unfortunately, the "actualizing" psychologists got mixed up with the human relations psychologists, and a new KITA emerged.

8. JOB PARTICIPATION

Though it may not have been the theoretical intention, job participation often became a "give them the big picture" approach. For example, if a man is tightening 10,000 nuts a day on an assembly line with a torque wrench, tell him he is building a Chevrolet. Another approach had the goal of giving the employee a *feeling* that he is determining, in some measure, what he does on his job. The goal was to provide a *sense* of achievement rather than a substantive achievement in his task. Real achievement, of course, requires a task that makes it possible.

But still there was no motivation. This led to the inevitable conclusion that the employees must be sick, and therefore to the next KITA.

9. EMPLOYEE COUNSELING

The initial use of this form of KITA in a

systematic fashion can be credited to the Hawthorne experiment of the Western Electric Company during the early 1930s. At that time, it was found that the employees harbored irrational feelings that were interfering with the rational operation of the factory. Counseling in this instance was a means of letting the employees unburden themselves by talking to someone about their problems. Although the counseling techniques were primitive, the program was large indeed.

The counseling approach suffered as a result of experiences during World War II, when the programs themselves were found to be interfering with the operation of the organizations; the counselors had forgotten their role of benevolent listeners and were attempting to do something about the problems that they heard about. Psychological counseling, however, has managed to survive the negative impact of World War II experiences and today is beginning to flourish with renewed sophistication. But, alas, many of these programs, like all the others, do not seem to have lessened the pressure of demands to find out how to motivate workers.

Since KITA results only in short-term movement, it is safe to predict that the cost of these programs will increase steadily and new varieties will be developed as old positive KITAs reach their satiation points.

HYGIENE VS. MOTIVATORS

Let me rephrase the perennial question this way: How do you install a generator in an employee? A brief review of my motivation-hygiene theory of job attitudes is required before theoretical and practical suggestions can be offered. The theory was first drawn from an examination of events in the lives of engineers and accountants. At least 16 other investigations, using a wide variety of populations (including some in the Communist countries), have

since been completed, making the original research one of the most replicated studies in the field of job attitudes.

The findings of these studies, along with corroboration from many other investigations using different procedures, suggest that the factors involved in producing job satisfaction (and motivation) are separate and distinct from the factors that lead to job dissatisfaction. Since separate factors need to be considered, depending on whether job satisfaction or job dissatisfaction is being examined, it follows that these two feelings are not opposites of each other. The opposite of job satisfaction is not job dissatisfaction but, rather, no job satisfaction; and, similarly, the opposite of job dissatisfaction is not job satisfaction, but no job dissatisfaction.

Stating the concept presents a problem in semantics, for we normally think of satisfaction and dissatisfaction as opposites-i.e., what is not satisfying must be dissatisfying, and vice versa. But when it comes to understanding the behavior of people in their jobs, more than a play on words is involved.

Two different needs of man are involved here. One set of needs can be thought of as stemming from his animal nature—the built-in drive to avoid pain from the environment, plus all the learned drives which become conditioned to the basic biological needs. For example, hunger, a basic biological drive, makes it necessary to earn money, and then money becomes a specific drive. The other set of needs relates to that unique human characteristic, the ability to achieve and, through achievement, to experience psychological growth. The stimuli for the growth needs are tasks that induce growth; in the industrial setting, they are the *job content*. Contrariwise, the stimuli inducing pain-avoidance behavior are found in the *job environment*.

The growth or *motivator* factors that are intrinsic to the job are: achievement, recognition for achievement, the work itself, responsibility, and growth or advancement. The dissatisfaction-avoidance or *hygiene* (KITA) factors that are extrinsic to the job include: company policy and administration, supervision, interpersonal relationships, working conditions, salary, status, and security.

A composite of the factors that are involved in causing job satisfaction and job dissatisfaction, drawn from samples of 1,685 employees, is shown in Figure 1. The results indicate that motivators were the primary cause of satisfaction, and hygiene factors the primary cause of unhappiness on the job. The employees, studied in 12 different investigations, included lower-level supervisors, professional women, agricultural ad-

ministrators, men about to retire from management positions, hospital maintenance personnel, manufacturing supervisors, nurses, food handlers, military officers, engineers, scientists, housekeepers, teachers, technicians, female assemblers, accountants, Finnish foremen, and Hungarian engineers.

They were asked what job events had occured in their work that had led to extreme satisfaction or extreme dissatisfaction on their part. Their responses are broken down in the exhibit into percentages of total "positive" job events and total "negative" job events. (The figures total more than 100 percent on both the "hygiene" and "motivators" sides because often at least two factors

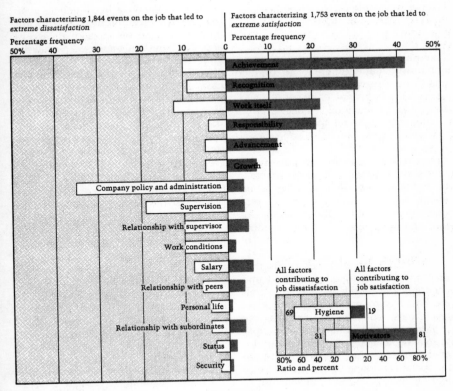

Figure 1
FACTORS AFFECTING JOB ATTITUDES, AS REPORTED IN
12 INVESTIGATIONS

can be attributed to a single event; advancement, for instance, often accompanies assumption of responsibility.)

To illustrate, a typical response involving achievement that had a negative effect for the employee was, "I was unhappy because I didn't do the job successfully." A typical response in the small number of positive job events in the Company Policy and Administration grouping was, "I was happy because the company reorganized the section so that I didn't report any longer to the guy I didn't get along with."

As the lower right-hand part of the exhibit shows, of all the factors contributing to job satisfaction, 81 percent were motivators. And of all the factors contributing to the employees' dissatisfaction over their work, 69 percent involved hygiene elements.

ETERNAL TRIANGLE

There are three general philosophies of personnel management. The first is based on organizational theory, the second on industrial engineering, and the third on behavioral science.

The organizational theorist believes that human needs are either so irrational or so varied and adjustable to specific situations that the major function of personnel management is to be as pragmatic as the occasion demands. If jobs are organized in a proper manner, he reasons the result will be the most efficient job structure, and the most favorable job attitudes will follow as a matter of course.

The industrial engineer holds that man is mechanistically oriented and economically motivated and his needs are best met by attuning the individual to the most efficient work process. The goal of personnel management therefore should be to concoct the most appropriate incentive system and to design the specific working conditions in a way that facilitates the most efficient use of the human machine. By structuring jobs in a manner that leads to the most efficient operation, the engineer believes

that he can obtain the optimal organization of work and the proper work attitudes.

The behavioral scientist focuses on group sentiments, attitudes of individual employees, and the organization's social and psychological climate. According to his persuasion, he emphasizes one or more of the various hygiene and motivator needs. His approach to personnel management generally emphasizes some form of human relations education, in the hope of instilling healthy employee attitudes and an organizational climate which he considers to be felicitous to human values. He believes that proper attitudes will lead to efficient job and organizational structure.

There is always a lively debate as to the overall effectiveness of the approaches of the organizational theorist and the industrial engineer. Manifestly they have achieved much. But the nagging question for the behavioral scientist has been: What is the cost in human problems that eventually cause more expense to the organization—for instance, turnover, absenteeism, errors, violation of safety rules, strikes, restriction of output, higher wages, and greater fringe benefits? On the other hand, the behavioral scientist is hard put to document much manifest improvement in personnel management, using his approach.

The three philosophies can be depicted as a triangle, as is done in Figure 2, with each persuasion claiming the apex angle. The motivation-hygiene theory claims the same angle as industrial engineering, but for opposite goals. Rather than rationalizing the work to increase efficiency, the theory suggests that work be *enriched* to bring about effective utilization of personnel. Such a systematic attempt to motivate employees by manipulating the motivator factors is just beginning.

The term *job enrichment* describes this embryonic movement. An older term, job enlargement, should be

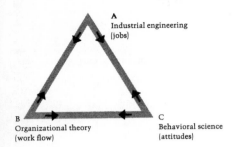

A
Industrial engineering
(jobs)

B
Organizational theory
(work flow)

C
Behavioral science
(attitudes)

Figure 2
"TRIANGLE" OF PHILOSOPHIES
OF PERSONNEL MANAGEMENT

avoided because it is associated with past failures stemming from a misunderstanding of the problem. Job enrichment provides the opportunity for the employee's psychological growth, while job enlargement merely makes a job structurally bigger. Since scientific job enrichment is very new, this article only suggests the principles and practical steps that have recently emerged from several successful experiments in industry.

JOB LOADING

In attempting to enrich an employee's job, management often succeeds in reducing the man's personal contribution, rather than giving him an opportunity for growth in his accustomed job. Such an endeavor, which I shall call horizontal job loading (as opposed to vertical loading, or providing motivator factors), has been the problem of earlier job enlargement programs. This activity merely enlarges the meaninglessness of the job. Some examples of this approach, and their effect are:

• Challenging the employee by increasing the amount of production expected of him. If he tightens 10,000 bolts a day, see if he can tighten 20,000 bolts a day. The arithmetic involved shows that multiplying zero by zero still equals zero.
• Adding another meaningless task to the existing one, usually some routine clerical activity. The arithmetic here is adding zero to zero.

• Rotating the assignments of a number of jobs that need to be enriched. This means washing dishes for a while, then washing silverware. The arithmetic is substituting one zero for another zero.
• Removing the most difficult parts of the assignment in order to free the worker to accomplish more of the less challenging assignments. This traditional industrial engineering approach amounts to subtraction in the hope of accomplishing addition.

These are common forms of horizontal loading that frequently come up in preliminary brainstorming sessions on job enrichment. The principles of vertical loading have not all been worked out as yet, and they remain rather general, but I have furnished seven useful starting points for consideration in Table 1.

A SUCCESSFUL APPLICATION

An example from a highly successful job enrichment experiment can illustrate the distinction between horizontal and vertical loading of a job. The subjects of this study were the stockholder correspondents employed by a very large corporation. Seemingly, the task required of these carefully selected and highly trained correspondents was quite complex and challenging. But almost all indexes of performance and job attitudes were low, and exit interviewing confirmed that the challenge of the job existed merely as words.

A job enrichment project was initiated in the form of an experiment with one group, designated as an achieving unit, having its job enriched by the principles described in Table 1. A control group continued to do its job in the traditional way. (There were also two "uncommitted" groups of correspondents formed to measure the so-called Hawthorne Effect—that is, to gauge whether productivity and attitudes toward the job changed artificially merely because employees sensed that the company was paying more attention to them in doing something different or novel. The results for these groups were substantially the same as for the control group, and for the sake of simplicity I do

Table 1
PRINCIPLES OF VERTICAL JOB LOADING

Principle	Motivators involved
A. Removing some controls while retaining accountability	Responsibility and personal achievement
B. Increasing the accountability of individuals for own work	Responsibility and recognition
C. Giving a person a complete natural unit of work (module, division, area, and so on)	Responsibility, achievement, and recognition
D. Granting additional authority to an employee in his activity; job freedom	Responsibility, achivement, and recognition
E. Making periodic reports directly available to the worker himself rather than to the supervisor	Internal recognition
F. Introducing new and more difficult tasks not previously handled	Growth and learning
G. Assigning individuals specific or specialized tasks, enabling them to become experts	Responsibility, growth and advancement

not deal with them in this summary.) No changes in hygiene were introduced for either group other than those that would have been made anyway, such as normal pay increases.

The changes for the achieving unit were introduced in the first two months, averaging one per week of the seven motivators listed in Table 1. At the end of six months the members of the achieving unit were found to be outperforming their counterparts in the control group, and in addition indicated a marked increase in their liking for their jobs. Other results showed that the achieving group had lower absenteeism and, subsequently, a much higher rate of promotion.

Figure 3 illustrates the changes in performance, measured in February and March, before the study period began, and at the end of each month of the study period. The shareholder service index represents quality of letters, including accuracy of information, and speed of response to stockholders' letters of inquiry. The index of a current month was averaged into the average of the two prior months, which means that improvement was harder to obtain if the indexes of the previous months were

low. The "achievers" were performing less well before the six-month period started, and their performance service

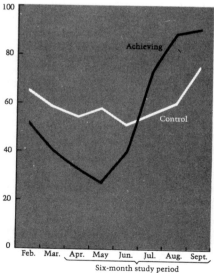

Performance index

Figure 3
SHAREHOLDER SERVICE INDEX
IN COMPANY EXPERIMENT
(Three-month cumulative average)

index continued to decline after the introduction of the motivators, evidently because of uncertainty over their newly granted responsibilities. In the third month, however, performance improved, and soon the members of this group had reached a high level of accomplishment.

Figure 4 shows the two groups' attitudes toward their job, measured at the end of March, just before the first motivator was introduced, and again at the end of September. The correspondents were asked 16 questions, all involving motivation. A typical one was, "As you see it, how many opportunities do you feel that you have in your job for making worthwhile contributions?" The answers were scaled from 1 to 5, with 80 as the maximum possible score. The achievers became much more positive about their job, while the attitude of the control unit remained about the same (the drop is not statistically significant).

How was the job of these correspondents restructured? Table 2 lists the suggestions made that were deemed to be horizontal loading, and the actual vertical loading changes that were in-

corporated in the job of the achieving unit. The capital letters under "Principle" after "Vertical loading" refer to the corresponding letters in Table 1. The reader will note that the rejected forms of horizontal loading correspond closely to the list of common manifestations of the phenomenon [under the subheading "JOB LOADING"].

STEPS TO JOB ENRICHMENT

Now that motivator idea has been described in practice, here are the steps that managers should take in instituting the principle with their employees [*italic first sentences not in original*]:

1. *Select those jobs in which (a) the investment in industrial engineering does not make changes too costly, (b) attitudes are poor, (c) hygiene is becoming very costly, and (d) motivation will make a difference in performance.*

2. *Approach these jobs with the conviction that they can be changed.* Years of tradition have led managers to believe that the content of the jobs is sacrosanct and the only scope of action that they have is in ways of stimulating people.

3. *Brainstorm a list of changes that may enrich the jobs, without concern for their practicality.*

4. *Screen the list to eliminate suggestions that involve hygiene, rather than actual motivation.*

5. *Screen the list for generalities, such as "give them more responsibility," that are rarely followed in practice.* This might seem obvious, but the motivator words have never left industry; the substance has just been rationalized and organized out. Words like "responsibility," "growth," "achievement," and "challenge," for example, have been elevated to the lyrics of the patriotic anthem for all organizations. It is the old problem typified by the pledge of allegiance to the flag being more important than contributions to the country—of following the form, rather than the substance.

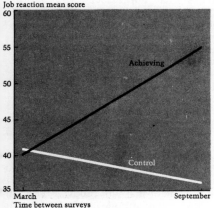

Figure 4
CHANGES IN ATTITUDES TOWARD TASKS IN COMPANY EXPERIMENT
(Changes in mean scores over six-month period)

Table 2

ENLARGEMENT VS. ENRICHMENT OF CORRESPONDENTS' TASKS
IN COMPANY EXPERIMENT

Horizontal loading suggestions (rejected)	Vertical loading suggestions (adopted)	Principle
Firm quotas could be set for letters to be answered each day, using a rate which would be hard to reach.	Subject matter experts were appointed within each unit for other members of the unit to consult with before seeking supervisory help. (The supervisor had been answering all specialized and difficult questions.)	G
The women could type the letters themselves, as well as compose them, or take on any other clerical functions.	Correspondents signed their own names on letters (The supervisor had been signing all letters.)	B
All difficult or complex inquiries could be channeled to a few women so that the remainder could achieve high rates of output. These jobs could be exchanged from time to time.	The work of the more experienced correspondents was proofread less frequently by supervisors and was done at the correspondents' desks, dropping verification from 100% to 10%. (Previously, all correspondents' letters had been checked by the supervisor.)	A
The women could be rotated through units handling different customers, and then sent back to their own units.	Production was discussed, but only in terms such as "a full day's work is expected." As time went on, this was no longer mentioned. (Before, the group had been constantly reminded of the number of letters that needed to be answered.)	D
	Outgoing mail went directly to the mailroom without going over supervisors' desks. (The letters had always been routed through the supervisors.)	A
	Correspondents were encouraged to answer letters in a more personalized way. (Reliance on the form-letter approach had been standard practice.)	C
	Each correspondent was held personally responsible for the quality and accuracy of letters. (This responsibility had been the province of the supervisor and the verifier.)	B, E

6. *Screen the list to eliminate any* horizontal [*emphasis in original*] *loading suggestions.*

7. *Avoid direct participation by the employees whose jobs are to be enriched.* Ideas they have expressed previously certainly constitute a valuable source for recommended changes, but their direct involvement contaminates the process with human relations hygiene and, more specifically, gives them only a *sense* of making a contribution. The job is to be changed, and it is the content that will produce the motivation, not attitudes about being involved or the challenge inherent in setting up a job. The process will be over shortly, and it is what the employees will be doing from then on that will determine their motivation. A sense of par-

ticipation will result only in short-term movement.

8. *In the initial attempts at job enrichment, set up a controlled experiment.* At least two equivalent groups should be chosen, one an experimental unit in which the motivators are systematically introduced over a period of time, and the other one a control group in which no changes are made. For both groups, hygiene should be allowed to follow its natural course for the duration of the experiment. Pre- and post-installation tests of performance and job attitudes are necessary to evaluate the effectiveness of the job enrichment program. The attitude test must be limited to motivator items in order to divorce the employee's view of the job he is given from all the surrounding hygiene feelings that he might have.

9. *Be prepared for a drop in performance in the experimental group the first few weeks.* The changeover to a new job may lead to a temporary reduction in efficiency.

10. *Expect your first-line supervisors to experience some anxiety and hostility over the changes you are making.* The anxiety comes from their fear that the changes will result in poorer performance for their unit. Hostility will arise when the employees start assuming what the supervisors regard as their own responsibility for performance. The supervisor without checking duties to perform may then be left with little to do.

After a successful experiment, however, the supervisor usually discovers the supervisory and managerial functions he has neglected, or which were never his because all his time was given over to checking the work of his subordinates. For example, in the R&D division of one large chemical company I know of, the supervisors of the laboratory assistants were theoretically responsible for their training and evaluation. These functions, however, had come to be performed in a routine, unsubstantial fashion. After the job enrichment program, during which the supervisors were not merely passive observers of the assistants' performance, the supervisors actually were devoting their time to reviewing performance and administering thorough training.

What has been called an employee-centered style of supervision will come about not through education of supervisors, but by changing the jobs that they do.

CONCLUDING NOTE

Job enrichment will not be a one-time proposition, but a continuous management function. The initial changes, however, should last for a very long period of time. There are a number of reasons for this:

- The changes should bring the job up to the level of challenge commensurate with the skill that was hired.
- Those who have still more ability eventually will be able to demonstrate it better and win promotion to higher-level jobs.
- The very nature of motivators, as opposed to hygiene factors, is that they have a much longer-term effect on employees' attitudes. Perhaps the job will have to be enriched again, but this will not occur as frequently as the need for hygiene.

Not all jobs can be enriched, nor do all jobs need to be enriched. If only a small percentage of the time and money that is now devoted to hygiene, however, were given to job enrichment efforts, the return in human satisfaction and economic gain would be one of the largest dividends that industry and society have ever reaped through their efforts at better personnel management.

The arguement for job enrichment can be summed up quite simply: If you have someone on a job, use him. If you can't use him on the job, get rid of him, either via automation or by selecting someone with lesser ability. If you can't use him and you can't get rid of him, you will have a motivation problem.

19. The Effect of Performance on Job Satisfaction*

EDWARD E. LAWLER III
LYMAN W. PORTER

The human relations movement with its emphasis on good interpersonal relations, job satisfaction, and the importance of informal groups provided an important initial stimulant for the study of job attitudes and their relationship to human behavior in organizations. Through the thirties and forties, many studies were carried out to determine the correlates of high and low job satisfaction. Such studies related job satisfaction to seniority, age, sex, education, occupation, and income, to mention a few. Why this great interest in job satisfaction? Undoubtedly some of it stemmed from a simple desire on the part of scientists to learn more about job satisfaction, but much of the interest in job satisfaction seems to have come about because of its presumed relationship to job performance. As Brayfield and Crockett have pointed out, a common assumption that employee satisfaction directly affects performance permeates most of the writings about the topic that appeared during this period of two decades.[1] Statements such as the following characterized the literature: "Morale is not an abstraction; rather it is concrete in the sense that it directly affects the quality and quantity of an individual's output," and "Employee morale—reduces turnover—cuts down absenteeism and tardiness; lifts production."[2]

It is not hard to see how the assumption that high job satisfaction leads high performance came to be popularly accepted. Not only did it fit into the value system of the human relations movement but there also appeared to be some research data to support this point. In the Western Electric studies, the evidence from the Relay Assembly Test Room showed a dramatic tendency for increased employee productivity to be associated with an increase in job satisfaction. Also, who could deny that in the Bank Wiring Room there was both production restriction and mediocre employee morale. With this background it is easy to see why both social scientists and managers believed that if job dissatisfaction could be reduced, the human brake on production could be removed and turned into a force that would increase performance.

PREVIOUS RESEARCH

But does the available evidence support the belief that high satisfaction will lead to high performance? Since an initial study, in 1932, by Kornhauser and Sharp, more than thirty studies have considered the relationship between these two variables.[3] Many of the earlier studies seemed to have assumed implicitly that a positive relationship existed and that it was important to demonstrate that it in fact did exist. Little attention was given to trying to understand *why* job satisfaction should lead to higher performance; instead, re-

*Source: From Industrial Relations (October 1967), vol. 7, pp. 20-28. Copyright © 1967 Industrial Relations. Reprinted by permission.

searchers contented themselves with routinely studying the relationship between satisfaction and performance in a number of industrial situations.

The typical reader of the literature in the early fifties was probably aware of the fact that some studies had failed to find a significant satisfaction-performance relationship. Indeed, the very first study of the problem obtained an insignificant relationship.[4] However, judging from the impact of the first review of the literature on the topic, by Brayfield and Crockett, many social scientists, let alone practicing managers, were unaware that the evidence indicated how little relationship exists between satisfaction and performance.[5] The key conclusion that emerged from the review was that "there is little evidence in the available literature that employee attitudes bear any simple—or, for that matter, appreciable—relationship to performance on the job." (The review, however, pointed out that job satisfaction did seem to be positively related, as expected, to two other kinds of employee behavior, absenteeism and turnover.)

The review had a major impact on the field of industrial psychology and helped shatter the kind of naive thinking that characterized the earlier years of the human relations movement. Perhaps it also discouraged additional research, since few post-1955 studies of the relationship between satisfaction and performance have been reported in scientific journals.

Another review, covering much of the same literature, was completed about the same time.[6] This review took a more optimistic view of the evidence:

> . . . there is frequent evidence for the often suggested opinion that positive job attitudes are favorable to increased productivity. The relationship is not absolute, but there are enough data to justify attention to attitudes as a factor in improving the worker's output. However, the correlations obtained in many of the positive studies were low.[7]

This review also pointed out, as did Brayfield and Crockett, that there was a definite trend for attitudes to be related to absenteeism and turnover. Perhaps the chief reasons for the somewhat divergent conclusions reached by the two reviews were that they did not cover exactly the same literature and that Brayfield and Crockett were less influenced by suggestive findings that did reach statistical significance. In any event, the one conclusion that was obvious from both reviews was that there was not the *strong, pervasive* relationship between job satisfaction and productivity that had been suggested by many of the early proponents of the human relations movement and so casually accepted by personnel specialists.

A more recent review of the literature by Vroom has received less attention than did the two earlier reviews,[8] perhaps because it is now rather generally accepted that satisfaction is not related to performance. However, before we too glibly accept the view that satisfaction and performance are unrelated, let us look carefully at the data from studies reviewed by Vroom. These studies show a median correlation of +.14 between satisfaction and performance. Although this correlation is not large, the consistency of the direction of the correlation is quite impressive. Twenty of the 23 correlations cited by Vroom are positive. By a statistical test such consistency would occur by chance less than once in a hundred times.

In summary, the evidence indicates that a low but consistent relationship exists between satisfaction and performance, but it is not at all clear *why* this relationship exists. The questions that need to be answered at this time, therefore, concern the place of job satisfaction both in theories of employee motivation and in everyday organizational practice. For example, should an organization systematically measure the level of employee satisfaction? Is it important for an organization to try to improve employee job satisfaction? Is there theoretical reason for believing that job satisfaction should be related to job behavior and if so, can it explain why this relationship exists?

WHY STUDY JOB SATISFACTION?

There are really two bases upon which to argue that job satisfaction is important. Interestingly, both are different from the original reason for studying job satisfaction, that is, the assumed ability of satisfaction to influence performance. The first, and undoubtedly the most straightforward reason, rests on the fact that strong correlations between absenteeism and satisfaction, as well as between turnover and satisfaction, appear in the previous studies. Accordingly, job satisfaction would seem to be an important focus of organizations which wish to reduce absenteeism and turnover.

Perhaps the best explanation of the fact that satisfaction is related to absenteeism and turnover comes from the kind of path-goal theory of motivation that has been stated by Georgopoulos, Mahoney and Jones; Vroom; and Lawler and Porter.[9] According to this view, people are motivated to do things which they feel have a high probability of leading to rewards which they value. When a worker says he is satisfied with his job, he is in effect saying that his needs are satisfied as a result of having his job. Thus, path-goal theory would predict that high satisfaction will lead to low turnover and absenteeism because the satisfied individual is motivated to go to work where his important needs are satisfied.

A second reason for interest in job satisfaction stems from its low but consistent association with job performance. Let us speculate for a moment on why this association exists. One possibility is that, as assumed by many, the satisfaction caused the performance. However, there is little

theoretical reason for believing that satisfaction can cause performance. Vroom, using a path-goal theory of motivation, has pointed out that job satisfaction and job performance are caused by quite different things:

... job satisfaction is closely affected by the amount of rewards that people derive from their jobs and ... level of performance is closely affected by the basis of attainment of rewards. Individuals are satisfied with their jobs to the extent to which their jobs provide them with what they desire, and they perform effectively in them to the extent that effective performance leads to the attainment of what they desire.[10]

RELATIONSHIP BETWEEN SATISFACTION AND PERFORMANCE

Vroom's statement contains a hint of why, despite the fact that satisfaction and performance are caused by different things, they do bear some relationship to each other. If we assume, as seems to be reasonable in terms of motivation theory, that rewards cause satisfaction, and that in some cases performance produces rewards, then it is possible that the relationship found between satisfaction and performance comes about through the action of a third variable—rewards. Briefly stated, good performance may lead to rewards, which in turn lead to satisfaction; this formulation then would say that satisfaction, rather than causing performance, as was previously assumed, is caused by it. Figure 1 presents this thinking in a diagrammatic form.

This model first shows that performance leads to rewards, and it distinguishes between two kinds of rewards and their connection to performance. A wavy line between performance and extrinsic rewards indicates that such rewards are likely to be imperfectly related to performance. By extrinsic rewards is meant such organizationally controlled rewards as pay, promotion, status, and security—

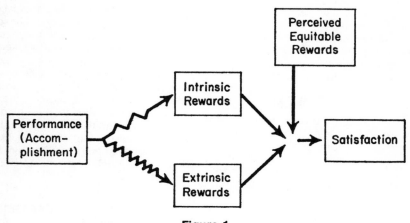

Figure 1
THE THEORETICAL MODEL

rewards that are often referred to as satisfying mainly lower level needs.[11] The connection is relatively weak because of the difficulty of tying extrinsic rewards directly to performance. Even though an organization may have a policy of rewarding merit, performance is difficult to measure, and in dispensing rewards like pay, many other factors are frequently taken into consideration. Lawler, for example, found a low correlation between amount of salary and superiors' evaluation for a number of middle and lower level managers.[12]

Quite the opposite is likely to be true for intrinsic rewards, however, since they are given to the individual by himself for good performance. Intrinsic or internally mediated rewards are subject to fewer disturbing influences and thus are likely to be more directly related to good performance. This connection is indicated in the model by a semiwavy line. Probably the best example of an intrinsic reward is the feeling of having accomplished something worthwhile. For that matter, any of the rewards that satisfy self-actualization needs or higher order growth needs are good examples of intrinsic rewards.

The model also shows that intrinsic and extrinsic rewards are not directly re-

lated to job satisfaction since the relationship is moderated by expected equitable rewards. This variable refers to the level or amount of rewards that an individual feels he *should* receive as the result of his job performance. Thus, an individual's satisfaction is a function both of the number and amount of the rewards he receives as well as what he considers to be a fair level of reward. An individual can be satisfied with a small amount of reward if he feels that it is a fair amount of reward for his job.[13]

This model would seem to predict that because of the imperfect relationship between performance and rewards and the importance of expected equitable rewards there would be a low but positive relationship between job satisfaction and job performance. The model also leads to a number of other predictions about the relationship between satisfaction and performance. If it turns out that, as this model predicts, satisfaction is dependent on performance, then it can be argued that satisfaction is an important variable from both a theoretical and a practical point of view despite its low relationship to performance. However, when satisfaction is viewed in this way, the reasons for considering it to be important are quite different from those that are proposed when satisfaction is considered to cause performance. But first, let us look at some of the predictions that are derivable from the model and at some data that were collected in order to test the predictions.

RESEARCH DATA

Usable data were collected from 148 middle and lower level managers in five organizations. One of the organizations was a large manufacturing company; the others were small social service and welfare agencies. As determined from the demographic data collected from each manager, the sample was typical of other samples of middle and lower level managers, with one exception—31 of the managers were female.

Two kinds of data were collected for each manager. Superior and peer rankings were obtained on two factors: (1) how hard the manager worked, and (2) how well the manager performed his job. Since a number of peers ranked each manager, the average peer's rankings were used for data analysis purposes. The rankings by the superiors and peers were in general agreement with each other, so the rankings met the requirements for convergent and discriminant validity. In addition to the superior and peer rankings each manager filled out an attitude questionnaire designed to measure his degree of satisfaction in five needed areas. This part of the questionnaire was identical to the one used in earlier studies by Porter.[14] It consists of 13 items in the following form:

The opportunity for independent thought and action in my management position:
(a) How much is there now?
   (min) 1 2 3 4 5 6 7 (max)
(b) How much should there be?
   (min) 1 2 3 4 5 6 7 (max)

The answers to the first of these questions (a) for each of the 13 items was taken as the measure of need fulfillment or rewards received. The answer to the second of the questions (b) was taken as a measure of the individual's expected equitable level of rewards. The difference in answers between the second and first of these questions was taken as the operational measure of need satisfaction. That is, the larger the difference between "should" and "is now" in our findings, the greater the dissatisfaction.[15]

The 13 items, though presented in random order in the questionnaire, had been preclassified into five types of needs that have been described by Maslow: security, social, esteem, autonomy, and self-actualization.

PREDICTIONS AND RESEARCH RESULTS

Let us now consider two specific predictions that our model suggests. The first is that an individual's degree of need satisfaction is related to his job performance as rated by his peers and by his superior. A second prediction is that this relationship is stronger for managers than for nonmanagers.

The basis for this second prediction can be found in the assumed connection between rewards and performance. It seems apparent that most organizations have considerably more freedom to reward their managers differentially than they do their often unionized rank-and-file employees (unless the latter are on incentive pay plans). Even in a nonunionized organization (such as a governmental unit), management jobs generally offer the possibility of greater flexibility in differential rewards, especially in terms of prestige and autonomy in decision-making. Management jobs also typically provide greater opportunities to satisfy higher order intrinsic needs. As the model shows, satisfaction of these higher order needs is more closely tied to performance.

SATISFACTION AND PERFORMANCE

Data collected from our sample of managers generally support the first two predictions. Job satisfaction (the sum of the difference scores for all 13 items) correlates significantly with both the superiors' rankings (r = .32, p < .01) and peers' rankings (r = .30, p < .01) of performance. Although the correlations are not large, they are substantially larger than the median correlation between satisfaction and performance at the level of rank-and-file workers (r = .14 as given in Vroom's review). It is possible that this higher relationship came about because we used a different measure of need satisfaction than has been typically used before or because we used a better performance measure. However, our belief is that it came about because the study was done at the management level in contrast to the previous studies which mainly involved nonmanagement employees. Neither our measure of job performance nor our measure of satisfaction would seem to be so unique that either could account for the higher relationship found between satisfaction and performance. However, future studies that use the same measure for both managers and nonmanagers are needed if this point is to be firmly established.

SATISFACTION AND EFFORT

An additional prediction from the model is that satisfaction should be more closely related to the rankings obtained on performance than to the rankings obtained on effort. The prediction is an important one for the model and stems from the fact that satisfaction is seen as a variable that is more directly dependent on performance than on effort. Others have pointed out that effort is only one of the factors that determines how effective an individual's performance will be. Ability factors and situational constraints are other obviously relevant determinants. It is also important to note that if we assume, as many previous writers have, that satisfaction causes performance then it would seem logical that satisfaction should be more closely related to effort than to performance. Satisfaction should influence an individual's performance

by affecting his motivation to perform effectively, and this presumably is better reflected by effort than by job performance.

The results of the present study show, in fact, a stronger relationship between the superiors' rankings of performance and satisfaction (r = .32), than between the superiors' rankings of effort and satisfaction (r = .23). Similarly, for the peer rankings there is a stronger relationship between performance and satisfaction (r = .30), than between effort and satisfaction (r = .20).

INTRINSIC AND EXTRINSIC REWARDS

The model suggests that intrinsic rewards that satisfy needs such as self-actualization are more likely to be related to performance than are extrinsic rewards, which have to be given by someone else and therefore have a weaker relationship between their reception and performance. Thus, the satisfaction should be more closely related to performance for higher than for lower order needs. Table 1 presents the data relevant to this point. There is a slight tendency for satisfaction of the higher order needs to show higher correlations with performance than does satisfaction with lower order needs. In particular, the highest correlations appear for self-actualization which is, of course, the highest order need, in the Maslow need hierarchy.

Overall, the data from the present study are in general agreement with the predictions based on the model. Significant relationships did appear between performance and job satisfaction. Perhaps even more important for our point of view, the relationship between satisfaction and performance was stronger than that typically found among blue-collar employees. Also in agreement with our model was the finding that satisfaction was more closely related to performance than to effort. The final prediction, which was supported by the data, was that the satisfaction of higher order needs would be the most

Table 1
PEARSON CORRELATIONS BETWEEN PERFORMANCE AND SATISFACTION IN FIVE NEED AREAS

Needs	Rankings by	
	Superiors	Peers
Security	.21[a]	.17[b]
Social	.23[a]	.26[a]
Esteem	.24[a]	.16[b]
Autonomy	.18[b]	.23[a]
Self-actualization	.30[a]	.28[a]

[a] $p < .01$
[b] $p < .05$

closely related to performance. Taken together then, the data offer encouraging support for our model and in particular for the assertion of the model that satisfaction can best be thought of as depending on performance rather than causing it.

IMPLICATIONS OF THE FINDINGS

At this point we can ask the following question: what does the strength of the satisfaction-performance relationship tell us about an organization? For example, if a strong positive relationship exists we would assume that the organization is effectively distributing differential extrinsic rewards based on performance. In addition, it is providing jobs that allow for the satisfaction of higher order needs. Finally, the poorer performers rather than the better ones are quitting and showing high absenteeism, since, as we know, satisfaction, turnover, and absenteeism are closely related.

Now let us consider an organization where no relationship exists between satisfaction and performance. In this organization, presumably, rewards are not being effectively related to performance, and absenteeism and turnover in the organization are likely to be equally distributed among both the good and poor performers. Finally, let us consider the organization where satisfaction and performance bear a negative relationship to

each other. Here absenteeism and turnover will be greatest among the best performers. Furthermore, the poor performers would be getting more rewards than the good performers.

Clearly, most organization theorists would feel that organizational effectiveness is encouraged by rewarding good performers and by restricting turnover to poorer performers. Thus, it may be desirable for organizations to develop a strong relationship between satisfaction and performance. In effect, the argument is that the less positive relationship between satisfaction and performance in an organization, the less effective the organization will be (certeris paribus). If this hypothesis were shown to be true, it would mean that a measure of the relationship between satisfaction and performance would be a helpful diagnostic tool for examining organizations. It is hardly necessary to note that this approach is quite different from the usual human relations one of trying to maximize satisfaction, since here we are suggesting trying to maximize the relationship between satisfaction and performance, rather than satisfaction itself.

One further implication of the model appears to warrant comment. It may well be that a high general level of satisfaction of needs like self-actualization may be a sign of organization effectiveness. Such a level of satisfaction would indicate, for instance, that most employees have interesting and involving jobs and that they probably are performing them well. One of the obvious advantages of providing employees with intrinsically interesting jobs is that good performance is rewarding in and of itself. Furthermore, being rewarded for good performance is likely to encourage further good performance. Thus, measures of higher order need satisfaction may provide good evidence of how effective organizations have been in creating interesting and rewarding jobs and, therefore, indirect evidence of how motivating the jobs themselves are. This discussion of the role of intrinsic rewards and satisfaction serves to highlight the importance of including measures of higher order need satisfaction in attitude surveys. Too often attitude surveys have focused only on satisfaction with extrinsic rewards, such as pay and promotion, and on the social relations which were originally stressed by the human relations movement.

In summary, we have argued that it is important to consider the satisfaction level that exists in organizations. For one thing, satisfaction is important because it has the power to influence both absenteeism and turnover. In addition, in the area of job performance we have emphasized that rather than being a cause of performance, satisfaction is caused by it. If this is true, and we have presented some evidence to support the view that it is, then it becomes appropriate to be more concerned about which people and what kind of needs are satisfied in the organization, rather than about how to maximize satisfaction generally. In short, we suggest new ways of interpreting job satisfaction data.

NOTES

1. Arthur H. Brayfield and Walter H. Crockett, "Employee Attitudes and Employee Performance," Psychological Bulletin, 52 (September, 1955), 396-424.

2. Ibid.

3. Arthur Kornhauser and A. Sharp, "Employee Attitudes: Suggestions From a Study in a Factory," Personnel Journal, 10 (1932), 393-401.

4. Ibid.

5. Brayfield and Crockett, op. cit.

6. Frederick Herzberg, Bernard Mausner, R. O. Peterson, and Dora F. Capwell, Job Attitudes: Review of Research and Opinion (Pittsburgh: Psychological Service, 1957).

7. Ibid., p. 103.

8. Victor H. Vroom, Work and Motivation (New York: Wiley, 1964).

9. Basil S. Georgopoulos, G. M. Mahoney, and N. W. Jones, "A Path-Goal Approach to Productivity," Journal of Applied Psychology, 41 (1957), 345-353; Vroom, op. cit.; Edward E. Lawler and Lyman W. Porter, "Antecedent Attitudes of Effective Managerial Performance," Organizational Behavior and Human Performance, 2 (May, 1967), 122-143. See also Lyman W. Porter and Edward E. Lawler, Managerial Attitudes and Performance (Homewood, Ill.: Irwin-Dorsey, in press).

10. Vroom, op. cit., p. 246.

11. Abraham H. Maslow, Motivation and Personality (New York: Harper, 1954). According to Maslow, needs are arranged in a hierarchy with physiological and security needs being the lowest level needs, social and esteem needs next, and autonomy and self-actualization needs the highest level.

12. Edward E. Lawler, "Managers' Attitudes Toward How Their Pay Is and Should Be Determined," Journal of Applied Psychology, 50 (August, 1966), 273-279.

13. Lyman W. Porter, "A Study of Perceived Need Satisfactions in Bottom and Middle Management Jobs," Journal of Applied Psychology, 45 (January, 1961), 1-10.

14. Ibid.

15. A third question about the importance of the various types of needs was also included, but the results based on it are not reported in the findings presented in this article.

20. Expectancy Theory*

JOHN P. CAMPBELL
MARVIN D. DUNNETTE
EDWARD E. LAWLER III
KARL E. WEICK, JR.

Expectancy theory, because of its greater potential relevance to managerial behavior, will be discussed more fully.

EARLY COGNITIVE THEORIES

Concomitant with the development of drive x habit theory, Lewin[1] and Tolman[2] developed and investigated cognitive, or expectancy, theories of motivation. Even though Lewin was concerned with human subjects and Tolman worked largely with animals, much of their respective theorizing contained common elements. Basic to the cognitive view of motivation is the notion that individuals have cognitive *expectancies* concerning the outcomes that are likely to occur as the result of what they do and that individuals have preferences among outcomes. That is, an individual has an "idea" about possible consequences of his acts, and he makes conscious choices among consequences according to their probability of occurence and their value to him.

Thus for the cognitive theorist it is the anticipation of reward that energizes behavior and the perceived value of various outcomes that gives behavior its direction. Tolman spoke of a *belief-value* matrix that specifies for each individual the value he places on particular outcomes and his belief that they can be attained.

Atkinson[3] has compared drive theory and expectancy theory. Although he points out some differences, he emphasizes that both theories are actually quite similar and contain many of the same concepts. Both include the notion of a reward or favorable outcome that is desired, and both postulate a learned connection contained within the organism. For expectancy theory this learned connection is a behavior-outcome expectancy, and for drive theory it is an *S-R* habit strength.

However, the theories differ in two ways which are important for research on motivation in an organizational setting. For example, they differ in what they state is activated by the anticipation of reward. Expectancy theory sees the anticipation of a reward as functioning selectively on actions expected to lead to it. Drive theory views the magnitude of the anticipated goals as a source of general excitement—a nonselective influence on performance.

Expectancy theory is also much looser in specifying how expectancy-outcome connections are built up. Drive theory postulates that *S-R* habit strengths are built up through repeated associations of stimulus and response;

*Source: From *Managerial Behavior, Performance, and Effectiveness*, pp. 343-348, by Campbell, et al. Copyright © 1970 by McGraw-Hill, Inc. Used with permission of McGraw-Hill Book Company. References converted to footnotes.

that is, the reward or outcome must actually have followed the response to a particular stimulus in order for the S-R connection to operate in future choice behavior. Such a process is sufficient but not necessary for forming expectancy-outcome relationships. An individual may form expectancies vicariously (someone may tell him that complimenting the boss's wife leads to a promotion, for example) or by other symbolic means. This last point is crucial since the symbolic (cognitive) manipulation of various S-R situations seems quite descriptive of a great deal of human behavior.

These two differences make the cognitive or expectancy point of view much more useful for studying human motivation in an organizational setting. In fact, it is the one which has been given the most attention by theorists concerned with behavior in organizations.

INSTRUMENTALITY-VALENCE THEORY

Building on expectancy theory and its later amplifications by Atkinson,[4] W. Edwards,[5] Peak,[6] and Rotter,[7] Vroom[8] has presented a process theory of work motivation that he calls instrumentality theory. His basic classes of variables are expectancies, valences, choices, outcomes, and instrumentalities.

Expectancy is defined as a belief concerning the likelihood that a particular act will be followed by a particular outcome. Presumably, the degree of belief can vary between 0 (complete lack of belief that it will follow) and 1 (complete certainty that it will). Note that it is the perception of the individual that is important, not the objective reality. This same concept has been referred to as subjective probability by others (e.g., W. Edwards).

Valence refers to the strength of an individual's preference for a particular outcome. An individual may have either a positive or a negative preference for an outcome; presumably, outcomes

gain their valence as a function of the degree to which they are seen to be related to the needs of the individual. However, this last point is not dealt with concretely in Vroom's formulation. As an example of these two concepts, one might consider an increase in pay to be a possible outcome of a particular act. The theory would then deal with the valence of a wage increase for an individual and his expectancy that particular behaviors will be followed by a wage increase outcome. Again, valence refers to the perceived or expected value of an outcome, not its real or eventual value.

According to Vroom, outcomes take on a valence value because of their instrumentality for achieving other outcomes. Thus he is really postulating two classes of outcomes. In the organizational setting, the first class of outcomes might include such things as money, promotion, recognition, etc. Supposedly, these outcomes are directly linked to behavior. However, as Vroom implicitly suggests, wage increases or promotion may have no value by themselves. They are valuable in terms of their instrumental role in securing second level outcomes such as food, clothing, shelter, entertainment, and status, which are not obtained as the direct result of a particular action.

According to Vroom, instrumentality, like correlation, varies between $+1.0$ and -1.0. Thus a first level outcome may be seen as always leading to some desired second level outcome $(+1.0)$ or as never leading to the second level outcome (-1.0). In Vroom's theory the formal definition of valence for a first level outcome is the sum of the products between its instrumentalities for all possible second level outcomes and their respective valences.

To sum up, Vroom's formulation postulates that the motivational force, or effort, an individual exerts is a function of (1) his expectancy that certain outcomes will result from his behavior (e.g., a raise in pay for increased effort) and (2) the valence, for him, of those outcomes. The valence of an outcome is in turn a function of its instrumentality for obtaining other outcomes and the valence of these other outcomes.

A HYBRID EXPECTANCY MODEL

Since his formulation first appeared, a number of investigators have attempted to extend Vroom's model to make it more explicit and more inclusive in terms of relevant variables (Graen;[9] L. W. Porter and Lawler[10]). Although we shall not discuss the contributions of these writers in detail, we would like to incorporate a number of their ideas in our own composite picture of an expanded expectancy model. However, any imperfections in what follows should be ascribed to us and not to them.

One major addition to Vroom's model is the necessity for a more concrete specification of the task or performance goals toward which work behavior is directed. Graen[11] refers to this class of variables as *work roles*, but we prefer to retain the notion of *task goals*. Task goals may be specified externally by the organization or the work group, or internally by the individual's own value system. Examples of task goals include such things as production quotas, time limits for projects, quality standards, showing a certain amount of loyalty to the organization, exhibiting the right set of attitudes, etc.

We would also like to make more explicit a distinction between first and second level outcomes. First level outcomes are outcomes contingent on on achieving the task goal or set of task goals. A potential first level outcome is synonymous with the term "incentive," and an outcome which is actually realized is synonymous with the term "reward." The distinction is temporal. Like task goals, first level outcomes may be external or internal. Some examples of external first level outcomes granted by the organization are job security,

pay, promotions, recognition, and increased autonomy. An individual may also set up his own internal incentives or reward himself with internally mediated outcomes such as ego satisfaction.

As pointed out in the discussion of Vroom's model first level outcomes may or may not be associated with a plethora of second level outcomes; that is, the externally or internally mediated rewards are instrumental in varying degrees for obtaining second level outcomes, such as food, housing, material goods, community status, and freedom from anxiety.

The concepts of valence for first and second level outcomes and the instrumentality of first for second level outcomes are defined as before, but the notion of expectancy decomposes into two different variables. First, individuals may have expectancies concerning whether or not they will actually accomplish the task goal if they expend effort (expectancy I); that is, an individual makes a subjective probability estimate concerning his chances for reaching a particular goal, given a particular situation. For example, a manufacturing manager may think the odds of his getting a new product into production by the first of the year are about 3 to 1 (i.e., expectancy I = 0.75). Perhaps the primary determiner of expectancy I is how the individual perceives his own job skills in the context of what is specified as his task goals and the various difficulties and external constraints standing in the way of accomplishing them. Certainly, then, an employee's perceptions of his own talents determine to a large degree the direction and intensity of his job behavior. This first kind of expectancy should be more salient for more complex and higher level tasks such as those involved in managing.

Second, individuals possess expectancies concerning whether or not achievement of specified task goals will actually be followed by the first level outcome (expectancy II). In other words, they form subjective probability estimates of the degree to which rewards are *contingent* on achieving task goals. The individual must ask himself what the probability is that his achievement of the goal will be rewarded by the organization. For example, the manufacturing manager may be virtually certain (expectancy II = 1.0) that if he does get the new product into production by the first of the year, he will receive a promotion and a substantial salary increase. Or, and this may be the more usual case, he may see no relationship at all between meeting the objective and getting a promotion and salary increase.

None of the authors cited so far have explicitly labeled these two kinds of expectancies. Indeed, in a laboratory or other experimental setting the distinction may not be necessary since the task may be so easy that accomplishing the goal is always a certainty (*i.e.*, expectancy I is 1.0 for everybody) or the contingency of reward on behavior may be certain and easily verified by the subject (*i.e.*, expectancy II is 1.0 for everybody). Vroom[12] defines expectancy as an action-outcome relationship which is represented by an individual's subjective probability estimate that a particular set of behaviors will be followed by a particular outcome. Since Vroom presents no concrete definitions for the terms "action" and "outcome," his notion of expectancy could include both expectancy I and expectancy II as defined above. Thus effort expenditure could be regarded as an action, and goal performance as an outcome; or performance could be considered behavior, and money an outcome. Vroom uses both kinds of examples to illustrate the expectancy variable and makes no conceptual distinction between them. However, in the organizational setting, the distinction seems quite necessary. Rewards may or may not be contingent on goal accomplishment, and the individual may or may not believe he has the wherewithal to reach the goal. A

schematic representation of this hybrid is shown in Figure 1.

We have purposely been rather vague concerning the exact form of the relationships between these different classes of variables. This schematic model is no way meant to be formal theory. To propose explicit multiplicative combinations or other configural or higher order functions is going a bit too far beyond our present measurement capability. Rather, we shall sum up the relationships contained in our expanded model as follows:

1. The valence of a first level outcome (incentive or reward) is a function of the instrumentality of that outcome for obtaining second level outcomes (need satisfactions) and the valences of the relevant second level outcomes.

2. The decision by an individual to work on a particular task and expend a certain amount of effort in that direction is a function of (a) his personal probability estimate that he can accomplish the task (ecpectancy I), (b) his personal probability estimate that his accomplishment of the task goal will be followed by certain first level outcomes or rewards (expectancy II), and (c) the valence of the first level outcomes.

3. The distinction between external and internal goals and rewards leads to a number of potential conflict situations for the individual. For example, an individual might estimate his chances for accomplishing a particular task is virtually certain (*i.e.*, expectancy = 1.0). However, the internal rewards which are virtually certain to follow (*i.e.*, expectancy = 1.0) may have a very low or even negative valence (e.g., feelings of extreme boredom or distants). If external rewards, such as a lot of money, have a very high valence, a serious stress situation could result from outcomes which have conflicting valences. It would be to an organization's advantage to ensure positive valences for both internal and external rewards. Other conflict situations could be produced by high positive valences for outcomes and low estimates of type I expectancies (*i.e.*, the individual does not think he can actually do the job).

Even though this kind of hybrid expectancy model seems to be a useful

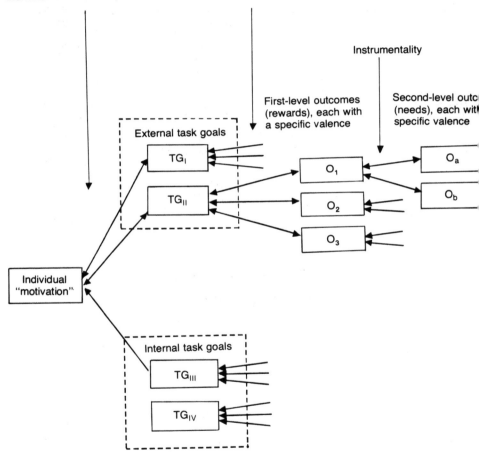

EXPECTANCY I
(perceived probability of goal
accomplishment, given a particular
individual and situation)

EXPECTANCY II
(perceived probability of receiving
first-level outcome, given
achievement of the task goal)

Instrumentality

First-level outcomes
(rewards), each with
a specific valence

Second-level outc
(needs), each wit
specific valence

External task goals

TG$_I$

TG$_{II}$

O$_1$

O$_2$

O$_3$

O$_a$

O$_b$

Individual
"motivation"

Internal task goals

TG$_{III}$

TG$_{IV}$

Figure 1
SCHEMATIC REPRESENTATION OF HYBRID EXPECTANCY MODEL OF
WORK MOTIVATION OUTLINING DETERMINANTS OF DIRECTION,
AMPLITUDE, AND PERSISTENCE OF INDIVIDUAL EFFORT.

way of looking at organizational behavior and even though we have devoted more space to it, the reader should keep in mind that it is not the only process theory that one could use. Equity theory is its major competitor. . . .

NOTES

1. K. Lewin, The Conceptual Representation and the Measurement of Psychological Forces (Durham, N.C.: Duke University Press, 1938).

2. E. C. Tolman, Purposive Behavior in Animals and Men (New York: Century. By permission of the University of California Press, 1932).

3. J. W. Atkinson, An Introduction to Motivation (Princeton, N.J.: Van Nostrand, 1964).

4. J. W. Atkinson (ed.), Motives in Fantasy, Action and Society (Princeton, N.J.: Van Nostrand, 1958).

5. W. Edwards, "The Theory of Decision Making," Psychological Bulletin, Vol. 51 (1954), pp. 380-417.

6. H. Peak, "Attitude and Motivation," in M. R. Jones (ed.) Nebraska Symposium on Motivation (Lincoln, Nebr.: University of Nebraska Press, 1955), pp. 149-188.

7. J. B. Rotter, "The Role of the Psychological Situation in Determining the Direction of Human Behavior," in M. R. Jones (ed.) Nebraska Symposium on Motivation (Lincoln, Nebr.: University of Nebraksa Press, 1955).

8. V. H. Vroom, Work and Motivation (New York: Wiley, 1964).

9. G. B. Graen, Work Motivation: The Behavioral Effects of Job Content and Job Context Factors in an Employment Situation. Unpublished doctoral dissertation (University of Minnesota, 1967).

10. L. W. Porter and E. E. Lawler, Managerial Attitudes and Performance (Homewood, Ill.: Dorsey-Irwin, 1968).

11. Graen, op. cit.

12. Vroom, op. cit.

21. Employee Reactions to Job Characteristics*

J. RICHARD HACKMAN

EDWARD E. LAWLER III

Researchers and managers alike are increasingly attending to the way jobs are designed as an important factor in determining the motivation, satisfaction, and performance of employees at work. This is not to say that jobs previously have been seen as irrelevant to organizational administration. On the contrary, earlier in this century when scientific management was in its prime, considerable research effort was expended to find ways that jobs could be simplified, specialized, standardized, and routinized. At the same time, industrial psychologists were developing rather complex and sophisticated procedures for describing and analyzing jobs in terms of their simplest components, as a means of evaluating the

*Source: From Journal of Applied Psychology, vol. 55 (June 1971), pp. 259-86. Copyright © 1971 by the American Psychological Association. Reprinted by permission. Footnotes renumbered.

skill levels required for different jobs. The results of job analyses have been used to establish fair rates of pay, for training purposes, and in personnel selection (see, e.g., Ghiselli & Brown, 1955; Lytle, 1946; Stigers & Reed, 1944). The general expectation of the scientific management approach was that by simplifying jobs, work could be carried out more efficiently; less-skilled employees would be required; the control of management over production would be increased; and, ultimately, organizational profits would be enhanced.

In recent years, numerous scholars have documented a number of unintended and unfortunate consequences of the trend toward work simplification (e.g., Argyris, 1964; Blauner, 1964; Davis, 1957; Friedmann, 1961; Guest, 1955; Herzberg, Mausner, & Snyderman, 1959; Walker, 1950; Walker & Guest, 1952). In brief, it has been shown that simple, routine nonchallenging jobs often lead to high employee dissatisfaction, to increased absenteeism and turnover, and to substantial difficulties in effectively managing employees who work on simplified jobs.[1] The expected increases in profitability from work simplification have not materialized as had been hoped, and the reasons apparently have very much to do with the human problems encountered when jobs are standardized and simplified.

Partially in response to the above findings, a number of researchers began experimentally enlarging various jobs to determine whether or not worker productivity and satisfaction would increase if jobs were designed so as to be more generally meaningful and challenging to employees. By and large, those job enlargement experiments which have been reported in the literature have been considered successful

(see, e.g., Biganne & Stewart, 1963; Conant & Kilbridge, 1965; Davis & Valfer, 1965; Ford, 1969; Kilbridge, 1960; Pelissier, 1965). With few exceptions, however, job enlargement experiments have been case studies and often have lacked appropriate experimental controls. Hulin and Blood (1968) review the research literature on job enlargement in some detail and are especially attentive to possible difficulties in procedure and methodology which may cast doubt on the generality or the validity of the findings reported.

Perhaps equally as disturbing as the uneven level of methodological rigor which has characterized job enlargement studies is the almost total absence of any systematic conceptual or theoretical basis for the studies which have been done. As a result, after dozens of experiments, little cumulative knowledge has been gained regarding the effects and effectiveness of job redesign. Job enlargement experiments, for example, typically have involved a number of simultaneous changes—such as in the amount of variety in the work, the amount of responsibility required, the degree to which working with others is an important part of the enlarged job, etc. Very little is known about which of these (or of other) aspects of the redesigned job are in fact responsible for observed behavioral and attitudinal changes. Further, the generality of job enlargement effects is largely unknown (e.g., whether they are effective only for certain types of workers or whether they are relevant only to certain kinds of jobs). More case studies are not likely to contribute very much to the development of answers to crucial questions such as these. Instead, what appears to be needed are conceptual frameworks which generate testable propositions about how job characteristics affect employees under various circumstances, and empirical research which is designed explicitly to test these propositions. This article proposes one way of conceptualizing the impact of job

---

1. These observations have not, however, gone unchallenged. See, for example, Kilbridge (1961) and MacKinney, Wernimont, and Galitz (1962).

characteristics on individual work behavior and attitudes. It then reports data
which were collected to provide a preliminary test of that conceptualization.

I

PREVIOUS THEORY AND
RESEARCH

Some progress toward the development of theory relevant to job design has
been made in recent years. The well-
known two-factor theory of Herzberg
(Herzberg, Mausner, & Snyderman,
1959; Herzberg, 1966), for example, can
be used to derive general propositions
regarding conditions on the job which
will be motivating and satisfying to employees. In particular, the theory suggests
that a job should enhance employee
motivation to the extent that it provides
opportunities for (a) achievement, (b)
recognition, (c) responsibility, (d) advancement, and (e) growth in competence. These principles have given rise to
a series of generally successful job enlargement experiments in the American
Telephone and Telegraph Company
(summarized by Ford, 1969).

Unfortunately, a number of researchers have been unable to provide empirical support for some of the major tenets
of the theory from which the principles
used in the AT&T studies were derived
(e.g., Dunnette, Campbell, & Hakel,
1967; Hinton, 1968; King, 1970), and
the general conceptual status of the
theory must presently be considered
uncertain. Further, the theory has not
yet been elaborated to specify how
characteristics of workers interact with
the presence or absence of the five
motivating conditions in determining
worker performance and satisfaction.
Finally, the theory in its present form
does not specify how the presence or
absence of the motivating conditions
can be measured for existing jobs. This
makes it very difficult to test the theory
and to generate unambiguous predictions from it about the effects of specific

changes which may be contemplated
for existing jobs.

The problem of measuring job
characteristics has been explicitly and
carefully dealt with by Turner and
Lawrence (1965). These authors developed operational measures of six "requisite task attributes" which, on the
basis of a review of existing literature
and an a priori conceptual framework,
were predicted to be positively related
to worker satisfaction and attendance.
The six attributes are: (a) variety, (b) autonomy, (c) required interaction, (d) optional interaction, (e) knowledge and
skill required, and (f) responsibility.
Scores on each attribute for each of 47
different jobs were obtained from field
observations and interviews by the researchers, and precise specification of
how scores on each of the attributes is
determined is provided. Examination of
the relationships among the six requisite
task attributes for the 47 jobs revealed
that the attributes were very closely related to one another. Therefore, Turner
and Lawrence developed a summary
measure called the Requisite Task Attribute Index (RTA Index) by formulating a linear combination of the six
separately measured attributes. This
summary index was then used in ascertaining the relationships between the attributes of the jobs and worker job satisfaction and attendance.

The authors' expectation that employees working on jobs which were
high on the RTA Index would have
higher job satisfaction and lower absenteeism was not fully supported. Instead,
it appeared that the predicted relationship between the RTA Index and employee reactions held only for workers
from factories located in small towns.
Workers in urban settings reported less
satisfaction with their jobs when the
jobs were high on the RTA Index, and
the RTA Index was unrelated to absenteeism for urban workers. Turner and
Lawrence (1965) argued that the obtained differences in reactions to good
(i.e., high RTA Index) jobs were substan-

tially moderated by differences in the cultural backgrounds of employees.

Blood and Hulin (1967) and Hulin and Blood (1968) provide additional data on the importance of subcultural factors in determining worker responses to the makeup of their jobs. These authors hypothesize that an important moderating factor is alienation from the traditional work norms which characterize the middle class. When employees hold traditional values regarding the value of work and achievement in work settings (as would be expected of the employees in small town factories in the Turner and Lawrence study), more complex jobs should be responded to positively. When employees are alienated from these norms (as might be expected of urban workers), more complex jobs should be responded to negatively. Blood and Hulin (1967) provide data supporting this general proposition and propose a three-dimensional response surface (Hulin & Blood, 1968) which specifies the expected interrelationships among worker alienation, job level, and satisfaction with work.

The data of Turner and Lawrence (1965) and of Blood and Hulin (1967) are sufficiently compelling that the generality of the strong proposition that enlarged jobs (in the sense of being high, e.g., on the dimensions which make up the RTA Index) lead to improved satisfaction, attendance, and/or performance on the job must be called into question. Instead, it appears that certain characteristics of the employees themselves must be taken into account simultaneously with the characteristics of their jobs in order to generate valid predictions about the behavioral and affective responses of employees at work.

If the above conclusion is accepted, thorny questions then arise about how the relevant differences among employees are to be conceptualized and measured. Both Turner and Lawrence (1965) and Hulin and Blood (1968) choose to deal with individual differences on a subcultural or sociological level (i.e., in terms of

differences between town and city workers or in terms of the alienation of city workers from middle-class work norms).

An alternative strategy would be to attempt to conceptualize and measure the relevant individual differences directly at the individual level of analysis. The town-city conceptualization assumes a substantial homogeneity of worker characteristics and response tendencies for employees within the two cultural settings. To the extent that there are substantial individual differences among town workers and among city workers, an attempt to measure relevant individual differences directly at the individual level would seem to have considerable merit. The difficulty in implementing this alternative approach, of course, is that it requires prior specification on a conceptual level of what specific differences among people are responsible for the results reported by Turner and Lawrence (1965) and Blood and Hulin (1967) (i.e., what it is about people that moderates the way they react to their jobs). In the following paragraphs, we will propose such a conceptualization, and derive from it a number of predictions about the effects of job characteristics on employee satisfaction and motivation.

JOBS AND INDIVIDUALS: A CONCEPTUAL FRAMEWORK

The present conceptualization of the interaction between job characteristics and individual differences is based primarily on the expectancy theory of motivation, as formulated by Lewin (1938) and Tolman (1959), and as applied to work settings by Vroom (1964), Porter and Lawler (1968), and others. In particular, five propositions based on expectancy theory are suggested below, which address the specific problem of how employee motivation can be enhanced through the design of jobs.

1. To the extent that an individual believes that he can obtain an outcome he values by engaging in some particular

behavior or class of behaviors, the likelihood that he will actually engage in that behavior is enhanced. Relevant valued outcomes can be both intrinsic (e.g., feelings of accomplishment or of personal worth) and extrinsic (e.g., material goods); the only requirement is that the outcomes be valued by the individual. When an individual anticipates obtaining some valued outcome as a result of a contemplated action or course of action, that outcome may be termed an incentive for engaging in the action.

2. Outcomes are valued by individuals to the extent that they satisfy the physiological or psychological needs of the individual, or to the extent that they lead to other outcomes which satisfy such needs or are expected by the individual to do so. Such need satisfaction need not, of course, be in the objective best interest of the individual. People frequently strive for satisfying states of affairs which are quite inconsistent with their long-term well-being (Locke, 1969). Nevertheless, if an outcome is not somehow linked to satisfaction, it will not continue to be valued and therefore cannot continue to serve as an incentive.

3. Thus, to the extent that conditions at work can be arranged so that employees can satisfy their own needs best by working effectively toward organizational goals, employees will in fact tend to work hard toward the achievement of these goals (McGregor, 1960).

4. Most lower level needs (e.g., physical well-being, security) can be (and often are) reasonably well satisfied for individuals in contemporary society on a continuing basis and, therefore, will not serve as motivational incentives except under unusual circumstances. This is not the case, however, for certain higher order needs (e.g., needs for personal growth and development or for feelings of worthwhile accomplishment). A person may experience higher order need satisfaction on a continuing basis without the strength of desire for additional satisfaction of these needs diminishing. Indeed, it may be that additional satisfaction of

higher order needs actually increases their strength (Alderfer, 1969). This is an important possibility since it suggests that the opportunity for the development of continuing (and possibly even increasing) motivation is much more a reality when higher order needs are engaged than in the case for more easily satisfied lower order needs. There is, of course, a major cost associated with any motivational approach in which higher order needs are central: Not all employees can or will respond to opportunities for the satisfaction of higher order needs, and thus motivational approaches based on these needs cannot be applied indiscriminantly. Maslow (1943, 1954) and Alderfer (1969, 1971) discuss in much more complete detail the nature of higher order needs and their motivational implications.

5. Individuals who are capable of higher order need satisfaction will in fact experience such satisfaction when they learn that they have, as a result of their own efforts, accomplished something that they personally believe is worthwhile or meaningful (see Argyris, 1964; Lewin, Dembo, Festinger, & Sears, 1944). Specifically, individuals who desire higher order need satisfactions should be most likely to obtain them when they work effectively on meaningful jobs which provide feedback on the adequacy of their personal work activities. To establish conditions for internal work motivation, then, it appears that a job must: (a) allow workers to feel personally responsible for an identifiable and meaningful portion of the work, (b) provide work outcomes which are intrinsically meaningful or otherwise experienced as worthwhile, and (c) provide feedback about performance effectiveness. The harder and better an individual works on such a job, the more opportunities he will have to experience higher order need satisfactions and the more incentive there can be for continued effective performance. Higher order need satisfactions, therefore, are seen both as (a) a result of (rather than a determinant of) effective per-

formance (Lawler & Porter, 1967), and (b) an incentive for continued efforts to perform effectively.[2]

The five propositions outlined above lead to the conclusion that it may be possible under specifiable conditions simultaneously to achieve high employee satisfaction and high employee effort toward organizational goals. Specifically, the long term congruence of high satisfaction and high effort is seen as depending upon (a) the existence of employee desires for higher order need satisfaction and (b) conditions on the job such that working hard and effectively toward organizational goals will bring about satisfaction of these needs.

CHARACTERISTICS OF MOTIVATING JOBS

The three general job characteristics identified above as central in developing a congruence between individual need satisfaction and organizational goal achievement must be describable in more measurable terms if the validity of the conceptualization proposed here is to be tested. In the following paragraphs, therefore, each of the three general characteristics are examined in somewhat more detail. In addition, it will be proposed that four of the requisite task attributes proposed by Turner and Lawrence (1965) are likely to be useful as measures of the three general job characteristics.

1. The job must allow a worker to feel personally responsible for a meaningful portion of his work. What is accomplished must be through the individual's own efforts. He must realize that the work he does is his own. And he must

believe that he personally is responsible for whatever successes and failures occur as a result of his work. Only if what is accomplished is seen as one's own can an individual experience a feeling of personal success and a gain in self-esteem. This does not mean, of course, that feelings of personal responsibility for work outcomes cannot occur in team projects; all that is required is for team members to feel that their own efforts are important in accomplishing the task at hand.

The autonomy dimension, as specified by Turner and Lawrence (1965), would seem to tap the degree to which workers feel personal responsibility for their work. In jobs high on measured autonomy, workers will tend to feel that they own the outcomes of their work; in jobs low on autonomy, a worker may more often feel that successes and failures on the job are more often due to the good work (or to the incompetence) of other workers or of his supervisor.[3]

2. The job must provide outcomes which are intrinsically meaningful or otherwise experienced as worthwhile to the individual. If a worker feels that the results of his efforts are not very important, it is unlikely that he will feel especially good if he works effectively. Instead, he must achieve something that personally feels is worthwhile and important if he is to be able to experience positive feelings about himself as a result of

---

2. It should be noted that only higher order satisfactions are predicted to be increased by effective work on a job with the characteristics outlined above; other satisfactions (e.g., pay satisfaction, satisfaction with supervision) may not be affected.

3. Having high autonomy on the job does not, of course, necessarily imply that one will have major control over the work outcomes achieved. There may be a number of factors in the work environment which affect the nature of work outcomes, over which the worker has little meaningful control. For example, a football quarterback has high autonomy in selecting plays but only a moderate level of personal control over the outcomes obtained from execution of the plays. Thus, work autonomy is probably best viewed as a necessary but not sufficient condition for feeling personal responsibility for work outcomes.

his efforts. It clearly is not possible to indicate for people in general what kinds of job characteristics will be likely to provide outcomes seen as meaningful and worthwhile; people differ too much in the kinds of things they value for any statement of such generality to be made. It is possible, however, to provide some such specifications for individuals who have high desires, for higher order need satisfaction and, of course, these are the individuals to whom the present conceptualization is intended to apply.

There are at least two ways that work can come to be experienced as meaningful for employees with relatively high desires for higher order need satisfaction. The first is for the job to be a sufficiently whole piece of work that the worker can perceive that he has produced or accomplished something of consequence. In terms of a Turner and Lawrence task attribute, this would be expected to be the case when a job is high on task identity. According to Turner and Lawrence (1965, p. 157), jobs high on task identity are characterized by (a) a very clear cycle of perceived closure—the job provides a distinct sense of the beginning and ending of a transformation process, (b) high visibility of the transformation to the worker, (c) high visibility of the transformation in the finished product, and (d) a transformation of considerable magnitude. For a worker who has high needs for developing and using his competence, a job with such characteristics generally would be expected to be experienced as highly meaningful and worthwhile.

In addition, the experienced meaningfulness of work may be enhanced when a job provides a worker with the opportunity to accomplish something by using skills and abilities which he personally values. For example, a strongly motivated duffer feels good when he hits a solid tee shot, even though the broader significance of this event is doubtful. His golfing skills are on the line when he steps to the tee; those skills are important to him; he

performs well—and that, in itself, is enough.

Jobs high on the Turner and Lawrence (1965) dimension of variety would be expected to provide opportunities for workers to experience this kind of meaningfulness on the job, since high variety jobs typically tap a number of different skills which may be important to the employee. Thus, working on high variety jobs may become personally meaningful to some employees through a process very analogous to that which makes golf meaningful to the duffer. It should be noted, however, that only variety which does in fact challenge the worker will be expected to be experienced as meaningful to workers with desires for higher order need satisfaction; screwing many different sizes of nuts on many different colors of bolts, if this could be considered variety, would not be expected to be experienced as meaningful.[4]

To summarize, it may be that jobs can come to be experienced as meaningful to employees to the extent that they involve doing a whole piece of work of some significance (i.e., have high task identity) and, at the same time, to the extent that they give employees the chance to use their valued skills and abilities (i.e., to be challenged) in doing the work. In many cases the latter condition may be met on jobs which have high variety.

3. The job must provide feedback about what is accomplished. Even if the two general conditions discussed above are met, an employee cannot experience

4. It is also possible, of course, for a job to have too much variety. Activation theory (e.g., Scott, 1966) suggests that when variety is too high, employees may experience a general state of muscular and mental hypertension which can greatly handicap performance effectiveness. In addition, Hall and Lawler (1970) found that among research scientists, high job variety can be associated with low job satisfaction, apparently because jobs with high variety also tended to be low in task identity and feedback.

higher order need satisfaction when he performs effectively unless he obtains some kind of feedback about how he is doing. Such feedback may come from doing the task itself (e.g., when a telephone operator successfully completes a long distance person-to-person call), but performance feedback also may come from some other person—an esteemed co-worker, a supervisor, etc. The crucial condition is that feedback be present in a form that is believable to the worker, so that a realistic basis exists for the satisfaction (or frustration) of higher order needs.

It should be emphasized that, for all of the job characteristics discussed above, it is not their objective state which affects employee attitudes and behavior, but rather how they are experienced by the employees. Regardless of the amount of feedback (or variety, or autonomy, or task identity) a worker really has in his work, it is how much *he perceives that he has* which will affect his reactions to the job. Objective job characteristics are important because they do affect the perceptions and experiences of employees. But there are often substantial differences between objective job characteristics and how they are perceived by employees, and it is dangerous to assume that simply because the objective characteristics of a job have been measured (or changed) that the way that job is experienced by employees has been dealt with as well.

In summary, then, it has been argued that the characteristics of jobs can establish conditions which will enhance the intrinsic motivation of workers who desire higher order need satisfaction. In particular, it has been suggested, in terms of a subset of the Turner and Lawrence (1965) dimensions, that such individuals will be able to obtain meaningful personal satisfaction when they perform well on jobs which they experience as high on variety, autonomy, task identity, and feedback. Further, the harder and better an individual performs on a job which is perceived as high on these dimensions (hereafter will be

called the four core dimensions), the more satisfaction he is likely to feel.

II

STRATEGY OF THE PRESENT RESEARCH

The conceptualization presented above provides the basis for the present empirical research on the relationships among job characteristics; individual differences in need strength; and employee motivation, satisfaction, performance, and absenteeism on the job. In particular, the research to be reported here follows the strategy steps listed below:

1. Measures of the following six job dimensions were developed:

    a) variety, the degree to which a job requires employees to perform a wide range of operations in their work and/or the degree to which employees must use a variety of equipment and procedures in their work;

    b) autonomy, the extent to which employees have a major say in scheduling their work, selecting the equipment they will use, and deciding on procedures to be followed;

    c) task identity, the extent to which employees do an entire or whole piece of work and can clearly identify the result of their efforts;

    d) feedback, the degree to which employees receive information as they are working which reveals how well they are performing on the job;

    e) dealing with others, the degree to which a job requires employees to deal with other people (either customers, other company employees, or both) to complete the work;

    f) friendship opportunities, the degree to which a job allows employees to talk with one another on the job and to establish informal relationships with other employees at work.

The latter two dimensions were included to permit exploration of the impact of the interpersonal characteristics of job design. These dimensions were adapted with very minor revision from the task attributes "required interaction" and "optional interaction" proposed by Turner and Lawrence (1965). They are not, however, directly relevant to the conceptualization about job-based work motivation proposed above, and no specific predictions regarding them were made. Thirteen different jobs were described on these six dimensions by the researchers, by employees who worked on the jobs, and by members of the management of the telephone company in which the research was carried out.

2. A measure was developed which was expected, on an a priori basis, to reflect the level of employee desire for the satisfaction of higher order needs.

3. Based on the mean scores of the employees on the measure of need strength, predictions were made regarding the expected relationships between the job characteristics as measured by the four core dimensions and the dependent variables: satisfaction, performance, and absenteeism. Relevant data were collected from 208 employees, and correlations between each of the four core dimensions and each of the dependent measures were computed.

4. The theory outlined above indicates that how a job is experienced or perceived by an individual employee should determine his reactions to it, rather than the objective characteristics of the job. This possibility can be examined by analyzing the relationship between the characteristics of a single job (as they are perceived by employees) and the behavioral and attitudinal reactions of individuals who hold that job. By restricting the scope of the analysis to individuals working on the same job, it is possible to rule out objective differences in jobs as an explanation for obtained empirical relationships—and, thereby, to address the possibility that the perceived characteristics of jobs affect employees in the same general fashion as do objectively measured characteristics. Therefore, relationships between perceived job characteristics and the dependent variables of interest were computed separately for employees who worked on each of the 13 objectively different jobs included in the study, and these relationships were compared to those obtained in the overall analyses involving all Ss and all 13 jobs.

5. The theory implies that satisfaction, performance, and attendance should be highest when all four of the core dimensions are present. That is, being high on, say, variety and task identity but low on autonomy and feedback should not provide the conditions that are necessary for positive behavioral and affective responses. Under such circumstances, a worker would be expected to have neither a sense of personal ownership of his work activities and outcomes (low autonomy) nor a trustworthy gauge of the adequacy of his performance (low feedback). The conditions for the development of internal work motivation specified earlier would therefore not be met. The importance of having all four core dimensions present was tested by comparing the dependent variable scores of employees who saw their jobs as moderately high on all four core dimensions both with the scores of employees who saw their jobs as high on some dimensions and low on others, and with the scores of employees who saw their jobs as moderately low on all four dimensions.

6. The theory states that individual differences in desire for higher order need satisfactions should moderate the relationships between job characteristics and the dependent variables. In order to test this possibility, relationships were computed separately and compared for the third of the employees highest on desire for higher order need satisfaction and for those employees lowest on desire for higher order need satisfaction.

7. Finally, exploratory analyses were made of the relationships between the two interpersonal job dimensions (deal-

ing with others, and friendship opportunities) and the dependent variables.

METHOD

RESEARCH SETTING AND SUBJECTS

The research was carried out in an eastern telephone company, and focused on employees who worked on 13 different jobs in the plant and traffic departments of the company. The jobs were selected so as to include (a) several varieties of operators, installers, central office repairmen, and cable splicers; (b) to range widely in complexity and in the level of employee skill required; and (c) to be located in both rural and urban settings.

Data were collected from 208 employees and 62 supervisors. Employees in the traffic department (about one-third of the sample) were female; all plant department employees were male.

PROCEDURE

All data were collected on site at each of the 13 job locations. One to three days were spent at each location, and all data were collected from each location before moving on to another location. Data were collected over a period of about nine months. At each location, the following five procedural steps were followed (although the order of the steps sometimes varied because of local circumstances).

1. Local second- or third-level management was visited to obtain permission to collect data from employees working on a particular job. When permission was secured (it was never denied), the managers were interviewed about the general nature of the job as they perceived it.

2. First-level supervisors on the local job were interviewed about the nature of the job and employees' reactions to it and were given a questionnaire which tapped the supervisors' perceptions of the employee job in a format similar to that used for obtaining the employees' own job perceptions.

3. Employees working on the job

were observed and interviewed informally. These observations and interviews were conducted by two researchers and continued until the researchers felt that they were no longer obtaining substantial new information about the job. Observation typically lasted approximately one working day. Ratings of the job characteristics by the researchers were made on the basis of these observations and interviews.

4. A questionnaire was administered to a sample of 15-20 employees on the job. The questionnaire took between ½-1 hour to complete and usually was administered to employees in groups of three or four. The general nature of the research was explained to each group of employees before they began work on the questionnaire, although the hypotheses of the study and the dependent variables to be analyzed were not mentioned. It was emphasized to each individual that participation was voluntary, and a few individuals did decline to participate. In addition, employees were told that putting their names on the questionnaires, while desirable for research purposes, also was voluntary. About 10 percent of the employees who participated declined to give their names.

5. Ratings of the performance of those employees who had taken the questionnaire and provided their names were made by first-line supervisors. Absence data were collected later from company records.

INSTRUMENTS AND MEASURES

● *Job descriptions.* Each of the 13 jobs examined in the research was described in terms of the six general dimensions described earlier (variety, autonomy, task identity, feedback, dealing with others, and friendship opportunities). The jobs were described on all six dimensions using four different methods: (a) a sample of employees on the job completed several questionnaire scales relevant to the six dimensions; (b) first- and second-level management on the job completed identical questionnaire scales; (c) the researchers, after observing the job and interviewing employees and supervisors, completed similar scales; and (d) the researchers utilized a set of objective coding procedures adapted from Turner and Lawrence (1965) to obtain a set of nonsubjective assessments of each job.

The job descriptions completed by employees and supervisors involved three separate questionnaire items for five of the six dimensions; two items were used for the dimension "dealing with others." One section of the questionnaire involved making direct ratings of the job on six 7-point scales. The scales used in this section of the employee questionnaire, together with the labels attached to each of the scale end points and the mid-point, are listed below.

a) How much *variety* is there in your job?

Very little; I do pretty much the same things over and over and use the same pieces of equipment and procedures almost all the time. (Scored 1)

Moderate variety. (Scored 4)

Very much; I do many different things and use a wide variety of equipment and procedures. (Scored 7)

b) How much *autonomy* do you have on your job; how much are you left on your own to do your own work?

Very little; I have almost no "say" about scheduling my work; the work and the procedures are all laid out for me in detail.

Moderate autonomy; I make some of the decisions about my work, but many of them are made for me.

Very much; I have almost all of the "say" about the scheduling of my own work; I alone decide what procedures will be used.

c) To what extent do you do a *"whole"* *piece of work* (as opposed to doing part of a job which is finished by some other employee)?

I do one small part of a job; there are many others who do other parts of the job; I may not see the final result.

I do a moderate size "chunk" of the

work; there are others involved too, but my contribution is clear.

I do an entire piece of work; I do the job from start to finish, and what is done is clearly "mine."

d) To what extent do you *find out how well you are doing* on the job as you are working?

Very little; I often work for long stretches without finding out how I am doing.

Moderately; sometimes I know how I am doing and other times I do not.

Very much; I get almost constant "feedback" on my performance as I work.

e) To what extent do you have the *opportunity to talk informally* with other employees while at work. (That is, is your job arranged so that you can chat with other workers while on the job—even though the job does not require you to talk to these people?)

Very little; there is almost no chance to talk to other employees except about "business."

Moderately; there is some chance to talk, but you may have to arrange it ahead of time.

Very much; there is almost always an opportunity to talk with other employees about non-business topics.

f) To what extent is *dealing with other people* a part of your job?

Very little; working with other people is *not* a very important part of my job.

Moderately; I have to deal with some other people, but this is not a major part of my job.

Very much; probably the single most important part of my job is working with other people.

A second section of the questionnaire asked employees on 7-point scales how much of the various job attributes was actually present on their jobs. These scales ranged from "none or a minimum amount" (scored 1) through "a moderate amount" (scored 4) to "a maximum amount" (scored 7). Scales which were used in this section of the questionnaire include:

a) For variety: The amount of variety in my job.

The opportunity to do a number of different things.

b) For autonomy: The opportunity for independent thought and action.

The freedom to do pretty much what I want on my job.

c) For task identity: The opportunity to do a job from the beginning to end (i.e., the chance to do a whole job).

The opportunity to complete work I start.

d) For feedback: The opportunity to find out how well I am doing in my job.

The feeling that I know whether I am performing my job well or poorly.

e) For dealing with others: The opportunity, in my job, to give help to other people.

f) For friendship opportunities: The opportunity in my job to get to know other people.

The opportunity to develop close friendships in my job.

The items described above were randomly spread throughout a 23-item section of the questionnaire which asked about the presence or absence of a number of heterogeneous aspects of the work setting.

Scores on all items describing each of the six job dimensions were averaged to arrive at a set of six summary scores from the employee ratings described above. The questionnaire items given to supervisors were identical in every respect, except that supervisors were asked to describe "the job you supervise" rather than "your job" as was the case for the employees.

Internal consistency reliabilities for the items making up each of the six job dimension scores are presented separately for employees and supervisors in Table 1. Also included are interjudge reliabilities for the researchers' assessments of the jobs. With the exception of supervisors' data on the dimension "dealing with others," the reliabilities are adequate.

TABLE 1

ESTIMATED RELIABILITIES OF THE SIX DESCRIPTIVE DIMENSIONS

Dimension	Source of ratings		
	Employees	Supervisors	Turner-Lawrence
Variety	.90	.91	.86
Autonomy	.77	.68	.89
Task identity	.77	.86	.95
Feedback	.75	.75	.97
Dealing with others	.47	.17	.88
Friendship opportunities	.43	.42	.92

Note.—Reported reliabilities for employee and supervisor ratings are estimated internal consistencies. Each dimension score for these ratings consists of the average of three questionnaire items, except for "dealing with others" which is the average of two items. The reliability reported for the Turner-Lawrence procedure is the estimated reliability of the average of two judges, adjusted by Spearman-Brown procedures. Ratings by the researchers (the fourth procedure used) were made collaboratively and reliability data are not available.

Comparison of the scores obtained for each job by the four rating procedures reveals high agreement on all but one of the dimensions. These correlations are presented in Table 2. There is no agreement about which jobs are high and which jobs are low on the feedback dimension. One possible source of confusion regarding this dimension is that some feedback is provided directly by the job as an employee works (e.g., an installer successfully installing and testing a telephone), while additional feedback may be provided by supervision (e.g., a foreman telling an installer that he has taken too long to do a particular job). It may be that employees, supervisors, and researchers were not attending to the same aspect of the feedback process in making their judgments, thereby lowering the level of agreement.

In addition to the problem with the feedback dimension, there is a tendency for correlations involving supervisors to be lower than others. This is especially true for the two dimensions involving interpersonal relationships: dealing with others, and friendship opportunities. Examination of the mean scores of employees and supervisors on these two jobs reveals no consistent differences. Supervisors did not see the jobs as having either consistently more or consis-

TABLE 2
CORRELATIONS AMONG THE FOUR RATING PROCEDURES

	Job dimensions					
Correlation between	Variety	Autonomy	Task identity	Feedback	Dealing with others	Friend-ship op-portuni-ties
Employees & supervisors	.87*	.85*	.65*	.09	.31	.49*
Employees & researchers	.94*	.94*	.79*	−.22	.91*	.73*
Employees & Turner-Lawrence	.89*	.72*	.63*	−.66	.95*	.52*
Supervisors & researchers	.94*	.79*	.63*	−.15	.37	.38
Supervisors & Turner-Lawrence	.84*	.49*	.62*	.23	.26	.35
Researchers & Turner-Lawrence	.90*	.80*	.69*	.16	.93*	.67*

Note.—N = 13 jobs.
* $p < .05$ (one-tailed test).

tently less of an interpersonal component than employees—they simply did not agree well with the employees (or with the researchers) about the extent of interpersonal activities relevant to the job. Part of the reason for this lack of agreement may be the low internal consistency reliability of supervisors on the dimension "dealing with others." In addition, on-site observations indicated that, by and large, supervisors were considerably more attentive to and concerned with the technical and production aspects of the jobs they supervised than with interpersonal issues. This tendency may partially account for both the unreliability of the supervisors on the "dealing with others" dimension and the low level of agreement between supervisors and the other raters on the two interpersonal dimensions.

Table 2 shows that employees themselves provide judgments of the characteristics of their jobs which, in general, agree quite well with those made by outsiders and (with the exceptions noted above) by their supervisors. It is not, of course, possible to demonstrate conclusively that the employee judgments are objectively accurate, because no unambiguous standard of accuracy is available. Nevertheless, the strong convergence of the employee judgments with the assessments obtained from the researchers, from supervisors, and from the Turner-Lawrence procedures does

suggest that the employees were able to provide generally nondistorted descriptions of the characteristics of their jobs. In most of the analyses reported in this article, employee judgments are used as the primary measures of job characteristics. This is appropriate and necessary, given that it was argued earlier that employees' perceptions of their jobs (rather than objective job characteristics) are causal in affecting the reactions of employees to their work. Fortunately, the data in Table 2 establish that employee perceptions have convergent validity as descriptors of jobs—and, therefore, that they are probably reasonably well-grounded in reality.

The relationships among the six job dimensions themselves are presented in Table 3. Although there is some tendency for the six dimensions to be positively related to one another, only two of the correlations are of substantial magnitude: jobs seen as having high variety also are seen as being high in autonomy and in friendship opportunities. The level of interrelationship among the six dimensions as measured in the present research is lower than that reported by Turner and Lawrence (1965), and does not mitigate against use of the six dimensions separately as descriptors of job characteristics.

Table 4 presents a listing of the 13 jobs studied, the number of employees on each job who participated in the re-

TABLE 3

Correlations among the Six Descriptive Dimensions: Employee Ratings

Dimensions	Variety	Autonomy	Task identity	Feedback	Dealing with others	Friendship opportunities
Variety	—					
Autonomy	.67*	—				
Task identity	.17	.24*	—			
Feedback	.11	.06	.12	—		
Dealing with others	.05	−.05	.19*	.26*	—	
Friendship opportunities	.41*	.21*	.07	.32*	.13	—

Note.—N = 208 employees.
* p < .01 (two-tailed test).

TABLE 4

Summary of the Characteristics of the Jobs Studied

Job description	Sex	N	$\bar{X}$ employee ratings of job characteristics					
			Variety	Autonomy	Task identity	Feedback	Dealing with others	Friendship opportunities
Director assistance (DA) operators	F	16	3.08	3.64	5.66	4.88	6.06	4.13
Toll operators	F	18	2.87	3.06	5.15	4.80	6.03	3.69
Combined DA & toll operators	F	17	3.97	3.29	5.87	5.59	6.32	5.02
Traffic service position (TSP) operators	F	18	2.78	2.91	5.06	5.09	6.14	4.23
TSP operators with "enriched" jobs	F	19	2.94	2.96	5.26	5.08	5.90	4.05
Tip & ring (residence) installers	M	18	4.78	5.23	6.38	4.41	5.23	4.14
Key (commercial) installers	M	19	5.72	5.06	6.26	4.87	5.60	4.85
Private branch exchange installers	M	15	6.31	5.61	5.25	4.11	5.07	4.87
Cable splicers	M	16	5.14	4.67	4.94	5.12	4.59	4.67
Combined tip & ring & key installers	M	17	4.94	5.09	6.11	4.23	4.85	4.45
Central office framemen	M	8	4.50	3.89	4.42	5.43	5.12	5.44
Central office repairmen: Step equipment	M	11	5.30	4.84	5.32	4.30	4.77	4.70
Central office repairmen: Crossbar equipment	M	16	5.91	4.92	5.03	5.15	5.47	5.19

search, and the mean employee ratings of the characteristics of each job.[5]

● Individual need strength. To obtain a measure of the degree to which Ss

were desirous of obtaining higher order need satisfactions from their work, a questionnaire was administered which asked how much of various oppor-

---

5. Descriptions of the 13 jobs on Turner-Lawrence dimensions are not included in Table 4 for two reasons. First, the Turner-Lawrence procedures were modified somewhat for use in the present study, and therefore the scores obtained are not directly comparable to those reported by Turner and Lawrence (1965) for their sample of 47 jobs. Second, the primary use of the Turner-Lawrence scores in the present research was to demonstrate the convergence of employee assessments of their jobs with more objec-

tively based job descriptions (see Table 2). Substantive analyses using the modified Turner-Lawrence scores are not reported, since the scores of specific jobs on the six dimensions are confounded both with traffic versus plant functions in the telephone company and with employee sex (see Table 4). It was concluded on these grounds that the sample of 13 jobs was not adequate for analysis of relations between objective job descriptions and mean dependent variable scores using jobs as observations.

tunities and attributes the employees "would like" to have on their job. In a space beside each item, employees entered a number ranging from 1 (would like to have none or a minimum amount) to 7 (would like to have a maximum amount). Content of the questionnaire ranged widely, and included items relevant to pay, promotion, security, working conditions, peer relationships, and supervisory relationships. Twelve of the items were judged on an a priori basis to measure desire for higher order need satisfactions. These items are:

a) The opportunity for personal growth and development on my job.
b) The opportunity for independent thought and action on my job.
c) The opportunity to find out how I am doing.
d) The opportunity to complete work I start.
e) The opportunity to do challenging work.
f) The feeling that I know whether I am performing my job well or poorly.
g) The opportunity to do a number of different things.
h) The opportunity to do a job from the beginning to the end (that is, the chance to do a whole job).
i) The freedom to do pretty much what I want on my job.
j) The amount of variety in my job.
k) The feeling of worthwhile accomplishment in my job.
l) The opportunity, in my job, for participation in the determination of methods, procedures, and goals.

Scores of each employee on the 12 items were summed to obtain an overall measure of the level of higher order need strength. Internal consistency reliability of the 12-item scale was .89.

● *Employee reactions to their jobs.* Four types of employee reactions to their jobs were obtained from the questionnaires employees completed, for use as dependent variable measures. The four types of reactions are described separately below.

1. Experienced work motivation: measures were derived from the questionnaire to reflect both the amount of intrinsic motivation employees experienced on the job and the focus of their motivation. The amount of intrinsic motivation was assessed by three questionnaire items: (a) I feel a great sense of personal satisfaction when I do my job well. (b) Doing my job well increases my feeling of self-esteem. (c) I feel bad when I do my job poorly. The items were placed on 7-point scales ranging from "strongly disagree" (scored 1) to "strongly agree" (scored 7). Scores on the three items were averaged to yield a score indicative of the degree to which an employee experiences positive affective outcomes when he performs well, and negative affective outcomes when he performs poorly (Lawler & Hall, 1970). Internal consistency reliability of this scale was .72.

The focus of employee motivation was tapped by three questionnaire items which addressed the kinds of internal pressures for performance which were experienced on the job. Three items were used, which dealt with three different (but not mutually exclusive) foci of work motivation: (a) Being personally responsible for what you do; checking your own work. (b) Producing a large quantity of work. (c) Doing high quality work. Each item was on a separate 7-point scale, which ranged from high experienced pressure (e.g., "It is extremely important for a worker on this job to do high quality work") to low experienced pressure (e.g., "It is not especially important for a worker on this job to do high quality work").

2. Job involvement: three questionnaire items, in the same format as the intrinsic motivation items, were averaged to yield a score indicative of the degree employees felt personally involved in their work. The items were selected from those used by Lodahl and Kejner (1965). Internal consistency reliability of the scale was .81. The three items are: (a) The most important things that happen to me involve my work. (b) I live, eat, and breathe my job. (c) I am

very much personally involved in my work.

3. General job satisfaction: employees completed three questionnaire items designed to tap overall job satisfaction. The three items also were in the same format as the intrinsic motivation items and were averaged to provide an index of general satisfaction. Internal consistency reliability of the 3-item scale was .76. The items are: (a) Generally speaking, I am very satisfied with my job. (b) I frequently think of quitting my job (reversed scoring). (c) Generally speaking, I am very satisfied with the kind of work I have to do on my job.

The nine items used in the general satisfaction, job involvement, and intrinsic motivation scales were randomly spread throughout a 23-item section of the employee questionnaire which addressed various types of reactions to work. Lawler and Hall (1970) have argued that it is useful, on a conceptual level, to treat satisfaction, involvement, and intrinsic motivation separately. In addition, they demonstrated that the three variables do have discriminant validity in predicting other employee attitudes and behaviors—even though the variables are moderately positively intercorrelated. The correlations obtained in the present research among intrinsic motivation, general satisfaction, and the three items reflecting the specific focus of employee motivation are included in Table 5.

4. Specific satisfaction items: Employees indicated on 12 questionnaire items the degree to which they were satisfied with particular aspects of their job. The items ranged from "extremely dissatisfied" (scored 1) to "extremely satisfied" (scored 7). The 12 items were not summed but were retained as separate indicators of specific satisfactions of the job. Median intercorrelation among the 12 items was .40. The items queried how satisfied employees were with:

a) The feeling of self-esteem or self-respect a person gets from being in my job.

b) The opportunity for personal growth and development in my job.

c) The prestige of my job inside the company (that is, the regard received from others in the company).

d) The amount of close supervision I receive.

e) The opportunity for independent thought and action in my job.

f) The feeling of security in my job.

g) The pay for my job.

h) The feeling of worthwhile accomplishment in my job.

i) The opportunity, in my job, for participation in the determination of methods, procedures, and goals.

j) The opportunity to develop close friendships in my job.

k) The opportunity for promotion.

l) The amount of respect and fair treatment I receive from my boss.

● *Performance measures.* Supervisors rated the performance of each employee on several dimensions, three of which are used in this report: (a) quantity of work produced, (b) quality of work produced, and (c) overall performance effectiveness.

The quantity and quality scores for each employee were obtained by averaging the ratings he received on 7-point rating scales from his supervisors (when more than one supervisory rating was available). The overall performance measure was obtained by summing average supervisory ratings across seven separate performance scales, including quantity and quality. Interjudge reliabilities of the quantity and quality scales were .71 and .79, respectively, and the internal consistency reliability of the overall performance effectiveness scale was .92. The correlation between the quantity and the quality scales was .63.

Anchors for the performance ratings were phrased in absolute terms, and supervisors were encouraged to assess each employee against the highest conceivable level of performance possible for the job in making his assessments. Nevertheless, the degree to which ratings made by different supervisors on

INTERCORRELATIONS AMONG DEPENDENT VARIABLES

Variable	X̄	SD	1	2	3	4	5	6	7	8	9	10	11	12	13	14	15	16	17	18	19	20	21	22
1. Level of intrinsic motivation	5.96	.87	—																					
Focus of motivation																								
2. Taking personal responsibility	6.39	.99	.30*	—																				
3. Doing large quantities of work	5.21	1.53	.01	.17*	—																			
4. Doing high quality work	5.22	1.09	.25*	.44*	.08	—																		
Rated performance																								
5. Quantity	5.24	1.45	.04	-.09	.09	-.05	—																	
6. Quality	5.24	1.27	.13	.05	.08	-.04	.63*	—																
7. Overall effectiveness	5.53	1.11	.18*	.02	.10	.06	.79*	.85*	—															
8. General job satisfaction	4.97	1.26	.39*	.18*	.01	.23*	.07	.08	.16*	—														
9. Job involvement	3.00	1.37	.39*	.20*	.04	.16*	.07	.07	.11	.44*	—													
10. Absenteeism (no. of times absent)	2.69	2.16	-.23*	-.14*	-.10	-.06	-.12	-.26*	-.33*	-.10	-.15*	—												
Specific satisfaction items																								
11. Self-esteem obtained from job	4.34	1.44	.23*	.04	-.01	.06	-.07	-.02	-.04	.49*	.34*	-.06	—											
12. Personal growth and development	4.33	1.48	.26*	.18*	.04	.11	.07	.03	.07	.58*	.38*	-.02	.66*	—										
13. Prestige of job inside company	3.95	1.44	.16*	-.01	.10	.04	-.09	-.03	-.03	.44*	.29*	-.09	.63*	.50*	—									
14. Amount of close supervision received	4.46	1.45	.25*	.14*	-.01	.13	.04	.06	.10	.28*	.25*	-.07	.31*	.45*	.30*	—								
15. Independent thought and action	4.62	1.58	.21*	.13	-.11	.10	.11	.12	.17*	.36*	.34*	-.09	.39*	.50*	.32*	.62*	—							
16. Security	5.32	1.47	.15*	.13	.02	.16*	-.01	.06	.09	.47*	.23*	-.08	.43*	.46*	.39*	.40*	.40*	—						
17. Pay	3.68	1.74	.07	.04	-.02	.10	-.06	-.13	-.11	.44*	.16*	.02	.41*	.43*	.39*	.21*	.15*	.45*	—					
18. Feeling of worthwhile accomplishment	4.82	1.61	.45*	.22*	.01	.19*	.09	.14*	.11	.58*	.39*	-.02	.58*	.58*	.41*	.32*	.49*	.53*	.42*	—				
19. Participation in job-related decisions	3.86	1.50	.23*	.08	.05	.13	.04	.04	.07	.31*	.28*	-.04	.38*	.52*	.39*	.37*	.46*	.30*	.31*	.50*	—			
20. Development of close friendships	4.78	1.28	.06	.06	-.11	-.02	-.09	-.04	-.14*	.19*	.05	.15*	.24*	.34*	.21*	.25*	.31*	.28*	.22*	.33*	.33*	—		
21. Promotion	3.98	1.64	.16*	.16*	.08	.15*	.07	-.04	.03	.39*	.34*	.09	.43*	.60*	.42*	.38*	.29*	.44*	.48*	.43*	.51*	.22*	—	
22. Respect and fair treatment from boss	5.34	1.47	.23*	.08	-.06	.14*	.10	.06	.15*	.33*	.10	-.07	.42*	.40*	.35*	.43*	.41*	.57*	.34*	.45*	.35*	.25*	.42*	—

Note.—$N = 208$.
* $p < .05$ (two-tailed test).

different jobs are directly comparable is open to question, and results involving the performance ratings must be interpreted with caution.

● *Absenteeism measure.* The number of occasions an employee was absent during the 12-month period during which the study took place was derived from company payroll records. Occasions absent rather than days absent were used to discount the effects of single long periods of absence. For example, if an employee were ill for a 2-week period, the data would show the event as one occasion of absence, rather than as 10 working days of absence.

● *Summary of measures.* The various measures used in the research are summarized below. The means, standard deviations, and intercorrelations of all dependent variable measures are presented in Table 5. The measures include:

(a) Job descriptions: variety, autonomy, task identity, feedback, dealing with others; and friendship opportunities. Descriptions were made by employees, by supervisors, by the researchers using the Turner-Lawrence procedures, and by the researchers subjectively after job observations and interviews. Because there was generally high convergent validity among the four sets of job descriptions, and because the conceptual basis of the study suggests that jobs as experienced by employees should be most directly causal of employee reactions to their jobs, the employee job descriptions are used in the analyses to be reported in subsequent sections.

(b) Level of higher order need strength of employees: a summary score of employee reactions to 12 need strength items.

(c) Employee reactions to their jobs and work. Questionnaire-derived measures of: the amount of intrinsic motivation experienced by employees, and the focus of their motivation; general job satisfaction; personal job involvement; and 12 specific satisfactions or dissatisfactions with the job or the work situation.

(d) Rated performance effectiveness of employees, in terms of quantity of work

produced, work quality, and overall performance effectiveness.

(e) Absenteeism, measured by the number of occasions an employee was absent during a 12-month period.

RESULTS

GENERAL RELATIONSHIPS BETWEEN JOB CHARACTERISTICS AND EMPLOYEE REACTIONS

According to the conceptual position outlined earlier, the nature of the relationships between job characteristics and employee reactions to their work (including satisfaction, performance, and absenteeism) will depend upon the need states of the employees. In particular, it was predicted that, if employees are desirous of higher order need satisfactions, there should be a positive relationship between the four core dimensions (variety, autonomy, task identity, and feedback) and motivation, satisfaction, performance, and attendance.

The mean score of the 208 telephone company employees on the 12-item scale indicative of higher order need strength was 6.01. Given that the maximum possible score on the scale is 7.0, it would appear that the employees who participated in the present research had strong higher order needs, or at least that they felt it was appropriate to express high desires for these need satisfactions. Therefore, generally positive relationships would be expected between job descriptions on the four core dimensions and the dependent variables.

Correlations between the six job description measures obtained from employees and the scores of employees on the dependent variable measures are presented in Table 6. Results are discussed below separately for the four core dimensions and the two interpersonal dimensions.

CORE DIMENSIONS: TOWARD INTERNAL MOTIVATION

In general, positive relationships were obtained between the four core dimen-

TABLE 6

GENERAL RELATIONSHIPS BETWEEN JOB CHARACTERISTICS AND EMPLOYEE REACTIONS

Dependent variable	Core dimension				Interpersonal dimension	
	Variety	Autonomy	Task identity	Feedback	Dealing with others	Friendship opportunities
Level of intrinsic motivation	.32*	.30*	.16*	.18*	.07	.09
Focus of motivation						
Taking personal responsibility	.14*	.12*	.19*	.06	.08	.05
Doing large quantities of work	−.10	−.12	.01	.02	.06	−.17
Doing high quality work	.16*	.12*	.13*	.10	.04	.12*
Rated performance						
Quantity	−.03	.13*	.05	.00	−.02	−.18
Quality	.17*	.16*	.07	.02	−.11	−.02
Overall effectiveness	.20*	.26*	.11*	−.03	−.07	−.09
General job satisfaction	.38*	.39*	.20*	.28*	.17*	.21*
Job involvement	.24*	.22*	.12*	.24*	.03	.16*
Absenteeism (no. of times absent)	.02	−.14*	−.22*	−.10	.01	−.05
Specific satisfaction items						
Self-esteem obtained from job	.32*	.32*	.15*	.35*	.15*	.27*
Personal growth and development	.36*	.34*	.14*	.31*	.11*	.29*
Prestige of job inside company	.30*	.25*	.15*	.35*	.14*	.28*
Amount of close supervision received	.31*	.35*	.13*	.30*	.07	.16*
Independent thought and action	.53*	.62*	.25*	.15*	.00	.25*
Security	.22*	.27*	.19*	.39*	.15*	.28*
Pay	.04	.05	.04	.34*	.25*	.24*
Feeling of worthwhile accomplishment	.29*	.32*	.28*	.42*	.23*	.31*
Participation in job-related decisions	.28*	.27*	.20*	.34*	.12*	.25*
Development of close friendships	.25*	.12*	.09	.29*	.09	.47*
Promotion	.17*	.20*	.15*	.34*	.21*	.19*
Respect and fair treatment from boss	.19*	.26*	.22*	.35*	.14*	.24*

Note.—$N = 208$.
* $p < .05$ (one-tailed test).

sions and dependent measures indicative of motivation, satisfaction, performance, and attendance.

Performance motivation and actual performance. The higher jobs are on the core dimensions, the more employees tend to report feeling internal pressures to take personal responsibility for their work and to do high quality work. And, in fact, when jobs are described as being higher on variety, autonomy, and task identity, employees are rated as doing higher quality work and as being generally more effective performers on the job.

Further, the data provide support for the interpretation of these relationships which was proposed earlier in this paper: when jobs are high on the core dimensions, employees report having higher intrinsic motivation to perform

well. That is, employees indicate that when they perform well on the job, they experience positive internal feelings, and when they perform poorly, they feel badly. Apparently jobs seen by employees as being high on the core dimensions do establish conditions on the job so that it is possible for workers to obtain personally rewarding experiences by doing well on the job. The data suggest, moreover, that "doing well" is interpreted in the job context as having much more to do with high quality performance than producing large quantities of work. The core dimensions do not relate either to felt pressure for high quantity production, or to the actual quantity of work which is produced. This is consistent with the notion that employees with strong higher order needs feel positively when they have "accomplished something that they feel is meaningful"; it is not unreasonable that such workers would see doing high quality work as much more of a meaningful "accomplishment" than simply turning out large quantities of work.

General satisfaction, job involvement, and absenteeism. The core dimensions are, as expected, strongly and positively related to overall job satisfaction and to the degree that employees feel personally involved in their work. It is not, therefore, surprising to find that employees whose jobs are seen as high on the core dimensions tend to have better absence records as well. Work apparently is a satisfying place to be for employees with jobs high on the four core dimensions, and one way they behaviorally demonstrate this is by coming to work regularly.

Specific satisfactions. Nearly all of the specific satisfaction items were significantly positively correlated with the descriptions of jobs on the core dimensions. This is to be expected from the fact that the core dimensions relate substantially to overall job satisfaction—since overall satisfaction is likely to be strongly influenced by satisfaction with the particular aspects of the work situation addressed by the 12 specific satisfaction items.

It is instructive, however, to note which of the specific satisfaction items are especially strongly related to the core dimensions, and which have negligible relationships. Items with consistently strong relationships to the core dimensions should be considered especially sensitive to differences on these dimensions, whereas those items with weak relationships should be considered not as responsive to differences in job design. These data should be helpful, therefore, in more fully understanding the kinds of effects that the core dimensions have on employees' reactions to their jobs.

The four specific satisfaction items most strongly related to the core dimensions are (in descending order): (a) The

opportunity for independent thought and action in my job. (b) The feeling of worthwhile accomplishment in my job. (c) The opportunity for personal growth and development in my job. (d) The self-esteem and self-respect a person gets from being in my job.

The four items least strongly related to the core dimensions are (in ascending order): (a) The pay for my job. (b) The opportunity to develop close friendships in my job. (c) The opportunity for promotion. (d) The amount of respect and fair treatment I receive from my boss.

It appears, as expected, that the four core dimensions seem to be most strongly related to the satisfaction of higher order needs. The satisfaction items which are most weakly related to the four core dimensions seem to be most relevant to the satisfaction of needs classified as lower-order in the hierarchies of Maslow (1943) and Alderfer (1969).

TWO INTERPERSONAL DIMENSIONS

Also included in Table 6 are the relationships between two primarily interpersonal job dimensions (dealing with others, and friendship opportunities) and the dependent variable measures. The nature of the relationships obtained are strikingly different from those obtained for the four core dimensions. The two interpersonal dimensions do not relate very consistently or strongly either to employee affective responses to the job, or to their actual work performance. There is no significant relationship between the dimension "dealing with others" and any measure of motivation, performance, or absenteeism.

Relationships involving the dimension "friendship opportunities" also are generally negligible. The dimension does not relate to the level of intrinsic motivation employees report, or to any measure of performance or absenteeism.

There are positive relationships (moderately large for friendship opportunities, small for dealing with others) between the two interpersonal dimensions and job satisfaction. The single largest relationship between any of the satisfaction items and either of the interpersonal job dimensions is not a very suprising one: The more friendship opportunities are present on a job, the more employees are satisfied with the chances they have to develop close friendships on the job. This relationship suggests that the kinds of consequences to be expected from having jobs with high interpersonal components (as measured in this research) are primarily social in nature—rather than being relevant to the performance and motivation of employees as is the case for jobs high on the core dimensions.

WITHIN-JOB RELATIONSHIPS BETWEEN JOB DIMENSIONS AND EMPLOYEE REACTIONS

It was proposed earlier that job design factors affect employee attitudes and behavior because of their impact on the perceptions employees have of their jobs. This may be represented schematically as follows:

Objective job $\xrightarrow{1}$ Perceived job $\xrightarrow{2}$ Work attitudes
characteristics   characteristics   and behavior

Data presented in Table 2 show that employee perceptions of their jobs have substantial convergence with the assessments of objective job characteristics made by the researchers and by company supervisors. If it is assumed that the assessments by the researchers and supervisors do reflect the "objective" character of the jobs, these data strongly sugggest that employee job perceptions are based (at least in major part) on objective job characteristics—the first link in the chain. Results reported in Table 6 and discussed immediately above show that employee job perceptions also are related to work attitudes and behavior—the second link in the chain. However, these latter analyses are based on job descriptions provided by employees who worked on

13 different jobs—jobs which have been shown (see Table 4) to vary substantially on the six job dimensions. These large objective differences among the 13 jobs may, therefore, have been primarily responsible for the relationships which were obtained. In other words, the results in Table 6 could have come about because the objective job characteristics directly caused both the perceived job characteristics and the employee reactions—and not because they caused the perceived job characteristics which, in turn, caused the reactions.

By examining the relationships between employee perceptions of their jobs and the dependent variables separately for workers on each of the 13 jobs, it is possible to determine if perceptual factors, largely uncontaminated by objective between-job differences, bear a significant relationship to the dependent variables. Such an analysis, therefore, would provide a relatively unconfounded test of the second link in the above diagram. Within-job relationships should, of course, be lower in magnitude than those obtained using all employees working on all jobs, since there is little meaningful variation in actual job characteristics when data are obtained only from a single job, and as a result the variance in employee perceptions should be severely attenuated.[6]

Thirteen matrices of relationships were obtained by correlating job de-

---

6. To the extent that there are differences in the actual jobs assigned to employees who work on the same objective job, the usefulness of within-job analyses for testing the impact of strictly perceptual factors on the dependent variables is limited. Although some differences in actual work assignments were noted by the researchers among employees working on the same objective job, these differences invariably were of little consequence. Therefore, the within-job analyses probably do reflect primarily differences in employee job perceptions rather than actual differences in job design.

scriptions and dependent variables separately for employees working on each of the 13 jobs. The median of the 13 correlations between each job dimension and each dependent variable was selected, and the matrix of median correlations is presented in Table 7.

As expected, the median within-job correlations generally are consistent with the correlations computed across all employees and jobs (see Table 6). The order of magnitude of the median within-job correlations, also as expected, is lower than that of the correlations based on data from all employees. These results suggest, therefore, that employees' perceptions of their jobs are of central importance in affecting job attitudes and behaviors, but that the major determinant of such perceptions is the objective make-up of the job itself.

EXPLORATION OF CONDITION FOR ENHANCING MOTIVATION AND SATISFACTION

Results presented in the preceding discussion indicate that when jobs are high on the core dimensions, employees who have strong desires for higher order need satisfaction will be highly motivated and well satisfied on the job. In the following discussion, two analyses will be reported which extend these findings and provide additional documentation of the conditions which seem necessary to enhance employee motivation and satisfaction through job design.

MUST JOBS BE HIGH ON ALL FOUR CORE DIMENSIONS?

The theory on which the present research is based specifies that when jobs

TABLE 7

MEDIAN WITHIN-JOB CORRELATIONS BETWEEN JOB CHARACTERISTICS AND EMPLOYEE REACTIONS

Dependent variable	Core dimension				Interpersonal dimension	
	Variety	Autonomy	Task identity	Feedback	Dealing with others	Friendship opportunities
Level of intrinsic motivation	.31	.23	.11	.35	.03	.06
Focus of motivation						
Taking personal responsibility	.00	.00	.18	.09	.15	.00
Doing large quantities of work	−.05	−.06	.10	.01	.07	−.07
Doing high quality work	.05	.22	.19	.05	.10	.06
Rated performance						
Quantity	.06	.21	−.10	−.05	−.02	−.18
Quality	.06	.18	.06	.03	−.10	−.05
Overall effectiveness	.12	.21	.06	.04	.00	−.11
General job satisfaction	.38	.48	.21	.39	.22	.21
Job involvement	.34	.28	.20	.19	.22	.04
Absenteeism (no. of times absent)	−.10	−.03	.03	.00	.17	.14
Specific satisfaction items						
Self-esteem obtained from job	.26	.31	.15	.44	.18	.27
Personal growth and development	.57	.40	.18	.34	.25	.21
Prestige of job inside company	.44	.44	.17	.42	.24	.26
Amount of close supervision received	.19	.39	.08	.31	.17	.07
Independent thought and action	.40	.55	.31	.30	.13	.20
Security	.21	.28	.28	.35	.11	.25
Pay	.24	.33	.17	.33	.19	.18
Feeling of worthwhile accomplishment	.40	.37	.41	.48	.25	.26
Participation in job-related decisions	.34	.34	.39	.31	.31	.25
Development of close friendships	.27	.07	.25	.35	.26	.51
Promotion	.19	.33	.13	.32	.26	.06
Respect and fair treatment from boss	.20	.29	.24	.35	.09	.30

Note.—Because the correlations reported in this table are medians, no indication of statistical significance is given.

TABLE 8

COMPARISON OF JOBS DESCRIBED AS HIGH ON ALL CORE DIMENSIONS, HIGH ON SOME CORE DIMENSIONS, AND LOW ON ALL CORE DIMENSIONS

| Dependent variable | F ratio | Dependent variable $\bar{X}$ | | |
		Jobs low on all core dimensions[a]	Jobs high on some core dimensions[b]	Jobs high on all core dimensions[c]
Level of intrinsic motivation	13.72**	5.28	5.99	6.46
Focus of motivation				
Taking personal responsibility	6.08**	5.90	6.40	6.88
Doing large quantities of work	.24	5.48	5.17	5.29
Doing high quality work	3.04*	6.00	6.20	6.71
Rated performance				
Quantity	.15	5.19	5.23	5.39
Quality	3.36*	4.97	5.57	5.89
Overall effectiveness	3.40*	5.14	5.54	5.94
General job satisfaction	28.97**	3.78	4.99	6.21
Job involvement	18.40**	2.30	2.94	4.43
Absenteeism (no. of times absent)	1.62	3.11	2.70	2.00
Specific satisfaction items				
Self-esteem obtained from job	27.06**	3.33	4.30	6.00
Personal growth and development	24.45**	3.43	4.27	6.00
Prestige of job inside company	21.65**	3.24	3.88	5.59
Amount of close supervision received	15.97**	3.57	4.44	5.65
Independent thought and action	31.66**	3.24	4.62	6.35
Security	9.75**	4.52	5.32	6.24
Pay	2.95	3.38	3.63	4.47
Feeling of worthwhile accomplishment	35.59**	3.05	4.88	6.41
Participation in job-related decisions	21.09**	2.81	3.85	5.29
Development of close friendships	9.56**	4.14	4.77	5.65
Promotion	13.98**	3.24	3.92	5.47
Respect and fair treatment from boss	14.64**	4.14	5.40	6.24

[a] $N = 21$.
[b] $N = 170$.
[c] $N = 17$.
* $p < .05$ (one-tailed test).
** $p < .01$ (one-tailed test).

are high on the core dimensions, employees have the opportunity to find out (feedback) that they personally (autonomy) have accomplished something meaningful (task identity and variety) when they perform well. The implication of this assertation is that, for maximum motivation, jobs should be high simultaneously on all four of the core dimensions.

To test this possibility, Ss were partitioned into three groups: (a) those who described their jobs as being above the 60th percentile on all four core dimensions; (b) those who described their jobs as being below the 40th percentile on all four core dimensions; and (c) the majority of Ss, who typically described their jobs as being high on some of the

core dimensions and low on others. A one-way, missing-data, unequal N analysis of variance was used to compare the mean scores of employees in the three groups on each of the dependent variables. Means and F ratios are presented in Table 8.

Results are consistent with those reported in Table 6 and, in addition, tend to be more substantial in magnitude and more statistically reliable.[7] It was expected that when jobs were described as high on all four core dimensions: (a)

7. The analytic procedures used, unfortunately, do not permit computation of the amount of variation controlled, for comparison with the correlational data reported earlier.

experienced pressures to take personal responsibility for one's work and to do high quality work would be high, (b) intrinsic motivation would be high, (c) rated performance quality and overall performance effectiveness would be high, (d) job satisfaction and involvement would be high, and (e) absenteeism would be low. All of these expectations were borne out substantially and statistically significantly, except for the one involving absenteeism. While absenteeism was lowest when jobs were seen as high on all four core dimensions, differences among the three groups were not statistically significant.

Although these results support the contention that motivation, satisfaction, and performance are enhanced when jobs are high simultaneously on all four core dimensions, they do not imply that a disjunctive model for combining the core dimensions is necessarily the optimal one. Therefore, the relative usefulness of other ways of combining the dimensions was explored. In particular, (a) an unweighted sum of the four dimensions was computed for each S and correlated with each of the dependent variables, (b) the four dimensions were used as independent variables in a multiple-regression analysis predicting each of the dependent variables, and (c) the product of the four dimensions (Variety × Autonomy × Task Identity × Feedback) was correlated with each of the dependent variables. The latter score is a continuous measure which is congruent with the disjunctive combinatory model specified by the theory. That is, for a product score to be high, all of the four core dimensions must be moderately high, and, therefore, the measure reflects the degree to which a job is high simultaneously on all four core dimensions. Correlations involving the product score were compared to those obtained using the other two combinatory models.

Correlations between the unweighted sum score and the dependent variables ranged from −.08 to .61, with a median

of .30. Multiple correlations ranged from .13 to .65, with a median of .37. Correlations using the product score ranged from −.05 to .60, and also had a median of .30. Since some shrinkage would be expected in the magnitude of the multiple correlations obtained upon cross-validation, it seems appropriate to conclude that the results did not meaningfully differentiate among the three means of combining the core dimensions. Thus, while the theory-specified disjunctive model is not disconfirmed by the data, neither has it been shown to represent a more adequate means of combining the dimensions than the other models tested.

DOES HIGH ORDER NEED STRENGTH MODERATE OBTAINED RELATIONSHIPS?

It has been maintained throughout this article that jobs which are high on the core dimensions should be motivating only to individuals who are desirous of the intrinsic rewards that the jobs provide, namely, higher order need satisfactions.

The analysis reported in this section tests the possibility that Ss differing in higher order need strength do in fact show differential responsiveness to jobs high on the core dimensions, despite the generally high mean of all Ss on the need strength measure. Correlations between each of the core dimensions and the dependent variables were computed separately for those employees whose higher order need strength scores were in the top one-third of the distribution of scores for all Ss, and for those employees whose scores were in the bottom one-third of the same distribution. The mean higher order need strength score for the employees in the top third was 6.78, and the mean score for employees in the bottom third was 5.09. Since 5.09 is still one full point above the midpoint of the scale, it was expected that even for these "low" need strength employees, relationships between the core dimensions and the dependent variables would be in the positive direction, but lower in magnitude than the relationships for Ss in the top third of the distribution. It also was expected that the relationship found for the top third should be stronger than those reported in Table 6 for all Ss. Results are presented in Table 9.

For variety, autonomy, and, to a lesser extent, feedback, the expectation of a differential relationship was confirmed. Relationships between these job dimensions and the dependent variables are larger, and often strikingly so, for the Ss with high higher order need strength than for Ss with moderate higher order need strength. Further, the correlations for higher need strength employees are typically larger than those reported in the general analysis involving all Ss (see Table 6), and the correlations based on the lower need strength Ss are typically lower than the general relationships.

The moderating effect of higher order need strength was not obtained for task identity. Part of the reason for this may have to do with the nature of the particular jobs included in this study. Among the jobs in this study which were high on task identity were those of telephone operators. By and large,

when an operator takes a toll call she does a "whole" piece of work. She is involved in the call from the time the customer comes on the line until the called party answers and confirms his identity. The operator will do and redo this task and similar tasks many times during a typical working day. Observations by the researchers strongly suggest that an operator with strong higher order need strength quickly becomes bored and impatient with so many repetitions of this small but "whole" piece of work. If this is so, then it should not be surprising to find that there is little difference in the relationship between task identity and the dependent variables for employees with high versus low higher order need strength.

Indeed, it would be expected from the theory that differences between high and low need strength employees should be maximized when jobs are moderately high on all four core dimensions. The job of the toll operator clearly does not meet this criterion: while it is reasonably high on task identity and feedback, it is very low on both variety and autonomy (see Table 4).

To examine the validity of this argu-

TABLE 9

MODERATING EFFECTS OF HIGHER ORDER NEED STRENGTH

Dependent variable	Variety		Autonomy		Task identity		Feedback	
	High strength	Low strength	High strength	Low strength	High strength	Low strength	High strength	Low strength
Level of intrinsic motivation	.56*	.15	.49*	.07	.19	.22*	.41*	.25*
Focus of motivation								
Taking personal responsibility	.41*	.00	.39*	.07	.30*	.23*	.21*	-.02
Doing large quantities of work	-.07	-.20	-.19	-.06	-.18	.03	.10	.09
Doing high quality work	.17	.19	.18	.03	.07	.01	.21*	.09
Rated performance								
Quantity	-.02	-.24	.09	-.09	.01	.15	.04	.23*
Quality	.15	.05	.17	-.05	-.02	.31*	.12	.03
Overall effectiveness	.09	.05	.16	-.01	.01	.26*	-.04	.06
General job satisfaction	.41*	.28*	.43*	.29*	.27*	.18	.17	.33*
Job involvement	.30*	.17	.35*	.19	.16	.26*	.30*	.15
Absenteeism (no. of times absent)	-.29*	-.18	-.24*	.01	.21	-.26*	.04	.06
Specific satisfaction items								
Self-esteem obtained from job	.48*	.06	.39*	.07	.38*	.12	.34*	.29*
Personal growth and development	.55*	.03	.47*	-.01	.34*	.04	.39*	.33*
Prestige of job inside company	.41*	.17	.32*	.07	.32*	.18	.41*	.24*
Amount of close supervision received	.33*	.15	.43*	.10	.06	.07	.45*	.28*
Independent thought and action	.62*	.42*	.75*	.45*	.28*	.29*	.37*	-.01
Security	.29*	.04	.38*	.08	.20*	.24*	.41*	.33*
Pay	.24*	-.10	.15	.09	.07	.03	.26*	.36*
Feeling of worthwhile accomplishment	.53*	.06	.49*	.15	.38*	.33*	.42*	.40*
Participation in job-related decisions	.41*	.20*	.32*	.18	.15	.22*	.41*	.25*
Development of close friendships	.56*	-.04	.40*	-.35*	.38*	-.03	.36*	.13
Promotion	.29*	-.09	.35*	-.10	.14	.10	.40*	.34*
Respect and fair treatment from boss	.39*	.06	.45*	.03	.21*	.22*	.38*	.38*

Note.—$N = 67$ in each group.
* $p < .05$ (one-tailed test).

ment, therefore, the product score (Variety × Autonomy × Task Identity × Feedback) described earlier was correlated with the dependent variables separately for the third of Ss highest in higher order need strength and for the third of Ss lowest in higher order need strength. Since the product score reflects the degree to which a job is seen as being simultaneously high on all four core dimensions, substantial differences would be expected in the magnitude of correlations obtained for high versus low need strength employees. Results are presented in Table 10.

TABLE 10

MODERATING EFFECT OF HIGHER ORDER NEED STRENGTH FOR JOBS HIGH ON ALL FOUR CORE DIMENSIONS

Dependent variable	High need strength	Low need strength
Level of intrinsic motivation	.54*	.23*
Focus of motivation		
Taking personal responsibility	.37*	.12
Doing large quantities of work	−.09	−.01
Doing high quality work	.21*	.12
Rated performance		
Quantity	.07	−.04
Quality	.23*	.02
Overall effectiveness	.15	.05
General job satisfaction	.48*	.40*
Job involvement	.45*	.28*
Absenteeism (no. of times absent)	−.26*	−.08
Specific satisfaction items		
Self-esteem obtained from job	.54*	.13▴
Personal growth and development	.57*	.16*
Prestige of job inside company	.50*	.26*
Amount of close supervision received	.48*	.27*
Independent thought and action	.70*	.45*▴
Security	.49*	.25*▴
Pay	.27*	.09
Feeling of worthwhile accomplishment	.59*	.32*▴
Participation in job-related decisions	.44*	.37*
Development of close friendships	.54*	−.19▴
Promotion	.45*	.08▴
Respect and fair treatment from boss	.48*	.20*▴

Note.—N = 67 in each group.
▴ The difference between the correlations for high need strength Ss and for low need strength Ss is significant at p < .05.
* p < .05 (one-tailed test).

Again, obtained relationships were much higher for Ss who were high in relevant need strength than for Ss low in need strength for nearly all of the measures of motivation, satisfaction, and performance, The difference between the correlations for high and low need strength Ss was tested for statistical significance, and these results are included in the table. Even though most of the correlations were positive (because of the relatively high mean need strength for even the "low" need strength em-

ployees), a number of pairs of correlations were significantly different from one another. All in all, the data make a strong case for the moderating effect of individual higher order need strength in determining the effects of job characteristics on employee behavior and attitudes at work.

III

DISCUSSION AND IMPLICATIONS

JOB DESIGN AND INDIVIDUAL DIFFERENCES

The results of this study suggest that there are important interdependencies among the characteristics of individuals and the characteristics of jobs which must be taken account of in the development of any full understanding of the impact of various kinds of job designs. Both the advocates of a "scientific management" approach to job design (make the work routine, simple, and standardized) and the more recent supporters of "job enlargement" (make the work complex, challenging, and demanding of individual responsibility and decision making) appear to have attached insufficient importance to individual-job interactions in determining affective and behavioral reactions to jobs. Those of the scientific management persuasion, for example, have tended to assume that the typical employee will be content, if paid judiciously for his cooperation, to work on jobs which provide little or no opportunity for personal feelings of accomplishment or achievement. Those of the job enlargement school, on the other hand, have tended to assume that most employees are desirous of such opportunities and will work hard and effectively when they have a job which provides them. The present research suggests that, depending on the characteristics of the workers involved, both points of view would lead to job design practices which are appropriate some of the time and inappropriate other times. The present findings and conclusions fit well with the previous research of Turner and Lawrence (1965) and Hulin and Blood (1968). In both of these studies a sociological-level variable (urban vs. rural background) was shown to moderate the relationship between job characteristics and employee satisfaction. The relationship between job level (i.e., jobs which would be high on the four core dimensions) and satisfaction was found to be high for rural workers and low for urban workers. The present study demonstrates that individual higher order need strength also moderates the relationship between job level and satisfaction (as well as the relationship between job level and other dependent variables). In particular, individuals with strong desires for higher order need satisfaction respond much more positively to high level jobs than do individuals who have weaker higher order needs.

It may be that urban workers desire higher order need satisfaction less than do rural workers—in which case the findings of the earlier studies and the present study would be highly congruent. This possibility was tested with the present data and a small difference in the expected direction was in fact found: workers with rural backgrounds were higher on higher order need strength than were workers with urban backgrounds ($t = 1.47$, $p < .10$). Thus, the present research has taken the previous finding regarding urban–rural differences from the sociological level to the psychological level, refined it, and successfully replicated it. The present results also substantially extend the previous results in that the moderating effect of individual differences has been shown to apply to a number of dependent variables in addition to job satisfaction (i.e., job involvement, work motivation, quality of performance). Presumably it now should be possible to make considerably more specific predictions about how different individuals will respond to jobs with various characteristics.

It has been assumed throughout the above discussion that job characteristics actually cause the differences in employee satisfaction, motivation, performance, and absenteeism which were observed. Although the predictions which were made (and confirmed by the data) were based on a conceptual framework which includes causal propositions, the study design was correlational and at no point were the causal links in the theory directly tested. There is, however, reason to believe that the causal directions specified in the theory may be correct. While the simple correlations between job characteristics and the dependent variables (see Table 6) are open to alternative causal interpretations, this appears to be much less the case for those data which support other, more specific, predictions of the theory. In particular, it is difficult even after the fact to imagine an alternative causal model which would predict simultaneously that (a) all four of the core dimensions need to be present to realize the most positive affective and behavioral reactions on the part of employees, and that (b) the strength of desire for higher order need satisfaction will substantially moderate the relationships between the core dimensions and the dependent variables. It appears, therefore, that a cautious interpretation of the results in terms of the causal impact of job characteristics may be reasonable. This does not deny the fact that any theory can best be tested by experimental alteration of the independent variables, and manipulation of the core dimensions in an experimental setting would seem to be a clear next step in research on job effects.

USE OF PERCEIVED JOB
CHARACTERISTICS

One of the major conceptual and methodological problems which pervades studies of task and job effects on behavior has to do with the differences between task materials as they exist in objective reality and as they are perceived by individual performers. Tasks and jobs are invariably redefined by the individuals who perform them, sometimes deliberately and sometimes without full awareness by the performers of the changes or re-emphases that are being made. Further, it is the redefined task rather than the objective task which the individual tries to perform, and thus only those aspects of tasks or jobs which are actually perceived or experienced by a performer can have an impact on his performance and attitudes. This would seem to argue for the use of task and job characteristics as described by the performers themselves in research aimed at ascertaining the effects of these characteristics on performance. Yet when such subjective assessments are used, many of the important conceptual and methodological advantages associated with the use of independently and objectively described independent variables are lost.[8]

There are at least two strategies for dealing with this problem in research on task and job effects on behavior. One, which was used in the present research, is to employ subjective assessments of the tasks or jobs by the performers themselves, but simultaneously to develop means of determining the relationship between these assessments and others, including objective measures when possible. Thus, in addition to employee descriptions of the characteristics of their jobs in the present study, jobs were rated by three other methods: by company managers, by the researchers, and by an adaptation of the Turner and Lawrence (1965) procedures for describing jobs in operational terms. As was shown in Table 2, there was high convergence among the four methods for all job dimensions except feedback. Thus, while the job descriptions used in the analyses are those actually experi-

enced by the employees (and thus presumably are more directly causal of their behavior than would be the case for objectively described characteristics), they also have been shown to have substantial convergent validity and to be based upon the objective job characteristics.

A second strategy for dealing with the redefinition problem has been proposed by Hackman (1970) and, while methodologically more difficult to implement, probably has more potential for the development of a general understanding of the effects of tasks and jobs. In essence, this strategy suggests that the redefinition process should be viewed as the first stage of the performance process itself, and the redefined task should be conceived of as a potentially measurable intervening variable in the causal chain between the objective task input and the dependent variables of interest (e.g., performance, satisfaction). Just as individual differences in need strength have been shown in this research to moderate the effects of job characteristics on employee behavior and attitudes, so would individual needs, values, and goals be expected to interact with the objective task or job in influencing task redefinition. It might be, for example, that individuals with a particular pattern of needs tend to redefine the tasks they perform to be more consistent with those needs than is actually the case. These individuals might then develop hypotheses about appropriate on-the-job behavior which they expect to lead to need-satisfying outcomes, but which, because of the lack of congruence between the objective and the redefined task, might in fact serve only to set the stage for disillusionment and frustration. In any case, it appears that research on the ways different individuals redefine tasks and jobs may have considerable potential for furthering general understanding of the effects of tasks and jobs on the behavior and attitudes of performers.

---

8. The conceptual and methodological implications of the task redefinition phenomenon are discussed in more detail elsewhere (Hackman, 1969b; Weick, 1965).

NATURE OF THE FOUR CORE DIMENSIONS

The results of the present research show that, in general, employees with moderately high desires for higher order need satisfaction tend to work harder and be more satisfied when they perceive their jobs as being relatively high on the four core dimensions. In addition, it was shown that for the most favorable outcomes, jobs need to be at least moderately high on all four of the dimensions.

Further refinement of the core dimensions and exploration of their impact on individuals clearly is called for by the research. For example, the relationship between variety and task identity needs further examination. In one sense, since both of these dimensions are viewed as enhancing the meaningfulness of the work (although by different means), it might be argued that it is not necessary for both to be present (i.e., that one can effectively substitute for the other). The finding of Hall and Lawler (1970), that jobs which were very high on variety and low in task identity are not associated with high quality performance among researchers, would tend to argue against this possibility, however. An alternative possibility which would not be contrary to the Hall and Lawler findings is that some moderate level of variety is essential simply to keep the employee from being bored with his work (Scott, 1966), and that once this is achieved, experienced meaningfulness of the work will vary directly with the amount of task identity present. Finally, it may be that increases in variety can serve two different functions, depending on the amount initially present on a given job. For low initial levels of variety an increase may serve mainly to decrease the monotony of the work and make it possible for perceived meaningfulness to vary as a function of the amount of task identity present, as suggested above. At some point, however, variety may assume a different function, namely, introducing challenge into the work which, when successfully dealt with, can be satisfying to many individuals. Clearly, additional research on the psychological impact of these dimensions is called for.

Additional work also needs to be done on the operationalization of the feedback dimension, since no convergence was obtained among the several methods for measuring this dimension. The fact that the dimension operated as predicted in the data analyses indicates that the employee judgments of the dimension have some validity, but because the various groups who rated the jobs did not agree on the amount of feedback present, the exact meaning of the dimension remains highly uncertain.

Finally, the generality of the moderately high correlation ($r = .67$) between variety and autonomy should be tested. The descriptions of the scales used to measure these two dimensions were quite dissimilar, and it may be that the high correlation was obtained simply because jobs which had high variety in the particular organization where the study took place also tended to be jobs which provided considerable autonomy. The fact that most telephone traffic jobs (i.e., various kinds of operators) were low on both variety and autonomy would certainly facilitate obtaining a positive correlation between the dimensions, and might suggest that the high correlation is to some extent organization specific. There is reason, however, to believe that the positive relationship between variety and autonomy is at least moderately general. Turner and Lawrence (1965) found an analogously high relationship between these two dimensions across 47 different jobs, and Alderfer (1967) obtained a very high correlation between variety and "decision time" (which has some conceptual similarity to autonomy) across a sample of 30 jobs which included management jobs. It appears well worth examining the possibility that the psychological meaning of the two dimensions is similar in ways that have not been attended to in the present conceptualization.

INTERPERSONAL COMPONENTS OF JOBS

The two job dimensions reflective of the interpersonal components of jobs (dealing with others, and friendship opportunities) did not relate to employee work motivation or performance. The dimensions did relate positively to certain kinds of satisfaction, but the relationships were not as substantial as those involving the four core dimensions.

According to the conceptualization on which the present study is based, the degree to which jobs require interpersonal activities should relate to work motivation only when (a) workers have high desires for the satisfaction of social needs, and (b) working hard on the job can lead to the satisfaction of these needs. Even those jobs which scored relatively high on the two interpersonal dimensions (e.g., some operators jobs) fail to meet the latter criterion. Operators reported in fact that they could obtain social satisfactions best when they were not "working hard" by company standards (i.e., completing a large number of calls), since when the load of calls was heavy they had little or no time for meaningful interpersonal activities with either customers or fellow employees.

Even if jobs were designed so that relating meaningfully to others was an integral part of doing the job well, there is reason to doubt whether such jobs would have long-term motivational payoffs. The reason for skepticism is the arguments of Maslow (1953) and of Alderfer (1971) (presented earlier in this article) that when individuals have had ample opportunities to satisfy their social needs, the level of desire for additional social satisfaction will decrease and the level of desire for higher order need satisfaction will increase. When this occurs, of course, then jobs should be high on the four core dimensions

(rather than high on an interpersonal dimension) to provide conditions for internal work motivation.

All of the above is not to suggest that the interpersonal aspects of work are unimportant. They do affect satisfaction and it is also possible that they affect other variables which were not considered in this study (e.g., problem-solving effectiveness, turnover). It should also be noted that all of the jobs in the present study were at least moderately high on the interpersonal dimensions; it is very likely that important negative reactions might be obtained from employees on jobs which were very low or totally lacking in interpersonal aspects. Further, the present data address only the degree to which the existing structure of jobs requires or provides opportunities for interpersonal activities. Alderfer (1967) has shown that when jobs are changed, interpersonal relationships (especially between the worker and his supervisor) are markedly affected, and that "relationship problems" clearly have the potential of negating or reversing increases in motivation and satisfaction which are anticipated as a result of job enlargement.

NATURE OF THE IMPACT OF JOBS ON BEHAVIOR

Until relatively recently, research attention given to jobs has focused mainly on the ways jobs can be designed for most efficient production, or on the analysis of jobs into component parts to facilitate employee selection, placement, and compensation. Since the mid-1950s, however, research attention gradually has shifted toward examination of the effects jobs can have on the people who do them, and how jobs can be designed so that these effects are desirable for both employees and organizations.

Many studies, including this one, have shown that jobs can and often do have a substantial impact on employee behavior and attitudes; this finding is by now rather well documented. It appears that additional understanding of the nature and implications of job effects will require more direct investigation of the process by which these effects take place.

The present study represents some progress in this direction, by providing data which show that certain job characteristics and certain individual differences interact in determining behavior and satisfaction. Apparently, individuals who are desirous of higher order need satisfactions will, when working on a job high on the core dimensions, gradually develop and/or verify the hypothesis that personally valued rewards can be obtained by working hard and effectively on the job. When this occurs, the job can be said to have influenced the behavior of these employees by affecting their personal hypotheses about what kinds of behaviors will lead to favorable outcomes. Thus, one general way that jobs can influence behavior is by creating conditions whereby employees are likely to develop and validate specific behavioral hypotheses about what they can do on the job to obtain work outcomes favorable to themselves (or to avoid unfavorable outcomes).

The general process outlined briefly above represents only one of several possible ways that jobs can influence behavior and attitudes on the job. For example, jobs also can affect behavior by influencing the level of activation of employees at work (Scott, 1966), or by arousing (or depressing) particular employee need states themselves. The general question of how jobs and tasks influence behavior is discussed in some detail by Hackman (1969a; 1970). The point of emphasis here is that job effects can and do come about via a number of different (albeit interrelated) psychological processes, only one of which was given focal attention in the present research. It is likely that sometimes these processes will operate simultaneously and will be mutually reinforcing; other times they may work at cross purposes. Further work toward a more general

understanding of the several processes by which jobs affect behavior and how they interact with individual differences would seem to be warranted.

IMPLICATIONS FOR ORGANIZATIONAL PRACTICE

Standard organizational selection and placement procedures attempt to match the skills and abilities of a prospective employee with the skill requirements of the job for which he is being considered. The results of the present research suggest that it may be equally critical for long-term organizational effectiveness to achieve a match between the psychological makeup of the prospective employee and the psychological demands and opportunities of the job. In particular, the present results suggest that individuals who desire higher order need satisfaction will be likely to contribute most effectively to organizational goals (and simultaneously to satisfy their own needs) if they are placed on jobs which are high on the four core dimensions. Other employees, of course, who may be neither desirous of higher order need satisfactions nor capable of dealing with complex jobs requiring considerable autonomy, would be ineffective on such jobs and dissatisfied with them.

It appears from research cited earlier in this article that many organizations err rather consistently by designing jobs which are too low on the core dimensions. The present study supports this conclusion. It suggests that there are many workers who want to obtain more higher order need satisfactions from their work, but few who are overwhelmed by the psychological demands of their jobs. The implication of this argument, of course, is that organizations might be well advised to consider redesigning many of their jobs.

When job enlargement is carried out, the question often arises whether the changes should be toward horizontal enlargement (i.e., increasing the number of different things an employee does) or toward vertical enlargement (i.e., increasing the degree to which an employee is responsible for making most major decisions about his work) or both. Lawler (1969) has reviewed the literature regarding the effects of vertical and horizontal job enlargement and concludes that simultaneous enlargement in both directions may be optimal in most cases. The results of the present study provide some support for this contention. Only if a job is enlarged vertically is an employee likely to feel personally responsible for his work outcomes; and only if a job has some amount of horizontal enlargement is he likely to experience his work as meaningful—although it should be kept in mind that too much horizontal enlargement apparently can cause problems. Simultaneous vertical and horizontal enlargement should increase the likelihood that a redesigned job will be high on all four of the core dimensions.

It should be re-emphasized in conclusion, however, that while jobs appear to be highly potent in determining employee motivation and satisfaction, there is no single best way to design a job. Instead, the results of the present research suggest that the substantial motivational potential of jobs can be realized only when the psychological demands and opportunities of jobs mesh well with the personal needs and goals of employees who work on them. This kind of matching can be developed through selection and placement of employees, through job redesign, or (perhaps optimally) by attempting to fit people to jobs and jobs to people simultaneously and continuously as both the organization and the characteristics of its employees change over time.

NOTES

Alderfer, C. P. An organizational syndrome. *Administrative Science Quarterly*, 1967, **12**, 440-460.

Alderfer, C. P. An empirical test of a new theory of human needs. *Organizational Behavior and Human Performance*, 1969, **4**, 142-175.

Alderfer, C. P. *Human needs in organizational settings.* New York: The Free Press of Glencoe, 1971.

Argyris, C. *Integrating the individual and the organization.* New York: Wiley, 1964.

Biganne, J. F., & Stewart, P. A. *Job enlargement: A case study.* (Research Series No. 25) State University of Iowa, Bureau of Labor and Management, 1963.

Blauner, R. *Alienation and freedom.* Chicago: University of Chicago Press, 1964.

Blood, M. R., & Hulin, C. L. Alienation, environmental characteristics, and worker responses. *Journal of Applied Psychology*, 1967, **51**, 284-290.

Conant, E. H., & Kilbridge, M. D. An interdisciplinary analysis of job enlargement: Technology, costs, and behavioral implications. *Industrial and Labor Relations Review*, 1965, **3**, 377-395.

Davis, L. E. Job design and productivity: A new approach. *Personnel*, 1957, **33**, 418-429.

Davis, L. E., & Valfer, E. S. Intervening responses to changes in supervisor job designs. *Occupational Psychology*, 1965, **39**, 171-189.

Dunnette, M. D., Campbell, J. P., & Hakel, M. D. Factors contributing to job satisfaction and job dissatisfaction in six occupational groups. *Organizational Behavior and Human Performance*, 1967, **2**, 143-174.

Ford, R. N. *Motivation through the work itself.* New York: American Management Association, 1969.

Friedmann, G. *The anatomy of work.* New York: The Free Press of Glencoe, 1961.

Ghiselli, E. E., & Brown, C. W. *Personnel and industrial psychology.* New York: McGraw-Hill, 1955.

Guest, R. H. Men and machines: An assembly-line worker looks at his job. *Personnel*, 1955, **31**, 3-10.

Hackman, J. R. Nature of the task as a determiner of job behavior. *Personnel Psychology*, 1969, **22**, 435-444. (a)

Hackman, J. R. Toward understanding the role of tasks in behavioral research. *Acta Psychologica*, 1969, **31**, 97-128. (b)

Hackman, J. R. Tasks and task performance in research on stress. In J. E. McGrath (Ed.), *Social and psychological factors in stress.* New York: Holt, Rinehart & Winston, 1970.

Hall, D. T., & Lawler, E. E., III. Job design and job pressures as facilitators of professional-organization integration. *Administrative Science Quarterly*, 1970, **15**, 271-281.

Herzberg, F. *Work and the nature of man.* Cleveland: World, 1966.

Herzberg, F., Mausner, B., & Snyderman, B. *The motivation to work.* New York: Wiley, 1959.

Hinton, B. L. An empirical investigation of the Herzberg methodology and two-factor theory. *Organizational Behavior and Human Performance*, 1968, **3**, 286-309.

Hulin, C. L., & Blood, M. R. Job enlargement, individual differences, and worker responses. *Psychological Bulletin*, 1968, **69**, 41-55.

Kilbridge, M. D. Reduced costs through job enlargement: A case. *Journal of Business of the University of Chicago*, 1960, **33**, 357-362.

Kilbridge, M. D. Turnover, absence, and transfer rates as indicators of employee dissatisfaction with repetitive work. *Industrial and Labor Relations Review*, 1961, **15**, 21-32.

King, N. A clarification and evaluation of the two-factor theory of job satisfaction. *Psychological Bulletin*, 1970, **74**, 18-31.

Lawler, E. E., III. Job design and employee motivation. *Personnel Psychology*, 1969, **22**, 426-435.

Lawler, E. E., III, & Hall, D. T. The relationship of job characteristics to job involvement, satisfaction and intrinsic motivation. *Journal of Applied Psychology*, 1970, **54**, 305-312.

Lawler, E. E., III, & Porter, L. W. Antecedent attitudes of effective managerial performance. *Organizational Behavior and Human Performance*, 1967, **2**, 122-142.

Lewin, K. *The conceptual representation of the measurement of psychological forces.* Durham: Duke University Press, 1938.

Lewin, K., Dembo, T., Festinger, L., & Sears, P. Level of aspiration. In J. McV. Hunt (Ed.), *Personality and the behavior disorders.* New York: Ronald Press, 1944.

Locke, E. A. What is job satisfaction? *Organi-*

zational Behavior and Human Performance, 1969, **4**, 309-336.

Lodahl, T. M., & Kejner, M. The definition and measurement of job involvement. *Journal of Applied Psychology*, 1965, **49**, 24-33.

Lytle, C. W. *Job evaluation methods.* New York: Ronald Press, 1946.

MacKinney, A. C., Wernimont, P. F., & Galitz, W. O. Has specialization reduced job satisfaction? *Personnel*, 1962, **39**, 8-17.

Maslow, A. H. A theory of human motivation. *Psychological Review*, 1943, **50**, 370-396.

Maslow, A. H. *Motivation and personality.* New York: Harper, 1954.

McGregor, D. *The human side of enterprise.* New York: McGraw-Hill, 1960.

Pelissier, R. F. Successful experience with job design. *Personnel Administration*, 1965, **28**, 12-16.

Porter, L. W., & Lawler, E. E., III. *Managerial attitudes and performance.* Homewood, Ill.: Irwin, 1968.

Scott, W. E. Activation theory and task design. *Organizational Behavior and Human Performance*, 1966, **1**, 3-30.

Stigers, M. F., & Reed, E. G. *The theory and practice of job rating.* New York: McGraw-Hill, 1944.

Tolman, E. C. Principles of purposive behavior. In S. Koch (Ed.), *Psychology: A study of a science.* Vol. 2. New York: McGraw-Hill, 1959.

Turner, A. N., & Lawrence, P. R. *Industrial jobs and the worker.* Boston: Harvard University Graduate School of Business Administration, 1965.

Vroom, V. H. *Work and motivation.* New York: Wiley, 1964.

Walker, C. R. The problem of the repetitive job. *Harvard Business Review*, 1950, **28**, 54-58.

Walker, C. R., & Guest, R. H. *The man on the assembly line.* Cambridge: Harvard University Press, 1952.

Weick, K. E. Laboratory experimentation with organizations. In J. G. March (Ed.), *Handbook of organizations.* Chicago: Rand-McNally, 1965.

22. Some Social and Psychological Consequences of the Longwall Method of Coal-Getting*

E. L. TRIST
K. W. BAMFORTH

I
INTRODUCTION:
A PERSPECTIVE FROM
RECENT INNOVATIONS

A number of innovations in work organization at the coal-face have been making a sporadic and rather guarded appearance since the change-over of the industry to nationalization. During the past two years the authors have been following the course of these developments. Though differing from each other, they have had the common effect of increasing productivity, at least to some extent, and sometimes the increase reported has reached a level definitely above the upper limit customarily achieved by good workmen using similar equipment under conventional conditions. They have been accompanied by impressive changes in the social quality of the work-life of face teams. Greater cohesiveness has appeared in groups, and greater personal satisfaction has been reported by individuals. Decreases have also been indicated in sickness and absenteeism.

These schemes have been initiated in pits where the quality of technical management and the level of group relationships, both within and with the executive, have been sufficiently high to give the security necessary for undertaking new developments. Many of the workmen concerned in the early stages have contributed substantially to the understanding of the issues. Though it is not uncommon for changes of this character to make their initial appearance in so selective a manner, the elite status of the pioneer units necessitates some caution in assessing their suitability for wider application.

For this reason, some of those most concerned regarded the proposed dissemination studies as premature, while the writers found their own first task to be that of making a detailed appraisal of the standard current work system, known as the "longwall" method. Two preliminary hypotheses suggested themselves: that the improvements recorded were to be ascribed to remarkable attributes possessed by the innovations; alternatively, that a considerable part of their effect was to be accounted for by social shortcomings in the longwall method itself, so that changes, modest in themselves, might easily produce the results obtained.

The content of the innovations suggested the greater likelihood of this second hypothesis; their common characteristic so far having been to take some step that has increased the group-

---

*Source: E. L. Trist and K. W. Bamforth, "Some Social and Psychological Consequences, of the Longwall Method of Coal-Getting," Human Relations, Vol. 4, No. 1 (1951), pp. 3-38.

relatedness of the face-worker in a basic respect, though by a simple means. Some have made use of possibilities of improving group relationships associated with "room-and-pillar" techniques, much advocated recently for work in thicker seams. Others have been concerned with altering the form of the work group at the longwall itself. On the "filling" shift, for example, "group sectionalization" has been tried in place of individual "stints." In the longwall method the total task of coal-getting is spread over three shifts, and the culminating activity of moving the coal on to the conveyor is known as "filling off." It is on this shift that most troubles appear to accumulate; and it is on this shift that the largest number of men is employed. Changes that might lessen its difficulties would be specially welcome. But steps of the type taken can scarcely be considered as in themselves "remarkable." Both the need to take them and the degree of their success point rather to a lack in the social quality of longwall organization in its present form—and to the importance of group relations in the underground situation.

Most competent authorities appear to be agreed that the "hand-got" methods which preceded the longwall provided face-worker with a social balance that has since been lost. But the reasons for this have remained obscure. Before nationalization their investigation tended to be side-tracked by the fact that the advent of mechanization coincided with the appearance in the coal-fields of economic depression and bitter exacerbation of the struggle between miners and owners. Only medical writers, such as Dickson[1] and Halliday,[2] concerned with the epidemic incidence of psycho-somatic disorders among miners working under mechanized conditions, stressed the independent importance of the psychological and sociological factors to be discussed in this report. A more recent medical survey has been made by Morris.[3] None of these writers, however, has traced in detail the connection between the health and productivity of the miner and the social structure of the work system that controls his relationships.

Since nationalization, displacement on to the economic struggle of troubles stemming from this source has tended to be replaced by their displacement on to problems of management-worker relationships; but difficulties in joint consultation are not likely to be lessened by carrying a surcharge that should be placed to the account of the longwall method. Faced with low productivity despite improved equipment, and with drift from the pits despite both higher wages and better amenities, those in authority have increased their interest in the organizational innovations that have been taking place. A point seems to have been reached where the industry is in a mood to question a method it has taken for granted. To assist evaluation of the new developments, the first information requiring dissemination is an account of the social and psychological consequences of the longwall method itself.

In the account to follow, the longwall method will be regarded as a technological system expressive of the prevailing outlook of mass-production engineering and as a social structure consisting of the occupational roles that have been institutionalized in its use. These interactive technological and sociological patterns will be assumed to exist as forces having psychological effects in the life-space of the face-worker, who must either take a role and perform a task in the system they compose or abandon his attempt to work at the coal-face. His own contribution to the field of determinants arises from the nature and quality of the attitudes and relationships he develops in performing one of these tasks and in taking one of these roles. Together, the forces and their effects constitute the psycho-social whole which is the object of study.

The method followed has been to

maintain relatively continuous contact over a period of two years with some twenty key informants who represented between them the various coal-face occupations and all of whom had wide and varied experience of the industry. With this group repeated discussions and long interviews have been held. On the management side, similar discussions and interviews have been held with all grades of personnel up to Area Manager. Group discussions were taken over periods of a fortnight at two Divisional schools for Colliery Managers. Other informants have included three psychiatrists with wide experience of miners' problems gathered in medical practice in colliery districts or in public health inquiries.

The earlier situation on the background of which the longwall method originally developed will first be described. Longwall procedure itself will then be discussed. Later sections will be concerned with special problems arising in the various occupational sub-groups.

II
THE CHARACTER OF THE PRE-MECHANIZED EQUILIBRIUM AND THE NATURE OF ITS DISTURBANCE

HAND-GOT SYSTEMS AND THE RESPONSIBLE AUTONOMY OF THE PAIR-BASED WORK GROUP

The outstanding feature of the social pattern with which the pre-mechanized equilibrium was associated is its emphasis on small group organization at the coal-face. The groups themselves were interdependent working pairs to whom one or two extra individuals might be attached. It was common practice for two colliers—a hewer and his mate—to make their own contract with the colliery management and to work their own small face with the assistance of a boy "trammer." This working unit could function equally well in a variety of engineering layouts both of the advance and retreat type, whether step-

wise or direct. Sometimes it extended its numbers to seven or eight, when three or four colliers, and their attendant trammers, would work together.[4]

A primary work-organization of this type has the advantage of placing responsibility for the complete coal-getting task squarely on the shoulders of a single, small, face-to-face group which experiences the entire cycle of operations within the compass of its membership. For each participant the task has total significance and dynamic closure. Though the contract may have been in the name of the hewer, it was regarded as a joint undertaking. Leadership and "supervision" were internal to the group, which had a quality of *responsible autonomy*. The capacity of these groups for self-regulation was a function of the wholeness of their work task, this connection being respresented in their contractual status. A whole has power as an independent detachment, but a part requires external control.

Within these pair-based units was contained the full range of coal-face skills; each collier being an all-round workman, usually able to substitute for his mate. Though his equipment was simple, his tasks were multiple. The "underground skill" on which their efficient and safe execution depended was almost entirely person-carried. He had craft pride and artisan independence. These qualities obviated status difficulties and contributed to responsible autonomy.

Choice of workmates posed a crucial question. These choices were made by the men themselves, sociometrically, under full pressure of the reality situation and with long-standing knowledge of each other. Stable relationships tended to result, which frequently endured over many years. In circumstances where a man was injured or killed, it was not uncommon for his mate to care for his family. These work relationships were often reinforced by kinship ties, the contract system and the small group autonomy allowing a close but spontaneous connection to be maintained between family and occupation, which avoided tying the one to the other. In segregated mining communities the link between kinship and occupation can be oppressive as well as supportive; against this danger, "exogamous" choice was a safeguard. But against too emotional a relationship, more likely to develop between non-kin associates, kinship barriers were in turn a safeguard.

The wholeness of the work task, the multiplicity of the skills of the individual, and the self-selection of the group were congruent attributes of a pattern of responsible autonomy that characterized the pair-based face teams of hand-got mining.

THE ADAPTABILITY OF THE SMALL GROUP TO THE UNDERGROUND SITUATION

Being able to work their own short faces continuously, these pair, or near pair, groups could stop at whatever point may have been reached by the end of a shift. The flexibility in work pace so allowed had special advantages in the underground situation; for when bad conditions were encountered, the extraction process in a series of stalls could proceed unevenly in correspondence with the uneven distribution of these bad conditions, which tend to occur now in one and now in another section along a seam. Even under good conditions, groups of this kind were free to set their own targets, so that aspirations levels with respect to production could be adjusted to the age and stamina of the individuals concerned.

In the underground situation external dangers must be faced in darkness. Darkness also awakens internal dangers. The need to share with others anxieties aroused by this double threat may be taken as self-evident. In view of the restricted range of effective communication, these others have to be immediately present. Their number therefore is limited. These conditions point to

the strong need in the underground worker for a role in a small primary group.

A second characteristic of the underground situation is the wide dispersal of particular activities, in view of the large area over which operations generally are extended. The small groups of the hand-got systems tended to become isolated from each other even when working in the same series of stalls; the isolation of the group, as of the individual, being intensified by the darkness. Under these conditions there is no possibility of continuous supervision, in the factory sense, from any individual external to the primary work group.

The small group, capable of responsible autonomy, and able to vary its work pace in correspondence with changing conditions, would appear to be the type of social structure ideally adapted to the underground situation. It is instructive that the traditional work systems, evolved from the experience of successive generations, should have been founded on a group with these attributes.

But to earn a living under hand-got conditions often entailed physical effort of a formidable order, and possession of exceptional skill was required to extract a bare existence from a hard seam with a bad roof. To tram tubs was "horsework." Trammers were commonly identified by scabs, called "buttons," on the bone joints of their backs, caused by catching the roof while pushing and holding tubs on and off "the gates." Hand-got conditions still obtain, for by no means all faces are serviced by conveyors and coal-cutters. In some circumstances this equipment is unsuitable. But hardness of work is a separate consideration from the quality of the group.

THE COUNTER BALANCE OF THE LARGE UNDIFFERENTIATED COLLECTIVITY

The psychological disadvantages of a work system, the small group organization of which is based on pair relationships, raises issues of a far-reaching kind only recently submitted to study in group dynamics.[5] It would appear that the self-enclosed character of the relationship makes it difficult for groups of this kind to combine effectively in differentiated structures of a somewhat larger social magnitude, though this inability does not seem to hold in respect of much larger collectivies of a simpler mass character. But in premechanized mining there was no technological necessity for intermediate structures, equivalent to factory departments, to make their appearance between the small pair-based primary units and the larger collectivities called into action by situations of crisis and common danger. To meet situations requiring the mobilization of the large mass group, mining communities have developed traditions generally recognized as above the norm commonly attained by occupational groups in our society. This supranormative quality was present also in the traditions of the small pair-based organizations. But between these extremes there was little experience.

Sociologically, this situation is not atypical of industries which, though large-scale, have experienced delay in undergoing mechanization. The pair-based face teams corresponded to the technological simplicity of the hand-got methods, with their short faces, autonomously worked and loosely co-ordinated on a district basis. The mass collectivities reflected the large-scale size of the pit as an overall industrial unit. Absent were structures at the level of the factory department, whose process-linked, fractionated role-systems, dependent on external supervision, were antithetical alike to the pattern of small group autonomy and to the artisan outlook of the collier.

In the pre-mechanized pattern, the pair-based primaries and the large relatively undifferentiated collectivities composed a dynamically interrelated system that permitted an enduring social balance. The intense reciprocities of the former, with their personal and family significance, and the diffuse identifications of the latter, with their community and class connectedness, were mutually supportive. The face teams could bear the responsibility of their autonomy through the security of their dependence on the united collectivity of the pit.

Difficulties arose largely from rivalries and conflicts between the various pairs and small teams. A common form of "graft" was to bribe the deputy in order to secure a good "benk," i.e., a "length" with a "rack roof," under which the coal was notoriously soft and easy to work. Trammers were encouraged to resort to sharp practices to obtain adequate supplies of tubs. As supplies were often short, the amount of coal a working pair could send up depended not a little on the prowess of their trammer. Going early to work, he would turn two or three tubs on their sides in his "gate," maintaining he had taken only one. Ensuing disputes caused frequent fights both underground and in the community. In the common saying, it was he who could lie, cheat, or bully the most who made the best trammer. All this was accepted as part of the system.

Inter-team conflict provided a channel for aggression that preserved intact the loyalties on which the small group depended. In the large group aggression received structured expression in trade union resistance. If the struggle was harsh, it was at least direct and understandable. It was not the insidious kind that knocked the bottom out of life, leaving those concerned without a sense of a scheme in things—the "anomie" described by Halliday[6] after the transition to the longwall. The system as a whole contained its bad in a way that did not destroy its good. The balance persisted, albeit that work was of the hardest, rewards often meager, and the social climate rough at times and even violent.

MECHANIZATION AND THE
PROBLEM OF INTERMEDIATE
ORGANIZATION

With the advent of coal-cutters and
mechanical conveyors, the degree of
technological complexity of the coal-
getting task was raised to a different
level. Mechanization made possible the
working of a single long face in place of
a series of short faces. In thin seams
short faces increase costs, since a large
number of "gates" (see Figure 1) have
to be "ripped" up several feet above the
height of the seam to create haulage
and travelling facilities. In British coal,
seams less than 4 feet in thickness are

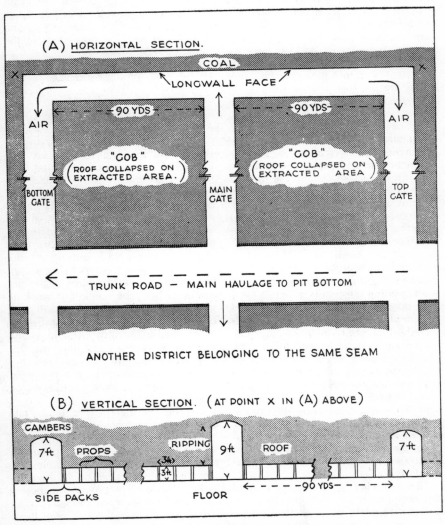

Figure 1
LAYOUT OF A DISTRICT, LONGWALL METHOD

common, so that there was a tendency to make full use of the possibility of working optimally long rather than optimally short faces. For this reason, and for others also, discussion of which is beyond present scope, the longwall method came into being. Applicable to thick as well as to thin seams, it became the general method of coal-getting in the British industry, enabling the average type of pit, which may contain three or four seams of different thickness, to work its entire coal economically, and to develop its layout and organize its production in terms of a single, self-consistent plan. In America, where thick seams are the rule, mechanization has developed in terms of shorter faces and room-and-pillar techniques.

The associated characteristics of mechanized complexity, and of largeness as regards the scale of the primary production unit, created a situation in which it was impossible for the method to develop as a technological system without bringing into existence a work relationship structure radically different from that associated with hand-got procedures. The artisan type of pair, composed of the skilled man and his mate, assisted by one or more labourers, was out of keeping as a model for the type of work group required. Need arose for a unit more of the size and differentiated complexity of a small factory department. A structure of intermediate social magnitude began therefore to emerge. The basic pattern round which the work relationships of the longwall production unit were organized became the cycle group of 40–50 men, their shot-firer and shift "deputies," who were responsible to the pit management for the working as a whole. Only in relation to this total cycle group could various smaller subgroups secure function and acquire social form.

This centring of the new system on a differentiated structure of intermediate social magnitude disturbed the simple balance that had existed between the very small and very large traditional groups, and impaired the quality of responsible autonomy. The psychological and sociological problems posed by the technological needs of the longwall system were those with respect to which experience in the industry was least, and towards which its traditions were antithetical. The consequences of this conflict between the demands of the new situation and the resources available from past experience will be taken up in the light of the detailed account, which will now be presented, of the longwall system itself.

THE LACK OF RECOGNITION OF THE NATURE OF THE DIFFICULTIES

No new equilibrium came into being. As was mentioned in the introduction, disturbances associated with industrial struggle and economic depression have tended to mask those associated with the coal-getting method. Though perception of these latter has begun to clarify since nationalization, shortcomings such as those in the haulage system, more readily appreciated in engineering terms, continue to attract the wider attention. It is only since the morale changes accompanying recent face-work innovations have begun actually to be experienced in working groups that the nature of longwall troubles is becoming manifest. That they require understanding in social and psychological terms is something that still remains largely unrecognized. Accounts so far appearing have presented recent changes almost exclusively in engineering terms.

Anyone who has listened to the talk of older miners who have experienced in their own work-lives the change-over to the longwall cannot fail to be impressed by the confused mourning for the past that still goes on in them together with a dismay over the present coloured by despair and indignation. To the clinical worker the quality of these talks has at times a ring that is familiar. Those with rehabilitation experience will recognize it as similar to the quality of feeling expressed by rehabilitees when ventilating the aftermath in themselves of an impairment accepted as irreversible.

Expectation was widespread that something magical would happen as a result of nationalization. But as one filler put it: "My coals don't wear any new look since Investment Day. They gave me a look as black as before." When some of these same men take on a new lease of life, perhaps exaggeratedly, after experiencing one of the new group methods and refuse to return to a conventional working having found a new spirit in themselves and their work-mates, strong clues are already to hand regarding the character of longwall deficiencies. But what has been intuitively grasped has still to become articulate. So close is the relationship between the various aspects that the social and the psychological can be understood only in terms of the detailed engineering facts and of the way the technological system as a whole behaves in the environment of the underground situation. These points will be taken up in the next two Sections.

III
FEATURES AND DIFFICULTIES OF THE LONGWALL PRODUCTION UNIT AS A WHOLE[7]

THE SCALE AND SPATIO-TEMPORAL STRUCTURE OF THE THREE-SHIFT CYCLE

In the longwall method, a direct advance is made into the coal on a continuous front; faces of 180-200 yards being typical, though longer faces are not uncommon. The work is broken down into a standard series of component operations that follow each other in rigid succession over 3 shifts of 7½ hours each, so that a total coal-getting cycle may be completed once in each 24 hours of the working week. The shift spread of the 40 workmen needed on an average face is: 10 each to the first

("cutting") and second ("ripping") shifts; 20 to the third ("filling") shift. The amount of coal scheduled for extraction varies under different conditions but is commonly in the neighbourhood of 200 tons per cycle. A medium-size pit with three seams would have 12-15 longwall faces in operation simultaneously.

These faces are laid out in districts as shown in Figure 1. Since the longwall method is specially applicable to thin seams, Figure 1 has been set up in terms of a 3-foot working. The face, extending 90 yards on either side of the main gate is within average limits for a seam of this thickness. The height of the face area—that of the 3-foot seam itself—may be contrasted with the 9 foot and 7 foot to which the main and side gates have been ripped and built up as permanent structures with cambers and side-packs. By regulation, props must be placed every 3 feet, and the line of props shown in Figure 1 (b) is that placed immediately against a coal-face waiting to be filled off. The area marked "Gob" (to use a term common in mining vernacular) indicates the expanse from which the coal has already been extracted. On this area the roof is left to collapse. Only the tunnels made by the main and side gates, which are used for ventilation and for haulage and travelling, are kept open. These tunnels may sometimes extend for distances of 2 miles, and even more, before the coal face itself is reached from the trunk road leading from the pit bottom.

In each coal-getting cycle the advance made into the coal is equal to the depth of the undercut. A cut of 6 feet represents typical practice in a thin seam with a good roof. All equipment has to be moved forward as each cycle contributes to the advance. The detail in the face area is represented in Figure 2, where the coal is shown cut and waiting for the shot-firer, whose task is the last to be performed before the fillers come on. The combined width of the lanes marked "New Creeping Track" and

"New Conveyor Track" equal the depth of 6 feet, from which the coal has been removed by the fillers on the last shift of the previous cycle. As part of the preparation work of the current cycle (before the fillers can come on again), the con-veyor has to be moved from its previous position in the "old Conveyor Track" to its present position, shown in Figure 2, in the "New Conveyor Track," against the face. At the same time the two lines of props on either side of the "Old

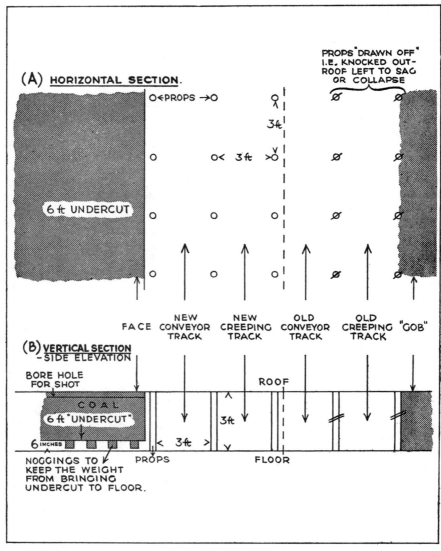

Figure 2
COAL FACE AS SET FOR FILLING SHIFT

Creeping Track" are withdrawn (allowing the roof to sag or collapse) and thrown over beside the conveyor for the fillers to use in propping up their roof as they get into the next 6 feet of coal. The term "creeping track" refers to the single, propped, 3-foot lane, adjacent to that occupied by the conveyor but on the side away from the coal. It allows free passage up and down the face, and is called a creeping track since in thin seams the low roof makes it necessary for all locomotion to take the form of "creeping," i.e., crawling on the hands and knees.

The mass-production character of the longwall operation necessitates a large-scale, mobile layout of the type described. But the spatio-temporal structure imposed by the long face and the shift sequence makes a difficult habitat when considered as a theatre in which effective communication and good working relationships must be maintained between 40 men, their shot-firer and shift deputies. On the one hand, the group is spread over 200 yards in a tunnel 2 yards wide and 1 yard high, cross-cut only by the main and side gates; on the other, it is spread over 24 hours and divided up in 3 successive shifts. The production engineer might write a simple equation: 200 tons equals 40 men over 200 yards over 24 hours. But there are no solutions of equivalent simplicity to the psychological and social difficulties raised. For psychological and social difficulties of a new order appear when the scale of a task transcends the limits of simple spatio-temporal structure. By this is meant conditions under which those concerned can complete a job in one place at one time, i.e., the situation of the face-to-face, or singular group.

Once a job is too big for a singular group, a multiple group comes into existence, composed of a number of subgroups of the singular type. In these differentiated organizations of intermediate social magnitude, problems of intergroup relationships are superimposed on, and inter-act with, the intra-group tensions of the primary components. In the longwall production unit, the scale of the task introduces the contradiction of spatio-temporal disintegration as a condition of multiple group integration.

THE DIFFERENTIATION AND INTERDEPENDENCE OF TASKS

Occupational roles express the relationship between a production process and the social organization of the group. In one direction, they are related to tasks, which are related to each other; in the other, to people, who are also related to each other. At workman level, there are seven of these roles in the longwall system—borer, cutter, gummer, belt-breaker, belt-builder, ripper, and filler—which are linked to the component tasks of the production process. In Table 1 the functions of these 7 categories in the interrelated technological and social structures are described in detail in a comprehensive table. For analytical purposes, however, it is necessary to treat separately these 2 different aspects of occupational roles; and, in this section, consideration will be given to the interdependence of component tasks in the production process, and to occupational roles so far as they are related to this. These tasks fall into 4 groups, concerned with (a) the preparation of the coal-face for shot-firing, (b) shifting the conveyor, (c) ripping and building up the main and side gates, and (d) moving the shot coal on to the conveyor.

The face preparation tasks are all performed on the first shift. They include boring holes for the shot-firer, with pneumatic or electrically operated drills, near the roof of the seam through to the depth of the undercut, at short distances (within each filler's "length") along the entire expanse of face; driving the coal-cutter so that the blade or "jib" makes an even undercut into the coal some 6 inches from the floor to whatever depth has been assigned, again along the entire expanse of face; taking

Table 1
OCCUPATIONAL STRUCTURE IN THE LONGWALL SYSTEM

Shift Sequence	Occupational Roles	No. of Men	Methods of Payment	Group Organization	Tasks	Skills	Status Differences and Ranking
First (usually called) "cutting" shift. Either night, 8 p.m.–3.30 a.m., or afternoon, 12 noon–7.30 p.m. (borers start an hour earlier). Though alternating between night and afternoon, personnel on the cutting shift are never on days.	Borer	2	Per hole	Interdependent pair on same note.	Boring holes for shot-firer in each stint to depth of under-cut.	Management of electric or pneumatic drills, placing of holes, judgment of roof, hardness of coal, etc.	4·5, equal in pair.
	Cutter	2	Per yard	Interdependent pair on same note, front man and back man.	Operating coal-cutter to achieve even cut at assigned depth the entire length of the face ; knocking out (front man), re-setting (back man) props as cutter passes. Back man inserts noggings.	Requires rather more "engineering" skill than other coal-face tasks. Mining skills in keeping cut even under changing conditions, watching roof control.	1, front man senior and responsible for cut ; back man assists ; cutting the key preparation task.
	Gummer	4	Day wage	Loose group attached to cutters, though front man without supervisory authority.	Cleaning out undercut, so that clear space for coal to drop and level floor for filler. The coal between undercut and floor is called "the gummings".	Unskilled, heavy manual task, which unless conscientiously done creates difficulties for filler, for when gummings left in, the shot simply blows out and coal is left solid.	7, equal in group ; some chance of promotion to cutter eventually.
	Belt-breaker	2	Per yard	Interdependent pair on same note.	Shifting belt-engine and tension-end into face clear of rippers ; breaking up conveyor in old track, placing plates, etc., ready in new track, drawing off props in old creeping track ; some packing as required.	Belt-breaking is a relatively simple engineering task ; engine shifting is awkward and heavy ; drawing off and packing involve responsibility for roof control and require solid underground experience.	4·5, equal in pair.
Second (usually called the "ripping" shift). Either night or afternoon alternating with cutting shift. Rippers may start rather later than builders. None of these personnel go on day shift proper.	Belt-builder	2	Per yard	Interdependent pair on same note.	Reassembling conveyor in new track ; positioning belt-engine and tension-end in line with this ; testing running of reassembled conveyor ; placing chocks ; packing as required.	As with breaking, the level of engineering skill is relatively simple ; inconvenience caused to fillers if belt out of position. The roof control responsibilities demand solid underground experience.	4·5, equal in pair.
	Ripper	8	Cubic measure	Cohesive functionally inter-related group on same note.	To "rip" "dirt" out of main and side gates to assigned heights ; place cambers and build up roof into a solid, safe structure ; pack-up the sides. The ripping team carries out all operations necessary to their task, doing their own boring. The task is a complete job in itself, seen through by the group within the compass of one shift.	This work requires the highest degree of building skill among coal face tasks. Some very heavy labour is entailed. Since the work is relatively permanent there is much pride of craft. On the ripper depends the safety of all gates and main ways.	2, the status of the "main ripper" is next to that of the front man on the cutter, but he is not separately paid. The group usually contains all degrees of experience and is egalitarian.
Third (usually called "filling" shift). Either day, 6 a.m.–1.30 p.m., or afternoon, 2 p.m.–9.30 p.m. Never night.	Filler	20	Weight—tonnage on conveyors.	Aggregate of individuals with equal "stints" ; all on same note ; fractionated relationships and much isolation.	The length of the "stint" is determined by the depth of the cut and the thickness of the seam. Using hand or air pick and shovel, the filler "throws" the "shot" coal on to the conveyor until he has cleared his length, i.e. "filled off". He props up every 2 ft. 6 in. as he works in.	The filler remains in one work place while conditions change. Considerable underground experience is required to cope with bad conditions. Each man is responsible for his own section of roof. Bad work on other shifts makes the task harder. It is heavy in any case and varies in different parts of the wall.	4·5, equal throughout the group ; "corner" men are envied, reputation of being good or bad workman is important.
3 shifts	7 roles	40 men	5 methods	4 types	The common background of "underground" skill is more important than the task differences.		Differences in status and weekly earnings are small, apart from the case of the gummers.

out the 6 inches of coal (called the "gummings") left in the undercut, so that the main weight of coal can drop and break freely when the shots are fired; placing supporting "noggings" underneath it so that this weight does not cause it to sag down to the floor while the "cut" is standing during the next shift. These tasks are performed in the order given. Three of the 7 work roles are associated with their execution, 2 men being fully occupied boring the holes, a further 2 in managing the coal-cutter, and 4 in clearing out the undercut.

The success of the shots fired at the end of the second shift to make the coal finally ready for the filler depends on the efficiency with which each of these interdependent preparation tasks has been carried out. Bad execution of any one of them diminishes, and may even cancel out, the effect of the shots, with consequent havoc in the lengths of the particular fillers where such breakdowns have occurred. Holes bored too low leave a quantity of coal, difficult to extract, clinging to the roof after the shots have been fired. If the roof is sticky, this gives rise to "sticky tops." Holes not bored through to the full depth of the undercut create the condition of "hard backs," the shots having no effect on this part of the coal. The coal-cutter only too frequently has a tendency to leave the floor and "get up into the coal," producing an uneven cut. This means less working height for the filler, and also less wages, since his tonnage is reduced. When the "gummings" are left in, the shot is wasted; the coal has nowhere to drop and the powder blows out of the hole (usually up the "cutting break" in the roof) so that the mass to be extracted is left solid. Failure to insert noggings, which leads to the cut sagging down, also renders useless the services of the shot-firer.

The group of operations concerned with the conveyor involves—since forward movement is blocked by props which must be left standing—breaking up the sections of belt in the old conveyor track and building them up in the new. Each of these tasks requires 2 men: the belt-breakers and belt-builders. The dismantling part is done on the first shift in the wake of the cutting operation. The reasons include the necessity of shifting belt-engines and tension-ends out of the gate areas (where they are positioned when the conveyor is working) in order to allow the ripping operation to proceed. The reassembly of the conveyor is the only task performed in the face area during the second shift. Unless the conveyor is properly jointed, set close to the new face, and accurately sighted in a straight line, a further crop of difficulties arise, and frequently stoppages may interfere with filling. The most modern types of belt, e.g., floor belts, avoid the labour of breaking up and reassembling plates. Belt-engines and tension-ends are cumbersome equipment, but they must nevertheless be shifted every day. Similarly, the last 2 lines of props have to be taken down and thrown forward.

The third group of tasks comprise those that entail ripping up the roof of the main and side gates to the depth of the undercut, and building them up with a stable roof and firmly packed sides so that haulage- and air-ways can advance with the face. Unless this work is expertly done, the danger of roof falls is acute, with the likelihood both of men and equipment being blocked in the face. This work is carried out by a team of 7-8 rippers.

Only when all these operations have been completed, can the shots be fired and the fillers come on. For the filling operation, the entire face is divided up into equal lengths—except that the corner positions are somewhat shorter in view of difficulties created by the proximity of belt-engines and tension-ends. In a 3-foot seam, lengths would be 8-10 yards, and some 20 fillers would be required, 10 in each half-face of 90-100 yards. Each filler is required to extract the entire coal from his length, going back to the depth of the 6-foot undercut. When he has thrown his last load on to the conveyor he has "filled off," *i.e.,* finished his "length" or "stint." As he progresses into his coal, he has the additional task of propping up his roof every 3 feet. As well as a handpick and shovel, his tool kit includes an air pick, used for dealing with some of the difficulties created by bad preparation, or in any case when his coal is hard.

At a later point there will be a discussion of the differential distribution of bad conditions among the lengths of a face. Here it may be noted that the face is not "filled off" until each and every length has been cleared, and that until this has been done, the new cycle cannot begin. Disorganization on the filling shift disorganizes the subsequent shifts, and its own disorganization is often produced by the bad preparation left by these teams. Every time the cycle is stopped, some 200 tons of coal are lost.

So close is the task interdependence that the system becomes vulnerable from its need for 100 percent performance at each step. The most sensitive interaction is between the face-preparation activities and filling, but it is in relation to this that social organization is weakest. This point will be taken up in later sections.

THE SEGMENTED QUALITY OF
THE SOCIAL ORGANIZATION

With respect to the way in which the work roles have been institutionalized as regards the person and groups concerned, a basic segregation of the various categories of workers from each other follows from the fact that it has been the traditional practice for a face-worker to be trained in only 1 of the 7 roles, and to spend all or most of his underground life in this one occupation. This basic segregation of roles is intensified by the 5 different methods of payment described in Table 1, and by the exaggeration of status differences,

despite the common background of "underground skill" and the equivalence of earnings (apart from the rather lower rate received by the gummers).

It is still further reinforced by the segregation of shifts. As will be seen from the shift time-tables, the 3 shifts never meet. Moreover, the 2 preparation groups alternate on the so-called "back shifts" while the fillers alternate on "days" and "afternoons," so that a far-reaching community, as well as work, split is effected between the fillers and the others. The "back shift" men are either going to or coming from work in the evening, so that they are cut off from normal community activities during the week. Even at weekends they are down the pit either on Saturday afternoon or Sunday evening.

As regards the primary work groups in which those performing the various roles participate, there are 4 radically different patterns: the series of interdependent pairsborers, belt-builders, and belt-breakers; the extended pair organization of the cutters and gummers; the self-sufficient group of 8 rippers; and the aggregate of 20 fillers spread out over the 200-yard face. The uneven social quality of these different types of primary group will be discussed in Sections V-VII, both with respect to intra- and inter-group relations. This unevenness, taken together with the role and shift segregation, works against the social integration of the cycle group as a whole. Yet, in view of the close interdependence of tasks, the social integration of the total work group is a first essential of the system.

It is submitted that the non-existence of the cycle group as a social whole in face of the interdependence of the component tasks is one of the major contradictions present in the longwall method. The social organization is a simple reflection of the "job breakdown." Because this latter is reintegrated into a technological whole by the task sequence it does not follow that the differentiated role-groups concerned are also and thereby reintegrated into a social whole. Differentiation gives rise to the need for social as well as technological integration. No attempt seems to have been made in the longwall method to achieve any living social integration of the primary and shift groups into which the cycle aggregate has been differentiated. This, of course, is a common omission in mass-production systems.

IV
THE STRESS OF MASS PRODUCTION IN THE UNDERGROUND SITUATION

THE INTERACTION OF BAD CONDITIONS AND BAD WORK

Differentiated, rigidly sequenced work systems, organized on mass-production lines to deal with large quantities of material on a multi-shift cycle, are a basic feature of the factory pattern. Even in the factory situation, their maintenance at a level which allows full and continuous realization of their technological potentialities creates a difficult problem of industrial management. In the underground situation these difficulties are of a higher order, it being virtually impossible to establish the kind of constant background to the task that is taken for granted in the factory. A very large variety of unfavourable and changing environmental conditions is encountered at the coal-face, many of which are impossible to predict. Others, though predictable, are impossible to alter.

The factory and underground situations are different with respect to the "figure-ground" relationship of the production process to its environmental background. In the factory a comparatively high degree of control can be exercised over the complex and moving "figure" of a production sequence, since it is possible to maintain the "ground" in a comparatively passive and constant state. But at the coal face,

there is always present the threat of some untoward activity in the "ground." The internal organization of the task "figure" is therefore much more liable to disorganization. The instability of the "ground" limits the applicability in the underground situation of methods derived from the factory.

Unfavourable natural conditions, as distinct from "bad work"—which is the result of human shortcomings—are referred to as "bad conditions." Some of the most dreaded, such as wet, heat, or dust, are permanent features of the working environment of certain faces. But other, less known outside the industry, may also make the production tasks of the face-worker both difficult and dangerous, even though the seam in which he is working is well ventilated, cool, and dry without being dusty. Rolls or faults may appear in the seam. Control may be lost over the roof for considerable periods. Especially in the middle of a long face, certain types of roof are apt to sag down. Changes may occur in the floor; the condition known as "rising floor" being not uncommon. Since some of these conditions, described in Table 2 and Figure 4, reduce working height, their appearance is particularly troublesome in thin seams. If the difference between working in 5 feet 6 inches and 5 feet may be of small account, that between working in 3 feet and 2 feet 6 inches may often produce intolerable conditions. Loss of roof-control is serious, whatever the working height. In general, bad conditions mean not only additional danger but additional labour. The need to insert packs to support a loose roof is a common example.

Special tasks of any kind, over and above the specific production operation for which a given category of face-worker receives his basic pay, are known as "bye-work." Though many bye-work tasks have gained the status of specially remunerated activities, the rates are such that the overall wage received at the end of a week during

Table 2

CUMULATIVE AND DIFFERENTIAL INCIDENCE OF BAD CONDITIONS AND BAD WORK IN THE FILLING SHIFT

(This table has been built up as a " model " of the situation from the experience of a group of face-workers who acted as informants. It relates the effect of bad conditions and bad work, traversing the face unevenly, to the unequal personal and group qualities of the fillers.)

x indicates local distribution of difficulty in typical examples of different kinds of bad conditions and bad work.

Types of Adverse Factor	Positions Across the Face of 20 Fillers																			
	1	2	3	4	5	6	7	8	9	10	11	12	13	14	15	16	17	18	19	20
Loose roof—roof broken up by weight or natural " slips " (cracks) making it difficult to support ; extra time required for timbering reduces that for filling.					x	x	x	x						x	x	x				
Faults—sudden changes in slope of seam either up or down, producing bad conditions capable of anticipation, possibly lasting over a considerable period.	x	x																		x
Rolls—temporary unevenness in floor or roof reducing working height and producing severely cramped conditions in thin seams. As above for anticipation and duration.	x				x										x					
Roof weight—roof sagging down—especially in middle positions along the face where weight is greatest ; not dissimilar to above in effect.				x	x	x								x	x	x				
Rising floor—from natural bad stone floor, or from the cut having been made into the coal so that the gas in the coal lifts up the floor, or from naturally inferior coal which is left down but which lifts (gas).					x	x								x	x					
Bad boring—holes bored short so that coal at the back of the undercut is unaffected by shot (hard backs) ; heavy extraction task with air pick at end of shift, when tired ; or holes too low, so that shot leaves coal clinging to roof (sticky tops). Both these conditions tend to occur through naturally hard coal and certain types of roof.										x		x					x			
Uneven cut—from the coal cutter having gone up into the coal. This reduces the filler's working height, cf. rolls, and the tonnage on which his wages depend. Also, as with rolls, faults, etc., it means that 3-ft. props have to be inserted in 2-ft. 6-in. height, which means sinking them in floor (dirting props) as an additional unremunerated task.	x				x					x	x							x		x
Gummings left in—failure on the part of the gummers to clear coal from undercut so that coal cannot drop and shot is wasted. The result is a solid mass of hard coal, requiring constant use of air pick and back-breaking effort. The amount left in varies.				x	x	x				x	x						x	x		x
Belt trouble—the belt may not have been set in a straight line, or bad joints may have been made, or it may not have been made tight enough. On top-delivery belts coal going back on the bottom belt very soon stops it. Belt stoppages may produce exceedingly awkward delays, especially if conditions are otherwise bad.				x	x	x	x													
* Total	3	1	-	3	7	5	2	1	-	3	2	1	-	3	4	2	2	2	-	3
** Skill	+			+								-	+		-		-			+
** Stamina				+		-									-			-	+	
** Conscientiousness				-											+		-			
*** Sub-group membership	a	a	a	I	b	b	I	c	c	c	d	d	I	e	e	e	e	I	f	f

* These numbers simply indicate the fact that several different kinds of things often go wrong in the same length. Severity varies. At one extreme there may be a series of minor nuisances, at the other one major interference. When conditions seriously deteriorate the interaction of factors and effects is such that some degree of disturbance is apt to be felt from most quarters at one or other point along the face.

** Plus or minus ratings have been given for supra- or infra-norm group status on the three attributes of skill, stamina and conscientiousness on the job, which represent the type of judgments of each other that men need to make, and do in fact make.

*** Members of the same informal sub-group are indicated by the same letter ; I = Isolate.

which a good deal of bye-work has been necessary is less than that which would have been received had the whole of the 5 shifts been available for production work. From the face-worker's point of view, bad conditions mean not only more danger and harder work but less pay; and they may also compel overtime. To stay behind an hour or sometimes three hours longer under bad conditions may involve a degree of hardship beyond the capacity of many face-workers to endure, especially if they are older, and if overtime demands are repeated in close succession.

"Bad conditions" tend to instigate "bad work." When they occur, the smooth sequence of tasks in the production cycle is more likely to be disturbed by faulty performance. Bad work can, and does, arise when conditions are good, from personal shortcomings and social tensions, in themselves independent of bad conditions; but difficulties arising from human failings are more readily—and conveniently—expressed when the additional difficulty, and excuse, of bad conditions is also present. The result is a tendency for circular causal processes of a disruptive character to be touched off. Unless rapidly checked by special measures, often of an emergency character, these, once started, threaten to culminate in the fillers not filling off, and the cycle being stopped. The system is therefore always to some extent working against the threat of its own breakdown, so that tension and anxiety are created.

THE MAGNIFICATION OF LOCAL DISTURBANCES

Under these conditions, the closeness of the functional interdependence of tasks tends to rebound on itself. Mistakes and difficulties made or encountered at one stage are carried forward, producing yet other difficulties in the next. The inflexible character of the succession gives no scope for proceeding with later tasks when hold-ups have occurred earlier,

and the temporal extension of the cycle increases the likelihood of interference from unpredictable events which are provided with 24 hours in which to occur. The aspects of mass-production engineering methods (rigid sequence, functional interdependence and spatio-temporal extension), which create vulnerability in the underground situation, all stem from the large-scale character of the longwall cycle. For it is the magnitude of the cycle, produced by the long expanse of face scheduled for clearance, that leads to the segregated treatment of the component tasks—in view of the large amount of work required on each—and thence to their fixed, extended succession. In an organization of this scale, local disturbances at specific points—resulting from the interaction of bad conditions and bad work—resonate through a relatively large social space, becoming magnified for this reason.

Stricter field theory formulation may assist the more dynamic description of this situation. The size of the bounded region in which the system exists as a whole, together with the high degree of differentiation in its unidirectional internal connectedness, first increases the number of points at which small disturbances may occur, and thereafter enlarges the scope of their effects to a scale proportional to the magnitude of the whole. Since these effects must be contained within a closed system, single events are, as the result of induction which takes place from the power field of the whole, endowed with the potentiality of disrupting the cycle. No matter that this potentiality is realized only in the extreme case; disturbance is always experienced to some extent under pressure of this potentiality. Stress arising from this pressure itself produces fresh disturbances. Measures necessary to prevent these from still further spreading absorb a correspondingly greater amount of the available concern and energy.

VARIATIONS IN THE LEVEL OF FUNCTIONING

It has been mentioned that a characteristic of bad conditions and bad work is their uneven distribution—not only between different faces, but also over different sections and among different tasks within the same face (see Table 2). The consequence is an uneven level of functional efficiency, more generally lowered also by the magnified resonances and induced pressures described above. The atmosphere of uncertainty thus created arouses the expectation in the individual that bad work done by someone else will increase his own difficulties, or that some untoward event will occur to keep him down at the end of his shift. The resulting attitudes and suspicions are ingrained in the culture of the longwall work group and adversely affect the entire pattern of relationships at the coal-face.

No systematic survey of the incidence of cycle stoppages was possible within the limits of the present study. But on one of the best faces known at first hand by the writers it was a matter of self-congratulation that the fillers had failed to fill off only 3 times during the past year. Experienced informants gave once in 2 months, or 5 or 6 times during the course of a year, as a more usual frequency, with instances of many more stoppages in "bad faces" in "bad pits." If one week's work is commonly lost in this way during a year, the overall loss in production would amount to some 2 percent. This relatively low figure expresses the extent of the efforts made to check disturbances short of the point where the cycle is stopped.

THE STRAIN OF CYCLE CONTROL

The main burden of keeping down the number of cycle stoppages falls on the deputy, who is the only person in the face area with cycle, as distinct from task, responsibility. Discussion with groups of deputies readily yields evidence of the strain involved. A common and reality-based complaint is that the

authority of the deputy is incommensurate with responsibility of this order. The background to this complaint is the fact, noted in the discussion of the hand-got systems, that, in view of the darkness and the spread out character of the work, there is no possibility of close supervision. Responsibility for seeing to it that bad work is not done, however bad the conditions, rests with the face-workers themselves. But the responsible autonomy of some, especially, of the occupational sub-groups has been impaired in the longwall method. This problem will be taken up in succeeding sections.

As a result, management complain of lack of support from the men, who are accused of being concerned only with their own fractional tasks and unwilling to take broader cycle responsibility. The parallel complaint of the workers is of being driven and tricked by management, who are resented as outsiders—intermittent visitors and "stick" men, who interfere without sharing the hard, physical work and in-group life of the face. On occasions, for example, the deputy is reduced to bargaining with the men as to whether they will agree to carry out essential bye-work. The complaint of the men is that deputies' promises are rarely kept, and that they have gone unpaid too often to be again easily persuaded. The deputy's answer is that the under-manager or manager has refused to uphold his case. Whether he presented it, how he presented it, or what reasons may have dictated the managerial view are a type of issue on which effective communication back to the man breaks down. The deputy has equally little chance of increasing the insight of the workmen into their own tendency to drive sharp bargains.

The strain of cycle control tends to produce a group "culture" of angry and suspicious bargaining over which both management and men are in collusion. There is displacement both upwards and downwards of the tensions generated. The "hell" that breaks loose in the under-manager's office when news comes in that the fillers are unlikely to fill off in one or more faces resounds through the pit.

THE NORM OF LOW PRODUCTIVITY

In all work at the coal-face 2 distinct tasks are simultaneously present; those that belong to the production cycle being always to some extent carried out on the background of a second activity arising from the need to contend with interferences, actual or threatened, emanating from the underground situation. The activity of the "ground" has always to be dealt with, and ability to contend with this second or background task comprises the common fund of underground skill shared alike by all experienced face-workers. This common skill is of a higher order than that required simply to carry out, as such, any of the operations belonging to the production cycle. For these, initial training is short, and may be measured in months; it is longest for those, such as cutting, where the engineering component is largest. But the specifically mining skill of contending with underground conditions, and of maintaining a high level of performance when difficulties arise, is developed only as the result of several years of experience at the face. A work-system basically appropriate to the underground situation requires to have built into its organization the findings of this experience. Unless this has been done, it will not only fail to engage the face-worker to the limit of his capabilities, but will restrict him to a level of performance below his potentiality.

The evidence suggests that the longwall method acts in this way. The crises of cycle stoppages and the stress of the deputy's role are but symptoms of a wider situation characterized by the establishment of a norm of low productivity, as the only adaptive method of handling, in the contingencies of the underground situation, a complicated, rigid, and large-scale work system, borrowed with too little modification from an engineering culture appropriate to the radically different situation of the factory. At the time the longwall method developed, there were no precedents for the adaptive underground application of a machine technology. In the absence of relevant experience in the mining tradition itself it was almost inevitable that heavy culture-borrowing of this kind should have taken place. There was also no psychological or sociological knowledge in existence at that time which might have assisted in lessening the difficulties.

As regards the special difficulties which stem from the large-scale character of the longwall production unit, it may be noted that less acute problems appear to have arisen at equal or even higher levels of mechanization, with room-and-pillar techniques. Here the scale of operations is less, in view of the shorter expanse of the faces; while adaptability to the changing circumstances of underground conditions appears to have been correspondingly greater. It must not, however, be inferred from room-and-pillar experience that the development of a high level of functional efficiency is impossible in a large-scale mechanized unit; rather, that the problems presented are more difficult. The difficulties occur very largely in the field of social organization. In the succeeding sections consideration will be given to problems of group relationships in the various occupational subgroups of the longwall system.

V
THE SPECIAL SITUATION OF THE FILLING SHIFT

ISOLATED DEPENDENCE

Relationships between members of the filling shift are characterized by an absence of functional interdependence, which arises from the absence of role differentiation in the 20 identical tasks performed by the shift aggregate. The filler is the modern version of the second collier of the older hand-got systems, whose hewer has departed to the cutting shift. While his former mate has acquired a new partner in the back man on the coal-cutter, and is serviced by a new group of labourers—gummers, as distinct from trammers—the filler is alone in his stint, the dimensions of which are those of the short face formerly worked in common. The advent of mechanization has changed but little the character of filling, except that the filler has, in his air pick, the assistance of one power-drive tool and, instead of a hand-pushed tub, a mechanically driven conveyor on to which to load his coal.

The effect of the introduction of mechanized methods of face preparation and conveying, along with the retention of manual filling, has been not only to isolate the filler from those with whom he formerly shared the coal-getting task as a whole, but to make him one of a large aggregate serviced by the same small group of preparation workers. In place of an actually present partner, who belonged to him solely as the second member of an interdependent pair, he has acquired an "absent group," whom he must share with 19 others. The temporal distance separating him from this absent group is increased by the interval of the ripping shift.

The preparation group itself is so loosely organized that its boundaries are difficult to determine. If thought of as centered on the 2 cutters, the extent of the filler's dependence on earlier activities is such that the cutting group must be expanded to include the 2 borers as well as the 4 gummers. Since in addition he is dependent on the beltmen, these latter, representing transformed but likewise absent versions of trammers formerly under his own eye, must also be included in his absent group. While, in the time perspective of the present, the filler has no relationships of functional interdependence with other fillers on his own shift, in the time perspective of the past he must contend with a complex set of dependent relationships with the entire series of preparation workers who have preceded him in the face. These relationships are dependent rather than interdependent since, within a given cycle period, they operate only in one direction.

Though, from the filler's point of view, preparation personnel form a total group in virtue of their common relation to him, they do not for this reason constitute an organized group with respect to each other. The structure of their own relationships is that of a series of self-enclosed interdependent pairs, whose connection with each other is small compared with their common connection with him. In this series the cutters form a pair of the extended type with the 4 gummers loosely attached. But gummings "left in" cause no difficulties for the cutters; and, though antecedent, the work of the borers also causes them no difficulties. On the next shift, the belt-builders complete the second part of an overall conveyor task begun by the breakers, but the work of this team is not affected by the level of performance of those who prepare the coal-face. A series of absent pairs, on each and all of whom one is dependent, but themselves not reciprocating this dependence and remaining relatively independent of each other, constitute a difficult group with whom to enter into a working relationship. This difficulty is increased by the fact that their services have to be shared among 19 others, who are in the position of rivals for the receipt of preferential attention.

Difficulties are increased still further by the fact that the concern of this succession of pairs is with the entire 180-200 yards of the face. For them the face is a single continuous region, whereas for the fillers it is differentiated into a series of short adjacent sections. For the individual filler it is the 8–10 yards of his own length. In the corner of this length he usually chalks up his name, but these chalk marks mean little more than just the name to traversing pairs, to whom individual fillers are personally little known. The structure of the preparation tasks as continuous activities covering the entire expanse of the face gives the succession of traversing pairs no functional relationship with the discrete tasks of individual fillers. The absent, internally disconnected group on which he is dependent takes no functional cognizance of the existence of the filler as an individual. In view of the far-reaching community, as well as work, separation that exists between the preparation and the filling shifts (produced by the time-table arrangements), actual cognizance tends also to be minimal. The pattern of these relationships is shown in Figure 3, where the picture presented is one in which, within the period of a given cycle, the fillers are left "alone with each other" and at the mercy of the rest.

UNEQUAL MEN WITH EQUAL STINTS UNDER UNEQUAL CONDITIONS

The fillers, as has been shown, have no secure relationships in face of the differential incidence of the bad conditions they may encounter or of the bad work they may inherit from the preparation workers on whom they are dependent. The men who face these unequal conditions are themselves unequal; but the lengths of face they clear are the same. The detailed implications of this situation are set out in Table 2, where the differential incidence of some of the most common types of bad conditions and of bad work, in the different lengths of a typical face, is shown in relation to the variations in skill, conscientiousness, and stamina in a typical group of fillers, fractionated into informal subgroups interspersed with isolates.

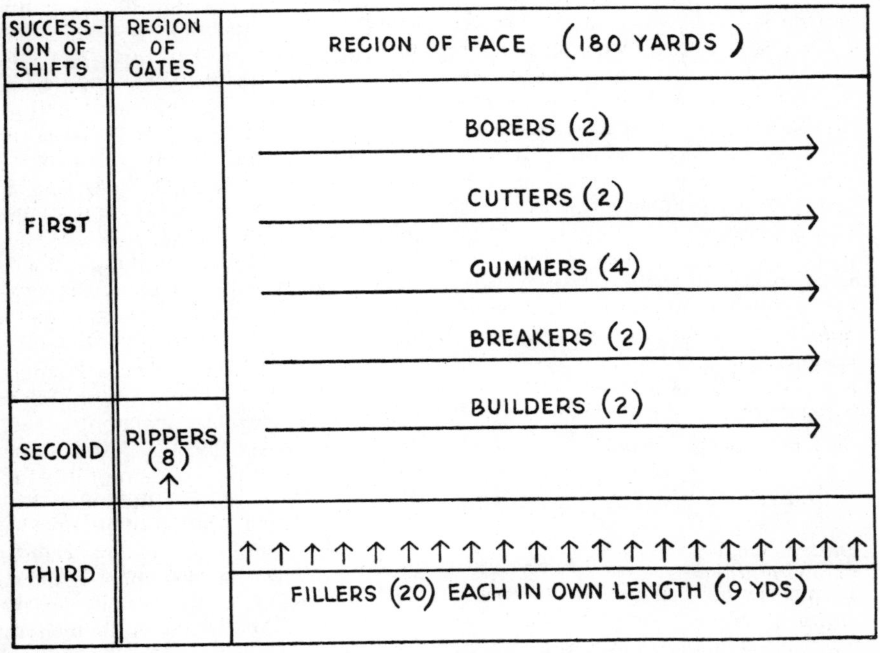

SUCCESS-ION OF SHIFTS	REGION OF GATES	REGION OF FACE (180 YARDS)
FIRST		BORERS (2) →
		CUTTERS (2) →
		GUMMERS (4) →
		BREAKERS (2) →
SECOND	RIPPERS (8) ↑	BUILDERS (2) →
THIRD		↑ FILLERS (20) EACH IN OWN LENGTH (9 YDS)

Figure 3
POSITION AND LOCOMOTION OF SUCCESSIVE
GROUPS OF FACE WORKERS ON THE LONGWALL

The local arrival of certain types of bad conditions, such as rolls that move across the face, can be anticipated, so that anxiety piles up. The passage across a face of a roll that continues for different periods of time in various lengths is shown in Figure 4. As regards bad work left by the other shifts, the filler is in the situation of never knowing what he may find, so that anxiety of a second kind arises that tends to produce chronic uncertainty and irritation. There is little doubt that these 2 circumstances contribute to the widespread incidence of psycho-somatic and kindred neurotic disorders among those concerned.

The degree of stress arising when men experience the full weight of this situation could have been explored only in a therapeutic relationship. But many instances were given of neurotic episodes occurring on shift—of men sitting in their lengths in stony silence, attacking their coal in towering rage, or leaving the face in panic. In a situation of dependent isolation with the odds unequal both as regards his own resources and what is required of him, the individual inevitably erects protective defences, and these are elaborated and shared in the work group. An account of the main pattern of group defences will now be given. These defences are reactive rather than adaptive. Their effectiveness therefore is only partial. But without them life at the longwall would be intolerable for all but those whose level of personal adjustment is rather better than that attained by most individuals in the course of their development.

VI
FOUR TYPES OF GROUP DEFENCE

INFORMAL ORGANIZATION

The functional isolation of the filler within his own group, which leaves him "officially" alone with his "coals," is met by an attempt to develop informal, small-group organization in which private arrangements to help each other out are made among neighbours, in 2s,

3s, or 4s. But these solely interpersonal arrangements are undependable and open to manipulation for anti-social and competitive as well as for mutually protective ends. A number of isolates is left over. The total face group is incapable, except defensively, of acting as a socially responsible whole, since not even private allegiances are owed outside the small informal groups. These in turn are without responsible autonomy; the absence of institutionalized mutual obilgation means that there are no statutory group tasks, and each individual can be held ultimately responsible only for clearing his own length. Internal "rows" the more easily break up the informal "coalitions," whose morale tends to be of the clique type.

Examples were, however, given to the writers of stable groups who stuck to each other and worked well over long periods. One informant said of these: "Here things are more like the old times in the pit." Groups of this kind were envied and also criticized for being "too close." They appeared sometimes to be held together by a natural leader, and at others to be made up of individuals of generally good personality. Most informants were agreed that there was a tendency for the extremes to sort themselves out; there were "good" and "bad" faces as well as "good" and "bad" cliques within a particular face aggregate. But all this happened as it might. There was no support from the system.

Isolates, it appears, are either individualists—who "won't even share timber"—or men with bad reputations, with whom others refuse to work. Amongst these are the unconscientious—who "won't help out at the end of a shift" and who are frequently absent—and the helpless—who "cannot learn to look after themselves under bad conditions." Others, whose stamina is deficient (whether through age, illness, or neurosis) and whose lengths are often uncleared in consequence, are dropped from the informal groups.

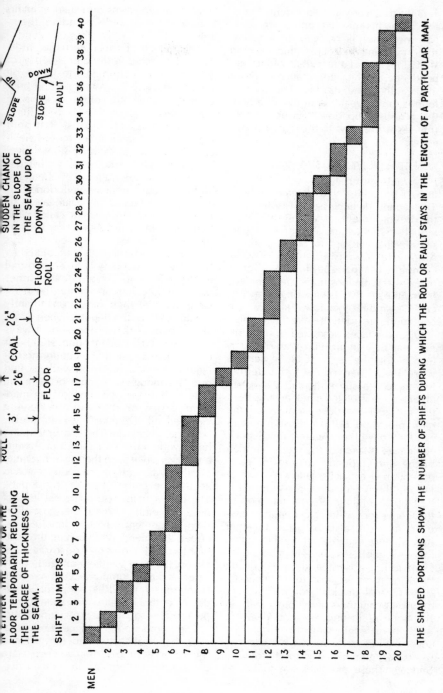

Figure 4

THE COURSE OF A ROLL OR FAULT ACROSS A LONGWALL FACE

Only to a very limited extent, therefore, does his informal group organization meet the filler's need for a secure role in a primary group within his own shift. In view of the extent of his dependence on the performance of those in the other 2 shifts, his need for this foundation is greater than that of any of the other occupational groups, while the resources available to him are fewer.

REACTIVE INDIVIDUALISM

His small group failing, the filler is thrown on to himself and against others. The second defence against isolation is the development of a reactive individualism, in which a reserve of personal secrecy is apt to be maintained. Among his own shift mates there is competitive intrigue for the better places—middle positions are avoided; from these "it is a long way to creep"—and for jobs in workings where conditions are good there is a scramble.

On some faces described to the writers, fear of victimization was rife, particularly in the form of being sent to work in a "bad place"; the deputy being more easily turned into a persecutor in view of the guilt arising from the intrigue and deception which the men practised both against him and against each other. Against the deputy, advantage is taken of the scope afforded in the underground situation for petty deception over such matters as time of leaving the pit, or the "measure that is sent up" (amounts of coal filled on to the conveyor). With the deputy, however, men are also prepared to enter into alliance against each other, often for very good reasons—to stop mates from going absent and by so doing throwing more work on to the others.

As regards outside groups, practices of bribing members of the other shifts in the hope of getting a "good deal" in one's own length were mentioned by several informants. Tobacco is taken to the cutter; gummers are stood a pint on Sunday. These practices are to be regarded as symptoms of a state of affairs rather than as widespread in themselves.

The effect of this defensive individualism is to reduce the sense of secure identification in the larger pit collectivity, which was the second principle on which the older equilibrium was based.

Nowhere is the mistrust that shift mates have of each other more in evidence than in controversies over bye-work "slipping off the note." On what is referred to as the "big note" is entered all the contract and bye-work done during the week by the shift aggregate. This note is issued to one man called "the number man" since he is identifed by his check-number. In no sense is this individual a representative appointed by his mates. Only rarely is he an informal leader. Customarily he is a "corner man," whose length adjoins the main gate, i.e., the man most conveniently within reach of the deputy. When asked about bye-work he does not always know what has been done at the far ends of the face and he is under no obligation to stop his own work to find out. But though a number of men will grouse about their pay being short, mentioning this or that item as having "slipped off the note," very few ever bother to check up. There are men who have worked on a face for 3 or 4 years and never once seen their own big note. Yet these are among the more ready to accuse the corner man or the deputy. The corner man is suspected at least of never forgetting to make the most of his own assignments. To the deputy is ascribed the intention of keeping the costs of his district down. Conspiracy between the two is often alleged. Only when a major rumpus occurs are such suspicions put to the test, but showdowns of this kind are avoided as apt to peter out in squabbles proving nothing.

The competition, intrigue, unwillingness to put allegations to the test and the reserve of personal secrecy, are parts of one pattern. Whatever their personal wishes, men feel under pressure to be out for themselves, since the social structure in which they work denies them membership in any group that can legitimize interdependence. In this respect reactive individualism makes a basic interpretation of the social structure of the filling shift and is the only form of authorized behaviour.

MUTUAL SCAPEGOATING

Fillers almost never see those who work on the "back shifts," and this absence of contact gives full scope for mutual and irresponsible scapegoating. When there is a crisis, and the filling shift is unable to fill off, the "buck" is passed to the other shifts—or vice versa if disorganization has occurred elsewhere. It is frequently also passed to the deputy, who is blamed for not finding substitutes, and to repair men, brought in, but too old to stand the pace.

For these to pass the buck back to the fillers is fruitless. As they do not exist as a responsible whole, they, as a group, are not there to take the blame, and the individual filler can always exempt himself. Since bad conditions and bad work interact so closely, it is usually difficult to pin blame specifically. Mutual scapegoating is a self-perpetuating system, in which nothing is resolved and no one feels guilty. For all concerned to remain in collusion with such a system is a defense which allows each to make his "anonymous contribution" to the "group mentality,"[8] which sabotages both the goal of cycle productivity and the needs of the individual for a membership in a satisfying work-group. So far as this pattern obtains, all strike at each other in a mock war in which no one is hurt yet all suffer.

This defence can also be seen as a "back-handed" attempt to recover the supportive unity lost through reactive individualism in a way that is consistent with it. For all to be "in the bad" together is at least a way of being together. If one's contribution to a group is to help carry the badness of others,

the group's contribution to oneself is to allow one to leave some of one's own badness in the group by being granted, for example, the privilege of withdrawal so that one's absence is sanctioned on a fair share of occasions. This "formula" provides a workable scheme since the tacit agreement is only too plausibly maintained that the badness both of the group and of the individual are exclusively effects of the system which the group is compelled to operate without having power to change, i.e., these effects are regarded as "induced" rather than also as "own" forces. The group and the individual can therefore deny and get rid of their own badness by ascribing it to the system. The good of the group becomes its power to preserve the good of individual members by limiting the degree of their exposure to the bad system. The alternative would be constructive limitation of its real deficiencies so that it might be operated with more productive results and a higher degree of mutual satisfaction.

Not that the system is felt as entirely bad since it is the means by which a living is earned. Moreover, under present conditions this living is a good one, both in terms of wages and of community status. But the benefits which these "goods" bring are not realized in the work activities of the group. They lie outside the work system. which is tolerated as a means to external ends rather than accepted also as an end in itself, worthy of wholehearted pursuit in virtue of the internal satisfactions it affords. When these different aspects of the matter are put together the expectation emerges of a balance being struck which would allow things to tick over, though with a degree of social illness costly alike to productivity and to personal well-being. This expectation accords with reality.

SELF-COMPENSATORY ABSENTEEISM

Withdrawal is the fourth form of defense, complementing mutual scapegoating, and absenteeism is to be regarded as a recognized social technique within this pattern. For example, one filler, returning from his week's holiday with pay, complained that the first two shifts had "knocked it all out of him." The gummings had been left in. His coal was solid. He had had the air-pick on all day. "I've tried cursing 'em but it's no use, and pleading with 'em but it's no use. I'll take a day off for this."

When conditions on a face deteriorate, especially in ways that are predictable, absenteeism among fillers sometimes piles up to a point where the remainder have to stay down an extra 2 or 3 hours in order to clear the face. Should this situation repeat itself for more than a day or two, those coming on shift often meet at the pit-head baths before presenting themselves for work. If less than a certain number arrive, all go home.

Absenteeism of this self-compensatory type, though carried out as an act of aggrieved defiance against a system, felt in these circumstances as persecutory, is an attempt on the part of the individual to prolong his work life at the coalface. For without the respite of occasional absences, he feels that he would soon become unable to carry on. In view of the accentuated differences both in wages and in status between face workers and repair, haulage, or surface personnel, the goal of remaining at the coal-face for as long as possible would appear to operate as a powerful motivational force in determining the behaviour of the ordinary face-worker.

The following is some of the material obtained in interviews and discussions. Fear of being "too old for the face at 40," or even 35, was a frequently expressed anxiety, made more acute by personal experience of the painful tensions in miners' families, where a father relegated to the surface at £5 19s. 3d. a week must face a son, still in his early 20s, earning more than twice this wage. Instances were reported of quarrels between brothers, among whom long-standing but mild neurotic rivalries had

existed, that severely disturbed the larger family when the older, through sickness, often of a psycho-somatic kind, had been forced to leave the face. In the culture of the mining family a face-worker husband is the object of special care on the part of his wife. There were men who felt that the privilege of this care, the emotional need for which was now stronger, was no longer merited once their elite position had been forfeited and their potency as breadwinners reduced. The dilemma of this situation is that fear of the loss of this care and acceptance of its continuing offer are both unbearable.

Absenteeism of this self-compensatory type is a socially structured activity operated in accordance with a complex code that governs both the occasions and amounts regarded as permissible. It is a psycho-social defence motivated by the wish to remain at the coal-face, and is a species of "institutional" conduct with a functional role in the total social system in which the longwall method plays a central part.

This, and the other 3 defences discussed, play a dynamically interrelated part in forming the culture[9] of the work group, though naturally the intensity to which the pattern is present varies widely, and there are faces where the group atmosphere remains for long periods relatively immune from these influences. These are apt, however, to be "fair-weather" faces.

The danger is that habituation to working in a bad system has the compensation of enabling those concerned to leave too much both of their own and of their group's "badness" in the system. It then ties them to it through the fact that it does this, despite their hatred of it. As well as its faults, it is their own hatred that they hate in the system—and there is usually stubborn refusal to recognize such projections in work- no less than in therapy-groups. A characteristic of faces with a bad group atmosphere is the protesting yet excited collusion of all concerned with the state of affairs.

This is in contrast to the more independently critical and realistic attitude of those in groups where the pattern is less complete and less intense.

VII
SOME PROBLEMS OF THE PREPARATION SHIFTS

THE ABSENCE OF AUTHORITY IN THE CUTTING TEAM

As it is on this preparation group—containing the front and back man on the cutter and the 4 gummers—that the filling shift is most specially dependent, there is special need for social organization to be sound at this point. But the cutting team does not exist officially as a group, since the cutters are on their own note, responsible for, and paid for, their cutting alone. The gummers are not under their authority, and no one except the deputy can take responsibility for any tendency they may have to leave some or all of the gummings in, in certain stints, as they traverse the face. As they are on day wage, they have nothing to lose unless they go too far—so, at least, the fillers feel in their bitterness on this score.

As the lowest paid and lowest prestige group on the face, doing the least skilled task, gummers are both an outcast and scapegoated group. Their work is arduous, dangerous, dusty—and awkward. Hostility in them towards "the system" and towards other face workers is almost inevitable and is most easily displaced on to the fillers, whom they never see but can severely annoy—not necessarily with conscious malice—by leaving in some of the gummings under conditions of fatigue or difficulty. A system that puts this power of interference into the hands of a potentially disgruntled, scapegoated group, with no effective social means of controlling it, fosters the hostile tendencies almost inevitably present. These difficulties are increased by the fact, among all face workers, status differences are greatest between cutters

and gummers and by the fact that the cutters are a closed pair. Tensions within this ambiguously organized group are apt to be sharp.

There are, of course, instances where effective leadership is exercised over the gummers by the front man, and some of these were quoted by informants. But it was stressed at the same time that management could hold the cutters responsible only for the cut, and that to exercise detailed supervision was an impossible task for a deputy, especially on "back shifts" where his territory of responsibility is apt to be more extensive than on day shift. In shift groups where a good spirit of co-operation obtains, the belt-breakers are often willing to help out the gummers. It was suggested that fewer lapses occurred when these interchanges took place. But the pattern of the cutting shift works against such co-operation, consisting, as it does, of 4 different categories of workers successively traversing the face at their own separately institutionalized component tasks, with no overall goal to bind them together and no functionally defined responsibilities to each other.

So closely tied, however, are the cutting and gumming operations that they cannot in practice be treated as separate. Hence arises the dilemma of the team that is at the same time not a team. Given a work system with a different type of culture there might be no problem, but given longwall separatism there would appear to be no solution—until new conceptions of relationship emerge.

Some instances were quoted of gummers being paid by the front man, who could therefore be penalized for gummings left in by having money stopped out of his contract. But it was pointed out that this sanction could be applied only in cases of the grossest kind which the deputy would in any case pick up, and that it tended to place cutters in the hands of their gummers. This suggests that the persistence or resuscitation of the old forms of contract are not in themselves enough to restore responsible autonomy.

THE SPLIT-OFF POSITION OF THE INTER-DEPENDENT PAIRS

Superficially, borers, belt-builders, and belt-breakers look like pair structures that echo those of pre-mechanized days. But whereas the pairs of hand-got coal-getting had craft status and an artisan type of independence in working their own face, with the satisfaction of seeing through the whole coal-getting job, these longwall pairs are restricted to work tasks of a singularly narrow component character.

The borers are off by themselves; and as regards the belt workers, since breakers and builders are on different shifts, neither can feel the satisfaction of accepting responsibility for the conveyor system as a whole.

The most fractionated tasks are therefore performed by those restricted to the narrowest relations. It would be difficult to imagine a situation in which they were more completely split off from any sense of belonging to a shift or total production group. But they are at least responsible to each other and are based on a stable, if narrow, relationship.

THE SOCIAL VIABILITY OF THE RIPPING TEAM

By contrast, the ripping team is a well-organized primary work group of 7 or 8 with an intelligible total task for which it carries complete responsibility. Rippers are frequently referred to by others as a "good crowd" who seldom "go absent on each other." Pride of craft is considerable. A main ripper and—usually—individuals of very varying experience compose the group, but it appears to manage its internal relationships without status difficulties. Here, responsible autonomy persists.

Unfortunately, like the other facework groups, it is a group by itself and there is as a result no transfer of its more stable morale to other groups in the sys-

tem. Working, as it does, in the main and side gates, it is felt to be a closed group very much apart from the main interaction between the preparation and filling operations carried out in the face itself.

In all essential respects the ripping team represents a survival of the hand-got past in the mechanical present. For the gates in which ripping parties of varying sizes operate are, as it were, their own "stalls", continuously and autonomously worked. All relevant operations are carried out within the group which completes them within the compass of one shift. Rippers have escaped from, rather than become part of, the longwall system, retaining intact their total task, their multiple skills, their artisan independence, and their small group organization. They work in the gates. Though part of the total layout, gates are not like a longwall face. In the gates the scale of the task remains small; the spatio-temporal structure is simple, and methods are unmechanized. Changes consequent on the introduction of power-driven tools, or of steel replacing wood, have been assimilated without essential re-structuring.

In the face, it was the introduction of machines (still foreign to the gates) that caused the appearance of a new order, changing the scale to mass production and bringing fractionation of tasks, extension of sequence, role and shift segregation, small group disorganization and inter-group dependence. In the gates the old order continues in a special setting. To compare the two one needs only to step from gates to face. Those in the face once fared as well as those in the gates.

VIII
CONCLUSIONS

The fact that the desperate economic incentives of the between-war period no longer operate means a greater intolerance of unsatisfying or difficult working conditions, or systems of organization, among miners, even though they may not always be clear as to the exact nature of the resentment or hostility which they often appear to feel. The persistence of socially ineffective structures at the coal-face is likely to be a major factor in preventing a rise of morale, in discouraging recruitment, and in increasing labour turnover.

The innovations in social organization of face-work groups, which have begun to appear, and the success of some of these developments, suggest that the organizational changes brought about by nationalization provide a not inappropriate opportunity for the experimental working through of problems of the types which have been indicated. It can certainly be said with some confidence that within the industry there exist the necessary resources and creativity to allow widespread constructive developments to take place.

As regards the longwall system, the first need is for systematic study and evaluation of the changes so far tried.[10] It seems to the present writers, however, that a qualitative change will have to be effected in the general character of the method, so that a social as well as a technological whole can come into existence. Only if this is achieved can the relationships of the cycle work-group be successfully integrated and a new social balance be created.

The immediate problems are to develop formal small-group organization on the filling shift and to work out an acceptable solution to the authority questions in the cutting team. But it is difficult to see how these problems can be solved effectively without restoring responsible autonomy to primary groups throughout the system and ensuring that each of these groups has a satisfying sub-whole as its work task, and some scope for flexibility in work-pace. Only if this is done will the stress of the deputy's role be reduced and his task of maintaining the cycle receive spontaneous support from the primary work group.

It is likely that any attempts in this direction would require to take advantage of the recent trend of training face-workers for more than one role, so that interchangeability of tasks would be possible within work teams. Moreover, the problem of shift segregation will not be overcome until the situation is altered in which one large group is permanently organised round the day shift and the others round the back shifts. Some interchange between roles in preparation and filling tasks would seem worth consideration. Once preparation workers and fillers could experience each other's situations, mutual understanding and tolerance would be likely to increase.

It is to be borne in mind that developments in room-and-pillar methods appear to be stressing the value of the strongly-knit primary work-group and that the most recent advances in mechanization, such as power loaders or strippers, both require work teams of this kind.

NOTES

1. D. E. Dickson, "The Morbid Miner," *Edin. Med. J.,* 1936, p. 696.

2. J. L. Halliday, *Psychosocial Medicine: A Study of the Sick Society* (London: Heinemann, 1949).

3. J. N. Morris, "Coal Miners," *Lancet,* Vol. II, 1947, p. 341.

4. Hand-got methods contained a number of variants, but discussion of these is beyond present scope.

5. W. R. Bion, "Experiences in Groups, III," *Human Relations,* Vol. II, No. 1, January, 1949, pp. 13-22.

6. Halliday, *op. cit.*

7. The procedure followed both in the text and in *Figures 1* and *2* and *Table I* has been to build up a model of the system in terms of the experience of a group of faces similarly run and well known at first hand. What follows is therefore an account of one version of the system, though the version is a common one. Faces exist that are twice as long as that given. In thick seams these may require 40-50 fillers alone (even more), apart

altogether from other personnel. In thin seams with high gates more than twice the number of rippers given may be employed, 8 or more on the main gate and some 6-4 on the side gates respectively. On shorter faces there may be only one borer and at least one gummer. Under some conditions packing and drawing-off are separated from belt-work, and loading-point personnel are included as face workers. There are differences in nomenclature in different areas, e.g., "dinters" for "rippers". Variations arise partly from differences in natural conditions (thickness of seam, hardness of coal, type of roof and floor, etc.), partly from preferences in the matter of lay-out, and partly from the amount and character of the equipment available or judged necessary. Though conveyor serviced, quite a long face may be hand-got if the coal is soft; alternatively, two cutting units may be employed if it is hard and the face exceptionally long. Belts are of several varieties ("floor", "plate", "top", etc.). Where the seam is thick enough to eliminate ripping an approximation may be made to a two-shift system. Productivity varies widely in accordance with these differences, as does smoothness of functioning

and the degree of stress experienced. Nevertheless, all are versions of one method. The basic pattern is the same.

8. Bion, *op. cit.*

9. The concept of "culture" as a psycho-social technique developed by a group in a structurally determined situation has been outlined by Trist, "Culture as a Psycho-Social Process", contributed to a symposium on The Concept of Culture, British Association, Section (H), Anthropology and Archeology, Birmingham Meeting, 1950. This viewpoint develops that of Curle, and Curle and Trist, "Transitional Communities and Social Re-connection", *Human Relations,* Vol. I, No. 1, pp. 42-68, and No. 2, pp. 240-288; and is akin to that of Ruesch, "Experiments in Psychotherapy, II: Individual Social Techniques", *The Journal of Social Psychology,* 1949, 29, 3-28; and Ruesch and Bateson, "Structure and Process in Social Relations", *Psychiatry,* 1949, Vol. XII, 2, pp. 105-124.

10. One of·the most interesting of these is "An Experiment in Continuous Longwall Mining at Bolsover Colliery", W. V. Sheppard, The Institution of Mining Engineers, Annual General Meeting, Jan. 1951.

23. Job Satisfaction Reconsidered*

WALTER R. NORD

Job satisfaction has been a favorite topic of American organizational psychologists. Locke (1976) estimated that by 1972, 3,350 articles (or dissertations) had been written on the subject. As a result of this voluminous research, many aspects of work life and job satisfaction have been thoroughly studied. However, despite the magnitude of effort, some of the most interesting characteristics of the existing research are revealed

not by the results of what has been studied but by an examination of the topics that have gone unanalyzed.

A number of major deficiencies in our study of job satisfaction stem from assumptions we have made about society, people, and organizations. One purpose of this paper is to examine these assumptions and the omissions in our work for which they appear to be responsible. If this effort is successful, it

Source: From *American Psychologist,* vol. 32 (December 1977), pp. 1026-35. Copyright © 1977 by the American Psychological Association. Reprinted by permission. Reference notes combined.

will stimulate the development of a more explicit and more adequate set of underlying assumptions and will expand the scope of approaches to job satisfaction.

COMMON ASSUMPTIONS ABOUT JOB SATISFACTION

A fairly common set of assumptions, many of which are latent, underlies and shapes our knowledge about job satisfaction.

DESIRABILITY OF ECONOMIC COMPETITION, GROWTH, AND UTILITARIANISM

Most students of job satisfaction have taken the values of economic competition, growth, and utilitarianism as givens and have ignored the limitations those values have upon the ability of organizations to provide satisfying work. However, if organizations are "open systems," the impact of the economic ideology of the society in which organizations exist can be substantial, because this ideology functions to legitimate specific roles for organizations and it induces certain criteria for organizational decisions. For example, in our society, many organizations are designed and managed to make a profit for their owners. As a result, economic logic often dominates all other considerations. As Schumacher (1973) observed:

> Economics plays a central role in shaping the activities of the modern world, inasmuch as it supplies the criteria of what is "economic" and what is "uneconomic," and there is no other set of criteria that exercises a greater influence over the actions of individuals and groups as well as over those of government. (p. 40) . . . In the current vocabulary of condemnation there are few words as final and conclusive as the word "uneconomic." (p. 41)

Besides, economic criteria that guide organizational decision makers are easily quantified. As Gross's (1968) phrase *number magic* suggests, objectives and actions that are easily quantified tend to achieve dominance over objectives and actions that are hard to quantify. Since job satisfaction is difficult to measure, its proponents seldom advocate it at the expense of economic criteria.

Again, economic growth, technological progress, and the satisfaction of consumer demands are accepted as desirable and legitimate goals. When, at a practical level, these ends conflict with gains in job satisfaction, seldom does the latter win out.

In short, organizational decision makers often relegate job satisfaction to a secondary role in relation to economic factors. And researchers in the field of job satisfaction have, for the most part, accepted management's hierarchy. Only rarely have psychologists studied, much less recommended, changes that would, in the long run, increase job satisfaction at the expense of the traditional economic criteria of organizational performance.

WORK AS A CENTRAL INTEREST IN LIFE

Typically, we have assumed that work is and/or ought to be a central life interest. Consistent with this assumption, much of our research has sought ways to promote job involvement. However, there is a growing body of support (Goldthorpe, 1966; Hulin & Blood, 1968; Tausky, 1969; Turner & Lawrence, 1965) for a contradictory view. Individuals do not seek more involving work. In fact, Fein (1976) reported that 85 percent of the work force rejects the notion that work can be an end in itself. Moreover, there is no more reason to suggest that work *ought* to be a central life interest than to assume the opposite. In fact, as Oates's (1971) concept of the workaholic implies, involvement in work is by no means a pure "good." The human and social costs incurred when individuals obtain an overwhelming component of their self-identity from their work can be substantial.

HUMAN NATURE AS INDIVIDUALISTIC

For the most part, modern approaches

to job satisfaction are based upon assumptions about the individualistic nature and goals of human development. The dominance of the individualistic perspective appears to be due more to the psychological roots of the researchers and the prevailing economic and political ideology than to a reasoned decision based on evidence. Other ideologies (e.g., cooperative, socialist) and research rooted in other disciplines (e.g., sociology) could lead to quite different (e.g., collectivistic) perspectives regarding job satisfaction.

Acceptance of individualism has helped to shape our discipline. For example, consider our treatment of independence and cooperation. We have stressed individual achievement, recognition, and productivity. While we have recognized interdependence among people as a necessity for achieving organizational goals, human cooperation itself has seldom been considered as a worthy goal. Interdependence among people has been viewed more as a necessary cost of achieving other goals. Rarely has human cooperation been considered as a direct source of job satisfaction.

SHARED, SUPERORDINATE GOALS

We have focused on nonzero-sum conflict and assumed that organizational participants seek similar goals. While a number of goals are shared, some goals are more commonly held than others. Thus, as long as organizations do not have enough resources to satisfy the wants of all constituents, zero-sum conflict among competing interests will occur. As a result, organizational participants are in constant struggle with each other and they use a number of tactics—manipulation, dishonesty, even violence—to satisfy their own interests. To the degree that our approaches to job satisfaction have underplayed the importance of zero-sum conflict, they have underestimated many problems in making organizations pleasant places in which to be.

MAINTENANCE OF THE EXISTING DISTRIBUTION OF POWER

Organizational psychologists have taken the existing distribution of power, which gives certain individuals the right to determine fundamental organizational goals and procedures, as given. Seldom have students of job satisfaction considered the possibility that improvements in the quality of work life might be facilitated by new institutional arrangements that would permit lower level participants to affect basic goals and policies. Consequently, possibilities for improving job satisfaction by changing the existing distribution of power have been ignored.

Our failure to consider alternate distributions of power is linked to what Ellerman (1975) labeled the "myth of the ownership of the firm." We have assumed that the ownership of capital conveys the right to govern economic enterprises and hence gives the owners the right to control significant aspects of the lives of employees. We have overlooked what Dahl (1970) and Pateman (1975) have described as a serious inconsistency between relatively authoritarian work organizations and a democratic society. In the lives of many people, significant personal contingencies are controlled by organizations; organizations have powerful effects on where people live, when they sleep, when they eat, when and whether they work, and what they do at work and even after work. As Pateman (1975) observed, the ability to influence these aspects of one's existence is a necessary condition of a democratic society. Not only might alternative systems of organizational control have positive consequences for job satisfaction and other aspects of a person's life, but they are necessary for a truly democratic society. By accepting the legitimacy of the existing distribution of power, students of job satisfaction have ignored matters of importance to the quality of work life and to the democratic character of our society.

IDEOLOGICAL CONSERVATISM

We have tended to accept the ideologies of the modern corporation leaders. Consequently, I believe Heilbroner's (1964) attack on modern business ideology is applicable to us as well. Heilbroner (1964) observed:

What is it, in the end, that deprives the business ideology of the quality of inspiration it seeks? In part, of course, it is the more or less transparent defense of privilege masquerading as philosophy, the search for sanction cloaked as a search for truth, the little evasions and whitewashings that cheapen what purports to be a fearless confrontation of great issues. And .yet, these are only surface flaws. At its core, the business ideology as a spiritual creed or as an historic beacon is vitiated by something that is missing—I cannot but think fatally missing—from its deepest conception. What it lacks is a grandiose image of society, a projection of human possibilities cast in a larger mold than is offered by today's institutions. (p. 35)

SUMMARY

We have approached job satisfaction without examining the influence of prevailing social, political, and economic values on the nature of work and work life. We may have overemphasized the individualistic as opposed to the cooperative potential of human beings. Furthermore, by ignoring the role of competing interests and conflicts in organizations, we have overlooked the limitations that scarce resources and the struggle for control of resources place on the ability of organizations to provide job satisfaction. Finally, our research has a management bias and a latent conservatism.

DEFICIENCIES OF CURRENT APPROACHES TO JOB SATISFACTION

To the degree that the assumptions discussed in the first section portray contemporary views on job satisfaction accurately, our current approaches are vulnerable to a number of crucial omis-

sions and distortions that render them both incomplete and unrealistic.

1. We have limited ourselves to an incomplete and biased set of dependent variables.
2. We have failed to recognize that organizations often have no incentives for experimenting with ways of increasing job satisfaction; in fact, they have good reasons for maintaining the present order.
3. We have failed to consider that job satisfaction is to some degree based on the quality of the product produced.
4. We have failed to give sufficient attention to such basic satisfactions as income, job security, treatment by one's boss, and the like.
5. We have failed to give sufficient attention to the relationship of power and control to job satisfaction and alienation.

BIASED AND LIMITED CHOICE OF DEPENDENT VARIABLES

The assumptions of shared goals and the acceptance of the current distribution of power and prevailing choices among competing goals have affected our selection of dependent variables. Basically, the goals of management, including reducing turnover and absenteeism, increasing productivity and work-involvement, and overcoming "resistance to change," are among the dependent variables we have studied most frequently.

The biased choice of a particular set of dependent variables has important consequences for the substance of research on job satisfaction. For example, if such outcomes as productivity or work involvement are taken as dependent variables, then it is likely that certain "causal" variables (e.g., pay or leadership) that influence them will be discovered. Collectively, the causal variables found to affect the dependent variables we choose to study become the essence of our discipline. Future research is designed to refine our knowledge on these topics; other independent variables remain unincorporated into our research and our knowledge. If, instead of productivity, our major de-

pendent variables were self-actualization, organizational democracy,
feelings of self-control and self-worth,
equity and justice, the essence of our
knowledge would be different. Our
major independent variables might include sources of managerial legitimacy,
alternative forms of ownership, and the
nature of the products produced.

The frequent choice of job satisfaction as a dependent variable appears to
be an exception to the managerial bias
in organizational psychology, because
the study of job satisfaction appears to
take the positive experiences of lower
level organizational members as major
goals. However, given the tendency to
confine interest in job satisfaction to
cases in which satisfaction and productivity go together, the importance of this
exception is reduced. Again, the emphasis on job involvement as a major
component of job satisfaction is a case
in point. Despite its humanistic conno-
tations, one outcome of work that is
psychologically involving is that the
worker may work harder and longer at
no apparent direct cost to management.
However, as suggested earlier, the
highly involved worker, his or her family, and society at large are not necessarily better off. The effects of involving
work on such outcomes as total life
satisfaction, the quality of family life,
and the enjoyment of leisure activities
have gone unstudied.

BARRIERS TO SATISFYING JOBS

Consider the incentives to enrich jobs.
For example, how does the payoff matrix appear to a manager who is considering enrichment of the work of his or
her subordinates? Generally speaking,
the payoffs for maintaining the status
quo are adequate and fairly certain; the
rewards for innovating are unknown
and their likelihood of occurrence is
uncertain. The redesign is often costly in
terms of energy, time, and material resources. In addition to being expensive,
the redesign of jobs often introduces
uncertainty.

A variety of elements contribute to
this uncertainty. First, it is unclear
whether employees really want "enriched" work. Moreover, adverse reaction of unions and technical problems
in redesign can be anticipated. Finally,
it is by no means certain that the redesign of work will either increase job
satisfaction or improve the effectiveness
or profitability of the organization. In
fact, Fein (1976) came to some very
negative conclusions on this matter:

> Attempts to enrich work so that it becomes
> meaningful to most workers have low pos-
> sibility of success. Production technology
> in the advanced industrialized countries
> has reduced the need for skilled craftsmen
> in the production process, with the bulk of
> work highly mechanized and routinized,
> requiring low skills and limited judgments.
> These jobs cannot be meaningfully en-
> riched. The production process cannot be
> reversed without tremendously increasing
> product costs, which no one would toler-
> ate. Proposals that jobs be enriched with
> additional responsibilities and skills are
> made through sheer ignorance of the pro-
> duction process. (p. 523)

Thus, job enrichment is a very risky venture to managers in many existing organizations.

As a second example, consider debureaucratization, about which Perrow
(1972) wrote,

> In my judgement, most organizations are,
> and will continue to be, moderately
> routine in terms of the tasks of most of the
> salaried and hourly work force. They are
> neither so routine as to permit full automa-
> tion nor so non-routine as to permit the
> decentralization of ends and democ-
> racy. . . . If moderate routineness continues
> to characterize almost all large organiza-
> tions in our society and most of the small
> ones, bureaucracy, with its centralized
> power in the hands of a few, will remain
> the dominant mode of organization. The
> only change will be that those few will
> command even greater resources and in-
> creasing political, social, and economic
> power. (p. 175)

Moreover, bureaucratic structures and
routine jobs have not been rendered obsolete by turbulent environments, as

many thought they would be. Consumer demands for inexpensive material goods and services force organizations to establish routine operations and to buffer them from sources of uncertainty. Technological advances in data processing and communications permit and encourage such systematization.

In fact, rather than discourage routinization, many current environmental pressures actually foster it. For example, selection, promotion, safety standards, product quality, production processes, and other internal functions of the organization have been increasingly subject to public scrutiny. As a result of government regulations, pressure groups, and legal actions, management is motivated to develop routines and procedures that are defensible to the public as well as in the courts.

If widespread gains in job satisfaction depend on job enrichment and debureaucratization, then organizations as they currently exist face major problems in attempting to provide satisfying work. Organizational survival, protection from environmental demands, satisfaction of consumer demands, and the contingencies faced by managers within organizations are, to a substantial degree, in conflict with the necessary innovations.

OMISSION OF ALTERNATIVE SOURCES
OF INTRINSIC SATISFACTION

Our assumptions about people and work have led us to view traditional craft work as a model of a satisfying job. However, these same assumptions, when coupled with our acceptance of management's goals, have induced us to emphasize certain aspects of traditional craftsmanship and to ignore others. In particular, we have considered mainly those aspects of craftsmanship related to the act of production and ignored the role of the product itself. To what degree is job satisfaction limited when a worker is called upon to use inferior materials to produce a poor product that, even when it works, serves merely peripheral human needs?

Although the influence of product quality upon job satisfaction has seldom been taken as problematic, there is some evidence that it is an important factor. Turner and Miclette (1962) reported that assembly workers attached great importance to their role in producing a needed, high-quality product. Similarly, Nord (1968) reported that furniture assemblers voiced strong dissatisfaction over their perceptions that management was "cheapening" the product. Moreover, the fact that some products and processes are actually harmful to potential users or to third parties is also a source of worker dissatisfaction. Terkel (1972) and Heilbroner et al. (1973) have reported that many employees are frustrated by the knowledge that their outputs are of trivial importance and may be dangerous to the user.

While individualistic models and a focus on management's goals encourage us to emphasize the act of production, a complete approach to job satisfaction must consider other aspects of work. As Marx pointed out, production affects the social relationships among human beings. Work relates *producers* to *users*, not just *producers* to *producers*.[1] A complete view of job satisfaction must be concerned with producer-user and producer-third-party relationships.

In addition to ignoring the influence of the nature of the product on job satisfaction, we have overlooked other sources of satisfaction that are part of the work *situation* as opposed to the work itself. For example, Maccoby

1. Some studies on job enrichment (Herzberg, 1968) have reported that having operatives handle consumer contacts directly and personally resulted in significant improvements in productivity and satisfaction. These results are usually attributed to feelings of increased responsibility of achievement as a result of changes in the act of production. However, they also could be due to the new nature of the relationship between the producer and user.

350 WALTER R. NORD

(1975) noted that union activity and social relationships provide satisfaction for many individuals. It is important to recognize that such things as union activities have the potential to provide all of Herzberg's (1968) "satisfiers." They are part of the total work situation but are usually ignored when management's goals are taken as the point of departure.

UNDEREMPHASIS ON EXTRINSIC SOURCES OF JOB SATISFACTION

Most theorists have assumed that satisfaction of the so-called "lower level" needs is necessary before intrinsic factors become important. Given this assumption and the fact that typically between 6 percent and 8 percent of the work force is unemployed and the earnings of several million others are so low that they must live below officially defined poverty levels, it is surprising that extrinsic sources of satisfaction have received so little attention recently in organizational psychology. There is a great deal of support for the proposition that money, job security, treatment by one's boss, and other such traditional factors are extremely important to a high percentage of American workers. A number of writers have documented the importance of economic aspects of work for many contemporary workers. Wool (1973) observed that many individuals (e.g., the 20 million workers holding nonfarm jobs that pay under $2.50 per hour) do not have their lower level needs satisfied. Tausky (1969) observed that "the economic payoff from work may frequently be the main focus of concern rather than rewards stemming from prestige or intrinsic content of work" (pp. 54-55). Similarly, Fein (1976) concluded, "What is really demeaning about low level skill jobs is that workers in these jobs cannot earn enough to achieve a level of living to which they aspire" (p. 523).

Even when the so-called basic needs are satisfied, economic aspects of work may still be crucial, because satisfaction with one's economic status is a social or relative phenomenon. As Jencks (1972) noted, the cost of living is not just the cost of buying a fixed set of goods and services: "It is the cost of participating in a social system. The cost of participating depends in large part on how much other people habitually spend to participate" (p. 5). Wool (1973) made a similar point:

One fallacy in the Maslow-Herzberg model of worker aspirations, as a guide to behavior, lies in its inherently static premises. Even though individual earnings and family incomes have increased steadily over the decades, the great majority of American workers certainly do not consider themselves as "affluent," when they relate their spendable income to their spending needs, for what they now consider an acceptable standard of living. (p. 42)

Moreover, even if pay is relatively high, job security is still a relevant concern for many individuals. Tausky (1969) observed that, for many people, crucial aspects of self-esteem are still derived from simply holding a job. General economic cycles, seasonal cycles, changes in consumer demands, plant relocation, and even the whims of employers and union leaders threaten the jobs of many workers. Some individuals, particularly older ones, members of minority groups, and people without critical skills, are vulnerable to periodic and often prolonged unemployment.

Foy and Gordon (1976) argued that the high unemployment tolerated in the United States has slowed innovations designed to increase worker satisfaction. Lower rates of unemployment in such nations as Sweden and Great Britain appear to have induced employers to make work life more satisfying. Foy and Gordon (1976) suggested that job security "on both a national and a company basis" (p. 82) is a precondition for greater worker participation in decisions and other changes in work.

Finally, other basic needs are still

threatened in many work situations. Most notably, physical safety is by no means assured. Not only do accidents threaten the short-term well-being of people, but noise, fumes, and other emissions from production processes threaten long-term health. In addition, it is probable that long-term health is also impaired by work-induced stress.

In sum, the so-called lower level needs and extrinsic sources of satisfaction are still important for many workers. In light of this fact, Strauss's (1963) charge that middle-class social scientists have inaccurately attributed certain needs to workers tells only half the story; the other half involves motives we *have failed* to attribute to others.

OMISSION OF THE POWERLESSNESS → ALIENATION HYPOTHESIS

While it is commonly acknowledged that organizational psychologists have not treated power adequately, little has been made of the fact that the concept of alienation has also been ignored. Greater attention to both of these concepts would have important effects on the job satisfaction literature because it would force a confrontation between the meaningless work → job dissatisfaction hypothesis and the powerlessness → alienation hypothesis.

The psychological literature has been dominated by the belief that meaningless work → dissatisfaction; it has been almost unaffected by the significant body of knowledge supporting the powerlessness → alienation hypothesis. As Israel (1971) has shown, the latter hypothesis has some important implications.

According to Israel, in a capitalistic society,

> Workers who experience themselves as exploited feel alienated because the means of production are in private hands, and because as employees they have no influence over the process of production. For them, the *conditions of power* are of decisive importance. Those workers, however, who are not happy with the work processes, and other conditions of their place

of work, are *not alienated* but only dissatisfied, or fail to experience "enjoyment of work." Thus, there should be a clear difference between alienation and dissatisfaction. The consequence is that only the politically conscious workers are able to experience alienation. (p. 254)

In other words, dissatisfaction is not the same thing as alienation. Moreover, the experience of alienation resulting from powerlessness is a positive outcome, because people who feel powerless under existing social arrangements are apt to be agents for social change. Thus, whereas the meaningful work → job satisfaction view leads to a focus on rearrangement of work within existing social structures, the powerlessness → alienation view induces a focus on the social structures themselves.

The powerlessness → alienation view has already stimulated some provocative empirical research. Based on Israel's concept of alienation, Shepard and Panko (1974) operationalized alienation as a power deficit. Power-deficit workers (i.e., those who felt they had less freedom and control on the job than they believed they should have) had a significantly greater instrumental orientation toward work and were more isolated from organizational goals than were individuals in the balanced- or surplus-power groups. Shepard and Panko concluded that power deficits were in tension with commitment to organizational goals and with intrinsic job interest. These findings are consistent with those of Seeman (1972) and Form (1975) in suggesting that the power individuals exercise over the situations that affect them, relative to their expectations of how much influence they should have, may be of greater importance in determining their experiences of alienation than is their work itself.

The powerlessness → alienation perspective also draws attention to the consequences of power inequalities within organizations upon the satisfaction and self-esteem of lower level participants. For example, Israel (1971) noted that inequalities in power induce powerful individuals to perceive others as objects or as means. Data reported by Kipnis (1972), Rosenhan (1973), and Kipnis, Castell, Gergen, and Mauch (1976) have provided clear support for Israel's assertion.

SUMMARY

Due to certain underlying assumptions, current psychologically based approaches to job satisfaction appear to be deficient. For the most part, these deficiencies are due to omissions in what topics have been taken as problematic and what ones have been generally ignored. Development of more adequate approaches will be aided by altered assumptions that will stimulate the study of those omitted factors.

NEW DIRECTIONS FOR STUDY AND ACTION

To date, psychological approaches to job satisfaction have been limited by our tendency to accept certain premises and our omission of a number of elements that contribute to job satisfaction and the quality of work life. Our general tendency has been to focus on those elements that contribute to job satisfaction *and* that simultaneously advance (or at least do not sacrifice) organizational goals as determined by managers and owners. Conversely, elements that might contribute to job satisfaction but that are in conflict with organizational goals have been ignored. How can organizational psychology develop more balanced and complete approaches to job satisfaction?

Based on the foregoing analysis, two general sets of changes seem worthy of consideration. One set of changes is primarily intellectual; the other set is more action oriented.

INTELLECTUAL CHANGES

At the level of theory and research, the implications are reasonably clear. First, the assumptions underlying current work need to be analyzed and expanded. Second, the topics that have been omitted from consideration deserve empirical study, and the results must be incorporated into our theories and policy recommendations.

First, the study of job satisfaction must be put into a broader social, political, and economic context. To date, we have tended to view the character of work as determined primarily by factors endogenous to the organization. Consequently, we have sought to improve job satisfaction within a powerful set of exogenous constraints. In contrast, a more comprehensive approach to job satisfaction would take such exogenous factors as social values and patterns of control as variables, not as givens. Under this approach, the task for students of job satisfaction would require considerable vision. Instead of attempting to design work that is maximally satisfying under an existing set of political, economic, and social structures, these structures must be viewed as variables whose effects on the nature of work and other aspects of organizational life are central to our analysis.

Second, the development of more complete approaches to job satisfaction requires a reduction in the strength of the management bias that has characterized existing research. The influence of management's definition of problems on the study of job satisfaction is so pervasive that it will be difficult to make our work relevant to other possible clients. Not only do many students of job satisfaction work for corporations, but many others work in business schools and/or have consulting and research pursuits linked to certain definitions of problems of alienation and job dissatisfaction. There are few incentives to attract applied psychologists to define their work in ways to serve lower level participants.

Moreover, without substantial effort, we may not even be able to give away our ideas and services to those who might benefit from them. Individuals and groups whom we could help may not trust us; leaders of established groups such as unions may see us more as a threat than as a useful resource and do not recognize that we have anything of value to offer them. We may need to make special efforts to establish working relationships with the relevant groups. Finally, at the present time, these groups may be right. Psychologists have little to offer them because the substance of our discipline has been shaped by other interest groups.

Our emphasis on intrinsic rather than extrinsic sources of satisfaction is a prime example of the irrelevance of our work to other possible interest groups and of some difficulties involved in serving new interests. As suggested earlier, we have tended to overlook the current importance that economic factors and job security have for many individuals. If we attempt to become relevant to these people, the definition of the problems of job satisfaction will change and so will our relations with management.

If such traditional elements as pay and job security *are* major factors affecting job satisfaction, those of us who would take job satisfaction as a primary goal may find ourselves in adversary roles vis-à-vis management. The provision of "dissatisfiers" is often more likely to involve zero-sum conflict than is provision of "satisfiers." Money is an obvious example—what is paid out to the lower level participants is not available for use elsewhere. Similarly, if we press for greater job security, we are apt to find ourselves in conflict with employers attempting to preserve their rights of hiring and firing. In short, as our work becomes more "relevant" to new clients, it may become less "relevant" to some old clients.

ACTION-LEVEL CHANGES

At the action level, the implications of this analysis must be very tentative. However, there is one theme running through many of the deficiencies in contemporary approaches to job satisfac-

tion. We have failed to consider how the existing patterns of organizational control influence the quality of work life through their effects upon priorities, intraorganizational patterns of interaction, and ultimately the psychological development of lower level participants.

In modern society, important sources of control come from the ability to influence the goals and behavior of organizations. As Perrow (1972) argued, organizations are one of the most important tools of control in contemporary society. As discussed earlier, a growing number of scholars (cf. Israel, 1971; Kohn & Schooler, 1973; Seeman, 1972) have suggested that control in the work place is a major factor shaping one's self-image and feelings of efficacy. Israel (1971) stated this argument well:

> The basic relations between men are those which exist in the process of production and (we may add after our analysis) in the process of distribution. Thus, if man's self, his own image, is the relation between himself and others, and if the most important relations are those occurring in the process of production and distribution, then those relations may have a profound influence on man. If man perceives himself as powerless in his relations to others, if he perceives himself as an object, then this perception will make him experience reification as the "normal state of affairs"—his consciousness will be a reified one. (p. 314)

Consequently, if work is to promote psychological development on these dimensions, new processes to help more people to exercise significant influence over organizations, at least on matters that concern them, are needed. A first step is to stimulate lower level participants' awareness of (a) the types of dissatisfaction they and their peers experience and (b) the leverage points through which they can attack the sources of their discontent. Ideally, this process must involve lower level participants in all phases in order to stimulate their awareness of needs and help them to develop skills and attitudes consistent with the exercise of control of their organization in an ongoing way. I call this strategy the "worker-consciousness" approach.

There are at least three major differences between the worker-consciousness approach and that of "participative management." The first is the degree of emphasis each gives to the concerns of the workers. While it is not at all clear that most lower level participants want to be involved in many aspects of managerial decision making, there is clear evidence that workers do want to have influence on certain decisions—the ones that affect them directly. For example, the history of "bread and butter" unions in the United States reveals a clear tendency of workers to be interested in a limited set of issues. More generally, Jenkins (1974) found that in Europe, where democratization of the workplace is a major trend, workers have not always opted for larger, more complex jobs but have welcomed the opportunity to decide upon this issue and others that affect them directly. The worker-consciousness view avoids dealing with abstract notions of participation about "peripheral" issues; instead, it begins by developing the concrete issues of the everyday work situation and stimulates "participation."

A second major contrast between this approach and participative management is that the strategy of the worker-consciousness approach is to institutionalize the process. In "participative management," the power to participate is "given" from above. Under a worker-consciousness approach, power is mobilized and "taken" from below. Power mobilized from below cannot be taken away as easily as power that has been "given" from above.

Third, a worker-consciousness strategy is, at least in some ways, more realistic than participative management. Underlying most participative-management approaches is the dubious assumption that managers who have fought hard to control various sources of

power are going to be willing to give them away. The worker-consciousness model does not rely on people giving valued resources away but relies on individuals and groups promoting their own interests.

The roles psychologists might play in this process are unclear, but some possibilities can be found in recent literature. Culbert (1974) outlined a series of steps that individuals and groups can take to move from their own discontents toward the exercise of greater control over their working lives. Argyris (1970) proposed action research as a strategy to involve full participation of organizational members in research design and implementation. Such involvement might well develop the capability of lower level participants to competently initiate, conduct, and act on, inquiry about the quality of their own work lives. Gorz (1967), Maccoby (1975), and Gordon (1976) have all proposed that such strategies focused on problems of interest to the worker lead not only to psychological development but also to the ability of individuals to exercise effective control in organizations. Further, although generalizing from his results to the American worker is hazardous, Young (1974) reported some support for the potential of this approach. He found that efforts by Chinese leaders to get lower level participants involved in research reduced the tendency of individuals to reify existing social practices.

CONCLUSIONS

Specific conclusions about the study of job satisfaction have already been presented. Analysis of latent assumptions and omissions has revealed the need for more explicit attention to our assumptions, to new areas for research, and to the possibility of new action steps. This work will contrast sharply with many attributes of current work on job satisfaction. It will be more macro in scope, take the express interests of lower level participants as a point of departure, and focus on ways to alter the existing distribution of power in organizations. In a word, it will be more radical.

Perhaps the most important implications to be derived from this analysis are not unique to the study of job satisfaction but are relevant to applied social science more generally. Caplan and Nelson (1973) observed that the social scientist who becomes "relevant" seldom questions existing problem definitions or the wisdom that leads to identification of the so-called problems. More recently, Dubin (1976) observed that the definition of problems studied by applied social scientists is influenced by the need for the results to "make sense" to practitioners who will consume the knowledge. If these writers are correct in their view that the essence of knowledge in applied science is strongly influenced by what makes sense to users, then there is a serious shortcoming of applied science qua science. An important element of scientific inquiry is the so-called self-correcting process through which errors in conceptualization and methods are assumed to be removed from the body of accepted knowledge. Unfortunately, if research in a particular field of study is continuously guided by a homogenous population of users, the conceptualization of problems is systematically constrained and insulated from corrective tendencies. However, the analysis of job satisfaction presented in this paper suggests a possible source of self-correction—client diversification.

As I have tried to show, our understanding of job satisfaction can be improved if we make a deliberate effort to serve the interests of lower level participants (i.e., to make them our customers too). If we can generalize from this particular case to other areas, applied science can be made more self-corrective by deliberately serving a diverse set of clients who have different conceptions of what "makes sense."

Finally, this process suggests a paradoxical outcome of Miller's (1969) strategy for improving society by giving psychology away. If the above reasoning is correct, at least for applied psychology, giving psychology away will not only improve society, it will improve psychology.

NOTES

Argyris, C. Intervention theory and method. Reading, Mass.: Addison-Wesley, 1970.

Caplan, N., & Nelson, S. D. On being useful: The nature and consequences of psychological research on social problems. American Psychologist, 1973, 28, 199-211.

Culbert, S. A. The organization trap. New York: Basic Books, 1974.

Dahl, R. A. After the revolution? Authority in a good society. New Haven, Conn.: Yale University Press, 1970.

Dubin, R. Theory building in applied areas. In M. D. Dunnette (Ed.), Handbook of industrial and organizational psychology. Chicago: Rand McNally, 1976.

Ellerman, D. The "ownership of the firm" is a myth. Administration and Society, 1975, 7, 27-42.

Fein, M. Motivation for work. In R. Dubin (Ed.), Handbook of work, organization, and society. Chicago: Rand McNally, 1976.

Form, W. H. The social construction of anomie: A four-nation study of industrial workers. American Journal of Sociology, 1975, 80, 1165-1191.

Foy, N., & Gordon, H. Worker participation: Contrasts in three countries. Harvard Business Review, 1976, 54, 71-83.

Goldthorpe, J. H. Attitudes and behavior of car assembly workers: A deviant case and a theoretical critique. British Journal of Sociology, 1966, 17, 227-244.

Gordon, G. Psychologist and the work. Paper presented at the meeting of the American Psychological Association, Washington, D.C., September 1976.

Gorz, A. Strategy for labor; A radical proposal. Boston: Beacon Press, 1967.

Gross, B. M. Organizations and their managing. New York: Free Press, 1968.

Heilbroner, R. L. The view from the top: Reflections on a changing business ideology. In E. F. Cheit (Ed.), *The business establishment.* New York: Wiley, 1964.

Heilbroner, R. L., Mintz, M., McCarthy, C., Ungar, S. J., Vandivier, K., Friedman, S., & Boyd, J. *In the name of profit.* New York: Warner, 1973.

Herzberg, F. One more time: How do you motivate employees? *Harvard Business Review,* 1968, **46**, 53-62.

Hulin, C. L., & Blood, M. R. Job enlargement, individual differences, and worker responses. *Psychological Bulletin,* 1968, **69**, 41-55.

Israel, J. *Alienation: From Marx to modern sociology.* Boston: Allyn & Bacon, 1971.

Jencks, C. *Inequality: A reassessment of the effect of family and schooling in America.* New York: Harper & Row, 1972.

Jenkins, D. Beyond job enrichment: Workplace democracy in Europe. *Working Papers For A New Society,* 1974, **2**(4), 51-57.

Kipnis, D. Does power corrupt? *Journal of Personality and Social Psychology,* 1972, **24**, 33-41.

Kipnis, D., Castell, P. J., Gergen, M., & Mauch, D. Metamorphic effects of power. *Journal of Applied Psychology,* 1976, **61**, 127-135.

Kohn, M. L., & Schooler, C. Occupational experience and psychological functioning: An assessment of reciprocal effects. *American Sociological Review,* 1973, **38**, 97-118.

Locke, E. A. The nature and causes of job satisfaction. In M. D. Dunnette (Ed.), *Handbook of industrial and organizational psychology.* Chicago: Rand McNally, 1976.

Maccoby, M. Changing work: The Bolivar project. *Working Papers For A New Society,* 1975, **3**(2), 43-55.

Miller, G. A. Psychology as a means of promoting human welfare. *American Psychologist,* 1969, **24**, 1063-1075.

Nord, W. R. Individual and organizational

conflict in an industrial merger. *Proceedings of the 11th Annual Academy of Management Conference, Midwest Division,* 1968, pp. 50-66.

Oates, W. E. *Confessions of a workaholic.* New York: World, 1971.

Pateman, C. A contribution to the political theory of organizational democracy. *Administration and Society,* 1975, **7**, 5-26.

Perrow, C. *Complex organizations: A critical essay.* Glenview, Ill.: Scott, Foresman, 1972.

Rosenhan, D. L. On being sane in insane places. *Science,* 1973, **179**, 250-258.

Schumacher, E. F. *Small is beautiful; Economics as if people mattered.* New York: Perennial Library, 1973.

Seeman, M. The signals of '68: Alienation in pre-crisis France. *American Sociological Review,* 1972, **37**, 385-402.

Shepard, J. M., & Panko, T. R. Alienation: A discrepancy approach. *Sociological Quarterly,* 1974, **15**, 253-263.

Strauss, G. Some notes on power equalization. In H. J. Leavitt (Ed.), *The social science of organizations.* Englewood Cliffs, N.J.: Prentice-Hall, 1963.

Tausky, C. Meanings of work among blue collar men. *Pacific Sociological Review,* 1969, **12**, 49-55.

Terkel, S. *Working.* New York: Avon Books, 1972.

Turner, A. N., & Lawrence, P. R. *Industrial jobs and the worker: An investigation of response to task attributes.* Cambridge, Mass.: Harvard University, Graduate School of Business Administration, 1965.

Turner, A. N., & Miclette, A. L. Sources of satisfaction in repetitive work. *Occupational Psychology,* 1962, **36**, 215-231.

Wool, H. What's wrong with work in America?—A review essay. *Monthly Labor Review,* 1973, **96**, 38-44.

Young, L. C. Mass sociology: The Chinese style. *American Sociologist,* 1974, **9**, 117-125.

VI

Engineering Psychology

Introduction. As mentioned in the preface, engineering psychology is not formally a field within I/O psychology, but it does overlap and share several common roots and has contributed significantly to its development. For example, the work of Frederick W. Taylor, as illustrated by his article in Section I, led to many of the activities that later formed the basis for engineering psychology. In addition, the issues of criterion development and performance appraisal (see Section II, particularly the article by Fleishman), training (Section IV, particularly the articles by Gagné and Goldstein), and job design (Section V) are as important to engineering psychologists as they are to I/O psychologists, and it is frequently impossible to categorize research on these issues in terms of one field or the other.

The first selection is the introductory chapter, "Applied Experimental Psychology," from the first published textbook on engineering psychology, written by Chapanis, Garner and Morgan (1949). This chapter provides a very readable summary of the history of the field and the problems of application shortly after World War II. The most important point to note is the seminal role of the military in stimulating engineering psychology research and application during the war.

Much of the literature following the war was concerned with the interaction of the operator with a machine system. Our next selection, the 1957 article by Franklin V. Taylor, entitled "Psychology and the Design of Machines," focuses on this problem. During the period, with the further support of the military, those involved in engineering psychology activities were concerned with the analysis and design of man–machine systems and the measurement of operator effectiveness in these systems. The Taylor article stresses the importance of taking into account human characteristics and the role of the operator in the design of the mechanical components of the system. He also describes the ways in which the psychologist can help the engineer—specifically, by studying the psychology of the human as a system component, by assisting the engineer in the experimental evaluation of prototypes, and by actively participating in the design of the hardware.

A number of post-war political and technological events further stimulated research and application during the late 1950s and 1960s. A number of them should be mentioned in order to put the remaining articles into perspective. First was the technological explosion in the electronics and computer industry. It was important because varied and extensive information could now be readily displayed to the operator of a machine system. Another was the technology explosion in propulsion systems for aircraft, which allowed the operator to travel at speeds heretofore unobtainable. The combination of speed and information posed realistic and critical problems for the engineer. Such issues as operator workload, information display and control design, and response capabilities of the operators were dominant. Engineering psychologists during that period were constantly queried by engineers on the type and nature of the information to be displayed, operator reaction time, performance limitations, etc. (see Ronco, 1966a and 1966b).

Military support of this research was strengthened during the late 1950s, as the U.S. public became increasingly aware of the "missile crisis" or "missile gap" with the Soviet Union. The initiation of crash efforts by the U.S. military and, in particular, the U.S. Air Force on complex missile and aircraft systems further underlined the importance of optimizing the operator's performance in complex military systems. The importance of such activity was reinforced when the Air Force made human factors issues a major consideration in the award of contracts for the design and development of aerospace systems. (The reader may be interested in reviewing the *Handbook of Instructions for Aerospace Personnel Subsystem Designers,* published in 1960, which delineates the responsibility of the contractor and the USAF in the development of a personnel subsystem from preliminary design through training and evaluation.)

Another influencing factor was the launch of Sputnik in 1957. This led to the U.S. commitment to land a man on the moon by 1970. The problems faced by engineers were formidable in terms of environmental unknowns, payload limitations, and the design of reliable telecommunications systems. Because of these concerns, one of the primary questions raised was the value and reliability of the operator in a space exploration system. In fact, there were a considerable number of very vocal and prominent engineers and scientists who argued that the inclusion of the operator in either an active or passive role would contribute nothing to space exploration. Further, their inclusion would place severe constraints on scientific payload and available funds. The major concern of this group was the physiological and psychological stress the operator would encounter during long space missions and the possible deterioration in mission performance that might result. Such factors as radiation, acceleration and deceleration, weightlessness, sensory deprivation, and isolation were cited as limiting and debilitating. Even if the operator were protected (at considerable cost) could he perform effectively, reliably, and continuously for the duration of the mission? The data required to answer this question were quite limited and many empirical and analytical studies were initiated to address this issue.

The next article, "Functions of Man in Complex Systems" by Paul Fitts, summarizes state-of-the art knowledge at the time and discusses in general the allocation of functions to the human operator in complex systems. He notes the major limitations and special capacities of humans and the implications they have for identifying the appropriate role for man in space flight. (Also see Jones, Youngling and McGee, 1966; Grodsky, Moore, and Flaherty, 1966; McRuer, Askenas, and Krendall, 1959.)

In recent years, the emphasis in engineering psychology has shifted from specific operator–machine interfaces to consideration of the human factor in large-scale, complex systems (e.g., see Parsons, 1972). In addition, the systems that have increasingly become the focus of engineering psychology research and application are decidedly non-military in nature and broadly societal in scope—transportation, health, urban, and educational, to name just a few (see DeGreene, 1970 and 1973). No doubt, "classic" work reflecting these more recent concerns will have emerged when the time comes to update this collection.

REFERENCES

DeGreene, K. B. (ed.). 1970. *Systems psychology.* New York: McGraw-Hill.
DeGreene, K. B. 1973. *Sociotechnical systems: Factors in analysis, design, and management.* Englewood Cliffs, N.J.: Prentice-Hall.
Grodsky, M. A., Moore, H. G., and Flaherty, T. M. 1966. Crew reliability during simulated space flight. *Journal of Spacecraft and Rockets,* **3**, 810-817.
Handbook of instructions for aerospace personnel subsystem designers (Part A). United States Air Force, October 1960.
Jones, E. R., Younglin, E. W., and McGee, D. W. 1966. Overall implications for future space missions. *Proceedings of the NASA symposium: The effects of confinement on long duration manned space flight.* Space Medicine, Office of Manned Space Flight, National Aeronautics and Space Administration.
McRuer, D. T., Askenas, I. L., and Krendall, E. S. 1958. A positive approach to man's role in space. *Aerospace Engineering,* **18(8).**
Parsons, H. I. 1972. *Man–machine system experiments.* Baltimore: Johns Hopkins.
Ronco, G. 1966a. *U.S. Army human factors engineering bibliographic series: Volume 1, 1940–1959 literature.* U.S. Army Human Engineering Laboratories, Aberdeen Proving Ground, Maryland.
Ronco, G. 1966b. *U.S. Army human factors engineering bibliographic series: Volume 2, 1960–1964 literature.* U.S. Army Human Engineering Laboratories, Aberdeen Proving Ground, Maryland.

24. Human Factors in Engineering Design*

ALPHONSE CHAPANIS
WENDELL R. GARNER
CLIFFORD T. MORGAN

In writing this book, the authors had three objectives in mind. The first is definition. What does *Applied Experimental Psychology* mean? What subject matter does the title cover, and in what area is the subject matter most useful? This first chapter attempts to provide a general definition of the field, even though we must recognize that a complete definition is possible only after the entire book has been read or at least skimmed.

The second objective is to introduce the reader to the most important experimental and statistical techniques in this field. Two chapters, therefore, are concerned solely with problems of methodology because there are some new techniques that are helpful in handling experimental problems in this field, and they are not too well known. Furthermore, the statistical methodology used in an experiment is more than a tool; it is a way of thinking rigorously about quantitative data. This "way of thinking" is particularly important for the scientist in this field.

The third and most important objective is to provide an introduction to the many facts that have been accumulated in this area during the past several years. The bulk of the book is, of course, devoted to this objective. Some of the facts we discuss are specific in the sense that they can be applied only in restricted situations; others are of a general nature and will be useful in many different situations. More time will be spent on general facts because of their greater usefulness, but, when general facts are not available in discussing a particular problem, we shall offer specific facts.

WHAT IS APPLIED EXPERIMENTAL PSYCHOLOGY?

Perhaps a good way to begin a general definition of the field is to mention some of the many names that have been used to describe the subject matter. The newness of the field has led to the use of many different terms, none of which seems to express all possible shades of meaning adequately. We have chosen to call it *Applied Experimental Psychology* for reasons we shall explain below. Other terms that have been used, however, are engineering psychology, human engineering, biomechanics, psychological problems in equipment design, the human factor in equipment design, applied psychophysics, and psychotechnology. Any of these terms could, with various degrees of precision, be used to describe the subject matter of this book. We shall frequently use many of these terms interchangeably. Particularly, we feel that the term

*Source: From *Applied Experimental Psychology: Human Factors in Engineering Design*, by Alphonse Chapanis, Wendell R. Garner, and Clifford T. Morgan, chapter 1, pp. 1-13 (New York: John Wiley & Sons, Inc., 1949). Copyright © 1949 by Wendell R. Garner. Reprinted by permission. Selection has been retitled.

engineering psychology is synonymous with applied experimental psychology and shall frequently use it as an equivalent term.

● *Psychology.* These many terms in themselves give some idea of our interests and point of view. In the first place, this field is psychological—it is concerned with the behavior of human beings. It is concerned, however, with only certain kinds of behavior—the behavior of human beings while working with machines or instruments. We want to know about the abilities and capacities of man because we want to know how well he can work with different kinds of machines.

● *Design of instruments.* But the applied experimental psychologist is also concerned with instruments and machines with which human beings work. His interest here, however, is in those characteristics of the machine which determine how well a man can use them. Is the machine designed in such a way that it can be used most efficiently by an operator? Can a better machine be designed—better in the sense that it can be used more easily? These are questions about the machine, but they are questions which have to do with the operation of the instrument or machine by human beings.

● *Man-machine relations.* Perhaps the best way of stating the whole problem is to say that we, as applied experimental psychologists, are interested in the interrelation between men and machines. We want to know the best way to design a machine so that a human being can use it. How should the dials be constructed and arranged? How should the controls be designed, so that the normal human being can use them easily and accurately? How should equipments be arranged in a group?

Our interest in the design of machines for human use runs the full gamut of machine complexity—from the design of single instruments to the design of complete systems of machines which must be operated with some degree of

coordination. In Chapter 5, for example, we consider some of the factors which determine how fast and accurately a single dial can be read. This is a relatively simple machine unit. But in Chapter 12, we discuss principles of the arrangement of whole units of equipments into a single integrated work area. Some of these systems—radar systems, for example—may involve groups of ten or more extremely complex machines with ten or more men working together as a team.

AN HISTORICAL APPROACH

No new branch of science suddenly springs from nowhere to become a full-fledged member of the scientific world. Science grows, and usually its growth can be traced. In the case of experimental psychology, or engineering psychology, there are three quite distinct lines of development which have led to the present status of this science. One of these developments stems from the engineering sciences; the other two have their roots in the history of psychology.

TIME-AND-MOTION ENGINEERING

One of the scientific developments that has led to the growth of engineering psychology is time-and-motion study. Time-and-motion study grew out of the engineering sciences, and the people who started it were engineers. There is a general distinction made between time studies and motion studies, in theory at least, although in practice it is often difficult to separate them.

● *Time study.* The time relations of motions and sequences of motion are the particular concern of time studies. The primary effort here has been to find out the best working rate in order to set the base rate on which pay should be scaled. Credit for the beginning of time study usually goes to Frederick W. Taylor, who made the first time studies in the machine shop about 1881. At present some industries use time study methods in determining wage rates. Unfortunately, people have often made the too ready assumption that the primary function of a time engineer is to get more work for less money out of the worker. That is not necessarily so.

• *Motion study.* Credit for the development of motion study is usually given to Frank B. Gilbreth, an engineer, and his psychologist wife, Lillian M. Gilbreth. Motion study, unlike time study, is concerned primarily with the manipulations or movements which a human operator must make in performing any job. It usually consists of an analysis of those movements in an attempt to get at the best way of doing a particular job by studying the various possible ways it can be done. Several techniques have been developed from motion study, some of which have been very useful to us. . . .

• *Job simplification.* Frequently, the time-and-motion engineer has been able to assume that the machine is already there and that his task is simply to determine the individual's best way of operating the machine. Sometimes this assumption of the prior existence and status of the machine has been necessary, and at other times it has been convenient. Nevertheless, many such engineers have realized that often the machine or the job arrangement is ill designed for the capabilities of the human operator. They have frequently found it necessary to change the machine of the job, instead of trying to make the behavior of the worker conform to characteristics that really do not match his capabilities. When they make such changes, they have become interested in some of the same kinds of problems that we, as applied experimental psychologists, are concerned with.

PERSONNEL SELECTION

One root of applied experimental psychology, then, goes back into time-and-motion engineering. Personnel selection, a second historical influence, comes from psychology.

• *Human similarities and differences.* It could be said that psychologists, in terms of their interests, fall into two general groups. Some are interested in human similarities, whereas others are interested mainly in human differences. Those concerned with similarities try to find out what the *average* person can see, feel, hear, or do under various circumstances. To such psychologists, the fact that all people are not precisely alike is simply an inconvenience. Those who work with human differences, however, consider *variability* as the problem. These two emphases have led to two different developments in psychology. The emphasis on human differences has given us the field of personnel selection as we know it today.

• *Intelligence selection.* From its official birth until the turn of the century, psychology was primarily a science of individual similarities. Individual differences were not considered much of a problem until a psychologist named Cattell became interested in the way people differ in reaction time, in the ability to see, hear, smell, move, and solve problems. Work on human differences developed strongly during the First World War when large numbers of people became available for testing. As a result of the work during the First World War, intelligence testing became a firmly established technique.

• *Development of tests.* The science of individual differences got the impetus it needed during the First World War, and psychologists did a tremendous amount of work on problems of personnel selection between the two wars. Industry began to use tests more and more. New tests were devised, tried out, revised, found good, and put to use. There were performance tests and paper-and-pencil tests, ability tests and interest tests, long tests, short tests, big tests, and little tests. Almost any one of them, if properly used, could be shown to have some useful selective function.

• *Selection of operators.* The development of selection techniques stressed another aspect of the general problem of human beings working with machines. This branch of psychology developed because it was recognized that there is a best man for every kind of job, and that there is a best job for every kind of man. Some people can do some jobs better than others, and how well a man can do one job does not necessarily determine how well he can do another.

● *Selection versus designed jobs.* There is no denying the very great significance of selection procedures. In studying and doing something about the human being in his working environment, personnel selection has been of outstanding importance. In *Applied Experimental Psychology*, however, we are not primarily interested in that aspect of the problem. We are not so much interested in selecting a particular man for the job as we are in designing the job so that the average man can perform efficiently.

● *Limits of selection.* We have decided not to present any systematic treatment of selection techniques, partly because this field is highly specialized and there are already many excellent books on that subject. But there is another reason for our emphasis on the design of the machine rather than the selection of the man. Selection of personnel can be profitable only when there is a reasonable number of people to select from—people who have the right abilities and capabilities. Many modern machines have become so complicated that no amount of selection will make it possible to get more out of the machine. When machines become so complex that none or only a very few people can work with them satisfactorily, selection is of no help. It is necessary then to turn our attention to some of the basic problems of human limitations and to study the machine in the light of these limitations.

EXPERIMENTAL PSYCHOLOGY

The third development leading to

applied experimental psychology is experimental psychology itself. Before we describe the interests and activities of the experimental psychologist, it might be well to point out that there are various kinds of psychology.

● *Nonexperimental psychologists.* Just as there are different kinds of engineers—electrical, civil, mechanical, chemical, and so forth—so psychologists are divided into various specializations. Some psychologists have a primary interest in personality and abnormal psychology. When they are particularly interested in the treatment of abnormal cases, they are called *clinical* psychologists.

Another kind of psychologist we have already mentioned is the *personnel* psychologist, who is interested in the selection of people for various jobs. Still another kind is interested in the social interaction of human beings, or the behavior of groups of humans. These *social* psychologists work with such things as public-opinion polls, scales for measuring attitudes, propaganda devices, group morale, and racial prejudice. There are also those interested in educational problems, who are called *educational* psychologists.

● *Experimental psychologists.* There are many other kinds of psychological specialists, but our interest is in *experimental* psychology, which is the oldest form of psychology. The usual date given for the birth of experimental psychology (at least in the laboratory) is 1879. This date like most such dates is not exact but indicates the general time when experimental psychology began to be a specialized science. In the past the experimental psychologist has been interested primarily in the behavior of the normal man—man as a perceiver and a doer—in vision, hearing, tactual sensitivity, motor behavior, and learning. He has worked mostly in university laboratories, since there were very few other places where he could apply his interests. With increased technical knowledge in other fields, however, and with increasingly technical machines, the interests of experimental psychologists became of practical importance and were put to use. Knowledge about the average human being's capabilities is now being applied in the design of instruments, and we have called this application *applied experimental psychology.*

Incidentally, it should be clear that many different types of psychologists do experiments. The name *experimental* started out to distinguish psychologists who were interested in an experimental science from those who were philosophically inclined. The name stuck to people interested in certain kinds of behavior, although since then many other psychologists have become experimental. But engineering psychology stems most directly from experimental psychology, not from the other types.

WARTIME DEVELOPMENTS

Although applied experimental psychology started at the turn of the century, scientific studies in this field during the next 40 years were rather few in number. The big impetus came during World War II when most psychologists were forced out of the academic laboratory and began to do much more practical research. The demands made during this war were so great that they could not be ignored. It was really during this time that experimental psychology merged with time-and-motion engineering to produce what we have called applied experimental psychology.

● *Human limitations.* This last war gave new importance to many things that were not important before. It imposed new demands on machines and on the men who operate these machines. New machines were developed, and these new machines made life more complicated for the man who had to operate them. Something had to be done to make man more efficient—or, to change our perspective 180 degrees, to make the machines more effi-

cient. Often the machine did not do what was expected of it, only because of the limitations of the humans who operated it.

We can make a machine that will do almost anything, given enough time and enough engineers. But man has limits to his development, at least as far as we can see it. When we think how much a single radar can do in a small fraction of a second, and then realize by comparison that even the simplest form of reaction for a human being requires about a fifth of a second, we realize what we are up against. Machines that demand superhuman performance will fail, and jobs that push man beyond the limits of his skill, speed, sensitivity, and endurance will not be done.

● *Physiological limitations.* The human limitations that we have run up against are of two kinds—physiological and psychological. We have developed modern aircraft so rapidly, for example, that we are now worried about not only whether a man can fly it but also whether he can live in it. With the tremendous speeds now being obtained in modern aircraft, the purely physiological limitations of the human organism become a cardinal consideration for designers and engineers—if they want the aircraft to be flown and returned.

● *Psychological limitations.* But we are more concerned with the psychological limitations, which we meet more frequently. Our problem is often: What can a man bear and still work? We are now reaching the point where, because of human limitations, better and better equipment does not necessarily insure better and better performance.

Even now it is surprising to remember that not until 1934 was anything done about the design of an airplane from the point of view of the individual who has to fly it, even though considerable attention was devoted to the selection of the pilots. The reasons for this are now easy to see. In the first place, the airplane of early days was fairly slow; it had only a few simple controls and instruments; and it did not fly very high. Second, there were only a few airplanes but many pilots to fly them. Selection procedures could thus work fairly well.

But during succeeding years the need for greater numbers of pilots arose. In order to get these pilots selection standards had to be lowered. In addition, the next few years produced revolutionary new aircraft, that flew so high and so fast and were so complex that many months of training were required for an ordinary man to learn to fly them. So not only were more pilots needed, but also the airplane had become more complicated. Both these factors changed the emphasis from selection of the pilot to better psychological design of the airplane.

● *Electronic instruments.* Aircraft were not the only machines that began to tax human limitations. The electronic equipment—radio communications systems, radar, sonar—which became so common during the war imposed new problems for the human operator. Many of these instruments, in their entirety, were so complex that it was almost impossible to get the most out of the machine. The full potentialities of radar, for example, lagged far behind physical developments because human operators could not master the complex operation of this machine system. We had to worry about such things as a new kind of visual signal—very small and not very bright. In sonar we had to worry about the limits of hearing. The communications equipment likewise had its own special problems.

Historically, then, much of experimental psychology was first applied during the war—because it had to be. Science had gotten so far ahead in physical developments that something had to be done about the human beings. Physical developments had begun to reach their limits, because human beings could not operate the machines efficiently after they were built. The job of the experi-

mental psychologist was to worry about designing these instruments so that human beings could operate them and get the most out of them.

SCIENCE AND APPLIED EXPERIMENTAL PSYCHOLOGY

In order to bring this subject into a little better perspective, it might be well to discuss for a moment the nature of science and its applications. Science can be approached from a fundamental or an applied point of view, and in *Applied Experimental Psychology* we are interested in both points of view. We are interested both in the acquisition of basic knowledge and in the application of that knowledge to engineering problems.

FUNDAMENTAL SCIENCE

Fundamental science is sometimes called "pure" science, and its general purpose is to determine basic relationships among phenomena. Scientists, for example, have been interested in discovering the basic relations among voltage, resistance, and current flow in electric circuits; the relationships among atoms in various sorts of chemical elements; the effect of extreme variations in temperature on human behavior; and so on.

● *Controlled experiments.* The emphasis of fundamental science is on discovery rather than on application. Fundamental scientists are research people, who spend their time accumulating information, usually by controlled experiments. Traditionally, the controlled experiment is arranged so that all factors are held constant except the one being investigated. Then that factor is systematically varied, and the result of that variation on just one other factor is measured. What is varied is called the independent variable, and what is measured is called the dependent variable. When the experiment is done, we know the relation between two phenomena—the independent and dependent variables. If we like, that relationship can be stated in mathematical terms, in a graph, or in a table.

In practice, of course, experiments are not always that simple. Actually sometimes, several things are varied all at once, but, when we are done, it is still necessary to know about the relation between just two things at a time. The experimental techniques for getting information this way can get quite complicated; . . .

• *Scientific laws.* After the scientist has assembled many specific relationships or facts, he attempts to catalog and sort them into meaningful groups and then to deduce from these many observations and relations some scientific laws or generalizations which describe all the relationships. A famous example of this sort is Newton's universal law of gravitation.

• *Generality of scientific laws.* An important thing to remember about scientific laws is that they really are general: they apply to any relevant situation. From basic scientific laws we can make many predictions about specific things. Newton's law, for example, accounts for the rise and fall of tides, the behavior of falling bodies, and the motion of the planets. These laws are general, and they do not change with time.

We can summarize the approach of the fundamental or pure scientist, then, as follows: (a) He makes many systematic observations on whatever he is interested in, (b) he collects and arranges his data, (c) he pores over these data with the idea of hitting upon (d) some generalization which, he at least hopes, will describe once and for all the general phenomena he has been studying.

• *Efficiency of general laws.* In any new area of science, such as engineering psychology, we look for these general relations. We look for them because they are the most efficient way of summarizing our knowledge of the field. Also, when experiments are done in such a way as to provide general

laws, the acquiring of knowledge is more efficient. General laws apply to many things. Specific relations apply only to the circumstances under which the relations were obtained.

APPLIED SCIENCE

But the scientist's job has not ended when the scientific laws are established. Science becomes of practical value only when these facts or principles are applied. There are, in general, two kinds of applications of fundamental science.

• *Applied research.* In the first place, the *techniques* of science—the research methods—can be used to find out specific information about specific things, if scientific laws do not predict what will happen in a particular instance. For example, we might want to determine which of two instruments is better in terms of an operator's ability to use them. We do a little experiment—called a test—and use the techniques of science to answer our immediate question.

• *Design.* The second application of science involves the use of basic knowledge in the design or evaluation of equipments and machines or systems of equipment. For example, if we have the basic information about the way human arms and legs work, we can probably do a better job of designing radar or aircraft controls. Basic information about visual acuity can be used in designing new instrument dials. This putting to use of basic science provides many problems of its own.

APPLICATIONS OF ENGINEERING PSYCHOLOGY

In order to make this discussion more specific, we shall point out several ways in which experimental psychology can be applied to engineering problems. Some of the applications are essentially applied research; others involve engineering and development.

• *Appraisals.* One very practical application is the testing of new equipment designs. A new design may be appraised by either comparing it to existing equipment or making a logical analysis of its characteristics. That is to say, we may be interested only in the relative value of the instrument, in which case we simply make a test comparing two or more instruments. On the other hand, if we want some absolute appraisal, we can rate the instrument in terms of its conformity to known principles of design.

● *Optimal methods of work.* Another application involves the determination of optimal methods of work with equipment that is already available. It is the classical time-and-motion approach. This kind of work is practical and immediately applicable. Sometimes research is needed; at other times a time-and-motion analysis may prove sufficient.

● *Design of instruments.* This is a development-engineering problem. After certain basic relations are determined, these principles are put to use in the design of new equipments. We have already stressed the importance of this type of work.

● *Design of tasks.* With this type of work we should be able to classify certain kinds of jobs and to establish certain principles for the classification of such jobs. In this way jobs can be made more efficient. This application is different from that involving optimal methods of work in that here we are interested in the design of the job before the machines are decided on. The design of the job involves the design and arrangement of the equipment with which a man works; we do not assume that the equipment is already there and must be used as is. The equipment is part of the total job.

● *Design of systems.* Last, but not least, we would like to determine the overall design of systems of equipment and systems of men operating the equipment. This is the problem of the coordination of machines with other machines, or men with men, when several people have to work together. It is not only the most difficult application but also, often, the most important. . . .

25. Psychology and the Design of Machines*

FRANKLIN V. TAYLOR

Psychologists have been helping engineers design machines for more than fifteen years. It all began during World War II with the rapid development of radars, sonars, aircraft control systems, and other similar devices. Previous to this time, the only role played by psychologists relative to military mechanisms was that of doing research and giving advice on the selection and training of the operators. However, very early in the war, it became apparent that these Procrustean attempts to fit the man to the machine were not enough. Regardless of how much he could be stretched by training or pared down through selection, there were still many military equipments which the man just could not be moulded to fit. They required of him too many hands, too many feet, or in the case of some of the more complex devices, too many heads.

Sometimes they called for the operator to see targets which were close

*Source: From *The American Psychologist*, vol. 12 (May 1957), pp. 249-58. Copyright © 1957 by the American Psychological Association. Reprinted by permission. Footnote deleted.

to invisible, or to understand speech in the presence of deafening noise, to track simultaneously in three coordinates with the two hands, to solve in analogue form complex differential equations, or to consider large amounts of information and to reach life-and-death decisions in split seconds and with no hope of another try. Of course the man often failed in one or another of these tasks. As a result, bombs and bullets often missed their mark, planes crashed, friendly ships were fired upon and sunk. Whales were depth-charged.

Because of these "human errors," as they were called, psychologists were asked to help the engineers produce machines which required less of the man and which, at the same time, exploited his special abilities. The story of what happened is sufficiently well known not to require any lengthy retelling here. In brief, the psychologists went to work, and with the help of anatomists, physiologists, and, of course, engineers they started a new interdiscipline aimed at better machine design and called variously human engineering, biomechanics, psychotechnology, or engineering psychology. The new field has developed rapidly in the seventeen or eighteen years of its existence, and it has now attained sufficient respectability to be accorded divisional status by the American Psychological Association. At the last meeting of the Council of Representatives, authorization was given for the founding of The Society of Engineering Psychologists as Division 21 of the APA.

It seems fitting, now that engineering psychology has been recognized as a viable entity, that we examine this new field to find out just what it is that psychology is doing for the design of machines. It is probably even more necessary that we also inquire into what the participation in the design of machines is doing for, or to, psychology. Many young people are being lured into human engineering by the abundant opportunities provided for advancement and the tantalizing salaries offered by commercial organizations. It has been suggested by an unassailable authority that a major breakthrough in the field of psychology in recent years has been the psychologists' discovery of money. It may be remarked that it was undoubtedly an engineering psychologist who first got wind of the find.

In all seriousness, however, psychologists who might otherwise conduct basic research may be attracted into this new applied area, and it is therefore important to know what it represents professionally and scientifically in order to evaluate its threat, or its promise. To decide what actions to take relative to encouraging the further development of the field, answers are needed to questions such as the following: To what extent is engineering psychology engineering, to what extent is it psychology, and to what extent is it neither? Is it a fruitful scientific area? Is it, indeed, a scientific area at all?

In the attempt to provide answers to these questions, let us look at psychologists caught in the act, so to speak, of doing human engineering. However, before we can meaningfully analyze the behavior of engineering psychologists, the concept of the man-machine system must be described. Human engineers have for some time now looked upon the man and the machine which he operated as interacting parts of one overall system. In Figure 1 is shown a paradigm of the concept. This may be viewed as a radar device, a pilot-aircraft control system, a submarine diving control station, the captain's station on the bridge of his ship, or, in fact, any man-machine system at all.

In essence, it represents the human operator as an organic data transmission and processing link inserted between the mechanical or electronic displays and controls of a machine. An input of some type is transformed by the mechanisms into a signal which appears on a display. Perhaps it is shown as a pointer reading, a pattern of lights, or a pip on a

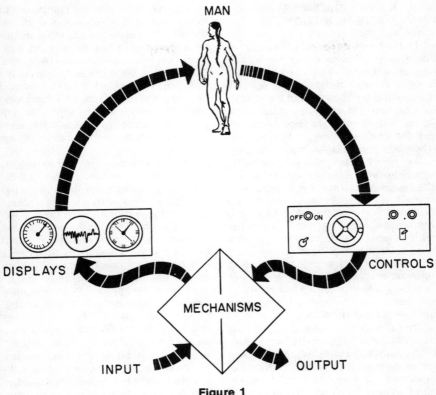

Figure 1
THE MAN–MACHINE SYSTEM

cathode ray tube. However it appears, the presented information is read by the operator, processed mentally, and transformed into control responses. Switches are thrown, buttons are pushed, or force is applied to a joy stick. The control signal, after transformation by the mechanisms, becomes the system output, and in some devices it acts upon the displays as well. These latter are called "closed-loop" systems in contrast to "open-loop" systems wherein the displays do not reflect the human's response.

When the man and the machine are considered in this fashion, it immediately becomes obvious that, in order to design properly the mechanical components, the characteristics of the man and his role in the system must be taken into full account. Human engineering seeks to do this and to provide as much assistance to the system designer as possible. Specifically, the psychologist tries to help his engineering colleague in three different ways. First of all, he studies the psychology of the human as a system component. Second, he assists the engineer in experimentally evaluating prototype man-machine systems. Finally, he teams up with engineers to participate actively in the design of machines. Each of these human engineering functions will be described in turn, beginning with the last and the least scientific activity.

HUMAN ENGINEERING TECHNOLOGY

The academic psychologist often forgets, or perhaps never knew, that human engineering is not only a science, it is also a technology; it not only tries to find out things about the interaction of men and machines, it builds the latter. And, surprisingly enough, it is not just the engineers who do the building. There are psychologists also, renegades to be sure but psychologists nevertheless, who are taking an active hand in the design of systems. It is true that with some their apostasy is venial, having progressed only to the stage of writing human engineering handbooks; but with others the defection is more serious, it having developed to the stage where they can spend anything up to full time in systems planning and design with only a twinge or two of longing for the serenity of the research laboratory and the comfort of statistics.

The aim of the human engineering technologist is to apply the knowledge of human behavior, which he and others have gained, to the structuring of machines. He seeks to translate scientific findings into electronic circuits and "black boxes" which in specific situations will compensate for the human's limitations or complement his abilities. Specifically, the practicing engineering psychologist works on an engineering team and participates in the design of man-machine systems. Using procedural analysis techniques, drawing upon his psychological knowledge and attitudes, and employing his common sense and creative ability, the human engineer proceeds to contribute to system development at three levels of complexity.

At the simplest, he designs individual displays, controls, or display-control relationships. At a somewhat more complex level, the human engineering technologist contributes to the design of consoles and instrument panels. At the highest level of complexity, he assists in structuring large systems composed of many mechanical elements and frequently several human beings. In this capacity he helps to determine what information must flow through the system, how it must be processed, how many men are required, what tasks they will perform, and what type of information each one will need. In short, the engineering psychologist helps at this level to determine the configuration of the system.

Human engineering technology is much more extensively practiced by psychologists than is generally recognized by those who are not closely identified with the field. The specific nature of each accomplishment and the difficulty of assigning individual credit for team effort conspire with security and proprietary considerations to keep the lay and psychological public in almost complete ignorance of the technological products of human engineering. However, literally hundreds of devices and systems have been affected to a greater or less extent during the last ten years by the efforts of engineering psychologists. Every major type of military equipment has received some attention, as have also certain nonmilitary products such as aircraft instruments and cabins, flight control towers, artificial limbs, semiautomatic post office sorting equipment, telephone sets, theodolites, experimental equipment for the earth satellite program, control panels for an atomic reactor, and numerous industrial machines.

Although there are no statistics available as to precisely how much time psychologists devote to technology, an informal estimate based on my own experience would suggest that approximately one-third of the engineering psychology effort in government and industry is devoted to the practice of equipment design.

Now, how does this practical activity tie in with psychology? Certainly it cannot be denied that in one sense of the term it is an area of applied psychology.

Facts about human behavior are being utilized in the design of machines. Yet in another sense it cannot be regarded as psychology at all, for certainly the design of machines is engineering, regardless of who does it or of the extent of interest on the part of the designer in human behavior. To deny this in favor of the view that system design is applied psychology because of its human reference, converts all engineers to psychologists the moment they take into account the behavior of the human for whom they are designing the machine. Certainly we do not customarily consider all occupations oriented toward human behavior to be psychology. If we did, the APA would undoubtedly be the largest professional society in the world, speaking for actors, school teachers, policemen, politicians, and members of the clergy, in addition to its present membership. So far as I know, such an expansion is not yet contemplated.

A second difficulty which stands in the way of incorporating the design aspects of human engineering under psychology arises from the nature of the goal of systems design. Whereas the primary aim of the practitioners of the more conventional applied psychologies is to control and influence people, the human engineering designer seeks to produce more effective machines. While psychology has, in the past, been applied to improving human performance by selecting, training, and motivating normal men, by curing mentally ill men, and by persuading both to buy toothpaste and television sets, human engineering aims first at building better systems and only secondarily at improving the lot of the operator. Thus, whereas conventional psychology, both basic and applied, is anthropocentric, human engineering is mechanocentric.

Because of these peculiarities of the new field, one is forced to the conclusion that it is of questionable profit to attempt to maintain that human engineering technology is a branch of psychology. Or if one still wishes to do so, it must be admitted that it is psychology most diluted and highly contaminated with physical science and engineering considerations. Although this, of course, does not reflect in any way upon the importance to society of human engineering, it does raise questions concerning the training and professional affiliation of those psychologists who decide to enter this exciting new trans-disciplinary technology.

MAN-MACHINE SYSTEMS EVALUATION

The second way in which the engineering psychologist assists in the design of machines is by taking part in systems evaluations. Like human engineering technology, evaluation studies require a sizeable effort yet receive scarcely any publicity. Evaluations have been performed on headphones, range finders, gunsights, fire control and missile control systems, radar sets, information plotting systems, combat information centers, aircraft control towers, and numerous assorted display and control components. In some instances, the experiments have been carried out in the laboratory with the system inputs being simulated. In other cases, the tests are conducted in the field. But in both situations, the attendant complexities and difficulties of statistical control make this necessary variety of research as trying as any in which psychologists are likely to participate.

The reason that psychologists were called upon in the first place to assist in these evaluations was that they possessed methods for dealing with human variability. In contrast, the engineers generally had worked only with time-stationary components and, therefore, found themselves at somewhat of a loss when they were called upon to assess the performance of devices which were being operated by men.

It is easy to see that psychologists have something definite to offer in regard to this aspect of systems design, and it is not surprising, therefore, that their services are often sought out and accepted. However, the question which we wish to pose, albeit a bit bluntly, is what are the psychologists getting out of it in turn, besides a living? Certainly they are making a contribution to the engineering of better systems, and the consciousness of this may be all that is required for the satisfaction of the individual. Yet, one might wish to know if there were any other returns—to science in general or to psychology in particular.

Admittedly, this is a difficult question which will be more easily answered fifty years from now than at present after only a few years of this activity. But one thing can be said right now about experiments performed on man-machine systems: if one's main object is to learn about human behavior, the use of a complex systems experiment is an uncommonly unwieldy way to go about it.

This may be illustrated with a preposterous, hypothetical systems evaluation. Suppose we wished to compare the performance of a boy on a bicycle with that of a boy hopping on a pogo stick. The main independent variable would be the nature of the boy-machine system; the dependent variable could be, for example, the length of time to travel a quarter mile.

Here we would have a perfectly proper systems test. At least it could be made proper through adequate attention to the training of the boys and to statistical precautions to overcome human variability. Also, the experiment would undoubtedly yield clear and unambiguous results. Assuming that the maintenance of the two conveyances was adequate to the point where neither broke down during the race, the boy-bicycle system would very likely prove to be superior to the boy-pogo stick complex. It is granted that, before positive recommendations could be made concerning the adoption of one vehicle system over the other as a general

means of boyish travel, other system criteria such as initial cost, cost of replacing parts, safety, maneuverability, ease of stowage, and consumer acceptance would have to be considered. But this is always true and constitutes no valid criticism of the evaluation. The test itself could have been highly successful; and, if so, we would have learned from it something about systems.

But what have we learned about boys? After all, we are psychologists and are interested in the laws of human behavior. What anthroponomic relationships are revealed by the study? It would seem clear that in our contrived example we have learned next to nothing of interest to psychology. Apart from finding out that boys can learn to operate both bicycles and pogo sticks, the test has disclosed nothing about the characteristics of the human operator. There are several reasons for this.

First of all, the dependent variable in the experiment is a measure of system performance, not human performance. It is perfectly apparent that the fact that one system is better than the other does not mean that the boy in the superior system is doing better in any real sense than the boy who loses the race. Quite the contrary might be true. The boy on the losing pogo stick may actually be doing a better job of pogo stick jumping than the bicycle rider is doing of his bicycle riding. As long as one is dealing with a system performance variable, the behavior of the human in the system can only be inferred, and often the inference is hazardous indeed.

This would not be a serious matter if it were always possible to find some other dependent variable which did directly reflect human behavior. But in many studies no meaningful, uncontaminated, human performance variable exists. Whenever the human responds through some variety of control, his response is inextricably tied up with the physical properties of the control itself. Thus, in our example, it is not possible to measure hopping independently of the physical characteristics of the pogo stick hopped on, nor pedaling in the absence of pedals. Try as one will, one cannot pedal a pogo stick nor effectively hop through the air on a bike. Since it is impossible to separate the manner in which the human applies force from the characteristics of the thing to which the force is applied, there is no way of getting a pure measure of man's behavior in many systems studies and, as a matter of fact, in many laboratory experiments not construed as dealing with systems.

The basic indeterminability of human response has, of course, been recognized for a long time. Philosophers and psychologists have pointed out repeatedly that behavior is an interaction among different kinds of things and that it is arbitrary and misleading to say that one of the things (usually the animate one) is doing the behaving while the others make up the environment. Thus, we say that we are studying the behavior of a man walking (Bentley, 1941) and not the behavior of the ground under his feet. Yet, of course, the walking behavior would be impossible without the ground, just as it would without the man. Both, and much else besides, are necessary for the walking to occur, and any measurement of the behavior reflects the characteristics of all of the interacting objects and forces.

Now all this is of very little consequence to psychology so long as the parts of the human's environment which interact with his motor output remain unchanged during an experiment. If, in the walking study, the ground underfoot was always of the same general firmness, levelness, and texture, its contribution to the behavior could be neglected. Similarly, if in a tracking investigation the S always uses the same joy stick working through the same system dynamics, it matters not a whit that the performance measured is that of the man-joy stick system and not of the man alone.

But let the properties of the objects to which the man applies force be varied, unknowingly or deliberately, and it becomes vital to recognize the contaminated nature of the performance measure. Change the ground from hard to muddy, or the tracking control from joy stick to handwheel, and the altered performance resulting is a composite of direct effects and man-environment interactions impossible to untangle without further research. When this is not recognized and the behavioral shift is attributed exclusively to the man, one blunders scientifically.

Conventional psychology has generally avoided this problem of confounded dependent variables by working much more frequently with sensory and state-of-the-organism parameters than with human output variables. Engineering psychology, however, has deliberately undertaken to work with system variables, with the result that performance measures are almost never pure human response scores. Although this repeated experience has alerted some of the experimenting human engineers to the inferential pitfalls of blindly equating system performance with human performance, there are still those who fall into the trap. One still occasionally hears said, for example, that human tracking performance is improved or degraded by changes in the nature of the control or by alterations in the control dynamics. Such statements may be true but they are certainly not justified, for tracking performance, as measured, is system behavior which can change radically as a result of altered dynamics without reflecting any comparable change on the part of the man.

But it is not only the dependent variable which gives the human engineer trouble in making psychological hay out of systems studies. The independent variables are often even more troublesome because they frequently embody many parameters. Consider the independent variable in our example. When the pogo stick is substituted for the bicycle,

actually four sets of dimensions are involved. First of all, the controls are
shifted: pedals and handlebars are
traded for a spring-mounted step and a
pole. Secondly, the system dynamics
are changed as they relate to the transformation of human energy into motion
along the ground. Third, the sensory inputs to the boys are modified (the displays are altered, so to speak): with the
pogo stick the visual world bobs up and
down, with the bicycle it glides by; with
the pogo stick the boy's weight is all
upon his feet, with the bicycle he feels
pressure from his seat. Finally, the
operator's task is completely transformed: the psychomotor performance
of hopping up and down along a Z axis
while simultaneously maneuvering
along X and Y coordinates, through
shifting balance around these axes, is an
entirely different stunt from controlling
in X through balancing around X, steering around Z, and pedalling around
Y—the latter is the task of the bicycle
rider.

Now even if one had a measure of
human performance as a dependent variable, which one does not, it is clear
that next to nothing of psychological
interest could be learned by manipulating this multiparameter, independent,
system variable. Since the displays, the
controls, the dynamics, and the
psychomotor task are all varied simultaneously, the logic of experiment is so
completely violated that it is impossible
to partial out the individual effects of
any of the components upon the performance of the system or of the man.
All that one can know in such a systems
test is the combined effects of the di-
mensionally massive, independent
variable—in other words, that one system is better than another. This is of
value in deciding between systems, but
it may be suggested that it is im-
poverished psychological research.

Of course, our example is a *reductio
ad absurdum* intentionally. In many systems experiments, the independent var-

iables are less complex than in the illustration. Yet it is almost always true that
system variables comprise more diverse
dimensions than do the variables customarily chosen for psychological analysis.

But it is not just the complexity and
dimensional confounding typical of system variables which make it hard to derive psychologically relevant facts from
man-machine systems tests. A further
difficulty stems from the shift in the
operator's task (already alluded to)
which so often results from the manipulation of the physical parameters of the
system. We have pointed out that the
psychomotor processes involved in riding a bicycle are entirely different from
those underlying hopping about on a
pogo stick. Similar radical differences in
the operator's task are often to be observed when real systems are compared.
One system may require the operator to
act analogously to a complex differential equation-solver, while another may
require of him nothing more than proportional responding. One radar warning system may require the operator to
calculate the threat of each target and to
indicate the most threatening; another
may compute the threat automatically
and place a marker around the target to
be signaled.

Clearly, the operator's tasks differ so
much from one of these systems to the
next that it would never have occurred
to a psychologist to compare them. The
differences are so gross, so obvious, that
they obscure the need for relating the
tasks, for placing them on some kind of
a useful continuum and for scaling the
distances in between. Yet these behaviors must be compared in some way
and the knowledge made available to
engineers if the human is to be
employed effectively in man-machine
systems. Changing the operator's task
from one of these complex psychomotor
processes to another may produce startling improvements in system performance, and the principles determin-

ing the substitution of the task must be discovered if systems design is to progress.

But can we consider this to be good psychology? Do those who regard themselves as scientific psychologists wish to spend their time comparing and analyzing vastly dissimilar psychomotor tasks? Is it sophisticated psychology to compare the speed of running with that of walking, or the ability to add in one's head with that of adding on a machine calculator, or the skill of playing a piano with that of operating a phonograph? I think that most psychologists would agree that, although these kinds of comparisons might be relevant to systems design, they are not quite the stuff out of which conventional psychology is made. Likewise, many would no doubt agree that the contaminated variables of systems research are to be avoided whenever possible in psychological investigations. Some might even go so far as to put the two together and suggest that the time spent by psychologists in evaluating systems is a dead loss to the science of psychology. Of such a view we will have more to say shortly.

ENGINEERING PROPERTIES OF THE MAN

The third and final way in which psychologists help in the design of machines is through studying, by conventional means, the behavior of the man as a machine operator. Although, as has just been remarked, psychologists have not yet quite brought themselves to making systematically the gross comparisons required by the system designers, they have undertaken to study selected aspects of the behavior of the man as a system component. The intent here is to provide the engineers or the technologically oriented psychologists with information concerning certain of the characteristics of the man in order

that the properties of the machine may be made to harmonize with them.

In contrast to the other two types of assistance furnished, this is precisely what psychologists would be expected to do. Furthermore, with the exception of some experiments on displays and controls which are actually masked systems tests employing confounded variables, the psychology is both satisfying and sanitary. The preponderance of the work is unambiguously directed toward discovering laws of human behavior, and it is as scientific as ever one could wish.

However, although the work in this domain of engineering psychology is every bit as respectable as that of the parent subject, it is far more limited. Whereas psychology in the generic sense embraces all manner of human action, engineering psychology deals with a much more restricted variety of behavior. This class of responses may be characterized in a number of different ways:

1. First off, as was pointed out at the very beginning, the human in a man-machine system can be considered as an information transmission and processing link between the displays and the controls of the machine. When so viewed, his behavior consists of reading off information, transforming it mentally, and emitting it as action on the controls. Thus, the performance may be described as of the type in which the operator's responses image in some way the pattern or sequence of certain of the input events. For example, the S signals when a tone comes on and withholds his response when he hears nothing, or he presses one key when he sees a red light and a different key when he sees a green one, he perceives the range and bearing of a radar target and identifies its location verbally, he moves a cursor to follow the motion of a target image. In all these cases, the essential interest in the behavior focuses upon the correlation in space and time between events in a restricted and predefined stimulus "space" and corresponding events in a preselected response "space."

2. Another way to characterize the behaviors studied in engineering psychology is to indicate that they are voluntary and task-directed or purposive. The operator of a man-machine system is always consciously trying to perform some task. Perhaps it is to follow on a keyboard the successive spatial positions of a signal light, perhaps to see a visual target imbedded in "noise" and to signal its position, possibly it is to watch a bank of displays in order to determine malfunction and to take action where necessary. In all cases, the operator is voluntarily trying to accomplish something specific; he is not just free associating, or living.

3. A third characteristic of the human operator's behavior emerges as a corollary of voluntary control. The class of human responses of interest to the engineering psychologist involves chiefly the striate muscles. Because it is through the action of this type of effector that men speak and apply force to levers and handwheels, it is these muscles which play the dominant role in the human's control of machines.

4. Finally, practical considerations dictate that vision and audition be the sense modalities most often supplying the input to the human transmission channel. Because of the nature and location of the eyes and ears and because of their high informational capacity, they are ideal noncontact transducers for signal energies emitted by the mechanical or electronic displays of machines.

These four characteristics define the human reactions investigated in engineering psychology as falling within the narrow confines of the classical category of "sensorimotor" or "psychomotor" behavior. But actually, the subject matter is even more limited than this. As was mentioned earlier, the main task of the psychologist-human engineer is to provide system-relevant facts concerning human behavior, and it must be emphasized that not all facts, even though they concern psychomotor performance, can meet this criterion. The hundreds of studies conducted with the pursuit-rotor, for example, have generated very few facts having the remotest relation to the design of systems.

Because it is recognized that not all

good sensorimotor psychology is necessarily good engineering psychology, steps are being taken to get at the kinds of behavioral information which the engineers really need. In order to do this, the concepts and models of orthodox psychology are beginning to be replaced by physical and mathematical constructs and engineering models. We have already encountered the notion of the man as an information channel. Systems psychologists also view him as a multipurpose computer and as a feedback control system. The virtue of these engineering models is that they furnish ready-made a mathematics which has already proved itself of value when applied to the inanimate portions of the man-machine system and which may turn out to be useful for the human element as well. In addition, they provide the behavioral scientist with a new set of system-inspired hypothetical constructs and concepts which may redirect his research and stimulate entirely novel lines of inquiry.

Whereas orthodox psychomotor psychology still speaks in a construct language consisting of terms like stimulus, response, sensation, perception, attention, anticipation, and expectancy, the new "hardware" school is rapidly developing a concept argot which, although quite unintelligible to outsiders, is providing considerable inspiration to the initiates. Human behavior for this psychological avantgarde is a matter of inputs, outputs, storage, coding, transfer functions, and bandpass.

And this is far more than a matter of language. The research itself is changing. Questions about human behavior are now being asked experimentally which were literally inconceivable a few years ago. Yet they are the very questions to which engineers desire answers. How stationary and linear is the man? What frequencies can he pass and how many bits per second can he transmit under a variety of different conditions? How does the human's gain

tion that human behavior and mechanical or electronic processes can be surrogates for each other provides an excellent reason for seeking to conceptualize men and machines in terms of the same models.

Engineering psychology has begun to do this as we have already seen. It is beginning to adopt engineering techniques, to ask experimentally how well men can differentiate or integrate or amplify, how their gains change or their frequency response characteristics shift. It is starting to apply to human behavior the trans-science concepts and methods of information theory and feedback servo analysis. It has begun to use cybernetics, not just talk about it.

In short, in starting to contribute to the design of machines, psychologists have begun theoretically and pragmatically to pull together the psychological and physicial sciences. Just how far they can be moved toward one another at the concept level has yet to be seen. Certainly today there are no physical or engineering models which are sufficiently complex to be used profitably with any but the most primitive of human behaviors. But, then, there are no models of any type, hardware or software, which are satisfactory.

One can only look at what has already been accomplished, apply his own hunches and prejudices, take a deep breath, and guess. My guess is that psychology, biology, and physics will some day all employ the same physicomathematical meta-language when describing the behavior of those particular system components which fall within their purview. Furthermore, should this ever come about, it will have resulted, at least in part, from the efforts of psychologists to design machines.

NOTE

Bentley, A. F. The behavioral superfice. *Psychol. Rev.*, 1941, **48**, 39-59.

26. Functions of Man in Complex Systems*

PAUL M. FITTS

The central issue in allocating functions to men in systems is the overall performance of the system, relative to cost, not what man does "better" than a machine, or vice versa. After discussion of the appropriate way to approach the question of man's role in complex systems, some of his major limitations and special capacities are considered. Low information-handling rate and inability to carry on parallel operations are perhaps his major limitations. Among the abilities which are found relatively uniquely in man are such things as versatility, ability to trade off time for accuracy, adaptive capacities, ability to estimate probabilities, ability to use judgment, and ability to devise heuristic procedures and to take action in the face of uncertainties. These considerations suggest certain roles for man in space flight, such as that of reprogram-

*Source: Reprinted with permission from the American Institute of Aeronautics and Astronautics, *Aerospace Engineering*, Volume 22, pp. 34-39. Copyright © 1962 by the American Institute of Aeronautics and Astronautics.

ing the system if unforeseen contingencies arise, and of scientific, hypothesis-forming, and testing activities.

ALTERNATE WAYS OF FORMULATING THE PROBLEM

It is becoming accepted practice for system design engineers to treat man as just another component which they may or may not use in a complex system. Fortunately, this implies a view of man that is similar to the one which has dominated scientific psychology for the last half-century. In this respect the psychologist seeks to specify man's characteristics in terms exactly analogous to those used by physical scientists in specifying the physical components of systems. As an illustration, the behavioral scientist often treats man as a complicated "black box," which must be specified in terms of its input-output relationships, such as signal-to-noise ratio, channel capacity, and filtering and smoothing properties.

In spite of the general acceptance of these views, however, there has been a good deal of confusion as to how to proceed in allocating functions between human and mechanical components in complex systems. This confusion is quite apparent in the way in which questions are asked regarding man's role in systems. Three widely different ways of stating the issue of man's role in complex systems are illustrated below. It is hoped that the discussion of these three questions may at least clear up some of the confusion regarding the nature of the problem.

CAN MAN PERFORM SOME FUNCTIONS BETTER THAN A MACHINE?

Stated in this way, the question is somewhat trivial and may even be misleading. Man, of course, can be viewed as a machine, although certainly a very special kind of machine. In order to understand how a man carries out a given function, and in order to specify his limitations and capabilities in performing

this function, we must develop a model, which characterizes the behavior in the same way that we specify the characteristics of any physical device or process. Therefore, if we understand how a man performs a function, we will have available a mathematical model which presumably should permit us to build a physical device or program a computer to perform the function in the same way as does the man (or in a superior manner). Inability to build a machine that will perform a given function as well as or better than a man, therefore, simply indicates our ignorance of the answers to fundamental problems of psychology. A more meaningful restatement of the question, therefore, would be "What human functions are understood well enough today so that mechanisms can be specified which will have similar capabilities? How complex would such mechanisms have to be?" We also need to ask such questions as, "How much would they cost? How much would they weigh? What would be their useful life expectancy?"

The question, "What can a man do better than a machine?" is, as we have noted, not only somewhat trivial, but it may be misleading, because even if the answer were known it would seldom be of any relevance to the design of complex man-machine systems. This is true for the obvious reason that it is seldom wise to select the "best" components for a given system. Instead, one usually wants to know what available components meet system requirements, so that the least expensive or the most readily available component that meets requirements can be used. In other words, system requirements seldom state that a given function must be performed by the best component available. This is probably self-evident, but a few examples will strengthen the point. We seldom use silver as an electric conductor, even though it has slightly less resistivity than copper. We do not arm policemen with submachine guns even though in some respects they are "better" weapons than police revolvers. And the advent of the digital computer has not eliminated the usefulness of slide rules. Thus, a little reflection makes it clear that the central issue in choosing components for a complex system is usually not so much which component will do a *better* job, as which component will do an *adequate* job for less money, less weight, less power, or with a smaller probability of failure and less need for maintenance.

WHAT FUNCTIONS DO MEN PREFER TO PERFORM IN SYSTEMS?

A meaningful question, but one that often is not asked by the system designer, has to do with man's preferences for, and his acceptance of, different roles and functions in complex systems. From a humanistic point of view, it is of course desirable to maximize man's satisfactions, including those derived from the work in which he is engaged. If we accept this goal in system design, we are led to consider the effects of automation and other technological changes on the worker, and the degree to which the roles assigned to a man enable him to find satisfaction in his work. These are legitimate issues for engineers to consider in designing systems.

It is important to consider human preferences for another reason. If the functions required of individuals in a system turn out to be ones which men refuse to accept willingly, then a great many undesirable by-products may result. These by-products include absenteeism, labor turnover, low re-enlistment rates, strong demands for side benefits, and often poor job performance. Thus, except in unusual circumstances, it is desirable—for economic and other practical reasons—for system designers to pay considerable attention to the degree to which a man will accept his proposed role in a new system.

WHAT ALLOCATION OF FUNCTIONS BETWEEN MEN AND MACHINES IS BEST FROM A SYSTEM VIEWPOINT?

This third statement of the problem treats man like any other potential system component, and is the way the present issue usually should be stated. In many instances, for example, even though a man may not perform a given function very well in an absolute sense, his performance may still easily meet system requirements. Thus, the function can be given to the man if he has time to devote to it, and if this will involve less cost than using a mechanical device.

In viewing man as a system component, the implication is that human limitations and capabilities can be described in precisely the same way in which the characteristics of any other component are specified. This is the goal of scientists such as engineering psychologists, who are interested in human-factor problems in system design. However, it is a goal that has not yet been fully attained with respect to the myriad range of potential human functions. Scientists would like to be able to specify how accurately and how reliably man can perform given functions, how long it will require him to complete each action, the extent to which this activity can be time-shared with other ongoing activities, and the limits of environmental conditions necessary for effective performance. In some areas, such as hearing and vision, human characteristics can be specified quite accurately. Other functions, such as reasoning and decision-making, can be specified only in the most general terms. Much progress is being made in specifying human performance characteristics, however. Due to man's great adaptive capacities, which will be discussed later, his characteristics must often be specified in terms of the range of task or input conditions over which he can function effectively.

The remainder of this article will deal

primarily with some of the general issues relating to this third question, the most effective use of people as components in complex systems, particularly in relation to what is known about human capacities.

SOME GENERAL CHARACTERISTICS OF MAN AS A SYSTEM COMPONENT

Some ten years ago, the present writer fell into the trap of trying to make a list of the ways in which man is superior to a machine and vice versa. Such a list was published[5] in a document dealing with human-engineering aspects of air traffic control. Similar lists have appeared in recent years in various other publications. In view of my present views regarding the trivial and somewhat misleading nature of this earlier effort, further comments on this general topic, will, I hope, be stated with sufficient reservations, and in answer to more appropriate questions. Fortunately, we can at least avoid the trap of trying to list the ways in which man is "better" than a machine, by emphasizing instead some fairly important things that are known about human capacities and limitations.

MAN'S LIMITED
INFORMATION-HANDLING CAPACITY

One of man's most general limitations is his low information-handling rate.[1, 6, 10] For any but the simplest and almost reflex-like activities, man is essentially a single-channel computer with a very low bandpass or channel capacity. If he is asked to perform several different functions at once, he must usually accomplish them serially—i.e., by some kind of alternation or time-sharing arrangement. He can drive an automobile in heavy traffic and talk to the person in the seat beside him only by a process of shifting his attention rapidly between the subject matter of the conversation, and the task of driving the car. If he is flying an airplane, he must read various instruments one at a time. There are many combined tasks that man cannot perform at all on such a time-sharing basis. For example, most people cannot carry on a conversation and solve a difficult problem in mathematics concurrently.

Even when he is engaged in a single task, man has a relatively low information-handling rate. Thus, estimates of peak performance rates vary from an upper limit not much above 25 bits per second in highly skilled activities such as reading or piano playing, down to lower limits of a few bits a second in many less highly skilled or less compatible tasks. In dealing with continuous signals, as in a tracking task, he can only deal adequately with input frequencies of a few cycles a second.

One of man's most serious limitations in handling information arises from his very limited buffer storage (or immediate memory) capacity. Thus, a task as simple as remembering a telephone number long enough to complete the dialing operation overtaxes the memory of a large proportion of people—i.e., they must refer back to the telephone book before completing the dialing. Man's ability to understand conversation, to recode information for more effective transmission, to look ahead and use anticipation while driving in traffic, and even his ability to learn simple associations, is seriously restricted by the amount of readily available information that he can retain in immediate memory. It should be noted, however, that this limitation definitely does not apply to man's capacity to retain information in long-term or permanent storage—as, for example, the ability of a test pilot to recall information needed in an emergency situation, or the ability of a chess player to recall some strategy employed in a championship match which he observed many years before.

MAN'S VERSATILITY

In marked contrast to his limited information-handling rate is man's ability to handle a great variety of different information-processing tasks. The number of different functions which a man is capable of performing almost defies enumeration, and undoubtedly is one of his greatest assets as a system component. Man's versatility even poses a considerable danger to system design, since it is always a temptation to assign to a man any and all miscellaneous functions which are left over after most of the rest of the system has been designed, assuming that after a short learning period he will be able to handle all such "simple" tasks equally well. In this connection, it is important to remember that although man is extremely versatile, and can, in fact, learn to perform a great number of different functions, he nevertheless performs some of these functions much better than others. As an illustration, his information-handling rate in bits per second varies by a factor of at least five to one, depending on how input and output information is coded. Thus man's information-handling capacity is usually lower when a binary code is employed, and is substantially higher when a large alphabet such as the alpha-numeric English alphabet is employed. As a further illustration, a typist, who uses all ten fingers, one at a time, can transmit information at a considerably higher rate than can a telegraph operator who uses only a single key; and a stenotype operator, who uses five fingers in many combinations, can record information at even higher rates. This ability to handle information at higher rates when using more complex input and output codes, is one of the interesting ways in which the conditions required for optimum human performance differ significantly from the requirements of a machine such as a digital computer.

ADAPTATION AND LEARNING

Closely related to man's versatility is his capacity for learning new skills, for long-term retention of important information, and for adaptation to the particular requirements of a new task or a new environment. This aspect of human capacity is so well-known that it hardly warrants further discussion. However, a few special characteristics of man's learning processes and their implications for system design do need to be emphasized.

In a system task, man tends to optimize his performance with respect to the requirements of the system, provided only that he is given proper feedback—i.e., has available information regarding the system input and system output which he needs in order to search for an optimum. Thus, rather than asking, "What is man's transfer function in a closed-loop system?" it is more appropriate to ask, "What are the limits within which man can change his transfer function in accordance with the demands for system optimization?"

After adequate training, man is capable of "reprograming" his activities— i.e., switching from one to a different function—in less than a second. Thus, a man who is thoroughly familiar with two languages can shift from conversing in one language to conversing in the other in the amount of time it takes to recognize the first word of a message. A single cue, a single word of warning, is often sufficient to call up an entire set of human expectancies appropriate to a particular situation, such as the adjustments necessary in changing from one airplane type to another, or in going from one conference to another. Such ability is not easily acquired, however, and it is easy to overlook the importance of the months and years of training that lie behind high levels of skill.

SPEED-ACCURACY TRADE-OFF

Man has unique ability to interchange speed for accuracy.[4, 6] He can solve an arithmetic problem quickly in his head by using approximations, or he can find the answer to any required number of decimal places by using paper and pencil. A typist can produce a rough draft very quickly, or she can produce a perfect copy in a longer time, depending on which is requested. Thus, in spite of man's low information-handling *rate*, given sufficient time he can perform certain functions that require a great deal of *precision*. Man's capacity to trade off time for accuracy has very important implications for system design.

HUMAN RELIABILITY

Space does not permit a detailed discussion of the issues of human reliability. Man's performance varies as a function of alertness, fatigue, and stress. Different people vary widely. In the present context, however, one point should be emphasized. Man can often increase his reliability to meet the demands of the task. In driving along a highway at 60 miles an hour, for example, it is obviously desirable to keep the automobile from straying into the opposite traffic lane. In this instance reliability is a life-or-death matter. Fortunately, it is a function which many individuals perform hundreds of times a day with small likelihood of a serious error within their lifetime. Elsewhere,[7] the present author has estimated that, given any two cars which are closing with a speed of 120 miles an hour and must pass with a clearance of 5 to 10 feet, the probability of a head-on collision is somewhere on the order of 10^{-9} or 10^{-10}. The generalizations about reliability hold, however, only if an individual realizes that reliable performance is required—as, for example, in the case of landing an airplane or passing another car.

SOME RELATIVELY UNIQUE AND LESS WELL UNDERSTOOD HUMAN CAPACITIES

As indicated earlier, some of the most unique human capacities are also those which are least well understood. (The implication, of course, is that once we thoroughly understand these capabilities, they will not seem as unique as they do today, and we may be able more easily to duplicate them with machines.) A few such abilities deserve special discussion.

JUDGMENT

Immediately prior to World War II, the author was involved in the development of tests for selecting aviation cadets. As a preliminary step in determining the abilities needed for success in pilot training, we interviewed experienced Air Corps pilots, and also analyzed reasons given by instructor pilots for eliminating cadets from pilot training. Both studies suggested that one of the most important traits of a good pilot was the ability to exercise good "judgment" in emergencies. Later research clearly confirmed this conclusion.[9] However, the nature of good judgment, and the development of measures of this ability, still remain something of an unsolved problem. Good judgment involves more than following a prescribed rule (deductive reasoning). It is more than the ability to remember and use practical information. It involves not only the ability to think clearly and logically, and to apply relevant previous experience, but also the ability to estimate probabilities and eventualities, to evaluate alternatives, and to perceive what is relevant in novel situations. In analyzing a critical situation afterward, it may appear that men may not always use the best possible judgment in critical situations. However, they nevertheless do remarkably well in such circumstances. They bring previous experience to bear on unique situations. They improvise, see relationships, select appropriate procedures, and usually arrive at decisions within the time and environmental limitations of the particular problem facing them at the moment. As a result, we often decide to include men in new systems because we assume that they will be able to react intelligently to situations which cannot be anticipated at the time the system is designed. Some recent progress has been made in writing adaptive computer programs and in designing adaptive control systems that can change their characteristics so as to optimize their performance in response to unpredicted environmental changes; however, man is still the chief component that is employed to provide judgment in novel situations.

PERCEPTUAL CAPACITIES

Human perception is based on unique organizing and selecting processes.[2] Man organizes his visual world, for example, into objects, into figure and background, into meaningful shapes and contours. He recognizes the faces of his friends, interprets printed and handwritten symbols, and performs a myriad of other similar classification functions. His ability to use language is certainly one of his most remarkable abilities. Many of man's unique perceptual abilities have been used routinely by system designers, and occasionally some unique human perceptual ability finds a new system use. As an illustration, it has recently been found that a man can listen to the video signal from a radar antenna and identify many of the characteristics of the target source. It has also been discovered that he can look at two photographs in a "blink comparator" and almost immediately pick out the one target in a large area which is new or which has changed position.

SMOOTHING, FILTERING, AND EXTRAPOLATING: DEALING WITH UNRELIABLE INFORMATION

Throughout his lifetime, man selects and smooths information, estimates probabilities, anticipates alternative outcomes, and in various other ways learns to make decisions in the face of excess, missing, or unreliable information.[3] These abilities have many implications with respect to functions which he can perform in complex systems.

Many of the perceptual functions discussed in the previous section involve selecting, smoothing, or filling gaps in information. Man is able to perform such functions by virtue of his knowledge of the statistical properties of noise

and of coherent signal sequences. Thus, man's knowledge of the redundancies of the English language helps him to converse with a friend in the presence of acoustic noise. He can reconstruct a jumbled English message, detect the possible presence of a submarine amidst a great many other water noises, and make intuitive estimates of probabilities. Since many modern man-machine systems must operate in environments that degrade information, man's ability to function effectively in the face of uncertainty often enables him to make an important contribution to the continued functioning of such systems.

USE OF HEURISTIC PROCEDURES

Many of the complex problems encountered in everyday life are such that analytic solutions have not yet been found. Examples include certain kinds of transportation, scheduling and personnel assignment problems, where the only sure way to find an optimum is systematically to try all possible combinations. In circumstances where he is faced with problems of this sort, man usually finds moderately efficient solutions. In their daily affairs executives, commanding officers, and business managers make a great many decisions of this sort. We do not yet have a very good understanding of the kinds of heuristics which people employ in solving such complex problems. Once we understand better how man uses heuristic procedures, we may be able to devise similar machine programs. In the meantime, however, it is often convenient to use people when heuristic methods are necessary. Thus the scheduling of work on production problems, where deadlines must be met and unexpected contingencies are likely to be encountered, is often a function which is assigned today to an experienced human manager (although the manager may use a computer to assist him in reaching decisions).

CONTINGENT PROGRAMING

Most of what has been said in this section in regard to some of the unique capabilities of man in performing system functions can be summarized under the general heading of contingent programing. The implication is that where contingencies cannot be completely anticipated, and thus where situations are likely to arise calling for judgment, for selectivity in processing information, for the use of estimates of probabilities, or for the devising of novel procedures, it is probably desirable to have people around who can change the rest of the system in accordance with their best judgment. This does not mean, of course, that system designers and computer programers should not make every effort to anticipate contingencies and to provide computer programs and mechanical devices for changing system characteristics under such novel circumstances. It is even desirable to attempt to provide adaptive mechanisms for handling certain classes of situations the exact nature of which cannot be anticipated. At present, however, there appears to be a definite limit to the extent to which we can turn over such reprograming functions to adaptive mechanisms. In summary, man may be expected to try to change his own behavior, relative to fixed system characteristics, and also to try to change the rest of the system, in both instances so as to maximize overall system performance.

IMPLICATIONS FOR THE ROLE OF MAN IN SPACE FLIGHT

Once the decision is made to build a manned space vehicle, much can be gained by using the crew to perform as many different functions as is feasible, since in many instances an additional function assigned to the crew results in a saving in weight. Thus one rule-of-thumb for assigning functions to human space crewmen might be: use man for as many different functions as is feasible, provided first, that these can be performed with the required time, accuracy, and other tolerances, and second,

that the function is performed at such times that man's information-handling rate will not be overloaded by this additional assignment of responsibility. This principle must certainly not be applied uncritically. As an illustration, men should probably not be required to perform functions where it is essential to remember to perform an operation at a precisely specified time, or where a very fast reaction time is essential in responding to an infrequent and unexpected event.

Many possibilities are open to the designer, due to the large amount of time available in space flight, for using crewmen to perform functions where high precision is required. As mentioned previously, a man is seriously limited with respect to the frequencies that he can cope with in a closed-loop control system. Thus, he cannot directly stabilize a highly underdamped system which tends to oscillate at frequencies above several cycles a second. However, a man can easily cope with disturbances whose rates are substantially less than one cycle per second, especially if he is provided with a properly "quickened" display, and if he can anticipate the time of onset of the disturbance. A man can even control a pure inertia system (such as a space vehicle) in three dimensions, provided the rates are sufficiently low in each dimension. As a further illustration, it is conceivable that a number of relatively simple (essentially paper-and-pencil) navigation procedures might be employed by a man in space flight, provided there were sufficient time to complete and check the computations before action had to be taken.

Man's ability to use general-purpose equipment, such as test instruments, for checking out electrical and mechanical systems, for making observations, or for computing purposes can possibly be exploited in space systems, even though these procedures might be highly inefficient if time were at a premium.

Lastly, of course, it should be mentioned that many of the points which have been emphasized in regard to man's versatility, his adaptive capacity, and his capacity for improvising and devising heuristic procedures, apply also to his potential role as a space scientist. Scientific work is highly creative in nature. A scientist is not just a person who makes routine observations in a fixed pattern—such forms of data collection can often be performed faster and more accurately by automatic devices. A scientist, rather, is a person who uses current information in forming hypotheses, who searches for new information on the basis of contingencies which have arisen in the course of his previous investigations. In space flight, where the time for communications is lengthened and the time required for a return trip is great, the availability of a trained scientist who can make on-the-spot decisions based on current information may lead to savings worth years of time and millions of dollars, provided space systems are designed so that man's full potential as a creative scientist can be exploited.

NOTES

1. Alluisi, E. A., Muller, P. F., and Fitts, P. M. An information analysis of responses in a forced-paced serial task. *J. Exper. Psych.*, 1958, **53**, 153-158.

2. Broadbent, D. E. *Preception and communication.* Pergamon Press, New York, 1958.

3. Edwards, W. The theory of decision making. *Psych. Bulletin*, 1954, **51**, 380-417.

4. Egan, J. P., Greenberg, G. Z., and Schuman, A. I. Operating characteristics, signal detectability, and the method of free response. *J. Acoustical Soc. Amer.*, 1961, **33**, 993-1007.

5. Fitts, P. M. (Ed.). *Human engineering for an effective air navigation and traffic control system.* National Research Council, Washington, D.C., 1951.

6. Fitts, P. M. The information capacity of the human motor system. *J. Exper. Psych.*, 1954, **47**, 381-391.

7. Fitts, P. M. Skill Maintenance Under Adverse Conditions. In B. E. Flaherty (Ed.), *Psychophysiological aspects of space flight.* Columbia University Press, New York, 1961.

8. Fitts, P. M., and Seegar, C. S-R compatibility: Spatial characteristics of stimulus and response codes. *J. Exper. Psych.*, 1953, **46**, 199-210.

9. Flanagan, J. C. *The aviation psychology program in the Army Air Forces.* Washington, U.S. GPO, 1948.

10. Miller, G. A. The magic number seven, plus or minus two: Some limits on our capacity for processing information. *Psychol. Rev.*, 1956, **63**, 81-97.

VII

Leadership

Introduction. Many might argue that the study of leadership should be the central concern of the I/O psychologist, because it has so much apparent relevance to the problems of society. Leadership appears to be related to the effective functioning of most of the social systems in our society, from the local chapter of the United Way to the government of the United States. It is this very relevance, however, that has made leadership such a difficult phenomenon to study. Leadership has been characterized as the "charisma" of a John F. Kennedy, the "great personality" of a Theodore Roosevelt, the "human relations" of a Sister Mary Theresa, and the "planning and organizing" of a General George Patton. The study of such a phenomenon is obviously complex and elusive. Attempts to define leadership in a rigorous, scientific fashion have been criticized for being too narrow, and the investigation of singular and isolated components of leadership has often led to insignificant results. Nevertheless, I/O psychology has attempted to define and analyze leadership into its component parts so that instances of leadership, effective and ineffective, can be observed, measured and related to organizational effectiveness. This brief Introduction attempts to identify some of the major theoretical and empirical developments in the study of leadership within I/O psychology and give an overview of selected readings that can be considered "classical" representations of these developments.

The earliest writings on leadership began by focusing on leadership in animal and primitive human societies (Blakmar, 1904; Mumford, 1906; Terman, 1904), perhaps because leadership functions in these settings tend to be simpler and hence easier to observe than the leadership functions in a more complex, industrial society. Since animals seemed to engage in group and leadership behavior, these investigators concluded that leadership was a universal function common to all stages of the social process, primitive and complex, involving the coordination of social interests within and between individuals and groups. Thus, these early works laid the foundation for viewing leadership as a process that guides the social phenomenon of cooperation whenever interactions among individuals and groups occur (Barnard, 1939, pp. 46–61).

It was not until the post-World War II era and the development of the empirical approach to psychological research that the study of leadership made significant advances beyond this early period. Perhaps the most significant work between 1900 and 1945 was done by Barnard (1939) who laid out a conceptual framework for describing the "functions of the executive" (pp. 215–236). While his work detailed many of the important functions and roles of leadership in organizations, the studies conducted by the Ohio State University group in the late 1940s and early 1950s are generally credited as the beginning of the "modern" era of leadership research.

The first entry in this section, "Leadership, Membership, and Organization" by Stogdill (1950), is one of the first published reviews of the early work of the Ohio State group. In this article, he sets forth a definition of leadership that has served as the classical definition for theorists and researchers for the last 30 years. Leadership is defined as a ". . . process (act) of influencing the activities of an organized group in its efforts toward goal setting and goal achievement" (p. 4). This definition relates leadership directly to the organized group and its goals and sets forth the minimum social conditions for leadership (i.e., a group of two or more persons, a common task, and differentiation of responsibility). Most importantly, this definition provided a framework for the systematic study of leadership in that: (1) any member of an organization could be studied in order to determine the extent of his or her influence, (2) every member of the organization could be considered a potential contributor to the leadership of the organization, and (3) the study of leadership required a small group (two or more persons) working on a specific task. Thus, leadership could be studied in any small group working towards a specific goal because anyone could be said to have the opportunity to exercise leadership at any time.

This small-group setting has become a standard format for the conduct of empirically based leadership research, and this format has come to be formally known as the Leaderless Group Discussion technique (LGD). The Bass (1954) article, "The Leaderless Group Discussion," serves as landmark review in tracing the history and describing the methodology and applicability of this technique to leadership assessment. The basic scheme of the LGD is to ask a group of persons to carry on a discussion about a specified task for a given period of time. A leader is not appointed, but leadership is allowed to emerge and may be exhibited in the form of different acts by different persons at various times during the discussion. The group members are rated by trained observers on the degree to which they exhibit specific leadership behaviors or acts. The LGD technique serves as a major research tool for I/O psychologists and has also been used extensively in business, industry, and government in the prediction and selection of persons with leadership potential (see also the discussion of Assessment Centers in Section II, Personnel Selection).

The other major development in leadership research in the early post-World War II period was the identification of specific behaviors, acts, and processes that are components of leadership. Representative classical works of two research traditions, the Ohio State and National Training Laboratory (NTL) groups have been included in this section. Both groups identified two behavioral clusters associated with effective leadership— leader behaviors concerned with task design structuring and accomplishment, on the one hand, and with human relations on the other. The reader may note the obvious historical ties to the earlier classic work of Frederick W. Taylor and Mayo as presented in Section I.

The NTL group was primarily concerned with leadership and small-group training. Their work distinguished itself from many prior attempts to train leaders by focusing on membership roles required for effective group growth and production. Thus, leadership was defined in terms of group member functions to be performed within a productive work group without making a sharp distinction between leadership and membership functions. Such an approach made their category system particularly applicable to the study of leaderless group discussions. The Benne and Sheats (1948) article, "Functional Roles of Group Members," presents an analysis of the group member roles developed in connection with the First National Training Laboratory in Group Development in 1947. Three sets of roles are identified: group task, group building and maintenance, and individual or non-participatory, inhibiting roles. These roles have served as one of the major category systems for leadership training and research for the last 30 years and are currently in use at such major leadership training centers as the Center for Creative Leadership, Greensboro, North Carolina (see Lombardo, 1976).

In contrast to the NTL work, the Ohio State group made use of a large data base and the statistical technique of factor analysis to identify what has become to be considered the two "classic" dimensions of leader behavior, "initiating structure" and "consideration." Although the Korman article, "Consideration, Initiating Structure, and Organizational Criteria—A Review," was published in 1966, it serves as a major review of the "structure" and "consideration" research which began in the late 1940s. "Initiating structure" is analogous to the task functions and "consideration" to the maintenance functions identified by the NTL group. The Ohio State group's work resulted in the development of a number of research instruments including the Leadership Opinion Questionnaire (Fleishman, 1957), and the Leader Behavior Description Questionnaire (Stogdill, 1957), both of which are designed to assess the dimensions of "consideration" and "initiating structure." These instruments are still in wide use by I/O researchers and practitioners today. Although this line of research has had a dramatic impact on the research in the field, the Korman article clearly shows that little evidence exists to support the contention that "initiating structure" or "consideration" are related to effective group and organizational performance. Thus, these two classes of leader acts seem to be important for defining leader behavior but not for predicting leader effectiveness.

A popular view throughout the history of leadership research has been that the most effective leaders are those with certain personality traits, and the view that effective leadership is a function of a unidimensional personality trait has been the starting point for much of this research. The unidimensional personality trait theory assumes that some trait is distributed throughout the population and that individuals vary in the amount of this trait they possess. The focus on personality has led many to write about the "Great Man Theory of Leadership," but, in general, the search to identify significant personality traits in leadership has been disappointing. The next article selected for this set of classics, "Some Findings Relevant to the Great Man Theory of Leadership" by Borgatta, Bales, and Couch (1954), is one of the few well designed empirical tests of this view. These authors, however, defined "great man" on the basis of exhibited leader behaviors in leaderless group discussion rather than on a score on a paper-and-pencil personality measure. This behavioral assessment technique appeared to predict effective leadership since persons scoring high on a composite set of leader behaviors ("great men") were found to direct more effective group performance. The findings reported in this article lend credence to the behavioral assessment techniques of the LGD, but these data do not account for the large body of insignificant and inconsistent literature on leader personality and effectiveness.

Since leadership research has found little consistent support for a unidimensional leadership trait related to group or organizational performance, most current leadership theorists and researchers have turned to developing more complex models which take account of the task or situation. Articles representing two of the major contributors to this more complex approach have been included as the final two selections in this section.

Fiedler's work on a Contingency Theory of Leadership, which began in the late 1940s and continues today, represents one of the most extensive lines of theoretical and empirical study of this topic to date. The selection presented here, "Engineer the Job to Fit the Manager," presents an eight-fold model that characterizes effective leadership in terms of leader personality and three situational factors—leader–member relations, task structure, and position power. The personality trait is a function of task (structure) and relations (consideration) activities. There is, however, a significant difference from the earlier Ohio State works in that Fiedler's "task" and "relations" dimensions are motivational preferences measured as relatively stable personality traits and relate to a person's desire to accomplish either the task or build positive socio-emotional relationships. Both types of leaders use some combination of "initiating structure" and "consideration" behaviors to accomplish their relative goals (i.e., task completion or the building of relations). However, each motivational type uses the most effective combination of these leader behaviors when the situation is appropriately "matched" to their style. Fiedler's work is of particular importance because it has received over 30 years of empirical support. Further, the model contains effective performance criteria not considered in much of the early work. The research to date on Fiedler's model is quite impressive, and the model also translates nicely into management training and practice (see Fiedler, 1976 and Fiedler, 1978).

The final selection in this section, "A New Look at Managerial Decision Making" by Victor Vroom (1974), presents another type of contingency model and is similar to Fiedler in that the use of a particular leadership style is contingent on the task, goal, or situation. However, Vroom's model differs from Fiedler's in that it does not rely on the measurement of a personality trait. Rather, Vroom concerns himself with the question of when leaders should make decisions alone versus with others. Vroom has established a set of detailed algorithms for telling leaders and managers the conditions under which they should use various types of decision styles. Vroom's model appears very practical and is a very carefully worked out logical analysis of the requirements for effective decision making. Because Vroom's model is much more recent than Fiedler's, it has not received the empirical support that Fiedler's has. Instead of competing with Fiedler's model, however, Vroom's model may complement it. That is, after managers have decided whether or not they should involve their subordinates in the decision, they need to diagnose the situation a la Fiedler to determine if there is a match between their style and the situation. If a match does not exist, the manager may have to modify the leader–member relations, task structure, or position power in a way to make the situation more compatible with his or her style. Even though Vroom's work is recent, it is the belief of these authors that his work will eventually pass the test of time necessary for a "genuine" classic in the leadership literature.

In summary, the early writings on leadership show an emphasis on conceptualizing and defining leadership, while empirical approaches did not begin until the late 1940s. From the beginning, the emphasis has been on explaining leadership as a phenomenon of social and group behavior. Initial conceptions focused on the leader as a "great personality" and on identifying components of leader behavior. The current conceptions focus on complex models of leader behavior involving interactions between leadership styles and situational characteristics. The most significant developments in the history of leadership research and theory within I/O psychology appear to be: (1) the classification of leader behavior into the "initiating structure" and "consideration" dimensions; (2) the use of the Leaderless Group Discussion technique to investigate and identify leadership potential; and (3) the contingency model approach, which characterizes leadership as an interaction between style and situation.

REFERENCES

Barnard, C. I. 1939. *Dilemmas of leadership in the democratic process.* Princeton, N.J.: Princeton University Press.

Blackmar, F. W. 1911. Leadership in reform. *American Journal of Sociology,* **16**, 626-644.

Fleishman, E. A. 1957. The leadership opinion questionnaire. In R. M. Stogdill and A. E. Coons, *Leader behavior: Its description and measurement.* Columbus, Ohio: Bureau of Business Research, Ohio State University.

Lombardo, N. M. 1976. *A seven-day leadership development program: Utilizing group resources.* Greensboro, N.C.: Center for Creative Leadership.

Mumford, E. 1906-07. The origins of leadership. *American Journal of Sociology,* **12**, 216-240 (Pt. I).

Stogdill, R. M. and Coons, A. E. (eds.). 1957. *Leader behavior: Its description and measurement.* Columbus, OH: Bureau of Business Research, Ohio State University.

Terman, L. M. 1904. A preliminary study of the psychology and pedagogy of leadership. *Pedagogical Seminary,* **11**, 413-451.

27. Leadership, Membership and Organization*

RALPH M. STOGDILL

The present paper is concerned with a point of view regarding the relation of leadership to group organization. It represents one attempt within the Ohio State Leadership Studies staff to clarify and systematize certain aspects of the leadership problem. Such clarification appears to be necessary as a preliminary step toward the development of an integrated program of research on leadership problems in formal organizations.

The pioneering work of Lewin (9), Moreno (10), and their followers has resulted in marked progress in the development of methods for studying leadership as a phenomenon of *groups*. However, comparable progress remains to be made in the development of methods for the study of leadership as an aspect of *organization*. Several factors appear to have operated as barriers to the development of scientific theory and method in this area. One is the lack of an adequate definition of leadership. A second is the fact that in much of the literature on leadership, the terms "group" and "organization" are used interchangeably or are defined in

*Source: From *Psychological Bulletin*, vol. 47 (January 1950), pp. 1-14. Copyright © 1950 by the American Psychological Association. Reprinted by permission. Footnotes deleted.

exactly the same terms. A third derives from two opposed theoretical approaches represented, on the one hand, by those theories of organization in which the leader is conceived as a symbol of authority or as an embodiment of superior personal traits, and on the other hand, by a type of group-oriented theory in which leadership appears to be regarded as a manifestation of social pathology. A fourth, and related obstacle, results from a reaction of social scientists against the authoritarian principles advanced in many discussions of organization. Some social theorists appear to reject all concepts of organization as authoritarian; and some researchers appear reluctant to deal experimentally with such concepts as responsibility, authority, stratification and similar phenomena related to organization. It is beyond the scope or purpose of this paper to portray the magnitude of the latter two difficulties. Nevertheless, it seems relevant to recognize the fact that they are present and act to the detriment of scientific work in the field.

The Ohio State Leadership Studies are being conducted on the basis of these assumptions: (1) that group organization is a recognizable social phenomenon in our culture; (2) that as such it is a legitimate subject for scientific study; and (3) that the variables of organization can be isolated and defined so as to permit their scientific study. It is the purpose of the present paper to examine various concepts relevant to leadership and organization, and to develop a formulation of the problem which will suggest hypotheses that can be subjected to experimental test.

GROUPS AND ORGANIZATIONS

Wilson (17) has reviewed the important sociological literature relating to concepts of the social group. He reports that in "current sociological literature one finds no consensus as to the meaning of the group," and concludes that much experimental work is yet to be done in order to delimit the group concept in any satisfactory manner. An important step in this direction has been made by Hemphill (5), who has devised scales for the measurement of such group dimensions as size, permeability, stability, viscidity homogeneity of membership, and the like.

The most satisfactory definition available at the present time appears to be that of Smith (15) who defines a *social group* as

> a unit consisting of a plural number of organisms (agents) who have collective perception of their unity and who have the ability to act/or are acting in a unitary manner toward the environment.

Krech and Crutchfield (8) present a similar view. They state that

> the criteria for establishing whether or not a given set of individuals constitutes a psychological group are mainly two: (1) all the members must exist as a group in the psychological field of each individual, *i.e.* be perceived and reacted to as a group; (2) the various members must be in dynamic interaction with one another.

A special kind of group is the *organization*. An organization may be defined as a social group in which the members are differentiated as to their responsibilities for the task of achieving a common goal.

Znaniecki (18) has reviewed the sociological literature relating to various concepts of organization. He stresses the fact that the terms *group* and *organization* are rather tenuous concepts, in that it is often difficult to determine whether a particular aggregate of persons constitutes a group, and that it may also be difficult at times to determine whether a particular group can be regarded as an organization. He points out that social organization

> ... can be realized only in a lasting "social group" or "association." Individuals belonging to such a group are aware that they will be regularly expected to perform certain actions, and some of them act as organizers, leaders, coordinators of the regular activities of others with reference to the common purpose. Not all of these

individuals need be continuously active; indeed, in many groups a considerable proportion remain passive, acting only in reaction to the actions of others. The common purpose of the organized actions may be simple or complex.

Some of the consequences of distinguishing between the terms "group" and "organization" are the following. First, there is nothing in the term "group" which gives any clue as to the nature of leadership. Second, there is nothing in the group definition which provides any foundation for integrating leadership with group phenomena, except at a superficial level of social perception or interaction. Third, the group orientation can suggest research methods relating to leadership only in so far as the social group is defined in terms of organization. The concept of organization, however, with its implications for the differentiation of responsibility roles, does permit the study of leadership as an aspect of the relationships between members who are coordinating their efforts for the achievement of common goals.

A group may or may not have leaders. If it does have leaders, it is an organization, for at least some of the members are thereby differentiated from the others as to responsibility, or role expectation in relation to some common purpose. The members of a group may or may not have mutual responsibilities for a common task. If the members do have differentiated responsibilities in relation to common goals then the group is an organization—a particular kind of group. The continued presence of leaders and of responsibility differentiations in relation to group goals are indicative of organization. It may not always be easy to determine the exact point at which a group emerges into an organization.

LEADERSHIP AS AN ASPECT OF ORGANIZATION

The following definition of leadership may serve as a starting point for discus-

sion. Leadership may be considered as the process (act) of influencing the activities of an organized group in its efforts toward goal setting and goal achievement. The definition of leadership relates it directly to the organized group and its goal. It would appear that the minimal social conditions which permit the existence of leadership are the following:

1. A group (of two or more persons).
2. A common task (or goal oriented activities).
3. Differentiation of responsibility (some of the members have different duties).

There are innumerable other group and situational factors which may influence leadership in varying degrees, but these appear to be the minimal conditions which will permit the emergence of leadership. There must be a group with a common task or objective, and at least one member must have responsibilities which differ from those of the other members. If all members perform exactly the same duties in exactly the same way there is no leadership. A leader then is a person who becomes differentiated from other members in terms of the influence he exerts upon the goal setting and goal achievement activities of the organization.

The foregoing discussion suggests that leadership cannot emerge unless the members of a group assume different responsibilities. It has been suggested that group organization also is founded upon differentiation of responsibility. It would then appear that leadership and organization are derived from a common factor or, viewed from a different light, that leadership is an aspect of group organization. This view has been expressed in various forms by writers in the field of business organization. Davis (3), for example, states that the

... development of organization structure is largely a problem in the division of responsibility, and involves two important problems: (1) the grouping of similar functions to form the various organization elements in a manner that will promote effective cooperation, and (2) the determination of the proper relationships between functional groups and organization elements, with a view to promoting both cooperation and effective executive leadership.

The definition of leadership does not specify how many leaders an organization shall have, nor whether the leadership influence of an individual is continuous or intermittent, nor whether the influence of the leader shall be for the welfare or detriment of the organization and its members. It merely specifies that leaders may be differentiated from other members in terms of the extent to which they influence the activities of the organization in its efforts toward the achievement of goals. The definition of effective and ineffective leadership is an additional problem.

ASPECTS OF RESPONSIBILITY

Brown (2) in a challenging analysis of organization maintains that "An enterprise is a mosaic of its individual responsibilities. The sum of them must exactly equal the whole requirement of administration." He continues, "Responsibility is that part in administration which is assigned to a particular member of an enterprise. Its definition is an act of organization."

Responsibility cannot be regarded as a simple or uncomplicated variable. Jucius (7) writes,

> By responsibility is meant, first, the obligation to do an assigned task, and, second, the obligation to someone for the assignment. But what is meant by obligation and how far does it extend? This implies a willingness to accept, for whatever rewards one may see in the situation, the burden of a given task and the risks which attend in the event of failure. Because of the rewards and penalties involved, it is highly essential to specify the limits of responsibility.

Formal organization can seldom define all the possible variations of responsibility and personal interaction to be expected of all members in all situations. Nevertheless, organization appears to be founded upon a basic sys-

tem of stable expectations regarding differential responsibilities and relationships among the members. This is not a one-way process. That is, it is not the organization alone which sets up role expectations for its members. The members set up expectations for each other and for the organization as a whole. It is assumed for purposes of the present discussion that this principle applies not only to stratified organizations, such as military and industrial establishments. It applies as well to membership in any organized group, whether it be a business, political, educational, religious, fraternal, or social organization and regardless of size, stratification, purpose, or member characteristics. The essential relationship which makes possible the conduct of organized group activities is a differentiation of responsibility roles among the members. Without this there is no possibility of coordination or of leadership toward goal achievement. The very process of organization defines the responsibilities of the members and thereby the formal leadership of the group. It is true that in some organized groups, such as recreational groups, the responsibilities of members may appear to be vaguely defined. However, this is not equivalent to saying that no responsibilities exist.

Responsibility, in its broadest scope, defines not only the duties for which a member is accountable; it defines also the persons to whom and for whom he is accountable in the discharge of his duties. In doing so, it also defines a member's formal status, or location in the organization hierarchy. Authority and formal status systems in organization are but aspects of the division of responsibility.

Responsibilities in a systematic organization are determined by the assignment of persons to particular positions, the duties of which are outlined in an organization manual or organization chart. In less systematic organizations the responsibilities of a particular job or position may be determined by on-the-spot instructions, by general hints or by unverbalized assumptions. In a systematic organization an individual's *work patterns* (the tasks he *actually* performs) will correspond fairly closely with his *responsibility patterns* (the tasks he *is supposed* to perform). However, as the mission and activities of the organization change there will be found in many instances an increasing discrepancy between the tasks being performed and the responsibilities originally outlined and defined.

ATTRIBUTES OF ORGANIZATION

The studies of Roethlisberger (12) and others have directed attention to the factor of informal groups within formal organization. Informal organization, as usually defined, refers to the friendship groups and cliques—based upon close association, mutual interests or antagonisms, and the like—which develop within formal organization. It has been pointed out by Homans (6) that this conception is too narrow, since what is informal in a factory may be formal in a primitive society. Firey (4), who defines informal organization in terms of schism, presents a more useful approach to the problem. He maintains that

> if we regard behavioral conformity, in which interactional processes are highly repetitive and synchronized, as the overt counterpart of a social system, then behavioral nonconformity may be taken as the overt counterpart of schism within a system.

An organization in operation seldom corresponds exactly with the organization model as charted. The intervention of human social factors and other influences result in the emergence of informal organization, that is, in the development of work patterns and interaction patterns which do not correspond with responsibility patterns.

It would appear then that there are two fundamental sets of variables which define the operations of an organized group. These are:

1. *Variables which define formal organization.* These are:
   a. Responsibility variables (the work one is expected to do).
   b. Formal interaction variables (the persons with whom one is expected to work).
2. *Variables which define informal organization.* These are:
   a. Work performance variables (the tasks one actually performs).
   b. Informal interaction variables (the persons with whom one actually works).

If we regard the variables listed above as basic variables of organization, we can also regard them as variables of membership and of leadership. In other words, an organization can be studied in terms of these four types of variables: responsibilities, work performances, formal interactions and informal interactions. Leadership can also be studied in terms of the same variables.

Responsibility variables define the duties that the members are expected to perform. The responsibilities of a given position may remain the same, whether A or B occupies the position. *Work performance* variables are defined by the tasks performed and by the methods of their performance. Individual A may accept a position previously occupied by B. The responsibilities as defined by organization charts and manuals may remain the same, but the tasks actually performed by A may differ somewhat from those performed by B, and the methods of performance may vary markedly.

Formal interaction variables define the persons to whom and for whom the members are accountable, as well as others with whom they are expected to cooperate, in the discharge of their responsibilities. *Informal interaction* variables are defined by the persons with whom the members actually work and cooperate in the performance of their tasks.

Informal organization comes about as

a result of the development of discrepancies (a) between work performance and responsibilities as defined and (b) between informal interactions and formally defined interactions. Thus leadership is ever confronted with the task of reconciling discrepancies— discrepancies between what ought to be done and what is being done, between goals and achievements, between organizational needs and available resources, between the needs of individual members and the requirements of organization, between formal lines of cooperation and informal patterns of cooperation.

An organization in action comprises a complex of many variables in interaction. In making a pictorial representation of a business organization, the usual procedure is to plot the division of formal responsibility on a two dimensional chart. The horizontal dimension of the chart shows the division of responsibility for various kinds of work. The vertical dimension of the chart shows the division of responsibility for different levels of decision-making, and indicates the persons to whom one is accountable and those for whose performance one is accountable in the discharge of duties. This dimension defines the formal authority and status systems of the organization. Level (position in the organization hierarchy) and function (kind of work performed) are not independent dimensions. Although functions tend to differ from level to level, there is considerable overlap. Results from the Ohio State Leadership Studies (13, 16) have shown that the functions of top leadership tend to be supported at each lower level in the leadership structure by increasingly more detailed and routine work in the same functions.

Personal interaction can also be conceived as varying in both horizontal and vertical directions. The horizontal dimension is defined by the range (number) of members with whom an individual interacts. Some persons tend to work alone or with single individuals, while others are observed to work with large numbers of persons. The vertical aspect of personal interaction is defined by the number of strata (echelons) above and below his own in which a member works with others. Some persons may be observed to work only with others at the same level in the organization. Others tend to work only with subordinates, and still others tend to work only with superiors. These tendencies may or may not represent expression of individual differences in social interaction patterns. Results obtained thus far in the Ohio State Leadership Studies suggest that these patterns of interaction may be determined in part by the functions served by various types of positions. Technical consultants and staff aides tend to spend more time with superiors. Members in supervisory positions are observed, as would be expected, to spend more of their time with assistants, and subordinates. Members in coordinative positions tend to spend time with superiors and subordinates, as well as with associates at the same level in the organization. A member's function or duties may determine to a considerable degree which persons in the organization he may influence, as well as the nature of the influence that he can exert.

GROUP ORGANIZATION DEFINES AND DELIMITS LEADERSHIP

The very process of defining responsibility serves to structure and delimit the role that the leader may play in the organization. He cannot perform all the duties of all the members. His own accomplishment is therefore dependent upon the performance of others. His responsibilities are circumscribed by the outlined procedures and delegated responsibilities necessary for the achievement of stated goals.

Each member must work within the organizational framework which defines the limits of his participation (how far he ought to go and beyond which he ought not to go) in performance of duties. It also sets the requirements for his cooperation with others and defines his relationships with his superiors and subordinates. This organizational structuring is not viewed alike by all persons. To some it appears as a barrier to participation or recognition. To others it appears as a prod and stimulus to greater effort and participation. For still others it provides a secure and comfortable sphere of activities and working relationships. Organization, therefore, in defining the responsibilities and working relationships of its members, sets up barriers to participation, as well as facilitating it.

Even as the organization sets boundaries by providing a framework within which members discharge their responsibilities, so the individual presents various barriers to the influence of the organization upon his own behavior and reactions. Some members may be limited in capacity to discharge their responsibilities, while others who are highly skilled in the techniques of their responsibilities are limited in capacity to interact with others. Each member carries into the organization his past experiences, his needs, ideals, personal goals, and commitments to other organizations, which may modify and determine his capacity for participation. It would appear that the extent to which the behavior of different members is determined by the characteristics of the group represents a continuum from little to great, and also, that the extent to which the behavior of the different individuals determines the behavior of groups may be conceived as representing a similar continuum.

It becomes apparent that a study in leadership represents a study of relationships, of variables in interaction. According to Pigors (11), a study of leadership must consider: (1) the leader, (2) the members as individuals, (3) the group as a functioning organization, and (4) the situation.

All organizations operate within a larger cultural and environmental framework. No organization can escape entirely the influence of the external situation. The organization may be influenced by the availability of resources, by changes in the social order of which it is a part, by competition of other organizations for the participation, resources or loyalty of its members, and by innumerable other factors outside the control of the organization itself. These factors also influence the leadership of the group.

LEADERSHIP AND EFFECTIVENESS OF ORGANIZATION

According to Barnard (1) the persistence of cooperation depends upon two conditions: (a) effectiveness, the accomplishment of cooperative purpose, and (b) efficiency, the satisfaction of individual motives. Thus, although in many situations it may appear desirable to effect a maximum of goal achievement with a minimum of organizational expenditure, such a procedure might jeopardize the welfare or morale of the members. It then becomes evident that there are many situations in which organization is confronted by a complex of contradictory factors which must be considered in arriving at a decision. It also becomes apparent that the effectiveness of an organization cannot always be evaluated in terms of the degree to which it has attained its objectives. It may be necessary first to evaluate the goals and objectives themselves or the cost of their attainment. A carefully thought out discussion of factors to be considered in setting organizational goals, arriving at decisions, and evaluating the success of an organization has been presented by Simon (14). He states,

The accomplishment by an administrative program of its organizational goals can be measured in terms of adequacy (the degree to which its goals have been reached) or of efficiency (the degree to which the goals have been reached relative to the available resources).

Simon, in agreement with Barnard, maintains that the criterion of adequacy alone is not valid as a measure of group accomplishment. He observes that "the fundamental criterion of administrative decision must be a criterion of *efficiency* rather than a criterion of *adequacy*. The task of administration is to maximize social values relative to limited resources."

If organizational goals are employed as reference points in evaluating effectiveness, then the goals themselves must be subject to evaluation. In addition, the cost (human or material) of goal attainment must be considered as a factor in evaluation. Both Barnard and Simon imply that organization cannot be regarded as a unit in isolation—or as a law unto itself. The motive of organization is the creation of social value or goods for its members, and these values bear some significant relation to the values of society in general.

Since leadership is related to the determination of group goals, it becomes apparent that the leader is seldom a free agent. In influencing the activities of the organization in its striving toward goal achievement he must consider certain social values, not only in relation to the members, but in relation to society as well. If he ignores the welfare of the members he is likely to lose their following. If he ignores the welfare of society he is likely to lead his group into difficulty. Thus leadership is subject to determination by factors which are external to the organization, as well as by internal group factors.

THE DEFINITION OF LEADERSHIP

The definition of leadership as a process of influencing the activities of an organized group in its task of goal setting and goal achievement should perhaps be reexamined. Does it define leadership? What are its implications? Admittedly, it defines only at a high level of generality. Certainly it does not include all social acts and influences, but it is nevertheless, an inclusive rather than a restrictive definition of leadership. Even so, it is more restrictive than most of those attempted in the recent literature. The definition restricts leadership to influence within the organized group. It does not imply domination or direction of others, nor any technique of influence; nor does it specify any particular member who should be regarded as a leader. The definition permits the study of any member of an organization to determine the extent of his leadership influence, and permits consideration of the possibility that every member may contribute toward determining the leadership of the organization.

The definition carries the implication that leadership may be not so much an attribute of individuals as an aspect of organization. In this respect it parallels the concept of authority. It is generally recognized that an executive in a business concern has authority in relation to his employees only during the time they are working as members of the organization. His authority does not extend outward into the direction of their personal or social lives. Nor does his position as an executive give him authority over other persons who are not members of his organization. In other words, authority is a relationship that exists between persons who are mutually participating as members of an organized enterprise. Authority is not an attribute of one or a few persons. Authority is an interactional process by means of which the organization defines for each individual the scope for action he has in making decisions, carrying out responsibilities, and enlisting the cooperation of others. The authority of any single individual will be largely circumscribed and defined by the authority of others, and at the same time, his own degree of authority will in part determine the authority of others.

Leadership appears also to be determined by a system of interrelationships.

As such it must be regarded as an aspect of organization, just as authority is a derivative of organization. If leadership is determined by a system of interacting variables, then each of the several dimensions of responsibility and personal interaction might be conceived as representing a gradient of influence. If so, then it should be possible to measure leadership influences in terms of these dimensions.

Some members may be regarded as rating higher than others in leadership by virtue of the fact that they have responsibility for making decisions which exert a marked influence upon the activities of the organization. Some members may influence the activities of the organization as a result of personal interaction with other members, even though they do not hold positions of high level responsibility. Some members may rate high in both types of influence. It would not be expected that any organization could be found in which all influence is exerted by a single member. It would rather be expected that all the members of the organization could be ordered or ranked to some degree in terms of the influence they exert in various dimensions. The proposal to measure leadership in terms of the influence exerted by individuals may appear to contradict the statement that leadership is an aspect of organization rather than an attribute of individuals. But this is not a necessary conclusion. It was pointed out that authority is generally understood to be an aspect of organization. However, it can be observed that some members exercise more authority than others. The judgment can also be made that some persons have "too much" or "too little" authority. Such observations indicate an evaluation of conditions relative to various factors in the organization. In the same way it can be observed that member A exerts more leadership influence in some situations; while members B, C, and D exert more influence in determining activities of the organization in other instances. It may

be that the leadership of A is circumscribed by the leadership of B, C, and D who are in competition with him; or it may be that the leadership of A is dependent upon the supporting leadership of B, C, and D. In either event, the leadership influence of any one member is determined in part by the leadership exerted by others, and the balance may change from time to time.

SUMMARY

An organization is composed of individuals. Its existence is dependent upon the cooperation and performance of individuals who play different roles. Measures of authority, leadership, and the like, are but measures of aspects of organization, even though the measurements are made in terms of members and the relationships among members. Leadership exists only in so far as individuals, as members of organization, are differentiated as to the influence they exert upon the organization; and the leadership influence of any one member will be determined to a large degree by the total leadership structure of the organization. It is for this reason that leadership has been here defined in terms of influence upon the activities of the organization, rather than in terms of influence upon persons.

The advantages of this formulation of the leadership problem are as follows: First, it removes leadership from the broad, vaguely defined realm of social interaction in general, and integrates it with the basic variables which describe an organized group. Second, and more important, is the fact that it suggests the development of methods for studying leadership as an aspect of work performance, work methods and working relationships.

An attempt is being made to develop such methods for the Ohio State Leadership Studies. For example, the goals and structure of organization and the responsibility patterns of members are determined by examining organization charts and manuals and by interviews with members of the organization. Work patterns are determined by modified job analysis procedures. Sociometric methods are employed to determine working relationships between the members and to chart the informal organization. The social values and role concepts of leaders and members are studied by means of attitude scales. These methods are supplemented by various check lists and rating scales.

In conclusion, a word of caution may be in order. The present paper has been concerned with a search for the minimal factors which will permit a functional integration of the concepts: leader, member and organization. In attempting to isolate these minimal common elements, many other important factors associated with leadership and group functioning have been excluded as not contributing to this central purpose. The present formulation represents merely one segment of a set of hypotheses to be subjected to experimental test.

NOTES

1. Barnard, Chester I. *The functions of the executive.* Cambridge: Harvard Univ. Press, 1938.
2. Brown, Alvin. *Organization of industry.* New York: Prentice-Hall, 1947.
3. Davis, Ralph C. *Industrial organization and management.* New York: Harper, 1940.
4. Firey, Walter. Informal organization and the theory of schism. *Amer. Social. Rev.,* 1948, **13,** 15-24.
5. Hemphill, John K. *Situational factors in leadership.* Ohio State Univ., Bur. Educ. Res. Monogr. 31, 1949.
6. Homans, G. C. A conceptual scheme for the study of social organization. *Amer. Social. Rev.,* 1947, **12,** 13-26.
7. Jucius, Michael J. *Personnel management.* New York: Irwin, 1947.
8. Krech, David, & Crutchfield, Richard S. *Theory and problems of social psychology.* New York: McGraw-Hill, 1948.
9. Lewin, Kurt, Lippitt, Ronald, & Escalona, Sybille K. *Studies in topological and vector psychology I.* Univ. Iowa Stud. Child Welf., **16,**(3), 1940.
10. Moreno, J. L. *Who shall survive?* Washington: Nervous and Mental Diseases Publ. Co., 1934.
11. Pigors, Paul. *Leadership or domination.* New York: Houghton Mifflin, 1935.
12. Roethlisberger, F. J., & Dickson, William J. *Management and the worker.* Cambridge: Harvard Univ. Press, 1939.
13. Shartle, Carroll L. Leadership and executive performance. *Personnel,* 1949, **25,** 370-380.
14. Simon, Herbert A. *Administrative behavior.* New York: Macmillan, 1947.
15. Smith, Mapheus. Social situation, social behavior, social group. *Psychol. Rev.,* 1945, **52,** 224-229.
16. Stogdill, Ralph M., & Shartle, Carroll L. Methods for determining patterns of leadership behavior in relation to organization structure and objectives. *J. Appl. Psychol.,* 1948, **32,** 286-291.
17. Wilson, Logan. Sociography of groups. In G. Gurvitch and W. E. Moore (Eds.), *Twentieth centruy sociology.* New York: Philosophical Library, 1945. Pp. 139-171.
18. Znaniecki, Florian. Social organization and institutions. In G. Gurvitch and W. E. Moore (Eds.), *Twentieth century sociology.* New York: Philosophical Library, 1945. Pp. 172-217.

28. The Leaderless Group Discussion*

BERNARD M. BASS

The purpose of this review is to describe the leaderless group discussion (LGD): its history, applicability, method of administration, and reliability and validity as a technique for assessing leadership potential. We shall discuss the major variants in procedure that have been tried, and indicate the effects of these variations on LGD reliability and validity. We shall not consider the initially leaderless discussion's role as a basic research tool for studying the development of leadership as it has been employed by investigators such as Carter (29, 30, 31, 32), Pepinsky, Siegel, and Vanatta (61), and Bell and French (24), although we will make use of their findings wherever they shed light on the LGD as an assessment device.

HISTORY OF THE LEADERLESS GROUP DISCUSSION

According to Ansbacher (2), the originator of the method was J. B. Rieffert, who directed German military psychology from 1920 to 1931. The technique, called by first users the *Schlusskolloquium* or *Rundgespräch*, was aimed at showing behavior "toward equal partners." The German Army used the procedure until about 1939, while the Navy continued employing it in their selection programs until late in World War II. Various German civilian agencies now appear to be employing the LGD as an assessment tool.

Influenced by the German developments in situational testing, by 1942 the British War Selection Board introduced such tests into their battery for selecting Army officer candidates. The basic series of leaderless group tests was evolved by Bion and included the LGD (41, 45, 70). A similar program was established by the British Navy (70).

At the end of the war, the LGD was employed by Fraser (39, 40) as a device for screening British management trainees, and by Vernon (68, 69) for testing British Civil Service applicants.

Similar developments took place in Australia (43, 65), South Africa (3), and Norway.[1]

The OSS Assessment Staff (59) appears to have initiated use of the LGD in the United States late in World War II. American federal and state civil service examiners began trying out the technique at the end of the war (5, 26, 27, 53).

Approximately 25 percent of the 190 Civil Service agencies surveyed by Fields (37) reported using the LGD. A Federal Civil Service manual appeared in 1952 (56). The LGD has also been employed by several American industrial and business firms. Its rapid acceptance has led both Meyer (58) and Douglas (35) to caution about overestimating its validity and utility.

---

1. Private Correspondence from V. C. Jahl, Chief Psychologist, Norwegian Armed Forces.

*Source: From *Psychological Bulletin*, vol. 51 (September 1954), pp. 465-92. Copyright © 1954 by the American Psychological Association. Reprinted by permission. Footnotes renumbered.

We attribute the use of the LGD primarily to its relative ease of administration compared to individual interviews, especially where large numbers of applicants are involved, as well as to its face validity compared to paper-and-pencil tests.

It may be that the face validity of the LGD really is what Gulliksen (44) has labeled *intrinsic* validity. A number of *extrinsic* validity studies are now available which may justify ex post facto the possibly widespread premature acceptance of the LGD as a valid measure of the tendency to display successful leadership.

Several investigators have assumed that the LGD is intrinsically valid as a means of appraising successful leadership behavior. Pepinsky, Siegel, and Vanatta (61) have used LGD performance as a criterion for evaluating the effects of counseling; Bell and French (24) and Carter and his associates (29, 30, 31, 32) have assumed that they are studying leader behavior when observing discussions.

Another reason for the continuing interest in employing situational tests to forecast or appraise leadership behavior may be due to the nature of leadership and psychometrics.

In reaction to the earlier emphasis on the effects of individual differences on leadership behavior, there has been, more recently, an emphasis on situational effects on leader behavior. That both sources of variance are important for leadership behavior can be accounted for fully only after analyzing the main effects and the interaction effects of situational differences and individual differences in motivation, behavioral history, and biological level (maturity, heredity, and integrity of the CNS).[2]

It follows that any test designed to

forecast leadership potential and intended to have some generality of application would need to: (a) share elements in common with a variety of situations; (b) vary directly with the situation for which predictions are to be made.

Most psychometric test procedures have been developed to meet only the first requirement, for many behaviors are relatively little influenced by situational changes. Thus, one's speed-of-arm movement or spatial visualization accuracy remains fairly constant over a wide range of situations. On the other hand, since the effects on leadership behavior of situational change are large, psychometric methods like the LGD, and other situational tests which meet both requirements, would appear to offer more promise initially as psychometric techniques for forecasting leadership behavior.

With reference to the first requirement, the LGD, in common with a range of other situations in which leader behavior is to be appraised or predicted, appears to share such elements as the need for would-be leaders: to communicate effectively, to overcome inertia, to solve various interaction problems, to meet deadlines, and to reach consensus.

With reference to the second requirement, the LGD and other situational tests, by their very construction and administration, tend to vary consistently with the nature of the examinees and the real-life situations for which personnel are being chosen. Candidates for positions of leadership are assessed among administrators by observing them solving abstracts of *administrative* problems *among administrative trainees*. Tests of the same individuals for positions as Army officers would involve studying them solving *military* problems during interaction with *officer candidates*. To some extent, therefore, situational tests may be able to take situational variations into account.

APPLICABILITY OF THE LEADERLESS GROUP DISCUSSION

According to published reports, the LGD has been used to assess candidates for many professions and occupations. The examinees have included: officer candidates (2, 41, 43, 45, 70, 71); OSS agent applicants (59); advanced Naval (31, 32), Air Force, and Army ROTC cadets (15); industrial management trainees (39, 40, 65); industrial executives and supervisors (21, 22); shipyard foremen (53); supervisory labor mediators (42); civil service supervisors and administrators (3, 54, 68, 69); applicants for foreign service (68, 69); graduate engineer trainee applicants (9, 10); sales trainee applicants (9, 10); public health physicians (5, 26, 27); teachers (47); visiting teachers (51); and social service workers (52).

DESCRIPTION OF THE LEADERLESS GROUP DISCUSSION

The basic scheme of the LGD is to ask a group of examinees, as a group, to carry on a discussion for a given period of time. No one is appointed leader. The examiners do not participate in the discussion, but remain free to observe and rate the performance of each examinee. To date, there has been little standardization by all examiners of the number of discussants per group, the length of testing time, type of problems, if any, presented to the candidates, and the directions given to them. Also, the number of raters has varied, as has the seating arrangement. Examiners have differed in the kinds of behavior they have observed and rated and in the extent to which their ratings have been attempts to describe the behavior they have observed, rather than attempts to make inferences about the personality of the candidates.

FACTORS RATED BY OBSERVERS

Unless otherwise indicated, the LGD results we shall describe are either based on observers' ratings of the amount of *successful* leadership displayed[3] in the discussion, or are inferences about the personalities of the candidates based on observations of this behavior.

In regard to personality inferences, Cough and Carter (34), following a factorial analysis of observers' inferences based on several kinds of situational tests including the LGD, found that three independent factors could be isolated which accounted for situational test ratings. The factors and the ratings with highest loadings on each factor were: (a) Individual Prominence (authoritarianism, confidence, aggressiveness, leadership, striving for recognition); (b) Group Goal Facilitation (efficiency, cooperation, adaptability, pointed toward group solution); (c) Group Sociability (sociability, adaptability, pointed toward group acceptance).

As will be pointed out later, many of these specific inferences by observers, such as those concerning authoritarian tendencies, may be valid only as descriptions of performance in leaderless groups and actually may be inversely related to attitudes and performance in real life.[4]

A similar factorial analysis of OSS situational test data by Sakoda (62) un-

---

3. A leadership act is said to occur when member A of a group behaves in a way directed toward changing another member, B's, behavior. More specifically, a leadership act occurs when A's behavior is directed toward: (a) changing the intensity and/or direction of B's motivation, and/or (b) restructuring B's abilities to cope with the situation and reduce B's needs (13).

All *attempted* leadership acts in which A reaches his goal of changing B are considered *successful leadership*. If B's change in behavior brought about by A's successful leadership leads to need satisfaction for B and for A (apart from A's satisfaction in being a successful leader), A's successful leadership act is considered effective (46).

4. For a discussion of leadership and authoritarianism, the reader is referred to Hollander (48).

covered three factors which resemble Couch and Carter's: (a) Physical Energy (energy and initiative, physical ability, leadership); (b) Intelligence (effective intelligence, observing and reporting, propaganda skills); (c) Social Adjustment (social relations, emotional stability, "security"). Carter (29) noted that similar factors appeared in several studies when real-life leader behavior was rated and factor analyzed.

In aiming to estimate successful leadership behavior, the descriptive check lists of behavior in leaderless discussions that evolved from various studies made by the author and associates appear to concern primarily what Hemphill (46) has labeled "Initiation of Structure," a factor which has emerged in several of the Ohio State Leadership Studies (e.g., 38) and which has similarities to Couch and Carter's "Group Goal Facilitation."

In the check list used in most studies by the author and his co-workers to assess leader behavior, raters are asked to indicate whether each candidate showed the following behaviors "a great deal" (4 pts.), "fairly much" (3 pts.), "to some degree" (2 pts.), "comparatively little" (1 pt.), or "not at all" (0 pts.): (a) Showed initiative; (b) was effective in saying what he wanted to say; (c) clearly defined or outlined the problems; (d) motivated others to participate; (e) influenced the other participants; (f) offered good solutions to the problem; (g) led the discussion. The sum of ratings received on all seven items is the examinee's performance score.

In an unpublished study by Pruitt and the author, seven items were rated which aimed at assessing the extent to which each LGD participant showed "consideration for the welfare of his associates"—a factor of leader behavior uncovered in various Ohio State Leadership Studies (38). This factor is similar to Couch and Carter's Group Sociability and Sakoda's Social Adjustment factors. The seven items included: (a) Engaged in friendly jokes and comments; (b) made others feel at ease; (c) complimented others; (d) helped others; (e) encouraged others to express their ideas and opinions; (f) had others share in making decisions with him; (g) helped settle conflicts. At the same time, a list of seven "Initiation" behaviors were observed and rated.

The intercorrelation between 80 LGD participants' Initiation and Consideration scores was .78, too high to warrant continued use of both assessments. More significantly, the mean rating on any single Initiation behavior was 2.2 points, while the mean rating on any single Consideration item was 0.75 points. Thus, although raters could assess reliably both types of leader behavior $(r_{,,} = .90, .85)$, much less Consideration behavior appeared, and most of it was exhibited by Initiators.

On the basis of this, and evidence to be presented later, we suspect that the LGD rating is more an assessment of the tendency to initiate structure in an initially unstructured social situation—one of several types of successful leadership behavior—than an assessment of tendencies to be considerate.

CONDITIONS AFFECTING LGD LEADERSHIP RATINGS AND PERFORMANCE

A number of variations have been systematically studied which may or may not seriously affect ratings of successful leadership in the LGD. These include: the size of the group, the seating arrangement, pretest coaching, the motivation of the participants specific to the situation, and member participation.

● *Effects of size.* As the size of the group increases from two to twelve, the mean LGD rating assigned is reduced approximately 50 percent. Eighty-three percent of the variance in ratings where members come from groups of 2, 4, 6, 8, and 12 is accounted for by size according to a study of 120 examinees by the author and Norton (19). It appears that the opportunity to display successful leadership is closely associated with the size of the group. We conclude that proper correction must be made in any LGD studies where different examinees have been tested in groups varying in size.

• *Effects of location of seat and seating arrangement.* Sixty-eight discussions among 467 participants were analyzed by the author and Klubeck (16) to determine the effects of the particular seat a participant held on the LGD rating he obtained. For both V-shaped arrangements and those in which members sat in parallel rows facing each other, members seated at the ends obtain slightly higher mean scores. In two sets of the seven studies included in this analysis, the results were significant at the 1 percent level. The effects tended to disappear when variations in the real-life esteem of the members were held constant. At any rate, the differences, statistically significant or not, associated with participants' location in the group were too small to be of much practical concern.

• *Pretest coaching.* If LGD performance can be greatly altered by means of brief coaching which does not reflect any real change in personality, its routine use by large organizations such as the Armed Forces for screening OCS applicants would be impossible. Therefore, Klubeck and the author (50) briefly coached the third highest and the sixth highest participants (among seven) of each of 20 leaderless discussions and then ran retests on each group of seven. An analysis of covariance led to the inference that while those who were fairly high in LGD score initially profited significantly from coaching, those who were initially low did not profit at all from the brief coaching. While the shift upward of the high ranking subjects was statistically significant, it was not very large in an absolute sense.

The investigators cited a number of reasons for rejecting the inference that the differential improvement was due to differential motivation, and concluded

that LGD behavior is a function of personality traits and needs which cannot be altered readily by brief coaching.

This interpretation was in agreement with Harris' (45) opinion that one could not "cram" for the leaderless group discussion. Harris suggested that priming a candidate, rather than help would most likely handicap him by "inhibiting his spontaneity."

In an unpublished study, Pruitt and the author gave the same part-directive, part-permissive coaching as Klubeck and the author had administered previously, but the groups receiving training were coached for 15 minutes while assembled as groups prior to undergoing the LGD. Directly in line with Harris' hypothesis, the five trained groups, each with six participants, showed significantly less "initiation" behavior than eight untrained control groups of six each. The trained groups exhibited only half as much "consideration" behavior as the untrained groups. Raters commented on the "freezing up" and the "increased nervousness and tensions" which characterized the trained groups; this was in line with Harris' hypothesis.

As pointed out by Klubeck and the author:

... long term training is obviously an entirely different matter. Thus, if an ineffective individual underwent psychotherapy successfully which led to favorable modifications in his needs and self-esteem, there is no reason to reject the possibility that he would exhibit improved performance on the LGD, but here the LGD would reflect real personality change (50, p. 71).

Actually, Pepinsky, Siegel, and Vanatta (61) carried out such long-term training with some success.

• *Effects of extrinsic motivation of participants specific to the situation.* Do momentary changes in the incentive to participate, unrelated to the personality of the participants, make much difference in LGD performance? An unpublished study completed by the author tentatively suggests that added extrinsic motivation is relatively unimportant in determining the behavior of LGD participants. Two small samples of a total of 31 college students were tested and retested in leaderless groups of seven to nine. The first sample was told that the first test was mere practice and had no bearing on class grades, but that the second test would count as an important grade determiner. The second sample took the "important" examination first and was then given the second test as a "check-up on the test" that would not affect them. The means of successful leadership displayed in both the motivated and unmotivated situations were practically identical. Moreover, the correlation between LGD performance in both situations was .86, indicating that the addition of incentives affected performance relatively and absolutely very little.

Needs more basic to the personality probably energize and sustain LGD behavior. These needs appear to be either openly denied or unconscious to a great extent. When 227 ROTC cadets, in an unpublished study by the author and Coates, were asked to indicate on a five-point scale how much they tried to do as well as possible on an LGD, a correlation of only .30 was found between reported effort and actual LGD scores obtained.

Analogous to performance on paper-and-pencil aptitude tests, increasing the extrinsic motivation of mature subjects does not serve to raise scores materially, since subjects usually perform near their maximum without such added incentive. Of course, we might succeed in lowering performance if we could sufficiently discourage subjects or increase tension beyond some optimum point.

It is possible that the LGD may be no more sensitive to variations in examinee's extrinsic motivation than most aptitude tests. It is probable that the LGD is less affected by such extrinsic motivation as the desire to obtain a job than is the usual undisguised personality test.

What is needed are comparative studies of operational, as opposed to experimental, validities of the LGD.

● *Amount of participation.* Analyses generally find a high correlation between the sheer amount of talk of LGD participants and the scores they earn for successful leadership. Time spent talking correlated .65 with ratings of success for 64 sales and management trainee candidates (10), .77 for 140 sorority girls (23), .93 for 20 college students (6), and .96 for 36 college students of an unpublished study by R. L. French.[5]

This high correlation is disturbing at first, since it suggests that LGD ratings primarily discriminate the verbose from the terse. However, the relationship can be shown by a series of deductions to logically follow if we assume that almost all participation in the LGD is *attempted* leadership behavior, that LGD ratings are assessments of *successful* leadership behavior, and that attempted leadership must occur in order for some of it to be judged successful. More detailed discussions of these relationships are presented elsewhere (6, 13).

● *Kind of participation.* Qualitative differences appear in the kinds of LGD participation engaged in by the successful leader and by those who participate and attempt leadership acts, but who nevertheless earn low scores as successful leaders. When the responses during leaderless discussions of 46 fraternity members were analyzed by the Bales technique (4), other judges' ratings of participants' successful leadership correlated .66 with frequency of *attempting answers*; .50 with frequency of *positive socioemotional responses*; .44 with frequency of *asking questions*; and .32 with frequency of *negative socioemotional responses* (12). The roles associated with successful leadership

---

5. French, R. L. Verbal output and leadership status in initially leaderless discussion groups. *Amer. Psychologist*, 1950, **5**, 310 (Abstract)

were initiator-contributor, opinion-giver, elaborator, compromiser, orient-er, evaluator, energizer, encourager, etc. (11). Only one type of participation, *attempting answers*, was associated (r = .48) with the real-life esteem of the participants.

In a study of 40 ROTC cadets, Carter, Haythorn, Shriver, and Lanzetta (32) found that LGD leaders were much more likely than nonleaders to diagnose the situation, ask for expressions of opinion, propose courses of action for others, support and defend their proposals, give information, express opinions, and argue with others.

RELIABILITY OF THE LEADERLESS GROUP DISCUSSION

The reliability of the LGD will be considered in two phases: rater agreement and test-retest reliability. Wherever possible we will indicate factors that systematically influence these reliability estimates.

RATER AGREEMENT

Table 1 displays the average agreement found between any two observers in rating the first LGD administered to the designated subjects. The results suggest that the refined 7-item check list and its predecessors of 9 and 14 items used in most of the studies by the author and associates (e.g., 15) yield a consistent rater correlation of between .82 and .84. LGD scores based on two raters using the check list method yield a satisfactory estimated reliability of .90 or above.

A number of factors influence the agreement between raters. These will be considered next.

• *Effects of discussion effectiveness.* A pronounced curvilinear relationship was found between the rated effectiveness of 67 leaderless discussions and the correlation between two observers' ratings for each discussion. Rater agreement was highest for discussions of average effectiveness and was lowest for dis-cussions which were either extremely effective or extremely ineffective. The average eta found for four subsamples of these 67 discussions was .68 (17). It may be that observers become too interested in the very effective discussions and too bored or detached from the very ineffective ones; or, the variance of LGD ratings may be reduced in discussions at either extreme of the distribution of effectiveness, which, in turn, will serve to reduce the reliability of the ratings.

• *Effects of size.* The number of participants in a given discussion appears to influence the extent to which observers will agree with each other. The author and Norton (19) tested five samples of 24 subjects each in discussions of two, four, six, eight, and twelve in size. Maximum agreement among observers was reached in groups of six (r = .89) and was lowest in groups of two (r = .72). Carter, et al. (31) found that mean observer agreement was only .70 for four-man groups, while it was .85 when the same men were retested in eight-man groups.

• *Effects of test or retest.* The last results cited can also be accounted for, in part, by the fact that observer agreement appears to increase when the same subjects are retested. Thus, when the 120 subjects of the author and Norton were all retested, observer agreement increased for groups of all sizes from a mean correlation of .82 to a mean correlation of .90.

• *Effects of the object of rating.* The data summarized in Table 1 suggest that rater agreement is higher where raters employ a check list in which they merely indicate the extent to which each of a number of items of leader behavior was exhibited by each candidate, rather than where they employ a single graphic rating, or where they attempt to make inferences about the standing of the examinees on intervening variables of personality or ability supposedly underlying the LGD behavior being observed. The median estimated reliability

TABLE 1
RELIABILITY OF LGD RATINGS ESTIMATED BY THE AVERAGE AGREEMENT
BETWEEN ANY TWO RATERS

Subjects	What Rated	Rating Method	Average Correlation between Any Two Observers	Estimated Reliability of LGD Rating Using Two Observers
1. 64 sales and mgt. trainee candidates (9)	Desirability for position	Paired comparison	.67	.80
2. 219 administrative trainee candidates (3)	Personality and ability (highly intercorrelated)	Graphic rating scale	.70	.82
3. 36 male college students (30)	Leadership performance	Graphic rating scale	.61	.75
4. 40 NROTC subjects (31)	Leadership, authoritarianism, initiative, and insight (highly intercorrelated)	Graphic rating scale	.53	.70
5. 20 mixed college students (6)	Successful leadership displayed	Check list (13-item)	.67	.80
6. 46 fraternity members (20)	Successful leadership displayed	Check list (14-item)	.82	.90
7. 120 mixed college students (19)	Successful leadership displayed	Check list (9-item)	.82	.90
8. 244 ROTC cadets (15)	Successful leadership displayed	Check list (9-item)	.83	.91
9. 88 fraternity pledges (72)	Successful leadership displayed	Check list (9-item)	.84	.91
10. 140 sorority members (23)	Successful leadership displayed	Check list (7-item)	.83	.91
11. 48 mixed college students*	Initiation of structure and interaction	Check list (8-item)	.90	.95
12. 48 mixed college students*	Consideration of others	Check list (8-item)	.85	.92

* Unpublished data.

of check list ratings is .90; the median estimated reliability of other types of ratings is .80.

TEST-RETEST RELIABILITY

The seven available test-retest reliability coefficients and the studies on which they are based are listed in Table 2 in order of the size of the coefficients. Listing them by size leads to the inference that test-retest reliability is higher the more similar the test and retest situations. The consistency of LGD behavior is higher the less group membership

TABLE 2

TEST-RETEST RELIABILITY OF RATINGS OF LEADERSHIP DISPLAYED IN LEADERLESS
GROUP DISCUSSIONS RANKED IN ORDER OF SIMILARITY OF TEST AND RETEST

Subjects	Rating Method	Differences between Test Situations	Interval between Tests	Test-Retest-Correlations
1. 120 mixed college students (19)	Check list (9-item)	None	Week	.90
2. 31 mixed college students*	Check list (9-item)	One "important exam," other not	Week	.86
3. 140 sorority members (23)	Check list (7-item)	Two members of each group of 7 given training between tests	Three hours	.75
4. 25 mixed college students (24)	Participants rank each other	Groups rearranged, six retests	Week	.75
5. 20 mixed college students (6)	Checklist (13-item)	Intervening LGD among leader or followers only before second test	Six weeks	.72
6. 23 mixed college students (21)	Check list (7-item)	Group rearranged, type of problem systematically varied: case history, no problem presented, and leader specification to be outlined	Two days to week	.58
7. 172 ROTC cadets (15)	Check list (9-item)	Groups rearranged; some subjects changed in "real-life" status more than others between tests; different raters	Year	.53
8. 36 male college students (30)	Rating scale	Six intervening situational tests in groups of two before second test	Three to four months	.39

* Unpublished data.

changes from test to retest; the less the problem changes; the less some members are increased in ability to lead; the less some members are increased in "real-life" status; the less observers are changed; and the less time between tests increases, permitting more random or biasing change to occur among participants. These results conform to the principle of consistency, proposed by the OSS Assessment Staff, that a subject will respond to similar environmental conditions in a similar manner (59).

Where changes in situation from test to retest are reduced to a minimum, a high test-retest reliability is found. It is probable that where behavior check lists describing participant behavior are used, the true test-retest reliability of the LGD is somewhere between .75 and .90.

• *Effects of size.* The number of participants in a group appears to determine the consistency of the behavior from test to retest. For, while the author and Norton (19) found groups from four to twelve in size to have an average test-retest reliability of above .90, groups of two had a corresponding reliability of only .46. These results suggest that two-man and probably three-man leaderless group discussions should not be used for assessment purposes.

VALIDITY OF THE LEADERLESS GROUP DISCUSSION

The construct validity of the LGD will be examined in this discussion. This requires both logical and empirical review.

Figure 1 diagrams the relationships among a group of variables of importance in the study of leadership. Using a set of postulates based primarily on learning theory, the author elsewhere

(13) has deduced these relationships, which may be summarized as follows:

1. The more a member *is able to solve the group's problems* because of personal characteristics (such as his capacity, achievement, responsibility, and participation), the more likely he is to exhibit successful leadership behavior in real life, in quasi-real situations, and in the leaderless group discussion. These personal characteristics are reflected in performance on various psychological tests of intelligence, proficiency, and personality.

2. The more a member exhibits successful leadership, the higher is his *esteem* among his associates—the extent to which he is regarded of worth as a member or leader to the group, regardless of his position—and the higher will be the merit ratings he receives as a successful leader or member. The higher his *esteem*, the more likely he is to be of further success as a leader among his associates.

3. The higher a member's *status*, as inferred from his rank or the worth of his *position* among his associates, the more likely he is to successfully lead his associates.

Further relations between variables noted in Figure 1 can be ignored here.

If ratings of LGD performance are actually valid measures of tendencies of individuals to differ in successful be-

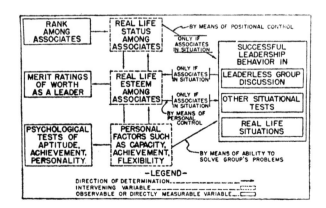

Fig. 1. Relations among Leadership
Variables

havior, and if we accept as a logical rule that variables with common determinants should correlate positively with each other, then following the outline of Figure 1, LGD scores should correlate:

1. With real-life rank (and hence real-life status) when the LGD is among associates of different ranks;
2. With real-life merit ratings (hence real-life esteem);
3. With leadership performance in other quasi-real situations;
4. With observations and indices of successful leadership performance in real-life situations;
5. With personal characteristics as measured by psychological tests and measurements commonly associated with success as a leader.

Any positive correlation between an LGD rating and these other specified measures should provide partial evidence of validity of the LGD performance rating—namely that it actually measures leadership potential or individual differences in tendency to be successful as a leader. Previously presented evidence indicates that the measurement of LGD performance is consistent with itself. The question still to be answered is whether or not it is consistent with the various other measurements associated with, described as, or defined as successful leadership behavior. Rated LGD performance should be associated with these other measures if it is an assessment of success as a leader.

We will now survey empirical investigations of the extent to which rated LGD performance was found associated with status and esteem in real-life, personal characteristics and leadership performance elsewhere.

STATUS (AS ESTIMATED BY RANK) AND LGD PERFORMANCE

A biserial correlation of .88 was found between the rank in the company of each of 131 oil refinery supervisors and their success as LGD leaders among their associates (22). The more the discussion problem concerned matters for which they had rank over their associates, the higher was this correlation (21). A corresponding correlation of .51 was found for 264 ROTC cadets.[6] The lower correlation in ROTC probably reflected the fact that rank differences were less vital to the cadets than to the industrial executives.

When 180 ROTC cadets were retested among their associates a year after an original test, those who rose during the year from cadet noncom to cadet first lieutenant or higher gained significantly more in LGD score on the retest compared to the test than those who received promotions to cadet second lieutenant only.[7]

ESTEEM AS ESTIMATED BY REAL-LIFE MERIT RATINGS AND LGD PERFORMANCE

Table 3 lists 17 correlations between LGD performance and esteem-in-real-life as estimated by merit ratings. It also shows when and how the ratings of merit were obtained. The median correlation is .39 and is raised to .51 when only the seven cases in which correction was made for the unreliability of esteem ratings are considered. As shown in Table 3, LGD scores have been found moderately predictive of merit as an ROTC cadet officer (15), sorority or fraternity member (20, 23, 72), civil service administrator (3, 69), shipyard foreman (55), foreign service administrator (69), and OCS cadet officer (71). The moderate correlations between LGD scores and real-life esteem for the studies that involved discussions among strangers suggest that a common source of variance among examinees, which exists beyond the effects of situation, underlies an examinee's merit among his real-life associates and his success as a leader among strangers. The relation-

6. Bass, B. M., & Coates, C. H. Situational and personality factors in leadership in ROTC. Unpublished manuscript.

7. See footnote 6.

TABLE 3
CORRELATION BETWEEN LGD PERFORMANCE AND "REAL-LIFE" ESTEEM AS ESTIMATED BY MERIT RATINGS BASED ON "REAL-LIFE" PERFORMANCE

Subjects	Tested With	Estimate of Esteem	Raters	When Esteem Data Collected in Reference to LGD	Correlation
1. 100 Army ROTC cadets (15)	Equal status associates	Rated merit as a cadet and officer	Campus cadet and tactical officer superiors	6 months before	.51†
2. 96 Army ROTC cadets (15)	Equal status associates	Rated merit as a cadet and officer	Campus cadet and tactical officer superiors	6 months after	.44†
3. 85 Army ROTC cadets (15)	Equal status associates	Rated merit as a cadet and officer	Summer camp tactical officer superiors	9 months after	.53†
4. 55 Air ROTC cadets (15)	Equal status associates	Rated merit as a cadet and officer	Campus cadet and tactical officers	6 months before	.68†
5. 52 Air ROTC cadets (15)	Equal status associates	Rated merit as a cadet and officer	Campus cadet and tactical officers	6 months after	.65†
6. 167 Army and Air ROTC cadets*	Equal status associates	Rated merit as a cadet and officer	Peer associates	Year after	.38
7. 46 fraternity members (20)	Equal status associates	Nominations for positions of leadership	Peer associates	Week before	.44
8. 65 fraternity pledges (72)	Strangers	Nominations for positions of leadership	Peer associates	6 months after	.47†
9. 140 sorority members (23)	Strangers	Nominations for positions of leadership	Peer associates	Same time	.39†
10. 168 administrator trainees (3)	Strangers	Potential capacity as administrator	Superior associates	Year after	.50
11. 84 shipyard foremen (54)	Equal status associates	Adequacy of foreman	Superior and peer associates	Not specified	.29
12. 123 foreign service personnel (69)	Strangers	Suitability in foreign service	Superior associates	2 years after	.33
13. 202 civil service administrators (69)	Strangers	General merit as administrator	Superior associates	2 years after	.36
14. 131 oil refinery supervisors (22)	Associates of varying status	Merit as supervisor	Superior associates	1 month to year before	-.06
15. 48 uncoached mixed college students*	Strangers of the same sex	Nominations as leader	Associates	1 to 4 weeks before	.00
16. 35 coached mixed college students*	Strangers of the same sex	Nominations as leader	Associates	5–7 weeks before	.33
17. 323 Air Force officer candidates (71)		Rated merit as a cadet and officer	OCS peers and faculty		.23

* Unpublished data.
† Corrected for criterion unreliability and/or for between subsample variations in criterion means and variances.

ship between esteem and LGD score cannot be attributed solely to the tendency of an examinee to display successful leadership among associates who esteem him. Thus, the LGD appears to assess attributes of the examinee that are not specific either to the test situation or to the group in which he is tested.[8]

● *Variables related to the correlation between esteem and LGD performance.* The total amount of successful leadership displayed in a leaderless discussion appears to reflect the average merit as leaders elsewhere of all the participants of the discussion. An analysis of 67 LGDs among fraternity pledges, sorority

---

8. Another interpretation of these findings has been offered by E. L. Kelly in the 1954 *Annual Review of Psychology* (Stanford, Calif.: Annual Reviews, Inc., p. 295). Kelly suggests that to some extent, the real-life merit raters may react in the same way to the same cues irrelevant to leadership success, as do the LGD raters. Both assessments are in agreement, but the source of agreement does not necessarily concern leadership potential. Thus, in a given situation, real-life merit raters and LGD raters both may tend to assign high ratings to thin men, and logic and the literature on the subject suggest that thinness should have no relation to leadership potential.

A counterargument is as follows: The real-life merit ratings, biased as they are, are a function of the extent to which the raters value or esteem the ratees. The evaluation tends to have consequences affecting the continuing success of the performance under evaluation. If seemingly irrelevant cues such as thinness influence merit ratings in real life, they will then tend to be associated with esteem and leadership potential. In reacting to the same biasing cues, the LGD observers are in error as far as logic or psychologists are concerned, but, despite this, their error is associated with real-life leadership potential as well as with the biased real-life merit ratings.

This same counterargument will not apply where merit ratings have no future consequences on the success of the actual performance being rated, such as in the case of appraising diagnostic proficiency of physicians.

members, and ROTC cadets found a correlation of .35 between the mean LGD score per discussion group and the mean esteem-in-real-life score of the participants of each group. Thus, there was a between-groups as well as a within-groups positive correlation between LGD ratings and esteem as estimated by merit ratings. In the same way, the LGD scores within a discussion correlated .20 with the merit scores among the participants of that discussion (17).

These results suggest that LGD ratings which depend solely on standards within a group discussion should suffer in validity as estimated by correlations with real-life merit ratings. Rating techniques with this disadvantage include the forced distribution rating, paired comparison, ranking, and any others which force the equalization of all discussion-group LGD score means and/or variances. Similarly, when tested among strangers, any ratings of each other by the participants themselves will be attenuated in validity as predictions of esteem, since they will depend solely upon standards based on observation of a single discussion.

This same analysis (17) indicated that a number of variables are associated with the variation from discussion to discussion in the correlation between real-life esteem of the members and their LGD performance. According to a Doolittle solution, these variables included: within-discussion variance in real-life esteem; within-discussion variance in LGD ratings; and group size. All relationships were positive except for size. Six-man groups were slightly more valid than larger ones as predictors of real-life esteem.

Status differences among members almost completely invalidate the LGD as an indicator of real-life esteem. Yet above and beyond these effects, the case history discussion appears more likely than other types of discussions to reflect differences in real-life esteem and personality. Where members of different rank were tested together, the case history discussion was the only one which yielded scores that correlated positively with merit ratings as refinery supervisors ($r = .28$). Furthermore, case history discussion performance correlated .54 with a supervisory aptitude test battery. Other types of discussion, in these circumstances, averaged .23 in correlation with supervisory aptitude test scores, and correlated negatively with ratings of esteem of these supervisors of different rank (21).

PERSONAL CHARACTERISTICS
ASSOCIATED WITH LEADERSHIP AND
LGD PERFORMANCE

According to Stogdill's survey of over one hundred studies, leaders tend to surpass nonleaders in certain personal characteristics such as *capacity* (intelligence, alertness, verbal facility, originality, and judgment), *achievement* (scholarship and knowledge), *responsibility and associated personality factors* (dependability, initiative, persistence, aggressiveness, self-confidence, desire to excel), and *participation* (activity, sociability, cooperation, and adaptability) (63). If these characteristics can be included under the broad concept of "abilities to solve group problems," then their relationship to leadership can be deduced as well (13). Performance in the LGD should be associated with these personal factors, if it is to be judged valid as a measure of individual differences in tendency to exhibit successful leadership behavior. Table 4 shows the correlations obtained between various measures of capacity and/or achievement and LGD performance. Table 5 shows the correlations between LGD performance and various personality variables that approximate the "responsibility" and "participation" clusters of Stogdill. The first three items of Table 7 may be regarded as further evidence of the correlation between participation and LGD performance. We shall briefly consider, in turn, the correlations between LGD performance and capacity, achievement, responsibility, and participation.

• *Capacity and leaderless group discussion performance.* While the correlation between LGD performance and verbal aptitude averages .30 or above, as might be expected, the correlation between LGD behavior and numerical aptitude is below .20. Intelligence test scores measuring verbal, numerical, and spatial factors tend to fall in between in correlation with LGD performance. Ability to solve the leaderless discussion group's problems appears to depend more on verbal than on other aptitude factors.

A factor analysis of 14 leadership and ability measures by the author and Coates[9] found that while rated performance in initially leaderless discussions correlated close to zero with one factor, Ability in Active Situations, it correlated .44 with another factor, Ability in Verbal Situations. Sakoda's (62) analysis of OSS data also noted that discussion ratings fell into a cluster with other ratings based on "verbal" situations. Carter, Haythorn, and Howell (30) arrived at the same conclusion following factorial analyses of several criteria of leadership. These findings may indicate the boundaries to the range of real-life situations in which leadership behavior can be forecast by rated LGD performance.

The 10 available correlations between intelligence and associated aptitude test scores and success in the LGD appear consistent with expectations. Yet, verbal aptitude only accounts for 10 to 15 percent of the variance in LGD, and so cannot be regarded as a more easily administered substitute for predicting success as a leader.

• *Achievement and leaderless group discussion performance.* Six studies are available of the correlation between LGD ratings and tested achievement, years of education, or grades in college.

---

9. See footnote 6.

TABLE 4

CORRELATION BETWEEN LGD PERFORMANCE AND MEASURES OF CAPACITY
AND ACHIEVEMENT

Subjects	Test of Capacity or Achievement	Factor(s) Most Probably Measured by Test or Measurement	Correlation
1. 140 sorority members (23)	ACE Linguistic	Verbal aptitude	.35
2. 66 fraternity pledges (72)	ACE Linguistic	Verbal aptitude	.32
3. 64 sales and management trainee candidates (10)	OSPE	Verbal aptitude	.25
4. 140 sorority members (23)	ACE Quantitative	Numerical aptitude	.17
5. 66 fraternity pledges (72)	ACE Quantitative	Numerical aptitude	.17
6. 180 ROTC cadets*	ACE Total	Verbal and numerical aptitude (intelligence)	.25
7. 202 administrator candidates (68)	South African Air Force test of mental alertness	Intelligence	.32†
8. 131 oil refinery supervisors (22)	Otis Gamma	Verbal, spatial, numerical, aptitude (intelligence)	.45
9. 123 foreign service candidates (69)	Cognitive Test Battery	Intelligence	.32
10. 202 administrator candidates (69)	Cognitive Test Battery	Intelligence	.20
11. 123 foreign service candidates (69)	Civil Service Qualifying Exam	Intelligence and scholastic achievement	.30
12. 202 administrator candidates (69)	Civil Service Qualifying Exam	Intelligence and scholastic achievement	.20
13. 140 sorority members (23)	Years of education	Scholastic achievement	.18
14. 131 oil refinery supervisors (22)	Years of education	Intelligence and scholastic achievement	.57†
15. 180 ROTC cadets	Average grade in college	Scholastic achievement	.16
16. 140 sorority members (23)	Average grade in college	Scholastic achievement	.31
17. 131 oil refinery supervisors (22)	Supervisory aptitude test	Supervisory aptitude	.30‡
18. 66 mixed college students (64)	How Supervise?	Supervisory knowledge	.46

* Unpublished data.
† Contaminated by the correlation between rank and test of measurement.
‡ Not affected by holding rank constant.

Again, the correlations are uniformly positive, ranging from .16 to .31, with a median of .25. If the unusually high correlation of .57 is ignored because it is contaminated by the correlation of rank with both education and LGD success, the median becomes .20.

Above and beyond the effects of rank, a correlation of .30 appears to exist between LGD performance and supervisory aptitude as measured by an optimally weighted battery of interest, biographical, and supervisory judgment tests.

How Supervise?, a fairly widely used test of knowledge of principles of supervision, which aims to predict success as an industrial supervisor, correlates .46

TABLE 5

CORRELATION BETWEEN LGD PERFORMANCE AND PERSONALITY TESTS OR MEASUREMENTS

	Subjects	Personality Test or Measurement	Trait Probably Measured	Correlation
1.	76 sorority members (18)	Guilford-Zimmerman Temperament Survey—G	General activity and energy	.15
2.	66 mixed college students (64)	Guilford-Zimmerman Temperament Survey—G	General activity and energy	.12
3.	20 sorority members highest and lowest on LGD (18)	Rorschach	Imagination, strongly interested in details, able to see larger aspects of things vs. conventionality, stereotypy, etc.	.60
4.	172 ROTC cadets (15)	UCPOC F scale	Authoritarianism, rigidity	.30†
5.	100 ROTC cadets*	Concealed Figures	Perceptual flexibility	.32
6.	67 ROTC cadets*	Gestalt Completion	Perceptual flexibility	.33
7.	140 sorority members (23)	Self-nominations for leadership positions in sorority	Self-esteem	.29
8.	18 sorority members highest and lowest on LGD (18)	W-A-Y interview	Self-esteem	‡
9.	76 sorority members (18)	Guilford-Zimmerman Temperament Survey—E	Emotional stability	.20
10.	66 mixed college students (64)	Guilford-Zimmerman Temperament Survey—E	Emotional stability	.17
11.	140 sorority members (23)	Peer ratings	Overt social adjustment	.28
12.	49 sorority members (18)	Guilford-Zimmerman Temperament Survey—F	Friendliness, agreeableness	-.23
13.	66 mixed college students (64)	Guilford-Zimmerman Temperament Survey—F	Friendliness, agreeableness	.04
14.	47 ROTC cadets*	Gordon Personal Profile—H	Freedom from hypersensitivity	-.40
15.	49 sorority members (18)	Guilford-Zimmerman Temperament Survey—O	Freedom from hypersensitivity	-.04
16.	66 mixed college students (64)	Guilford-Zimmerman Temperament Survey—O	Freedom from hypersensitivity	.29
17.	49 sorority members (18)	Guilford-Zimmerman Temperament Survey—P	Cooperativeness	.14
18.	66 mixed college students (64)	Guilford-Zimmerman Temperament Survey—P	Cooperativeness	.13
19.	76 sorority members (18)	Guilford-Zimmerman Temperament Survey—P	Sociability	.27

TABLE 5—*Continued*

	Subjects	Personality Test or Measurement	Trait Probably Measured	Correlation
20.	66 Mixed college students (64)	Guilford-Zimmerman Temperament Survey—S	Sociability	.31
21.	47 ROTC cadets*	Gordon Personal Profile—S	Sociability	.07
22.	47 ROTC cadets*	Gordon Personal Profile—R	Responsibility	-.29
23.	49 sorority members (18)	Guilford-Zimmerman Temperament Survey—T	Thoughtfulness, reflectiveness	.19
24.	66 mixed college students (64)	Guilford-Zimmerman Temperament Survey—T	Thoughtfulness, reflectiveness	.26
25.	76 sorority members (18)	Guilford-Zimmerman Temperament Survey—A	Ascendency	.44
26.	66 mixed college students (64)	Guilford-Zimmerman Temperament Survey—A	Ascendency	.25
27.	47 ROTC cadets*	Gordon Personal Profile—A	Ascendency	.02
28.	66 mixed college students (64)	A-S Reaction Test	Ascendency	-.02
29.	140 sorority members (23)	Ratings of motivation for various offices	Motivation to lead	-.05
30.	46 uncoached college students*	Check list descriptions	Parental initiation	-.08
31.	30 coached college students*	Check list descriptions	Parental initiation	.19
32.	46 uncoached college students*	Check list descriptions	Parental consideration	-.07
33.	30 coached college students*	Check list descriptions	Parental consideration	.07
34.	39 uncoached college students*	Kerr Empathy Test	Social knowledge	.16
35.	29 coached college students*	Kerr Empathy Test	Social knowledge	-.19
36.	22 coached college students*	Dymond Empathy Test (modified)	Accuracy of estimated self-ratings of others	-.07
37.	22 coached college students*	Dymond Empathy Test (modified)	Accuracy of estimated group ratings of self	.36
38.	22 coached college students*	Dymond Empathy Test (modified)	Accuracy of estimated group ratings of others	.19
39.	49 sorority members (18)	Guilford-Zimmerman Temperament Survey—M	Masculinity-femininity	-.02
40.	66 mixed college students (64)	Guilford-Zimmerman Temperament Survey—M	Masculinity-femininity	-.01

with the LGD success of 66 college students (64).

● *Personality and leaderless group discussion performance.* We shall now consider correlations obtained between LGD performance and the specific personality traits found to be associated with leadership according to Stogdill.

Stogdill cites five studies in which leaders are found to be more energetic than nonleaders. For the LGD, a correlation of .15 was found between general activity and energy as assessed by the Guilford-Zimmerman Temperament Survey for 76 sorority girls. A corresponding correlation of .12 was found for 66 college students (64). Also, LGD leaders were more often characterized in a Rorschach analysis as highly energetic, while LGD nonleaders more often were described as lazy or passive (18).

Stogdill uncovered a large number of studies that found successful leadership associated with originality, soundness of judgment, and ability to evaluate situations. Rorschach analysis characterized LGD leaders as strongly imaginative, strongly interested in details, and able to see the larger aspects of things, and LGD nonleaders as stereotyped or conventional in thoughts and perceptions, as unclear, plodding, and confused thinkers, and as unimaginative. A study of 172 ROTC cadets found an eta of .30 between the F scale of authoritarianism and LGD performance. Highly authoritarian—hence stereotyped and rigid—personalities did extremely poorly in the discussion, while equalitarian—but not too equalitarian—cadets earned the highest LGD scores. Among samples of 100 and 67 of these same cadets, Pearson correlations of .32 and .33 were found between LGD performance and Thurstone's Concealed Figures and Gestalt Completion tests—tests of perceptual flexibility.[10]

Self-assurance and absence of modesty were uniformly associated with leadership in 17 studies cited by Stogdill. Similarly, self-esteem as measured by 140 self-nominations for sorority leadership positions correlated .29 with LGD performance. An analysis of interviews with nine LGD leaders and nine LGD nonleaders from a total of 140 subjects using the Who-Are-You technique (28) showed that compared with nonleaders, LGD leaders more frequently regard in a more favorable light themselves, their effects on others, and other persons' effects on them.

Discrepancies between Stogdill's conclusions concerning leadership in general and LGD personality correlations arise when we consider personality characteristics such as emotional stability, sociability, ascendency, and responsibility.

Eleven studies have found emotional stability to be associated with leadership, although the evidence is not uniformly positive (63). Similarly, LGD performance correlated .20 and .17 with emotional stability as measured by the Guilford-Zimmerman inventory (18, 64). Rorschach analysis likewise characterized more LGD leaders than nonleaders as emotionally stable. Overt social adjustment based on peer ratings correlated .28 with LGD performance. On the other hand, five correlations found between LGD performance and the inventoried traits of freedom from hypersensitivity and hostility ranged from −.40 to .29 with a median of −.04 (18, 64).

Responsibility was uniformly reported by Stogdill to be associated with leadership. But a correlation of −.29 was found for 47 ROTC cadets between LGD ratings and responsibility as measured by the Gordon Personal Profile, while correlations of .19 and .26 were found in two analyses of the relations between thoughtfulness as assessed by the Guilford-Zimmerman and LGD performance (18, 64).

Evidence concerning the relation between extroversion, ascendency, and

---

10. See footnote 6.

leadership in general is contradictory according to Stogdill (63). Ascendency as measured by the Guilford-Zimmerman Temperament Survey correlated .44 with LGD performance of 76 sorority girls (18) and .25 with LGD performance of mixed college students (64); but ascendency as measured by the Gordon Personal Profile and the A-S Reaction Test correlated only .02 and −.02, respectively, with LGD performance.

Sociability as measured by the Guilford-Zimmerman in two studies (18, 64) correlated .27 and .31, respectively, with LGD performance; similar correlations between cooperativeness and LGD success were .14 and .13, while sociability as measured by the Gordon Personal Profile correlated close to zero with LGD performance.

Finally, while Stogdill found ambition and desire to excel important attributes of leadership, an average correlation of −.05 was found between LGD performance and expressed desire to hold sorority or university student offices (23).

It may be inferred that some consistency exists between Stogdill's generalizations of the relations between leadership in general and such personality traits as energy, flexibility of judgment, and self-esteem, and the relations between these traits and LGD performance. Contradiction or lack of uniformity appears when we consider such traits as responsibility, emotional stability, ascendency, and sociability.[11]

---

11. Part of this lack of uniformity may be due to variations among techniques used to measure the various personality traits, and variations in the sex composition of the samples studied.

The responsibility, ascendency, sociability, and freedom from hypersensitivity scales of the Gordon Personal Profile, a forced-choice personality inventory, administered to samples of men only, tended to correlate zero or negatively with LGD success. Corresponding Guilford-Zimmerman scales with the same or

• *Participation and LGD performance.* According to Stogdill, leaders, in general, tend to be more talkative, more industrious, and more likely to participate in group activities. The same appears to be true of high scorers on the LGD who, compared with low scorers, were found to make 1.5 times as many responses in a personal interview, and to give 1.6 as many responses to the Rorschach (18). LGD success also has been found, for 140 sorority members, to correlate .36 with the number of university student leadership positions held per semester, and .10 with the number of sorority positions held per semester (23).

• *Parental leadership and LGD performance.* It is expected that childhood experiences and memories of them should play a significant role in adolescent or adult leadership behavior (13).

---

similar names—of the traditional self-report type—tended to correlate positively with the LGD success of a sample of women only (18) and with the LGD success of mixed men and women (64).

Assuming the Gordon's forced-choice procedure is less subject to distortion than the Guilford-Zimmerman, and assuming that the measurement techniques rather than the samples were a significant source of variance, one might speculate that LGD performance tends to be associated with a participant's concept of himself, but only where the participant is free to distort the description to suit himself.

To go one step further, it may be that LGD success is related to the way a participant likes to see himself, but not to the way he actually sees himself when forced to make discriminations over which he has less control.

Neither of these self-inventoried evaluations actually meets the requirements of the original hypothesis that the more able member is more likely to be esteemed and be successful as a leader. The crucial evaluations of ability for leadership and esteem are those based not on self-evaluation, but on other group members' judgments of the participant, or on objective *tests* of personality (as contrasted with inventories).

In an unpublished study, the author hypothesized that LGD performance would be a function of the participants' perception of how they had been led by their parents. Examinees used modified Ohio State Leadership Studies behavior check lists (38) to describe the extent to which their mothers and fathers initiated structure for them and were considerate of them. The average and range of correlations between such descriptions and LGD performance suggested that no consistent relationship existed between parental descriptions and LGD performance.

• *Empathy and LGD performance.* A series of studies (e.g., 33, 67) has found a moderate relationship between empathic ability and leadership. The results have not been uniformly positive, mainly because the measure of empathy has varied greatly from one investigation to another. Elsewhere (13), the author has deduced that the more a person can accurately estimate the *needs* of others, the more likely he is to successfully lead others. Chowdry and Newcomb (33) have come closest to testing this hypothesis, and have obtained positive results.

Kerr and Dymond Empathy test data collected on a small sample (N's = 22 to 39) of students by Stolper (64) were correlated by the author with LGD performance scores, as shown in Table 5. The correlation of .36 between *accuracy of estimations of group ratings of self* on the Dymond test and LGD performance was somewhat artifactual since LGD leaders probably led in the Dymond test also, and *all* members of a group are likely to agree more closely on leaders' ratings compared to nonleaders, according to an earlier study by the author (6).

LEADERSHIP PERFORMANCE IN OTHER QUASI-REAL SITUATIONS AND LGD PERFORMANCE

According to Figure 1, leadership in other quasi-real situations is governed by the same individual factors as performance in the LGD. Therefore, the two should correlate fairly highly with each other if successful leadership is being measured in these other situations, and if ratings of LGD performance are valid as leadership ratings. Similar deductions can be made about LGD performance and success as a leader in real life.[12]

Table 6 summarizes the 17 available correlations between leadership or "desirability for leadership positions" ratings based on LGDs and other situational tests. The correlations are almost uniformly highly positive, but many are contaminated because the same raters were used to assess candidates during the LGD and the other situations.

The median correlation between interview and LGD ratings is .70. Where ratings are made by different raters in each situation, the correlation drops to .45 (9).

Correlations of .37 and .67 were found between ratings based on assigned leadership and leaderless discussion (3, 59). Correlations between the LGD and other verbal situational tests, such as debates and committee work, are almost as high as between the LGD and its retest, averaging .70. As the other situations involve less discussion and more mechanical or athletic activity, the median correlation between the LGD and these other situational tests is reduced to around .52.

Leadership ratings based on the leaderless group discussion alone correlated .64 with the final leadership ratings based on the entire OSS battery of situational tests (59).

LEADERSHIP PERFORMANCE IN REAL-LIFE SITUATIONS AND LGD PERFORMANCE

Table 7 summarizes the correlations between LGD performance and real-life

---

12. The same alternative interpretation and rebuttal apply here as are presented in footnote 5.

TABLE 6

CORRELATION BETWEEN PERFORMANCE IN OTHER QUASI-REAL SITUATIONS
AND IN THE LGD

Subjects		Other Quasi-Real Situational Tests	Trait Measured	Corre-lation
1. 223–442	OSS applicants (59)	Interview	Leadership	.48
2. 123	foreign service candidates (69)	Interview	Desirability for job	.75
3. 202	administrator candidates (69)	Interview	Desirability for job	.78
4. 64	sales management trainees (9)	Interview with different raters	Desirability for job	.45
5. 14	shoe factory trainee executive candidates (65)	Interview and tests	Desirability for job	.70
6. 223–442	OSS applicants (59)	Assigned leadership	Leadership	.37
7. 219	administrator candidates (3)	Assigned leadership	"Personality and ability"	.67
8. 223–442	OSS applicants (59)	Debate	Leadership	.56
9. 223–442	OSS applicants (59)	Brook	Leadership	.47
10. 223–442	OSS applicants (59)	Construction	Leadership	.30
11. 40	NROTC subjects (31)	Leaderless Mechanical Assembly—4-man	Leadership	.37
		Leaderless Mechanical Assembly—8-man	Leadership	.58
		Leaderless Group Reasoning Task—4-man	Leadership	.62
		Leaderless Group Reasoning Task—8-man	Leadership	.78
12. 123	foreign service candidates (69)	Other situational tests such as committee work	Desirability for job	.75
13. 202	administrator candidates (69)	Other situational tests such as committee work	Desirability for job	.70

leadership performance.[13] While LGD ratings correlate somewhat with the tendency to hold leadership offices, they appear to be associated more with the tendency in real life to initiate structure and interaction among associates and subordinates ($r = .32$). On the contrary, a low negative correlation exists between LGD performance and the tendency in real life to be considerate of the welfare of subordinates and associates ($r = -.25$).[14]

13. An attempt has been made in this article to treat separately from the more numerous studies of LGD performance correlated with merit ratings of real-life performance (Table 3), studies of the LGD correlated with objective indices of real-life leadership performance or fairly nonevaluative descriptions of real-life leadership performance. While usually empirically related, merit rating of performance is considered conceptually independent of actual performance or descriptions of performance.

STUDIES OF FACTORS ASSOCIATED WITH LGD PERFORMANCE

Two factorial studies analyzing LGD test

14. See footnote 6.

TABLE 7

CORRELATION BETWEEN LGD PERFORMANCE AND REAL-LIFE BEHAVIOR

Subjects	Method of Measurement	Real-Life Behavior Measured	Correla-tion
1. 140 sorority girls (23)	Extent of extracurricular activities	Participation in social groups	.32
2. 140 sorority girls (23)	Number of university leadership positions held	Real-life leadership performance	.36
3. 140 sorority girls (23)	Number of sorority leadership positions held	Real-life leadership performance	.10
4. 140 sorority girls (23)	Extent peers know her well enough to rate	Visibility among associates	.24
5. 180 ROTC cadets*	Final cadet rank achieved	Future success as a leader	.27†
6. 133 ROTC cadet officers*	Ratings of subordinates and peer associates	Degree of "consideration of subordinates"	−.25
7. 133 ROTC cadet officers*	Ratings of subordinates and peer associates	Degree of initiation of structure and interaction among associates and subordinates	.32
8. 32 sales trainee candidates (9)	Number of leadership positions held previously	Real-life leadership performance	‡

* Unpublished data.
† Eta (curvilinear relationship).
‡ Significant difference at 15 per cent level between LGD score of experienced leaders and those without experience as leaders.

TABLE 8

ORTHOGONAL FACTORS CORRELATED WITH OVER-ALL LGD PERFORMANCE

Factor	Correlation in Sororities (23)	Factor	Correlation in ROTC*
I. Leadership Potential (Esteem)	.24	I. Esteem	.30
II. Ascendency-Sociability	.39	II. Tendency to Initiate Structure	.53
III. Verbality	.51	III. Ability in Verbal Situations	.44
IV. Intellectualism	.21		

* Unpublished data.

and retest scores in a correlation matrix of real-life, situational test, and psychological test measures are available. The first (23) was based on 41 measurements of 140 sorority girls; the second concerned 14 measures made of 66 to 244 ROTC cadets.[15] Table 8 lists the

loadings of the LGD test and retest on the factors that accounted for most of the variance of the LGD.

In line with propositions stated earlier, ratings based on LGD performance appear to assess the extent to which an individual initiates structure or is socially bold in ambiguous situations. Esteem, or personal worth, and verbal ability are also involved. On the basis of

15. See footnote 6.

these studies it may be inferred that there exist three independent sources of variance underlying leaderless group discussion performance:

    I. Tendency to Initiate Structure
    II. Tendency to Be Esteemed or of Value to a Group
    III. Ability in Verbal Situations.

Little specific varience is left when the common variance accounted for by these factors is extracted.

SUMMARY

The history, applicability, reliability, and validity of the leaderless group discussion as a means of assessing variations among persons in the tendency to exhibit successful leadership behavior have been considered. While the procedure was originated as a psychological technique in Germany over 30 years ago, it is only in the last decade that systematic reliability and validity studies have appeared.

High interrater agreement and high test-retest reliabilities have been reported consistently, especially where descriptive behavior check lists have been used as the rating technique.

Group size, length of testing time, type of problem presented, directions, seating arrangement, number of raters, and rating procedure influence to a greater or lesser extent performance in the LGD as well as the reliability and validity of LGD ratings. Studies of the effects of many of these have appeared since 1950.

According to both deductive and inductive evidence, a valid assessment of the tendency to display successful leadership should correlate with: (a) status as measured by rank, when the assessment is based on performance among associates of different rank; (b) esteem in real life as estimated by merit ratings; (c) successful leadership performance in other quasi-real and real-life situations; (d) personal characteristics as measured by psychological tests, such as capacity, proficiency, responsibility, and partici-

pation. On the whole, ratings based on performance in the LGD tend to do this. Therefore, it is inferred that they have some validity as assessments of the tendency to display successful leadership, i.e., leadership potential.

Other evidence suggests that the successful leadership behavior observed in the LGD concerns primarily initiation of structure rather than consideration of the welfare of others.

The preceding analysis, coupled with recommendations made by others working in the field of situational tests, such as Weislogel (71), leads us to the following hypotheses:

1. To maximize the reliability and validity of the LGD and other situational tests, scoring techniques should minimize reliance on the ability of observers to infer differences in personality traits and future tendencies among examinees. Observers should merely report or evaluate the immediate behavior they observe. For example, in an unpublished study, the author found that two Army colonels' estimates of the potential as Army officers of ROTC examinees were less valid as predictors of the merit ratings of the examinees than were the colonels' check list descriptions of who initiated structure during the LGD. Similar results were noted in a study of fraternity members reported by the author and White (20).

When the observer makes an inference about the future behavior of an examinee from the observations of the examinee during the LGD, several potential errors are likely. The observer may err in deciding on which dimensions to make inferences; he may err in collating his observations with the future behavior to be predicted; and finally, the dimensions on which the inferences are made may be private ones which cannot be shared with other observers. The errors may be constant, variable, or both. Lack of knowledge and control over such errors disappears when raters are merely asked to describe what they observed and these descriptions are used as predictors.

Further reduction of uncontrolled raters' errors may be made in the following ways:

    a. Objective criteria for describing specific behaviors can be used (71). In the LGD, the actual number of times a participant suggests a new approach to a problem can be noted instead of rating "to what extent did the participant suggest new approaches to problems."

b. Forced-choice check lists can be used instead of present check lists. Otis' (60) recent successful application of the forced-choice technique to interviewer ratings indicates promise for applying the same procedure to the LGD.

2. To maximize validity, problems that are equally ambiguous to all participants, and that require the initiation of structure for their solution, should be used. Where interest is in forecasting leader behavior in real life, the structure to be set up should approximate the real-life setting as much as possible.

3. Since the LGD correlates fairly highly with most other intellectual or verbal situational tests, the use of many situational tests in a battery to forecast leadership potential is of doubtful utility. Thus, leadership ratings based on a one-hour LGD correlated above .60 with leadership assessments based on the three days of OSS situational testing (59). A similar correlation between the LGD and an entire battery of situational tests was found by Vernon (69). However, a significant proportion of the variance in over-all potential as a successful leader, unaccounted for by LGD, may be predicted by a fairly pure active or mechanical, initially leaderless, situational test which minimizes variance due to verbal ability.

4. Compared to paper-and-pencil techniques, the LGD is expensive; compared to the individual interview, in many locales, it may prove economical. The LGD appears feasible administratively, especially in military programs screening OCS or advanced ROTC applicants, in civil service examinations, in screening college seniors who are to be assessed at their colleges for management trainee positions, and anywhere else where "boards" have been used traditionally, such as in the selection of public school teachers.

5. While the LGD appears to have some validity as a predictor of the tendency to be a successful leader in a number of situations, especially in comparison to other assessment techniques, tailor-made batteries of paper-and-pencil tests will undoubtedly yield higher validities in designated situations. However, it may be that just as the brief intelligence test is applicable for pre-

dicting trainability for many skilled occupations, so the LGD will provide a general technique for partially assessing potential success as a leader in a relatively wide range of situations.

6. A number of situations in which the LGD is less likely to be successful may include the following:

a. The LGD is less likely to be valid for measuring or forecasting esteem or leadership potential when examinees can be tested only among others of different rank. In such a case, status—and not esteem or personality—will determine who succeeds in the LGD.

b. The LGD is less likely to be useful where factors peculiar to the situation block initiation of structure where no structure exists. Conceivably, in certain military settings for example, the examinees may be imbued with the dictum "never volunteer for anything." However, exactly how this would affect LGD validities is unknown.

c. Another unknown is the effect of the average verbal aptitude and educational status of the participants on the validity and utility of the LGD. It is expected that where this mean falls below a certain minimum, LGD forecasting efficiency may suffer.[16]

d. Since achievement and intelligence appear to correlate with LGD performance as well as with success as a leader in real life, any restriction in the range of intelligence or achievement of LGD participants would be likely to reduce the forecasting efficiency of the LGD. Conversely, the greater the variance in intelligence and achievement of participants, the more likely is the LGD to accurately assess leadership potential.

e. Finally, the less the leadership situation for which we are selecting leaders requires verbal communication or verbal problem solving, the less likely is the LGD to be useful as a measure or predictor of the tendency to exhibit successful leadership.

---

16. Subsequent to the preparation of this manuscript, the author found no systematic correlation between mean ACE scores and the validity (as estimated by correlation with real-life esteem) of 64 leaderless group discussions among college students.

NOTES

1. Adorno, T. W., Frenkel-Brunswik, Else, Levinson, D. J., & Sanford, R. N. *The authoritarian personality.* New York: Harper, 1950.
2. Ansbacher, H. L. The history of the leaderless group discussion technique. *Psychol. Bull.*, 1951, **48**, 383-390.
3. Arbous, A. G., & Maree, J. Contribution of two group discussion techniques to a validated test battery. *Occup. Psychol.*, 1951, **25**, 1-17.
4. Bales, R. *Interaction process analysis.* Cambridge: Addison Press, 1950.
5. Barnard, M. A., & Brody, W. A. A new method of selecting health officers-in-training. *Amer. J. Publ. Hlth*, 1946, **37**, 716.
6. Bass, B. M. An analysis of the leaderless group discussion. *J. Appl. Psychol.*, 1949, **33**, 527-533.
7. Bass, B. M. Selecting personnel by observation. *Personnel*, 1950, **26**, 269-272.
8. Bass, B. M. The leaderless group discussion technique. *Personnel Psychol.*, 1950, **3**, 17-32.
9. Bass, B. M. Situational tests: I. Individual interviews compared with leaderless group discussions. *Educ. Psychol. Measmt.*, 1951, **11**, 67-75.
10. Bass, B. M. Situational tests: II. Variables of the leaderless group discussion. *Educ. Psychol. Measmt.*, 1951, **11**, 196-207.
11. Bass, B. M. Discussion and external leadership status related to roles played in initially leaderless group discussions. *Amer. Psychologist*, 1951, **6**, 486. (Abstract)
12. Bass, B. M. Differential response patterns in initially leaderless discussions related to discussion and external status. *Amer. Psychologist*, 1951, **6**, 511. (Abstract)
13. Bass, B. M. A psychological theory of leadership. Mimeographed manuscript, Louisiana State Univer., Baton Rouge, 1953.
14. Bass, B. M. Symposium on situational performance tests: the leaderless group discussion as a leadership evaluation technique. *Personnel Psychol.*, in press.
15. Bass, B. M., & Coates, C. H. Forecasting officer potential using the leaderless group discussion. *J. Abnorm. Soc. Psychol.*, 1952, **47**, 321-325.
16. Bass, B. M., & Klubeck, S. Effects of seating arrangement on leaderless group discussions. *J. Abnorm. Soc. Psychol.*, 1952, **47**, 724-727.
17. Bass, B. M., Klubeck, S., & Wurster, C. R. Factors influencing the reliability and validity of leaderless group discussion assessment. *J. Appl. Psychol.*, 1953, **37**, 26-30.
18. Bass, B. M., McGehee, C. R., Hawkins, W. C., Young, P. C., & Gebel, A. Personality variables related to leaderless group discussion behavior. *J. Abnorm. Soc. Psychol.*, 1953, **48**, 120-128.
19. Bass, B. M., & Norton, F. T. M. Group size and leaderless discussions. *J. Appl. Psychol.*, 1951, **6**, 397-400.
20. Bass, B. M., & White, O. Situational tests: III. Observers' ratings of leaderless group discussion participants as indicators of external leadership status. *Educ. Psychol. Measmt.*, 1951, **11**, 355-361.
21. Bass, B. M., & Wurster, C. R. Effects of the nature of the problem on LGD performance. *J. Appl. Psychol.*, 1953, **37**, 96-99.
22. Bass, B. M., & Wurster, C. R. Effects of company rank on LGD performance of oil refinery supervisors. *J. Appl. Psychol.*, 1953, **37**, 100-104.
23. Bass, B. M., Wurster, C. R., Doll, P. A., & Clair, D. J. Situational and personality factors in leadership among sorority women. *Psychol. Monogr.*, 1953, **67**, No. 16 (Whole No. 366).
24. Bell, G. B., & French, R. L. Consistency of individual leadership position in small groups of varying membership. *J. Abnorm. Soc. Psychol.*, 1950, **45**, 764-767.
25. Benne, K. D., & Sheats, P. Functional roles of group members. *J. Soc. Issues*, 1948, **4**(2), 41-49.
26. Brody, W. Judging candidates by observing them in unsupervised group discussion. *Personnel*, 1947, **26**, 170-173.
27. Brody, W., & Powell, N. J. A new approach to oral testing. *Educ. Psychol. Measmt.*, 1947, **7**, 289-298.
28. Bugental, J. F. T., & Zelen, S. L. Investigations into the 'self-concept.' I. The

W-A-Y technique (Who are you?). *J. Pers.*, 1950, **18**, 483-498.

29. Carter, L. F. Recording and evaluating the performance of individuals as members of small groups. *Amer. Psychologist*, 1953, **8**, 464. (Abstract)

30. Carter, L., Haythorn, W., & Howell, Margaret. A further investigation of the criteria of leadership. *J. Abnorm. Soc. Psychol.*, 1950, **45**, 350-356.

31. Carter, L., Haythorn, W., Shriver, Beatrice, & Lanzetta, J. The relation of categorizations and ratings in the observation of group behavior. *Hum. Relat.*, 1951, **4**, 239-253.

32. Carter, L., Haythorn, W., Shriver, Beatrice, & Lanzetta, J. The behavior of leaders and other group members. *J. Abnorm. Soc. Psychol.*, 1951, **46**, 589-595.

33. Chowdry, K., & Newcomb, T. M. The relative abilities of leaders and non-leaders to estimate opinions. *J. Abnorm. Soc. Psychol.*, 1952, **47**, 51-57.

34. Couch, A. S., & Carter, L. F. A factorial study of the rated behavior of group members. *Amer. Psychologist*, 1952, **7**, 537. (Abstract)

35. Douglas, A. G. Shall civil service endorse science or novelty? *Publ. Adm. Rev.*, 1950, **10**, 78-86.

36. Fields, H. The group interview test: its strength. *Publ. Personnel Rev.*, 1950, **11**, 139-146.

37. Fields, H. An analysis of the use of the group oral interview. *Personnel*, 1951, **27**, 480-486.

38. Fleishman, E. A. The description of supervisory behavior. *J. Appl. Psychol.*, 1953, **37**, 1-6.

39. Fraser, J. M. An experiment with group methods in the selection of trainees for senior management positions. *Occup. Psychol.*, 1946, **20**, 63-67.

40. Fraser, J. M. New-type selection boards in industry. *Occup. Psychol.*, 1947, **21**, 170-178.

41. Garforth, G. I. de la P. War officer selection boards. *Occup. Psychol.*, 1945, **19**, 97-108.

42. Gellhorn, W., & Brody, W. Selecting supervisory mediators through trial by combat. *Publ. Adm. Rev.*, 1948, **8**, 259-266.

43. Gibb, C. A. The principles and traits of leadership. *J. Abnorm. Soc. Psychol.*, 1947, **42**, 267-284.

44. Gulliksen, H. Intrinsic validity. *Amer. Psychologist*, 1950, **5**, 511-517.

45. Harris, H. *The group approach to leadership-testing.* London: Routledge & Kergan-Paul, 1950.

46. Hemphill, J. K. Leadership in small groups. Multilithed manuscript, Personnel Research Board, The Ohio State Univer., 1952.

47. Herbert, L. A. Case study of a group selection procedure for selecting candidates for teacher's training. *Hum. Relat.*, 1951, **4**, 77-94.

48. Hollander, E. P. Authoritarianism and leadership choice in a military setting. *Amer. Psychologist*, 1953, **8**, 368. (Abstract)

49. Kelley, H. H. Communication in experimentally created hierarchies. *Hum. Relat.*, 1951, **4**, 39-56.

50. Klubeck, S., & Bass, B. M. Differential effects of training on persons of different leadership status. *Hum. Relat.*, 1954, **7**, 59-72.

51. Landry, H. A., Krugman, M., & Wrightstone, J. W. *Validation study of the group oral interview test.* New York: Bd. of Educ., 1951.

52. Lang, H. A. A statement on the practical application of role playing in the group interview technique by the Washington State Personnel Board. *Sociometry*, 1951, **14**, 63-68.

53. Mandell, M. M. The group oral performance test. *Publ. Personnel Rev.*, 1946, **4**, 209-212.

54. Mandell, M. M. Testing for administrative and supervisory positions. *Publ. Personnel Rev.*, 1948, **9**, 190-193.

55. Mandell, M. M. Validation of group oral performance test. *Personnel Psychol.*, 1950, **3**, 179-185.

56. Mandell, M. M. The group oral performance test. Multilithed manuscript, U.S. Civil Service Commission, 1952.

57. Mandell, M. M. The group oral performance test. *Personnel Adm.*, 1953, **15**, 11-17.

58. Meyer, C. A. The group interview test: its weakness. *Publ. Personnel Rev.*, 1950, **11**, 147-154.

59. OSS Assessment Staff. *Assessment of men.* New York: Rinehart, 1948.

60. Otis, J. J. The effectiveness of the selection interview in appraising personality of salesmen. *Amer. Psychologist*, 1953, **8**, 468. (Abstract)

61. Pepinsky, H. B., Siegel, L., & Vanatta, A. The criterion in counseling: a group participation scale. *J. Abnorm. Soc. Psychol.*, 1952, **47,** 415-419.

62. Sakoda, J. M. Factor analysis of OSS situational tests. *J. Abnorm. Soc. Psychol.*, 1952, **47,** 843-852.

63. Stogdill, R. M. Personal factors associated with leadership: a survey of the literature. *J. Psychol.*, 1948, **25,** 31-75.

64. Stolper, R. An investigation of some hypotheses concerning empathy. Unpublished master's thesis, Louisiana State Univer., 1953.

65. Taft, R. Use of the "group situation observation" method in the selection of trainee executives. *J. Appl. Psychol.*, 1948, **32,** 587-594.

66. Taft, R. Some correlates of the ability to make accurate social judgments. Unpublished doctor's dissertation, Uni-

ver. of California, Berkeley, 1950.

67. Van Zelst, R. H. Empathy test scores of union leaders. *J. Appl. Psychol.*, 1952, **36,** 293-295.

68. Vernon, P. E. The validation of civil service observation method in the selection of trainee executives. *Occup. Psychol.*, 1948, **32,** 587-594.

69. Vernon, P. E. The validation of civil service selection board procedures. *Occup. Psychol.*, 1950, **24,** 75-95.

70. Vernon, P. E., & Parry, J. B. *Personnel selection in the British Forces.* London: Univer. of London Press, 1949.

71. Weislogel, R. L. The development of situational performance tests for various types of military personnel. *Amer. Psychologist*, 1953, **8,** 464. (Abstract)

72. Wurster, C. R., & Bass, B. M. Situational tests: IV. Validity of leaderless group discussions among strangers. *Educ. Psychol. Measmt.*, 1953, **13,** 122-132.

29. Functional Roles of Group Members*

KENNETH D. BENNE
PAUL SHEATS

THE RELATIVE NEGLECT OF MEMBER ROLES IN GROUP TRAINING

Efforts to improve group functioning through training have traditionally emphasized the training of group leadership. And frequently this training has been directed toward the improvement of the skills of the leader in transmitting information and in manipulating groups. Little direct attention seems to have been given to the training of group members in the membership roles required for effective group growth and production. The present discussion is based on the conviction that both effective group training and adequate research into the effectiveness of group training methods must give attention to the identification, analysis, and practice of leader *and* member roles, seen as co-relative aspects of over-all group growth and production.

Certain assumptions have undergirded the tendency to isolate the leadership role from membership roles and to neglect the latter in processes of group training. 1) "Leadership" has been identified with traits and qualities inherent within the "leader" personality. Such traits and qualities can be developed, it is assumed, in isolation from the functioning of members in a group setting. The present treatment sees the leadership role in terms of functions to be performed within a group in helping that group to grow and to work produc-

*Source: From *Journal of Social Issues*, vol. 4, no. 2 (1948), pp. 41-49. Copyright © 1948 Society for the Psychological Study of Social Issues. Reprinted by permission.

tively. No sharp distinction can be made between leadership and membership functions, between leader and member roles. Groups may operate with various degrees of diffusion of "leadership" functions among group members or of concentration of such functions in one member or a few members. Ideally, of course, the concept of leadership emphasized here is that of a multilaterally shared responsibility. In any event, effectiveness in the leader role is a matter of leader-member relationship. And one side of a relationship cannot be effectively trained in isolation from the retraining of the other side of that relationship. 2) It has been assumed that the "leader" is uniquely responsible for the quality and amount of production by the group. The "leader" must see to it that the "right" group goals are set, that the group jobs get done, that members are "motivated" to participate. On this view, membership roles are of secondary importance. "Membership" is tacitly identified with "followership." The present discussion assumes that the quality and amount of group production is the "responsibility" of the group. The setting of goals and the marshalling of resources to move toward these goals is a group responsibility in which all members of a mature group come variously to share. The functions to be performed both in building and maintaining group-centered activity and in effective production by the group are primarily member roles. Leadership functions can be defined in terms of facilitating identification, acceptance, development and allocation of these group-required roles by the group. 3) There has frequently been a confusion between the roles which members enact within a group and the individual personalities of the group members. That there are relationships between the personality structures and needs of group members and the range and quality of group membership roles which members can learn to perform is not denied. On the contrary, the importance of

studies designed to describe and explain and to increase our control of these relationships is affirmed. But, at the level of group functioning, member roles, relevant to group growth and accomplishment, must be clearly distinguished from the use of the group environment by individuals to satisfy individual and group-irrelevant needs, if clear diagnosis of member-roles required by the group and adequate training of members to perform group-required roles are to be advanced. Neglect of this distinction has been associated traditionally with the neglect of the analysis of member roles in group growth and production.

A CLASSIFICATION OF MEMBER ROLES

The following analysis of functional member roles was developed in connection with the First National Training Laboratory in Group Development, 1947. It follows closely the analysis of participation functions used in coding the content of group records for research purposes. A similar analysis operated in faculty efforts to train group members in their functional roles during the course of the laboratory.[1]

The member-roles identified in this analysis are classified into three broad groupings.

(1) *Group task roles.* Participant roles here are related to the task which the group is deciding to undertake or has undertaken. Their purpose is to facilitate and coordinate group effort in the selection and definition of a common problem and in the solution of that problem.

(2) *Group building and maintenance roles.* The roles in this category are oriented toward the functioning of the group as a group. They are designed to alter or maintain the group way of working, to strengthen, regulate and perpetuate the group as a group.

(3) *Individual roles.* This category does not classify member-roles as such, since the "participations" denoted here are directed toward the satisfaction of the "participant's" individual needs. Their purpose

is some individual goal which is not relevant either to the group task or to the functioning of the group as a group. Such participations are, of course, highly relevant to the problem of group training, insofar as such training is directed toward improving group maturity or group task efficiency.

GROUP TASK ROLES

The following analysis assumes that the task of the discussion group is to select, define and solve common problems. The roles are identified in relation to functions of facilitation and coordination of group problem-solving activities. Each member may of course enact more than one role in any given unit of participation and a wide range of roles in successive participations. Any or all of these roles may be played at times by the group "leader" as well as by various members.

a. The *initiator-contributor* suggests or proposes to the group new ideas or a changed way of regarding the group problem or goal. The novelty proposed may take the form of suggestions of a new group goal or a new definition of the problem. It may take the form of a suggested solution or some way of handling a difficulty that the group has encountered. Or it may take the form of a proposed new procedure for the group, a new way of organizing the group for the task ahead.

b. The *information seeker* asks for clarification of suggestions made in terms of their factual adequacy, for authoritative information and facts pertinent to the problem being discussed.

c. The *opinion seeker* asks not primarily for the facts of the case but for a clarification of the values pertinent to what the group is undertaking or of values involved in a suggestion made or in alternative suggestions.

d. The *information giver* offers facts or generalizations which are "authoritative" or relates his own experience pertinently to the group problem.

e. The *opinion giver* states his belief or opinion pertinently to a suggestion made or to alternative suggestions. The emphasis is on his proposal of what should become the group's view of pertinent values, not

primarily upon relevant facts or information.

f. The *elaborator* spells out suggestions in terms of examples or developed meanings, offers a rationale for suggestions previously made and tries to deduce how an idea or suggestion would work out if adopted by the group.

g. The *coordinator* shows or clarifies the relationships among various ideas and suggestions, tries to pull ideas and suggestions together or tries to coordinate the activities of various members or sub-groups.

h. The *orienter* defines the position of the group with respect to its goals by summarizing what has occurred, points to departures from agreed upon directions or goals, or raises questions about the direction which the group discussion is taking.

i. The *evaluator-critic* subjects the accomplishment of the group to some standard or set of standards of group-functioning in the context of the group task. Thus, he may evaluate or question the "practicality," the "logic," the "facts" or the "procedure" of a suggestion or of some unit of group discussion.

j. The *energizer* prods the group to action or decision, attempts to stimulate or arouse the group to "greater" or "higher quality" activity.

k. The *procedural technician* expedites group movement by doing things for the group—performing routine tasks, e.g., distributing materials, or manipulating objects for the group, e.g., rearranging the seating or running the recording machine, etc.

l. The *recorder* writes down suggestions, makes a record of group decisions, or writes down the product of discussion. The recorder role is the "group memory."

GROUP BUILDING AND MAINTENANCE ROLES

Here the analysis of member-functions is oriented to those participations which have for their purpose the building of group-centered attitudes and orientation among the members of a group or the maintenance and perpetuation of such group-centered behavior. A given contribution may involve several roles and a member or the "leader" may perform various roles in successive contributions.

a. The *encourager* praises, agrees with and accepts the contribution of others. He indicates warmth and solidarity in his attitude toward other group members, offers commendation and praise and in various ways indicates understanding and acceptance of other points of view, ideas and suggestions.

b. The *harmonizer* mediates the differences between other members, attempts to reconcile disagreements, relieves tension in conflict situations through jesting or pouring oil on the troubled water, etc.

c. The *compromiser* operates from within a conflict in which his idea or position is involved. He may offer compromise by yielding status, admitting his error, by disciplining himself to maintain group harmony, or by "coming half-way" in moving along with the group.

d. The *gate-keeper and expediter* attempts to keep communication channels open by encouraging or facilitating the participation of others ("we haven't got the ideas of Mr. X yet," etc.) or by proposing regulation of the flow of communication ("why don't we limit the length of our contributions so that everyone will have a chance to contribute?", etc.).

e. The *standard setter* or *ego ideal* expresses standards for the group to attempt to achieve in its functioning or applies standards in evaluating the quality of group processes.

f. The *group-observer* and *commentator* keeps records of various aspects of group process and feeds such data with proposed interpretations into the group's evaluation of its own procedures.

g. The *follower* goes along with the movement of the group, more or less passively accepting the ideas of others, serving as an audience in group discussion and decision.

"INDIVIDUAL" ROLES

Attempts by "members" of a group to satisfy individual needs which are irrelevant to the group task and which are non-oriented or negatively oriented to group building and maintenance set problems of group and member training. A high incidence of "individual-centered" as opposed to "group-centered" participation in a group always calls for self-diagnosis of the group. The diagnosis may reveal one or several of a number of conditions—low level of skill-training among members, including the group leader; the prevalence of "authoritarian" and "laissez faire" points of view toward group functioning in the group; a low level of group maturity, discipline and morale; an inappropriately chosen and inadequately defined group task, etc. Whatever the diagnosis, it is in this setting that the training needs of the group are to be discovered and group training efforts to meet these needs are to be defined. The outright "suppression" of "individual roles" will deprive the group of data needed for really adequate self-diagnosis and therapy.

a. The *aggressor* may work in many ways—deflating the status of others, expressing disapproval of the values, acts or feelings of others, attacking the group or the problem it is working on, joking aggressively, showing envy toward another's contribution by trying to take credit for it, etc.

b. The *blocker* tends to be negativistic and stubbornly resistant, disagreeing and opposing without or beyond "reason" and attempting to maintain or bring back an issue after the group has rejected or bypassed it.

c. The *recognition-seeker* works in various ways to call attention to himself, whether through boasting, reporting on personal achievements, acting in unusual ways, struggling to prevent his being placed in an "inferior" position, etc.

d. The *self-confessor* uses the audience opportunity which the group setting provides to express personal, non-group oriented, "feeling," "insight," "ideology," etc.

e. The *playboy* makes a display of his lack of involvement in the group's processes. This may take the form of cynicism, nonchalance, horseplay and other more or less studied forms of "out of field" behavior.

f. The *dominator* tries to assert authority or superiority in manipulating the group or certain members of the group. This domination may take the form of flattery, of asserting a superior status or right to attention, giving directions authoritatively, interrupting the contributions of others, etc.

g. The *help-seeker* attempts to call forth "sympathy" response from other group members or from the whole group, whether through expressions of insecurity, personal confusion or depreciation of himself beyond "reason."

h. The *special interest pleader* speaks for the "small business man," the "grass roots" community, the "housewife," "labor," etc., usually cloaking his own prejudices or biases in the stereotype which best fits his individual need.

THE PROBLEM OF MEMBER ROLE REQUIREDNESS

Identification of group task roles and of group building and maintenance roles which do actually function in processes of group discussion raises but does not answer the further question of what roles are required for "optimum" group growth and productivity. Certainly the discovery and validation of answers to this question have a high priority in any advancing science of group training and development. No attempt will be made here to review the bearing of the analyzed data from the First National Training Laboratory in Group Development on this point.

It may be useful in this discussion, however, to comment on two conditions which effective work on the problem of role-requiredness must meet. First, an answer to the problem of optimum task role requirements must be projected against a scheme of the process of group production. Groups in different stages of an act of problem selection and solution will have different role requirements. For example, a group early in the stages of problem selection which is attempting to lay out a range of possible problems to be worked on, will probably have relatively less need for the roles of "evaluator-critic," "energizer" and "coordinator" than a group which has selected and discussed its problem and is shaping to decision. The combination and balance of task role

requirements is a function of the group's stage of progress with respect to its task. Second, the group building role requirements of a group are a function of its stage of development—its level of group maturity. For example, a "young" group will probably require less of the role of the "standard setter" than a more mature group. Too high a level of aspiration may frustrate a "young" group where a more mature group will be able to take the same level of aspiration in its stride. Again the role of "group observer and commentator" must be carefully adapted to the level of maturity of the group. Probably the distinction between "group" and "individual" roles can be drawn much more sharply in a relatively mature than in a "young" group.

Meanwhile, group trainers cannot wait for a fully developed science of group training before they undertake to diagnose the role requirements of the groups with which they work and help these groups to share in such diagnosis. Each group which is attempting to improve the quality of its functioning as a group must be helped to diagnose its role requirements and must attempt to train members to fill the required roles effectively. This describes one of the principal objectives of training of group members.

THE PROBLEM OF ROLE FLEXIBILITY

The previous group experience of members, where this experience has included little conscious attention to the variety of roles involved in effective group production and development, has frequently stereotyped the member into a limited range of roles. These he plays in all group discussions whether or not the group situation requires them. Some members see themselves primarily as "evaluator-critics" and play this role in and out of season. Others may play the roles of "encourager" or of "energizer" or of "information giver" with only small sensitivity to the role requirements of a given group situation. The development of skill and insight in diagnosing role requirements has already been mentioned as an objective of group member training. An equally important objective is the development of role flexibility, of skill and security in a wide range of member roles on the part of all group members.

A science of group training, as it develops, must be concerned with the relationships between the personality structures of group members and the character and range of member roles which various personality structures support and permit. A science of group training must seek to discover and accept the limitations which group training per se encounters in altering personality structures in the service of greater role flexibility on the part of all members of a group. Even though we recognize the importance of this caution, the objective of developing role flexibility remains an important objective of group member training.

METHODS OF GROUP MEMBER TRAINING

The objectives in training group members have been identified. Some of the kinds of resistances encountered in training group members to diagnose the role requirements of a group situation and to acquire skill in a variety of member roles have been suggested. Before analyzing briefly the methods used for group member training in the First National Training Laboratory, a few additional comments on resistances to member training may be useful. The problem of group training is actually a problem of re-training. Members of a training group have had other group experiences. They bring to the training experience attitudes toward group work, more or less conscious skills for dealing with leaders and other members, and a more or less highly developed rationale of group processes. These may or may not support processes of democratic operation in the training group. Where they do not, they function as resistances to retraining. Again, trainees are inclined to make little or no distinction between the roles they perform in a group and their personalities. Criticism of the role a group member plays is perceived as criticism of "himself." Methods must be found to reduce ego-defensiveness toward criticism of member roles. Finally, training groups must be helped to make a distinction between group feeling and group productivity. Groups which attain a state of good group feeling often perceive attempts to diagnose and criticize their level of productivity as threats to this feeling of group warmth and solidarity.

(1) Each Basic Skill Training group in the Laboratory used self-observation and diagnosis of its own growth and development as a primary means of member training.

(a) Sensitization to the variety of roles involved in and required by group functioning began during the introduction of members to the group. In one BST group, this early sensitization to member role variety and role requiredness began with the "leader's" summarizing, as part of his introduction of himself to the group, certain of the member roles in which he was usually cast by groups and other roles which he found it difficult to play, even when needed by the group. He asked the group's help in criticizing and improving his skill in those roles where he felt weakest. Other members followed suit. Various members showed widely different degrees of sensitivity to the operation of member roles in groups and to the degree of their own proficiency in different roles. This introduction procedure gave the group a partial listing of member roles for later use and supplementation, initial self-assessments of member strengths and weaknesses and diagnostic material concerning the degree of group self-sophistication among the members. The training job

434 KENNETH D. BENNE & PAUL SHEATS

had come to be seen by most members as a re-training job.

(b) A description of the use of training observers in group self-evaluation sessions is given in the next paper in this issue. At this point, only the central importance which self-evaluation sessions played in member training needs to be stressed. Research observers fed observational data concerning group functioning into periodic discussions by the group of its strengths and weaknesses as a group. Much of these data concerned role requirements for the job the group had been attempting, which roles had been present, which roles had probably been needed. "Individual" roles were identified and interpreted in an objective and non-blaming manner. Out of these discussions, group members came to identify various kinds of member roles, to relate role requiredness to stages in group production and in group growth and to assess the range of roles each was able to play well when required. Out of these discussions came group decisions concerning the supplying of needed roles in the next session. Member commitments concerning behavior in future sessions also came out of these evaluations. These took the form both of silent commitments and of public commitments in which the help of the group was requested.

(c) Recordings of segments of the group's discussion were used by most Basic Skill Training groups. Groups listened to themselves, diagnosed the member and leader functions involved and assessed the adequacy of these.

(2) Role-played sessions in each group, although they were pointed content-wise to the skills of the change-agent, offered important material for the diagnosis of member roles and of role-requiredness. These sessions offered an important supplement to group self-diagnosis and evaluation. It is easier for members to get perspective on their participation in a role-played episode of group process than it is on their own participation in a "real"

group. The former is not perceived as "real." The role is more easily disengaged for purposes of analysis and evaluation from the person playing the role. Ego-defensiveness toward the role as enacted is reduced. Role-playing sessions also provided practice opportunity to members in a variety of roles.

(3) Practice by group members of the role of *observer-commentator* is especially valuable in developing skill in diagnosing member roles and in assessing the role requirements of a group situation. In several groups, each member in turn served as observer, supplementing the work of the research observers in evaluation sessions. Such members worked more or less closely with the anecdotal observer for the group on skill-problems encountered. Practice opportunity in the *observer-commentator* role was also provided in clinic group meetings in the afternoon.

SUMMARY

Training in group membership roles requires the identification and analysis of various member roles actually enacted in group processes. It involves further the analysis of group situations in terms of roles required in relation both to a schema of group production and to a conception of group growth and development. A group's self-observation and self-evaluation of its own processes provides useful content and practice opportunity in member training. Practice in enacting a wider range of required roles and in role flexibility can come out of member commitment to such practice with help from the group in evaluating and improving the required skills. Member training is typically re-training and resistances to re-training can be reduced by creating a non-blaming and objective atmosphere in group self-evaluation and by using role-playing of group processes for diagnosis and practice. The training objectives of developing skill in the diagnosis of group role requirements and developing role flexibility among members also indicate important research areas for a science of group training.

NOTE

1. A somewhat different analysis of member-participations, in terms of categories used by interaction-observers in observation of group processes in the First National Training Laboratory, is described in the *Preliminary Report* of the laboratory, pages 122-132. The number of categories used by interaction observers was "directed primarily by limitations of observer load."

30. "Consideration," "Initiating Structure," and Organizational Criteria—A Review*

ABRAHAM K. KORMAN

INTRODUCTION

Among the several large-scale psychological research programs on leadership which developed after World War II, one of the most significant was that at Ohio State University during the years 1946-1956 (approximately). While this program was responsible for a variety of significant findings, it is quite likely that the most important contribution was isolation of "Consideration" and "Initiating Structure" as basic dimensions of leadership behavior in the formal organization. These variables were identified as a result of a series of investigations which attempted to determine, through factor-analytic procedures, the smallest number of dimensions which would adequately describe leader behavior, as perceived by the leader's subordinates and as the leader himself perceived his own attitudes toward his role. The result, in both cases, was the isolation of two identical dimensions which were named "Consideration" and "Initiating Structure" and which were defined in the following manner (Fleishman & Peters, 1962):

Initiating Structure (S): Reflects the extent to which an individual is likely to define and structure his role and those of his subordinates toward goal attainment. A high score on this dimension characterizes individuals who play a more active role in directing group activities through planning, communicating information, scheduling, trying out new ideas, etc.

Consideration (C): Reflects the extent to which an individual is likely to have job relationships characterized by mutual trust, respect for subordinates' ideas, and consideration of their feelings. A high score is indicative of a climate of good rapport and two-way communication. A low score indicates the supervisor is likely to be more impersonal in his relations with group members.

These dimensions in the industrial situation are now measured by two separate questionnaires, depending on the nature of the responding population (Fleishman, 1953a, 1953b). The *Leadership Opinion Questionnaire* is a Likert-type attitude scale which attempts to assess how the supervisor thinks he should behave in his leadership role, while the *Leader Behavior Description Questionnaire* typically measures sub-

Source: From *Personnel Psychology*, vol. 19, no. 4 (Winter 1966), pp. 349-361. Copyright © 1966 by Personnel Psychology, Inc. Reprinted by permission.

ordinate perceptions of supervisory behavior. (This latter questionnaire can, however, theoretically be completed by other observers of the supervisor's behavior.)

Since these original descriptive developments, attention has turned to an examination of the relationship between variations on these dimensions and various effectiveness criteria with the result that there has now accumulated a significant number of studies of this type. The purpose of this paper is to provide a review of these studies and to suggest some possible implications for further research. While no claim is made that the coverage of this review is complete, all those journals which would be expected to carry research of this nature were examined for criterion-oriented studies of "Consideration" and "Initiating Structure," and private correspondence was engaged in with those psychologists who are prominently associated with research on these dimensions in order to uncover unpublished studies, if any. It should be noted that research on "C" and "S" as dependent variables in training studies, etc. (cf. Fleishman, Harris & Burtt, 1955; Barrett, 1965) were not of concern here and are not included in this review. The sole interest was in reviewing the obtained relationships of these dimensions to specific independent organizational criteria, i.e., in the traditional "experimental" sense, we were interested in them only as independent variables. In addition, this review is not concerned with other studies relating leader characteristics to effectiveness, since these other leader characteristics have not been defined in the same way nor are they subjected to the same type of measurement procedures (cf. Likert [1961] for a review of these other studies).

RESULTS

Tables 1 and 2 provide summary review of the relationships between vari-

ous criteria and the Leadership Opinion Questionnaire and the Leader Behavior Description Questionnaire, respectively.

In addition to the studies detailed in these tables, there are at least two other non-correlational published reports which are relevant to the concerns of this paper. Rambo (1958) has reported the development of a questionnaire which is explicitly designed to measure the "Consideration" and "Initiating Structure" dimensions analogously to the Leader Behavior [Description] Questionnaire. In the same paper, Rambo reports that there was no relationship between scores on his questionnaire and superior ratings. In another paper, Hills (1963) in a study of 53 school principals, found that those who were high on both dimensions on the Leader Behavior [Description] Questionnaire were also rated significantly higher by their subordinates on various attitude dimensions. They were also rated higher by their supervisors, but not significantly.

DISCUSSION

Since the studies reported in Tables 1 and 2 were done under a wide number of conditions and in a host of different circumstances, a tabular summary of the results would be somewhat meaningless and will not be attempted here. Nevertheless, the general pattern of the results are such that several implications seem clear, both in terms of interpreting the data presented and in suggesting directions for further research.

First, looking at Table 1, most of the correlations are insignificant for both variables. Whatever trend that does exist seems to indicate that consideration might have some relation to a "pleasantly affective" work situation as it is rated both by self (Oaklander & Fleishman, 1964) and by subordinates (Parker, 1963). However, this conclusion is mitigated by the fact that, in the former case, predictor and criterion ratings were made by the same people who might be seeking some kind of "balanced" situation. Thus, for example, lack of "intra-unit stress" might lead the supervisor to consider himself as more considerate, while the reverse might also be true. The results in Table 1 for "Initiating Structure" are quite inconsistent and no discernible pattern appears except for the prevalence of low correlations.

Studies of the Leader Behavior Description Questionnaire tend to show a slightly more consistent pattern of Consideration being related to effective performance positively and Initiating Structure negatively, but there is a great degree of inconsistency (cf. Bass, 1957; Hemphill, 1955), even among studies using somewhat similar populations (Halpin & Winer, 1957; Halpin, 1957). Similarly, the tendency to design studies where the same people make both predictor and criterion ratings is a problem here also since, again, the rater might distort one (or both) of his perceptions in order to attain a more "balanced" cognition (cf. Halpin, 1957).

What seems most apparent, however, is that there is very little evidence that leadership behavioral and/or attitudinal variation, as defined by scores on the Leadership Behavior [Description] and Leadership Opinion Questionnaire, are predictive of later effectiveness and/or satisfaction criteria. The writer was unable to locate any studies in the literature where "Consideration" and/or "Initiating Structure" were experimentally varied in order to determine criterion outcomes, and there are only two predictive field studies (Bass, 1956, 1958), both with relatively small samples and both of which support a relationship (moderate) for "Consideration" only. The great preponderance of concurrent validity studies provide no evidence whatsoever, even in those cases of positive relationships, that variation on these scales is a predictor of different kinds of worker behavior since, as we have argued above, the reverse could very easily be the case. For example, Vroom (1964) has pointed out that a supervisor might be more considerate of a superior subordinate than one who is not an effective performer, thus reversing the causal relationship usually hypothesized. This hypothesis by Vroom is similar to one proposed by Kipnis (1960) who argued on the basis of a literature review that supervisors rate higher those individuals who are supportive of the supervisor. Similarly, one could also argue that a supervisor has to exhibit more "S" with a low performing group than high performers. Thus, it seems that a justifiable conclusion would be that there is a great need for experimental research and predictive studies oriented toward determining the predictive significance of variation in Leader "Consideration" and "Initiating Structure" before they are utilized further as dependent variables in applied training programs, etc.

A second conclusion which seems inescapable concerns the design of the concurrent validity studies reviewed. While a few of those actively involved in this area have emphasized constantly that the effects of "Consideration" and "Initiating Structure" on performance would depend on various situational variables (cf. Fleishman, 1953a; Oaklander & Fleishman, 1964), in most cases the researchers have made little attempt to either conceptualize situational variables which might be relevant and/or measure them. Instead, the researchers have tended almost always to follow the two-variable design which consists simply of correlating the test variable with the criterion variable, with little appreciation of the possible situational variables which might be moderating these relationships. A good example of a more satisfactory approach is that by Vroom and Mann (1960) who showed that the acceptability of certain kinds of supervisory behavior varied according to the size of the organizational units involved. Thus authoritarian (high F-scale) leaders were more accepted by workers in large units than were those low on this variable

TABLE 1
Validity Studies of the Leadership Opinion Questionnaire

Investigator	Type of Sample	Type of Validity	Type of Criteria	Correlation with Consideration	Correlation with Initiating Structure	N
I. Objective Measures of Performance as Criteria						
Parker (1963)	Supervisors	Concurrent	Group Productivity	.13	.07	80
			Order-Filling Errors Group	−.11	.15	80
			Order-Pricing Errors Group	−.10	.23*	80
Spitzer & McNamara (1964)	Various Mgmt. Levels	Concurrent	Corrected Salary—Sample A	.02	.09	51
			Corrected Salary—Sample B	.14	−.05	51
II. Superior Ratings as Criteria			*Rating*			
Bass (1956)	Supervisors	Predictive	Over-All	.29*	−.09	53
Bass (1958)	Supervisors	Predictive	Over-All	.32*	.05	42
Fleishman & Peters (1962)	Various Mgmt. Levels	Concurrent	Over-All	.02	−.02	35
Oaklander & Fleishman (1964)	Large Hospital Mgmt.	Concurrent	Inter-Unit Stress Sample A	.16	.06	60
	Medium Hospital Mgmt.		Inter-Unit Stress Sample B	.19	−.39**	36
	Small Hospital Mgmt.		Inter-Unit Stress Sample C	.15	−.30	22
Spitzer & McNamara (1964)	Various Mgmt. Levels	Concurrent	Over-All—Sample A	.04	−.07	51
			Over-All—Sample B	−.06	.13	51

III. Peer Ratings As Criteria

Study	Group	Type	Criterion			N
Spitzer & McNamara (1964)	Various Mgmt. Levels	Concurrent	Over-All Ratings Sample A	-.17	.14	51
			Over-All Weighted Ratings—Sample A	-.12	.15	51
			Over-All Rankings Sample A	-.09	.04	51
			Over-All Ratings Sample B	.03	-.11	51
			Over-All Weighted Ratings—Sample B	.01	-.09	51
Fleishman (1957)	OCS Group	Concurrent	Over-All Rankings Sample B	-.02	-.01	51
			Over-All Ratings	-.01	.03	116
			Over-All Ratings	-.02	.08	247

IV. Self-Ratings As Criteria

Study	Group	Type	Criterion			N
Oaklander & Fleishman (1964)	Large Hospital Mgmt.	Concurrent	Intra-Unit Stress Sample A	-.37**	-.41**	60
	Medium Hospital Mgmt.	Concurrent	Intra-Unit Stress Sample B	-.46**	-.07	36
	Small Hospital Mgmt.	Concurrent	Intra-Unit Stress Sample C	-.02	.45*	22

V. Subordinate-Ratings As Criteria

Study	Group	Type	Criterion			N
Parker (1963)	Supervisors	Concurrent	Attitudes Toward Supervisor	.51*	.22*	80
			Supervisory Recognition	.45**	.05	80
			Performance Instrumentality	.24*	.18	80

* $p < .05$.
** $p < .01$.

TABLE 2
Validity Studies of the Leader Behavior Description Questionnaire

Investigator	Type of Sample	Type of Validity	Type of Criteria	r with Consideration	r with Initiating Structure	N
I. Objective Measures of Performance as Criteria						
Fleishman (1953)	Supervisors	Concurrent	Work Group Grievances	-.43	.23	23
Fleishman, Harris & Burtt (1955)	Production Supervisors	Concurrent	Work Group Absenteeism	-.49**	.27*	72
			Work Group Accidents	-.06	.15	72
			Work Group Grievances	-.07	.45**	72
			Work Group Turnover	.13	.06	72
Fleishman, Harris & Burtt (1955)	Non-Production Supervisors	Concurrent	Work Group Absenteeism	-.38	-.06	23
			Work Group Accidents	-.42*	.18	23
			Work Group Grievances	.15	.23	23
			Work Group Turnover	.04	.51*	23
Fleishman & Harris (1962)	Supervisors	Concurrent	Work Group Grievances	-.51**[1]	.71**[1]	57
			Work Group Turnover	-.69**[1]	.63**[1]	57
II. Superior Ratings As Criteria						
			Rating			
Halpin & Winer (1957)	Air Crew Commanders	Concurrent	Technical Competence	-.38*[2]	.36*	29
			Effectiveness of Working with Crew Members	-.33	.40*	29
III. Combined Peer-Subordinate Ratings As Criteria						
Hemphill (1955)	Academic Department Heads	Concurrent	Administrative Reputation	.36	.48*	18

IV. Peer Ratings As Criteria

Study	Sample	Type	Criteria			N
Bass (1957)	Sales Supervisors —Sample A	Concurrent	Visibility	-.04	-.11	34
			Popularity	.06	.12	34
			Value to Company	.08	.10	34
			Problem-Solving Ability	.05	-.06	34
			Ability to Influence Rater	-.18	.15	34
Bass (1957)	Sales Supervisors —Sample B	Concurrent	Visibility	-.03	.25	28
			Popularity	-.09	-.04	28
			Value to Company	-.11	-.09	28
			Problem-Solving Ability	.00	.14	28
			Ability to Influence Rater	-.09	.15	28

V. Subordinate Ratings as Criteria

Study	Sample	Type	Criteria			N
Halpin & Winer (1957)	Air Crew Commanders	Concurrent	Satisfaction	.57**[a]	-.03	29
			Conformity to Standard Operating Procedures	-.52**	.54**	29
			Performance Under Stress	.24	.26	29
			Attitude & Motivation to be Effective	-.50**	.42*	29
			Over-All	-.46*	.48**	29
Halpin (1957)	Aircraft Commanders	Concurrent	Technical Competence	.09	.30**	87
			Effectiveness in Working with Others	.18	.28**	87
			Conformity to Standard Procedures	-.03	.32**	87
			Performance under Stress	.18	.32**	87
			Attitude & Motivation	.03	.29	87
			Over-All Effectiveness	.17	.30**	87

TABLE 2—*Cont.*

V. Subordinate Ratings as Criteria—*Cont.*

Investigator	Type of Sample	Type of Validity	Type of Criteria		*r* with Consideration	*r* with Initiating Structure	*N*
				Rating			
Fleishman, Harris & Burtt (1955)	Production Foremen	Concurrent	Over-All		−.31**	.47**	72
Fleishman, Harris & Burtt (1955)	Non-Production Foremen	Concurrent	Over-All		.28	−.19	23
Bass (1957)	Sales Supervisors —Sample A	Concurrent	Merit		−.02	−.05	34
	Sales Supervisors —Sample B	Concurrent	Merit		.02	.15	28
Halpin (1957)	Air Craft Commanders	Concurrent	Confidence & Proficiency		.69**	.68**	84
			Friendship & Cooperation		.84**	.51**	84
			Morale		.27**	.28**	84
			Satisfaction		.75*	.47**	88

[1] These are correlation ratios. All other correlations in Tables 1 and 2 are Pearson *r*'s.

[2] All predictor-criterion correlations reported for the Halpin and Winer (1957) study are partial *r*'s with the effect of the other predictor-criterion correlation removed. Unlike most studies, "Consideration" and "Initiating Structure" were highly negatively related for this sample.

[3] See Footnote 2 above.

* *p* < .05.

** *p* < .01.

whereas the reverse was true for those in small units. This kind of "situational variable," it seems, is only one of the kinds of situational variables which might moderate the relationships between "Consideration" and "Initiating Structure" and performance variables, with another being the "organizational climate" of the company (cf. Fleishman, Harris & Burtt, 1955), and perhaps some others. What is needed, however, in future concurrent (and predictive) studies is not just recognition of this factor of "situational determinants" but, rather, a systematic conceptualization of situational variance as it might relate to leadership behavior and a research program designed to test derivations from such a conceptualization so that direction might be given to the field. The piecemeal accumulation of "two-variable" studies such as that detailed in Tables 1 and 2 does not provide the kinds of direction needed. One start in this direction has been made by Katzell et al. (Katzell, Barrett & Parker, 1961), who have suggested that the effectiveness of particular kinds of leadership practices might be moderated by such variables as the size of the company and the degree of urbanization where the company is located. On the other hand, a different kind of situational moderator has been proposed by Vroom (1964) who feels that the degree of acceptance which particular kinds of supervisory practices receive might be determined by the wishes and expectancies of the subordinates, and who cites research by himself and others in support of this hypothesis. Korman (1966), however, has provided evidence which indicates that the Vroom hypothesis may hold only for high self-esteem individuals. It seems apparent that the possible situational moderators which might be operating in a given instance as a determinant of the effectiveness of a given leadership style are quite large in number, yet their importance cannot be underestimated. It would seem crucial that research on "C" and

"S" move in this direction if we are to be able to accurately assess the effects of variation on these dimensions, if any. More approaches of this type are needed.

A third implication from these data which seems to be of possible significance concerns the very high curvilinear r's reported in the Fleishman and Harris study of automobile company supervisors (1962). It has been suggested by these writers and others that future work should move in this direction and the results do appear more promising. Before such a movement appears, however, it would seem that some of the problems involved in postulating a more complex relationship as opposed to a simple linear one be kept in mind. The major problem, and one related to our argument in the previous paragraph, concerns the specification of those score ranges on these scales which are unrelated to criterion variance and those score ranges which are related; a disparity of conditions which Fleishman and Harris seem to indicate might be the rule in understanding the effect of these variables. Undoubtedly, such score ranges are related to specific situational parameters, i.e., those parameters that we know little about as yet and which still do not seem to be the subject of serious investigation. Yet, if the curvilinearity hypothesis is to be of value theoretically and practically, it would seem that it is of extreme importance to determine those scores which "make a difference" and those which do not, and when a condition does not hold to the same degree when a linear hypothesis is assumed.

CONCLUSIONS

Despite the fact that "Consideration" and "Initiating Structure" have become almost bywords in American industrial psychology, it seems apparent that very little is now known as to how these variables may predict work group performance and the conditions which affect such predictions. At the current time, we cannot even say whether they have any predictive significance at all. Research is needed of a systematic nature to answer these most basic questions, since it is only in the answers to such questions that the most useful applications can take place.

SUMMARY

The purpose of this paper was to review the research literature on the relationship between "Consideration," "Initiating Structure," and organizational criteria. The results show a predominance of low to moderate correlations, but almost all of a concurrent validity nature. There is as yet almost no evidence on the predictive validity of "Consideration" and "Initiating Structure" nor on the kinds of situational moderators which might affect such validity.

REFERENCES

Barrett, R. "Impact of the Executive Program on the Participants." *Journal of Industrial Psychology,* III (1965), 1-14.

Bass, B. "Leadership Opinions as Forecasts of Supervisory Success." *Journal of Applied Psychology,* XL (1956), 345-346.

Bass, B. "Leadership Opinions and Related Characteristics of Salesmen and Sales Managers." In Stogdill, R. M. and Coons, A. E. (Eds.), *Leader Behavior: Its Description and Measurement.* Columbus, Ohio: Bureau of Business Research, 1957.

Bass, B. "Leadership Opinions as Forecasts of Supervisory Success: A Replication." *Personnel Psychology,* II (1958), 515-518.

Fleishman, E. A. "The Description of Supervisory Behavior." *Journal of Applied Psychology,* XXXVII (1953), 1-6. (a)

Fleishman, E. A. "The Measurement of Leadership Attitudes in Industry." *Journal of Applied Psychology,* XXXVII (1953), 153-158. (b)

Fleishman, E. A. "A Leader Behavior Description for Industry." In Stogdill, R. M. and Coons, A. E. (Eds.), *Leader Behavior: Its Description and Measurement.* Colum-

bus, Ohio: Bureau of Business Research, 1957.

Fleishman, E. A. and Harris, E. F. "Patterns of Leadership Behavior Related to Employee Grievances and Turnover." *Personnel Psychology,* XV (1962), 43-56.

Fleishman, E. A., Harris, E. F., and Burtt, H. E. *Leadership and Supervision in Industry.* Columbus, Ohio: Bureau of Educational Research, Ohio State University, 1955.

Fleishman, E. A. and Peters, D. A. "Interpersonal Values, Leadership Attitudes, and Managerial Success." *Personnel Psychology,* XV (1962), 127-143.

Halpin, A. W. "The Leader Behavior and Effectiveness of Aircraft Commanders." In Stogdill, R. M. and Coons, A. E. (Eds.), *Leader Behavior: Its Description and Measurement.* Columbus, Ohio: Bureau of Business Research, 1957.

Halpin, A. W. and Winer, B. J. "A Factorial Study of the Leader Behavior Description." In Stogdill, R. M. and Coons, A. E. (Eds.), *Leader Behavior: Its Description and Measurement.* Columbus, Ohio: Bureau of Business Research, 1957.

Hemphill, J. K. "Leadership Behavior Associated with the Administrative Reputation of College Departments." *Journal of Educational Psychology,* XLVI (1955), 385-401.

Hills, R. J. "The Representative Function: Neglected Dimension of Leadership Behavior." *Administrative Science Quarterly,* VIII (1963), 83-101.

Katzell, R. A., Barrett, R. S., and Parker, T. C. "Job Satisfaction, Job Performance, and Situational Characteristics." *Journal of Applied Psychology,* XLV (1961), 65-72.

Kipnis, D. "Some Determinants of Supervisory Esteem." *Personnel Psychology,* XIII (1960), 377-392.

Korman, A. K. "The Self-Esteem Variable in Vocational Choice." *Journal of Applied Psychology,* in press.

Likert, R. *New Patterns of Management.* New York: McGraw-Hill Book Company, 1961.

Oaklander, H. and Fleishman, E. A. "Patterns of Leadership Related to Organizational Stress in Hospital Settings." *Administrative Science Quarterly,* VIII (1964), 520-532.

Parker, T. C. "Relationships Among Measures of Supervisory Behavior, Group Behavior and Situational Characteristics." *Personnel Psychology,* XVI (1963), 319-334.

Rambo, W. W. "The Construction and Analysis of a Leadership Behavior Rating

Form." *Journal of Applied Psychology*, XLII (1958), 409-415.

Spitzer, M. E. and McNamara, W. J. "A Managerial Selection Study." *Personnel Psychology*, XVII (1964), 19-40.

Vroom, V. *Work and Motivation.* New York: John Wiley & Sons, 1964.

Vroom, V. and Mann, F. C. "Leader Authoritarianism and Employee Attitudes." *Personnel Psychology*, XIII (1960), 125-140.

31. Some Findings Relevant to the Great Man Theory of Leadership*

EDGAR F. BORGATTA

ROBERT F. BALES

ARTHUR S. COUCH

A central area of research and theory in social psychological science, particularly in group dynamics and small group research, is that of "leadership." The interest apparently lies in the expectation that the "effectiveness" of group performance is determined in large part by the leadership structure of the group. Effective performance is usually defined by the joint occurrence of high task accomplishment and high satisfaction of members of the group.

There are at least six types of thinking about the optimum leadership structure of the group for effective performance.[1]

1) The most effective group is the one which has the most adequate all-around leader ("great man").

2) The most effective group is the one in which all members have been chosen according to ability for the specific task.

3) The most effective group is the one in which members are selected on the basis of their sociometric choices of each other as co-workers.

4) The most effective group is the one in which the various qualities of task ability and social ability are distributed among the members to allow or encourage role differentiation and division of labor.

5) The most effective group is one in which members are similar in values or some critical area of values.

6) The most effective group is the one in which members are selected primarily on the basis of compatibility of personality characteristics, such as authoritarianism, major mechanisms of defense, ascendance-submission, and the like.

Our concern here is with exploring some aspects of the first principle which we arbitrarily call the "great man theory of leadership." This is probably the oldest of the six theories and one which has received attention throughout the centuries. Such attention is understandable when one considers that history is frequently written from the reference point of "great men." It is equally understandable in terms of the implicit ease with which manipulation is possible if the organizational performance is determined by the single person in the top position. Much psychological research, assuming the great man theory, has been oriented to the problems of selecting persons who are best fitted for a top position of leadership. However, tests of the great man theory which in-

*Source: From *American Sociological Review*, vol. 19 (1954), pp. 755-59. Copyright © 1954 American Sociological Association. Reprinted by permission.

volve the performance of groups rather than the consistency of the leader's behavior are relatively absent in the literature.

PROCEDURE

The data to be presented, bearing on the great man theory, are based on 166 sessions of three man groups.[2] The subjects (N = 126) were male enlisted Air Force personnel assigned to the research project on temporary duty. They were recruited from different organizations, and acquaintance was minimal. The purpose of the testing was represented to the subjects as being the observation of how small groups work together, and presumably, this observation was to take place when they did some role playing. However, they were also observed in periods during which they planned the role playing session and periods of informal participation. It is these data which are analyzed in this experiment. Each of these 166 sessions was 24 minutes long. Every person participated in four sessions with two new co-participants in each session. The differences in enlisted grade were controlled by assignment of subject to session with persons of their own status.

DESIGN

Couch and Carter[3] have demonstrated in a factor analysis of the rated behavior of individuals in group interaction that three orthogonal factors account for the major portion of the variance in these ratings. The factors have been identified as: (1) *Group goal facilitation;* (2) *Individual prominence;* and (3) *Group sociability.* More simply, the factors may be identified as Task ability, Individual assertiveness and Social acceptability. For this study, using the Couch and Carter experience, along with that accrued from other sources, we attempted to measure the factors as follows:

Factor I. *Task ability*—(a) leadership rating received from co-participants on a task

criterion; (b) the I.Q. score as measured by the Science Research Associates Primary Mental Abilities.

Factor II. *Individual assertiveness*—the total activity rate of the individual in terms of the number of initiated acts per unit of time (using Bales' category system).[4]

Factor III. *Social acceptability*—the sociometric popularity as determined by choices received on a criterion of "enjoyed participation with."

It is our notion that a *great man* would need to possess each of the three independent qualities to a substantial degree. With this *fusion of qualities* the great man is able to satisfy the major role demands and personality needs of group members. In this study, we have defined the great man in terms of a product of the four measures mentioned above. The product of the scores is used rather than a sum to emphasize the requirement of a *simultaneous* occurrence of the qualities. Some sample computations of the product index used are shown in Table 1.

Great men were selected on the basis of their performance in the first session. The top eleven such persons were chosen, each participating in a separate group. That is, there was no case of two great men together in a first session. Our choice of eleven persons was arbitrary and based on the assumption that only about the top tenth of the total sample would satisfy the criterion of "greatness." In the three subsequent sessions when two great men participated together, that three man group was eliminated from the sample; this reduced our number from 33 to 25. We did this because the term "great man group" implies a group with a *single* great man as all-around leader.

Before examining other hypotheses, a point of concern for this study is whether a person who performs as a great man in the first session does so by virtue of the particular composition of his group, or whether it is a function of relatively stable characteristics of his personality which determine his "greatness" in any group in which he partici-

Table 1
SOME SAMPLE FACTOR PRODUCT INDICES

Subject Identification (Ordered By Index)	Factor I Task Ability		Factor II Individual	Factor III Social	Product Index
	(a) Leadership	(b) I.Q. (Percentile)	(c) Assertiveness	(d) Acceptability	(a)(b)(c)(d) (in 1,000's)
1	4	97	161	2	124.9
2	4	96	145	2	111.4
3	4	93	126	2	98.8
4	4	81	152	2	98.5
5	4	78	151	2	94.2
6	3	88	175	2	92.4
7	4	78	135	2	84.2
8	4	96	105	2	81.4
9	4	68	144	2	78.3
10	4	70	121	2	67.8
11	4	54	145	2	62.6
• • •					
102	1	4	117	2	0.9
103	3	2	94	1	0.6
104	1	4	46	2	0.4
105	1	1	99	2	0.2
106	0	8	75	0	0.0*
107	0	1	25	1	0.0
108	0	12	16	0	0.0
• • •					

*There were twenty-one persons with a product-index of 0.

pates. If there is no stability in performance, our subsequent hypotheses are meaningless.

We have no post-meeting estimates of productivity or satisfaction. However, we have indices of interaction in the group which have face validity as bearing on productivity and satisfaction.

a) For the satisfactory performance of a group in relation to a complex or general task, a large number of suggestions which are acceptable to the group must be made. An index which is a reasonable a priori estimate of this kind of task facilitation is the simultaneous presence of high rates of giving suggestion and showing agreement in the group as a whole. Again, for this index we use a product relationship so that both must be high in order for the index to be

high. The total number of suggestions was multiplied by the total number of agreements (Bales' category 4 times category 3). This gives a rough measure of the degree to which a given group reaches consensus on proposed solutions to the task problem.

b) A high rate of showing tension (Bales' category 11) is a fairly direct indication of difficulty in the interaction process. It is usually a sign of anxiety and withdrawal from participation by the individual. High rates of showing tension in the group are probably associated with low satisfaction, although the relationship may not be linear.

c) An indication of a friendly atmosphere in a group is a high rate of interaction in the positive social emotional categories—showing solidarity and showing tension release. In this case, our measure is the sum of these (Bales' category 1 plus category 2), indicating the amount of warmth expressed in the group.

HYPOTHESES

Hypothesis (1). *Great men* will tend to remain *great men* over a series of sessions.

Hypothesis (2). Sessions in which *great men* participate will have a higher product rate of suggestion and agreement (index: time rate of giving suggestion times rate of giving agreement).

Hypothesis (3). Sessions in which *great men* participate will have lower time rates of showing tension than those in which they do not participate.

Hypothesis (4). Sessions in which *great men* participate will have higher time rates of showing solidarity and tension release than those in which they do not participate.

RESULTS

Hypothesis (1). The top eleven persons (of a total sample of 123) defined by the product index of the first session were followed through the subsequent sessions, and the frequency with which they appeared within the top eleven ranks of the product index in the second, third and fourth sessions was noted. Of the eleven persons, eight were in the top ranks in the second and third sessions, and seven were still in top rank in the fourth session, which is a remarkably stable performance. This pattern, based on chi-square tests, is significant beyond .001 level. The hypothesis is emphatically supported.

The results of the remaining hypotheses are presented in Table 2.

Hypothesis (2). When the first sessions in which the great men participated were examined, it was found that they were significantly higher than the residual category of first sessions in terms of the product rate of agreement and suggestion. When subsequent sessions in which they participated were examined, it was found that the product index of agreement and suggestion for the sessions remained significantly

Table 2

MEAN RATES OF INTERACTION FOR GREAT MAN GROUPS AND NON GREAT MAN GROUPS: IDENTIFICATION OF GREAT MEN BASED ON FIRST SESSION

Interaction	Session 1	Sessions 2,3,4
Product Rate of Giving Suggestion and Agreement:		
Great Man Groups	867 (N=11)	530 (N=25)
Non Great Man Groups	566 (N=31)	362 (N=95)
(value of t)	(5.98)*	(2.43)*
Rate of Showing Tension		
Great Man Groups	9.4 (N=11)	11.7 (N=25)
Non Great Man Groups	14.1 (N=31)	16.4 (N=95)
(value of t)	(1.41)	(1.79)*
Rate of Showing Solidarity and Tension Release		
Great Man Groups	39.6 (N=11)	28.6 (N=25)
Non Great Man Groups	19.7 (N=31)	22.2 (N=95)
(value of t)	(3.98)*	(1.65)*

*$a \leq .05$, one-tail test.

higher than those in which the great men did not participate. The hypothesis is emphatically supported.

Hypothesis (3). Sessions from which great men were selected showed less tension than the residual first sessions as expected. The difference in the predicted direction was significant when subsequent sessions in which great men participated were compared to those in which they did not. The hypothesis is supported.

Hypothesis (4). When the first sessions in which great men participated were compared with the remaining first sessions with regard to amount of positive effect shown, it was found that the "great man" sessions were significantly higher. In the subsequent sessions, the difference remained significant. The hypothesis is emphatically supported.

DISCUSSION

The stability with which great men, chosen on the basis of their first session performance, retain top position in subsequent groups is impressive. One is encouraged to believe that a single session may be adequate for the selection of great men.

To the extent that our hypotheses are supported, it is suggested that great men selected on the basis of their first session continue to have an influence on the relatively superior performance of the groups in which they subsequently participate.

The evidence is quite clear that those groups containing a great man have higher product-rates of giving suggestions and agreements. Insofar as one has any reason to believe that this is related to the quality of solutions, the "productivity" of these groups is likely to be increased relative to the groups without great men.

To the extent that a lack of showing tension is an indication of smooth functioning, groups with great men appear to show less inhibited response to the task situation with less anxiety and

withdrawal from active participation. This may indicate greater satisfaction with the group. Further evidence of this is seen by the greater amount of positive social emotional behavior, reflecting friendly interpersonal relationships among the members of the group.

Thus, it may be said that great men tend to make "great groups" in the sense that both major factors of group performance—productivity and satisfaction of the members—are simultaneously increased.

CONCLUSION

In general, the great man principle of group composition appears to have much to recommend it. Further study[5] should focus on testing some of the underlying assumptions of the various principles of group composition, especially in terms of the differential effort of the leadership structures on group performance.

NOTES

1. The classification of the six types represents our abstraction in this complex field. Thus each position may be represented without sufficient qualification. It is also probable that these positions may actually overlap in the thinking of various social scientists. Aspects of (1), the great man theory, will be found discussed in such different, recent sources as: F. Redl, "Group Emotion and Leadership," *Psychiatry*, 5 (November, 1942), pp. 573-596 and M. Weber, *The Theory of Social and Economic Organization*, New York: Oxford, 1947 (Chapter 3, the section on Charismatic Authority). The second theory (2) is probably that which underlies the situational concept of leadership. Sophisticated forms of this theory are found in: R. B. Cattell, "New Concepts for Measuring Leadership in Terms of Group Syntality," *Human Relations*, 4 (1951), pp. 161-184; and L. F. Carter, "Some Research on Leadership in Small Groups," in H. Guetzkow, *Groups, Leadership and Men*, Carnegie Press, 1951. The sociometric position (3) will be found considered in: J. L. Moreno, *Who Shall*

Survive? Beacon, N. Y.: Beacon House, Inc., 1953; and Helen H. Jennings, *Leadership and Isolation,* New York: Longmans Green, 1950. The role differentiation theory (4) is considered in: E. Durkheim, *The Division of Labor in Society,* Glencoe, Ill.: The Free Press, 1947; and R. F. Bales and P. E. Slater, "Role Differentiation in Small Groups" (In press). The fifth (5) is usually implied in the theory that a group needs a "common culture base" in order to achieve adequate integration. At a general level, this theory underlies many of the clinical approaches, and it is evident in cultural anthropology. Such studies as those of national character also fit this theoretical position. See: A. Inkeles and D. Levinson, "National Character: The Study of Modal Personality and Sociocultural Systems," in G. Lindzey, *Handbook of Social Psychology,* Cambridge: Addison-Wesley Press, 1954. The personality compatibility theory (6) is considered in: W. Haythorn, A. S. Couch, P. Langham, D. Haefner and L. F. Carter, "A Study of the Behavior of the Authoritarian and Equalitarian Personalities" (forthcoming), and W. Schutz, "Construction of High Productivity Groups," *Studies in Group Behavior,* Medford, Mass: Tufts College, 1953. Several other theories of leadership presented themselves in our consideration but are not classed here. For example, there is a group-centered approach built around a concept of no leadership. It is clear that a classification of leadership types and group structure requires additional attention.

2. Other aspects of this research have been reported in other papers. Problems of reliability of scoring and consistency of sub-ject performance were discussed in: E. F. Borgatta and R. F. Bales, "The Consistency of Subject Behavior and the Reliability of Scoring in Interaction Process Analysis," *American Sociological Review,* 18 (October, 1953), pp. 566-569. Problems concerning the effect of task differences of experience, and the "accumulation of a common culture" are discussed in: E. F. Borgatta and R. F. Bales, "Task and Accumulation of Experience as Factors in the Interaction of Small Groups," *Sociometry,* 16 (August, 1953), pp. 239-252. The effects of participation with various types of co-participants, and a rationale for reconstituting groups are presented in: E. F. Borgatta and R. F. Bales, "Interaction of Individuals in Reconstituted Groups." *Sociometry,* 16 (November, 1953), pp. 302-320. The relationships among sociometric measures, interaction performance, ratings by superiors, intelligence, and selected variables are discussed in: E. F. Borgatta, "Analysis of Social Interaction and Sociometric Perception," *Sociometry,* 17 (February, 1954), pp. 7-32.

3. See: L. F. Carter, "Leadership and Small Group Behavior," in M. Sherif and M. O. Wilson, *Group Relations at the Crossroads,* New York: Harper, 1953.

4. The observation system used was that of: R. F. Bales, *Interaction Process Analysis,* Cambridge: Addison-Wesley Press, 1950.

5. A study is now in progress under the direction of Robert F. Bales in which groups composed according to the role differentiation principle will be compared with groups composed according to the great man rationale.

32. Engineer the Job to Fit the Manager*

FRED E. FIEDLER

What kind of leadership style does business need? Should company executives be decisive, directive, willing to give orders, and eager to assume responsibility? Should they be human relations-oriented, nondirective, willing to share leadership with the men in their group? Or should we perhaps start paying attention to the more important problem of defining under what conditions each of these leadership styles works best and what to do about it?

The success or failure of an organization depends on the quality of its management. How to get the best possible management is a question of vital importance; but it is perhaps even more important to ask how we can make better use of the management talent which we already have.

To get good business executives we have relied primarily on recruitment, selection, and training. It is time for businessmen to ask whether this is the only way or the best way for getting the best possible management. Fitting the man to the leadership job by selection and training has not been spectacularly successful. It is surely easier to change almost anything in the job situation than a man's personality and his leadership style. Why not try, then, to fit the leadership job to the man?

Executive jobs are surprisingly pliable, and the executive manpower pool is becoming increasingly small. The luxury of picking a "natural leader" from among a number of equally promising or equally qualified specialists is rapidly fading into the past. Business must learn how to utilize the available executive talent as effectively as it now utilizes physical plant and machine tools. Your financial expert, your top research scientist, or your production genius may be practically irreplaceable. Their jobs call for positions of leadership and responsibility. Replacements for these men can be neither recruited nor trained overnight, and they may not be willing to play second fiddle in their departments. If their leadership style does not fit the job, we must learn how to engineer the job to fit their leadership style.

In this article I shall describe some studies that illuminate this task of job engineering and adaptation. It will be seen that there are situations where the authoritarian, highly directive leader works best, and other situations where the egalitarian, more permissive, human relations-oriented leader works best; but almost always there are possibilities for changing the situation around somewhat to match the needs of the particular managers who happen to be available. The executive who appreciates these differences and possibilities has knowledge that can be valuable to him in running his organization.

To understand the problems that a new approach would involve, let us look first at some of the basic issues in organizational and group leadership.

STYLES OF LEADERSHIP

Leadership is a personal relationship in which one person directs, coordinates, and supervises others in the performance of a common task. This is especially so in "interacting groups," where men must work together cooperatively in achieving organizational goals.

In oversimplified terms, it can be said that the leader manages the group in either of two ways. He can:

• Tell people what to do and how to do it.

• Or share his leadership responsibilities with his group members and involve them in the planning and execution of the task.

There are, of course, all shades of leadership styles in between these two polar positions, but the basic issue is this: the work of motivating and coordinating group members has to be done either by brandishing the proverbial stick or by dangling the equally proverbial carrot. The former is the more orthodox job-centered, autocratic style. The latter is the more nondirective, group-centered procedure.

Research evidence exists to support both approaches to leadership. Which, then, should be judged more appropriate? On the face of it, the first style of leadership is best under some conditions, while the second works better under others. Accepting this proposition immediately opens two avenues of approach. Management can:

• Determine the specific situation in which the directive or the nondirective leadership style works best, and then select or train men so that their leadership style fits the particular job.

• Or determine the type of leadership style which is most natural for the man in the executive position, and then change the job to fit the man.

The first alternative has been discussed many times before; the second has not. We have never seriously considered whether it would be easier to fit the executive's job to the man.

NEEDED STYLE?

How might this be done? Some answers have been suggested by a research program on leadership effectiveness that I have directed under Office of Naval Research auspices since 1951. This program has dealt with a wide variety of different groups, including basketball teams, surveying parties, various military combat crews, and men in open-hearth steel shops, as well as members of management and boards of directors. When possible, performance was measured in terms of objective criteria—for instance, percentage of games won by high school basketball teams; tap-to-tap time of open-hearth shops (roughly equivalent to the tonnage of steel output per unit of time); and company net income over a three-year period. Our measure of leadership style was based on a simple scale indicating the degree to which a man described, favorably or unfavorably, his least-preferred co-worker (LPC). This co-worker did not need to be someone he actually worked with at the time, but could be someone the respondent had known in the past. Whenever possible, the score was obtained before the leader was assigned to his group.

The study indicates that a person who describes his least-preferred co-worker in a relatively favorable manner tends to be permissive, human relations-oriented, and considerate of the feelings of his men. But a person who describes

his least-preferred co-worker in an unfavorable manner—who has what we have come to call a low LPC rating—tends to be managing, task-controlling, and less concerned with the human relations aspects of the job. It also appears that the directive, managing, and controlling leaders tend to perform best in basketball and surveying teams, in open-hearth shops, and (provided the leader is accepted by his group) in military combat crews and company managements. On the other hand, the nondirective, permissive, and human relations-oriented leaders tend to perform best in decision- and policy-making teams and in groups that have a creative task—provided that the group likes the leader or the leader feels that the group is pleasant and free of tension.

CRITICAL DIMENSIONS

But in order to tell which style fits which situation, we need to categorize groups. Our research has shown that "it all depends" on the situation. After reviewing the results of all our work and the findings of other investigators, we have been able to isolate three major dimensions that seem to determine, to a large part, the kind of leadership style called for by different situations.

It is obviously a mistake to think that groups and teams are all alike and that each requires the same kind of leadership. We need some way of categorizing the group-task situation, or the job environment within which the leader has to operate. If leadership is indeed a process of influencing other people to work together effectively in a common task, then it surely matters how easy or difficult it is for the leader to exert his influence in a particular situation.

• *Leader-Member Relations.* The factor that would seem most important in determining a man's leadership influence is the degree to which his group members trust and like him, and are willing to follow his guidance. The trusted and well-liked leader obviously does not require special rank or power in order to get things done. We can measure the leader-member relationship by the so-called sociometric nomination techniques that ask group members to name in their group the most influential person, or the man they would most like to have as a leader. It can also be measured by a group-atmosphere scale indicating the degree to which the leader feels accepted and comfortable in the group.

● *The Task Structure.* The second important factor is the "task structure." By this term I mean the degree to which the task (a) is spelled out step by step for the group and, if so, the extent to which it can be done "by the numbers" or according to a detailed set of standard operating instructions, or (b) must be left nebulous and undefined. Vague and ambiguous or unstructured tasks make it difficult to exert leadership influence, because neither the leader nor his members know exactly what has to be done or how it is to be accomplished.

Why single out this aspect of the task rather than the innumerable other possible ways of describing it? Task groups are almost invariably components of a larger organization that assigns the task and has, therefore, a big stake in seeing it performed properly. However, the organization can control the quality of a group's performance only if the task is clearly spelled out and programmed or structured. When the task can be programmed or performed "by the numbers," the organization is able to back up the authority of the leader to the fullest; the man who fails to perform each step can be disciplined or fired. But in the case of ill-defined, vague, or unstructured tasks, the organization and the leader have very little control and direct power. By close supervision one can ensure, let us say, that a man will correctly operate a machine, but one cannot ensure that he will be creative.

It is therefore easier to be a leader in a structured task situation in which the work is spelled out than in an unstruc-

tured one which presents the leader and his group with a nebulous, poorly defined problem.

● *Position Power.* Thirdly, there is the power of the leadership position, as distinct from any personal power the leader might have. Can he hire or fire and promote or demote? Is his appointment for life, or will it terminate at the pleasure of his group? It is obviously easier to be a leader when the position power is strong than when it is weak.

MODEL FOR ANALYSIS

When we now classify groups on the basis of these three dimensions, we get a classification system that can be represented as a cube; see Exhibit I. As each group is high or low in each of the three dimensions, it will fall into one of the eight cells.

From examination of the cube, it seems clear that exerting leadership influence will be easier in a group in which the members like a powerful leader with a clearly defined job and where the job to be done is clearly laid out (Cell 1); it will be difficult in a group where a leader is disliked, has little power, and has a highly ambiguous job (Cell 8).

In other words, it is easier to be the well-esteemed foreman of a construction crew working from a blueprint than it is to be the disliked chairman of a volunteer committee preparing a new policy.

I consider the leader-member relations the most important dimension, and the position-power dimension the least important, of the three. It is, for instance, quite possible for a man of low rank to lead a group of higher-ranking men in a structured task—as is done when enlisted men or junior officers conduct some standardized parts of the training programs for medical officers who enter the Army. But it is not so easy for a disrespected manager to lead a creative, policy-formulating session well, even if he is the senior executive present.

EXHIBIT I. A MODEL FOR CLASSIFYING
       GROUP-TASK SITUATIONS

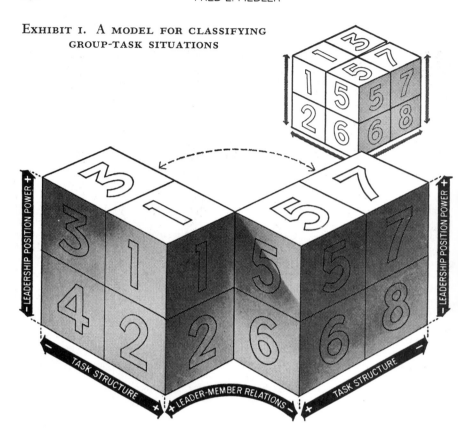

VARYING REQUIREMENTS

By first sorting the eight cells according to leader-member relations, then task structure, and finally leader position power, we can now arrange them in order according to the favorableness of the environment for the leader. This sorting leads to an eight-step scale, as in Exhibit II. This exhibit portrays the results of a series of studies of groups performing well but (a) in different situations and conditions, and (b) with leaders using different leadership styles. In explanation:

The *horizontal* axis shows the range of situations that the groups worked in, as described by the classification scheme used in Exhibit I.

The *vertical* axis indicates the leadership style which was best in a certain situation, as shown by the correlation coefficient between the leader's LPC and his group's performance.

A positive correlation (falling above the midline) shows that the permissive, nondirective, and human relations-oriented leaders performed best; a negative correlation (below the midline) shows that the task-controlling, managing leader performed best. For instance, leaders of effective groups in situation categories 1 and 2 had LPC-group performance correlations of −.40 to −.80, with the average between −.50 and −.60; whereas leaders of effective groups in situation categories 4 and 5

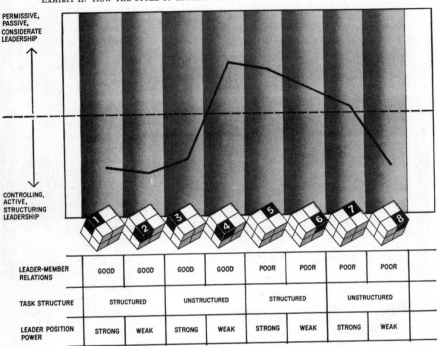

LEADER-MEMBER RELATIONS	GOOD	GOOD	GOOD	GOOD	POOR	POOR	POOR	POOR
TASK STRUCTURE	STRUCTURED		UNSTRUCTURED		STRUCTURED		UNSTRUCTURED	
LEADER POSITION POWER	STRONG	WEAK	STRONG	WEAK	STRONG	WEAK	STRONG	WEAK

had LPC-group performance correlations of .20 to .80, with the average between .40 and .50.

Exhibit II shows that both the directive, managing, task-oriented leaders and the nondirective, human relations-oriented leaders are successful under some conditions. Which leadership style is the best depends on the favorableness of the particular situation for the leader. In very favorable or in very unfavorable situations for getting a task accomplished by group effort, the autocratic, task-controlling, managing leadership works best. In situations intermediate in difficulty, the nondirective, permissive leader is more successful.

This corresponds well with our everyday experience. For instance:

• Where the situation is very favorable, the group expects and wants the leader to give directions. We neither expect nor want the trusted airline pilot to turn to his crew and ask, "What do you think we ought to check before takeoff?"

• If the disliked chairman of a volunteer committee asks his group what to do, he may be told that everybody ought to go home.

• The well-liked chairman of a planning group or research team must be nondirective and permissive in order to get full participation from his members. The directive, managing leader will tend to be more critical and to cut discussion short; hence he will not get the full benefit of the potential contributions by his group members.

The varying requirements of leadership styles are readily apparent in organizations experiencing dramatic changes in operating procedures. For example:

• The manager or supervisor of a routinely operating organization is expected to provide direction and supervision that the subordinates should follow. However, in a crisis the routine is no longer adequate, and the task becomes ambiguous and unstructured. The typical manager tends to respond in such instances by calling his principal assistants together for a conference. In other words, the effective leader changes his behavior from a directive to a permissive, nondirective style until the operation again reverts to routine conditions.

• In the case of a research planning group, the human relations-oriented and permissive leader provides a climate in which everybody is free to speak up, to suggest, and to criticize. Osborn's brainstorming method[1] in fact institutionalizes these procedures. However, after the research plan has been completed, the situation becomes highly structured. The director now prescribes the task in detail, and he specifies the means of accomplishing it. Woe betide the assistant who decides to be creative by changing the research instructions!

PRACTICAL TESTS

Remember that the ideas I have been describing emanate from studies of real-life situations; accordingly, as might be expected, they can be validated by organizational experience. Take, for instance, the dimension of leader-member relations described earlier. We have made three studies of situations in which the leader's position power was strong and the task relatively structured with clear-cut goals and standard operating procedures. In such groups as these the situation will be very favorable for the leader if he is accepted; it will be progressively unfavorable in proportion to how much a leader is disliked. What leadership styles succeed in these varying conditions? The studies confirm what our theory would lead us to expect:

• The first set of data come from a study of B-29 bomber crews in which the criterion was the accuracy of radar bombing. Six degrees of leader-member relations were identified, ranging from those in which the aircraft commander was the first choice of crew members and highly endorsed his radar observer and navigator (the key men in radar bombing), to those in which he was chosen by his crew but did not endorse his key men, and finally to crews in which the commander was rejected by his crew and rejected his key crew members. What leadership styles were effective? The results are plotted in Exhibit III.

• A study of anti-aircraft crews compares the 10 most chosen crew commanders, the 10 most rejected ones, and 10 of intermediate popularity. The criterion is the identification and "acquisition" of unidentified aircraft by the crew. The results shown in Exhibit III are similar to those for bomber crew commanders.

• Exhibit III also summarizes data for 32 small-farm supply companies. These were member companies of the same distribution system, each with its own board of directors and its own management. The performance of these highly comparable companies was measured in terms of percentage of company net income over a three-year period. The first quarter of the line (going from left to right) depicts endorsement of the general manager by his board of directors and his staff of assistant managers; the second quarter, endorsement by his board but not his staff; the third quarter, endorsement by his staff but not his board; the fourth quarter, endorsement by neither.

As can be seen from the results of all three studies, the highly accepted and strongly rejected leaders perform best if they are controlling and managing, while the leaders in the intermediate acceptance range, who are neither rejected nor accepted, perform best if they are permissive and nondirective.

Now let us look at some research on organizations in another country:

Recently in Belgium a study was made of groups of mixed language and cultural composition. Such teams, which are becoming increasingly frequent as international business and governmental activities multiply, obviously present a difficult situation for the leader. He must not only deal with men who do not fully comprehend one another's language and meanings, but also cope with the typical antipathies, suspicions, and antagonisms dividing individuals of different cultures and nationalities.

EXHIBIT III. HOW EFFECTIVE LEADERSHIP STYLES VARY DEPENDING ON GROUP ACCEPTANCE

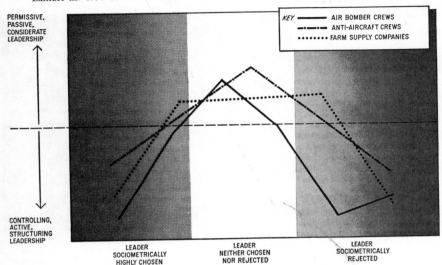

At a Belgian naval training center we tested 96 three-man groups, half of which were homogeneous in composition (all Flemish or all Walloon) and half heterogeneous (the leader differing from his men). Half of each of these had powerful leader positions (petty officers), and half had recruit leaders. Each group performed three tasks: one unstructured task (writing a recruiting letter); and two parallel structured tasks (finding the shortest route for ships through 10 ports, and doing the same for 12 ports). After each task, leaders and group members described their reactions—including group-atmosphere ratings and the indication of leader-member relations.

The various task situations were then arranged in order, according to their favorableness for the leader. The most favorable situation was a homogeneous group, led by a well-liked and accepted petty officer, which worked on the structured task of routing a ship. The situation would be especially favorable toward the end of the experiment, after the leader had had time to get to know his members. The least favorable situation was that of an unpopular recruit leader of a heterogeneous group where the relatively unstructured task of writing a letter came up as soon as the group was formed.

There were six groups that fell into each of these situations or cells. A correlation was then computed for each set of six groups to determine which type of leadership style led to best team performance. The results, indicated in Exhibit IV, support the conclusions earlier described.

Of particular interest is the fact that the difficult heterogeneous groups generally required controlling, task-oriented leadership for good performance. This fits the descriptions of successful leader behavior obtained from executives who have worked in international business organizations.

CONCLUSION

Provided our findings continue to be supported in the future, what do these results and the theory mean for executive selection and training? What implications do they have for the management of large organizations?

SELECTION & TRAINING

Business and industry are now trying to attract an increasingly large share of exceptionally intelligent and technically well-trained men. Many of these are

EXHIBIT IV. EFFECTIVE LEADERSHIP STYLES AT BELGIAN NAVAL TRAINING CENTER

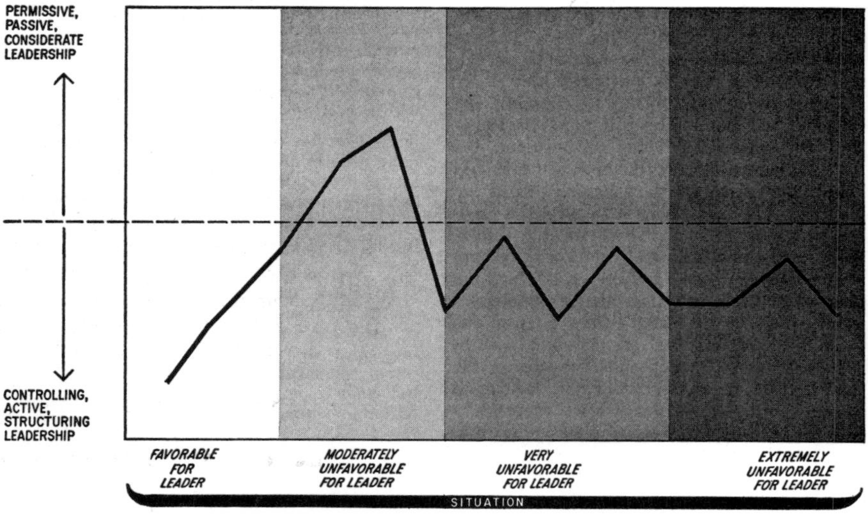

specialists whose talents are in critically short supply. Can industry really afford to select only those men who have a certain style of leadership in addition to their technical qualifications? The answer is likely to be negative, at least in the near future.

This being the case, can we then train the men selected in one leadership style or the other? This approach is always offered as a solution, and it does have merit. But we must recognize that training people is at best difficult, costly, and time-consuming. It is certainly easier to place people in a situation compatible with their natural leadership style than to force them to adapt to the demands of the job.

As another alternative, should executives learn to recognize or diagnose group-task situations so that they can place their subordinates, managers, and department heads in the jobs best suited to their leadership styles? Even this procedure has serious disadvantages. The organization may not always happen to have the place that fits the bright young man. The experienced executive may

not want to be moved, or it may not be possible to transfer him.

Should the organization try to "engineer" the job to fit the man? This alternative is potentially the most feasible for management. As has been shown already, the type of leadership called for depends on the favorableness of the situation. The favorableness, in turn, is a product of several factors. These include leader-member relations, the homogeneity of the group, and the position power and degree to which the task is structured, as well as other, more obvious factors such as the leader's knowledge of his group, his familiarity with the task, and so forth.

It is clear that management can change the characteristic favorableness of the leadership situation; it can do so in most cases more easily than it can transfer the subordinate leader from one job to another or train him in a different style of interacting with his members.

POSSIBILITIES OF CHANGE

Although this type of organizational engineering has not been done systematically up to now, we can choose from several good possibilities for getting the job done:

1. *We can change the leader's position power.* We can either give him subordinates of equal or nearly equal rank or we can give him men who are two or three ranks below him. We can either give him sole authority for the job or require that he consult with this group, or even obtain unanimous consent for all decisions. We can either punctiliously observe the channels of the organization to increase the leader's prestige or communicate directly with the men of his group as well as with him in person.

2. *We can change the task structure.* The tasks given to one leader may have to be clarified in detail, and he may have to be given precise operating instructions; another leader may have to be given more general problems that are only vaguely elucidated.

3. *We can change the leader-member relations.* The Belgian study, referred to earlier, demonstrates that changing the group composition changes the leader's relations with his men. We can increase or decrease the group's heterogeneity by introducing men with similar attitudes, beliefs, and backgrounds, or by bringing in men different in training, culture, and language.

The foregoing are, of course, only examples of what could be done. The important point is that we now have a model and a set of principles that permit predictions of leadership effectiveness in interacting groups and allow us to take a look at the factors affecting team performance. This approach goes beyond the traditional notions of selection and training. It focuses on the more fruitful possibility of organizational engineering as a means of using leadership potentials in the management ranks.

NOTE

1. See Alex F. Osborn, *Applied Imagination* (New York: Charles Scribner's Sons, 1953).

33. A New Look at Managerial Decision Making*

VICTOR H. VROOM

All managers are decision makers. Furthermore, their effectiveness as managers is largely reflected in their "track record" in making the "right decisions." These "right decisions" in turn largely depend on whether or not the manager has utilized the right person or persons in the right ways in helping him solve the problem.

Our concern in this article is with decision making as a social process. We view the manager's task as determining how the problem is to be solved, not the solution to be adopted. Within that overall framework, we have attempted to answer two broad sets of questions: What decision-making processes should managers use to deal effectively with the problems they encounter in their jobs? What decision-making processes

*Source: Reprinted, by permission of the publisher, from *Organizational Dynamics*, Spring 1973, pp. 66-80. Copyright © 1973 by AMACOM, a division of American Management Associations. All rights reserved.

do they use in dealing with these problems and what considerations affect their decisions about how much to share their decision-making power with subordinates?

The reader will recognize the former as a normative or prescriptive question. A rational and analytic answer to it would constitute a normative model of decision making as a social process. The second question is descriptive, since it concerns how managers do, rather than should, behave.

TOWARD A NORMAL MODEL

About four years ago, Philip Yetton, then a graduate student at Carnegie-Mellon University, and I began a major research program in an attempt to answer these normative and descriptive questions.

We began with the normative question. What would be a rational way of deciding on the form and amount of participation in decision making that should be used in different situations?

We were tired of debates over the relative merits of Theory X and Theory Y and of the truism that leadership depends upon the situation. We felt that it was time for the behavioral sciences to move beyond such generalities and to attempt to come to grips with the complexities of the phenomena with which they intended to deal.

Our aim was ambitious—to develop a set of ground rules for matching a manager's leadership behavior to the demands of the situation. It was critical that these ground rules be consistent with research evidence concerning the consequences of participation and that the model based on the rules be operational, so that any manager could see it to determine how he should act in any decision-making situation.

Table 1 shows a set of alternative decision processes that we have employed in our research. Each process is represented by a symbol (e.g., AI, CI, GII) that will be used as a convenient method of referring to each process. The first letter in this symbol signifies the

Table 1
TYPES OF MANAGEMENT DECISION STYLES

AI	You solve the problem or make the decision yourself, using information available to you at that time.
AII	You obtain the necessary information from your subordinate(s), then decide on the solution to the problem yourself. You may or may not tell your subordinates what the problem is in getting the information from them. The role played by your subordinates in making the decision is clearly one of providing the necessary information to you, rather than generating or evaluating alternative solutions.
CI	You share the problem with relevant subordinates individually, getting their ideas and suggestions without bringing them together as a group. Then *you* make the decision that may or may not reflect your subordinates' influence.
CII	You share the problem with your subordinates as a group, collectively obtaining their ideas and suggestions. Then *you* make the decision that may or may not reflect your subordinates' influence.
GII	You share a problem with your subordinates as a group. Together you generate and evaluate alternatives and attempt to reach agreement (consensus) on a solution. Your role is much like that of chairman. You do not try to influence the group to adopt "your" solution and you are willing to accept and implement any solution that has the support of the entire group.

(GI is omitted because it applies only to more comprehensive models outside the scope of the article.)

basic properties of the process (A stands for autocratic; C for consultative; and G for group). The Roman numerals that follow the first letter constitute variants on that process. Thus, AI represents the first variant on an autocratic process, and AII the second variant.

CONCEPTUAL AND EMPIRICAL BASIS OF THE MODEL

A model designed to regulate, in some rational way, choices among the decisions processess shown in Table 1 should be based on sound empirical evidence concerning the likely consequences of the styles. The more complete the empirical base of knowledge, the greater the certainty with which we can develop the model and the greater will be its usefulness. To aid in understanding the conceptual basis of the model, it is important to distinguish among three classes of outcomes that bear on the ultimate effectiveness of decisions. These are:

   1) The quality or rationality of the decision.

   2) The acceptance or commitment on the part of subordinates to execute the decision effectively.

   3) The amount of time required to make the decision.

The effects of participation on each of these outcomes or consequences were summed up by the author in *The Handbook of Social Psychology* as follows:

The results suggest that allocating problem solving and decision-making tasks to entire groups requires a greater investment of man hours but produces higher acceptance of decisions and a higher probability that the decision will be executed efficiently. Differences between these two methods in quality of decisions and in elapsed time are inconclusive and probably highly variable . . . It would be naive to think that group decision making is always more "effective" than autocratic decision making, or vice versa; the relative effectiveness of these two extreme methods depends both on the weights attached to quality, acceptance and time variables and on differences in amounts of these out-

comes resulting from these methods, neither of which is invariant from one situation to another. The critics and proponents of participative management would do well to direct their efforts toward identifying the properties of situations in which different decision-making approaches are effective rather than wholesale condemnation or deification of one approach.

We have gone on from there to identify the properties of the situation or problem that will be the basic elements in the model. These problem attributes are of two types: 1) Those that specify the importance for a particular problem of quality and acceptance, and 2) those that, on the basis of available evidence, have a high probability of moderating the effects of participation on each of these outcomes. Table 2 shows the problem attributes used in the present form of the model. For each attribute a question is provided that might be used by a leader in diagnosing a particular problem prior to choosing his leadership style.

In phrasing the questions, we have held technical language to a minimum. Furthermore, we have phrased the questions in Yes-No form, translating the continuous variables defined above into dichotomous variables. For example, instead of attempting to determine how important the decision quality is to the effectiveness of the decision (attribute A), the leader is asked in the first question to judge whether there is any quality component to the problem. Similarly, the difficult task of specifying exactly how much information the leader possesses that is relevant to the decision (attribute B) is reduced to a simple judgment by the leader concerning whether or not he has sufficient information to make a high quality decision.

We have found that managers can diagnose a situation quickly and accurately by answering this set of seven questions concerning it. But how can such responses generate a prescription concerning the most effective leadership

Table 2
PROBLEM ATTRIBUTES USED IN THE MODEL

Problem Attributes	Diagnostic Questions
A. The importance of the quality of the decision.	Is there a quality requirement such that one solution is likely to be more rational than another?
B. The extent to which the leader possesses sufficient information/expertise to make a high-quality decision by himself.	Do I have sufficient information to make a high-quality decision?
C. The extent to which the problem is structured.	Is the problem structured?
D. The extent to which acceptance or commitment on the part of subordinates is critical to the effective implementation of the decision.	Is acceptance of decision by subordinates critical to effective implementation?
E. The prior probability that the leader's autocratic decision will receive acceptance by subordinates.	If you were to make the decision by yourself, is it reasonably certain that it would be accepted by your subordinates?
F. The extent to which subordinates are motivated to attain the organizational goals as represented in the objectives explicit in the statement of the problem.	Do subordinates share the organizational goals to be obtained in solving this problem?
G. The extent to which subordinates are likely to be in conflict over preferred solutions.	Is conflict among subordinates likely in preferred solutions?

style or decision process? What kind of normative model of participation in decision making can be built from this set of problem attributes?

Figure 1 shows one such model expressed in the form of a decision tree. It is the seventh version of such a model that we have developed over the last three years. The problem attributes, expressed in question form, are arranged along the top of the figure. To use the model for a particular decision-making situation, one starts at the left-hand side and works toward the right asking oneself the question immediately above any box that is encountered. When a terminal node is reached, a number will be found designating the problem type and one of the decision-making processes appearing in Table 1. AI is prescribed

for four problem types (1, 2, 4, and 5); AII is prescribed for two problem types (9 and 10); CI is prescribed for only one problem type (8); CII is prescribed for four problem types (7, 11, 13, and 14); and GII is prescribed for three problem types (3, 6, and 12). The relative frequency with which each of the five decision processes would be prescribed for any manager would, of course, depend on the distribution of problem types encountered in his decision making.

RATIONALE UNDERLYING THE MODEL

The decision processes specified for each problem type are not arbitrary. The model's behavior is governed by a set of principles intended to be consistent with existing evidence concerning the

Figure 1.
DECISION MODEL

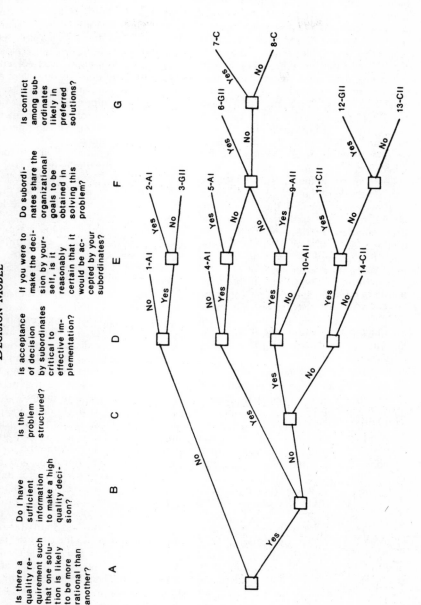

consequences of participation in decision making on organizational effectiveness.

There are two mechanisms underlying the behavior of the model. The first is a set of seven rules that serve to protect the quality and the acceptance of the decision by eliminating alternatives that risk one or the other of these decision outcomes. Once the rules have been applied, a feasible set of decision processes is generated. The second mechanism is a principle for choosing among alternatives in the feasible set where more than one exists.

Let us examine the rules first, because they do much of the work of the model. As previously indicated, the rules are intended to protect both the quality and acceptance of the decision. In the form of the model shown, there are three rules that protect decision quality and four that protect acceptance.

1. *The Information Rule.* If the quality of the decision is important and if the leader does not possess enough information or expertise to solve the problem by himself, AI is eliminated from the feasible set. (Its use risks a low-quality decision.)

2. *The Goal Congruence Rule.* If the quality of the decision is important and if the subordinates do not share the organizational goals to be obtained in solving the problem, GII is eliminated from the feasible set. (Alternatives that eliminate the leader's final control over the decision reached may jeopardize the quality of the decision.)

3. *The Unstructured Problem Rule.* In decisions in which the quality of the decision is important, if the leader lacks the necessary information or expertise to solve the problem by himself, and if the problem is unstructured, i.e., he does not know exactly what information is needed and where it is located, the method used must provide not only for him to collect the information but to do so in an efficient and effective manner. Methods that involve interaction among all subordinates with full knowledge of the problem are likely to be both more efficient and more likely to generate a high-quality solution to the problem. Under these conditions, AI, AII, and CI are eliminated from the feasible set. (AI does not provide for him to collect the necessary information, and AII and CI represent more cumbersome, less effective, and less efficient means of bringing the necessary information to bear on the solution of the problem than methods that do permit those with the necessary information to interact.)

4. *The Acceptance Rule.* If the acceptance of the decision by subordinates is critical to effective implementation, and if it is not certain that an autocratic decision made by the leader would receive that acceptance, AI and AII are eliminated from the feasible set. (Neither provides an opportunity for subordinates to participate in the decision and both risk the necessary acceptance.)

5. *The Conflict Rule.* If the acceptance of the decision is critical, and an autocratic decision is not certain to be accepted, and subordinates are likely to be in conflict or disagreement over the appropriate solution, AI, AII, and CI are eliminated from the feasible set. (The method used in solving the problem should enable those in disagreement to resolve their differences with full knowledge of the problem. Accordingly, under these conditions, AI, AII, and CI, which involve no interaction or only "one-on-one" relationships and therefore provide no opportunity for those in conflict to resolve their differences, are eliminated from the feasible set. Their use runs the risk of leaving some of the subordinates with less than the necessary commitment to the final decision.)

6. *The Fairness Rule.* If the quality of decision is unimportant and if acceptance is critical and not certain to result from an autocratic decision, AI, AII, CI, and CII are eliminated from the feasible set. (The method used should maximize the probability of acceptance as this is the only relevant consideration in de-

termining the effectiveness of the decision. Under these circumstances, AI, AII, CI, and CII, which create less acceptance or commitment than GII, are eliminated from the feasible set. To use them is to run the risk of getting less than the needed acceptance of the decision.)

7. *The Acceptance Priority Rule.* If acceptance is critical, not assured by an autocratic decision, and if subordinates can be trusted, AI, AII, CI, and CII are eliminated from the feasible set. (Methods that provide equal partnership in the decision-making process can provide greater acceptance without risking decision quality. Use of any method other than GII results in an unnecessary risk that the decision will not be fully accepted or receive the necessary commitment on the part of subordinates.)

Once all seven rules have been applied to a given problem, we emerge with a feasible set of decision processes. The feasible set for each of the fourteen problem types is shown in Table 3. It can be seen that there are some problem types for which only one method

Table 3

PROBLEM TYPES AND THE FEASIBLE SET OF DECISION PROCESSES

Problem Type	Acceptable Methods
1.	AI, AII, CI, CII, GII
2.	AI, AII, CI, CII, GII
3.	GII
4.	AI, AII, CI, CII, GII*
5.	AI, AII, CI, CII, GII*
6.	GII
7.	CII
8.	CI, CII
9.	AII, CI, CII, GII*
10.	AII, CI, CII, GII*
11.	CII, GII*
12.	GII
13.	CII
14.	CII, GII*

*Within the feasible set only when the answer to question F is Yes.

remains in the feasible set, others for which two methods remain feasible, and still others for which five methods remain feasible.

When more than one method remains in the feasible set, there are a number of ways in which one might choose among them. The mechanism we have selected and the principle underlying the choices of the model in Figure 1 utilizes the number of man-hours used in solving the problem as the basis for choice. Given a set of methods with equal likelihood of meeting both quality and acceptance requirements for the decision, it chooses that method that requires the least investment in man-hours. On the basis of the empirical evidence summarized earlier, this is deemed to be the method furthest to the left within the feasible set. For example, since AI, AII, CI, CII, and GII are all feasible as in Problem Types 1 and 2, AI would be the method chosen.

To illustrate application of the model in actual administrative situations, we will analyze four cases with the help of the model. While we attempt to describe these cases as completely as is necessary to permit the reader to make the judgments required by the model, there may remain some room for subjectivity. The reader may wish after reading the case to analyze it himself using the model and then to compare his analysis with that of the author.

● CASE I. You are a manufacturing manager in a large electronics plant. The company's management has recently installed new machines and put in a new simplified work system, but to the surprise of everyone, yourself included, the expected increase in productivity was not realized. In fact, production has begun to drop, quality has fallen off, and the number of employee separations has risen.

You do not believe that there is anything wrong with the machines. You have had reports from other companies that are using them and they confirm this opinion. You have also had representatives from the firm that built the machines go over them and they report that they are operating at peak efficiency.

You suspect that some parts of the new work system may be responsible for the change, but this view is not widely shared among your immediate subordinates who are four first-line supervisors, each in charge of a section, and your supply manager. The drop in production has been variously attributed to poor training of the operators, lack of an adequate system of financial incentives, and poor morale. Clearly, this is an issue about which there is considerable depth of feeling within individuals and potential disagreement among your subordinates.

This morning you received a phone call from your division manager. He had just received your production figures for the last six months and was calling to express his concern. He indicated that the problem was yours to solve in any way that you think best, but that he would like to know within a week what steps you plan to take.

You share your division manager's concern with the falling productivity and know that your men are also concerned. The problem is to decide what steps to take to rectify the situation.

Analysis

Questions—
 A (Quality?) = Yes
 B (Managers Information?) = No
 C (Structured?) = No
 D (Acceptance?) = Yes
 E (Prior Probability of Acceptance?) = No
 F (Goal Congruence?) = Yes
 G (Conflict?) = Yes
Problem Type—12
Feasible Set—GII
Minimum Man-Hours Solution (from Figure 1)—GII
Rule Violations—
 AI violates rules 1, 3, 4, 5, 7
 AII violates rules 3, 4, 5, 7
 CI violates rules 3, 5, 7
 CII violates rule 7

● CASE II. You are general foreman in charge of a large gang laying an oil pipeline and have to estimate your expected rate of progress in order to schedule material deliveries to the next field site.

You know the nature of the terrain you will be traveling and have the historical data needed to compute the mean and variance in the rate of speed over that type of terrain. Given these two variables, it is a simple matter to calculate the earliest and latest times at which materials and support facilities will be needed at the next site. It is important that your estimate be reasonably accurate. Underestimates result in idle foremen and workers, and an overestimate results in tying up materials for a period of time before they are to be used.

Progress has been good and your five foremen and other members of the gang stand to receive substantial bonuses if the project is completed ahead of schedule.

Analysis

Questions—
 A (Quality?) = Yes
 B (Manager's Information?) = Yes
 D (Acceptance?) = No
Problem Type—4
Feasible Set—AI, AII, CI, CII, GII
Minimum Man-Hours Solution (from Figure 1)—AI
Rule Violations—None

● CASE III. You are supervising the work of 12 engineers. Their formal training and work experience are very similar, permitting you to use them interchangeably on projects. Yesterday, your manager informed you that a request had been received from an overseas affiliate for four engineers to go abroad on extended loan for a period of six to eight months. For a number of reasons, he argued and you agreed that this request should be met from your group.

All your engineers are capable of handling this assignment and, from the standpoint of present and future projects, there is no particular reason why anyone should be retained over àny other. The problem is somewhat complicated by the fact that the overseas assignment is in what is generally regarded as an undesirable location.

Analysis

Questions—
  A (Quality?) = No
  D (Acceptance?) = Yes
  E (Prior Probability of Acceptance?) = No
  G (Conflict?) = Yes
Problem Type—3
Feasible Set—GII
Minimum Man-Hours Solution (from Figure 1)—GII
Rule Violations—
  AI and AII violate rules 4, 5, and 6
  CI violates rules 5 and 6
  CII violates rule 6

● CASE IV. You are on the division manager's staff and work on a wide variety of problems of both an administrative and technical nature. You have been given the assignment of developing a standard method to be used in each of the five plants in the division for manually reading equipment registers, recording the readings, and transmitting the scorings to a centralized information system.

Until now there has been a high error rate in the reading and/or transmittal of the data. Some locations have considerably higher error rates than others, and the methods used to record and transmit the data vary among plants. It is probable, therefore, that part of the error variance is a function of specific local conditions rather than anything else, and this will complicate the establishment of any system common to all plants. You have the information on error rates but no information on the local practices that generate these errors or on the local conditions that necessitate the different practices.

Everyone would benefit from an improvement in the quality of the data; it is used in a number of important decisions. Your contacts with the plants are

through the quality-control supervisors who are responsible for collecting the data. They are a conscientious group committed to doing their jobs well, but are highly sensitive to interference on the part of higher management in their own operations. Any solution that does not receive the active support of the various plant supervisors is unlikely to reduce the error rate significantly.

Analysis

Questions—
  A (Quality?) = Yes
  B (Manager's Information?) = No
  C (Structured?) = No
  D (Acceptance?) = Yes
  E (Prior Probability of Acceptance?) = No
  F (Goal Congruence?) = Yes
Problem Type—12
Feasible Set—GII
Minimum Man-Hours Solution (from Figure 1)—GII
Rule Violations—
  AI violates rules 1, 3, 4, and 7
  AII violates rules 3, 4, and 7
  CI violates rules 3 and 7
  CII violates rule 7

SHORT VERSUS LONG-TERM MODELS

The model described above seeks to protect the quality of the decision and to expend the least number of man-hours in the process. Because it focuses on conditions surrounding the making and implementation of a particular decision rather than any long-term considerations, we can term it a short-term model.

It seems likely, however, that the leadership methods that may be optimal for short-term results may be different from those that would be optimal over a longer period of time. Consider a leader, for example, who has been uniformly pursuing an autocratic style (AI or AII) and, perhaps as a consequence, has subordinates who might be termed "yes men" (attribute E) but who also cannot be trusted to pursue organizational goals (attribute F), largely because the leader has never bothered to explain them.

It appears likely, however, that the manager who used more participative methods would, in time, change the status of these problem attributes so as to develop ultimately a more effective problem-solving system. A promising approach to the development of a long-term model is one that places less weight on man-hours as the basis for choice of method within the feasible set. Given a long-term orientation, one would be interested in the possibility of a trade-off between man-hours in problem solving and team development, both of which increase with participation. Viewed in these terms, the time-minimizing model places maximum relative weight on man-hours and no weight on development, and hence chooses the style farthest to the left within the feasible set. A model that places less weight on man-hours and more weight on development would, if these assumptions are correct, choose a style further to the right within the feasible set.

We recognize, of course, that the minimum man-hours solution suggested by the model is not always the best solution to every problem. A manager faced, for example, with the problem of handling any one of the four cases previously examined might well choose more time-consuming alternatives on the grounds that the greater time invested would be justified in developing his subordinates. Similar considerations exist in other decision-making situations. For this reason we have come to emphasize the feasible set of decision methods in our work with managers. Faced with considerations not included in the model, the manager should consider any alternative within the feasible set, not opt automatically for the minimum man-hours solution.

As I am writing this, I have in front of me a "black box" that constitutes an electronic version of the normative model discussed on the preceding

pages. (The author is indebted to Peter Fuss of Bell Telephone Laboratories for his interest in the model and his skill in developing the "black box.") The box, which is small enough to fit into the palm of one hand, has a set of seven switches, each appropriately labeled with the questions (A through G) used in Figure 1. A manager faced with a concrete problem or decision can "diagnose" that problem by setting each switch in either its "yes" or "no" position. Once the problem has been described, the manager depresses a button that illuminates at least one or as many as five lights, each of which denotes one of the decision processes (AI, AII, etc.). The lights that are illuminated constitute the feasible set of decision processes for the problem as shown in Table 3. The lights not illuminated correspond to alternatives that violate one or more of the seven rules previously stated.

In this prototype version of the box, the lights are illuminated in decreasing order of brightness from left to right within the feasible set. The brightest light corresponds to the alternative shown in Figure 1. Thus, if both CII and GII were feasible alternatives, CII would be brighter than GII, since it requires fewer man-hours. However, a manager who was not under any undue time pressure and who wished to invest time in the development of his subordinates might select an alternative corresponding to one of the dimmer lights.

TOWARD A DESCRIPTIVE MODEL OF LEADER BEHAVIOR

So far we have been concerned with the normative questions defined at the outset. But how do managers really behave? What considerations affect their decisions about how much to share their decision-making power with their subordinates? In what respects is their behavior different from or similar to that of the model? These questions are but a few of those that we attempted to answer in a large-scale research program aimed at gaining a greater understanding of the factors that influence managers in their choice of decision processes to fit the demands of the situation. This research program was financially supported by the McKinsey Foundation, General Electric Foundation, Smith Richardson Foundation, and the Office of Naval Research.

Two different research methods have been utilized in studying these factors. The first investigation utilized a method that we have come to term "recalled problems." Over 500 managers from 11 different countries representing a variety of firms were asked to provide a written description of a problem that they had recently had to solve. These varied in length from one paragraph to several pages and covered virtually every facet of managerial decision making. For each case, the manager was asked to indicate which of the decision processes shown in Table 1 they used to solve the problem. Finally, each manager was asked to answer the questions shown in Table 2 corresponding to the problem attributes used in the normative model.

The wealth of data, both qualitative and quantitative, served two purposes. Since each manager had diagnosed a situation that he had encountered in terms that are used in the normative model and had indicated the methods that he had used in dealing with it, it is possible to determine what differences, if any, there were between the model's behavior and his own behavior. Second, the written cases provided the basis for the construction of a standard set of cases used in later research to determine the factors that influence managers to share or retain their decision-making power. Each case depicted a manager faced with a problem to solve or decision to make. The cases spanned a wide range of managerial problems including production scheduling, quality control, portfolio management, personnel allocation, and research and development. In each case, a person could readily assume the role of the manager described and could indicate which of the decision processes he would use if he actually were faced with that situation.

In most of our research, a set of thirty cases has been used and the subjects have been several thousand managers who were participants in management development programs in the United States and abroad. Cases were selected systematically. We desired cases that could not only be coded unambiguously in the terms used in the normative model but that would also permit the assessment of the effects of each of the problem attributes used in the model on the person's behavior. The solution was to select cases in accordance with an experimental design so that they varied in terms of the seven attributes used in the model and variation in each attribute was independent of each other attribute. Several such standardized sets of cases have been developed, and over a thousand managers have now been studied using this approach.

To summarize everything we learned in the course of this research is well beyond the scope of this paper, but it is possible to discuss some of the highlights. Since the results obtained from the two research methods—recalled and standardized problems—are consistent, we can present the major results independent of the method used.

Perhaps the most striking finding is the weakening of the widespread view that participativeness is a general trait that individual managers exhibit in different amounts. To be sure, there were differences among managers in their general tendencies to utilize participative methods as opposed to autocratic ones. On the standardized problems, these differences accounted for about 10 percent of the total variance in the decision processes observed. These differences in behavior between managers, however, were small in comparison with differences within managers. On the standardized problems, no manager has indicated that he would use the same decision process on all problems or decisions, and most use all five methods under some circumstances.

Some of this variance in behavior within managers can be attributed to widely shared tendencies to respond to some situations by sharing power and others by retaining it. It makes more sense to talk about participative and autocratic situations than it does to talk about participative and autocratic managers. In fact, on the standardized problems, the variance in behavior across problems or cases is about three times as large as the variance across managers!

What are the characteristics of an autocratic as opposed to a participative situation? An answer to this question would constitute a partial descriptive model of this aspect of the decision-making process and has been our goal in much of the research that we have conducted. From our observations of behavior on both recalled problems and on standardized problems, it is clear that the decision-making process employed by a typical manager is influenced by a large number of factors, many of which also show up in the normative model. Following are several conclusions substantiated by the results on both recalled and standardized problems: Managers use decision processes providing less opportunity for participation (1) when they possess all the necessary information than when they lack some of the needed information, (2) when the problem that they face is well-structured rather than unstructured, (3) when their subordinates' acceptance of the decision is not critical for the effective implementation of the decision or when the prior probability of acceptance of an autocratic decision is high, and (4) when the personal goals of their subordinates are *not* congruent with the goals of the organization as manifested in the problem.

So far we have been talking about relatively common or widely shared ways of dealing with organizational problems. Our results strongly suggest that there are ways of "tailoring" one's approach to the situation that distinguish managers from one another. Theoretically, these can be thought of as differences among managers in decision rules that they employ about when to encourage participation. Statistically, they are represented as interactions between situational variables and personal characteristics.

Consider, for example, two managers who have identical distributions of the use of the five decision processes shown in Table 1 on a set of thirty cases. In a sense, they are equally participative (or autocratic). However, the situations in which they permit or encourage participation in decision making on the part of their subordinates may be very different. One may restrict the participation of his subordinates to decisions without a quality requirement, whereas the other may restrict their participation to problems with a quality requirement. The former would be more inclined to use participative decision processes (like GII) on such decisions as what color the walls should be painted or when the company picnic should be held. The latter would be more likely to encourage participation in decision making on decisions that have a clear and demonstrable impact on the organization's success in achieving its external goals.

Use of the standardized problem set permits the assessment of such differences in decision rules that govern choices among decision-making processes. Since the cases are selected in accordance with an experimental design, they can indicate differences in the behavior of managers attributable not only to the existence of a quality requirement in the problem but also in the effects of acceptance requirements, conflict, information requirements, and the like.

The research using both recalled and

standardized problems has also enabled us to examine similarities and differences between the behavior of the normative model and the behavior of a typical manager. Such an analysis reveals, at the very least, what behavioral changes could be expected if managers began using the normative model as the basis for choosing their decision-making processes.

A typical manager says he would (or did) use exactly the same decision process as that shown in Figure 1 in 40 percent of the situations. In two thirds of the situations, his behavior is consistent with the feasible set of methods proposed in the model. In other words, in about one third of the situations his behavior violates at least one of the seven rules underlying the model.

The four rules designed to protect the acceptance or commitment of the decision have substantially higher probabilities of being violated than do the three rules designed to protect the quality or rationality of the decision. One of the acceptance rules, the Fairness Rule (Rule 6) is violated about three quarters of the time that it could have been violated. On the other hand, one of the quality rules, the Information Rule, (Rule 1) is violated in only about 3 percent of occasions in which it is applicable. If we assume for the moment that these two sets of rules have equal validity, these findings strongly suggest that the decisions made by typical managers are more likely to prove ineffective due to deficiencies of acceptance by subordinates than due to deficiencies in decision quality.

Another striking difference between the behavior of the model and of the typical manager lies in the fact that the former shows far greater variance with the situation. If a typical manager voluntarily used the model as the basis for choosing his methods of making decisions, he would become both more autocratic and more participative. He would employ autocratic methods more

frequently in situations in which his subordinates were unaffected by the decision and participative methods more frequently when his subordinates' cooperation and support were critical and/or their information and expertise were required.

It should be noted that the typical manager to whom we have been referring is merely a statistical average of the several thousand who have been studied over the last three or four years. There is a great deal of variance around that average. As evidenced by their behavior on standardized problems, some mangers are already behaving in a manner that is highly consistent with the model, while others' behavior is clearly at variance with it.

A NEW TECHNOLOGY FOR LEADERSHIP DEVELOPMENT

The investigations that have been summarized here were conducted for research purposes to shed some light on the causes and consequences of participation in decision making. In the course of the research, we came to realize, partly because of the value attached to it by the managers themselves, that the data collection procedures, with appropriate additions and modifications, might also serve as a valuable guide to leadership development. From this realization evolved an important by-product of the research activities—a new approach to leadership development based on the concepts in the normative model and the empirical methods of the descriptive research.

This approach is based on the assumption stated previously that one of the critical skills required of all leaders is the ability to adapt their behavior to the demands of the situation and that one component of this skill involves the ability to select the appropriate decision-making process for each problem or decision he confronts.

Managers can derive value from the

model by comparing their past or intended behavior in concrete decisions with that prescribed by the model and by seeing what rules, if any, they violate. Used in this way, the model can provide a mechanism for a manager to analyze both the circumstances that he faces and what decisions are feasible under these circumstances.

While use of the model without training is possible, we believe that the manager can derive the maximum value from a systematic examination of his leadership style, and its similarities to and dissimilarities from the model, as part of a formal leadership development program.

During the past two years we have developed such a program. It is not intended to "train" participants in the use of the model, but rather to encourage them to examine their own leadership style and to ask themselves whether the methods they are using are most effective for their own organization. A critical part of the program involves the use of a set of standardized cases, each depicting a leader faced with an administrative problem to solve. Each participant then specifies the decision-making process that he would use if faced with each situation. His responses are processed by computer, which generates a highly detailed analysis of his leadership style. The responses for all participants in the course are typically processed simultaneously, permitting the economical representation of differences between the person and other participants in the same program.

In its present form, a single computer printout for a person consists of three 15" x 11" pages, each filled with graphs and tables highlighting different features of his behavior. Understanding the results requires a detailed knowledge of the concepts underlying the model, something already developed in one of the previous phases of the training program. The printout is accompanied by a manual that aids in explaining results and provides suggested steps

to be followed in extracting full meaning from the printout.

Following are a few of the questions that the printout answers:

1. How autocratic or participative am I in my dealings with subordinates in comparison with other participants in the program?

2. What decision processes do I use more or less frequently than the average?

3. How close does my behavior come to that of the model? How frequently does my behavior agree with the feasible set? What evidence is there that my leadership style reflects the pressure of time as opposed to a concern with the development of my subordinates? How do I compare in these respects with other participants in the class?

4. What rules do I violate most frequently and least frequently? How does this compare with other participants? On what cases did I violate these rules? Does my leadership style reflect more concern with getting decisions that are high in quality or with getting decisions that are accepted?

5. What circumstances cause me to behave in an autocratic fashion; what circumstances cause me to behave participatively? In what respects is the way in which I attempt to vary my behavior with the demands of the situation similar to that of the model?

When a typical manager receives his printout, he immediately goes to work trying to understand what it tells him about himself. After most of the major results have been understood, he goes back to the set of cases to re-read those on which he has violated rules. Typically, managers show an interest in discussing and comparing their results with others in the program. Gatherings of four to six people comparing their results and their interpretation of them often for several hours at a stretch, were such a common feature that they have recently been institutionalized as part of the procedure.

We should emphasize that the method of providing feedback to managers on their leadership style is just one part of the total training experience, but it is an important part. The program is sufficiently new so that, to date, no long-term evaluative studies have been undertaken. The short-term results, however, appear quite promising.

CONCLUSION

The efforts reported in this article rest on the conviction that social scientists can be of greater value in solving problems of organizational behavior if their prescriptive statements deal with the complexities involved in the phenomena with which they study. The normative model described in this paper is one step in that direction. Some might argue that it is premature for social scientists to be prescriptive. Our knowledge is too limited and the issues too complex to warrant prescriptions for action, even those that are based on a diagnosis of situational demands. However, organizational problems persist, and managers cannot wait for the behavioral sciences to perfect their disciplines before attempting to cope with them. Is it likely that models that encourage them to deal analytically with the forces impinging upon them would produce less rational choices than those that they now make? We think the reverse is more probable—reflecting on the models will result in decisions that are more rational and more effective. The criterion for social utility is not perfection but improvement over present practice.

VIII

Organizational Communications and Decision Making

Introduction. The papers selected for this section are concerned with organizational communications and decision making. These two topics represent the basis of interaction among work units, environments, and the formal organizational structure. Thus, they are important considerations if the organization is to be effective and efficient. It should be noted that there is not a generally accepted model of decision making and communication for organizations. Rather, there exists a collection of studies and quasi-models which provide guidance to the manager in establishing structures for effective communication and decision making and methods for evaluation of their payoffs.

The Bavelas and Barrett article, "An Experimental Approach to Organizational Communication," suggests a general structure for the evaluation of communication within an organizational context. They argue that communication "is the essence of organized activity and is the basic process out of which other functions derive" (1951, p. 368). Organizational effectiveness is then a function of the quality and availability of information within the organization. The reader should pay particular attention to the patterns of communication discussed in this article.

The article by Herbert Simon, "On the Concept of Organizational Goal," represents the introduction of the concept of organizational goal into organizational theory. Simon argues that decision making in organizations is discovering courses of action that satisfy a *set* of constraints rather than any particular member of that set. This "satisficing" of the set of constraints is the goal. He further argues that the term organizational goal is most appropriately used to refer to sets of constraints imposed by organizational role rather than the personal motives of the individual. Finally, he argues that different constraints define the different positions or specialized units within an organization. In this article, Simon has provided a partial model for describing the structure of organizational decision making and how goals help determine courses of action.

The third selection, "Interpersonal Barriers to Decision Making" by Chris

Argyris, discusses certain barriers to decision making by executives. This well conceived analysis raises individual personality issues as enhancing or detracting from effective organizational decision making. The importance of motivation and feedback on the effectiveness of decisions is stressed. The assumption is made that no member of a group will knowingly make a poor decision. Instead, a poor decision results from a lack of awareness of the outcome.

The next selection, "Assets and Liabilities in Group Problem Solving: The Need for an Integrative Function" by Norman R. F. Maier, reviews the factors influencing group and individual problem solving. The paper stresses the importance of the nature of the problem, communication, the type of solution, and the skill of the group leader in selecting the particular mode of problem solving. Maier argues that if one can overcome some of the liabilities of group problem solving, this approach has more potential than individual problem solving. The key appears to be the role of the leader.

The last article, a chapter from Irving Janis' book *Victims of Groupthink* (1972), concerns the phenomenon of "groupthink." This phenomenon has been characterized by Janis as a process leading to certain decision based upon the cohesive characteristics of the group. One of the major characteristics is concurrence-seeking behavior. While Janis' discussion on the prevention of groupthink utilizes examples in the public policy area, it should be applicable to other contexts as well. He provides some "prescriptions" that, with careful application, may reduce the probability of groupthink. Along with Maier (1967) he stresses the importance of the group leader.

The reader interested in the general area of organizational decision making should consider the work of Janis and Mann (1977). This is an excellent summary of some key issues, models, and strategies of decision making.

REFERENCES

Bavelas, A., and Barrett, D. 1951. An experimental approach to organizational communication. *Personnel, 27*, 366-371.

Janis, I. L. 1972. *Victims of groupthink.* Boston: Houghton-Mifflin.

Janis, I. L. and Mann, L. 1977. *Decision making: A psychological analysis of conflict, choice and commitment.* New York: Free Press.

34. An Experimental Approach to Organizational Communication*

ALEX BAVELAS
DERMOT BARRETT

Communication as a critical aspect of organization has been attracting more and more attention. If one may judge from articles and speeches, much of the current thinking on communication centers around categories of problems which arise in day-to-day operations— "getting management's point of view to the workers," "stimulating communication up the line as well as down," "obtaining better communication with the union," "establishing more effective communication within management, and especially with the foremen." Knowing how such questions usually arise, it is not surprising that their discussion invariably resolves itself into considerations of *content* and *technique:* on the one hand, analyses of what management ought to be saying to the worker, the union, the foreman; on the other hand, descriptions of devices which can best say it—bulletin boards, letters, films, public address systems, meetings, etc. In its extreme form this approach becomes one of searching for a specific remedy for a specific ill. Helpful and practical as this may be, it is doubtful that such activity can lead to the discovery and understanding of the basic principles of effective organizational communication. Breakdowns and other difficulties at some point of a communication system are often only superficially related to the local conditions which appear to have produced

them. They may, rather, be cumulative effects of properties of the entire communication system taken as a whole. But what are these properties, if, indeed, they exist?

FORMAL AND INFORMAL SYSTEMS

An organizational system of communication is usually created by the setting up of formal systems of responsibility and by explicit delegations of duties. These categories include statements, often implicitly, of the nature, content, and direction of the communication which is considered necessary for the performance of the group. Students of organization, however, have pointed out repeatedly that groups tend to depart from such formal statements and to create other channels of communication and dependence. In other words, informal organizational systems emerge. One may take the view that these changes are adaptations by the individuals involved in the direction of easier and more effective ways of working, or, perhaps, not working. It is no secret that informal groups are not always viewed by managers as favorable to the goals of the larger body. Also, it is by no means obvious that those informal groupings which evolve out of social and personality factors are likely to be more efficient (with respect to organ-

*Source: Reprinted, by permission of the publisher, from *Personnel,* March 1951, pp. 366-71. Copyright © 1951 by American Management Association, Inc. All rights reserved.

izational tasks) than those set up formally by the managers. Altogether, if one considers how intimate the relations are between communication channels and control, it is not surprising that the managers of organizations would prefer explicit and orderly communication lines.

Fig. 1

IS THERE "ONE BEST WAY"?

Unfortunately, there seems to be no organized body of knowledge out of which one can derive, for a given organization, an optimal communication system. Administrative thinking on this point commonly rests upon the assumption that the optimum system can be derived from a statement of the task to be performed. It is not difficult to show, however, that from a given set of specifications one may derive not a single communication pattern but a whole set of them, all logically adequate for the successful performance of the task in question. Which pattern from this set should be chosen? The choice, in practice, is usually made either in terms of a group of assumptions (often quite untenable) about human nature, or in terms of a personal bias on the part of the chooser. The seriousness of this situation is illustrated by the following example.

Let us assume that we have a group of five individuals who, in order to solve a problem, must share as quickly as possible the information each person possesses. Let us also assume that there are reasons which prevent them from meeting around a table, and that they must share this information by writing notes. To avoid the confusion and waste of time of each person writing a message to each of the others, a supervisor decides to set up channels in which the notes must go. He strikes upon the pattern shown in Figure 1.

In this arrangement each individual can send to and receive messages from two others, one on his "left" and one on his "right." Experiments actually per-

formed with this kind of situation show that the number of mistakes made by individuals working in such a "circle" pattern can be reduced by fully 60 percent by the simple measure of removing one link, thus making the pattern a "chain" as shown in Figure 2. The relevance of such a result to organization communication is obvious, simple though the example is. The sad truth, however, is that this phenomenon is not clearly derivable either from traditional "individual psychology" or from commonly held theories of group communication.

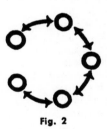

Fig. 2

AN INTEGRAL PROCESS OF ORGANIZATION

Perhaps some headway can be made by approaching the general problem from a somewhat different direction. In the affairs of organizations, as well as in the affairs of men, chance always plays a part. However good a plan may be, however carefully prepared its execution, there is a point beyond which the probability of its success cannot be increased. With the firmest of intentions, agreements and promises may be impossible to carry out because of unforeseen events. Nevertheless, an organization whose functioning is too often interrupted by unforeseen events is looked upon with suspicion. Bad luck is an unhappy plea, and it may well be that the "unlucky" organization is more to be avoided than the simply incompetent one. On the other hand, few things about an organization are more admired and respected than the ability to "deliver" despite widely varying conditions and in the face of unusual difficulties.

In a very broad sense, it may be argued that the principal effort of organizational activities is the making of favorable conditions for the achievement of certain goals. In other words, an effort is made to increase, as much as the economics of the situation will permit, the probabilities of succeeding. This is the essence of the manager's job. The development of training and selection programs, the improvement of methods and the specification of techniques, the organization of research and development activities, the designation of responsibility and the delegation of duties—all these processes have one organizationally legitimate purpose: to increase the chances of organizational success. Upon this point rest almost all of the notions by which we are accustomed to evaluate organizations—in part or as a whole.

An organization is, in short, a social invention—a kind of "machine" for increasing certain sets of probabilities. (Which sets of probabilities are given to it to increase, which it chooses, how freely and by what means will not be discussed here. These problems, although they lie well within the scope of this subject, are outside the range of this paper. We will confine ourselves to a consideration of the process by which an accepted set of probabilities is optimized.) Probabilities of success are increased, however, only by taking relevant and appropriate actions. For the manager, these actions reduce in most instances to the gathering and evaluat-

ing of information in the form of reports, schedules, estimates, etc. It is entirely possible to view an organization as an elaborate system for gathering, evaluating, recombining, and disseminating information. It is not surprising, in these terms, that the effectiveness of an organization with respect to the achievement of its goals should be so closely related to its effectiveness in handling information. In an enterprise whose success hinges upon the coordination of the efforts of all its members, the managers depend completely upon the quality, the amount, and the rate at which relevant information reaches them. The rest of the organization, in turn, depends upon the efficiency with which the managers can deal with this information and reach conclusions, decisions, etc. This line of reasoning leads us to the belief that communication is not a secondary or derived aspect of organization—a "helper" of the other and presumably more basic functions. Rather it is the essence of organized activity and is the basic process out of which all other functions derive. The goals an organization selects, the methods it applies, the effectiveness with which it improves its own procedures—all of these hinge upon the quality and availability of the information in the system.

PATTERNS OF COMMUNICATION

About two years ago a series of studies was begun whose purpose was to isolate and study certain general properties of information handling systems. The first phase of this research program[1] is directed at a basic property of all communication systems, that of connection or "who can talk to whom."

This property of connection can be conveniently expressed by diagrams. The meaning of the picture in Figure 3 is obvious. Individuals A and B send messages to C but they can receive messages from no one; C and D can exchange messages; E can receive messages from D, but he can send messages

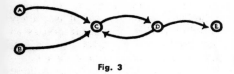

Fig. 3

to no one. The pattern shown in Figure 3, however, is only one of the many that are possible. A group of others is shown in Figure 4. An examination of these patterns will show that they fall into two classes, separated by a very important difference. Any pair of individuals in each of the patterns d, e, and f can exchange messages either directly or indirectly over some route. No pair of individuals in each of the patterns a, b, and c can exchange messages. Patterns like a, b, and c obviously make any coordination of thought or action virtually impossible; we will be concerned from this point on only with patterns like d, e, and f.

Since the individuals in any connected pattern like d, e, and f can share ideas completely, should we expect that the effectiveness of individuals in performing group tasks or solving group problems would be the same in patterns d, e, and f except for differences in ability, knowledge, and personality? Should

we expect differences in quality and speed of performance? Is it likely that the individuals working in one pattern would show significantly better morale than the individuals working in a different pattern? Sidney Smith and Harold J. Leavitt conducted a series of experiments[2] which yielded very definite answers to these questions. An experimental design was used which made it possible to equate the difficulty of the tasks which the groups performed, and which permitted the cancelling of individual differences by randomizing the assignment of subjects to patterns. Also, the experiment was repeated with different groups enough times to establish the consistency of the results. A brief summary of the findings is given in Figure 5. The use of qualitative terms in Figure 5 in place of the quantitative measurements which were actually made blurs the comparison somewhat, but it gives a fair picture of the way these patterns performed. Since the original experiments were done by Smith and Leavitt, this experiment has been repeated with no change in the findings.

The question very properly arises here as to whether these findings can be "explained" in the sense of being related to the connection properties of the

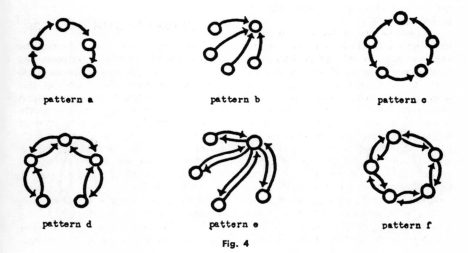

Fig. 4

Speed	slow	fast	fast
Accuracy	poor	good	good
Organization	no stable form of organization	slowly emerging but stable organization	almost immediate and stable organization
Emergence of Leader	none	marked	very pronounced
Morale	very good	poor	very poor

Fig. 5

patterns themselves. The answer to this question is a qualified yes. Without developing the mathematical analysis, which can be found in Leavitt's paper, the following statements can be made:

For any connected pattern, an *index of dispersion* can be calculated. Relative to this index, there can be calculated *for each position in each pattern* an *index of centrality,* and an *index of peripherality.* The data suggest strongly that the rapidity with which organization emerges and the stability it displays are related to the gradient of the indices of centrality in the pattern. In Figure 6 these indices are given for each position. It should be added at this point that in the patterns in which leadership emerged, the leader was invariably that person who occupied the position of highest centrality.

The index of peripherality appears to be related strongly to morale. In Figure 7 the indices of peripherality are given by position. Those individuals who occupied positions of low or zero peripherality showed in their actions as well as in self-ratings (made at the end of the experiments) that they were satisfied, in high spirits, and generally pleased with the work they had done. Those individuals who occupied positions of high peripherality invariably displayed either apathetic or destructive and uncooperative behavior during the group effort, and rated themselves as dissatisfied and critcal of the group's operation.

A word of caution should be given concerning the slow, inaccurate, but happy "circle" pattern. Subsequent experiments by Sidney Smith indicate that this pattern possesses unusual abilities

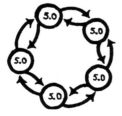 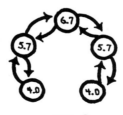 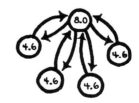

Fig. 6

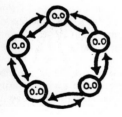 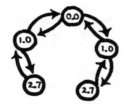 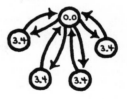

Fig. 7

for adaptation to sudden and confusing changes of task—a quality lacking in the other two patterns.

A PROMISING FIELD FOR RESEARCH

Clearly, these experiments are only the beginning of a long story. The findings, although they promise much, settle nothing; but they do suggest that an experimental approach to certain aspects of organizational communication is possible and that, in all probability, it would be practically rewarding. As the characteristics of communication nets and their effects upon human performance *as they occur in the laboratory* become better understood, the need will grow for systematic studies of actual operating organizations. The job of mapping an existing net of communications even in a relatively small company is a complicated and difficult one, but it is not impossible. Some work is beginning on the development of field methods of observation. The importance of bridging the gap between the simple, directly controlled experiment and the very complex, indirectly controlled social situation cannot be overestimated.

NOTES

1. These studies are supported jointly by the Rand Corporation and the Research Laboratory of Electronics at M.I.T.

2. Harold J. Leavitt reports these experiments in detail in the January, 1951, issue of the *Journal of Abnormal and Social Psychology.*

35. On the Concept of Organizational Goal*

HERBERT A. SIMON

Few discussions of organization theory manage to get along without introducing some concept of "organization goal." In the classical economic theory of the firm, where no distinction is made between an organization and a single entrepreneur, the organization's goal—the goal of the firm—is simply identical with the goal of the real or hypothetical entrepreneur. In general, it is thought not to be problematical to postulate that individuals have goals. If it is not, this solution raises no difficulties.

When we are interested in the internal structure of an organization, how-

*Source: From *Administrative Science Quarterly*, vol. 9 (June 1964), pp. 1-22. Copyright © 1964 *Administrative Science Quarterly*. Reprinted by permission. Footnotes renumbered.

ever, the problem cannot be avoided in this way. Either we must explain organizational behavior in terms of the goals of the individual members of the organization, or we must postulate the existence of one or more organization goals, over and above the goals of the individuals.[1]

The first alternative is an attractive one. It protects us from the danger of reifying the organization, of treating it as a superindividual entity having an existence and behavior independent of the behavior of its members. The difficulty with this alternative is that it is hard to carry off. The usual way it is attempted is by identifying the phrase "organization goals" with "goals of the firm's owners" or, alternatively, "goals of the firm's top management," or "goals of those who hold legitimate authority to direct the organization."

But this solution raises new difficulties, for we often have occasion to observe that the goals that actually underlie the decisions made in an organization do not coincide with the goals of the owners, or of top management, but have been modified by managers and employees at all echelons. Must we conclude, then, that it is the goals of the latter—of subordinate managers and employees—that are governing organizational behavior? Presumably not, because the kinds of behavior taking place are not those we would expect if the managers and employees were consulting only their personal goals. The whole concept of an informal organization, modified by, but not identical with, the goals either of management or of individual employees, becomes hazy and ambiguous if we follow this path.

Let us see if we can find a way between this Scylla and the Charybdis of reification. The first step toward clarification is to maintain a distinction between goals, on the one hand, and motives, on the other. By *goals* we shall mean value premises that can serve as inputs to decisions. By *motives* we mean the causes, whatever they are, that lead individuals to select some goals rather than others as premises for their decisions. In the next section we shall develop the concept of goal, defined as above. In subsequent sections we shall undertake to explicate the notion of *organization goal* and to clarify the relations between organization goals and personal motives.

Before we can define "organization goals" we shall have to be clear on what we mean by "goals of an individual." We shall begin by considering the latter question.

GOALS AND DECISIONS: MULTIPLE CRITERIA

Our discussion of goals will be much simplified if we have a definite model before us of the situation we are considering. In recent years in the field of management science or operations research, we have learned to build formal models to characterize even quite elaborate and complex decision situations, and to use these models to reach "optimal" decisions. Since many of these models make use of the tool of linear programming, we will employ a linear programming framework to describe the decision situation. No mathematical knowledge will be assumed beyond the ability to read algebraic notation.[2]

The optimal diet problem is a typical simple linear programming problem. We are given a list of foods, and for each item on the list its price, its calory content, and its proportions of each of the minerals and vitamins relevant to nutrition. Then we are given a set of nutritional requirements, which may include statements about minimum daily intake of minerals, vitamins, and calories, and may also put limits on maximum intake of some or all of these components.

The diet problem is to find that sublist of foods and their quantities that will meet the nutritional requirements at least cost. The problem can be formalized as follows:

Let the various foods be numbered from 1 through N, and the various nutritional components from 1 through M. Let x_i be the quantity of the ith food in the diet, y_j be the total quantity of the jth nutritional component in the diet, and p_i the price of the ith food. Let a_{ij} be the amount of the jth nutritional component in a unit quantity of the ith food; let b_j be the minimum requirement of the jth nutritional component, and c_j the maximum allowance. (Some of the b_j's may be zero, and some of the c_j's infinite.) Then:

(1) $\sum_i a_{ij}x_i = y_j,$ for $j = 1, \ldots, M;$

i.e., the total consumption of the jth nutritional element is the sum of the quantities of that element for each of the foods consumed. The nutritional requirements can be stated:

(2) $c_j \geq y_j \geq b_j,$ for $j = 1, \ldots, M;$

i.e., the total quantity of the jth element must lie between b_j and c_j. The quantity of each food consumed must be nonnegative, although it may be zero:

(3) $x_i \geq 0,$ $i = 1, \ldots, N.$

Finally, the total cost of the diet is to be minimized; we are to find:

(4) $\underset{x}{\text{Min}} \sum_i x_i p_i.$

A diet (the solution is not necessarily unique) that satisfies all the relations (2), (3), (4) is called an *optimal* diet. A diet that satisfies the inequalities (2) and (3) (called *constraints*), but which is not necessarily a minimum cost diet, is called a *feasible* diet.

What is the goal of the diet decision? It would be an appropriate use of ordinary language to say that the goal is to minimize the cost of obtaining an adequate diet, for the condition (4) is the criterion we are minimizing. This criterion puts the emphasis on economy as the goal.

Alternatively, we might direct our attention primarily to the constraints, and in particular to the nutritional requirements (2). Then we might say that the goal is to find a nutritionally satisfactory diet that is economical. Although we still mention costs in this statement, we have clearly shifted the emphasis to the adequacy of the diet from a nutritional standpoint. The primary goal has now become good nutrition.

The relation between the criterion function (4) and the constraints (2) can be made even more symmetrical. Let us replace the criterion (4) with a new constraint:

(5) $\sum_i x_i p_i \leq k,$

that is to say, with the requirement that the total cost of the diet not exceed some constant, k. Now the set of feasible diets has been restricted to those that satisfy (5) as well as (2) and (3). But since the minimization condition has been removed, there is apparently no basis for choosing one of these diets over another.

Under some circumstances, we can, however, restrict the set of diets that deserve consideration to a subset of the feasible set. Suppose that all the nutritional constraints (2) are minimal constraints, and that we would always prefer, *ceteris paribus*, a greater amount of any nutritional factor to a smaller amount. We will say that diet A is dominated by diet B if the cost of diet B is no greater than the cost of diet A, and if diet B contains at least as much of each nutritional factor as does diet A, and more of at least one factor. We will call the set of diets in the feasible set that is undominated by other diets in that set the Pareto optimal set.

Our preference for one or the other of the diets in the Pareto optimal set will depend on the relative importance we assign to cost in comparison with amounts of nutritional factors, and to the amounts of these factors in relation with each other. If cost is the most important factor, then we will again choose the diet that is selected by criterion (4). On the other hand, if we attach great importance to nutritional factor j, we will generally choose a quite different feasible diet—one in which the quantity of factor j is as great as possible. Within the limits set by the constraints, it would be quite reasonable to call whatever criterion led us to select a particular member of the Pareto optimal set our goal. But if the constraints are strong enough, so that the feasible set and, a fortiori, the Pareto optimal set is very small, then the constraints will have as much or more influence on what diet we finally select than will the goal, so defined. For example, if we set one or more of the nutritional requirements very high, so that only a narrow range of diets also satisfy the budget constraint (5), then introducing the cost minimization criterion as the final selection rule will have relatively little effect on what diet we choose.

Under such circumstances it might be well to give up the idea that the decision situation can be described in terms of a simple goal. Instead, it would be more reasonable to speak of a whole set of goals—the whole set, in fact, of nutritional and budgetary constraints—that the decision maker is trying to attain. To paraphrase a familiar epigram: "If you allow me to determine the constraints, I don't care who selects the optimization criterion."

MULTIPLE CRITERIA IN ORGANIZATIONS

To show the organizational relevance of our example it is only necessary to suppose that the decision we are discussing has arisen within a business firm that manufactures commercial stock feeds, that the nutritional requirements are requirements for hogs and the prices

those of available feed ingredients, and that the finished feed prices facing the firm are fixed. Then minimizing the cost of feed meeting certain nutritional standards is identical with maximizing the profit from selling feed meeting those standards. Cost minimization represents the profit-maximizing goal of the company.

We can equally well say that the goal of the feed company is to provide its customers with the best feed possible, in terms of nutritional standards, at a given price, i.e., to produce feeds that are in the Pareto optimal set. Presumably this is what industry spokesmen mean when they say that the goal of business is not profit but efficient production of goods and services. If we had enlarged our model to give some of the prices that appear in it the status of constraints, instead of fixing them as constants, we could have introduced other goals, for example, the goal of suppliers' profits, or, if there were a labor input, the goal of high wages.[3]

We may summarize the discussion to this point as follows. In the decision-making situations of real life, a course of action, to be acceptable, must satisfy a whole set of requirements, or constraints. Sometimes one of these requirements is singled out and referred to as the goal of the action. But the choice of one of the constraints, from many, is to a large extent arbitrary. For many purposes it is more meaningful to refer to the whole set of requirements as the (complex) goal of the action. This conclusion applies both to individual and organizational decision making.

SEARCH FOR A COURSE OF ACTION

Thus far, we have assumed that the set of possible actions is known in advance to the decision maker. In many, if not most, real-life situations, possible courses of action must be discovered, designed, or synthesized. In the process of searching for a satisfactory solution, the goals of the action—that is, the constraints that must be satisfied by the solution—may play a guiding role in two ways. First, the goals may be used directly to synthesize proposed solutions (alternative generation). Second, the goals may be used to test the satisfactoriness of a proposed solution (alternative testing).[4]

We may illustrate these possibilities by considering what goes on in the mind of a chess player when he is trying to choose a move in a game. One requirement of a good move is that it put pressure on the opponent by attacking him in some way or by preparing an attack. This requirement suggests possible moves to an experienced player (alternative generation). For example, if the opponent's king is not well protected, the player will search for moves that attack the king, but after a possible move has been generated in this way (and thus automatically satisfies the requirement that it put pressure on the opponent), it must be tested against other requirements (alternative testing). For example, it will not be satisfactory if it permits a counterattack that is more potent than the attack or that can be carried out more quickly.

The decisions of everyday organizational life are similar to these decisions in chess. A bank officer who is investing trust funds in stocks and bonds may, because of the terms of the trust document, take as his goal increasing the capital value of the fund. This will lead him to consider buying common stock in firms in growth industries (alternative generation). But he will check each possible purchase against other requirements: that the firm's financial structure be sound, its past earnings record satisfactory, and so on (alternative testing). All these considerations can be counted among his goals in constructing the portfolio, but some of the goals serve as generators of possible portfolios, others as checks.[5]

The process of designing courses of action provides us, then, with another source of asymmetry between the goals that guide the actual synthesis and the constraints that determine whether possible courses of action are in fact feasible. In general, the search will continue until one decision in the feasible set is found, or, at most, a very few alternatives. Which member of the feasible set is discovered and selected may depend considerably on the search process, that is, on which requirements serve as goals or generators, in the sense just defined, and which as constraints or tests.

In a multiperson situation, one man's goals may be another man's constraints. The feed manufacturer may seek to produce feed as cheaply as possible, searching, for example, for possible new ingredients. The feed, however, has to meet certain nutritional specifications. The hog farmer may seek the best quality of feed, searching, for example, for new manufacturers. The feed, however, cannot cost more than his funds allow; if it is too expensive, he must cut quality or quantity. A sale will be made when a lot of feed is feasible in terms of the requirements of both manufacturer and farmer. Do manufacturer and farmer have the same goals? In one sense, clearly not, for there is a definite conflict of interest between them: the farmer wishes to buy cheap, the manufacturer to sell dear. On the other hand, if a bargain can be struck that meets the requirements of both—if the feasible set that satisfies both sets of constraints is not empty—then there is another sense in which they do have a common goal. In the limiting case of perfect competition, the constraints imposed by the market and the technology actually narrow down the feasible set to a single point, determining uniquely the quantity of goods they will exchange and the price.

The neatness and definiteness of the limiting case of perfect competition should not blind us to the fact that most real-life situations do not fit this case exactly. Typically, the generation of alternatives (e.g., product invention, development, and design) is a laborious, costly process. Typically, also, there is a practically unlimited sea of potential alternatives. A river valley development plan that aims at the generation of electric power, subject to appropriate provision for irrigation, flood control, and recreation will generally look quite different from a plan that aims at flood control, subject to appropriate provision for the other goals mentioned. Even though the plans generated in both cases will be examined for their suitability along all the dimensions mentioned, it is almost certain that quite different plans will be devised and proposed for consideration in the two cases, and that the plans finally selected will represent quite distinct points in the feasible set.

In later paragraphs we shall state some reasons for supposing that the total sets of constraints considered by decision makers in different parts of an organization are likely to be quite similar, but that different decision makers are likely to divide the constraints between generators and tests in quite different ways. Under these circumstances, if we use the phrase organization goals broadly to denote the constraint sets, we will conclude that organizations do, indeed, have goals (widely shared constraint sets). If we use the phrase organization goals narrowly to denote the generators, we will conclude that there is little communality of goals among the several parts of large organizations and that subgoal formation and goal conflict are prominent and significant features of organizational life. The distinction we have made between generators and tests helps resolve this ambiguity, but also underlines the importance of always making explicit which sense of goal is intended.

MOTIVATION FOR GOALS

If by motivation we mean whatever it is that causes someone to follow a particular course of action, then every ac-

tion is motivated—by definition. But in most human behavior the relation between motives and action is not simple; it is mediated by a whole chain of events and surrounding conditions.

We observe a man scratching his arm. His motive (or goal)? To relieve an itch.

We observe a man reaching into a medicine cabinet. His motive (or goal)? To get a bottle of lotion that, his wife has assured him, is very effective in relieving the itch of mosquito bites. Or have we misstated his motive? Is it to apply the lotion to his arm? Or, as before, to relieve the itch? But the connection between action and goal is much more complex in this case than in the previous one. There intervenes between them a means-end chain (get bottle, apply lotion, relieve itch), an expectation (that the lotion will relieve the itch), and a social belief supporting the expectation (that the wife's assurance is a reliable predictor of the lotion's efficacy). The relation between the action and the ultimate goal has become highly indirect and contingent, even in this simple case. Notice that these new complications of indirectness are superimposed on the complications we have discussed earlier—that the goal is pursued only within limits imposed by numerous side constraints (don't knock over the other bottles in the medicine cabinet, don't brush against the fresh paint, and so on).

Our point is identical with the point of the venerable story of the three bricklayers who were asked what they were doing. "Laying bricks," "Building a wall," "Helping to erect a great cathedral," were their respective answers. The investment trust officer whose behavior we considered earlier could answer in any of these modes, or others. "I am trying to select a stock for this investment portfolio." "I am assembling a portfolio that will provide retirement income for my client." "I am employed as an investment trust officer." Now it is the step of indirectness between the second and third answers that has principal interest for organization theory. The investment trust officer presumably has no "personal" interest in the retirement income of his client, only a "professional" interest in his role as trust officer and bank employee. He does have, on the other hand, a personal interest in maintaining that role and that employment status.

ROLE BEHAVIOR

Of course, in real life the line of demarcation between personal and professional interests is not a sharp one, for personal satisfactions may arise from the competent performance of a professional role, and both personal satisfactions and dissatisfactions may result from innumerable conditions that surround the employment. Nevertheless, it is exceedingly important, as a first approximation, to distinguish between the answers to two questions of motive: "Why do you keep (or take) this job?" and "Why do you make this particular investment decision?" The first question is properly answered in terms of the personal motives or goals of the occupant of the role, the second question in terms of goals that define behavior appropriate to the role itself.

Corresponding to this subdivision of goals into personal and role-defined goals, organization theory is sometimes divided into two subparts: (1) a theory of motivation explaining the decisions of people to participate in and remain in organizations; and (2) a theory of decision making within organizations comprised of such people.[6]

In the motivational theory formulated by Barnard and me, it is postulated that the motives of each group of participants can be divided into *inducements* (aspects of participation that are desired by the participants) and *contributions* (aspects of participation that are inputs to the organization's production function but that generally have negative

utility to participants). Each participant is motivated to maximize, or at least increase, his inducements while decreasing his contributions, and this motivation is a crucial consideration in explaining the decision to join (or remain). But "joining" means accepting an organizational role, and hence we do not need any additional motivational assumptions beyond those of inducements-contributions theory to explain the ensuing role-enacting behavior.

I hasten to repeat the caveat, introduced a few paragraphs above, that in thus separating our consideration of organizational role-enacting behavior from our consideration of personal motivation—allowing the decision to join as the only bridge between them—we are proposing an abstraction from the complexities of real life. A good deal of the significant research on human relations and informal organization, which has contributed heavily in the last generation to our understanding of organizational behavior, has been concerned specifically with the phenomena that this abstraction excludes. Thus, desire for power and concern for personal advancement represent an intrusion of personal goals upon organizational role, as do the social and craft satisfactions and dissatisfactions associated with work.

To say that the abstraction is sometimes untenable is not to deny that there may be many situations in which it is highly useful. There are, first of all, many organizational decisions that simply do not affect personal motives at all—where organizational goals and personal goals are orthogonal, so to speak. As a trivial example, the secretary's inducement-contribution balance is generally in no whit affected by the choice between typing a letter to A or a letter to B or by the content of the letter. Second, personal motives may enter the decision process as fixed constraints (only courses of action that satisfy the constraints are considered, but the constraints have no influence on the choice of action within the set). Thus, the terms of the employment contract may limit work to a forty-hour week but may have little to say about what goes on during the forty hours.[7]

The abstraction of organizational role from personal goals turns out to be particularly useful in studying the cognitive aspects of organizational decision making, for the abstraction is consonant with some known facts about human cognitive processes. Of all the knowledge, attitudes, and values stored in a human memory, only a very small fraction are evoked in a given concrete situation. Thus, an individual can assume a wide variety of roles when these are evoked by appropriate circumstances, each of which may interact only weakly with the others. At one time he may be a father, at another a machinist, at another a chess player. Current information processing theories of human cognition postulate that there is only modest overlap of the subsets of memory contents—information and programs—that are evoked by these several roles. Thus, we might postulate that the day-to-day organizational environment evokes quite different associations out of the memory of the participant from those evoked when he is considering a change of jobs. To the extent this is so, it provides a further explanation of why his "personal" system of inducements and contributions, i.e., the utilities that enter into the latter decisions, will have no effect on his "organizational" decisions, i.e., those that are made while the first set is evoked.

The ability of a single individual to shift from one role to another as a function of the environment in which he finds himself thus helps explain the extent to which organizational goals become internalized, that is, are automatically evoked and applied during performance of the role. By whatever means the individual was originally motivated to adopt the role in the first place, the goals and constraints appro-

priate to the role become a part of the decision-making program, stored in his memory, that defines his role behavior.

INTERPERSONAL DIFFERENCES

Although the considerations introduced in the last section show that the uncoupling of organizational role from personal goals need not be complete, it may be useful to indicate a little more specifically how differences among individuals can affect their behavior in roles that are identical from an organizational standpoint.

A role must be understood not as a specific, stereotyped set of behaviors, but as a *program* (as that word is understood in computer technology) for determining the courses of action to be taken over the range of circumstances that arise. In previous sections we have given examples of such programs and have shown that they can be highly complex; for instance, a single decision may be a function of a large number of program instructions or premises.

Thus, while we may conceive of an ideal type of role that incorporates only organizational goals among its premises, the roles that members of organizations actually enact invariably incorporate both organizational and personal goals. We have already seen how both can be part of the total system of constraints.

But interpersonal differences in the enactment of roles go far beyond the incorporation of personal goals in the role. Role behavior depends on means-end premises as well as goal premises. Thus, particular professional training may provide an individual with specific techniques and knowledge for solving problems (accounting techniques, legal techniques, and so on), which are then drawn upon as part of the program evoked by his role. In this way, a chief executive with an accounting background may find different problem solutions from a chief executive, in the same position, with a legal background.

An individual may incorporate in his role not only a professional style but also a personal style. He may bring to the role, for example, habits and beliefs that provide him with crucial premises for his handling of interpersonal relations. Thus, an authoritarian personality will behave quite differently from a more permissive person when both are in the same organizational role and pursuing the same organizational goals.

The leeway for the expression of individual differences in role behavior is commonly narrowest in the handling of those matters that come to the role occupant at the initiative of others and is commonly broadest in his exercise of initiative and in selecting those discretionary matters to which he will attend and give priority. In terms used in earlier paragraphs, premises supplied by the organizational environment generally control alternative selection more closely than alternative generation.

THE ORGANIZATIONAL DECISION-MAKING SYSTEM

Let us limit ourselves for the present to situations where occupational roles are almost completely divorced from personal goals and pursue the implications of this factoring of the behavior of organizational participants into its personal and organizational components. If we now consider the organizational decision-making programs of all the participants, together with the connecting flow of communication, we can assemble them into a composite description of the organizational decision-making system—a system that has been largely abstracted from the individual motives that determine participation.

In the simplest case, of a small, relatively unspecialized organization, we are back to a decision-making situation not unlike that of the optimal diet problem. The language of "goals," "requirements," "constraints," that we applied there is equally applicable to similarly uncomplicated organizational situations.

In more complicated cases, abstracting out the organizational decision-making system from personal motives does not remove all aspects of interpersonal (more accurately, interrole) difference from the decision-making process. For when many persons in specialized roles participate in making an organization's decisions, the total system is not likely to be monolithic in structure. Individual roles will differ with respect to the number and kinds of communications they receive and the parts of the environment from which they receive them. They will differ with respect to the evaluative communications they receive from other roles. They will differ in their search programs. Hence, even within our abstraction, which neglects personal motives, we can accommodate the phenomena of differential perception and subgoal formation.

To make our discussion more specific, let us again consider a specific example of an organizational decision-making system—in this case a system for controlling inventory and production. We suppose a factory in which decisions have to be made about (1) the aggregate rate of production, that is, the work force that will be employed and the hours employees will work each week, (2) the allocation of aggregate production facilities among the several products the factory makes, and (3) the scheduling of the sequence in which the individual products will be handled on the production facilities. Let us call these the aggregate production decision, item allocation decision, and scheduling decision, respectively. The three sets of decisions may be made by different roles in the organization; in general, we would expect the aggregate decision to be handled at more central levels than the others. The real world situation will always include complications beyond those we have described, for it will involve decisions with respect to shipments to warehouses, decisions as to which products to hold in warehouse inventories, and many others.

Now we could conceive of an omniscient Planner (the entrepreneur of classical economic theory) who, by solving a set of simultaneous equations, would make each and all of these interrelated decisions. Decision problems of this kind have been widely studied during the past decade by management scientists, with the result that we now know a great deal about the mathematical structures of the problems and the magnitude of the computations that would be required to solve them. We know, in particular, that discovery of the optimal solution of a complete problem of this kind is well beyond the powers of existing or prospective computational equipment.

In actual organizational practice, no one attempts to find an optimal solution for the whole problem. Instead, various particular decisions, or groups of decisions, within the whole complex are made by specialized members or units of the organization. In making these particular decisions, the specialized units do not solve the whole problem, but find a "satisfactory" solution for one or more subproblems, where some of the effects of the solution on other parts of the system are incorporated in the definition of "satisfactory."

For example, standard costs may be set as constraints for a manufacturing executive. If he finds that his operations are not meeting those constraints, he will search for ways of lowering his costs. Longer production runs may occur to him as a means for accomplishing this end. He can achieve longer production runs if the number of style variations in product is reduced, so he proposes product standardization as a solution to his cost problem. Presumably he will not implement the solution until he has tested it against constraints introduced by the sales department—objections that refusal to meet special

requirements of customers will lose sales.

Anyone familiar with organizational life can multiply examples of this sort, where different problems will come to attention in different parts of the organization, or where different solutions will be generated for a problem, depending on where it arises in the organization. The important point to be noted here is that we do not have to postulate conflict in personal goals or motivations in order to explain such conflicts or discrepancies. They could, and would, equally well arise if each of the organizational decision-making roles were being enacted by digital computers, where the usual sorts of personal limits on the acceptance of organizational roles would be entirely absent. The discrepancies arise out of the cognitive inability of the decision makers to deal with the entire problem as a set of simultaneous relations, each to be treated symmetrically with the others.[8]

An aspect of the division of decision-making labor that is common to virtually all organizations is the distinction between the kinds of general, aggregative decisions that are made at high levels of the organization, and the kinds of specific, item-by-item decisions that are made at low levels. We have already alluded to this distinction in the preceding example of a system for controlling inventory and production. When executives at high levels in such a system make decisions about "aggregate inventory," this mode of factoring the decision-making problem already involves radical simplification and approximation. For example, there is no single, well-defined total cost associated with a given total value of aggregate inventories. There will generally be different costs associated with each of the different kinds of items that make up the inventory (for example, different items may have different spoilage rates or obsolescence rates), and different probabilities and costs associated with stock-outs of each kind of item. Thus, a given aggregate inventory will have different costs depending on its composition in terms of individual items.

To design a system for making decisions about the aggregate work force, production rate, and inventories requires an assumption that the aggregate inventory will never depart very far from a typical composition in terms of individual item types. The assumption is likely to be tolerable because subsidiary decisions are continually being made at other points in the organization about the inventories of individual items. These subsidiary decisions prevent the aggregate inventory from becoming severely unbalanced, hence make averages meaningful for the aggregate.

The assumption required for aggregation is not unlike that made by an engineer when he controls the temperature of a tank of water, with a single thermometer as indicator, knowing that sufficient mixing of the liquid in the tank is going on to maintain a stable pattern of temperature relations among its parts. Without such a stable pattern it would be infeasible to control the process by means of a measurement of the average temperature.

If one set of decisions is made, on this approximate basis, about aggregate work force, production rate, and inventories, then these decisions can be used as constraints in making detailed decisions at subsidiary levels about the inventory or production of particular items. If the aggregate decision has been reached to make one million gallons of paint next month, then other decisions can be reached as to how much paint of each kind to make, subject to the constraint that the production quotas for the individual items should, when added together, total one million gallons.[9]

This simple example serves to elucidate how the whole mass of decisions that are continually being made in a complex organization can be viewed as an organized system. They constitute a

system in which (1) particular decision-making processes are aimed at finding courses of action that are feasible or satisfactory in the light of multiple goals and constraints, and (2) decisions reached in any one part of the organization enter as goals or constraints into the decisions being made in other parts of the organization.

There is not guarantee that the decisions reached will be optimal with respect to any over-all organizational goal. The system is a loosely coupled one. Nevertheless, the results of the over-all system can be measured against one or more organizational goals, and changes can be made in the decision-making structure when these results are adjudged unsatisfactory.

Further, if we look at the decision-making structure in an actual organization, we see that it is usually put together in such a way as to insure that the decisions made by specialized units will be made in cognizance of the more general goals. Individual units are linked to the total system by production schedules, systems of rewards and penalties based on cost and profit goals, inventory limits, and so on. The loose coupling among the parts has the positive consequence of permitting specific constraints in great variety to be imposed on subsystems without rendering their decision-making mechanisms inoperative.

THE DECISION-MAKING SYSTEM AND ORGANIZATIONAL BEHAVIOR

In the previous sections great pains were taken to distinguish the goals and constraints (inducements and contributions) that motivate people to accept organizational roles from the goals and constraints that enter into their decision making when they are enacting those organizational roles. On the one hand, the system of personal inducements and contributions imposes constraints that the organization must satisfy if it is to survive. On the other hand, the constraints incorporated in the organizational roles, hence in what I have called here the organizational decision-making system, are the constraints that a course of action must satisfy in order for the organization to adopt it.

There is no necessary *logical* connection between these two sets of constraints. After all, organizations sometimes fail to survive, and their demise can often be attributed to failure to incorporate all the important motivational concerns of participants among the constraints in the organizational decision-making system. For example, a major cause of small business failure is working capital shortage, a result of failure to constrain actions to those that are consistent with creditors' demands for prompt payment. Similarly, new products often fail because incorrect assumptions about the inducements important to consumers are reflected in the constraints that guide product design. (It is widely believed that the troubles of the Chrysler Corporation stemmed from the design premise that car purchasers were primarily interested in buying a good piece of machinery.)

In general, however, there is a strong empirical connection between the two sets of constraints, for the organizations we will usually observe in the real world—those that have succeeded in surviving for some time—will be precisely those which have developed organizational decision-making systems whose constraints guarantee that their actions maintain a favorable balance of inducements to contributions for their participants. The argument, an evolutionary one, is the same one we can apply to biological organisms. There is no logical requirement that the temperatures, oxygen concentrations, and so on, maintained in the tissues of a bird by its physiological processes should lie within the ranges required for its survival. It is simply that we will not often have opportunities for observing birds whose physiological regulators do not

reflect these external constraints. Such birds are soon extinct.[10]

Thus, what the sociologist calls the functional requisites for survival can usually give us good clues for predicting organizational goals; however, if the functional requisites resemble the goals, the similarity is empirical, not definitional. What the goals are must be inferred from observation of the organization's decision-making processes, whether these processes be directed toward survival or suicide.

CONCLUSIONS

We can now summarize our answers to the question that introduced this paper: What is the meaning of the phrase "organizational goal"? First, we discovered that it is doubtful whether decisions are generally directed toward achieving a goal. It is easier, and clearer, to view decisions as being concerned with discovering courses of action that satisfy a whole set of constraints. It is this set, and not any one of its members, that is most accurately viewed as the goal of the action.

If we select any of the constraints for special attention, it is (a) because of its relation to the motivations of the decision maker, or (b) because of its relation to the search process that is generating or designing particular courses of action. Those constraints that motivate the decision maker and those that guide his search for actions are sometimes regarded as more "goal-like" than those that limit the actions he may consider or those that are used to test whether a potential course of action he has designed is satisfactory. Whether we treat all the constraints symmetrically or refer to some asymmetrically as goals is largely a matter of linguistic or analytic convenience.

When we come to organizational decisions, we observe that many, if not most, of the constraints that define a satisfactory course of action are associated with an organizational role and hence only indirectly with the personal motives of the individual who assumes that role. In this situation it is convenient to use the phrase organization goal to refer to constraints, or sets of constraints, imposed by the organizational role, which has only this indirect relation to the motives of the decision makers.

If we examine the constraint set of an organizational decision-making system, we will generally find that it contains constraints that reflect virtually all the inducements and contributions important to various classes of participants. These constraints tend to remove from consideration possible courses of action that are inimical to survival. They do not, of course, by themselves, often fully determine the course of action.

In view of the hierarchical structure that is typical of most formal organizations, it is a reasonable use of language to employ organizational goal to refer particularly to the constraint sets and criteria of search that define roles at the upper levels. Thus it is reasonable to speak of conservation of forest resources as a principal goal of the U.S. Forest Service, or reducing fire losses as a principal goal of a city fire department. For high-level executives in these organizations will seek out and support actions that advance these goals, and subordinate employees will do the same or will at least tailor their choices to constraints established by the higher echelons with this end in view.

Finally, since there are large elements of decentralization in the decision making in any large organization, different constraints may define the decision problems of different positions or specialized units. For example, "profit" may not enter directly into the decision making of most members of a business organization. Again, this does not mean that it is improper or meaningless to regard profit as a principal goal of the business. It simply means that the decision-making mechanism is a loosely coupled system in which the profit constraint is only one among a number of constraints and enters into most subsystems only in indirect ways. It would be both legitimate and realistic to describe most business firms as directed toward profit making—subject to a number of side constraints—operating through a network of decision-making processes that introduces many gross approximations into the search for profitable courses of action. Further, the goal ascription does not imply that any employee is motivated by the firm's profit goal, although some may be.

This view of the nature of organization goals leaves us with a picture of organizational decision making that is not simple. But it provides us with an entirely operational way of showing, by describing the structure of the organizational decision-making mechanism, how and to what extent over-all goals, like "profit" or "conserving forest resources" help to determine the actual courses of action that are chosen.

NOTES

1. The present discussion is generally compatible with, but not identical to, that of my colleagues, R. M. Cyert and J. G. March, who discuss organizational goals in chapter 3 of *A Behavioral Theory of the Firm* (Englewood Cliffs, N.J., 1963). Their analysis is most germane to the paragraphs of this paper that treat of motivation for goals and organizational survival.

2. There are now a substantial number of elementary discussions of linear programming in the management science literature. For a treatment that develops the point of view proposed here, see A. Charnes and W. W. Cooper, *Management Models and Industrial Applications of Linear Programming* (New York, 1961), chapter 1. See also Charnes and Cooper, "Deterministic Equivalents for Optimizing and Satisfying under Chance Constraints," *Operations Research*, 11 (1963), 18-39.

3. See "A Comparison of Organization Theories," in my *Models of Man* (New York, 1957), pp. 170-182.

4. For further discussion of the role of

generators and tests in decision making and problem solving, see A. Newell and H. A. Simon, "The Processes of Creative Thinking," in H. E. Gruber, G. Terrell, and M. Wertheimer, eds., Contemporary Approaches to Creative Thinking (New York, 1962), particularly pp. 77-91.

5. G. P. E. Clarkson, "A Model of Trust Investment Behavior," in Cyert and March, op. cit.

6. For further discussion and references, see J. G. March and H. A. Simon, Organizations (New York, 1958), chapter 4.

7. See "A Formal Theory of Employment Relation," in Models of Man, op. cit.

8. For some empirical evidence, see D.

C. Dearborn and H. A. Simon, "Selective Perception: A Note on the Departmental Identification of Executives," Sociometry, 21 (1958), 140-144.

9. A system of this kind is developed in detail in "Determining Production Quantities under Aggregate Constraints," in C. Holt, F. Modigliani, J. Muth, and H. A. Simon, Planning Production, Inventories, and Work Force (Englewood Cliffs, N.J., 1960).

10. The relation between the functional requisites for survival and the actual constraints of the operating system is a central concept in W. R. Ashby's notion of a multistable system. See his Design for a Brain (2d ed.; New York, 1960).

36. Interpersonal Barriers to Decision Making*

CHRIS ARGYRIS

• The actual behavior of top executives during decision-making meetings often does not jibe with their attitudes and prescriptions about effective executive action.

• The gap that often exists between what executives say and how they behave helps create barriers to openness and trust, to the effective search for alternatives, to innovation, and to flexibility in the organization.

• These barriers are more destructive in important decision-making meetings than in routine meetings, and they upset effective managers more than ineffective ones.

• The barriers cannot be broken down simply by intellectual exercises. Rather, executives need feedback concerning their behavior and opportunities to develop self-awareness in action. To this end, certain kinds of questioning are valuable; playing back and analyzing tape recordings of meetings has proved to be a helpful step; and laboratory education programs are valuable.

These are a few of the major findings of a study of executive decision making

in six representative companies. The findings have vital implications for management groups everywhere; for while some organizations are less subject to the weaknesses described than are others, all groups have them in some degree. In this article I shall discuss the findings in detail and examine the implications for executives up and down the line. (For information on the company sample and research methods used in the study, see the opposite page.)

WORDS VS. ACTIONS

According to top management, the effectiveness of decision-making activities depends on the degree of innovation, risk taking, flexibility, and trust in the executive system. (Risk taking is defined here as any act where the executive risks his self-esteem. This could be a moment, for example, when he goes

NATURE OF THE STUDY

❧ The six companies studied include: (1) an electronics firm with 40,000 employees, (2) a manufacturer and marketer of a new innovative product with 4,000 employees, (3) a large research and development company with 3,000 employees, (4) a small research and development organization with 150 employees, (5) a consulting-research firm with 400 employees, and (6) a producer of heavy equipment with 4,000 employees.

❧ The main focus of the investigation reported here was on the behavior of 165 top executives in these companies. The executives were board members, executive committee members, upper-level managers, and (in a few cases) middle-level managers.

❧ Approximately 265 decision-making meetings were studied and nearly 10,000 units of behavior analyzed. The topics of the meetings ranged widely, covering investment decisions, new products, manufacturing problems, marketing strategies, new pricing policies, administrative changes, and personnel issues. An observer took notes during all but 10 of the meetings; for research purposes, these 10 were analyzed "blind" from tapes (i.e., without ever meeting the executives). All other meetings were taped also, but analyzed at a later time.

❧ The major device for analyzing the tapes was a new system of categories for scoring decision-making meetings.* Briefly, the executives' behavior was scored according to how often they —

> . . . owned up to and accepted responsibility for their ideas or feelings;
>
> . . . opened up to receive others' ideas or feelings;
>
> . . . experimented and took risks with ideas or feelings;
>
> . . . helped others to own up, be open, and take risks;
>
> . . . did not own up; were not open; did not take risks; and did not help others in any of these activities.

❧ A second scoring system was developed to produce a quantitative index of the *norms* of the executive culture. There were both positive and negative norms. The positive norms were:

1. *Individuality*, especially rewarding behavior that focused on and valued the uniqueness of each individual's ideas and feelings.

2. *Concern* for others' ideas and feelings.

3. *Trust* in others' ideas and feelings.

The negative norms were:

1. *Conformity* to others' ideas and feelings.

2. *Antagonism* toward these ideas and feelings.

3. *Mistrust* of these ideas and feelings.

❧ In addition to our observations of the men at work, at least one semistructured interview was conducted with each executive. All of these interviews were likewise taped, and the typewritten protocols served as the basis for further analysis.

* For a detailed discussion of the system of categories and other aspects of methodology, see my book, *Organization and Innovation* (Homewood, Illinois, Richard D. Irwin, Inc., 1965).

against the group view; when he tells someone, especially the person with the highest power, something negative about his impact on the organization; or when he seeks to put millions of dollars in a new investment.)

Nearly 95 percent of the executives in our study emphasize that an organization is only as good as its top people. They constantly repeat the importance of their responsibility to help themselves and others to develop their abilities. Almost as often they report that the qualities just mentioned—motivation, risk taking, and so on—are key characteristics of any successful executive system. "People problems" head the list as the most difficult, perplexing, and crucial.

In short, the executives vote overwhelmingly for executive systems where the contributions of each executive can be maximized and where innovation, risk taking, flexibility, and trust reign supreme. Nevertheless, the *behavior* of these same executives tends to create decision-making processes that are *not*

very effective. Their behavior can be fitted into two basic patterns:

Pattern A—thoughtful, rational, and mildly competitive. This is the behavior most frequently observed during the decision-making meetings. Executives following this pattern own up to their ideas in a style that emphasizes a serious concern for ideas. As they constantly battle for scarce resources and "sell" their views, their openness to others' ideas is relatively high, not because of a sincere interest in learning about the point of view of others, but so they can engage in a form of "one-upmanship"—that is, gain information about the others' points of view in order to politely discredit them.

Pattern B—competitive first, thoughtful and rational second. In this pattern, conformity to ideas replaces concern for ideas as the strongest norm. Also, antagonism to ideas is higher—in many cases higher than openness to ideas. The relatively high antagonism scores usually indicate, in addition to high competitiveness, a high degree of conflict and pent-up feelings.

Exhibit I summarizes data for four illustrative groups of managers—two

EXHIBIT I. MANAGEMENT GROUPS WITH PATTERN A AND PATTERN B CHARACTERISTICS

	PATTERN A				PATTERN B			
TOTAL NUMBER OF UNITS ANALYZED*	GROUP 1 198		GROUP 2 143		GROUP 3 201		GROUP 4 131	
UNITS CHARACTERIZED BY:	NUMBER	PERCENT	NUMBER	PERCENT	NUMBER	PERCENT	NUMBER	PERCENT
OWNING UP TO OWN IDEAS	146	74	105	74	156	78	102	78
CONCERN FOR OTHERS' IDEAS	122	62	89	62	52	26	56	43
CONFORMITY TO OTHERS' IDEAS	54	27	38	26	87	43	62	47
OPENNESS TO OTHERS' IDEAS	46	23	34	24	31	15	25	19
INDIVIDUALITY	4	2	12	8	30	15	8	6
ANTAGONISM TO OTHERS' IDEAS	18	9	4	3	32	16	5	4
UNWILLINGNESS TO HELP OTHERS OWN UP TO THEIR IDEAS	5	2	3	2	14	7	4	3

* A unit is an instance of a manager speaking on a topic. If during the course of speaking he changes to a new topic, another unit is created.

groups with Pattern A characteristics and two with Pattern B characteristics.

PRACTICAL CONSEQUENCES

In both patterns executives are rarely observed:

- taking risks or experimenting with new ideas or feelings;
- helping others to own up, be open, and take risks;
- using a style of behavior that supports the norm of individuality and trust as well as mistrust;
- expressing feelings, positive or negative.

These results should not be interpreted as implying that the executives do not have feelings. We know from the interviews that many of the executives have strong feelings indeed. However, the overwhelming majority (84 percent) feel that it is a sign of immaturity to express feelings openly *during decision-making meetings.* Nor should the results be interpreted to mean that the executives do not enjoy risk taking. The data permit us to conclude only that few risk-taking actions were *observed* during the meetings. (Also, we have to keep in mind that the executives were always observed in groups; it may be that their behavior in groups varies significantly from their behavior as individuals.)

Before I attempt to give my views about the reasons for the discrepancy between executives' words and actions, I should like to point out that these results are not unique to business organizations. I have obtained similar behavior patterns from leaders in education, research, the ministry, trade unions, and government. Indeed, one of the fascinating questions for me is why so many different people in so many different kinds of organizations tend to manifest similar problems.

WHY THE DISCREPANCY?

The more I observe such problems in different organizations possessing different technologies and varying greatly in size, the more I become impressed with the importance of the role played by the values or assumptions top people hold on the nature of effective human relationships and the best ways to run an organization.

BASIC VALUES

In the studies so far I have isolated three basic values that seem to be very important:

1. *The significant human relationships are the ones which have to do with achieving the organization's objective.* My studies of over 265 different types and sizes of meetings indicate that executives almost always tend to focus their behavior on "getting the job done." In literally thousands of units of behavior, almost none are observed where the men spend some time in analyzing and maintaining their group's effectiveness. This is true even though in many meetings the group's effectiveness "bogged down" and the objectives were not being reached because of interpersonal factors. When the executives are interviewed and asked why they did not spend some time in examining the group operations or processes, they reply that they were there to get a job done. They add: "If the group isn't effective, it is up to the leader to get it back on the track by directing it."

2. *Cognitive rationality is to be emphasized; feelings and emotions are to be played down.* This value influences executives to see cognitive, intellectual discussions as "relevant," "good," "work," and so on. Emotional and interpersonal discussions tend to be viewed as "irrelevant," "immature," "not work," and so on.

As a result, when emotions and interpersonal variables become blocks to group effectiveness, all the executives report feeling that they should *not* deal with them. For example, in the event of an emotional disagreement, they would tell the members to "get back to facts" or "keep personalities out of this."

3. *Human relationships are most effectively influenced through unilateral direction, coercion, and control, as well as by rewards and penalties that sanction all three values.* This third value of direction and control is implicit in the chain of command and also in the elaborate mana-

gerial controls that have been developed within organizations.

INFLUENCE ON OPERATIONS

The impact of these values can be considerable. For example, to the extent that individuals dedicate themselves to the value of intellectual rationality and "getting the job done," they will tend to be aware of and emphasize the intellectual aspects of issues in an organization and (consciously or unconsciously) to suppress the interpersonal and emotional aspects, especially those which do not seem relevant to achieving the task.

As the interpersonal and emotional aspects of behavior become suppressed, organizational norms that coerce individuals to hide their feelings or to disguise them and bring them up as technical, intellectual problems will tend to arise.

Under these conditions the individual may tend to find it very difficult to develop competence in dealing with feelings and interpersonal relationships. Also, in a world where the expression of feelings is not valued, individuals may build personal and organizational defenses to help them suppress their own feelings or inhibit others in such expression. Or they may refuse to consider ideas which, if explored, could expose suppressed feelings.

Such a defensive reaction in an organization could eventually inhibit creativity and innovation during decision making. The participants might learn to limit themselves to those ideas and values that were not threatening. They might also decrease their openness to new ideas and values. And as the degree of openness decreased, the capacity to experiment would also decrease, and fear of taking risks would increase. This would reduce the *probability* of experimentation, thus decreasing openness to new ideas still further and constricting risk taking even more than formerly. We would thereby have a closed circuit which could become an impor-

tant cause of loss of vitality in an organization.

SOME CONSEQUENCES

Aside from the impact of values on vitality, what are some other consequences of the executive behavior patterns earlier described on top management decision making and on the effective functioning of the organization? For the sake of brevity, I shall include only examples of those consequences that were found to exist in one form or another in all organizations studied.

RESTRICTED COMMITMENT

One of the most frequent findings is that in major decisions that are introduced by the president, there tends to be less than open discussion of the issues, and the commitment of the officers tends to be less than complete (although they may assure the president to the contrary). For instance, consider what happened in one organization where a major administrative decision made during the period of the research was the establishment of several top management committees to explore basic long-range problems:

As is customary with major decisions, the president discussed it in advance at a meeting of the executive committee. He began the meeting by circulating, as a basis for discussion, a draft of the announcement of the committees. Most of the members' discussion was concerned with raising questions about the wording of the proposal:

- "Is the word *action* too strong?"
- "I recommend that we change 'steps can be taken' to "recommendations can be made.'"
- "We'd better change the word 'lead' to 'maintain.'"

As the discussion seemed to come to an end, one executive said he was worried that the announcement of the committees might be interpreted by the people below as an implication "that the executive committee believes the organization is in trouble. Let's get the idea in that all is well."

There was spontaneous agreement by all executives: "Hear, hear!"

A brief silence was broken by another executive who apparently was not satisfied with the concept of the committees. He raised a series of questions. The manner in which it was done was interesting. As he raised each issue, he kept assuring the president and the group that he was not against the concept. He just wanted to be certain that the executive committee was clear on what it was doing. For example, he assured them:

- "I'm not clear. Just asking."
- "I'm trying to get a better picture."
- "I'm just trying to get clarification."
- "Just so that we understand what the words mean."

The president nodded in agreement, but he seemed to become slightly impatient. He remarked that many of these problems would not arise if the members of these new committees took an overall company point of view. An executive commented (laughingly), "Oh, I'm for motherhood too!"

The proposal was tabled in order for the written statement to be revised and discussed further during the next meeting. It appeared that the proposal was the president's personal "baby," and the executive committee members would naturally go along with it. The most responsibility some felt was that they should raise questions so the president would be clear about *his* (not *their*) decision.

At the next meeting the decision-making process was the same as at the first. The president circulated copies of the revised proposal. During this session a smaller number of executives asked questions. Two pushed (with appropriate care) the notion that the duties of one of the committees were defined too broadly.

The president began to defend his proposal by citing an extremely long list of examples, indicating that in his mind "reasonable" people should find the duties clear. This comment and the long list of examples may have communicated to others a feeling that the president was becoming impatient. When he finished, there was a lengthy silence. The president then turned to one of the executives and asked directly, "Why are you worried about this?" The executive explained, then quickly added that as far as he could see

the differences were not major ones and his point of view could be integrated with the president's by "changing some words."

The president agreed to the changes, looked up, and asked, "I take it now there is common agreement?" All executives replied "yes" or nodded their heads affirmatively.

As I listened, I had begun to wonder about the commitment of the executive committee members to the idea. In subsequent interviews I asked each about his view of the proposal. Half felt that it was a good proposal. The other half had reservations ranging from moderate to serious. However, being loyal members, they would certainly do their best to make it work, they said.

SUBORDINATE GAMESMANSHIP

I can best illustrate the second consequence by citing from a study of the effectiveness of product planning and program review activities in another of the organizations studied:

It was company policy that peers at any given level should make the decisions. Whenever they could not agree or whenever a decision went beyond their authority, the problem was supposed to be sent to the next higher level. The buck passing stopped at the highest level. A meeting with the president became a great event. Beforehand a group would "dry run" its presentation until all were satisfied that they could present their view effectively.

Few difficulties were observed when the meeting was held to present a recommendation agreed to by all at the lower levels. The difficulties arose when "negative" information had to be fed upward. For example, a major error in the program, a major delay, or a major disagreement among the members was likely to cause such trouble.

The dynamics of these meetings was very interesting. In one case the problem to present was a major delay in a development project. In the dry run the subordinates planned to begin the session with information that "updated" the president. The information was usually presented in such a way that slowly and carefully the president was alerted to the fact that a major problem was about to be announced. One could hear such key phrases as:

- "We are a bit later than expected."
- "We're not on plan."
- "We have had greater difficulties than expected."
- "It is now clear that no one should have promised what we did."

These phrases were usually followed by some reassuring statement such as:

- "However, we're on top of this."
- "Things are really looking better now."
- "Although we are late, we have advanced the state of the art."
- "If you give us another three months, we are certain that we can solve this problem."

To the observer's eyes, it is difficult to see how the president could deny the request. Apparently he felt the same way because he granted it. However, he took nearly 20 minutes to say that this shocked him; he was wondering if everyone was *really* doing everything they could; this was a serious program; this was not the way he wanted to see things run; he was sure they would agree with him; and he wanted their assurances that this would be the final delay.

A careful listening to the tape after the meeting brought out the fact that no subordinate gave such assurances. They simply kept saying that they were doing their best; they had poured a lot into this; or they had the best technical know-how working on it.

Another interesting observation is that most subordinates in this company, especially in presentations to the president, tended to go along with certain unwritten rules:

1. Before you give any bad news, give good news. Especially emphasize the capacity of the department to work hard and to rebound from a failure.

2. Play down the impact of a failure by emphasizing how close you came to achieving the target or how soon the target can be reached. If neither seems reasonable, emphasize how difficult it is to define such targets, and point out that because

the state of the art is so primitive, the original commitment was not a wise one.

3. In a meeting with the president it is unfair to take advantage of another department that is in trouble, even if it is a "natural enemy." The sporting thing to do is say something nice about the other department and offer to help it in any way possible. (The offer is usually not made in concrete form, nor does the department in difficulty respond with the famous phrase, "What do you have in mind?")

The subordinates also were in agreement that too much time was spent in long presentations in order to make the president happy. The president, however, confided to the researcher that he did not enjoy listening to long and, at times, dry presentations (especially when he had seen most of the key data anyway). However, he felt that it was important to go through this because it might give the subordinates a greater sense of commitment to the problem!

LACK OF AWARENESS

One of our most common observations in company studies is that executives lack awareness of their own behavioral patterns as well as of the negative impact of their behavior on others. This is not to imply that they are completely unaware; each individual usually senses some aspects of a problem. However, we rarely find an individual or group of individuals who is aware of enough of the scope and depth of a problem so that the need for effective action can be fully understood.

For example, during the study of the decision-making processes of the president and the 9 vice presidents of a firm with nearly 3,000 employees, I concluded that the members unknowingly behaved in such a way as *not* to encourage risk taking, openness, expression of feelings, and cohesive, trusting relationships. But subsequent interviews with the 10 top executives showed that they held a completely different point of view from mine. They admitted that negative feelings were not expressed, but said the reason was that "we trust each other and respect each other." According to 6 of the men, individuality was high and conformity low; where conformity was agreed to be high, the reason given was the necessity of agreeing with the man who is boss. According to 8 of the men, "We help each other all the time." Issues loaded with conflict were not handled during meetings, it was reported, for these reasons:

- "We should not discuss emotional disagreements before the executive committee because when people are emotional, they are not rational."
- "We should not air our dirty linen in front of the people who may come in to make a presentation."
- "Why take up people's time with subjective debates?"
- "Most members are not acquainted with all the details. Under our system the person who presents the issues has really thought them through."
- "Pre-discussion of issues helps to prevent anyone from sandbagging the executive committee."
- "Rarely emotional; when it does happen, you can pardon it."

The executive committee climate or emotional tone was characterized by such words as:

- "Friendly."
- "Not critical of each other."
- "Not tense."
- "Frank and no tensions because we've known each other for years."

How was I to fit the executives' views with mine? I went back and listened to all the interviews again. As I analyzed the tapes, I began to realize that an interesting set of contradictions arose during many of the interviews. In the early stages of the interviews the executives tended to say things that they contradicted later; Exhibit II contains examples of contradictions repeated by 6 or more of the 10 top executives.

What accounts for these contradictions? My explanation is that over time the executives had come to mirror, in their behavior, the values of their culture (e.g., be rational, nonemotional, diplomatically open, and so on). They

had created a culture that reinforced their own leadership styles. If an executive wanted to behave differently, he probably ran the risk of being considered a deviant. In most of the cases the executives decided to forego this risk, and they behaved like the majority. These men, in order to live with themselves, probably had to develop various defenses and blinders about their acquiescence to an executive culture that may not have been the one they personally preferred and valued.

Incidentally, in this group there were two men who had decided to take the other route. Both men were viewed by the others as "a bit rough at the edges" or "a little too aggressive."

To check the validity of some of the findings reported, we interviewed the top 25 executives below the executive committee. If our analysis was correct, we knew, then they should tend to report that the members of the executive committee were low in openness to uncomfortable information, risk taking, trust, and capacity to deal with conflicts openly, and high in conformity. The results were as predicted (see Exhibit III).

BLIND SPOTS

Another result found in all organizations studied is the tendency for executives to be unaware of the negative feelings that their subordinates have about them. This finding is not startling in view of the fact that the executive problem-solving processes do not tend to reward the upward communication of information about interpersonal issues that is emotionally laden and risky to communicate. To illustrate:

In one organization, all but one of the top executive committee members reported that their relationships with their subordinates were "relatively good to excellent." When asked how they judged their relationships, most of the executives responded with such statements as: "They do everything that I ask for willingly," and "We talk together frequently and openly."

The picture from the middle management men who were the immediate subor-

EXHIBIT II. CONTRADICTORY STATEMENTS

DURING ONE PART OF THE INTERVIEW AN EXECUTIVE SAID:	YET LATER IN THE SAME INTERVIEW HE SAID:
The relationship among the executive committee members is "close," "friendly," and based on years of working together.	I do not know how [my peers] feel about me. That's a tough question to answer.
The strength of this company lies in its top people. They are a dedicated, friendly group. We never have the kinds of disagreements and fights that I hear others do.	Yes, the more I think of it, the more I feel this is a major weakness of the company. Management is afraid to hold someone accountable, to say, "You said you would do it. What happened?"
I have an open relationship with my superior.	I have no direct idea how my superior evaluates my work and feels about me.
The group discussions are warm, friendly, not critical.	We trust each other not to upset one another.
We say pretty much what we think.	We are careful not to say anything that will antagonize anyone.
We respect and have faith in each other.	People do not knowingly upset each other, so they are careful in what they say.
The executive committee tackles all issues.	The executive committee tends to spend too much time talking about relatively unimportant issues.
The executive committee makes decisions quickly and effectively.	A big problem of the executive committee is that it takes forever and a day to make important decisions.
The members trust each other.	The members are careful not to say something that may make another member look bad. It may be misinterpreted.
The executive committee makes the major policy decisions.	On many major issues, decisions are really made outside the executive committee meetings. The executive committee convenes to approve a decision and have "holy water" placed on it.

EXHIBIT III. HOW THE EXECUTIVE COMMITTEE WAS RATED BY 25 EXECUTIVES BELOW IT

CHARACTERISTIC RATED	NUMBER OF MANAGERS RATING THE COMMITTEE AS:		
	LOW	MODERATE	HIGH
OPENNESS TO UNCOMFORTABLE INFORMATION*	12	6	4
RISK TAKING	20	4	1
TRUST	14	9	2
CONFORMITY	0	2	23
ABILITY TO DEAL WITH CONFLICTS	19	6	0

* Three executives gave a "don't know" response.

dinates was different. Apparently, top management was unaware that:

- 71 percent of the middle managers did not know where they stood with their superiors; they considered their relationships as ambiguous, and they were not aware of such important facts as how they were being evaluated.
- 65 percent of the middle managers did not know what qualities led to success in their organizations.
- 87 percent felt that conflicts were very seldom coped with; and that when they were, the attempts tended to be inadequate.
- 65 percent thought that the most important unsolved problem of the organization was that the top management was unable to help them overcome the intergroup rivalries, lack of cooperation, and poor communications; 53 percent said that if they could alter one aspect of their superior's behavior, it would be to help him see the "dog eat dog" communication problems that existed in middle management.
- 59 percent evaluated top management effectiveness as not too good or about average; and 62 percent reported that the development of a cohesive management team was the second most important unsolved problem.
- 82 percent of the middle managers wished that the status of their function and job could be increased but doubted if they could communicate this openly to the top management.

Interestingly, in all the cases that I have observed where the president asked for a discussion of any problems that the top and middle management men present thought important, the problems mentioned above were never raised.

Rather, the most frequently mentioned problem (74 percent of the cases) was the overload problem. The executives and managers reported that they were overloaded and that the situation was getting worse. The president's usual reply was that he appreciated their predicament, but "that is life." The few times he asked if the men had any suggestions, he recieved such replies as "more help," "fewer meetings," "fewer reports," "delay of schedules," and so on. As we will see, few of these suggestions made sense, since the men were asking either for increases in

costs or for a decrease in the very controls that the top management used to administer the organization.

DISTRUST & ANTAGONISM

Another result of the behavior patterns earlier described is that management tends to keep promotions semisecret and most of the actual reasons for executive changes completely secret. Here is an example from an organization whose board we studied in some detail over a period of two years:

The executives complained of three practices of the board about which the board members were apparently unaware: (1) the constant alteration of organizational positions and charts, and keeping the most up-to-date versions semiconfidential; (2) shifting top executives without adequate discussion with all executives involved and without clearly communicating the real reasons for the move; and (3) developing new departments with product goals that overlapped and competed with the goals of already existing departments.

The board members admitted these practices but tended not to see them as being incompatible with the interests of the organization. For example, to take the first complaint, they defended their practice with such statements as: "If you tell them everything, all they do is worry, and we get a flood of rumors"; "The changes do not *really* affect them"; and, "It will only cut in on their busy schedule and interrupt their productivity."

The void of clear-cut information from the board was, however, filled in by the executives. Their explanations ranged from such statements as "They must be changing things because they are not happy with the way things are going" to "The unhappiness is so strong they do not tell us." Even the executives who profited from some of these moves reported some concern and bewilderment. For example, three reported instances where they had been promoted over some "old-timers." In all cases they were told to "soft-pedal the promotion aspect" until the old-timers were diplomatically informed. Unfortunately, it took months to inform the latter men, and in some cases it was never done.

There was another practice of the

board that produced difficulties in the organization:

Department heads cited the board's increasing intervention into the detailed administration of a department when its profit picture looked shaky. This practice was, from these subordinates' view, in violation of the stated philosophy of decentralization.

When asked, board members tended to explain this practice by saying that it was done only when they had doubts about the department head's competence, and then it was always in the interests of efficiency. When they were alerted about a department that was not doing well, they believed that the best reaction was to tighten controls, "take a closer and more frequent look," and "make sure the department head is on top of things." They quickly added that they did not tell the man in question they were beginning to doubt his competence for fear of upsetting him. Thus, again we see how the values of de-emphasizing the expression of negative feelings and the emphasizing of controls influenced the board's behavior.

The department heads, on the other hand, reported different reactions. "Why are they bothered with details? Don't they trust me? If not, why don't they say so?" Such reactions tended to produce more conformity, antagonism, mistrust, and fear of experimenting.

Still another board practice was the "diplomatic" rejection of an executive's idea that was, in the eyes of the board, offbeat, a bit too wild, or not in keeping with the corporate mission. The reasons given by the board for not being open about the evaluation again reflected adherence to the pyramidal values. For example, a board member would say, "We do not want to embarrass them," or "If you really tell them, you might restrict creativity."

This practice tended to have precisely the impact that the superiors wished to avoid. The subordinates reacted by asking, "Why don't they give me an opportunity to really explain it?" or "What do they mean when they suggest that the 'timing is not right' or 'funds are not currently available'?"

PROCESSES DAMAGED

It is significant that defensive activities like those described are rarely observed during group meetings dealing with minor or relatively routine decisions. These activities become most noticeable when the decision is an important one in terms of dollars or in terms of the impact on the various departments in the organization. *The forces toward ineffectiveness operate most strongly during the important decision-making meetings.* The group and organizational defenses operate most frequently when they can do the most harm to decision-making effectiveness.

Another interesting finding is that the more effective and more committed executives tend to be upset about these facts, whereas the less effective, less committed people tend simply to lament them. They also tend to take on an "I told them so" attitude—one of resignation and noninvolvement in correcting the situation. In short, it is the better executives who are negatively affected.

WHAT CAN BE DONE?

What can the executive do to change this situation?

I wish that I could answer this question as fully as I should like to. Unfortunately, I cannot. Nevertheless, there are some suggestions I can make.

BLIND ALLEYS

First, let me state what I believe will *not* work.

Learning about these problems by listening to lectures, reading about them, or exploring them through cases is not adequate; an article or book can pose some issues and get thinking started, but—in this area, at least—it cannot change behavior. Thus, in one study with 60 top executives:

Lectures were given and cases discussed on this subject for nearly a week. A test at the end of the week showed that the executives rated the lecturers very high, liked the cases, and accepted the diagnoses. Yet when they attempted to apply their new-found knowledge outside the learning situation, most were unable to do so. The major problem was that they had not learned how to make these new ideas come to life in their behavior.

As one executive stated, pointing to his head: "I know up here what I should do, but when it comes to a real meeting, I behave in the same old way. It sure is frustrating."[1]

Learning about these problems through a detailed diagnosis of executives' behavior is also not enough. For example:

I studied a top management group for nearly four months through interviews and tape recordings of their decision-making meetings. Eventually, I fed back the analysis. The executives agreed with the diagnosis as well as with the statement by one executive that he found it depressing. Another executive, however, said he now felt that he had a clearer and more coherent picture of some of the causes of their problems, and he was going to change his behavior. I predicted that he would probably find that he would be unable to change his behavior—and even if he did change, his subordinates, peers, and superiors might resist dealing with him in the new way.

The executive asked, "How can you be so sure that we can't change?" I responded that I knew of no case where managers were able to alter successfully their behavior, their group dynamics, and so forth by simply realizing intellectually that such a change was necessary. The key to success was for them to be able to show these new strategies in their behavior. To my knowledge, behavior of this type, groups with these dynamics, and organizational cultures endowed with these characteristics were very difficult to change. What kind of thin-skinned individuals would they be, how brittle would their groups and their organizations be if they could be altered that easily?

Three of the executives decided that they were going to prove the prediction to be incorrect. They took my report and studied it carefully. In one case the executive asked his subordinates to do the same. Then they tried to alter their behavior. According to their own accounts, they were unable to do so. The only changes they reported were (1) a softening of the selling activities, (2) a reduction of their aggres-

sive persuasion, and (3) a genuine increase in their asking for the subordinates' views.

My subsequent observations and interviews uncovered the fact that the first two changes were mistrusted by the subordinates, who had by now adapted to the old behavior of their superiors. They tended to play it carefully and to be guarded. This hesitation aggravated the executives, who felt that their subordinates were not responding to their new behavior with the enthusiasm that they (the superiors) had expected.

However, the executives did not deal with this issue openly. They kept working at trying to be rational, patient, and rewarding. The more irritated they became and the more they showed this irritation in their behavior, the more the subordinates felt that the superiors' "new" behavior was a gimmick.

Eventually, the process of influencing subordinates slowed down so much that the senior men returned to their more controlling styles. The irony was that in most cases the top executives interpreted the subordinates' behavior as proof that they needed to be needled and pushed, while the subordinates interpreted the top managers' behavior as proof that they did not trust their assistants and would never change.

The reason I doubt that these approaches will provide anything but temporary cures is that they do not go far enough. If changes are going to be made in the behavior of an executive, if trust is to be developed, if risk taking is to flourish, he must be placed in a different situation. He should be helped to (a) expose his leadership style so that he and others can take a look at its true impact; (b) deepen his awareness of himself and the dynamics of effective leadership; and (c) strive for these goals under conditions where he is in control of the amount, pace, and depth of learning.

These conditions for learning are difficult to achieve. Ideally, they require the help of a professional consultant. Also, it would be important to get away from the organization—its interruptions, pressures, and daily administrative tensions.

CHRIS ARGYRIS

VALUE OF QUESTIONS

The executive can strive to be aware that he is probably programmed with a set of values which cause him to behave in ways that are not always helpful to others and which his subordinates will not discuss frankly even when they believe he is not being helpful. He can also strive to find time to uncover, through careful questioning, his impact on others. Once in a while a session that is focused on the "How am I doing?" question can enlighten the executive and make his colleagues more flexible in dealing with him.

One simple question I have heard several presidents ask their vice presidents with success is: "Tell me what, if anything, I do that tends to prevent (or help) your being the kind of vice president you wish to be?" These presidents are careful to ask these questions during a time when they seem natural (e.g., performance review sessions), or they work hard ahead of time to create a climate so that such a discussion will not take the subordinate by surprise.

Some presidents feel uncomfortable in raising these questions, and others point out that the vice presidents are also uncomfortable. I can see how both would have such feelings. A chief executive officer may feel that he is showing weakness by asking his subordinates about his impact. The subordinate may or may not feel this way, but he may sense that his chief does, and that is enough to make him uncomfortable.

Yet in two companies I have studied where such questions were asked, superiors and subordinates soon learned that authority which gained strength by a lack of openness was weak and brittle, whereas authority resting on open feedback from below was truly strong and viable.

WORKING WITH THE GROUP

Another step that an executive can take is to vow not to accept group ineffectiveness as part of life. Often I have heard people say, "Groups are no damned good; strong leadership is what is necessary." I agree that many groups are ineffective. I doubt, however, if either of the two leadership patterns described earlier will help the situation. As we have seen, both patterns tend to make the executive group increasingly less effective.

If my data are valid, the search process in executive decision making has become so complicated that group participation is essential. No one man seems to be able to have all the knowledge necessary to make an effective decision. If individual contributions are necessary in group meetings, it is important that a climate be created that does not discourage innovation, risk taking, and honest leveling between managers in their conversations with one another. The value of a group is to maximize individual contributions.

Interestingly, the chief executive officers in these studies are rarely observed making policy decisions in the classic sense, viz., critical selections from several alternatives and determination of future directions to be taken. This does not mean that they shy away from taking responsibility. Quite the contrary. Many report that they enjoy making decisions by themselves. Their big frustration comes from realizing that most of the major decisions they face are extremely complex and require the coordinated, honest inputs of many different executives. They are impatient at the slowness of meetings, the increasingly quantitative nature of the inputs, and, in many cases, their ignorance of what the staff groups did to the decision inputs long before they received them.

The more management deals with complexity by the use of computers and quantitative approaches, the more it will be forced to work with inputs of many different people, and the more important will be the group dynamics of decision-making meetings. If anyone doubts this, let him observe the dry runs subordinates go through to get a presentation ready for the top. He will observe, I believe, that much data are included and excluded by subordinates on the basis of what they believe those at the top can hear.

In short, *one of the main tasks of the chief executive is to build and maintain an effective decision-making network.* I doubt that he has much choice *except* to spend time in exploring how well his group functions.

Such explorations could occur during the regular workday. For example:

> In one organization the president began by periodically asking members of his top group, immediately after a decision was made, to think back during the meeting and describe when they felt that the group was not being as effective as they wished. How could these conditions be altered?
>
> As trust and openness increased, the members began to level with each other as to when they were inhibited, irritated, suppressed, confused, and withholding information. The president tried to be as encouraging as he could, and he especially rewarded people who truly leveled. Soon the executives began to think of mechanisms they could build into their group functioning so they would be alerted to these group problems and correct them early. As one man said, "We have not eliminated all our problems, but we are building a competence in our group to deal with them effectively if and when they arise."

UTILIZING FEEDBACK

Another useful exercise is for the superior and his group members to tape-record a decision-making meeting, especially one which is expected to be difficult. At a later date, the group members can gather and listen to the tape. I believe it is safe to say that simply listening to the tape is an education in itself. If one can draw from skilled company or outside help, then useful analyses can be made of group or individual behavior.

Recently, I experimented with this procedure with an "inside" board of directors of a company. The directors met once a month and listened to tape recordings of their monthly board meetings. With my help they analyzed their behavior, trying to find how they could improve their individual and group effectiveness. Listening to tapes became a very involving experience for them. They spent nearly four hours in the first meeting discussing less than ten minutes of the tape.

● *'Binds' created.* One of the major gains of these sessions was that the board members became aware of the "binds" they were creating for each other and of the impact they each had on the group's functioning. Thus:

> Executive A was frequently heard antagonizing Executive B by saying something that B perceived as "needling." For example, A might seem to be questioning B's competence. "Look here," he would say, "anyone who can do simple arithmetic should realize that. . . ."
>
> Executive B responded by fighting. B's way of fighting back was to utilize his extremely high capacity to verbalize and intellectualize. B's favorite tactic was to show A where he missed five important points and where his logic was faulty.
>
> Executive A became increasingly upset as the "barrage of logic" found its mark. He tended to counteract by (a) remaining silent but manifesting a sense of being flustered and becoming redfaced; and/or (b) insisting that his logic *was* sound even though he did not express it in "highfalutin language" as did B.
>
> Executive B pushed harder (presumably to make A admit he was wrong) by continuing his "barrage of logic" or implying that A could not see his errors because he was upset.
>
> Executive A would respond to this by insisting that he was not upset. "The point you are making is so simple, why, anyone can see it. Why should I be upset?"
>
> Executive B responded by pushing harder and doing more intellectualizing. When Executive A eventually reached his breaking point, he too began to shout and fight.
>
> At this point, Executives C, D, and E could be observed withdrawing until A and B wore each other out.

● *Progress achieved.* As a result of the meetings, the executives reported in interviews, board members experienced fewer binds, less hostility, less frustration, and more constructive work. One member wondered if the group had lost some of its "zip," but the others disagreed. Here is an excerpt from the transcript of one discussion on this point:

Executive A: My feeling is, as I have said, that we have just opened this thing up, and I for one feel that we have benefited a great deal from it. I think I have improved; maybe I am merely reflecting the fact that you [Executive B] have improved. But at least I think there has been improvement in our relationship. I also see signs of not as good a relationship in other places as there might be.

I think on the whole we are much better off today than we were a year ago. I think there is a whole lot less friction today than there was a year ago, but there's still enough of it.

Now we have a much clearer organization setup; if we were to sit down here and name the people, we would probably all name exactly the same people. I don't think there is much question about who should be included and who should not be included; we've got a pretty clean organization.

Executive B: You're talking now about asking the consultant about going on with this week's session?

Executive A: It would be very nice to have the consultant if he can do it; then we should see how we can do it without him, but it'd be better with him.

Executive B: But that's the step, as I understand it, that should be taken at this stage. Is that right?

Executive A: Well, I would certainly favor doing something; I don't know what. I'm not making a specific recommendation; I just don't like to let go of it.

Executive C: What do you think?

Executive D: I'm not as optimistic as A. I wonder if anybody here agrees with me that maybe we haven't made as much progress as we think. I've personally enjoyed these experiences, and I'd like to see them continued.

Executive A: Would you like to venture to say why I think we have made progress and why I might be fooled?

Executive D: Well, I think maybe you are in the worst position to evaluate prog-

ress because if the worst possible thing that can happen is for people to no longer fight and struggle, but to say, "yes, sir," you might call that progress. That might be the worst thing that could happen, and I sort of sense some degree of resignation—I don't think it's progress. I don't know. I might be all alone in this. What do you think?

Executive C: On one level it is progress. Whether it is institutional progress and whether it produces commensurate institutional benefits is a debatable question. It may in fact do so. I think it's very clear that there is in our meetings and in individual contact less heat, less overt friction, petulance, tension, than certainly was consistently the case. Do you agree?

Executive D: Yes, I think so.

Executive C: It has made us a great deal more aware of the extent and nature of the friction and clearly has made all of us intent on fighting less. There's some benefit to it; but there are some drawbacks.

Executive A: Well, if you and D are right, I would say for that reason we need more of the program.

LABORATORY TRAINING

Another possibility is for the executive to attend a program designed to help increase competence in this area, such as laboratory education and its various offshoots ("T-groups," the "managerial grid," "conflict management labs," and so on[2]). These learning experiences are available at various university and National Training Laboratory executive programs. They can also be tailor-made for the individual organization.

I believe outside programs offer the better way of becoming acquainted with this type of learning. Bear in mind, though, that since typically only one or two executives attend from the same organization, the biggest payoff is for the individual. The inside program provides greater possibilities for payoff to the organization.

At the same time, however, it should also be kept in mind that in-house programs can be dangerous to the organization. I would recommend that a thorough study be made ahead of time to ascertain whether or not a laboratory educational experience would be helpful to company executives individually and to the organization.

OPEN DISCUSSION

I have never observed a group whose members wanted it to decay. I have never studied a group or an organization that was decaying where there were not some members who were aware that decay was occurring. Accordingly, one key to group and organizational effectiveness is to get this knowledge out into the open and to discuss it thoroughly. The human "motors" of the group and the organization have to be checked periodically, just as does the motor of an automobile. Without proper maintenance, all will fail.

NOTES

1. See Chris Argyris, "Explorations in Interpersonal Competence II," *Applied Behavioral Science*, Vol. 1, No. 3, 1965, p. 255.

2. For detailed discussions of such variations see Chris Argyris, "T-Groups for Organizational Effectiveness," HBR March-April 1964, p. 60; R. R. Blake, J. S. Mouton, L. B. Barnes, and L. E. Greiner, "Breakthrough in Organization Development," HBR November-December 1964, p. 135; and Edgar Schein and Warren Bennis, *Personal and Organizational Change Through Laboratory Methods* (New York, John Wiley & Sons, 1965).

37. Assets and Liabilities in Group Problem Solving: The Need for an Integrative Function*

NORMAN R. F. MAIER

A number of investigations have raised the question of whether group problem solving is superior, inferior, or equal to individual problem solving. Evidence can be cited in support of each position so that the answer to this question remains ambiguous. Rather than pursue this generalized approach to the question, it seems more fruitful to explore the forces that influence problem solving under the two conditions.[1] It is hoped that a better recognition of these forces will permit clarification of the varied dimensions of the problem-solving process, especially in groups.

The forces operating in such groups include some that are assets, some that are liabilities, and some that can be either assets or liabilities, depending upon the skills of the members, especially those of the discussion leader. Let us examine these three sets of forces.[2]

GROUP ASSETS

GREATER SUM TOTAL OF KNOWLEDGE AND INFORMATION

There is more information in a group than in any of its members. Thus problems that require the utilization of knowledge should give groups an advantage over individuals. Even if one member of the group (e.g., the leader) knows much more than anyone else, the limited unique knowledge of lesser-informed individuals could serve to fill in some gaps in knowledge. For example, a skilled machinist might contribute to an engineer's problem solving and an ordinary workman might supply infor-

*Source: From *Psychological Review*, Vol. 74, No. 4 (July 1967), pp. 239–249. Copyright © 1967 by the American Psychological Association. Reprinted by permission.

mation on how a new machine might be received by workers.

GREATER NUMBER OF APPROACHES TO A PROBLEM

It has been shown that individuals get into ruts in their thinking.[3] Many obstacles stand in the way of achieving a goal, and a solution must circumvent these. The individual is handicapped in that he tends to persist in his approach and thus fails to find another approach that might solve the problem in a simpler manner. Individuals in a group have the same failing, but the approaches in which they are persisting may be different. For example, one researcher may try to prevent the spread of a disease by making man immune to the germ, another by finding and destroying the carrier of the germ, and still another by altering the environment so as to kill the germ before it reaches man. There is no way of determining which approach will best achieve the desired goal, but undue persistence in any one will stifle new discoveries. Since group members do not have identical approaches, each can contribute by knocking others out of ruts in thinking.

PARTICIPATION IN PROBLEM SOLVING INCREASES ACCEPTANCE

Many problems require solutions that depend upon the support of others to be effective. Insofar as group problem solving permits participation and influence, it follows that more individuals accept solutions when a group solves the problem than when one person solves it. When one individual solves a problem he still has the task of persuading others. It follows, therefore, that when groups solve such problems, a greater number of persons accept and feel responsible for making the solution work. A low-quality solution that has good acceptance can be more effective than a higher-quality solution that lacks acceptance.

BETTER COMPREHENSION OF THE DECISION

Decisions made by an individual, which are to be carried out by others, must be communicated from the decision-maker to the decision-executors. Thus individual problem solving often requires an additional stage—that of relaying the decision reached. Failures in this communication process detract from the merits of the decision and can even cause its failure or create a problem of greater magnitude than the initial problem that was solved. Many organizational problems can be traced to inadequate communication of decisions made by superiors and transmitted to subordinates, who have the task of implementing the decision.

The chances for communication failures are greatly reduced when the individuals who must work together in executing the decision have participated in making it. They not only understand the solution because they saw it develop, but they are also aware of the several other alternatives that were considered and the reasons why they were discarded. The common assumption that decisions supplied by superiors are arbitrarily reached therefore disappears. A full knowledge of goals, obstacles, alternatives, and factual information is essential to communication, and this communication is maximized when the total problem-solving process is shared.

GROUP LIABILITIES

SOCIAL PRESSURE

Social pressure is a major force making for conformity. The desire to be a good group member and to be accepted tends to silence disagreement and favors consensus. Majority opinions tend to be accepted regardless of whether or not their objective quality is logically and scientifically sound. Problems requiring solutions based upon facts, regardless of feelings and wishes, can suffer in group problem-solving situations.

It has been shown that minority opinions in leaderless groups have little influence on the solution reached, even when these opinions are the correct ones.[4] Reaching agreement in a group often is confused with finding the right answer, and it is for this reason that the dimensions of a decision's acceptance and its objective quality must be distinguished.[5]

VALENCE OF SOLUTIONS

When leaderless groups (made up of three or four persons) engage in problem solving, they propose a variety of solutions. Each solution may receive both critical and supportive comments, as well as descriptive and explorative comments from other participants. If the number of negative and positive comments for each solution are algebraically summed, each may be given a valence index.[6] The first solution that receives a positive valence value of 15 tends to be adopted to the satisfaction of all participants about 85 percent of the time, regardless of its quality. Higher quality solutions introduced after the critical value for one of the solutions has been reached have little chance of achieving real consideration. Once some degree of consensus is reached, the jelling process seems to proceed rather rapidly.

The critical valence value of 15 appears not to be greatly altered by the nature of the problem or the exact size of the group. Rather, it seems to designate a turning point between the idea-getting process and the decision-making process (idea evaluation). A solution's valence index is not a measure of the number of persons supporting the solution, since a vocal minority can build up a solution's valence by actively pushing it. In this sense, valence becomes an influence in addition to social pressure in determining an outcome.

Since a solution's valence is independent to its objective quality, this group factor becomes an important liability in group problem solving, even when the value of a decision depends upon objective criteria (facts and logic). It becomes a means whereby skilled manipulators can have more influence over the group process than their proportion of membership deserves.

INDIVIDUAL DOMINATION

In most leaderless groups a dominant individual emerges and captures more than his share of influence on the outcome. He can achieve this end through a greater degree of participation (valence), persuasive ability, or stubborn persistence (fatiguing the opposition). None of these factors is related to problem-solving ability, so that the best problem solver in the group may not have the influence to upgrade the quality of the group's solution (which he would have had if left to solve the problem by himself).

Hoffman and Maier found that the mere fact of appointing a leader causes this person to dominate a discussion.[7] Thus, regardless of his problem-solving ability a leader tends to exert a major influence on the outcome of a decision.

CONFLICTING SECONDARY GOAL: WINNING THE ARGUMENT

When groups are confronted with a problem, the initial goal is to obtain a solution. However, the appearance of several alternatives causes individuals to have preferences and once these emerge the desire to support a position is created. Converting those with neutral viewpoints and refuting those with opposed viewpoints now enters into the problem-solving process. More and more the goal becomes that of winning the decision rather than finding the best solution. This new goal is unrelated to the quality of the problem's solution and therefore can result in lowering the quality of the decision [footnote omitted].

FACTORS THAT SERVE AS ASSETS OR LIABILITIES, DEPENDING LARGELY UPON THE SKILL OF THE DISCUSSION LEADER

DISAGREEMENT

The fact that discussion may lead to disagreement can serve either to create hard feelings among members or lead to a resolution of conflict and hence to an innovative solution.[9] The first of these outcomes of disagreement is a liability, especially with regard to the acceptance of solutions; while the second is an asset, particularly where innovation is desired. A leader can treat disagreement as undesirable and thereby reduce the probability of both hard feelings and innovation, or he can maximize disagreement and risk hard feelings in his attempts to achieve innovation. The skill of a leader requires his ability to create a climate for disagreement which will permit innovation without risking hard feelings. The leader's perception of disagreement is one of the critical factors in this skill area.[10] Others involve permissiveness,[11] delaying the reaching of a solution,[12] techniques for processing information and opinions,[13] and techniques for separating idea-getting from idea-evaluation.[14]

CONFLICTING INTERESTS VERSUS MUTUAL INTERESTS

Disagreement in discussion may take many forms. Often participants disagree with one another with regard to solutions, but when issues are explored one finds that these conflicting solutions are designed to solve different problems. Before one can rightly expect agreement on a solution, there should be agreement on the nature of the problem. Even before this, there should be agreement on the goal, as well as on the various obstacles that prevent the goal from being reached. Once distinctions are made between goals, obstacles, and solutions (which represent ways of overcoming obstacles), one finds increased opportunities for cooperative problem solving and less conflict.[15]

Often there is also disagreement regarding whether the objective of a solution is to achieve quality or acceptance,[16] and frequently a stated problem reveals a complex of separate problems, each having separate solutions so that a search for a single solution is impossible.[17] Communications often are inadequate because the discussion is not synchronized and each person is engaged in discussing a different aspect. Organizing discussion to synchronize the exploration of different aspects of the problem and to follow a systematic procedure increases solution quality.[18] The leadership function of influence discussion procedure is quite distinct from the function of evaluating or contributing ideas.[19]

When the discussion leader aids in the separation of the several aspects of the problem-solving process and delays the solution-mindedness of the group,[20] both solution quality and acceptance improve; when he hinders or fails to facilitate the isolation of these varied processes, he risks a deterioration in the group process.[21] His skill thus determines whether a discussion drifts toward conflicting interests or whether mutual interests are located. Cooperative problem solving can only occur after the mutual interests have been established and it is surprising how often they can be found when the discussion leader makes this his task.[22]

RISK TAKING

Groups are more willing than individuals to reach decisions involving risks.[23] Taking risks is a factor in acceptance of change, but change may either represent a gain or a loss. The best guard against the latter outcome seems to be primarily a matter of a decision's quality. In a group situation this depends upon the leader's skill in utilizing the factors that represent group assets and avoiding those that make for liabilities.

TIME REQUIREMENTS

In general, more time is required for a group to reach a decision than for a single individual to reach one. Insofar as some problems require quick decisions, individual decisions are favored. In other situations acceptance and quality are requirements, but excessive time without sufficient returns also represents a loss. On the other hand, discussion can resolve conflicts, whereas reaching consensus has limited value.[24] The practice of hastening a meeting can prevent full discussion, but failure to move a discussion forward can lead to boredom and fatigue-type solutions, in which members agree merely to get out of the meeting. The effective utilization of discussion time (a delicate balance between permissiveness and control on the part of the leader), therefore, is needed to make the time factor an asset rather than a liability. Unskilled leaders tend to be too concerned with reaching a solution and therefore terminate a discussion before the group potential is achieved.[25]

WHO CHANGES

In reaching consensus or agreement, some members of a group must change. Persuasive forces do not operate in individual problem solving in the same way they operate in a group situation; hence, the changing of someone's mind is not an issue. In group situations, however, who changes can be an asset or a liability. If persons with the most constructive views are induced to change the end-product suffers; whereas if persons with the least constructive points of view change the end-product is upgraded. The leader can upgrade the quality of a decision because his position permits him to protect the person with a minority view and increase his opportunity to influence the majority position. This protection is a constructive factor because a minority viewpoint influences only when facts favor it.[26]

The leader also plays a constructive role insofar as he can facilitate communications and thereby reduce misunderstandings.[27] The leader has an adverse effect on the end-product when he supresses minority views by holding a contrary position and when he uses his office to promote his own views.[28] In many problem-solving discussions, the untrained leader plays a dominant role in influencing the outcome, and when he is more resistant to changing his views than are the other participants, the quality of the outcome tends to be lowered. This negative leader-influence was demonstrated by experiments in which untrained leaders were asked to obtain a second solution to a problem after they had obtained their first one.[29] It was found that the second solution tended to be superior to the first. Since the dominant individual had influenced the first solution, he had won his point and therefore ceased to dominate the subsequent discussion which led to the second solution. Acceptance of a solution also increases as the leader sees disagreement as idea-producing rather than as a source of difficulty or trouble.[30] Leaders who see some of their participants as trouble-makers obtain fewer innovative solutions and gain less acceptance of decisions made than leaders who see disagreeing members as persons with ideas.

THE LEADER'S ROLE FOR INTEGRATED GROUPS

TWO DIFFERING TYPES OF GROUP PROCESS

In observing group problem solving under various conditions it is rather easy to distinguish between cooperative problem-solving activity and persuasion or selling approaches. Problem-solving activity includes searching, trying out ideas on one another, listening to understand rather than to refute, making relatively short speeches, and reacting to differences in opinion as stimulating. The general pattern is one of rather complete participation, involvement, and interest. Persuasion activity includes the selling of opinions already formed, defending a position held, either not listening at all or listening in order to be able to refute, talking dominated by a few members, unfavorable reactions to disagreement, and a lack of involvement of some members. During problem solving the behavior observed seems to be that of members interacting as segments of a group. The interaction pattern is not between certain individual members, but with the group as a whole. Sometimes it is difficult to determine who should be credited with an idea. "It just developed," is a response often used to describe the solution reached. In contrast, discussions involving selling or persuasive behavior seem to consist of a series of interpersonal interactions with each individual retaining his identity. Such groups do not function as integrated units but as separate individuals, each with an agenda. In one situation the solution is unknown and is sought; in the other, several solutions exist and conflict occurs because commitments have been made.

THE STARFISH ANALOGY

The analysis of these two group processes suggests an analogy with the behavior of the rays of a starfish under two conditions; one with the nerve ring intact, the other with the nerve ring sectioned.[31] In the intact condition, locomotion and righting behavior reveal that the behavior of each ray is not merely a function of local stimulation. Locomotion and righting behavior reveal a degree of coordination and interdependence that is centrally controlled. However, when the nerve ring is sectioned, the behavior of one ray still can influence others, but internal coordination is lacking. For example, if one ray is stimulated, it may step forward, thereby exerting pressure on the sides of the other four rays. In response to these external pressures (tactile stimulation), these rays show stepping responses on the stimulated side so that locomotion successfully occurs without the aid of neural coordination. Thus integrated behavior can occur on the basis of external control. If, however, stimulation is applied to opposite rays, the specimen may be "locked" for a time, and in some species the conflicting locomotions may divide the animal, thus destroying it.[32]

Each of the rays of the starfish can show stepping responses even when

sectioned and removed from the animal. Thus each may be regarded as an individual. In a starfish with a sectioned nerve ring the five rays become members of a group. They can successfully work together for locomotion purposes by being controlled by the dominant ray. Thus if uniformity of action is desired, the group of five rays can sometimes be more effective than the individual ray in moving the group toward a source of stimulation. However, if "locking" or the division of the organism occurs, the group action becomes less effective than individual action. External control, through the influence of a dominant ray, therefore can lead to adaptive behavior for the starfish as a whole, but it can also result in a conflict that destroys the organism. Something more than external influence is needed.

In the animal with an intact nerve ring, the function of the rays is coordinated by the nerve ring. With this type of internal organization the group is always superior to that of the individual actions. When the rays function as a part of an organized unit, rather than as a group that is physically together, they become a higher type of organization—a single intact organism. This is accomplished by the nerve ring, which in itself does not do the behaving. Rather, it receives and processes the data which the rays relay to it. Through this central organization, the responses of the rays become part of a larger pattern so that together they constitute a single coordinated total response rather than a group of individual responses.

THE LEADER AS THE GROUP'S CENTRAL NERVOUS SYSTEM

If we now examine what goes on in a discussion group we find that members can problem-solve as individuals, they can influence others by external pushes and pulls, or they can function as a group with varying degrees of unity. In order for the latter function to be maximized, however, something must be introduced to serve the function of the nerve ring. In our conceptualization of group problem solving and group decision,[33] we see this as the function of the leader. Thus the leader does not serve as a dominant ray and produce the solution. Rather, his function is to receive information, facilitate communications between the individuals, relay messages, and integrate the incoming responses so that a single unified response occurs.

Solutions that are the product of good group discussions often come as surprises to discussion leaders. One of these is unexpected generosity. If there is a weak member, this member is given less to do, in much the same way as an organism adapts to an injured limb and alters the function of other limbs to keep locomotion on course. Experimental evidence supports the point that group decisions award special consideration to needy members of groups.[34] Group decisions in industrial groups often give smaller assignments to the less gifted.[35] A leader could not effectually impose such differential treatment on group members without being charged with discriminatory practices.

Another unique aspect of group discussion is the way fairness is resolved. In a simulated problem situation involving the problem of how to introduce a new truck into a group of drivers, the typical group solution involves a trading of trucks so that several or all members stand to profit. If the leader makes the decision the number of persons who profit is often confined to one.[36] In industrial practice, supervisors assign a new truck to an individual member of a crew after careful evaluation of needs. This practice results in dissatisfaction, with the charge of *unfair* being leveled at him. Despite these repeated attempts to do justice, supervisors in the telephone industry never hit upon the notion of a general reallocation of trucks, a solution that crews invariably reach when the decision is theirs to make.

In experiments involving the introduc-

tion of change, the use of group discussion tends to lead to decisions that resolve differences.[37] Such decisions tend to be different from decisions reached by individuals because of the very fact that disagreement is common in group problem solving and rare in individual problem solving. The process of resolving difference in a constructive setting causes the exploration of additional areas and leads to solutions that are integrative rather than compromises.

Finally, group solutions tend to be tailored to fit the interests and personalities of the participants; thus group solutions to problems involving fairness, fears, face-saving, etc., tend to vary from one group to another. An outsider cannot process these variables because they are not subject to logical treatment.

If we think of the leader as serving a function in the group different from that of its membership, we might be able to create a group that can function as an intact organism. For a leader, such functions as rejecting or promoting ideas according to his personal needs are out of bounds. He must be receptive to information contributed, accept contributions without evaluating them (posting contributions on a chalk board to keep them alive). Summarize information to facilitate integration, stimulate exploratory behavior, create awareness of problems of one member by others, and detect when the group is ready to resolve differences and agree to a unified solution.

Since higher organisms have more than a nerve ring and can store information, a leader might appropriately supply information, but according to our model of a leader's role, he must clearly distinguish between supplying information and promoting a solution. If his knowledge indicates the desirability of a particular solution, sharing this knowledge might lead the group to find this solution, but the solution should be the group's discovery. A leader's contributions do not receive the same treatment as those of a member of the group.

Whether he likes it or not, his position is different. According to our conception of the leader's contribution to discussion, his role not only differs in influence, but gives him an entirely different function. He is to serve much as the nerve ring in the starfish and to further refine this function so as to make it a higher type of nerve ring.

This model of a leader's role in group process has served as a guide for many of our studies in group problem solving. It is not our claim that this will lead to the best possible group function under all conditions. In sharing it we hope to indicate the nature of our guidelines in exploring group leadership as a function quite different and apart from group membership. Thus the model serves as a stimulant for research problems and as a guide for our analyses of leadership skills and principles.

CONCLUSIONS

On the basis of our analysis, it follows that the comparison of the merits of group versus individual problem solving depends on the nature of the problem, the goal to be achieved (high quality solution, highly accepted solution, effective communication and understanding of the solution, innovation, a quickly reached solution, or satisfaction), and the skill of the discussion leader. If liabilities inherent in groups are avoided, assets capitalized upon, and conditions that can serve either favorable or unfavorable outcomes are effectively used, it follows that groups have a potential which in many instances can exceed that of a superior individual functioning alone, even with respect to creativity.

This goal was nicely stated by Thibaut and Kelley when they

> wonder whether it may not be possible for a rather small, intimate group to establish a problem solving process that capitalizes upon the total pool of information and provides for great interstimulation of ideas without any loss of innovative creativity due to social restraints.[38]

In order to accomplish this high level of achievement, however, a leader is needed who plays a role quite different from that of the members. His role is analogous to that of the nerve ring in the starfish which permits the rays to execute a unified response. If the leader can contribute the integrative requirement, group problem solving may emerge as a unique type of group function. This type of approach to group processes places the leader in a particular role in which he must cease to contribute, avoid evaluation, and refrain from thinking about solutions or group *products*. Instead he must concentrate on the group *process*, listen in order to understand rather than to appraise or refute, assume responsibility for accurate communication between members, be sensitive to unexpressed feelings, protect minority points of view, keep the discussion moving, and develop skills in summarizing.

NOTES

1. L. R. Hoffman, "Group Problem Solving," in *Advances in Experimental Social Psychology*, vol. 2, ed. L. Berkowitz (New York: Academic Press, 1965), pp. 99-132. H. H. Kelley and J. W. Thibaut, "Experimental Studies of Group Problem Solving and Process," in *Handbook of Social Psychology*, ed. G. Lindzey (Cambridge, Mass.: Addison Wesley, 1954), pp. 735-85.

2. The research reported here was supported by Grant No. MH-02704 from the United States Public Health Service. Grateful acknowledgment is made for the constructive criticism of Melba Colgrove, Junie Janzen, Mara Julius, and James Thurber.

3. K. Duncker, "On Problem Solving," *Psychological Monographs*, 1945, 58 (5, Whole No. 270). N. R. F. Maier, "Reasoning in Humans. I. On Direction," *Journal of Comparative Psychology* 10 (1930): 115-43. M. Wertheimer, *Productive Thinking* (New York: Harper, 1959).

4. N. R. F. Maier and A. R. Solem, "The Contribution of a Discussion Leader to the Quality of Group Thinking: The Effective Use of Minority Opinions," *Human Relations* 5 (1952): 277-88.

5. N. R. F. Maier, *Problem Solving Discussions and Conferences: Leadership Methods and Skills* (New York: McGraw-Hill, 1963).

6. L. R. Hoffman and N. R. F. Maier, "Valence in the Adoption of Solutions by Problem-Solving Groups: Concept, Method, and Results," *Journal of Abnormal and Social Psychology* 69 (1964): 264-71.

7. L. R. Hoffman and N. R. F. Maier, "Valence in the Adoption of Solutions by Problem-Solving Groups: II. Quality and Acceptance as Goals of Leaders and Members," mimeographed (1967).

8. Footnote omitted; unclear reference in original.

9. L. R. Hoffman, "Conditions for Creative Problem Solving," *Journal of Psychology* 52 (1961): 429-44. L. R. Hoffman, E. Harburg, and N. R. F. Maier, "Differences and Disagreement as Factors in Creative Group Problem Solving," *Journal of Abnormal and Social Psychology* 64 (1962): 206-14. L. R. Hoffman and N. R. F. Maier, "Quality and Acceptance of Problem Solutions by Members of Homogeneous and Heterogeneous Groups," *Journal of Abnormal and Social Psychology* 62 (1961): 401-07. N. R. F. Maier, *The Appraisal Review* (New York: Wiley, 1958). Maier, *Problem* . . . (1963). N. R. F. Maier and L. R. Hoffman, "Acceptance and Quality of Solutions as Related to Leaders' Attitudes toward Disagreement in Group Problem Solving," *Journal of Applied Behavioral Science* 1 (1965): 373-86.

10. *Ibid.*

11. N. R. F. Maier, "An Experimental Test of the Effect of Training on Discussion Leadership," *Human Relations* 6 (1953): 161-73.

12. N. R. F. Maier and L. R. Hoffman, "Quality of First and Second Solutions in Group Problem Solving," *Journal of Applied Psychology* 44 (1960): 278-83. N. R. F. Maier and A. R. Solem, "Improving Solutions by Turning Choice Situations into Problems," *Personnel Psychology* 15 (1962): 151-57.

13. Maier, *Problem* . . . (1963). N. R. F. Maier and L. R. Hoffman, "Using Trained 'Developmental' Discussion Leaders to Improve Further the Quality of Group Decisions," *Journal of Applied Psychology* 44 (1960): 247-51. N. R. F. Maier and R. A. Maier, "An Experimental Test of the Effects of

'Developmental' vs. 'Free' Discussions on the Quality of Group Decisions," *Journal of Applied Psychology* 41 (1957): 320-23.

14. N. R. F. Maier, "Screening Solutions to Upgrade Quality: A New Approach to Problem Solving under Conditions of Uncertainty," *Journal of Psychology* 49 (1960): 217-31. Maier, *Problem* . . . (1963). A. F. Osborn, *Applied Imagination* (New York: Scribner's, 1953).

15. L. R. Hoffman and N. R. F. Maier, "The Use of Group Decision to Resolve a Problem of Fairness," *Personnel Psychology* 12 (1959): 545-59. Maier, "Screening . . ." (1960). Maier, *Problem* . . . (1963). Maier and Solem, "Improving . . ." (1962). A. R. Solem, "1965: Almost Anything I Can Do, We Can Do Better," *Personnel Administration* 28 (1965): 6-16.

16. N. R. F. Maier and L. R. Hoffman, "Types of Problems Confronting Managers," *Personnel Psychology* 17 (1964): 261-69.

17. Maier, *Problem* . . . (1963).

18. Maier and Hoffman, "Using . . ." (1960). Maier and Maier, "An Experimental . . ." (1957).

19. N. R. F. Maier, "The Quality of Group Decisions as Influenced by the Discussion Leader," *Human Relations* 3 (1950): 155-74. Maier, "An Experimental . . ." (1953).

20. Maier, "The Appraisal . . ." (1958). Maier, *Problem* . . . (1963). Maier and Solem, "Improving . . ." (1962).

21. Solem, "Almost . . ." (1965).

22. N. R. F. Maier, *Principles of Human Relations* (New York: Wiley, 1952). Maier, *Problem* . . . (1963). N. R. F. Maier and J. J. Hayes, *Creative Management* (New York: Wiley, 1962).

23. M. A. Wallach and N. Kogan, "The Roles of Information, Discussion and Concensus in Group Risk Taking," *Journal of Experimental and Social Psychology* 1 (1965): 1-19. M. A. Wallach, N. Kogan, and D. J. Bem, "Group Influence on Individual Risk Taking," *Journal of Abnormal and Social Psychology* 65 (1962): 75-86.

24. Wallach and Kogan, "The Roles . . ." (1965).

25. Maier and Hoffman, "Quality . . ." (1960).

26. Maier, "The Quality . . ." (1950). Maier, *Principles* . . . (1952). Maier and Solem, "The Contribution . . ." (1952).

27. Maier, *Principles* . . . (1952). Solem, 1965. . . .

28. Maier and Hoffman, "Quality . . ." (1960). N. R. F. Maier and L. R. Hoffman,

"Group Decision in England and the United States," Personnel Psychology 15 (1962): 75-87. Maier and Solem, "The Contribution . . ." (1952).

29. Maier and Hoffman, "Using . . ." (1960).

30. Maier and Hoffman, "Acceptance . . ." (1965).

31. W. F. Hamilton, "Coordination in the Starfish. III. The Righting Reaction as a Phase of Locomotion (Righting and Locomotion)," Journal of Comparative Psychology 2 (1922): 81-94. A. R. Moore, "The Nervous Mechanism of Coordination in the Crinoid Antedon rosaceus," Journal of Genetic Psychology 6 (1924): 281-88. A. R. Moore and M. Doudoroff, "Injury, Rec very and Function in an Aganglionic Central Nervous System," Journal of Comparative Psychology 28 (1939): 313-28. T. C. Schneirla and N. R. F. Maier, "Concerning the Status of the Starfish," Journal of Comparative Psychology 30 (1940): 103-10.

32. W. J. Crozier, "Notes on Some Problems of Adaptation," Biological Bulletin 39 (1920): 116-29. Moore and Doudoroff, "In-

jury . . ." (1939).

33. Maier, Problem . . . (1963).

34. Hoffman and Maier, "The Use . . ." (1959).

35. Maier, Principles . . . (1952).

36. Maier and Hoffman, "Group . . ." (1962). N. R. F. Maier and L. F. Zerfoss, "MRP: A Technique for Training Large Groups of Supervisors and Its Potential Use in Social Research," Human Relations 5 (1952): 177-86.

37. Maier, Principles . . . (1952). Maier, "An Experimental . . ." (1953). N. R. F. Maier and L. R. Hoffman, "Organization and Creative Problem Solving," Journal of Applied Psychology 45 (1961): 277-80. N. R. F. Maier and L. R. Hoffman, "Financial Incentives and Group Decision in Motivating Change," Journal of Social Psychology 64 (1964): 369-78. N. R. F. Maier and L. R. Hoffman, "Types of Problems Confronting Managers," Personnel Psychology 17 (1964): 261-69.

38. J. W. Thibaut and H. H. Kelley, The Social Psychology of Groups (New York: Wiley, 1961), p. 268.

38. Preventing Groupthink*

IRVING L. JANIS

A PRETZEL-SHAPED QUESTION

One obvious way to prevent groupthink is simply to make one person responsible for every important decision, eliminating all the problems of group dynamics from the outset. But clearly this solution would be self-defeating. Only the most authoritarian of leaders fails to recognize the peril in relying solely on his own deliberations.

For constructive thinking to go on, a group must have a fairly high degree of like-mindedness about basic values and mutual respect. The members must forego trying to score points in a power

struggle or to obtain ego gratification by deflating rivals. These basic conditions are not likely to be created until the policy-making group becomes at least moderately cohesive. But then the quality of the group's deliberations may deteriorate as a result of the concurrence-seeking tendency that gives rise to the symptoms of groupthink. Consequently, the problem of preventing costly miscalculations and lapses from rational thinking in decision-making bodies is complicated: How can policy-makers benefit from the cohesiveness of their group without suffering serious losses from groupthink? This sort of intricate

*Source: Irving L. Janis, Victims of Groupthink, chapter 9, pp. 207-224. Copyright © 1972 by Houghton Mifflin Company. Reprinted by permission.

psychological issue has been called a
pretzel-shaped question and it may require pretzel-shaped answers.

THEREFORE, WHAT?

The difficulties of making inferential
leaps from generalizations about the
conditions that foster groupthink to
concrete proposals for preventive action
are essentially the same for our pretzel-
shaped problem as for any other complicated social problem, such as environmental pollution. F. Kenneth Hare
has pointed out that although life scientists have accumulated considerable
knowledge about the causes and consequences of air pollution and other forms
of environmental contamination, the
scientists with the greatest expertise do
not have the competence single-
handedly to prescribe public policies for
preventing eco-catastrophes:

> the greatest hazard in our path is inherent
> in Lyndon Johnson's acid query "There-
> fore, what?" which he is said to have
> thrown at a group of professors who had
> just briefed him on the Middle Eastern
> situation. The political interest in the envi-
> ronment demands proposals for *action*. . . .
> At present, we are not equipped to make
> such proposals.

The same must be said even more
emphatically about the problem of
counteracting the psychological pollution of groupthink, for much less is
known about the causes and consequences of concurrence-seeking behavior than is known about environmental contaminants. Yet, as Hare
points out, the researchers who have the
deepest understanding of the problems
are not acting in a socially responsible
way if they attempt to withdraw completely from the arena of practical reform. Hare argues that "no important
social problem is ever simple and none
ever lies fully within the competence of
a single academic discipline." He recommends that instead of evading the
issue by repeating that "this is an interdisciplinary problem," everyone who
knows something relevant should par-

ticipate in developing a new discipline
that will tackle the social and technical
engineering problems. So great is the
need for synthesis and multivariate
analysis of theoretical and applied problems in all disciplines, according to
Hare, that a marked change is to be expected in the trend of basic sciences.
Whereas the past century has been the
era in which each subdiscipline dissect-
ed reality in fine detail, Hare foresees
that in the next century scientists will try
to understand how complex systems
work and how they can be changed.

If we are to overhaul the machinery
of policy-making in complex governmental, industrial, and welfare organizations, we must certainly apply
Hare's advice and stop complaining
about the interdisciplinary complexities
of the problems and start creating a new
discipline that synthesizes whatever is
relevant from them all. What is urgently
needed is a new type of intervention research, in which experienced executives familiar with the policy-making
system from the inside and a variety of
specialists familiar with various
decision-making processes from the
outside collaborate to develop viable
improvements. If this type of enterprise
materializes, one line of intervention research might be devoted to testing
plausible recommendations, inferred
from tentative generalizations about the
conditions under which groupthink
flourishes, for improving the quality of
executive decision-making.

My answer to the acid-test question
"Therefore, what?" is heavily influenced by many prior social psychological experiments and detailed observations bearing on group dynamics,
including my own studies of task-
oriented groups. In this field of research,
we become sensitized to the vagaries of
human response to seemingly straightforward treatments for improving the
quality of group products—vagaries that
often force the investigator to conclude
that the remedy is worse than the disease. Furthermore, even if free from un-

desirable side effects, the new treatments are undoubtedly a long way from providing a complete cure. In most cohesive groups, concurrence-seeking tendencies are probably much too powerful to be subdued by administrative changes of the type to be proposed. At best, those changes might somewhat decrease the strength of concurrence-seeking tendencies, thereby reducing the frequency of error. But is it worthwhile, then, for an organization to expend effort, time, and money to try to introduce and assess improvements with such limited potentialities? The answer depends partly on how much damage can be expected from collective miscalculations by an organization's policy-making group. When there is no known antibiotic to cure a virulent respiratory disease, it is still worthwhile during an epidemic to find out whether some elementary precautions, such as staying away from crowded places, will lower significantly the chances of being infected. The prescriptions I am proposing are perhaps like those elementary precautions; they may sometimes help to keep us out of danger while the search for an effective cure continues. It is with considerable ambivalence, therefore, that I offer my suggestions for preventing groupthink.

THREE PRESCRIPTIONS AND THEIR UNDESIRABLE SIDE EFFECTS

The three suggestions for preventing groupthink presented at the end of Chapter 7 have major drawbacks. One reason for dwelling on the drawbacks is to underline the fact that these prescriptive hypotheses, as well as others to be discussed shortly, must be validated before they can be applied with any confidence. In my opinion, despite potential drawbacks, they warrant the trouble and expense of being tested as potentially useful means for partially counteracting groupthink whenever a small number of executives in any organiza-

tion meet with their chief executive to work out new policies. Certain of the anti-groupthink procedures might also help to counteract initial biases of the members, prevent pluralistic ignorance and eliminate other sources of error that can arise independently of groupthink.

1. *The leader of a policy-forming group should assign the role of critical evaluator to each member, encouraging the group to give high priority to airing objections and doubts. This practice needs to be reinforced by the leader's acceptance of criticism of his own judgments in order to discourage the members from soft-pedaling their disagreements.*

If the proposed practice is wholeheartedly approved and reinforced by the chief executive and the other top executives in the organization's hierarchy, it might help to counteract the spontaneous group pressures that give rise to a premature consensus. This will not happen, however, unless the leader conveys to the members by his own actions that the task of critical appraisal is to be given precedence over maintaining traditional forms of deference. It is difficult for the members of an amiable executive group to adopt such a norm, but without this basic change in orientation, no other recommendation for improving the quality of group decision-making is likely to be successful because each can easily be subverted by a group intent on pleasing the leader. The leader must demonstrate that he can be influenced by those who disagree with him. He will fail to reinforce the new norm if he shows his displeasure by terminating a discussion when it is not moving in the direction he wants or if his facial expressions and other nonverbal communications belie his words.

The proposed leadership practice has some potential disadvantages that must be taken into account. Prolonged debates within the group can sometimes be costly when a rapidly growing international crisis requires an immediate policy solution in order to avert catastrophe.[1] Open criticism can also lead to damaged feelings when the members resolutely live up to their role as critical evaluators and take each other's proposals over the bumps. Feelings of rejection, depression, and anger might be evoked so often when this role assignment is put into practice that it could have a corrosive effect on morale and working relations within the group. The critical-evaluator role assignment might have to be supplemented by an in-service training program to give executives special skills for avoiding the pitfalls of uninhibited debate. Further, a judicious chairman would be needed, one whose talents as a mediator enable him to head off disruptive quarrels and demoralizing stalemates.

The effectiveness of a group of critical evaluators will depend on the background and personality of the members. A policy-making group of bristling curmudgeons might waste their time on endless reiterations of clashing points of view. Seldom, if ever, do we find in a policy-making committee the ideal type of genuinely reasonable people who can be counted on to function as constructive discussants, to take account of their colleagues' points of view, and to make judicious but principled compromises when the time comes for consensus. Nevertheless, many policy-making groups are probably made up of people who are capable of functioning more effectively in the desired direction if norms that foster critical evaluation are adopted.

2. *The leaders in an organization's hierarchy, when assigning a policy-planning mission to a group, should be impartial instead of stating preferences and expectations at the outset. This practice requires each leader to limit his briefings to unbiased statements about the scope of the problem and the limitations of available resources, without advocating specific proposals he would like to see adopted. This allows the conferees the opportunity to develop an atmosphere of open inquiry and to explore impartially a wide range of policy alternatives.*

The expected benefit of this leadership practice is that it avoids setting a group norm that will evoke conformity with the leader's views. Among the hazards, however, is a potential cleavage between the leader and the members, which could become a disruptive power struggle if the chief executive regards the emerging consensus among the members as anathema to him.[2] Having lost the opportunity at the outset to steer the group, an inflexible chief might fight with the others, reject their consensus, or disband the group entirely. Even if no rift develops, the chief may feel so frustrated that he becomes more directive than ever. Perhaps the proposed nondirective leadership practice will work only when the chief can be genuinely open-minded in all stages of decision-making and values the judgment of the group sufficiently to abstain from using his power when the others reach a consensus that displeases him.

3. *The organization should routinely follow the administrative practice of setting up several independent policy-planning and evaluation groups to work on the same policy question, each carrying out its deliberations under a different leader.*

This practice—which many specialists in administrative sciences advocate for other reasons—would prevent insulation of an executive in-group from challenging information and independent judgments by well-qualified outsiders. Many executives object to it, however, on the grounds that the more people consulted, the greater is the risk of a security leak. This risk would have to be tolerated, or the security problem would have to be solved by adopting measures that could be applied to a larger number of participants without being inordinately costly in time, money, efficiency, and morale. Another drawback is that the more organizational units involved in policy formation, the greater is the opportunity for intraorganizational politics to play a determining role. Harold Wilensky has emphasized this drawback in *Organizational Intelligence*:

> President Eisenhower . . . made the National Security Council "the climax of a ponderous system of boards, staffs and interdepartmental committees through which national security policy was supposed to rise to the top" [Schlesinger wrote in *A Thousand Days*]. As a result, the NSC was converted into a forum for intramural negotiations; what Dean Acheson called "agreement by exhaustion" blurred policy discord. An ironic feature of such a system is that men of good will are moved to obfuscate their positions and overstate agreements with their rivals, on behalf of an ultimate consensus. . . . When they cannot cope with issues by glittering generalities representing the lowest common denominator of agreement, such supercommittees avoid controversial issues entirely, delay decisions, refer issues to other committees, or engage in logrolling, as when the Navy trades off support for more Air Force wings in return for Air Force support for more Navy carriers. Sharp questions, cogent arguments, minority positions, a clear calculation of gains and costs are lost to view.

Furthermore, when many different planning and evaluation groups deliberate, none of them feels responsible for making a careful assessment of the policy's drawbacks. These are the circumstances that encourage a "let George do it" attitude and the even more pervasive presumption that "George must have already done it." Warren Weaver speaks of an organization whose top administrators take great pride in the series of scheduled steps that each new proposal has to go through before reaching them, without realizing that they are allowing responsibility to be so diffuse that no one actually takes on the task of making a careful evaluation:

> By the time the proposal reaches the higher levels of responsibility, the number of examinations and successive interim approvals is so impressive that there is an almost overwhelming temptation to assume that the real decision has already been made.

To minimize the risks, guidelines might be formulated that specify the responsibilities of each group and define the role of each participant, emphasizing that primary loyalty is expected to the organization as a whole rather than to a local unit. Further, it may be possible to select statesmen-like executives capable of surmounting the chronic rivalries that plague every large bureaucracy—men who can be counted on to assess objectively the potential gains and losses for each policy alternative without always giving priority to the special interests of their own unit in its power struggles within the organization. The ultimate success of a multiple-group procedure probably depends on whether these and other safeguards can be introduced. Otherwise the multiple-group antidote to groupthink could spawn a virulent form of politicking that is a worse disease than the one it is supposed to prevent.

MORE PRESCRIPTIONS TO OFFSET INSULATION

Additional prescriptive hypotheses based on inferences from the generalizations stated in chapter 8 concerning the conditions under which groupthink is least likely to occur might help prevent groupthink. The costs and potential losses are essentially the same as those just described for the first three prescriptions; the reader will undoubtedly think of additional ones. Suffice it to say that all the recommendations pose obvious risks: The proposed procedures may lower group cohesiveness and correspondingly lower the morale of the participants, as consensus continues to elude them. They may also prove to be prohibitively costly in taking up the precious time of already overburdened executives. Nevertheless, these prescriptions seem to hold the promise of somewhat reducing the chances of groupthink at a moderate cost, if they are implemented flexibly by sensible executives who do not suffer fools gladly and who do not gladly allow themselves to be made into fools. Like the first three, the additional prescriptions offer only a partial cure.

The next three prescriptions take account of the need to offset the potentially adverse effects of insulation of the policy-making group; they would be especially applicable when the multiple-group structure cannot be implemented.

4. *Throughout the period when the feasibility and effectiveness of policy alternatives are being surveyed, the policy-making group should from time to time divide into two or more subgroups to meet separately, under different chairmen, and then come together to hammer out their differences.*

The formation of subgroups might reduce the chances that the entire group will develop a concurrence-seeking norm and increase the chances that illusory assumptions will be critically examined before a consensus is reached. Subgrouping was one of the procedures used by the Executive Committee during the Cuban missile crisis, and it appears to have contributed to the effectiveness of that group's critical appraisals.

5. *Each member of the policy-making group should discuss periodically the group's deliberations with trusted associates in his own unit of the organization and report back their reactions.*

Here I am assuming that each policy-maker's circle of associates can be trusted to adhere to the security regulations that govern the policy-makers. I also assume that each circle will include men with somewhat different types of expertise, outlooks, and values, so that they can be expected to make independent criticisms and perhaps offer some fresh solutions. In order for the home-office meetings to be effective, each policy-maker would have to conduct them in a nondirective style that encourages free discussion, taking

on the role of information-seeker rather than of proselytizing boss. When reporting back to the group, each policy-maker would have to take on the role of information-transmitter and try to describe accurately all varieties of reactions, not specially singling out those that support his own views.

Consider what would have happened at the Bay of Pigs planning sessions if, instead of restricting discussion to the small group of advisers dominated by the two CIA leaders who had evolved the plan, Secretary Rusk had conducted a genuine evaluation meeting with trusted associates in the State Department, Secretary McNamara had done the same in the Defense Department, and each of the others had done likewise in his home office. Chances are that the members of the planning group would have been rudely shaken out of their complacency as they encountered strong negative reactions like the horror that Chester Bowles is reported to have experienced at the one planning session he attended. When Bowles submitted his criticisms in a memorandum and spoke privately to Rusk, his objections were quickly brushed aside; Rusk did not permit the memorandum to be shown to the President or to anyone else. Wouldn't a member of a policy-making group be much less likely to protect the group from such outside influence, to take on the functions of a mindguard, if he were to encounter strong objections to a preferred policy alternative from more than one colleague, especially when he knew that the policy-making group was expecting him to report back on what was actually said at the meetings in his home office?

6. *One or more outside experts or qualified colleagues within the organization who are not core members of the policy-making group should be invited to each meeting on a staggered basis and should be encouraged to challenge the views of the core members.*

In order to counteract a false sense of complacency about risky decisions, the visitors would have to be trustworthy associates carefully selected because of their capacity to grasp new ideas quickly, perspicacity in spotting hidden catches, sensitivity to moral issues, and verbal skill in transmitting criticism. Such outsiders were, in fact, deliberately brought into the Executive Committee's meetings during the Cuban missile crisis, and they were urged to express their objections openly. This atmosphere was quite different from the one that prevailed throughout the Bay of Pigs planning sessions, where, with rare exceptions, the discussants at every meeting were always the same men.

Additional safeguards might be needed to ensure that the objective of inviting well-qualified visitors is not neutralized or subverted. First, visitors who are likely to raise debate-worthy objections should be invited long before a consensus has been reached, not after most of the core members have made up their minds, as was the case when Senator Fulbright was invited to participate in the Bay of Pigs deliberations. Second, each visitor should be asked to speak out about his qualms and not brood silently, as Bowles felt constrained to do when he attended a Bay of Pigs planning session. Third, after the visitor speaks his piece, the chairman should call for open discussion of his objections instead of moving on to other business, as President Kennedy did after Senator Fulbright gave his rousing speech at the final planning session about the undesirable political and moral consequences of the Bay of Pigs invasion plan.

MORE PRESCRIPTIONS TO OFFSET LEADERSHIP BIAS

These prescriptions are designed to help offset leadership practices that bias the group's deliberations and that establish concurrence-seeking as an informal group norm.

7. *At every meeting devoted to evaluating policy alternatives, at least one member should be assigned the role of devil's advocate.*

Whenever assigning the role of critical evaluator to every member of the group is not feasible, assigning the devil's advocate role to one or two members may be of some limited value. In recent years, however, use of a devil's advocate has become popular among high-level executives, and many go through the motions without any apparent effect. For example, President Johnson and other leading members of his Tuesday Lunch Group claimed that they had devil's advocates in their midst each time they decided to intensify the air war against North Vietnam. But those devils were not very devilish. James C. Thomson has informed us, on the basis of his observations during several years of service on the White House staff, that the devil's advocates in Johnson's inner circle quickly became domesticated and were allowed by the President to speak their piece only as long as they remained within the bounds of what he and other leading members of the group considered acceptable dissent. George Reedy, who was President Johnson's press secretary for a time, adds that within Johnson's councils "[the official devil's advocate's] objections and cautions are discounted before they are delivered. They are actually welcomed because they prove for the record that decision was preceded by controversy." Alexander George also comments that, paradoxically, the institutionalized devil's advocate, instead of stirring up much-needed turbulence among the members of a policy-making group, may create the "comforting feeling that they have considered all sides of the issue and that the policy chosen has weathered challenges from within the decision-making circle." He goes on to say that after the President has fostered the ritualized use of devil's advocates, the top-level officials may learn nothing more than how to enact their policy-making in such a way as to meet the informed public's expectation about how important decisions should be made and "to project a favorable image into the 'instant histories' that will be written shortly thereafter."

The problem, then, is how to avoid tokenism on the part of the chief executive, how to inject a genuine effort that will not belie the instant historians' reassuring picture of healthy controversy. If the leader genuinely wants the group to examine opposing arguments, he will have to give the devil's advocate an unambiguous assignment to present his arguments as cleverly and convincingly as he can, like a good lawyer, challenging the testimony of those advocating the majority position. This does not mean that the leader has to transform the meetings with his policy advisers into a kind of formal debate or that the devil's advocate should be strident, rude, or insolent in pressing for an alternative point of view. The most effective performers in the role are likely to be those who can be truly devilish by raising new issues in a conventional, low-key style, asking questions such as, "Haven't we perhaps overlooked . . ?" "Shouldn't we give some thought to . . ?" The chief executive must make it clear by what he says and does that the listeners are expected to pay close attention to all the devilish arguments and to take them up one by one for serious discussion. The group might adopt essentially the same supplementary procedures suggested for dealing with the points raised by outsiders who introduce fresh notes into the group's deliberations.

During the Cuban missile crisis, President Kennedy gave his brother, the Attorney General, the unambiguous mission of playing devil's advocate, with seemingly excellent results in breaking up a premature consensus. But the vehemence with which Robert Kennedy plunged into the role may have cost him a considerable amount of popularity among his colleagues on the Executive Committee, and had he not been the President's brother, this might have damaged his government career. Perhaps rotating the role among the most talented role-players in the group would help solve this problem and hamper the build-up of subtle pressures that induce domestication of the role. With one fresh contender after another on hand to challenge the consensus of the majority, the devil could get his due at the meetings and not afterward.

8. *Whenever the policy issue involves relations with a rival nation or organization, a sizable block of time (perhaps an entire session) should be spent surveying all warning signals from the rivals and constructing alternative scenarios of the rivals' intentions.*

To counteract the members' shared illusions of invulnerability and their tendency to ignore warning signals that interfere with complacency, the leader may have to exert special efforts to induce himself and his colleagues to pay sufficient attention to potential risks to make realistic contingency plans. Even when men have a role assignment requiring them to be vigilant, they are likely to disregard intelligence reports and warnings about a potential danger if there is a pre-existing consensus among members of their reference group that the particular threat is improbable. Thomas Schelling speaks of the "poverty of expectations" that prevented the military commanders at Pearl Harbor from considering that the warning signals they were receiving during 1941 might point to an oncoming Japanese attack. "Unlike movies," he points out, "real life provides no musical background to tip us off to the climax."

When participants in a policy-planning group are being briefed about their rival's latest moves, audio-visual aids that provide the equivalent of melodramatic background music might overcome their poverty of expectations, especially when their complacency is grounded in unanimous agreement that the warning signals point only to minor threats that can be safely ignored.

Setting aside a block of time for thorough consideration of the potential risks probably has to be made an institutionalized requirement; otherwise any bearer of ill tidings is likely to meet the fate of Cassandra, whose accurate prophecies of catastrophe were never taken seriously. Briefings by intelligence specialists might be supplemented by films or illustrated talks prepared by a skilled scenario writer who deliberately takes on the role of Cassandra's advocate, calling attention as vividly as possible to alarming interpretations of the evidence at hand that might otherwise be overlooked.

I am not proposing that Hollywood-like productions become standard fare in high government counsels, which could bring us closer to the day when the Pentagon will routinely commission horror films for use along with other forms of scare propaganda to persuade congressional committees to increase their appropriations to the armed forces. What I have in mind is an occasional presentation of multiple scenarios as a stimulant to the imagination of the members of a policy-making group, which could arouse a state of constructive vigilance in an inert group that has been reposing in tranquil overconfidence. Perhaps the model for the presentation of multiple scenarios should be the great Japanese film Rashomon, directed by Akira Kurosawa. This film presents four entirely different scenarios successively, each explaining the same events (a sexual assault and a murder) in a different way, attributing entirely different motivations to the principals, yet accounting equally well for the known facts.

Of course if the most ominous interpretation of an enemy's activities is presented convincingly, a group of government policy-makers might overreact to relatively innocuous events and become all too ready to launch a preemptive first strike. In the series of Rashomon-like alternative scenarios there should always be at least one that plausibly attributes benign intentions to the enemy; this might help prevent such overreactions. To ensure careful weighing of the evidence, additional safeguards against precipitous judgment might be needed. For example, after bringing in outside experts to brief the policy-making group, the leader might assign several members the task of evaluating all warning messages and information about risks that need to be taken into account for contingency planning. In carrying out this task, the participants might find it useful to assume that there is some truth and also some exaggeration in every unwelcome message, before they begin any discussion that moves in the direction of either acting on it or dismissing it as irrelevant.

Psychodramatic role-play exercises might also be used to overcome the influence of stereotypes and to facilitate understanding of the rivals' warnings, enabling the group to predict more accurately the probable responses to one or another course of action. For example, after intelligence experts have given a factual briefing on, say, the Chinese Communists' ambiguous threats during a new international crisis in the Far East, the members of a foreign policy planning group who are most familiar with the beliefs and values of the Chinese leaders might try out a psychodramatic procedure in which they assume the role of their opposite numbers in Peking. The psychodrama might be enacted as a meeting during which the Chinese leaders talk over their options for dealing with the crisis and the countermoves they might make if the United States takes a hard line versus an ameliorative stance. Had this type of role-play exercise been conducted by Truman's advisers in the fall of 1950, they might have taken much more seriously the repeated warnings from Communist China and become reluctant to approve General MacArthur's catastrophic policy of pursuing the North Korean army to the Manchurian border.

The same type of role-playing might be useful in overcoming complacency in a group that collectively judges a series of warnings to be inapplicable and sees no reason to prepare contingency plans for dealing with the potential danger. Suppose that a role-play exercise had been carried out by the group of United States Navy commanders in Hawaii on December 2, 1941, the day that Admiral Kimmel, after being informed by the chief of naval intelligence that no one in the Navy knew where the Japanese aircraft carriers were, jokingly asked if they could be heading straight for Hawaii. If the exercise of playing the role of Japan's supreme military command had been carried out seriously, isn't it likely that at least a few of the high-ranking naval officers responsible for the defense of Hawaii would have argued against the prevailing view that the war warnings they had been receiving during the past week did not warrant the expense of a full alert at Pearl Harbor or a 360-degree air patrol around the Hawaiian Islands?

9. *After reaching a preliminary consensus about what seems to be the best policy alternative, the policy-making group should hold a "second chance" meeting at which every member is expected to express as vividly as he can all his residual doubts and to rethink the entire issue before making a definitive choice.*

In order to prevent a premature consensus based on unwarranted expectations of invulnerability, stereotypes about the enemy, and other unexamined assumptions shared by members of the group, the second-chance session should be held just before the group takes a definitive vote or commits itself in any other way. At this special meeting, every member should be encouraged to become the devil's advocate and Cassandra's advocate, challenging his own favorite arguments and playing up all the risks. Everyone should deliberately set himself the task of presenting to the group any objections he can think of that have not yet been adequately discussed. In order to stimulate a freewheeling, open discussion in which residual doubts are frankly expressed, the members might be asked to read in advance an eloquent document presenting opposing arguments prepared by opponents of the chosen policy. In giving out such an assignment on occasions when a consensus has been reached rapidly, the leader might take as his model the statement made by Alfred P. Sloan, a former chairman of General Motors who reportedly announced at a meeting of his fellow policy-makers:

> Gentlemen, I take it we are all in complete agreement on the decision here. . . . Then I propose we postpone further discussion of this matter until our next meeting to give ourselves time to develop disagreement and perhaps gain some understanding of what the decision is all about.

To encourage members to reveal vague forebodings, it might not be a bad idea for the second-chance meeting to take place in a relaxed atmosphere far from the executive suite, perhaps over drinks (as sometimes happens spontaneously anyhow). According to a report by Herodotus dating from about 45 B.C., whenever the ancient Persians made a decision following sober deliberations, they would always reconsider the matter under the influence of wine. Tacitus claimed that during Roman times the Germans too had a custom of arriving at each decision twice, once sober, once drunk. Some moderate, institutionalized form of allowing second thoughts to be freely expressed before the group commits itself might be remarkably effective for breaking down a false sense of unanimity and related illusions, without endangering anyone's reputation or liver.

TOOLING UP FOR INNOVATIONS

Recognizing that each innovation in policy-making procedures can introduce new sources of error that might be as bad as or worse than groupthink, we can see why public administrators and executives in large private organizations might have solid reasons for resisting any change in their standard procedures. Nevertheless, innovative executives who know their way around the organizational maze may be able to figure out how to apply one or another of the prescriptions successfully, without producing harmful side effects. If they were to invite well-qualified behavioral scientists to collaborate with them, they might obtain something more than academic advice from the sidelines. Some behavioral scientists (though, alas, not many) possess that rare set of skills required for developing and making objective assessments of new administrative procedures. A few specialists in administrative science, for example, have developed ways of applying the most sophisticated methods of assessment used in engineering and the behavioral sciences to problems that arise in connection with executive functions in large organizations. They know a great deal about obtaining data from field studies to evaluate innovations for coordinating the operations of the specific units of an organization so as to determine whether the proposed changes will achieve the goals of the organization as a whole. Research teams of specialists from several different behavioral science disciplines have dealt with management problems such as the allocation of available resources, the scheduling of sequential tasks, the replacement of facilities, and the development of effective steps for carrying out information searches that will supply policy-makers with the information they need at the lowest cost and with the fewest errors. The same systematic methods used by research teams to deal with these problems— evaluating the effects of changing a given procedure in one unit of the organization on every other aspect of the unit's functioning and on the organization as a whole—might be applied to

problems concerning the procedures used by an executive committee making its policy decisions.

Imaginative workers in the new field of research on policy-making procedures might be able to develop the equivalent of a wind tunnel for a series of trial runs to pretest various anti-groupthink procedures before going to the expense of setting up a field test. For example, in recent studies of political gaming, small groups of middle-level executives (who are thought to have the potential for eventually becoming top-level executives) are given decision-making exercises in simulated crises. In one exercise, conducted during a three-day period at the Center for International Studies at the Massachusetts Institute of Technology, two teams of executives met separately to arrive at policy decisions in a simulated clash between the United States and the Soviet Union centering around a Communist revolt in an underdeveloped country, similar to the situations that led to United States intervention in Korea and Vietnam. Both sides initially tried to avoid intervention and a direct confrontation, but these cautious strategies gradually gave way to military policies involving considerable risks, just as in real life. While these decisions were being made, it was clear that each side was misunderstanding the intentions of the other and was drawing incorrect inferences because of stereotyped images and unexamined preconceptions about how the rival group would react. This too resembles what has happened in groups making real-life decisions.

One of the limitations of political game-playing is that it does not generate the severe stress and intense need for social support that arise in real international crises. Nevertheless, some symptoms of groupthink may regularly appear when group decision-making exercises are carried out in the context of simulated international crises. It should be possible to use them to try out various anti-groupthink prescriptions to see what the problems are, to find out how the problems can most easily be eliminated, and then to evaluate the success in preventing the worst effects of groupthink. The political gaming exercises might also be useful for training executives. Briefing sessions could be held afterward to enable them to become aware of symptoms of groupthink and other manifestations of group dynamics.

A collaborative team made up of practical-minded men from inside the organization working with behavioral scientists who spend enough time tooling up to understand what the insiders tell them ought to be able to find a relatively painless way to carry out field studies to assess the long-run effectiveness of the most promising innovative procedures. The objective evaluations made by a team of administrators and behavioral scientists could weed out ineffective and harmful procedures and provide solid evidence to keep the good ones going. By accumulating systematic evidence, they could contribute to the transformation of rational policy-making from a haphazard art into a cumulative science. In the absence of sound evaluation studies, improvements in decision-making procedures have a chancy existence and often get lost in the shuffle of changing personnel at the top of the organization. Consider the promising innovations introduced by President Kennedy after the humiliation of the Bay of Pigs fiasco. We have seen that he made several major changes along the lines of some of the foregoing prescriptions for counteracting groupthink and improved the quality of decision-making on subsequent occasions, including the Cuban missile crisis. What happened to those innovations after Kennedy's death? Evidently they were regarded simply as part of Kennedy's personal style of leadership and were promptly dropped by his successor, who had his own way of doing things. If a solid body of evidence had been available to show that those pro-

cedures would generally be effective in various policy-making bodies headed by men other than John Kennedy, there might have been strong pressures to retain the innovations. The better the evidence showing that a given innovation is effective in a variety of different organizations and at all levels of management, the more confidence everyone can have that the prescription is a valid generalization and the better the chances are that it will be retained when new top executives replace those who initiated the change.

THE ETHICAL ISSUE

The type of innovation I have been discussing confronts us with a rather painful ethical issue that is a source of embarrassment for anyone who would like to see improvements in the policy-making procedures in our society: Suppose that knowledge about how to prevent groupthink turns out to have practical value for improving the effectiveness of policy-making groups. Who will benefit? Will it be good or bad for the Jews? For the Christians? For the blacks? For the whites? For the hawks? For the doves? For the men in power? For the oppressed who are striving for power? All along, I have assumed that many people are inadvertently victimized when war-and-peace decisions are dominated by groupthink, that many lives are unintentionally sacrificed as a result of ill-conceived nationalistic policies. In the back of my mind has been the expectation (and hope) that improving the efficiency of policy-making groups will increase the chances that they will fulfil their humanitarian goals along with their other goals.

But, of course, there is a rub. Suppose that a policy-making body talks about humanitarianism only for window dressing, while secretly believing that whatever is good for "our group" will be good for mankind. For any exploitative, totalitarian, or criminalistic gang, wouldn't the prevention of groupthink be contributing to evil rather than good by helping them to be more successful? Yes, of course. Any improvement in the cure for evils intentionally perpetrated by a policy-making group, any more than a cure for the bedsores afflicting patients in a cancer ward will restore them to full health.

Where does that leave us? My answer is that a cure for staphylococcus infection can be worthwhile even if it does not cure cancer. The evils that are deliberately perpetrated by policy-making groups must be fought as people have always fought them, through persistent political confrontations that challenge the legitimacy of bad policies and through concerted efforts to change public attitudes to win the support of large constituencies for good policies. This struggle is often carried out by small groups of dedicated men and women who are deeply committed to democratic and humanitarian values. One hopes that these groups are open to innovation and will want to avoid the unfortunate consequences of groupthink. Similarly, the policy-making groups in large organizations that take democratic and humanitarian values seriously might be less hidebound than those striving primarily to maintain traditional bureaucratic or conventional values. Maybe there are grounds, therefore, for being somewhat optimistic about the possibility that some groups with good values will take seriously the techniques for preventing groupthink in their own policy-making deliberations and make good use of those techniques.

Most of what I have just been saying boils down to a simple truism: Improving the quality of decision-making by eliminating certain sources of error that prevent a group from achieving its goals can be expected to have good social consequences for policy-making groups that have good goals; otherwise not. I hope that behavioral scientists will keep this in mind when they are deciding whether or not to collaborate with executives who want them to help improve the effectiveness of an organization's policy-making.

IS A LITTLE KNOWLEDGE OF GROUPTHINK A DANGEROUS THING?

Even if we had more than a little knowledge of groupthink, my answer to this question would be a categorical "yes" if we have in mind a naive person in a position of power who might be led to believe that groupthink is the only major source of error in policy-making and therefore that decisions can be made better by just one man (notably himself) than by a group of colleagues. I would also answer "yes" if I thought that a substantial number of policy-makers might be misled into believing that preventing groupthink should be given high priority, so that all sorts of safeguards should be introduced into the decision-making process without regard for hidden costs. Finally, I would wearily say "yes" if I discovered that many executives were being subjected to a lot of nonsense from overly eager faddists on their staffs who were taking up precious time trying to introduce some kind of group therapy in the conference room, like an earlier generation of faddists who tried to inflict parlorroom psychoanalysis on their friends.

But my answer is "no" for anyone who takes the trouble to examine the fragmentary evidence on which I have drawn inferences about the conditions that give rise to groupthink. My two main conclusions are that along with other sources of error in decision-making, groupthink is likely to occur within cohesive small groups of decision-makers and that the most corrosive effects of groupthink can be counteracted by eliminating group insulation, overly directive leadership practices, and other conditions that foster premature consensus. Those who take these conclusions seriously will probably find that the little knowledge they have about groupthink increases their understanding of the causes of erroneous group decisions and sometimes even has some practical value in preventing fiascoes. (If I didn't think so, I wouldn't have bothered to write this chapter.)

A little knowledge of groupthink might be valuable for anyone who participates in a group that makes policy decisions, whether it is the executive committee of an international organization, an ad hoc committee set up by a government agency, the steering committee of a local business, professional, or political organization, or a student committee at a college. Such knowledge can be especially useful if it inclines the participants to consider introducing antidote prescriptions, provided, of course, that they are aware of the costs in time and effort and realize that there are other disadvantages they must also watch out for before they decide to adopt any of them as a standard operating procedure.

Sometimes it may even be useful for one of the members of the group to ask, at the right moment, before a decision is definitely made, "Are we allowing ourselves to become victims of groupthink?" I am not proposing that this question should be placed on the agenda or that the members should try to conduct a group therapy session. Rather, I have in mind making salient the realization that the desire for unity within the group can be discussed frankly and that agreement within the group is not always desirable. This open acknowledgment may enable some members to adopt a psychological set that inclines them to raise critical questions whenever there are signs of undue complacency or a premature consensus. One such question has to do with the consensus itself. A leader or a member who is aware of the symptoms of groupthink, for example, might ask to hear from those who have not yet said anything, in order to get all points of view onto the table before the group makes a

final decision. In addition to this common-sense application, some ingenious procedures may be worked out or spontaneously improvised so that the symptoms of groupthink are counteracted by participants who know about the groupthink hypothesis, without constantly reminding the group of it.

With these considerations in mind, I suggest that awareness of the shared illusions, rationalizations, and other symptoms fostered by the interaction of members of small groups may curtail the influence of groupthink in policy-making groups, including those that meet in the White House. Here is another place where we can apply George Santayana's well-known adage: "Those who cannot remember the past are condemned to repeat it." Perhaps a better understanding of group dynamics among government leaders will help them avoid being condemned to repeat the fiascoes of the recent past described in this book.

NOTES

1. In a crisis the use of decision-making procedures that take up a great deal of time and lead to hesitation when rapid decisions may be urgently required can be disadvantageous and even disastrous. However, all the fiascoes discussed in this book were actually planned piecemeal over a long period of time, often with one small commitment growing out of another. Ironically, of all the foreign policy crises I have studied, the one that put the policy-makers under the greatest time pressure was the Cuban missile crisis. The policy-makers knew that if United States action was delayed, the installations would be completed and the missiles would be armed with atomic warheads, posing a tremendous threat to American cities. Nevertheless, the group debated the issues thoroughly and examined critically many alternatives. This suggests that if the members of a policy-making group give priority to critical scrutiny of alternatives, they can somehow find the time to do so during a crisis.

2. A leader who absents himself from

some of the meetings, as President Kennedy did during the Cuban missile crisis, might become somewhat perturbed when he returns to discover that the group has moved toward a consensus on adopting a policy alternative to which he objects. This puts him on the spot because if he feels strongly that the group's judgment is wrong, he is at a disadvantage at that late date in trying to persuade the members otherwise, unless he glaringly uses his power, which might impair his relations with his advisers and even create a permanent rift with those who feel resentful that the chief has devalued their judgment. After one traumatic experience of this type, a chief executive might thereafter attend all meetings and try to steer his advisers in the direction he wants them to go.

IX

Organizational Assessment and Change

Introduction. In recent years, numerous authors have argued that adapting to change may be the most significant problem facing organizations today (e.g., Daniel Bell, 1973; Peter Drucker, 1968; and Warren Bennis, 1969). Some of these changes include major economic, political, and technological factors, as well as the associated psychological dimensions of values, motives, and interpersonal relations between men and women, minorities and middle-class whites, and workers and employers. In fact, some writers (Kranzberg and Geis, Chapter 1, 1975; Ogburn, 1979) describe the period from the Industrial Revolution to modern times as a series of cycles initiated by the introduction of technological, economic, and/or political changes having major impacts on the organization of work (e.g., the introduction of the modern factory system in 18th-century England). These changes have then resulted in profound social and psychological disruptions such as the breakdown of the worker's family life and feelings of anomie, leading in turn to government regulation such as child labor and worker health and safety laws in an attempt to ameliorate these disruptions. This process can best be described as one of action and reaction between organizations and various parts of society. The alternative, of course, is a proactive approach in which organizations assess environmental demands and internal resources and then make planned responses to current and anticipated changes.

Unfortunately, it has been only in the last twenty years that the knowledge base in I/O psychology has reached the level of complexity and sophistication necessary to aid organizations in their planned responses to such environmental changes. The first major step was the development of a broad conceptual framework for understanding how organizations interact with their environments. This step has come to be known as the "open systems concept," and it is elaborated in the third reading in this section, "Organizations and the System Concept" by Katz and Kahn (originally published in 1966 and revised in 1978 edition). The "systems" concept has led to a general view that organizations are most effective when they

533

have the capacity to innovate—that is, to make decisions that increase the organization's ability to adapt to changing conditions. The "open system" presented by Katz and Kahn describes the relationship between organizations and their environments. In an "open system," "inputs" to the organization from the environment are "transformed" into products and exported to the environment as "output" resulting in further changes in the environment. "Feedback" about those changes is then cycled back to the organization at the "input" phase. The most important concepts are "transformation" and "feedback," because the former process embodies the planning and decision making capacities of the organization and the latter process enables the organization to resist a tendency for all systems to move toward disintegration by making use of information that enables the system to correct for its own breakdowns and for changes in the environment. In this way, organizations can reach a "steady-state" relative to the environment and make effective planned transactions with the environment such that the organization remains on a relatively even "keel" with respect to its own growth, differentiation, and response to environmental changes.

I/O psychology has come to view organizations operating as "open systems" as having "innovative capacity," which is primarily a function of the organization's human resources. Rensis Likert, in his article, "Measuring Organizational Performance," which is the first selection of this section, addresses the definition, assessment, and development of such human resources within an organization characterized as an "open system." Likert was clearly one of the early pioneers in the specialty within I/O psychology that focuses on systematic assessment and planned change in organizations. In particular, Likert raises the question of whether or not top management's emphasis on a rapid return on investment may encourage division managers to emphasize earnings and cost reductions at the expense of the organization's human assets. The traditional view, which focuses assessment on end results and outputs, is criticized as limited and typical of "closed system thinking." According to Likert, if the real innovative capacity of the organization is to be improved, then organizations must focus on what Likert terms "intervening factors." These factors include characteristics of individuals in the organization, such as responsibility, skill, motivation and the capacity for effective interaction, communication, and decision making. These are the key factors that transform the resources available at the input phase into quality resources the organization puts back into the environment. Once the basic theoretical framework is set forth, Likert presents a series of rather convincing studies showing that increases in the retention and capacity of these human factors have direct results in terms of organizational outputs and productivity.

Robert Blake is also considered one of the early pioneers in this area, and the second selection describes the approach of Blake and his colleague, Jane Mouton, in their article, "Grid Organization Development." The Grid approach was one of the first large-scale and systematic approaches to organizational assessment and change, and it is used widely today in many organizations after a 20-year history of implementation and testing. These authors characterize their approach as "organization development," a term encompassing the complimentary processes of diagnosis, implementation, and assessment of results. The Grid program is aimed at management development and training. Executives are taught how to diagnose their current management style and its effectiveness. Then, they are taught a more effective leadership style. This optimum management style involves a high concern for people with an equally high concern for task production (see also Section VII on Leadership). Following the training, the manager's effectiveness in his or her "home" organization is evaluated. The article thus describes a step-by-step approach involving the assessment of organizational problems, the training of managers in the concepts and techniques of the Grid, and the final evaluation of the manager's effectiveness. Like Likert, the primary focus is on the development of the human potential required to transform resources at input to high quality products at output.

The last selection acknowledges the proliferation of organizational assessment and change models since 1960 and the resultant need for some way of classifying the models and comparing their relative potential for producing effective planned change. Sashkin, Morris, and Horst, in the last article in this section, "A Comparison of Social and Organizational Change Models: Information Flow and Data Use Processes," do a comparative analysis of five "classic" models of social and organizational change by examining the generation and flow of change-related information. The five models considered are: Research, Development and Diffusion; Social Interaction and Diffusion; Intervention Theory and Method; Planned Change; and Action Research. For each model, the major theoretical assumptions and the key questions and issues with which their approach attempts to deal are outlined, examples of the model's use in studies on organizational assessment and change are provided, and finally, major problems with the approach are identified. Most interestingly, the authors develop a general framework based on open systems theory that can be used to compare the relative effectiveness of each model in enabling organizations to make effective plans for dealing with the rapid pace of contemporary social and organizational change.

Before reading the actual selections, the reader should note that systematic knowledge about organizational assessment, change, and development is relatively new within I/O psychology and certainly promises to be one of the major new directions of the field. It is precisely because "organization development" is so new that it has been particularly difficult to identify true classics in the field. Nonetheless, the relatively small set of selected articles are representative of the current state of knowledge and its historical origins because they provide a description of the early conceptions of how organizations effectively respond to a changing environment and they identify the major behavioral science approaches to systematic social and organizational change.

REFERENCES

Bell, D. 1973. *The coming of post-industrial society: A venture in social forecasting.* New York: Basic Books, Inc.

Bennis, W. G. 1969. *Organization development: Its nature, origins, and prospects.* Reading, MA: Addison-Wesley.

Drucker, P. F. 1969. *The age of discontinuity: Guidelines to our changing society.* New York: Harper & Row.

Kranzberg, M. and Geis, J. 1975. *By the sweat of thy brow: Work in the western world.* New York: G. P. Putnam's Sons.

Ogburn, W. F. 1979. Technology as environment. In Burke, J. G. & Eakin, M. C. *Technology as change.* San Francisco: Boyd & Fraser Publishing Company.

39. Measuring Organizational Performance*

RENSIS LIKERT

• Does top management's emphasis on immediate earnings, production, cost reduction, and similar measures of end results encourage division managers to dissipate the organization's human assets?

• What measurable changes occur in the productivity, loyalty, attitudes, and satisfactions of an organization where decision levels are pushed down and group methods of leadership are employed? What measurable changes occur in an organization where decision levels are pushed upward and close control is exercised at the top? How do the results of each type of management compare in the short and long run?

• What qualities of an organization can and should be measured for the purposes

of appraising the leadership of division managers and others to whom authority is delegated?

Decentralization and delegation are powerful concepts based on sound theory. But there is evidence that, as now utilized, they have a serious vulnerability which can be costly. This vulnerability arises from the measurements being used to evaluate and reward the performance of those given authority over decentralized operations.

This situation is becoming worse. While companies have during the past decade made greater use of work measurements and measurements of end results in evaluating managers, and also greater use of incentive pay in rewarding them, only a few managements have regularly used measurements that deal directly with the human assets of the organization—for example, measurements of loyalty, motivation, confidence, and trust. As a consequence, many companies today are encouraging managers of departments and divisions to dissipate valuable human assets of the organization. In fact, they are rewarding these managers well for doing so!

NEW MEASURES NEEDED

The advocates of decentralization recognize that measurements play a particularly important function. Ralph J. Cordiner, one of the most articulate spokesmen, has stated his views on the question as follows:

> Like many other companies, General Electric has long felt a need for more exact measurements and standards of performance, not only to evaluate past results, but to provide a more accurate means for planning future activities and calculating business risks. The traditional measures of profits such as return on investment, turnover, and percentage of net earnings to sales provide useful information. But they are hopelessly inadequate as measures to guide the manager's effectiveness in planning for the future of the business—the area where his decisions have the most important effects.
>
> When General Electric undertook the thorough decentralization. . . , the need for more realistic and balanced measurements became visibly more acute. For with the decentralization of operating responsibility and authority to more than a hundred local managerial teams, there was a need for common means of measuring these diverse business operations as to their short-range and long-range effectiveness. . . .
>
> It was felt that, if a system of simple, common measurements could be devised, they would have these important values. . . .
>
> 1. Common measurements would provide all the managers of each component, and the individual contributors in the component, with means to measure and plan their own performance, so that their individual decisions could be made on the basis of knowledge and informed judgment.
>
> 2. Common measurements would provide each manager with a way of detecting deviations from established standards in time to do something about it—the feedback idea, in which current operations themselves provide a means of continuous adjustment of the operation.
>
> 3. Common measurements would provide a means of appraisal, selection, and compensation of men on the basis of objective performance rather than personality judgments, which is better for both the individual and the Company.
>
> 4. Common measurements would provide an important motivation for better performance, since they made clear on what basis the individual is to be measured and give him a way of measuring his own effectiveness.
>
> 5. Common measurements would simplify communications by providing common concepts and common language with which to think and talk about the business, especially in its quantitative aspects.
>
> You will notice that all these points are directed at helping each decentralized manager and individual contributor measure and guide his own work, through self-discipline; they are not designed as a way for others to 'second-guess' the manager of a component or the workers in his component. When measurements are designed primarily for the 'boss' rather than for the man himself, they tend to lose their objectivity and frequently become instruments of deception.
>
> An adequate system of common measurements, moreover, would have the additional advantage of providing the company's executives with a way of evaluating performance in some hundred different businesses without becoming involved in the operational details of each of them.[1]

TRADITIONAL THEORY

These specifications point to serious inadequacies in the measurements now being obtained. Virtually all companies regularly secure measurements which deal with such end results as production, sales, profits, and percentage of net earnings to sales. The accounting procedures of most companies also reflect fairly well the level of inventories, the investment in plant and equipment, and the condition of plant and equipment.

But much less attention is given to what might be called "intervening factors," which significantly influence the end results just mentioned. These factors include such qualities of the human organization that staffs the plant as its loyalty, skills, motivations, and capacity for effective interaction, communication, and decision making. At present there is not one company, to my knowledge, that regularly obtains measurements which adequately and accurately reflect the quality and capacity of its human organization. (But in two companies experimental programs are underway to develop measurements of this kind.)

There are two principal reasons for this situation: (1) The traditional theory of management, which dominates current concepts as to what should be measured, largely ignores motivational and other human behavior variables. (2) Until recently the social sciences were not developed enough to provide methods for measuring the quality of the human organization.

The traditional theory of management is based on scientific management, cost accounting and related developments, and general administrative concepts taken from military organizational theory. As a consequence, it calls for measurements that are concerned with such end result variables as profits and costs, or with such process variables as productivity.

Substantial research findings show, however, that the managers in business and government who are getting the best results are systematically deviating from this traditional theory in the operating procedures which they use.[2] The general pattern of these deviations is to give much more attention to motivation than the traditional theory calls

for. High-producing managers are not neglecting such tools and resources provided by scientific management as cost accounting; quite to the contrary, they use them fully. But they use these quantitative tools in special ways—ways that achieve significantly higher motivation than is obtained by those managers who adhere strictly to the methods specified by the traditional theory of management.

MODIFIED THEORY

The exact principles and practices of high-producing managers have been integrated into a modified theory of management, which has been discussed elsewhere.[3] What I am interested in discussing here are the implications of this modified theory for control. Management needs to make extensive changes in the measurements now being obtained. It should take into account such factors as the levels of confidence and trust, motivation, and loyalty, and the capacity of the organization to communicate fully, to interact effectively, and to achieve sound decisions.

It is important for all companies to obtain these new kinds of measurements to guide their operations, but it is especially important for companies making extensive use of decentralization to do so. The logic of decentralization and the underlying theory on which it is based point to the need for this. In the absence of the new measurements, as we shall see presently, many managers are enabled and may even be encouraged to behave in ways which violate the logic of decentralization and which run contrary to the best interests of their companies.

It is easy to see why. Managers, like all human beings, guide their behavior by the information available to them. The measurements which a company provides them as a basis for decision making are particularly important. They are used by top management not only to judge the performance of departmental and division heads but also, through promotions, bonus compensation, and similar devices, to reward them. If the measurements which companies use for these purposes ignore the quality of the human organization and deal primarily with earnings, production, costs, and similar end results, managers will be encouraged to make a favorable showing on those factors alone.

MANAGEMENT & PRODUCTIVITY

Let us examine the evidence for these statements. A central concept of the modified theory is (1) that the pattern of interaction between the manager and those with whom he deals should always be such that the individuals involved will feel that the manager is dealing with them in a supportive rather than a threatening manner. A related concept is (2) that management will make full use of the potential capacities of its human resources only when each person in an organization is a member of a well-knit and effectively functioning work group with high interaction skills and performance goals.

A test of these concepts, and thereby of the modified theory, was made recently using attitudinal and motivational data collected in 1955 in a study done by the Institute for Social Research, University of Michigan:

Data are from a company that operates nationally. The company comprises 32 geographically separated units, varying in size from about 15 to over 50 employees, which perform essentially the same operations, and for which extensive productivity and cost figures are available continuously.

A single score was computed for the manager in charge of each of the 32 units. These scores, based on seven questions in the managers' questionnaire, measure the manager's attitude on the two concepts which represent the modified theory. These two concepts were found to be highly related, and consequently have been handled in the analysis as a single combined score—labeled, for convenient reference, attitude toward men. The results obtained are shown in Exhibit I.

This study demonstrates clearly that

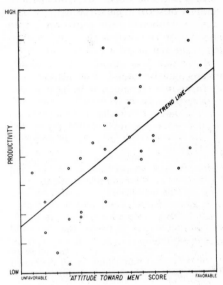

Exhibit i. Relationship of attitude toward men score of manager to unit's productivity

those managers who, as revealed in their questionnaires, have a favorable attitude toward men score achieve significantly higher performance than those managers who have an unfavorable score. Managers who have a supportive attitude toward their men and endeavor to build them into well-knit teams obtain appreciably higher productivity than managers who have a threatening attitude and rely more on man-to-man patterns of supervision. (The correlation coefficient is 0.64.)

Information obtained from the non-supervisory employees under these managers confirms the supervisory pattern reported by the managers. The material from the employees also confirms the character of the important intervening human variables contributing to the better productivity of the high-performance units. The men in those units in which the manager has an above-average attitude toward men score differ in their descriptions of their supervision and experience from the men in units whose managers are below average in their *attitude toward men* score. More specifically, the men in units whose managers had a favorable *attitude toward men* score are more likely than the men in the other units to indicate that:

(1) The supervision of their unit is of a supportive character. This involves such supervisory behavior as being more interested in the men, friendlier, more willing to go to bat for them, and being less threatening, less punitive, less critical, and less strict (but still have high performance expectations).

(2) There is more team spirit, group loyalty, and teamwork among the men and between the men and management.

(3) The men have more confidence and trust in management and have higher motivation. Moreover, there is better communication between the men and management.

(4) The men work under less sense of pressure, feel much freer to set their own work pace, and yet produce more.

The findings from this study are consistent with the results obtained in a number of other studies in widely different industries.[4] These other studies have also yielded evidence showing important differences in the way the managers of high- and low-producing units conceive of their job and deal with their subordinates:

• The units achieving the best performance are much more likely than the poor performance units to have managers who deal with their subordinates in a supportive manner and build high group loyalty and teamwork.

• The poor performance units are much more likely than the best units to have managers who press for production and treat their subordinates as "cogs in a machine."

• The supportive managers tend to supervise by establishing goals and objectives for their subordinates; in contrast, the pressure-oriented managers tend to focus on the processes they want their employees to carry out in order to achieve the objectives of the manager.

DANGERS OF PRESSURE

These research findings, therefore, provide a pattern of results which confirms central concepts of the modified theory of management. These results demonstrate that, on the average, *pressure-oriented, threatening, punitive management yields lower productivity, higher costs, increased absence, and less employee satisfaction than supportive, employee-centered management which uses group methods of supervision coupled with high-performance expectations.*

Since the supportive pattern of supervision tends to yield the best results, clearly this is the pattern which boards of directors and top company officials should foster in all situations including those that involve decentralization and delegation. Company officers believe, no doubt, that they are achieving this pattern of management in their operations. But, unfortunately, the performance measurements now being used by most top managements put pressures on lower levels of management to behave otherwise.

What often confuses the situation is that pressure-oriented, threatening supervision can achieve impressive *short-run* results, particularly when coupled with high technical competence. There is clear-cut evidence that for a period of at least one year supervision which increases the direct pressure for productivity can achieve significant increases in production. However, such increases are obtained only at a substantial and serious cost to the organization.

TESTING PERFORMANCE

To what extent can a manager make an impressive earnings record over a short-run period of one to three years by exploiting the company's investment in the human organization in his plant or department? To what extent will the quality of his organization suffer if he does so?

CONTRASTING PROGRAMS

On this further question, we also have some concrete evidence from an important study conducted by the Institute for Social Research in a large multidivision corporation:

The study covered 500 clerical employees in four parallel divisions. Each division was organized in the same way, used the same technology, did exactly the same kind of work, and had employees of comparable aptitudes.

Productivity in all four of the divisions depended on the number of clerks involved. The work was something like a billing operation; there was just so much of it, but it had to be processed as it came along. Consequently, the only way in which productivity could be increased under the existing organization was to change the size of the work group.

The four divisions were assigned to two experimental programs on a random basis. Each program was assigned at random a division that had been historically high in productivity and a division that had been below average in productivity. No attempt was made to place a division in that program which would best fit its habitual methods of supervision used by the manager, assistant managers, supervisors, and assistant supervisors.

The experiment at the clerical level lasted for one year. Beforehand, several months were devoted to planning, and there was also a training period of approximately six months. Productivity was measured continuously and computed weekly throughout the year. Employee and supervisory attitudes and related variables were measured just before and after the period.

Turning now to the heart of the study, in two divisions an attempt was made to change the supervision so that the decision levels were pushed *down*. More *general* supervision of the clerks and their supervisors was introduced. In addition, the managers, assistant managers, supervisors, and assistant supervisors of these two divisions were trained in group methods of leadership, which they endeavored to use as much as their skill would permit during the experimental year. (To this end we made liberal use of methods developed by the National Training Laboratory in Group

Development). For easy reference, the experimental changes in these two divisions will be labeled the "participative program."

In the other two divisions, by contrast, the program called for modifying the supervision so as to increase the closeness of supervision and move the decision levels *upward*. This will be labeled the "hierarchically controlled program." These changes were accomplished by a further extension of the scientific management approach. For example, one of the major changes made was to have the jobs timed by the methods department and to have standard times computed. This showed that these divisions were overstaffed by about 30 percent. The general manager then ordered the managers of these two divisions to cut staff by 25 percent. This was to be done by transfers without replacing the persons who left; no one was to be dismissed.

As a check on how effectively these policies were carried out, measurements were obtained for each division as to where decisions were made. One set of these measurements was obtained before the experimental year started, and the second set was obtained after the completion of the year. The attempts to change the level at which decisions were made were successful enough to develop measurable differences. In the hierarchically controlled program a significant shift upward occurred; by contrast, a significant shift downward occurred in the levels at which decisions were made in the participative program. Also, in the participative program there was an increase in the use of participation and in the extent to which employees were involved in decisions affecting them.

CHANGES IN PRODUCTIVITY

Exhibit II shows the changes in salary costs per unit of work, which reflect the changes in productivity that occurred in the divisions. As will be observed, the hierarchically controlled program increased productivity by about 25 percent. This was a result of the direct orders from the general manager to reduce staff by that amount. Direct pressure produced a substantial increase in production.

A significant increase in productivity

EXHIBIT II. CHANGES IN PRODUCTIVITY

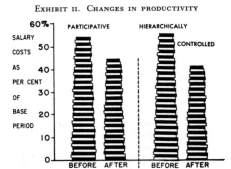

of 20 percent was also achieved in the participative program, but this was not so great an increase as in the hierarchically controlled program. To bring about this improvement, the clerks themselves participated in the decision to reduce the size of the work group. (They were aware, of course, that productivity increases were sought by management in making these experiments.) Obviously, deciding to reduce the size of a work group by eliminating some of its members is probably one of the most difficult decisions for a work group to make. Yet the clerks made it. In fact, one division in the participative program increased its productivity by about the same amount as each of the two divisions in the hierarchically controlled program. The other participative division, which historically had been the poorest of all of the divisions, did not do so well and increased productivity by only about 15 percent.

CHANGES IN ATTITUDES

Although both programs had similar effects on productivity, they had significantly different results in other respects. The productivity increases in the hierarchically controlled program were accompanied by shifts in an *adverse* direction in such factors as loyalty, attitudes, interest, and involvement in the work. But just the opposite was true in the participative program.

For example, Exhibit III shows that

when more general supervision and increased participation were provided, the employees' feeling of responsibility to see that the work got done increased. Again, when the supervisor was away, they kept on working. In the hierarchically controlled program, however, the feeling of responsibility decreased, and when the supervisor was absent, the work tended to stop.

EXHIBIT III. EMPLOYEES' FEELING OF RESPONSIBILITY TO SEE THAT WORK GETS DONE

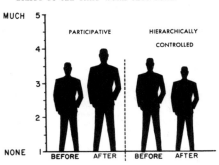

Another measurement of the extent to which an employee feels involved in his work is his attitude toward workers who are high producers. The changes in attitudes toward the high producer by the employees in the two programs are shown in Exhibit IV. Here again there was a statistically significant shift in opposite directions. In the participative

EXHIBIT IV. EMPLOYEE ATTITUDES TOWARD HIGH PRODUCER

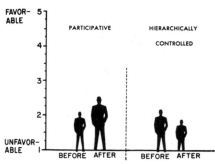

program the attitudes became more favorable, and there was less pressure to restrict production. In the hierarchically controlled program the opposite effect occurred.

In industrial organizations that are effective in achieving their objectives, extensive research in a variety of organizations shows that superiors and subordinates are linked by loyalty, a mutual feeling of understanding and closeness, and a feeling that influence and communication (both upward and downward) function well.[5] How are these attitudes and feelings achieved? Our study of the four divisions throws some light on the answer.

As Exhibit V shows, the employees in the participative program at the end of the year felt that their manager and assistant manager were "closer to them" than at the beginning of the year. The opposite was true in the hierarchically controlled program. Moreover, as Exhibit VI shows, employees in the participative program felt that their superiors were more likely to "pull" for them, or for the company *and* them, and not be solely interested in the company; while in the hierarchically controlled program, the opposite trend occurred.

EXHIBIT V. HOW CLOSE MANAGER AND ASSISTANT MANAGER WERE FELT TO BE TO EMPLOYEES

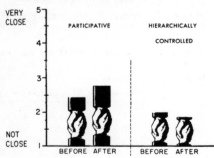

As might be expected from these trends, a marked shift in opposite directions showed up during the year in the employees' feeling of satisfaction with

EXHIBIT VI. EMPLOYEE OPINIONS AS TO EXTENT TO WHICH SUPERIORS "PULLED" FOR COMPANY ONLY OR FOR EMPLOYEES AND COMPANY

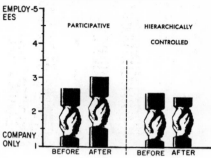

their superiors. Exhibit VII shows the shifts in employees' feelings as to how well their superiors communicated upward and influenced management on matters which concerned them. Once again the participative program showed up better than the hierarchically controlled program. One significant aspect of the changes in attitude in the hierarchically controlled program was that the employees felt that their superiors were relying more at the end of the year on rank and authority to get the work done than was the case at the beginning of the year. "Pulling rank" tends to become self-defeating in the long run because of the hostilities and counterpressures it evokes.

The deterioration under the hierarchically controlled program showed up in several other ways. For instance, turnover increased. Employees began to quit because of what they felt to be excessive pressure for production. As a consequence, the company felt it desirable to lessen the pressure. This happened toward the end of the experimental year.

Unfortunately, it was not possible to conduct the participative and hierarchically controlled programs for more than one year because of changes in the over-all operations of the company. However, the significant trends in opposite directions which occurred in these two programs are the trends which

Exhibit vii. Employees' satisfaction with superiors as representatives

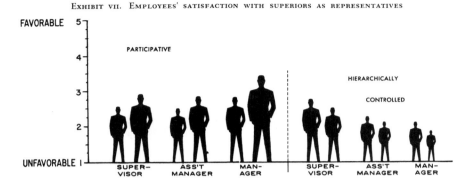

Left figure in each pair = BEFORE
Right figure in each pair = AFTER

would be expected in the light of the studies cited earlier in the article. The attitudes which improved the most in the participative program and deteriorated the most in the hierarchically controlled program are those which these studies have consistently shown to be most closely related *in the long run* to employee motivation and productivity. This gives us every reason to believe that had the clerical experiment been continued for another year or two, productivity and quality of work would have continued to increase in the participative program, while in the hierarchically controlled program productivity and quality of work would have declined.

IMPLICATIONS FOR POLICY

What are the implications of all this for management policy—particularly in the company that is decentralizing its operations or otherwise delegating a good deal of authority to various managers?

TREATMENT OF HUMAN ASSETS

To begin with, most executives will readily agree that it costs money to hire and train personnel. And, after personnel have been hired and trained, it takes additional time and money to build them into a loyal, well-knit effectively

functioning organization with well-established goals. Most businessmen will also agree with the research findings which show that the more supportive the supervision and the better the organization (in terms of loyalty, level of performance goals, communication, motivation, and so forth), the greater is its capacity for high-quality performance at low cost.

If we make these assumptions, we can come, I believe, to only one conclusion. As was demonstrated in the hierarchically controlled program of the experiment, putting pressure on a well-established organization to produce can yield substantial and immediate increases in productivity. *This increase is obtained, however, at a cost to the human assets of the organization.* In the company we studied, for example, the cost was clear: hostilities increased, there was greater reliance upon authority, loyalties declined, and motivations to produce decreased while motivations to restrict production increased. In other words, the quality of the human organization deteriorated as a functioning social system.

If the company had had an accounting procedure which showed the investment in the human organization, it would have shown that in the two divisions in the hierarchically controlled program the value of the human organization was less at the end of the experimental year than at the beginning. In other words, some of the increased productivity was achieved actually by liquidating part of the investment which the company had in the human organization in these divisions. The increase in productivity should have been charged with this cost.

On the other hand, had the company's accounting records reflected the value of the company's investment in the human organization in the two divisions in the participative program, they would have shown an opposite picture. During the year, the value of this investment increased. The management of the two divisions had been of such a character as to increase the productive capacity of the organization as a functioning social system: loyalties had increased, hostilities had decreased, communication was improved, decisions were better since they were based on more accurate and adequate information, and production goals and motivations to produce were increasing.

While a company's investment in its human organization is less tangible than the investment in plant and equipment, and therefore has not yet been given the kind of evaluation an accountant would give it, it can be measured approximately with the methods now available. These methods can enable management to size up present trends, analyze their relationships, and guide company operations accordingly.

QUANTITATIVE CONTROLS

Companies are very careful not to let managers of decentralized plants show spurious profits and earnings by juggling inventory or by failing to maintain plant and equipment. Their accounting procedures measure and report regularly on inventory and condition of plant and equipment. "Earnings" achieved by liquidating the assets represented in the human organization are just as spurious as though achieved by liquidating the

investment in plant. Yet they are encouraged by compensation formulas that urge managers to press unduly for immediate production, cost reduction, and similar goals; by the present-day emphasis on measuring only the end results of the activities of the lower echelons or of decentralized operations; and by job evaluations focused on the immediate contribution to earnings and profits.

In the long run, of course, such measurements are valid. The executive who "milks the human franchise" today will not be in a position to show good profit-and-loss figures tomorrow. The catch is that, by the time the symptoms of trouble are clear, the human organization has deteriorated to a point where steps to correct it are difficult and costly. As a practical matter, moreover, there is often so much rotation in executive responsibilities, and so much change in the conditions of business, that short-run tests which will provide adequate measures of current performance, including trends in the human organization, are worth much more than long-run evaluations.

There is only one solution to this problem, and it does not yet lie in more precise accounting data. The solution is to obtain adequate periodic measurements of the character and the quality of the human organization. Judgment alone is notoriously inaccurate and tends to be most inaccurate in those situations which are unsatisfactory or deteriorating. Measurements and compensation formulas are needed which will penalize managers financially and otherwise when they permit the quality of the human organization under them to deteriorate, and reward them when they improve the quality of this organization.

Identically the same point can be made with regard to consumer attitudes, good will, and confidence in the company, in its products, and in its service. A manager of a decentralized operation can substantially increase current earnings by reducing the product quality with low-cost, shoddy output. However, the immediate earnings shown on the company books would be spurious and would actually represent a substantial liquidation of the investment made in developing consumer confidence and acceptance. Therefore, periodic measurements of consumer perceptions, attitudes, and acceptance should be made not only for the usual purposes, such as to provide directions in product development and to guide advertising and marketing, but also to protect the company's investment in consumer good will.

ADEQUATE APPRAISALS

It is not sufficient merely to measure morale and the attitudes of employees toward the organization, their supervision, and their work. Favorable attitudes and excellent morale do not necessarily assure high motivation, high performance, and an effective human organization. A good deal of research indicates that this relationship is much too simple. Favorable attitudes may be found, for example, in situations where there is complacency and general contentment but where production goals are low and there is little motivation to achieve high performance.

Similarly, measurements of behavior which reflect the past condition of the human organization, while useful, are also inadequate for current appraisals. Such measurements as absence, turnover, and scrap loss tend not only to be insensitive measurements but also to reflect changes in the human organization *after* they have become substantial. More sensitive and more current measurements than those are needed.

Progress in the social sciences in recent years enables any company which so desires to obtain measurements needed for adequate appraisals of the quality and performance capacity of its human organization. Instruments to measure many of the important vari-

ables are now available; for those variables for which measuring instruments are not now available, the basic methodology now exists to develop the necessary tools. The organization for which these measurements are obtained can be an entire corporation or any of its divisions.

The following illustrate the kinds of variables which are now being measured in some companies or for which satisfactory measuring instruments can be developed:

1. Extent of loyalty to and identification with the institution and its objectives.

2. Extent to which members of the organization at all hierarchical levels feel that the organization's goals are consistent with their own needs and goals, and that the achievement of the company's goals will help them achieve their own.

3. Extent to which the goals of units and of individuals are of a character to enable the organization to achieve its objectives.

4. Level of motivation among members of the organization with regard to such variables as:

    a. Performance, including both quality and quantity of work done;

    b. Concern for elimination of waste and reduction of costs;

    c. Concern for improving product;

    d. Concern for improving processes.

5. Degree of confidence and trust among members of the organization in each other and in the different hierarchical levels.

6. Amount and quality of teamwork in each unit of the organization and between units.

7. Extent to which people feel delegation is being effectively achieved.

8. Extent to which members feel that their ideas, information, knowledge of processes, and experience are being used in the decision-making processes of the organization.

9. Level of competence and skill of different groups in the organization to interact effectively in solving problems and other tasks.

10. Efficiency and adequacy of the communication process upward, downward, sidewise.

11. Level of the leadership skills and abilities of supervisors and managers, in-

cluding their basic philosophy of management and orientation toward the processes of leadership.

12. Aptitude scores of the members of the organization. If aptitude scores are obtained as people join the organization, then trends in these scores will show whether the current management is improving the basic quality of the personnel through its hiring practices or is letting quality deteriorate through unfavorable turnover.

JOB FOR EXPERTS

The measurement of these variables is a complex process and requires a high level of scientific competence. It cannot be done by an untrained person, no matter how intelligent he is. Nor can it be done simply by asking people questions that have not been pretested or by handing them a ready-made questionnaire. Few companies trust cost figures obtained by inexperienced personnel. It is equally dangerous to trust the untrained to obtain measurements of the state of a human organization.

CONCLUSION

Industry needs more adequate measures of organizational performance than it is now getting. Progress in the social sciences now makes these measurements possible. As a consequence, new resources are available to assist company presidents in their responsibility for the successful management of their companies.

The president's responsibility requires that he build an organization whose structure, goals, levels of loyalty, motivation, interaction skills, and competence are such that the organization achieves its objectives effectively. As tools to assist him and the other members of management, a president needs a constant flow of measurements reporting on the state of the organization and the performance being achieved. The measurements proposed here would provide a president with data which he needs to fill the current serious gap in the information coming to him and to his organization.

NOTES

1. Ralph J. Cordiner, *New Frontiers for Professional Managers* (New York, McGraw-Hill Book Company, Inc., 1956), pp. 95-98. This volume comprises the McKinsey Lectures, which Mr. Cordiner delivered in 1956 at the Graduate School of Business, Columbia University.

2. See, for example, R. Likert, "Motivational Dimensions of Administration," *America's Manpower Crisis* (Chicago, Public Administration Service, 1952), p. 89, and "Developing Patterns of Management," *General Management Series*, No. 178 (New York, American Management Association, 1955), pp. 32-51; and D. Katz and R. Kahn, "Human Organization and Worker Motivation," *Industrial Productivity*, edited by L. Reed Tripp (Madison, Industrial Relations Research Association, 1952), p. 146.

3. R. Likert, "Developing Patterns of Management: II," *General Management Series*, No. 182 (New York, American Management Association, 1956), pp. 3-29.

4. R. Kahn, "The Prediction of Productivity," *Journal of Social Issues*, Vol. 12, No. 2, 1956, p. 41. D. Katz, N. Maccoby, G. Gurin, and L. G. Floor, "Productivity, Supervision and Morale among Railroad Workers," *SRC Monograph Series No. 5* (Ann Arbor, Institute for Social Research, 1951). D. Katz, N. Maccoby, and N. Morse, "Productivity, Supervision and Morale in an Office Situation," *SRC Monograph Series No. 2* (Ann Arbor, Institute for Social Research, 1950). R. Likert, "Motivation: The Core of Management," *Personnel Series A155* (New York, American Management Association, 1953), pp. 3-21.

5. R. Kahn, F. Mann, and S. Seashore, Editors, "Human Relations Research in Large Organizations, II," *Journal of Social Issues*, Vol. 12, No. 2, 1956, p. 1. D. Katz and R. Kahn, "Some Recent Findings in Human Relations Research in Industry," *Readings in Social Psychology*, edited by E. Swanson, T. Newcomb, and E. Hartley (New York, Henry Holt and Company, 1952), p. 650.

40. Grid Organization Development*

ROBERT R. BLAKE
JANE S. MOUTON

Organizations are changing today, often dramatically. The changes are taking place in business organizations, in hospitals and institutions of various kinds, in local, state, and federal government bodies. Change in industrial organizations has been spurred by competition. New moves toward diversification of product lines have heightened change. Profit squeezes and steadily rising operating costs have stimulated it. Automation, computers, and improved methods of analysis have eroded the traditional ways of doing business. Efforts to capitalize on opportunities for moving into new forms of business have further energized change. In government, change has been spurred by the recognition of the need for efficiency in the use of tax dollars, by the emergence of new programs, and by demands for better management of programs. The public has demanded streamlining in government, the kind of change that makes for greater effectiveness.

All this has created new requirements for over-all effectiveness of organization. Yesterday's management practices are being challenged. New ways to achieve organization effectiveness are being pioneered and are having a wide impact on many segments of contemporary life.

BLUEPRINT FOR EFFECTIVENESS

Sound management can meet the challenge of change, even accelerate it.

But a blueprint is needed to describe an organization so well managed that it can grasp opportunity from the challenge of change. What would such an organization be like?

1. *Its objectives would be sound, strong, and clear.* Its leaders would know where it was headed and how to get there. Its objectives would also be understood and embraced by all members of the management body. These persons would strive to contribute because the organization's objectives and their own goals would be consistent. There would be a high level of commitment to organization goals as well as to personal goals. Commitment would be based on understanding. To be understood, goals would be quite specific.

Every business has as an objective "profit." But this is too vague to motivate persons to greater effectiveness. Profit needs to be converted into concrete objectives. One might be, "To develop a position in the plastic industry which will service 20 percent of this market within the next 5 years." In a government organization, a specific objective might be "To establish six urban renewal demonstration projects distributed by regions and by city size within 10 months." Government objectives would be implemented through program planning and budgeting rather than the profit motive.

2. *Standards of excellence would be high.* Managers would be thoroughly acquainted with their areas of operation. A premium would be placed on knowledge and thorough analysis rather than on opinion and casual thought.

3. *The work culture would support the work.* It would be an organization culture in which the members would be highly

*Source: From *Personnel Administration* (January-February 1967). Reprinted by permission of the International Personnel Management Association, 1850 K Street, N.W., Washington, DC 20006. Copyright © 1967 International Personnel Management Association.

committed to achieving the goals of the organization, with accomplishment at the source of individual gratification.

4. *Teamwork would increase individual initiative.* There would be close cooperation within a work team, each supporting the others to get a job done. Teamwork would cut across department lines.

5. *Technical business knowledge needed for valid decision-making and problem-solving would come through coaching, developmental assignments, on-the-job training, and special courses.*

6. *Leadership would be evident.* With sound objectives, high standards of excellence, a culture characterized by high commitment, sound teamwork, and technical know-how, productivity would increase.

The way of life or culture of an organization can be a barrier to effectiveness. Barriers may stem from such elements of culture as the attitudes or traditions present in any unit of the organization. Culture both limits and guides the actions of the persons in the organization. Because of traditional ways and fear of change, an organization's leaders may be reluctant to apply modern management science. Yet, the need for change may be quite evident.

CRITERIA FOR CHANGE

A sound approach to introducing change and improvement is an Organization Development effort. It should:

1. *Involve the widest possible participation of executives, managers, and supervisors* to obtain a common set of concepts about how management can be improved.

2. *Be carried out by the organization itself.* The development of subordinates is recognized as part of the manager's job. When organization members from the line become the instructors, higher management's commitment, understanding, and support for on-the-job application and change are insured.

3. *Aim to improve the skills of executives and supervisors who must work together to improve management*—the skills of drawing on each other's knowledge and capacities, of making constructive use of disagreement, and of making sound decisions to which members become committed.

4. *Aim to improve the ability of all*

managers to communicate better so that genuine understanding can prevail.

5. *Clarify styles of management* so that managers learn how the elements of a formal management program (e.g., planned objectives, defined responsibilities, established policies) can be used without the organization's becoming overly formal and complex or unduly restricting personal freedom and needed individual initiative.

6. *Aid each manager to investigate his managerial style* to understand its impact and learn to make changes to improve it.

7. *Provide for examination of the organization's culture* to develop managers' understanding of the cultural barriers to effectiveness and how to eliminate them.

8. *Constantly encourage managers to plan and introduce improvements* based on their learnings and analysis of the organization.

ONE WAY TO GET THERE

Grid Organization Development is one way of increasing the effectiveness of an organization, whether it is a company, a public institution, or a government agency. The behavioral science concepts on which Organization Development is based reach back more than 50 years. Because Organization Development itself is only a decade or so old, those unfamiliar with its rationale may look upon it with doubt or skepticism, see it as a mystery or a package, a gimmick or a fad. Experience pinpoints which behavioral science concepts are tied to the struggle for a more effective organization. This has done much to help managers apply the pertinent concepts to everyday work.

There are several questions preceding the definition of Organization Development as it is applied to raise an organization's capacity to operate by using behavioral science concepts. One question is, "What is an organization?" Another is, "What is meant by development?" Finally, "What is it that Organization Development adds to the organization, that it lacks without it?"

SEVEN PROPERTIES OF AN ORGANIZATION

Because an organization is a complex entity, definitions often lap over into the abstract, becoming too vague to be useful. A meaningful way to define an organization is to list its properties. Seven properties of an organization are: purpose, structure, wherewithal, know-how, human interaction, culture, and results. If any are missing, the entity termed an organization probably cannot truly qualify as such.

PURPOSE

Purpose is the unifying principle around which human energy clusters in the organization. It defines direction. Any decision made can be tested against purpose to see if it makes the organization more effective or less so. Purpose is more complex than such simple statements as "to realize a fair return on investment" would suggest. Rarely is such a statement specific enough to help an organization improve. To be useful, a statement of purpose must be specific and operational, clearly understandable, and able to provide a direction. It must be realistic and practical, acceptable and meaningful to those running the organization. It must arouse the motivation to move forward.

STRUCTURE

Every member of the organization is not expected to do all the kinds of work required within it. Instead, there is a division of labor. Related work is lumped under organizational units. A way to coordinate efforts between the units is determined. The structure of a large organization is subdivided into regions or functional activities. It may be further subdivided within each of these into departments, divisions, sections, or units of various kinds. These vary widely from one organization to the next and depend to a great extent on purpose. Small organizations are likely to have more simple structures. All organizations, regardless of size, contain elements of structure.

FINANCIAL RESOURCES

Present in every organization is a financial system enabling it to invest in new efforts or withdraw its investments from less successful activities. Financial resources are important. Without them the organization would not be able to carry out its activities.

KNOW-HOW

To carry out the purposes of the organization its members supply technical skills and competence—know-how. No matter how clearly defined, how realistic, and how sound an organization's purposes may be, if its leaders are not competent to see that the purposes are obtained, the organization will flounder.

HUMAN INTERACTION

The human interaction property of the organization exists because the persons manning it must of necessity interact. They must exchange information, implement decisions made, and coordinate their efforts.

ORGANIZATION CULTURE

In any organization, over a period of time, a set of practices builds up. A way of organizational life become accepted. A climate is created; established practices become traditional. Everyone in the organization is expected to conform. Nonconformists may be punished. The punishment varies in kind as well as in degree. Sometimes it is very subtle. It may simply take the form of isolation of the person deviating from established practice, the cultural norm.

RESULTS

A seventh property of every organization is the generation of results that are in some way measurable in terms of organization purpose. If results show a loss, the major reason for sustaining the organization is absent and bankruptcy may be expected. Unless it provides a useful service that is in the public interest, in time the organization will go out of existence.

If the conglomeration of persons and equipment is truly an organization, it will have a realistic *purpose* clearly understood by all to provide a direction to their efforts; a *structure* that provides the necessary coordination of interlocking parts; access to *financial resources* needed to support decisions that enable it to obtain its purposes; the necessary technical skill and *know-how* among its personnel; a *human interaction process* supporting sound decision-making with a minimum of waste; a *culture* thoroughly understood and controlled which is an asset and not a liability; and, finally, an ability to achieve *results* so as to be effective within the free enterprise objective of realizing an acceptable return on investments. Results may also be in the form of a service that is in the public interest.

THE MEANING OF DEVELOPMENT

Once the meaning of "organization" is clear, "development" needs to be clarified. What characterizes an organization that is fully developed? The biggest task of an organization is integration. As used in relation to an organization, integration denotes the highest degree of attainment of these seven properties that can be achieved. Many fall short in development of one or more. They experience an endless parade of trials and troubles, ups and downs, low morale, resistance to needed change, and disregard by members of the problem of achieving results. Such organizations can be described as poorly integrated, for they have not achieved integration of the properties of organization.

*The goal of Organization Development is to increase operational effectiveness by increasing the degree of integration of the seven properties of organization. Three of the seven prop-*erties are critical for development. They are purpose, human interaction, and organization culture. The others are more likely to be under managerial control and less likely to need attention through an Organization Development effort. It is not that one property is less important than the others, but that organizations usually insure the presence of the other four, whereas purpose, human interaction, and culture receive less attention.

It seems almost self-evident that everyone in an organization would have a clear idea of the *purpose* toward which its efforts were being directed. Yet this is seldom true. For many persons, an organization's purpose is fuzzy, unrealistic, and with little force as a motivator. A major Organization Development contribution is to clarify organization purposes and identify individual goals with them to increase efforts toward their attainment.[1,2]

As for the *human interaction* process, some styles of managing may decrease a person's desire to contribute to the organization's purpose. The kind of supervision exercised not only fails to make a subordinate feel "in" but even serves to make him feel "out." His efforts are alienated rather than integrated. This may hold true in the coordination of efforts between organized units. Relationships between divisions, for example, may deteriorate into the kind of disputes that can be reconciled only through arbitration by higher levels of management. At best, they are likely to encourage attitudes of appeasement and compromise.[3]

Finally, the organization's *culture*, its history, its traditions, its customs and habits which have evolved from earlier interaction and have become norms regulating human actions and conduct may be responsible for many of the organization's difficulties and a low degree of integration within it.

The basic theme of Organization Development is that the key to organization integration lies within the three organization properties, *purpose, human* interaction process, and organization culture. The executive who is trying to ferret out the source of problems in his organization may look at other properties. He may look to structure as preventing integration of effort and search for ways to change the organization chart. Organization structure far more often turns out to be a symptom of the integration problem than its cause. Or the executive may look at technical skills and know-how as the area of difficulty and search for better trained personnel. This area of technical competence often turns out to be a blind alley in which much effort is spent tracking down a problem. Second-rate human performance may be widespread but is not likely to be the cause of ineffectiveness. Competence is often present but poorly utilized. Finally, he may seize upon the absence of positive results as a difficulty and jump into finding ways to achieve greater earnings by cutting costs, meanwhile oblivious to the possibility that the organization's troubles might be in its culture or the interaction process. The concentration upon results may also be treating the symptom rather than finding the causes of the problem, which are probably rigidities of interaction, lack of clarity of purpose, and low morale of organization members who feel "out" rather than identified with the organization.

Organization Development deliberately shifts the emphasis away from the organization's structure, from human technical skill, from wherewithal and results per se as it diagnoses the organization's ills. Focusing on organization purpose, the human interaction process, and organization culture, it accepts these as the areas in which problems are preventing the fullest possible integration within the organization. Once an organization has moved to the point at which the three key properties are fully developed, the problems that originally seemed to be related to the others are more easily corrected.

SIX-PHASE APPROACH

How, specifically, does one go about Organization Development? The Managerial Grid is one way of achieving it. The six-phase approach provides the various methods and activities for doing so.

The Managerial Grid is a description of various approaches men use in managing. It is used to summarize management practices and compare them with behavioral science findings. It identifies five kinds of managerial behavior based on two key variables—concern for results and concern for people. (See Exhibit 1.)

Phase 1 of the six-phase approach involves study of The Managerial Grid. Managers learn the Grid concepts in seminars of a week's length.

These seminars are conducted both on a "public" and on an internal basis. They involve hard work. The program requires 30 or more hours of guided study before the beginning of the seminar week. A seminar usually begins Sunday afternoon, and participants work morning, afternoon, and evening through the following Friday.

The sessions include investigation by each man of his own managerial approach and alternative ways of managing which he is able to learn, experiment with, and apply. He measures and evaluates his team effectiveness in solving problems with others. He also studies methods of team action. A high point of Grid Seminar learning is when he receives a critique of his style of managerial thought and performance from other members of his team. The emphasis is on his style of managing, not on his character or personality traits. Another high point of the Grid Seminar is when the manager critiques the style of his organization's culture—its traditions, precedents, and past practices—and begins to consider steps for increasing the effectiveness of the whole organization.

EXHIBIT 1
THE MANAGERIAL GRID

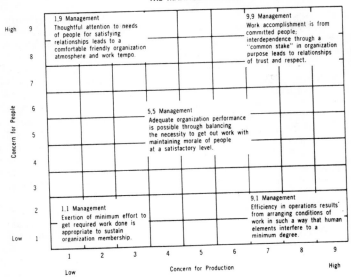

A participant in a Grid Seminar can expect to gain insight into his own and other managerial approaches and develop new ways to solve managerial problems. He can expect to improve his team effectiveness skills. He will on completion of Phase 1 have new standards of candor to bring to work activities and a greater awareness of the effects of his company's culture upon the regulation of work.

Comments are often heard to the effect, "The Grid has helped me to better understanding and is useful in many aspects of my life." But the vital question is in the use made of Phase 1 learning. The test for the manager is usefulness on the job. To direct this usefulness to the work situation, and incidentally enhance it from a personal point of view, one proceeds to Phase 2.

Phase 2 is Work Team Development. As the title suggests, work team development is concerned with development of the individual and the work team. Phases 1 and 2 are often viewed

as *management* development, while Phases 3 through 6 move into true *Organization* Development. The purpose of Phase 2 is to aid work team members to apply their Phase 1 learning directly to the operation of their team.

Individual effort is the raw material out of which sound teamwork is built. It cannot be had just for the asking. Barriers that prevent people from talking out their problems need to be overcome before their full potential can be realized.

Work Team Development starts with the key executive and those who report to him. It then moves down through the organization. Each supervisor sits down with his subordinates as a team. They study their barriers to work effectiveness and plan ways to overcome them.

An important result to be expected from the Phase 2 effort is teamwide agreement on ground rules for team operation. The team may also be expected to learn to use critique to improve teamwork on the job. Teamwork is increased through improving communication, control, and problem solving. Getting greater objectivity into work behavior is vital to improved teamwork. A team analysis of the team culture and operating practices precedes the setting of goals for improvement of the team operation along with a time schedule for achieving these goals. Tied into the goal-setting for the team is personal goal-setting by team members. This might be a goal for trying to change aspects of behavior so as to increase a member's contribution to teamwork. Setting standards for achieving excellence are involved throughout the process.

Phase 3 is Intergroup Development. It represents the first step in Grid OD that is applied to organization components rather than to individuals. Its purpose is to achieve *better problem-solving between groups through a closer integration of units that have working interrelationships.*

Managers examine and analyze these working relationships to strengthen and unify the organization across the board. Some dramatic examples of successful Phase 3 applications between labor and management groups are on record.[4] Other units that might appropriately be involved in Phase 3 would be a field unit and the headquarters group to whom it reports, or two sections within a division, or a region and its reporting parent group. It is the matter of coordination between such units that is the target of Phase 3. Problems of integration may be problems of function or merely problems in terms of level.

Management is inclined to solve the problem of functional coordination by setting up systems of reporting and centralized planning. Misunderstandings or disagreements between levels are often viewed as "a communications problem." Phase 3, in recognition that many problems are relationship problems, seeks closer integration of units through the exchange and comparison of group images as set forth by the members of

two groups. Areas of misunderstanding are identified while conditions are created to reduce such intergroup problems and plan steps of operational coordination between the groups. Only groups that stand in a direct, problem-solving relationship with one another and share a need for improved coordination participate in Phase 3 intergroup development. And only those members with key responsibilities for solving the coordination problem are participants.

The activities of Phase 3 naturally follow Phase 2 because when there is conflict between working teams, if the teams themselves have already had the opportunity to solve their internal problems, they are prepared to engage in activities designed to solve their problem of working together. Phase 3 also can be expected to clear the decks for Phases 4 and 5. Any past intergroup problems that were barriers to coordinated effort are solved before the total Organization Development effort is launched in the latter phases. A successful Phase 3 will link groups vertically and horizontally and reduce intergroup blockages. This increases the problem-solving between departments, divisions, and other segments wherever coordination of effort is a vital necessity. Persons who have participated in Phase 3 report improved intergroup relationships and express appreciation of the team management concept, pointing out that it reverses the traditional procedure in which criticism flows from one level of management down to the next.

Phase 4 calls for the Production of an Organization Blueprint. If Phases 1, 2, and 3 represent pruning the branches, Phase 4 gets at the root structure. A long-range blueprint is developed to insure that the basic strategies of the organization are "right." The immediate goal is to set up a model that is both realistic and obtainable for an organization's system for the future. How is this done? The existing corporate entity is momentarily set aside while an ideal concept is drawn up representing how it would be organized and operated if it were truly effective. The optimal organization blueprint is produced as a result of a policy diagnosis based on study of a model organization culture. The blueprint is drawn up by the top team and moves down through lower levels. The outcome is organization-wide understanding of the blueprint for the future.

It can be expected that as a result of Phase 4, the top team will have set a direction of performance goals to be achieved. Individuals and work teams will have developed understanding and commitment to both general and specific goals to be achieved.

Phase 5 is *Blueprint Implementation*. That is, Phase 5 is designed for the carrying out of the organizational plan through activities that change the organization from what it "is" to what it "should be." A Phase 5 may spread over several years, but as a result there comes about the effective realization of the goals that have been set in Phase 4 and specific accomplishments, depending on concrete issues facing the organization. During Phase 5, the members who are responsible for the organization achieve agreement and commitment to courses of action that represent steps to implement the Phase 4 blueprint for the future.

Phase 6 is *stabilization*. It is for reinforcing and making habitual the new patterns of management achieved in Phases 1 through 5. Organization members identify tendencies to slip back into

the older and less effective patterns of work and take corrective action. Phase 6 involves an over-all critique of the state of the OD effort for the purpose of replanning for even greater effectiveness. It is not only to support and strengthen the changes achieved through earlier activities, but also to identify weaknesses and plan ways of eliminating them. By the time Phase 6 is under way, the stabilization of new communication, control, and problem-solving approaches should be evident. Moreover, there should be complete managerial confidence and competence in resisting the pressures to revert to old managerial habits.

NOTES

1. "Breakthrough in Organization Development." Robert R. Blake, Jane S. Mouton, L. B. Barnes and L. E. Greiner, *Harvard Business Review*. Soldiers Field, Massachusetts; November-December 1964.

2. "Management Training for Organization Development." Bernard Portis, *The Business Quarterly*. London, Canada; Summer 1965.

3. *Managing Intergroup Conflict in Industry*. Robert R. Blake, Herbert A. Shepard, and Jane S. Mouton. Houston: Gulf Publishing Company; 1964.

4. Blake, R. R., Mouton, J. S., & Sloma, R. L., "The Union-Management Intergroup Laboratory." *Journal of Applied Behavioral Science*, Jan.-Mar. 1965.

41. Organizations and the System Concept*

DANIEL KATZ
ROBERT L. KAHN

The aims of social science with respect to human organizations are like those of any other science with respect to the events and phenomena of its domain. Social scientists wish to understand human organizations, to describe what is essential in their form, aspects, and functions. They wish to explain cycles of growth and decline, to predict organizational effects and effectiveness. Perhaps they wish as well to test and apply such knowledge by introducing purposeful changes into organizations—by making them, for example, more benign, more responsive to human needs.

Such efforts are not solely the prerogative of social science, however; common-sense approaches to understanding and altering organizations are ancient and perpetual. They tend, on the whole, to rely heavily on two assumptions: that the location and nature of an organization are given by its name; and that an organization is possessed of built-in goals—because such goals were implanted by its founders, decreed by its present leaders, or because they emerged mysteriously as the purposes of the organizational system itself. These assumptions scarcely provide an adequate basis for the study of organizations and at times can be misleading and even fallacious. We propose, however, to make use of the information to which they point.

THE DEFINITION AND IDENTIFICATION OF ORGANIZATIONS

The first problem in understanding an organization or a social system is its location and identification. How do we know that we are dealing with an organization? What are its boundaries? What behavior belongs to the organization and what behavior lies outside it? Who are the individuals whose actions are to be studied and what segments of their behavior are to be included?

The common-sense answer to such questions begins with the organizational name. The fact that popular names exist to label social organizations, however, is both a help and a hindrance. These labels represent socially accepted stereotypes about organizations and do not specify their role structure, their psychological nature, or their boundaries. On the other hand, these names help in locating the area of behavior in which we are interested. Moreover, the fact that people both within and without an organization accept stereotypes about its nature and functioning is one determinant of its character.

The second key characteristic of the common-sense approach to understanding an organization is to regard it simply as the epitome of the purposes of its designer, its leaders, or its key members. The teleology of this approach is again both a help and a hindrance. Since human purpose is deliberately built into organizations and is specifically recorded in the social compact, the by-laws, or other formal protocol of the undertaking, it would be inefficient not to utilize these sources of information. In the early development of a group, many processes are generated that have little to do with its rational purpose, but over time there is a cumulative recognition of the devices for ordering group life and a deliberate use of these devices.

Apart from formal protocol, the primary mission of an organization as perceived by its leaders furnishes a highly informative set of clues for the researcher seeking to study organizational functioning. Nevertheless, the stated purposes of an organization as given by its by-laws or in the reports of its leaders can be misleading. Such statements of objectives may idealize, rationalize, distort, omit, or even conceal some essential aspects of the functioning of the organization. Nor is there always agreement about the mission of the organization among its leaders and members. The university president may describe the purpose of the institution as turning out national leaders; the academic dean sees it as imparting the cultural heritage of the past, the academic vice-president as enabling students to move toward self-actualization and development, the graduate dean as creating new knowledge, the dean of students as training young people in technical and professional skills which will enable them to earn their living, and the editor of the student newspaper as inculcating the conservative values that will preserve the status quo of an outmoded capitalistic society.

The fallacy here is equating the purposes or goals of organizations with the purposes and goals of individual members. The organization as a system has an output, a product or an outcome, but this is not necessarily identical with the individual purposes of group members. Though the founders of the organization and its key members do think in teleological terms about organizational objectives, we should not accept such practical thinking, useful as it may be, in place of a theoretical set of constructs for purposes of scientific analysis. Social science, too frequently in the past, has been misled by such shortcuts and has equated popular phenomenology with scientific explanation.

In fact, the classic body of theory and thinking about organizations has assumed a teleology of this sort as the easiest way of identifying organizational structures and their functions. From this point of view an organization is a social device for efficiently accomplishing through group means some stated purpose; it is the equivalent of the blueprint for the design of a machine that is to be created for some practical objective. The essential difficulty with this purposive approach is that an organization characteristically includes more and less than is indicated by the design of its founder or the purpose of its leader. Some of the factors assumed in the design may be lacking or so distorted in operational practice as to be meaningless, while unforeseen embellishments dominate the organizational structure. Moreover, it is not always possible to ferret out the designers of the organization or to discover the intricacies of the design which they carried in their heads. The attempt by Merton (1957) to deal with the latent function of the organization in contrast with its manifest function is one way of dealing with this problem. The study of unanticipated consequences as well as anticipated consequences of organizational functioning is a similar way of handling the matter. Again, however, we are back to the purposes of the creators or leaders, dealing with unanticipated consequences on the assumption that we can discover the consequences anticipated by them and can lump all other outcomes together as a kind of error variance.

It would be much better theoretically,

however, to start with concepts that do not call for identifying the purposes of the designers and then correcting for them when they do not seem to be fulfilled. The theoretical concepts should begin with the input, output, and functioning of the organization as a system and not with the rational purposes of its leaders. We may want to employ such purposive notions to lead us to sources of data or as subjects of special study, but not as our basic theoretical constructs for understanding organizations.

Our theoretical model for the understanding of organizations is that of an energic input-output system in which the energic return from the output reactivates the system. Social organizations are flagrantly open systems in that the input of energies and the conversion of output into further energic input consist of transactions between the organization and its environment.

All social systems, including organizations, consist of the patterned activities of a number of individuals. Moreover, these patterned activities are complementary or interdependent with respect to some common output or outcome; they are repeated, relatively enduring, and bounded in space and time. If the activity pattern occurs only once or at unpredictable intervals, we could not speak of an organization. The stability or recurrence of activities can be examined in relation to the *energic input* into the system, the *transformation of energies within the system*, and the *resulting product or energic output*. In a factory the raw materials and the human labor are the energic input, the patterned activities of production the transformation of energy, and the finished product the output. To maintain this patterned activity requires a continued renewal of the inflow of energy. This is guaranteed in social systems by the energic return from the product or outcome. Thus the outcome of the cycle of activities furnishes new energy for the initiation of a renewed cycle. The company that produces automobiles sells

them and by doing so obtains the means of securing new raw materials, compensating its labor force, and continuing the activity pattern.

In many organizations outcomes are converted into money and new energy is furnished through this mechanism. Money is a convenient way of handling energy units both on the output and input sides, and buying and selling represent one set of social rules for regulating exchange. Indeed, these rules are so effective and so widespread that there is some danger of mistaking the business of buying and selling for the defining cycles of organization. It is a commonplace executive observation that businesses exist to make money, and the observation is usually allowed to go unchallenged. It is, however, a very limited statement about the purposes of business.

Some human organizations do not depend on the cycle of selling and buying to maintain themselves. Universities and public agencies depend rather on bequests and legislative appropriations, and in so-called voluntary organizations the output reenergizes the activity of organization members in a more direct fashion. Member activities and accomplishments are rewarding in themselves and tend therefore to be continued without the mediation of the outside environment. A society of bird watchers can wander into the hills and engage in the rewarding activities of identifying birds for their mutual edification and enjoyment. Organizations thus differ on this important dimension of the source of energy renewal, with the great majority utilizing both intrinsic and extrinsic sources in varying degree. Most large-scale organizations are not as self-contained as small voluntary groups and are very dependent upon the social effects of their output for energy renewal.

Our two basic criteria for identifying social systems and determining their functions are (1) tracing the pattern of energy exchange or activity of people as it results in some output and (2) ascertaining how the output is translated into energy that reactivates the pattern. We shall refer to organizational functions or objectives not as the conscious purposes of group leaders or group members but as the outcomes that are the energic source for maintenance of the same type of output.

The problem of identifying the boundaries of an organization is solved by following the energic and informational transactions as they relate to the cycle of activities of input, throughput, and output. Behavior not tied to these functions lies outside the system. Many factors are related to the intake of materials into a structure but only those activities concerned with the actual importation of energy or information are part of that structure. Similarly, many processes are associated with the reception of outputs by the environment, but only those activities having to do with export of products are behavioral patterns of the organization. Obviously there is less difficulty in identifying the patterns of behavior responsible for the throughput of the system than for the boundary subsystems that deal with the environment. These subsystems do not always have clearly identifiable borders. Nor can the problem be handled by regarding any behavior of an organizational member as organizational behavior. A person in a boundary role may interact with members of another system as if he or she belonged to that system. Even the production worker's behavior, although physically taking place within the factory, at times may be social interaction with friends unrelated to the work role. In searching for criteria to define the boundaries of a system one looks for some qualitative break in the nature of the behavior pattern under scrutiny or some sudden quantitative change. These changes can be noted as the same people step out of their organizational roles and behave in radically different fashion or as we move to different people operating in different role systems.

This model of an energic input-output system is taken from the open system theory as promulgated by von Bertalanffy (1956). Theorists have pointed out the applicability of the system concepts of the natural sciences to the problems of social science. It is important, therefore, to examine in more detail the constructs of system theory and the characteristics of open systems.

System theory is basically concerned with problems of relationships, of structure, and of interdependence rather than with the constant attributes of objects. In general approach it resembles field theory except that its dynamics deal with temporal as well as spatial patterns. Older formulations of system constructs dealt with the closed systems of the physical sciences, in which relatively self-contained structures could be treated successfully as if they were independent of external forces. But living systems, whether biological organisms or social organizations, are acutely dependent on their external environment and so must be conceived of as open systems.

Before the advent of open system thinking, social scientists tended to take one of two approaches in dealing with social structures; they tended either (1) to regard them as closed systems to which the laws of physics applied or (2) to endow them with some vitalistic concept like entelechy. In the former case they ignored the environmental forces affecting the organization and in the latter case they fell back upon some magical purposiveness to account for organizational functioning. Biological theorists, however, have rescued us from this trap by pointing out that the concept of the open system means that we neither have to follow the laws of traditional physics, nor in deserting them do we have to abandon science. The laws of Newtonian physics are correct generalizations but they are limited to closed systems. They do not apply in the same fashion to open systems which maintain themselves through constant commerce with their environment, that is, a continuous inflow and outflow of energy through permeable boundaries.

The essential difference between closed and open systems can be seen in terms of the concept of entropy and the second law of thermodynamics. According to the second law of thermodynamics, a system moves toward equilibrium; it tends to run down, that is, its differentiated structures tend to move toward dissolution as the elements composing them become arranged in random disorder. For example, suppose that a bar of iron has been heated by the application of a blowtorch on one side. The arrangement of all the fast (heated) molecules on one side and all the slow molecules on the other is an unstable state, and over time the distribution of molecules becomes in effect random, with the resultant cooling of one side and heating of the other, so that all surfaces of the iron approach the same temperature. A similar process of heat exchange will also be going on between the iron bar and its environment, so that the bar will gradually approach the temperature of the room in which it is located, and in so doing will elevate somewhat the previous temperature of the room. More technically, entropy increases toward a maximum and equilibrium occurs as the physical system attains the state of the most probable distribution of its elements. In social systems, however, structures tend to become more elaborated rather than less differentiated. The rich may grow richer and the poor may grow poorer. The open system does not run down, because it can import energy from the world around it. Thus the operation of entropy is counteracted by the importation of energy and the living system is characterized by negative rather than positive entropy.

COMMON CHARACTERISTICS OF OPEN SYSTEMS

Though the various open systems have common characteristics by virtue of being open, they differ in other characteristics. If this were not the case, we would be able to obtain all our basic knowledge about social organizations through studying biological organisms or even through the study of a single cell.

The following ten characteristics seem to define all open systems.

1. IMPORTATION OF ENERGY

Open systems import some form of energy from the external environment. The cell receives oxygen from the bloodstream; the body similarly takes in oxygen from the air and food from the external world. The personality depends on the external world for stimulation. Studies of sensory deprivation show that a person placed in a darkened sound-proof room, with minimal visual and auditory stimulation, develops hallucinations and other signs of mental stress (Solomon et al., 1961). Deprivation of social stimulation also can lead to mental disorganization (Spitz, 1945). In other words, the functioning personality is heavily dependent upon the continuous inflow of stimulation from the external environment. Similarly, social organizations must draw renewed supplies of energy from other institutions, or people, or the material environment. No social structure is self-sufficient or self-contained.

2. THE THROUGHPUT

Open systems transform the energy available to them. The body converts starch and sugar into heat and action. The personality converts chemical and electrical stimuli into sensory qualities, and information into thought patterns. The organization creates a new product, or processes materials, or trains people, or provides a service. These activities entail some reorganization of input. Some work gets done in the system.

3. THE OUTPUT

Open systems export some product into the environment, whether it be the invention of an inquiring mind or a bridge constructed by an engineering firm.

Even the biological organism exports physiological products such as carbon dioxide from the lungs, which helps to maintain plants in the immediate environment. Continuing to turn out a system product depends on the receptivity of the environment. The stuff that is pumped into the environment may not be absorbed—either the primary product which surfeits the market or the secondary product which pollutes the surrounding air and water.

4. SYSTEMS AS CYCLES OF EVENTS

The pattern of activites of the energy exchange has a cyclic character. The product exported into the environment furnishes the sources of energy for the repetition of the cycle of activities. The energy reinforcing the cycle of activities can derive from some exchange of the product in the external world or from the activity itself. In the former instance, the industrial concern utilizes raw materials and human labor to turn out a product which is marketed, and the monetary return is used to obtain more raw materials and labor to perpetuate the cycle of activities. In the latter instance, the voluntary organization can provide expressive satisfactions to its members so that the energy renewal comes directly from the organizational activity itself.

System structure, or the relatedness of parts, can be observed directly when the system itself is physically bounded and its subparts are also bounded within the larger structure. The human body and its various organs constitute such a system. But how do we deal with social structures, where physical boundaries in this sense do not exist? The genius of F. H. Allport (1962) contributed the answer, namely that the structure is to be found in an interrelated set of events that return upon themselves to complete and renew a cycle of activities. It is events rather than things which are structured, so that social structure is a dynamic rather than a static concept. Activities are structured so that they comprise a unity in their completion or closure. A simple linear stimulus-response exchange between two people would not constitute social structure. To create structure, the responses of A would have to elicit B's reactions in such a manner that the responses of the latter would stimulate A to further responses. Of course the chain of events may involve many people, but their behavior can be characterized as showing structure only when there is some closure to the chain by a return to its point of origin, with the probability that the chain of events will then be repeated. The repetition of the cycle does not have to involve the same set of phenotypical happenings. It may expand to include more subevents of exactly the same kind or it may involve similar activities directed toward the same outcomes. In the individual organism the eye may move in such a way as to have the point of light fall upon the center of the retina. As the point of light moves, the movements of the eye may also change but to complete the same cycle of activity, that is, to focus upon the point of light.

A single cycle of events of a self-closing character gives us a simple form of structure. But such single cycles can also combine to give a larger structure of events or an event system. An event system may consist of a circle of smaller cycles or hoops, each one of which makes contact with several others. Cycles from other types of subsystems may also be tangential to one another. The basic method for the identification of social structures is to follow the energic chain of events from the input of energy through its transformation to the point of closure of the cycle.

5. NEGATIVE ENTROPY

To survive, open systems must reverse the entropic process; they must acquire negative entropy. The entropic process is a universal law of nature in which all forms of organization move toward disorganization or death. Complex physical systems move toward simple random distribution of their elements and biological organisms also run down and perish. In the long run all open systems are subject to the law of entropy; they lose inputs or the ability to transform them, and die. While they live, however, the entropic process is arrested or reversed. The cycle of input, transformation, and output is essential to system life, and it is a cycle of negative entropy.

Open systems vary in their ability to survive even brief interruptions in this cycle. Some storage capacity, however, is characteristic. By importing more energy from its environment than it expends, the open system can store energy and acquire negative entropy. Within the limits of its storage capacity, an open system tends to maximize its ratio of imported to expended energy, to survive and, even during periods of crisis, to live on borrowed time. Prisoners in concentration camps on a starvation diet will carefully conserve the expenditure of energy, in order to make the limited food go as far as possible (Cohen, 1954). Social organizations will seek to improve their survival position and to acquire in their reserves a comfortable margin of operation.

The entropic process asserts itself in all biological systems as well as in closed physical systems. The energy replenishment of the biological organism cannot maintain indefinitely the complex organizational structure of living tissue. Social systems, however, are not anchored in the same physical constancies as biological organisms and so are capable of almost indefinite arresting of the entropic process. Nevertheless the number of organizations that go out of existence every year is large.

6. INFORMATION INPUT, NEGATIVE FEEDBACK, AND THE CODING PROCESS

The inputs into living systems do not consist only of energic materials that become transformed or altered in the work that gets done. Inputs are also informative in character and furnish signals to the structure about the environment and about its own functioning in relation to the environment. Just as we recognize the distinction between cues and drives in individual psychology, so must we distinguish between informational and energic inputs for all living systems.

The simplest type of informational input found in all systems is negative feedback. Information feedback of a negative kind enables the system to correct its deviations from course. The working parts of the machine feed back information about the effects of their operation to some central mechanism or subsystem which acts on such information to keep the system on target. The thermostat that controls the temperature of the room is a simple example of a regulatory device which operates on the basis of negative feedback. The automated power plant would furnish more complex examples. Miller (1955) emphasizes the critical nature of negative feedback in his proposition: *"When a system's negative feedback discontinues, its steady state vanishes, and at the same time its boundary disappears and the system terminates"* (p. 529). If there is no corrective device to get the system back on its course, it will expend too much energy or it will ingest too much energic input and no longer continue as a system.

The reception of inputs into a system is selective. Not all energic inputs can be absorbed into every system. The digestive system of living creatures assimilates only those inputs to which it is adapted. Similarly, systems can react only to those information signals to which they are attuned. The general term for the selective mechanisms of a system by which incoming materials are rejected or accepted and translated for the structure is coding. Through the coding process the "blooming, buzzing confusion" of the world is simplified into a few meaningful and basic categories for a given system. The naire of the functions performed by the system determines its coding mechaisms, which in turn perpetuate this pe of functioning.

THE STEADY STATE AND DYNAMIC ꞀOMEOSTASIS

ꞇe importation of energy to arrest enꞷpy operates to maintain some conꞷancy in energy exchange, so that open ꞇstems that survive are characterized ꝡ a steady state. A steady state is not a ꞇotionless or true equilibrium. There is continuous inflow of energy from the ꭗternal environment and a continuous ꭗport of the products of the system, but ꞇe character of the system, the ratio of ꞇe energy exchanges and the relations ꞇtween parts, remains the same. The ꞇtabolic and anabolic processes of tisꞇe breakdown and restoration within ꞇe body preserve a steady state so that ꞇe organism from time to time is not ꞇe identical organism it was but a ꞇghly similar organism. The steady ꞇate is seen in clear form in the ꞷmeostatic processes for the regulation ꞇ body temperature; external condiꞷns of humidity and temperature may ꞇry, but the temperature of the body ꞇmains the same. The endocrine glands ꞇe a regulatory mechanism for preservꞷg an evenness of physiological funcꞷning. The general principle here is ꞷat of Le Châtelier (see Bradley and ꞷalvin, 1956), who maintains that any ꞷternal or external factor that threatens ꞷ disrupt the system is countered by ꞷrces which restore the system as ꞷosely as possible to its previous state. ꞇrech and Crutchfield (1948) similarly ꞷld, with respect to psychological orꞷanization, that cognitive structures will ꞷact to influences in such a way as to ꞷsorb them with minimal change to ꭗisting cognitive integration. The initial ꞇjustment to such disturbances is typiꞷlly approximate rather than precise. If ꞇ is insufficient, further adjustment in ꞇe same direction will follow. If it is ꭗcessive, it will be followed by a counꞷradjustment. The iterative process will

then continue to the point of equilibrium or until the process is broken by some further disruptive event. A temporal chart of activity will thus show a series of ups and downs instead of a smooth curve. Moreover, the system itself is in motion. Its equilibrium, as Lewin (1947) put it, is quasi-stationary, more like the constant depth of a flowing river than a still pond. *The basic principle is the preservation of the character of the system.*

The homeostatic principle must be qualified in one further respect in its application to complex living systems: in counteracting entropy these systems move toward growth and expansion. This apparent contradiction can be resolved, however, if we recognize the complexity of the subsystems and their interaction in anticipating changes necessary for the maintenance of an overall steady state. Stagner (1951) has pointed out that the initial disturbance of a given tissue constancy within the biological organism will result in mobilization of energy to restore the balance, but that recurrent upsets will lead to actions to anticipate the disturbance:

> We eat before we experience intense hunger pangs . . . energy mobilization for forestalling tactics must be explained in terms of a *cortical tension* which reflects the visceral-proprioceptive pattern of the original biological disequilibration. . . . *Dynamic homeostasis* involves the maintenance of tissue constancies by establishing a constant physical environment—by reducing the variability and disturbing effects of external stimulation. Thus the organism does not simply restore the prior equilibrium. A new, more complex and more comprehensive equilibrium is established. (p. 5)

Growth is one form of this tendency toward equilibria of increasing complexity and comprehensiveness. In preserving its character, the system tends to import more energy than is required for its output, as we noted in discussing negative entropy. To insure survival, systems operate to acquire some margin of safety beyond the immediate level of existence. The body will store fat, the social organization will build up reserves, the society will increase its technological and cultural base. Miller (1955) has formulated the proposition that the rate of growth of a system—within certain ranges—is exponential if it exists in a medium that makes available unrestricted amounts of energy for input.

In adapting to their environment, systems will attempt to cope with external forces by ingesting them or acquiring control over them. The physical boundedness of the single organism means that such attempts to control the environment affect the behavioral system rather than the biological system of the individual. Social systems will move, however, toward incorporating within their boundaries the external resources essential to survival. Again the result is an expansion of the original system.

Thus, the steady state, which at the simple level is one of homeostasis over time, at more complex levels becomes one of preserving the character of the system through growth and expansion. The basic system does not change directly as a consequence of expansion. The most common growth pattern is a multiplication of the same type of cycles or subsystems—a change in quantity rather than in quality. Animal and plan species grow by multiplication. A social system adds more units of the same essential type as it already has. Haire (1959) has studied the ratio between the sizes of different subsystems in growing business organizations. He found that though the number of people increased in both the production subsystem and the subsystem concerned with the external world, the ratio of the two groups remained constant. Qualitative change does occur, however, in two ways. In the first place, quantitative growth calls for supportive subsystems of a specialized character not necessary when the system was smaller. In the second place, there is a point where quantita-

tive changes produce a qualitative di ference in the functioning of a system. small college that triples its size is n longer the same institution in terms (the relation between its administratio and faculty, relations among the variou academic departments, or the nature (its instruction.

In short, living systems exhibit growth or expansion dynamic in whic they maximize their basic characte They react to change or they anticipat change through growth which assim lates the new energic inputs to the n; ture of their structure. In terms of Lev in's quasi-stationary equilibrium, th ups and downs of the adjustive proces do not always result in a return to th old level. Under certain circumstances solidification or freezing occurs durir one of the adjustive cycles. A new bas line is thus established and successiv movements fluctuate around this leve which may be either above or belo* the previous plateau of operation.

8. DIFFERENTIATION

Open systems move in the direction (differentiation and elaboration. Diffus global patterns are replaced by mor specialized functions. The sense orgar and the nervous system evolved a highly differentiated structures from th primitive nervous tissues. The growth (the personality proceeds from primitive crude organizations of mental functior to hierarchically structured and wel differentiated systems of beliefs and fee ings. Social organizations move towar the multiplication and elaboration (roles with greater specialization of fun(tion. In the United States today medic; specialists now outnumber the gener; practitioners.

One type of differentiated growth i systems is what von Bertalanffy (195€ terms progressive mechanization. finds expression in the way in which system achieves a steady state. Th early method is a process that involve an interaction of various dynami forces, whereas the later development entails the use of a regulatory feedback mechanism. He writes:

It can be shown that the *primary* regulations in organic systems, that is, those which are most fundamental and primitive in embryonic development as well as in evolution, are of such nature of dynamic interaction. . . . Superimposed are those regulations which we may call *secondary*, and which are controlled by fixed arrangements, especially of the feedback type. This state of affairs is a consequence of a general principle of organization which may be called progressive mechanization. At first, systems— biological, neurological, psychological or social—are governed by dynamic interaction of their components; later on, fixed arrangements and conditions of constraint are established which render the system and its parts more efficient, but also gradually diminish and eventually abolish its equipotentiality. (p. 6)

9. INTEGRATION AND COORDINATION

As differentiation proceeds, it is countered by processes that bring the system together for unified functioning. Von Bertalanffy (1956) spoke of progressive mechanization in the regulatory processes of organic systems, the replacement of dynamic interaction by fixed control arrangements. In social systems, in contrast to biological systems, there are two different paths for achieving unification which Georgopoulos (1975) calls coordination and integration.[1] Coordination is analogous to von Bertalanffy's fixed control arrangements. It is the addition of various devices for assuring the functional articulation of tasks and roles—controlling the speed of the assembly line, for example. Inte-

gration is the achievement of unification through shared norms and values.

In organisms, hormonal and nervous subsystems provide the integrating mechanisms. In social systems, without built-in physical mechanisms of regulation, integration is often achieved at the small group level through mutually shared psychological fields. . . . For large social organizations, coordination, rather than integration, is the rule for providing orderly and systematic articulation—through such devices as priority setting, the establishment and regulation of routines, timing and synchronization of functions, scheduling and sequencing of events.

10. EQUIFINALITY

Open systems are further characterized by the principle of equifinality, a principle suggested by von Bertalanffy in 1940. According to this principle, a system can reach the same final state from differing initial conditions and by a variety of paths. The well-known biological experiments on the sea urchin show that a normal creature of that species can develop from a complete ovum, from each half of a divided ovum, or from the fusion product of two whole ova. As open systems move toward regulatory mechanisms to control their operations, the amount of equifinality may be reduced.

SOME CONSEQUENCES OF VIEWING ORGANIZATIONS AS OPEN SYSTEMS

Like most innovations in scientific theory, the open system approach was developed in order to deal with inadequacies in previous models. The inadequacies of closed system thinking about organizations became increasingly apparent during the midcentury decades of rapid societal change. The limitations of empirical research based on closed system assumptions also pointed up the need for a more com-

---

1. This distinction is similar to the one formulated by Nancy Morse on *binding-in* and *binding-between* functions—the binding-in referring to the involvement of people in the system, the binding-between referring to the ties between system parts. (Unpublished manuscript.)

prehensive theoretical approach. The consequences, or rather the potentialities, of dealing with organizations as open systems can best be seen in contrast to the limitations and misconceptions of closed system thinking. The most important of these misconceptions, almost by definition, is the failure to recognize fully the dependence of organizations on inputs from their environment. That inflow of materials and energy is neither constant nor assured, and when it is treated as a constant much of organizational behavior becomes unexplainable. The fact that organizations have developed protective devices to maintain stability and that they are notoriously difficult to change or reform should not be allowed to obscure their dynamic relationships with the social and natural environment. Changes in that environment lead to demands for change in the organization, and even the effort to resist those demands results in internal change.

It follows that the study of organizations should include the study of organization-environment relations. We must examine the ways in which an organization is tied to other structures, not only those that furnish economic inputs and support but also structures that can provide political influence and societal legitimation. The open-system emphasis on such relationships implies an interest in properties of the environment itself. Its turbulence or placidity, for example, limits the kinds of relationships that an organization can form with systems in the environment and indicates also the kinds of relationships that an organization will require to assure its own survival.

The emphasis on openness is qualified, however, there is a duality to the concept of open system; the concept implies openness but it also implies system properties, stable patterns of relationships and behavior within boundaries. Complete openness to the environment means loss of those properties; the completely open organization would no longer be dif-

ferentiated from its environment and would cease to exist as a distinct system. The organization lives only by being open to inputs, but selectively; its continuing existence requires both the property of openness and of selectivity. and of selectivity.

The open system approach requires study of these selective processes, analysis of those elements in the environment that are actively sought, those disregarded, and those kept out or defended against. The basis of these choices, the means employed for their implementation, and the consequences for organizational effectiveness and survival becomes topics for research. In well-established organizations the internal arrangements for making and implementing such choices are highly developed, a fact that often allows such organizations to withstand environmental turbulence better than the reform or revolutionary movements that seek to displace them. Sustained supportive inputs are less predictable for groups attempting social change.

A second serious deficiency in closed system thinking, both theoretical and pragmatic, is overconcentration on principles of internal functioning. This could be viewed as merely another aspect of disregard for the environment, but it has consequences of its own. Internal moves are planned without regard for their effects on the environment and the consequent environmental response. The effects of such moves on the maintenance inputs of motivation and morale tend not to be adequately considered. Stability may be sought through tighter integration and coordination when flexibility may be the more important requirement. Coordination and control become ends in themselves, desirable states within a closed system rather than means of attaining an adjustment between the system and its environment. Attempts to introduce coordination in kind and degree not functionally required tend to produce new internal problems.

Two further errors derive from the characteristic closed system disregard of the environment and preoccupation with internal functions—the neglect of equifinality and the treatment of disruptive external events as error variance. The equifinality principle simply asserts that there are more ways than one of producing a given outcome. In a completely closed system, the same initial conditions must lead to the same final result; nothing has changed and therefore nothing changes. In open systems, however, the principle of equifinality applies; it holds true at the biological level, and it is more conspicuously true at the social level. Yet in practice most armies insist that there is one best way for all recruits to assemble their guns; most coaching staffs teach one best way for all baseball players to hurl the ball in from the outfield. And in industry the doctrine of scientific management as propounded by Taylor and his disciples begins with the assumption of the one best way: discover it, standardize it, teach it, and insist on it. It is true that under fixed and known conditions there is one best way, but in human organizations the conditions of life are neither fixed nor fully known. Such organizations are better served by the general principle, characteristic of all open systems, that there need not be a single method for achieving an objective.

The closed system view implies that irregularities in the functioning of a system due to environmental influences are error variances and should be treated accordingly. According to this conception, they should be controlled out of studies of organizations. From the organization's own operations they should be excluded as irrelevant and should be guarded against. The decisions of officers to omit a consideration of external factors or to guard against such influences in a defensive fashion, as if they would go away if ignored, is an instance of this type of thinking. So is the now outmoded "public be damned" attitude of business executives toward the clientele upon whose support they depend. Open system theory, on the other hand,

would maintain that environmental influences are not sources of error variance but are integral to the functioning of a social system, and that we cannot understand a system without a constant study of the forces that impinge upon it.

Finally, thinking of organizations as closed systems results in failure to understand and develop the feedback or intelligence function, the means by which the organization acquires information about changes in the environment. It is remarkable how weak many industrial companies are in their market research departments when they are so dependent on the market. The prediction can be hazarded that organizations in our society will increasingly move toward the improvement of the facilities for research in assessing environmental forces. We are in the process of correcting our misconception of the organization as a closed system, but the process is slow.

Open system theory, we believe, has potentialities for overcoming these defects in organizational thinking and practice. Its potentialities, however, cannot be realized merely by acknowledging the fact of organizational openness; they must be developed. Open is not a magic word, and pronouncing it is not enough to reveal what has been hidden in the organizational cave. We have begun the process of specification by discussing properties shared by all open systems. We turn next to the special properties of human organizations, as one category of such systems.

SUMMARY

The open system approach to organizations is contrasted with commonsense approaches, which tend to accept popular names and stereotypes as basic organizational properties and to identify the purpose of an organization in terms of the goals of its founders and leaders.

The open system approach, on the other hand, begins by identifying and mapping the repeated cycles of input, transformation, output, and renewed input which comprise the organizational pattern. This approach to organizations represents the adaptation of work in biology and in the physical sciences by von Bertalanffy and others.

Organizations as a special class of open systems have properties of their own, but they share other properties in common with all open systems. These include the importation of energy from the environment, the throughput or transformation of the imported energy into some product form that is characteristic of the system, the exporting of that product into the environment, and the reenergizing of the system from sources in the environment.

Open systems also share the characteristics of negative entropy, feedback, homeostasis, differentiation, coordination and equifinality. The law of negative entropy states that systems survive and maintain their characteristic internal order only as long as they import from the environment more energy than they expend in the process of transformation and exportation. The feedback principle has to do with information input, which is a special kind of energic importation, a kind of signal to the system about environmental conditions and about the functioning of the system in relation to its environment. The feedback of such information enables the system to correct for its own malfunctioning or for changes in the environment, and thus to maintain a steady state or homeostasis. This is a dynamic rather than a static balance, however. Open systems are not at rest but tend toward differentiation and elaboration, both because of subsystem dynamics and because of the relationship between growth and survival. Finally, open systems are characterized by the principle of equifinality, which asserts that systems can reach the same final state from different initial conditions and by different paths of development.

Traditional organizational theories have tended to view the human organi-

zation as a closed system. This tendency has led to a disregard of differing organizational environments and the nature of organizational dependency on environment. It has led also to an overconcentration on principles of internal organizational functioning, with consequent failure to develop and understand the processes of feedback which are essential to survival.

NOTES

1. Allport, F. H. 1962. A structuronomic conception of behavior: individual and collective. I. Structural theory and the master problem of social psychology. *Journal of Abnormal and Social Psychology*, **64**, 3-30.
2. Bradley, D. F., and M. Calvin. 1956. Behavior: imbalance in a network of chemical transformations. *General Systems*. Yearbook of the Society for the Advancement of General System Theory, **1**, 56-65.
3. Cohen, E. 1954. *Human behavior in the concentration camp*. London: Jonathan Cape.
4. Georgopoulos, B. S. 1975. *Hospital organization research: review and source book*. Philadelphia: W. B. Saunders.
5. Haire, M. 1959. Biological models and empirical histories of the growth of organization. In M. Haire (Ed.) *Modern organization theory*. New York: Wiley, 272-306.
6. Krech, D., and R. Crutchfield. 1948. *Theory and problems of social psychology*. New York: McGraw-Hill.
7. Lewin, K. 1947. Frontiers in group dynamics. *Human Relations*, **1**, 5-41.
8. Merton, R. K. 1957. *Social theory and social structure*, rev. ed. New York: Free Press.
9. Miller, J. G. 1955. Toward a general theory for the behavioral sciences. *American Psychologist*, **10**, 513-531.
10. Solomon, P., et al. (Eds.) 1961. *Sensory deprivation*. Cambridge, Mass: Harvard University Press.

(the communication medium, method, and time) for the innovation or new knowledge which will result in user acceptance?

• *Example.* The National Aeronautics and Space Administration (NASA) has sponsored much basic and applied research related to technical problems faced by the United States space program.[1] Much of the knowledge produced in this effort could be useful to organizations in a wide variety of fields, particularly industrial and manufacturing firms (many of which support internal research efforts) but including many other types of organizations as well, since some NASA-sponsored research relates to management and organizational functioning, not merely technological innovation. Consider a moderate-size industrial organization, producing high-pressure valve fittings (among other items). Suppose a major customer has asked for an improved fitting which will withstand pressures several times greater than will the presently produced item, for use in a new truck air-brake system. The firm may subscribe to NASA *Tech Briefs,* short announcements of innovations, new concepts, devices, or techniques, which can be subscribed to by category. The supervisor of a development team might examine these notes in the company library, finding a specific description of high-strength valve fittings developed for use in rocket fueling. He could then request detailed information from NASA's Office of Technology Utilization, and if the information seemed appropriate order a Technical Support Package which would provide complete details for using the innovation. The development team would then proceed to adapt this innovation for their customer.

The above example concerns the adoption of a specific technological innovation. While the type of information flow and data use process contained in the research, development, and diffusion model is, as we noted above, particularly oriented toward this type of information content, changes of more interest to social scientists—changes in the functioning of the client-user system—are also conceivable. Consider, again, the industrial firm described above. The manager of research and development might be faced with the problem of managing, controlling, and coordinating numerous development programs with somewhat competing resource needs. By reviewing NASA *Tech Briefs* on research management, he would find one reporting a new systems control process for multiple project management. By ordering the Technical Support Package, he would receive all needed details for planning and implementing this new control technique.[2]

• *Problems.* Havelock et al. (1969) have noted that the research, development, and diffusion model is "over-rational, over-idealized, excessively research-oriented, and inadequately user-oriented, [pp. 11-17]." Perhaps the most serious problem is that while the process described by the research, development, and diffusion model does seem to take place, the model lacks sophistication in that major aspects of the actual communication (and change) process are ignored. Specifically, the model seems to describe communication and subsequent adoption of innovation accurately but only over a very long time period, perhaps 20 to 40 years. By ignoring the detail of the process as well as the reasons for this extreme dissemination-to-use time lag we cannot determine how the lag might be avoided. Any failure must be attrib-

---

1. These examples were developed on the basis of discussion with Elizabeth Markowitz; we are grateful to her for sharing with us her information resources. The second example is based on specific, actual cases.

2. NASA actually uses a variety of knowledge diffusion approaches; some are quite sophisticated but all are basically within the research, development, and diffusion approach.

uted to improper packaging or transmission, but due to the immense number of alternative packaging designs and transmission methods such a conclusion is not very helpful to the disseminator who must repeat the process looking for the error or proceed by a trial-and-error approach. Of course, such failures must be seen as failures in the application of the model, rather than the results of possible defects in the model itself. Research on the model, while possible, seems rarely attempted by users of the research, development, and diffusion model. For example, despite extensive and sophisticated applications of the research, development, and diffusion model, NASA does not engage in any scientific research evaluation of the effectiveness of their efforts.

SOCIAL INTERACTION AND DIFFUSION

There are three sources for this approach to social change. The earliest stems from studies in rural sociology, investigating the processes by which farmers adopted technological innovations such as hybrid corn (e.g., Lionberger, 1953). Research along the same lines was continued by Menzel and Katz (1955-1956) in examining the ways in which new drugs were adopted by physicians. The latter researchers had the advantage of the two other research approaches: first, Lazarsfeld, Berelson, and Gaudet's (1948) work on voting behavior which introduced the concept of "opinion leaders" (individuals who influenced the voting choice of peers by direct personal contact); and, second, the work of Lewin (1947a, 1947b) and his associates on changing food habits, which introduced the notion of the "gatekeeper" (persons—such as housewives—who control the flow of physical or informational materials by opening and closing hypothetical "gates" through which the materials must pass on the way from sources—such as markets—to destinations—such as dinner tables). Katz (1957) refined his

model as the "two-step flow of communication." In that model, information was said to pass, selectively, from mass media, through opinion leaders, to users. Katz and Lazarsfeld (1955) also collaborated to create a general model of personal influence or "opinion leadership."

● *Assumptions.* (a) Data exist and have been generated by persons other than the (potential) users. (b) There exists a natural process of data flow via personal influence on users by key persons called "opinion leaders" or "gatekeepers." (c) This natural process can be used by a change agent to introduce new information into a social system. Use of the process (by a change agent) will naturally lead to active application of the information.

● *Key question.* How can the "opinion leaders" or "gatekeepers" be identified and used to channel the information that the change agent wants to convey to the potential users of the information?

● *Example.* At the state medical school, new and refined treatments for particular blood diseases are continually being developed. There is, however, a considerable time lag before practicing physicians who treat blood diseases, particularly those other than board-certified hematologists, know about and use these new treatments. A change agent helping the medical school to increase the effectiveness of its postgraduate continuing education program would identify those physicians in a group of participating hospitals who are the "opinion leaders" or "gatekeepers" in the information-flow process. The change agent would determine which physicians in the hospitals read more than others, attend more conferences and conventions, participate more often in continuing education programs in hematology, and are seen more often by their colleagues as primary consultants for new information. After doing this, the change agent would create a special education program for just these "gatekeepers" in the different hospitals, knowing that this approach would lead to widespread and more rapid acceptance of the new treatments by the total community of physicians. Thus, the change agent uses the natural process of data flow through key persons in the client system to produce significant changes in that system.[3]

• *Problems.* Havelock (1968) has pointed out some basic problems with the social interaction and diffusion approach. He notes that three important assumptions—(a) that there are two steps, (b) that only the personal interaction channel of communication is relevant, and (c) that those persons who are opinion leaders are in fact influenced by the mass media (are media oriented)—have all been contradicted by empirical research. The more general problems are (a) that the social interaction and diffusion approach sees the target of change as the individual, thus ignoring much of the most important work of Lewin (1947a, 1947b) and his students (e.g., Cartwright, 1951), and does not, therefore, adequately deal with problems of changes in organized social systems; and, (b) that the user or user system remains a passive consumer, as in the research, development, and diffusion model, rather than taking any active role in the dissemination and use process.

INTERVENTION THEORY AND METHOD

Since the early 1950s, Argyris has been engaged in research and practice on organizational change. He has recently (Argyris, 1970) developed his comprehensive model, called "intervention theory." In contrast to the approaches to change discussed above, Argyris concentrates on *internal* changes in an organization. The model is focused on the flow and use of information within the

system. Basically, Argyris argues that organizational problems are not solved because the people in the system do not know how to (a) generate problem-relevant data, (b) use the data to obtain solution alternatives and make decisions, and (c) communicate a shared commitment to the decisions. These three activities are the three primary tasks of the interventionist. As the interventionist models these actions, in the context of real and relevant problems, the client system learns to use and eventually internalizes the information flow process Argyris believes is critical for organization effectiveness.

While other approaches recognize the importance of problem solving, decision making, and action taking by the client, without undue influence by the change agent, Argyris places major emphasis on this factor. He prefers the term "interventionist" to the label "change agent" because, he argues, the creation of specific changes is *not* one of the primary tasks of the interventionist. This is an important point, for Argyris is making a significant clarification here. That is, the interventionist *is* attempting to change the client system, in a major and basic way. He is trying to alter the basic *processes* of information flow and data use within the client system. The interventionist, however, is not trying to implement specific "content" decisions or changes; that is, specific recommendations concerning problem solutions are not made. Indeed, if this were done, the interventionist would effectively nullify any impact he might have on changing the basic information processes: people who are given solutions, or a range of solutions to choose from, do not have to learn how to gather data or how to use those data to generate their own solutions.

• *Assumptions.* (a) Needed data are in the client system. (b) Problems are due to blockages in the communication system or a lack of linkages in the communication network within the client

---

3. This example is based on research by Morris (1970).

system. (c) Data are not being adequately generated, appropriately disseminated, and effectively used within the client system.

• *Key questions.* How can the interventionist remove blocks, add linkages, and generally support an increased flow of information throughout the client system? How can the interventionist develop awareness of data implications and promote the use of data to solve problems and take actions, without exerting major influence over decisions, choices, and actions?

• *Example.* Consider the classical case of a rigid bureaucratized organization, in which formalized procedures have made it increasingly difficult for top-level authorities to gain the information needed to make effective operating decisions. Those at lower levels, who possess the necessary information, do not have decision-making authority. This rather extreme example would call for the interventionist to (a) help the client generate data regarding specific problems, as well as data regarding the organizational processes in use; (b) assist groups in using these data to evaluate specific problems (as well as the more general problems related to the organizational climate) and to make action decisions based on the data; and (c) help develop commitment to those decisions on the part of the decision makers. A specific problem an interventionist might be working with could be illustrated by the following situation. A case of intergroup conflict may have led to the virtual isolation from one another of two interdependent groups. The interventionist must then help generate a flow of information which the parties can use to understand and in some way resolve their conflict. Intervention activities might include some form of intergroup confrontation meeting to generate data and information flow. This would be followed by analysis of the information and decision making. Finally, the interventionist would attempt to develop open commitment to whatever

decisions were made about actions to be taken (if any).

• *Problems.* Underlying Argyris' model is a set of assumptions about the way information is generated, shared, and used in effective organizations. Argyris does not offer any research evidence regarding the validity of these assumptions. While the assumptions do generate testable hypotheses and although Argyris (1970) greatly emphasizes the need for research on change, the model itself seems to use research more as a client-training process for the development of skills in generating valid data. Although research is emphasized within the client system, on the state of the system as well as (to a lesser degree) on the effects of action changes, Argyris' approach to analysis of the model itself is more on the order of the clinical case study. Thus, the evidence presented to support the model is quite difficult to evaluate. Much research evidence is needed before Argyris' model can be accepted by behavioral scientists, especially including comparative studies of similar and different organizations.

This need presents yet another type of problem, for Argyris has conceptually and operationally developed an alternative, "organic" research model as part of intervention theory and method. While this model shares significant overlap with traditional "rigorous" models, the differences may dissuade some behavioral scientists from considering the possibility of valid research on intervention theory and method. Not only has Argyris developed a model of applied social system change which requires empirical validation, he has also created a research model, integral to the use of his change model, which *also* requires validation. As mentioned, this new research model seems far more oriented toward client training than toward research on change, the change process, or the intervention theory and method model itself. We should, however, note that Argyris' (1970) presentation is only partial—complete treatment of the model will be achieved with publication of a planned second volume.

PLANNED CHANGE

Perhaps the first integrated, systemic, and comprehensive model of change in social systems was developed by Lippitt, Watson, and Westley (1958). In *The Dynamics of Planned Change*, these authors drew on behavioral science knowledge from fields as diverse as psychoanalysis, sociology, and social activism. This knowledge was integrated across system levels, from "individual" through "community." The approach which emerged is a theory of planned change which is applicable to social systems in general. Lippitt et al. presented a theory which is focused on the process of planned change, expanding Lewin's (1947a) three-stage model of change (unfreezing-moving-refreezing) into seven phases (establishing a need for change; establishing a change relationship between client and change agent; data collection and diagnosis; action planning; action implementation; generalization and stabilization of change; termination of the change relationship). There are two primary principles concerning information flow and data use: (a) all information must be openly shared between client and change agent, including information about the values and methods of each; (b) information is useful only insofar as it can be translated directly into action.

● *Assumptions.* (a) Data exist within the client system or can be provided (linked into the system from the outside) by the change agent. (b) Data must be directly translated (or translatable) into action steps which generate further data. Thus, data generation, diagnosis, action planning, and action implementation are elements of a sequential and continuous process of change. (c) Mechanisms and commitments can be developed to stabilize (support) the changes which have been made.

● *Key questions.* How does the change agent determine what data are relevant? How does the change agent gather and present these data to the client and help the client to use them? How does the change agent create procedures and commitments for the continuation (stabilization) of the changes made?

● *Example.* In a school, faculty have problems around the issue of collaboration in decision making (a process problem) concerning the development of an experimental curriculum (a content problem). The change agent may show client system members how information on curriculum development can be retrieved from an ERIC (Educational Resources Information) center. The change agent could then work with the faculty as a group to review these data and derive action implications relevant to their own situation. In the process of doing this the change agent would be demonstrating personal values and specific methods of collaboration, attempting to "resocialize" client sytem members to these values and train them in the use of the methods.[4] The change agent would help the clients assemble further data about their own problems (content and process) and implement selected actions (derived from the ERIC data and their own) which are aimed at certain specific problems (e.g., curriculum decision issue, decision-making process issues, etc.). Plans would also be made for evaluation of the effects of the actions. By successive iterations of the data gathering-diagnosis-action planning-implementation-evaluation cycle, specific problems would be resolved. This would involve the development of a set of internal supports—methods, procedures, commitments, and norms—which would insure the con-

4. Note that in this case the change agent is a "methodological-process advocate"— actively *advocating* a set of values and methods for the client system to adopt, which would result in changes in the basic processes of the client system.

tinuance of effective action changes after the change agent leaves.

• *Problems.* Although the planned change model aims at the ultimate internalization of the planned change process within the client system, this goal is not operationally specified. Rather, the emphasis is on solving specific problems and creating specific changes. Perhaps more serious is the fact that while the model is extensively grounded in theory and research evidence, there is little emphasis on research measurement and evaluation of results and no significant treatment of research designed to validate the model.

ACTION RESEARCH

The action-research model derives from the work of Lewin (1947a, 1947b, 1948) and is a major factor in the Lippitt et al. (1958) planned change model which was discussed above. The action-research model does, however, differ enough to deserve separate treatment. It is primarily a *process* model, focused on the development of the action-research process within the client system. The action-research model has received most use in applications involving social problems (Lewin, 1948) and educational systems (Corey, 1953), but it has recently been considered as a major element in organization development (French & Bell, 1973; see also Frohman, Sashkin, and Kavanagh[5]). Essentially, the model emphasizes the link between research and action. Data gathering, analysis, and diagnosis (research phases) lead to action planning and action implementation (action), the results of which are carefully evaluated (research). This evaluation provides data for further diagnosis and action. Thus, a continuous cycle of research and action provides a general model for problem solving and change. A further factor in this model is the concern for research knowledge which can be added to the general fund of behavioral science knowledge and then be put into practice by other applied behavioral scientists in new situations.

• *Assumptions.* (a) Research (data gathering and analysis) is an action intervention in a client system and is the basis for diagnosing problems and planning and implementing changes. Research data are also collected after changes are made in order to evaluate the effectiveness of the changes and to serve as a basis for planning and taking further action. Action research is a continuous process of research and action, inextricably linked. (b) The client learns this process by applying it, with the assistance of a change agent/researcher, to real, specific problems. (c) In the context of the action-research process, knowledge is gained relevant to more general social or organizational problems.

• *Key questions.* How can the change agent/researcher design the data collection and action experiment processes so that the *specific* problem of concern to the client is attacked in detail while producing behavioral science knowledge of a more general utility? How can the change agent/researcher demonstrate the continuous nature of the action-research process (thus providing the client with the opportunity to learn and internalize the process) while using the process to help the client solve a specific problem? How can the change agent provide the client with the skills needed to keep the action-research cycle going after the consultant-client relationship is terminated?

• *Example.* Action-research studies tend to be complex and data rich. Whyte and Hamilton (1964), for example, presented a book-length report of one such project involving a hotel in Chicago. A classic example can be seen in Coch and French's (1948) study on overcoming resistance to change in a

---

5. M. A. Frohman, M. Sashkin, and M. J. Kavanagh. Action research as an organization development approach. Unpublished manuscript, 1973.

pajama factory, which resulted not only in the development of specific techniques for the effective introduction of technological change but also produced significant increments in theoretical and practical knowledge about the change process. A more recent action-research example, involving the same organization Coch and French worked with, is given by Marrow, Bowers, and Seashore (1967).[6]

In 1961 the Harwood company acquired Weldon, one of its major competitors. It quickly became evident that the Weldon organization was in dire straits, operating at a loss with multiple and severe personnel and production problems. These problems were confirmed and detailed by extensive initial measures of organizational processes (e.g., coordination and communication) and of attitudes of client system members. In a two-year program, the action-research team (consisting of persons internal and external to the client system) assisted client system members in developing, implementing, and evaluating a wide variety of specific actions. The changes were planned on the basis of both theoretical understanding of the dynamics of effective organizations (such as Harwood) and the extensive data collected. The eight major action changes were:

(a) a new production system, involving the creation of semiautonomous work groups and corresponding changes in layout, work flow, production methods, and equipment:
(b) a training program for new employees;
(c) intensive coaching and training for substandard workers;
(d) training seminars in interpersonal relations for supervisors and staff;
(e) institution of work group problem-solving meetings;
(f) a blanket wage increase;

(g) the development and use of personnel selection tests;
(h) firing chronic poor performers.

While these actions clearly had interactive effects, the net result being a 30 percent production increase in less than one year, careful research methods enabled estimation of the impact of each action in this overall improvement. For example, the program of training for substandard employees was estimated to account for 11 percent of the 30 percent productivity increase, while weeding out low performers and interpersonal relations training each represented a 5 percent gain. Measurement, was, of course, not limited to before-after comparison but was continuous throughout the change program since information was used to alter action changes which were not showing desirable results. There were also multiple types of measures used, although we have mentioned only the final outcome measure of overall performance in terms of productivity. As of 1964, the changes appeared significant and stable.

An extensive remeasurement in 1969 (Seashore & Bowers, 1970) showed not only that the changes had been lasting but that organizational improvement had continued, in many areas, and significantly so.

The text report of this effort involved written analyses, not only from the external researchers and internal change team members but from individual client system members as well, thus vividly demonstrating that client system members had indeed developed the understanding required for future applications of the action-research model. The report also added to knowledge about organizational change, perhaps the most significant point here being increased theoretical and practical understanding of how "support systems" for change can be designed and implemented. This reflects the emphasis on the interaction of specific changes as well as the internalization of the action-research change process.

---

6. Our discussion of this study is, in large part, based on Seashore and Bowers' (1970) report.

Seashore and Bowers (1970) noted particularly the importance of consistent and interdependent changes in organization structure and technology which are also consistent with desirable psychological conditions (e.g., the values and motives of individuals).

● *Problems.* The change agent/researcher has multiple roles here, which may sometimes be in conflict. Hired to help the client with a problem and to help the client learn to solve problems more effectively, in general, the change agent must also teach the client how to *evaluate* the results of action, which may not always reflect well upon the choices he has helped them make. He must also serve as scientist, adding to the knowledge of his field, yet sometimes protecting the identity and perhaps even the ideas of the client. It may not, in some cases, be possible to operationalize these roles unless more than one person is involved as change agent. Effective application of the model also requires considerable commitment and effort on the part of the client, more perhaps than the client is willing or can afford to give. Finally, the model is focused on the process of change, not on specific changes or types of change, and thus requires a "technology" of change, a set of tools, to effectively implement specific changes. Since the field of organization development itself developed more around various tools and techniques (see, e.g., Fordyce & Weil, 1971), the recent emphasis on action research as an organization development approach may be an excellent match.

COMPARATIVE ANALYSIS

CHANGE AGENT ROLES

We can compare the five models of change described above by considering the *roles* taken by the change agent using each model, with respect to information flow and data use processes. The change agent may fulfill one or more of the three basic roles we now define.[7]

● *Consulting.* The change agent may be a *consultant* to the client, placing the client in touch with data from outside the client system or helping the client to generate data from within the system. In either case, the purpose is to help the client find, through analysis of valid data, solutions to existing organizational problems, or to make the client aware of new ideas which would, if used, result in increased effectiveness of the organization, in terms of both internal operations and output or product.

● *Training.* In addition to being a consultant, the change agent may take the role of *trainer*. In this respect the change agent is interested in helping the client learn how to use data to bring about change. The concern is twofold. First, the change agent is aware that simply making data available to the client will not insure that the data are used to benefit the client system. The purpose, then, becomes one of helping the client derive implications for action from the data and building and testing action plans to be used in the client system. Second, the change agent wishes to leave the client with a new set of *skills*, skills which the client can then use to retrieve, translate, and use data to solve future problems more effectively, even after the change agent has terminated his relationship with the client.

● *Research.* Finally, the change agent may also take on the role of *researcher*. There are two aspects to this role. First, the change agent may model the role of researcher for the purpose of training the client in the skills needed for accurate evaluation of the effects and effectiveness of action plans which have been implemented. This element of the researcher role overlaps, then, with the

---

7. This analysis is, in part, based on a discussion by Bennis, Benne, and Chin (1961, Chap. 11).

role of the change agent as trainer. Second, the change agent may be concerned with adding to the general knowledge of his profession—applied behavioral science. His purpose in this case is to design the data use process so that it includes, as an integral part, a thorough evaluation component which is addressed to problems or research questions more general than the specific problem the client system is trying to solve. For example, the change agent may want to know whether a particular process for translating research data into client action steps, a process which he has trained his client to use, really works or works better than alternative processes and should therefore be reported to other professional workers in his field. To determine this, the change agent must include an evaluation design as part of his activity and must in addition compare the outcome with similar evaluations of alternative processes in similar systems with similar problems. He may also, of course, actually train other (but similar) clients, or other parts of the client system, in alternative processes and compare the results. Here, however, we are getting into the elements of research design, which is not our primary topic (see Campbell & Stanley, 1963.)

● *Change agent roles in the five models of change.* Each of the five models for data use we have described can be viewed in relation to the above activities which the change agent may perform: consulting, training, research, or some combination of these. In our view, the complete change agent performs all three of these activities in the data use process. Table 1 summarizes what we believe to be the major activities emphasized by the change agent in each of the five orientations to data use.

Looking at Table 1, we see that all five models emphasize consultation as a change agent activity. They do, however, differ here in emphasis on data sources. For the research, development, and diffusion and the social interaction and diffusion models, the data source to be used is generally outside the client system. For intervention theory and method, the source is internal to the client system. Finally, in both the planned change and the action-research models the data source is *both* inside and outside the client system.

Only three of the models, intervention theory and method, planned change, and action research, focus on *training* clients to use data to answer needs and solve problems. The change agent using any of these models aims to leave the client with new expertise in data use and problem solving.

These same three models all include *research* activities, of different types. Intervention theory and method notes the importance of a variety of research activities but operationalizes and strongly emphasizes only the training of the

Table 1
CHANGE AGENT ACTIVITIES EMPHASIZED IN THE FIVE MODELS

Model	Consulting	Training	Research
Research, development, and diffusion	Yes (External data sources)	No	No, but possible
Social interaction and diffusion	Yes (External data sources)	No, but possible	Possibly, but not integral to the model
Intervention theory and method	Yes (Internal data sources)	Yes	Probably, but limited and not integral to the model
Planned change	Yes	Yes	Yes, but implicit and limited
Action research	Yes	Yes	Yes

client in research skills and methods for the purpose of internalizing an effective data generation and use process. There is some question as to whether research activities involving the evaluation of change agent interventions, research on the intervention theory and method model itself, and research on the change process in general are really integral to the model. The planned change model, while perhaps less clearly operationalized by Lippitt et al., is explicitly concerned with research evaluation of the effects of knowledge use and research on change agent actions and the model itself. Only the action-research model is explicit on all three of the research activities we define as of primary importance: evaluation of the effects of knowledge use; evaluation of the model itself and the change agent's actions within the model; and, research on change in general, on the processes and problems of change.

We would, therefore, conclude that the action-research model is the most complete and sophisticated of the five we have considered, with respect to the information flow and data use processes the change agent follows. We conclude this discussion with a model of change agent data use activities, focusing on the overall role of the change agent as a "knowledge linker."

• The linking function of the change agent in information flow and data use. The change agent can be thought of as a "linker" in information flow and data use processes. The activities of the change agent in this process of helping clients retrieve and use data for themselves and their organization can take several different forms. Figure 1 illustrates these activities as they relate to the retrieval and flow of data in a client system, to the three change agent roles, and to the five models of change.

As a consultant the change agent en-

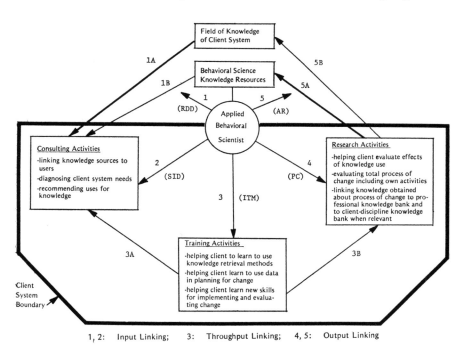

1, 2:   Input Linking;   3:   Throughput Linking;   4, 5:   Output Linking

Fig. 1. Data use and linking activities of the applied behavioral scientist.

gages in linking activities between *sources* and *users* of knowledge. Arrows 1 and 2 in Figure 1 represent the change agent's control over this linking, information flow activity, which we call "input linking." That is, the change agent is linking external information sources into the client system.

Let us consider a brief example. A group of private landowners who grow Christmas trees may be aware that research is being done on tree types, land use, and insect control. They may not, however, be aware that the U.S. Forest Service is the major knowledge source in these areas. As a consultant, the change agent would help link the growers to previous research knowledge in these areas and, perhaps, to individual researchers in specific locations accessible to the growers (Arrow 1A). In the process of doing this, the change agent is applying certain behavioral science knowledge (Arrow 1B). He might also help translate the research findings into usable ideas—action implications—to help the growers improve their practices. This latter activity is illustrated by Arrow 2 in Figure 1.

All models of change we have discussed *except* research, development, and diffusion include such activities. The research, development, and diffusion model assumes automatic adoption of properly packaged information and is, therefore, oriented almost entirely to the first, external part of input linking (Arrows 1A and, to a limited extent, 1B). The social interaction and diffusion model is, however, *primarily* focused on the change agent activity indicated by Arrow 2, an aspect of input linking which takes into account the specific characteristics of the client system as part of the input linking process.

In the intervention theory and method model, the consulting role of the interventionist is limited to problems involving internal information flow and data use processes. As a consultant, the interventionist would examine existing information linkages within the system,

between data sources and users, would demonstrate the inadequacy or dysfunction of present linkages, and would help the client in designing and implementing more effective linkages. In addition, external behavioral science knowledge might be explicitly brought into the system.

As a *trainer* the change agent is also performing a linking function. In this case the change agent is a linker between the *client user* and the *methods and skills of effective data use*. In this sense, the change agent is engaging in "throughput linking." That is, the change agent is intervening in the information flow and data use processes internal to the client system, trying to help the client learn to modify these processes and thus build more effective *throughput* linkages.

To continue the example of the tree growers, the change agent/trainer might conduct workshop sessions for the growers' association to help them develop skills in retrieving research data and putting these data to practical use. The change agent/trainer might, for example, teach the growers how to obtain, read, evaluate, and use U.S. Forest Service research report data. This training role is shown by Arrow 3 in Figure 1. The skills developed on the part of the clients would be useful after the change agent leaves the system, indicated by Arrows 3A and 3B.

While the planned change and action-research models would both fit our example, thus far, the intervention theory and method model does so in a more limited way. That is, throughput linking is greatly emphasized, but only for data internal to the client system. These data would be concerned with internal problems and processes. We noted earlier that the planned change model puts the change agent in the role of a "methodological-process advocate," committed to changing the basic methods and processes by which the client obtains and uses information. In intervention theory and method, this aim receives primary emphasis. The planned change and action-research models promote change in internal processes by demonstrating the use of alternative, more functional, processes in a variety of specific problem situations. Intervention theory and method specifies one general problem, this being the use of certain dysfunctional (or the lack of specific functional) data generation, dissemination, and use processes. Thus, the action-research or planned change trainer would probably engage in all of the training activities mentioned above with respect to the tree growers example, but the intervention theory and method trainer would focus on how the growers share information and their data use (decision making) processes. The research, development, and diffusion and social interaction and diffusion models, of course, involve none of these activities.

Finally, as a *researcher* the change agent links the *outcomes of practice* to external *knowledge banks*. That is, the change agent translates new information, gained by means of the first two linking activities, into general knowledge available to other scientists, usually applied behavioral scientists but possibly scientists working in the discipline of the client system. This activity could be termed "output linking," for the change agent is acting to link the knowledge output of his own consulting and training activities into the general bank of knowledge available to other applied behavioral scientists.[8]

8. We might note that the behavioral science disciplines, seen as social systems, focus almost exclusively on the research, development, and diffusion and social interaction and diffusion approaches for transmitting new knowledge to users (other behavioral scientists). While considerable research has been done during the past decade (e.g., Garvey & Griffith, 1971), action changes seem to involve variations on these two approaches (e.g., the Experimental Publication System and the Journal Supplement Abstract Service).

Concluding the example of the tree growers, the change agent/researcher is concerned with evaluation and measurement. The growers would receive help in developing means of evaluating the results of the applications they made based on the data they retrieved. If the measures showed that the outcomes were beneficial, this would provide support for both the specific changes and for the processes used to create the changes. If the results were neutral or negative, the change agent would help the client determine the causes, whether due to inadequate actions or to faulty use of the methods the change agent was trying to train the clients to use.

The change agent/researcher might, however, go further in evaluating the process of change that was used with this group of Christmas tree growers. By doing this, the change agent will be able to inform professional colleagues that the model and methods used do or do not work as expected, are valuable or should be avoided.

These activities are summarized in Figure 1 under "research activities." The first such activity, helping the client evaluate the effects of knowledge use, is clearly specified by the intervention theory and method, planned change, and action-research models and is emphasized in intervention theory and method in large part due to the trainer-research role overlap in this activity. That is, the primary reason for the first research activity, in intervention theory and method, is to train the client in evaluation skills. Thus, mostly out of concern for client use of evaluation skills and methods, indicated by Arrow 3B in Figure 1, the first research activity receives considerable emphasis in the intervention theory and method model. This is a significant factor in planned change and action research, but the change agent researcher using those models would be equally interested in this activity as it relates to and is necessary for the other two activities: evaluating the total process of change, and linking the knowledge obtained to professional knowledge banks.

The second research activity might also be performed by an interventionist using the intervention theory and method model, but this does not seem to necessarily follow from the model, as it now stands. The planned change model, however, places a fair degree of emphasis on evaluation of the overall change process—in effect an evaluation of whether the model was properly applied as well as of the adequacy of the model itself.

As for the third research activity, the primary activity of output linking, only the action-research model is explicit in making this a part of the change process (Arrow 5). Most often, such output linking would take place with respect to the field of behavioral science knowledge (Arrow 5A), but it is also possible that knowledge could be generated which would be of value to researchers and practitioners in the specific discipline related to the technology of the client system (Arrow 5B). The action researcher might, then, share with professional colleagues the specific results of three somewhat different intervention methods that were used with the Christmas tree growers association, as well as an evaluation, for this type of client system, of the utility of the change model. In addition, the change agent might help these tree growers share with other growers certain improved methods of planting, developed in the context of the change effort, which resulted in greater crop yield.

DISCUSSION AND CONCLUSION

We have not, of course, exhausted the range of possible comparisons among the five models. Some, like intervention theory and method, are focused almost exclusively on the *process* of change, while others, such as the research, development, and diffusion model, are concerned primarily with the *technical content* of innovation. The other three models fall between these extremes. We have neglected this and other comparisons because they do not bear directly upon the issue of information flow and data use.

Another omission is more serious. We have spoken very little of relevant research evidence regarding the five models. Of course, some research data exist concerning each of the models; generally that research has been performed by behavioral scientists who have been instrumental in developing the model being tested. We do not, however, mean to cast aspersions on such validation studies. In fact, we would suggest that each of the models can be applied with positive results in certain circumstances. However, we also believe that some of these models are more generally effective and useful than others, particularly considering the increasing rate of and need for effective response to change by organizations of all types. Effective, problem-solving changes require effective flow of information and use of data. While the research, development, and diffusion and social interaction and diffusion models may be useful in certain, rather limited, situations, the latter three models, intervention theory and method, planned change, and action research, should form the basic repertoire of change agent approaches. It is generally recognized that effective change agents are familiar with and able to use a variety of different approaches (e.g., see Beckhard, 1969; Bennis, 1969). While the action-research model provides the only complete change process model (in terms of our analysis of the information flow and data use roles of the change agent), to the extent that a recent text defines action research as one of the bases of organization development (French & Bell, 1973), the intervention theory and method and planned change models should also, we believe, be of general use to the applied behavioral scientist. In addition, as noted above, the research, development, and diffusion and social interaction and diffusion models may prove useful in certain circumstances and should not simply be disregarded. However, the circumstances which indicate the use of one model over the others remain to be determined. This leads us to consideration of needed research areas.

RESEARCH DIRECTIONS

Our analysis implies at least three significant areas of needed research. First, a comparative analysis of the effects and effectiveness of the five models in similar and different situations would prove most valuable. Second, the three change agent roles and the three linking activities should be examined. Third, research is needed on the viability of individual and team operationalization of the three roles.

All three research areas require comparative analyses—involving similar and different client systems—and longitudinal measures. We briefly consider each of the suggested areas as follows.

• *Comparison of models.* Obviously, a primary research direction is the determination of the conditions under which one model is more useful than another. Despite the difficulties associated with comparative field studies (e.g., Seashore, 1964), possibilities do exist.

As an example, Morris has proposed a research design[9] to test three of the data use models in health care delivery systems concerned primarily with the delivery of ambulatory care. In this design three different change models would be tested in each of four types of practice setting. Practice Setting 1 would be composed of medical groups who charge fees for service given as the service is used; Setting 2 would be groups who are of the prepaid membership type; Setting 3 would be urban neighborhood centers; the fourth would

be grouped "solo" practitioners, delivering office care.

Within each practice setting three identical groups of physicians, who provide the type of care defined by that setting, would be formed. Thus, four provider groups, in four different settings, would receive the social interaction and diffusion treatment. Similarly, four provider groups, one from each setting, would receive the planned change treatment and four other groups would receive the research, development, and diffusion treatment.

In each of the provider groups, ambulatory care criteria would be established, and data from provider records would be collected relating to the performance of provider group practitioners. In the planned change treatment the data would be returned to each of the four groups in seminars; action derivation sessions would be held; goals for actions would be set; and several reinforcement visits and short events would be conducted by the change agent over a nine-month period. For the social interaction and diffusion treatment two information "gatekeeper" physicians would be recruited from each of the four provider groups; a data use seminar would be held with these eight persons; action plans would be developed; and the change agent would meet periodically with each provider gatekeeper pair over the nine-month period. In the research, development, and diffusion model application, the change agent would prepare a complete package of the data for each of the four groups and mail or deliver the package to them, with some suggestions on how it was to be used.

At the beginning of the second year a complete data collection process would take place for the second time, and the three data use processes would be repeated for the second year with data collection again at the beginning of the third year. At the close of this three-year study, we should be able to determine fairly clearly and predict with reason-

---

9. This example is based on an actual research design proposal. Various details have been altered.

able certainty which of the three data use processes had and will have the most influence on the use of performance criteria to improve the quality of patient care. From this kind of design, it is possible to isolate the main effects of practice setting, type of data use (change model) process, and their interactions.

• *Change agent roles.* Research in this area must focus on the way different change agents operationalize the three roles we have defined (consulting, training, research) and the three linking activities (input, throughput, output), in terms of information flow and data use processes. Such a study would not be fully compatible with the example given above, comparing different models, since a change agent operating primarily in a consultant, or consultant and trainer, role could not be expected to fulfill the researcher role, as well. Perhaps the most logical approach here would be the identification and role categorization (in terms of the three roles and the three linking activities) of a number of different change agent practitioners involved with similar client systems. This would be followed by research observation, data collection, and evaluation by independent researchers. In this way, it could be determined whether the roles and activities, as we have defined them, do exist and are effectively used, and in what situations certain roles and activities should be emphasized or deemphasized, for maximal effectiveness of the change effort. Such a project would also be useful in determining the extent to which the models we have defined are actually used, explicitly or implicitly. In addition, operational combinations of change models might well be found, and still other, different, models may be discovered. Such findings would be of particular value in improving the analytic framework developed here.

• *Role operationalization.* We have noted, earlier, that the full operationalization of the three change agent roles may require a team approach; the complexity of the role responsibilities and interactions may be too much for one person. While change agent/researcher teams are no longer uncommon (e.g., Blake, Mouton, Barnes, & Greiner, 1964; Frohman & Water, 1969; Marrow et al., 1967), such studies have not examined the role variables and interactions defined here. Research in this area would probably be more difficult than in the two areas previously discussed. The first area requires primarily an extensive application of current research methods; the second, the cooperation and collaboration of numerous applied behavioral scientists. Investigations in this third area, however, require not only numerous, similar client systems and the collaborative efforts of numerous practitioners but the deliberate formation of different types of teams, a clear definition of and control over the role activities of team members, and, in effect, research on research since some overall research design would be needed to explore, compare, and evaluate the operationalization of the three role activities, one of which is that of researcher.

While it may be unrealistic to call for extensive research in this area, it would be possible, to some extent, to examine certain issues in role operationalization in the context of either of the research areas defined above. At the very least, it would seem possible to compare individual with team approaches for a given model involving the same, carefully defined, change agent role activities.

CONCLUSION

The present analysis adds to our understanding of change processes by integrating several change approaches, with rather different foci, in terms of a common frame of reference: the linking activities of the change agent or applied behavioral scientist with respect to information flow and data use. While our analysis is limited, it does serve to compare, contrast, and integrate a variety of approaches in terms of the rather basic element of communication. While our analysis is but a beginning, such integration seems of considerable importance in a field which is of great relevance to the continued and more effective functioning of society.

In general, we conclude that the action-research model provides the best basis for the effective attainment of adaptive change in social systems, not only because it is the only one of the models we have discussed which is, in our terms, "complete," but because it seems to afford the greatest probability of adding to our knowledge about the change process and problems of change.

NOTES

Argyris, C. Intervention theory and method. Reading, Mass.: Addison-Wesley, 1970.

Beckhard, R. Organization development: Strategies and models. Reading, Mass.: Addison-Wesley, 1969.

Bennis, W. G. Organization development: Its nature and origins. Reading, Mass.: Addison-Wesley, 1969.

Bennis, W. G., Benne, K. D., & Chin, R. The planning of change. New York: Holt, Rinehart & Winston, 1961.

Blake, R. R., Mouton, J. S., Barnes, L. B., & Greiner, L. E. Breakthrough in organization development. Harvard Business Review, 1964, 42(6), 133-155.

Campbell, D. T., & Stanley, J. C. Experimental and quasi-experimental designs for research. Chicago: Rand McNally, 1963.

Cartwright, D. Achieving change in people: Some applications of group dynamics theory. Human Relations, 1951, 4, 381-392.

Coch, L., & French, J. R. P., Jr. Overcoming resistance to change. Human Relations, 1948, 1, 512-532.

Corey, S. M. Action research to improve school practices. New York: Columbia University, Teachers College, Bureau of Publications, 1953.

Fordyce, J. K., & Weil, R. Managing with people. Reading, Mass.: Addison-Wesley, 1971.

French, W. L., & Bell, C. H., Jr. Organization development. Englewood Cliffs, N.J.: Prentice-Hall, 1973.

Frohman, M. A., & Waters, C. A. Building internal resources for organizational development. Paper presented for the staff of the Institute for Social Research, University of Michigan, 1969.

Garvey, W. D., & Griffith, B. C. Scientific communication: Its role in the conduct of research and creation of knowledge. American Psychologist, 1971, 26, 349-362.

Havelock, R. G. Dissemination and translation roles. In T. L. Eidell & J. M. Kitchell (Eds.), Knowledge production and utilization in educational administration. Eugene, Ore.: University Council for Educational Administration, and Center for the Advanced Study of Educational Administration, University of Oregon, 1968.

Havelock, R. G., Guskin, A. E., Frohman, M. A., Havelock, M., Hill, M., & Huber, J. Planning for innovation. Ann Arbor, Mich.: University of Michigan, Institute for Social Research, 1969.

Katz, E. The two-step flow of communication—an up-to-date report on an hypothesis. Public Opinion Quarterly, 1957, 21, 61-78.

Katz, E., & Lazarsfeld, P. Personal influence. Glencoe, Ill.: Free Press, 1955.

Lazarsfeld, P., Berelson, B., & Gaudet, H. The people's choice. (2nd ed.) New York: Columbia University Press, 1948.

Lewin, K. Frontiers in group dynamics. Human Relations, 1947, 1, 5-42. (a)

Lewin, K. Group decision and social change. In T. M. Newcomb & E. L. Hartley (Eds.), Readings in social psychology. New York: Holt, Rinehart & Winston, 1947. (b)

Lewin, K. Resolving social conflict. New York: Harper's, 1948.

Lionberger, H. F. Some characteristics of farm operators sought as sources of farm information in a Missouri community. Rural Sociology, 1953, 18, 327-338.

Lippitt, R., Watson, J., & Westley, B. The dynamics of planned change. New York: Harcourt, Brace & World, 1958.

Marrow, A. J., Bowers, D. G., & Seashore, S. E. Management by participation. New York: Harper & Row, 1967.

Menzel, H., & Katz, E. Social relations and innovation in the medical profession: The epidemiology of a new drug. Public Opinion Quarterly, 1955-1956, 19, 337-352.

Morris, W. C. The information influential

physician: The knowledge flow process among medical practitioners. Unpublished doctoral dissertation, University of Michigan, 1970.

Ruesch, J., & Batson, G. Communication: The social matrix of psychiatry. New York: Norton, 1951.

Seashore, S. E. Field experiments with formal organizations. Human Organization, 1964, 23, 164-170.

Seashore, S. E., & Bowers, D. G. Durability of organizational change. American Psychologist, 1970, 25, 227-233.

Whyte, W. F., & Hamilton, E. L. Action research for management. Homewood, Ill.: Irwin-Dorsey, 1964.

standards
FOR EDUCATIONAL & PSYCHOLOGICAL TESTS

Prepared by a joint committee of the
American Psychological Association
American Educational Research Association
National Council on Measurement in Education
Frederick B. Davis, *Chair*

Published by the
AMERICAN PSYCHOLOGICAL ASSOCIATION, INC.

INTRODUCTION

In March, 1954, the American Psychological Association issued the *Technical Recommendations for Psychological Tests and Diagnostic Techniques*, endorsed by the American Educational Research Association and the National Council on Measurement in Education. In January, 1955, the latter two organizations published a further document, *Technical Recommendations for Achievement Tests*. Subsequently, a joint committee of the three organizations consolidated, modified, and revised the two documents and in 1966, through the American Psychological Association, published the *Standards for Educational and Psychological Tests and Manuals*. The present document is both a revision and an extension of the 1966 *Standards*. It presents standards for test use as well as for test manuals; it is intended to guide both test developers and test users.

A test user is one who chooses tests, interprets scores, or makes decisions based on test scores. (People who do only routine administration or scoring of tests are not included in this definition, although test users often do both.) Test users include clinical or industrial psychologists, research directors, school psychologists, counselors, employment supervisors, teachers, and various administrators who select or interpret tests for their organizations. The audience for the *Standards* is, therefore, broad and cuts across publics with varying backgrounds and different training in measurement and statistics.

those related to validity and reliability, are necessarily technical. These two sections should be meaningful to readers who have training approximately equivalent to a level between the master's degree and the doctorate in education or psychology. However, the remaining sections—the greater part of the document—are generally nontechnical and may be read with profit by all users.

The authors of the 1966 *Standards* declared that a test producer has an obligation to provide enough information about a test so that a qualified user will know what reliance can safely be placed on it; they also provided statements of consensus concerning the information that should be in a manual. It now appears desirable to provide similar statements of consensus concerning competency in testing practices.

Part of the stimulus for revision is an awakened concern about problems like invasion of privacy or discrimination against members of groups such as minorities or women. Serious misuses of tests include, for example, labeling Spanish-speaking children as mentally retarded on the basis of scores on tests standardized on "a representative sample of American children," or using a test with a major loading on verbal comprehension without appropriate validation in an attempt to screen out large numbers of blacks from manipulative jobs requiring minimal verbal communication.

These are specific examples of a

priateness. A test score describes but it does not explain a level of performance. Test performance may be influenced by many factors such as amount and quality of certain kinds of training, distractions during testing, sensory defects, inability to hear instructions because of poor administration, inappropriate language in instructions or in the test, inability to read, brain damage, motivation level, illumination level, cultural background of the examinee, or test-taking strategies.

Some unfairness may be built into a test, for example, requiring an inordinately high level of verbal ability to comprehend the instructions for a nonverbal test. Many of the social ills attributed to tests, however, seem more a result of the ways in which tests have been used than of characteristics of the tests themselves; for example, errors in administration, failure to consider the appropriateness of normative data, failure to choose an appropriate procedure, use of incorrect assumptions about the causes of a low or deviant test score, or administrative rigidity in using test scores for making decisions.

Tests and Test Uses to Which These Standards Apply

It is intended that these standards apply to any assessment procedure, assessment device, or assessment aid; that is, to any systematic basis for making inferences about characteristics of people.

A test is a special case of an assessment procedure. It may be thought of as a set of tasks or questions intended to elicit particular types of behavior when presented under standardized conditions and to yield scores that will have desirable psychometric properties such as high reliability and high validity.

Tests include standardized aptitude and achievement instruments, diagnostic and evaluative devices, interest inventories, personality inventories, projective instruments and related clinical techniques, and many kinds of personal history forms. It was pointed out in the 1966 Standards that the same general types of information are needed for all these varieties of published diagnostic, prognostic, and evaluative devices. It is equally appropriate to point out that unpublished assessment devices can be better used if the same kind of information is available to users.[1]

[1] It is sometimes suggested in response to perceptions of test abuse and unfair uses of tests that a moratorium on testing be observed until better and more appropriate instruments are developed and more equitable instruments can be constructed. The suggestion of such an extreme measure may be indicative of the growing sense of frustration group members who sense that testing has had a disproportionately negative impact on their opportunities for equal access to success in education and employment. This suggestion, although well intended, seems futile for several reasons:

First, it fails to consider unfairness resulting from the misuses of tests. If new and better tests were subject to the same sorts of misuse, they might well produce the same sorts of errors for rejecting the same magnitudes) in the decisions based on them.

Second, it requires a corresponding but unlikely moratorium on decisions. Employers will continue to make employment decisions with or without standardized tests. Colleges and universities will still select students, some elementary pupils will still be recommended for special education, and boards of education will continue to evaluate the success of specific programs. If

There are wide variations in the sophistication of assessment techniques. At one extreme is the test that has gone through several revisions based on many research studies. Such a test may provide normative data based on thousands of cases classified into dozens of subpopulations. At the other extreme is the casual interview that provides assessments based on varying and unsystematically observed cues.

These standards are written specifically to apply to standardized tests. They apply in varying degrees, however, to the entire range of assessment techniques. If it is required that a relationship be demonstrated between scores (assessments) on an employment test and subsequent performance on a job, the requirement should in principle also apply to the judgments (assessments) of the employment interviewer. It may not be possible to apply the standards with the same rigor, but the kind of judgments the interviewer is to make can be identified; the time and procedures for developing and recording them can be standardized; and they can be validated in the same ways that scores are validated. When someone who makes personnel decisions developes his own assessment techniques (a practice not discouraged intentionally in these stan-

those responsible for making decisions do not use standardized assessment techniques, they will use less dependable methods of assessment.

Third, tests are often useful for *finding* talent but are too often used only as devices for rejecting those with low scores; they can also be used to discover potential for performance that might not otherwise be observed. In this way, the use of tests may sometimes improve the prospects of minority group members and women.

There are many dimensions along which measuring instruments can be classified. Some are designed to measure abilities, some to measure accomplishments, others to measure attitudes or interests. Some are inventories, interview aids, biographical data forms, and experimental diagnostic devices, and are not called tests. Generally, however, the word "test" is used in these standards to apply to all kinds of measurement. What these different kinds have in common is that scores with desirable psychometric properties may be derived from each.

These standards also apply to *criterion measures*. Studies evaluating uses of well-developed tests too often employ inadequate criterion data. A criterion measure should have the psychometric properties expected of any other measurement, such as validity, including in special instances some form of criterion-related validity, for example, the relationship of an intermediate criterion measure to an intermediate or more nearly ultimate measure. Criterion development should be guided by the standards guiding test development.

Some assessment techniques are used as interview aids. The intent of such use

dards), he will find the standards useful guides for developing information similar to that in good test manuals; the principles are as relevant to him as to the professional test developer. If he chooses to use a test that has been developed by someone else, he may find the standards helpful in evaluating alternatives from which he may choose; moreover, the standards may help in developing a program of application.

is an idiographic analysis of an individual—an approach to assessment which places special reliance on the skill of the clinician. It is often argued that this use is so unlike the use of other testing procedures that it cannot be judged by essentially psychometric standards. The qualitative nature of the assessment is less the point at issue than the distinction that can be made between clinical and actuarial prediction. When tests, projective or otherwise, are used as aids to an interviewer's assessment, the interviewer is himself the final assessment device, and his assessments become the "scores." These assessments can and should be validated like other psychometric measures.

Component bits of information may be analyzed somewhat as items are analyzed. Proposals for arriving at idiographic interpretations are almost always based partially upon a nomothetic premise; for example, that a Rorschach determinant correlates with a specified internal factor. The usual standards can be applied to premises of this kind. Therefore, although interview aids can present unusual problems, their user requires the same information about them that he requires for any test score, and his use of them is subject to some of the same psychometric considerations (e.g., reliability) applicable to other test scores.

The developer of such an interview aid need not indicate his test's validity by correlating it with any simple criterion. But if he goes so far as to make any generalization about what "most people see" or what "schizo-

statistical claim and should be held to the usual rules for supporting it. Moreover, when on the basis of projective test data, biographical information, or various behavioral cues elicited during an interview the interviewer makes a statement such as "this man will fail or be subject to severe depression if placed in this situation," he is making a prediction based on his assessment and should be held to the standards for demonstrating the validity of his prediction.

A comment also seems appropriate about hidden tests (such as an interviewer's systematic attempt to assess a trait within the context of the interview) or other unobtrusive or observational measures. Some of these may raise ethical problems, but they do not differ, in principle, from other tests, and the standards apply as much to these unseen or unrecognized tests as to those more clearly perceived by the examinee. Therefore, the psychologist who counts examples of a specific type of response in a behavior-modification setting is as much responsible for the validity of his interpretations of change or the basic reliability of his observations as is any other test user.

In short, the standards are intended to be widely applicable both to standardized tests and a wide variety of other assessment techniques. The degree of applicability of individual standards to nontest assessments will vary; developers and users of such assessment procedures should at least observe the spirit of the standards.

Tests are used for basic research purposes as well as for practical purposes. Although these standards were not writ-

qualified investigator should be able to determine the manner in which they apply to his research.

These standards cannot replace instructional material on test development; therefore, there are no specific statements directly related to such procedures as item writing or item analysis.

Information Standards as a Guide to Test Developers

For each test there should be a test manual, perhaps with supplements, to provide enough information for a qualified user to make sound judgments regarding the usefulness and interpretation of test scores. Research is required prior to the release of the test or test scores for operational use.

A manual is to be judged not merely by its literal truthfulness, but by the impression it leaves with the reader. If the typical professional user for whom the manual is prepared is likely to obtain an inaccurate impression of the test from the manual, the manual is poorly written. The standards apply to the spirit and tone of the manual (or supplemental publication) as well as to its literal statements.

A manual must often communicate information to many different groups. Many tests are used by people with limited training in testing. These users may not follow technical discussion or understand detailed statistical information. Other users are measurement specialists; they seek information on which to judge the technical adequacy of the test. Sometimes

in a supplementary handbook. Whatever the form, the prospective test user must have available to him the information needed for making whatever judgments his use of the test requires. Even when the test (or test battery) is developed for use within a single organization, a manual can often be helpful; preparation of a manual helps the test developer organize his thinking, codify his procedures, and communicate his ideas and intentions to his assistants.

It is not appropriate for this publication to call for a particular level of validity or reliability, or otherwise to establish technical test specifications for specific tests, but it is appropriate to ask that any test manual provide the information necessary for a test user to decide whether the consistency, relevance, or standardization of a test makes it suitable for his purpose. These standards need not prescribe minimum statistical specifications. Rather, their intent is to describe in an explicit and conveniently available form the information required by test users. In arriving at those requirements, it has been necessary to judge what is a reasonable compromise between pressures of cost and time, on the one hand, and the ideal, on the other. The test producer ordinarily spends large sums of money in developing and standardizing a test. Insofar as these recommendations indicate the kind of information that is most valuable to test users, authors and publishers can more efficiently allocate funds for gathering and reporting data of greatest value. Some provisions are more applicable than others in any specific case. The completion of predictive validity studies essential before a vocational interest inventory can be used properly, but it may be only desirable for a values inventory and irrelevant for an inventory designed to diagnose mental disorders. These standards, therefore, represent an attempt to state what type of studies should be completed before a test is ready for release to the profession. They can serve as a similar guide for those who are developing tests for their own use.

Procedural Standards as a Guide to Test Users

The test user, in selecting, administering, scoring, or interpreting a test, should know his purposes, what he is doing to achieve those purposes, and their probable consequences. It is not enough to have benign purposes; the user must know the procedures necessary to maximize effectiveness and to minimize unfairness in test use. He must evaluate the many factors that may have influenced test performance in light of his purposes. Where he finds that certain factors would unfairly influence performance, his procedures for using the test and interpreting the scores should be designed to minimize such influences.

Competence in test use is a combination of knowledge of psychometric principles, knowledge of the problem situation in which the testing is to be done, technical skill, and some wisdom. Although it is not appropriate to tell a test user that he needs particular levels of validity and reliability, it is appropriate to ask him to ascertain that his procedures result in reasonably valid predictions or reliable clas-sifications, or otherwise conform to the purposes of his testing. These standards of practice are written more as guidelines than as commandments. It is as necessary to make cost-benefit compromises in test use as in test development. These standards provide useful guidelines for test users as well as for test developers.

Three Levels of Standards

Manuals can never give all the information, and test users can never follow all the procedures that might be desirable. At the same time, restricting this statement of recommendations solely to essential or indispensable information and practices might tend to discourage development and reporting of additional information. The standards are, therefore, grouped in three levels: Essential, Very Desirable, and Desirable. Each proposed requirement is judged based on its importance and the feasibility of attaining it.

The statements listed as Essential are intended to represent the consensus of present-day thinking concerning what is normally required for competent use of a test. Any test or testing situation may present some unique problems; it is undesirable for the standards to be treated as unduly rigid; for example, they should not bind the producer of a novel test to an inappropriate procedure or form of reporting. The Essential standards indicate what information or practices will be needed for most tests in most applications. When a test developer or test user fails to satisfy these requirements, he should do so only as a considered judgment. In any single test or testing situation, there may be some Essential standards that do not apply. It should be noted that many of these standards require thought rather than specific action as an outcome of thought; for example, "A test user should consider...." In most cases, such statements are listed as Essential.

If some type of Essential information is not available on a given test, it is important to help the reader recognize that the research on the test is incomplete in this respect. A test manual should include clear statements of what research has been done and avoid misleading statements.

The category Very Desirable is used to draw attention to types of information or practices that contribute greatly to the user's understanding of the test and to competence in its use. Standards in this category have not been listed as Essential if their usefulness is debatable.

The category Desirable includes information and practices that are helpful but not Essential or Very Desirable.

When a test is widely used, the developer has a greater responsibility for investigating it thoroughly and providing more extensive reports about it than when the test is limited in use. Large sales make research financially possible. Therefore, the developer of a popular test can add information in subsequent editions of the manual. For tests having limited sales, it is unreasonable to expect that as much information will be furnished.

some function and in some situations, but even the best test can have damaging consequences if used inappropriately. Therefore, the primary responsibility for the improvement of testing continues to rest on the shoulders of test users. It is hoped that these standards will be used to extend the professional training of many test users who are not now being trained appropriately. Professional training of personnel managers, school administrators, and classroom teachers should prepare them to better understand information about tests, test interpretations, and these standards. Such training will do much to improve the quality of test use and to minimize the extent of test misuse. The standards draw attention to recent developments in thinking about tests, test analysis, and test use. A comparison of these standards with those in earlier editions should remind test developers and test users that testing is a stable but not a static enterprise and that, in fact, there is room for improvement in the quality of assessments that are being made.

Tests are often developed and used in circumstances that lead to maintaining less than the highest standards of technical excellence. We do not intend to discourage those who must make assessments of people from doing the best they can with whatever training and collaborative resources are available to them. These standards, however, are written to promote excellence. They provide a kind of checklist of factors to be considered in designing, standardizing, validating, scoring, and interpreting tests. They may help test developers and test users decide what studies are needed and how those

Cautions To Be Exercised in the Use of These Standards

Almost any test can be useful for

studies might best be recorded in manuals or in validation reports. Test users who are not going to do independent research on a test should refer to these standards for guidance in the choice, administration, scoring, and interpretation of tests.

It is conceivable that a test developer could fulfill most of the standards presented and still produce a test that would fall short of his intended or stated objectives. Care should be exercised to adhere, both in test development and test use, to the spirit as well as to the letter of these standards. Because of the possibility of misunderstanding or misinterpretation, it would not be appropriate for test developers or test users to state that a manual or procedure "satisfies" or "follows" these standards. There would be no objection to a statement that one has "taken into account or considered" these standards.

A final caveat is necessary in view of the prominence of testing issues in litigation. This document is prepared as a technical guide for those within the sponsoring professions; it is *not* written as law. What is intended is a set of standards to be used in part for self-evaluation by test developers and test users. An evaluation of their competence does not rest on the literal satisfaction of every relevant provision of this document. The individual standards are statements of ideals or goals, some having priority over others. Instead, an evaluation of competence depends on the degree to which the intent of this document has been satisfied by the test developer or user.

STANDARDS FOR TESTS, MANUALS, AND REPORTS

Tests vary in the amount of knowledge and research required to develop them. Much background work is needed for a test that is published or otherwise distributed for widespread use. Less work need be done for a test developed for local use. At any level, however, better tests and testing can be expected where test developers have been guided by fundamental considerations and have demonstrated this in writing.

A test user needs information describing a test's rationale, development, technical characteristics, administration, and interpretation. Such information is ordinarily expected in a test manual or in its supplements. This information is also needed by those using a test or test battery that has not been published but which is used within an organization to aid in making decisions. For these uses, a properly prepared manual reports to local users and to other interested persons (colleagues in other organizations, representatives of governmental agencies, representatives of citizen's groups, etc.) the procedures followed in construction of the test, in its use, and in the interpretation of scores derived from it. In certification or selection programs, a manual can present information about the program as a whole as well as about component tests. Data supporting claims for the program, procedures followed, kinds of tests used, and related information should be recorded not only to provide an adequate basis for the proper use of tests but also to make the information available for public scrutiny.

The development of a test or testing program is based on research; the report of that research is often contained in a manual. These standards, therefore, concentrate on the manual (and any supplementary publication) as the full and proper report of what was done in test development; they specify standards of reporting from which one may infer standards for research.

A. Dissemination of Information

A test user needs information to help him use the test in standard ways and to evaluate a test relative to others he might select for a given purpose. The information that he needs to select a test or to use it must come, at least in part, from the test developer. Practices of authors and publishers in furnishing information have varied. Sometimes the test manual offers only vague directions for administering and scoring, norms of uncertain origin, and perhaps nothing more. In contrast, some manuals furnish extensive information on test development, validity, reliability, bases for normative information, appropriate kinds of interpretations and uses, and they present all such information in detail.

A1. When a test is published or otherwise made available for operational use, it should be accompanied by a manual (or other published or readily available

Information) that makes every reasonable effort to follow the recommendations of these standards and, in particular, to provide the information required to substantiate any claims that have been made for its use. Essential

[Comment: The term "operational use" refers to making practical decisions about the evaluation or handling of individuals, groups, curricula, therapeutic treatments, and so on.

The term "manual" refers to documents describing procedures of test development, use, interpretation, relevant research, normative data, and related information. Depending on such things as the amount of information to report and the diversity of uses and users, the term may designate a document entirely within one cover or a series of separately bound pamphlets. This term might also be extended to include procedural manuals governing the use of tests or of test batteries in, for example, selection situations; the wording and importance of many of these standards would be different for a procedural manual, but the principles applicable to test manuals would at least, therefore, be analogous.

Not all of the standards in this report will apply to any one particular test. A standard may be ignored if it is irrelevant in light of the purpose of the test and the claims made for it, but it may not be ignored merely because it is difficult to meet or has not usually been met by a similar test.]

A1.1. If information needed to support interpretations suggested in the manual cannot be presented at the time the manual is published, the manual should satisfy the intent of standard A1 by pointing out the absence and importance of this information. Essential

A1.2. Where the information is too extensive to be fully reported in the manual, the essential information should be summarized and accompanied by references to other sources of information, such as technical supplements, articles, or books. Very Desirable

[Comment: Developers of some well-known tests provide extensive technical manuals, make further research data available through other sources (such as the Education Resources Information Center), prepare annotated bibliographies, or include relevant information in technical books which users are encouraged to consult. In other instances, the essential information is given in the manual sold with the instrument, along with references to other useful sources.

Publications by persons other than the author of the test frequently fulfill many functions of a manual. If a book about a test is designed to serve as a manual, its author and publisher have the same responsibility in preparing it as do the author and publisher of a test.]

A1.2.1. When information about a test is provided in a separate publication, that publication should meet the same standards of accuracy and freedom from misleading impressions that apply to the manual. Essential

A1.2.2. Promotional material for a test should be accurate and should not give the reader false impressions. Essential

[Comment: One publisher presents an extensive and complete bibliography, without comment or annotation, of research involving a test; he does not mention that many of the entries are studies with negative findings. The impression is one of extensive use, not of limitations to the usefulness of the test.]

A1.2.3. Informational material distributed within a using organization should be accurate, complete for the purposes of the reader's need, and written in language that will not give the reader a false impression. Essential

[Comment: Such information is often given in brief memoranda. In preparing these brief reports, the technical capability of the readers may be kept in mind, but this does not suggest that essential information be either omitted or distorted in the interest of simplicity. Where a reader may be expected to receive such reports regularly, efforts can be made to increase his ability to understand technical detail.]

A2. A test manual should describe fully the development of the test: the rationale, specifications followed in writing items or selecting observations, and procedures and results of item analysis or other research. Essential

A2.1. Data gathered during the process of developing a test before it is in final form should be clearly distinguished from data pertaining to the test in final form. Essential

A2.2. A test manual should specify the need for maintaining necessary test security. Very Desirable

[Comment: For example, a manual might describe some acceptable coaching practices. If so, it would be appropriate to add warnings against unacceptable practices that might jeopardize test security.]

A2.3. A test manual or supplementary document should provide representative sample items and a statement of the intended purpose of the test in a form that can be made available to those concerned about the nature and quality of a testing program. Very Desirable

[Comment: The evaluation of a test may not fall exclusively to those who are technically trained. Examinees, members of citizen panels, civil rights advocates, and parents are among those who may have reason to make judgments about the appropriateness of a test. Their right to do so need not conflict with the necessity to maintain test security if descriptive and explanatory materials are made available.

One publisher of educational tests has published descriptive material in nontechnical language for a wide variety of tests; pamphlets include information on test development and rationale as well as examples of items and suggestions on test-taking strategies.]

A2.4. The identity and professional qualifications of item writers and editors should be described in instances where they are relevant; for example, when adequacy of coverage of a subject-matter achievement test cannot appropriately or practically be measured against any external criterion. Desirable

A3. The test and its manual should be revised at appropriate intervals. The time for revision has arrived whenever changing conditions of use or new research data make any statements in the manual incorrect or misleading. Very Desirable

[Comment: The technical characteristics and the appropriateness of a test may change as social conditions and attitudes, job definitions, educational pressures, or the composition of relevant school populations change.]

A3.1. Competent studies of the test following its publication, whether the results are favorable or unfavorable to the test, should be taken into account in revised editions of the manual or its supplementary reports. Pertinent studies by investigators other than the test authors and publishers should be included. Very Desirable

[Comment: The developer of one test has published a comprehensive review of validity studies of the test covering a 15-year period.]

A3.2. When the test is revised or a new form is issued, the manual should be suitably revised to take those changes into account. In addition, the nature and extent of the revision and the comparability of data from the old test and the revised test should be explicitly stated. Essential

[Comment: It is useful for publishers to identify revisions of test manuals in their catalogs and to take other steps to increase the probability that test users have current information.]

A3.2.1. If a short form of a test is prepared by reducing the number of items or organizing a portion of the test into a separate form, new evidence should be obtained and reported for that shorter test. Essential

[Comment: It is especially important to report the reliability and other technical data for the test in its shorter form, since placing items in a new context may alter responses to them.

In the manual for one test that has two alternate forms, the validity data presented were obtained using the sum of the scores of the two forms. It would have been more appropriate to have presented the data for each form independently.]

A3.2.2. When a short form is prepared from an established test, the manual should present evidence that the items in the short form represent the items in the long form or measure the same characteristics as the long form. Very Desirable

[Comment: When no short form of a test has been prepared but there is reason to believe that it is commonly used in a shortened form, the manual should remind the reader that data in the manual may not be applicable to results of administration of a shortened form.

One revision of a long-established achievement test battery illustrates a desirable practice by listing all previous editions and then describing in detail the relation of the new revision to the previous editions.]

B. Aids to Interpretation

The responsibility for making inferences about the meaning and legitimate uses of test results rests primarily with the user. In making such judgments, however, he must depend in part on information about the test made available by its developer.

The manual or report form from a scoring service cannot fully prepare the user for interpreting the test. He will sometimes have to make judgments that have not been substantiated by published evidence. Thus, the vocational counselor cannot expect to have validity data available for each job about which he makes tentative predictions from test scores. The counselor or employment interviewer will have examinees who do not fit into any group for which normative or validity data are available. The teacher will have to evaluate the content of an achievement test in terms of his instructional goals and emphasis. The clinician must bring general data and theory into his interpretation of data from a personality inventory. The degree to which the manual can be expected to prepare the user for accurate interpretation and effective use of the test varies with the type of test and the purpose for which it is used. It is the test developer's responsibility to provide the information necessary for good judgment; in fact, developers should make tests as difficult to misuse and to misinterpret as they can.

B1. The test, the manual, the record forms, and other accompanying material should help users make correct interpretations of the test results and should warn against common misuses. Essential

B1.1. Names given to published tests, and to parts within tests, should be chosen to minimize the risk of misinterpretation by test purchasers and subjects. Essential

[Comment: It is desirable that names carry no unwarranted suggestion as to the characteristics measured. Such descriptions as "culture-free," "intelligence," "introversion," "creativity," "primary mental abilities," or "productivity quotients" are questionable for published tests, unless there is appropriate evidence of construct validity, since they may suggest interpretations going beyond the demonstrable meaning of the scores.]

B1.1.1. Devices for identifying interests and personality traits through self-report should be entitled "inventories," "questionnaires," or "checklists" rather than "tests." Very Desirable

[Comment: In referring to such instruments in textual material, however, as in these standards, the word "test" may be used to simplify the language even where it is properly avoided in the title.]

B1.2. The manual should draw the user's attention to data that especially need to be taken into account in the interpretation of test scores. Very Desirable

[Comment: Many test manuals point out variables that should be considered in the interpretation of a test score, such as information about school record, recommendations, or clinically relevant history.

A personality assessment manual may provide data to show that the psychologist should consider such facts as the sex and age of the subject, whether his parents are dead or separated, the ages and sexes of his siblings, or his vocational or marital status.]

B1.3. The manual should call attention to marked influences on test scores known to be associated with region, socioeconomic status, race, creed, color, national origin, or sex. Essential

[Comment: Social or cultural factors known to affect performance on the test differentially, administrator errors that are frequently repeated, examiner-examinee differences, and other factors that may result in spurious or unfair test scores should, for example, be clearly and prominently identified in the manual.]

B1.4. The manual should draw attention to, and warn against, any serious error of interpretation that is known to be frequent. Essential

[Comment: Some users of general intelligence tests think of the score as a direct measure of inherent native ability, given and unchanging; manuals of such tests may be expected to caution against this interpretation and to do so with reference to appropriate data. They should clearly warn users against unwarranted assumptions about the generality of normative data, particularly avoiding the impression that national norms are genuinely representative when in fact they are not. Manuals for interest inventories can apply this standard by stressing the fact that interest does not necessarily imply ability and is only one of many factors to be considered in choosing among occupations.]

B2. The test manual should state explicitly the purposes and applications for which the test is recommended. Essential

[Comment: A clear statement of a test's purposes will help prevent the misapplication of test scores. It will alert the user to the kind and extent of evidence he should expect to find in the manual in support of the claims made for the test by the author and publisher. For example, if an achievement test is recommended as a survey test of what students know, an accurate description of its content is important. If, on the other hand, it is recommended as a diagnostic test or one that predicts performance, data on its relationship with one or more criteria are required. See Section E on validity.]

B2.1. If a test is intended for research use only and is not distributed for operational use, that fact should be prominently stated in the accompanying materials. Essential

[Comment: If the developer of a new device (e.g., for studying personality) releases his instrument for studies by other investigators before he considers it ready for operational use, it is appropriate to print "distributed for research use only" on the test package, on the cover of the booklet of directions, and in any catalog where it is listed. This cautions against premature use of the instrument in guidance or selection.]

B3. The test manual should describe clearly the psychological, educational, or other reasoning underlying the test and nature of the characteristic it is intended to measure. Essential

[Comment: There ordinarily are explicit reasons for setting up the test as it has been done; it may be assumed that certain psychological processes are required in taking the test and that certain traits are being measured as a result. The identification of these processes may be based on a theory, empirical research, or empirical processes internal to the test itself. In any case, a clear description of the construct or content and of the manner of measurement enables a user to judge the test by its conformity to his own psychological or educational insight as well as by statistical evidence of its efficacy.]

B3.1. In the case of tests developed for content-referenced interpretation, special attention should be given to defining the content domain in operational terms. In the case of a mastery test, the test developer's rationale for any cutting score that he suggests should be specified, or the procedures that the user might employ to establish mastery levels should be described. Essential

[Comment: The test user needs such information so that he can compare his concept of mastery or competence with that of the test author.]

B4. The test manual should identify any special qualifications required to administer the test and to interpret it properly. Essential

[Comment: One manual differentiates psychologists who work with children from those who work only with adults in identifying qualifications needed to use an individually administered test for children. Another offers specifications for administering the test to non-English-speaking students.

User qualifications might be described in terms of special training generally thought necessary to achieve competence. It may be possible for some test manuals to identify the most frequent sources of error in test use and to specify the kind of user training necessary to eliminate these common errors.

B4.1. The test manual should not imply that a test is "self-interpreting." It should specify information to be given about test results to persons who lack the training usually required to interpret them. Essential

[Comment: It is not ordinarily desirable to entrust interpretation of scores to an untrained person. There are, of course, tests that can be scored by the examinee, and it is often useful to give scores to students or parents. Where these practices are followed, the sense of this standard is that interpretative aids should also be given.

The manual should indicate what may be done by untrained persons and what should not be done. The manual for one well-known interests test, for example, indicates that examinees may perform the mechanics of scoring their own tests but properly stresses that they need the help of a trained teacher or counselor in making interpretations and future plans.]

B4.2. Where a test is recommended for a variety of purposes or types of inference, the manual should indicate the amount of training required for each use. Essential

B4.3. The manual should draw the user's attention to references with which he should become familiar before attempting to interpret the test results. Very Desirable

[Comment: The references might be to books or articles dealing with related psychological theory or with the particular test in question.]

B5. Evidence of validity and reliability, along with other relevant research data, should be presented in support of any claims being made. Essential

[Comment: Standards for validity and reliability are extensive. Moreover, they are as applicable to research reports prepared by test users as to test manuals. For these reasons, and because of their overreaching importance, a major section of this document presents standards for reports of research on validity and reliability. Adherence to the intent of this standard requires adherence to the appropriate standards in that section.]

B5.1. Statements in the manual reporting relationships are by implication quantitative and should be stated as precisely as the data permit. If data to support such statements have not been collected, that fact should be made clear. Essential

[Comment: Writers sometimes say, for example, "Spatial ability is required for architectural engineering." or, "Bizarre responses may indicate schizophrenic tendencies." Such statements by themselves are quantitatively inadequate. In what proportion of cases giving bizarre responses has schizophrenia been shown to develop? How much has architectural success been found to depend upon spatial ability? Numerical data relating the test scores to definite criteria would help to provide the answers.]

B5.2. Statistical procedures that are well known and readily interpreted should be preferred for reporting any quantitative information. Any uncommon statistical techniques should be explained, and references to descriptions of them should be given. Essential

[Comment: Publishers need not uniformly adhere to the procedures commonly used for reporting data, but terminology and procedures should be sufficiently common in practice to permit adequate judgment by reasonably competent users.]

This standard is an elaboration of the principle that data presented in a manual should not be misleading. For example, it is misleading to show the value of combining tests in a battery in a regression equation by using data where intercorrelations are lower than those reported elsewhere in the manual.]

B5.3. When the statistical significance of a relationship is reported, the statistical report should be in a form that makes clear the sensitivity or power of the significance test. Essential

[Comment: Statistical significance that has no practical usefulness can often be obtained by using a very large number of cases. For example, a well-known inventory yields statistically significant differences between large samples of males and of females, but the differences are too small to be of practical importance. Conversely, one who uses an insensitive statistical test can falsely conclude that there is no difference of practical importance. In general, it is more appropriate in reporting test data to state a confidence interval or the likelihood function for the parameter of interest than to report only that the null hypothesis can or cannot be rejected.]

B5.4. The manual should differentiate between an interpretation that is applicable only to average tendencies of a group and one that is applicable to an individual within the group. Very Desirable

B5.5. The manual should state clearly what interpretations are intended for each subscore as well as for the total test. Essential

[Comment: Where subscores are obtained only for convenience in scoring the test, and no interpretation is intended, this should be made clear. For some tests, keys are provided for subscores that have possible research use but are not intended to be interpreted; this should be made clear.]

B6. Test developers or others offering computer services for test interpretation should provide a manual reporting the rationale and evidence in support of computer-based interpretations of scores. Essential

[Comment: A computer makes possible the storage and recall of large amounts of data; test interpretation can be greatly assisted by the use of computer data banks. Computer scoring services may provide lengthy printouts of descriptive and prognostic information from individual profiles on a test battery or personality inventory. The user of such printouts needs to know the reasoning and the evidence supporting the suggested interpretations because they are as fallible as other subjective interpretations.]

C. Directions for Administration and Scoring

Interpretations of test and measurement techniques, like those of experimental results, are most reliable when the measurements are obtained under standardized or controlled conditions. To be sure, there are circumstances in testing where it may be important to change conditions systematically for maximum understanding of the performance of an individual. For example, an examiner may systematically modify procedures in successive readministrations of a test to explore the limits of a child's mastery of a specific content area such as a set of concepts. Nevertheless, the test developer should provide a standard procedure from which modifications can be made. Without standardization, the quality of interpretations will be reduced to whatever extent differences in procedure influence performance.

For most purposes, great emphasis is properly placed on strict standardization of procedures for administering a test and reciting its instructions. If a test is to be used for a wide range of subpopulations, these procedures should be wholly comprehensible to all examinees in each subpopulation.

C1. The directions for administration should be presented in the test manual with sufficient clarity and emphasis so that the test user can duplicate, and will be encouraged to duplicate, the administrative conditions under which the norms and the data on reliability and validity were obtained. Essential

[Comment: Because persons administering tests in schools and industry sometimes may not follow instructions rigidly and may not understand the need for doing so, it is necessary that the manual be insistent and persuasive on this point. Some tests are fully administered by tape recordings to insure standardization of procedure.]

C1.1. The directions published in the test manual should be complete enough that persons tested will understand the task as the author intended. Essential

[Comment: For example, in a personality inventory, it may be intended that the subject give the first response that occurs to him. If so, this expectation should be made clear in the directions read by or to the subject. Directions for interest inventories should specify whether the person is to mark what things he would ideally like to do or whether he is also to consider the possibility that he would have the opportunity and ability to do them. Likewise, the directions should specify whether the person is to mark those things he would like to do and does oc-casionally, or only those things he would like to do and does regularly.]

C1.1.1. The directions should clearly point out such critical matters as instructions on guessing, time limits, and procedures for marking answer sheets. Essential

C1.1.2. The directions to the test administrator should include guidance for dealing with questions from examinees. Very Desirable

C1.2. If expansion or elaboration of instructions described in the test manual is permitted, the conditions under which this may be done should be clearly stated either in the form of giving general rules or in terms of giving numerous examples, or both. Essential

C2. Instructions should prepare the examinee for the examination: Sample material, practice use of answer sheets or punch cards, sample questions, etc., should be provided. Desirable

[Comment: The extent and nature of such material depends on expected levels of knowledge among examinees. For example, extensive practice material might be wasteful if developed for frequently tested school children and for a commonly encountered type of test; it may be very important for a novel test format to be administered to older job applicants.]

C3. The procedures for scoring the test should be presented in the test manual with a maximum of detail and clarity to reduce the likelihood of scoring error. Essential

C3.1. The test manual should furnish scoring instructions that maximize the accuracy of scoring an objective test by outlining a procedure for checking the obtained scores for computational or clerical errors. Very Desirable

C3.2. Where subjective processes enter into the scoring of a test, evidence on the degree of agreement between independent scorings under operational conditions should be presented in the test manual. If such evidence is not provided, the manual should draw attention to scoring variations as a possible significant source of errors of measurement. Very Desirable

C3.2.1. The bases for scoring and the procedures for training scorers should be presented in the test manual in sufficient detail to permit other scorers to reach the level of agreement reported in studies of scorer agreement given in the manual. Very Desirable

C3.2.2. If persons having various degrees of supervised training are expected to score the test, studies of the interscorer agreement at each skill level should be presented in the test manual. Desirable

C3.3. If the test is designed to use more than one method for the examinee's recording of his reponses, such as hand-scored answer sheets, or entering of responses in the test booklet, the test manual should report data on the degree to which results from these methods are interchangeable. Essential

[Comment: The different amounts of time required for responding to items in forms adapted to different scoring methods may affect the reliability or validity of the test or the applicability of the test norms.]

C3.4. If an unusual or complicated scoring system is used, the test manual should indicate the approximate amount of time required to score the test. Desirable

C3.5. "Correction-for-guessing" formulas should be used with multiple-choice and true-false items when the test is speeded. Desirable

D. Norms and Scales

Interpretations of test scores traditionally have been *norm referenced*; that is, an individuals score is interpreted in terms of comparisons with scores made by other individuals. Alternative interpretations are possible. *Content-referenced* interpretations are those where the score is directly interpreted in terms of performance at each point on the achievement continuum being measured. *Criterion-referenced* interpretations are those where the score is directly interpreted in terms of performance at any given point on the continuum of an *external* variable. An external criterion variable might be grade averages or levels of job performance.[2]

[2]Current usage in educational measurement commonly refers to "criterion-referenced" interpretations for *both* alternatives to interpretations requiring norms. The different meanings of the word "criterion," however, produce some confusion; some measurement specialists have therefore turned to the term "content referenced" and this usage is adopted here. The word "criterion," as it is used in the phrase "criterion-related" validity (that is, an external variable) has suggested a similar but distinguishable alternative to normative interpretation; therefore, "content-referenced" and criterion-referenced" are not interchangeable terms as used in this document.)

The standards in this section refer principally to tests intended for norm-referenced test interpretations rather than for content-referenced interpretations.

D1. Norms should be published in the test manual at the time of release of the test for operational use. Essential

D1.1. Norms should be established even for a test developed only for local use or only for predictive purposes. Desirable

[Comment: It is sometimes forgotten that norms tables provide information useful for purposes other than comparing one individual with group data. For example, a test user can derive information from a normative table at which the score levels at which the discrimination power of the measurement is good or poor.]

D1.2. Even though a test is expected to be used primarily with local norms, the test manual should nevertheless provide normative data to aid the interpreter who lacks local norms. Very Desirable

[Comment: The manual for one instrument designed to measure employee aptitude stresses the value of local norms but also includes norms based on a wide variety of occupational and educational classifications.]

D2. Norms presented in the test manual should refer to defined and clearly described populations. These populations should be the groups with whom users of the test will ordinarily wish to compare the persons tested. Essential

[Comment: It should be noted that "populations" are plural; in nearly all instances of tests developed for other than purely local use, the user needs to know the applicability of the test to different groups. For tests developed with a view to widespread use in schools or industry, information is needed about differences or similarities of normative data for appropriate subgroups such as sex, ethnic, grade, or age groups. Users need to be alert to situations when norms are less extensive for one group than another.

For example, the manual for an occupational interest inventory, or for an aptitude test particularly useful in certain occupations, should point out that a person who has a high degree of interest or aptitude in a curriculum or occupation when compared to people in general will usually have a lower degree of interest or aptitude compared to persons actually engaged in that field. Thus, a high percentile score on a scale reflecting musical interest, in which the examinee is compared with people in general, may be equivalent to a low percentile where the examinee is compared with professional musicians.]

D2.1. Care should be taken to avoid misleading impressions about the generality of normative data. Essential

[Comment: Truly representative national norms, for example, are rarely if ever obtained; normative data collected from people or schools with specific characteristics, however, are frequently used as if they were taken from a representative national group. Thus, we have test users who may say that an examinee's performance is at a "tenth-grade reading level," without qualification when the norms are in fact obtained only from superior schools voluntarily participating in the test research. It is an error of interpretation to assume that the norms of the volunteer group of schools apply to schools in general; the incidence of such errors may be reduced by manuals that clearly define the characteristics of the normative populations.]

D2.1.1. The test manual should report the method of sampling from the population of examinees and should discuss any probable bias in this sampling procedure. Essential

D2.1.2. Norms reported in any test manual should be based on well-planned samplings rather than on data collected primarily because it is readily available. Any deviations from the plan should be reported along with descriptions of actions taken or not taken with respect to them. Essential

[Comment: Occupational and educational test norms have often been based on scattered groups of test papers, for authors sometimes have requested that all users mail in results for use in subsequent reports of norms. Distributions so obtained are subject to unknown degrees and types of biases. Hence, the methods of obtaining such samples should be clearly described.]

D2.1.3. In addition to reporting the number of individuals in a set of normative data, the manual should also report the number of sampling units from which those individuals were drawn along with the numbers of individuals in each unit. Essential

D2.2. The description of the norms group in the test manual should be complete enough so that the user can judge its appropriateness for his use. The description should include number of cases, classified by one or more of such relevant variables as ethnic mix, socioeconomic level, age, sex, locale, and educational status. If cluster sampling is employed, the description of the norms group should state the number of separate groups tested. Essential

[Comment: Manuals often use too gross a classification system in describing their normative data. For example, the manual for one employee aptitude test provides a variety of normative data for many occupational and educational groupings. However, the lack of information as to sex, ethnic origins, age, education, and experience levels within these groupings considerably reduces the usefulness of the norms.]

D2.2.1. The populations upon which the psychometric properties of a test were determined and for which normative data are available should be *clearly and prominently described* in the manual. Any accompanying report forms should provide space for identifying the normative groups used in interpreting the scores. Essential

[Comment: The intent of this standard is to provide a warning to consumers (users and examinees) against unwarranted interpretations. If a standard report form results in percentile-rank or standard-score interpretations by consistently using the same normative population, the definition of that population, with an indication of the time period of data collection, would be sufficient.]

D2.3. If the sample on which norms are based is small or otherwise undependable, the user should be cautioned explicitly in the test manual regarding the possible magnitude of errors arising in the interpretation of scores. Very Desirable

D2.4. Norms on subtests or groups of test items should be reported in the test manual only if the validity and reliability of such subtests or groups of items are also indicated. Essential

[Comment: The test user is justified in assuming that, when norms are given for part of a test, the author implies their usefulness for interpreting performance. The reliability and validities of such scores should be reported.]

D2.5. The significant aspects of conditions under which normative data were obtained should be reported in the test manual. Essential

[Comment: Some tests are standardized on job-applicant groups, others on groups that have requested vocational guidance, and, still others, on groups that realized that they were experimental subjects. While precise description of levels is probably not always possible, motivation for taking tests, test-taking attitudes, abilities, and personality characteristics often differ within these groups and from group to group.]

D3. In reporting norms, test manuals should use percentiles for one or more appropriate reference groups or standard scores for which the basis is clearly set forth; any exceptional type of score or unit should be explained and justified. Measures of central tendency and variability always should be reported. Essential

D3.1. In the case of tests used for prediction, expectancy tables or experience tables translating obtained scores into probabilities of success or into proficiency levels should be included whenever possible. Desirable

D4. Local norms are more important for many uses of tests than are published norms. A test manual should suggest using local norms in such situations. Very Desirable

D5. Derived scales used for reporting scores should be carefully described in the test manual to increase the likelihood of accurate interpretation of scores by both the test interpreter and the examinee. Essential

[Comment: It would be helpful if the number of kinds of derived scales could be reduced to a few with which testers can become familiar. The present variety makes description necessary in each manual. In part the problem is that many different systems are now used that have no logical advantage over others; some may have outlived their usefulness. New scaling methods may be used in attempts to overcome presumed difficulties with older ones. The variety of scales for reporting test scores can create confusion and misinterpretation unless the scales recommended for a given test are clearly and fully explained.]

D5.1. Derivation of any scale from normative data should be clearly and unambiguously described in terms likely to prevent user misinterpretations or overgeneralization. Essential

[Comment: Derived scores can be very useful for drawing inferences. Too often, however, they are treated as if they had absolute meaning independent of a particular test or normative population. An example is the IQ; it is often simply a standard score, but it is frequently refied and interpreted as representing an unchanging and unchangeable characteristic of the person tested. Grade-equivalent scores or even percentile ranks may also be misinterpreted as absolute entities unless the manual makes clear the reference group on which they were based.]

D5.2. When standard scores are used, the system should be consistent with the purposes for which the test is intended and should be described in detail in the test manual. The reasons for choosing one scale in preference to another should also be made clear in the manual. Very Desirable

D5.2.1. The manual should specify whether standard scores are linear transformations of raw scores or are normalized. Essential

D5.2.2. The choice of a standard scale should be based upon either the standard error of measurement of raw scores or on some other basis that is clearly defined. Desirable

[Comment: There are many standard-score scales in use. The scale for reporting scores on one widely used test is so designed that each unit of the scale is equal to about one thirtieth of the overall standard error of measurement; a different test used for similar purposes is scaled so that one unit is equal to about one third the overall standard error of measurement. The former scale suggests a greater degree of precision than the latter, but this implication is unwarranted.]

D5.2.3. Interpretive scores that lend themselves to gross misinterpretations, such as mental-age or grade-equivalent scores, should be abandoned or their use discouraged. Very Desirable

[Comment: When, despite this recommendation, such scores are included in a manual, their relationship to standard scores or percentile ranks, within each category and within an appropriate norm group, should also be provided in tabular form. For example, the table might show, in addition to a grade-equivalent score, the corresponding percentile rank within the examinee's own age or grade level for each raw score. At the high school level, norms within courses (for example, second-year Spanish) may be more appropriate than norms within grades.]

D5.3. When it is suggested in the test manual that percentile ranks are to be plotted on a profile sheet, the profile sheet should be based on the normal probability scale or some other appropriate nonlinear transformation. Very Desirable

D5.4. Normative data should be provided in a form that emphasizes the fallibility of an obtained score. Very Desirable

[Comment: Some publishers provide norms showing ranges of standard scores or percentile ranks that have designated probability levels including the true score. A norms table might show for each raw score, not only the associated standard score or percentile rank but also the values for raw scores at plus and at minus one standard error of measurement for each raw score.

D6. If scales are revised, new forms added, or other changes made, the revised test manual should provide tables of equivalence between the new and the old forms. This provision is particularly important in cases where data are recorded on cumulative records. Desirable

[Comment: New forms of a test should be equated to *recently determined* standard-score scales of other forms, in order that the user may be confident that the scores furnished by the new forms are comparable with those of earlier forms.]

D6.1. When a new form is equated with an older form of a test, the revised manual should describe the content of both old and new forms and the nature of the norms group for each form. Essential

[Comment: Changes in knowledge, technology, or curricula may require that new editions of a test differ in important respects from earlier editions, and the demand for continuity may require that the scales for reporting scores be equated. There is some doubt as to whether meaningful comparability of scores is possible with changed content, however, and a user should be able to evaluate claims of equivalency in terms of the kinds of content changes that have occurred.]

D6.2. The manual should describe the method used to establish equivalent or comparable scores and should include an assessment of the accuracy of the equating procedure. Very Desirable

D7. Where it is expected that a test will be used to assess groups rather than individuals (i.e., for schools or programs), normative data based on group summary statistics should be provided. Essential

[Comment: For example, it is inappropriate to evaluate schools by using norms developed for the evaluation of individuals. It is also inappropriate to compute group means for nonlinear scales such as percentile ranks derived for individual norms.

STANDARDS FOR REPORTS OF RESEARCH ON RELIABILITY AND VALIDITY

A test developer must provide evidence of the reliability and validity of his test; it is usually reported in the test manual. Many test users should do similar research on their own application of the test. Their reports often differ from those in test manuals by being more detailed or more specific to a particular problem, or by validating test batteries rather than individual tests. Despite such differences, the standards of research, and of research reporting, should be generally similar in the two situations.

E. Validity

Questions of validity are questions of what may properly be inferred from a test score; validity refers to the appropriateness of inferences from test scores or other forms of assessment. The many types of validity questions can, for convenience, be reduced to two: (a) What can be inferred about what is being measured by the test? (b) What can be inferred about other behavior?

The first question inquires into the intrinsic nature of the measurement itself. The measuring instrument is an operational definition of a specified domain of skill or knowledge, or of a trait, of interest to the test developer or user. The essential problem in this context is to reach some conclusion as to how faithfully the scores represent that domain, and it is appropriate to speak of the validity of the measurement.

The second question inquires into the usefulness of the measurement as an indicator of some other variable as a predictor of behavior. In this context, the essential problem is to reach some conclusion about how well scores on the test are related to some other performance, and it is appropriate to speak of the closeness of the relationship.

The two questions are not necessarily independent. For example, where the test is a sample of the "other behavior," the answer is the same for either question. Moreover, answers to both questions may require a knowledge of the interrelationships between the test scores and other variables. A thorough understanding of validity may require many investigations. The investigative processes of gathering or evaluating the necessary data are called validation. There are various methods of validation, and all, in a fundamental sense, require a definition of what is to be inferred from the scores and data to show that there is an acceptable basis for such inferences.

It is important to note that validity is itself inferred, not measured. Validity coefficients may be presented in a manual, but validity for a particular aspect of test use is inferred from this collection of coefficients. It is, therefore, something that is *judged* as adequate, or marginal, or unsatisfactory.

The kinds of validity depend upon the kinds of inferences one might wish to draw from test scores. Four interdependent kinds of inferential interpretation are traditionally described to summarize most test use: the *criterion-related* validities (*predictive* and *concurrent*); *content* validity; and *construct* validity.[3] (So-called "face" validity, the mere appearance of validity, is not an acceptable basis for interpretive interferences from test scores.)

These aspects of validity can be discussed independently, but only for convenience. They are interrelated operationally and logically; only rarely is one of them alone important in a particular situation. A thorough study of a test may often involve information about all types of validity. In developing or choosing a test for prediction, one should first postulate the constructs likely to provide a basis for useful prediction of the variable of interest; the measures chosen should have adequate construct validity. The information about construct validity may make a test more useful. To

---

[3]Many other terms have been used. Examples include synthetic validity, convergent validity, job-analytic validity, rational validity, and factorial validity. In general, such terms refer to specific procedures for evaluating validity rather than to new kinds of interpretive inferences. Any specially-named procedures, including these examples, should meet the standards of investigation contained in this section. These standards apply generally to the various statistics or procedures that might be used in support of one or more classes of inferences from test scores.

evaluate construct validity, all knowledge regarding validity is relevant. A reading comprehension test, for example, may be used and validated for all three types of inference: how well it predicts future academic performance, how well it samples a defined content area of material to read, and how well it measures the construct of comprehension.

Criterion-Related Validities

Criterion-related validities apply when one wishes to infer from a test score an individual's most probable standing on some other variable called a criterion. Statements of predictive validity indicate the extent to which an individual's future level on the criterion can be predicted from a knowledge of prior test performance; statements of concurrent validity indicate the extent to which the test may be used to estimate an individual's present standing on the criterion. The distinction is important. Predictive validity involves a time interval during which something may happen (e.g., people are trained, or gain experience, or are subjected to some treatment). Concurrent validity reflects only the status quo at a particular time. Under appropriate circumstances, data obtained in a concurrent study may be used to estimate the predictive validity of a test. However, concurrent validity should not be used as a substitute for predictive validity without an appropriate supporting rationale.

For many test uses, such as for selection decisions or assignment to treatment, predictive validity provides the appropriate model for evaluating the use of a test or test battery. In employment testing, for example, use of

any procedure implies prediction to some degree. Whether one uses a carefully developed test or casual judgments of interviewers, their use for selection purposes assumes that applicants who obtain high scores will become better employees than applicants who obtain low scores.

Other forms of validity are not substitutes for criterion-related validity. In choosing a test to select people for a job, for example, an abundance of evidence of the construct validity of a test of flexibility in divergent thinking, or of the content validity of a test of elementary calculus, is of no predictive value without reason to believe that flexibility of thinking or knowledge of calculus aids performance on that job. The *model* of predictive validity should guide thinking about validity in such applications even where circumstances preclude an actual criterion-related validation study. Whatever other validity information a manual may include, one or more studies of criterion-related validity must be included for any test developed for prediction and for many tests intended for diagnosis; otherwise, such tests can only be regarded as experimental.

Many factors may make a single, obtained validity coefficient questionable. First, the conditions of a validation study are never exactly repeated. Rapidly changing conditions may limit the usefulness of a predictive study. The logic of predictive validation assumes that conditions existing at the start of the time sequence will exist again after the study is completed. Second, the logic of criterion-related validity assumes that the criterion possesses validity. All too often, tests

are validated against any available criterion with no corresponding investigation of the criterion itself. The merit of a criterion-related validity study depends on the appropriateness and quality of the criterion measure chosen. In applied research, the criterion should be chosen with reference to the problem at hand, and the test or other assessment technique should be chosen with reference to the criterion. If the study is done primarily to enhance understanding of what a test measures, criteria should be selected in terms of beliefs about the nature of the construct reflected by the test scores. In either case, the adequacy of the study depends on the adequacy of the criterion. Criterion-related validity studies based on the "criterion at hand," chosen more for availability than for a place in a carefully reasoned hypothesis, are to be deplored.

Third, the logic of criterion-related validity assumes that the sample is truly representative of the population for which the later inferences are to be drawn. In practice, samples are often nonrepresentative because of, for example, restricted range, preselection, or attrition before a predictive study can be completed.

Fourth, in many practical situations validity studies cannot be done with adequate numbers of cases, and the investigators must do the best they can with the data at hand. It may be better to try to investigate criterion-related validity, even if imperfectly, than to accept totally untested hypotheses. However, "doing something" is not necessarily better than doing nothing; the results of an inadequate study may be quite misleading. Results of validation studies with severely restricted ranges or small Ns are especially open to question.

Content Validity

Evidence of content validity is required when the test user wishes to estimate how an individual performs in the universe of situations that the test is intended to represent. Content validity is most commonly evaluated for tests of skill or knowledge; it may also be appropriate to inquire into the content validities of personality inventories, behavior checklists, or measures of various aptitudes. The present discussion will be directed toward the more typical case of achievement testing.

To demonstrate the content validity of a set of test scores, one must show that the behaviors demonstrated in testing constitute a representative sample of behaviors to be exhibited in a desired performance domain. Definitions of the performance domain, the users' objectives, and the method of sampling are critical to claims of content validity. An investigation of content validity requires that the test developer or test user specify his objectives and carefully define the performance domain in light of those objectives. The definition should ordinarily specify the results of learning rather than the processes by which learning is either acquired or demonstrated. It should be sufficiently detailed and organized to show the degree to which component tasks make up the total domain.

Definition of the performance domain is relatively simple where it is finite and unambiguous, as in a simple test of addition for elementary-school use. Depending upon instructional

objectives, the performance domain might be defined as *all* addition problems of three to five single-integer addends. The total number of problems and the relative frequency of occurrence of specific integers or pairs of integers within that total are known, and the representativeness of any sample of such problems can be easily judged.

If a test is used to estimate achievement in American history in Grade 12, the performance domain is less objectively defined. Given agreement on instructional objectives, it could be defined in terms of the types and quantities of the skills, facts, and concepts of American history, as determined by the pooled judgments of authorities, experienced teachers, and competent curriculum makers in that field. A definition of the total universe might well be tempered by the specific instructional objectives accepted by the panel. A definition appropriate for evaluation of performance at the end of the year of study would differ from the definition appropriate for developing an examination over knowledge of the colonial period. Within such limits, the performance domain requires definition so carefully detailed that rules for item writing will assure appropriate representation of all facets of the definition. It should be noted that an achievement test so constructed would not necessarily constitute a representative sample of the skills, facts, and concepts taught by any particular teacher during any particular year. Consequently, a definition of the performance domain of interest must always be provided by a test user so that the content of a test may be checked against an appropriate task universe.

It is appropriate to inquire into the content validity of many employment tests. Examples would include tests of typing skill, driving ability, or knowledge of certain regulatory laws. The performance domain for published tests might be defined by the pooled judgments of job designers, incumbents, and supervisors. Test users might define the performance domain of interest to them in terms of judgments of similar people in their own organizations or, preferably, in terms of appropriately detailed and comprehensive job analyses. The question of objectives would again enter into the definition; unless only fully trained and experienced people are to be hired, applicants cannot be expected to demonstrate proficiency in all facets of a job. The performance domain would need definition in terms of the objectives of measurement, restricted perhaps only to critical, most frequent, or prerequisite work behaviors.

It should be clear that content validity is quite different from face validity. Content validity is determined by a set of operations, and one evaluates content validity by the thoroughness and care with which these operations have been conducted. In contrast, face validity is a judgment that the requirements of a test merely *appear* to be relevant. The writing of items in terms used in a particular job or by a particular subgroup of the population may give an appearance of relevance while contributing nothing to content validity or indeed to any other useful validity information (although such items may serve a useful public-relations function).

In defining the content universe, a

test developer or user is accountable for the adequacy of his definition. An employer cannot justify an employment test on grounds of content validity if he cannot demonstrate that the content universe includes all, or nearly all, important parts of the job.

Construct Validity

A psychological construct is an idea developed or "constructed" as a work of informed, scientific imagination; that is, it is a theoretical idea developed to explain and to organize some aspects of existing knowledge. Terms such as "anxiety," "clerical aptitude," or "reading readiness" refer to such constructs, but the construct is much more than the label; it is a dimension understood or inferred from its network of interrelationships.[4] It may be necessary to postulate several different constructs to account for the variance in any given set of test scores. Moreover, different constructs may be required to account for the variance in different tests of the same general type, or a given test may provide evidence relating to several constructs. For example, given proper evidence, scores on vocabulary tests might be used to infer (a) the level of present vocabulary; (b) the existence of pathology, interests, or values; or (c) intellectual capacity.

Construct validity is implied when one evaluates a test or other set of operations in light of the specified construct. Judgments of construct

---

[4]This is an admittedly restricted statement of the nature of scientific constructs, which may include entities as well as dimensions. Constructs of interest in the present context are, however, primarily quantitative.

validity are useful in efforts to improve measures for the scientific study of a construct. They are also useful when a test developer or test user wishes to learn more about the psychological qualities being measured by a test than can be learned from a single criterion-related validity coefficient.

Evidence of construct validity is not found in a single study; rather, judgments of construct validity are based upon an accumulation of research results. In obtaining the information needed to establish construct validity, the investigator begins by formulating hypotheses about the characteristics of those who have high scores on the test in contrast to those who have low scores. Taken together, such hypotheses form at least a tentative theory about the nature of the construct the test is believed to be measuring. In a full investigation, the test may be the dependent variable in some studies and the independent variable in others. Some hypotheses may be "counterhypotheses" suggested by competing interpretations or theories.

Such hypotheses or theoretical formulations lead to certain predictions about how people at different score levels on the test will behave on certain other tests or in certain defined situations. If the test measures about what the test measures is essentially correct, most of his predictions should be confirmed. If they are not, he may revise his definition of the construct, or he may revise the test to make it a better measure of the construct he had in mind. Through the process of successive verification, modification, or elimination of hypo-

theses, the investigator increases his understanding of the qualities measured by the test. Through the process of confirmation or disconfirmation, test revision, and new research on the revised instrument, he improves the usefulness of the test as a measure of a construct.

It is important to note in this that the investigation of construct validity refers to a specific test and not necessarily to any other test given the same label.

Evidence of construct validity may also be inferred from the procedures followed in developing a test. For example, in a measure of mechanical interest, a double item analysis may be used to reduce the effect of verbal ability. A preliminary item analysis might be done using a standard verbal-comprehension test as an external criterion. Those items with a very low discrimination index in this analysis could then be subjected to a second item analysis, a conventional internal-consistency analysis. Only those items with a low discrimination index in the first analysis and a high discrimination index in the second analysis would be included in the final item pool.

Although evidence of construct validity may be developed on the basis of a series of criterion-related studies, it is important to note that evidence of the construct validity of a test is *not* adequate evidence of the usefulness of the construct in specific further hypotheses. In the selection of hypotheses, for example, it is often hypothesized that success is a function of sociability. If one has a measure of sociability with generally acceptable evidence of its validity as a measure of sociability, he may expect to find it

useful as a predictor of sales success; perhaps some of the evidence of the construct validity of that measure came, in fact, from confirmation of such an expectation. However, the test may have no predictive validity against the criterion of success in an engineering sales job. In such a case it is not the construct validity of the sociability measure that is to be questioned.

General Principles

A test developer, or anyone who conducts validation research, should provide as much validity information as possible so the user can evaluate the test or the research for his own purposes. A test manual can provide evidence that will enable the user to evaluate the appropriateness of the item content, to determine whether the test is an acceptable measure of a specified construct, and to decide whether the test has provided useful predictive validities in situations similar to his own. An adequate research report can help the user decide whether to go ahead with the use of the test or to seek another predictor.

research reported elsewhere, either by the test developer or by others. Preferably, the manual will report on individual studies and provide summaries of validity data for various kinds of interpretations or inferences.]

E1.1. Statements about validity should refer to the validity of particular interpretations or of particular types of decisions. Essential

[Comment: It is incorrect to use the unqualified phrase "the validity of the test." *No test is valid for all purposes or in all situations or for all groups of individuals.* Any study of test validity is pertinent to only a few of the possible uses of or inferences from the test scores.

If the test is likely to be used incorrectly for certain areas of decision, the manual should include specific warnings. For example, the manual for a writing-skills test stated that the test apparently was not sufficiently difficult to discriminate among students "at colleges that have selective admissions."]

E1. A manual or research report should present the evidence of validity for each type of inference for which use of the test is recommended. If validity for some suggested interpretation has not been clearly indicated, that fact should be made clear. Essential

[Comment: Validation studies are a part of the process of test development; test users expect them to be reported in detail by the developer, preferably in the manual itself. At the very least, the manual should summarize competent

E1.2. Wherever interpretation of subscores, score differences, or profiles is suggested, the evidence justifying such interpretation should be made explicit. (See also B5.5.) Essential

E1.2.1. If the manual suggests that the user consider an individual's responses to specific items as a basis for assessment, it should either present evidence supporting this use or call attention to the absence of such data. The manual should warn the reader that inferences based on responses to single items are subject to extreme error. Hence, they should be used only to direct further inquiry, perhaps in a counseling interview. Essential

E1.3. To insure the continued correct interpretation of scores, the validity of suggested interpretations should be rechecked periodically; test developers should report results in subsequent editions of the manual. Very Desirable

[Comment: Job duties, conditions of work, and the types of individuals entering an occupation often change materially with the passage of time. Similarly, the meanings of clinical categories, the nature of therapeutic treatment, and the objectives of academic programs change. The difficulty and psychological meaning of test items will also change. Hence, the reader should be in a position to judge the extent to which tests are obsolete.]

E1.3.1. If factors that may affect test performance or the validity of a suggested test interpretation have changed, and validity studies have not been repeated for the changed conditions, the test should be withdrawn from general sale and distributed, if at all, only to persons who will conduct their own validity studies. Very Desirable

[Comment: It should be noted that no specific time interval is mentioned. Test developers and publishers should know the relevant conditions and should be able and willing to obtain new validity information when such conditions have changed. It is not necessary to repeat every part of the validation; what is needed is a repetition of those studies most likely to have been rendered obsolete. In the case of some inventories and biographical-data forms, scoring keys should be reevaluated after relatively brief periods of time.]

E1.4. Correlations of item scores with total scores on the test in which the item is included (or a parallel form of that test) may be presented as item-discrimination coefficients, but they should not be presented or used as item-validity coefficients. Essential

[Comment: Item-discrimination coefficients are useful in reasoning about construct validity, and such information is appropriately included in a manual. However, they are indicators of internal consistency, not of validity.]

E2. A test user is responsible for marshalling the evidence in support of his claims of validity and reliability. The use of test scores in decision rules should be supported by evidence. Essential

[Comment: It is a basic responsibility of a test user to read, understand, and evaluate the manual, the research, and the literature to show the appropriateness of the test for the intended use. A large-scale user may have the added responsibility for empirical research bearing on his claims of test validity. Evidence of validity is needed for all bases for decision, not merely those that are easy to study. It is a peculiar paradox that many employers and schools are abandoning the use of standardized tests and are turning instead to casual assessment techniques likely to be less valid. Many employers use procedures with no validity, or biased selection procedures of unknown validity rather than objective procedures for which evidence of validity could have been assembled.]

E2.1. Test users are responsible for gathering data on the validity and reliability of their assessment techniques. Very Desirable

[Comment: For many individual test users, this may be a nearly impossible requirement. It would seem, however, that a test user has an obligation to gather data, at least on an informal basis, in an effort to evaluate his work. In even the most difficult circumstances, a test user can be alert to data suggesting possible lack of validity.]

E2.2. If a user wants to use a test in a situation for which the use of the test has not been previously validated, or for which there is no supported claim for validity, he is responsible for validation. Very Desirable

[Comment: He who makes the claim for validity is responsible for providing the evidence. Evidence of validity sufficient for test use may often be obtained in a well-documented manual. If the test user wishes to claim that the validity generalizes beyond the evidence for the kinds of situations reported in the manual, it is his responsibility to demonstrate it.]

E2.3. When a test user plans to make a substantial change in test format, instructions, language, or content, he should revalidate the use of the tests for the changed conditions. Essential

Criterion-Related Validity

E3. All measures of criteria should be described completely and accurately. The manual or research report should comment on the adequacy of a criterion. Whenever feasible, it should draw attention to significant aspects of performance that the criterion measure does not reflect and to irrelevant factors likely to affect it. Essential

[Comment: Desirable practices are illustrated in a manual for a test designed to measure abstract intelligence. Several validity studies relating this instrument to criteria are reported, some involving concurrent measures and others involving predictions over periods of time. Limitations of the studies are recognized, and it is stated that "no one criterion is uniquely appropriate." The value of local norms is stressed, and an example of a local expectancy table is provided.

In the case of interest measures, it is sometimes not made clear whether the criterion indicates satisfaction, success, or merely continuance in the activity under examination. When criterion groups include people in a given occupation and when a comparison of such groups is made to people in general, the manual should point out the distinction between working in an occupation and success in it or satisfaction with it.]

E3.1. When the validity of a test for predicting occupational performance is reported, the manual should describe the duties of the workers as well as give their job titles. Very Desirable

[Comment: The principle is that information should be given from which the reader can make judgments of the relevance of the criterion. The description of a criterion is often incomplete without such information.

E3.1.1. Where a wide range of duties is subsumed under a given occupational label, the test user should be warned against assuming that only one pattern of interests or abilities is compatible with the occupation. Essential

E4. A criterion measure should itself be studied for evidence of validity and that evidence should be presented in the manual or report. Very Desirable

[Comment: Criterion measures are forms of assessment and are subject to the same standards governing the development and use of any assessment technique. For many employment and educational purposes, the ideal criterion may be an achievement test or work sample judged acceptable in terms of content validity. Supervisory or instructor ratings are more common but may be questioned in terms of construct validity. For example, a rating of proficiency may be defined to include elements of both speed and accuracy, but to exclude elements of dependability. A judgment of acceptable construct validity might be based on evidence of high correlations of the ratings with production data or work samples and of independence from seniority or attendance data.]

E4.1. Particular attention should be given to potential sources of criterion contamination; results of investigations of contamination should be reported. Essential

[Comment: Results of such investigations are often ambiguous, and readers should be warned of this fact. For example, an investigation of possible sex differences in criterion ratings might show significant differences between men and women. That fact in itself, however, is not sufficient evidence of criterion contamination; it might reflect actual sex differences in performance.]

E4.1.1. The criterion score should be determined independently of test scores. The manual should describe precautions taken to avoid contamination of the criterion or should warn the reader of possible contamination. Essential

[Comment: When the criterion is based on judgment, the manual should state whether the test data were available to the judge or were capable of influencing the judgments in any other way. If the test data could have influenced the criterion rating, the user should be warned that the reported validities are likely to be spuriously high.]

E4.2. The basis for judgments of criterion relevance should be clearly set forth. Essential

E4.3. Criterion-related validation should ordinarily consider more than a single global criterion. Very Desirable

[Comment: In most situations where decision rules based on testing are worthwhile, performance falls along many dimensions that may be independent. Combining unrelated aspects of behavior into a single composite criterion may obscure important relationships and reduce a test user's opportunity to identify and understand valid test interpretations. A problem exists in that single decisions must frequently be made on multivariate bases. Nevertheless, it is preferable to find a decision rule for combining predictions than to use a decision rule for combining predictors of ambiguous validity.]

E4.4. In criterion-related validation, it is important that the criterion measure have substantial reliability. Very Desirable

[Comment: Since corrections for unreliability of a criterion can be made with generally reasonable statistical assumptions, the degree of reliability of a criterion is perhaps less important than the degree of reliability of the predictor. Nevertheless, reliability is not a trivial consideration; reasonable effort should be made to assure a level of reliability such that statistical corrections are unlikely to change interpretations markedly.]

E4.4.1. Since the criterion measure is a sample of all possible measures of the same criterion construct, reliability should be reported in terms of the agreement of that sample with other similar samples where feasible. If such evidence cannot be given, the author should make this clear and should discuss the probable extent of agreement of the sample with other samples as judged from indirect evidence. Very Desirable

[Comment: When validity is measured by agreement of the test with psychiatric judgment, for example, the degree of agreement among judges should be described. Where a published achievement test is used as a criterion measure, the form-to-form agreement or the reliability reported by the test's author may be used as a basis for evaluating the criterion. due regard being given to the effect of differences between the present sample of persons and the original sample.]

E4.4.2. When validity is appraised by agreement of test results with psychiatric diagnoses, the diagnostic terms or categories should be defined specifically and described clearly. Very Desirable

[Comment: For example, "paranoid schizophrenia, chronic" is preferable as a category to "schizophrenia." Since the types of patients included in specific diagnostic classifications depend to some extent on the point of view of the classifying psychiatrist, an amplified description of each diagnostic category used in the validity study should be presented.]

E4.4.3. When validity is appraised by the agreement of test results with psychiatric judgments, the training, experience, and professional status of the judge(s) should be stated, and the nature and extent of his contacts with the patients and other factors influencing the interaction should be reported. Very Desirable

E.5. The manual or research report should provide information on the appropriateness of or limits to the generalizability of validity information. Very Desirable

E5.1. A test manual should report evidence of validity for each type of criterion about which a recommendation is made. If validity for some recommended interpretation has not been tested, that fact should be made clear. Essential

[Comment: This principle should not be interpreted as license to present as valid, any information various correlations with irrelevant variables. Data should be presented with reference to recommended interpretations, either supporting those interpretations or suggesting limitations to them.]

E5.2. For any type of prediction, a test manual should report criterion-related validities for a variety of institutions or situations. Where validity studies have been confined to a limited range of situations, the manual should remind the reader of the risks involved in generalizing to other types of situations. Essential

E5.2.1. Validity coefficients are specific to the situations in which they are obtained. If the manual is to suggest generalization of validity for prediction of a given kind of criterion construct, it must present data suggesting the limits of generalizability regarding population or sample characteristics, situational context variables, or variations in criterion measurement. Very Desirable

E5.2.2. Local collection of evidence on criterion-related validity is frequently more useful than published data. In such cases the manual should suggest appropriate emphasis on local validity studies; and test users should, where feasible, conduct such studies. Desirable

[Comment: In cases where criteria differ from one locality to another or from one institution to another, no published validity data can serve all localities. For example, the validity of a certain test for predicting grades at a college with a unique kind of curriculum may be quite different from the published validities of the same test based on a more conventional curriculum.

Some publishers have made available advice on local validation studies, including information on the preparation of expectancy tables.]

E6. The sample employed in a validity study and the conditions under which testing is done should be consistent with recommended test use and should be described sufficiently for the reader to judge its pertinence to his situation. Essential

E6.1. Any selective factor determining the composition of the validation sample should be indicated in a manual or research report. The sample should be described in terms of those variables known as thought to affect validity, such as age, sex, socioeconomic status, ethnic origin, residential region, level of education, or other demographic or psychological characteristics. Essential

[Comment: If a validity study uses patients as subjects, the diagnoses of the patients would usually be important to report. The severity of the diagnosed condition should be stated when feasible. For tests used in industry the employment status, occupational experience, and the sex and ethnic composition of the sample should be described. For tests used in educational settings, relevant information may include community characteristics or any selection policies.]

E6.1.1. Evidence of validity should be obtained for subjects who are of the same age or in the same educational or vocational situation as the persons for whom the test is recommended. Any deviation from this requirement should be described in the manual or research report. Essential

[Comment: Validity information for tests intended for guidance should generally be determined on subjects tested prior to or near the time when they are making educational or vocational choices.

One interest inventory was first standardized on men currently employed in the occupation in question. The ability of these scales to differentiate between occupational groups did not, in and of itself, warrant using the inventory in the counseling of high school or college students. Better evidence was obtained later by administering the inventory to students, determining the nature of their later employment, and then establishing the relation between preoccupation score and later occupation.

If an interest inventory uses a criterion of enrollment or nonenrollment in a certain occupation, the sample used in its validation should include only the range of mental ability appropriate to the occupational group. For example, college students are not suitable subjects with whom to estimate the validity of an inventory of interest in manual skills, even though some of them later enter manual occupations.]

E6.1.2. If an ability test is to be used for educational or occupational selection, its validity should be established using subjects who are actual candidates and who are therefore ordinarily motivated to perform well. If the subjects used in a validity study are volunteers or were told that their test scores would not be used in making decisions about them, this fact should be made clear. Very Desirable

[Comment: Widespread use is made in industrial selection of the "present-employee method" of validation. Typically, this involves administering the tests to present employees who are told that their performance on the test will not influence their employment situation. The motivational difference may distort sample characteristics in that it introduces a completely new variable to the testing situation.]

E6.2. Basic statistics should be reported in describing the sample, including numbers of cases (and the reasons for any eliminated cases) and measures of central tendency and variability. A description of the distribution, perhaps with measures of skewness and kurtosis, should also be included. Very Desirable

[Comment: The smaller the number of cases in a validation sample, the less reliable the statistics. Consider, for example, the effect of the number of cases on the 95% confidence interval when the obtained correlation coefficient is .30. With 250 pairs of observations, the interval runs from .18 to .41. Where $N = 50$, the interval runs from .02 to .53; where $N = 25$, the interval runs from $-.10$ to $+.62$.]

When N is very small, an obtained correlation coefficient of zero may result in the erroneous rejection of a valid test.]

E6.2.1. If the distribution of test scores in a validation sample is markedly different from the distribution of scores in the group with whom the test is ordinarily used, data based on these scores, including estimates of population parameters, should be interpreted with great caution. Reports of parameter estimates should cite the original statistics, the distribution characteristics used in making the new estimate, and the statistical procedures employed. Essential

[Comment: The reader of the manual or research report needs to evaluate any adjustments made because of atypical sample characteristics. The assumptions underlying such adjustments are frequently ignored; the resulting errors are of undetermined size and direction. Despite such difficulties, an estimate of the appropriate statistic is often needed. The reported validity coefficient, for example, should reflect the predictive power of a test in the group to which it will be applied.]

E6.2.2. Statistical corrections, such as those for restriction of range, should not be made in situations where mean performance in the sample is in the validation study is so different from the mean performance of the population in which it is to be used as to suggest differences in parent populations. Very Desirable

[Conment: A validation study was conducted on a sample of applicants

hired in a period when the rejection ratio was very high, resulting in a serious restriction of range. However, the passage of time brought with it changes in performance standards and in recruiting activities; the variance was greater and the mean was lower in a new sample than in the sample used in the validation study. The situational and psychometric facts together identify a change in groups more important than differences in variance alone, and a "correction" based on sample variances is therefore inappropriate.

In this situation it would be more appropriate to replicate the study with the new applicant population than to "correct" data obtained from the old population for restriction of range.]

E7. The collection of data for a validity study should follow procedures consistent with the purposes of the study. Essential

E7.1. Where feasible, a test should not be used as a basis for decision while its proposed use is being validated. Desirable

[Comment: In many practical situations, decisions must be made whether or not there is a validated basis for them. In some circumstances, high costs may necessitate the use of a test even though it has not been validated, but great caution should then be exercised. In a selection situation, for example, decisions should not be so highly selective that restriction of range makes discovery of validity impossible. Wherever possible, at least some validation research should be done before a test is put to use as a decision

instrument, and further data should be gathered subsequently.]

E7.2. If the validity sample is made up of records accumulated haphazardly or voluntarily submitted by test users, this fact should be stated in the manual or research report, and the test user should be warned that the group is not a systematic or random sample of any specifiable population. Probable selective factors and their presumed influence on the test variable should be stated. Essential

[Comment: While it is entirely appropriate to include in the manual such phrases as "the author and publisher of this test would welcome additional data derived from its use," it is difficult to judge the quality and representativeness of most of the resulting reports.]

E7.3. In collecting data for a validity study, the person who interprets the test results should have only that information about the examinees that is ordinarily expected to be available in practical use of the test, or he should be sufficiently trained and disciplined disregard information ordinarily not available to him. If there is any possible contamination associated with prior favorable or unfavorable knowledge about the examinees, the manual should discuss its effect on the outcome of the study. Very Desirable

E7.4. The time elapsing between the test administration and the collection of criterion data should be reported in the manual. If the criterion data are collected over a period of time, beginning and ending dates should be included. Essential

E7.4.1. Validation reports should be clearly dated, with the time interval given during which the data were collected. Essential

[Comment: Validity may deteriorate over time; in employment testing, for example, changes in jobs, work aids, and in the ability levels of applicant populations tend to change the circumstances in which validity information is developed.]

E7.4.2. In general, a test user should be cautious in making long-term predictions. Essential

[Comment: Short-term predictions are much more likely to be valid than are long-term predictions because they are less subject to influences other than the characteristics measured.]

E7.4.3. If a test is recommended for long-term predictions, but comparisons with concurrent criteria only are presented, the manual should emphasize that the validity of long-term predictions is undetermined. Essential

E7.4.4. The amount and kind of any experience or training received by the subjects between the time of testing and the time of criterion measurement should be stated. Very Desirable

E7.4.5. When validity for predicting grades in a course is reported, reasonably clear information should be provided regarding the types of performance required in the course, the nature of the instructional method, and the way in which performance is measured. If the test was administered after the course was started, this fact should be made clear. Very Desirable

E8. Any statistical analysis of criterion-related validity should be reported in the manual in a form that enables the reader to determine how much confidence is to be placed in judgments or predictions regarding the individual. Essential

E8.1. A report of criterion-related validity should give full information about the statistical analysis and should ordinarily include, in addition to such basic descriptive statistics as means and standard deviations, one or more of the following: (a) one or more correlation coefficients of a familiar type, (b) descriptions of the efficiency with which the test separates criterion groups, (c) expectancy tables, or (d) charts that graphically illustrate the relationship between test and criterion. Essential

[Comment: Full information includes data on the reliability, the strength, and the nature of the relationship. In correlational terms, this would imply information about the statistical significance and magnitude of the correlation coefficient and about the regression equation.

Reports solely of differences between group means give inadequate information regarding validity; if variance is large, classification may be inaccurate even if means differ considerably. The strength of the relationship may be indicated by describing the amount of misclassification or of overlapping. Expectancy tables may provide information about the nature of the predictions.

In general, since manuals and research reports are often directed to test users who have limited statistical knowledge, every effort should be made to communicate validity information clearly.]

E8.1.1. Errors of prediction should be estimated and reported; a validity coefficient should be supplemented with reports of the regression slope and intercept and of the standard error of estimate. Very Desirable

[Comment: The required information could be presented in an expectancy table showing the range of possible criterion values for each of several points on the score range. The standard error of estimate at different points along the score range is often helpful.

For a dichotomous criterion, this objective might be achieved by indicating the proportion of hits, misses, and false inclusions at various cutting scores.]

E8.1.2. For some users, analysis of test variance according to the following sources is appropriate: variance relevant to the criterion, variance explained as form-to-form or trial-to-trial inconsistency, and a reliable but irrelevant remainder. Very Desirable

[Comment: Such an analysis is more complete and less subject to misinterpretation than a correlation coefficient, including even a "corrected" validity coefficient, or a comparison of group means.]

E8.1.3. The method of statistical analysis should be chosen with due consideration of the characteristics of the data and of the assumptions of the method. Essential

[Comment: Data may often depart from the assumed characteristics with little ill effect. Some violation of assumptions may, however, be seriously misleading. For example, the use of predictions based on the assumption of a normal bivariate correlation surface may seriously overestimate the mean performance of high-scoring candidates if the data are markedly heteroscedastic (as in triangular scatter distributions). In such cases, a method of analysis not based on assumptions about the bivariate distribution would present a more accurate statement of validity.]

E8.2. If validity coefficients are corrected for errors of measurement in the criterion, the computation of the reliability coefficient of the criterion should be explained, and both corrected and uncorrected coefficients should be reported. Essential

[Comment: Coefficients corrected for errors of measurement in the test are not estimates of the criterion-related validity for the existing test and should not be reported. Corrections for attenuation are very much open to misinterpretation, especially if based on obtained correlation coefficients that are very low or from a small or otherwise inappropriate sample; if misinterpreted, they give an unjustifiably favorable impression of the validity of the test scores. The hazard is illustrated in the manual for an adjustment inventory. The author reported correlation coefficients between inventory scores and criterion ratings; also reported were estimated coefficients between "true" inventory and criterion scores. He then commented that the augmented correlation coefficients "are as high as those often secured between college aptitude tests and college grades." The

comparison is improper, in part, because the test author compared augmented coefficients with uncorrected coefficients for ability tests.]

E8.2.1. Where correlation coefficients are corrected for attenuation or restricted range, full information relevant to the correction should be presented. If such corrections are made, significance tests should be made with the uncorrected correlation coefficients. Essential

[Comment: Corrections should be applied only to obtained coefficients. It is ordinarily unwise to make sequential corrections, as in applying a correction for attenuation to a coefficient already corrected for restriction of range. Chains of corrections may be useful in considering possible further research, but their results should not be seriously reported as estimates of population correlation coefficients.]

E8.3. If validity is demonstrated by comparing groups that differ on the criterion, the manual should report whether and by how much the groups differ on other available variables that are relevant. Very Desirable

[Comment: Since groups that differ on a criterion may also differ in other respects, the test may be discriminating on a quality other than that intended. Types of mental disorders, for instance, are associated with age, education, and length of time in the hospital. Confounding of this sort should be taken into account when the usefulness of a test for diagnosis is appraised.]

E8.3.1. If a test is suggested for the differential diagnosis of patients, the manual should include evidence of the test's ability to place individuals in diagnostic groups rather than merely to separate diagnosed abnormal cases from the normal population. Essential

[Comment: When a test is recommended for the purpose of assigning patients to discrete categories, such statistics as contingency coefficients, phi coefficients, or discriminant functions should be supplemented by a table of misclassification rates giving, for example, the proportion of patients falsely included in a category or falsely excluded from it. Such proportions should be compared with base rates, that is, the proportions of correct classifications made possible by a mere knowledge of the sizes of the categories.]

E8.3.2. If validity is demonstrated by comparing groups that differ on the criterion (e.g., where one group is identified as a high-performance group and another as a low-performance group), all cases should be assigned to one or the other of the groups. Very Desirable

[Comment: The most reliable statistics are obtained if all cases are used; validity coefficients derived from extreme groups may be misleading. In some situations, analyses using extreme groups may be useful for identifying predictors, but generally the validity reported for any given predictor should be based on all cases. If the use of extreme groups is deemed necessary or appropriate to a particular study, appropriate estimates of correlation should be used. The typical product-moment and biserial estimates are not appropriate in this situation.]

E8.4. When information other than the test scores is known to have an appreciable degree of criterion-related validity and is ordinarily available to the prospective test user, the user should consider both the validity of the other information and the resulting multiple correlation when the new test information is combined with it. Essential

[Comment: Whether a test should be used for prediction and classification when other information is readily available sometimes depends not on the validity of the test but on its "incremental validity," that is, what it adds to the soundness of the judgment that would otherwise be made.

For a questionnaire intended to predict marital success, delinquency, and similar behavioral variables, the investigator should find out how much the questionnaire enhances prediction over that provided by base rates developed from demographic variables such as socioeconomic status.]

E8.5. Where more than one test is to be used, validity information should report the validity of the combination actually used. Where composite scores are developed, the basis for weighting (e.g., multiple regression equations) should be given. Essential

[Comment: In one organization, a composite was developed and validated by multiple regression in which the optimal weighting of one test was negative. Nevertheless, the organization added unweighted scores to form a different composite for use in making decisions. The multiple correlation coefficient did not, therefore, describe the validity of the test battery as it was actually used. Where a given method of combination is to be used, that method should be validated.

When multiple regression is used and one predictor in a battery is evaluated, the beta weight is a better index of its contribution to the validity of the test in that combination than is its original validity coefficient.]

E9. A test user should investigate the possibility of bias in tests or in test items. Wherever possible, there should be an investigation of possible differences in criterion-related validity for ethnic, sex, or other subsamples that can be identified when the test is given. The manual or research report should give the results for each subsample separately or report that no differences were found. Essential

[Comment: For many uses, regulations published pursuant to civil rights legislation require that validity studies be performed separately on samples differing in national origin, race, sex, or religious affiliation, when technically feasible.

The concept of fairness may involve other sources of inappropriate discrimination. For example, placing a hand-dexterity test on a low table may unfairly bias the test against tall people. The test user should try to identify potentially unfair influences on test scores in his situation. Variables which may contribute inappropriate variance may be used for subgrouping in investigation of fairness.

However, caution must be exercised in evaluating the possibility of bias. A simple difference in group means does not by itself identify an unfair test, although it should stimulate research to explore the question of fairness. Evidence of differential validity is developed by comparing, for example, regression correlation coefficients, regression equations, and means and variances for each variable.

The proper statistical test for such a difference is, for any parameter, the test of the hypothesis of no true difference between the groups, for example, a test of no difference between correlation coefficients, slopes, or intercepts. Some investigators have attempted to examine such differences by comparing in each subgroup independently the validity statistic (e.g., the correlation coefficient) to a postulated true value of zero. This is not a proper procedure; it does not answer the question at issue of differences in the characteristics of validity. It is impossible to demonstrate such differences by showing that one correlation coefficient, for example, is significantly different from zero while the other is not.

Users should routinely investigate differences in validity when it is technically feasible to do so, that is, when N's are sufficient for reliable comparisons and when criteria are reasonably valid in each group. Users should be aware, however, that a too-hasty acceptance of bias or of differential validity, if used in decision making, may be as likely to produce unfair test use as is failure to consider the possibility.

For example, to avoid unfairness in test use for blacks, an employer may investigate the possibility of differential validity and find not only differences in means between black and white applicants but also differences in intercepts of the regression. Some definitions of fairness require that predictions for applicants in either group should be based on the regression line developed for his own group. If the differences in intercepts are statistical artifacts (due, for example, to unreliability), the result might be considered unfair to blacks (if they have the lower regression line) since their performance might be systematically under predicted. The effect can, of course, work both ways depending on the direction of differences in regression.

It is important to recognize that there are different definitions of fairness, and whether a given procedure is or is not fair may depend upon the definition accepted. Moreover, there are statistical and psychometric uncertainties about some of the sources of apparent differences in validity or regression. Unless a difference is observed on samples of substantial size, and unless there is a reasonably sound psychological or sociological theory upon which to explain an observed difference, the difference should be viewed with caution.

Bias is not necessarily detected by criterion-related validity alone; cf. E12.12).

E10. When a scoring key, or the weighting of items, or the selection of tests is based on one sample, the manual should report validity coefficients based on data obtained from one or more independent cross-validation samples. Validity statements should not be based on the original sample. Essential

E10.1. If the user recommends certain regression weights for combining scores on a test or for combining the test with other variables, the statement of the validity of the composite should be based on a crossvalidation sample. Essential

[Comment: Cross-validation is particularly necessary when the number of predictors entering the study (not the final equation) is greater than 4 or 5 and when the sample size is less than 200.]

E10.1.1. When the scoring of tests in a battery is based on regression coefficients, negative scoring weights should be used only if they have been verified by cross-validation in large samples and if their use will not be invalid (and thus unfair) to one or more subgroups in the population to be tested. Essential

E10.2. If it is proposed that decisions be based on a complex nonlinear combination of scores, it should be shown that this combination has greater validity than a simpler linear combination, that the equation can be logically explained, and that the procedures for combining scores have been cross validated. Essential

[Comment: The use of "moderator variables," for example, is to be recommended only where a moderator is shown to produce a clear improvement in validity in a cross-validation sample. Similarly, when it is proposed that some pattern of scores (e.g., high standing in scores on both Variables 2 and 5) is an indicator of success, it is necessary to show that the proportion of successful persons in the group so identified is higher than would be expected from the regression of frequency of success on a linear combination of Variables 2 and 5.]

E11. To the extent feasible, a test user who intends to continue employing a test over a long period of time should develop procedures for gathering data for continued research. Desirable

[Comment: Validity data may become obsolete. The relationship between test performance and criterion performance may be influenced by many factors, such as changes in populations, recruiting sources, the economy, organizational characteristics, processes, or tasks. Moreover, validity studies are often based on relatively few cases. A plan for the systematic collection of further data after the test has been placed into operational use may be useful both for the development of a more reliable data base and for information on changes in the trends of relationships over time.

Operational use may, however, result in severe restriction of range. Continuing research may be less necessary if the original data are based on a relatively large sample, if the bases for generalizing validity are well established, and if evidence shows a relatively slight rate of change in variables likely to limit the generizability of validity information. When these favorable conditions do not exist, it may be possible to plan for small replications from time to time rather than for a continuous program of research.]

Content Validity

E12. If test performance is to be interpreted as a representative sample of performance in a universe of situations, the test manual should give a clear definition of the universe represented and describe the procedures followed in the sampling from it. Essential

[Comment: The definition of the universe of tasks represented by the test scores should include the identification of that part of the content universe represented by each item. The definition should be operational rather than theoretical, containing specifications regarding classes of stimuli, tasks to be performed and observations to be scored. The definition should not involve assumptions regarding the psychological processes employed since these would be matters of construct rather than of content validity.]

E12.1. When experts have been asked to judge whether items are an appropriate sample of a universe or are correctly scored, the manual should describe the relevant professional experience and qualification of the experts and the directions under which they made their judgments. Very Desirable

E12.1.1. When items are selected by experts, the extent of agreement among judges should be reported. Desirable

E12.1.2. Test content should be examined for possible bias. Essential

[Comment: Bias may exist where items do not represent comparable tasks and therefore do not sample a common performance domain for the various subgroups (cf. B1.3). One may investigate such bias in terms of carefully developed expert judgments; studies of the attitudes or interpretations of items in different subgroups might also present useful information (although care must be taken to assure that the investigation is clearly directed to an analysis of content in relation to an adequately defined performance domain). The judgment of bias may itself be biased; the principle here is that, when it is possible, such judgments should be supported by data.]

E12.2. In achievement tests of educational outcomes, the manual should report the classification system used for selecting items. Desirable

E12.2.1. When an achievement test has been prepared according to a two-way content-by-process outline, that outline should be presented in the manual, with a list of the items identified with each cell of the outline. Very Desirable

E12.3. Any statement in the manual of the relation of items to a course of study (or other source of content) should mention the date when the course of study was prepared. Essential

[Comment: In achievement testing, it is frequently the practice to identify significant topics for items by a careful sampling from textbooks. Textbooks and courses of study change, however, and the test that was once an excellent sample becomes out of date. The manual might therefore report such information as the range and median of copyright dates of the textbooks examined, or the date at which the items to be judged the items to be judged representative.

One checklist concerns problems common to students. The manual for this checklist properly reports the date when the list was assembled. From time to time, it will be necessary to determine whether student problems have changed and, if so, to change the test accordingly.

It should be recognized that this standard implies that definitions of a content universe are subject to change as jobs, society, or curricula change.]

E12.4. When a test is represented as having content validity for a job or class of jobs, the evidence of validity should include a complete description of job duties, including relative frequency, importance, and skill level of such duties. Essential

Construct Validity

E13. **If the author proposes to interpret scores on a test as measuring a theoretical variable (ability, trait, or attitude), his proposed interpretation should be fully stated. His theoretical construct should be distinguished from interpretations arising on the basis of other theories.** Essential

[Comment: For example, if a test is intended to measure the construct of anxiety, the test author should distinguish his formulation of the construct from other possible meanings of the term and should relate his concept to measures of anxiety discussed in the literature.

The description of a construct may be as simple as the identification of "creativity" with "making many original contributions." Even this definition provides some basis for judging whether various pieces of empirical evidence support the proposed interpretation. Ordinarily, however, the test author will have a more elaborate conception. He may wish to rule out such originality as derives only from a large and varied store of information. He may propose explicitly to identify the creative person as one who produces numerous ideas, whether of high or low quality. He may propose to distinguish the ability to criticize ideas from the ability to be "creative." He may go on to hypothesize that the person who shows originality in identifying or describing pictures will also have unconventional preferences in food and clothing. All such characterizations or hypotheses are part of the author's concept of "what the test measures" and are needed in designing and in drawing conclusions from empirical investigations of the psychological interpretation of the construct.]

E13.1. The manual should indicate the extent to which the proposed interpretation has been substantiated and should summarize investigations of the hypotheses derived from the theory. Essential

E13.1.1. Each study investigating a theoretical inference regarding the test should be summarized in a way that covers both the operational procedures of the study and the implications of the results for the theory. Very Desirable

E13.1.2. The manual should report correlations between the test and other relevant tests for which interpretations are relatively clear. Very Desirable

E13.2. The manual should report evidence about the extent to which constructs other than those proposed by the author account for variance in scores on the test. Very Desirable

[Comment: Although it is unreasonable to require a test author to anticipate or to include every counterinterpretation in a test manual, he ought to present data relevant to those counterhypotheses most likely to account for variance in the test scores.]

E13.2.1. The manual for any specialized test or inventory used in educational selection and guidance should report the correlation of scores derived from it with well-established measures of verbal and quantitative ability in an appropriately representative population. Very Desirable

[Comment: Verbal and quantitative abilities are specified here because their importance in educational performance is recognized, because they often account for much of total test variance, and because numerous tests of these abilities are already available. To be of practical value, a new test designed to measure other constructs (e.g.,spatial abilities) must not closely duplicate the measurement of verbal and quantitative ability.]

E13.2.2. If a test has been included in factorial studies that indicate the proportion of the test variance attributable to widely known reference factors, such information should be presented in the manual. Desirable

E13.2.3. For inventories such as personality, interest, or attitude measures, evidence should be presented of the extent to which scores are susceptible to an attempt by the examinee to present a socially desirable.

conforming, or false picture of himself, or to which the scores may reflect other response sets or styles. Such response patterns should be studied for identifiable subgroups rather than for a more general sample. Very Desirable

[Comment: Correlational or experimental studies might be reported. Appropriate evidence of acquiescence might, for example, be the proportion of the total test variance in the number of yes responses to the test, or by the correlation of the test scores with one or more independent measures of the acquiescence tendency, or by experimental procedures designed to induce acquiescence.]

E13.2.4. If a test given with a time limit is to be interpreted as measuring a hypothetical psychological attribute not specifically related to speed, evidence should be presented in the manual concerning the effect of speed on the test scores and on their correlation with other variables. Essential

[Comment: The most complete evidence of the effect of speed would be the comparison of scores on one form, using the usual time limit, with scores on another form having unlimited time. The correlation of scores at the end of the usual time with scores obtained with extra time on the same trial is of limited meaning because the two scores are not independent. Less complete evidence would consist of data on the percentage of examinees who attempt the last item or some item very near the end of the test. If the percentage is below 90, a more penetrating study is needed to show that individual differences on the test do not reflect speed to any great extent.]

E13.2.5. Where differences in test-taking strategies that might influence the interpretation of scores are associated with identifiable subgroup characteristics, this information should be clearly presented or its absence clearly noted. Very Desirable

E13.2.6. Where a low correlation or small difference between groups is advanced as evidence *against* some counterinterpretation, the manual should report the confidence interval for the parameter. The manual should also correct for or discuss any errors of measurement that may have lowered the apparent relationship. Desirable

F. Reliability and Measurement Error

Reliability refers to the degree to which the results of testing are attributable to systematic sources of variance. Classical methods of estimating reliability coefficients call for correlating at least two sets of similar measurements.

One method of obtaining the two sets of measurements is by retesting with the identical test. Aside from practical limitations, theoretically, retesting is not ordinarily a desirable method of estimating reliability because the examinee may remember his or her responses to items from one testing to the next. Hence, memory becomes a systematic source of variance and the correlation of the two sets of scores may be higher than the correlation of two sets of scores based on two different but parallel sets of items drawn from the population of items in the same way.

If we want to eliminate memory as a systematic source of variance and to include the effects of item sampling and response variation over time as sources of variance, we may use two sets of items developed or selected according to the same specifications. These are called parallel forms of the test.

If the effect of content sampling *alone* is sought without the effects of memory or response variability over time, or if it is not practical to administer two parallel forms with separate time limits, reliability can be estimated from a single administration of an unspeeded test. The test may be divided into two sets of items of equal, or approximately equal, length that are judged by competent authorities to sample as nearly as possible the same functions. Any items based on the same source of data (such as a reading passage) must be assigned to the same set. Then the correlation between scores on the two parallel halves is a matched-half coefficient from which an estimate of the parallel-forms reliability coefficient for the total test may be obtained by a procedure that does not assume that the numbers of items or the variances of the two sets are exactly equal.

Estimates of reliability from a single administration may also be obtained by analysis-of-variance procedures. Such estimates will be spuriously high if the test is speeded or if the items are not independent of each other. On the other hand, for unspeeded tests, such estimates will tend to be lower than matched-half coefficients because they constitute, given certain assumptions, the mean of coefficients obtained by correlating scores on all possible pairs of halves of the test.

From the preceding discussion, it is clear that *different methods of estimating reliability take account of different sources of error*. Thus, from one testing to the other, the result is affected not only by random response variability and changes in subjects over time but also by differences in administration (especially if different persons administer the test on the two occasions). Reliability coefficients based on a single administration of a test exclude response variability over time; these effects on scores do not appear as errors of measurement. Hence, "reliability coefficient" is a generic term. It can be based on various types of evidence; each type of evidence suggests a different meaning. It is essential that any method used to estimate reliability be clearly described.

The estimation of score variance is the most informative outcome of a reliability study, both for the test developer wishing to improve the reliability of his instrument and for the user desiring to interpret test scores with maximum understanding. The analysis of score variance calls for the use of an appropriate experimental design. There are many different multivariate designs that can be used in reliability studies; the choice of design for studying a particular test is determined by its intended interpretation and by practical limitations.

It is recommended that test authors describe the meanings of any coefficients they report as accurately and precisely as possible. It is informative to say, for example, "This coefficient indicates the stability of measurement of equivalent scores based on parallel forms of the test administered 7 days apart, without intervening practice or instruction." Although lengthy, such a description is reasonably free from ambiguity.

Reliability coefficients have limited practical value for test users. The standard error of measurement ordinarily is more useful; it has great stability across populations since it is relatively independent of range of talent, and it may be used to identify limits that have a defined probability of including the true score. Test users may use reliability coefficients in comparing tests, but they use standard errors of measurement in interpreting test scores. Information in a test manual about a standard error of measurement may often be more important than information about a reliability coefficient.

General Principles

F1. The test manual or research report should present evidence of the reliability, including estimates of the standard error of measurement, that permits the reader to judge whether scores are sufficiently dependable for the intended uses of the test. If any of the necessary evidence has not been collected, the absence of such information should be noted. Essential

[Comment: It is most helpful to the user when several types of reliability estimates are reported. Reports of standard errors of measurement in different groups are also helpful.]

F1.1. The test manual should furnish, insofar as feasible, a quantitative analysis of the total inconsistency of measurement into its major identifiable components; namely, inconsistency in responses of the subject; inconsistency or heterogeneity within the sample of test content (such as the stimulus items, questions, and situations); inconsistencies in administration of the test; inconsistency among scorers, raters, or units of apparatus; and mechanical errors of scoring. Desirable

[Comment: In general, the desired analysis will not be feasible unless scores are expressed in quantitative, as distinguished from categorical or nonparametric, terms and the design of data collection includes the necessary controls.

With group tests of school achievement, the principal sources of error to be evaluated usually include: (a) inconsistency of test content; (b) inconsistencies in test administration; and (c) inconsistency in responses of the examinee over time, that is, instability. The collection of data should be designed to permit evaluation of these three factors. Fluctuation or inconsistency in the responses of the subject may be an important variable by itself; it is often a major source of random error to be evaluated. Inconsistency among scorers or raters should also be evaluated.]

F1.2. Standard errors of measurement and reliability coefficients should be provided for every score, subscore, or combination of scores (such as a sum, difference, or quotient) that is recommended by the test manual (either explicitly or implicitly) for other than merely tentative or pilot use. Essential

F1.3. For instruments that yield a profile having a low reliability of differences between scores, the manual should explicitly caution the user against interpretation of such differences, except as a source of tentative information requiring external verification. Essential

F1.4. The manual should state the minimum difference between two scores ordinarily required for statistical significance at a designated level. Very Desirable

[Comment: A nomograph or table for determining the significance of any given score difference would be a very useful addition to a test manual. "Change" or "growth" scores require careful attention to Standards F1.3 and F1.4.]

F2. The procedures and samples used to determine reliability coefficients or standard errors of measurement should be described sufficiently to permit a user to judge the applicability of the data reported to the individuals or groups with which he is concerned. Essential

[Comment: The mean and variance of the sample and information about its composition should be provided. Reliability data should be obtained from "natural" groups such as examinees of a single age or grade level. Estimates of the reliability of a test to be used in selecting employees should be based on scores of applicants for positions rather than scores obtained by testing college students or workers already employed.

If a test claims to be appropriate for groups from the fourth grade through graduate school, the manual should provide reliability data for each grade or age level.]

F2.1. Any identifying characteristics of the sample that may be related to consistency of performance on the test should be described in the test manual. Essential

[Comment: Demographic information, such as distributions of the subjects with respect to age, sex, socioeconomic level, intellectual level, locale, employment status or history, and minority group membership should be given in the test manual. For standardized tests, the samples used to compute reliability coefficients and standard errors of measurement should be drawn at random from the norms groups.]

F2.2. If reliability coefficients are corrected for restriction of range, both the uncorrected and the corrected coefficients should be reported in the test manual together with the standard deviations of the group actually tested and of the group to which the corrected coefficients are applicable. Essential

[Comment: When variances differ and there seem to be other justifications for such a correction, the superiority of the standard error of measurement should be noted; it is largely unaffected by differences in variance.]

F2.3. When a test is recommended or ordinarily employed in homogeneous subsamples, the reliability and standard error of measurement should be independently investigated within each subsample and reported in the test manual. Essential

[Comment: The mechanical reasoning section of a well-known aptitude test yields scores that have significantly different reliability coefficients for boys and for girls. The manual reports the reliability coefficients for each sex in each grade.]

F2.3.1. At least one estimate of the standard error of measurement should be provided in the manual for every group for which reliability data are given. Essential

[Comment: When it is specifically recommended that scores be transformed to a particular metric, the standard errors should be presented in that metric.]

F2.3.2. The test manual should report the standard errors of measurement at different score levels. Desirable

[Comment: The manual for one test of college aptitude reports standard errors of measurement for three score levels: the mean, one standard deviation above the mean, and one standard deviation below the mean. Since more important changes in the standard error of measurement are associated with extreme scores, it might be better to use more widely separated score levels if the number of cases available justifies this action.

F2.4. Item statistics (such as difficulty or discrimination indices, etc.) should be presented in at least summary form in a test manual. Desirable

F3. Reports of reliability studies should ordinarily be expressed in the test manual in terms of variances of error components, standard errors of measurement, or product-moment reliability coefficients. Unfamiliar expressions of data should be clearly described, with references to their development. Essential

[Comment: Test authors and publishers should avoid unconventional statistics unless conventional statistics are inappropriate. If unusual statistical analyses are presented, explanations should minimize the likelihood of misinterpretation.]

Comparability of Forms

F4. If two or more forms of a test are published for use with the same examinees, information on means, variances, and characteristics of items in the forms should be reported in the test manual along with the coefficients of correlation among their scores. If necessary evidence is not provided, the test manual should warn the reader against assuming equivalence of scores. Essential

[Comment: Information to be examined would include a summary of item statistics for each form, such as a frequency distribution of item difficulties and of indices of item discrimination. Content analyses of each of the forms should be presented. Thus, both frequency distributions of item statistics and a tabulation of items by categories of subject-matter content and of behavioral or instructional objectives should be furnished.

The forms should represent different samples of items within each category of content. Insofar as one's concern is for error arising from sampling a content universe, the forms to be compared should have been developed from a common universe according to an appropriate plan. An artificially close similarity between forms will result from item-by-item matching or by creating a second form merely by rephrasing items on a first form. A reliability coefficient based on forms created in this way will be spuriously high because it does not properly take into account sampling error in drawing items from the universe of items.]

Internal Consistency

F5. Evidence of internal consistency should be reported for any unspeeded test. Very Desirable

[Comment: Internal consistency is important if items are viewed as a sample from a relatively homogeneous universe, as in a test of addition with integers, a test of general high school vocabulary, or a test presumed to measure introversion. Nevertheless, estimates of internal consistency should not be regarded as a substitute for other measures.]

F5.1. Estimates of internal consistency should be determined by matched-half or random-half methods or by analysis or variance procedures, if these can properly be used with the data. Any additional measure of internal consistency that the author wishes to report should be carefully explained in the test manual. Very Desirable

[Comment: Matched-half coefficients reflect expert judgment and tend to be higher in value than random-half coefficients. Analysis of variance procedures tend to yield lower values than matched-half procedures. In unusual circumstances, special coefficients may provide useful information; if used, such coefficients should be described so the reader will be able to understand them in relation to more conventional estimates.]

F5.2. Internal reliability estimates should not be obtained for highly speeded tests. Essential

F5.3. When a test consists of separately scored parts or sections, the correlation between the parts or sections should be reported in the test manual along with relevant reliability estimates, relevant means, and relevant standard deviations. Very Desirable

F5.3.1. If a test manual reports the correlation between a subtest and a total score, it should call attention to the fact that the coefficient is spuriously high because it is based partly on the perfect correspondence of identical errors of measurement in the subtest and in the total score. Essential

F5.4. If several questions within a test are experimentally linked so that the reaction to one question influences the reaction to another, the entire group of questions should be assigned to one of the two halves of the test when random-half or matched-half procedures are used. Very Desirable

[Comment: In a reading test, several questions about the same paragraph are ordinarily experimentally dependent. All of these questions should be placed in the same half test in using the split-half method. The fact that the test halves do not have exactly equal numbers of items need not be troublesome if an appropriate step-up procedure is used.

Comparisons Over Time

F6. The test manual should indicate to what extent test scores are stable, that is, how nearly constant the scores are likely to be if a parallel form of a test is administered after time has elapsed. The manual should also describe the effect of any such variation on the usefulness of the test. The time interval to be considered depends on the nature of the test and on what interpretation of the test scores is recommended. Essential

[Comment: For many purposes, reliability coefficients and standard errors of measurement should be based on parallel-forms procedures, with a period of perhaps 2 to 4 weeks elapsing between the administration of two parallel forms. In some situations, when test scores are obtained for changing characteristics of individuals, reliability coefficients or standard errors of measurement based on the administration of parallel forms on successive days or weeks may be desirable. A reading-readiness test used only for initial tentative assignment of first-grade pupils to instructional groups is an example. In experiments on the effects of drugs, it may be desirable to measure changes in two sets of test scores obtained before and after a time lapse of only a few minutes.

It seems reasonable to require an assessment of stability for projective techniques and other devices for assessing personality dynamics, even though it is recognized in some instances that low stability of scores over a substantial period may reflect true trait fluctuation. Clinical practice rarely presumes that the inferences from projective tests are to be applied on the very day the test is given. Realistically, one must recognize that pragmatic decisions are being made from test data which are meaningful only in terms of at least days, and usually weeks or months of therapy. If scores on a certain test are found to be highly unstable from day to day, this evidence casts doubt upon the utility of the test for most purposes, even if some fluctuation might be explained by the hypothesis of trait inconstancy. An investigator may be concerned with a psychological characteristic or educational effect which changes rapidly over a short period of time. In this instance it is important not to confuse the inconstancy of the trait with the instability of the measuring instrument.]

F6.1. Determination of the stability of scores by repeated testing should make use of parallel forms of the test to minimize recall of specific answers, especially if the time interval is short. Very desirable

F6.2. The report in a test manual of a study of consistency of scores over time should state what period of time elapsed between tests and should give the mean and standard deviation of scores at each testing as well as the correlation coefficient. Essential

F6.3. If it is reasonable to expect scores on a test to change significantly over some time interval in response to developmental or educational influences, the manual should call the test user's attention to this possibility and advise care in the use of old scores. Very Desirable

[Comment: Since some schools administer aptitude, achievement, or interest tests only at intervals of 2 or 3 years, the manual for such tests should report correlations and changes in means and standard deviations between tests administered 1 year apart, 2 years apart, and 3 years apart. From these data the user can learn how rapidly test records become obsolete with the passage of time.]

F6.3.1. In reporting on stability, the test manual should describe relevant experience, education, or treatment intervening between administrations of the test, if known. Desirable

F6.4. Where a test is to be used to compare groups rather than individuals, standard errors and standards errors of measurement of group means and related statistics should be presented. Essential

STANDARDS FOR THE USE OF TESTS

There are many kinds of test use. As one example, test scores are used for decisions to select or to reject applicants for jobs, schools, or other opportunities. In such use, the test score is a basis for a prediction, one that is either explicit or strongly implied. The test score is used to estimate or predict a likely level of performance on some criterion variable external to the test itself.

Another use is as a prescriptive aid where different scores imply different treatments. For example, elementary school pupils may be classified according to reading ability on the basis of test scores; they may be assigned to different books or to different kinds of instruction. Job applicants may be classified as marginally employable and assigned to programs of remedial vocational training on the basis of test scores. Disturbed persons with one profile of scores may be assigned to treatments different from those for people with different profiles. Each of these examples implies a hypothesis that people with a specific set of attributes will perform a task or achieve a goal more effectively with one form of treatment than with another. The test user in an applied setting may not have the power, the resources, or the training to carry out the necessary experimental work for testing these hypotheses; he may simply accept them as part of the prevailing scientific or professional body of knowledge and use tests accordingly.

A test score may be used to certify that an individual has met some designated standard, that a person is qualified to perform certain skilled tasks, that a child is qualified for a remedial program, or that a defendant can stand trial.

The basic use of tests is descriptive or evaluative. A test score provides a description of the individual who obtained it and can help the test user to understand, analyze, or help that individual. Test scores may be used by a counselor to help a student make a vocational choice or to help a couple in marriage counseling communicate more clearly with each other. They may help a teacher work more effectively with a pupil. These are clinical, diagnostic, and individualistic uses of tests in a continuing relationship between a test user and an individual. Because the relationship is a continuing one, tentative decisions or judgments can be modified as new information is accumulated.

Test scores may constitute the dependent variable or criterion measure in an institutional research study. A program may be continued or terminated on the basis of test results; an institution may receive more or less funding because of test results; test results may be considered in organizational analysis or in making program changes. These *Standards* do not deal fully with these problems; their emphasis is more on the interpretation of scores of individuals. A companion volume is planned dealing with standards for test use in program evaluation, policy-related research, and curriculum evaluation; it will also address issues of research design and of data analysis.

The standards in the present volume are to varying degrees directed to all forms of use. As the use of tests moves along a continuum from the description of a single individual, in a situation allowing for corrections of erroneous interpretations, making decisions about large numbers of people, the test user must apply more of the standards and, perhaps, apply them more rigorously. Such decisions may profoundly influence the lives of those tested, such as decisions for employment or for attendance at college, or decisions to assign a person to one treatment or opportunity rather than to another (e.g., tracking in a school system), or decisions to continue or terminate a program or to regulate its funds. The cost of error, in money and in human suffering, may be great. A test user cannot abdicate the responsibilities described in these standards by subscribing to external testing services or test suppliers.

The standards of test use may not have to be so rigidly followed when the purpose of testing is the understanding of an individual. Sometimes such testing is less standardized than is usually recommended. For example, a school counselor may be interested in assessing the maximum performance capability of a single student. To get a full understanding of that student, he must be able to elicit new information, perhaps even through an embellishment of a standardized test, to seek the broadest possible understanding of the level of mastery and of the generalizability of the situations in which mastery can be demonstrated. Interpretation of test scores in such cases is not made in terms of norms but in terms of a counselor's analysis of what mastery of a particular skill entails (even a social skill, not likely to be measured by tests ordinarily used for content-referenced interpretations). In short, exploration of an individual case is different from standardized testing. *The user who develops test embellishments must know the difference;* that is, he must have a clear rationale for what he is doing when he departs from standard procedure, and he must be able to apply that rationale consistently and sensibly. Such individualized testing does not require less skill than does testing broadly for institutional decisions; it requires a different kind of skill (cf. II).

The standards necessary for using tests for making decisions are not different from the standards necessary when tests are used simply for understanding, but the emphasis within a standard may be different. A test user should be familiar with the standards governing test use in general, and he should pay particular attention to those standards most nearly fitting his own specific type of application.

In doing so, he should realize that the standards are intended to apply, in principle, to *all forms* of assessment. In choosing from alternative methods of assessment, the test user should consider the differences in the ease of applying these standards.

G. Qualifications and Concerns of Users

Assessing others is an occupational activity for teachers, parents, clergymen, shopkeepers, correction officers, etc. Some people assess with remarkable skill; others are inept and have little or no training to help them. Users of educational and psychological tests in schools, places of employment, clinics, laboratories, prisons, and other places where educators and psychologists work should have had at least some formal training.

A test user, for the purposes of these standards, is one who chooses tests, interprets scores, or makes decisions based on test scores. He is not necessarily the person who administers the test following standard instructions or who does routine scoring. Within this definition, the basic user qualifications (an elementary knowledge of the literature relating to a particular test or test use) apply particularly when tests are used for decisions, and such uses require additional technical qualifications as well. A recurring phrase in discussions about testing is "the legitimate uses of a test." One cannot competently judge whether his intended use is among those that are "legitimate" (however defined) without the technical skill and knowledge necessary to evaluate the validity of various types of inferences.

G1. A test user should have a general knowledge of measurement principles and of the limitations of test interpretations. Essential

[Comment: The required level of knowledge will vary with the complexity of the evaluations to be made and the responsibility of the user. At a minimum, the user must be knowledgeable about testing principles, understand the concept of measurement error, and be able to interpret an obtained test score. He should realize that there are alternative explanations for a given score and should have a pool of knowledge from which to evaluate some of the alternatives.]

G1.1. A test user should know his own qualifications and how well they match the qualifications required for the uses of specific tests. Essential

G2. A test user should know and understand the literature relevant to the tests he uses and the testing problems with which he deals. Very Desirable

[Comment: A broad connotation is intended for this standard. The test user should have some acquaintance with the relevant findings of behavioral sciences, such as those related to the roles of heredity and environment, when using aptitude tests; some understanding of physiology is useful when one is using tests of motor skills. A very narrow interpretation of "the literature relevant to the test" is inadequate.

Unfortunately, it seems that ignorance of the literature requires that old information be rediscovered. For over 40 years, for example, it has been known that children with limited or restricted cultural exposure, such as children on canal boats or in isolated mountain communities, make low scores on intelligence tests standardized on more advantaged populations. The point has been made repeatedly, in research reports and textbooks. Nevertheless, many black and Spanish-speaking children with limited cultural exposure who receive low scores on intelligence tests standardized on more advantaged groups are improperly classified as mentally retarded.]

G3. One who has the responsibility for decisions about individuals or policies that are based on test results should have an understanding of psychological or educational measurement and of validation and other test research. Essential

[Comment: A test user should have acquired the technical understanding appropriate to his responsibilities. Test users within organizations or regulatory agencies should have enough technical knowledge to be able to evaluate competently the tests and testing procedures relevant to the decisions they must make. If their technical training is limited, they should seek refresher training or work under the guidance of another test user whose training is adequate.]

G3.1. The principal test users within an organization should make every effort to be sure that all those in the organization who are charged with responsibilities related to test use and interpretation (e.g., test administrators) have received training appropriate to those responsibilities. Essential

[Comment: Serious misuse and distortion in interpretation may occur when people are not properly trained to carry out their responsibilities. The level of training needed varies with the complexity of a testing program, the level of the individual's responsibility for it, and the nature and intensity of possible adverse consequences. Test users should provide at least a basic orientation for administrators or executives who decide whether to test or not to test, to approve or to disapprove specific assessment procedures, to appropriate funds for necessary research, or to decide how test or research results will be used in the organization. Similar knowledge is needed by compliance officers who may have a detrimental influence on testing programs because of unreasoned and unreasoning demands for interpretation of data, who might disapprove of a testing program without adequate consideration of the alternatives, or who might approve faulty and unfair uses of tests out of ignorance.]

G3.1.1. A test user should have sufficient technical knowledge to be prepared to evaluate claims made in a test manual. Very Desirable

[Comment: A test user must accept some responsibility for the choice when a test is chosen. The user must also be able to exercise some judgment concerning descriptions of intended populations that appear in a manual. If he is using the test to evaluate a remedial program for low-performing pupils in the fourth grade, it is not necessarily appropriate to select a test standardized on "children in Grades 4 through 6."]

G3.2. Anyone administering a test for decision-making purposes should be competent to administer that test or class of tests. If not qualified, he should seek the necessary training regardless of his educational attainments. Essential

[Comment: Some tests are easily administered, and a brief explanation of the instructions and of the necessity for standardization may be sufficient training for administering them. The use of other tests or assessment procedures may require more specific or unique kinds of training, for example, individually administered intellectual or personality measures or some work samples. It should be recognized that the administration and scoring of a test may not require any specific academic degree; conversely, possession of a degree is not necessarily evidence of qualifications to administer a particular test.]

G4. Test users should seek to avoid bias in test selection, administration, and interpretation; they should try to avoid even the appearance of discriminatory practice. Essential

[Comment: This is a difficult standard to apply. Sources of item or test bias are neither well understood nor easily avoided. The very definition of bias is open to question. The competent test user will accept the obligation to keep abreast of developments in the literature and, at the very least, to demonstrate a sensitivity to the problem and to the feelings of examinees.]

G5. Institutional test users should establish procedures for periodic internal review of test use. Essential

[Comment: The competent use of tests and test scores requires regular review of procedures and of concepts that may change with the advent of new knowledge. A practice that might have been considered acceptable or appropriate at an early period may be found to be either harmful or ineffective in light of subsequent findings in psychometric theory or criticisms of test use. The review should examine the soundness of procedures used in test administration, the modes of assessment, the bases for inferences drawn from test scores, and the relative quality of various validation strategies.]

H. Choice or Development of Test or Method

Standardized tests constitute one class of assessment procedures available to the user. He may also choose various kinds of ratings, personal history information, reference information, or "unobtrusive measures." He may also elect to develop his own tests. His choice depends upon what is available for assessing the characteristics of concern, ethical considerations, and his own knowledge and competency. Among standardized tests there are usually many alternatives: different dimensions to be measured, different methods of measurement, and different forms of tests. Choices should be made as deliberately and carefully as circumstances permit; test users should not use habitually the same test or method of assessment for all purposes; neither should they assess only those characteristics that are easily or conveniently assessed and fail to consider other, possibly more important, characteristics. Standards refer to the process of choice, not to the choices themselves.

H1. The choice or development of tests, test batteries, or other assessment procedures should be based on clearly formulated goals and hypotheses. Essential

[Comment: There is usually an assumption that one's goals are good, and that the method of assessment chosen will help one achieve those goals. In choosing or building a test one should be able to articulate such assumptions and values. As a general rule, the assumptions take the form of at least an implicit hypothesis: "If I come to a clearer understanding of this individual, in terms of the characteristic or set of characteristics assessed, I will be able to infer something about his vocational success, or his academic problems, or his prognosis in marriage, or whatever."

The use of a test in a decision context implies a hypothesis of the form that a designated outcome is a function of the test variable. A test user should be able to state clearly the desired outcome, the nature of the variables believed to be related to it, and the probable effectiveness of alternative methods of assessing those variables.

The purpose of administering a test should be explicit. In some school systems, it has been alleged, tests are routinely administered with no purpose other than an apparent hope that they will someday be useful. Such routine testing is unwise.]

H1.1. The test user should formulate goals clearly enough so that he can later evaluate his success in achieving them and can communicate that evaluation to other qualified persons. Very Desirable

[Comment: In a clinical or counseling situation, there is a continuing relationship with a person who has been tested. If a test user has clear purposes, later events can provide evidence of some success in achieving goals or information for changing inferences or procedures. Without a clear idea of what is to be learned about a person, and why, there will be no clear direction in the counseling relationship.

One's purposes in developing a testing program define his criteria, and the nature of the criteria should suggest to the informed user hypotheses, that is, test variables, that might be associated with them. Such hypotheses should be reasonable. There is no clear reason, for example, to use a mechanical-aptitude test to try to predict performance in English classes. Similarly, it is not easy to see what purpose is intended when a vocabulary test is adopted for use in the selection of rolling-mill employees.

Some hypotheses are much more easily justified than others. Few people will quarrel with the suggestion that applicants who type rapidly with few errors will become preferred employees in a stenographic pool. The hypotheses that those who are likely to work with greater persistence at a routine, manipulative task can be identified by scores on a very long but easy perceptual speed and accuracy test may require a more detailed explanation of the logic and background data.]

H1.2. The test user should consider the possibility that different hypotheses may be appropriate for people from different populations. Essential

H2. A test user should consider more than one variable for assessment and the assessment of any given variable by more than one method. Essential

[Comment: For most purposes, the evaluation of a person requires description that is both broad and precise; a single assessment or assessment procedure rarely provides all relevant facets of a description.

Decisions about individuals should ordinarily be based on assessment of more than one dimension; when feasible, all major dimensions related to the outcome of the decision should be assessed and validated. This is the principle of multivariate prediction; where individual predictors have some validity and relatively low intercorrelations, the composite is usually more valid than prediction based on a single variable. It is not always possible to conduct the empirical validation study (certainly not in working with problems of individuals one at a time), but the principle can be observed.

In any case, care should be taken that assessment procedures focus on important characteristics; decisions are too often based on assessment of only those dimensions that can be conveniently measured with known validity. For example, mental retardation is often defined as both deficiency in tested intelligence and poor adaptive behavior. If both parts of this definition are accepted, then both variables should be considered in deciding whether an individual is to be classified as a mental retardate, even though it is much more difficult to measure adaptive behavior than to find an acceptable scale for testing intelligence.

Test users should also consider more than one method of assessment. Even a test yielding generally valid scores may in an individual case be susceptible to idiosyncratic errors of interpretation, and a pattern of confirming or modifying assessments may be useful. Confidence in inferences drawn from assessments may be increased by varying the sources and increasing the amount of information on which the inferences are made. In addition to tests, one might consider ratings, references, observations of actual performance, etc. Of these, a test is probably most valid. If the others add to the validity of an assessment, they should be systematically considered in statistical prediction; otherwise, they should be ignored. Frequently, however, one will not have enough confidence in test interpretations to justify overlooking other data. In particular, when using a given test with minorities, one may question the validity of test inferences for those populations and want to get as much additional information as possible before making decisions.]

H2.1. In choosing a method of assessment, a test user should consider his own degree of experience with it and also the prior experience of the test taker. Essential

[Comment: Inexperience of the test user can be alleviated by reading, practice, and training. Warm-up tests or other methods of acclimatization are advocated to alleviate the inexperience of test takers. In addition, attention should be given to the degree of interaction between test user and test taker; there may be special sources of anxiety in situations where they are of different cultural or ethnic background.]

H2.2. The choice or development of a test or test procedure, or the addition of a test or test procedure to existing assessments, should involve consideration of the relationship between the cost of the choice and the benefit expected. Very Desirable

[Comment: Both costs and benefits may involve broader considerations than the specific problem at hand. Although quantification may be difficult and even unreliable, costs and benefits to the individuals tested and to the broader society should enter into consideration.]

H3. In choosing an existing test, a test user should relate its history of research and development to his intended use of the instrument. Essential

[Comment: A school system was faced with the necessity of reducing its faculty. Reductions in force, according to policy, were to be based on teacher competence. However, decisions were in fact based on scores on a test that had been developed to evaluate the educational backgrounds of new teachers-college graduates. Nothing about the test established its validity as a measure of classroom effectiveness, nor was any local research conducted on this point. Its choice was, therefore, inappropriate.

In a different situation, a decision had been made to use a standard achievement test to evaluate pupil progress. Upon investigation of the test's development, it was found inconsistent with the curriculum objectives of that school. Other tests were examined and an alternative test was chosen that more closely matched the curriculum content. (In some cases, closely matching curriculum content may not be advantageous since it prevents one from knowing the extent to which pupils may be deficient in skills or knowledge not deliberately specified in the local curriculum objectives.)

This standard calls for a general evaluation of the validity of the proposed use of a test. Such an evaluation includes evaluation of the procedures followed in the development of the test and of the quality and relevance of the research that has been done with it.]

H4. In general a test user should try to choose or to develop an assessment technique in which "tester-effect" is minimized, or in which reliability of assessment across testers can be assured. Essential

[Comment: In general, the less the influence of the tester on scores, the fairer the test. The influence of the tester is obviously greater in an unstructured interview than in a structured one, and there may be more tester effect in a structured interview than in a structured personal history form. Tester effect is most likely to be minimized by standardized testing. In using tests, some organizations have turned to tape-recorded instructions in an effort to minimize further possible tester effect.]

H5. Test scores used for selection or other administrative decisions about an individual may not be useful for individual or program evaluation and vice versa. Desirable

[Comment: The purposes of institutional testing and of evaluative testing are not always compatible. Whereas the typical evaluative use is intended to help the individual (or program), institutional decisions frequently have the apparent effect of hurting, even if the decision may have unseen long-term benefits to the individual (such as avoidance of an unnecessary failure experience). These seemingly contradictory functions may prevent effective interpretation in either instance.]

I. Administration and Scoring

A test user may delegate to someone else the actual task of administering or scoring tests, but he retains the responsibility for these activities. In particular, he has the responsibility for ascertaining the qualifications of such agents. Standards for administration apply not only to the act of testing but also to more general matters of test administration. The basic principle is standardization; when decisions are based on test scores, the decision for each individual should be based on data obtained under circumstances that are essentially alike for all.

I1. A test user is expected to follow carefully the standardized procedures described in the manual for administering a test. Essential

[Comment: It may in rare cases be necessary to modify procedures. When there is any deviation from standard practice, it should be duly noted, and interpretations of scores should not be made in terms of normative data provided in the manual. Modifications may be standardized for specific purposes. For example, modifications were necessary for testing a group of deaf mutes, but the modified procedures were applied in the same way to all children in the group.

Standardization of procedure is particularly important when decisions are based on test scores. Nevertheless, known examples of failure to follow

standardized procedures are numerous. In one organization, when test supplies were depleted, mimeographed versions of uneven quality were prepared. (In addition to being a violation of copyright laws, the result was a markedly changed set of stimulus materials). One test administrator tried to relieve the monotony of the repeated verbatim instructions by giving a shorter and varied version.]

I1.1. A test user must fully understand the administrative procedures to be followed. Essential

[Comment: The test user should be fully trained to do whatever is required for competent administration of the test. The administration of many tests requires nothing more than the ability to read and understand routine instructions, that of others requires extensive supervised practice. Whatever the requirement, the test user lacking such training should seek it.]

I1.2. A test user should maintain consistent conditions for testing. Very Desirable

[Comment: Situational variables should be reasonably controlled. For example, there should be no great variation in temperature or humidity; noises and other distractions should be as nearly eliminated as possible. Interadministrator reliability should be high. In general, testing conditions should minimize variations in the testing procedure.]

I1.3. A test user should make periodic checks on material, equipment, and procedures to maintain standardization. Essential

[Comment: This standard refers, for example, to the constancy of graphics and of printing, or the accuracy of stop watches. It also seeks the elimination of bad habits that may creep into administrative procedures. It applies particularly to any testing procedures that make use of physical equipment which is subject to wear. Such equipment should be regularly examined to assure that its characteristics remain within acceptable tolerances; for example, a pegboard should be replaced if holes become enlarged or beveled through use.]

I2. The test administrator is responsible for establishing conditions, consistent with the principle of standardization, that enable each examinee to do his best. Essential

[Comment: In a negative sense, the goal of this standard is that conditions inhibiting maximum performance should be avoided. The principle can be followed in part simply by being sure that all materials—such as answer sheets, pencils, and erasers—are on hand and that precautions have been taken to avoid distractions. In a more positive sense, the administrator should be sure that the examinee understands the tasks involved in taking the test: what kinds of responses are to be made and on what answer sheets, the implications for test-taking strategy of erasures or multiple marking or guessing, and how to know whether the test has been completed.

The tester should try to create a nonhostile environment; standardized procedures are impersonal, but the test administrator must avoid being either patronizing or unresponsive to the

examinees, especially when the tester and the examinee differ in race, sex, or status. A testing situation contains elements that are nonrecurring and unique to the persons tested. Although these may have negligible effects on test reliability, they may include events perceived as denigrating or questioning of the worth of the individual. A complete catalog of such events is not possible or easily described. In general, however, the social amenities of respect, politeness, and due regard for extenuating circumstances are relevant guides for insuring the dignity of persons. While it may not be demonstrated that abuse of these principles leads to poor test performance, such abuse is not likely to enhance performance.

It is often difficult to maximize the motivation of the examinees. The attempt is important; a major source of error may arise when examinees do not like or trust the test, tester, or test situation, and therefore make no special effort to do well in it.]

I2.1. Procedures manuals should be prepared for use in organizations when there is repeated testing. Very Desirable

[Comment: Just as a manual is needed for a test, a manual is needed for a testing program. Changes in personnel or lapses in memory make a record of procedures developed and followed necessary for standardization. Such a manual might indicate appropriate circumstances for testing or for referral for testing, standard sequences of tests, or guides to interpretations of test batteries in addition to instructions for administering and scoring tests tal en or adapted from individual test manuals.]

13. A test user is responsible for accuracy in scoring, checking, coding, or recording test results. Essential

[Comment: Any agent of the user shares this responsibility. The clerk who scores a test must understand and accept the necessity for accuracy. The test user, who may or may not do the actual scoring, nevertheless has the responsibility to be sure that procedures are established and followed for verifying accuracy. It is unfair to individuals or organizations when decisions are based on avoidable error.]

13.1. When test scoring equipment is used, the test user should insist on evidence of its accuracy; when feasible, he should make spot checks against hand scoring or develop some other system of quality control. Essential

[Comment: The frequency of such checks will depend on what is known of the procedures on checking within the scoring service. Commercial scoring services may be queried about their procedures if they have not already announced them; if the procedures seem well designed, such spot checks may be needed only infrequently. Some computer services, on the other hand, may be less meticulous, and some hand scoring may be required in each batch of tests scored by machine. One test user in a certification program, where machine analysis of answers not only yields individual scores but also supplies data for analysis prior to revisions, has adopted the policy of hand scoring as well as machine scoring each test. This assures the accuracy of every score used in individual decisions, and it also assures the accuracy of the computer data used in the continuing research program.]

13.2. When test scoring requires judgment, the test user should determine interscorer or intrascorer reliability. Very Desirable

[Comment: When the test user does his own scoring, he should make periodic comparisons of scores he has determined against scores on the same sets of responses determined by other scorers or by himself at other times.]

14. If specific cutting scores are to be used as a basis for decisions, a test user should have a rationale, justification, or explanation of the cutting scores adopted. Essential

[Comment: When a cutting score is adopted, the effect is to reduce scoring to a scale of only two points: pass and fail. The validity of the test scored in this way is different at different cutting scores and, in general, is different from the validity found with continuous scores.

The test user should have some justifiable reason for the adoption of a given cutting score. Many kinds of arguments might be used. In a content-referenced interpretation of a mastery test, such a score might be determined as the obtained score at which one can reject, at a preselected level of probability, the hypothesis that a predesignated confidence interval for that score includes the perfect score on the test. If interpretations are referenced against an external criterion, the cutting score might be one where there is a designated probability of achieving a specified level of success (e.g., "We do not admit students who have less than a 30 per-cent chance of graduating"). Decision theory principles can be used to find a cutting score that will maximize the discrimination between high- and low-criterion groups. One might base the cutting score simply on a distribution of scores in a "predicted-yield" situation; for example, the proportion of job applicants who accept offered employment, the number of new employees who will be needed, predictions of growth or reduction in force, and related information can be used to determined the "predicted yields" of new employees at different cutting scores. The determination of a cutting score on this basis may result in using the test in a range where it is less than maximally effective; its validity should be determined in light of its actual use.

This standard does not attempt to recommend a specific procedure for developing cutting scores where they are to be used. The intent is to recommend that test users avoid the practice of designating purely arbitrary cutting scores they can neither explain nor defend. Cutting scores adopted with reference to those used in another organization or for another purpose, or by a casual glance at normative tables, are usually unsatisfactory.]

14.1. A validity coefficient for each criterion for which a predictor test is recommended should be provided at each one of several points on the score continuum that may be used as cutting scores. Very Desirable

14.1.1. If examinees are to be selected on the basis of a set of scores that displays different regression lines for use in predicting the same criterion in different subgroups of an applicant population, cutting scores should be established with great caution to avoid unfairness to members of one or more of the subgroups. Essential

[Comment: There are many defensible definitions of "unfairness" in the literature, and techniques have been developed for setting cutting scores to minimize "unfairness" as defined in these ways. Test users should keep abreast of the rapidly developing literature on this topic.]

15. The test user shares with the test developer or distributor a responsibility for maintaining test security. Essential

[Comment: Test security is a problem whenever a lapse in security can result in changing an individual's score without making a change in his true score. For some kinds of tests a lapse of security would not be serious. If one is to be tested for achieved skill, for example, knowing and practicing the test samples might be highly recommended. In many cases, however, prior knowledge of test items or scoring procedures could destroy validity. The problem is not simply one of cheating. Security may be compromised where examinees have had much prior experience with a popular test, have been taught specific test items, or have heard a lot about the test.

15.1. Where a probable breach of security may invalidate test inferences, the test user should employ other methods of assessment; that is, he should seek a basis for more valid inferences. Very Desirable

15.2. All reasonable precautions

should be taken to safeguard test material. Essential

[Comment: The use of locked files is a minimal requirement in maintaining test security. It is important to know the recipient whenever tests are out of the filing cabinets. In a test-taking situation, examinees should be proctored. When a test is mailed out to other locations, the recipient should be known and trusted. The ubiquitous copying machine has intensified the problem of safeguarding test materials.]

15.3. The test user should avoid basing decisions on scores obtained from insecure tests. Very Desirable

[Comment: A test may be designated insecure because it is known that unauthorized copies have gone astray. Another test might be considered insecure because it is so widely used that a test taker may have had ample opportunity to practice it in other test-taking situations previously and be able to recognize items. Some employment tests, for example, are so widely used that a job applicant may have taken them several times while applying to various employers.]

J. Interpretation of Scores

Standards in this section refer to the interpretation of a test score by the test user and to reports of interpretations. Reports may be made to the person tested, to his agent, or to other affected people: Teachers, parents, supervisors, and various administrators and executives.

J1. A test score should be interpreted as an estimate of performance under a given set of circumstances. It should not be interpreted as some absolute characteristic of the examinee or as something permanent and generalizable to all other circumstances. Essential

J1.1. A test user should consider the total context of testing in interpreting an obtained score before making any decisions (including the decision to accept the score). Essential

[Comment: The standard is that one must avoid the abdication of responsibility by relying exclusively on an obtained score. Users should, in particular, look for contaminating or irrelevant variables that may have influenced obtained scores; for example, in testing to classify school children, scores may be influenced by behavior problems, visual or hearing defects, language problems, and racial or cultural factors, as well as by ability.]

J2. Test scores should ordinarily be reported only to people who are qualified to interpret them. If scores are reported, they should be accompanied by explanations sufficient for the recipient to interpret them correctly. Desirable

[Comment: There are difficult problems associated with the question of who should have access to test scores within an organization. Certainly, curious peers should not have access to them. An individual who must make the ultimate decision to admit or to reject, or to hire or to reject, or to certify or not to certify, must have the interpretation. One useful (and unanswered) question is whether such a person who lacks the training necessary for the interpretation of scores should be given that training or should be given only the interpretations of scores.]

J2.1. An individual tested (or his agent or guardian) has the right to know his score and the interpretations made. In some instances, even scores on individual items should be made known. Desirable

[Comment: Strictly speaking, this is an ethical standard rather than a standard of competent test use; it is stated here because it conflicts with technical considerations of test security. If the standard is followed, test interpretations and their foundations will be made available to those with a "need to know"; certainly, the individual whose future is affected by the decision is among those with a "need to know." The test user should take any precautions he can, when the demand for information is severe, to protect test security, but he should not do so at the expense of an individual's right to understand the bases for decisions that affect him adversely. Such understanding may be better promoted, with less threat to test security, by using qualified persons sympathetic to the individual's interests. For example, when there is a civil-rights issue, it would be most useful to have items examined by a qualified testing specialist who is known to be both concerned and knowledgeable.]

J2.2. A system of reporting test results should provide interpretations. Essential

[Comment: Although the form of a report will differ for different audiences (examinees, teachers, parents, supervisors), it should communicate the interpretation in a form that will be clear and easily understood.]

J2.2.1. Scores should ordinarily be interpreted in light of their confidence intervals rather than as specific values alone. Very Desirable

J2.3. In general, test users should avoid the use of descriptive labels (e.g., retarded) applied to individuals when interpreting test scores. Desirable

[Comment: The standard applies to the use of summary diagnoses in general. For nearly all purposes, it is better to describe behavior and to differentiate such description from inferences treated as if they were descriptions.

The use of a summary label generally connotes value judgments; unfortunately, most are words used in everyday language and therefore subject to inaccurate interpretation. A test maker may know precisely what he means when he uses the term "retarded," but he has no influence over the interpretation of the same word by a judge, teacher, parent, or child.]

33. The test user should recognize that estimates of reliability do not indicate criterion-related validity. Essential

[Comment: Reliability is a necessary but not a sufficient condition of validity. Reliability coefficients are pertinent to validity in the negative sense that unreliable scores cannot be valid; but reliable scores are by no means *ipso facto* valid.]

34. A test user should examine carefully the rationale and validity of computer-based interpretations of test scores. Essential

[Comment: The user of a special service has the obligation to be thoroughly familiar with the principles on which such interpretations are derived, and he should have the ability to evaluate a computer-based interpretation of test performance in light of other evidence he may have.

J5. In norm-referenced interpretations, a test user should interpret an obtained score with reference to sets of norms appropriate for the individual tested and for the intended use. Essential

[Comment: The reverse is also a standard of competent test use: The test user ordinarily should not interpret an obtained score with reference to a set of norms that is inappropriate for the individual tested or for the purposes of the testing. This is a relatively simple standard to state, but it often is difficult to apply. Contemporary social problems suggest that men and women or members of different ethnic groups should for some purposes be evaluated in terms of several norms groups. For other purposes, such as vocational counseling, students should know how they stand relative to those in or entering a relevant occupation, regardless of their ethnic background. Of course, women or members of minority groups should not be counseled to avoid nontraditional occupations (e.g., women in engineering) merely for lack of appropriate norms.

It is by no means certain that sex or race is the crucial variable in interpreting a given score. It may well be that more important variables for differential norms would be breadth of cultural exposure (or degree of cultural isolation), skill and experience in the use of standard English, interests, or similar variables which may seem to be related to sex or racial differences in test performance.]

J5.1. It is usually better to interpret scores with reference to a specified norms group in terms of percentile ranks or standard scores than to use terms like IQ or grade equivalents that may falsely imply a fully representative or national norms group. Essential

J5.2. Test users should avoid the use of terms such as IQ, IQ equivalent, or grade equivalent where other terms provide more meaningful interpretations of a score. Essential

[Comment: Such scores are objectionable for several reasons. Most important, they generally involve spurious projections of growth. They involve an interpretation which is at best awkward. (To illustrate: It is much simpler to ask, in interpreting a score, "Where does this person stand in relation to specific norm groups?" than to ask, "What group is this person's performance like the average of?" The semantic awkwardness of the latter question illustrates its psychometric awkwardness as well.) They are labels to which the general public attaches many different inappropriate meanings.

Some of these scores, such as mental age or grade equivalent scores, involve severe technical problems. For example, serious misinterpretations occur when grade levels are extrapolated beyond the range for which the test is designed. Moreover, it should be recognized that the standard error of measurement for some widely used standardized achievement tests may be equal to one grade level.

If a test user, either because of his own limitations or because of rigid institutional policies, feels that he must use such terms, he should be sure that interpretations are also given in standard scores or percentile ranks with reference to the specific norms group used in deriving them. The specific test, test form, time of testing, and nature of the test situation should be included in the statement.]

J5.3. A test user should examine differences between characteristics of a person tested and those of the population on whom the test was developed or norms developed. His responsibility includes deciding whether the differences are so great that the test should not be used for that person. Essential

J5.3.1. If no standardized approach to the desired measurement or assessment is available that is appropriate for a given individual (e.g., a child of Spanish-speaking migrant workers), the test user should employ a broad-based approach to assessment using as many methods as are available to him. Very Desirable

[Comment: The standard is to do the best one can. This may perhaps include the use of a test, even though no appropriate normative data are available, simply as a means of finding out how the individual approaches the task of the test. It might include references, extensive interviews, or perhaps some *ad hoc* situational tasks. Efforts to help solve educational or psychological problems should not be abandoned simply because of the absence of an appropriate standardized instrument.]

J5.4. Local normative data or expectancy tables should ordinarily be developed, if possible, when administrative decisions are based on test scores. Very Desirable

[Comment: Expectancy tables may be more useful than norms. When decisions are based on test scores (with the possible exception of content-referenced interpretations), the test user has ordinarily hypothesized that some outcome on an external criterion is related to performance on the test. Decision makers will have a more useful interpretation of a test score if it is expressed in terms of an expected level of performance on the criterion than if it is expressed in terms of relative standing.]

J5.5. Ordinarily, normative interpretations of ability-test scores should not be made for scores in the chance range. Essential

[Comment: On one reading test for elementary school students, a child who cannot read, and therefore gives truly random responses, would be most likely to obtain a grade-equivalent score, according to the norms, of 2.2; that is, second month of second grade. Quite apart from the usual difficulties with grade-equivalent scores, the example demonstrates the impropriety of trying to make a normative interpretation of a test score obtained in a chance range. One test manual for a widely used test of general mental ability has provided a useful guide to the interpretation of "range-of-chance" scores.]

J6. Any content-referenced inter-

pretation should clearly indicate the domain to which one can generalize. Essential

J7. The test user should consider alternative interpretations of a given score. Essential

[Comment: In a sense, a test-score interpretation implies the hypothesis that the score obtained is a function of the trait level "really" possessed. Alternative hypotheses can be suggested. The obtained score might be a function of anxiety, prior knowledge of the test, inadequate understanding of the instructions, a general sort of test wiseness, deliberate faking, or any of several other possibilities. The test user needs to consider more than the obvious interpretation and to have the skill and sensitivity necessary to develop alternative explanations and to evaluate them.]

J7.1. Where cutting scores are established as guides for decision, the test user should retain some degree of discretion over their use. Desirable

[Comment: The point bears repeating that a test user cannot abdicate the responsibility for the decision to use the test. In most circumstances, there are alternatives. Despite the fact that a given test may have a high predictive validity for a specific function, it may represent a trait which is not the only path to success in the predicted venture; and its validity for a given individual, tested at a particular time and under particular circumstances, may be in doubt.

This standard may not be taken as a license to discriminate; it is to be used sparingly in recognition that excessive subjectivity can reduce rather than enhance validity. The intent is to avoid a mechanical rigidity in using test scores of imperfect validity. See also H2.]

J7.2. A person tested should have more than one kind of opportunity to qualify for a favorable decision. Desirable

[Comment: In some situations, a candidate might be given the option to qualify on the basis of characteristics other than those measured by the test. If a person with a score so low that his best prognosis is academic failure, nevertheless succeeds in college, he may have demonstrated qualities necessary for success other than those measured by the test, and the fact might well be considered.

Again, the standard must be judiciously applied. In general, the most valid methods available should guide decisions; the subjective use of information not validated can reduce validity. When compelling information exists, however, it should not be ignored in individual cases. It should be noted that it would be unethical as well as invalid to invoke this principle in the application of particular biases of the test user.]

J7.3. A procedure for reporting test results should include checks on accuracy and make provision for retesting. Desirable

[Comment: Errors in procedures and in test scoring occur; procedures should be available for checking. Retesting is one form of checking results. There should be some limits to a retesting provision. The number of allowable retests may be limited by the number of parallel forms available. Certain types of assessments (e.g., personal-history data) are inappropriate for "retesting." Moreover, a true score is likely to be closer to the mean than is its corresponding obtained score. This fact has important implications for extremely low scores; they will tend to be increased in a retest.

In general, however, opportunities for retesting should be permitted without major obstacles. The principle is that no one should be a victim, without recourse, of an adverse decision on the basis of faulty and correctable psychological assessment. Nor should such decisions be permanent; over a period of time, individuals should have a chance for reevaluation on the basis of new learning or new experience.]

J8. The test user should be able to interpret test performance relative to other measures. Very Desirable

[Comment: For many uses, one should be able to interpret test scores in terms of external criteria. The necessary data may be in a test manual; manuals for some academic aptitude tests provide expectancy charts useful for such interpretations. When an assessment of performance on an external criterion is also available, and when there is a wide discrepancy between actual and predicted criterion performance, the test user should investigate possible reasons for the discrepancy. Furthermore, there should be no a priori assumption that either the test or the criterion is the instrument in error.]

J8.1. A test user should . . .

statistical significance of differences between scores. Very Desirable

[Comment: A test user may observe differences in scores made by two individuals on the same test. There may be differences in the scores made by an individual on a pretest and a posttest after some intervening treatment or training. He may be interested in comparing the individual's performance on one test with the same person's performance on still another test. In such cases, the test user should know how much confidence to place in an observed score difference.]

J9. A test user should develop procedures for systematically eliminating from data files test-score information that has, because of the lapse of time, become obsolete. Essential

[Comment: Data should not even be available for consideration in decision making after an invalidating period of time. Scores on early achievement tests in areas where later learning or forgetting is to be expected (e.g., an old typing-test score) are no longer likely to be valid.

Not all data are equally susceptible to obsolescence. Information of a highly subjective nature might be judged to become obsolete in a shorter time than more objective items of information. Information about young children might be judged to become obsolete in a shorter period of time than comparable kinds of information about adults.

In the case of data that have potential value for research or for survey purposes, the purging may consist of destroying the link between a person's name and the information relevant to

NOTES

NOTES

NOTES

NOTES